Nineteenth-Century Literature Criticism

Guide to Gale Literary Criticism Series

For criticism on	Consult these Gale series
Authors now living or who died after December 31, 1999	*CONTEMPORARY LITERARY CRITICISM (CLC)*
Authors who died between 1900 and 1999	*TWENTIETH-CENTURY LITERARY CRITICISM (TCLC)*
Authors who died between 1800 and 1899	*NINETEENTH-CENTURY LITERATURE CRITICISM (NCLC)*
Authors who died between 1400 and 1799	*LITERATURE CRITICISM FROM 1400 TO 1800 (LC)* *SHAKESPEAREAN CRITICISM (SC)*
Authors who died before 1400	*CLASSICAL AND MEDIEVAL LITERATURE CRITICISM (CMLC)*
Authors of books for children and young adults	*CHILDREN'S LITERATURE REVIEW (CLR)*
Dramatists	*DRAMA CRITICISM (DC)*
Poets	*POETRY CRITICISM (PC)*
Short story writers	*SHORT STORY CRITICISM (SSC)*
Literary topics and movements	*HARLEM RENAISSANCE: A GALE CRITICAL COMPANION (HR)* *THE BEAT GENERATION: A GALE CRITICAL COMPANION (BG)*
Asian American writers of the last two hundred years	*ASIAN AMERICAN LITERATURE (AAL)*
Black writers of the past two hundred years	*BLACK LITERATURE CRITICISM (BLC)* *BLACK LITERATURE CRITICISM SUPPLEMENT (BLCS)*
Hispanic writers of the late nineteenth and twentieth centuries	*HISPANIC LITERATURE CRITICISM (HLC)* *HISPANIC LITERATURE CRITICISM SUPPLEMENT (HLCS)*
Native North American writers and orators of the eighteenth, nineteenth, and twentieth centuries	*NATIVE NORTH AMERICAN LITERATURE (NNAL)*
Major authors from the Renaissance to the present	*WORLD LITERATURE CRITICISM, 1500 TO THE PRESENT (WLC)* *WORLD LITERATURE CRITICISM SUPPLEMENT (WLCS)*

ISSN 0732-1864

Volume 129

Nineteenth-Century Literature Criticism

Criticism of the
Works of Novelists, Philosophers, and Other
Creative Writers Who Died between 1800
and 1899, from the First Published Critical
Appraisals to Current Evaluations

Lynn M. Zott
Project Editor

GALE®

THOMSON
™
GALE

Detroit • New York • San Diego • San Francisco • Cleveland • New Haven, Conn. • Waterville, Maine • London • Munich

THOMSON

GALE

Nineteenth-Century Literature Criticism, Vol. 129

Project Editor
Lynn M. Zott

Editorial
Jessica Bomarito, Jenny Cromie, Kathy D. Darrow, Elisabeth Gellert, Edna M. Hedblad, Jelena O. Krstović, Michelle Lee, Thomas J. Schoenberg, Lawrence J. Trudeau, Maikue Vang, Russel Whitaker

Research
Nicodemus Ford, Sarah Genik, Tamara C. Nott, Tracie A. Richardson

Permissions
Shalice Shah-Caldwell

Imaging and Multimedia
Robert Duncan, Lezlie Light, Kelly A. Quin

Composition and Electronic Capture
Carolyn Roney

Manufacturing
Stacy L. Melson

LIBRARY OF CONGRESS CATALOG CARD NUMBER 84-643008

ISBN 0-7876-6917-2
ISSN 0732-1864

Printed in the United States of America
10 9 8 7 6 5 4 3 2 1

Contents

Preface

Since its inception in 1981, *Nineteeth-Century Literature Criticism* (*NCLC*) has been a valuable resource for students and librarians seeking critical commentary on writers of this transitional period in world history. Designated an "Outstanding Reference Source" by the American Library Association with the publication of is first volume, *NCLC* has since been purchased by over 6,000 school, public, and university libraries. The series has covered more than 450 authors representing 33 nationalities and over 17,000 titles. No other reference source has surveyed the critical reaction to nineteenth-century authors and literature as thoroughly as *NCLC*.

Scope of the Series

NCLC is designed to introduce students and advanced readers to the authors of the nineteenth century and to the most significant interpretations of these authors' works. The great poets, novelists, short story writers, playwrights, and philosophers of this period are frequently studied in high school and college literature courses. By organizing and reprinting commentary written on these authors, *NCLC* helps students develop valuable insight into literary history, promotes a better understanding of the texts, and sparks ideas for papers and assignments. Each entry in *NCLC* presents a comprehensive survey of an author's career or an individual work of literature and provides the user with a multiplicity of interpretations and assessments. Such variety allows students to pursue their own interests; furthermore, it fosters an awareness that literature is dynamic and responsive to many different opinions.

Every fourth volume of *NCLC* is devoted to literary topics that cannot be covered under the author approach used in the rest of the series. Such topics include literary movements, prominent themes in nineteenth-century literature, literary reaction to political and historical events, significant eras in literary history, prominent literary anniversaries, and the literatures of cultures that are often overlooked by English-speaking readers.

NCLC continues the survey of criticism of world literature begun by Gale's *Contemporary Literary Criticism* (*CLC*) and *Twentieth-Century Literary Criticism* (*TCLC*).

Organization of the Book

An *NCLC* entry consists of the following elements:

- The **Author Heading** cites the name under which the author most commonly wrote, followed by birth and death dates. Also located here are any name variations under which an author wrote, including transliterated forms for authors whose native languages use nonroman alphabets. If the author wrote consistently under a pseudonym, the pseudonym will be listed in the author heading and the author's actual name given in parenthesis on the first line of the biographical and critical information. Uncertain birth or death dates are indicated by question marks. Single-work entries are preceded by a heading that consists of the most common form of the title in English translation (if applicable) and the original date of composition.

- The **Introduction** contains background information that introduces the reader to the author, work, or topic that is the subject of the entry.

- A **Portrait of the Author** is included when available.

- The list of **Principal Works** is ordered chronologically by date of first publication and lists the most important works by the author. The genre and publication date of each work is given. In the case of foreign authors whose works have been translated into English, the list will focus primarily on twentieth-century translations, selecting those works most commonly considered the best by critics. Unless otherwise indicated, dramas are dated by first performance, not first publication. Lists of **Representative Works** by different authors appear with topic entries.

- Reprinted **Criticism** is arranged chronologically in each entry to provide a useful perspective on changes in critical evaluation over time. The critic's name and the date of composition or publication of the critical work are given at the beginning of each piece of criticism. Unsigned criticism is preceded by the title of the source in which it appeared. All titles by the author featured in the text are printed in boldface type. Footnotes are reprinted at the end of each essay or excerpt. In the case of excerpted criticism, only those footnotes that pertain to the excerpted texts are included. Criticism in topic entries is arranged chronologically under a variety of subheadings to facilitate the study of different aspects of the topic.

- A complete **Bibliographical Citation** of the original essay or book precedes each piece of criticism.

- Critical essays are prefaced by brief **Annotations** explicating each piece.

- An annotated bibliography of **Further Reading** appears at the end of each entry and suggests resources for additional study. In some cases, significant essays for which the editors could not obtain reprint rights are included here. Boxed material following the further reading list provides references to other biographical and critical sources on the author in series published by Gale.

Indexes

Each volume of *NCLC* contains a **Cumulative Author Index** listing all authors who have appeared in a wide variety of reference sources published by the Gale Group, including *NCLC*. A complete list of these sources is found facing the first page of the Author Index. The index also includes birth and death dates and cross references between pseudonyms and actual names.

A **Cumulative Nationality Index** lists all authors featured in *NCLC* by nationality, followed by the number of the *NCLC* volume in which their entry appears.

A **Cumulative Topic Index** lists the literary themes and topics treated in the series as well as in *Classical and Medieval Literature Criticism, Literature Criticism from 1400 to 1800, Twentieth-Century Literary Criticism,* and the *Contemporary Literary Criticism* Yearbook, which was discontinued in 1998.

An alphabetical **Title Index** accompanies each volume of *NCLC*, with the exception of the Topics volumes. Listings of titles by authors covered in the given volume are followed by the author's name and the corresponding page numbers where the titles are discussed. English translations of foreign titles and variations of titles are cross-referenced to the title under which a work was originally published. Titles of novels, dramas, nonfiction books, and poetry, short story, or essay collections are printed in italics, while individual poems, short stories, and essays are printed in roman type within quotation marks.

In response to numerous suggestions from librarians, Gale also produces an annual paperbound edition of the *NCLC* cumulative title index. This annual cumulation, which alphabetically lists all titles reviewed in the series, is available to all customers. Additional copies of this index are available upon request. Librarians and patrons will welcome this separate index; it saves shelf space, is easy to use, and is recyclable upon receipt of the next edition.

Citing *Nineteenth-Century Literature Criticism*

When citing criticism reprinted in the Literary Criticism Series, students should provide complete bibliographic information so that the cited essay can be located in the original print or electronic source. Students who quote directly from reprinted criticism may use any accepted bibliographic format, such as University of Chicago Press style or Modern Language Association style.

The examples below follow recommendations for preparing a bibliography set forth in *The Chicago Manual of Style,* 14th ed. (Chicago: The University of Chicago Press, 1993); the first example pertains to material drawn from periodicals, the second to material reprinted from books:

Guerard, Albert J. "On the Composition of Dostoevsky's *The Idiot.*" *Mosaic: A Journal for the Interdisciplinary Study of Literature* 8, no. 1 (fall 1974): 201-15. Reprinted in *Nineteenth-Century Literature Criticism.* Vol. 119, edited by Lynn M. Zott, 81-104. Detroit: Gale, 2003.

Berstein, Carol L. "Subjectivity as Critique and the Critique of Subjectivity in Keats's *Hyperion.* In *After the Future: Post-modern Times and Places,* edited by Gary Shapiro, 41-52. Albany, N. Y.: State University of New York Press, 1990. Reprinted in *Nineteeth-Century Literature Criticism.* Vol. 121, edited by Lynn M. Zott, 155-60. Detroit: Gale, 2003.

The examples below follow recommendations for preparing a works cited list set forth in the *MLA Handbook for Writers of Research Papers,* 5th ed. (New York: The Modern Language Association of America, 1999); the first example pertains to material drawn from periodicals, the second to material reprinted from books:

Guerard, Albert J. "On the Composition of Dostoevsky's *The Idiot.*" *Mosaic: A Journal for the Interdisciplinary Study of Literature* 8. 1 (fall 1974): 201-15. Reprinted in *Nineteenth-Century Literature Criticism.* Ed. Lynn M. Zott. Vol. 119. Detroit: Gale, 2003. 81-104.

Berstein, Carol L. "Subjectivity as Critique and the Critique of Subjectivity in Keats's *Hyperion. After the Future: Post-modern Times and Places.* Ed. Gary Shapiro. Albany, N. Y.: State University of New York Press, 1990. 41-52. Reprinted in *Nineteeth-Century Literature Criticism.* Ed. Lynn M. Zott. Vol. 121. Detroit: Gale, 2003. 155-60.

Suggestions are Welcome

Readers who wish to suggest new features, topics, or authors to appear in future volumes, or who have other suggestions or comments are cordially invited to call, write, or fax the Project Editor:

Project Editor, Literary Criticism Series
The Gale Group
27500 Drake Road
Farmington Hills, MI 48331-3535
1-800-347-4253 (GALE)
Fax: 248-699-8054

Acknowledgments

The editors wish to thank the copyright holders of the excerpted criticism included in this volume and the permissions managers of many book and magazine publishing companies for assisting us in securing reproduction rights. We are also grateful to the staffs of the Detroit Public Library, the Library of Congress, the University of Detroit Mercy Library, Wayne State University Purdy/Kresge Library Complex, and the University of Michigan Libraries for making their resources available to us. Following is a list of the copyright holders who have granted us permission to reproduce material in this volume of *NCLC*. Every effort has been made to trace copyright, but if omissions have been made, please let us know.

COPYRIGHTED MATERIAL IN *NCLC*, VOLUME 129, WAS REPRODUCED FROM THE FOLLOWING PERIODICALS:

American Quarterly, v. 40, June, 1988. Copyright 1988, American Studies Association. Reproduced by permission of The Johns Hopkins University Press.—*British Critic*, v. 20, August, 1802.—*Canadian Slavonic Papers*, v. 41, June, 1999. Copyright ©, Canadian Slavonic Papers, Canada, 1999. Reproduced by permission of the publisher.—*Charles Lamb Bulletin*, v. 5, January, 1974; v. 58, April, 1987; v. 108, October, 1999. Copyright 1974, 1987, 1999 by *The Charles Lamb Bulletin*. All reproduced by permission.—*Essays in Literature*, v. 3, Fall, 1976. Copyright 1976 by Western Illinois University. Reproduced by permission.—*Italian Quarterly*, v. 70, 1974. Copyright © 1974 by *Italian Quarterly*. Reproduced by permission.—*Italica*, v. 72, Spring, 1995; v. 77, Autumn 2000. Copyright © 1995, 2000 by The American Association of Teachers of Italian. Both reproduced by permission.—*Journal of European Studies*, v. 29, March, 1999. Copyright 1999 by the *Journal of European Studies*. Reproduced by permission.—*New York History*, v. 25, July 1944. Copyright 1944 by New York History. Reproduced by permission.—*Poetics Today*, v. 4, 1983. Copyright © 1983 by Duke University Press, Durham, NC. Reproduced by permission.—*The Polish Review*, v. 24, 1979. Copyright 1979 by *The Polish Review*. Reproduced by permission.—*Proceedings of the British Academy*, v. 53, 1967. Copyright 1967 by the *Proceedings of the British Academy*. Reproduced by permission.—*Rivista di Studi Italiani*, v. 16, December, 1998. Copyright 1998 by *Rivista di Studi Italiani*. Reproduced by permission.—*Romance Studies*, v. 19, Winter, 1991. Copyright 1991 by *Romance Studies*. Reproduced by permission.—*Slavic and East European Journal*, v. 21, Fall 1977; v. 39, Spring, 1995. © 1977, 1995 by AATSEEL of the U.S., Inc. Both reproduced by permission.—*South Atlantic Bulletin*, v. 41, May, 1976. Copyright 1976 by the South Atlantic Modern Language Association. Reproduced by permission.—*Wordsworth Circle*, v. 29, 1998. © 1998 Marilyn Gaull. Reproduced by permission of the editor.

COPYRIGHTED MATERIAL IN *NCLC*, VOLUME 129, WAS REPRODUCED FROM THE FOLLOWING BOOKS:

Adams, M. Ray. From *Studies in the Literary Backgrounds of English Radicalism; with Special Reference to the French Revolution*. Franklin and Marshall College Studies, Number Five, 1947.—Baehr, Stephen. From "Is Moscow Burning? Fire in Griboedov's *Woe From Wit*," in *Russian Subjects: Empire, Nation, and the Culture of the Golden Age*. Edited by Moinka Greenleaf and Stephen Moeller-Sally. Northwestern University Press, 1998. Copyright © 1998 by Northwestern University Press. All rights reserved. Reproduced by permission.—Baym, Nina. From *American Women of Letters and the Nineteenth-Century Sciences: Styles of Affiliation*. Rutgers University Press, 2001. Copyright © 2001 by Nina Baym. All rights reserved. Reproduced by permission.—Bini, Daniela, From *A Fragrance from the Desert: Poetry and Philosophy in Giacomo Leopardi*. ANMA Libri & Co., 1983. Copyright © 1983 by ANMA Libri & Co. All rights reserved. Reproduced by permission of the publisher and the author.—Bonadeo, Alfredo. From "Leopardi's Concept of Nature," in *The Two Hesperias: Literary Studies in Honor of Joseph G. Fucilla on the Occasion of His 80th Birthday*. Edited by Americo Bugliani. José Porrúa Turanzas, S. A., 1977. Copyright © 1977 by Americo Bugliani. All rights reserved. Reproduced by permission.—Brown, William Edward. From *A History of Russian Literature of the Romantic Period, Volume One*. Ardis, 1986. Copyright © 1986 by Ardis Publishers. All rights reserved. Reproduced by permission.—Faherty, Duncan. From "The Borderers of Civilization: Susan Fenimore Cooper's View of American Development," in *Susan Fenimore Cooper: New Essays on Rural Hours and Other Works*. Edited by Rochelle Johnson and Daniel Patterson. The University of Georgia Press, 2001. Copyright © 2001 by the University of Georgia Press. All rights reserved. Reproduced by permission.—Gershkovich, Alexander. From "Russian Romantic Drama: The Case of Griboedov," in *Romantic Drama*. Edited by Gerald Gillespie. John Benjamin's Publishing Company, 1994. Copyright © 1994 by John Benjamin's B. V./Association Interna-

PHOTOGRAPHS AND ILLUSTRATIONS APPEARING IN *NCLC*, VOLUME 129, WERE RECEIVED FROM THE FOLLOWING SOURCES:

Literary Criticism Series Advisory Board

Susan Fenimore Cooper
1813-1894

American essayist, novelist, and short story writer.

INTRODUCTION

Credited as the first female nature writer in America, Cooper is best known for *Rural Hours* (1850), a journal based on her observations of nature and community life written over the course of two years in rural Cooperstown, New York. Cooper was a self-effacing woman who rejected notions of equality for women, and as the devoted daughter of James Fenimore Cooper, she was often overshadowed by her more famous father.

BIOGRAPHICAL INFORMATION

The second child of Susan De Lancey and James Fenimore Cooper, Susan Cooper was born in Scarsdale, New York, on April 17, 1813. Her older sister Elizabeth died soon after Cooper was born, and a few months later the family moved to Cooperstown, the village founded by Cooper's paternal grandfather. It was here that Cooper's two sisters, Caroline and Anne, were born and Cooper's father began his literary career. The family, which grew to include another daughter and two sons, one of whom died at the age of two, moved to New York City in 1822 and Cooper was enrolled in private school. From 1826 to 1833 the Coopers lived abroad, based in Paris, but traveling throughout Europe. During this period Cooper attended a boarding school in France and was privately tutored during the two years that the family spent in Italy. She was educated in both America and European literature, was skilled in languages and the arts, and gained a basic understanding of botany and zoology. The family again took up residence in New York City when they returned from Europe and then permanently settled in Cooperstown three years later.

Cooper and her father were very close; she served as his literary secretary and later as his editor. It is believed that the senior Cooper discouraged his daughter from marrying by finding every potential suitor—the inventor Samuel F. B. Morse among them—unworthy of Susan. Although Cooper wrote a novel and numerous stories, biographical sketches, and essays focused on nature, her own career always took second place to that of her father's. After his death, she took charge of

his literary estate and reputation, editing his diaries and unpublished articles and writing introductions to the reprints of his many novels. Cooper also edited and annotated an American edition of nature writer John Leonard Knapp's *Country Rambles in England, or Journal of a Naturalist* (1853). In addition, she assembled and edited a biography of missionary William West Skiles and the volume of folklore *The Rhyme and Reason of Country Life* (1854). Despite her literary prowess, Cooper was never given to self-promotion, so she was not as rigorous in securing her own literary reputation as she was in sustaining her father's. As a result, most of her stories and essays were never collected and published beyond their initial appearance in popular magazines.

In addition to her literary pursuits, Cooper devoted herself to a variety of philanthropic causes. Using the skills and social contacts she had acquired while managing her father's literary affairs, Cooper became an effective fund-raiser for a wide variety of community projects.

She was instrumental in founding a hospital, a school for under-privileged children, a charity home for poor families, and an orphanage that served as many as one hundred children. Cooper died December 31, 1894, in her sleep.

MAJOR WORKS

Cooper's first major publication is a domestic novel, *Elinor Wyllys; or, The Young Folk of Longbridge* (1846), which she published with some assistance from her father. In the tradition of nineteenth-century sentimental fiction, Cooper's story involves an unattractive but virtuous country girl as the title character. Elinor is an orphan whose betrothed travels to Europe, falls in love with her more attractive friend, and abandons Elinor, only to be abandoned himself by the friend. He eventually returns, however, and he and Elinor are reconciled. The novel was not as well received as other works of domestic fiction.

Cooper's most famous text is *Rural Hours,* a seasonal nature journal consisting of a year's worth of observations of the flora and fauna of upstate New York and the community life of the village of Cooperstown. Like Henry David Thoreau's *Walden,* to which it is frequently compared, *Rural Hours* was condensed from journal entries that actually covered two years of observations and notes. Although Cooper's book appeared four years earlier than Thoreau's, it has been overshadowed by the later work. The two nature journals differ in their approach to the relationship between humans and the natural world and the degree to which the authors tend to anthropomorphize natural phenomena. According to Rochelle Johnson (see Further Reading), "Thoreau's *Walden* tends toward exploring nature's symbolic meanings for humans. Nature as it is represented in *Rural Hours,* however, has more autonomy: its meaning exceeds its reflection of human needs and values." Johnson cites as evidence of Thoreau's "more anthropocentric imagination" his famous passage on loons—wherein he attributes to the birds his own love of Walden Pond—and compares it to Cooper's passage on loons, which consists of a description of their behavior and patterns with no human-centered explanation offered. Vera Norwood, however, suggests that Cooper also tended to anthropomorphize wild creatures, particularly birds, with which she felt an especially strong affinity. According to Norwood, "she gave the birds' home a domestic arrangement similar to her own," and often used the exemplary behavior of mother birds as models for human mothers.

CRITICAL RECEPTION

Although her novel was poorly received, Cooper's *Rural Hours* was well known in its time and is still considered by many critics to be her masterpiece and only noteworthy work. Several scholars, among them Anna K. Cunningham, have lamented the fact that, despite her considerable talent and extensive literary background, Cooper was apparently unable to produce anything of equal merit throughout the remainder of her long career. Cunningham lists the other texts in Cooper's bibliography, but dismisses them all as "mere word-chopping, in no way comparable to the freshness, grace and originality of *Rural Hours.*" Lucy B. Maddox has also considered Cooper's failed potential, suggesting that the young author was fearful of competing with her father. Maddox notes that although Cooper published her own work anonymously or under a pseudonym, she signed her full name to the introductions she wrote for her father's works. Nonetheless, *Rural Hours* was enormously popular at the time of its publication, and had gone through six printings before the more famous *Walden* reached its second. It fell out of favor later in the nineteenth century and throughout most of the twentieth. However, interest in environmental writing in general and in *Rural Hours* in particular has increased dramatically in recent years. A new edition of the work appeared in 1998 along with a number of critical essays, most praising Cooper as one of the first American environmentalists and the first American woman to write essays on nature. Richard M. Magee credits Cooper with combining the sentimental elements of her domestic fiction with the environmental and community concerns of her nature writing to create a new subgenre he calls "sentimental ecology." Magee suggests that the enduring value of Cooper's work may be found in the way "she uses her domestic voice to convince us of the intellectual and moral value of the landscape and the responsibility we have to perpetuate this value."

PRINCIPAL WORKS

Elinor Wyllys; or, The Young Folk of Longbridge. A Tale [as Amabel Penfeather] (novel) 1846
Rural Hours. By a Lady [anonymous] (journal) 1850; revised and enlarged 1887
The Rhyme and Reason of Country Life [editor] (folklore) 1854
Rural Rambles. By a Lady [editor] (essays) 1854
Mount Vernon, a Letter to the Children of America (essay) 1859
"Small Family Memories" (memoirs) 1922

CRITICISM

Anna K. Cunningham (essay date July 1944)

SOURCE: Cunningham, Anna K. "Susan Fenimore Cooper—Child of Genius." *New York History* 25 (July 1944): 339-50.

[*In the following essay, Cunningham provides an overview of Cooper's writing career, attempting to explain her status as a minor figure in nineteenth-century American literature despite her considerable talent and early promise.*]

In the summer of 1813 young James Cooper (the Fenimore was not formally added until an act of the New York State Legislature in 1826) drove with his wife and infant daughters, Elizabeth and Susan Augusta, from Mamaroneck up to Cooperstown, the settlement founded by his father, Judge William Cooper. James Cooper brought his little family over the old Cherry Valley Turnpike down into Otsego in a carriage which he called—in the vocabulary of a seafaring man,[1]—the "rasée". The little party in the rasée, drawn by a team of greys, stopped to rest at Cherry Valley. There the elder of the two little girls, Elizabeth, was fed some over-ripe strawberries and she died in Cooperstown shortly after from food poisoning. And so a journey that was to prove eventful had a sad note. It brought an end to a short life for the firstborn child of James Fenimore Cooper, and it brought to Cooperstown as an infant a woman who left an impress on the community that is strong today, one hundred and thirty-one years later. For Susan Cooper was to be a leading spirit in the founding of Thanksgiving Hospital, so named in gratitude for the close of our own Civil War, and from Thanksgiving Hospital has grown, at least in inspiration, Cooperstown's Mary Imogene Bassett Hospital.

But Cooperstown is, after all, only a small community and the Bassett Hospital, outstanding though it be, a memorial limited in influence for one who once gave promise of a career to rival, if not outshine, her father's. Listen to what William Cullen Bryant said of Susan Fenimore Cooper's first work *Rural Hours* when it appeared (1850): "It is a great book—the greatest of the season." In a sense it was to be expected that the judgment of Susan's fond father would be favorable but his opinion is phrased in terms so considered that they show him almost leaning over backwards in an effort to be fair. Writing to his wife in Cooperstown from his New York publisher's office in March, 1850, Cooper said:[2]

> I have written to Sue how much I am pleased with her book. It is not strong, perhaps, but is so pure, and so elegant, so very feminine and charming, that I do not

doubt now, of its eventual success—I say "eventual", for, at first, the world will not know what to make of it. Let her be at ease—I shall do all I can for her. She has struggled nobly, and deserves success. At any rate she has pleased us, and that is a great deal for so dear a child.

To his daughter he had written a day or two previously, evidently in acknowledgment of her submitting the galley to him and to reassure her fear that he might find the work "disjointed and tame":[3]

> I cannot let the occasion pass without expressing to you the great satisfaction I have had in reading the sheets [*Rural Hours*]. So far from finding them disjointed and tame, they carried me along with the interest of a tale. The purity of mind, the simplicity, elegance, and knowledge they manifest, must, I think, produce a strong feeling in your favor with all the pure and good. I have now very little doubt of its ultimate success, though at first the American world will hesitate to decide.

There is in this approval a temperance, almost a reluctance, that indicate here speaks Cooper, the craftsman skilled in his trade, as much as Cooper, father of the author.

But we do not need to depend on the opinion of Cullen Bryant nor Fenimore Cooper, honored though those opinions be. Take up *Rural Hours* today, and its quality is still strong, its flavor distinct. Few books of ninety years ago, certainly not, it must be admitted, the works of Susan's "dearest Father" have as clearly that timeless readability that marks good, not to say great, work. Susan Cooper stands the test of time.

As Cooper noted, *Rural Hours* carries one along with the interest of a work of fiction. The book is divided into the four seasons: Spring, Summer, Autumn and Winter; these seasons in turn are broken down into the days and dates of the month, as, for example "Sunday, March 6th"; the year, however, is a synoptic one summarizing the experiences of many years. In substance the volume is a series of reports—on the weather, the activities of the family circle and the life of the village of Cooperstown. The year's slow round on the woody shores of the Glimmerglass is Susan Cooper's province: the melting snows of spring, the first robin, housecleaning, walks in the May woods, the lushness of full summer, the autumn air spiced with burning leaves and the brightness of the autumn sky, the county fair, grey November, family gaiety at Christmas and the round of New Year's calls. The emphasis is on the natural background against which man plays his little part. Four years before Thoreau published *Walden* Susan Cooper spoke of nature with something of the same understanding. Sometimes her account is written with considerable elaboration and sometimes as tersely as her father's 1848 Journal (which was rarely more than three or four lines a day, with the inevitable last sentence "Played chess with Mrs. C. tonight as usual."). There may be an entry for "Monday, July 8th" with the haze of heat and the harvest of hay in the Otsego Hills told of so clearly and beautifully that one turns the page in delighted haste but, alas, the next entry is a dry little note for "Saturday, August 18th!"

This quality of casualness is at one and the same time the strength and the weakness of Susan Cooper's work. It is the charm which makes a book, primarily of nature lore and one which treated differently might easily be dull and heavy, so universal. And it is perhaps the key to the enigma of why a writer possessed of so rich a native talent should have remained a minor figure in American letters. For so Susan Cooper did remain. *Rural Hours,* this beginning so promising, proved not the prelude to greater achievements but the utmost peak she was ever to achieve. True, she kept on with her writing, if such elegantly bound and illustrated scrapbooks as *The Rhyme and Reason of Country Life* (an anthology of rural lore ranging from Virgil on the keeping of bees to old German carols) and *Pages and Pictures* (clippings from her father's works) can be dignified by the name of writing. Her complete bibliography would include also an American edition of *Country Rambles* by John Leonard Knapp (1853), *Rural Rambles* (1854), *Mount Vernon, a Letter to the Children of America* (1859), *William West Skiles, a Sketch of Missionary Life in Valle Crucis in Western North Carolina, 1842-1862* (1890), the **"Small Family Memories"** which was unfinished at her death and which her nephew, another James Fenimore Cooper, was to use as the introduction to his edition of his grandfather's correspondence, and prefaces to the Household Edition of Cooper's works. All these, however, were mere word-chopping, in no way comparable to the freshness, grace and originality of *Rural Hours.* The question then stands, why did Susan Fenimore Cooper, possessed of her literary heritage and fine capacity, equipped too with entrée into literary circles both in America and abroad, remain a woman of one book? An able writer with an unusually clear, observant eye for color, detail, and dramatic quality, reared with the smell of printer's ink continually in her nostrils, gives to the world but a single major work. We ask why was this? Why did not Susan Cooper reach the literary stature to which her father aspired for her? Today, we search for the factors that muted her talents and kept her only a dilettante of letters.

The riddle is hard to read, for Susan Cooper is today, despite the abundant and obvious evidence of her good works, an elusive figure. There is enough written into the record for us to know that she was a dynamic personality and a leader in her circle, but we must imagine

the little lady—she was very slight and very deaf in age—waving away with a deprecating hand any suggested memorials which would have helped today's searcher. She was born at Scarsdale, New York, April 17, 1813. In *The Story of Cooperstown,* we find this picture of her.[4]

> A memorial window in Christ Church idealizes in form and color the spirit of this noble woman, without attempting portraiture. A real likeness of Miss Cooper, as she appeared in her ripest years, would recall a sweet face framed in dangling curls, a manner somewhat prim, but always gentle and placid, a figure slight and spare, with a bonnet and Paisley shawl that are all but essential to the resemblance. She would best be represented in the midst of orphan children whom she catechises for the benefit of some visiting dignitary, while the little rascals, taking advantage of her growing deafness, titter forth the most palpable absurdities in reply, sure of her benignant smile and commendatory, "Very good; very good indeed!"

We know a little more from the **"Small Family Memories."** Fenimore Cooper remained with his family in Cooperstown from 1813 until 1817. Then the family—there were two other little sisters to make the return trip with Susan Augusta, Caroline and Anne Charlotte—returned to Westchester County, the home of the De Lanceys, Mrs. Cooper's people. It was there, at Angevine, that Cooper on a day tossed aside one of Mrs. Opie's novels, just in on a packet from England, with the statement that he could write a better book himself. Sue Cooper tells[5] of playing with her dolls one day under a table completely covered with a deep heavy cloth and of the novelist and his wife entering the room and sitting down to read aloud a chapter of *Precaution.* The little girl became so sad over the fate of the hero at one particular point that she began to sob aloud and was dragged out from under the table by the astonished author. She tells again of driving with her mother and the burgeoning novelist to Bedford, home of the Jay family, close friends, with *Precaution* in manuscript. There a group listened to the reading of it with only one or two being told the authorship. So intimate was the little girl with the beginnings of literary fame.

Then, after a few years spent in the vicinity of the De Lancey estate at Westchester and in New York City, Cooper secured an appointment through the good offices of DeWitt Clinton as United States Consul for the city of Lyons in France. The family sailed for Europe aboard the *Hudson* on June 1, 1826, and remained abroad until 1833.

Miss Cooper's description of the family's first days on the Continent as they traveled by calèche from Rouen to Paris is like an old-fashioned nosegay, pungent and nostalgic:[6]

> At the end of a few weeks we left Southampton for Havre, in a small, rickety, jerky, dirty steamboat. On a bright moonlight night we landed on the soil of Nor-

mandy, the native province of our Huguenot ancestors, the de Lancés. At Havre everything was desperately foreign. After a few days we embarked for Rouen in a tugboat. Great was our delight in the views of the banks, the open unfenced farms, the compact dark villages, and the ruined castles. At Rouen we passed several days under the shadow of the grand old Cathedral. . . .

Our dear Father bought a travelling calèche at Rouen, and we were soon climbing the hill of St. Catherine, where we greatly enjoyed the fine view. A Norman *paysanne,* in winged white cap and wooden sabots, was walking up the hill, as well as ourselves; a dark village of some size lay among the open patch-work fields below; my Father asked its name of the young woman. "Je ne suis pas de ce pays là, Monsieur," she replied. She did not live in the village, and therefore did not know its name!

A Yankee girl would have known the name of every village in sight, remarked Papa. We were travelling post, the most charming of all ways of travelling, stopping at different points of interest. . . .

We were soon in Paris, and the first afternoon our dear Mother was enticed out for a walk on the Boulevards by Papa. A few days more and we had left the Hotel de Montmorency and were regularly installed in a temporary home of our own, as *bourgeois de Paris,* in the narrow, gloomy Rue St. Maur, with its muddy gutter in the centre, and a melancholy oil lamp swinging from a rope, above the gutter. Our first Paris home was in a pleasant furnished apartment, *au second,* in a fine old hotel, once occupied by a ducal dignitary of the day of Louis XIV. Towards the street it was a most gloomy looking building, blank gray walls. But, once within the *porte-cochére,* all was changed; there was a lovely garden of more than an acre, with other adjoining gardens, all surrounded with stone walls at least twelve feet high, while groves of fine trees appeared above the walls. The hotel itself was on a grand scale—a noble stone stairway, with elaborate iron railing, rooms with very high ceilings, wide doorways, with pictured panels above and gilt lines on the woodwork—large windows, and parquet floors, of course.

The years that followed were far from dull for the Coopers. Cooper was lionized to a considerable degree, the family was intimate with such important personages as Lafayette and the Princess Galitzin. In writing for her nieces and nephews, Miss Cooper says:[7]

> The Princess Galitzin was an elderly lady, very clever, a very kind friend of your grandmother and grandfather. Madame de Terzè, the Princess' daughter, gave a brilliant affair, I remember, to which we four little sisters were invited. Another child's party was given by Madame de Vivien for her granddaughters, Mesdemoiselles de Lostange. The whole Hotel was open, and brilliantly lighted, and a company of cuirassiers in full uniform were on guard in the court and adjoining street, to keep order among the coachmen and footmen. That was the most brilliant affair of the kind that I ever attended, in my childish days.

So we know that the young Miss Sue Cooper who returned from Europe in October of 1833 after two years spent in Paris at the school of Madame Trigant de le Tour and Madame Kautz and five years in Italy and travelling on the Continent of Europe was an accomplished young person. We know too that she had great psychic power—she frequently would move an inverted dining-table with a heavy man seated on a pile of books on it. This must have been an accomplishment of her salad days, however, for we are told that in later life, the sincerely devout Miss Cooper gave up this practice.[8] It is apparent also that the returning young lady was possessed of a clear, incisive mind; her letters show her shrewd and observant.

That such a woman, with her background, should turn to the pen was inevitable. The circumstances which dictated her choice of a theme for **Rural Hours** she herself attributes to her earliest years:[9]

> I often drove with my Grandfather De Lancey about his farms and into his woods [while she lived at Angevine] and it was my duty to jump out and open all the gates. In these drives he taught me to distinguish the different trees by their growth, and bark, and foliage— this was a beech, that an oak, here was an ash, yonder a tulip-tree. He would point out a tree and ask me to name it, going through a regular lesson in a very pleasant way. Such was the beginning of my **Rural Hours** ideas.

Her father's influence was strong in this, too, as in so many other things. She says:[10]

> In his own garden he took very great pleasure, passing hours at a time there during the summer months . . . It was his great delight to watch the growth of the different plants, day by day. His hot beds were always among the earliest in the village.

But the publication of **Rural Hours** was soon followed by what may well have been the severest cross in *Susan Cooper's* life, her father's death one day before his sixty-second birthday, on September 14, 1851. At any rate, from then on the Mary in her character, concentrated on the business of literature, seems to have yielded to the Martha, busied about many things. Her energy was diffused in numerous charities: the Hospital, a Home for Old Women, and, perhaps most important of all, the Orphan House of the Holy Savior, founded in 1873. Beginning with five inmates, the latter prospered so under her guidance that in 1881 the local paper recorded, "Miss Cooper began this Fall to solicit subscriptions for a fund to be used in the erection of a new Orphan House, the building now occupied being much too small." By its tenth anniversary the institution could boast a plant sufficient for the housing and education of a hundred boys and girls. Besides these more effective philanthropies, Susan Cooper's interest in the affairs of the town which had alternately cherished and differed with the family of its founder ranged so widely that on one occasion it is even entered on the record that she took up cudgels to prevent the moving of the graves out of a local churchyard when this was contemplated!

Perhaps the absorption in doing good that Susan Cooper manifested after 1851, a busyness that seems almost a form of escapism from the hard concentration and inner growth that would have been necessary to pursue the path on which she had set her foot with *Rural Hours,* was a reflection of the disgust with literature and the literary life her father had been feeling in his later years. This might account for a curious episode that occurred before the novelist's death, for which we are still paying heavily today. In the words of her nephew:[11]

> Shortly before his death, while sitting on a sofa beside his eldest child, Susan Augusta, he [the novelist] said to her that he wished his family not to authorize the publication of any biography. There was even then a difference of opinion in the family as to the extent of the prohibition intended; some members believing that it was only a temporary one prompted by the bitterness still felt toward Cooper by much of the press of the country on account of his libel suits. Acting on the other theory, however, his eldest daughter, before she died, destroyed a great deal of the material which could have been used in the preparation of a biography, and had buried with her the most interesting of his Journals.

Or perhaps the clue to Susan Cooper's failure to face the obligations of her talent is to be found farther back, in her childhood and early youth. There is a hint to the solution in a letter written by Mrs. Cooper from Paris to her sister in Westchester, dated 4 March, 1827, in which we read:[12]

> Sue goes on very well with her painting. And they all dance very prettily; on Monday next they are to be at a little party at the Marquise de Terzè's, where there is to be a show of magic lantern. You must not be alarmed— this will only be the second time they have been out this winter, excepting their School ball.

And again and again throughout her correspondence we find Mrs. Cooper reassuring her sisters and her father that the girls have not been exposed to dancing on Sunday or other similar evils then current in European Society.

Those were the days when even Mother didn't know best. That prerogative was still almost exclusively Father's. And so from the Cooper parental pen comes our knowledge of romance in the life of young Sue Cooper. Writing to his nephew, Richard Cooper, in Cooperstown from Paris in 1833, he said:[13]

> You speak of some report as in connexion with Mr. Morse and your eldest cousin. Surely they who speak of such a thing can have no idea of the fitness of things. Mr. Morse is an old friend of mine, but neither of my daughters would dream of making a husband of him. Morse is an excellent man, but not just the one to captivate a fine young woman of twenty. I had proposals for Susan, last week, coming from a Frenchman of good fortune, noble family, and very fair looks, but the thing would not do. We mean to continue Americans. These things, however, ought always to be respected as family secrets. You can contradict the silly report about Mr. Morse, with confidence.

The "Mr. Morse" in question is Samuel F. B. Morse, inventor of the telegraph, and long an intimate friend of the novelist and his family. How different might this whole story have been if Fenimore-Cooper had been "willing to yield so fair a prize" to either Morse or the young Frenchman of "very fair looks."

The Cooper girls were members of a family group that was particularly close and devoted to one another. No one of them probably ever questioned, nor had any right to question, but that she was born into the best of all families and the finest of all days. But they were reared in the stern French Huguenot (De Lancey) tradition in the first quarter of the Nineteenth Century, a time when woman's place, if not exclusively in the home, was still in homely pursuits. We found the word "prim" in a description of Miss Cooper earlier in this article and that is perhaps the solution to our puzzle. Neither her immediate family circle nor the century into which she was born gave a woman freedom to develop creative talents. Some women might, and did, break their fetters to achieve largely but Susan Cooper was not aggressive for herself, only for others. That, in all likelihood, is the reason why no great stream of books flowed from her pen, no living, lusty children of her brain stepped forth to tread the hills where Leatherstocking roamed and sail the waters Judith and Hetty Hutter knew.

Perhaps it is true that "the fault . . . is in ourselves, that we are underlings" but the same wise pen wrote that "the time is out of joint." Certainly for Susan Cooper's gentle talent it was so.

Notes

1. Susan Fenimore Cooper, "Small Family Memories," Cooper, ed., *Correspondence of James Fenimore-Cooper* (New Haven, 1922), I, 10-11.

2. J. F. Cooper, ed., *Correspondence of James Fenimore Cooper* (New Haven, 1922), II, 673-674.

3. *Ibid.,* II, 671-672.

4. Ralph Birdsall, *The Story of Cooperstown* (New York, 1925) 334-335.

5. S. F. Cooper, *op. cit.,* 38-39.

6. *Ibid.,* 62-63.

7. *Ibid.,* 66.

8. J. F. Cooper, *Legends and Traditions of a Northern County,* (New York, 1921), 44.

9. S. F. Cooper, *op. cit.*, 32-33.

10. J. F. Cooper, *The Crater* (Household Edition, 1880), preface, 10-11.

11. J. F. Cooper, [grandson] *op. cit.*, I, 3.

12. *Ibid.*, I, 122.

13. *Ibid.*, 314.

Lucy B. Maddox (essay date June 1988)

SOURCE: Maddox, Lucy B. "Susan Fenimore Cooper and the Plain Daughters of America." *American Quarterly* 40, no. 2 (June 1988): 131-46.

[*In the following essay, Maddox examines Cooper's relationship with her famous father and the way it informed her writings, particularly her novel,* Elinor Wyllys, *and her nature journal,* Rural Hours.]

The story of the way James Fenimore Cooper began his career as a novelist has by now entered the folklore of American literature. Readers who first encounter Cooper in an anthology are likely to learn from the introduction that his first novel was written in response to his wife's challenge: to write something better and more interesting than the imported novel of English manners he was in the process of reading aloud to his family. The eventual result of that challenge was the Leatherstocking novels, a series that was to earn him his reputation as the originator of an American hero-myth and the author of an American tradition in fiction. The source of the famous anecdote was Cooper's oldest daughter, Susan Fenimore Cooper, the only one of his five children to follow him in becoming a writer, and the person he chose to be his literary executor. While her own career as a writer was briefer and much more modest than that of her father, it illustrates in an especially personal and focused way the complex constraints on the woman writer in mid-nineteenth century America, writing within a space that has already been defined for her by the literary fathers. In all of her published writing, Susan Cooper revealed a self-conscious sense of her identity as the inheritor and guardian of her father's vision of America, in which the role of the daughter is defined as crucially important to the future of the nation.

Fenimore Cooper had set out that vision most effusively in *Notions of the Americans*,[1] in which he argued explicitly for the superiority of American culture to the exhausted European culture that the new country was, in his view, designed by nature to replace. The book consists of a series of responses to the American scene by a fictitious travelling bachelor, identified only as European, who is visiting the new republic for the first time. In the opening scenes of the book, the bachelor and his American companion, Cadwallader, make the acquaintance of a young American girl named Isabel. The girl presents "a simple picture, in which delicacy, feminine beauty, and the most commendable ingenuousness, were admirably mingled" (1:25). The two gentlemen escort the young lady to her home, where she is greeted with happy tears all around; once her "foot was on the threshold of her father's house . . . nature was awakened in all its best and sweetest sympathies" (1:31). Observing this scene leads Cadwallader to remark that "Notwithstanding all that the old world has said of itself on this subject, . . . you are now in the true Paradise of women" (1:49). The bachelor soon begins to understand the full import of what he has seen and heard:

> After all, what nobler or more convincing proof of high civilization can be given than this habitual respect of the strong for the weak? The condition of women in this country is solely owing to the elevation of its moral feeling. . . . To me, woman appears to fill in America the very station for which she was designed by nature. In the lowest conditions of life she is treated with the tenderness and respect that is due to beings whom we believe to be the repositories of the better principles of our nature. Retired within the sacred precincts of her own abode, she is preserved from the destroying taint of excessive intercourse with the world. . . .
>
> (1:104-05)

The sophisticated European is thus ushered into the moral heart of America by the young female, the daughter whose natural place is the home of her father. Cooper offers her as a kind of official greeter for the new country, toward which the eyes of the rest of the civilized world are turned with skeptical curiosity. Her "condition" is both an advertisement for the moral and cultural health of the country and, not incidentally, an implicit protection against the "manly interest" of the foreign bachelor.

Cooper's sunny image of the daughter who freely chooses to inhabit exactly that domestic, patriarchal place "for which she was designed by nature" is indeed a "simple picture" and a familiar one, largely indistinguishable from the many other sentimentalized portraits of woman as "the moral guardian for all society"[2] that were produced by both male and female writers in nineteenth-century America. Behind Cooper's flattened image of the young Isabel, however, lie his rather complex theories about the origin and evolution of American culture, theories which are dramatized over and over in his novels—especially in the Leatherstocking series—in terms of the relationships between fathers and daughters. In those novels, Cooper attempted the inscription of an American daughter-myth to complement the masculine hero-myth embodied in the figure of the childless man of the woods, Natty Bumppo.

The centrality of the father-daughter relationship to Cooper's interpretation of the American past is suggested by the opening scenes of *The Pioneers*, the first of the Leatherstocking novels.[3] The book begins as the widowed father, Judge Temple, is escorting his daughter and only heir, Elizabeth, to the home he has built in the frontier settlement of Otsego, New York. Elizabeth, who has been living in the city while she completed the "juvenile labors" (*Leatherstocking*, 1:17) of getting an education, returns to the frontier prepared both to inherit the extensive estate of her father and to understand the nature of the sacrifices, physical and moral, that were required of the father in his work of establishing a settlement. The appearance in the opening scene of the two old men of the woods, the white Natty Bumppo and the Indian Chingachgook, reminds Elizabeth and the reader that the land was inhabited by others before settlers like the Temples arrived and that, no matter how legal the process of acquisition has been, the land that Elizabeth will inherit has, undeniably, "been wrested by violence from others" (34). It is also clear from the beginning that the work of settlement has worn the Judge physically; as he will explain to Elizabeth later, "pain, famine, and disease" were all part of the price he and others paid, a price that newcomers are likely to overlook: "No, Bess, . . . he who hears of the settlement of a country, knows but little of the toil and suffering by which it is accomplished. Unimproved and wild as this district now seems to your eyes, what was it when I first entered the hills!" (233, 236). The daughter listens with sympathy and responds with gratitude; she understands that the father has had to sacrifice both his body and his moral integrity to a battle with the wilderness in order to prepare a place that the daughter can inherit, a place in which moral and physical violence are no longer necessary.

In her study of the diaries and journals of women who moved to the American frontier, Annette Kolodny concludes that "women avoided male anguish at lost Edens and male guilt in the face of the raping of the continent" by imagining the frontier primarily as a potential garden and themselves as its potential cultivators.[4] In Cooper's novels, the woman who comes to cultivate the cleared space is not only avoiding the male experience but providing its moral justification as well. When Elizabeth Temple marries at the end of *The Pioneers*, she and her husband establish themselves in the father's house and say a tearful farewell to the now displaced woodsman, Natty Bumppo. In the moral scheme of the book, Elizabeth is Natty's heir as well as the Judge's; by replacing Natty, Elizabeth moves the moral center of the book (and the settlement) indoors, relocating it in the heart of the patriarchal family. Her continuing presence in the father's home will, Cooper implies, eventually redeem the father's crimes against the woods and the woodsmen.

The pattern of inheritance that Cooper dramatized in detail in *The Pioneers* is reflected repeatedly in the other novels. The fathers enter the wilderness as soldiers, hunters, or even (like Old Hutter of *The Deerslayer*) as fugitive criminals, to begin the violent process of settlement. The daughters follow, and it is their vulnerability that both necessitates and justifies the violence of the fathers. The space that the daughters are to occupy must first be cleared if the daughters are not to be destroyed—morally or physically—by contact with the wilderness and its savage inhabitants. The crucial importance of the father's success in clearing a space is indicated by the fate of the two Ruths, mother and daughter, of *The Wept of Wish-Ton-Wish*.[5] The first Ruth lives happily in a stockaded frontier farm built by her father-in-law, a retired soldier and fierce Puritan (the setting of the novel is "less than half a century" after the Plymouth landing [1]). Ruth thrives in the protected space provided by the stern patriarch: "Her situation was one eminently fitted to foster the best affections of woman, since it admitted of few temptations to yield to other than the most natural feelings" (100). The fate of the second Ruth, her daughter, is much less happy. When the responsibility for the family passes from the fierce old man to his weaker son, the Indians also return across the cleared space to invade the stockade and carry off the female child. This Ruth is restored to the family years later, but when she returns she brings with her the half-breed infant son that is, for Cooper, the tangible symbol of her irrevocable alienation from her natural place within the white family: "She stood . . . in the centre of the grave, self-restrained group of her nearest kin, like an alien to their blood, resembling some timid and but half-tamed tenant of the air" (349). Because of the father's failure, the daughter becomes a victim of the wilderness, dispossessed of family and of selfhood. The Indians and white hunters, like Natty Bumppo, find their natural home in the moral freedom of the wilderness; but the wilderness must eventually give way to the cleared, enclosed space, since it is only there that the inheritors of the American place, the white daughters, can survive.

Given this evidence of Cooper's efforts to create a myth of the inheriting daughter that would be as compelling as the accompanying myth of the childless man of the woods, it is entirely appropriate that the writer who took over the daughter myth most directly and developed it most explicitly was his own daughter, Susan. The extent to which both Coopers saw the daughter as the right successor to the father is suggested by his appointment of her as his literary executor, at a time when his reputation as a writer had become thoroughly embattled. Susan Cooper was more than dutiful in publicly defending her father's work after his death, not only providing prefaces to editions of his novels, a reverential memoir to accompany her anthology of extracts from his novels, and a biography of his lifelong friend,

Commodore William Branford Shubrick, but also frequently paraphrasing her father's words in her own writing:

> In no country is the protection given to woman's helplessness more full and free—in no country is the assistance she receives from the stronger arm so general—and nowhere does her weakness meet with more forebearance and consideration. . . . The position accorded to her is favorable; it remains for her to fill it in a manner worthy her own sex, gratefully, kindly, and simply. . . .[6]

Susan Cooper's gratitude to her father is most visibly documented in the work she produced as his literary executor, but the more complex aspects of her relationship to him are reflected in the writing she produced in an effort to become the first of his successors—specifically in her novel, *Elinor Wyllys* (1846); her journal of a year in Cooperstown, published as *Rural Hours* (1850); her edition of John Leonard Knapp's *Country Rambles in England* (1853); and her anthology of nature writing, *The Rhyme and Reason of Country Life* (1854).

George Henry Lewes declared in 1852 that "to write as men write is the aim and besetting sin of women; to write as women is the real task they have to perform."[7] Susan Cooper's writing illustrates the special situation that arises when the woman defines herself primarily as daughter, and particularly when she defines herself as the daughter of a writing father whose own successful work enshrines the virtuous daughter and projects her role as the one most crucial to the healthy growth of a young nation. The situation for Susan Cooper was complicated by her awareness that Fenimore Cooper had successfully taken on himself the role of one of the principal "fathers" of an emerging tradition in American literature. For her, that role entitled him to special deference and respect, especially from his female heirs—both literal and figurative. In a small book she wrote about Mount Vernon, the home of another important national "father," Susan Cooper noted that "the solemn guardianship of the home, and of the grave, of George Washington is now offered to us, the women of the country."[8] That emphasis on the American woman's duty as inheritor and guardian of the legacy left by the pioneering males constitutes the strongest theme in all of Susan Cooper's writing.

Susan Cooper's situation was further complicated, in a more personal way, by the nature of her father's attitude toward the oldest of his four daughters. Fenimore Cooper's correspondence suggests that he was well pleased with his daughters, finding them "all that I could desire—natural, simple, sincere, obedient and intelligent."[9] Susan, however, he singled out for special praise, in part because she was the daughter with the strongest inclination to remain under the paternal roof. When she was nineteen, he noted approvingly that "[Susan] has

the good sense to know that this is the time to work, and I do not know that I ever heard her express a desire to go into the world."[10] The father's implied fear that the daughter might marry and leave home became more explicit as they both grew older:

> I had proposals for Susan last week, coming from a Frenchman of good fortune, noble family, and very fair hopes, but the thing would not do. We mean to continue Americans.
>
> I am horribly afraid for [Susan]. She is so pretty and good, and engaging, and all that, I fear some fellow will be after her.[11]

This last and most anxious remark was written in 1851, the year of Fenimore Cooper's death, when Susan was thirty-eight.

The most curious aspect of Fenimore Cooper's paternal possessiveness appears in his attempt to find in Susan an adequate replacement for his sister Hannah, who was killed in a riding accident when Cooper was eleven. The strength of his attachment to Hannah, or at least to her memory, is indicated by his heated reaction to a reader's suggestion that Hannah was the model for Elizabeth Temple, the heroine of *The Pioneers*. Cooper declared himself wounded by the implication "that one whom he regarded with a reverence that surpassed the love of a brother, was converted by him into the heroine of a work of fiction."[12] He repeated the disclaimer in a footnote in the revised edition of *The Pioneers,* and concluded the note by asserting that "few of her sex and years were . . . more universally beloved, than the admirable woman who thus fell a victim to the chances of the wilderness" (*Leatherstocking,* 1:234n). The phrasing of the note is suggestive of what may have been a powerful psychological motivation behind his repeated fictional portraits of vulnerable young women whose susceptibilities to the "chances of the wilderness" require the constant protection of strong males. It may also suggest a reason for Cooper's possessive attitude toward his own favorite daughter. His private correspondence indicates clearly that if he was loath to use his perfect sister as the model for a fictional heroine, he was not at all reluctant to reincarnate her in his real daughter:

> How I love that child! Her countenance is that of a sister I lost, by a fall from a horse, half a century since, and her character is very much the same. They were, and are, as perfect as it falls to the lot of humanity to be. I am in love with Sue, and have told her so, fifty times. She refuses me, but promises to live on in gentle friendship, and, my passion not being at all turbulent, I do not see but this may do.[13]

The tone of this remarkable protestation is difficult to decipher, especially since it was written by the sixty-year-old Cooper to a young girl (Sarah Heyward

Cruger), the daughter of a family friend. No matter how whimsical or avuncular the tone was meant to be, however, certain implications are clear; the father was willing to offer his daughter as a model of the perfect generic female—sister, child, lover, and friend—whose weakness entitles her to protection and whose stainless moral character entitles her to be beloved.

There is no evidence that Susan Cooper openly resisted the formidable psychological burden imposed on her by her father. As Stephen Railton has observed, "Devoted is probably not too strong a word" to describe her behavior toward him.[14] As a writer, however, she necessarily put herself in the difficult position of threatening to compete with her father. Her efforts to find an accommodating position are suggested by the names she used to sign her writing: when she wrote as her father's literary executor, supplying prefaces to his novels or an account of his life, she signed that writing with the name of the daughter—Susan Fenimore Cooper. When she wrote her own books, however, and thus implied competition with her father, she did not use the identifiable name. The novel **Elinor Wyllys** was published under the protectively self-deprecating pseudonym "Amabel Penfeather"; **Rural Hours,** an account of Cooperstown that could invite comparison with her father's fictional account of the village in *The Pioneers,* was identified only as the work of "a lady"; and her introduction to **The Rhyme and Reason of Country Life** is signed "the author of **Rural Hours,** etc." By omitting the father's name, Susan Cooper could put herself on an equal footing with other "ladies" writing, pseudonymously or not, in the middle of the nineteenth century; furthermore, by concealing the presence of the demanding father, she could give additional force to her public choice of the role of the good American daughter.

The father was pleased with the daughter's work: in writing to Susan about the manuscript of **Rural Hours,** he praised it for its "purity of mind" and "simplicity"[15]; in writing to his wife he was more candid:

> I have written to Sue to say how much I am pleased with her book—it is not strong, perhaps, but is so pure, and so elegant, so very feminine and charming that I do not doubt, now, of its eventual success—I say *eventual,* for, at first, the world will not know what to make of it. . . . She has struggled nobly, and deserves success. At any rate, she has pleased us, and that is a great deal for so dear a child.[16]

While Cooper does not explain the reasons for his concern about the reception of the book, it makes sense that he would consider "the world" still puzzled by the kind of daughter's book for which his own work had so carefully prepared the way. In another letter, Fenimore Cooper predicted to his friend William Branford Shubrick that **Rural Hours** "will make [Susan] *the* Cooper, at once."[17] The comment suggests that the father had in

his own mind designated as his natural successor the daughter whose "purity of mind" and "simplicity" fit her to occupy the space provided by the father, and whose feminine lack of strength would prevent her from ever overshadowing the father.

Susan Cooper not only accepted her father's idea that simplicity is a requirement for the good daughter, she urged it. The implications of this idea for her are suggested by her uses of the Old Testament story of Ruth—a model of the life of the exemplary woman that Fenimore Cooper had also alluded to in his portrait of Ruth Heathcote, the faithful daughter-in-law of *The Wept of Wish-Ton-Wish.* In **Rural Hours,** Cooper describes the account of Ruth as a "wholly beautiful" story that is "all pure simplicity, nature and truth, in every line" (258). Significantly, Cooper is insistent that a full appreciation of the story requires our assumption that Ruth was herself a *physically* plain woman. Since "it is nowhere said that Ruth was beautiful," then should we not "please ourselves with believing that Ruth was not beautiful; that she had merely one of those faces which come and go without being followed, except by those that know and love them?" (260-61) The beauty of Ruth's story is in her faithfulness and constancy as a daughter-in-law to Naomi. In this case the dutifulness of Ruth is rewarded in a striking way: she is noticed by her elder kinsman Boaz, who praises her publicly and approves so much of her virtue that he marries her. In the King James version, which was surely Susan Cooper's source, Boaz addresses Ruth twice as "my daughter" and specifically praises her because she "followedst not young men." The narrative that Cooper offers as an illustration of both moral and aesthetic beauty thus becomes, in addition, a story of the plain daughter's rewards for simplicity and restraint: she earns her entry into the home of the elder kinsman, the surrogate father, who demonstrates his approval not only by marrying her but also by establishing her public reputation.

Elinor Wyllys,[18] Susan Cooper's only published novel, is in some ways a recasting of the Ruth story, with the additions and adjustments required by the American setting. The action of the novel moves in and out of a place called Longbridge, which is, like Cooperstown, a small community in upstate New York. The configuration of characters at the beginning of the novel is a variation of the ideal Ruth-Naomi-Boaz grouping: living together at Wyllys-Roof, the paternal home, are the amiable father, Mr. Wyllys; his unmarried, middle-aged daughter Agnes; and the eponymous Elinor, an orphan granddaughter of Mr. Wyllys who has been taken in by her grandfather and aunt. Like Ruth, Elinor is far from beautiful; her family acknowledges that she is "plain," while strangers more bluntly call her ugly. In this opening arrangement, the role of the daughter is split into two of its most predictable psychological components: Elinor is the good child who is willingly received into the father's household, while the older Agnes assumes the position of the father's wife in caring for the child. This arrangement is threatened only by the potentially disruptive presence of the eligible young male cousin, Harry Hazlehurst, who is presented immediately as an appropriate future husband for Elinor. The agenda of the novel is to accomplish the assimilation of the young male into the patriarchal household without either displacing the father or estranging the daughters from him.

In its general contours, *Elinor Wyllys* fits a familiar pattern, taking its place quietly among the other "books from the pens of women" that Lydia Maria Child noted were being "poured forth by hundreds" in the America of 1848.[19] In her survey of this body of mid-century fiction by American women, Nina Baym concludes that the many novels finally tell one basic story over and over: "In essence, it is the story of a young girl who is deprived of the supports she had rightly or wrongly depended on to sustain her throughout life and is faced with the necessity of winning her own way in the world."[20] The young female protagonist, Baym points out, is usually an orphan who has to struggle within a highly socialized environment, and whose problems can only be satisfactorily resolved through marriage. The happy marriage is then a frequent ending to the woman novelist's story, "which is in most primitive terms the story of the formation and assertion of a feminine ego."[21] Susan Cooper's Elinor, the orphan who achieves a happy marriage at the end of the novel, seems thus to have been drawn to fit and even reinforce a popular sentimental formula. Where Cooper's novel departs from the formula, however, is in imaging the defining role of the American female as daughter rather than as potential wife; as daughter, her identity, or "feminine ego," is already formed and needs only an appropriate space in which to flourish. Like her father, Susan Cooper is much less concerned with examining the psychology of her female characters than with delineating their fixed place within a changing social environment. There is, therefore, no sign in her novel of the "deep discontent" that Mary Kelley finds underlying the patterns of mid-century women's fiction and that leads her to conclude that "the fiction of the sentimentalists is, finally, expressive of a dark vision of nineteenth-century America, and not, as they wished, of the redemptive, idyllic, holy land."[22] Susan Cooper's heroine, like her father's, plays a redemptive role simply by her presence; what is required of her is only the patience to wait until the rest of the world—including her potential husband—comes around to valuing the quiet plainness that, for both Coopers, makes the good daughter the most appropriate symbol of the new state of the American place.

Cooper makes it clear from the beginning that Elinor is so completely and perfectly *at home* as a daughter at Wyllys-Roof as to seem almost an organic extension of the place. The house itself is a "comfortable, sensible-looking place, . . . such as were planned some eighty or a hundred years since, by men who had fortune enough to do as they pleased, and education enough to be superior to all pretension" (1:7). Surrounding this patriarchal structure is an appropriately feminine adjunct, a simple border of native flowers: "There was not a hybrid among them, not a single blossom but what bore a plain, honest name; . . . they were the commonest varieties only" (1:8-9). In this rather fiercely American place, the orphan Elinor, the plain daughter whose "appearance exposed her to be entirely overlooked and neglected by strangers" (1:41), can grow like a native plant or a native house, combining the natural simplicity of the former with the sensible sturdiness of the latter: "Her whole manner, indeed, was always natural; its simplicity was its great charm, for one felt confident that her grace and sweetness, her ease and quiet dignity, flowed readily from her character itself" (2:109).

Elinor's moral education is essentially complete at the opening of the novel, since her physical plainness has prevented any interference with the natural development of her authentic nature: her "pleasing manner, . . . so frank, yet so feminine, so simple, yet so graceful, was only the natural result of her character, and her very want of beauty" (1:148). The course of Harry Hazlehurst's moral education, however, is slower and rockier—in part because as a young male with no settled home he is free (unlike Elinor) to wander away from the steadying American environment. His first excursion is to France, in the company of another young man from Longbridge, Charlie Hubbard. Both young Americans are dazzled by their sudden confrontation with the aesthetic richness of French culture, which presents a striking contrast to the simple prettiness of Longbridge. Charlie Hubbard's introduction to European art has a salutary effect, in that it confirms his decision to become a painter. He returns home with a more sophisticated ability to recognize the peculiar beauty in the simplicity of the American landscape. He now "looks with a painter's eye at the country; the scenery is of the simplest kind, yet beautiful" (2:7-8). Harry also has his eyes opened by his stay in France, but because he is not an artist himself, his excitement at discovering beauty in so many new forms is quickly misdirected into a passion for his beautiful *other* cousin, Jane Graham: "This course of aesthetics gradually carried Harry so far, that after a profound study of the subject in general, and of Jane's features in particular, he became a convert to the opinion of the German philosopher, who affirms that 'the Beautiful is greater than the Good'" (1:73). Fortunately, the lovely Jane refuses Harry and thus initiates another "course of aesthetics," this time a long one that will eventually bring him back to Longbridge with a mature appreciation of the simple dignity to be found in the American landscape, in

American art (particularly landscape art), and especially in his plain American cousin, Elinor.

One of the more curious signs of Harry's healthy conversion on his return to America is that he begins collecting books, especially botanical works. The significance of this odd detail becomes clear when one contrasts Harry's attraction to nature writing with the literary inclinations of some of the other characters. Among the silliest and most pretentious of the young married ladies of Longbridge, for example, is a Mrs. Hilson, whose credulous reading of foreign novels is the immediate cause of her scandalous flirtation with a visiting French dandy. Mrs. Hilson has never been to Europe, but has gotten her "silly ambition of playing the fine lady" from reading "certain European novels" (2:192). The seductive novels convince Mrs. Hilson that the true paradise of women is to be found not in democratic America but in aristocratic Europe:

> What is it that makes the patrician orders so delightful in Europe?—all those who know anything about it, will tell you that it is because the married women are not slaves; they have full liberty, and do just as they fancy, and have as many admirers as they please; this very book that I am reading says so. That is the way things are managed in high life in Europe.
>
> (2:195)

Under the influence of her European novels, Mrs. Hilson adopts a Parisian coiffure and a vaguely British accent and proceeds to assert her liberty by publicly parading her genuine French admirer. As a result, she not only destroys her marriage, but—more importantly for Susan Cooper—she "filled with the bitterest grief, the heart of an indulgent father" (2:195).

The unhappy fate of Mrs. Hilson, who disgraces herself with both husband and father through her impressionable reading of foreign books, casts an interesting light on Susan Cooper's sense of her own function as a writer. The discussion of the social and moral implications of what women read suggests that Cooper accepted her responsibility, as a writing daughter, to produce the kind of books that could keep the Mrs. Hilsons of America within the patriarchal home rather than enticing them out of it. Considered abstractly, the ideal texts might be the botanical works that Harry comes to value (at the same time he comes to value Elinor and America), since in these the subject is unadorned nature itself, but the Mrs. Hilsons require more than botanical description and Latin nomenclature. Women readers, the implication is, look for models—just as Susan Cooper seems to have found her model in the story of Ruth and in the heroines of her father's fiction. As we have seen, *Elinor Wyllys* clearly offers such a model, with its reinforcing rewards, in the natural simplicity of Elinor; in *Rural Hours,* Cooper moves from the fictional model to a non-fictional demonstration of her own comfortable assimilation into the American patriarchal place, miniaturized in the father's home at Cooperstown.

Rural Hours was actually the third book about Cooperstown published by a member of the Cooper family. Susan's grandfather, William Cooper, had compiled an account of his participation in founding the village, which he published in 1810 as *A Guide to the Wilderness.* Fenimore Cooper then incorporated his father's experiences into his fictional account of the settlement in *The Pioneers*—the novel that ends with the daughter's inheritance of the estate her male progenitors have carved out of the wilderness. *Rural Hours* thus completes a pattern, providing final documentation of the moral and cultural significance of the great undertaking that begins with the grandfather's confrontation of the wilderness and ends with the daughter's inheritance of a place that is no longer wild but comfortably rural. In her introduction to *The Rhyme and Reason of Country Life,* published four years after *Rural Hours,* Cooper concluded that "the moment has come when in American society many of the higher influences of civilization may rather be sought in the fields, when we may learn there many valuable lessons of life, and particularly all the happy lessons of simplicity."[23] The lessons of simplicity in *Rural Hours* are themselves rather complex lessons which constantly return, implicitly, to the central issues of the daughter's location in the domesticated landscape of America and the voice that she can use to speak from, and about, that place.

One object of the daughter's voice in *Rural Hours* is to continue the process of domesticating the American language, making it as simple and functional as the American objects it describes. The failure to achieve an indigenous language is, for Susan Cooper, the equivalent of displacement from one's psychological home. In the introduction to her edition of John Leonard Knapp's *Country Rambles,* Cooper describes the problem this way:

> We are still, in some sense, half aliens to the country Providence has given us; there is much ignorance among us regarding the creatures which held the land as their own long before our forefathers trod the soil, and many of which are still moving about us, living accessories of our existence, at the present hour. On the other hand, again, English reading has made us very familiar with the names, at least, of those races which people the old world. . . . Thus it is that knowing so little of the creatures in whose midst we live, and mentally familiar by our daily reading with the tribes of another hemisphere, the forms of one continent and the names and characters of another, are strangely blended in most American minds. And in this dream-like phantasmagoria, where fancy and reality are often so widely at variance, in which the objects we see, and those we read of are wholly different, and where bird and beast undergo metamorphoses so strange, most of us are content to pass through life.[24]

The language that Americans acquire from their "English reading" is therefore as artificial and disorienting as is the image of woman's happiness that Mrs. Hilson absorbs from her reading of European novels—and in both cases, the result is separation from the patriarchal place. Since the problem is best addressed by replacing English books with American books written in an American idiom—especially books for women readers—Susan Cooper's contribution in **Rural Hours** can be seen as the daughter's continuation, on a modest scale, of the more revolutionary efforts to liberate Americans from their dependence on England that were initiated by the fathers—through the settlement of a continent, the waging of a war, or the authoring of a native literary tradition.

Part of the daughter's work as a writer is to supply the particular names and details that will anchor the patriarchal tradition in a specific local landscape. Susan Cooper's references to the "creatures" of that landscape in her introduction to Knapp appear to include the Indians, those who once "held the land as their own," as well as native plants and animals. The signatures of the Indians remain on the land primarily in the names of things; repeatedly in **Rural Hours** Susan Cooper evokes the Indians as the original namers of the components of the American landscape. Her language at times comes close to equating the Indians with the plants they lived among, presenting them both as the pure, uncorrupted, organic products of a special place:

> The wild natives of the woods grow there willingly, while many strangers, brought originally from over the Ocean, steal gradually onward from the tilled fields and gardens, until at last they stand side by side upon the same bank, the European weed and the wild native flower. These foreign intruders are a bold and hardy race, driving away the prettier natives. . . . It is remarkable that these troublesome plants have come very generally from the Old World; they do not belong here, but following the steps of the white man, they have crossed the ocean with him.
>
> (81)

The specific identity of these native people and plants who once shared the American place Cooper finds to be disappearing from the American consciousness, chiefly through the loss of names. Cooper deplores her neighbors' ignorance of "the common names of plants they must have seen all their lives" (135), just as she deplores the practice of replacing the Indian names with the absurd names supplied by "Yankee nomenclature" (484). The retention of Indian place-names has a moral as well as a practical justification, since the stability of the names is both a reminder and a measure of the Indians' loyalty to their own patriarchs: "Shall we, in a Christian land, claim to have less of justice, less of decency and natural feeling, than the rude heathen whose place on the earth we have taken; a race who carefully

watched over the burial-places of their fathers with unwavering fidelity?" (291) The good daughter can therefore use her voice to reaffirm both the linguistic authority of the Indian names and the moral authority of the Indians' fidelity to their fathers: "A name is all we leave them, let us at least preserve that monument to their memory" (485).

There are many indications in **Rural Hours** that Cooper saw the reaffirmation of both kinds of authority as an appropriate form of woman's work, primarily because, she implies, the woman is instinctively responsive to the world of nature—the ultimate source of both linguistic and moral authority. She is therefore the one best prepared to recognize and translate the moral lessons provided by nature. In the rose, for example, she recognizes a symbol of modesty, "and modesty in every true-hearted woman is, like affection, a growth of her very nature, whose roots are fed with her life's blood" (123). The American house-wren, in addition to being sweet and cheerful, is a model of monogamous fidelity; the arbutus, which blooms predictably in the same place and at the same time each year, is an example of the virtue of constancy, "which has a reward above all that fickle change can bestow, giving strength and purity to every affection of life, and even throwing additional grace about the flowers which bloom in our native fields" (49). Nature therefore offers women simple models that confirm the virtues to which they are instinctively drawn, just as the women of Cooper's village are "attracted by the wildflowers" (135): in return, the woman as writer can restore to the natural objects in the American landscape the simple, plain, unaffected names that are the only accurate ones.

One of the few "dramatic" passages in **Rural Hours** is an account of the surprise visit made by three Oneida women to the Cooper home. Cooper uses the appearance of these "half-civilized" women to extend her implied argument that the moral virtues of the fully civilized woman are not learned but are hers *by nature*. She describes the Indian women as speaking to each other in a "wild but musical tone"; the voice of one is as "low and melancholy as the note of the whip-poor-will" (176). Their quiet demeanor is natural and winning: "their manners were so gentle and womanly, so free from anything coarse or rude in the midst of their untutored ignorance, that we were much pleased with the visit" (177). A return visit to the Indians' camping-place reveals that what is true for the women is not at all true for the men: they are lethargic, spiritless, marked by "the stamp of vice" (177). The contrast leads Cooper to conclude that the very naturalness and simplicity of the women make them better equipped to benefit from their contact with civilization:

> In the savage state, the women appear very inferior to the men, but in a half-civilized condition, they have much the advantage over the stronger sex. They are

rarely beautiful, but often very pleasing; their gentle expression, meek and subdued manner, low, musical voices, and mild, dark eyes, excite an interest in their favor, while one turns with pain and disgust from the brutal, stupid, drunken countenances too often seen among the men.

(180)

The gentleness, mildness, and plainness of the Indian women are taken as signs of their successful, natural evolution from the "savage" state toward the "civilized"—that is, toward the fully evolved state of the white woman in America. The women can move easily "from field labors to household tasks" (180) (just as Cooper's favorite, Ruth, moved gracefully from gleaning in Boaz's fields to being the mistress of his household). Presumably, for Cooper and for those of her readers who are "content to await the natural order of things" (23), these signs predict for the Indian women a full assimilation into the American "Paradise of women" and thus a full participation in the culture represented by the American daughter. The moral irreproachability of that culture could, eventually, justify even the slaughtering of "savages" that marked its beginnings.

This discussion of **Rural Hours** has focused on the book's definition of the territory inherited by the American daughter and its illustration of the possible uses of her voice. To present the book in this way is necessarily limiting, since much of it is actually taken up with a descriptive record of life in and around Cooperstown, arranged as journal entries for a calendar year. The entry for July 18, to take one example, consists entirely of brief descriptions of the plants that might be found blooming in the Cooperstown woods on that day of the year. When Cooper gives her full attention to descriptions of plant and animal life, she is as accurate and interesting an observer as any American naturalist writing before or since. Her writing in these descriptive passages contrasts sharply with the forced and almost formulaic quality of the more didactic passages; it is frequently reminiscent of the writing of Gilbert White, the English naturalist whose *Natural History of Selborne* Cooper described (along with Knapp's *Country Rambles*) as belonging to the "choice class" of books "which have opened spontaneously, one might almost say unconsciously, from the author's mind."[25] One interesting question for a contemporary reader is why Cooper did not limit her book to description, especially since her descriptive passages have exactly the quality of comfortable spontaneity that she admired in the male naturalists White and Knapp.

The answer to that question has everything to do with Cooper's consciousness of her position as a writing woman and especially as a writing daughter. Her books announce their special status as a daughter's books,

thereby removing them from competition with the father's books and fitting them up to meet the expectations imposed on them from without, especially from the father. One of the most crucial of those expectations is that the daughter's book will be artless, giving at least the appearance of the spontaneity that she admired in White and Knapp, but with this difference: since as a woman she is one of the "repositories of the better principles of our nature," then her writing must be not only "natural" but principled as well. She must, that is, dispense moral precepts and display a set of principles as if they were hers *by nature*. For the daughter to write a book that did not assume an overt moral stance would be, in short, unnatural. Susan Cooper's father had written that the eyes of all Europe, as well as the eyes of the American fathers, were on the daughters of America; in **Elinor Wyllys,** Susan Cooper had demonstrated her acceptance of the writing daughter's obligation to produce plain American books to replace the foreign novels that can turn the daughters away from their fathers. By using her writing to confirm the daughter's place as the natural heir and guardian of the American patriarchy, Cooper could not only demonstrate her gratitude and secure the father's approval; if she were modest and unassuming enough, she could, ironically, perhaps help to accomplish the final justification of the fathers.

Notes

1. James Fenimore Cooper, *The Travelling Bachelor: or, Notions of the Americans,* 2 vols. (New York, 1852). Hereafter page numbers cited in text.

2. Mary Kelley, "The Sentimentalists: Promise and Betrayal in the Home," *Signs* 4 (Spring 1979): 441.

3. James Fenimore Cooper, *The Leatherstocking Tales,* 2 vols. (New York, 1985). Hereafter page numbers cited in text.

4. Annette Kolodny, *The Land Before Her: Fantasy and Experience of the American Frontier, 1630-1860* (Chapel Hill, 1984), 7.

5. James Fenimore Cooper, *The Wept of Wish-Ton-Wish,* Leatherstocking ed. (New York: Putnam's, n.d.). Hereafter page numbers cited in text.

6. Susan Fenimore Cooper, *Rural Hours* (New York, 1850), 484. Hereafter page numbers cited in text.

7. George Henry Lewes, "The Lady Novelists," *Westminster Review* 58 (July 1852): 72.

8. Susan Fenimore Cooper, *Mount Vernon: A Letter to the Children of America* (New York, 1859), 70.

9. James Fenimore Cooper, *The Letters and Journals of James Fenimore Cooper,* ed. James Franklin Beard, 6 vols. (Cambridge, Mass., 1968), 2: 176.

10. Ibid.

11. Ibid., 2:375 and 6: 258-59.

12. Quoted in Susan Fenimore Cooper, *Pages and Pictures from the Writings of James Fenimore Cooper* (New York, 1861), 62-63.

13. Cooper, *Letters,* 6: 99.

14. Stephen Railton, *Fenimore Cooper: A Study of His Life and Imagination* (Princeton, 1978), 56.

15. Cooper, *Letters,* 6: 149.

16. Ibid., 6: 151.

17. Ibid., 6: 195.

18. Amabel Penfeather [Susan Fenimore Cooper], *Elinor Wyllys, or, The Young Folks of Longbridge,* ed. James Fenimore Cooper, 2 vols. (New York, 1846). Hereafter page numbers cited in text.

19. Lydia Maria Child, *Letters from New York,* 2nd ser. (New York, 1848), 106.

20. Nina Baym, *Woman's Fiction: A Guide to Novels by and about Women in America 1820-1870* (Ithaca, 1978), 11.

21. Ibid., 12.

22. Kelley, "The Sentimentalists," 436, 446.

23. Susan Fenimore Cooper, *The Rhyme and Reason of Country Life* (New York, 1854), 33-34.

24. John Leonard Knapp, *Country Rambles in England: or Journal of a Naturalist* (Buffalo, 1853), 16-17.

25. Ibid., 11.

Vera Norwood (essay date 1993)

SOURCE: Norwood, Vera. "Pleasures of the Country Life: Susan Fenimore Cooper and the Seasonal Tradition." In *Made from this Earth: American Women and Nature,* pp. 25-53. Chapel Hill: University of North Carolina Press, 1993.

[*In the following essay, Norwood discusses Cooper's entry into the male-dominated arena of nature writing, the specific gender issues she brought to the genre, and her continuing influence on women's nature writing well into the twentieth century.*]

We are none of us very knowing about the birds in this country, unless it be those scientific gentlemen who have devoted their attention especially to such subjects. The same remark applies in some measure to our native trees and plants; to our butterflies and insects. But little attention has yet been given by our people generally, to these subjects . . . Had works of this kind been as common in America as they are in England, the vol-

ume now in the reader's hands would not have been printed . . . But such as it is, written by a learner only, the book is offered to those whose interest in rural objects has been awakened, a sort of rustic primer, which may lead them, if they choose, to something higher.

—Susan Fenimore Cooper, *Rural Hours*

With the publication of her seasonal journal—*Rural Hours*—in 1850, Susan Fenimore Cooper stepped into the charmed circle of American writers who created and popularized the nature essay. Although there were a few precedents, such as William Bartram's late eighteenth-century *Travels,* not until the early nineteenth century did American writers and artists give voice to the beauties of the American landscape. William Cullen Bryant and Susan's father, James Fenimore Cooper, had written nature poems and novels based on the American country landscape for only a little more than twenty-five years. Ralph Waldo Emerson's *Nature* appeared in 1835. Henry David Thoreau had published his first essay only four years earlier and was still four years away from the introduction of *Walden.* John Burroughs's popular essays on birds would not appear for another fifteen years.[1] Obviously, all of these writers were men, although their adult reading public consisted of both men and women. Susan Cooper was the first woman to enter this company.[2] Her appearance not only sets the stage for women nature essayists, but also raises the question of how she and the men whose world she entered handled this new woman's public voice. For she also grew to womanhood during a very restrictive period in American women's history, when many northeastern, middle-class, Euro-American women were confined to the home and domesticity. Her life mirrored the picture of proper womanhood touted in ladies magazines and sentimental novels of the time.[3]

James Fenimore Cooper believed that members of the female sex were most suited to the privacies of home and needed the thoughtful protection of their men. Discouraged by both parents from marrying, Susan, the oldest daughter, never left the family home. Early in life she took on the role of assistant to her father's writing career.[4] Her parental fidelity was also instrumental to her education. Her family taught her to love the plants and animals of her native New York and exposed her to some of the premier naturalists and tastemakers of her day. In **"Small Family Memories,"** an autobiographical essay, she fondly remembers a flower garden kept by her Grandmother Cooper. Her maternal grandfather first introduced her to botanizing as he took her on drives throughout his property. Her father was an avid gardener and followed the new American landscape aesthetic espoused by Andrew Jackson Downing. Susan often rode with him around their Otsego properties, consulting with him on landscape design. James Fenimore Cooper's father, Judge William Cooper, had written one of the first American texts on the agricultural potential of the wilderness. His son retained an interest in the natural history of the region. Not only did father and daughter read widely in natural history; they had as visitors to their home such luminaries as Downing and Dr. James De Kay, author of an early New York zoology.[5] By the mid-nineteenth century such interest in nature was a socially condoned way for middle-class American women to display their civility. Susan received her training within the approved bounds of home under a watchful paternal eye. The effort signified her rejection of the frivolous materialism so much a threat to city women.

Cooper's writing career further demonstrates the importance of gender-role expectations in her life. Before the publication of *Rural Hours,* she had tried her hand at the domestic novel, a genre that was popular among female writers by mid-century. In 1846, under the pseudonym Amabel Penfeather, she published *Elinor Wyllys; or, The Young Folks of Longbridge* with her father's blessing and help. When the manuscript of *Rural Hours* was complete, James took on the public role of choosing a publisher and negotiating the financial deal. Susan remained secluded in the country, safe from the potentially coarsening impact of such city doings. The anonymity of *Rural Hours* attested to a fitting modesty. The mechanisms behind the publication of Susan Cooper's works mirror strategies of the women writers of the time, women Mary Kelley has dubbed "literary domestics." The content of her writing also fits the mold. Literary domestics brought the scenes and values of middle-class homes to a wide readership. They handled the tensions involved in such an effort by "disparaging and dismissing" their talent and by couching their literary role as an expansion of their domestic duty.[6]

Although her own domestic novel did not garner Cooper the kind of fame others achieved, *Rural Hours* did place her on the public stage. William Cullen Bryant and Washington Irving both knew of the book; Bryant wrote a favorable review. Downing encouraged Fredrika Bremer to read it as an example of American women's nature writing. And Henry David Thoreau cited her comments on loons in his journals.[7] Prefacing *Rural Hours* with a disclaimer, Cooper alerted the reader that she had written a "simple record" of the "little events" of her life that have slight "merit of their own" and "make no claim to scientific knowledge" (v). With such language, she carefully maintained female propriety. As the literary domestics centered around home, so she focused her nature essay on the family grounds. Such tactics upheld the social codes bounding Susan Cooper's public voice.

Rural Hours also benefited from changing ideas about the value of the native American landscape. Hans Huth has shown how the development of a strong set of nationalistic ideas in early nineteenth-century America al-

tered artists' and writers' portrayal of the natural landscape. Exemplifying this trend, the landscape painter, Thomas Cole, in 1835 wrote about the importance of familiarity with the "home" scene. Responding to Europeans' image of Americans living in a wilderness that contained no civilized history, Cole urged his countrymen and countrywomen to adopt the American landscape as a true and worthwhile domicile. James Fenimore Cooper was himself one of the early proponents of the value of sparsely settled, rural America over European cities. Encouraged to locate their homes in nature, Americans incorporated images of that landscape into their homes. Huth documents the rise of landscape painting and the frequent appearance of regional landscapes on such domestic appurtenances as glassware and wallpaper. Further, as the century progressed, the value of rural life increased as an antidote to America's own increasingly urban character. Country traditions in the old homestead—in touch with the seasons, the birds, and the trees—were inherently more moral than a life dominated by the artificial environment of the city.[8]

Who could better tell the story of America domestica than an individual whose own life mirrored what was most valuable in the national character? Secluded from urban corruption, often situated in the suburbs or the country, women like Susan Cooper lived in households within the larger home that was nature. Collecting and identifying the common flowers of their gardens and local woods, studying natural history in order to adequately educate their children as well as nurture their own moral character, women were primed to participate in the burgeoning celebration of the American environment. Unique though it was, *Rural Hours* was actually a predictable occurrence. Conjoining women's roles as domesticator and the American landscape's new image as home, Susan Cooper found a space in which to write a classic naturalist's essay. In so doing, she framed the context in which many American women have produced such works from her day to the present.

Rural Hours grew out of the perfectly centered Cooper family home in Otsego. From her ancestral base, Susan Cooper describes the changing, seasonal landscape in an area within walking distance, or occasionally a day's carriage ride from this spot. All the important elements of the biophysical environment exist in this space. Her book, though written over a two-year period, recounts one year in her life roaming the gardens, fields, and woods of her region of New York. Divided by the four seasons, beginning with spring and ending in winter, the text takes the form of a diary that documents how the details of her own domestic life are embedded in the natural round. Although the restriction of her rambles to home and environs, and of her voice to that of the common woman's diary, marks this as a female genre, precedents existed among male naturalists for just this approach.

Two of Cooper's favorite authors, and two men who influenced the circle of American nature writers, were the Englishmen Gilbert White and John Leonard Knapp. White inaugurated the natural history essay with the appearance in 1789 of his *Natural History of Selborne.* Knapp looked to him as a mentor when in the early nineteenth century he published *Country Rambles.* Susan Cooper served as the American editor of Knapp's text when it was reprinted in America in 1853; her introduction praises both Knapp and White for their work.[9] These Englishmen focused their nature study on the landscape of their homes. White's text consists of letters sent to colleagues. Although not as tightly structured around the seasons as Cooper's *Rural Hours,* both books cover the seasonal round. Such harmonies between her role as a nineteenth-century female writer and the traditional nature essay style enhanced Cooper's ability to appeal to a broad readership.

In *Rural Hours,* Cooper speaks to a mixed-sex public in the voice of a woman with an interest in the national issues of her day. Although her identity was meant to be a secret, her gender was not. On the title page is the descriptor "By a Lady." References to the utility of a parasol in a lady's adventurous walks around local terrain reinforce her status. Throughout, Cooper's lady is very clear on appropriate behavior for women. Observing women laboring in a hayfield or behind a plow in her neighborhood, she imagined them newly arrived from Europe, for American men would never expect such work of their wives and daughters (171-72). Although she bemoaned the harsh life of these poor rural women, she did not celebrate the ease of more middle-class village dwellers. Concerned that young village girls were too materialistic—"these are often wildly extravagant in their dress"—she offered farm wives of a certain class as better models. Making their own domestic goods kept farmers in their proper domain: "it is certainly pleasant to see the women busy in this way, beneath the family roof, and one is much disposed to believe that the home system is healthier and safer for the individual, in every way. Home, we may rest assured, will always be, as a rule, the best place for a woman; her labors and interests, should all centre there, whatever be her sphere of life" (161-62).

Cooper stated here a set of conservative values that she clung to for the rest of her life. Unlike some women of her time, she never shifted from her commitment to the woman's sphere to argue for women's rights. Cooper resisted feminism, preferring to end her days performing the sort of charitable work common to women's maternal associations. Unlike some of her literary sisters, she did not doubt that the dominant culture paid serious attention to the values of home. This did not mean, however, that the domestic round offered no corrective to American public life. On the contrary, women's different voice in *Rural Hours* serves just the purpose it should in recalling her readers to their republican roots in the unassuming country life.[10]

Although well read in the naturalists of her day, not all Susan Cooper learned met with her approval. She found the new specialists somewhat too willing to take over knowledge of nature from the common folk. *Rural Hours* contains a long discussion of the perils of the Latinate system for naming plants. Its author bemoaned the loss of common names for wildflowers. She felt that many American plants never had a chance of receiving a common English name, discovered as they were by traveling naturalists who proceeded to dub them "Batschia, Schoberia, Buchnera, Goodyeara," and the like. Such practices denied nature its poetry (and female muses): "Can you picture to yourself . . . maidens, weaving in their golden tresses, *Symphoricarpus vulgaris, Tricochloa, Tradescantia, Calopogon?*" (138-40). Further, scientific naming removed nature study from the home: "if we wish those who come after us to take a natural, unaffected pleasure in flowers, we should have names for the blossoms that mothers and nurses can teach children" (141).

Expanding on women's duty to use nature study for moral education throughout her text, Cooper used plants and animals she saw in nature as a springboard for religious meditation and moral instruction.[11] Critical of scientists' tendency to forget the moral aspect of their studies, she reminded her readers that "every new science introduced into the school-room brings with it an additional weight of moral responsibility" (366). So, parasol in hand, Susan Cooper sallied forth from her domestic hearth to the gardens and woods of her home to speak to all Americans about their native land, in a voice blending lessons from the woman's sphere with knowledge garnered from the scientist-naturalists whose company she kept and books she read.

The home-dwelling, semirural women among whom Cooper counted herself shared in the national effort to define America and Americans. She counseled her compatriots to cherish the rural life and native plants and animals of their locale, rather than looking back to Europe for models of landscape beauty. This emphasis on the virtues of the bucolic American scene continued throughout Cooper's writing career. In her sentimental novel *Elinor Wyllys,* the female protagonist is a country dweller whom her male counterpart comes to love only after rejecting the lures of Europe; one of the other sympathetic characters is an American landscape painter. Her appendix to Knapp's *Country Rambles* mostly distinguishes American flora and fauna from that described by Knapp. In her preface to the same volume, she states that many Americans, through their familiarity with English writers, have more knowledge of the British outdoors than their own. She exhorts readers to "open [your] eyes to the beautiful and wonderful realities of the world we live in . . . Americans are peculiarly placed in this respect; . . . their native soil being endued with the . . . deeper interest of home affections."[12]

Cooper knew that English literature, particularly that penned by the romantics, relied on images from nature for its effect. British flora and fauna provided most nature symbolism for English and American writers. Yet America, she argued, could now provide the stage for new achievements in literature about nature. If the English bard James Thomson had established the standard for poetry of this type in "Seasons," American poets could create their own national literature writing about the unique seasonal round of their new homeland.[13] Cooper envisioned that ultimately Americans would surpass the English in nature writing, making her country the standard-bearer of romantic nature poetry (335). At the heart of this new writing was the rural landscape in the fall, seen in *Rural Hours* as the essential American homescape: "At this very moment, . . . the annual labors of the husbandman are drawing to a close, . . . the first light frosts ripen the wild grapes in the woods, and open the husks of the hickory-nuts, bringing the latest fruits of the year to maturity . . . [these] are the heralds which announce the approach of a brilliant pageant—the moment chosen by Autumn to keep the great harvest-home of America is at hand" (337-38).

As a rural woman, Cooper conserved traditional American country life because the gardens and woods of Otsego were an extension of her domestic sphere. As a public figure, and as the daughter and granddaughter of men who helped define what it meant to be an American, she wanted to protect America domestica—those aspects of nature widely perceived by mid-century as the American heritage. Throughout her descriptions of the plants and animals of her home, these two positions—as native daughter and as member of the new breed of American nature writer—intermingle to create a text that speaks from the personal experience of a rural lady in a voice tinged with the public duty of a well-educated scion of an influential family and class.[14]

By the middle 1800s the Northeast had been settled and cultivated by many generations of Euro-Americans. As James Fenimore Cooper well knew, the location for the classic American tale of confrontation with the wilderness was shifting further west along a moving frontier. To describe America as home, however, required something more than awesome accounts of newly discovered terrain. In striking contrast to the frontier tales of families who kept moving west over the course of the century, and to her father's parallel motion of Leatherstocking's escape to the same wilderness terrain, Susan Cooper and other native nature writers wrote stories of a landscape in which they had deep roots. Because generations of Euro-Americans had lived in the same spot

for many years, they could experience American history in a way that more mobile Americans and visitors from Europe could not. As Europeans were reminded of the history of their civilization upon viewing their cathedrals, so Americans could now find a record of their achievements in the land they had domesticated.[15]

On seeing flowering thorn trees while out for an afternoon drive, Susan was reminded of the Revolution: "during the war . . . the long spines of the thorn were occasionally used by the American women for pins . . . probably it was the cockspur variety, which bears the longest and most slender spines, and is now in flower" (121). She went on to note that though there was no longer any need for such improvisation, the thorn tree still was useful to rural women for storing yarn (122). Americans did not have to build monuments, or constantly seek new territory, to create a national identity. As Cooper knew, they read their history in the common, everyday plants around and in their towns and villages. As she shows here, knowledge of natural history—of the difference between one kind of tree from another—is integral to the construction of national history. One gathers knowledge by settling in one place, becoming familiar with its native flora and fauna.

A mixture of wild and tame plants constituted a chief virtue in Cooper's rural landscape. Domesticating the wilderness did not necessarily eradicate it. For Cooper, the original natural landscape before Euro-American settlement remained an integral part of the country's heritage and appeared in the terrain around her home. A stand of forest pines at the top of a hill overlooking her village represented a crucial aspect of American history as surely as a ruined castle contained symbolic meaning for an Englishwoman. In describing such a stand of aged trees, Cooper labored to give them an exact and unique past similar to the history found in buildings. This specific pine grove could not be cut down and replanted with young trees to grow back over time. Rather, like a historic monument, the forest pines were creatures of a particular time and place. Losing them meant losing American history: "no other younger wood can ever claim the same connection as this, with a state of things now passed away forever; they cannot have that wild, stern character of the aged forest pines" (194). As the thorn tree reminded her of the Revolution, the pine stand contained memories of the "tenants of the wilderness"—the "wild creatures" and the "red man" (190). In taming the land, Cooper asserted, Americans had a responsibility to preserve as historic monuments those features of its original face, for without them her country would be in danger of losing its knowledge of the past. In this way, wilderness became part of a homescape rather than some far and fearsome frontier threatening civilization.

In Susan Cooper's time and place, wilderness had been, at least for her, subsumed under a new class—the native. Used to define a distinctive American character, the native usually was elevated over the imported.[16] Original American forest was not so much wild as it was indigenous; in this lay its merit. Cooper realized that she and her compatriots were most knowledgeable about the plants and animals of England. She also knew a good deal about their importation to America. Although appreciating many of the changes wrought by these foreigners, she consistently encouraged her readers to value the bounty of their own land. Much of her journal celebrates patches of native growth surprised among recently cultivated fields around home. Following a path through a meadow, she led her readers into a hidden runnel "filled with native plants; on one side stands a thorn-tree, whose morning shadow falls upon grasses and clovers brought from beyond the seas, while in the afternoon, it lies on gyromias and moose-flowers, sarsaparillas and cahoshes, which bloomed here for ages, when the eye of the red man alone beheld them. Even within the limits of the village spots may still be found on the bank of the river, which are yet unbroken by the plough, where the trailing arbutus, and squirrel-cups, and May-wings tell us so every spring" (148-49).

With the negative connotations of wilderness controlled in the celebration of the native, Cooper offered her audience a bountiful nature functioning as the mid-nineteenth-century home was meant to function—as a place of harmony where citizens found security, contentment, and civility. This domestic haven arose not only from the tended crops, but equally from the native plants and animals of the region. On her daily walks, Cooper often gathered food from wild-growing plants— various berries were a particular source of pleasure. Other plants, such as the pumpkin, transplanted easily into the country garden. In fact, the whole landscape appears to have been incredibly fecund, created as a sort of Eden for the new settlers: "Year after year, from the early history of the country, the land has yielded her increase in cheerful abundance; the fields have been filled with the finest of wheat, and maize, and rice, and sugar; the orchards and gardens, aye, the very woods and wastes, have yielded all their harvest of grateful fruits . . . like the ancient people of God, we may say, that fountains of milk and honey have flowed in upon us" (392). In a landscape revealing little difference between tilled fields and the "woods and wastes," where terrain served the same purpose as another room in their household, settlers rightly preserved all aspects of nature.

Finally, American readers discovered that, for all the blessings peculiar to their new home, their land was really but one room in the greater household of earth: "The mandrakes, or May-apples, are in flower . . . This common showy plant growing along our fences, and in many meadows, is said also to be found under a different variety in the hilly countries of Central Asia. One

likes to trace these links, connecting lands and races, so far apart, reminding us, as they do, that the earth is the common home of all" (91). With language culled from religious texts, and from the emerging ecological understanding of the naturalists, Cooper constructed an all-encompassing household, placing a heavy duty on its human tenants to make their individual homes in keeping with the terms of the environment.

Cooper encouraged her readers to change their confrontational attitude toward their home. For all her glowing reports of the fecundity of the American landscape, *Rural Hours* also documents declining populations. Animal life suffered the most obvious loss. Cooper wrote little about animals until the winter, when she had less to say about the plant world. Spending more time indoors, writing from her reading, she reported on the decline in fish and game birds; on the disappearance of deer, bear, and beaver from her region; and on rare sightings of otter, of whom she could only report that "it is said that they actually slide down hill on the snow, merely for amusement . . . One would like to see them at their play" (499). She called for the enactment of laws to protect certain animals before hunting and settlements eradicated them from the area (306, 376).

In the plant kingdom, her major concern was the devastation of the forests, and here the home imagery came to the fore. Arguing for the preservation of native forests, Cooper appealed to a variety of interests—some pragmatic, some aesthetic, some moral and religious. All centered, however, on the understanding that Euro-Americans could no longer behave as though they were just passing through, on their way back to the old home across the ocean or to the new on the western frontier. First, she counseled those who profited from the land to remember that trees constituted a large part of the country's current and future wealth (214). Then, moving on to the moral value of trees (conjoining the good with the beautiful here), she declared that preservation of trees around the home signified advanced civilization and looked better than expensive coats of paint on the walls or columns around the porch (items often purchased with funds earned by cutting down native timber) (215).

She argued that the wanton cutting of trees displayed "careless indifference to any good gift of our gracious Maker, shows a want of thankfulness, . . . betrays a reckless spirit of evil" (217). If we are to live here, it is our responsibility to act with restraint and nurturance toward the woods: "thinning woods and not blasting them; clearing such ground as is marked for immediate till-age; preserving the wood on the hill-tops and rough side-hills; . . . permitting bushes and young trees to grow at will along the brooks and water courses; sowing, if need be, a grove on the bank of the pool" (216). Much of creation could be lost with the devastation of the forest. Understanding that "the dullest insect crawling about these roots lives by the power of the Almighty; and the discolored shreds of last year's leaves wither away upon the lowly herbs in a blessing of fertility" (203) obligated citizens to protect all of the forest and its denizens as it would its own family.

Her religious belief in a divinely created, static nature, in which humanity's responsibility was to preserve an assumed status quo, informed Cooper's understanding of a rudimentary sort of ecology. Yet, in her arguments for the conservation of nature, hers was one of the early voices warning Americans about the dangers of their profligate use of resources. Certainly, some of her insight sprang from her father's tutoring and from her reading of the naturalists. But *Rural Hours* remains one of the few popular texts of the time containing a holistic comprehension of nature, calling for the protection not only of certain plants and animals, but also of the household in which these individuals flourished.[17] Her father sensed the uniqueness of her work when he observed that he had "very little doubt of its ultimate success, though at first the American world will hesitate to decide."[18] Actually, her words were perfectly timed. The journal sold well, reflecting increasing interest in such conservation activities as Arbor Day and the rise of the popular essay celebrating amateur birding.[19]

In the public arena, Cooper's linkage of America and home served broad political purposes. Home also meant a private, secluded space for which she, as a woman of her time, had special responsibility. But seclusion did not mean a life restricted to domestic interiors. Protected from the physical and psychic threats of the city, the proper country home allowed women spatial freedom to seek outdoor pleasures and nature studies. An idealized version of the country house and grounds appears in the home of Cooper's hero in *Elinor Wyllys*: "The grounds were of the simplest kind. The lawn which surrounded the house was merely a better sort of meadow, from which the stones and briars had been removed with more care than usual, and which, on account of its position, received the attention of one additional mowing in the course of the summer. A fine wood, of a natural growth, approached quite near to the house on the northern side, partially sheltering it in that direction, while an avenue of weeping elms led from the gate to the principal entrance."[20] For urban apartments or the new suburban houses on modest lots, the dividing line between private and public began at either the family's front door or the edge of the lot. Country houses had the luxury of more expansive surroundings. The yard and local woods and fields of Otsego were merely extensions of Cooper's (and her imaginary hero's) domestic round.[21] Thus, in describing her personal circumstances in *Rural Hours,* she made no distinction between the supposedly secluded domain of her father's house and the natural world outside her door.

Her life exemplified the interconnections and interdependencies between humans and the rest of the natural world that she espoused in her book.[22]

Confined to the house on a blustery day, longing for early spring flowers, she consoled herself by surveying the nature imagery in the wallpaper, rugs, furniture, and glassware of her home:

> here, winter as well as summer, we find traces enough of the existence of that beautiful part of creation, the vegetation; winter and summer, the most familiar objects with which we are surrounded, which hourly contribute to our convenience and comfort, bear the impress of the plants and flowers in their varied forms and colors. We seldom remember, indeed, how large a portion of our ideas of grace and beauty are derived from the plants, how constantly we turn to them for models . . . Branches and stems, leaves and tendrils, flowers and fruits, nuts and berries, are everywhere models.
>
> (504-5)

Cooper was a proponent of Andrew Jackson Downing's rustic style. Her sense of oneness with nature's aspects, however, was not merely a fashionable fancy. Generally unconcerned in *Rural Hours* with the interior of her home, she mentions it only at this point, when it serves as a surrogate for the outdoors. As the flowers on the wallpaper were reflections of nature's model, so her house and its domesticity mirrored the lives of plants and animals living on the Cooper grounds. Their nests and dens, their responses to various forms of domestication, offered corollaries to her own experience as a female in a very traditional household.[23]

Excepting the coldest part of winter, Cooper usually took one and sometimes two daily walks or drives around Otsego. On these excursions she surveyed the state of agriculture and engaged in amateur naturalizing—seeking flowers or birds new to her. She often considered how other forms of life provide models or cautions for human behavior. She was consumed with understanding what nature suggests about female roles and family responsibilities, and how gender definitions and familial arrangements help people comprehend what they see in nature. Birds specifically interested Cooper, as she, and apparently many of her generation, subscribed to Alexander Wilson's contention that humans and birds share common habits and emotions.[24] Her comments about birds exemplify the influence of gender roles on her ideas about nature.

Cooper felt a strong sense of fellowship with her bird neighbors. On one chilly fall day she hoped that they would come in her windows for "they would be very welcome to warm themselves and fly away at will" (320-21). Equally as willing to open her house to their view as they were to display theirs for her, she spent long hours watching their domestic round:

late evening hours are not the most musical moments with the birds; family cares have begun, and there was a good deal of the nursery about the grove of ever-greens in the rear of the house, to-night. It was amus-ing to watch the parents flying home, and listen to the family talk going on; there was a vast deal of twittering and fluttering before settling down in the nest, husband and wife seemed to have various items of household information to impart to each other, and the young nestlings made themselves heard very plainly; one gath-ered a little scolding, too, on the part of some mother robins.

(77)

Anthropomorphizing at will, she gave the birds' home a domestic arrangement similar to her own, breathing in-dividuality into the creatures with her tale of domestic dissent.

Sometimes birds serve as models of excellent behavior; rather than our equals, they then become our betters. A mother on the nest offered one exemplar. Her "volun-tary imprisonment" "hour after hour, day after day, upon her unhatched brood, warming them with her breast—carefully turning them—that all may share the heat equally, and so fearful lest they should be chilled, that she will rather suffer hunger herself than leave them long exposed" is "a striking instance of that gen-erous enduring patience which is a noble attribute of parental affection" (39-40). Of course, not all birds merit such high praise. Cooper was quick to distinguish between the more reliably "domestic" ones and such animals as the "cow-pen black-bird." A terrible mother, she laid her eggs in other birds' nests, abandoning her young to their care (408). Wherever possible, however, Cooper urged her readers to view the domestic arrange-ments of birds as comparable to and part of nature's great, enveloping household.

Birds were not the only creatures subject to this sort of empathetic regard for their maternal doings. Almost any other creature she observed or about which she had read enough to have a sense of its family arrangements received similar treatment. Her discussion in *Rural Hours* of the "upholsterer bee" she had seen in England provides a case in point. The bee was associated with a red poppy, whose leaves the animal used in construct-ing a nest. Cooper provided an extravagant vision of the "careful mother" cutting a bit of "the scarlet flower" for her nest, where she "spreads it on the floor like a carpet" and makes "handsome hangings" for the "bril-liant cradle" of "one little bee" (199). As with the birds, such an encapsulated domestic scene gives the insect a moral character comparable to that of a human mother. John Leonard Knapp, who also wrote about these bees, took little notice of the insect's domesticity. Knapp and Cooper also parted company in describing the English hedgehog. Both saw it as a harmless animal subjected to much mistreatment by humans. But whereas Knapp

described a generic hedgehog, focusing on its physical features and habits, Cooper, in her addition to his text, tells a touching tale of a mother hedgehog's fidelity, even unto death, to her young.[25] For Susan Cooper, gen-der and the family responsibilities of females in particu-lar were significant aspects of hedgehog, bee, and bird character.

One commentator on *Rural Hours* has argued that, as a woman of her time, Cooper had to "dispense moral pre-cepts and display a set of principles," whereas Knapp and Gilbert White could freely engage in "spontaneous" nature description.[26] Although Cooper admired White, as did most of the budding nature essayists in England and America from the 1830s on, she and Knapp wrote about nature in rather different circumstances than White. As Donald Worster has shown, for White, nature study was an "integral part of the curate's life." White's work became important fifty years after its publication, when the pressures of industrialization engendered a search for the old pastoral landscape of White's Sel-borne.[27] Writers like Knapp and Cooper described na-ture with an eye to morally improving a people who were sorely threatened by the materialism of the city, thus taking a more principled tone than White. The more basic, gender-coded difference between Cooper and her male predecessors is Cooper's focused interest in family life and female behavior in plants and ani-mals. That many important moral lessons sprang from nature's domestic affairs obviously supported the valu-able contribution women (who viewed themselves as most attuned to family life) could make to nature study and appreciation.

Knapp and White gave little thought to what nature, or nature/human interactions, had to say about gender roles. On one occasion Knapp chided his countrymen for killing hedgehogs to prove their manhood, but on the whole his moralizing took a more general tone.[28] Nor was nature thought of as home in the same way in the men's writings. Knapp and White open their texts with a loving description of their home regions but present themselves primarily as researchers into na-ture's secrets. They collected plants and animals, ex-perimented with them, and corresponded with scientific colleagues about their findings. Nature's household was not commensurate with their own. Neither pondered what their findings suggested about their roles as fa-thers and husbands.

Susan Cooper always considered what her knowledge and her actions had to say about her womanly role, par-ticularly as keeper of the home. Although she might join in pronouncements with men when public concerns mirrored domestic affairs, she was conscious of her sta-tus as a lady. In *Rural Hours,* we never see Cooper en-gaged in collecting specimens for the microscope. She collected flowers for ornament and berries for dinner.

When, as in her comments on bird families, bees, and hedgehogs, she addressed her audience as a private woman describing her feeling for nature, rather than as an American converting the landscape from wilderness to household, Cooper spoke specifically to a female readership about the particular interests of women.

The plant kingdom also provided opportunities for commenting on human gender divisions and sexual differences. Aware of the language of flowers and schooled enough in botany to distinguish among plant types, Cooper showed her female readers how a close observation of flowering plants taught the proper female virtues of modesty, constancy, and sisterhood. When she observed the birds, she found her family; when she looked at flowers, she saw images of the female sex. Laying to rest men's fears that Linnaean botany, with its emphasis on sexual characteristics of plants, was too coarse a subject for female sensibilities, Cooper emphasized the emotional connotations of femininity that flowers called forth. In the spring, she found violets "growing in little sisterhoods" in the fields and forests (78). The regular appearance of these violets as well as arbutus, squirrel cups, and ground laurels offered a lesson in constancy: "How pleasant it is to meet the same flowers year after year! If the blossoms were liable to change—if they were to become capricious and irregular—they might excite more surprise, more curiosity, but we should love them less" (48). She found all of these flowers in her walks. They were not hothouse plants secluded in an artificial environment. Such hardiness was a positive attribute in both plants and women thriving freely and openly in the healthy rural atmosphere of Otsego.

While Cooper celebrated indigenous plants as part of her encouragement to Americans to make their home among the natives of the continent, she also believed that such plants were important sources of virtuous lessons to American women. Echoing Fredrika Bremer's fear of pampering, Cooper counseled her sisters to resist over-cultivation—both in themselves and in their flowers. The wild rose was much lovelier than the grafted tree roses popular in some gardens. Grafted roses lacked modesty: "[they] remind one of the painful difference between the gentle, healthy-hearted daughter of home, the light of the house, and the meretricious dancer, tricked out upon the stage to dazzle and bewilder, and be stared at by the mob. The rose has so long been an emblem of womanly loveliness, that we do not like to see her shorn of one feminine attribute; and modesty in every true-hearted woman is, like affection, a growth of her very nature, whose roots are fed with her life's blood" (123). If women were like roses, then it was their duty to protect the roselike quality of their nature as well as the nature of the rose.

Mirroring her public concern for the loss of morality in science, Cooper, speaking from the domestic sphere in a voice consciously female, reminded her readers that women, as conservators of tradition, had a responsibility to resist ambitious manipulation of God's creation.[29] Like the families who sold their native pines to buy ostentatious paint for their houses, women who bought such artificial plants as the grafted rose forgot their republican roots.[30] Such behavior endangered nature, American society, and women's status as moral standard-bearers. Linking woman's nature to the indigenous plants of America, Cooper framed women's appreciation, nurturance, and protection of such plants and their environments as a function of gender. By the late nineteenth century many women had picked up on her suggestion and were writing books grounded in their sense of the particular bond between themselves and nature.

Among the many traits these later texts share with Cooper's, the most striking is their emphasis on the gender of the writer. All are self-consciously nature studies by a woman who writes from within the domestic confines of her home about the seasonal round of plant and animal life. Among the earliest to follow Cooper were investigators who added to our knowledge of American flora and fauna. Often connected to the scientific community, these women saw themselves marking out a bit of experimental territory peculiarly suited to their gender. They included Mary Treat (*Home Studies in Nature*), Olive Thorne Miller (*In Nesting Time*), and Florence Merriam (*A-Birding on a Bronco*), all of whom published before the turn of the twentieth century. They lived middle-class, intellectual lives in much the same domestic circumstances as Susan Cooper. Nature study fulfilled their obligation to use their leisure in a productive, nonfrivolous manner that would be beneficial to society.

In ***Rural Hours*** Cooper encouraged Americans to learn more about insects, a neglected and misunderstood category of animal life. Mary Treat, of Vineland, New Jersey, took her up on the suggestion. In the 1880s she began publishing accounts of her experiments with spiders in her self-constructed "insect menagerie" at home. Whereas Susan Fenimore Cooper had a rank amateur's understanding of science and never proposed to conduct experiments, Treat—enjoying women's increasing involvement in science—worked at her research.[31] She provided detailed studies of birds, spiders, ants, wasps, and insectivorous plants, referring the reader to her articles in various scientific and popular journals, quoting from her correspondence with Asa Gray and Charles Darwin, and pointing out her own contributions in the field. She viewed nature as much less static than did Cooper. Aware of the explosion in theory attendant upon the publication of Darwin's *On the Origin of Species* (1859), Treat argued against human supremacy in a hierarchical natural world created in one stroke by God. She urged her readers to marvel instead at the constantly changing environment in which they lived. Along with others of this early generation of Darwinists, she saw evidence of evolution all around her.[32]

Mary Treat was, however, much more Susan Cooper's soul mate than she was Charles Darwin's colleague. Most of her experiments and her work centered around the domestic landscapes of her home in Vineland, with the rest resulting from winter excursions to Florida. In her most comprehensive work, *Home Studies in Nature,* she argued that to the true nature lover, "the smallest area around a well-chosen home will furnish sufficient material to satisfy all thirst of knowledge through the longest life" (6). Throughout the text she commented on the virtues of observations and experiments made in this more restricted sphere. If most women could not (and perhaps should not) join male naturalists on heroic journeys of exploration, they could make another sort of journey traveling the familiar round of home, garden, and local neighborhood. In this round, too, one could contribute to the public effort to understand the natural world.

For all its scientific voice, *Home Studies in Nature* is clearly a woman's book. Beginning, as had Cooper, with a description of her home and gardens, Treat highlighted the domestic life of animals. Her studies of birds emphasize family habits and read gender-coded meaning into nesting behavior. Treat's most fulsome consideration of animal life concerns an unlikely specimen—the spider. The spider habitat she built served as both a scientific laboratory and a domestic garden, surrounded by an arborvitae hedge, with a centered maple tree, "ornamental plants," and a couple of bird baths (113). Particularly interested, as she was with birds, in spider architecture, she offered lyric observations of the maternal instincts of various specimens/pets. One ground spider, whose carefully contrived home tower Treat described in some detail, evinces model domesticity in caring for her young. In one session, the babies crawl over the mother and she picks them up, holding them in front of her and "perhaps giving them a homily on manners. Soon she gently releases them" (105). Shedding their skins, the children dispose of their "baby dresses" (107). When the little ones are old enough to leave the nest, the mother "behaves much in the same way that the higher animals do in weaning their young" (107). Treat stressed not only her status as a woman at home engaging in nature study, but also how nature functions as a home akin to the human home.

Like Cooper, Treat found little difference between outdoors and indoors, or wild and domestic. As well as building a garden for watching wild spiders, she brought them into her study, housed in glass cases, where she could observe them throughout the seasons. Domesticating an animal meant accommodating it to her presence. In her terminology, wild birds were domesticated when they used her bird bath while she sat quietly watching. Although she was aware of the importance of struggle and competition in Darwin's model of evolution, she chose not to dwell on this aspect of life. Treat saw all of nature as a household, with each plant and animal playing a cooperative, harmonious part.[33] Nature "red in tooth and claw" receives short shrift in her work, whereas images of cooperative behavior predominate. This is particularly true in her comments on preserving bird populations. Aware that many agriculturists held deep prejudices against certain birds, she underlined their dependence on the birds for insect control (41-42). More sophisticated in her ecological understanding than Susan Cooper, she explained in more detail how the organic system operates.

Mary Treat's nature studies provide a missing link in accounting for the explosion of women naturalists studying birds in the late nineteenth century. In most nineteenth-century histories, women appear as individualized voices only once—as participants in these late-century bird preservation movements. During this period, a group of women writers produced many books on birds. Some were scientific studies of bird behavior, some were amateur naturalist accounts of birding, and some were children's books written to encourage the next generation to preserve bird populations. Trying to account for this phenomenon, historians have noted that by this time women had a long tradition of working on social issues through voluntary organizations. Much of the impetus for the "bird ladies" came from the rise of the Audubon clubs, often headed by men but whose members were primarily female amateurs trained in women's colleges.[34] Although such reasoning explains the mechanism by which women came to speak publicly for birds, it does not tell us much about the value they placed on these animals or about the nature of their interest. As the language of flowers provided early nineteenth-century women with entrée into botany, so the image of birds as microcosms of human domesticity offered women later in the century a rationale for their study.

Two of the most prolific bird authors, who were also political activists in the fight to save birds from their commercial use in women's hats and from hunters, were Olive Thorne Miller and Florence Merriam. Their works are typical of the sort of book produced by women during this period. Miller (born in 1831) upheld traditional gender-role expectations. She began publishing her bird books only after raising four children and then wrote under a pseudonym. Merriam (born in 1863) was of the next generation, contributing both to the more humanistic nature writing of the time and to the burgeoning science of ornithology. She was the first woman to win the Brewster Medal (for *Birds of New Mexico*), awarded for original work in ornithology. Merriam has received praise as well for her courage and stamina, when, in

1899, after marrying the naturalist Vernon Bailey, she traveled with him throughout the West surveying birds. Regardless of these differences, Miller and Merriam were close friends. Merriam's library contained inscribed copies of Miller's books, and Merriam occasionally mentions Miller in her own work. Their texts reveal a common language of birds, one concerned with female metaphors of domesticity.[35]

Both women wrote books featuring local birds. Miller's *In Nesting Time* details her efforts to make her home a home to birds. She kept one room in the house separate for her bird studies. In this room she housed birds in cages, but she also encouraged them to roam free. Thus, the room became a large aviary and she just one of the tenants. Generally, the birds were not house pets. After a brief season indoors, they were freed in her yard or the surrounding woods. Whereas Susan Fenimore Cooper, stranded inside in the winter, could locate nature only in the patterns on her rug, Miller entertained herself by watching a brown thrush peel the wallpaper in the bird room: "First came a little tear, then a leap one side, another small rent, another panic; and so he went on til he had torn off a large piece which dropped to the floor, while I sat too much interested in the performance to think of saving the paper. (The room and its contents are always secondary to the birds' comfort and pleasure, in my thoughts)."[36] Befitting her book's title, *In Nesting Time,* Miller concentrates on the mating and nesting habits of birds she kept indoors and those she spied on outdoors. As usual, the primary metaphors for describing behaviors come from her own female duties: "I discovered very soon that mocking-bird babies are brought up on hygienic principles, and have their meals with great regularity" (46). Bird mothers, like human mothers, subscribed to the newest trends in domestic science.

Not only did she write as a woman, she exhorted women readers to enter the field of ornithology. Noting that the old days of killing, dissecting, nest robbing, and mounting were over, that "all that can be learned with violence" has been learned, she asserted that the next phase of bird study required field observation of their habits, "infinite patience, perseverance, untiring devotion, and . . . a quick eye and ear, and a sympathetic heart" (16). Who among her readers shared these qualities better than women? "This is the pleasant path opening now, and in some ways it is particularly suited to woman with her great patience and quiet manners" (18). Florence Merriam, arriving a generation later, shared some of the qualities of the so-called New Woman, who had a much more visible and diverse public role and was less likely to marry and have children. Yet Merriam couched her interest in birds in exactly the gendered terms that Miller envisioned.[37]

Although Merriam wrote standard handbooks on western birds, full of straight, scientific information, in these texts and in more personal publications about her life among the birds, her tone differs little from that of Miller, Treat, or Cooper. Merriam patiently watched her subjects, with no more threatening weapons than a parasol and a consuming interest in courtship and family behavior. A good companion book to Miller's *In Nesting Time* is Merriam's *A-Birding on a Bronco,* written while the author was in California recuperating from tuberculosis.[38] For all the title suggests a woman escaping the confines of home for adventure in the rugged West, Merriam stays close to home, rambling around on her trusty horse until she knows the ranch as well as her own home back east. *A-Birding on a Bronco*'s precursor is not the high adventure of a John James Audubon lost in unknown territory, but Susan Cooper's **Rural Hours.**

The center of Merriam's interest was the home—the nest—which made nature worth studying. Riding through a eucalyptus grove, she commented on the importance of the domestic scene: "How one little home does make a place habitable! From bare silent woods it becomes a dwelling place. Everything seemed to centre around this little nest, then the only one in the grove; the tiny pinch of down became the most important thing in the woods."[39] Merriam regarded birds as persons, with rights to tenancy on her land and deserving of the same respect due human neighbors (65). As persons, they were interesting in their domestic arrangements. She spent much time speculating about the meaning of their family life. Occasionally, the questions that the women of her time were raising about gender roles informed her descriptions of bird life. Reflecting the New Woman's challenge to some of the constraints of patriarchy, Merriam lamented the classification system that science applied to birds. Female birds had to "bear their husband's names, however inappropriate . . . Here an innocent creature with an olive-green back and yellowish breast has to go about all her days known as the black throated warbler, just because that happens to describe the dress of her spouse."[40] Such a comment suggests somewhat more awareness of women's rights issues than either Cooper or Miller demonstrated. It does not, however, call into question the valuable lessons learned when female naturalists turn their gendered interest on the study of nature. Like Cooper, Merriam found within woman's different culture a source for correcting a form of scientific hubris and drawing a social lesson from nature's domestic arrangements.

Her interest in male/female roles created some difficulties when a bird's sex was not so easily determined by its plumage. Trying to figure which of a pair of gnatcatchers was the female, she realized that certain nesting behaviors could, using the human model, be attributed to either gender (51). Nevertheless, such questions did not lead her to violent methods. Unable to identify an elusive bird family, she was advised to shoot a specimen and send it to "the wise men." But her familiarity with their domestic scene made this impossible: "after knowing the little family in their home it would have been like raising my hand against familiar friends. Could I take their lives to gratify my curiosity about a name?" (141). *A-Birding on a Bronco* studies a natural world that is home, not a foreign terrain from which the explorer feels he has a right and an obligation to bring back plunder. As Miller had encouraged, Merriam found in the branch of ornithology emphasizing observational fieldwork a space appropriate to women's conservationist role.

The works of Treat, Miller, and Merriam share one other similarity with the earlier generation's study of the language of flowers. Just as botany was proper only insofar as plant sexuality camouflaged behind a mask of gentility, bird behavior had one taboo arena. With all the emphasis on mating and nesting, the reader might expect occasional descriptions of sexuality. Each author provides some details—describing, for example, a male bird's showy courting dance—but all avoid any mention of the sexual act. Female birds always act modestly as they are being wooed, and a pair invariably retreats to the cover of a handy tree at the point of mating, re-emerging ready to build their nest and get on with family affairs. As the struggle to survive is touched upon lightly, so too is the procreative act. Birds, like their female observers, have too much taste to reveal such matters to the public eye.[41]

The reticence and gentle quality of the bird books produced by women in the latter part of the century no doubt contribute to their contemporary critical reputation. While women are acknowledged to have had an important impact on wildlife preservation during the period for educating the popular readership in the virtues of birds, they have been dismissed by at least one historian from a secure place in the literary naturalist canon in part because of this emphasis on domesticity: "the special perceptions they brought to the study of birds were more valuable in giving instruction than in providing inspiration; they bestowed the gift of sight rather than insight."[42] Of course, the question such a comment raises is to whom, and in what context, these women were writing.

Between the publication of Susan Fenimore Cooper's **Rural Hours** in 1850 and Florence Merriam's *A-Birding on a Bronco* in 1896, the nature essay had become standard fare in many popular magazines. Specialized journals for nature lovers were common. With the appearance of Henry David Thoreau's *Walden* and John Burroughs' *Wake-Robin*, literary writing about nature entered the mainstream.[43] Thoreau and Burroughs developed the same theme Susan Cooper mined in writing about the American environment as home. These men and women shared a preference for the rural life, an

anti-materialist bias, a strong sense of the respect due to all life, and more interest in the ecological system than in tales of struggle and dominance. The men's images of home, however, are less focused on the domestic round than the representations of Cooper and the other women considered here.

Men and women developed somewhat different voices for writing about nature, but one wonders if, to the readership of the time, one voice was any less inspirational than the other. Certainly, the women were successful: they published a great deal and their texts enjoyed many printings. There is little in male naturalists' comments of the period to suggest that they found women less capable; in fact, in certain instances men cited women's works to settle public debates.[44] The reason for women's tenuous rank in the canon of literary nature writers probably lies in particular trends in the literary world and the scientific establishment during the late nineteenth and early twentieth centuries.

As Ann Douglas has shown, Victorian literary fashion was in many ways defined by the combined forces of middle-class women and the clergy. Disturbed by the feminization of culture, some writers criticized what they saw as excessive sentimentalism in women's literature, while more popular male novelists turned to producing works supportive of a burgeoning "crusade for masculinity."[45] As Margaret Rossiter has shown, the newly emerging scientific establishment was grappling with a concurrent explosion of women seeking and finding training in various fields. Certain areas, such as botany, appeared completely feminized. Reflecting this incursion of women into previously male domains was their membership in naturalist groups like the Audubon societies. As well as their work in these activist organizations, women sought entrance into scientific societies and edited scientific journals. The scientific establishment began a series of efforts to limit control and predominant membership in such institutions to men. For example, Florence Merriam became the first female member of the American Ornithological Union in 1885, but she was listed only as an associate.[46]

For the nature essayists, such a climate produced predictable results. On the literary side, the home-based tradition established by Gilbert White and carried on in America by Susan Fenimore Cooper, Henry David Thoreau, John Burroughs, Olive Thorne Miller, and Florence Merriam was eclipsed by more virile tales of the wilderness challenge popularized by Teddy Roosevelt, Jack London, and Edgar Rice Burroughs. Thrilling stories of wild animal hunting expeditions (with either gun or camera) held more interest than women's domestic tales of patient watching by the nest of a common yard bird. Although men and women had written the first nature essays, the privilege granted heroic exploration effectively silenced women's voices, while prominent men in the home-based tradition were rehabilitated and lauded for those aspects of their work that fit the new mold.[47] In the developing hierarchy of the scientific professions, women's names disappeared from the leadership; assigned associate roles, they appeared less influential—capable of "sight but not insight." Thus, the disappearance of women's voices from the canon was more a function of the end-of-the-century effort to reestablish masculine control of scientific and literary culture than any generalized defect in their ability as observers and writers.

Nothing in the accounts of women nature writers during this period suggests that they either repudiated their traditional form or recognized the threats to their status. In fact, the tradition begun by Cooper, Treat, Miller, Merriam, and others continued into the twentieth century and flourishes today. Throughout this century, writers have produced books in which their individual round as women in a country setting exemplifies a mode of living in keeping with the natural environment. Around the turn of the century, women more directly connected to agricultural or backcountry life began to publish. The narratives of these women continue Susan Cooper's belief that rural life avoids the excesses of materialism. Cooper looked to farm women as models of modesty and frugality; the chronicles of twentieth-century farm women repeat her theme. Martha McCulloch-Williams's *Next to the Ground* (1902), Louise Rich's *We Took to the Woods* (1942), Sue Hubbell's *A Country Year* (1986), and Maxine Kumin's *In Deep* (1987) all echo Cooper's practical interest in what the environment yields for human survival and how women may use and preserve nature's bounty.

These authors also reiterate the conservationist role that Cooper and Miller saw as women's responsibility, including pointed messages about women's duty to preserve and protect the plants and animals of home. McCulloch-Williams's protagonist in 1902 was given the task of nursing injured birds brought in from the field while her brother and father went shooting. Eighty years later Kumin argues that women, because of gender socialization, are more successful than men at working with problem horses.[48] Like Cooper, the twentieth-century writers believe that the city and, later, the suburbs trivialize women's lives. Both Rich in 1942 and Hubbell in 1986 argue that scraping out a living in the backcountry is preferable to the consumerist existence each had led as urban women.[49] And, finally, although these books from the farmlands speak consciously from within a woman's round, that sphere also offers a corrective to the public excesses of the day—be they the terrors of world war in Rich's 1942 narrative or the problems of "survival, of hunger and genocide" in Kumin's account.[50] As did Susan Cooper in 1850, the

contemporary nature essayists have found room to write from within the private domestic spaces of their lives about public, political issues facing Americans.

By the turn of the century, women were also immersed in conservation and preservation efforts developing out of the Progressive Era's reformist agenda. Reflecting the broadening national interest in safeguarding America's wilderness landscapes, key figures in this movement came from all over the country. During the first three decades of the twentieth century, Mary Hunter Austin, a midwesterner transplanted to the deserts of the Southwest, served as a leading female voice in the effort to protect arid regions from overdevelopment. Inspired in part by John Muir's call to preserve natural landscapes, Austin worked on political campaigns to conserve and appropriately use water in the West. Her talent as a nature writer, however, made more impact on American environmental values. Following in Cooper's tradition, Austin tracked seasonal variations in the flora and fauna around her homes in the California and Nevada deserts and the mountains of New Mexico. She earned her reputation as the most famous female nature writer of the period from such books as *The Land of Little Rain* (1903), *The Flock* (1906), and *The Land of Journey's Ending* (1924). Austin forms a link between the nineteenth-century birders and the women nature essayists who published in the 1960s and 1970s.[51]

Mary Austin and her literary daughters champion ways of living holistically in keeping with nature, seeking a way back into the endangered wild landscape. In Austin's *Land of Little Rain*, Helen Hoover's *The Gift of the Deer* (1965), Josephine Johnson's *The Inland Island* (1969), and Ann Zwinger's *Beyond the Aspen Grove* (1970), women naturalists have picked up the thread Cooper began in her pleas for the preservation of native forests and their plants and animals. The late twentieth-century reader of ***Rural Hours*** is struck by the devastation of animal populations more than one hundred years ago, particularly when Cooper recounts the sad death of one of the last deer in the area or the almost mythical sightings of an elusive "panther" near Otsego (240-44, 422). In the century since publication of Cooper's work, public concern for the preservation of wilderness areas has blossomed; with that concern has come an interest in living in the shadow of the forest (or, in Austin's case, on the edge of the desert).[52] Whereas Cooper and her family retired to a semidomesticated, rural landscape, this more contemporary group of female writers locates itself beyond the agricultural fringe, in the last pockets of American wilderness. Here its members seek an experience, however, much akin to that of Cooper, Treat, Miller, Merriam, and their more recent agricultural sisters. They establish a domestic life that makes room for the native plants and animals of the land.

Although twentieth-century writers do not share the nineteenth-century burden of constantly demonstrating the propriety of their work on the public stage by emphasizing their ties to home, their voices are clearly female. Sometimes being female in the twentieth century mirrors the nineteenth-century experience; at other times it does not. Hoover presents "Pretty," a female deer of the herd, in proper women's makeup. Zwinger writes about flora as though they are children and her daughters as though they are fauna. Johnson finds herself engrossed in a female passion to "tidy, tidy, tidy, tidy— lives . . . leaves . . . trees . . . emotions . . . house . . . endless sweeping, clipping, washing, arranging."[53] Whereas Cooper replaced the wild with the native in order to make indigenous plants preferable to the fancy hothouse flower, modern writers reinvest the native with connotations of the wild. Links between natural women and native landscape remain, but they have begun to reflect less gentility and more ambiguity than in Cooper's day.

While she struggled in her own life with early twentieth-century feminism, Austin created a free, sensuous female landscape and desert women invigorated by contact with the wilderness. Austin was of the same generation as Florence Merriam. Like Merriam and the other female nature writers of her day, the message she heard in nature reinforced her understanding of women's proper role. But Austin also spoke in the voice of the second wave of New Women who more openly questioned the meaning of women's sexuality. Her sensitivity to emerging women's issues rendered hers a lone female voice among the nature essayists in the early twentieth century when she suggested that there were connections between male domination of nature and women's oppression. Wilderness offered a clear lesson of the true freedom at the heart of both the natural world and women's nature: "If the desert were a woman, I know well what like she would be: deep breasted, broad in the hips, tawny . . . eyes sane and steady as the polished jewel of her skies . . . passionate, but not necessitous, patient—and you could not move her, not if you had all the earth to give, so much as one tawny hair's breadth beyond her own desires. If you cut very deeply into the soul that has the mark of the land on it, you find such qualities as these."[54]

Austin's sensitivity to female oppression was not picked up in women's nature essays until much later in the twentieth century. As inheritors of the feminist movement of the 1960s and 1970s, contemporary writers often question some of the constraints in their domestic inheritance. Reminding her readers of the distance of middle-class nineteenth-century women from the sexual content of nature, Maxine Kumin finds her own delicate aversion to intimate knowledge of horse foaling offensive and proudly celebrates her initiation into "a hardy band, a secret cell" of those able to attend such a birth.[55] Nineteenth-century women located positive reinforcement for their domesticity in images of middle-class

animal families; Josephine Johnson performs an ironic twist on that tradition when she describes her meeting with a female fox. Recognizing that few female animals, whether fox or human, lead a life of ease and tranquility, she faced a vixen whose imagined life symbolized freedom to Johnson and discovered "her as she really was—small, thin, harried, heavily burdened—not really free at all. Bound by instinct as I am bound by custom and concern."[56] In such imagery, twentieth-century naturalists reinvest native plants and animals with a wildness suppressed by the domestic cults of the nineteenth century. However, as nineteenth-century women located messages about human gender codes in the nesting habits of birds, so twentieth-century women continue to find models of their own female lives in the other animals with whom they live.

Over time, female nature writers have continually resisted constraints on women's round that artificially separated them from nature. The definition of appropriate limits has, of course, changed from 1850 to the present. As women's sphere has broadened, so too has their understanding of nature's domestic round and their image of the landscape of home. Throughout, however, women nature writers have warned against forces that would diminish or falsify the moral quotient of woman's sphere. If Susan Cooper located the threat in women's relegation to the hothouse and Maxine Kumin saw it in their exclusion from the barn, both did so in the belief that the domestic life, fully experienced, offered a necessary corrective to the social dislocations of their time.

In twentieth-century authors' identification of their own nature with the natural round, they too find a reason to act as conservators and protectors of the environment. In *The Land of Little Rain,* Mary Austin criticized the arrogant development of arid landscapes. Her home and its surrounding fields appear literally at the center of her book, critiquing by example domination of the land. She contrasts her attempt to coax various wild plants and animals into her yard from a neglected field next door with her neighbor's plan to turn the field into town lots. Austin, better acquainted with the field than he, argues: "though the field may serve a good turn in those days it will hardly be happier. No, certainly not happier."[57] *The Land of Little Rain* served as a cautionary tale to twentieth-century settlers in the Southwest, and the narrator achieved the right to speak as a result of her own adaptation to the place. Ann Zwinger built a cabin in the rugged Colorado mountains so she might learn how to fit her life into the ecology of the terrain, teach her daughters to do the same, and write books in support of public appreciation of the web of life. Similar to the bird writers before her, Helen Hoover became a spokesperson for the rights of deer, using as her weapon highly charged accounts of their family life in the forest around her Minnesota cabin.

Josephine Johnson, whose *Inland Island* is one of the finest nature essays ever written, captures perfectly (and with some humor) the role of female protector each of these twentieth-century writers embodies. Johnson and her husband lived outside Cincinnati on farmland that they encouraged the native plants and animals to reclaim: "This place, with all its layers of life, from the eggs of snails to the eyes of buzzards, is my home, as surely as it is the wild bird's or the woodchuck's home. I'll defend it if I have to patrol it with a bow and arrow—an old lady, like a big woodchuck in a brown coat, booting up and down these knife-cut hills, shouting at the dogs and hunters, making a path through that encroaching ecology we were told would come inevitably as the tides, and faster."[58] It may seem a long way from Susan Fenimore Cooper, planning for the salvation of old stands of pine as she strolls through the countryside of Otsego, to Josephine Johnson, angrily defending her island from destructive humans. However, the urge to preserve a native landscape contains the same appeal to women's special responsibility as wives, mothers, and teachers of the moral lessons derived from the domestic round. The most basic thread running from Susan Cooper's **Rural Hours** in 1850 to Ann Zwinger's *Beyond the Aspen Grove* in 1970 is the act of homing in on one spot, living with it through the seasons until the rocks, flowers, trees, insects, birds, deer, panthers, and coyotes are family. Enfolded within women's family, carrying the emotional weight of home, American flora and fauna are due the same consideration as human members of the household.

Having established a continuous, coherent tradition in women's writing on nature, I wondered why the century-old story these women composed has gone for so long unnoticed. Ann Zwinger provided one answer in a speech to the Thoreau Society in 1983. Her talk responded to a comment Thoreau made about a young woman's attempt to live alone in a cabin in the woods. In Thoreau's opinion, "her own sex, so tamely bred, only jeer at her for entertaining such an idea."[59] Based on this and other disparaging remarks about women in Thoreau's *Journals,* Zwinger concluded that he believed women were incapable of writing well about nature. She then refuted his finding by pairing quotations from various women naturalists with similar writings by men, proving that the women were as skilled as the men.

Zwinger is singular among nature writers in suggesting that, almost from the beginning, male writers subordinated women's work to their own and did not (contrary to Susan Cooper's hope) listen with equal attention to women. Although female nature essayists consistently pose women's images of nature as a critique of certain male behaviors, they have done so in the full confidence that they and their male compatriots ultimately share the same public stage and often have the same goals. Their history of joint endeavors suggests a large degree of overlap in nature study and appreciation. Cooper helped popularize Knapp, Treat did the same with Darwin, Florence Merriam worked companionably alongside her husband Vernon Bailey, Mary Austin supported John Muir's preservationist agenda, and Ann Zwinger returned to Thoreau's rivers in the company of Edwin Way Teale.[60] The happy congruence of Gilbert White's seasonal journal with Susan Cooper's daily diary set the stage for such male-female collaboration and for a flourishing nature writing tradition among American women. But the genre was White's to begin with; it developed out of the male-controlled naturalist tradition. As the history of women's disappearance from the literary naturalist canon after the turn of the century suggests, men have continued to control the field. It is as though a door of opportunity opened with the ornithologists in the nineteenth century and quickly closed again as the pantheon of nature essayists firmly cohered around a select group of men. Signifying the effectiveness of that canon, not only men but also women have neglected the work of writers like Susan Fenimore Cooper, Mary Treat, Florence Merriam Bailey, and Josephine Johnson.[61] Ann Zwinger is the first female nature writer to recognize the loss and speak for those who have been silenced. With her encouragement, the door once more opens and we discover that, in fact, the natural round has provided much inspiration to women who "recorded for their own or another's pleasure the tilt of the earth and the slant of the sky."[62]

Notes

1. On the early history of the nature essay, see Hanley, *Natural History in America,* 16-31, 103-19, 176-92, 224-38; Huth, *Nature,* 14-54, 87-105; Welker, *Birds and Men,* 91-149.

2. Margaret Fuller's account of her own travels through the West, *Summer on the Lakes,* contained much nature description, but nature study was secondary to Fuller's narrative of human society on the frontier.

3. On the cult of domesticity, see Cott, *Bonds of Womanhood*; Welter, *Dimity Convictions.*

4. On James's attitudes toward women as evidenced in his fiction, see Bradsher, "Women in the Works of James Fenimore Cooper." The standard biography of Susan is Cunningham, "Susan Fenimore Cooper." On the strong influence of her father on her life and work, see Maddox, "Susan Fenimore Cooper."

5. The primary source for information on Susan's family history is her "Small Family Memories," in J. F. Cooper, *Correspondence, 1:9-72.* William Cooper's *Guide in the Wilderness,* although not a natural history, contains much information on the lay of the land around Cooperstown. On the land-

scape aesthetic of Downing, see Leighton, *American Gardens,* 163-72. Susan thanks "Dr. De Kay and Mr. Downing . . . for their kindness in directing her course on several occasions" (*Rural Hours,* 406). All further references to *Rural Hours* are cited parenthetically in the text.

6. Kelley, *Private Woman,* xi, 248.

7. Her father's role in the publication of *Rural Hours,* and Bryant's and Irving's responses to the book, are documented in two published sets of correspondence: J. F. Cooper, *Letters and Journals,* 6:131, 216-17, 232, 234, and *Correspondence,* 3:640-41, 671-72, 681, 685-86, 690-92. Thoreau's interest in the book is reported by David Jones in his introduction to the 1968 reprint of *Rural Hours* (Syracuse: Syracuse University Press), xxxvii. On Downing's suggestion to Bremer, see the first chapter of this book.

8. Huth, *Nature,* 34, 48, 51, 89. For a focused study on the meaning of this sort of middle-landscape life during the century, see Stilgoe, *Borderland.* Stilgoe is one of the first commentators to emphasize Susan Fenimore Cooper's contribution to the celebration of country life (24).

9. Knapp, *Country Rambles,* 11. For an excellent discussion of Gilbert White's work and influence in mid-nineteenth-century America, see Worster, *Nature's Economy,* 3-25.

10. On the development of a middle-class ideal of domestic retirement and its connections to maternal associations, see Cott, *Bonds of Womanhood,* 149-59. In 1870 Cooper published an antisuffrage article, "Female Suffrage: A Letter to the Christian Women of America." On her later charitable work, see Cunningham, "Susan Fenimore Cooper." Here Cooper parted company with many of the most popular literary domestics, who, Kelley argues, felt "mocked" by their culture, found women "betrayed" in the home, and supported the call to women's rights (*Private Woman,* 309, 335).

11. Kurth notes that in the 1887 edition of *Rural Hours,* Cooper deleted a good deal of this moralizing, religious material in deference to different reader preferences of the day ("Susan Fenimore Cooper," 137-38).

12. Knapp, *Country Rambles,* 18.

13. On the influence of Thomson on Cooper's text, see Kurth, "Susan Fenimore Cooper," 144.

14. Her role here fits into a similar sort of "noblesse oblige" that Kelley identifies among the literary domestics who shared Cooper's station in life (*Private Woman,* 295).

15. Of course, the Euro-Americans had not been the first to domesticate the region, although they presented themselves as doing so. For accounts of the American Indians' impact on land in the Northeast, see Cronon, *Changes in the Land;* Merchant, *Ecological Revolutions.*

16. Stilgoe, *Borderland,* 115.

17. Huth pinpoints the rise of the conservationist impulse in America in the publication, in 1864, of George Perkins Marsh's *Man and Nature,* noting that prior to this date conservationist voices were isolated and few (*Nature,* 167-69).

18. J. F. Cooper, *Letters and Journals,* 6:149.

19. On the rise of Arbor Day in America in the early 1870s, see Huth, *Nature,* 171. On the development of the bird essay, see Welker, *Birds and Men,* 177-99; Brooks, *Speaking for Nature,* 133-81.

20. S. F. Cooper, *Elinor Wyllys,* 7-8.

21. On the search for privacy and seclusion from the city in the suburbs, and the restricted size of the grounds in the less expensive subdivisions, see G. Wright, *Building the Dream,* 98-113; Stilgoe, *Borderland,* 152-53. Wright comments on the urge in the last half of the century to bring nature indoors and open the house to the out-of-doors with added windows and living rooms decorated with dried leaves, but women engaged in such an endeavor were still restricted to the space inside or directly contiguous to their home. The suburbs of the majority did not contain within their round the varied natural landscape just outside Susan Cooper's door.

22. Susan shared this landscape aesthetic with her father. For a description of his views on the subject, see Nevius, *Cooper's Landscapes.*

23. The sentiment expressed here both reflects and extends the distinctions Victorian middle-class women made between "conspicuous housekeeping" and "homekeeping." Gillian Brown argues that such women converted market commodities purchased for the home into personal possessions through family use, building up emotional attachments to objects over time (*Domestic Individualism,* 47). Cooper suggests that the best such possessions are those that draw us closer to nature by modeling organic forms. She here contrasts frivolous consumerism to responsible domesticity. Her lack of interest in her home's interior amenities also forms a subtle critique of women who would spend more time arranging the parlor furniture than admiring nature's artifacts out in the fresh air.

24. For Wilson's influence on bird lore, see Huth, *Nature,* 25. Cooper had read Wilson and mentions him in *Rural Hours,* 347.

25. On the upholsterer bee, see Knapp, *Country Rambles,* 53, 284-85. On hedgehogs, see ibid., 97-98, 296-97. In support of her description of the bee, Cooper quoted from "Acheta Domestica," the name Miss L. M. Budgen used in publishing her *Episodes of Insect Life,* 3:86-88. Budgen explained that the purpose of her book was to build sympathy for insects by associating "them as much as possible with our domestic habits,—the summer's stroll,—the winter's walk" (vii). Her text includes charming illustrations of insects behaving as humans, offered in part to teach moral lessons through close observation. She often presents herself—the male "Acheta Domestica"—as a well-dressed grasshopper or cricket studying the habits of insects.

26. Maddox, "Susan Fenimore Cooper," 145.

27. Worster, *Nature's Economy,* 11-20.

28. Knapp, *Country Rambles,* 97-98.

29. Cooper no doubt garnered the general values expressed here from John Ruskin and his American followers; but, as with most every other idea she had about nature, she then looked for the application to woman's sphere. On Ruskin's influence on the popularization of wildflowers, see Blunt, *Art of Botanical Illustration,* 231; Foshay, *Reflections of Nature,* 37.

30. Gillian Brown argues that a number of nineteenth-century women shared Cooper's suspicion of much such consumerist display (*Domestic Individualism,* 46-47).

31. Rossiter demonstrates how important the years 1870 to 1890 were for women's participation in natural history (*Women Scientists,* 86). For biographies of Treat, see Harshberger, *Botanists of Philadelphia,* 298-302; Weiss, "Mrs. Mary Treat," 258-73. Treat groups spiders and wasps together under the general heading "insects" in *Home Studies.*

32. Like many scientists of the time, including Darwin in his later years, Treat was convinced that evolution could be triggered by geography. See her comments on the potential for development of a new species of cow as a result of the consumption of a certain plant in *Home Studies,* 220. For a good history of the development of evolutionary ideas, see Eiseley, *Darwin's Century.* All further references to *Home Studies* are cited parenthetically in the text.

33. I am not suggesting that Treat was somehow ahead of her time. As Donald Worster has demonstrated, Darwin's evolutionary theory could be read two ways—one that sanctioned violence and dominance and one that saw in natural selection an im-age of human immersion into the web of nature. Worster argues that Darwin himself came around to this second view in his later years. My point is that, having a choice, Mary Treat, for reasons partially connected to women's culture, was in the biocentric camp at a time when many of her compatriots were not. See Worster, *Nature's Economy,* 178-87.

34. See Welker, *Birds and Men,* 178-208; Brooks, *Speaking for Nature,* 105; Dunlap, *Saving America's Wildlife,* 13-16. Ainley argues, in addition, that ornithology has been less professionalized than other branches of science, leaving an opening for women amateurs not available in other fields ("Field Work and Family," 60). For a general history of women's work in clubs during this period, including conservation activities, see Blair, *Clubwoman as Feminist,* 119.

35. Schmitt discusses the general tendency of this literature, men's and women's, to engage in "Christian ornithology"—the application of moral lessons to bird behavior—but he does not discuss the women's application of such morals to lessons about gender (*Back to Nature,* 36-38).

36. O. T. Miller, *In Nesting Time,* 152. All further references are cited parenthetically in the text.

37. On the relationships between the New Woman, the True Woman, and the cult of domesticity, see Smith-Rosenberg, *Disorderly Conduct,* 173-76; Blair, *Clubwoman as Feminist,* 99-100. Merriam married late and pursued her own research throughout her life. The most complete biography is Kofalk, *No Woman Tenderfoot.* Most of the women ornithologists, Miller included, drew a line between songbirds and such predators as hawks and owls. They, along with male Audubon members, advocated eradicating such destroyers of family life. In this, they were as likely to take up a gun as their male colleagues (Dunlap, *Saving America's Wildlife,* 15).

38. In addition to Kofalk's biography of Merriam, see Brooks, *Speaking for Nature,* 171-75.

39. Merriam, *A-Birding on a Bronco,* 218. All further references are cited parenthetically in the text.

40. Quoted in Kofalk, who also reports that Merriam published under her maiden name after her marriage (*No Woman Tenderfoot,* 51).

41. Smith-Rosenberg notes that those in the first wave of New Women—Merriam's generation—remained tied to Victorian romantic vocabularies in describing their own sexuality, even while the next generation was openly flaunting their sexual behavior (*Disorderly Conduct,* 284). Some of this

reticence clearly informed what the nature writers had to say about bird behavior.

42. Welker, *Birds and Men*, 190. Paul Brooks is to be credited for first recognizing the women's achievements as both insightful and inspirational in *Speaking for Nature*, 163-81.

43. See Huth, *Nature*, 95-104; Welker, *Birds and Men*, 176-84.

44. For a history of the "nature fakers" argument between Burroughs and Earnest Thompson Seton in which Mabel Osgood Wright's observations play a key role, see Brooks, *Speaking for Nature*, 213. For full treatments of the nature fakers battles, see Dunlap, *Saving America's Wildlife*, 27-31; Schmitt, *Back to Nature*, 45-56.

45. Douglas, *Feminization of American Culture*, 397. Douglas argues that the sentimental novelists were pawns of industrial society, espousing "passivity" as a virtue that ultimately denied them real power (and literary greatness). In her study she does not consider literary naturalists or discuss how their work might have been painted with the large brush of masculine dismissal that occurred near the end of the century. Gillian Brown has recently countered Douglas's image of these writers as passive consumers (of things and ideas), posing some domestic novelists as engaged in a sophisticated critique of patriarchy, including the corrupting effects of the marketplace on domestic values (*Domestic Individualism*, 17-18).

46. Rossiter, *Women Scientists*, 79; Welker, *Birds and Men*, 206.

47. Nash chronicles the rise of the "cult of wilderness" in America (*Wilderness*, 141-60). He includes Burroughs and Thoreau as precursors to this masculinized cult. My reading of their contribution suggests that, at different points in their careers (and to fit different needs in cultural history), they have been claimed by both camps.

48. McCulloch-Williams, *Next to the Ground*, 139-40; Kumin, *In Deep*, 75.

49. Rich, *We Took to the Woods*, 319-20; Hubbell, *Country Year*, 120-21.

50. Kumin, *In Deep*, 178.

51. Merchant, "Women of the Progressive Conservation Movement." The standard biography of Austin is Stineman, *Mary Austin*. On her reputation as a nature essayist and her work as a conservationist, see Brooks, *Speaking for Nature*, 183-92; Blend, "Mary Austin." Austin admired Muir. In *Land of Little Rain* (152), she contrasted his approach to nature with that of scientific professionals who fail to see the moral precepts in their developing understanding of the biophysical environment.

52. Nash, *Wilderness*, 200-271.

53. Hoover, *Gift of the Deer*, 114; Zwinger, *Beyond the Aspen Grove*, 68, 80; J. Johnson, *Inland Island*, 53.

54. The quotation is from Austin's stories of women's lives in the Mojave (*Lost Borders*, 10-11). On her contradictory attitudes toward feminism, see Stineman, *Mary Austin*, 129-30. On her support for the younger generation's struggle for a female sexual vocabulary, see Smith-Rosenberg, *Disorderly Conduct*, 284-85. On her differences with other Progressive Era women (including naturalists) on the meanings of home and domesticity, see Blend, "Mary Austin," 14, 31-32. For a full discussion of female imagery in her work, see Norwood, "The Photographer and the Naturalist."

55. Kumin, *In Deep*, 87.

56. J. Johnson, *Inland Island*, 90.

57. Austin, *Land of Little Rain*, 88.

58. J. Johnson, *Inland Island*, 9.

59. Zwinger, "Thoreau on Women," 3 (Thoreau's quotation).

60. See Zwinger and Teale's account of their journey in *A Conscious Stillness*.

61. Women (and men) who write about nature refer primarily to male authorities, both for scientific proof and for sensitive evocations of flora and fauna. That I chose not to include Annie Dillard in my discussion of contemporary female nature essayists shows how effectively such silencing sometimes works. Dillard's *Pilgrim at Tinker Creek* has earned more recognition than any of the books discussed in this chapter. Dillard is a skilled nature writer, but no more so than Josephine Johnson. That Dillard is female enters rarely into her account of the seasonal round of her cabin. Nor does the cabin itself bear the emotional meanings of home. Dillard has stated that she wrote *Tinker Creek* off 1,103 note cards in a library carrel. Rachel Carson receives a brief mention, in a chapter including references to Joseph Wood Krutch, Rutherford Platt, Edwin Way Teale, and Arthur Stanley Eddington (162-84). Describing the books she reads as including men and women, Dillard names only the men: "Knud Rasmussen, Sir John Franklin, Peter Freuchen, Scott, Peary, and Bird; Jedediah Smith, Peter Skene Ogden, and Milton Sublette; or Daniel Boone" (43). Based as it is in Dillard's education, *Tinker Creek* reflects

our contemporary inheritance of that late nineteenth-century effort to remasculinize science and nature writing. *Tinker Creek*'s fame rests in part on its appeal to that tradition. On her writing method, see Major, "Pilgrim of the Absolute," 363.

62. Zwinger, "Thoreau on Women," 3.

Bibliography

Ainley, Marianne Goszwingertonyi. "Field Work and Family: North American Women Ornithologists, 1900-1950." In *Uneasy Careers and Intimate Lives,* edited by Pnina G. Abir-Am and Dorinda Outram, 60-77.

Austin, Mary. *The Land of Little Rain.* 1903. Reprint. Albuquerque: University of New Mexico Press, 1974.

———. *Lost Borders.* New York: Harper and Brothers, 1909.

Blair, Karen J. *The Clubwoman as Feminist: True Womanhood Redefined, 1868-1914.* New York: Holmes and Meier, 1980.

Blend, Benay. "Mary Austin and the Western Conservation Movement: 1900-1927." *Journal of the Southwest* 30 (Spring 1988): 12-34.

Blunt, Wilfrid. *The Art of Botanical Illustration.* New York: Charles Scribner's Sons, 1951.

Bradsher, Frieda Katherine. "Women in the Works of James Fenimore Cooper." Ph.D. dissertation, University of Arizona, 1979.

Bremer, Fredrika. *The Homes of the New World: Impressions of America.* 2 vols. Translated by Mary Howitt. New York: Harper and Brothers, 1853.

Brooks, Paul. *Speaking for Nature: How Literary Naturalists from Henry Thoreau to Rachel Carson Have Shaped America.* Boston: Houghton Mifflin, 1980.

Brown, Gillian. *Domestic Individualism: Imagining Self in Nineteenth-Century America.* Berkeley and Los Angeles: University of California Press, 1990.

Budgen, Miss L. M. *Episodes of Insect Life.* 3 vols. New York: J. S. Redfield, Clinton Hall; Boston: B. B. Mussey and Co., 1851-52.

Cooper, James Fenimore. *Correspondence of James Fenimore Cooper.* Edited by his grandson, James Fenimore Cooper. 2 vols. New Haven: Yale University Press, 1922.

———. *The Letters and Journals of James Fenimore Cooper.* Edited by James Franklin Beard. 6 vols. Cambridge: Harvard University Press, 1968.

Cooper, Susan Fenimore [pseud. Amabel Penfeather]. *Elinor Wyllys; or, The Young Folk of Longbridge.* Anon. 2 vols. Philadelphia: Carey and Hart, 1846.

———. "Female Suffrage: A Letter to the Christian Women of America." *Harper's New Monthly Magazine* 41 (August, September 1870): 438-46, 594-600.

———. *Rural Hours.* By a Lady. New York: George P. Putnam, 1850.

Cooper, William. *A Guide in the Wilderness.* New York: Gilbert and Hodges, 1810.

Cott, Nancy F. *The Bonds of Womanhood: Woman's Sphere in New England, 1780-1835.* New Haven: Yale University Press, 1977.

Cronon, William. *Changes in the Land: Indians, Colonists, and the Ecology of New England.* New York: Hill and Wang, 1983.

Cunningham, Anna K. "Susan Fenimore Cooper—Child of Genius." *New York History* 25 (July 1944): 339-50.

Dillard, Annie. *Pilgrim at Tinker Creek.* New York: Bantam Books, 1975.

Douglas, Ann. *The Feminization of American Culture.* New York: Alfred A. Knopf, 1977.

Dunlap, Thomas R. *Saving America's Wildlife.* Princeton, N.J.: Princeton University Press, 1988.

Eiseley, Loren. *Darwin's Century: Evolution and the Men Who Discovered It.* Garden City, N.Y.: Doubleday, 1958.

Foshay, Ella M. *Reflections of Nature: Flowers in American Art.* New York: Alfred A. Knopf in association with the Whitney Museum of American Art, 1984.

Fuller, Margaret. *Summer on the Lakes, in 1843.* Boston: Little and Brown, 1844.

Hanley, Wayne. *Natural History in America: From Mark Catesby to Rachel Carson.* New York: Quadrangle/New York Times Book Co., 1977.

Harshberger, John W. *The Botanists of Philadelphia and Their Work.* Philadelphia: T. C. Davis and Son, 1899.

Hoover, Helen. *The Gift of the Deer.* 1965. Reprint. Boston: Houghton Mifflin, 1981.

Hubbell, Sue. *A Country Year: Living the Questions.* New York: Random House, 1986.

Huth, Hans. *Nature and the American Mind: Three Centuries of Changing Attitudes.* Berkeley and Los Angeles: University of California Press, 1957.

Johnson, Josephine. *The Inland Island.* Columbus: Ohio State University Press, 1969.

Kelley, Mary. *Private Woman, Public Stage: Literary Domesticity in Nineteenth-Century America.* New York: Oxford University Press, 1984.

Knapp, John Leonard. *Country Rambles in England; or, Journal of a Naturalist, with notes and additions by the author of "Rural Hours."* 1829. Reprint. Edited and annotated by Susan Fenimore Cooper. Buffalo, N.Y.: Phinney and Co., 1853.

Kofalk, Harriet. *No Woman Tenderfoot: Florence Merriam Bailey, Pioneer Naturalist.* College Station: Texas A&M University Press, 1989.

Kumin, Maxine. *In Deep: Country Essays.* Boston: Beacon Press, 1987.

Kurth, Rosaly Torna. "Susan Fenimore Cooper: A Study of Her Life and Works." Ph.D. dissertation, Fordham University, 1974.

Leighton, Ann. *American Gardens of the Nineteenth Century: "For Comfort and Affluence."* Amherst: University of Massachusetts Press, 1987.

McCulloch-Williams, Martha. *Next to the Ground: Chronicles of a Countryside.* New York: McClure, Phillips and Co., 1902.

Maddox, Lucy B. "Susan Fenimore Cooper and the Plain Daughters of America." *American Quarterly* 40 (June 1988): 131-47.

Major, Mike. "Pilgrim of the Absolute." *America* 138 (May 6, 1978): 363-64.

Merchant, Carolyn. *Ecological Revolutions: Nature, Gender, and Science in New England.* Chapel Hill: University of North Carolina Press, 1989.

———. "Women of the Progressive Conservation Movement, 1900-1916." *Environmental Review* 8 (Spring 1984): 57-86.

Merriam, Florence A. *A-Birding on a Bronco.* Boston: Houghton Mifflin, 1896.

Miller, Olive Thorne. *In Nesting Time.* Boston: Houghton Mifflin, 1888.

Nash, Roderick. *Wilderness and the American Mind.* New Haven: Yale University Press, 1967 (3d ed., 1982).

Nevius, Blake. *Cooper's Landscapes: An Essay on the Picturesque Vision.* Berkeley and Los Angeles: University of California Press, 1976.

Norwood, Vera. "The Photographer and the Naturalist: Laura Gilpin and Mary Austin in the Southwest." *Journal of American Culture* 5 (Summer 1982): 1-29.

Rich, Louise Dickinson. *We Took to the Woods.* Philadelphia: J. B. Lippincott Co., 1942.

Rossiter, Margaret W. *Women Scientists in America: Struggles and Strategies to 1940.* Baltimore: Johns Hopkins University Press, 1982.

Schmitt, Peter J. *Back to Nature: The Arcadian Myth in Urban America.* 1969. Reprint. Baltimore: Johns Hopkins University Press, 1990.

Smith-Rosenberg, Carroll. *Disorderly Conduct: Visions of Gender in Victorian America.* New York: Alfred A. Knopf, 1985.

Stilgoe, John R. *Borderland: Origins of the American Suburb, 1820-1939.* New Haven: Yale University Press, 1988.

Stineman, Esther Lanigan. *Mary Austin: Song of a Maverick.* New Haven: Yale University Press, 1989.

Treat, Mary. *Home Studies in Nature.* New York: Harper and Brothers, 1885.

Welker, Robert Henry. *Birds and Men: American Birds in Science, Art, Literature, and Conservation, 1800-1900.* Cambridge: Harvard University Press, 1955.

Welter, Barbara. *Dimity Convictions: The American Woman in the Nineteenth Century.* Athens: Ohio University Press, 1976.

Worster, Donald. *Nature's Economy: A History of Ecological Ideas.* Cambridge: Cambridge University Press, 1977.

Wright, Gwendolyn. *Building the Dream: A Social History of Housing in America.* New York: Pantheon Books, 1981.

Zwinger, Ann. *Beyond the Aspen Grove.* New York: Random House, 1970.

———. "Thoreau on Women." *Thoreau Society Bulletin,* no. 164 (Summer 1983): 3-7.

Zwinger, Ann, and Edwin Way Teale. *A Conscious Stillness: Two Naturalists on Thoreau's Rivers.* Amherst: University of Massachusetts Press, 1984.

Rochelle Johnson (essay date 1999)

SOURCE: Johnson, Rochelle. "James Fenimore Cooper, Susan Fenimore Cooper, and the Work of History." In *James Fenimore Cooper: His Country and His Art,* Papers from the 1999 Cooper Seminar (no. 12), edited by Hugh C. MacDougall, pp. 41-5. Oneonta, N.Y.: The State University of New York College at Oneonta, 1999.

[*In the following excerpt, Johnson asserts that Susan Fenimore Cooper's writing reflects a desire to preserve the natural environment for its cultural and historical significance, while her father's works suggest an acquiescence to the necessary loss of landscape in the name of progress.*]

In the Introduction to her 1853 edition of John Leonard Knapp's *Country Rambles,* Susan Fenimore Cooper wrote, "We Americans . . . are still, in some sense, half aliens to the country . . . there is much ignorance among us regarding the creatures which held the land as their own long before our forefathers trod the soil, and many of which are still moving about us, living accessories of our existence, at the present hour" (16). Even a cursory look at Susan Cooper's publishing career reveals her interest in curbing this ignorance; in addition to writing *Rural Hours* and seeing it through nine editions, and then preparing a "revised," much shortened version, she wrote a number of essays devoted to natural history and undertook some substantial editorial projects that contributed to the genre. She also wrote quite a few articles about history in general; and her correspondence suggests that she nearly—if not entirely—completed a historical narrative about indigenous peoples. I would like to explore briefly here Susan Cooper's particular construction of history and, specifically, how the sense of national consciousness that emerges from her writings differs fundamentally from that of her father. By exploring Susan Cooper's specific uses of history in conjunction with her interests in natural history and in the various life forms present on the North American continent prior to European settlement, I hope to demonstrate that her writings work to revise the dominant national-historical myth of nineteenth-century America.

Lawrence Buell has suggested that part of what reveals the difference between Susan and James's environmental visions is Susan's emphasis on the natural world. Buell notes that throughout *Rural Hours,* Susan Cooper privileges nature to such a degree that one comes away from her book with the sense that she hoped to lead her readers toward a specific belief—namely, that human society would benefit from a more meaningful relationship with its natural surroundings.[1] Indeed, Cooper suggests throughout her volume that natural history is integral to human society. She also suggests, however, that natural history is integral to human history, and, more specifically, to American culture's sense of its presence on—and development of—a particular landscape.

For example, as she discusses in an often-anthologized section of *Rural Hours* the various significances of a stand of old-growth trees, she explains that it holds a value beyond its aesthetic and potential economic benefits to humans; it is, she asserts, valuable also in a historic sense. The trees are "a monument of the past," the only stand left in "the fields of the valley," for "their nearer brethren have all been swept away" (116). Cooper explains that "[t]here is no record to teach us" all that these trees have witnessed, but then, as if to demonstrate their historical significance, she uses them as a means to a speculative historical record of all that they have witnessed. That is, she imagines history from the perspective of the stand of trees. Through this perspective, she gains insight into what Philip Fisher has called the "moment just before beginning"—the period immediately preceding the formalization of European colonization (Fisher 26). By looking back in time through the

trees, as it were, and into the "pre-history" of America that they witnessed, Cooper is able to share with her readers the changes that the landscape underwent preceding the period of discovery, during exploration, and then during early settlement.

Cooper's use of this single stand of old-growth trees as a symbol of an earlier, idealized time, as well as of a vanished wilderness, is quite typical of her period. As Fisher explains, during this period in American letters, "The wilderness is always understood as vanishing or threatened" (10)[2]; furthermore, "the historical consciousness of the 1840s" was "fixed" on this "moment just before [the] beginning" of America's founding (26). Yet Fisher's analysis asserts that most mid-nineteenth-century authors used this trope of the vanishing wilderness as a means of "collaps[ing]" pre-history (26)—as a means, that is, of obviating the need to consider fully the destructive nature of European settlement. Susan Cooper, however, does not seem to use the trope in this way. Rather than invoking pre-history in order to "[train] resignation" or depict "forces as beyond control" (18), as Fisher explains other writers do, Cooper invokes pre-history by means of the old trees, specifically in order to call this pre-history to readers' attention—to remind readers that "forces" are not "beyond control" but, instead, are a matter of human control. "The aspect of the wood," she writes, "tells its own history" (118); and the trees ought to be preserved, she claims, precisely because of their ability to remind readers of a time prior to America—and prior, even, to the *idea* of America (119-20). She criticizes "the stout arm so ready to raise the axe to-day" (120) and expresses her gratitude at the individual who "has so long preserved them" (119). Americans' resignation thus seems to be a problem for Cooper, not an inevitable outcome of the country's development.

The stand of old-growth trees is significant to Cooper, then, both for what it can remind Americans of—namely, their comparatively short occupation of this land and their displacement of both human and nonhuman presences on the land—and for its power to serve a certain function of history. Without the presence of this natural life form, Cooper herself would seemingly lose her imaginative access to the historical "record" that the trees signify. Their physical presence, that is, enables her natural history. The demise of the trees, on the other hand, would weaken the culture's knowledge of its land by removing this symbol of pre-history. The small stand of pines conveys "the spirit of the forest" (120), a spirit that younger trees could not possibly convey, because they were not alive during the forest's reign. Without these trees, then, American history—the nation's sense of its presence on the land—is incomplete and, therefore, in the mind of Cooper, inadequate.

This passage from *Rural Hours* thus makes an implicit argument for the importance of preservation as a means of reconstructing natural history.

Susan Cooper undertakes in this entry for Monday, July 23, a brief essay in "natural history," then, in two senses of that term. First, she provides the history of a natural life form; and, second, she puts "history"—usually thought of in terms of humans—into "natural" terms—or, into the terms of nature—by providing a history from the trees' perspective. Her entry, of course, also has the effect of commemorating the stand of trees—of communicating its very presence on her valley floor, for, needless to say, it is now gone. This brief essay serves to mark the trees in her culture's memory. Finally, then, we can see the July 23 entry as an attempt to document a changing landscape and to inform future readers of the importance of preserving life forms that pre-date European settlement. *Rural Hours*—like the pines themselves—thus serves as a "record" of history, a chart of change.

Interestingly, stands of old pine trees reappear in one of Cooper's later essays, one which helps us understand that she herself conceived of *Rural Hours* as a record of history. This later essay also helps us realize Cooper's own refusal to sanction an ideology that deemed the disappearance of species "inevitable." This later essay appears in the August, 1893, *Harper's New Monthly Magazine,* and opens with a description of "a stern crest of spearlike pines" which stood forty years ago atop the hills along the Susquehanna ("Lament" 472). Cooper describes the trees and those that lived around them, but concludes her opening paragraph with a terse, but not all that surprising, announcement of their death: "The tall old pines have fallen beneath the axe" (427). With these words, Cooper establishes the theme of the essay: loss. In the essay, titled **"A Lament for the Birds,"** Cooper lists birds which have now vanished from her area, much like the old pines. She uses the pines to segue to the now-absent birds; as she describes a couple of species that likely "floated on Lake Otsego" in years past—the white pelican and wild swan—she invokes the July 23 entry from *Rural Hours* and she makes a connection between the absent birds and the absent trees. She suggests that "those wild old pines could have told us a strange tale of bird life connected with the past" (472). Her memory of the trees serves, as the trees themselves did in *Rural Hours,* as a means to history.

Cooper then shifts, however, from birds whose past presence in her region she surmises to those of whose previous habitation she is certain; as she explains, she has access to "a clear record of bird life" during her current century. Here she discusses the wild pigeon at length, and then she turns to specific moments when the passenger pigeons visited Cooperstown. Her references

demonstrate to us that we can see *Rural Hours* functioning as her record of bird history. Later in **"A Lament for the Birds,"** she describes, for example, an early morning one summer day—June 8, 1847—when "a large flock of wild-pigeons became bewildered in the fog, and lost their way" (473), an event which she had described in *Rural Hours,* where, however, she gives the date as June 7 (68). Later in the essay, Cooper lists a number of birds that "never failed in years past to bring joy with them to our lawns and meadows" but which now, in 1893, "are rare visitors." She describes seeing, in years past, "twenty merry goldfinches . . . clustered in eager company on a single tall thistle," and those familiar with her September 27 entry in *Rural Hours* will recall Cooper witnessing a flock of "several hundred" birds, many of which were "goldfinches" (*Rural Hours* 191); that day, she had seen groups of birds hanging onto one thistle stalk. She confesses in *Rural Hours* to having seen "six or eight" birds on one stalk, however, not twenty (*Rural Hours* 192). Cooper similarly makes use of her record of environmental history in *Rural Hours* when she refers to walking "about the village streets and not[ing] the deserted nests" after the birds have left for the winter. As she says, "Frequently there were two, three, and occasionally even four and five nests in the same tree" (474).[3] Indeed, in *Rural Hours* she records that on one February 22, she had counted "one hundred and twenty-seven nests" on one afternoon walk (324). "To-day," she writes for *Harper's,* "you may perhaps discover one or two nests in a dozen trees" (474).

These examples of Cooper's 1893 essay drawing on *Rural Hours* help us make meaning of her 1850 volume as a record of natural history and environmental change. Preservation was clearly a moral imperative for Cooper, not simply for utilitarian or even for eco-centric reasons, but for reasons pertaining to America's cultural memory. As Margaret Welch has recently demonstrated, American natural history seems to have adapted in the late eighteenth and early nineteenth centuries to the rapidly changing American landscape by making lamentations for disappearing species a staple of the genre;[4] and we can see Cooper's lament for the trees as evidence of this shift in natural history. She turns her attention in *Rural Hours* repeatedly to disappearing life forms: in addition to lamenting trees, she writes about animal species that were locally extinct, about plant and animal species that were dwindling in her region, and about weeds and other indigenous plants that were giving way to nonnative species.[5] Through her discussions of these subjects, she calls attention to the ways in which the landscape is being re-written and revised by European life forms.

Cooper clearly felt the need to document what she seems to have realized was a quickly vanishing American landscape, and her documentation serves not as a means of sanctioning change or progress, but as a means of providing Americans ignorant of their environments—as well as future Americans—a record of their material world. In this way, Susan's writing differs from her father's.

James Fenimore Cooper had, of course, also given ample attention to a disappearing landscape—and specifically to the "vanishing" race of Native Americans. Numerous scholars, including Philip Fisher, Carolyn Karcher, and Richard Slotkin, have pointed to the ways in which Cooper's Leatherstocking Tales in particular reflect the tensions in nineteenth-century America between nature and civilization, between sacrifice and progress, and between despoliation and development.[6] And numerous scholars have interpreted Cooper's resolutions of these conflicts as participating in an ideology of conquest. Philip Fisher, for example, explains that Cooper's main genre—the historical romance—is itself "a device for practicing how to meet a certain but postponed future. . . . [It] trains resignation and gives an elevated moral tone to stoic regret. It pictures forces as beyond control, already underway, and creates central figures who embody processes they do not control" (18). While James Fenimore Cooper lamented a vanishing wilderness and the rapid demise of a native culture, he also deemed the changes brought about by American progress inevitable.

We see this sense of inevitability even in his Native American characters' outlooks as, for example, Tamenund in the final sentences of *The Last of the Mohicans* seems to sanction his own culture's demise: "The pale-faces," he exclaims, "are masters of the earth, and the time of the red-men has not yet come again" (350). While Tamenund's words seem to promise hope for the "red-men"—their time may "come again"—the plot of the novel all but assures readers of the disappearance of the native presence: the last of the Mohicans is, after all, dead. And, as if to confirm the Natives' demise and indicate their complicity in their own cultural genocide, Cooper has Tamenund say, "My day has been *too* long" (350, my emphasis); apparently, he wants to go. As Lucy Maddox argues, Cooper perpetuates the "master narrative" of the period, which portrays and sanctions the "inevitable" vanishing of both the "savage" red man and the American wilderness (*Removals* 49). The sense of history that results from Cooper's narratives is a history shaped by a ratifying of the progress of America, a history destined to a specific and certain end—an end that clearly requires a seriously adapted natural world and the removal, largely, of Native populations.

Susan Cooper, however, as we have seen, tries to create a memory for an immanent material loss. She records a life that has importance outside of human concerns, and in so doing, she calls attention to the prehistory of America. Doing so expands the prevalent mid-nineteenth-century concept of "history" to include natural—or environmental—history. By foregrounding an America that will be seriously diminished through the loss of natural life forms, Susan also reveals her interest in preserving the landscape as part of the cultural memory. We can see her as working against her culture's tendency to see nature as a backdrop for human affairs, to conceive of the natural world as a metaphoric and ideological confirmation of American progress, or simply as a symbolic place for retreat from the growing urban and industrial centers. She urges readers to see the natural world as a reality—as a place rich in native life forms and therefore valuable, and, finally, as a place reflecting history.

However, she also urges readers—through her example—to recognize their humble position in the natural world. Scholars have pointed to Cooper's humility and have explained her humble narrative stance through discussions of her gender, her specific role as a fairly privileged woman in mid-nineteenth rural America, her adherence to traditional natural theology, and her position as the daughter of the nation's most prominent novelist.[7] However, we have not yet explained the fact that her most pronounced humility often occurs precisely in the face of nature, and often in passages that have nothing to do with God or religion. When she discusses forests and laments their rapid demise at the hand of the ax, for example, she emphasizes to readers that the culture largely neglects to consider humanity's humble position in relation to the natural world. Trees—and other natural life forms—are a means to a historical perspective for Cooper, and that perspective is a means to a humility that she values and finds necessary to the nation's morality. That humility, in turn, acts as a corrective to a nationalistic ideology of conquest which sanctions the demise of various forms of life. It appears that Cooper's relation to nature—and her belief in its historical and cultural importance—led her to challenge her country's national myth of progress and manifest destiny in part because that dominant ideology failed to endorse her experience of humility in nature.

We have in American literary scholarship a prominent tradition of tracing "nature" as symbol or myth, or as a dominant ideological cultural force. We find these themes addressed in some of the most influential monographs of the twentieth century. Clearly analyses of the public myths surrounding nature are essential to our understandings of American literary, environmental, and cultural history. And arguably, of course, scholars attend to a tradition of symbolic representations of nature because this is precisely what the literature provides.

Susan Fenimore Cooper's attention to the literal natural world, however, and to her humble stance in relation to it, seems to invite us to expand this tradition in critical praxis and to consider how literary attention to the physical environment—not as ideological force or mythic construction—but as daily reality and material presence, complicates our understanding of nature's function in American literature and culture. For it seems that Susan Cooper, like her father, envisioned her publications as having historical as well as aesthetic value. And like her father, she wishes to preserve for readers aspects of the natural world and the American landscape. Unlike her father, however, Susan called attention to disappearing physical life forms rather than to the myth that, for many Americans, signified and explained away an America vanishing in the name of "progress."[8] Indeed, as Susan states in her 1868 preface to **Rural Hours,** "Progress . . . is not always improvement."

Notes

1. In Buell's words, Susan Cooper "valorizes the natural by incorporating it into a vision of society brought closer to nature" (48).

2. Lucy Maddox (*Removals*) and Lee Clark Mitchell also analyze the nineteenth-century discourse of a "vanishing" America.

3. Cooper's phrasing in her "Lament for the Birds" essay suggests that she quite likely had a copy of *Rural Hours* in front of her as she composed: for example, in "Lament," she writes, "Frequently there were two, three, and occasionally even four and five nests in the same tree" (474); in *Rural Hours,* she had written, "In several instances this afternoon, we saw two, three, and even four nests in one tree. . . ." (323).

4. Welch explains, "Natural history had begun to act as a record for the disappearance of species" (43). Lee Clark Mitchell also notes the prevalent impulse to lament a "vanishing" America during this period; he refers specifically to "the impulse to fix a record" of disappearing life forms—the Native American and the wilderness in particular (xiv).

5. See pages 49-50, 64-67 and 76-77. The "prettier natives" (50), she states, are giving way to the nonnative "strangers to the soil" (64).

6. These dichotomies are articulated by Lee Clark Mitchell (45).

7. See Buell (especially 47), Levin, Norwood, and Maddox.

8. My reading of Susan Cooper's challenge to her father's ideology differs from Lucy Maddox's reading of the same; see Maddox's "Susan Fenimore Cooper and the Plain Daughters of America."

Works Cited

Buell, Lawrence, *The Environmental Imagination: Thoreau, Nature Writing, and the Formation of American Culture.* Cambridge: Harvard University Press, 1995.

Cooper, James Fenimore, *The Last of the Mohicans* [1826]. New York: Penguin, 1986.

Cooper, Susan Fenimore, "A Lament for the Birds." *Harper's New Monthly Magazine* 87 (August 1893), 472-474.

————, Introduction to *Country Rambles in England: Or, Journal of a Naturalist: With Notes and Additions, By the Author of "Rural Hours".* By John Leonard Knapp. Buffalo: Phinney, 1853, 11-20.

————, Preface to *Rural Hours.* New York: Putnam, 1868.

————, *Rural Hours* [1850]. Ed. Rochelle Johnson and Daniel Patterson. Athens, Ga.: University of Georgia Press, 1998.

Fisher, Philip, *Hard Facts: Setting and Form in the American Novel.* New York: Oxford University Press, 1987.

Jehlen, Myra, *American Incarnation: The Individual, the Nation, and the Continent.* Cambridge: Harvard University Press, 1986.

Karcher, Carolyn L., Introduction to *Hobomok and Other Writings on Indians.* Ed. Karcher. New Brunswick: Rutgers University Press, 1986, ix-xxxviii.

Kolodny, Annette, *The Lay of the Land: Metaphor as Experience and History in American Life and Letters.* Chapel Hill: University of North Carolina Press, 1975.

Levin, Susan, "Romantic Prose and Feminine Romanticism." *Prose Studies* 10.2 (1987), 178-195.

Maddox, Lucy, *Removals: Nineteenth-Century American Literature and the Politics of Indian Affairs.* New York: Oxford University Press, 1991.

————, "Susan Fenimore Cooper and the Plain Daughters of America." *American Quarterly* 40.2 (1988), 131-146.

Marx, Lee, *The Machine in the Garden: Technology and the Pastoral Ideal in America.* New York: Oxford University Press, 1964.

Mitchell, Lee Clark, *Witnesses to a Vanishing America: The Nineteenth-Century Response.* Princeton: Princeton University Press, 1981.

Norwood, Vera, *Made From this Earth: American Women and Nature.* Chapel Hill: North Carolina University Press, 1993.

Rosenthal, Bernard, *City of Nature: Journeys to Nature in the Age of American Romanticism.* Newark: University of Delaware Press, 1980.

Slotkin, Richard, *The Fatal Environment: The Myth of the Frontier in the Age of Industrialization, 1800-1890.* New York: Atheneum, 1985.

Smith, Henry Nash, *Virgin Land: The American West as Symbol and Myth*. New York: Vintage, 1950.

Tichi, Cecelia, *New World, New Earth: Environmental Reform in American Literature from the Puritans through Whitman*. New Haven: Yale University Press, 1979.

Welch, Margaret, *The Book of Nature: Natural History in the United States 1825-1875*. Boston: Northeastern University Press, 1998.

Rochelle Johnson (essay date 2000)

SOURCE: Johnson, Rochelle. "*Walden, Rural Hours*, and the Dilemma of Representation." In *Thoreau's Sense of Place: Essays in American Environmental Writing*, edited by Richard J. Schneider, pp. 179-93. Iowa City: University of Iowa Press, 2000.

[*In the following essay, Johnson compares Cooper's nature journal with Thoreau's* Walden, *attempting to account for the very different response each received from American readers.*]

> Mere facts & names & dates communicate more than we suspect.
>
> —Henry David Thoreau's *Journal*

When Barry Lopez, surely one of this century's most gifted nature writers, posed the question, "What is a dignified response to the land?," he raised an issue that has been central to nature writers for well over a century.[1] How best to represent a physical place, its various and interdependent life forms, and an individual human's response to this place are crucial and central issues for many. Place-based nature writing necessitates representing observation, perception, and experience, and while language has served as a solution of sorts to this dilemma of representation, the effectiveness of language to respond to a place—let alone in a "dignified" manner—has been called into question by writers even as they have relied on language as a means to that representation. We recall the now-famous words from Henry David Thoreau's *Walden* which reflect this very issue: "I desire to speak somewhere *without* bounds," he writes, "for I am convinced that I cannot exaggerate enough even to lay the foundation of a true expression." For Thoreau, the "truth" of words "is instantly *translated*," and so the dilemma of representing place deepens.[2] This is, then, not only a problem of developing a dignified response to the land, but also a problem of conveying observation and perception, and of cultivating an effective means of representation. Indeed, for many nature writers—and certainly for many of us familiar with the dictums of poststructural theory—the pronounced and problematic divisions between self, language, and place pose fundamental challenges to a satisfying union of human perception and physical reality.

It is, perhaps, partly because Susan Fenimore Cooper's *Rural Hours* (1850), the first book of nature writing published by an American woman, does not reveal its author's struggle with these issues that Cooper's text has been largely dismissed in the twentieth century. While *Rural Hours* was praised in the nineteenth century for the "simple earnestness" of Cooper's "style" and as "delightful reading,"[3] critics in the twentieth century have, until quite recently, found the very simplicity of *Rural Hours* to be indicative of its literary weakness.[4] Just one manner in which Cooper's prose may seem simpler than Thoreau's is its absence of direct attention to the inadequacies of language to represent perception of the natural world. Of course, there are other differences between these two mid-nineteenth-century authors, and I will discuss some of them further, but this one seems especially important since many critics have come to privilege just this dimension of place-based nature writing. In *Rural Hours*, Cooper avoids the reliance on figurative language that characterizes Thoreau's *Walden* prose and through which he most clearly struggles with the dilemma of representation. As she records in journal form the seasonal changes and varieties of life that she witnesses in her Lake Otsego region of New York state, Cooper creates a record of her place that suggests her faith in literal description. That is, she casts her observations in a style that suggests she sees no disparity between her perception, her object of description, and her linguistic representation. Whereas Thoreau exhibits many times in *Walden* his recognition of the potential ineffectiveness of language and his awareness of the difficulties inherent in representing his experience of place in words, Cooper's prose reflects her trust that her language will result in a dignified response to the land. Thus, the very quality that Peter Fritzell has attributed to the "best American nature writers"—an overt interest in the relationship between the self and language—does not appear in one of the most widely read works of nature writing in the nineteenth century.[5]

And yet, despite their differences, *Walden* and *Rural Hours* have similar purposes. Each author sought to present a specific place to readers, and each described his or her surroundings with the hopes of affecting readers' environmental sensibilities. These are projects not only of perception and observation, but also of connection. Cooper and Thoreau both sought cultural change, and they hoped that their literary projects would perform the cultural work of leading people to consider more seriously their connections to natural places.

That these two volumes of nature writing appeared within four years of each other, pursued similar goals, and met with markedly different responses from American readers suggests that their authors' styles and methods affected the reading public in quite distinct ways. Robert Kuhn McGregor has said of Thoreau's contemporaries and of their lack of enthusiasm for *Walden* upon its publication in 1854, "America was not prepared to find spirit in rocks and trees."[6] And yet, **Rural Hours** had faced a similar audience, having been published just four years before, and the nine nineteenth-century editions of Cooper's book suggest that her conveyance of the "spirit" in nature found many ready readers. Of special interest to us here, then, both for explaining the different receptions of these books and, more importantly, for exploring the dilemma of representation seemingly inherent in nature writing, are the contrasting methods Cooper and Thoreau employ in hopes of reaching their goals—specifically, how they represent their perception and experiences in order to bridge the gap between word and place and as a means of leading readers to a subtler recognition of the physical environment.

In this essay, I analyze these authors' differing means of encouraging cultural change, and demonstrate that by considering *Walden* in relation to **Rural Hours** we achieve a fuller understanding of the ways in which mid-nineteenth-century writers employed language on behalf of nature. Through these contemporaneous representations of place, we gain insight into the different theories of representation that circulated in this period, and we thereby acquire a more accurate understanding of Thoreau's place in the history of American nature writing. We also come to recognize that to judge a work of nature writing by the degree to which it exhibits its author's concern about issues of representation is to impose anachronistically a specific conception of language—one which may demonstrate our own complicity in an ideology privileging the metaphysical over the literal, or the philosophical over the material. Finally, this understanding of our own predicament may enable us to address the dilemma of representation still very much alive in our own environmental crisis.

The radical difference between Thoreau's and Cooper's descriptions of their narrative selves offers a quick and telling look at their distinctive narrative postures and methods. Clearly, place-based nature writing offers to some degree an anthropocentric view of its subject, simply because a writer brings a human perspective to the project; yet Thoreau's celebration of his "brag[ging] as lustily as Chanticleer in the morning . . . if only to wake my neighbors up" (84) seems markedly more self-assured and self-centered than Cooper's description of herself, sans metaphor, as a "rustic bird-fancier" who has completed a "simple record" of "trifling observations" on "the seasons in rural life."[7] Thoreau's use of metaphor here typifies his rhetorical strategies throughout *Walden,* where he often relies on metaphor not only to communicate his purposes in representing his Walden experiment but also to convey many aspects of his physical surroundings. Cooper, on the other hand, points critically to the use of this rhetorical device in describ-

ing her place. Whereas Thoreau claims of Walden Pond that he is "thankful that this pond was made deep and pure for a symbol" (287), Cooper, when admiring her village's Lake Otsego, remarks, "we are *all but cheated* into the belief that the waters know something . . . of our own hearts" (69, emphasis added). By drawing attention to the symbolic interpretation that Americans conventionally apply to a body of water, Cooper reminds readers of the human tendency to conceive of natural things metaphorically and thus anthropocentrically. For we may imagine the lake's sympathy, but the lake knows nothing "of our own hearts." Nature exists independently of human conceptions of it. Cooper thus appears intent on encouraging and maintaining a cautious awareness of the appropriative tendencies of the human imagination.

One result of Cooper's preference in this regard is that she seems to employ a more "objective" rhetoric; by avoiding symbolism or allegory, she maintains a distinction of sorts between her imagination and nature. While her lack of figurative language and philosophical debates may make her prose appear simple, Cooper's writing nonetheless enables a humble approach to place.[8] Cooper's reliance on a journal format augments this effect by connecting her observations to specific times and locales, thereby suggesting the prominence of the objects of her literary attention—most often natural objects and phenomena—over both her persona and her necessarily human orientation toward place. Her rhetorical posture seems thus designed to represent a non-appropriative environmental ethic.

In his Journal, Thoreau wrote increasingly in an "objective" style; this, along with his attention to the dilemmas of composition in his Journal, suggests that he came to believe that to represent place most effectively, and in the least appropriative manner, one must move beyond a metanarrative of representation—a prose overtly conscious of its inevitable inability to convey natural phenomena, individual perception, and experience—and toward a prose that represents these things as accurately—and as literally—as possible. Despite Thoreau's apparent discovery in this regard, however, readers and critics in the twentieth century are drawn to *Walden*'s depiction of place—despite the abstract qualities of that depiction. *Walden* exhibits the slipperiness of representing perception, for even while it attempts to discourage an anthropocentric view of place, Thoreau seems to get caught up in a style that seems, by its very nature, appropriative. In *Walden,* Thoreau engages the dilemma of representation in two particularly clear ways: by reworking his Journal writings in order to present his related thoughts in a form more unified, coherent, and polished than they appear in the Journal, and by using metaphor as a means of granting the Concord wilds a meaning more accessible to those readers living citified lives of quiet desperation. Yet even as

Thoreau reworked his *Walden* manuscript for publication, we find in his Journal his concern precisely with these methods of conveying his experience and perception. Even as he increasingly metaphorized his prose, for example, he speculated in 1852, "Mere facts & names & dates communicate more than we suspect."[9] And as he argued even amid *Walden*'s copious figurative language, "we are in danger of forgetting the language which all things and events speak without metaphor" (111). Further, as he mined his Journal entries, taking episodes and thoughts out of their original contexts, Thoreau mused, "Perhaps I can never find so good a setting for my thoughts as I shall thus have taken them out of" (*PJ* 4:296).

What these approaches to representing perception risk, Thoreau seems to recognize, is further encouraging an anthropocentric view of one's place in the natural world, one implication of which was the appropriative and utilitarian ethic that the majority of Thoreau's neighbors embraced and against which he wrote. However, the famous loon passage in *Walden* provides one instance in which Thoreau's use of metaphor implicitly encourages the appropriative perspective of nature and wilderness that he worked so hard elsewhere to discourage. Further, through an examination of the construction of this passage, we realize that Thoreau's revision process could—in wrenching his observations out of context—diminish significantly his recognition of nature's otherness.

The loon passage has two fairly distinct parts: preceding Thoreau's two-and-a-half-page account of chasing the loon appears a one-paragraph commentary on the Concord hunters' predations. This published, two-part passage merges two distinct episodes in Thoreau's writings: the first portion, commenting on the Concord hunters' pursuit of loons in autumn, Thoreau wrote in the fall of 1845, and it appears in the original manuscript version of *Walden* (*PJ* 2:213-14).[10] The second and major portion of the passage, however, is a reworded Journal entry from October 8, 1852, a passage which records his actual encounter with a loon on the surface of the pond (*PJ* 5:367-69). Combining the passages in *Walden*, however, makes Thoreau's loon chase appear as a metaphoric rendering of the hunters' pursuit, especially since the two parts of the passage have similar structures and repeat key phrases and images. The "Mill-dam sportsmen," like Thoreau on his pond, "are on the alert" to the loon's "wild laughter" (233). Whereas the hunters arrive at the pond "with patent rifles and conical balls and spy-glasses" (233), Thoreau's chase of the loon on the water begins with his arming himself with oars: "I pursued with a paddle" (234). While Thoreau's tools for pursuit clearly pose less danger to the bird, he nonetheless emphasizes the parallel aspects of the hunt and his own pursuit, and thereby suggests the consumptive dimension of his pursuit of his "adversary" (235).

This passage has been interpreted as one of Thoreau's most effective representations of his simultaneous yearning for the wild and feeling of ultimate separation from the world of nature. Indeed, while Thoreau's literal characterizations of the loon's wild voice and skilled diving emphasize his distinction from it,[11] his rendering of the loon as symbolic of pure wildness allows readers to interpret his chase of the loon as a quest for wildness itself. Through his complex rhetorical maneuvers, he underscores both his own struggle for accurate perception of the wild and the very difficulty of representing an aspect of nature in language. And yet, even while Thoreau communicates his distance from the loon and hence, implicitly, his humility in the face of the natural world, his consumptive desire for the loon rivals his humility. That is, while Thoreau's passage demonstrates his separateness from the loon, the passage also—especially through its reliance on the metaphor of hunting—risks promoting an anthropocentric perception of place, or of nature more generally. Certainly while this may not have been Thoreau's intent, what emerges from his published encounter with the loon is a representation of an encounter with wildness that is guilty of diminishing the very wildness *Walden* seeks to represent. Thus, Thoreau's use of metaphor—as a means of representing and advocating his perception of natural phenomena and his less appropriative environmental ethic—fails him.

In addition to ascribing the metaphor of the hunt to his encounter with the loon, Thoreau alters the tone of his earlier 1845 passage on the hunting of loons and waterfowl generally by removing from the published version a key passage. In the 1845 Journal, Thoreau had written of a waterfowl who had lost its mate to hunters: "And the silent hunter emerges into the carriage road with ruffled feathers at his belt. . . . And for a week you hear the circling clamor clangor of some solitary goose through the fog—seeking its mate—peopling the woods with a larger life there than they can hold" (*PJ* 2:214). When this passage does appear in slightly revised form in *Walden,* it rests in an entirely different context, quite far removed from Thoreau's original clear condemnation of hunting. Originally it conveyed both Thoreau's and the goose's disorienting and wrenching sense of loss, emphasizing both humans' disregard for natural life and their inability to recognize or conceive of nature's distinctly nonhuman version of loss and passion. In its reincarnation in the "Spring" chapter of *Walden,* amid signs of spring's birth, it becomes much more a celebratory statement of the powers of the wild—a symbol of both the force of life and of nature's will to regeneracy (313). Thus, the *Walden* paragraph on the loon hunters originates in a passage centered on and powerfully lamenting the varieties of hunting in autumn; the published version, however, greatly diminishes this mourning tone.

These revisions effectively demonstrate the problematic rupturing of perception involved in Thoreau's representation of his original experience. In fact, the famous loon passage could be said—somewhat paradoxically—to be as much about the difficulty of representing the natural as it is an enactment of that difficult representation. As Daniel Peck notes, "the loon insists upon its separateness from its observer" and thus illustrates for both reader and Thoreau the intractable distance between human and nonhuman.[12] And yet Thoreau's hunting metaphor conveys and mimics the process by which he appropriates the loon in his linguistic representation. Ultimately, then, his representation may be seen to have failed, in that his "hunt" for the loon fails, but as a lesson in consumptive perception, it may be seen to succeed, emphasizing in its final, published version individual transcendence over any call for an end to the destruction of loons or over a celebration of the uninhibited wildness of an individual loon.

Finally, Thoreau's prevalent use of metaphor in *Walden* suggests not only the limitations of human language, but also the limitations of Thoreau's own perception of place. SueEllen Campbell writes, "As [Aldo] Leopold says, 'The outstanding characteristic of perception is that it entails no consumption and no dilution of any resource.' Of course, how we see will often direct what we do."[13] Thoreau's view reflects his own struggle with his culture's appropriative ethic. While "Thoreau's refusal to organize the Walden landscape tidily for his readers may be one sign of his intent to get us lost in it,"[14] Thoreau's method emphasizes the "getting lost" over the literal "landscape" and, as such, further complicates the already slippery and complex task of representing one's perception of place. The landscape at Walden Pond is finally, for most readers, an abstract and philosophical landscape. As Thoreau claims in his "Conclusion," "The universe is wider than our views of it" (320); Thoreau's record of his place and life at Walden Pond perhaps ironically reveals that the dilemma of representing place concerns waking human perception to an awareness of its tendency toward a narrow view.

Like *Walden,* Susan Cooper's **Rural Hours** engages the cultural work of reshaping readers' perception of place; however, in a complex way, Cooper's critique of her culture is much more understated than Thoreau's, and this complexity results as much from Cooper's humble narrative stance as it does from her lack of overt attention to matters of representation. Cooper's prose is characterized by a somewhat paradoxical, humble assertiveness. Given the near absence of discussions of her purpose in recording her observations, Cooper appears to assume an inherent value to her descriptions. While she offers readers brief mentions of the varieties of birds returning to Cooperstown as spring settles in, for instance, she offers no developed discussion of their

significance—neither to herself nor to the place; she merely notes their return (e.g., 11). She similarly notes the plants appearing and blooming (e.g., 12, 28-29); and she mentions the seasonal return of insects: "The fire-flies are gleaming about the village gardens this evening—the first we have seen this year" (70). In addition, she notes the presence of food on the table that reflects the changes in season: on Tuesday, June 19, for example, she writes, "Fine strawberries from the fields this evening for tea" (75). Her narrative's distinction stems from its absence of self-consciousness, as it were; Cooper's use of language suggests her assurance that readers would discern a purpose for such straightforward representation. Her essential disregard for the gap that Thoreau so clearly regarded as persisting between object and subject implies her belief that readers could share in her place and its life forms merely through reading her record of them.

From Cooper's essay **"Small Family Memories,"** which she wrote in 1883, well after the publication of **Rural Hours,** we may discern a clue to how she intended **Rural Hours** to affect readers. For Cooper, **Rural Hours** represented an outgrowth of her devotion to nature, which had its origins in her childhood experiences with her maternal grandfather: "Grandfather [De Lancey] soon commenced my botanical education—being the eldest of the little troop, I often drove with him, in the gig, about his farms and into his woods, and it was my duty to jump out and open all the gates. In these drives he taught me to distinguish the different trees by their growth, and bark, and foliage. . . . He would point out a tree and ask me to name it, going through a regular lesson in a very pleasant way. Such was the beginning of my **Rural Hours** ideas."[15] While this passage presents a number of intriguing insights into the development of Cooper's nature study, its emphasis on naming provides a particularly significant context for Cooper's **"Rural Hours ideas."** In much of **Rural Hours,** Cooper dedicates herself to naming her surroundings, that is, to recording the natural life forms and seasonal changes; and she does so in a prose so removed from metaphysical and representational concerns that it seems—to modern readers—simple. However, Cooper's interest in "naming" her surroundings suggests her adherence to an eighteenth-century understanding of natural history.[16] Her faith in language's ability to represent nature reflects the natural historian's faith in the "relation between things and the human eye," a relation which Michel Foucault explains "defines [eighteenth-century] natural history."[17] The simplicity and naïveté that readers have found in Cooper's prose are best understood not as evidence of her poor writing, but as evidence of Cooper's adherence to a fast-fading conception of language. Foucault has explained that the "apparent simplicity, and that air of naïveté [that natural history] has from a distance" belie the complexity of its underlying philosophy of representation, and we can, by extension, say the same of Cooper's nature writing.[18] The "apparent simplicity" of *Rural Hours* proves to be its complex bridging of subject and object and its confidence in representing perception. As Foucault explains, eighteenth-century natural history *is* the "fundamental articulation of the visible." Its purpose, method, and emphasis are *naming*: "its construction requires only words applied, without intermediary, to things themselves." Whereas today—and this was increasingly so throughout the nineteenth century—we recognize "not the sovereignty of a primal discourse, but the fact that we are already, before the very least of our words, governed and paralysed by language," in the eighteenth and early nineteenth centuries, "Natural history [found] its locus in the gap that is now opened up between things and words."[19]

Cooper thus held a faith not so much in language as in representation—that is, she believed that "things and words . . . communicate in a representation," to borrow Foucault's words.[20] And given her unwavering Protestant faith, which she exhibits in *Rural Hours* and which was clearly informed by the tenets of natural theology, Cooper likely believed that giving language to her place was tantamount to spreading the word of God. Through her project of naming her surroundings and the seasonal changes, her "science" and religion would collaborate. By devoting a volume to descriptions of the life and natural phenomena of her village environs, Cooper thus shared with readers both the wonders of the creation and a model, offered through herself, of an individual closer to God through her very attentiveness to her environment. Through this understanding of Cooper's faith in representation, we realize that she had lofty goals indeed for *Rural Hours*; by means of her apparently simple descriptions, she reconstituted the natural environment before her readers' eyes. Moreover, this understanding of the cultural context of *Rural Hours* further explains her humble narrative posture. To be anything but humble in approaching the natural environment—God's domain—would be nothing less than blasphemous. Finally, for Cooper to concern herself with the efficacy of language was as unnecessary as it would be distracting.

Interestingly, Cooper's reliance on this understanding of representation serves partly to enable her to call attention to the changes she witnesses in her surrounding landscape. Many passages in *Rural Hours* suggest that Cooper realized that as the physical environment was altered, Americans' sense of history would change as well. And this concerned Cooper, because she believed that a failure to perceive nature's alteration would result in both an ill-conceived sense of American history and blind adherence to an ethic of "progress," which would inevitably damage the physical environment. Since Cooper recognized the negative effects of this ethic of progress, however, she hoped to convey her belief that

cultural memory, or a sense of history, is tied to perception, and that America's prevailing inattentiveness to the natural environment would result in a misrepresentation of the environment in the cultural memory. One obvious result of this would be a history that failed to account fully for the changes in the land. But a more disturbing implication of this distortion in cultural memory was that it would enable and encourage a disregard and even an apathy for environmental destruction. If Americans could not notice the perceptible changes in their environments, they could not represent these changes or their results in the national consciousness. Cooper sought to reverse this tendency by representing in *Rural Hours* the remnants of natural and cultural history she observed in her surroundings. Through her attention to the history revealed in landscape, she seeks both to enlarge her readers' capacities for perception and to call attention to the dangers of destroying nature—and, thereby, history. Cooper's faith that language adequately represents place aids this project.

Two passages in *Rural Hours* particularly manifest this potential of Cooper's faith in literal description. In the midst of a passage in which she describes her local forests—their aesthetic values, their support of diverse life forms, and the varieties of trees found therein—Cooper notes, "The forest lands of America preserve to the present hour something that is characteristic of their wild condition, undisturbed for ages" (128). Her detailed representation of old-growth forests, when placed alongside this remark, indicates that Cooper values the forests for their historical significance. They testify, she explains, to a history fading from her culture's memory. This remark could serve merely to remind readers of their quick and impressive "improvements" to the American landscape; however, Cooper points out to readers that while the forests provide "a sweet quiet, a noble harmony, [and] a calm repose, which we seek in vain elsewhere" (127), they are rapidly disappearing. Her impassioned call for preservation, which appears amid her discussion of forests (131-35), thus emphasizes that Americans risk losing this aspect of the "wild" in their cultural memory. She therefore shares her perception of the forest in order to suggest that the trees "are connected in many ways with the civilization of [the] country" (133), and that one crucial way in which they are connected to America's civilization is that they stand as a testament to a history that will be forever altered should the trees disappear. The American landscape now tells its own history, and this history must remain available to observation. Without the old-growth trees, we lose this sign of change, this evidence of the land's life preceding European colonization. Without the trees, Americans lose a reminder of the American wilderness.

Given the lamentative tone of passages like this one, Cooper's remark in **Rural Hours** that "a stranger moving along the highway looks in vain for any striking signs of a new country" (88)—that is, of a wilderness condition—takes on new weight. If Americans cannot discern the history of the land from the land itself—that is, if alterations to the environment prevent its revelation of its history of development—then Americans cannot perceive their destruction of nature. And with this lack of perception comes, of course, a lack of representation. Americans cannot know what they have displaced if their environment offers no record of the displacement. Thus, not only will America's natural environment suffer from large-scale development, but American culture will, as well, because of both its ignorance and its perceptual distance from the environment.

Cooper therefore instructs her readers in how to "read" the landscape, teaching them to develop as keenly as possible their perceptive powers. As she looks out over a "few miles of country in sight at the moment," she describes her view; and, typically, using the plural pronoun, she reveals that a scrupulous eye can perceive many stages of cultivation in the area: "we amused ourselves by following upon the hill-sides the steps of the husbandman, from the first rude clearing, through every successive stage of tillage, all within range of the eye at the same instant" (89). She points to the "pine stumps" as evidence of recent cultivation; to other signs of some "fallen forest"; and to "traces of water-work" (90, 92). She further differentiates areas, explaining that "those wild pastures upon hill-sides, where the soil has never been ploughed, look very differently from other fallows" (91). And she points to the "softer touches" that "[tell] the same story of recent cultivation": "It frequently happens, that walking about our farms, among rich fields, smooth and well worked, one comes to a low bank, or some little nook, a strip of land never yet cultivated, though surrounded on all sides by ripening crops of eastern grains and grasses." She foregrounds her close knowledge of botany as she explains, "One always knows such places by the pretty native plants growing there," as opposed to the nonindigenous plants that she finds frequently elsewhere (91). Here, then, Cooper encourages a finely tuned perception even as she expands cultural memory by surveying the evidences of natural history available even from one point of observation.

Thus, Cooper saw clear and deep value in "mere" description. In addition to bringing her readers as close as she could to her place, she employed descriptive language as a means of preserving her landscape and of preserving the history that her continent had undergone prior to—and during the early stages of—European settlement. Cooper's particular conception of language thus enabled her to recognize an important new purpose for the genre of nature writing. By recording her place in language, she might literally preserve it for readers; she might also, however, encourage her culture toward a much more acute environmental sensibility by calling attention to her country's path of widespread natural destruction. In relying on language to convey both place and history, she hoped to encourage a humbler ethic in her culture.

Cooper's emphasis on description granted her prose an important quality in a nature writer—humility. Lawrence Buell reminds readers that this is a quality that Thoreau seems to have sought later in his career; whereas in **Rural Hours** Cooper "managed to cultivate a nonegoistic, ecocentric sensibility," this was a narrative posture "toward which Thoreau had to grope his way laboriously."[21] In Robert Kuhn McGregor's view, we see this change begin during Thoreau's first spring at Walden Pond, as he records spring's arrival in his Journal: "No morals, no transcendental lessons accompany the journal entries describing these visions. Simply a lump in the throat in watching nature's overawing beauty."[22] As McGregor demonstrates, we arrive at a very different view of Thoreau's environmental sensibility if we consider *Walden* not the culmination of Thoreau's environmental career, but rather a mere "progress report"[23] in the development of Thoreau's environmental consciousness, a mere step in his long-term quest to convey what Barry Lopez calls "a dignified response to the land." However, our picture of environmental literary history is further complicated if we consider his quest alongside Cooper's 1850 record of her "ecocentric sensibility."

McGregor's demonstration that Thoreau moved toward a more biocentric view of the world during the 1850s suggests clearly that as Thoreau became increasingly familiar with his natural environment, his own humility in the presence of nature increased. Yet even in 1854, Thoreau asserts, "There is no such thing as pure *objective* observation. Your observation, to be interesting, *i.e.* to be significant," and—he might have added—to be possible at all, "must be *subjective*."[24] In 1852, he questions his method of mining the Journal for passages and thus presenting materials somewhat out of context, as he did with the lone goose crying out in his "Spring" chapter: "I do not know but thoughts written down thus in a journal might be printed in the same form with greater advantage—than if the related ones were brought together into separate essays. They are now allied to life—& are seen by the reader not to be far fetched—It is more simple—less artful" (*PJ* 4:296). Simplicity, as Thoreau realized, allowed for the written word to be more closely "allied to life," and less allied to art—or, we might say, more closely allied to nature and less so to human reformulating. As Thoreau had written in 1851, "We see too soon to ally the perceptions of the mind to the experience of the hand—to prove our gossamer truths practical—to show their connexion [*sic*] with our every day life (better show their distance from our every day life)" (*PJ* 4:223). This is clearly what Thoreau worked toward in his later years; indeed, as Frank Stewart notes, Thoreau's life work can be interpreted as a "process of perpetually seeking a truth in nature and a way to render it that would betray neither nature nor language."[25] Thus, while he was clearly cognizant and leery of the problems inherent in representation, the form he worked toward was one in which he humbled himself as narrator and recorded more deliberately "mere facts & names & dates." This is not to say, of course, that Thoreau embraced the conceptions of representation or of natural history that Cooper held, but rather to suggest that even with his more "modern" concerns about perception and representation, he recognized that the most powerful means of understanding his place was to focus more on it, and less on problematizing his means of representation: language. In his later writings, Thoreau worked to create nature's narrative.

Cooper, through her acceptance of a fading theory of language, achieves through her text a representation of her place's natural phenomena. In the perceptive words of one mid-nineteenth-century reviewer, the only story of **Rural Hours** is "the story of the earth."[26] Today, readers in Cooperstown consult this book in order to check in on the progress or cycle of this story, comparing Cooper's descriptions of a day's natural phenomena against the phenomena they witness around them. We might say, then, that in spite of its weak presence in literary history throughout much of the twentieth century, **Rural Hours** has achieved its ultimate goal by leading readers to notice the natural surroundings of a specific place. Clearly, Cooper preserved not herself through her prose, but the passage of time and her environment in Cooperstown. Paradoxically, then, her inability to conceive of a failure of language allowed her to create the story that encouraged "a dignified response to the land."

This mid-nineteenth-century struggle over the issue of representation becomes especially significant when we consider recent theorists' insights into the relation between narrative representation and our environmental predicament. According to Richard Kerridge, the environmental crisis results in part from a dilemma of representation: "The real, material ecological crisis," he argues, "is also a cultural crisis, a crisis of representation. The inability of political cultures to address environmentalism is in part a failure of narrative."[27] We simply do not have narrative structures that can convey or contain the depth and degree of our predicament. Clearly, the shape of narratives available to a given culture largely determines the range of its potential responses to nature, the kinds of nature people can imagine, and the choices for representation available to writers. Exploring the history of nature writers' representations might enable us to expose the ways in which our own narrative forms repeat and endorse an aesthetics of representation which has, in this century, dangerously privileged the philosophical and theoretical at the expense of the literal and material world.

Notes

1. Lopez and Wilson, "Ecology and the Human Imagination," 29.

2. Thoreau, *Walden,* 324, 325. Subsequent page references are cited parenthetically in the text.

3. Downing, review [of *Rural Hours*], 232; Sanborn, *Abandoning an Adopted Farm,* 110.

4. See David Jones, introduction to *Rural Hours,* by Susan Fenimore Cooper, esp. xxxvii-xxxviii; and Edward Halsey Foster, *The Civilized Wilderness: Backgrounds to American Romantic Literature, 1817-1860,* 100.

5. Fritzell, *Nature Writing,* 11.

6. McGregor, *A Wider View of the Universe,* 119.

7. Cooper, *Rural Hours,* 72, 3. Subsequent page references are cited parenthetically in the text.

8. Lawrence Buell has also made this observation in *The Environmental Imagination: Thoreau, Nature Writing, and the Formation of American Culture,* 177.

9. Thoreau, *Journal, Vol. 4: 1851-1852,* 296. Subsequent volume and page references to the Princeton edition of the Journal are cited parenthetically with *PJ.*

10. See also "The First Version of *Walden,*" in J. Lyndon Shanley, *The Making of Walden,* 193.

11. H. Daniel Peck observes, "The entire scene emphasizes the independence of object from subject" (*Thoreau's Morning Work,* 120).

12. Ibid., 120.

13. Campbell, "The Land and Language of Desire," 130.

14. Buell, *Environmental Imagination,* 135.

15. Cooper, "Small Family Memories," 32-33.

16. For discussions of relevant changes in natural history, see Michel Foucault, *The Order of Things: An Archaeology of the Human Sciences,* and Ernst Mayr, *The Growth of Biological Thought: Diversity, Evolution, and Inheritance. Rural Hours* provides ample evidence of Cooper's familiarity with the natural history writings of John James Audubon, Georges Cuvier, Alexander von Humboldt, Charles Lyell, Thomas Nuttall, John Torrey, and Alexander Wilson, among others.

17. Foucault, *Order of Things,* 133.

18. Ibid., 132.

19. Ibid., 134, 131, 298, 129-30.

20. Ibid., 130.

21. Buell, *Environmental Imagination,* 177.

22. McGregor, *Wider View of the Universe,* 68.

23. Ibid., 120.

24. Thoreau, *Journal of Henry David Thoreau,* ed. Torrey and Allen, vol. VI, 236-37.

25. Stewart, *Natural History of Nature Writing,* 11.

26. Downing, review, 231.

27. Kerridge, introduction to *Writing the Environment,* 4.

Works Cited

Buell, Lawrence. *The Environmental Imagination: Thoreau, Nature Writing, and the Formation of American Culture.* Cambridge, Mass.: Harvard University Press, 1995.

Campbell, SueEllen. "The Land and Language of Desire: Where Deep Ecology and Post-Structuralism Meet." *Western American Literature* 24, 3 (November 1989): 199-211.

Cooper, Susan Fenimore. *Rural Hours.* 1850. Reprint edited by Rochelle Johnson and Daniel Patterson. Athens: University of Georgia Press, 1998.

Downing, Andrew Jackson. Review [of *Rural Hours*]. *Horticulturalist* 5, 5 (November 1850): 232.

Foster, Edward Halsey. *The Civilized Wilderness: Backgrounds to American Romantic Literature, 1817-1860.* New York: Free Press, 1975.

Foucault, Michel. *The Order of Things: An Archeology of the Human Sciences.* Translation of *Les Mots et les choses.* New York: Vintage, 1970.

Fritzell, Peter A. *Nature Writing and America: Essays upon a Cultural Type.* Ames: Iowa State University Press, 1990.

Jones, David. Introduction to *Rural Hours,* by Susan Fenimore Cooper. Syracuse, N.Y.: Syracuse University Press, 1968.

Kerridge, Richard. Introduction to *Writing the Environment: Ecocriticism and Literature,* edited by Richard Kerridge and Neil Sammells. New York: Zed Books, 1998.

Lopez, Barry, and Edward O. Wilson. "Ecology and the Human Imagination." In *Writing Natural History: Dialogues with Authors,* edited by Edward Lueders, 7-35. Salt Lake City: University of Utah Press, 1989.

Mayr, Ernst. *The Growth of Biological Thought: Diversity, Evolution, and Inheritance.* Cambridge, Mass.: Belknap Press of Harvard University Press, 1982.

McGregor, Robert Kuhn. *A Wider View of the Universe: Henry Thoreau's Study of Nature.* Urbana: University of Illinois Press, 1997.

Peck, H. Daniel. *Thoreau's Morning Work: Memory and Perception in "A Week on the Concord and Merrimack Rivers," the Journal, and "Walden."* New Haven, Conn.: Yale University Press, 1990.

Sanborn, Kate. *Abandoning an Adopted Farm.* New York: D. Appleton & Co., 1894.

Shanley, J. Lyndon. *The Making of* Walden. Chicago: University of Chicago Press, 1957.

Stewart, Frank. *A Natural History of Nature Writing.* Washington, D.C.: Island/Shearwater, 1995.

Thoreau, Henry David. *Journal. Vol. 4: 1851-1852.* Edited by Leonard N. Neufeldt and Nancy Craig Simmons. Princeton, N.J.: Princeton University Press, 1992.

————. *The Journal of Henry David Thoreau.* 14 vols. Edited by Bradford Torrey and Francis H. Allen. Boston: Houghton Mifflin, 1906.

————. *Walden.* Edited by J. Lyndon Shanley. Princeton, N.J.: Princeton University Press, 1971.

Nina Baym (essay date 2001)

SOURCE: Baym, Nina. "Susan Fenimore Cooper and Ladies' Science." In *American Women of Letters and the Nineteenth-Century Sciences,* pp. 73-90. New Brunswick: Rutgers University Press, 2001.

[*In the following essay, Baym depicts Cooper's nature writing as a means to present to women readers a rural life that reflects an educated, class-conscious, progressive society.*]

Susan Fenimore Cooper's **Rural Hours** (1850) showed how scientific knowledge contributed to an ideal of gracious country living for women.[1] The book's anonymous publication "by a Lady"—at a time when anonymous authorship had gone out of style—quaintly made the point that the author's name mattered less than her class affiliation.[2] The book is shaped as a journal kept almost daily throughout a year, beginning and ending in spring. It merges accounts of excursions in the Cooperstown environs with associated material pieced together from a huge array of print sources, most of them scientific.

Modern editors of **Rural Hours** describe the book as "a dynamic interplay of science and literary nature writing" (xi). Lawrence Buell calls Cooper a "literary bioregionalist" with an "encyclopedic passion for bringing bibliographical resources to bear" on her "native township" (406). Both descriptions point to Cooper's interweaving of the literary, the scientific, and the sheerly descriptive; but in confining the focus to Cooperstown ("literary bioregionalism") they overlook the way in which Cooper's use of scientific texts remakes the township as an item in a global survey, with the result that excursions in Cooperstown become a gateway to the world. Bibliographic allusions place the native township on a map that, in turn, is clearly shown to be the product of reading in the library. *Rural Hours* signals its intertextual intentions as early as the second entry (March 7), when the sighting of a loon introduces observations by Charles Lucien Bonaparte (probably from his 1838 *Comparative List of the Birds of Europe and North America*) about loons in the Alps and Apennines (4-5).

The reason for elevating nature into textuality involves, one might surmise, Susan Cooper's practical awareness that country life was rather dreaded than welcomed by genteel women. As an acute natural observer and inveterate reader, Cooper presents a way of being in the rural world that shows other elite women how to make rural life—in Sarah Ripley's phrase cited in chapter 1—"supportable," and quite specifically supportable to "fine ladies" (Goodwin, "Botanic Mania," 20). As Cooper says in a late footnote, the book, written "by a learner only," is offered "to those whose interest in rural subjects has been awakened" as "a sort of rustic primer, which may lead them, if they choose, to something higher" (330).

Behind Ripley's comment, and behind Cooper's book as well, one senses the writers' awareness that "ladies" usually hated rural life because it was boring and boorish. Cooper wants to change that perception, in part by changing the character of rural life itself. She writes in her introduction to *The Rhyme and Reason of Country Life* that she wants to contribute, and help other women contribute, to the "national progress" toward "country life in its better form" (31, 30). By "better form" she means a country life suitable for, and reflective of, genteel cultivation. Where Sarah Hale or Almira Phelps urged science on women as a means to attain and demonstrate their rationality, Cooper urges it on them as a way to attain and demonstrate that they had class.

This work on behalf of rational rural gentility had particular relevance to the decades when the appurtenances of leisured country life increasingly became signifiers of class status. Thanks to such emerging social markers as summer homes, weekend retreats, landscaped grounds, gentlemen's farming, recreational hunting, and scenic tourism, a group of urbanites with newly disposable income were being enticed back to a countryside whose poverty perhaps they or their parents had fled.[3]

There had of course been from classical times a tradition of literary pastoral countering urban corruption with ideals of rural simplicity; but practically speaking, the harsh conditions of early national rural life did not support facile associations between the country and cultivated leisure.

There are many ways to account for the increasing reconstitution, in antebellum America, of vacant country real estate as adult playgrounds; the point is that people who well knew the harshness and sordidness of country life needed to be coaxed back to nature by learning to see it differently. It was no accident that the vogue for natural history in England and the United States arose just as access to country life became a status marker in both nations.[4] This coincidence may also help account for the success of *Rural Hours,* which was both fully aware of changing times and specifically directed toward women readers. The purpose of Cooper's work is to model country life as a constant intellectual, civilized, rational pleasure and therefore to show ladies a rational, civilized way of being ladylike. Country ladies demonstrate their class by reconstituting their rustic surroundings through a combination of literary and scientific knowledge.

In earlier chapters I have alluded to the function of school geography as a protoscience. The geographical approach to terrain in *Rural Hours* would not seem unfamiliar to readers, nor would its journal-like structure, which they would have encountered in the many biography-memoir hybrids published in the nineteenth century. The book obviously synthesizes these forms, along with models drawn from English writing about rural life.[5] Yet, the immediate inspiration for *Rural Hours* was probably the example of the well-known traveler and inventor of the science of physical geography (arguably, the construer of geography itself as a science), Alexander von Humboldt.[6] The first two volumes of Humboldt's magisterial and immensely popular multivolume *Cosmos* appeared in English in 1848, just when Cooper began her own project. Their publication led to the reissue of some of his earlier travel writings; the 1840s had also been the great decade of U.S. scientific exploration, including the Fremont land expedition and the Wilkes naval expedition.

Although *Rural Hours* does not resemble *Cosmos* in form, Humboldt's excitement about the huge world out there waiting to be catalogued, every individual item of which had some (perhaps as yet unknown) relation to the whole, could easily motivate a project whose aim is less to catalogue the locale accurately than to perceive its relation to the global. To be sure, Humboldt really traveled to all the places he wrote about, while in *Rural Hours* Cooper does her voyaging beyond Cooperstown through print resources. But this is exactly the point of *Rural Hours*; it shows how the judicious use of print resources allows country ladies to experience their surroundings as a cosmopolitan adventure.[7] ***Rural Hours*** may thus be thought of as a book of travels in which the use of scientific texts turns the local into the global while making travel a textual affair. Cooper shows repeatedly that even local terrain is unintelligible without the text-based interpretation. There is simply no recognizing the plant or bird one has sighted without consulting a guidebook; among diverse printed sources, none serve her purposes better than scientific works of natural history.

Because Cooper thinks that knowing where one is in the world requires textual knowledge rather than intuition, she collapses the distinction between reality and textuality just as she blurs the boundary between real and armchair travel. This is not to say that ***Rural Hours*** has no grounding in the real world. According to David Jones, the modern editor of the 1887 revision, her botanical identifications are of a caliber that "perhaps only a trained botanist can fully appreciate" (xxx). Yet, to the extent that the book is an instructed record of observations, it necessarily calls on texts. Anything but the artless, spontaneous record of walks and drives it sometimes pretends to be, ***Rural Hours*** thoughtfully refracts the notes on which it is based, which may have been recorded initially to be the basis for a book.[8]

Entries in Cooper's virtual journal vary from brief descriptions of the day's weather to extended set pieces, essays sometimes running to six thousand words or more. The connection between these essays and the day's outing is sometimes quite tenuous, suggesting that they might have been written independently of their position in the book. When bad weather precludes excursions, especially in winter, Cooper chooses sometimes to describe what she sees outside the window, sometimes to concentrate entirely on summarizing and commenting on books. Some of her many topics are botanical and ornithological identifications, the habitats of undomesticated flora and fauna, agriculture, horticulture, sylvaculture, milling, mining, political economy, rural technologies, local architecture, hunting, fishing, folkways, holidays, and biblical exegesis. Among her print sources are books of natural history, including the official surveys of New York State and some of the New England states; journal, pamphlet, and newspaper items; statistical reports; geographies; scientific travels; histories; and the Bible.

As she connects the terrain with the library, Cooper emerges as an exemplar of female rationality and decorous piety whose combination of scientific amateurism with Christian orthodoxy would not have been out of place twenty-five years earlier than the actual publication year of ***Rural Hours.*** No Transcendental intuitionist, she believes in the biblical God of Christian Revelation, who has authored nature but is not resident in it.

As a devout Episcopalian, she derived orthodox homilies from natural observation; these, scattered here and there in ***Rural Hours,*** are arguably the book's weakest segments. She writes for example on May 16: "At hours like these, the immeasurable goodness, the infinite wisdom of our Heavenly Father, are displayed in so great a degree of condescending tenderness to unworthy, sinful man, as must appear quite incomprehensible—entirely incredible to reason alone—were it not for the recollection of the mercies of past years, the positive proofs of experience" (45).

If the whole book read like this, there would be little reason to open it now. But the persona also represents a contemporary revision of the English amateur scientist and gentleman perambulator, a sort of nationalized, feminized, and updated Gilbert White. Cooper writes in ***The Rhyme and Reason of Country Life*** that it is the union of Christianity with a "general diffusion of a high degree of civilization which has led us to a more deeply felt appreciation of the works of the creation," such that "the verse of the fields—the rural hymn,—becomes the last form of song, instead of being the first" (27, 29).[9]

As she construes country living as an opportunity for women readers to develop themselves as genteel ladies, she hopes to disrupt the traditional association of women *with* physical nature by showing them how to think *about* physical nature, so as to perform themselves as intellectual beings. This is a common motif among all advocates of a scientific education for women. But Cooper nuances the work of the previous generation of scientific affiliates, who argued that women should be proficient in science to demonstrate their possession of reason, by proposing that possession of scientific knowledge also testifies to their possession of class.[10]

There is much in ***Rural Hours*** about the shortcomings of uneducated folk; that Cooper is no rustic boor is something she is at pains to clarify, less perhaps because of any insecurity she might feel than because of the likely insecurities of her readers. She approaches country people themselves less as conservators of useful local knowledge than as a population in need of instruction. She often asks for the whereabouts of a plant she is seeking, or for the name of a plant she has found, only to encounter entrenched ignorance:

> It is really surprising how little the country people know on such subjects. Farmers and their wives, who have lived a long life in the fields, can tell you nothing on these matters. The men are even at fault among the trees on their own farms, if these are at all out of the common way; and as for the smaller native plants, they know less about them than Buck or Brindle, their own oxen. . . . The women have some little acquaintance with herbs and simples, but even in such cases they frequently make strange mistakes; they also are at-

tracted by the wild flowers; they gather them, perhaps, but they cannot name them.

(83)

In the context of pervasive rustic ignorance, Cooper's emphasis on right naming has obvious class implications. Her chief strategy in every botanical excursion in *Rural Hours*—to see what is there at a particular point in the calendrical year, to identify and interpret it according to the best authorities—is something other than the desire to know nature as it really is. It is rather to know nature as the educated, enlightened, and well-bred know it. Whether she goes in quest of a particular natural object or takes what she finds, her proceedings always require names. The knowledge of the natural world she desires already translates the natural world into taxonomy. The concept of the "same" plant implies a standard. One cannot assert, or know, that the "same" plant is being differently named in different places or that "different" plants are getting the same name in different places without a stable point of reference. This stable point can only be imposed, top down, by scientific botany. The marsh marigold, for example, is a "handsome" flower called cowslip by the "country people"—"though different entirely from the true plant of that name" (30). She wants the name to be "true" to the "true" plant because she wants to integrate the particular with the general, the local with the global, under the sign of an Enlightenment universal science that is chiefly concerned to identify discrete species correctly so as to compile a comprehensive planetary inventory of the creation.[11]

But if, on the one hand, Cooper installs a distinction between herself and the rural population, or more generally between herself and those who needed to earn their own livings, she also installs one between herself and the sciences on which she relies to elevate herself above country and working people. She says her book, written "by a learner only," makes "no claim whatever to scientific knowledge" (3). In calling herself a learner only, she may be distancing herself from the financially needy women textbook writers whom she might otherwise seem to resemble. At any rate, she portrays herself as sitting gratefully at the feet of such notable natural historians as James Ellsworth De Kay (330), or "Professor S. F. Baird, Major Le Conte, and Mr. M. A. Curtis," who are thanked for personal help in her edition of Knapp (20). De Kay compiled the zoology and ichthyology volumes of the New York State natural history survey; the zoologist Spencer Baird helped amass the Smithsonian's natural history collections; John Eatton Le Conte, an army topographical engineer, produced an elegant North American lepidoptera; Moses Curtis was a botanist and ornithologist. All these men were family friends.

Yet her admiration for these experts is carefully balanced by a recognition that their professional work needs translation to suit the needs of amateurs in the country. Except for a few self-conscious Linnaean footnotes, she uses vernacular names, because they are attractive and accessible, and therefore (for an audience that must be persuaded to her project rather than commanded) useful. Although in many ways as eager as Almira Phelps to conscript women for science and use science for disciplinary purposes, for her audience the pedagogical stance of a Phelps or Catharine Beecher would be counterproductive. She chooses to present herself as a student for whom continuing with her science is a refined intellectual entertainment. Science merges with esthetics; Cooper suggests even that Linnaean taxonomy as such is merely the arbitrary nomenclature of scientists rather than anything inherent in the species or genus. She has, of course, no smidgen of a constructionist attitude toward scientific professionalism; it is simply that her old-style Natural Theology maintained that in relation to the mind of God, all systems of human naming are necessarily artificial.

Because names are artifices, even though they are necessary, Cooper feels free to use those best suited to her purposes, which are to make nature scientific and make science attractive to an esthetically sensitive group of genteel women. The best choice for this group is the English vernacular. She rejects Native American names with considerable vehemence as unpronounceable and, of course, ungenteel. The combined plainness and picturesqueness of English vernacular names are esthetically pleasing; using them at once makes clear that the user has no professional scientific pretensions and is of English descent. The focus on the esthetic comports with the Natural Theology idea that God's goodness and wisdom are evident in his making nature beautiful, which gives people pleasure and prepares them to admire it as evidence of the divine government of the cosmos. All this is at stake in one of the book's set pieces (June 23), which complains specifically about Latinate botanical nomenclature:

> What has a dead language to do on every-day occasions with the living blossoms of the hour? Why should a strange tongue sputter its uncouth, compound syllables upon the simple weeds by the wayside? If these hard words were confined to science and big books, one would not quarrel with the roughest and most pompous of them all; but this is so far from being the case, that the evil is spreading over all the woods and meadows, until it actually perverts our common speech.
>
> (83)

The rationale for common names asserts itself soon after this passage: "If we wish those who come after us to take a natural, unaffected pleasure in flowers, we should have names for the blossoms that mothers and nurses can teach children before they are 'in Botany'" (87).

Because she wants to make her subject attractive, Cooper is interested in esthetics. But because attractiveness has its use, esthetics is more than a luxury. Taking pleasure in rural scenery, and pointing to the beauties that have caused that pleasure, become elements of a rationalized, systematized approach to surroundings. Cooper may well have thought of esthetics itself as a nascent science. Several discourses already recognized as scientific—notably optics and acoustics, divisions of natural philosophy, or physics—involved reciprocal interactions between human perceptual apparatus (eye and ear) and environment. Drawing and painting were both increasingly defined as professional, teachable skills requiring systematic knowledge of geometry (for drawing), chemistry (for pigments and solvents in painting), and physics (for understanding color and light and the optics of perception). Cooper's **Elinor Wyllys,** which features a character who wants to be an artist, contains several discussions about the optics and chemistry of painting light.

"Taste," too, had been a major target of Enlightenment efforts to systematize esthetic response. Cooper's language of "pleasing effect" throughout **Rural Hours** assumes the existence of universally accepted standards that can be transmitted, as for example through Andrew Jackson Downing's best-selling treatise on landscape architecture. Working from Edmund Burke and other theorizers of the sublime and picturesque, along with the work of English landscapers like John Loudon, Downing—a close associate of the Cooper family whom Cooper cites—describes taste as an inalienable, objective attribute of natural objects, from which position his prescriptions for constructing and appreciating country surroundings were made to seem entirely objective.[12]

In between the beginning and end of scientific perception, for both of which Cooper require a stabilized name, she connects named objects in a scientific web of other names. Even the most apparently unmediated entry turns out on closer examination to be thoroughly, adroitly comparative. Take trees, for example. Before the end of May (the journal begins on March 4) she has identified local varieties of alder, ash, aspen, bass-wood, beech, birch, butternut, chestnut, elm, hemlock ("Some of the hemlocks have a much closer and more compressed upright growth than those commonly met with; so that one is almost tempted to believe there are two distinct varieties" [51]), hickory, locust ("always the last to open its leaves" [50]), maple, oak, pine (we have "but one pine," she will write later on, "though that one is the chief of its family; the noble white pine" [129]), poplar (but not "the great northern or balsam poplar," which "is found at Niagara and on Lake Champlain, but the farmers about here seem to know nothing of it" [43]), spruce, sumac, tamarack (an easy find, since "there are many planted in the village, and in summer they are a very pleasant tree, though inferior to the European larch" [30]), walnut, and golden willow ("the weeping willow is not seen here, our winters are too severe for it" [31]).

Cooper's method of authenticating her identifications follows guidebook convention; it notes the distinctive features of the species, that is, the features that differentiate it. Accordingly she must inform readers about a great deal that she does *not* see: not the great northern or balsam poplar, not the European larch, not the weeping willow. She also explains why she knows some things to be what they are rather than something else— for example, because local winters are too severe for weeping willows, the willow one sees is another kind. Sighting meadowlarks on July 30, she writes that "climate seems to affect them but little, for they reach from the tropics to 53° north latitude, and they are resident birds in the lower countries of our own State" (136)— information with no basis in anything that Cooper could actually have seen. In the course of observing and identifying a total of approximately fifty species of local birds, Cooper describes a much larger number of species. One bird leads to another—the sight of a white-bellied swallow (the tree swallow) invites discussion of other kinds of swallows: the bank swallow, "entirely a stranger here, though found on the banks of lakes and rivers at no great distance; we have seen them, indeed, in large flocks among the sandhills near the Susquehannah, just beyond the southern borders of the county" (36); the cliff swallow, "also a stranger here," the first pair of which only appeared in New York State in 1824 (37). Blue jays lead to "another kind of jay—the Canada jay—sometimes seen in this State" (193); a pair of golden-winged woodpeckers to other woodpeckers— "we frequently see the downy woodpecker, and the hairy woodpecker, in the village" as well as the "handsome red-head, one of the migratory woodpeckers" now "much more rare in our neighborhood than it used to be" and the pileated woodpecker, "said to have been occasionally seen here of late years; but we have never observed it ourselves" (187).

Two paragraphs about naturalized weeds name sixty-six of the "most common," which are "now choking up all our way-sides" (64-65)—a remark suggesting to a rapid reader that she saw and recognized this astonishing number of species during just a few walks. Closer attention suggests however that she is simply summarizing material from a systematic botany: "others still might be added to the list" (65). When she says that "the shepherd's-purse, with others, is common in China, on the most eastern coast of Asia" and "the gimson weed, or Datura, is an Abyssinian plant, and the Nicandra came from Peru" (65), she is not really describing the weed in her own locale. She has abstracted it from the immediate place and reconstructed it as a datum in the global picture. Although she calls "foreign" weeds "troublesome," "noxious," an "evil" requiring "patient care and toil" to keep within bounds, making it "the chief labor of the month to wage war upon their tribe," there is no sign that she recognizes why foreign weeds might easily overcome the indigenous. Her interpretation of the fact is strictly theological: "These noxious plants have come unbidden to us, with the grains and grasses of the Old World, the evil with the good, as usual in this world of probation. . . . The useful plants produce a tenfold blessing upon the labor of man, but the weed is also there, ever accompanying his steps, to teach him a lesson of humility" (66).[13]

The passage makes conventional use of natural phenomenon to construct a Christian homily (what Buell calls "homiletic naturism" [402]). If, however, Cooper sermonizes from natural history, so too does she attempt to understand the Bible itself as a scientific document. Just as she wants to get the name right for local plants, she wants to get the names right for biblical references to flora and fauna. The entry for May 1 contains a long discussion of the likely species of willow referred to in Psalm 137: "When we read of those willows of Babylon, in whose shade the children of Israel sat down and wept, thousands of years ago, we naturally think of the weeping willow which we all know to be an Asiatic tree. But the other day, while reading an observation of a celebrated Eastern traveller, the idea suggested itself, that this common impression might possibly be erroneous" (31). (Readers who "naturally" think of the weeping willow when they read Psalm 137 because they "all know" it to be an Asiatic tree comprise an ideally educated audience.) Now, having been provoked by Sir Robert Ker Porter's reference to the gray ozier willows of Palestine, she consults "several" travel books and finds no reference in any of them to the weeping willow. "The assertion, that it is the tree of the Psalmist is universally made, but we have never yet seen a full and complete account of the grounds for this opinion; and, so far as we can discover, no such statement has yet been published" (32).

This passage makes it once again abundantly clear how much **Rural Hours** is about translating nature into information through which it can be intellectually and instrumentally known. In winter, when bad weather keeps her housebound and few species are to be observed through the window, Cooper often works up descriptive lists of birds and animals that she has never seen but that have been spotted in the region (the parakeet! the ibis!). Winter is also the time to write at length about the great mammals who have disappeared from the region. The social value of all these facts for Cooper is their transformation of rural life into an intellectual text, which makes the provincial into a cosmopolitan and translates bleak days into mental festivals.

The seasonal approach in **Rural Hours** is itself another sign of Cooper's belief that nature requires translation and abstraction to be comprehensible. She recognizes that, while the seasons are facts of nature independent of the human, they are apprehended in human, that is, instrumental terms by human beings. Being able to pre-

dict and prepare for seasonal change in whatever climate one resides is the basic fact of human survival and hence of human history. The sciences of natural history recognized this fact; all official surveys were inventories of resources for present or future exploitation. Natural historians frequently referred to Linnaeus's recommendation that farmers should chart natural growth for agricultural purposes. In Howitt's *Book of the Seasons,* Linnaeus is quoted as saying that every farmer should "diligently mark the time of budding, leafing, and flowering of different plants" and "also put down the days on which his respective grains were sown" so that, "by comparing these two tables for a number of years, he will be enabled to form an exact calendar for his spring corn" (101-102).

Samuel Deane's well-known and often reissued *New England Farmer,* which from its first appearance in 1797 was calling for an Enlightened—experimental— rather than traditional approach to farming, urged "naturalists" to chart blossoming along with leafing on a local level. Because vegetation "is not equally forward, in each degree of latitude," they should list

> a considerable number of trees and shrubs, which are common, and near at hand; carefully watch their appearances, and minute the times of the first opening of their leaves, and also of their blossoming. . . . When these accounts are obtained, let trials be made by sowing a certain kind of seed before, at, and after the foliation, or the flowering, of some particular plant, and the produce compared. Let accurate experiments of this kind be yearly repeated, with all the most useful spring plants; by this, in a few years, complete kalendars may be obtained for every degree of latitude in this country. The consequence will be, that the farmer will be able infallibly to read the true times of sowing, by casting his eye upon the trees and shrubs that are about him.
>
> (236-237)

Deane wants similar "kalendars" of weather, winds, and "state of the atmosphere" made for "every climate in this country" (486).

The purpose here is not to know nature in the Thoreauvian sense (although Thoreau also prided himself in *Walden* for making the earth say beans instead of grass and in his late journals aspired to compile just such calendars, which he even spelled with a *k*), but to enable humans to use the earth for their own sustenance. Susan Cooper believed that this connection of people to the earth was divinely ordained, and therefore, as Johnson and Patterson observe, that it "is consistent with God's will" that "humans convert the wilderness into a land that is shaped and cultivated" (xix).

> The hand of man generally improves a landscape. The earth has been given to him, and his presence in Eden is natural; he gives life and spirit to the garden. Where there is something amiss in the scene, it is when there

is some evident want of judgment, or good sense, or perhaps some proof of selfish avarice, or wastefulness, as when a country is stripped of its wood to fill the pockets or fill the fires of one generation.

("Dissolving View," 82)

Because Cooper thought the earth had been given to humankind, she also thought the human presence could always be discerned on it. She likes to make the landscape reveal its human history.[14] For example, in **Rural Hours** for June 27: "While observing, this afternoon, the smooth fields about us, it was easy, within the few miles of country in sight at the moment, to pick out parcels of land in widely different conditions, and we amused ourselves by following upon the hill-sides the steps of the husbandman, from the first rude clearing, through every successive stage of tillage, all within range of the eye at the same instant" (89).

A habit of superimposing landscapes for purposes of topographical history is especially visible in Cooper's essay **"A Dissolving View,"** published in an 1852 anthology about American scenery, *The Home Book of the Picturesque.* The essay culminates with an overlaying of "merrie England" on a prospect of Cooperstown as she observes it from a nearby height. Wooden bridge, courthouse, seven taverns, a dozen stores, churches, and a hundred houses disappear; the town "dwindles to a mere hamlet" with "low, picturesque thatched cottages," an old church, a tavern, "two or three small, quiet-looking shops," and a stone bridge. Surrounding hills are "shorn of wood," hedges divide the fields and line the roads, there are country houses, a castle, a former convent, and no fewer than nine similar hamlets in view (91-92). The "same" topography cannot be the "same" when it has a different human history; scenery always represents and reflects national character, national history, and the national economy.[15]

The significance of human history for the landscape is so compelling to Cooper that in **"Dissolving View"** she even takes issue with Louis Agassiz's claim that America is, geologically speaking, an old land compared to Europe (thereby disclosing, of course, that she was up to date on her Agassiz). "He tells us that in many particulars our vegetation, our animal life, belong to an older period than those of the eastern hemisphere"; but "without doubting this theory"—of course one does not openly challenge an expert!—"still there are many peculiarities which give to this country an air of youth beyond what is observed in the East. There are many parts of Europe, of Asia, of Africa, which have an old, worn-out, exhausted appearance; sterile mountains, unwooded moors, barren deserts and plains" (90).

Here Cooper is not talking about the cultural superiority of the United States, or even its political promise; she is talking about deforestation and depletion of resources.

Her concerns are land use and overuse—concerns that have led Johnson and Patterson among others to identify her as protoenvironmentalist. Far more important than the picturesqueness of the stone bridge in this English picture is the fact that it, like the other structures described, is made of stone. The hills shorn of wood mark a historical point in the economic development of a society when wood is no longer available, a point exactly and dangerously coincident with increased population. In Cooperstown, by contrast, all the structures are wooden, and there are plenty of trees around. That England is an "old" country and the United States a "new" one, in human terms, is written in the amount of forested land.

But Cooperstown is in process, just like any other place on the globe. The English story is destined to become the American story as well. Today, Cooper writes in **Rural Hours** (July 28), a person fond of the forest, "by picking his way, and following a winding course, may yet travel a long mile over a shady path, such as the red man loved." Already it takes work and imagination to fantasize the locale as wholly forested; "another half century may find the country bleak and bare." This phrasing suggests regret, and there is some of that; but she also describes deforestation as a "wonderful change" (128), having awakened a land that "lay slumbering in the twilight of the forest. Wild dreams made up its half-conscious existence" (127). In the context of Cooper's drive to intellectualize, phrases like "slumbering" and "half-conscious" are negatives. Understanding the productive capacity of the earth and exploiting it are positive goods; misuse of the earth, always possible, is understood not in terms of nature itself as an absolute good, but in terms of exhausting a resource that the human population depends on.

Insofar as human consumption of the earth's products marks the end point of Cooper's rationale for understanding nature in scientific terms, the market enters her account. For example, in **Rural Hours** a long section on maple sugar (April 1) begins with two socioeconomic facts: "Fresh maple sugar offered for sale to-day; it is seldom brought to market early as this" (13). From this starting point Cooper moves to a full description of rural sugar-making technology: "A hole is first bored into the trunk, from one to three feet from the ground"; a small trough is inserted, "usually made of a branch of alder or sumach, which is sharpened at one end and the pith taken out for two or three inches"; the sap drips into buckets, "a regular article of manufacture in the country," made of pine "or at times of bass-wood," and selling "at twenty cents a piece" (14). That local maple sugar is mainly produced for farm use—not for village sale—is explained as the market outcome of cane sugar's being "produced so easily, and so cheap, from the West Indies and the southern part of our own country, that there is little motive for making that of the maple

RURAL HOURS.

BY

MISS COOPER,

" And we will all the pleasures prove
That valleys, groves, or hills, or field,
Or woods, and steepy mountains yield."
MARLOW.

IN TWO VOLUMES.

VOL. I.

LONDON:
RICHARD BENTLEY, NEW BURLINGTON STREET.
1850.

an article of commerce. Maple sugar sells in the village this year for nine cents a pound, and good Havana for six cents" (15-16). At the end of her discussion, Cooper abandons the village food mart for the global intellectual mart, via the natural history and geography that always returns her to print; "Many other trees are tapped for their juices in different parts of the world. . . . They prepare from the sap of the Palm of Chili, a syrup of the consistency of honey, using it as an article of food. In Northern Europe, the birch sap is made into a drink which they call birch-wine. . . . In the Crimea, the Tartars regularly make sugar from the fine walnut-trees on the shores of the Black Sea. So says Dr. Clarke in his Travels." The entry ends with statistics offered for no apparent reason other than that statistics are good to know: "According to the last general Census, the whole amount of maple sugar made during one year in this county, with a population of 49,658, was 351,748 pounds, or nearly eight pounds to each individual. The whole amount of sugar made in the State, was 10,048,109 pounds" (16).

In the longest set piece in the book, about disappearing forests (July 28, 125-135), Cooper channels trees

through pietistic, esthetic, and moral discourses before settling into the blended statistical, scientific, and commercial approaches that fundamentally characterize *Rural Hours.* "What a noble gift to man are the forests!" she begins, romantically enough; but practicality enters immediately: "What a debt of gratitude and admiration we owe for their utility and their beauty!" (125). She thanks the Creator; expatiates Bryant-like on the mingled signs of life and death in the forest; invokes a formulaic prehistory of vanished Indians. Then her inventory begins: "Perhaps two-fifths of the woods in our neighborhood are evergreens, chiefly pine and hemlock. . . . Neither the yellow, the pitch, nor the red pine is known here. . . . The oak of several varieties, white, black, the scarlet, and the red; the beech, the chestnut; black and white ashes; the lime or bass-wood; the white and the slippery elms; the common aspen, the large-leaved aspen; the downy-leaved poplar, and the balm of Gilead poplar; the white, the yellow, and the black birches, are all very common" (129).

After several paragraphs like this she starts to lament—not however over lost trees as an environmentalist might expect, but over rustic ignorance:

> One would think that by this time, when the forest has fallen in all the valleys—when the hills are becoming more bare every day—when timber and fuel are rising in prices, and new uses are found for even indifferent woods—some forethought and care in this respect would be natural in people laying claim to common sense. . . . Our people seldom remember that the forests, while they provide food and shelter to the wildest savage tribes, make up a large amount of the wealth of the most civilized nations. . . . Our fields are divided by wooden fences; wooden bridges cross our rivers; our village streets and highways are being paved with wood; the engines that carry us on our way by land and by water are fed with wood; the rural dwellings without and within, their walls, their floors, stairways, and roofs are almost wholly of wood; and in this neighborhood the fires that burn on our household hearths are entirely the gift of the living forest.
>
> (132-133)

True to her class, Cooper blames this waste on "the people" and suggests that those with long-term investments in land—owners as opposed to tenants—are more apt to conceive of trees as a renewable market crop as well as in "an intellectual and in a moral sense" (133). These things go together. "There is also something in the care of trees which rises above the common labors of husbandry, and speaks of a generous mind" (134). Only when the entire population becomes highly civilized—and "time is a very essential element, absolutely indispensable, indeed, in true civilization"—will ordinary farmers recognize that "a large shady tree in a door-yard is much more desirable than the most expensive mahogany and velvet sofa in the parlor" (133). Interchanging the tree with furniture, equating the esthetic with the civilized, attaching a literal cash value to the esthetic (and hence to the civilized), Cooper fuses esthetics and cash: "How easy it would be to improve most of the farms in the country by a little attention to the woods and trees, improving their appearance, and adding to their market value at the same time!" (134).

Many passages in *Rural Hours* show appreciation of country ways, but at best these are graciously patronizing or amusedly nostalgic. Cooper's distinction between herself and the country folk allows her to consider them as though they too are part of nature, are objects for her imperial gaze. One of the most extended set pieces in the book (July 3) describes a visit to a farm where the interconnections between old-fashioned virtues and agricultural practices are exhibited. Cooper assures her perhaps skeptical readers that one "who goes to enjoy and not to criticise, will find enough to please him about any common farm, provided the goodman be sober and industrious, the housewife be neat and thrifty" (96). "We went into her little buttery; here the bright tin pans were standing full of rich milk; everything was thoroughly scoured, beautifully fresh, and neat" (97). An encounter with local schoolchildren whose clothes are neatly patched (October 31) produces a celebration of the patch as evidence of old-fashioned prudence, simplicity, good sense, class awareness, and industry; it shows that the wearer is "not ashamed of honest poverty, and does not seek to parade under false colors," and it is "honorable to that man or woman to whom Providence has appointed the trial of poverty" (226).

As she thinks about how these patched children are being educated, she produces a deeply conservative critique of contemporary U.S. pedagogy for encouraging self-expression ("impulse") rather than "restraint," which ought to be "more especially the moral point in education." Where instruction in restraint is absent, she writes, "discipline and self-denial are wanting, with all the strength they give to integrity, and honor, and true self-respect, with all the decencies of good manners which they infuse into our daily habits" (228). Cooper need not say directly, indeed must not say directly since that would be indecorous, what is nevertheless redundantly clear in her self-presentation: that she herself exemplifies the outcome of an education in restraint, and that the scientific languages through which she mediates her encounters with nature exemplify the constant disciplining of her intellect.

To sum up: For Cooper the highest form of human relation to the created world is devotional, but *Rural Hours* is only occasionally a devotional book. It is a secular work privileging natural science above other forms of knowledge as a way to connect with one's surroundings and connect one's surroundings to the information web that is reconstituting human understanding. The book elaborates and updates a republican ideal of a lady's

life that detaches her from idleness, frivolity, and extravagance and turns her into an industrious worker on behalf of developing her own intellectuality through acquisition of information, thereby raising the civilized tone of rural society. Cooper's special work for the sciences is to show that they are the epitome of socially desirable knowledge, and thereby to translate them into items for genteel consumption. As I have been showing, the Enlightenment goal of construing women as mental beings took on special force when connected to science. Cooper clarifies what might always have been the class implications of this argument by making the lady who does science in amateur fashion into the highest development of the human female. Raising the social tone by assimilating science into the lady's repertoire becomes Cooper's special mission and gives the lady herself a mission as she comes to occupy the amateur position vacated by male professionals.

As she successively revised *Rural Hours* to keep it cogent in a changing world, Cooper interestingly shifts the balance between nature and science. In her preface to the lightly revised 1868 version of *Rural Hours,* Cooper alludes to changes in rural life brought about by the telegraph, gaslight, and railroad. These have made some of the work she had done to connect Cooperstown to the wider world superfluous. The country, if distant from the city, was no longer isolated from it. Concurrently, primitive rurality begins to assume a nostalgic charm. Despite the inroads of modernity, she assures readers, we still "may be as rustic as we please. The hills, and the woods, and the lake, may still afford us true delight" (xxvii). In 1850, in contrast, she had aimed to move the rustic world into the modern age.

The revision of 1887 is far more drastic. Removing her preface of 1868, Cooper also deletes about a quarter of the 1850 text. Deletions include entries that merely mention the weather, all biblical exegesis, dated criticism of local practices, obsolete statistics, global natural history, and, in fact, most of the scientific materials. The residual book contains little more than accounts of the excursions, so that the descriptions of natural phenomena appear much less mediated and contextualized than they had in 1850. Now, too, the book is published as Cooper's, not as an anonymous lady's.

It would appear that the lady herself, and her mission as well, have become obsolete in the late nineteenth century. With no lady in the title, and no criticism of the locals for their ignorance, *Rural Hours* is far more egalitarian in 1887 than it had been in 1850. The disappearance of the science is related, of course, to the vanished lady, because its role had been predicated on representing a specific kind of gentility.

By this point, too, the wilderness ethos had become far more powerful in American thinking about nature after the Civil War, as the West was "opened" and the idea of national parks as preserves of pristine nature took hold. The wilderness myth produced a corresponding form of imaginative nature writing, the one we know today—a form idealizing unmediated communion with an imagined untouched nature, a nature lacking human history and detached from the scientific understanding that humans had imposed on it.[16]

Without its panoply of scientific references, **Rural Hours** in 1887 looks much more like this newer sort of nature writing than did Cooper's book of 1850. From this angle one might call the 1887 **Rural Hours** a gesture of disaffiliation from science. Although Cooper would never go so far as to construct her natural world as a form of anti-science, or claim that Cooperstown was wilderness, or blame science and technology for the distresses of modernity, the late version of the book clearly intimates that one ought to approach local flora and fauna not for their value as natural history or global inventory, but as items useful for imagining a wilderness that exists, perhaps, somewhere else. Because she is no longer writing as a midcentury lady, Cooper has abandoned her science.

Notes

1. *Rural Hours* went through seven editions in five years; it was revised and reissued in 1868, and again in 1887. There is no biography of Susan Cooper; Beard's summary in *NAW* [*Notable American Women,*] is useful. The Cooper family, including three younger sisters and a brother, was close-knit. Susan and her father, James Fenimore Cooper, were especially close. He accompanied her on the excursions described in *Rural Hours* and helped get the book published. Susan Cooper never married; she continued to live in Cooperstown from the time the family moved there in 1836, when she was twenty-three, until her death in 1894. Following the publication of *Rural Hours* (an earlier novel, *Elinor Wyllys* [1846], had not been successful) she wrote essays, edited an English nature journal in 1853 (John Knapp's *Country Rambles in England*), and compiled and annotated a belletristic anthology, *The Rhyme and Reason of Country Life* (1855). From the late 1850s onward she put most of her literary energies into preserving and enhancing her father's reputation. *Pages and Pictures from the Writings of James Fenimore Cooper* (1861) was a lavishly produced, beautifully illustrated anthology of extracts from Cooper's novels interspersed with her astute biographical and critical commentary. She also wrote the introductions to volumes in the Household Edition of his novels (1876-1884). For analysis of *Elinor Wyllys* see Maddox.

2. Although one might suppose that Cooper published anonymously so as not to presume on her famous father, the dedication—"to the author of 'The Deerslayer' very respectfully, gratefully, and most affectionately"—obviously implied a close kinship between author and dedicatee. All the Cooper acquaintances knew the authorship from the start. James Fenimore Cooper wrote home excitedly from New York soon after publication, "Right and left, I hear of *Rural Hours*. I am stopped in the street, a dozen times a day to congratulate me" (quoted in the Johnson-Patterson edition of *Rural Hours,* xiii). Throughout my discussion of Cooper's *Rural Hours,* I cite this edition of the 1850 text.

3. For the gentrification of country life after 1840, see Huth; Marx; Stilgoe, *Borderlands*; Thornton. Among important New York writers publicizing an upscale rural style of life were Nathaniel P. Willis (*Rural Letters,* 1849), J. T. Headley (*The Adirondack, or Life in the Woods,* 1849), and the Hudson River Valley horticulturalist and landscape architect Andrew Jackson Downing. For the class aspirations of the Cooper family—and their interest in the value of real estate—see Taylor.

4. See chapter 2 and Keeney for the vogue of natural history, especially botany, in the United States; for Great Britain, see Allen, Barber.

5. Likely English models for Cooper's work include Leigh Hunt's perambulatory almanac *The Months* (London, 1821); William Howitt's calendrical *Book of the Seasons,* published in London in 1831 and in Philadelphia soon thereafter; Howitt's sociological *Rural Life of England* (London, 1838); John Knapp's *Country Rambles, or Diary of a Naturalist,* published in London in 1829 and edited for Americans in an 1853 edition by Cooper herself, brought out by a publisher in Buffalo; Gilbert White's *Natural History and Antiquities of Selborne,* first published in London in 1789 and many times reprinted; and Mary Russell Mitford's five volumes of popular sketches, *Our Village,* published between 1824 and 1832 in London and New York.

6. Humboldt's history of attitudes toward nature in the first volume of *Cosmos* is heavily mined by Cooper for her introduction to *The Rhyme and Reason of Country Life.* For an excellent popular biography of Humboldt, see Botting. For Humboldt's impact on scientific practice in England and the United States, see Bowen, Bruce, Cannon, Livingstone, Slotten.

7. Of course Thoreau's *Walden* comes to mind here, with its challenging insistence that traveling a great deal in Concord is equivalent to world voyaging and its truculent finale about the superficiality of actual travel as opposed to inward explora-

tion. Thoreau cites Cooper's work in his journals, and many discussions of *Rural Hours* deviate at some point into discussions of Thoreau. Some scholars propose that Thoreau got *Walden*'s seasonal form from Cooper. But, if she was his model, she was also his challenge; his masculine farmer's persona neatly counters her genteel femininity as a model of how to live in the country. For a development of this point, see Baym, "English Nature"; for the influence of Humboldt on Thoreau's own scientific writing, see Walls.

8. Neither the original journals nor the book manuscript seem to have survived; using local weather records, Hugh MacDougall has shown that she combined materials from at least 1848 and 1849, and perhaps 1850 as well, incongruously—and perhaps fatally for any project demanding scientific environmental accuracy—interweaving a very wet summer (1848) with a very dry one (1849). If the book is meant as an example, not a reliable scientific document, this compression does not matter. There is no evidence that Cooper kept a comparable journal at any other time in her life, for which reason—along with the evidence of *Elinor Wyllys* that she aspired to a literary career—I theorize that she kept this journal in the first place to make a book. Her preface, however, makes the ladylike disclaimer that she embarked on the project only for her own amusement (3) and *Rural Hours* editors Johnson and Patterson take her at her word (x).

9. Cooper follows Humboldt only up to a certain point in her history of human attitudes toward nature. In *Cosmos,* Humboldt declares that attitudes toward nature show increasing enlightenment, and Cooper agrees; but he also says that science has superseded poetry as the educated approach to nature, and here Cooper disagrees. She maintains the Natural Theology position that one eventually works up through nature to nature's God, who is outside nature. Her introduction to the *Rhyme and Reason of Country Life* draws on the orthodox Anglican John Keble for the phrase "last form of song." *Rural Hours,* however, is less focused than *Rhyme and Reason* on the theological implications of nature study.

10. Because much recent interest in *Rural Hours* has centered on its contribution to, even initiation of, a distinct women's form of nature writing in the United States, I emphasize that I see the book as an example neither of nature writing that rejects intellection for unmediated communion with nature (see, e.g., Finch and Elder, 19-30; Murray, passim) nor of nature writing that assumes the inherent sacredness of the earth and accepts, even celebrates, the traditional earthiness of women.

For this contrasting approach to Cooper, see Norwood, 25-53; for more general issues in ecofeminism and ecocriticism, see Gaard and Murphy; Glotfelty and Fromm; Mellor.

11. Cooper's annotations to John Knapp's journal mainly instruct American readers who might picture the wrong natural object when reading an English book—for example the American, not the English, robin.

12. A huge bibliography, far exceeding my scope in this study, exists of works on English esthetics, the role of discourses about the sublime and the beautiful in creating scenic tourism, and in the political bearings of ideologies of the picturesque.

13. Buell interestingly reads Cooper's hostility to naturalized weeds as a sign of ecological nationalism (407). Possibly the sentence about waging war against weeds inspired Thoreau to depict weeding in *Walden* as epic combat.

14. Ecologists and environmentalists, as well as adherents of the so-called New Geography, increasingly feature the constructedness of the wilderness ideal in U.S. culture. For the idea of all landscape as shaped by the human, and for the idea of landscape itself as a human construction, see especially Cronon, *Changes, Uncommon Ground*; Glacken; Oelschlager; Rackham; Stilgoe, *Common Landscape*; Michael Williams; Worster.

15. Stilgoe says that in this essay Cooper "worried that the rural scenery surrounding her home in Cooperstown, New York, stood a poor second to that of England" (*Borderlands*, 23).

16. For the emergence of, and rationale for, the national parks, see Runte, Sellars. Among denunciations of scientific taxonomy as an attempt to impose Western thinking on an indigenous nature that encompasses traditional cultures, Pratt's *Imperial Eyes* has become a classic.

Works Cited

Allen, David Elliston. *The Naturalist in Britain: A Social History.* Princeton: Princeton University Press, 1994.

Barber, Lynn. *The Heyday of Natural History.* Garden City, N.Y.: Doubleday, 1980.

Baym, Nina. "English Nature, New York Nature, and *Walden*'s New England Nature." In Charles Capper and Conrad Wright, eds., *Transient and Permanent: The Transcendentalist Movement and Its Contexts,* 168-189. Boston: Massachussetts Historical Society, 1999.

Beard, James Franklin. "Cooper, Susan Augusta Fenimore." In James, *Notable American Women,* 1:382-383.

Botting, Douglas. *Humboldt and the Cosmos.* New York: Harper and Row, 1973.

Bowen, Margarita. *Empiricism and Geographical Thought: From Francis Bacon to Alexander von Humboldt.* Cambridge: Cambridge University Press, 1981.

Bruce, Robert V. *The Launching of Modern American Science, 1846-1876.* New York: Knopf, 1987.

Buell, Lawrence. *The Environmental Imagination: Thoreau, Nature Writing, and the Formation of American Culture.* Cambridge: Harvard University Press, 1995.

Cannon, Susan Faye. *Science in Culture: The Early Victorian Period.* New York: Dawson and Science History Publications, 1978.

Cooper, James Fenimore. *Pages and Pictures, from the Writings of James Fenimore Cooper, with Notes by Susan Fenimore Cooper.* New York: W. A. Townsend, 1861.

Cooper, Susan Fenimore. "A Dissolving View." In *The Home Book of the Picturesque: or, American Scenery, Art, and Literature,* 79-94. New York: G. P. Putnam, 1852.

————. *Rural Hours.* Edited by Rochelle Johnson and Daniel Patterson. Athens: University of Georgia Press, 1998.

————. *Rural Hours.* Rev. ed., 1887. Reprint, edited by David Jones, Syracuse: Syracuse University Press, 1968.

————, ed. *Country Rambles in England; or, Journal of a Naturalist, by John Knapp.* Buffalo: Phinney, 1853.

————. *The Rhyme and Reason of Country Life.* New York: G. P. Putnam, 1855.

Cronon, William. *Changes in the Land: Indians, Colonists, and the Ecology of New England.* New York: Hill and Wang, 1983.

————, ed. *Uncommon Ground: Towards Reinventing Nature.* New York: W. W. Norton, 1995.

Deane, Samuel. *The New-England Farmer; or Georgical Dictionary.* 3d ed. Boston: Wells and Lilly, 1822.

Finch, Robert, and John Elder, eds. *The Norton Book of Nature Writing.* New York: W. W. Norton, 1990.

Gaard, Greta, and Patrick D. Murphy, eds. *Ecofeminist Literary Criticism: Theory, Interpretation, Pedagogy.* Urbana: University of Illinois Press, 1998.

Glacken, Clarence J. *Traces on the Rhodian Shore: Nature and Culture in Western Thought from Ancient Times to the End of the Eighteenth Century.* Berkeley: University of California Press, 1967.

Glotfelty, Cheryll, and Harold Fromm, eds. *The Ecocriticism Reader: Landmarks in Literary Ecology.* Athens: University of Georgia Press, 1996.

Goodwin, Joan W. "A Kind of Botanic Mania." *Arnoldia* 56 (1996-97): 17-24.

————. *The Remarkable Mrs. Ripley: The Life of Sarah Alden Bradford Ripley.* Boston: Northeastern University Press, 1998.

Howitt, William. *The Book of the Seasons; or, The Calendar of Nature.* London: Henry Colburn and Richard Bentley, 1831.

Humboldt, Alexander von. *Cosmos.* Translated by E. C. Otte. 2 vols. New York: Harpers, 1850.

Huth, Hans. *Nature and the Americans: Three Centuries of Changing Attitudes.* Berkeley: University of California Press, 1957.

Keeney, Elizabeth B. *The Botanizers: Amateur Scientists in Nineteenth-Century America.* Chapel Hill: University of North Carolina Press, 1992.

Livingstone, David N. *The Geographical Tradition: Episodes in the History of a Contested Enterprise.* Oxford: Blackwell, 1992.

Maddox, Lucy B. "Susan Fenimore Cooper and the Plain Daughters of America." *American Quarterly* 40 (1988): 131-146.

Marx, Leo. *The Machine in the Garden: Technology and the Pastoral Ideal in America.* New York: Oxford University Press, 1964.

Mellor, Mary. *Feminism and Ecology.* New York: New York University Press, 1997.

Murray, John A. *The Sierra Club Nature Writing Handbook.* San Francisco: Sierra Club Books, 1995.

Norwood, Vera. *Made from This Earth: American Women and Nature.* Chapel Hill: University of North Carolina Press, 1993.

Oelschlaeger, Max. *The Idea of Wilderness: From Prehistory to the Age of Ecology.* New Haven: Yale University Press, 1991.

Pratt, Mary Louise. *Imperial Eyes: Travel Writing and Transculturation.* London: Routledge, 1992.

Rackham, Oliver. *The History of the Countryside.* London: J. M. Dent, 1986.

Runte, Alfred. *National Parks: The American Experience.* 2d ed. Lincoln: University of Nebraska Press, 1987.

Sellars, Richard West. *Preserving Nature in the National Parks: A History.* New Haven: Yale University Press, 1997.

Slotten, Hugh Richard. *Patronage, Practice, and the Culture of American Science: Alexander Dallas Bache and the U.S. Coast Survey.* Cambridge: Cambridge University Press, 1994.

Stilgoe, John R. *Borderland: Origins of the American Suburb, 1820-1939.* New Haven: Yale University Press, 1988.

―――. *The Common Landscape of America, 1580-1845.* New Haven: Yale University Press, 1982.

Taylor, Alan. *William Cooper's Town: Power and Persuasion on the Frontier of the Early American Republic.* New York: Alfred A. Knopf, 1995.

Thornton, Tamara Plakins. *Cultivating Gentlemen: The Meaning of Country Life among the Boston Elite, 1785-1860.* New Haven: Yale University Press, 1989.

Walls, Laura Dassow. *Seeing New Worlds: Henry David Thoreau and Nineteenth-Century Natural Science.* Madison: University of Wisconsin Press, 1995.

Williams, Michael. *Americans and Their Forests: A Historical Geography.* Cambridge: Cambridge University Press, 1988.

Worster, Donald. *Nature's Economy: A History of Ecological Ideas.* 2d ed. Cambridge: Cambridge University Press, 1994.

Richard M. Magee (essay date 2001)

SOURCE: Magee, Richard M. "Sentimental Ecology: Susan Fenimore Cooper's *Rural Hours.*" In *Such News of the Land: U.S. Women Nature Writers,* edited by Thomas S. Edwards and Elizabeth A. De Wolfe, pp. 27-36. Hanover, N.H.: University Press of New England, 2001.

[*In the following essay, Magee examines Cooper's role as one of the earliest American nature writers, claiming that she combined elements of domestic fiction and natural history to create a sub-genre that Magee calls "sentimental ecology."*]

Susan Fenimore Cooper, the daughter of the famous novelist, was an early voice in the tradition of American nature writing, publishing her nature journal *Rural Hours* four years before Thoreau's *Walden* appeared.[1] This journal of her life in rural Cooperstown is vastly important in the tradition of American nature writing, as it was one of the first American natural histories and the first written by a woman. She acknowledges her thematic debt to male European writers such as Gilbert White and John Leonard Knapp, but claims the genre both for American writers and for women writers.[2] Before writing *Rural Hours,* Cooper tried her talents in a more traditional forum for women writers with her domestic-sentimental novel *Elinor Wyllys; or, The Young Folk of Longbridge.* Many of the concerns, themes, and tropes in this novel prefigure the passionate reverence for nature's beauties that informs much of

Rural Hours, a foreshadowing that tells us much about the motivating forces and structure of the environmental genre. For Cooper, rural values and domestic values are congruent, if not always identical. Domestic values are brought into the wilderness by enlightened and concerned men and women and are passed on largely through the educational efforts of mothers who use nature as a lesson or guide for their children. Thus, domestic values are enhanced by the wilderness, which is moderated but not urbanized.

Susan Cooper's interest and participation in the two genres—the domestic/sentimental and the natural history/environmental—suggest that the overlap in her writings may be more than historical coincidence. Certainly, the most popular and economically successful books written during the middle of the nineteenth century were those written by and for women—Hawthorne's "d―――d mob"—so Cooper's entry into the market with *Elinor Wyllys* is not unusual. On the other hand, her subsequent entry into the natural history or environmental genre was without precedent. Ironically, the novel, in spite of its firm grounding in the popular sentimental mode, did very poorly, while *Rural Hours* was successful enough to warrant numerous editions, including a "fine" gift edition with color illustrations. What makes Cooper's foray into domestic fiction important to students of environmental literature is the dramatic manner in which the language of the sentimental informs so much of her later work, so that any study of Cooper's nature writing that ignores her domestic writing is incomplete. Her domestic-influenced nature writing, in fact, indicates an important sub-genre, which I call sentimental ecology, whereby the demands of community and domestic life are intertwined, much like models of ecosystems, with the demands of the natural environment.

Susan Cooper's voice or author's persona also places *Rural Hours* firmly within the sentimental narrative of community, to use Sandra Zagarell's term. Throughout the journal, she consistently uses the "we" rather than the "I" to talk about her observations; this marked difference between Cooper and Thoreau, says Lawrence Buell, makes her eye "public, not merely idiosyncratic."[3] By creating this more public persona, Cooper offers an alternative to the narrative of self, an alternative whereby the "self exists . . . as a part of the *interdependent network* of the community rather than as an individualistic unit."[4] The narrative "we" constructs a linguistic counterpart to the ecological formulation that all life forms a complex web of interrelations dependent upon each other for survival. Arcadian ecology, the scientific notion expounded by Gilbert White at the end of the eighteenth century, states that "each organism, no matter how insignificant to human eyes or in the human economy, [has] a role to play in nature's economy."[5] White's view was still current at the time that Cooper was writing, and accurately reflects her attitude toward the natural world that surrounded her at Cooperstown. The connection between the sentimental ethos of human networks and the ecological ethos of bio-networks is reinforced by Cooper's participation in both genres, domestic or sentimental literature and nature writing.

Cooper's narrative also participates in what Buell terms the first major work of American bioregionalism, a subgenre related to local color or regional realism.[6] The "finely calibrated environmental sense" of *Rural Hours* is manifested by the variety of environmental goods that are uniquely products of the Otsego County area and include maple sugaring, rural housekeeping, and local farming.[7] Although Cooper was keenly interested in the regional products of her home, we would be wrong to mistake this interest for provincialism. On the contrary, she believes that Americans should be aware of the wider world but should use this awareness better to appreciate the "variety of the world God had given them."[8] Bioregionalism thus operates in a number of ways: It values the natural products of the land and, by extension, the land; it values the American over the foreign; and it values the community as much as the individuals within the community.

Cooper's journal was written over a two-year span but covers only one year, just as Thoreau's *Walden* did. She begins her entries on March 4 and concludes February 28 of the following year, with the entries further grouped according to the seasons. Cooper's seasonal ordering of her observations does not present any new or unique challenges; such reliance on seasonal change as a literary trope extends back at least as far as Virgil. The cyclical nature of changing seasons is, aside from the day and night cycle, the "most perceptible in everyday life."[9] *Rural Hours,* though, uses the seasonal cycle for reasons other than to denote the passage of time or to express an Ecclesiastes-like hymn to the cyclical nature of life. Instead, the book's awareness of the seasons serves to reinforce the environmental as well as nationalistic concerns that occupied a part of Susan Cooper's life. This first becomes evident in the manner in which she divides the seasons and the passages in her book. The book opens with an entry for early March that begins the "Spring" section of Cooper's observations. The "Summer" section begins on June 1 and ends the last day of August, while "Autumn" covers September through November, and "Winter," December through February. These divisions do not correspond to strict, calendrical definitions of the seasons: March 4 is actually still in winter; spring begins on March 21. Cooper's divisions, then, mark a more natural perception of the changing seasons based on observation and an empathetic feel for and understanding of the yearly cycle in her own region.

The first two entries in the book illustrate this point very well. As with many of her observations, Cooper begins with a brief note about the weather, and the first line of *Rural Hours* observes that everything "looks thoroughly wintry still, and fresh snow lies on the ground to the depth of a foot."[10] Her next entry, for Tuesday, March 7, indicates that she is eagerly anticipating spring weather when she begins, "Milder; thawing." She also points out in this entry that she has seen loons moving northward while walking near the river. The keen observer of birds' migratory patterns soon checks herself, though, saying, "It is early for loons, however, and we may have been deceived." Whether the birds are loons is not so important as what the migrating birds represent: nature moves at its own, mysterious, non-human pace, and humans may only observe but may not set constraints on the change. Furthermore, any date that we set for the advent of spring is necessarily arbitrary; the birds, who have a much better and more empathetic connection to nature, are better equipped to mark seasonal change than a date on a calendar.[11]

Another passage, again involving birds, further emphasizes this point. In the 1868 edition of *Rural Hours,* Susan Cooper added a chapter entitled "Later Hours," which takes the observations of the *Rural Hours* year and adds a greater perspective of time. Here she notes that, on June 26, a pair of robins has nested between deer antlers that hang over the door of her verandah. A year later the avian couple returns to build the nest on May 14, and a year after that on June 1. In the "New and Revised" edition of 1887, Cooper notes that the robins are still building in the same spot, having made their 1886 arrival on an unspecified day in May. Although the exact date the robins choose to build their nests never varies by much—except for the anomalous June 26, they are within two weeks—the different calendar dates of the nest-building indicates that nature will not be tied to arbitrary human demarcations.

Arbitrary human demarcations, though, are inevitable, and Cooper recognizes their importance in establishing a link between the natural and the human. According to Buell, "polite culture" and "popular culture" intersect in the almanac tradition through the shared trope of seasonal change: both "polite" poetry such as Thomson's "Seasons" and "popular" culture such as the almanac rely on the trope.[12] Cooper furthers the connective qualities of the almanac by noting its importance to farmers and other country people as a literary piece and as a mediator between humans and nature. On Tuesday, July 3, Cooper describes in detail the visit she takes to a local Farmer B——'s house, where she notes the prominent position of the "well-fingered almanac, witty and wise as usual."[13] She goes on to say that the almanac printers had, a year or two previously, decided to leave out the weather prognostications, but the resulting book sold so poorly that the printers had to resume the weather in subsequent editions. For country people, farmers especially, some knowledge of the weather is crucial, and the almanac helps mediate between wild nature and a domestic pastoral. Farmers can use the information about nature contained within the almanac to create a better, more comfortable living situation working within nature.[14] In a sense, then, Cooper's book itself is an almanac, both for its seasonal awareness and for its attempts to bridge natural and domestic concerns.

Cooper's visit to Farmer B——creates an extended narrative of community and rural values that is sustained longer than any other single episode in the book. For Cooper, the small details of daily rural life constitute a microcosm and ideal form of her national heritage. Her opening exclamation about the farmhouse sets the tone: "How pleasant things look about a farm-house! There is always much that is interesting and respectable connected with every better labor, every useful or harmless occupation of man."[15] She continues to list all of the products of human labor and nature's bounty that occupy the farm house and make it a prime model of domestic satisfaction, and she is particularly impressed by the dairy the wife keeps.[16] While on the visit at Farmer B——'s, Susan and her unnamed companion (her sister) admire the domestic accoutrements and comestibles, all of which are "almost wholly the produce of their own farm."[17] The farm wife is the model of self-sufficiency and the model of proper domestic roles; she is one who can take the goods of nature and produce comfort, food, and clothing. Interestingly, although Susan Cooper resisted feminism, she did feel that the domestic was a corrective and "recall[ed] her readers to their republican roots in the unassuming country life."[18]

Later, in an entry dated Friday, September 29, Cooper describes going to town for the local fair and market day. She again lists the various items crafted by the men and (mostly) women of Otsego County. The goods available range from woven and rag rugs, flannels, leather goods, woolen stockings, and table linens to "very neat shoes and boots, on Paris patterns."[19] Cooper is not content to list these items and let her readers draw their own conclusions, but must add her editorial, saying "Every one must feel an interest in these fairs; and it is to be hoped they will become more and more a source of improvement and advantage in everything connected with farming, gardening, dairy-work, manufacturing, mechanical, and household labors."[20] Here and elsewhere Cooper's agenda is clear: she wishes to perpetuate a rural lifestyle that values industry as it is practiced by the agrarian community. Such a lifestyle, performed in such a community, reflects her ideal of nationalism. A large part of this community is, of course, the industry of the farmer's wife, and such highly valued household industries as weaving, sewing, butter and cheese making, as well as other domestic duties.

One of the most important domestic duties is that of providing a moral education for the children in the family, and this task generally falls to the mother or other women in the household. In this case, the natural environment plays a crucial role, as the study of natural history provides a forum and excellent examples for teaching morality to children. Susan Cooper found herself writing in the natural history tradition, "conjoining women's roles as domesticator and the American landscape's new image as home."[21] Cooper was operating within a system of natural history writing that had been domesticated and sentimentalized already, most notably by Charlotte de la Tour's *La Langage des Fleurs,* published in France in 1819. This book purported to teach women botany, but mostly consisted of images of personified flowers and a set of symbols to communicate feelings.[22] The close scrutiny that Cooper gives to her natural surroundings had thus been mediated already by this and other quasi-scientific works that potentially undermined any serious study of botany or nature.

Cooper, however, resists being neatly pigeonholed as simply a woman writer participating in the sentimental floral tradition, as the preceding argument has already established.[23] Her own language further refutes any easy dismissal of her writings. Some of her most sustained and passionate passages in *Rural Hours* deal with complex botanical subjects, most importantly the naming of plants. She begins her June 23 diatribe with a complaint that too many country people cannot identify the plants, trees, and flowers that grow on their land, going on to say that the women sometimes know the names of herbs or simples but they often make strange mistakes. This sad state of education is troubling for two primary reasons. First, if women are to use botanical knowledge to inculcate moral knowledge in their children, they must have some understanding of what they are teaching, and the ignorant women who do not know the names of the plants are not rising to the challenge demanded and are not teaching well. Second, for a nation to grow and prosper, its citizens must understand their own landscape. The domestic pastoral ideal cannot exist when the rural inhabitants cannot identify the elements that contribute to the health and vitality of the ideal. As a corollary to this, those who do not understand the natural world are not as likely to value it, and, consequently, the stability of nature is jeopardized.

Susan Cooper's demand for a clear understanding of nature led to her great problem with the Latinate, specifically Linnaean process for naming plants. According to her domestic pastoral ideology, Latin appellations are clumsy and "very little fitted for every-day uses, just like the plants of our gardens, half of which are only known by long-winded Latin polysyllables, which timid people are afraid to pronounce."[24] One possible reason for so many of the native plants having such unfriendly nomenclature is that the American continent was settled after Linnaean taxonomy took root and names were given by botanists before the common people could give common names. More likely, though, is the possibility that Cooper, through her Linnaean critique, is defending her turf as an amateur botanist. Vernacular botanical names were in common usage, but Cooper sees the scientific language as encroachment from without the community by professionals. The danger of this is clear: professional botanists come from outside the community and thus have no stake in it. When the privilege of naming the land's bounty is removed, the inhabitants of the countryside are also removed from a crucial relationship with the land.[25] Furthermore, the spread of Latinate terms "actually perverts our common speech, and libels the helpless blossoms, turning them into so many *précieuses ridicules*."[26]

The reluctance and even antipathy that Cooper felt toward Latinate nomenclature is consistent with a sentimental ethos. As Annie Finch points out, many scholars feel that sentimental art is threatening because it becomes too close and intimate with its reader, and, "worse, sentimental art accomplishes this aim by reversing the crucial hierarchy of reason over emotion."[27] This reversal in some ways parallels Susan's balking at an overly scientific system of naming, if we take Latinate nomenclature as representative of reason and a fondness for common names as emotion. More importantly, though, Cooper is seeking, through this more emotional naming process, a closer, more vital connection between nature and the people who inhabit the bounds of nature. This real and vital connection to nature is at the heart of sentimental ecology.

When the native flowers have complicated and difficult Latinate names thrust upon them by botanists with no stake in the region, poets also suffer because of an inability to create an aesthetically pleasing poem incorporating these uncommon names. This problem, in fact, seems to be most troubling to Cooper, and she spends several pages railing against the unpoetic sound of Latinate names. She asks, "Can you picture to yourself *such* maidens, weaving in their golden tresses *Symphoricarpus vulgaris, Tricochloa, Tradescantia, Calopogon?*"[28] Her answer to this is "No, indeed!" and the reasons for this resounding denial are not as simple as aesthetic distaste. If one of the purposes of landscape and nature poetry is to help create a national American literature and, by extension, a national American identity, both of which help foster the sense of community crucial to the domestic scene, then American poets become ineffectual when their language becomes distanced and foreign.[29] Furthermore, a distinctly American literature would need to be written in a distinctly American idiolect or "ecolect" in order to be truly representative of

the new country.[30] An imposed language, particularly a foreign, distant, and lofty language like Latin, undermines the nationalistic or regionalistic tendencies of poetry.

Cooper's defense of the local extends beyond nomenclature to the uniqueness of American seasons, where it takes on a fiercely patriotic tone as she unfavorably compares European nature or seasonal poetry to American. In a long entry dated Wednesday, October 11, Cooper begins by saying that "[a]utumn would appear to have received generally a dull character from the poets of the Old World." She goes on to criticize in one of her longer entries the poor presentation of autumn by various European poets, remarking on many specific passages. Shakespeare, she points out, links "*chilling autumn*" with "angry winter," while Collins calls the colorful season "*sallow*" and Wordsworth dismisses it as a "melancholy wight."[31] Not content to chastise merely the English poets, Cooper displays her European education to good advantage by quoting several French poets in the original before moving on to her critique of German and Italian poets.[32] All of these European poets lack the ability to see the majesty and beauty of autumn that Cooper spends so much time praising. Not only are the poets factually wrong—she attacks Thomson, Spenser, and Keats for wrongly placing the summer wheat harvest in the autumn—but they are also blind to the beauties of the changing colors, seeing impending winter rather than multicolored autumn.[33] Cooper does admit, however, that the European leaf season is not so colorful, saying, "[h]ad the woods of England been as rich as our own, their branches would have been interwoven among the masques of Ben Jonson and Milton; they would have had a place in more than one of Spenser's beautiful pictures. All these are wanting now."[34] The American landscape, then, is not only more "rich" but it can provide an example for American poets to create works that must by association be more rich as well, which, in turn, allows for a superior setting of domestic/didactic possibilities.

Cooper's motivation for connecting the colorful autumn season and a national literature comes almost as an afterthought following her critique of the Europeans. She notes "the march of Autumn through the land is not a silent one—it is already accompanied by song. Scarce a poet of any fame among us who has not at least some graceful verse."[35] The poets "among us," the American poets, stand in clear contrast to the Europeans who fail to write anything "graceful" about autumn, and so the Americans have an advantage in their access to more colorful and more poetic subject matter. Cooper's confidence in her fellow American writers is remarkable as she says "year after year the song must become fuller, and sweeter, and clearer."[36] This confident optimism contrasts dramatically with Emerson's vain search for his ideal poet. "We have yet had no genius in America . . . which knew the value of our incomparable materials," Emerson says.[37] However, Cooper, though she does not cite American examples to support her claim, recognizes both the "incomparable materials" and the poets who know their value. The richness of the American environment seems to make the rise of rich, sweet, and clear poetry inevitable.

The narrative of community, which crucially informs the sentimental ecology of Cooper's work, culminates in an environmental awareness that transcends aesthetic appreciation to become a conservationist ethos. Cooper's construction of her community is marked by an inclusiveness that sets her apart from her father and illustrates her attempts to link community and environment. Susan Cooper first creates a narrative of community in her domestic sentimental novel, *Elinor Wyllys; or, The Young Folk of Longbridge.*[38]

The argument for labeling this a work of nature writing can be summed up as a complex form of environmental synecdoche. Rosaly Torna Kurth dismisses the novel in extremely harsh terms, saying that it "possesses as much or, rather, as little of artistic merit as do the novels of the later domestic writers," noting that the plot is "not plausible nor . . . unified," with too much emphasis on "domestic matters."[39] These very points, however, when viewed in another light, make it an important work of environmental writing. Cooper knew from her frequent nature walks that one action or event in a field, meadow, or forest could have larger reverberations elsewhere, just as she knew from her own social contacts that no member of society lives in a vacuum. Thus when she describes in detail the social climbing vulgarity of the seemingly minor character Mr. Clapp early in the novel, she does so because this unpleasant man and his morally suspect ambitions will have implications for Hazlehurst later. At least four subplots reveal themselves throughout the novel, and each one has some significant influence on the others. Her novel, then, is a model of interrelationships, a sort of sentimental ecosystem. The few subplots are representatives or synecdoches of the larger social environment.

While James Fenimore Cooper creates a moderately favorable portrait of Native Americans, his daughter goes further in her claims of sharing communal values with the Indians.[40] Susan Cooper notes the Indians' degradation as her father does, but differs from him by noting that civilization is responsible for it. The Indian women, Susan argues, are less likely to become corrupted by the influences of civilization and remain "gentle and womanly" while the braves are marked by the "heavy, sensual, spiritless expression, the stamp of vice."[41] The gender-dependent differences that Susan Cooper notes illustrate the most important manner in which she dis-

agrees with her father's point of view. To Susan, the "domestic qualities," which her father mentioned, are much more important, and she is better able not only to see this importance but to see the underlying causes for the disruption of these important qualities. As a woman intent on perpetuating a domestic ideal, she is able to diagnose the problem. Her diagnosis is based largely on a feminine sympathy, which her father seems to lack.

Susan Cooper's sympathy for the Indians is an important aspect of her sentimental ecology because she is sharing an emotional bond by sympathizing. The sympathetic bond is crucial in creating the interdependent links of the sentimental ecosystem. In one encounter with the Indians, she says: "The first group [of Indians] that we chance to see strike us strangely, appearing as they do in the midst of a civilized community with the characteristics of their wild race still clinging to them; and when it is remembered that the land over which they now wander as strangers in the midst of an alien race, was so lately their own—the heritage of their fathers—it is impossible to behold them without a feeling of particular interest."[42] This passage is remarkable for Susan's ability to imagine the Indian point of view, to place herself and her entire community as "alien," as other. By so doing, Susan's language is in some ways "at odds" with the dominant discourse, forming a Kristevan "semiotic discourse" which, rather than an "infantile fusion with the mother," indicates a fusion with the Indians *as* a mother.[43]

We can add another dimension to this maternal language after looking at a related passage that occurs some pages later. Still discussing the Indians, Susan Cooper says: "It is easy to wish these poor people well; but surely something more may justly be required of us—of those who have taken their country and their place on the earth. The time seems at last to have come when their own eyes are opening to the real good of civilization, the advantages of knowledge, the blessings of Christianity. Let us acknowledge the strong claim they have upon us, not in word only, but in deed also."[44] Here, Cooper is even more emphatic in her critique of white civilization. While still maintaining the supremacy of white civilization—its "blessings" and "advantages"—Cooper nevertheless acknowledges the displacement and alienation the Indians have a right to feel, as well as the debt that white Americans owe them. Significantly, this debt is not described in pecuniary terms, but in moral, specifically Christian, terms. It would not be overemphasizing the point to say that Cooper's idea of a debt is here a sentimental one: The debt may be paid, Cooper implies, by providing the means for the Indians to reap the "real good of civilization."

Cooper's next comment about the plight of the Indians points even more forcefully to the domestic or sentimental social awareness that the author brings to the observations of her community. She notes that "perhaps the days may not be distant when men of Indian blood may be numbered among the wise and the good, laboring in behalf of our common country.[45] The most striking idea expressed here is Susan Cooper's emphasis on the "common country" and her willingness—one might even say eagerness—to give a voice to the Indian. Though we might discern a note of condescension in her tone by her dismissal of any possibility that the Indians might already be wise, as well as the notion that Indians can only achieve social mobility through the generous and charitable efforts of whites, it is still notable that she stresses the importance of commonality and community. Her emphasis on community contrasts with her father's "more favorable picture of the redman than he deserves" and his understanding of the Indian as other and therefore not capable of being part of the same society that the Coopers inhabit. Susan, though, seeks to bring the Indians into her home, as she does literally in *Rural Hours,* figuratively in the national sense, and symbolically as a part of her domestic community in nature.

Perhaps the best-known entry in *Rural Hours* is a long description of a stand of old-growth pines, untouched by the threat of the axe, situated on the edge of town, which Cooper uses to illustrate the passage of natural epochs and the very short time white settlers have been on the land.[46] In this short time, the white settlers have radically altered the natural landscape in a manner that had never happened before. She concludes the passage by meditating on the fate of the forests, speculating that "[a]nother half century may find the country bleak and bare."[47] Her tone, however, is hopeful, because "as yet the woods have not all been felled" and we are left with the impression that such a calamity may be avoided. Cooper goes on to urge conservation and systematically refutes arguments in favor of clear-cutting the forests. The final value of a tree, she vehemently tells us, lies not merely in the "market price of dollars and cents," but in the "intellectual and . . . moral sense."[48] Here Cooper brings her notions of conservation back to the moral value of the landscape and nature.

Her tone as she discusses the unsparing logging in her community is very critical, even angry. She derides early colonists for looking on trees as enemies, and chastises their descendants for maintaining the same reckless spirit. "One would think," she notes wryly, "that by this time, when the forest has fallen in all the valleys . . . some forethought and care in this respect would be natural in people laying claim to common sense."[49] The brutal but understated sarcasm of her tone is consistent with other times she sees people not acting in the best interests of nature and the community. This is the same sarcasm that creeps into her voice as she chastises country women for not knowing the names of plants, and stands as a stark contrast to her warm approval of people such as Farmer B——'s wife, who recognizes the role of nature in her domestic life.

Cooper's overall tone throughout *Rural Hours,* though, is generally more positive, and she cannot sustain her anger long before she provides examples of her neighbors' care for the environment. She begins with a story of horrible degradation in the "wilds of Oregon," where a government scouting party comes across a huge tree that had been felled and left to rot. The man who cut the tree, she speculates, claimed, "no doubt, to be a civilized being."[50] Cooper compares this act to one committed by one of "the horde of Attila," and goes on to offer a counter-example that happened, "happily," near her own neighborhood. On the banks of the Susquehannah [*sic*], a large elm tree was left standing in spite of the fact that it stood in the way of the highway. Although the tree stands where a "thorough-going utilitarian would doubtless quarrel with it," its beauty rendered it safe from the axe.[51] Cooper applauds the decision of her neighbors to keep the tree and their ability to recognize that its moral and aesthetic value far outweighed any merely practical or utilitarian concerns. Environmentalism, Cooper's modern readers are led to see, is a community value that transcends mundane concerns and elevates the moral strength.

The final value of Susan Fenimore Cooper's work may be found in something other than the "market value" of her collection of natural observations, just as she insists that the final value of environmental health transcends the market. She uses her domestic voice to convince us of the intellectual and moral value of the landscape and the responsibility we have to perpetuate this value. By continuing her sentimental ethos from her novel and elaborating upon the themes of the domestic pastoral in the natural landscape, Cooper creates a sentimental ecology that illustrates the interconnectedness of all creatures on earth.

Notes

1. Susan Fenimore Cooper, *Rural Hours,* eds. Rochelle Johnson and Daniel Patterson (1850; reprint, Athens: University of Georgia Press, 1998). First published in the summer of 1850, the book was so much a success that her father negotiated with Putnam, the publisher, at the end of November 1850 to obtain a better bargain and higher percentage per copy. See *Rural Hours,* ed. David Jones (1887; reprint, Syracuse: Syracuse University Press, 1968), xxiv. The book eventually went through five more American and one more English edition, including a "fine" volume complete with color plates of local birds. Susan Cooper produced a new edition in 1868 with a new preface,

and a "new and revised" edition in 1887, which condensed a great deal of the original.

2. Susan Fenimore Cooper edited the 1853 American edition of John Leonard Knapp's *Country Rambles in England; or Journal of a Naturalist* (Buffalo, N.Y.: Phinney And Co., 1853).

3. Lawrence Buell, *The Environmental Imagination: Thoreau, Nature Writing, and the Formation of American Culture* (Cambridge, Mass.: Harvard University Press, 1995), 266.

4. Sandra Zagarell, "Narrative of Community: The Identification of Genre," *Signs: Journal of Women in Culture and Society* 13, no. 3 (1988): 499. My emphasis.

5. Max Oelschlaeger, *The Idea of Wilderness* (New Haven: Yale University Press), 104.

6. Buell, *Environmental Imagination*, 406.

7. Alan Taylor, *William Cooper's Town: Power and Persuasion on the Frontier of the Early American Republic* (New York: Vintage, 1995), 119. William Cooper, Susan's grandfather and the founder of Cooperstown, began heavily promoting Otsego County as a major source of maple sugar in June of 1789. In *The Pioneers* (1823; reprint New York: Signet, 1964, 1980), James Cooper's most environmentally informed novel, Judge Marmaduke Temple forbids the burning of maple wood in his estate's fireplaces both because maple trees are "precious gifts of nature," and because they are "mines of comfort and wealth" (101). Thus we can see maple sugar in terms of an important economic commodity, as a product of the Otsego region, and as an ecological treasure.

8. Buell, *Environmental Imaginations,* 407.

9. Ibid., 220.

10. *Rural Hours,* 4. Most references to *Rural Hours* are from the 1850 edition, reprinted in 1998 and edited by Rochelle Johnson and Daniel Patterson (Athens: University of Georgia Press, 1998). References to Cooper's later additions such as "Later Hours" are from the 1887 edition, reprinted in 1968 and edited by David Jones (Syracuse: Syracuse University Press, 1968). References are cited parenthetically in the text.

11. Thoreau also "questions seasonal categorization rigorously" by seeking to "free himself 'from the tyranny of chronological time,' to redefine November for example from a 'calendrical unit' to a 'phenomenological category of thought.'" Buell, *Environmental Imagination,* 228.

12. Buell, *Environmental Imagination,* 223.

13. *Rural Hours,* 98.

14. The importance of the almanac in creating the domestic pastoral also appears in Nathaniel Hawthorne's short story "Roger Malvin's Burial," in *Mosses From an Old Manse: The Centenary Edition of the Works of Nathaniel Hawthorne,* vol. X [n.p.] (Ohio State University Press, 1974), 337-60. When the family leaves the settlement to travel into the unknown wilderness, they carry with them "the current year's Massachusetts Almanac, which, with the exception of an old black-letter Bible, comprised all the literary wealth of the family" (354). These two literary works help the family in attempting to bring domestic comfort into the wilds, and thus also mediate between civilization and wild nature.

15. *Rural Hours,* 96.

16. The spotless dairy the mistress keeps rivals that of Aunt Fortune in Susan Warner's domestic sentimental novel, *The Wide Wide World,* and the industry in the dairy is mirrored by the other household duties.

17. *Rural Hours,* 100.

18. Vera Norwood, *Made from This Earth: American Women and Nature* (Chapel Hill: University of North Carolina Press, 1993), 29-30.

19. *Rural Hours,* 194.

20. Ibid.

21. Norwood, *Made from This Earth,* 28.

22. Ibid., 12.

23. Many of the pseudo-scientific works for women were condescending at best. One French author (L. F. Raban) avoids scientific terms because of their difficulty. Norwood, *Made from This Earth,* 13. Other books reduced their scientific goals even more, completely giving up any pretense of being scientific and provided "simplified codes for love, flattery, jealousy, motherhood, and nationalism." Norwood, *Made from This Earth,* 18.

24. *Rural Hours,* 83.

25. The relationship between stewardship and naming is clear in Genesis, when Adam is given the task of naming. By naming the plants and animals, Adam not only gains sovereignty but also undertakes a strong measure of responsibility at the same.

26. *Rural Hours,* 83.

27. Annie Finch, "The Sentimental Poetess in the World: Metaphor and Subjectivity in Lydia Sigourney's Nature Poetry," *Legacy* 5, no. 2 (1988): 5.

28. *Rural Hours,* 86. Cooper's italics.

29. Ann Bermingham, in *Landscape and Ideology: The English Rustic Tradition, 1740-1860* (Berkeley: University of California Press, 1986), proposes that "there is an ideology of landscape" that "embodied a set of socially and, finally, economically determined values" (3). The ideology of landscape as represented by both painters and poets reflects national concerns because the landscape is the face of the country. In developing a set of expressions and techniques to understand and manipulate landscape representations, artists and writers participate in the creation of a national identity.

30. James McKusick, "'A language that is ever green': The Ecological Vision of John Clare," *The University of Toronto Quarterly* 61, no. 2 (1991 Winter): 242. McKusick's term is perhaps more apt in this instance. His neologism, "ecolect," is used to describe the poetry of the British rustic poet John Clare, and refers to an idiolect that is specifically rooted in the local landscape. Because of the intimate connection between nature or landscape poetry and the natural environment, this term has more resonance.

31. *Rural Hours,* 202. (Cooper's italics.)

32. The Coopers lived in Paris from 1826 until 1833 (Jones xiv).

33. *Rural Hours,* 222-23.

34. Ibid., 209.

35. Ibid.

36. Ibid., 210.

37. Ralph Waldo Emerson, "The Poet," *Selections from Ralph Waldo Emerson,* ed. Stephen E. Whicher (Boston: Houghton, 1957), 238.

38. The novel centers around a young woman, Elinor, who lives with her doting grandfather and aunt in a rural village, probably a fictionalized Cooperstown, about "fifteen years since," or in the late 1820s and early 1830s. Elinor, who is often described as "plain," or, worse yet, ugly, is pleasant, kind, and popular among the upper classes in Longbridge. As the action begins, Elinor accepts a proposal of marriage from her long-time friend, Harry Hazlehurst, and seems to be on the path toward domestic happiness. Harry, though, soon falls in love with another family friend, a beautiful but shallow woman whose morals, sense, and intelligence pale beside Elinor's. This shallow woman, Jane, is not interested in Hazlehurst but marries a young rake who leads her to the brink of financial ruin before he dies. In the meantime, a presum- ably long-lost heir arrives in Longbridge to challenge Harry's right to his fortune. Harry eventually triumphs over the impostor, regains his inheritance, and finally marries Elinor by the end of the novel. While these events are transpiring, myriad subplots are unraveling. Another young friend of the Wyllys family, Charlie Hubbard, determinedly pursues his passion for landscape painting, becoming an important practitioner and advocate of American art before his untimely death in a boating accident. Other minor characters marry, make fortunes, lose fortunes, or fall into scandal and disrepute. Although the number of characters and plot developments can be a distraction, each event and person has a distinct effect on Elinor, and Elinor's family often influences other characters in important ways.

39. Rosaly Torna Kurth, "Susan Fenimore Cooper: A Study of Her Life and Works" (Ph.D. diss., Fordham University, 1974), 124, 112.

40. In the "Preface to the Leatherstocking Tales," which opens *The Deerslayer,* James Cooper addresses critics who claim that he has presented a "more favorable picture of the redman than he deserves." He goes on to say, "The critic is understood to have been a very distinguished agent of the government, one very familiar with Indians, as they are seen at the councils to treat for the sale of their lands, where little or none of their domestic qualities come in play, and where indeed, their evil passions are known to have fullest scope" (x). Here Cooper seems to understand the Indians, and is able to make excuses for their "evil passions," but he fails to see that the Indians have been wronged in any way. Instead, they are at a disadvantage in the councils, so their lesser nature comes in play.

41. *Rural Hours,* 209.

42. Ibid., 108.

43. Susan M. Levin, "Romantic Prose and Feminine Romanticism" *Prose Studies* 10, no. 2 (Sept. 1987): 178-95. Levin points out that "romantic women writers find the forms of conventional language at odds in some way with the realities their writing presents," which in turn creates this Kristevan discourse (185). As Levin notes, this discourse contradicts standard language by its infantile search for a maternal figure and appears "without discernible contours" (186). I propose taking this further by saying that Susan Cooper does not want to fuse with the mother in this example, but wants to become the nurturing figure.

44. *Rural Hours,* 112.

45. Ibid.

46. Walter Levy and Christopher Hallowell, the editors of the eco-conscious textbook reader, *Green Perspectives,* have chosen this passage as the first excerpt.

47. *Rural Hours,* 128.

48. Ibid., 133.

49. Ibid., 132.

50. Ibid., 135.

51. Ibid.

Rochelle Johnson and Daniel Patterson (essay date 2001)

SOURCE: Johnson, Rochelle and Daniel Patterson. Introduction to *Susan Fenimore Cooper: New Essays on* Rural Hours *and Other Works,* edited by Rochelle Johnson and Daniel Patterson, pp. xi-xxvii. Athens: The University of Georgia Press, 2001.

[*In the following excerpted introduction, Johnson and Patterson provide a detailed overview of Cooper's career, including a discussion of some of the author's more obscure works.*]

It was the tremendous swell of interest in environmental writing that provided the conditions needed for a new edition of Susan Fenimore Cooper's **Rural Hours** in 1998.[1] However, Cooper herself would not have missed the irony that our late-twentieth-century ability to appreciate her accomplishment as a nature writer was completely dependent upon our continued degradation of the planet. Nevertheless, that edition has brought **Rural Hours** more readers and Susan Cooper's career closer scrutiny by scholars. The breadth, complexity, and quality of her literary production have rewarded the investigations of numerous scholars, and this volume was conceived in order to make public the fruits of much of that effort. Indeed, the Susan Cooper who emerges from this collective work is one of the premier nature writers of the United States, but for fifty years she was also an accomplished writer and editor in several other genres.

Susan Fenimore Cooper (April 17, 1813-December 31, 1894) had begun writing with publication in mind by the mid-1840s. By the time of her death she had published a romance; a book of bioregional nature writing; an anthology of nature poetry; an edition of the journal of a British naturalist; a number of short stories for adults and children; a theoretical essay on American landscapes; a tract to solicit donations for the restoration of Mount Vernon; several selections from her father's unpublished manuscripts; one book-length biography and several biographical essays; a lengthy philosophical essay against female suffrage; at least seven magazine articles treating aspects of the natural environment; fifteen substantial introductions to the "Household Edition" of her father's novels; an almanac, which she edited; numerous historical essays; and an array of other magazine and newspaper articles. . . . In addition, Cooper prepared at least two other book-length manuscripts for publication.

Susan Cooper was also the daughter of James Fenimore Cooper, a fact that often helped her publishing career while she was alive. Nearly every time her contemporaries mention her in reviews, they note her relation to "the American Scott" or "the famous novelist." But since her death, her father's shadow has more often obscured her own literary achievement. One purpose of the present volume is to consider that achievement in direct light.

SUSAN FENIMORE COOPER'S LITERARY CAREER: FIRST FICTION

Following Susan Cooper's first thirteen years in Cooperstown, Westchester County, and New York City and following her European residence with her family from the summer of 1826 until the autumn of 1833, she began her literary career, not surprisingly, by writing fiction.[2] The earliest evidence we have showing that she was writing for publication is a letter from her father dated September 22, 1843, in which he promises to sell an undisclosed number of unidentified "tales": "I make no doubt of getting one or two hundred dollars for the whole." The successful author seems to imagine easily his daughter's future as a professional author herself: "A name will sell the remainder, and a little habit will set you up."[3] It is not clear, however, whether any of these tales was ever published.

It does seem clear, however, that these short fictions became pilots for the full-blown novel she then produced. By August 1844, Cooper had completed the manuscript of her 575-page *Elinor Wyllys,* which her father carried to New York City, had stereotyped, and sold to both Richard Bentley in London and Carey and Hart in Philadelphia (*Letters and Journals,* 4:470-71, 5:15, 25, 79, 82, 98, 101). From her late teens through her twenties, the author's father seems to have ushered her past several discussions and proposals of marriage, and at the end of that decade, she produced a novel in which the plain or even ugly young heroine is rewarded for her intelligence and goodness by the plot structure of the romance with a happy and financially secure marriage.

If the nonfictional dutiful daughter was unhappy to be unwed, no direct evidence survives. Certainly, Fenimore Cooper was a protective parent, and he may have had selfish motives, but his expressions of love for "dear little Suzy, meek little Suzy" strike one as genuine (*Letters and Journals*, 6:95). In the following words written in December 1849, just after he negotiated the terms of publication for *Rural Hours*, he even casts himself as a potential lover who settles for friendship: "How I love that child! Her countenance is like that of a sister I lost . . . by a fall from a horse, half a century since, and her character is very much the same. They were, and are, as perfect as it falls to the lot of humanity to be. I am in love with Sue, and have told her so, fifty times. She refuses me, but promises to live on in gentle friendship, and, my passion not being at all turbulent, I do not see but this may do" (*Letters and Journals*, 6:99). Three months later, we hear her expressing devotion to her father: "To satisfy yourself, and my dear Mother, has always been a chief object of my authorship, and hitherto I have met with little enough of encouragement from other quarters."[4] Their high regard for one another motivated them both and seems extremely important to the daughter's impetus to write.

Cooper's **"The Lumley Autograph"** was completed no later than November 1848 (*Letters and Journals*, 5:390). This is a playful but poignant variation on a device used by her father in his *Autobiography of a Pocket Handkerchief* (1841). Cooper was, however, already making studied observations of the plant and animal species native to her Otsego Lake region and planning a writing project in a genre her father would struggle to comprehend.

RURAL HOURS AND EARLY ENVIRONMENTAL PROJECTS

In her preface to **Rural Hours,** Cooper tells us that she began recording her field observations "in the spring of 1848," but in a memoir dated January 25, 1883, she suggests that the quality of mind that would conceive a nature-writing project had much earlier origins. Recalling childhood days in Westchester County with her maternal grandfather, she writes:

> Our Grandfather De Lancey must have been a charming companion—he was very amusing with his grandchildren, and told us many pleasant things, as he drove us about in his gig and farm-waggon. . . . And my dear Grandfather soon commenced my botanical education—being the eldest of the little troop, I often drove with him, in the gig, about his farms and into his woods, and it was my duty to jump out and open all the gates. In these drives he taught me to distinguish the different trees by their growth, and bark, and foliage—this was a beech, that an oak, here was an ash, yonder a tulip-tree. He would point out a tree and ask me to name it, going through a regular lesson in a very pleasant way. Such was the beginning of my **Rural Hours** ideas.[5]

The author also, however, attributes shaping influences to the knowledge and experiences of three women in her family. Cooper recalls from her childhood, for instance, a walk during which her mother, Susan Augusta De Lancey Cooper (whose namesake she was), "picked up a broken branch of raspberry and set it in the ground, telling me that it would take root and grow." Cooper evaluates this early bit of botanical knowledge as "a fact which greatly surprised my infant mind" (**"Small Family Memories,"** 10). Thus, more than seventy years after the event, the daughter paid homage in her 1883 memoir to the mother's presence at the birth of her affinity for plant life. She also fondly associates her grandmother De Lancey with her early awareness of plants: "She took great delight in flowers, and the south end of the long hall was like a greenhouse in her time. . . . Her flower garden was at the South of the house, and was considered something wonderful for the variety of flowers. There is a delicate little vine, called the Alleghany vine, Adlumia, growing in our hills; this was a favorite of hers" (**"Small Family Memories,"** 12-13). From her aunt Pomeroy, Cooper recalls hearing accounts of the abundance of large mammal species living near Otsego Lake: "the Lake was almost entirely surrounded with forest. Game was still abundant, and on that occasion [that is, of the first lake party] the gentlemen of the party pursued and killed a deer in the Lake. Bears and wolves were common then, and panthers also. The bears would lie dormant in the caves on the hillsides. And my Aunt said she had often heard the wolves howl on the ice in the Lake, in winter" (**"Small Family Memories,"** 18). In Cooper's record of these memories, written for her family members, it is clear that not only the patriarchs in her life but also the matriarchs contributed to her early conception of the flora, fauna, and environmental history of her native region.

Inspired and enabled by these early experiences, she found herself maturing as a writer amid dramatic alterations to her beloved landscape, and she composed **Rural Hours** to sway the human inhabitants of her place toward a wise restraint in their treatment of the physical environment: "No perfection of tillage, no luxuriance of produce can make up to a country for the loss of its forests; you may turn the soil into a very garden crowded with the richest crops, if shorn of wood, like Sampson shorn of his locks, it may wear a florid aspect, but the noblest fruit of the earth, that which is the greatest proof of her strength, will be wanting" (**Rural Hours,** 139). What we now call "nature writing" became, for this new author, a tool of suasion, a genre by which she could present her vivid plea for a human presence in her landscape that would be sustainable indefinitely into the future.

Her father wisely observed that the success of **Rural Hours** would be "eventual, for, at first, the world will not know what to make of it" (*Letters and Journals*, 6:151). Nevertheless, it was reviewed widely and favorably and appeared in nine editions and one abridgment over the next thirty-seven years. It became the work for which she was best known.

Two works from the beginning of the 1850s have disappeared and probably never were printed. In a letter to her father some four months before the July 1850 publication of *Rural Hours,* Cooper asks him to retrieve from a publisher "the M.S. of *Devotions for the Sick.*" She had no other copy of it and speculated, "Perhaps our Sunday School Publisher may take it one of these days."[6] This may be the work Fenimore Cooper refers to in May 1850: "I have not offered Susy's religious book to any one. I have thought it better to wait for *R[ural] Hours,* which will give value to all she does" (*Letters and Journals,* 6:187). No other reference to this manuscript is known.

The other lost work appears to have been at least partially in press at Putnam's. In George Putnam's letter to Susan Cooper dated December 2, 1851, he states that he has just received from Cooper "proofs of . . . '*The Shield.*'" He closes by assuring her that he "shall proceed with . . . *The Shield* as rapidly as possible— presuming you can furnish the copy as rapidly as it is wanted."[7] In an August letter to Richard Bentley, the London publisher of *Rural Hours,* Cooper had provided the following description of *The Shield*:

> The good success I have had in America has led me to prepare another work for the press, which will shortly be printed. It is called *The Shield, a Narrative*; and relates to the habits, and life of the red man, before his intercourse with the whites, or rather to his condition at the period of the discovery. Many historical essays, giving information on the antiquities and customs of the race, when first seen by the Europeans, have appeared here lately, and it is to embody these in a characteristic tale that the narrative has been written. It seems to me likely that in this case the tables may be turned, and *The Shield* from the nature of the subject may proove more interesting [*sic*] in the old world than a record of our simple rural life. Should such proove ti [*sic*] to be the fact it will also help the sale of *Rural Hours.* I have taken much pains to give the book accuracy in all its details. In your June letter you proposed to take the work on the same terms as *Rural Hours,* and I now wish to know if such are still your views. The first chapters will probably be printed within a month.[8]

Prior to this, in May of the same year, Fenimore Cooper had already characterized *The Shield* for Bentley as follows: "My daughter is preparing for Mr Putnam another book which will contain some of the surplus matter of *Rural Hours,* with large additions, in the same style; but the whole rendered more imaginative by a connection with a simple Indian story. It will be of about the size of *Rural Hours.* I should like to have an offer for it and that as soon as convenient as the work will shortly go to press" (*Letters and Journals,* 6:273-

74). Although *The Shield* was advertised by both Putnam and Bentley, no copy of the book has been found, and no subsequent references to it appear.[9]

This large work's disappearance and the ensuing silence create an intriguing mystery, but we can draw several tenable conclusions from its author's characterization of it: she was interested in the history of Native Americans before European contact; she devoted a significant amount of time and creative energy following the publication of *Rural Hours* to a narrative based on historical essays she took to be factual; she hoped to become better known in Europe; and, to some extent, she conceived and designed the project so that it would enhance her reputation as an author and bring her some royalties.

Cooper's publications throughout the three years that follow her father's death on September 14, 1851, seem to spring from the concern with the human relationship to the natural environment that informs her *Rural Hours* work. In **"A Dissolving View,"** an essay published in an expensive gift-book by Putnam in which she shares prominence with her father, William Cullen Bryant, and Washington Irving, Cooper meditates on a New England autumn landscape and provides a succinct statement of a premise that informs much of her environmental writing: "The hand of man generally improves a landscape. The earth has been given to him, and his presence in Eden is natural; he gives life and spirit to the garden. It is only when he endeavors to rise above his true part of laborer and husbandman, when he assumes the character of creator, and piles you up hills, pumps you up a river, scatters stones, or sprinkles cascades, that he is apt to fail."[10] As in *Rural Hours,* here she assumes a providential universe in which human restraint in the landscape is rewarded with success and in which the hubris of modern engineering is aligned with the sinful and ungodly.

Amid the early success of *Rural Hours,* Cooper continued to focus on the natural by writing an introduction and extensive natural history notes for an American edition of John Leonard Knapp's *Country Rambles in England* (1829).[11] She opens the introduction by placing Knapp's volume alongside Gilbert White's *The Natural History of Selborne* (1788) as among "the standards of English literature" (*Country Rambles,* 11). It seems clear that Cooper hopes her readers will place her own *Rural Hours* on this same shelf, since she associates her book with the nature writing of White and Knapp, whose books belong to that "choice class . . . written neither for fame nor for profit, but which have opened spontaneously, one might almost say unconsciously, from the author's mind" (*Country Rambles,* 11). The ornamented title page also encourages this association by presenting the title *Rural Hours* in the same style and size of rustic, bold lettering used for *Country*

Rambles. And Cooper's introduction itself, while paying sincere homage to a fellow nature writer, finally implies that Americans ought to read books about American nature: "As a people, we are still, in some sense, half aliens to the country Providence has given us; there is much ignorance among us regarding the creatures which held the land as their own long before our forefathers trod the soil; and many of which are still moving about us, living accessories of our existence, at the present hour" (*Country Rambles,* 16). Because of "English reading," Americans habitually assume that plant and animal species are identical on both sides of the Atlantic simply because they have the same names: "And in this dream-like phantasmagoria, where fancy and reality are often so widely at variance . . . most of us are content to pass through life" (*Country Rambles,* 18). The bulk of her numerous natural history notes to Knapp's text are designed to remedy this particular ignorance. She wants her American readers to realize how lucky they are: "the nature of both hemispheres lies open before them, that of the old world having all the charm of traditional association to attract their attention, that of their native soil being endued with the still deeper interest of home affections" (*Country Rambles,* 18). Humbly and subtly, she works in this volume to prepare a readership and a market for American nature writing, works like *Rural Hours.*

In 1854 the Philadelphia publisher Willis P. Hazard brought out an illustrated edition of *Rural Hours,* keeping the attribution "By a Lady," which Cooper preferred. In the same year, Hazard also published *Rural Rambles; or, Some Chapters on Flowers, Birds, and Insects* with the same attribution, "By a Lady." There is, however, no clear proof that Cooper is the "Lady" who wrote, compiled, and edited this now-rare volume. Nonetheless, since the work is "generally credited to Susan Fenimore Cooper," it is worthwhile to consider *Rural Rambles* here.[12]

Nothing in the volume suggests that Cooper could not have been the compiler; on the contrary, all the qualities and features of the book seem completely consistent with those that inform her other work. *Rural Rambles* assembles a mix of natural history, personal observation, and poetry throughout its six main sections, each of which bears the name of a flower. Within each main section, the compiler focuses on various insects, birds, and flowers, bringing together poems, natural history findings, anecdotes, and her own observations on, as examples, "The Butterfly," "The Ant Lion," and "The Owl." The overall purpose of *Rural Rambles* is to bring readers closer to the pleasures and insights the compiler valued in native flora and fauna. The prose in its phrasing, tone, and meaning is also consistent with Cooper's other published prose:

> Next to the resolving of flowers into their component parts, and determining their species, genera, &c., the most delightful of all botanical pursuits is that of Floral Geography. The inquiring mind beholds in every nook where a flower can find room to open its delicate leaves, some new tribute to the unerring providence of God. Every leaf and bud suggest new thoughts, and in viewing the wonderful structure of the vegetable kingdom, the mind begins to form an adequate idea of that Being who not only supplies man with all the necessaries of life, but scatters beauty along his path, and speaks to him of hope and mercy, through the fragrant cups and emerald leaves of the flowers that blossom everywhere.[13]

Various aspects of this passage—the fluid clarity and measured pace of the prose, the avoidance of hyperbole and excess of sentiment, the advocacy of botany, the goal of training readers to perceive Providence in common flora—cause one to wonder whether this and other passages in the work might have their originals in the lost manuscript, *Devotions for the Sick.* Nevertheless, despite the circumstantial evidence, *Rural Rambles* remains an open question in Cooper's career.

THE RHYME AND REASON OF COUNTRY LIFE, 1855

Certainly one of the earliest collections of poems about nature and rural life published in the United States, *The Rhyme and Reason of Country Life* reflects Cooper's desire to continue the cultural work she had begun in *Rural Hours.*[14] This anthology reflects her faith in the power of literature to influence—even change—minds; and it complements her earlier and later offerings of environmental prose by bringing poetry to the work of shaping the thoughts of Americans about nature and how human society—which she grants is also natural—ought to relate to it. Her introduction to this volume—more so possibly than any other single document—teems with insights into her thought and suggests how she understood her place in her culture and her work as a writer. For example, she theorizes about the motive behind nature writing. The ancient Greeks, she writes, did not write directly about their beautiful environment because they did not see themselves as independent of or distinguishable from nature. Americans in her day, by contrast, are motivated to write about nature by a "fear that she should fail them" (*Rhyme and Reason,* 14). Cooper also suggests that rural nature writers have one of the highest places in her culture. Whereas in past ages, the most important writers worked from within cities because only there were people educated (with the result that the "tastes and habits" of the culture were "necessarily . . . more or less artificial"), in Cooper's young nation, the much wider dissemination of education and the other advantages of civilization free the "rustic population" from the urban perception that they are "only fit for ridicule and burlesque" (*Rhyme and Reason,* 26). Instead, the American intellectual or artist can work effectively from rural settings: "He may read and he may write there with pleasure and with impunity. A wide horizon for observation opens about him to-day in the fields, as elsewhere." With general education "daily enlarging the public audience . . . [n]o single literary class is likely . . . to usurp undue authority over others—to impose academical fetters on even the humblest of its cotemporaries [*sic*]. Whatever is really natural and really worthy, may therefore hope in the end for a share of success" (*Rhyme and Reason,* 26-27).

The humbling influence of Christianity, however, is essential to the rustic writer whom Cooper would consider worthy of his or her place in the culture. We quote at length because of the importance of the following passage and because so few have a copy of the text at hand:

> No system connects man by more close and endearing ties, with the earth and all its holds, than Christianity, which leaves nothing to chance, nothing to that most gloomy and most impossible of chimeras, fate, but refers all to Providence, to the omniscient wisdom of a God who is love; but at the same time she warns him that he is himself but the steward and priest of the Almighty Father, responsible for the use of every gift; she plainly proclaims the fact, that even here on earth, within his own domains, his position is subordinate. . . . Look at the simple flower of the field; behold it blooming at the gracious call of the Almighty, beaming with the light of heavenly mercy, fragrant with the holy blessing, and say if it be not thus more noble to the eye of reason, dearer to the heart, than when fancy dyed its petals with the blood of a fabled Adonis or Hyacinthus? Go out and climb the highest of all the Alps, or stand beside the trackless, ever-moving sea or look over the broad, unpeopled prairie, and tell us whence it is that the human spirit is so deeply moved by the spectacle which is there unfolded to its view. Go out at night—stand uncovered beneath the star-lit heavens, and acknowledge the meaning of the silence which has closed your lips. Is it not an overpowering, heart-felt, individual humility, blended with an instinctive adoration or acknowledgment in every faculty of the holy majesty of the One Living God, in whom we live, and move, and have our being?
>
> (*Rhyme and Reason,* 28-29)

In Cooper's subsequent cultural analysis, America becomes the site of literature's full maturity, and the rural poet of nature becomes the culture's most important artist. The main distinguishing characteristic of American poetry, Cooper claims, is "a deeply-felt appreciation of the beauty of the natural world" (*Rhyme and Reason,* 31). This national affinity for the natural becomes for Americans a moral guide past the "follies of idle ostentation and extravagant expenditure" encouraged and cultivated by the cities, the centers of commerce and manufacture (*Rhyme and Reason,* 32). By contrast, in America "[t]he influences which surround the countryman are essentially ennobling, elevating, civilizing, in fact" (*Rhyme and Reason,* 33). She concludes: "It can

scarcely, therefore, be an error of judgment to believe that while in past generations the country has received all its wisdom from the town, the moment has come when in American society many of the higher influences of civilization may rather be sought in the fields, when we may learn there many valuable lessons of life, and particularly all the happy lessons of simplicity" (*Rhyme and Reason,* 33-34). Cooper's discussion in *Rural Hours* of the recent move to greater realism and accuracy in "descriptive writing, on natural objects" implies that literary representations of the natural can contribute to the "moral and intellectual progress" of the culture (*Rural Hours,* 208). Cooper's introduction to *The Rhyme and Reason of Country Life* provides a scholarly and philosophical analysis of her reasons for saying so.

The *Rhyme and Reason* introduction concludes a period of approximately six years during which Cooper devoted her literary labors exclusively to the cultural work of nature writing. Nearly five years pass before her next publication. The only other comparable gap—that between 1861 and 1868—includes the years of the Civil War. The fact that her first publications after the five-year silence were written in the service of other people—that is, a brief tract intended to encourage schoolchildren to donate funds for the restoration of Mount Vernon and a large memorial to her father's work—suggests that despite her earlier success, Cooper did not yet conceive of herself as—or commit herself to being—an independent, self-expressive author. She seems not to have any other nature-writing projects in mind; instead, she turns to the keeping—and shaping—of her father's literary reputation and to the establishment of a hospital and an orphanage in her town.

NEW DIRECTIONS: WRITING FOR FATHER AND SOCIETY

Susan Cooper's commentaries in *Pages and Pictures, from the Writings of James Fenimore Cooper* (1861) begin her active public efforts to maintain her father's place in American letters. With the approach of the Civil War, however, her community would have other concerns, and she turned her intelligence and influence to the philanthropy that would eventually result in the Thanksgiving Hospital (dedicated on Thanksgiving Day, 1867) and in the Orphan House of the Holy Saviour (incorporated in March 1870).[15] Even as she announced the publication of *Pages and Pictures* to Rear Adm. William Branford Shubrick, the longtime family friend to whom she dedicated the volume, Cooper's focus was divided between her devotion to her father's memory and the imminence of war. She wrote to Shubrick on December 7, 1860:

> May the volume serve, my dear Commodore, to remind you of the heart-felt and life-long affection, borne you

by my dear Father and may it remind you also occasionally of those who have so fully inherited that feeling!

These are solemn days for us all, dearest Commodore. Charlotte and I from our quiet womanly home have been watching sadly, the dark clouds gathering over the country, and which all who have the good of the country truly at heart must so deeply deplore. Loyalty to the Union[,] fidelity to the interests of the country in every high, and generous sense of the word[,] we could never forget without treachery to the name we bear. Were he whom we mourn still with us his clear tones might now be heard, the influence of his powerful pen might be widely felt in this crisis. But there is scarcely any symptom of the present condition of public affairs so discouraging as the want of a sound healthful moral tone, of clear, and vigorous, and generous reasoning in behalf of great Truths, of disinterested devotion to the service of the nation, in the full meaning which that word should ever convey. The prominent public men, whether politicians, or writers, are to-day widely different in character . . . from those who have gone before them.

Cooper's high regard for her father here seems called up by her sadness and by her perception of the decline of effective national leadership. In the sympathetic company of her Commodore, she can comfortably lament, from her "quiet womanly home," the diminished character of the day's "prominent public men." This must have been a powerful letter for Shubrick. He was a native South Carolinian from Charleston and at the time of this letter was resisting great pressure to abandon his "Loyalty to the Union." South Carolina seceded on December 20, thirteen days after Cooper wrote these words describing qualities of leadership now absent from her nation. It is possible that Cooper intended her words to encourage Shubrick, forced now to be seen as disloyal to his native South. In her biographical sketch of Shubrick after his death in 1874, the traits of leadership she describes here are precisely echoed.

With the close of the war and with the establishment of the hospital and orphanage, Cooper's publishing career resumed. In the very first year of *Putnam's Magazine* (1868), she published excerpts from her father's diary in two separate issues. Having established this relationship with the magazine, she became a fairly active magazine writer and published at least thirty-five article-length pieces over the next twenty-five years in several of the nation's most reputable magazines.

The most clearly polemical of her writings from this period is her **"Female Suffrage: A Letter to the Christian Women of America,"** published in *Harper's New Monthly Magazine* in August and September 1870. This is a carefully reasoned and logically developed argument against female suffrage, and it reflects the benevolence with which men treated Cooper throughout her life. Cooper argues that by divine creation, woman (with some rare exceptions) is physically and intellectually inferior to man and so must accept a subordinate position; woman, however, must always "connect self-respect and dignity with true humility, and never, under any circumstances . . . sink into the mere tool and toy of man."[16] While her argument rests mostly on Christian doctrine and the authority of centuries of past practice, she does mix in an element of essentialism:

[T]he great mass of women can never be made to take a deep, a sincere, a discriminating, a lasting interest in the thousand political questions ever arising to be settled by the vote. They very soon weary of such questions. On great occasions they can work themselves up to a state of frenzied excitement over some one political question. At such times they can parade a degree of unreasoning prejudice, of passionate hatred, of blind fury, even beyond what man can boast of. But, in their natural condition, in everyday life, they do not take instinctively to politics as men do.

("**Female Suffrage,**" 445)

This is an unusual moment in Cooper's oeuvre; here in her late fifties, she expresses a personal indignation that drives her nearly to the brink of satire. She did not, however, return to this subject for publication.

Outside of magazine writing, a major project she undertook beginning in the mid-1870s was a series of largely biographical introductions to Houghton Mifflin's "Household Edition" of her father's novels. Since her death, she has probably been best known as the rather silent author of these introductions. In 1876 the editions of the five Leatherstocking Tales appeared, and in 1881-84 editions of the ten other novels included in the series were published. Much research and labor went into preparing these introductions, and they consistently illuminate the history of the novels' compositions, settings, and characterizations. Cooper's commitment to this large and time-consuming project reveals her continuing devotion to her father's memory. When the last of these volumes was published, she was seventy-one years old, and her father had been dead thirty-one years. Some three years later, in February and October 1887, Cooper published two essays in the *Atlantic Monthly* that provide some biographical context for the composition and publication of three novels not included in the "Household Edition": *The Spy, The Wept of Wish-ton-Wish,* and *The Bravo.*[17] She was then seventy-four years old and did not again write about her father or his work for publication.

At nearly the same time that she completed the first five "Household" introductions in 1876, Cooper published two interesting biographical sketches, one of the national hero and her father's friend William Branford Shubrick and one of a Revolutionary War hero's wife, Mrs. Philip Schuyler. The Shubrick piece provides the readers of *Harper's* with a detailed chronology of this naval hero's life, emphasizing through vivid narrative his accomplishments during the War of 1812, during the war against Mexico, and at the beginning of the Civil War. Cooper's depiction of Shubrick's final visit to her dying father eulogizes a family friend but serves also to reflect some of Shubrick's light on her father's memory. Cooper's sketch of the life of Catharine Schuyler, **"Mrs. Philip Schuyler,"** frames a memorial to womanly dutifulness and courage within a memorial to a local (that is, from Albany) male hero of the American Revolution.

"OTSEGO LEAVES," 1878

Cooper produced a remarkable series of four essays published in *Appletons' Journal* under the collective title **"Otsego Leaves."** Since 1854 she had practically abandoned nature writing as a genre, but in 1878 she produced this rather nonchalant tour de force that is likely to be regarded, when it is more widely known, as her most mature and most fully realized contribution to American environmental writing. The four essays comprising **"Otsego Leaves"** are entitled **"Birds Then and Now," "The Bird Mediæval," "The Bird Primeval,"** and **"A Road-side Post-office."** The last of these consists of a sketch of a coach ride that focuses exclusively on the behavior and qualities of the human inhabitants of her region and is a compelling sketch of rural life. The first three essays, however, compose a work of literary ornithology and will establish for Cooper a place in the history of that popular science in the United States, ornithology, which was second only to botany in Cooper's century.

She begins the series, in **"Birds Then and Now,"** by documenting the decline of several of the most common bird species over the preceding two decades. She describes the bird populations of her region as they existed "Then," twenty years before, and then characterizes their reduction in numbers "Now." In her discussion of the causes of the decline, however, she becomes one of the earliest American voices trying to discern the reasons for a diminished biodiversity. The most tangible evidence of the decline in bird populations is Cooper's continuous counts over twenty and more years of bird nests: "When the leaves fall in November, the nests are revealed, and after snow has fallen, and each nest takes a tiny white dome, they become still more conspicuous." Because she has surveyed the same areas and been familiar with the same trees over many years, Cooper's conclusion seems sound: in the past, "you were never out of sight of some one nest, and frequently half a dozen could be counted in near neighborhood. To-day it may be doubted if we have more than one-third of the number of these street-nests which could be counted twenty years ago."[18] By modeling this method of monitoring bird populations in one area over many years, Cooper anticipates Aldo Leopold's encourage-

ment of amateur ornithology in the 1930s. She moves beyond mere lament when she delineates the causes of the declining populations (that is, boys kill them, girls wear them on their hats, and travelers dine upon them in southern resorts). She writes now as an amateur ornithologist and engages readers in the possibility of restoring the reduced bird populations by understanding the causes and by ceasing the destructive practices.

In the second essay, **"The Bird Mediæval,"** she models for her readers her method of culling environmental history from earlier Colonial texts. The opening dream-vision of bird life "about the homes of the early colonists" gives way to an unforgettable account of a visit to a Dutch farm on the "Upper Hudson," where she observed the many alliances the "Dutch negroes" kept with the birds. Central to her description of items set out in the spring as nesting places for the returning birds (old hats, gourds, some built bird houses, even the adorned skulls of domesticated mammals) is the image of the great barn and of the human and bird lives led there:

> Seventy of those brown nests, many old, others new, and still unfinished, might have been counted clinging to the vast, sloping roof, or clustering on the beams. In and out through the great doors, in and out through smaller openings, high over the roof without, low over the broad river beyond, in shadow and sunshine, now grazing the heads of the noisy negroes, now gliding over the quiet cattle in the stalls, now whirling among the doves and martins, which also haunted that vast, hospitable barn-roof, were the sprite-like swallow-people. Yes, the great barn was full of merry, cheery life, in which the negroes, old and young, filled the largest space, no doubt, but in which the birds far outnumbered them.[19]

This vivid narrative of a human lifestyle that completely accommodates the needs of bird species becomes an antidote to the avian "holocaust" she exposes in the first essay.

She opens the third essay, **"The Bird Primeval,"** with her regret that so much environmental history is irrecoverable; she then offers a narrative reconstruction of the life history of a three-hundred-year-old elm that occupied a slope overlooking Otsego Lake before Europeans first came to North America. The narrative center of this "history" is the image of the great hollow trunk of the storm-blasted elm and the scores of chimney swifts who build their nests in its shelter:

> About the old elm there was more of winged life and movement than elsewhere on the mountain-side, but it was a noiseless life. One by one small, dark birds of a dull-brown color came wheeling above the old crow, their long wings and short bodies darting through the air with wonderful rapidity, and with scarcely a vibration of the wings, whirling, diving, darting to and fro, and vanishing, as it were, one by one, each diving with

a singular rapidity and precision into the heart of the old elm. That aged trunk was hollow for some fifty feet downward from the open rift above. At the height of a man from the root it would have required three stalwart savage hunters to embrace the trunk in its outward girth. Within, the hollow space, at its widest point, measured twice the length of a man's arm in diameter. The entire hollow column was crowded with those singular birds, and had been their summer-house for half a century.[20]

These "primeval" swifts flourished in and experienced a state of nature now largely lost, as Cooper subtly explains to her readers. Her final maneuver in this essay is to lead readers from her image of the ancient elm's teeming trunk to their own chimneys, where the swifts of unrecorded history now nest and carry on their ancient survival.

Just as James Fenimore Cooper worked to give his country people a sense of *human* history, Susan Fenimore Cooper worked in **"Otsego Leaves"** to give her country people a sense of *environmental* history. She worked to deepen Americans' knowledge of and thereby their affinity with the other-than-human environment. The style of her nature writing had matured beyond that of the late 1840s and early 1850s. She had developed a slower pace and a more thorough attention to detail, as well as a more authoritative voice, reflecting perhaps a greater confidence that these essays might have the desired effect on her culture.

EPISCOPAL HISTORY AND A CLOSING "LAMENT"

Nevertheless, Cooper did not return to nature writing for some fifteen years, during which time she produced one of the most thoroughly researched works of her career, **"Missions to the Oneidas,"** a series of magazine articles relating the efforts of Episcopalian missionaries among the Oneida people in the region of Oneida Lake (near present-day Syracuse, New York). She was a devout Episcopalian her entire life, and her interest in the history of her church apparently increased in her final decade. Her adulatory biography of William West Skiles (1890) narrates the first establishment of her church in the most remote region of western North Carolina at midcentury. Although the title page presents Cooper as the book's editor, the narrative is so fluid and engaging that it seems clear that the "materials" she gathered from five ministers and one layman passed through much more than mere editorial changes. Her representations of the wild Appalachian settings show her affinity for nature description and provide further evidence that she authored—rather than merely edited—this book.

A short piece published in *Harper's* just over a year before her death, **"A Lament for the Birds,"** while not the last of her published writings, evokes for us Cooper's lifelong interest in environmental history. This essay makes rather emphatically the point that from the time when she conceived of her ***Rural Hours*** project in the late 1840s until her death half a century later, the mind of Susan Cooper was focused radically on the natural environment and on the human impact upon it. This closing lament literally echoes concerns expressed in **"Otsego Leaves"** and in ***Rural Hours,*** and in paraphrasing observations first published in the 1850 book, she transforms that book into a source of the environmental history she argues is needed if humans are to stop or even slow their destruction of plant and animal species. By associating the disappearance of white pelicans with the disappearance of the original human inhabitants of her region, she makes her **"Lament for the Birds"** into a lament for all her region's vanished inhabitants. It is a beautiful, lyrical essay, but it sings no song of hope: "Alas for the vanished birds!"

If the phrase "EDITED BY" preceding Cooper's name on the title page of her last published book, the Skiles biography, is an understatement, so too is the epithet "author of '***Rural Hours,***' ETC., ETC." Cooper has been remembered affectionately but neither fully nor accurately. The work is now under way to gather the pieces of and understand her considerable literary accomplishments. . . .

Notes

1. Susan Fenimore Cooper, *Rural Hours,* ed. Rochelle Johnson and Daniel Patterson (Athens: University of Georgia Press, 1998). Hereafter cited in text.

2. Rosaly Torna Kurth weaves a convenient narrative from the primary biographical data. See her "Susan Fenimore Cooper: A Study of Her Life and Works" (Ph.D. diss., Fordham University, 1974), esp. 1-103.

3. James Franklin Beard, ed., *The Letters and Journals of James Fenimore Cooper,* 6 vols. (Cambridge, Mass.: Harvard University Press, 1960-68), 4:411. Hereafter cited in text as *Letters and Journals.*

4. Letter to James Fenimore Cooper, Cooperstown, March 3, 1850, Yale Collection of American Literature, Beinecke Rare Book and Manuscript Library, Yale University, New Haven, Connecticut. Hereafter cited as Beinecke Library.

5. Susan Fenimore Cooper, "Small Family Memories," in *Correspondence of James Fenimore Cooper,* ed. James Fenimore Cooper, 2 vols. (New Haven, Conn.: Yale University Press, 1922), 1:32-33. Hereafter cited in text.

6. Letter to James Fenimore Cooper, Cooperstown, March 3, 1850, Beinecke Library.

7. G. P. Putnam, letter to Susan Fenimore Cooper, New York City, December 2, 1851, Beinecke Library.

8. Letter to Richard Bentley, Cooperstown, August 6, 1851, Beinecke Library.

9. See Jacob Blanck, *Bibliography of American Literature*, 9 vols. (New Haven, Conn.: Yale University Press, 1955-91), 2:312. Two letters to George Putnam among the Putnam papers at the New York Public Library refer to "The Shield." On August 27, 1851, Susan Cooper tells Putnam that she does not think the "new book" can be ready for publication by October 1. In a rather wordy excuse, she attributes her delay to the irregularity of "our mails" and to her inability to visit New York City that autumn because of her father's illness. A few weeks later, on October 11, Cooper again explains her delay: "As regards my own book, *The Shield* I have not been very well, and scarcely fit for composition; the delay in sending the first chapters, however, has proceeded from another cause, they contain various allusions to items of natural history, and fearful of making some mistake I was anxious to confirm what had been written by examining one or two other books. My cousin M. De Lancey promises that I shall have the information desired very shortly, and as soon as these points are settled you shall have the first Chapters."

10. Susan Fenimore Cooper, "A Dissolving View," in *The Home Book of the Picturesque; or, American Scenery, Art, and Literature* (New York: Putnam, 1852; reprint, Gainesville, Fla.: Scholars' Facsimiles & Reprints, 1967), 82.

11. [John Leonard Knapp], *Country Rambles in England; or, Journal of a Naturalist with Notes and Additions, by the Author of "Rural Hours," Etc., Etc.*, ed. Susan Fenimore Cooper (Buffalo: Phinney & Co., 1853). Hereafter cited in text.

12. Blanck, *Bibliography of American Literature*, 2:312.

13. [By a Lady], *Rural Rambles: or, Some Chapters on Flowers, Birds, and Insects* (Philadelphia: Willis P. Hazard, 1854), 10-11.

14. *The Rhyme and Reason of Country Life; or, Selections from Fields Old and New*, ed. Susan Fenimore Cooper (New York: Putnam, 1855). Hereafter cited in text.

15. "The Thanksgiving Hospital" and "Orphan House of the Holy Saviour," in *A Centennial Offering. Being a Brief History of Cooperstown, with a Biographical Sketch of James Fenimore Cooper*, ed. S. M. Shaw (Cooperstown, N.Y.: Freeman's Journal Office, 1886), 180-82, 182-84.

16. "Female Suffrage: A Letter to the Christian Women of America," *Harper's New Monthly Magazine* 41 (August 1870): 440.

17. "A Glance Backward," *Atlantic Monthly* 59 (February 1887): 199-206; and "A Second Glance Backward," *Atlantic Monthly* 60 (October 1887): 474-86.

18. "Otsego Leaves I: Birds Then and Now," *Appletons' Journal* 4 (June 1878): 530.

19. "Otsego Leaves II: The Bird Mediæval," *Appletons' Journal* 5 (August 1878): 165.

20. "Otsego Leaves III: The Bird Primeval," *Appletons' Journal* 5 (September 1878): 274.

Duncan Faherty (essay date 2001)

SOURCE: Faherty, Duncan. "The Borderers of Civilization: Susan Fenimore Cooper's View of American Development." In *Susan Fenimore Cooper: New Essays on* Rural Hours *and Other Works*, edited by Rochelle Johnson and Daniel Patterson, pp. 109-26. Athens: The University of Georgia Press, 2001.

[*In the following essay, Faherty illustrates Cooper's advocacy of landscape and emerging New World culture as primary influences upon American architectural development through a discussion of* Rural Hours *and* "A Dissolving View."]

Within her best-known work, ***Rural Hours*** (1850), and in an important but long-neglected essay **"A Dissolving View"** (1852), Susan Cooper calls for the development of uniquely American cultural forms reflective of the nation's democratic doctrines. Intimately linked to this appeal was her description of nature as essential nourishment for the national imagination. Implicit in her argument was a second call: for the necessity of preserving this resource. By becoming familiar with their native environment, Americans would locate foundations for institutions in harmony with the landscape around them. As part of a broad-based cultural movement away from the commodification of nature that was a hallmark of the Jacksonian era, Susan Cooper charged Americans to stop imitating European cultural models, urging her generation to form a new national identity grounded in American nature.[1] Within these two texts, which need to be considered in tandem to appreciate fully her conception of American development, she argued that the absence of inherited architectural forms liberated Americans from the obstacles that faced their contemporaries in the Old World. European social development was subject to the constraints imposed by previous architectural productions. While Americans had not yet devised cultural forms to embody their democratic values, they had also not irrevocably altered their environment in ways that would prohibit them from so doing.

Susan Cooper firmly believed that cultural values were products of the combination of material culture (the entire shaped human environment) and the landscapes in and upon which it was fashioned. Petitioning Americans to pause before making further mistakes, she contemplates the delusory effects on American social development if the nation fails to rectify its current architectural practices.[2] She proposes the scrutiny of new building plans prior to construction, for "[t]here is a certain fitness in some styles of architecture which adapts them to different climates" (*Rural Hours,* 297). By obscuring the natural negotiation between man and his specific environment, architectural failures threaten the stability of the culture. She teases out meaning on a local level, confining her examination to Cooperstown to illustrate her vision of national amelioration. Susan Cooper transforms Cooperstown into a "city upon a hill" to construct a jeremiad that decries current cultural practice, arguing that it mirrors much of the nation in economic and social progress at midcentury: "The growth of the inland region, to which our valley belongs, will prove, in most respects, a good example of the state of the country generally. The advance of this county has always been steady and healthful; things have never been pushed forward with the unnatural and exhausting impetus of speculation." Being spared the "unnatural" consequences of rampant speculation because of its geographical position, the environment of Cooperstown was shaped by the "industry of [its] population" and thus had grown "steadily and gradually" (*Rural Hours,* 318).[3]

As a post-Revolutionary War settlement largely unaltered by the rampant upheaval of Jacksonian commodification, Cooperstown reflected the social conditions of many rural American settlements. By recording its natural history, Susan Cooper hoped to teach others to respect the demands of the environment so that they might optimally arrange the human presence. Fashioned as a seasonal journal of observations of nature, *Rural Hours* catalogs the attempts of individuals in Cooperstown to shape and utilize their environment. The wealth of data collected in *Rural Hours* functions as source material for her more pointed arguments in **"A Dissolving View."**

In the "Autumn" section of *Rural Hours,* Susan Cooper considers the impact of the American wilderness on the writing of natural history. She describes a process of cross-pollination through which Europeans reconceived their environment in light of a new respect for American scenery, asserting that "all descriptive writing, on natural objects, is now much less vague and general than it was formerly; it has become very much more definite and accurate within the last half-century."

Cooper notes the popularity of landscape painting and the propensity for a "natural style in gardening" as possible causes of this transition. But, she contends, social patterns are rarely altered by discrete factors: "It is seldom, however, that a great change in public taste or opinion is produced by a single direct cause only; there are generally many lesser collateral causes working together, aiding and strengthening each other meanwhile, ere decided results are produced" (*Rural Hours,* 208). Cooper's caveat forestalls reading cultural trends reductively, revealing her deep concern with tracing the complexity of alterations in social attitudes. Furthermore, it underscores her concern with how "causes" combine to produce change.

Susan Cooper employed the languages of both natural history and social refinement to interrogate the current state of her society. The question of American social maturation was intrinsically tied to natural history for Susan Cooper: she perceived that the Republic's social structures had grown out of the management of its natural resources. Cooper's nuanced understanding of the "collateral causes" that collectively shape "public taste" exhibits her attempt to refine various disparate narratives in circulation. In *Rural Hours* and **"A Dissolving View,"** she promulgated the notion that American cultural behavior, both in practice and planning, ought to take into account and somehow represent America's environmental uniqueness. Familiar as she was with nineteenth-century natural histories, her own work deploys these source texts, and ideas derived from them, to deliberate about America's social, architectural, and cultural practices.

Susan Cooper's refusal to admit a "single direct cause" as responsible for cultural transformations reminds us that for most of her contemporaries the embrace of nature as model for culture was not intended to transcend their material lives but to complement them. Cooper's conception of nature and the patterns nature offered represents a paradigm shift in the way natural history writing was understood in the early nineteenth century. This shift emancipated treatments of American nature from the confines of eighteenth-century European descriptions of New World nature. Liberated from the restraints of such residual practice, Susan Cooper demanded that Americans, in order to define themselves, turn toward nature rather than continue to reject its primacy.

Susan Cooper's connections with her locale were deeply rooted; she understood that the natural environment and social development of Cooperstown were tied directly to her familial history. Susan Cooper was the third Cooper to describe the natural environment of central New York State, following both her grandfather Judge William Cooper and her father, the novelist James Fenimore Cooper.[4] The views expressed by these three authors, writing of the same region over a forty-year period (1810-50), document significant shifts in the history of American attitudes toward nature. William Cooper held a primarily utilitarian vision of wilderness: writing to attract Europeans contemplating immigration, he described the economic possibilities of New York State. James modified his father's vision by questioning his predecessor's interaction with nature, while simultaneously claiming the American wilderness as a setting for the historical romance. Susan Cooper infused her writing with a scientific consciousness absent in her forefathers' writings. Thus the movement from William to Susan Cooper mirrors developments in American natural history writing while also suggesting the great depth of her intellectual rootedness in her region.

By the mid-nineteenth century, when Susan launched her career as a writer, Americans—at least those who lived in New York—were no longer burdened either with fashioning a civilization out of wilderness or with validating their enterprise to a skeptical European audience. For the first post-Revolutionary generation of American writers, including Charles Brockden Brown, James Fenimore Cooper, and Washington Irving, the wilderness offered a fictive realm where they might rehearse the tensions that the formation of a national identity evoked. Empowered by developments in natural history and by the successful literary foundations of their predecessors, midcentury American authors employed nature toward very different ends. For this later generation of writers, nature was not an uncultured realm but an arena unfettered by the constraints of dogma. Freed from the need to defend American art, Susan Cooper figured nature not as a symbolic trope but as an element that evinced social life.

Born in 1813, Susan Cooper came of age in an America very different from that of her father. A mythic reinterpretation of the War of 1812 created a heretofore unknown sense of national cohesion that rapidly supplanted, in the popular imagination, the fact that the conflict had come perilously close to dissolving the union.[5] After weathering several challenging collapses and panics, the American economy had, by the 1840s, largely stabilized, transforming the nation from an economically stratified society to one with capital held predominantly by an emergent middle class.[6] Popular iconography figured America as the nation of the future, and youth and possibility became central themes of the new American narrative. Moving beyond an earlier tendency to measure American achievement against European models, Susan Cooper grounds her consideration of national identity in the determining role of the natural environment.

Throughout the 1830s and 1840s efforts to locate the sources of national identity were manifested in a broad-based interrogation of the institutions of the Republic

and their effects in forming post-Revolutionary subjectivities.[7] Beginning in the 1830s, America witnessed a massive increase in the publication of advice manuals and conduct guides.[8] Coupled with this trend was an increased attention to domestic economy, registered in the novels of Susan Warner, Harriet Beecher Stowe, and Maria Susanna Cummins, in handbooks by Lydia Maria Child and Catharine Beecher, and in popular journals such as *Godey's Lady's Book* (1836) and the *Home Journal* (1846).[9] The abundance and success of these publications speak retrospectively to a cultural desire for instruction on matters of identity formation. These texts responded to a Jacksonian cultural anxiety concerning the effects social migration and the commodification of nature—caused by the shift away from an agriculturally based economy—might have on the construction of a national culture. If Americans secured their identity through a primary connection to nature, what would be the cost of urban expansion and industrialization? Linked to this attention to the domestic was an increasing interest in forming scientific and educational associations dedicated to the study of natural history. The creation of these institutions responded to the emerging belief in a correlation between the natural environment and character development.

The advent of gentility in America during the mid-nineteenth century was, as Richard Bushman notes, yoked to a "beautification campaign," which insisted that "everything from houses to barns to village streets was to be made beautiful; every scene was to be turned into a picture."[10] In *Rural Hours* Susan Cooper argues for the congruence of interiors and exteriors by unearthing "how large a portion of our ideas of grace and beauty are derived from the plants, how constantly we turn to them for models" (316). Look at "all the trifling knick-knacks in the room," Cooper directs, "and on all these you may see, in bolder or fainter lines, a thousand proofs of the debt we owe to the vegetable world" (*Rural Hours,* 316). Cooper urges the incorporation of interior decorations that match America's exterior environments, rather than relying on foreign models. While Cooper's remarks recall the tenets of European *Naturphilosophie,* they are more properly read as a careful adaptation of that doctrine. Susan Cooper shuns the idealization of nature, insisting instead that Americans adopt realistic forms from their immediate environment.[11]

As Rochelle Johnson and Daniel Patterson note in their introduction to *Rural Hours,* Susan Fenimore Cooper avidly read natural history. Cataloging the volumes she is believed to have consulted, they document Cooper's repeated requests that her father purchase for her specific scientific and protoscientific texts. Familiar with the works of Louis Agassiz, Andrew Jackson Downing, and Charles Lyell, Susan Cooper also immersed herself in the writings of John James Audubon, François Chateaubriand, Georges Cuvier, Alexander von Humboldt, DeWitt Clinton, Thomas Jefferson, Alexander Wilson, and other natural historians.

Chief among these new natural historians was Charles Lyell, whose scientific discoveries had considerable impact on natural history writing in the United States after the publication of his *Principles of Geology* (1830-33). Lyell toured the Republic in 1841, lecturing to overcrowded halls in most of the nation's major cities.[12] In his speeches and writings, Lyell observed that the age of the earth far exceeded previous understandings, implying that European pride in its "ancient" civilization was misplaced. If the heritage of the West was dwarfed by the reality of the earth's age, then the relative youth of the Republic was inconsequential. By lengthening the frame of history, introducing what Foucault calls "the irruptive violence of time," Lyell indirectly helped assuage American anxiety about national identity.[13]

Lyell contended that the entirety of the past could be successfully interpreted by examining forces still operant in nature.[14] Such a reconceptualization reversed the prevalent Whig notion of progress, liberating the present from a deterministic past by inverting the figures in the equation. If, to understand the past, one must scrutinize the present, then America's failure to attain some prescribed plateau was irrelevant. These developments in natural history, spearheaded by the work of Lyell, enabled midcentury American writers to imagine nature not simply in a unidirectional relationship with cultivated European landscapes but as a fragment of a much older, more intricate picture. As a result of this recalibration of the earth's age, Susan Cooper could investigate the correlation between the society of the Republic and New World nature without privileging European social structures as the primal scene.

Lyell's American tour sparked a turn during the 1840s toward science as a vehicle for explaining the state of American culture. The first publication of *Scientific American* (1845) was followed in short order by the establishment of the Smithsonian Institution (1846). Harvard sought to rival European centers of learning by hiring Louis Agassiz and promoting his work through the foundation of the Lawrence Scientific School (1847). While such highbrow activities might seem divorced from the popular success of texts concerned with domestic economy, these trends were intrinsically connected with the creation of a uniquely American style of interior design, with landscape composition, and with stylistic developments in architecture. Intriguingly, Susan Cooper registers this phenomenon by speculating on the linkages between terra-forming strategies and social structures.

A major influence on Susan Cooper's conception of landscape aesthetics was Andrew Jackson Downing, whose widely celebrated *Treatise on the Theory and Practice of Landscape Gardening, Adapted to North America* (1841) was the first American work devoted to landscape design.[15] In Downing's work Susan Cooper found a voice that counseled patience and the cultivation of nature as the optimal means of advancing American cultural development. In a nation searching for domestic instruction, Downing quickly rose to prominence. Promulgating the cultivation of gentility, Downing argued that as nature could be shaped and husbanded, so too could social practices, and that alterations in the landscape would provoke shifts in cultural habit.

In an editorial in the *Horticulturist,* a journal Downing edited from 1846 until his death in 1852, he cautioned that "to live in the new world" meant leaving foreign preconceptions behind.[16] Downing called for moderation in the cultivation of the landscape rather than the typical American "goaheadism," urging his readers to have reasonable expectations and to appreciate the impossibility of forming a picturesque garden overnight. If America was to develop a refined native culture (autonomous, yet comparable to European society); then its citizens must proceed with caution. For Downing, landscape and social structure were directly linked. The cultural institutions Americans created must be grounded in an interior and exterior architecture that represented the democratic tenets of the Republic, for as Downing advanced in *The Architecture of Country Houses,* "different styles of Domestic Architecture" were "nothing more than expressions of national character."[17]

Immediately after the Revolution and well into the first quarter of the nineteenth century, American artists were largely ignored when they mourned the landscape's destruction. In an earlier appeal for preserving the American forest, Thomas Cole enumerated the glories of the New York wilderness, pointing out that it had yet to be "destroyed or modified" to "accommodate the tastes and necessities of a dense population."[18] In the 1830s, the United States was only beginning to confront the consequences of development, and Cole enjoined his audience to moderate the rate of progress, for "the ravages of the axe are daily increasing" and "the most noble scenes are made destitute." Writing during the height of large-scale terra-forming projects in New York, Cole realized that "such is the road society has to travel," yet he hoped this would "lead to refinement in the end."[19] Jacksonian America was not preoccupied with maintaining picturesque views but with improving market access and building a workable infrastructure. Over a decade later, after the American economy had stabilized and capital was more equally distributed, Downing's popular pleas for patience and preservation—which Susan Cooper echoed—found a more receptive audience. Cooper's arguments about American development were more pointed than Downing's, for the consequences she envisioned were not abstract but extremely personal.

In *Rural Hours* Susan Cooper investigated American social mores as an extension of the Republic's relationship to its natural environment. In a pivotal essay that appeared two years later, she advanced her argument more specifically, mapping the historical terrain of American architecture and its connection to the landscape. In **"A Dissolving View,"** which appeared in the handsome 1852 gift-book *The Home Book of the Picturesque,* Cooper entreated readers to emancipate themselves from received practice, to imagine their own location in nature as the central experience of their worldview. In **"A Dissolving View,"** she recapitulates residual conceptions of American social evolution and considers how emerging interests in natural history and landscape aesthetics departed from that inherited tradition.

Dedicated to Asher Durand, president of the National Academy of Fine Arts, *The Home Book of the Picturesque* sought to capitalize on cultural preoccupations with natural history and interior design, while also contributing to the cultivation of an American aesthetic.[20] The dedication underscores this intention by stating that the volume was "an initiatory suggestion for popularizing some of the characteristics of American Landscape and American Art."[21] Aspiring to fulfill consumer demand, Putnam undertook the volume "as an experiment," asserting that it would provide an American alternative to popular European gift books by illustrating "the picturesque beauties of American landscape."[22] Both nationalist and market-conscious, Putnam's editors canonized the productions of American artists while advancing an argument about the picturesque aesthetic.

On the title page of *The Home Book of the Picturesque,* the editors at G. P. Putnam list their contributors in ranking order. Susan Cooper's is the fourth name on that page, preceded only by Washington Irving, William Cullen Bryant, and her father, James Fenimore Cooper. Susan Cooper's prominent listing is not surprising, since Putnam's published *Rural Hours* as its 1850 presentation volume and profited from its considerable success. Susan Cooper's relation to the writers whose names precede hers on Putnam's title page is not, however, simply a matter of contemporary literary reputation. Her essay, **"A Dissolving View,"** conveys its readers from the landscape aesthetic of Irving, Bryant, and her father to a more localized and less romantic conception of American scenery.

America's foremost popularizer of "the Picturesque," Andrew Jackson Downing, defined that aesthetic mode as "an idea of beauty or power strongly and irregularly expressed," as opposed to "the Beautiful," which is "calmly and harmoniously expressed."[23] In creating a picturesque scene, Downing observes, "everything depends on *intricacy* and *irregularity.*" He began from an assumption that nature was not inherently picturesque but required arrangement and embellishment to be formed, and that this shaping "springs naturally from a love" for the terrain. To express a wild yet cultivated nature, landscape gardening must be tailored to its region. In America the progress of landscape gardening was not impeded by a lack of resources but by a failure to adapt European ideals to the demands of America's geographical and historical particularities: "Even those who are familiar with foreign works on the subject in question labor under many obstacles in practice, which grow out of the difference in our soil and climate, or our social and political position."[24] Downing's equation of regional differences with sociopolitical factors demonstrates how closely linked are these seemingly divergent agendas. A landscape aesthetic must reflect the demands of a given environment while representing a nation's heritage. It is precisely this new vision of a landscape aesthetic that informs the creation of *The Home Book of the Picturesque* and, in particular, Susan Cooper's **"A Dissolving View."**

Susan Cooper situates **"A Dissolving View"** during autumn in Cooperstown. Her choice of season grounds her essay within (as she conceives it) the paradigmatic American season. Beginning in *Rural Hours,* Cooper argues that America's autumnal palate offers unrivaled vistas. "Our native writers, as soon as we had writers of our own, pointed out very early both the sweetness of the Indian summer, and the magnificence of the autumnal changes," which uncovered, Cooper continues, "the precise extent of the difference between the relative beauty of autumn in Europe and in America: with us it is quite impossible to overlook these peculiar charms of the autumnal months," whereas in Europe "they remained unnoticed, unobserved, for ages" (*Rural Hours,* 209). While it is customary to associate nature with vernal scenes, the explosion of color during an American autumn affords a spectacle unfamiliar to Europeans. These diverse tints are the most difficult to reproduce, for "there is no precedent for such coloring as nature requires here among the works of old masters, and the American artist must necessarily become an innovator" (*Rural Hours,* 215). Autumn is, Cooper argues, an unworked genre, delivering American artists from the constraints of unfavorable comparisons with the artistic conventions of Europe. Representing American autumn required painstaking attention to fleeting scenery. The best vantage point a seeker of picturesque scenes could have is in "the hanging woods of a mountainous country" where the "trees throwing out their branches, one above another, in bright variety of coloring and outline" sufficiently frame the intricacy of the scene (*Rural*

Hours, 211). Susan Cooper's narrator occupies such a position at the opening of her meditation on the development of Cooperstown.

Cooper opens **"A Dissolving View"** with a familiar account of the beauty of the autumnal American landscape. That rendering is complicated when she describes autumn as protean. During fall an observer is unbalanced, never knowing "beforehand exactly what to expect," for "there is always some variation, occasionally a strange contrast." Yet Cooper quickly reveals that the human transformation of the multihued landscape generates the picturesque: "I should not care to pass the season in the wilderness," for while "a broad extent of forest is no doubt necessary to the magnificent spectacle," there "should also be broken woods, scattered groves, and isolated trees." She continues, "it strikes me that the quiet fields of man, and his cheerful dwellings, should also have a place in the gay picture." Fall contains "a social spirit," for its "brilliancy" draws attention to the human presence in the landscape (**"A Dissolving View,"** 80, 82, 81).

Cooper locates her narrator on the trunk of a fallen pine tree that "overlooked the country for some fifteen miles or more," framing her field of vision and enabling her perception of the picturesque. A nearby "projecting cliff" and "the oaks whose branches overshadowed" the narrator's seat, creating a natural Claude glass, guide her vision, imparting a graduated scale to the objects in the background.[25] Situated within the forest, Cooper's narrator overlooks a cultivated landscape that figures the progressive development of American settlement: "the lake, the rural town, and the farms in the valley beyond, lying at our feet like a beautiful map." From this topological position, the favorite perch of the Hudson River school, Cooper's narrator witnesses—and records—the history of American social evolution while ruminating on the consequences of all human development.[26] She concludes that although "the hand of man generally improves a landscape," there is a danger that terra-forming projects partake of the hubristic. In such work, man "endeavors to rise above his true part of laborer and husbandman," assuming "the character of creator" (**"A Dissolving View,"** 81, 82).

For Cooper, this hubristic inclination has contaminated architecture since its advent. Europe is replete with architectural projects that compete with nature rather than harmonize with it: "Indeed it would seem as if man had no sooner mastered the art of architecture, than he aimed at rivalling the dignity and durability of the works of nature which served as his models; he resolved that his walls of vast stones should stand in place as long as the rocks from which they were hewn; that his columns and his arches should live with the trees and branches from which they were copied; he determined to scale the heavens with his proud towers of Babel" (**"A Dis-**

solving View," 84). While such "imposing" ancient piles stir up wonder in viewers, they also recall the combative cultures out of which they arose.[27] The "very violence" of the past and its "superstitious nature" created monuments to dissolute empires and forged structures to withstand the continual danger of eradication (**"A Dissolving View,"** 86).

Should Americans mourn the absence of ancient edifices redolent of antagonistic cultural values? If a cultivated landscape should epitomize the specific social and cultural values of its population, as Cooper believes, then is it tragic that the United States lacks monuments to monarchies and feudalism? European cities are burdened by buildings that were formed by the "prevalence" of a "warlike spirit." These medieval buildings "are likely" to "outlast modern works of the same nature," for those who built them imagined a future dedicated to the same principles that governed them: "They not only built for the future, in those days, but they expected posterity to work with them; as one generation lay down in their graves, they called another generation to their pious labor." While Americans are "in some measure influenced by those days of chivalry and superstitious truth," they are not bound by them (**"A Dissolving View,"** 86-87).

Susan Cooper recognized just how much materiality matters in shaping a coherent social philosophy. By affirming agency, Cooper extends her contention that European architecture is ill suited for America; like the effect of a canopy formed by towering trees, the shadows of the past prohibit new growth from taking root. "Thus it is that there is not in those old countries," she observes, "a single natural feature of the earth upon which man has not set his seal." Cooper finds a triumphant strength in "how different from all this" the "fresh civilization of America" is. Within the United States, "there is no blending of the old and the new," for "there is nothing old among us" (**"A Dissolving View,"** 88-89). Much of the Republic's nature remains wild, and thus for Cooper, Americans fashioning a modern nation are not burdened by the detrimental decisions of their ancestors.

Critical of the current state of national life, Cooper complains that Americans are "the reverse of conservators," failing to preserve markers of their own history. Here Cooper's position reproduces contemporary, class-based arguments against the depredations of laissez-faire capitalism. Yet for Cooper there is freedom in Americans being "the borderers of civilization," for that position enables them to "act as pioneers." She extends her examination of American society by freighting the landscape with predictive power; Cooper observes that "the peculiar tendencies of the age are seen more clearly among us than in Europe" (**"A Dissolving View,"** 89). The unfolding of the American scene—measured by its architecture, its landscape design, and its consequent social refinements—is a matter of more than local interest. It is a barometer of the age, a register of the future.

Inheritors of Western social tradition, yet free from the constraints of modern Europe's determining environment (for "many parts" of the Old World "have an old, worn-out, exhausted appearance"), the United States should fashion an architecture suited to the more "subtle" nineteenth century. America's historic monuments are not to be found in man-made ruins but within nature itself. Paraphrasing Louis Agassiz, Cooper notes that "as the surface of the planet now exists, North America is, in reality, the oldest part of the earth," simultaneously more ancient and more vigorous than the natural environment of Europe (**"A Dissolving View,"** 89, 90). While Americans failed as historic conservationists, they have not yet irrevocably denuded their landscape and so can still alter their interaction with it.

Cooper continues by returning to Agassiz, who "tells us that in many particulars our vegetation, and our animal life, belong to an older period than those" of Europe (**"A Dissolving View,"** 90). Agassiz believed that vegetation that existed only in a fossil state in Europe continued to flourish in North America. By the 1850s, Agassiz was the most prominent natural historian in the United States, and Cooper's citation of his work testifies to her familiarity with contemporary natural history.[28] Agassiz wanted to understand nature through, as Edward Lurie suggests, "the perceptions provided by direct experience." While Agassiz straddled "the two worlds of empiricism and idealism," he also knew "that nature, if it meant anything at all, was to be understood as a whole, a historical and contemporary unit of experience."[29] Agassiz's conception of nature, which dominated natural history prior to Darwin's 1859 publication of his *Origin of Species,* rested on the assumption that local environments were shaped by divine power for particular ends. Advancing this notion of separate creations, he argued in *Lake Superior* (1850) that "the geographical distribution of organized beings displays more fully the direct intervention of a Supreme Intelligence in the plan of Creation, than any other adaption in the physical world."[30] Agassiz's sense of the uniqueness of each territory's natural history undergirds Cooper's promotion of a specific American architecture or interaction with the landscape. If, as Agassiz maintains, nature is separately created for a particular, divine purpose, then Americans, who have not completely disrupted their environment, are positioned to interpret properly their physical world. And by accurately reading their landscape, they can build dwellings in harmony with their surroundings.

Cooper ends her essay with an enigmatic turn. Seizing a "sprig of wych-hazel," Cooper's narrator plays a "game of architectural consequences" in which she imagines the landscape as it might have appeared if the culture that had formed it had been driven by different forces. The inroads of civilization disappear, and with a wave of the wand the landscape is restored to wilderness. But "merely razing a village" and restoring the valley to its virginal state "did not satisfy the whim of the moment," and so the spell is cast again until she "beheld a spectacle which wholly engrossed" her attention (**"A Dissolving View,"** 91-92).

The conjuring wand produces the valley as it would have appeared "had it lain in the track of European civilization during past ages; how, in such a case, would it have been fashioned by the hand of man?" In the midst of this reverie, in which everything is "so strangely altered," the narrator requires "a second close scrutiny to convince [herself] that this was indeed the site of the village which had disappeared a moment earlier." Only through an intense examination of "all the natural features of the landscape" is she assured that it is the valley, and not herself, that has been recast. Noting the geographically appropriate vegetation and recognizing the familiar contours of the lake shore, she understands that it is the history of cultural production that has mutated the landscape. Quickly, "all resemblance ceased," for the "hills had been wholly shorn of wood," and the "position of the different farms and that of the buildings was entirely changed." The little town "dwindled to a mere hamlet" (**"A Dissolving View,"** 92-93).

The valley is now dominated by two structures, the church and an "old country house" that give the surrounding habitations their meaning, or at least arrange them in "various grades of importance." The church and manor house define the social structure of this European village: all its citizens share one religion, and just as clearly, they are cast into a delineated social hierarchy based upon architectural style. Cooperstown's bustling industry becomes, in the "European" hamlet, "two or three small, quiet-looking shops"; its wooden bridge is replaced by a "massive stone" one guarded by "the ruins of a tower" (**"A Dissolving View,"** 93).

By recomposing the scene in the form of a European village, Cooper underscores the difference between American and European society. While the denuded European landscape contains buried "ancient coins" and the ruins of "feudal castles," the relationship of its current occupants to their environment is entirely predetermined (**"A Dissolving View,"** 93). Unlike the less-ordered American scene, the social roles of Europeans are always already fixed. In sharp contrast, the current state of architecture and civic planning in the United States permits the natural proliferation and change of the social relations of Americans.

The narrator's reverie is disrupted by "a roving bee, bent apparently on improving these last warm days, and harvesting the last drops of honey" (**"A Dissolving View,"** 94). As Washington Irving reminds us, bees were widely perceived as "the heralds of civilization, steadfastly preceding it as it advanced from the Atlantic borders."[31] The bee, cast here as a symbol of an intrusive market economy, quite literally stings the narrator out of her Hudson River fancy and reminds her that the rural location from which she views the American scene might soon fall victim to the energies of regnant capitalism. Or, perhaps, having imagined the appearance of the valley as if it had been shaped by European cultural advancement, readers of her essay would have understood the danger of choosing foreign models as social guides.

Prior to her wych-hazel fancy, Cooper contemplates the current state of American architecture, suggesting that "it is yet too unformed, too undecided to claim a character of its own, but the general air of comfort and thrift which shows itself in most of our dwellings, whether on a large or a small scale, gives satisfaction in its own way" (**"A Dissolving View,"** 91). This critique is not melancholic; rather, it is framed as a recognition that America is a nation whose identity will be decided in the present, a borderland between a determining past and an unknown future. While American architecture may lack a character of its own, that absence will not obstruct the progress of future generations. She encourages a movement toward preservation that would enable the development of an American aesthetic cognizant of the particular character of the nation's environment. By registering the vulnerability of older aesthetic perspectives that proceed from a reliance on European cultural models, she argues for their rejection. Anything built on such foreign foundations was doomed to collapse; alien to New World soil, they could never take root without damaging the natural environment. At the same time, she maintains that Americans need not pursue heedlessly forms of architectural and landscape design capable of reflecting a democratic cultural order.

Only by considering her two texts in tandem can a reader fully appreciate Susan Cooper's conception of the linkage between cultural forms and nature as dependent upon the imagination. Instead of further damaging their environment by constructing badly designed buildings, Americans, she argues, should imagine the consequences of their choices before plunging ahead, working with—rather than in opposition to—their natural environments. Since assembled aesthetic failures encumber the formation of a national culture by articulating inappropriate social codes, she promotes the imagination (and not the landscape) as the arena for testing the consequences of any new construction. Moving beyond residual aesthetics, requiems for an America that failed to import European cultural models, Susan Cooper makes a case for preserving the wild as the locus of the imagination.

Notes

1. Susan Cooper's distaste for the importation of European cultural forms registers in her critique of the unfortunate practice of naming American settlements after European cities. See Susan Fenimore Cooper, *Rural Hours,* ed. Rochelle Johnson and Daniel Patterson (Athens: University of Georgia Press, 1998), 298-309. Hereafter cited in the text. References to "A Dissolving View" are to *The Home Book of the Picturesque; or, American Scenery, Art, and Literature* (New York: Putnam, 1852; reprint, Gainesville, Fla.: Scholars' Facsimiles & Reprints, 1967), 79-94. Hereafter cited in text.

2. Cooper's interest in architecture as a record of American social practice reflects its status during the first half of the nineteenth century. Prior to its professionalization in the last quarter of the century, considering architecture one of the fine arts was a common practice, as even the Library of Congress (following Jefferson's cataloging schema) shelved architectural treatises along with works of poetry, fiction, and other artistic texts. Susan Cooper was also most likely familiar with Andrew Jackson Downing's *The Architecture of Country Houses* (1850), in which he argued that the aim of architecture, like that of "every fine art is the art of so treating objects as to give them a moral significance" ([New York: Dover, 1969], 38). Additionally, Cooper would have been familiar with her father's own speculations on this question, figured most prominently in *Home as Found* (1838) and *The American Democrat* (1838).

3. Cooperstown's distance from both the Erie Canal and existing railroads in the 1850s meant that it was relatively unaffected by the boom-and-bust economy of the Jacksonian period.

4. William Cooper published his study of Cooperstown, *A Guide in the Wilderness; or, The History of the First Settlements in the Western Counties of New York with Useful Instructions to Future Settlers* (Dublin: Gilbert and Hodges, 1810), at the close of the century's first decade, while James Fenimore Cooper repeatedly explored the terrain of New York State in his fiction starting in the 1820s.

5. The best critical accounts of the nationalist myths born from Jackson's victory at New Orleans remain Marvin Meyers, *The Jacksonian Persuasion: Politics and Belief* (Stanford, Calif.: Stanford University Press, 1957) and John William Ward, *Andrew Jackson: Symbol for an Age* (New York: Oxford University Press, 1955).

6. For a discussion of this economic phenomenon nationally, see Charles Sellers, *The Market Revo-*

lution: Jacksonian America, 1815-1846 (New York: Oxford University Press, 1991). For more specifically regional examinations, see Paul E. Johnson, *A Shopkeeper's Millennium: Society and Revivals in Rochester, New York 1815-1837* (New York: Hill and Wang, 1978) and Mary Ryan, *Cradle of the Middle Class: The Family in Oneida County, New York, 1790-1865* (New York: Cambridge University Press, 1981).

7. For an extended discussion of the shifting representation of America's Revolutionary heritage, see Michael Kammen, *A Season of Youth: The American Revolution and the Historical Imagination* (New York: Knopf, 1978).

8. For examinations of the effects of this increase in the publication of manuals and guides, see Karen Halttunen, *Confidence Men and Painted Women: A Study of Middle Class Culture in America, 1830-1870* (New Haven, Conn.: Yale University Press, 1982).

9. Among the key critical studies of the emergence of the cult of domesticity are Gillian Brown, *Domestic Individualism: Imagining Self in Nineteenth-Century America* (Berkeley: University of California Press, 1990); Ann Douglas, *The Feminization of American Culture* (New York: Doubleday, 1977); and Jane Tompkins, *Sensational Designs: The Cultural Work of American Fiction, 1790-1860* (New York: Oxford University Press, 1985).

10. Richard L. Bushman, *The Refinement of America: Persons, Houses, Cities* (New York: Vintage, 1993), xiv.

11. Consistently in *Rural Hours,* Cooper suggests that Americans manufacture interior decorations based upon the superior variety of colors and shades found in nature around them rather than continue to follow foreign trends.

12. For a detailed discussion of Lyell's importance in the United States, see Leonard G. Wilson, *Lyell in America: Transatlantic Geology, 1841-1853* (Baltimore, Md.: Johns Hopkins University Press, 1998).

13. Michel Foucault, *The Order of Things: An Archaeology of the Human Sciences* (New York: Vintage, 1994), 132.

14. See Stephen Jay Gould, *Time's Arrow, Time's Cycle: Myth and Metaphor in the Discovery of Geological Time* (Cambridge, Mass.: Harvard University Press, 1987).

15. Downing's influence reached into other aspects of rural life: see, as examples, his *Fruits and Fruit Trees of America* (1845), *Cottage Residences* (1842), and *The Architecture of Country Houses* (1850). For in-depth treatments of Downing's influence, see Judith K. Major, *To Live in the New World: A. J. Downing and American Landscape Gardening* (Cambridge, Mass.: MIT Press, 1997); David Schuyler, *Apostle of Taste: Andrew Jackson Downing 1815-1852* (Baltimore, Md.: Johns Hopkins University Press, 1996); and Adam Sweeting, *Reading Houses and Building Books: Andrew Jackson Downing and the Architecture of Popular Antebellum Literature, 1835-1855* (Hanover: University Press of New England, 1996).

16. As quoted by Major, *To Live in the New World,* 2.

17. Downing, *The Architecture of Country Houses,* 26.

18. Thomas Cole, "Essay on American Scenery," in *Thomas Cole: The Collected Essays and Prose Sketches,* ed. Marshall Tym (St. Paul: John Colet Press, 1980), 8.

19. Ibid., 17.

20. The dedication to Durand is testimony to his prominence, but possibly the editors were also trying to invoke the spirit of one of his most famous paintings, *Kindred Spirits* (1849). Commissioned to paint a portrait of Thomas Cole and William Cullen Bryant, Durand depicted them in *Kindred Spirits* in complete harmony with the American wilderness. For a sense of the reception of Durand's painting, see Barbara Novak, *Nature and Culture: American Landscape Painting 1825-1875* (New York: Oxford University Press, 1980) and James T. Callow, *Kindred Spirits: Knickerbocker Writers and American Artists, 1807-1855* (Chapel Hill: University of North Carolina Press, 1967).

21. From the title page of *The Home Book of the Picturesque.*

22. Ibid., 7.

23. Andrew Jackson Downing, *Landscape Gardening and Rural Architecture* (1852; New York: Dover, 1991), 54. This volume is a reprint of the seventh edition of *A Treatise on the Theory and Practice of Landscape Gardening* (1852).

24. Ibid., 82, 19, 7.

25. A familiar tool for those searching for the picturesque, the Claude glass (named for the French landscape artist Claude Lorraine) was a convex mirror used to concentrate the features of a landscape. Here Cooper suggests that the cliff and trees create a natural frame for her vision.

26. Employing a tactic familiar to Hudson River school painters, Cooper locates her narrator within

wild nature but casts her field of vision into a settled landscape. See Angela Miller's reading of Cole's *The Oxbow* (1836) in *The Empire of the Eye: Landscape Representation and American Cultural Politics, 1825-1875* (Ithaca, N.Y.: Cornell University Press, 1993), 39-48.

27. Cooper in particular singles out the architectural styles of Babylon, Greece, and Rome for their fortitude in surviving numerous attacks at the hands of "savages" and "barbarians."

28. The best account of Agassiz's importance is Edward Lurie, *Louis Agassiz: A Life in Science* (Baltimore, Md.: Johns Hopkins University Press, 1988), see esp. chaps. 4 and 5.

29. Ibid., 82, 52, 50.

30. Louis Agassiz, *Lake Superior: Its Physical Character, Vegetation, and Animals, Compared with Those of Other and Similar Regions* (1850; New York: Arno Press, 1970), 144.

31. Washington Irving, *A Tour of the Prairies* (1832; Norman: University of Oklahoma Press, 1956), 50. Cooper would have also been familiar with her father's treatment of this myth in his novel *The Oak Openings; or, The Bee-Hunter* (1848).

Jessie Ravage (essay date 2001)

SOURCE: Ravage, Jessie. "In Response to the Women at Seneca Falls: Susan Fenimore Cooper and the Rightful Place of Woman in America." In *Susan Fenimore Cooper: New Essays on* Rural Hours *and Other Works,* edited by Rochelle Johnson and Daniel Patterson, pp. 249-65. Athens: The University of Georgia Press, 2001.

[*In the following essay, Ravage surveys Cooper's conservative response to the women's suffrage movement, detailing the subtle ways in which the author reinforces traditional female roles in* Rural Hours.]

The July 14, 1848, number of the *Seneca County Courier* contained the following short announcement:

Seneca Falls Convention

WOMAN'S RIGHTS CONVENTION.—A convention to discuss the social, civil, and religious condition and rights of woman, will be held in the Wesleyan Chapel, at Seneca Falls, N.Y., on Wednesday and Thursday, the 19th and 20th of July, current; commencing at 10 o'clock A.M. During the first day the meeting will be exclusively for women, who are earnestly invited to attend. The public generally are invited to be present on the second day, when Lucretia Mott, of Philadelphia, and other ladies and gentlemen, will address the convention.[1]

Buoyed by the support for the sentiments expressed at the meeting in Seneca Falls, the leaders—Elizabeth Cady Stanton, Lucretia Mott, and Mary and Elizabeth McClintock—held a second one in Rochester on August 2. Like a pair of thunderclaps in the still heat of that drought-ridden summer, these conventions stirred a storm of comment in newspapers far and wide.

That same summer, Susan Fenimore Cooper, daughter of novelist James Fenimore Cooper and an aspiring writer in her own right, was visiting her aunts in Geneva, New York, a stone's throw from Seneca Falls.[2] By the summer of 1848, she was writing journal entries that would be collected and published in 1850 as *Rural Hours,* in which she discussed many issues confronting Americans. Her occasional commentary on the rightful place of woman in American society in this text is especially interesting because it is among the earliest discussions of the subject, pro or con, in the post-Seneca Falls era.[3]

For most late-twentieth-century students of mid-nineteenth-century American history and literature, the conditions under which women then lived seem unbearably constricted. In 1848 American women had virtually no legal standing and no political power, at least through the electoral process. A Philadelphia newspaper, the *Public Ledger and Daily Transcript,* summed up a common attitude of the time in its response to the woman's rights conventions of 1848, saying, "A woman is nobody. A wife is everything. A pretty girl is equal to ten thousand men, and a mother is, next to God, all powerful" (*History of Woman Suffrage,* 804). Readers of Susan Fenimore Cooper are often disappointed that she, a single woman published and acknowledged for her intellectual ability, did not support efforts to allow her financial autonomy and a role in electing governors who would support her right to equal treatment under the law. Instead, she wielded her pen to oppose the effort led by Stanton, Mott, Anthony, and others to provide women with equal rights under the law and the right to vote. Her opposition to the rights-of-woman arguments expounded in these early conventions was subtle. However, as it became apparent that gentle suasion would not quell the rising sentiment for female suffrage, Miss Cooper's arguments against it grew pointed and specific in the post-Civil War period.[4]

While her position seems an inherently contradictory position to readers in our own time, it did not seem so to many women writing in the middle decades of the nineteenth century. Other influential women writers, notably, the Beecher sisters and Sarah Josepha Hale, editor of *Godey's Lady's Book,* advocated roles for women that kept them in the home, fortifying it and, by extension, fortifying, even barricading, the nation as the collective home from foreign and potentially malevolent influences. It has also been argued that these women writers, by defining the home and women's role in it, made it possible for women to move outside the home, most notably into print.[5] Thus, Susan Fenimore Cooper's **Rural Hours** could be viewed as defining America's domestic natural history as part of America's identity, setting it aside from foreign species. Using American natural history as a springboard, Miss Cooper went on to discuss many issues facing America at the time. Among these, she expressed sentiments mirroring those laid out in what late-twentieth-century writers have dubbed the "cult of domesticity."

Domesticity was but one response to the considerable turbulence of the second quarter of the nineteenth century throughout Europe and North America. Writing in the *New York Herald,* the paper's proprietor, James Gordon Bennett, alluded to the numerous political upheavals in Europe in 1848, a year eventually called the "Year of Revolutions":

> This is the age of revolutions. To whatever part of the world the attention is directed, the political and social fabric is crumbling to pieces; and changes which far exceed the wildest dreams of the enthusiastic Utopians of the last generation, are now pursued with ardor and perseverance. . . . By the intelligence, however, which we have lately received, the work of revolution is no longer confined to the Old World, nor to the masculine gender. The flag of independence has been hoisted, for the second time on this side of the Atlantic; and a solemn league and covenant has just been entered into by a Convention of women at Seneca Falls, to "throw off the despotism under which they are groaning, and provide new guards for their future security." Little did we expect this new element to be thrown into the cauldron of agitation which is now bubbling around us with such fury.
>
> (Quoted in *History of Woman Suffrage,* 805)

In his comments on the Seneca Falls meeting, Bennett acknowledged the correspondingly charged atmosphere of the United States at the same period. Having led the way in political revolution in 1776, America was following up with economic, industrial, social, and religious revolutions of varying scope and scale. Westward migration, industrialization, urbanization, immigration, increased social mobility, and economic turbulence caused by an indecisive banking system and trade imbalances all engendered social upheaval, and well before the midcentury, progressive ideas posited by reformers of many stripes were receiving considerable attention.

Central New York State, where Susan Fenimore Cooper spent virtually all of her adult life, was called "the burned-over state" during the 1830s and 1840s for the numerous religious revivals and camp meetings held in the region. These appealed deeply to people displaced by so many new and conflicting forces. While evangelical preachers ranted about hellfire and damnation, other potentially disturbing ideas about social reorganization arose. Utopian groups, especially the Fourierists at New Phalanx, New Jersey, and the Perfectionists at Oneida, New York, threatened the hierarchical, patriarchal order posited by mainstream American theologians of the period. Like the Shakers earlier, these peculiarly American groups offered different roles within an altered power structure, especially for women. Communal child rearing, work outside of traditional domestic management, and inclusion in the community power structure offered potential fulfillment for women displaced within American society.[6]

The mainly female audience of two hundred who attended the two-day convention held in the sweltering July heat of a central New York State summer in 1848 demonstrated the agitation felt by at least a certain cadre of women. The Declaration of Sentiments read at the meeting and signed by sixty-eight attendees used the revolutionary Declaration of Independence written seventy-two Julys before as its model. The Declaration of Sentiments described the injustice to woman practiced by man through the American legal system. While relatively local papers failed to comment on the events of the meeting at Seneca Falls, the *Rochester Democrat* noted with derision, possibly tinged with concern lest those standing for the rights of woman might receive a fair hearing:

> This has been a remarkable Convention [held in Rochester on August 2, 1848]. It was composed of those holding to some of the various *isms* of the day, and some, we should think, who embraced them all. . . . The great effort seemed to be to bring out some new, impracticable, absurd, and ridiculous proposition, and the greater its absurdity the better. In short, it was a regular *emeute* of a congregation of females gathered from various quarters, who seem to be really in earnest in their aim at revolution, and who evince entire confidence that "the day of their deliverance is at hand." Verily, this a progressive era!
>
> (Quoted in *History of Woman Suffrage,* 804)

"Insurrection among the Women," the title of an article in the *Worcester (Massachusetts) Telegraph,* also reveals the concern with which the women's conferences were viewed (see *History of Woman Suffrage,* 803).

In mid-nineteenth-century America, the predominant editorial, literary, religious, and political voices generally worked to avoid open insurrection among any of the young nation's disaffected and, for the most part, disenfranchised populations, including Native Americans, African Americans, new immigrants, the growing industrial poor, and, after 1848, women. Thus in 1848 and 1849, when Susan Fenimore Cooper was composing the journal entries that she would publish as **Rural Hours** in 1850, the rights-of-woman issue was new and the discourse varied, but the rhetoric and activity of reform ideas of all kinds as an alternative to upheaval were well established in America. Miss Cooper, herself, was the promising scion of two American families—the Coopers and the Delanceys—who had played important roles in developing a new republic at once linked with its European forebears and traditions and separate from them. Her grandfather William Cooper had established Cooperstown, New York, where his granddaughter lived and set *Rural Hours*. In *A Guide in the Wilderness*, William outlined his plan for the successful settlement of the American wilderness, breaking with tradition by establishing free-hold tenure rather than tenancy. Miss Cooper's father, James Fenimore Cooper, was arguably America's best-known writer in the mid-1800s. Emotionally rooted in the landscape surrounding Otsego Lake, James became a student of the Romantic movement as a young man. He melded Romanticism with his sense of the American past to create some of the nation's most enduring stories. These helped define and elaborate America's past for the young and uncertain republic.

Susan Fenimore Cooper wrote with a consciousness of her role within that family and within American intellectual society. She continued her father's exploration of the relative merits of aspects of the emerging American culture and the meaning of being American. Though Miss Cooper prefaced *Rural Hours* as "the simple record of those little events which make up the course of the seasons in rural life," a careful reading suggests that she intended to cut much wider and deeper than that disclaimer suggests.[7] In *Rural Hours* we find commentary on a broad range of issues relating not only to American nature but also to facets of American culture. She was well aware of the social and economic turbulence of the time and almost certainly recognized the potential appeal that many reform ideas—among them the rights of woman and female suffrage—had for people displaced by a variety of economic and social forces.

Among the displaced were Native American people, whom she discusses in considerable detail in her entry for July 17. She notes: "There are already many parts of this country where an Indian is never seen. There are thousands and hundreds of thousands of the white population who have never laid eyes upon a red man. But this ground lies within the former bounds of the Six Nations, and a remnant of the great tribes of the Iroquois still linger about their old haunts, and occasionally cross our path" (*Rural Hours*, 108). As prominent citizens of the village of Cooperstown and the occupants of one of the village's largest houses, the Coopers received many visitors. She recalled one visit by three Iroquois men, among them the Reverend Mr. Kunkerpott. Of them she wrote: "when no longer warriors and hunters, [they] lose their native character; the fire of their savage energy is extinguished, and the dull and

blackened embers alone remain. Unaccustomed by habit, prejudice, hereditary instinct, to labor, they cannot work, and very generally sink into worthless, drinking idlers" (*Rural Hours*, 111). While her judgmental tone reveals a distaste for the men's current demeanor, she acknowledges their displacement through the disappearance of their traditional tribal culture. She is, however, quite taken with three Oneida women who visit. They are "meek in countenance, with delicate forms and low voices" (*Rural Hours*, 108). Miss Cooper perceives them as positioned between untamed nature and her own civilized culture and suggests that they retain the essential, perhaps natural, gentleness of the female sex despite being heathens and savage (*Rural Hours*, 109). She proposes that woman has a natural reticence and gentleness embodied in these Oneida women, who are barely exposed to the temptations available to the girls of her own village or of the larger towns. The native women are vessels containing true female virtue, preserving their own domestic ways in the face of loss of tribal lands and the ensuing disappearance of the Iroquois way of life. As white middle-class women were cast in the role of protector of domestic virtue and exemplary lights of the home, so too are these Oneida women protecting their own domestic virtue from outside forces. Miss Cooper praises their continued wearing of clothes related to their traditional costume, saying, "[T]hey seem to be the only females in the country who do not make a profound study of the monthly fashion-plates" (*Rural Hours*, 112).

The native gentleness and lack of concern for material goods among the Oneida women differed from that of girls living in towns, or even in the rural village of Cooperstown, whom Miss Cooper describes in a passage dated July 3:

> Those [girls] who live in our large towns, where they buy even their bread and butter, their milk and radishes, have no idea of the large amount of domestic goods, in wool and cotton, made by the women of the rural population of the interior, even in these days of huge factories. Without touching upon the subject of political economy, although its moral aspect must ever be a highly important one, it is certainly pleasant to see the women busy in this way, beneath the family roof, and one is much disposed to believe that the home system is healthier and safer for the individual, in every way. Home, we may rest assured, will always be, as a rule, the best place for a woman; her labors, pleasures, and interests, should all centre there, whatever be her sphere of life.
>
> (*Rural Hours*, 99-100)

Increasing industrialization, especially in textile manufacturing, had made serious inroads on what observers like Miss Cooper perceived to be the predominant way of life of the early Republic. Mills opened up wage labor to girls and young women, as well as boys and young men, and by the late 1840s numerous farm-bred girls worked in textile mills in New York and New England.[8] Many girls were dislocated from the traditional pattern of living at home until they married and developed interests and concerns unrelated to the rural pattern of life esteemed by Susan Fenimore Cooper.

Though an innovative thinker on issues relating to the conservation of American nature, Miss Cooper deplored the potential changes in traditional American family and community structure that might further result from some reformers' ideas. She noted in an 1874 manuscript opposing female suffrage that women had "much higher and noble work to do than dabbling in politics."[9] Woman, as wife and mother, was the "light of the home" who exerted a gentle, civilizing influence on brutish man. She was the spiritual flame around which children and husband gathered like moths in a lamp's glow. Miss Cooper compared "the gentle, healthy-hearted daughter of the home, the light of the house," to the naturally beautiful wild rose, in contrast to the clipped and hybridized garden roses, which reminded her of "the meretricious dancer tricked out upon the stage to dazzle and bewilder, and be stared at by the mob" (**Rural Hours,** 75). But the light of the home could be easily sullied by the world outside the door of her family home; she could so easily lose her spiritual strength and endanger the souls of husband and children entrusted to her.[10]

The argument was familiar; journalists expressed these sentiments in vigorously antagonistic terms following the women's conventions of 1848. In Albany the *Mechanic's Advocate* stated that meeting the demands made at Seneca Falls "would set the world by the ears, make 'confusion worse confounded,' demoralize and degrade from their high sphere and noble destiny, women of all respectable and useful classes, and prove a monstrous injury to all mankind" (quoted in *History of Woman Suffrage,* 803). The *Lowell (Massachusetts) Courier* served up the same rhetoric with mockery:

> The women folks have just held a Convention up in New York State, and passed a sort of "bill of rights," affirming it their right to vote, to become teachers, legislators, lawyers, divines, and do all and sundries, the "lords" may, of right now do. They should have resolved at the same time, that it was obligatory also upon the "lords" aforesaid, to wash dishes, scour up, be put to the tub, handle the broom, darn stockings, patch breeches, scold the servants, dress in the latest fashion, wear trinkets, look beautiful, and be as fascinating as those blessed morsels of humanity whom God gave to preserve that rough animal man, in something like a reasonable civilization.

> (Quoted in *History of Woman Suffrage,* 804)

The message was clear. Woman was incapable of filling her God-given role if she cluttered her mind with politics. Susan Fenimore Cooper noted on December 16 that "[t]he position of an American housewife is rarely, indeed, a sinecure" (**Rural Hours,** 268). Rather, she had the care of the souls of her household to see to, and so her domestic sphere, set aside from the male political one, was divinely ordained, purposed to protect home and heart from incursion.

Susan Fenimore Cooper drew many examples from nature, the stuff of America's individuality, to support her views of woman's domestic role in America. Nature, the product of the Creation, the dwelling place of the deity, and the mainspring of the American imagination, was divinely ordained and so the perfect source of lessons in correct behavior. Like a clergyman crafting a homily, she drew lessons from nature illustrating family life and maternal devotion to support her views on American behavior, including the domestic role of woman in the young nation. An avid birdwatcher, she observed the family behaviors of songbirds. Of the nuthatch, she remarks, he "is a remarkably good husband, taking a vast deal of pains to feed and amuse his wife, and listening to all her remarks and observations in the most meritorious manner" (**Rural Hours,** 20). Husbands were to respect and care for their wives, who played important roles in organizing the home and raising the children. Orioles, she notes, "are just as well behaved as robins—harmless, innocent birds, bearing an excellent character. We all know how industrious and skilful they are in building; both work together at weaving the intricate nest, though the wife is the most diligent" (**Rural Hours,** 21). Husband and wife were to build a home together, though the woman's task was to work most diligently in furnishing and developing the family's domestic life, while the man worked beyond the home to support its continued smooth running. Nesting birds also provided inspiration for maternal devotion and selflessness:

> By nature the winged creatures are full of life and activity, apparently needing little repose, flitting the live-long day through the fields and gardens, seldom pausing except to feed, to dress their feathers, or to sing;—abroad, many of them, before dawn, and still passing to and fro across the darkening sky of the latest twilight;—capable also, when necessary, of a prolonged flight which stretches across seas and continents. And yet there is not one of these little winged mothers but what will patiently sit, for hour after hour, day after day, upon her unhatched brood, warming them with her breast—carefully turning them—that all may share the heat equally, and so fearful lest they should be chilled, that she will rather suffer hunger herself than leave them long exposed.

> (**Rural Hours,** 23)

Woman's most important job was that of mother. Her individual needs and desires must necessarily be subjugated for the good of her children and the home they required. Perhaps the upholsterer bee's homemaking impressed her most. This Old World insect, according to her description, painstakingly builds a subterranean nest for a single egg, lines it with a brilliant red upholstery of poppy petals, and supplies it with food. Then "the careful mother replacing the earth as neatly as possible" seals up the nest to await the birth of the new generation (*Rural Hours,* 123). For a single offspring, this insect expends virtually all of its life energy. Through self-sacrifice, woman achieved power. In the words of the *Public Ledger and Daily Transcript,* "a mother is, next to God, all powerful" (quoted in *History of Woman Suffrage,* 804). A woman's quintessential identity was in creating, maintaining, and defending the home and her offspring against invasion of all sorts.

Miss Cooper also suggests that women who "trifl[e] with their own characters" by giving in to their own desires and going beyond their God-given role would necessarily lose the respect of their community and their own self-esteem. She parallels the behavior of the "cowpen black-bird," or brown-headed cowbird, with such women in yet another lesson from nature:

> It is well known that the cow-pen black-bird lays her eggs in the nest of other birds; and it is remarked that she generally chooses the nest of those much smaller than herself, like the summer yellow-bird, the bluebird, song-sparrow, among our nicest and best behaved birds. One might almost fancy, that like some unhappy women who have trifled with their own characters, the cowbird is anxious that her daughters should be better behaved than herself, for she is careful to choose them the best foster-mothers; happily, such a course has often succeeded with human mothers, but with the bird it seems to fail. There is no such thing as reformation among them.
>
> (*Rural Hours,* 255)

Miss Cooper notes that, unlike woman, who has free will and may make choices, the bird is guided only by biological destiny. Woman may, by her choices, improve or diminish herself. Woman must choose her proper Christian role, illustrated by nature and by the Bible. In so doing, she accepts domestic roles, for which she is best suited, in exchange for man's protecting her from harm.

This exchange was based partly on the perceived necessity to protect woman because she was thought naturally inferior in both physical and mental strength. If she was to exert power within the home, thus acting in the best interests of the American nation, she must not be overpowered by malevolent forces. Writing of her travels in America in 1837, Harriet Martineau felt this was carried too far. She observed that middle-class American women got little physical or mental exercise, noting, "The ladies plead that they have much exercise within doors, about their household occupations."[11] Martineau opposed this claim, saying that if American women would only get out and walk, they might not

feel so physically weary or be so mentally dull. Even though Susan Fenimore Cooper was a vigorous and intrepid walker, as a review of her routes in the Cooperstown area reveals, she nevertheless described women generally as weak and incapable of taking care of themselves. On July 11 she comments:

> We American women certainly owe a debt of gratitude to our countrymen for their kindness and consideration for us generally. Gallantry may not always take a graceful form in this part of the world, and mere flattery may be worth as little here as elsewhere, but there is a glow of generous feeling toward woman in the hearts of most American men, which is highly honorable to them as a nation and as individuals. In no country is the protection given to woman's helplessness more full and free—in no country is the assistance she receives from the stronger arm so general—and nowhere does her weakness meet with more forbearance and consideration.
>
> (*Rural Hours,* 106)

This follows a discussion about women doing field chores in which Miss Cooper notes how unusual it was to see women in the fields in her region but that female gleaners were commonplace in Europe. Furthermore, in Germany she had even seen a woman and a cow yoked together pulling a plough while the husband drove the team. These scenes, which might illustrate woman's potential hardiness, shocked Miss Cooper's sensibilities. For at least one leader at Seneca Falls, however, similar scenes led to different conclusions. Elizabeth Cady Stanton remarked:

> Let us now consider man's claim to physical superiority. Methinks I hear some say, surely, you will not contend for equality here. Yes, we must not give an inch, lest you take an ell. We cannot say what the woman might be physically, if the girl were allowed the freedom of the boy in romping, climbing, swimming, playing whoop and ball. . . . The Croatian and Wallachian women perform all the agricultural operations in addition to their domestic labors, and it is no uncommon sight in our cities, to see the German immigrant with his hands in his pockets, walking complacently by the side of his wife, whilst she bears the weight of some huge package or piece of furniture upon her head. Physically, as well as intellectually, it is us that produces growth and development.[12]

Like Martineau, Stanton thought that American women might not be physically weak if they only got exercise.

Susan Fenimore Cooper's arguments for the roles she advocated for women, even those derived from nature, are amplifications of ones commonly held by Christian theologians of the period. As a devout Episcopalian, Miss Cooper was inclined to rely on the interpretations of scripture presented to her by her clergymen, rather than acting as her own interpreter. Lucretia Mott, a Quaker and a believer in the Quaker doctrine of the priesthood of the self, declared that women "had all got our notions too much from the clergy, instead of from the Bible" (quoted in *History of Woman Suffrage,* 76). Thus when Episcopalian Susan Fenimore Cooper presented the Old Testament story of Ruth and Boaz, it was in terms typical of Christian theologians of the time. She wrote, "One never thinks of gleaning without remembering Ruth. How wholly beautiful is the narrative of sacred history in which we meet her! . . . her history is all pure simplicity, nature and truth, in every line" (**Rural Hours,** 160). Ruth, a young widow, returns to Bethlehem, her husband's native city, with her widowed mother-in-law. We see Ruth "*cleaving* to the poor, and aged, and solitary widow. . . . from that instant we love Ruth" (**Rural Hours,** 161). Ruth works to maintain the domestic circle even after her husband's death. When she discovers that Boaz, the wealthy man who owns the fields where she is gleaning, is related to her husband, she follows Jewish law and lies at Boaz's feet when he is sleeping to remind him of his duty to protect her as a woman of his family by marriage. Boaz accepts the responsibility. Thus Ruth, by appealing for protection following the law rather than "following young men," preserves her dignity and earns protection within the domestic sphere of her husband's family. Indeed, Susan Fenimore Cooper notes of her peers generally, "[I]t must be woman's own fault if she be not thoroughly respected also. The position accorded to her is favorable; it remains to her to fill it in a manner worthy of her own sex, gratefully, kindly, simply; with truth and modesty of heart and life; with unwavering fidelity of feeling and principle; with patience, cheerfulness, and sweetness of temper—no unfit return to those who smooth the daily path for her" (**Rural Hours,** 106). Woman's selflessness is a fair exchange for the effort man takes to protect and care for her.

By the time she published **Rural Hours** in 1850, Susan Fenimore Cooper had clearly formed strong views about the correct behavior of the American woman and her place in America. In **Rural Hours** she focused her argument on women's behavior and the forces—especially the increasing tendency of girls to leave home—she perceived as altering traditional values. While she never discusses female suffrage in **Rural Hours,** it seems certain that she was responding to many other issues discussed at the Seneca Falls conventions and subsequent meetings. Her discussion of some issues and not others mirrors the character of the women's conventions from the late 1840s through the 1850s and into the 1860s. The meetings of this period provided a forum for discussion, and so women with wide-ranging views and concerns came. Not all supported female suffrage; at Seneca Falls only a third of those attending signed the Declaration of Sentiments.[13] The *Mechanics Advocate* of Albany, New York, described their activities, activities common to all reform efforts of the early nineteenth century: "The women who attend these meet-

ings, no doubt at the expense of their more appropriate duties, act as committees, write resolutions and addresses, hold much correspondence, make speeches, etc., etc." (quoted in *History of Woman Suffrage,* 802). A second paper noted that "they design, in spite of all misrepresentations and ridicule, to employ agents, circulate tracts, petition the State and National Legislatures, and endeavor to enlist the pulpit and the press in their behalf" (quoted in *History of Woman Suffrage,* 803).

The women who led these conventions had developed these skills in other reform efforts, most notably abolition, and, in fact, abolition and the rights-of-woman issue remained closely linked for nearly two decades. During that period, the leaders of the women's conventions maintained a more-or-less united front and kept the issues of the rights of woman, including suffrage, more or less in the public eye, and a range of opinions was voiced from within this loosely organized group of reformers. Events in 1867, however, divided the group, and later writings on the subject of the rights of woman must be viewed in relation to the schism caused by the Kansas referenda on black and female suffrage of that year. Suffrage for neither group was permitted in national elections, but states could choose to allow them to vote at the state and local levels. The young Republican party, the party of Lincoln and of the emancipation of African-American slaves, sought to expand its supporters and feared linking black suffrage to female suffrage, a far more volatile issue that might alienate potential supporters. In hopes of improving their support, the Republican legislature divided female and black suffrage into two separate referenda. Neither passed, but the split resulting among women willing to support black suffrage before female suffrage and those insisting that the issues remain linked to achieve universal suffrage divided the leaders of the rights-of-woman movement for good.

Under the leadership of Elizabeth Cady Stanton and Susan B. Anthony, female suffrage became the leading and most highly visible argument. Susan Fenimore Cooper noted in her 1870 **"Letter to the Christian Women of America,"** published in *Harper's Monthly,* that this new group "claim[ed] for woman absolute social and political equality with man. And they seek to secure these points by conferring on the whole sex the right of elective franchise, female suffrage being the first step in the unwieldy revolutions they aim at bringing about. These views are no longer confined to a small sect. They challenge our attention at every turn. We meet them in society; we read them in the public prints; we hear of them in grave legislative assemblies."[14] The discourse had changed in both emphasis and volume, becoming more focused on female suffrage and better publicized. In 1867 John Stuart Mill, the English philosopher, published his essay "The Social and Political

Dependence of Women," calling for female suffrage following a series of petitions for female suffrage in Parliament.[15] In her **"Letter,"** Miss Cooper cites Mill's essay and rebuts his ideas by expounding the predominant clerical view on woman's rightful place in society and opposing female suffrage.

In her **"Letter,"** Susan Fenimore Cooper argues that woman, as a sex, will always be subordinate because of her inferiority to man in physical strength and intellect. Further, she recommends Christianity as the belief system that best provides for woman's well-being, saying:

> No system of philosophy has ever yet worked out in behalf of woman the practical results which Christianity has conferred on her. Christianity has raised woman from slavery and made her the thoughtful companion of man; it finds her the mere toy, or the victim of his passions, and it places her by his side, his truest friend, his most faithful counselor, his helpmeet in every worthy and honorable task. It protects her far more effectually than any other system. It cultivates, strengthens, elevates, purifies all her highest endowments, and holds out to her aspirations the most sublime for that future state of existence, where precious rewards are promised to every faithful discharge of duty, even the most humble. But, while conferring on her these priceless blessings, it also enjoins the submission of the wife to the husband, and allots a subordinate position to the whole sex while here on earth. No woman calling herself a Christian, acknowledging her duties as such, can, therefore consistently deny the obligation of a limited subordination laid upon her by her Lord and His Church.[16]

The subordination inherent in domesticity becomes power because woman's work is as important as man's, because it is a Christian duty. Miss Cooper goes on to detail the "gendered spheres" argument, concluding it by saying, "Women have thus far been excluded from the suffrage . . . from the conviction that to grant them this particular privilege would, in different ways, and especially by withdrawing them from higher and more urgent duties, and allotting to them other duties for which they are not so well fitted, become injurious to the nation, and, we add, ultimately injurious to themselves, also, as part of the nation."[17] Thus, gendered spheres and the domestic role of woman continued to be an issue of national importance, possibly national survival, in the post-Civil War era. American women must exert their powers to protect and enhance the home and insure America's future.

In both the **"Letter"** and a manuscript dated 1874, Susan Fenimore Cooper worried that most women would misuse their votes if they were granted the elective franchise. She wrote in 1874 that most women were both above political interest and incapable of using their vote wisely and would thus compromise the stability of the nation:

> Let us hope that the wild theories which demand Female Suffrage may never be carried into effect in this our good State of New York. Our women have already much higher and more noble work to do than dabbling in politics. To force the vote upon them would be to *degrade* them. If unhappily Female Suffrage should ever become a legal measure the downfall of Free Institutions would follow inevitably—the amount of political corruption would then become utterly unendurable. It would be *the beginning of the end.* Bribery would increase a thousandfold. Not that women are so mercenary. They are less mercenary than men. But they care little for political questions as a rule—their minds are filled with other matters—they would give their votes thoughtlessly, or the ignorant and unprincipled would sell them as a matter of course. The demagogues would be more powerful than ever. Mostly[?] female voters would trifle away their votes, and what good would it do that the remaining ten in every hundred would vote more wisely, and conscientiously than most men do?[18]

The 1874 manuscript reiterates the noble calling of domesticity for middle-class American women and insists on a difference in interests and abilities between man and woman. In her 1870 **"Letter,"** Miss Cooper expanded on this idea, writing, "Men are born politicians; just as they are born masons, and carpenters, and soldiers, and sailors. Not so women. Their thoughts and feelings are given to other matters. The current of their chosen avocations runs in another channel than that of politics. . . . The interest most women feel in politics is secondary, factitious, engrafted on them by the men nearest them. Women are not abortive men; they are a distinct creation."[19] As distinct creations, women have distinct, divinely ordained tasks. Suffrage is not among them.

As the discourse of the rights of woman shifted from a loose discussion among a variety of concerned citizens in the 1840s and 1850s to a set of more specifically argued agendas held by different groups in the late 1860s, the most vocal and visible being those calling for female suffrage, so too did Susan Fenimore Cooper's writing on the issues. Thus she moved from her more general discussion on the rightful place of woman in American society posited in several entries in *Rural Hours* in 1850 to an argument focused mainly on opposing female suffrage using the clerically based doctrine of the difference between the sexes by the 1870s. Her entries in *Rural Hours* are especially interesting because, unlike contemporary journalistic commentary, they are a woman's gentle, reasoned discussion of opposing and widely held views. Couched within the larger issue of American domesticity presented in the rural journal and so gently introduced, the subject of the rightful place of woman might be missed by a casual reader. In 1850 the issue was so new and considered by many so laughable that its potential threat must have seemed easy to quell, and the text can be read as a kind admonishment to women to reinforce their important domestic role in American society for the good of the young nation. But the call for legal and political rights for woman was not so easily put down; rather, it grew and was refined, and its supporters had to be addressed directly in reasoned terms. Miss Cooper's **"Letter"** of 1870 and her manuscript of 1874 can be seen as refinements and elaborations of the themes she first discussed in **Rural Hours,** to which she returned in light of the shift in the discussion of the call for the rights of woman, especially female suffrage. Miss Cooper never changed her mind on the subject of votes for women. When she died in 1894, women in some Western states could vote in state and local elections, but national suffrage was still many years away.

Notes

1. Elizabeth Cady Stanton, Susan B. Anthony, and Mathilda Joslyn Gage, *History of Woman Suffrage, Volume I, 1848-1861* (New York: Arno and the New York Times, 1969), 67. Hereafter cited in text. Though a potentially biased source, this history of the fight for female suffrage collects many useful and rather ephemeral sources, including numerous newspaper clippings.

2. James Fenimore Cooper to Mrs. Charles Jarvis Woolson (Hannah Cooper Pomeroy), June 1, 1848, in James Franklin Beard, ed., *The Letters and Journals of James Fenimore Cooper,* 6 vols. (Cambridge, Mass.: Harvard University Press, 1960-68), 5:368-69.

3. During the nineteenth century, literature of the suffrage movement referred to the rights of "woman" rather than "women," apparently in contrast to "man" rather than "men." This essay uses the nineteenth-century term in most instances.

4. While it is unusual to refer late in the twentieth century to a maiden lady as "Miss," Susan Fenimore Cooper would, I believe, have been surprised at the very least to be referred to as "Cooper." She would have thought of herself as "Miss Cooper," and so she is referred to in this essay in this way.

5. For a discussion of these arguments, see Amy Kaplan, "Manifest Domesticity," *American Literature* 70 (September 1998): 581-606.

6. See Dolores Hayden, *Seven American Utopias: The Architecture of Communitarian Socialism, 1790-1975* (Cambridge, Mass.: MIT Press, 1976) for encapsulated discussions of these groups as well as others and their relationship to their buildings and planned landscapes.

7. Susan Fenimore Cooper, *Rural Hours,* ed. Rochelle Johnson and Daniel Patterson (Athens: University of Georgia Press, 1998), 3. Hereafter cited in text.

8. See Rosalynn Baxandall, Linda Gordon, with Susan Reverby, *America's Working Women: A Documentary History, 1600 to the Present* (New York: W. W. Norton, 1976) for a discussion of the changes in work patterns for woman in the early nineteenth century.

9. Susan Fenimore Cooper, Manuscript, April 7, 1874, Chicago Historical Society, Archives and Manuscripts, Chicago, Illinois.

10. See Harvey Green, *The Light of the Home: An Intimate View of the Lives of Women in Victorian America* (New York: Pantheon Books, 1983) for a discussion of the light of the home and the cult of domesticity.

11. Harriet Martineau, *Society in America* (New York: Saunders and Otley, 1837), 262.

12. Elizabeth Cady Stanton, "Address Delivered at Seneca Falls, July 19, 1848," in Ellen Carroll DuBois, *Elizabeth Cady Stanton and Susan B. Anthony: Correspondence, Writings, and Speeches* (New York: Schocken Books, 1981), 31.

13. For discussion especially of this early period of the movement, see Ellen Carroll DuBois, *Feminism and Suffrage: The Emergence of an Independent Women's Movement in America, 1848-1869* (Ithaca, N.Y.: Cornell University Press, 1978). For more general discussions, see Miriam Gurko, *The Ladies of Seneca Falls: The Birth of the Woman's Rights Movement* (New York: Macmillan, 1974); and Christine Bolt, *The Women's Movements in the United States and Britain from the 1790s to the 1920s* (Amherst: University of Massachusetts Press, 1993).

14. Susan Fenimore Cooper, "Female Suffrage. A Letter to the Christian Women of America," *Harper's New Monthly Magazine* (August 1870): 440.

15. John Stuart Mill, the English political philosopher, published his long essay, "The Social and Political Dependence of Women," in 1867. It went through numerous printings and was read on both sides of the Atlantic.

16. Cooper, "Letter," 439.

17. Ibid., 442.

18. Cooper, Manuscript.

19. Cooper, "Letter," 445-46.

FURTHER READING

Biography

Kimball, Sue Laslie. "Susan Augusta Fenimore Cooper." In *American National Biography,* Vol. 5, edited by

John A. Garraty and Mark C. Carnes, pp. 460-61. New York: Oxford University Press, 1999.

> Brief biographical sketch of Cooper's family life, education, and writing career.

Criticism

Allibone, S. Austin. "Miss Susan Fenimore Cooper." In *A Critical Dictionary of English Literature and British and American Authors Living and Deceased,* Vol. 1, p. 427. 1858. Reprint, Detroit: Gale Research, 1965.

> Contains a brief entry on Cooper, including excerpts from contemporary reviews of her books.

Baym, Max I., and Percy Matenko. "The Odyssey of *The Water-Witch* and a Susan Fenimore Cooper Letter." *New York History* 51 (January 1970): 32-41.

> Details the Cooper family's European years and James Fenimore Cooper's writing and publication of *The Water Witch,* including Susan Fenimore Cooper's comments on the work.

Baym, Nina. Review of *Rural Hours* by Susan Fenimore Cooper, edited by Rochelle Johnson and Daniel Patterson. *New England Quarterly* 73, no. 1 (March 1999): 130-34.

> Praises the 1998 edition of Cooper's nature journal, citing its textual accuracy and suggesting that it will introduce a new generation of readers to an important American text.

Johnson, Rochelle. "Placing *Rural Hours.*" In *Reading under the Sign of Nature: New Essays in Ecocriticism,* edited by John Tallmadge and Henry Harrington, pp. 64-84. Salt Lake City: University of Utah Press, 2000.

> Discusses Cooper's *Rural Hours* in the context of contemporary nature writing, most notably Thoreau's *Walden,* and within the tradition of nineteenth-century women's writing.

Kurth, Rosaly Torna. "Susan Fenimore Cooper: An Annotated Checklist of Her Writings." *New York History* 58 (1977): 173-93.

> Provides a brief biography of Cooper and an annotated list of her writings, including introductions she produced for her father's novels.

Additional coverage of Cooper's life and career is contained in the following sources published by the Gale Group: *American Nature Writers*; *Dictionary of Literary Biography,* **Vols. 239, 254;** *Literature Resource Center.*

George Dyer
1755-1841

English essayist, historian, biographer, critic, and poet.

INTRODUCTION

Dyer is principally known for his influence on important Romantic writers and from the comic portrait of him in the essays of Charles Lamb. His doctrine of benevolence advised a moral obligation to the poor during a time of burgeoning interest in the plight of the lower classes, and impacted the literature of contemporaries such as William Godwin. He also gave critical and moral support to Samuel Taylor Coleridge and other young writers. Though Dyer was regarded as a mediocre poet by these and other Romantic authors, recent scholarship highlights his contribution to their ideals.

BIOGRAPHICAL INFORMATION

Dyer was born in 1755 in London's working-class Wapping District where his father was a shipwright. At seven he enrolled as a charity student at Christ's Hospital, the same school of a younger generation of writers whom he was to meet later—Coleridge, Lamb, and Leigh Hunt. Excelling in the classics, he attended Emmanuel College at Cambridge, earning his B.A. in 1778. As tutor to the children of a Cambridge Dissenter, Robert Robinson, he became part of a Unitarian circle with such liberal thinkers as William Frend, Joseph Priestley, and Anna Barbauld. From 1792 Dyer lived in Clifford's Inn, London, barely supporting himself by writing for periodicals like Leigh Hunt's *Reflector,* Robert Southey's *Annual Anthology,* and *The Monthly Magazine.* He wrote biographies, sketches, and histories as well as philosophical tracts in support of liberal causes. Influential in the radical circles of London that included such luminaries as Godwin and the young William Wordsworth and Coleridge, he was respected as a benevolent man of letters. Dyer had a lifelong passion for poetry, publishing his first volume in 1792. About the time Coleridge and Wordsworth were collaborating on *Lyrical Ballads,* Dyer was also thinking about the importance of poetry in its ability to teach humane values. He published occasional verse, odes, and critical articles in 1797, 1802, and 1812. His friend, Charles Lamb, made him into an unforgettable character in his *Elia* essays, creating Dyer's fame as a lovable but absentminded scholar. His strenuous studies contributed to

Dyer going blind in his later years. A widow in his boarding house, taking pity on his condition, married him at the age of fifty-nine. He died in 1841 at the age of eighty-five.

MAJOR WORKS

Dyer is best known for his radical tracts in the wake of the French Revolution. *Inquiry into the Nature of Subscription to the Thirty-Nine Articles* (1789) condemned subscription as inconsistent with natural rights and the principles of the British constitution. He rejected a state church and argued that the education of youth is a natural right, later supporting a scheme for national education. *Complaints of the Poor People of England* (1793) is a humanitarian description of the plight of the poor and their rights in which he laid responsibility for their ignorance on the government. A sequel, *A Dissertation on the Theory and Practice of Benevolence* (1795), is an attempt to stimulate the spirit and practice of benevolence through various relief societies. Dyer's liberalism was criticized by contemporaries as being comparatively soft spoken and "sober," as he called it, avoiding the more passionate outcries of fellow radicals who ended up in prison. *Memoirs of the Life and Writings of Robert Robinson* (1796) gave Dyer an opportunity to eulogize his Unitarian mentor, a preacher who was important to the Cambridge radical tradition. Dyers last attempts to espouse his political philosophy include *An Address to the People of Great Britain on the Doctrine of Libels and the Office of Juror* (1799) and *Four Letters on the English Constitution* (1812). *An Address* encourages a free press, while *Four Letters* reaffirms his stance against divine right and his belief in the primacy of universal reason and sovereignty of the people.

Dyer focused on poetry later in his career. He published his first volume of poetry, *Poems,* in 1792. *The Poet's Fate: A Poetical Dialogue* (1797) treats the plight of poets in a hostile society and is considered his most interesting poetic work. Dyer caused a stir with the publication of *The Poet's Fate* by praising Coleridge's and Southey's pantisocracy scheme, a commune-based social organization ideology that failed to materialize. *Poems* (1801) contains critical essays and lyrics, odes, miscellaneous and occasional poems. A reviewer of his *Poems and Critical Essays* (1802) in the *British Critic* claimed the poems "never rise to any extraordinary vigour . . . but [exhibit] a considerable share of taste, harmony, and feeling." *Poetics* (1812) received a similar lukewarm response by a reviewer in *The Gentleman's Magazine* who thought the poetry "better than mediocre." Dyer's voluminous and unremarkable poetry in an age that saw the rise of the major Romantic poets made him an old-fashioned figure to his younger contemporaries, such as Lamb and Coleridge. Dyer's scholarly output is represented by his *History of the University and Colleges of Cambridge* (1814), a description of his beloved Cambridge, particularly the dissenting community, and a study of its lifelong influence on his work and character.

CRITICAL RECEPTION

In the 1790s, during the English debate on the French Revolution, George Dyer was in the camp of Godwin and Paine, contributing to the republican cause through his writing and support of other writers. Wordsworth admired his biography of Robert Robinson as one of the finest in English. Outside his scholarly and philosophical output, however, Dyer was taken less seriously by his contemporaries as a poet and critic, and is known today as a minor writer in the Romantic circle. In fact, as Lamb's biographer E. V. Lucas has said, Lamb conferred immortality on Dyer, who would be unknown today without the *Elia* essays, "Oxford in the Vacation" and "Amicus Redivivus." His reputation as an altruistic but bumbling intellectual was set by Lamb's humorous portraits in essays and letters, and also by Coleridge's annotations ridiculing Dyer's literary criticism. Dyer's reputation in the field of poetry has not improved much with time. J. R. Watson concludes that Dyer's poems are no more than "traditional exercises in an eighteenth-century mode." Robin Jarvis, on the other hand, while agreeing that Dyer is no more than a "bronze" poet, asserts that Dyer's Romantic radicalism is manifest in poems like those from his "Pedestrian Tour" of Scotland, published in 1798 in *The Monthly Magazine*. Dyer's reputation as a serious and influential liberal in Godwin's London was revived by M. Ray Adams. Adams investigates Dyer's political ideas in relation to the thinkers of the day and his influence on Wordsworth, Coleridge, and Southey. Nicholas Roe's chapter on Dyer in *The Politics of Nature: Wordsworth and Some Contemporaries* shows Dyer to have been an important model for Wordsworth and Coleridge in the way he brought politics to bear on the poetry of nature and imagination. Dyer's influence represents for Roe the answer to current historicists who believe that the Romantics turned their backs on history in their search for a transcendent nature.

PRINCIPAL WORKS

An Inquiry into the Nature of Subscription to the Thirty-Nine Articles (essay) 1789; revised edition, 1792

Poems (poetry) 1792

The Complaints of the Poor People of England (essay) 1793

A Dissertation on the Theory and Practice of Benevolence (essay) 1795

Memoirs of the Life and Writings of Robert Robinson (biography) 1796

The Poet's Fate. A Poetical Dialogue (poetry) 1797

An Address to the People of Great Britain on the Doctrine of Libels and the Office of Juror (essay) 1799

Poems (poetry) 1801

Poems and Critical Essays. 2 vols. (poetry and criticism) 1802

Four Letters on the English Constitution (letters) 1812

Poetics, or a Series of Poems and Disquisitions on Poetry (poetry and criticism) 1812

History of the University and Colleges of Cambridge. 2 vols. (history) 1814

Academic Unity (essay) 1827

CRITICISM

British Critic (review date August 1802)

SOURCE: Review of George Dyer's *Poems. British Critic* 20 (August 1802): 121-25.

[*In the following anonymous review, the critic finds Dyer's poetry more noteworthy than his political sentiments.*]

In p. 590, of our seventeenth volume, the reader will find an account of a first book of **Poems** by this author, of which these were to have been a continuation, and consecrated *Divæ Libertati*! Mr. Dyer has been induced, partly by the advice of friends, and partly by the *hints of booksellers,* who, as he truly says, are the *best judges* in these matters, to alter the arrangement of his plan. We are now presented with two volumes of Lyric Poetry, on miscellaneous subjects, in which however the poet's favourite goddess is not neglected; these are introduced by a long **"Prefatory Essay on Lyric Poetry,"** in which are many pleasing sentiments and judicious observations. Mr. Dyer's pursuits and talents must indeed be various; for we find him at one time composing Sonnets, and Translations from Anacreon, and at another books of Biography, and tracts on Juries. We are however strongly inclined to suppose, that the character in which he will appear most acceptable and interesting is that of a Poet.

These compositions are distinguished by the usual character of the author's pen; they never rise to any extraordinary vigour, have none of the *ardentia verba,* but a considerable share of taste, harmony, and feeling. The following is an agreeable specimen.

"To the Cam."

Soon shall the young ambrosial spring
Wanton forth, in garlands gay,
And, spreading soft her virgin wing,
Shall wed the Lord of Day.
Soon shall reviving Nature homage yield,
And, breathing incense, lead her tuneful train
O'er hill and dale, soft vale, and cultur'd field;
The bard, the lover, and the jocund swain,
Their new-born joys shall sing; earth, sea, and sky,
All wake for thee, fair Spring, their sweetest minstrelsy.

2.

What though the winds, and sleety shower,
May seem awhile to hush the grove?
Soon, wak'd by Nature's living power,
Shall breathe the voice of love!
The lark gay mount, to hail the purple dawn,
And its clear matin carol thro' the sky,
The throstle's mellow warblings cheer the morn,
The linnet softly trill on hawthorn nigh;
The mists shall vanish soon, and soon the breeze
Kiss every glowing flower, and fan the trembling trees.

3.

I, too, the cheering warmth shall feel,
And join the rapturous choral song,
Musing smooth numbers, as I steal,
O Cam! thy banks along.
Tho' near thy banks no myrtle breathe perfume,
No rose unfold its blushing beauties near,
Tho' here no stately tulip spread its bloom,
Nor towering lily deck the gay parterre:
(Inclos'd within the garden's fair domain,
These all, in eastern pride, shall hold their golden reign:)

4.

Yet wild flowers o'er the fruitful scene,
Warm'd by the touch of gentle May,
Shall rise, obedient to their queen,
In simple beauty gay.
To me the violet sheds the richest sweet,
To me the king-cup shines with brightest hues;
The primrose pale, like modest virtue neat,
E'en the meek daisy, can instruct the Muse;
Roving with silent eyes, she loves to stand,
And in the field-flow'r views a more than master's hand.

5.

E'en now the sun-beam, dazzling bright,
Quick dances on the crisped stream;
And soft, tho' fleeting gales invite
The fond poetic dream.
Nor does in vain the swan majestic sail,
Nor glittering insect range the rushy brink;
Nor the fish sporting down the current steal,
And the light songsters on the margin drink;
Then, wild with bliss, shiver the painted wing,
And to their feather'd loves their sweetest wood-notes sing.

6.

Yet must we leave thy blooming reign:—
And short that reign, thou lovely Spring—
What time Fate's high decrees ordain,
Or wills the soveregn King!
Yes, all thy shadowy clouds, thy rainbow hues,
Thy flowers, and songs, thy gales, and glossy bloom,
All must be left, tho' friendly to the Muse;
And man, poor man, lie down in cheerless gloom;
That season cold of death shall chill his tongue,
Nor beauty's smile return, that wak'd the vernal song.

7.

But speed the hours on restless wing?
Must love's light season flit away?
Then hail, O man, the coming spring,

And seize the sweets of May;
Where now the bard of Camus' classic stream,
The skilful hand that wak'd th' Æolian lyre?
Ah! sleeps with him the spring enamour'd theme;
From him the loves, and "Venus' train" retire,—
He too, who trac'd the crystal streams of light,
And Nature's spacious fields, great Newton, sleeps in
night.

8.

No more he treads this hallow'd ground,
Nor tracks in thought yon boundless sky;
Ah! Science can but gaze around,
Then like the Muse, shall die.
Oh! quit then, Fancy, queen of songs and wiles,
The pearl-enamell'd grot, the moss-grown cell,
Thy many thousand hills, and purple isles,
And deign, oh! deign, near sedgy Cam to dwell;
Still let the song of love the valleys cheer,
And blooming Science spread fair spring-time all the
year.

At p. 55, of Vol. I. is an **"Essay on Elegiac Poetry,"** in which Mr. Dyer discusses the speculative question, whether blank verse is as capable of expressing sublime and tender sorrow as the most harmonious rhyme. He thinks it is; we think it unnecessary to decide such a question. Sublime and excellent examples may be produced in both forms; and a poetical mind, strongly impressed, may perform wonders in either way.

The second volume is, like the first, divided into two books, and, like that also, contains a mixture of prose and verse. It begins with an Essay on representative Poetry, in which there is much to please, and but little that is objectionable. The first Poem which succeeds this Essay is very poetical.

"The Love Poet."

Oh! Love, fair Nature's child, undeck'd by art,
Whom should I call, but thee, in every clime,
    The poet's mighty God?
Harmonious power! To whom all beings raise
    Gay songs, and gratulations meet,
For thine it is thro air, earth, sea to range,
    Wing'd with desire, and warm with life;
Thine the perennial fires, that renovate the world!

Have I not on thy altars duly pour'd
The pure libation, following it with sighs,
    And resignation meet?
To thee have I not paid, at morn and eve,
    The pray'r too big for words, a priest,
That greatly felt, and silently ador'd?
    Oh! then thy vot'ry's trembling heart
Touch with the living coals, that on thine altar burn.

But spare, oh! spare me now: assume no more
The form terrific, fire-red eyes and darts,
    Thy darts of living steel;
Nor bring with thee thy train of thousand ills,
    The sleepless night, the day of care,

Follies and wanderings, griefs, and fears, and smarts,
    Pale melancholy, pining shame,
That lead the vagrant heart to lab'rinths of despair.

Be but my Muse, what other shall I need?
Give me but that sweet music of the soul,
    Can I then want a lyre?
Oh! tune my heart-strings;—so the passions all
    Shall to my song sing jubilant:
So shall the seasons, in alternate dance,
    Pass smiling by, each herb, fruit, flow'r,
Be redolent of sweets, and every gale inspire!

True to thy name, now wear thy loveliest form
Dimples and smiles, and pity-beaming eyes,
    And soul-enliven'd mirths:
And bring the flower of bliss without the thorn,
    Delights that last, and cares that please,
With meek benevolence, but taught by thee;
    So from my heart, by thee attun'd,
Sweet melodies shall rise, and dignify my song.

At p. 83, vol. ii. will be found **"Cursory Remarks on Readers, and the Nature of Poetry; on Dreams and Visions."** This Essay places the writer in a new point of view, and shows him to possess talents for humour. Some Poetical Dreams succeed, which exhibit much power of fancy. **"The Padlocked Lady"** has many charming stanzas; but the catastrophe is ridiculous and false; intimating that, in this country, Liberty has a Padlock on her lips. Mr. Dyer himself has more than once exhibited a memorable example, how much may be said and written in this nation without reprehension or restraint. It is much to be lamented, that more of these whiners about Liberty, do not go and make their experiments in those happier lands, which are the subjects of their praise and envy. The punishment of those who have done so, has usually been exemplary.

We have, however, on the whole, no scruple in declaring, that these two volumes have afforded us more entertainment than any of Mr. Dyer's preceding publications, either in verse or prose.

E. V. Lucas (essay date 1920)

SOURCE: Lucas, E. V. "George Dyer." In *The Life of Charles Lamb*, Vol. 1, pp. 174-203. London: Methuen, 1920.

[*In the following excerpt, Lucas discusses the circumstances surrounding Dyer's second volume of poetry, and the reworked preface for it, as well as other observations on Dyer's oeuvre.*]

Dyer's principal work was scholarly or serious; but he had his lighter moments too, when he wrote verses, some of them quite sprightly, and moved socially from house to house. In the letter to Southey on page 172 we have seen something of George Dyer's attitude to poetry. The subject is continued in a letter to Wordsworth, some years later. "To G. D. a poem is a poem. His own as good as anybodie's, and God bless him, anybodie's as good as his own, for I do not think he has the most distant guess of the possibility of one poem being better than another. The Gods by denying him the very faculty itself of discrimination have effectually cut off every seed of envy in his bosom. But with envy, they excided Curiosity also, and if you wish the copy again, which you destined for him, I think I shall be able to find it again for you—on his third shelf, where he stuffs his presentation copies, uncut. . . ." Lamb adds that he recently gave Dyer his *Works,* and without any scruple rescued the copy after a little while and made it over to John Stoddart.

Dyer's principal verses are to be found in his *Poems,* 1800. This book originally was to consist of two volumes, one containing poetry and the other criticism; but its author altered and changed his plan, and it was ultimately sent to the printers in one volume with sixty-eight pages of preface. And then occurred a tragedy, for just after the book was ready Dyer suddenly realised that he had committed himself in this preface to a principle in which he did not really believe. Lamb tells the story in a letter to Manning in December, 1800:—

"At length George Dyer's phrenesis has come to a crisis; he is raging and furiously mad. I waited upon the heathen, Thursday was a se'nnight; the first symptom which struck my eye and gave me incontrovertible proof of the fatal truth was a pair of nankeen pantaloons four times too big for him, which the said Heathen did pertinaciously affirm to be new.

"They were absolutely ingrained with the accumulated dirt of ages; but he affirmed them to be clean He was going to visit a lady that was nice about those things, and that's the reason he wore nankeen that day. And then he danced, and capered, and fidgeted, and pulled up his pantaloons, and hugged his intolerable flannel vestment closer about his poetic loins; anon he gave it loose to the zephyrs which plentifully insinuate their tiny bodies through every crevice, door, window or wainscot, expressly formed for the exclusion of such impertinents. Then he caught at a proof sheet, and catched up a laundress's bill instead—made a dart at Blomfield's Poems, and threw them in agony aside. I could not bring him to one direct reply; he could not maintain his jumping mind in a right line for the tithe of a moment by Clifford's Inn clock. He must go to the printer's immediately—the most unlucky accident—he had struck off five hundred impressions of his *Poems,* which were ready for delivery to subscribers, and the Preface must all be expunged. There were eighty pages of Preface, and not till that morning had he discovered that in the very first page of said Preface he had set out

with a principle of Criticism fundamentally wrong, which vitiated all his following reasoning. The Preface must be expunged, although it cost him £30—the lowest calculation, taking in paper and printing! In vain have his real friends remonstrated against this Midsummer madness. George is as obstinate as a Primitive Christian—and wards and parries off all our thrusts with one unanswerable fence;—'Sir, it's of great consequence that the *world* is not *misled*!'". . . .

The history of Dyer's unfortunate poetical project is, I think, worth telling with some precision. The first notification that I can find is in the *Monthly Magazine* for October, 1796, where this statement occurs:—

> Mr. George Dyer, with whose poetical talents the public are well acquainted, is preparing a course of publications—satires, odes, and elegies; two of which will shortly make their appearance, under the titles of *Poets' Fate* and **"Poetic Sympathies."**

That was at the beginning of Lamb's acquaintance with G. D. Two years later, in November, 1798, the same magazine contained this announcement:—

> Mr. Dyer, in consequence of unforeseen engagements, and the advice of his friends, has been obliged to alter the plan of his Poetical Publication:—instead of three volumes at a guinea, two only, consisting of poems and poetical essays, will be published at twelve shillings. The first volume will appear next month.

Further delay occurred. No volumes, either at three for a guinea or two for twelve shillings, made their appearance; instead, in the *Monthly Magazine* for June, 1799, the following letter was printed:—

> G. Dyer presents respects to the subscribers to his poems, and informs them, with great concern, that the publication is delayed till the winter season. All the reasons of this delay could not with propriety be announced here, but shall be fully detailed in the preface to his poems. For the present, he must content himself with saying, that by unforeseen engagements, and by extending his plan beyond his original intention, he cannot get out the first volume, till the greater part of his subscribers will have left town for the summer; a time very inauspicious to publications of this nature. After mature deliberation, therefore, he thinks it most adviseable to print his two volumes at the same time; and his criticisms, extended as they are to an unexpected length, will form a distinct volume, comprehending free remarks on every species of poetry, and illustrations from the mythology of different nations. This arrangement, he apprehends, will less encumber the poems, and be more useful and agreeable to those persons for whose service this volume is intended. Such persons, however, as are not pleased with this arrangement may have their subscription-money returned, if they will have the goodness to apply to the bookseller where any subscription has been paid, or to the author himself, if the money was paid to him. Such other persons as choose to favour this work with their encouragement, are informed, that names are still received by the booksellers announced in his advertisement.
>
> *"Clifford's Inn, May* 20, 1799."

Dyer was now pledged to two volumes of poetry and preface, and we must suppose him actively engaged upon them thenceforward, for in 1800 the first volume was ready. **"Poems by George Dyer"** was the simple title. It was the preface to this volume which, when 500 copies were printed, suddenly confronted its author with a fallacy that led to his phrenesis. The half-burnt cancelled preface (Lamb called Dyer "Cancellarius Major"), bound up with the *Poems, 1801,* and other works, from Lamb's shelves, is in the British Museum, where the curious may study it. "Snatch'd out of the fire" is Lamb's comment in the margin. I am entirely at a loss to discover what the fallacy is, for the first page is practically reproduced in its entirety in the revised preface of 1802. Nor does a comparison of the two prefaces otherwise yield any discrepancy amounting (to the best of my belief, but such researches are very difficult to make thoroughly) to a false principle. The first omitted passage, on the second (not the first) page of the 1800 preface, is this:—

> A sufficient degree of generosity is found in the world to encourage a useful pursuit, and even an attempt to please: the violence of party cannot controul it; nor will it be overrated by the manœuverings of pride, or the feebleness of ignorance.

Can it be this benevolent opinion which poor G. D. discovered to be a fatal error?

The result at any rate was the suppression of the edition; surely one of those pacific acts of heroism which never receive recognition. Comic as the situation is—the flat, impossible poet declaring that the world must not be misled—it has its nobility, too, and very real pathos.

The luckless preface is very long and very discursive. It examines the nature of lyrical poetry, it analyses the poetic character, it exposes falsehoods told of Dyer by the critics and quidnuncs, it explains Dyer's attitude to his friends. One passage I must quote:—

> "With regard to the ladies, whose names are mentioned in this or a former volume, let it be publicly understood, as it has always been privately, that my language has been the expression of simple, though sincere, respect. To a powerful affection, many years indulged, and to a fondness for retirement, I am certainly indebted for a revival of some poetical feelings: when the heart is most subdued, it sometimes loves to worship in silence. These feelings may, perhaps, since have broken out into verse; but while immediately under the influence of that softness, I made no rebuses, and sent about no poetical billets doux; a confession, it is true, not of a very gallant poet: but reasons present themselves for my acknowledging, that, in print, just enough is delivered to secure me from the imputation of insin-

cerity, and no more. The mention of names may, perhaps, by some be considered imprudent; but the moral and intellectual qualities that entitle one sex to respect or esteem, will, also, justly entitle the other: and where a writer acts not without reasons, and where, by the parties concerned, those reasons are not disapproved, there is no ground for censure."

The volume, without its preface, appeared again in 1801, and again publication was interrupted. At last, in 1802, the waiting world had the work—in two small volumes, with the original preface in much the same form, and the following explanation of the change of shape:—

> "It was distantly suggested by friends, well qualified to have spoken with more freedom, that the undertaking to write *three* volumes of poems, and those mostly *lyrical,* would prove at once very arduous, and very unprofitable; and, that I had set myself no easy task, I could not be quite ignorant; well aware as I was, that through the whole range of poetry, no form required such frequent sacrifice to the graces, as what I was then attempting. The extent of the plan, also, was at least equal to the degree of elegance required in the treatment of the subject. In the ardour of my pursuit, the arts and sciences were made to pass in review before me. Statesmen, patriots, and heroes, poets, critics, and private friends, were each to receive some tribute of esteem, or some expressions of respect: and even amid these flights of fancy, critical remarks were intended on every branch of poetic composition. Thus extensive was the plan! So little do we know our weakness!"

Of Dyer's poetry there is little to say. It is just so many sober words in metre. His **"Stanzas Meditated in the Cloisters of Christ's Hospital,"** from which Lamb quotes at the end of his first essay on the school (in the *Gentleman's Magazine* in 1813), is among his best poems. The farthest swing of his poetical pendulum in the other direction is perhaps the comic paean, in the sapphic measure, in praise of snuff and tobacco, beginning:—

> I've gŏt th' hēad-āche: gīve mĕ thĕn, bōy thĕ snūff-
>   box,
> Fĭll'd wĭth Hōare's bēst snūff, ă rĕvīvĭng mīxture,
> Bēst ŏf āll snūffs: thăt wĭll rĕlīeve mĕ mōre than
>   Strāsbŭrgh ōr Hārdham's.

Ode VIII. in Book IV. of Dyer's *Poetics,* 1812, has a certain simple charm, but is chiefly interesting as exhibiting its author in nautical attire. I quote two stanzas:—

"The Sailor"

The author expresses grateful feelings to an honest landlady and her daughter, for kind attentions during his short stay with them near Hamilton, in Argyleshire; but pleads against their solicitations for his longer continuance. He wore the dress of a Sailor at this time, and writes under that character.

> My dame, you view a sailor brave,
>   Hastening far hence to plough the seas,
> To quit for the rude boisterous wave,
>   The babbling bourn, the whispering trees:
> The mavis calls; the laverocks ring
>   Their music thro' the heav'ns so clear:
> Nature's full chorus seems to sing,
>   Still, happy loiterer, linger here.
> But, dame, you view a sailor brave,
> And he must plough the ocean wave. . . .
> Your Peggy's eye is dew-drop bright;
>   Her smiling cheek is lily fair;
> Her feet as hare's move soft and light,*
>   Her voice as blackbird's loud and clear:
> Oh! she goes near to wound my heart,
>   As oft she sings her "*Highland Laddie*":
> So quickly, dame, must I depart,
>   And keep my heart still tight and steady:
> For, dame, you view a sailor brave;
> Quick he must plough the ocean wave.

Footnotes were a special weakness of Dyer's. Here is the last stanza, with its additaments, of a poem on **"The Triumph of Poetry,"** in his *Poetics*:—

> Oh! might I view again, with ravish'd sight,
>   As when with candid Anderson[1] I stray'd,
>   And all the wonder-varying scene survey'd,
> Sea, hills, and city fair, from Calton's[2] height;
>   And hear (for Scotland's rhimes, ah! soon may fail[3]),
>   Some Ednam bard awake the trembling string;[4]
>   Some tuneful youth[5] of charming Tiviotdale;
>   Some Kelso songstress[6] love's dear raptures sing.
> Language may fail, but love shall never die,
> Till beauty fails to charm, till love forgets to sigh.
>   . . . . .

* It is scarcely necessary to observe here, than an allusion is made to the *barefooted* lasses of Scotland:

> "Here view *two barefoot beauties* clean and clear."

> ALLAN RAMSAY'S "GENTLE SHEPHERD."

[1] Dr. Robert Anderson, Editor of the Works of the British Poets and author of a valuable Life of Dr. Smollet.

[2] Calton Hill, whence a view, at once romantic and sublime, is taken of the city of Edinburgh, of the Firth of Forth, and the hills of Fifeshire on the opposite coast.

[3] Such, at least, is the opinion of some judicious persons in Scotland.

[4] Ednam is near Kelso, in Berwickshire, near which the little river Eden flows, from which the village takes its name. Ednam is the native place of Thomson, the author of the Seasons.

[5] Alludes to a pedestrian tour made in this pastoral and truly classical country, and in some part of the north of England, with a gentleman of great talents, now eminently distinguished at Calcutta, for his extraordinary skill in the Asiatic languages. See an Essay on the Languages and Literature of the Indo-Chinese Nations, in Vol. X. of the ASIATIC RESEARCHES, by John Leyden, M.D.

[6] The Scotch melodies, sung to the Scotch airs, and by the female voice, constitute, as must be supposed, one of the charms of this delightful country.

I wonder which of his poems Dyer read to the other patients at Dr. Graham's earth-bath establishment (as he did when he was being treated there), his audience, like himself, being half-buried in the garden, all around him. What a picture!

Best among Dyer's prose works were his ***Memoirs on the Life and Writings of Robert Robinson*** and his *History of the University and Colleges of Cambridge*. He wrote, moreover, countless articles, reviews and biographies for periodicals, pamphlets on religious questions, and "all that was original" in James Valpy's edition of the classics, in 141 volumes, 1809-1831. He also travelled from library to library collecting materials for a bibliographical work, which was never published. Dyer showed Hazlitt "with some triumph" two fingers of which he had lost the use in copying out manuscripts of Procrus and Plotinus in a fine Greek hand.

W. C. Hazlitt recorded that Miss Lamb and Mrs. Hazlitt once made a plan pleasantly to surprise Dyer by mending his arm-chair, which had a hundred holes in it. These they sewed up. Dyer's horror may be imagined when it is recorded that in every one of those gaping wounds he kept a book.

"He hangs," said William Hazlitt, "like a film and cobweb upon letters, or like the dust on the outside of knowledge, which should not too rudely be brushed aside." And Lamb summed up his labours in the following words in "Oxford in the Vacation" in 1820: "D. has been under-working for himself ever since;—drudging at low rates for unappreciating booksellers,—wasting his fine erudition in silent corrections of the classics, and in those unostentatious but solid services to learning, which commonly fall to the lot of laborious scholars, who have not the art to sell themselves to the best advantage. . . . If his muse of kindness halt a little behind the strong lines, in fashion in this excitement-craving age, his prose is the best of the sort in the world, and exhibits a faithful transcript of his own healthy natural mind, and cheerful innocent tone of conversation."

M. Ray Adams (essay date 1947)

SOURCE: Adams, M. Ray. "George Dyer and English Radicalism." In *Studies in the Literary Backgrounds of English Radicalism,* pp. 227-66. Lancaster, Pa.: Franklin and Marshall College Studies, no. 5, 1947.

[*In the following excerpt, Adams corrects the image of Dyer as a lovable fool by investigating his religious and political ideals in relation to his contemporaries.*]

To see the gentle George Dyer placed among even the milder radicals will surprise those acquainted with him only as the friend of Charles Lamb (and there are few who know him otherwise); for Lamb has immortalized him by dwelling almost exclusively upon the unconscious comedy of his outer life. The oddities of his character have likewise been the engrossing topic of his other friends and of those of our own time who have written about him.[1] The only recognition of George Dyer's extensive contribution to the liberal thought of his time which I have been able to find in all that has been written about him, is contained in a single sentence of the obituary notice in the *Gentleman's Magazine* for May 1841: "His kind heart most warmly sympathized at all times with the cause of civil and religious liberty, which he uniformly espoused by his writings, more especially by his work on *The Theory and Practice of Benevolence* and a treatise entitled *Complaints of the Poor.*"But this gives little idea of the range of his thinking. Lamb has explored his heart for us, but has left no adequate intellectual estimate of him. In fact, by his minute chronicling of Dyer's harmless foibles he has spoiled the perspective upon his work. There is not a line of appreciation in Lamb about his political and religious philosophy. To Lamb, George Dyer was primarily a queer specimen in the laboratory of human nature. And yet he undoubtedly loved him; he wrote that he never spoke of him "except *con amore.*" Lamb's respect and even reverence for Dyer, it is true, have been often discounted because he so frequently made his friend the object of raillery, but his playfulness was always at the expense of the accidents, not of the essence, of Dyer's character. He was a convenient butt for good-natured ridicule and the tolerant object of some of the most delightful humour that has ever graced the English tongue. So perhaps more literature has been made about Dyer than he made himself. His many eccentricities are sauce to the bare facts of his uneventful life: his unassailable innocence, his amazing credulity, his bookishness, his absentmindedness, his slovenliness, his economy pushed to the point of denying himself proper nourishment, were sources of endless amusement to his friends and provided Lamb especially a constant temptation.

Lamb said that a biography of Dyer would be as interesting as any novel, and that he planned to put him in a novel if he outlived him. Strange to say, the biography has never been written. Even his autobiography, which in the blindness of his old age he dictated during the last seven years of his life, has been unfortunately lost, though there is an extract from it in the obituary sketch of the *Gentleman's Magazine.* So the records of his always laborious and generous-hearted and sometimes distinguished endeavors lie scattered in the lumber-rooms of literature. It is the hope of the author of this study, though he has had to accept the handicap of writing soberly about a man whose lack of humour was said to "amount to a positive endowment," to show that George Dyer was a respectable force in the progressive thought of his time and that, though he shines now in the reflected light of the genius of greater men who were his friends, the light of his own genius kept him, while living, from being obscured in contact with them.

Dyer's political and religious philosophy was steadied by the ballast of his great classical learning, in which, like his radical friend, Gilbert Wakefield, he was a marvel of industry. His works all have the air of serious scholarship. Lamb pays tribute to his "fine erudition." The simplicity upon which so many have remarked involved no lack of knowledge but was limited to his personal relations, though his scholarship was multifarious rather than profound. Leigh Hunt calls him "an angel of the dusty bookstalls and of the British Museum." Hazlitt has left us an engaging portrait of him as an unworldly bibliophile:

> He hangs like a film and cobweb upon letters, or is like the dust upon the outside of knowledge, which should not be too rudely brushed aside. He follows learning as its shadow, but as such he is respectable. He browzes on the husks and leaves of books. . . . The legend of good women is to him no fiction. When he steals from the twilight of his cell, the scene breaks upon him like an illuminated missal, and all the people he sees are but so many figures in a *camera obscura.* . . . His mind cannot take the impression of vice; but the gentleness of his nature turns gall to milk. . . . He draws the picture of mankind from the guileless simplicity of his own heart.[2]

Much of what Dyer wrote is buried under anonymity in the mere projects of booksellers or in such magazines as the *Analytical Review,* the *Critical Review,* the *Gentleman's Magazine,* and the *Monthly Magazine.* Circumstances condemned him to much hard literary labour without inspiration and left the blight of dullness upon much of his literary output. However, when dealing with subjects in which his convictions were enlisted, like most of the great public questions of the early period of the French Revolution, he wrote with vigour and perspicuity and often with grace. And he never reached the borders of rant. Upon matters of political and religious controversy he seemed to feel, like Godwin, what Wordsworth has called "the central calm subsisting at the heart of endless agitation." In fact, few men have delivered themselves of radical ideas with more soberness. As a writer in the *Monthly Review* notes, his use of obsolete phrases gives his prose "the air of an old sermon of the seventeenth century." But there is in his pages little of the unconsciously mirth-provoking qualities that sauced his conversation, and Lamb praised some of his prose.

Dyer's poetry naturally suffers more than his prose from the pervasive soberness of his nature. E. V. Lucas writes that it is "just so many sober words in metre." The epigram of Crabb Robinson's friend Reid was considered just by many:

> The world all say, my gentle Dyer,
> Thy odes do very much want fire.
> Repair the fault, my gentle Dyer,
> And throw thy odes into the fire.[3]

Lamb's ridicule of Dyer's critical pretensions and of his poetical discrimination has led to the complete neglect of his poetry and even to an imperfect knowledge of its extent.[4] But Lamb's opinions themselves are to be discounted to some degree from the very fact that he himself was incapable of soberness and that he always so warmed to his subject when he spoke of "G. D." that what went into him fact did not always come out truth. The denial to Dyer of a cultivated taste is not so well justified as the denial to him of imaginative vigour. Pegasus, it is true, generally "runs restive" with our poet. There can be little imaginative glow in poems full of borrowed sentiments conscientiously acknowledged in ubiquitous footnotes. But a careful reading of his essays published in *Poems, 1802,* on "representative," lyric, and elegiac poetry, indicates poverty neither of knowledge nor of discrimination. Unlike the average of his early contemporaries, he was no abject follower of Pope. He sometimes achieves the unaffected simplicity of Wordsworth's blank verse, and he is full of the humanitarian fervour of the early romantic poets.[5]

We now turn to pertinent facts about George Dyer's career, especially those of his association with the leaders of liberal thought.

The association of the name of Dyer with Lamb begins with their attendance at Christ's Hospital, which was the early intellectual nurse also of their friends Coleridge and Leigh Hunt. Through the kindness of "some charitable dissenting ladies" Dyer was sent to the famous charity school at nine. He stayed there twelve years and was for some time at the head with the rank of Grecian. But he had left long before Lamb entered in 1782, and had graduated in 1778 at Emmanuel College, Cambridge.[6] Upon taking his degree he submitted to subscription, though with misgivings sufficient, it is thought, to have caused him to be denied a fellowship. Soon afterward he was sent by the Baptist Fund in London as a pupil to the Rev. Robert Robinson in Cambridge, presumably to be trained for the dissenting ministry. Robinson, a brilliant man with whom Dyer had first become acquainted while an undergraduate and whose life he was later to write, was destined to run the whole gamut of dissent. Through Robinson's influence Dyer was led to Unitarianism and, it seems, to political free-thinking as well. Robinson was an admirer of Voltaire and Rousseau. About 1780 he founded the Cambridge branch of the Society for Constitutional Information, a society for political reform which was later very sympathetic toward French revolutionary principles. In this society Robinson preached civil and religious liberty, at the same time carrying his message to "a little society of dissenters at Oxford." Dyer, though he did not join the society, undoubtedly approved of its purpose. His political interest was probably stimulated about this time too through his acquaintanceship with the doughty political reformer, "Citizen" Earl Stanhope, in whose home he was for a while[7] a tutor and who, upon his death in 1816, made Dyer, with Fox and others, one of his executors and left him a handsome legacy.

In 1781 Dyer tried preaching, serving a dissenting congregation at Oxford, probably the "little society" to which his friend Robinson had preached the gospel of liberty the year before. But he soon returned again to Cambridge, where he took residence among the fellows; attracted the attention of Priestley, Wakefield, and Mrs. Barbauld; and for the next ten years was one of that influential group of Cambridge Dissenters which for more than thirty years made a valiant fight for the removal of political and religious disabilities. Besides Robert Robinson, this group included at various times Robert Tyrwhitt, John Jebb, William Frend, Robert Hall, and Benjamin Flower.[8] During the preceding twenty-five years the Dissenters had not without patience won a certain amount of respect at Cambridge.[9] However, while the atmosphere of Cambridge was in the 1780's more conducive to freedom of thought than that of Oxford (Oxford required subscription for entrance; Cambridge, for graduation), even there Dissenters were looked upon with suspicion and dislike. But Dyer was hopeful. He wrote of the period in 1793:

> From the temper of the studies pursued at Cambridge as well as from the great degree of liberality possessed by many of its members, there were not wanting those who hoped a disposition might prevail there to rectify some of its more glaring impositions begotten originally by tyranny and nursed by weakness.[10]

Accordingly, in 1789 he threw himself into the then much accelerated agitation against all the disabilities of Dissenters with his *Inquiry into the Nature of Subscription to the Thirty-nine Articles.* Robinson and Capel Lofft drew up the plan of a college for Dissenters at Cambridge in which it was their desire that Dyer should become a tutor, but Robinson died in 1790 before it was realized.

After a short period of teaching at Southampton with the father of Charles Cowden Clark in 1791, Dyer, apparently seeking a wider field of intellectual endeavor,[11] went to London in the next year and in 1795 settled at Clifford's Inn, where, as Lamb puts it, "like a dove in an asp's nest" he lived "in calm and sinless peace" for the remaining forty-six years of his life.

The main part of the record of these forty-six years will be found in his books. It has to do almost exclusively with adventures of the mind. His outward activity was practically narrowed to exertions on behalf of his friends, nearly all of whom were at one time or another closely identified with the forward-looking movements of the age. He became a member of the Chapter House Coffee Club, to which belonged many of the celebrities of the day. Before the campaign for the suppression of the revolutionary societies became so violent in 1792, he attended several of them and "almost constantly attended one of their committees formed by delegates from various societies."[12] In 1790 Gilbert Wakefield, his contemporary at Cambridge, came to teach in the dissenting college at Hackney, from which he loosed the tumult of his soul upon the government. They indulged together "some kindred likings and some kindred scorns" and when Wakefield's fanaticism brought the ire of officialdom down upon his head and sent him to prison in 1799, Dyer defended his friend's principles. After his expulsion from Cambridge in 1793, the reformer William Frend joined Dyer in London and continued to his death, only a few days before Dyer's, the close association begun at the university. As we shall see, Dyer's sympathy for men persecuted for opinion's sake in 1793 and 1794—Winterbotham, Muir, Palmer, Walker, Gerrald, Hodgson, Hardy, Tooke, Thelwall, Holcroft, Joyce—was openly expressed. . . .

We pass now to an analysis and estimate of that large part of Dyer's writings which links him with the revolutionary tradition.

An Inquiry into the Nature of Subscription to the Thirty-nine Articles was the first of Dyer's publications. It was originally issued in pamphlet form in 1789, but was not advertised for sale and was circulated only among a few friends. In the first edition he did not even allude to affairs in France, since they were then "suspended on the edge of contingencies." The second edition, "corrected, altered and much enlarged," came from the press of the radical bookseller Joseph Johnson in 1792. It is a book of 439 pages which, in the words of a reviewer in the *Monthly Review,*[13] "exposes, perhaps more fully than any former publication has done, the apprehended absurdities and mischiefs attending religious tests." It was, in fact, the culmination of the arguments in support of the proposal for the repeal of the obnoxious Corporation and Test Acts, the long fight against which had been given an extraordinary impetus during the early period of the French Revolution. He tells us in the preface that he had planned to make further "copious remarks" on the part of Burke's *Reflections* connected with his subject, but that he had desisted, "recollecting . . . that as he had been sufficiently confuted on the subject of French politics by Mr. Paine and since by Mr. Christie and Mr. Mackintosh, he had also been ably replied to on those matters which took my attention by Dr. Priestley and others."[14] So he dismisses Burke as "a writer whose flashy rather than correct style has gained him some admirers, but whose principles are approved by few who have no interest in being deceived."[15] The book, however, is multifarious enough in its range of subject-matter. All the political and religious ramifications of subscription are traced. Its style is marked by diffuse eloquence rather than by close logic. But the weight of Dyer's learning is carried with more grace and spirit than he usually shows.

In the four parts of the *Inquiry* he condemns subscription as inconsistent with natural rights, with the free exercise of the intellectual powers, with the principles of the British constitution, and with the doctrines of Christianity, respectively. We are here primarily concerned with the first two.

Dyer's conception of natural rights is little related to Rousseau's. Dyer defines them as "claims arising out of our present situation, our mutual relation, and our common equality." He thus confuses Rousseau's natural and civil rights.[16] With Rousseau, natural rights do not arise from a civilized social condition or mutual relations but are anterior to the social state. According to Dyer, government protects civil rights and at the same time helps to preserve the true equality of the state of nature. Rousseau would not have subscribed to such a statement as this: "As the wants of mankind are the foundation of society and as society gives birth to government, government is dictated by nature." Natural rights, Dyer tells his readers, are determined, not by a blanket fiat of our Creator, but by "the soil where ye received your origin." The natural rights of the enlightened Englishman will, then, admit him to higher privileges than those of an American Indian or of a Chinese, though the rights of the Englishman are not more real.

Among these natural rights which religious tests deny are the right to occupy offices of public trust, the right to educate children on any national endowment, the right to publish opinion, and the right to the free use of reason especially in regard to religion. Such rights have a priority over systems of law and religion: "As there is a primitive reason from whence proceed those relations which constitute law, there are also rights prior to any form of religion which are the foundation of liberty."[17] Therefore, any scheme of religion which deprives men of them is to be condemned.

Considering the education of youth as a natural right, Dyer launches into an attack upon the aristocratic element and intolerance in the universities. His respect for man is stronger than his regard for the society of scholars. He hopefully looks forward to the establishment of national education, which will follow the revolution in the principles of education introduced by "the spirit of modern politics." He hails the establishment of the dissenting college at Hackney as a move toward this liberation of education. The comprehensive scheme of his educational toleration takes in even the Jews, whose admission to the universities he advocates. The statutes of the medieval founders of the universities, where they involve intolerance toward the Dissenters, must "submit to an interpretation which the age can bear."

To the objection that the state must have "a just and permanent security," Dyer replies that government provides its own security by guarding the social compact and that mutual consent establishes the principles according to which just government is regulated. Like all revolutionary thinkers, he pitches his plea against subscription above the level of little groups of opinionative men upon the immovable basis of first principles:

> These reasonings which plead the cause of mankind are not the partial arguments of a dissenter against a churchman . . . , but the unsophisticating and, I think, the unanswerable plea of human nature against every domineering influence. For I am very much mistaken if there be not a secret corner in the human heart, where sophistry cannot enter, into which, would we condescend to look, . . . subscription . . . will appear abhorrent from the first principles of natural justice and of common benevolence.[18]

In his examination of the inconsistency between subscription and the powers of the human mind, he accepts the Hartleian refinement of Locke's sensationalism, though, as we shall see, he seems to baulk at the system of materialism towards which it leads. One corollary of sensationalism which he fully accepts is disbelief in mysteries. We can have no ideas about things concealed from us. To ask one to believe such incomprehensible mysteries as consubstantiation and transubstantiation, or even original sin, the trinity, and grace, by laying aside the reason, is like asking one to see without eyesight. Faith can result only from evidence. Moreover, mystery itself is too often the cloak of knavery. As the path to political salvation is less complicated than lawyers make it seem, so the path to heaven is plainer than theologians make it appear. Again, following the sensationalists, Dyer does not admit free-will "in the philosophical sense." Accepting the idea that "the mind is the effect of the organization of matter," he believes that "the will follows irresistibly and necessarily the most powerful impressions." But the darker implications of the ideas of predestination and election yield to those of infinite benevolence. He thinks that "the grace of God will at length prevail over all, it being impossible that infinite benevolence should be defeated of its own gracious intentions."[19] Hence all will eventually be "made happy in God." All are predestined to salvation: how could universal benevolence decree otherwise?

So much for Dyer's theory of the operations of the mind and the control of destiny. What about the relations between subscription and intellectual integrity? It is impossible for the average man to subscribe with integrity to the truth of thirty-nine propositions, involving metaphysical distinctions, all the leading church doctrines held since the establishment of Christianity, and all the multifarious matters of church ceremony and faith on which the church has legislated. "Such articles," he declares moreover, "will become standards to which we shall appeal as oracles of truth rather than guides to help us in our inquiries after it."[20] The variety of the human understanding, which becomes more and more evident with intellectual improvement, is irreconcilable with the uniformity of faith imposed by subscription.

Of the primacy of reason Dyer is an uncompromising advocate. He is convinced that all propositions to which people are asked to subscribe should be pursued to "self-evident truths or the principles of common sense," and that otherwise they are not binding. If revelation counteracts the principles of reason, he can hardly be convinced that it is divine. "If our establishments or even Christianity itself throw impediments in the way of the human understanding, . . . I shall not scruple to give them all up." True intellectual freedom and a reverence for the understanding, then, will not endure any kind of subscription.

> Subscription to any articles cannot be justified on any principle of reason; whatever be their number and wherever they be fabricated, . . . all alike tend to enslave the understanding and to retard the progress of truth.[21]

On historical grounds Dyer denies that the clergy are represented in Parliament as an ecclesiastical body and that the church is an essential part of the English constitution. Parliamentary assemblies of the clergy have their origin in the accumulation of large temporal possessions by the bishops and clergy from the people in payment for spiritual services. Under William the Conqueror the tenures of the clergy underwent the same changes as the tenures of the nobles; that is, they have been held since "by barony," not "in free alms." Hence the bishops sit in the House of Lords as barons rather than as representatives of the clergy, and the clergy as an organized ecclesiastical body are not only no estate in Parliament but are not represented except in common with the laity, who are freeholders. This reasoning denies the bishops the presumption that they have the power to speak or legislate for the rank and file of the church. The church is no primary part of the English constitution; for the fundamental maxims of the English government are antecedent to the establishment just as the natural rights of mankind, which the fundamental maxims of the English government express, are "antecedent to any particular regimen of religion." There is nothing in the constitution, therefore, to render the union of church and state indissoluble.

But more revealing of the real nature of Dyer's thinking in the *Inquiry* than such scholarly historical arguments are the frequently startling revolutionary sentiments which light up the sober colouring of his dispassionate pages and which he shares with the more outright contemporary radicals and agitators.

In his private convictions he went along quite a distance with his more explosive friend Wakefield. He professed the same personal aversion to public worship and believed that it gave a bias to religious inquiry. However, he does not go the length of Wakefield in contending that social worship is incompatible with the Christian religion. He commends Wakefield's and Geddes's translations of the New Testament as liberal yet accurate versions, which, unlike the King James version, do not "give countenance to the claims of high church authority" or "follow the expectations of a system."

His speculative ideas on the lineage of absolute government and on the sovereignty of the people show the influence of the bold mind and trenchant pen of Thomas Paine. "All monarchies, properly so called," Dyer declares, "originated in violence or corruption and their continuance depends upon the same principles which gave them their existence."[22] The sovereignty of the people makes the monarch "a public functionary only," and the divinity which hedges kings builds a sconce not only against the wall of heaven but against the very palladium of public liberty.

> When Europeans speak of a sovereign lord, of a sacred majesty, of a defender of the faith, and the Lord's anointed, mankind are misled. The former term savours of conquest; the next of theological claims, the third of superstition, if not something worse; the last is the incense of priests to the pride of kings.[23]

Here the sober temper of the inquirer gives way to the spleen of the agitator. In his ideas on hereditary legislators and the system of aristocracy, he alludes with approval to the *Rights of Man,* but they have more of the temperance of statement which makes it possible to reason with him than Paine's. He also cites Paine's and Joel Barlow's teachings about prelates and privileged orders; and he sees their ideas provoked by the inattention to distress, the tendency toward persecution, and the opposition to claims of conscience among the ruling classes. He sets up a hypothetical radical reformer behind whose downrightness he thinly conceals his own convictions. These words, for example, purport to be typical of the agitators, but the thoughts none the less are George Dyer's:

> Prelates are by office enemies to liberty and obstacles to the progress of truth. . . . Prelacy is founded in error and perpetuated by worldly policy. . . . "Admit only the original unadulterated truth that all men are equal in their rights, and the foundation of everything is laid. To build the superstructure requires no effort but that of natural deduction."[24]

The most open instance of his alignment with the radicals then being suspected or hunted down by the government is his appending with approval in a long note the declaration of the revolutionary Society of United Irishmen at Dublin, signed by its notorious secretary Tandy. This declaration, Dyer writes, "presents a model worthy of imitation in England." In the same connexion he advocates the distribution of radical political pamphlets among "the lower ranks of people," including "cheap editions of Mr. Paine's *Rights of Man.*" He also recommends to parents Locke's *Treatise on Education* and Mary Wollstonecraft's *Vindication of the Rights of Woman.* In the latter he hails the advent of the rational woman. Finally, the revolutionary radical's contempt for the past and his belief in the perfectibility which enfranchised man will achieve in the future, when "reason has supplanted enthusiasm," are expressed with the true Godwinian temper:

> Politics are capable of unknown degrees of improvement. Political wisdom is not wont to show itself in imitation, but . . . in rescuing truth from the rubbish of Gothic antiquity and political knavery. . . . The object in her eye is Man. . . . As present times come forward to her survey . . . , she sees liberty in the train while antiquity retires from her eye and vanishes in a point. Too well instructed to admire defects for their antiquity or to overlook improvement because incomplete, she advances with prudence yet with intrepidity, with humility yet with perseverance, with modesty yet with success. Happy to admit mistakes as well as to pursue discoveries, she yields without meanness and conquers without insolence; and thus never rests till she gains perfection. This, this is political wisdom.[25]

Dyer's first volume of poems came from Johnson's press the same year as the revised and enlarged edition of the *Inquiry.* It was a thin volume in pamphlet form, dedicated to William Frend to express his respect for him "as a man of letters and, what I value more, as a man of virtue and a friend to liberty." **"Ode on Peace, written in Jesus College Garden"** contains tributes to Tyrwhitt, Frend, and Wakefield—the Cambridge reformers, who as "steady friends of man" formed various generous plans for broadening liberty. An extensive portion of the **"Ode on Liberty"** is dedicated to such defenders of the French Revolution as John Jebb, Richard Price, Samuel Parr, John Aikin, Thomas Paine, Mary Hays, Helen Maria Williams, and Mary Wollstonecraft; and there are added long notes explaining in more detail their connexions with the cause of liberty. The stanza on Paine, written at the time when the *Rights of Man* was being acclaimed and condemned in such wholesale fashion, brought down upon the author the displeasure of the *Critical Review.*[26]

The following year (1793) brought the publication of Dyer's *Complaints of the Poor People of England.* The spirit and purpose of this production had been anticipated in the preface to the *Inquiry,* where he describes himself as more interested in and better fitted for humanizing the order of society by the peaceful penetration of political knowledge among "the outcasts of political society, the common people" than for more boldly "abashing venal statesmen and startling unfeeling oppressors." Again his title does not indicate the comprehensiveness of his book, which touches upon practically every matter of political agitation then stirring the country. Still, in a special way, it is a document instinct with humanitarian sentiment, a deep solicitude for the rights of the poor, and a sincere desire to lead them into a more abundant life. It is no speculative or doctrinaire performance, but a record of the observations and convictions of a man who has become as one of the poor to learn their problems and to appreciate their hardships. In spirit it is the most modern of all his productions.

The main defect of the English government from the point of view of the poor is the imperfect representation which denies them any share in the making of laws. Only about 12,000 people of a population of approximately 8,000,000 were eligible to vote for members of the House of Commons. The basis of representation had not been changed materially for more than a hundred years. The new growing industrial centres where the poor were concentrated were practically without representation, while the borough of Midhurst in Sussex, for example, though it had not then a single house, sent two members to parliament. Dyer fully outlines the consequences to the poor in tyranny and injustice. Responsibility for their ignorance is laid upon the government. Again he advocates a plan for national education, but calls it "a romantic idea." That the children of the rich and the poor should be taught in the same schools was a bold opinion in 1793. As Barlow had already pointed out in his *Advice to the Privileged Orders,* Dyer shows that the poor people are kept in ignorance of the

laws largely by the fact that they are printed in the old German character, which few can read, and sold at such a price that few can afford to buy. The tyranny of the game and penal laws, the extravagance of crown and church expenditure, and the ignoring of the rights of the poor in the administration of the army and navy, are dwelt upon—sometimes with high-spirited scorn, sometimes with deep indignation. To give to the poor the independence to which their rights as men entitle them, Dyer advocates the turning over of waste land to them and the establishment of life annuities according to a plan of Dr. Price. The abolition of certain oppressive feudal rights, such as primogeniture, which have survived into an age whose enlightened spirit they constantly violate, will also contribute to the reduction of poverty.

"An Address to the Friends of Liberty," the title which Dyer gives to the fourth part of his book, is a bold protest against the government's policy of suppression and a vigorous defence of the aims of the revolutionary societies. He declares his willingness to obey the laws in making which the majority have no share, but his inability to respect such a government. He asserts that the proclamations used to hamper the meeting of such organizations as the Constitutional and Corresponding societies are not laws, since they have not been ratified by Parliament. He denies that the societies have any designs on property, commending Major Cartwright and Lord Daer for their solicitude, in forming some of the societies, about the security of property. But he defends the suspected correspondence carried on by some of them with the French revolutionary bodies, since it was in response to the invitation of the National Assembly to give their advice about the new French constitution. He ends the book with a reaffirmation of his faith in the French Revolution:

> Yes, with few exceptions I approved and still approve the doctrines of the Rights of Man; and the French Revolution I contemplated and still contemplate as the most important era in the history of nations.[27]

A Dissertation on the Theory and Practice of Benevolence, published in 1795, was intended as a sequel to the *Complaints of the Poor.* It is not in part, as the title might imply, a metaphysical examination of the origin of our moral feelings. It is primarily an attempt "unconnected with the science of casuistry" to stimulate the spirit of benevolence by presenting objects for which it may be exercised: charity schools, workhouses, and various relief societies. Surely George Dyer comes nearer than any of the thinkers of the day to personifying that "universal benevolence" of which the revolutionary philosophers so glibly talked.[28] At the same time he is careful not to suggest any radical interference with the system of property. In fact, he thinks benevolence must be relied upon to correct the inequalities and imperfections inseparable from the social state. Among the objects of benevolence proposed are the defendants in the state trials of 1794. Without their solicitation, he gives particular accounts of these sufferers in the cause of freedom. He is careful, however, to stress, not the political, but the moral point of view—"moral, not in regard to the justice or injustice of putting these persons on their trials nor to the principles or characters of the accusers, matters upon which he had his private opinions, but in regard to the inconveniences and losses sustained by the defendants."[29] Even the ordinarily unsympathetic *Critical Review* was moved by admiration of Dyer's "humane and sensible strictures" of the treatment of the men who had lately been indicted for treason and sedition.

Dyer's liberality of mind made him peculiarly fit to write the life of Robert Robinson, whose spirit of eager inquiry early led his disciple to venture into the field of rational religion. *Memoirs of the Life and Writings of Robert Robinson* was published in 1796. Dr. Parr and Wordsworth thought it one of the best biographies in English. It also had the distinction of being translated into German. The book is examined here primarily for its reflection of Dyer's more liberal ideas: there are many independent reflections on the spirit of the age and on ecclesiastical and political affairs.

In the preface there is one of the most outright avowals of revolutionary ideas to be found in the whole range of Dyer's writings. The occasion, which seems rather incommensurate with the fervour of the philosophical comment which it engenders, is his decision not to use titles with the names of people in the *Memoirs.*

> The language of equality is adopted in this volume; it is the language of truth and soberness. . . . In my intercourse with society I conform to its language; but in publications, at least for such as I am responsible, I will abide by the language of equality. In the latter case I bear a testimony to liberty: in the former I leave the reader to smile at my inconsistency. But, to speak the truth, these titles present a caricature of man, while every inch of ground he treads on, . . . every propensity of the human heart, whether virtuous or vicious, proves the deception and mocks our pride. . . . France has emancipated mankind from these attempts at false greatness. By bursting the bars which imprison truth, she has aggrandized her species.[30]

The plainness of his style in the book is largely explained by the fact that he is willing to appear "among writers as a native of Botany Bay."

Dyer's sympathy with Robinson's various political and religious heresies is implicit when not expressed. He writes with evident satisfaction of Robinson's Rousseauistic belief in the pristine purity of human nature and of his general approbation of the French Revolution. The little respect Dyer shows for the arcana of political science would have pleased the subject of his biography also. Like Paine, Dyer thinks that government has been made a matter of mystery by designing men who have used religion to bolster tyranny and have thus obscured the plain path of public happiness by a "wilderness of turnpike gates." His usual philosophic composure deserts him completely on this subject, and he writes as if he had just risen from a perusal of Paine:

> There exists a class of lofty politicians by whom government is treated as priests treat religion, like a science too profound to be fathomed by common intellects or like a fabric too elegant and too sacred to be touched by the unclean, the unhallowed hands of the vulgar. The comprehension of political science, the arrangement and establishment of political institutions, are, according to these men appointed by a divine invisible agent and transferred to the administration of a transcendent personage, his vice-gerent in this lower world. To augment the splendour of this august character, inferior dignities are called in, enclosed with the bright emblazonry of hereditary greatness, and decorated with the exterior pomp of official magnificence. These sagacious speculatists, like the ancient Epicureans who maintained that the liberty of the will flows from a right line out of a curve, reverse the interests and claims of a community, and become advocates of the crooked manoeuverings of a few lucky spirits, fortunate by birth or blessed with affluence. In comparison with these politicians, how mere a novice was Aristotle! This philosopher did but resign the reins of government to such as nature had endowed with talents corresponding to the character of a governor. The other men possessed the holy oil by which even fools were made Solomons. The doctrine of Jus Divinum established tyranny and slavery by a commission from heaven.[31]

With little short of an implication of approval he quotes Paine's description of government as "an evil that the wickedness of mankind renders necessary" and seems to agree with Godwin in doubting its positive blessing.

The year 1797 is marked by two attempts at verse satire. *The Poet's Fate,* a plea for a more liberal patronage of writers, is a rhymed dialogue between a neglected poet and his friend. Among the writers of radical tendency mentioned as ill repaid by the world for their exertions in its behalf are Parr, Aikin, Geddes, Frend, and Wakefield. The following are two of several alternatives suggested by the despairing Muse:

> Take poor repast;
> For such as needs must learn to fast;
> Take moderate exercise and keep upstairs;
> When hungry, smoke your pipe or say your prayers;
> Or plough in learned pride the Atlantic main,
> Join Pantisocracy's harmonious train;
> Haste where young Love still spreads his brooding
>   wings,
> And freedom digs and ploughs and sings.

In a note to the above Dyer compliments Southey and Coleridge for their "ardent love of liberty" and "the softer feelings of benevolence," and singles out Wordsworth, Lloyd, and Lamb for poetical distinction. In the same year he published **"An English Prologue and Epilogue to the Latin Comedy of Ignoramus with a Preface and Notes relative to modern Times and Manners."[32]** In the epilogue there is one of his rare indulgences in personal satire. The lines on the established clergy are biting and offensive enough:

> Churchmen you think are *sacred*—be they so—
> Witchcraft was sacred some few years ago . . .
> Should some fools, and fools are often grave,
> With solemn cant affect my soul to save;
> With cheeks as fat as brawn, as soft as down,
> With nothing reverend save the band and gown,
> With eyes so full they cannot hold a tear,
> And heads that never ached, except with beer;
> Whose slender knowledge tells them to obey,
> Dull idle souls who only preach and pray; . . .
> Yes, I would claim as I have claimed before,
> As fair a right to laugh as you to snore.
> Peace on the Reverend head, however dull;
> Go, honest man, enjoy your empty skull.

These productions, in general, confirm, however, what might have been concluded otherwise—that George Dyer was constitutionally unfit to be a satirist. There was too much kindness in his nature for him to satirize often with great effectiveness. In its review of **The Poet's Fate,** the *Monthly Review*[33] observes:

> If it be possible for a satirist to be void of a single particle of ill-will toward any man breathing, or for a complainant against the times to be perfectly satisfied with his own lot, we firmly believe the humble and benevolent George Dyer to be that man.

An Address to the People of Great Britain on the Doctrine of Libels and the Office of Juror is a pamphlet of 120 pages occasioned by the various prosecutions of radicals by the government for public libel but specifically by the charges brought against Gilbert Wakefield and his publisher Johnson in 1799. Its publication, however, was delayed by Dyer's usual lack of promptness until after Wakefield's conviction and so did him no good. While, according to the title, it purports to deal with doctrines of law, its first concern is the persecution of opinion which the government was then carrying on. The most impassioned part is his appeal for a free press. It took courage to write this in 1799:

> Some who admit that thought is free are backward to allow that man should be free to publish his thoughts. But who are the men who propagate this doctrine? . . . They are selfish and narrow divines, artful politicians, corrupt lawyers. . . . Shackle opinion, restrain the press—and what will you effect? You will give confidence to absurdity and degrade wisdom. The principle goes to throw such philosophers as Bacon and Locke into shade; to silence such moralists as Helvetius, Hume, and Rousseau; it would encourage babes to prattle and triflers to dogmatize.[34]

But public opinion was by this time too much inflamed against the radicals for many to listen to reason in their defence. Even the *Monthly Review*[35] was seized with concern, criticizing him for choosing the radical philosophers as the moralists to whom mankind is most indebted, especially "at this time and in this country," though it recommended the **Address** as "good reading." But the *Gentleman's Magazine* in its hostility threw amenities to the winds in this vicious and supercilious thrust:

> As friends to this bold and disappointed writer, we see with concern that he is but too well versed in the *theory,* if not the *practice,* of libels. . . . To allow men to say what they please of each other . . . must finally lead to their doing what they please to each other. . . . No *honest* man in this country and in these times would wish to set himself as a rival of Voltaire and a propagator of opinions whose influence has been so severely felt.[36]

The two volumes of **Poems,** published in 1802 and including four critical essays, are of a very miscellaneous character in both versification and subject-matter. There are lyrics, elegies, odes, occasional poems, anacreontics, and pieces of a philosophical cast. Some of them show a lively fancy, but it does not always free itself from the trammels of mere learning. His poetry here is more rarely made the vehicle of his liberal sympathies than in the former volumes. **"On Visiting the Tomb of David Hume"** is one of his many tributes of deep respect to the great sceptic:

> . . . sagacious moralist,
> Whose lessons shine not only in thy works,
> Thy life was moral; and may I condemn
> The man of searching mind, who systems weighed
> In judgment's nicer scale, and yielded not
> His weight of faith, when he durst not believe.

"The Padlocked Lady," a long poem of thirty-three pages, is written in a happy vein for our poet, but signally fails to affect the reader at the emotional climax. It treats of the restraints put on British liberty during the war with France. The author represents himself as pursuing Freedom through the world under the conventional image of a fair woman, only at last to find her with her eyes bound by a golden bandage, her ears stopped to human cries,

> While from her lips, to seal her tongue,
> A vile, inglorious padlock hung.

The spirit of the larger patriotism is also breathed through the banalities of **"The Citizen of the World."**

By the beginning of the century it appears that practically all of Dyer's ideas which connect him with the revolutionary tradition had been written out. He seems at this time to have entered upon that long era of "calm and sinless peace" about which Lamb writes and during which most of his time was given to various scholarly endeavours, to laborious but generally unimportant projects for the booksellers, to the amenities of a bibliophile, and to the social claims of Lamb's famous literary fraternity. In fact, the ineffectiveness of reform propaganda was so conclusively shown during the early years of the century that few even of the most radical writers persisted.

In 1812 he published his *Four Letters on the English Constitution,* the last production of consequence as an expression of his political philosophy. In this book he reviews, without abating a jot of his earlier convictions, his previously expressed opinions about the principle of divine right, the sovereignty of the people, the unrepresentative status of bishops in the House of Lords, the priority of the constitution to the establishment, the defects in representation, the evils of the Corporation and Test Acts, and the fundamental simplicity of good government. He commends the suppressed reform societies for their promotion of enlarged views of the representative system and their fight for the liberty of the press. Believing with Godwin that only arbitary government can give permanence to error, Dyer is confident that with the establishment of an impartial administration of justice these societies will be restored to their former influence. He still does not hesitate to align himself openly with revolutionary political thinkers in some matters. For example, he accepts with little modification Paine's definition of a constitution as "a thing antecedent to government and laws," though he thinks Paine goes to ridiculous lengths in denying the existence of the English constitution altogether. But this is pure Paine:

> Those principles which ought to govern societies of men are deducible only from our wants, and appeal to *that divine light that lighteth every man that cometh into the world,* the primitive reason: they are not difficult to ascertain nor difficult to be understood.

He writes with his old indignation of the *Reflections,* whose author pleaded "for power against liberty, for the usurpations of establishments against the laws of nature."[37]

But for all the unadulterated radicalism of many of his ideas, George Dyer was generally very careful not to flout the English government on immediate questions of policy. The shades of speculation were more inviting to him than the platform of propaganda. Though he was intellectually hospitable toward the radical agitators, he shrank from much active participation in reform. He preferred, like Godwin, to manufacture the intellectual artillery for the radicals rather than to command a battery.

This outward caution meets us very frequently in the *Inquiry.* He does not openly advocate immediate disestablishment; in fact, he sometimes admits the expediency of an establishment. He is wary in letting his readers know just where he parts company with his intemperate friend Wakefield:

> Mr. Wakefield's sentiments on the office of the civil magistrate and on the tendency of religious establishments are, I am persuaded, the same as mine; nor do I here mean to drop any reflections on the present ruling powers.[38]

He is careful not to charge the government with the disorders against Dissenters at Birmingham in 1791, but he writes that he is "far from thinking they were not prompted by men who supposed themselves complying with the wishes of government."[39] At the conclusion of his discussion of the constitutional objections against subscription, he declares: "I am no political reformer, but an inquirer after truth." He disclaims any resentment against "the persons of our governors." He makes the admission, without being driven to it, that he has "to take shame that the hand that now writes against subscription has yet subscribed itself."

In his other writings his circumspection can be clearly traced. Sometimes his outward discretion is in amusing contrast with his inner convictions. In a passage on titles from a communication on the peculiarities of Quakers to the *Monthly Magazine,* there is a studied and almost ludicrous effort to tread the narrow path between offence to the government and faithfulness to his own convictions:

> Blackstone's comparison of a particular *form of government* to a pyramid with a broad strong base and terminating at length in a point, has been much admired. It is elegant but it is sophistical, though the excellency of his form of government I neither affirm nor deny. The same comparison has been applied to *titles,* where the sophism is still more transparent. The proper way to expose it in both cases is to appeal to nations the most enlightened, to societies the best regulated, to families the most orderly and harmonious: to inquire into the origin of titles and to trace their effects. Of the French I say nothing.[40]

In the *Address on Libels,* he is fearful lest he be thought in his defence of Wakefield "to arraign courts of justice" when his aim is "to interest the friend to humanity." Here also he tells us that, while he approves the purposes of the Constitutional Society, he "never had the honour of belonging to it." To escape the imputation of being a political undesirable, it appears that he was sometimes willing to thin his political philosophy down to the mildest kind of liberalism, as the following passage from a letter to Rickman in 1801 shows:

> How dare you call me a railer at Governments! My opinion is, I think, both modest and *generous,* viz.: that some govern too much, and too much government, sooner or later, defeats its own purposes and brings on troubles. Rulers therefore . . . should understand that

if their interest and the interest of the people are not the same, they are, so far, not standing on good and solid ground.[41]

The growth of his caution during the revolutionary decade is shown in the abridged version of the **"Ode on Liberty"** included in the *Poems* of 1802. The glowing passages on Paine and seven other contemporary radicals are omitted, while the tributes to Locke, Milton and Algernon Sidney are retained. In the later version a prayer of the version of 1792 to Liberty to aid the counsels and fight the battles of France is made to refer to England: but the tribute to the Polish patriots under Kosciusko remains. At least, his radicalism was becoming more English and less French. He was, by 1802, learning to moderate it more into conformity with the necessities of a prudential world. In **"To an Enthusiast,"**[42] he asks:

> What avail, O man, fantastic flights?
> Why muse ideal deeds,
> Heedless of what is true?

George Dyer did not stand at Armageddon and battle for the radicalism of the revolutionary era, but in his writings he did hold aloft its banner in days when its adherents were without honour in their own country. The residuum of his radicalism, after the tests to which reaction against the French Revolution exposed it, comprised much more than the mere benevolence with which his name has been so exclusively associated. He deserves an honourable place in the traditions of English liberty.

Notes

1. See the following: Mary and Charles Cowden Clarke, *Recollections of Writers* (New York, 1878), pp. 11-13. *Letters of Samuel Taylor Coleridge,* edited by Ernest Hartley Coleridge (Boston, 1895), I, 84, 93, 316-17, 363; II, 748-50. *Unpublished Letters of Samuel Taylor Coleridge,* edited by Earl Leslie Griggs (London, 1932), I, 21-2, 32-4, 102, 125. Barry Cornwall, *An Autobiographical Fragment* (Boston, 1877), pp. 77-80 and *Charles Lamb, A Memoir* (London, 1866), pp. 69-71. Joseph Cottle, *Reminiscences of Samuel Taylor Coleridge and Robert Southey* (London, 1847), pp. 155-7. William Hazlitt, *On the Look of a Gentleman* and *On the Conversation of Authors.* Leigh Hunt, *Autobiography* (New York, 1850), I, 70. *Letters of Charles and Mary Lamb,* edited by E. V. Lucas (London, 1921), I, 33, 134-5, 176, 180-3, 186-9, 209-10, 218, 234-40, 309-10, 523-4, 530, 547-8; II, 673-4, 710, 741, 847, 864-5, 925-6, 942, 975. Charles Lamb, *Oxford in the Vacation* and *Amicus Redivivus. Diary, Reminiscences, and Correspondence of Henry Crabb Robinson,* edited by Thomas Sadler (Boston, 1869), I, 39-40, 239-40; II,

472, 519. *Selections from the Letters of Robert Southey,* edited by J. W. Warter (London, 1856), I, 33, 335. T. N. Talfourd, *Final Memorials of Charles Lamb* (Philadelphia, 1855), pp. 250-2, 261-3. Orlo Williams, *Life and Letters of John Rickman* (Boston, 1912), pp. 7, 59, 82.

For modern accounts of Dyer see the following: E. V. Lucas, *Life of Charles Lamb* (London, 1921), Chapter XIV. Dudley Wright, "Charles Lamb and George Dyer," *English Review,* XXXIX, 390-7 (September 1924). G. A. Anderson, "Lamb and the Two G. D.'s," *London Mercury,* XI, 371-87 (February 1925). Edmund Blunden, "Elia's G. D.," *London Nation and Athenaeum,* XLIII, 138-9 (May 5, 1928). A. Edward Newton, *George Dyer* (1938), a privately printed brochure.

2. "On Conversations with Authors," *Collected Works of William Hazlitt,* edited by Waller and Glover (London, 1902-6), VII, 43-4.

3. *Diary, Reminiscences, and Correspondence of Henry Crabb Robinson,* I, 40.

4. Dudley Wright, for example, leaves the impression that he published only two volumes of poetry (*op. cit.,* p. 395). He published four. On George Dyer as a poet and critic, see *Letter of Charles and Mary Lamb,* edited by E. V. Lucas (New Haven, 1935), I, 141, 201, 205, 211-12, 217, 247; II, 242.

5. Good examples of both these qualities will be found in his poem "To Mr. Arthur Aikin, on taking Leave of him after a Pedestrian Tour" (*Monthly Magazine,* V, 121-3, February 1798).

6. The mistaken impression was long received that Lamb and Dyer were schoolfellows at Christ's Hospital. It seems to have been originally given by Lamb himself in a letter to Dyer 22 February 1831: "I don't know how it is, but I keep my rank in fancy still since schooldays. I can never forget that I was a deputy Grecian! And writing to you, or to Coleridge, besides affection, I feel a reverential deference as to Grecians still." Lamb, looking back upon Christ's Hospital forty-three years after, associates his deference as a deputy Grecian for Coleridge, who was a contemporary Grecian (Coleridge became a Grecian in 1788; Lamb left the school in 1789), with that for Dyer, who was a Grecian before Lamb was born. Talfourd confirmed the error by writing that Dyer "had attained the stately rank of Grecian in the venerable school of Christ's Hospital when Charles entered it" (*Op. cit.,* p. 261). Leslie Stephen repeated it after him in his article on Dyer in the *Dictionary of National Biography.*

7. Just when is uncertain. The obituary notice in the *Gentleman's Magazine* states that he engaged in "private tutoring" before he entered the home of Robinson.

8. Dyer has left us interesting observations on the reforming activities of these men in the chapter on "Dissentients" of his *History of the University and Colleges of Cambridge, including Notices relating to the Founders and Eminent Men* (1814), I, 114-29, and in his *Privileges of the University of Cambridge* (1824), II, 99, 107.

9. Dyer tells us that in the beginning of Robinson's ministry in 1757 Dissenters were regarded as "degraded characters" at Cambridge. The undergraduates were given to interrupting the meetings of Dissenters about the town so much that one parish prosecuted the offenders. On one occasion about 1769 in St. Andrew's Church "prostitutes paraded the aisles in academic habits" (*Memoirs of the Life and Writings of Robert Robinson*, p. 72).

10. *Complaints of the Poor People of England*, p. 94.

11. For the circumstances of the severance of his connexion with the dissenting society at Cambridge, to most of whom his unitarianism and his political views seemed extreme, see appendix to the second edition of the *Inquiry*.

12. *Op. cit.*, p. 81.

13. X, 77 (January 1793).

14. Thomas Christie's *Letters on the French Revolution*, James Mackintosh's *Vindiciae Gallicae*, and Joseph Priestley's *Letters to Burke* were, next to Paine's *Rights of Man*, all of which had been published in the early months of 1791, the most vigorous and able of the scores of answers to Burke's *Reflections*.

15. P. VII of the preface of the second edition. All the quotations from the *Inquiry* are taken from this edition. To Burke's contemptuous reference to the "intriguing philosophers" and "theological politicians" among the Dissenters Dyer retorts: "If under such a government as that of England, there were not among the Dissenters men of the above description, Dissenters would be contemptible pietists, dreaming monks, spiritless slaves, or unmanly sycophants" (p. 287).

16. *Cf.* Joel Barlow's idea that "a perfect state of society is a perfect state of nature."

17. Pp. 16, 13, 14, 19-22, 45. The references to the quotations above are given in the order of the quotations, since they relate to the same general theme. The same is true of the grouped references which follow.

18. Pp. 60-1.

19. P. 330.

20. P. 70.

21. Pp. 127-8, 131.

22. P. 152.

23. P. 263. On the last point he quotes with approval Mrs. Catherine Macaulay, who at the time was pursuing radical ideas with as keen a mind and as irrepressible a vigour as Mary Wollstonecraft: "That the people might learn to kiss the rod of power with devotion and, becoming slaves by principle, learn to reverence the yoke, priests were instructed to teach speculative despotism and graft on religious affections systems of civil tyranny" (p. 438).

24. Pp. 350-4. The last sentence is quoted from Barlow's *Address to the Privileged Orders*. Dyer accedes also to Barlow's quoted opinion that "the church in all ages . . . hath aimed to establish spiritualism on the ruins of civil order" (p. 400).

25. P. 254.

26. See second series, VII, 270-2.

27. P. 84.

28. Lamb has left us, in his *Oxford in the Vacation*, an inimitable tribute to this all-embracing and selfless charity of his friend: "With G. D., to be absent from the body is sometimes (not to speak it profanely) to be present with the Lord. At the very time when personally encountering thee, he passes on with no recognition or, being stopped, starts like a thing surprised—at that moment, reader, he is on Mount Tabor or Parnassus or cosphered with Plato or with Harrington, framing "immortal commonwealths," devising some plan of amelioration to thy country or thy species—peradventure meditating some individual kindness or courtesy to be done to *thee thyself*, the returning consciousness of which made him to start at thy obtruded personal presence."

29. *The Pamphleteer*, XIV, 75. The quotation is from a later printing of the *Dissertation* in *The Pamphleteer* for 1818 and 1819.

30. Pp. VII-IX.

31. Pp. 221-2.

32. The comedy was written by George Ruggles to ridicule the pedantic and barbarous cant of lawyers and was acted for the first time at Cambridge in 1614. Dyer wrote the prologue for delivery at its presentation at Westminster School in 1794.

33. XX, 472 (August 1796).

34. Pp. 114-15.

35. XXIX, 87 (May 1799).

36. LXIX, Part I, 320 (April 1799).

37. Pp. 121, 115. The quotations are taken from the third edition with additions, 1817.

38. Preface of the *Inquiry,* p. xx.

39. P. 288. The house of Joseph Prestley with the most valuable laboratory in England was burned in these riots.

40. VI, 342 (November 1798).

41. Orlo Williams, *Life and Letters of John Rickman,* p. 59.

42. *Poems,* 1802, I, 12.

Kenneth Kendall (essay date 1971)

SOURCE: Kendall, Kenneth E. "Other Contributors to the *Reflector.*" In *Leigh Hunt's* Reflector, pp. 123-58. The Hague: Mouton, 1971.

[*In the following excerpt, Kendall asserts that Dyer was not the naïve man of Lamb's essays, and that his writing in the* Reflector *is pedantic but reveals social criticism on par with Leigh Hunt's. Dyer's major articles in that publication are listed and summarized.*]

Dr. Aikin and George Dyer were the oldest of the several contributors to the *Reflector,* both belonging to a generation older than that of Lamb and Hunt. Both were minor men of letters who were ready at all times to break into print, so that a new magazine would be welcome to them. Both were well known if not prominent, and they moved in fairly broad literary circles. Dyer was an old Bluecoat boy, a fact which gave him a common background with the other alumni, but his friendship with Lamb and Coleridge and his personal nature as a "character" have given him an enduring place on the fringes of the circle of the immortals of his day. . . .

The first-hand verbal pictures of Dyer by his contemporaries depict a naïve but kindly man, an unkempt, absent-minded bookworm who wrote much but said little. He was a lovable man, but sadly in need of an influence for orderliness. After reading his 150 pages in the *Reflector,* one may be a little bored, since much of what he writes is no longer of interest. But nowhere do we get the impression of a fumbling, disordered or naïve old man. He is as sensitive to the shortcomings of the society of his day as was Leigh Hunt, yet he is more restrained and detached about them. Sometimes his points are made with less clarity than is expected in expository writing. The abundance of allusions and quotations gives his essays a pedantic cumbersomeness. Footnoting was his weakness, and the many allusions, quotations, and references attest to his bibliographical zeal.

Nine of Dyer's eleven essays in the *Reflector* are signed "An Observer", a common signature among letters to editors, and eight of them are credited to "G. Dyer" in the British Museum copy of the *Reflector.* His essays are strictly informative and in the first person, but they are unrelated to the personal essay. They usually begin with a long generalization (also a Hunt habit) before they launch into their subject matter. Dyer is never polemical but is straightforward and objective, depending for the most part on the "right reason" which he mentions and which he probably acquired, along with some of his other ideas, from Hartley. Two articles by Dyer are neither signed by him nor credited to him by Hunt.

Volume I, Number 1: "On Defects and Abuses in Public Institutions" (Signed "An Observer")

"On Opinions Respecting the English Constitution" (Signed "An Observer")

"On the Catholic Claims" (Unsigned)

Volume I, Number 2: "On the English Constitution (Continued)" (Signed "An Observer")

"On the Easiest Mode of Learning the Greek and Latin Languages, with occasional Strictures on the Greek and Latin Grammars taught in Public Schools" (Signed "An Observer")

"On the Connections and the mutual Assistance of the Arts and Sciences, and the Relation of Poetry to them all" (Signed "An Observer")

"On the Independence of Judges" (Unsigned)

Volume II, Number 3: "Defects in the English Constitution" (Signed "Observer")

Miscellaneous: "On the Bodleian Library" (Signed "An Observer")

Volume II, Number 4: "Why Are There so Few Excellent Poets?" (Signed "An Observer")

"On the best Means of promoting the Fundamental Principles of the English Constitution" (Signed "An Observer")

Dyer's first essay in the *Reflector* (I, 72-81) records some of his observations in schools and hospitals over a period of years and is probably all that was published of a projected work on the prisons and libraries of England.[1] After an introduction giving the etymology of the word *hospital* and a history of such institutions in England, he lists some of the abuses: Flogging in the public schools, charging entrance fees at free hospitals, intolerable conditions at lunatic hospitals, and the lack of full-time resident physicians at many public institutions. He is pleased to notice the recent abolition of the slave trade and the prevailing spirit of reform.

Dyer's second essay (I, 82-86) turns from defects in public institutions to defects in the English Constitution and is the first of the four *Reflector* essays which Dyer reprinted in book form in 1812 under the title *Four Letters on the English Constitution*. The essay is a collection of opinions about the Constitution, concluding that it is difficult to define because of its latent faults and because of abuse and corruption. The second installment (I, 283-297) traces the growth of the Constitution from the laws of Ethelbert in 561, the Anglo-Norman laws, and those of James I; he draws on such writers as Spelman, Cotton, William Penn, Thomas Paine, and William Blackstone. He maintains that the Constitution is no less real because it is intangible; that, since the Constitution existed before the Church of England, the Church is not part of the Constitution and citizens of all faiths should receive equal protection under it. Kingship is a trust given to one who governs by law under a contract, and the source of power is in the people. Thus Dyer follows Locke in his principle that "As men, we have a natural claim to existence, to liberty, to religion, to whatever comes under the denomination of personal rights; as members of a civil society, to frame the laws by which those rights are to be administered" (I, 287). The **"Defects in the English Constitution"** (II, 31-43) in the third of the series are two: It is defective in political liberty and in its lack of a clear statement of the prerogatives of the kingly office, an especially timely observation since George III was incapacitated and the Prince of Wales had recently taken over as Prince Regent. The fourth essay (II, 274-298) asserts that he does not wish to involve himself with reform, but since a fundamental principle of the Constitution is civil liberty, the Catholic claims should be recognized, the government should cease encroaching on the liberties of the people by bringing informations *ex officio* for libel, the Prince Regent should work for the common good rather than joining with self-seeking politicians, and the public should be assured of having full liberty of the press in reporting debates and expressing opinions. Dyer's contribution to the constitutional debates of 1812 probably caused few ripples in that already choppy sea upon which stronger crafts were being launched every day. Like Dyer, the essays are very mild, lost as he was amidst personalities more forceful, more willing to plunge into the rough waters of controversy.

Dyer's two unsigned articles, **"On the Catholic Claims"** (I, 174-207) in the first issue and **"On the Independence of Judges"** (II, 21-25) in the third are closely related to the Constitution articles, with many similarities that clearly indicate that Dyer is the author. In only one respect do these articles differ from those with his "Observer" signature: They speak with an air of authority and assume a firmness made possible, perhaps, by anonymity. But the diction, style, and ideas are Dyer's. **"On the Catholic Claims"** begins with a paragraph very similar to the opening of **"On the Defects and Abuses in Public Institutions"**. Both speak of improvements in society such as reform and the abolition of the slave trade, and they are identical in style and tone. Two phrases near the beginning of the article sound like the mild-mannered Dyer of other articles. He writes that his remarks are submitted with diffidence and he modestly asserts that "the cause of civil and religious liberty cannot be materially injured by the occasional deficiency of its advocates" (I, 174). The plethora of footnotes and citations is a Dyer characteristic. Favorite words and expressions tie this article to the rest of Dyer's contributions: "the welfare of the rising religion cemented with their blood" is a figure of speech repeated in the last of the Constitution series: "Civil and religious liberty . . . is the true cement of the English Constitution" (I, 179; II, 295). Civil liberty is the foundation upon which he bases the validity of the Catholic claims in this article and which is also stated in the final article of the serial. Finally, Dyer has a fondness for the word *nugatory*. In the article **"Defects of the English Constitution"** he uses the phrase "The political liberty of which constitution, in short, must be nugatory" (II, 35); in the present article he uses the word in the same manner three times.

The same word is one of the connecting links with the unsigned article in the third issue, **"On the Independence of Judges"**. Though the article is much shorter than most of Dyer's essays, it is Dyer in style and content and is actually an expansion of a part of his final article of the serial which said that judges and lawyers have been encroaching on the liberty of the people, especially in public libels, because of an obligation to the Crown. But Dyer says the impartiality of a judge comes from his character, not his office, and the public must depend upon juries for complete impartiality.

Except for the short piece in the third issue on the Bodleian Library (II, 209-211), the rest of Dyer's essays concern the fine arts. In the second issue (I, 332-345) he proposes **"The Easiest Mode of Learning the Greek and Latin Languages"**. He advises the student to begin with Greek because it is the older and sweeter of the two languages. Pronunciation should come first, after which one should learn the grammar and vocabulary simultaneously. **"The Connection and the Mutual Assistance of the Arts and Sciences, and the Relation of Poetry to Them All"** (I, 346-360) has a good summary of the article in its title, although his short discussion of imagination is interesting since the subject was a favorite with the Romantics. "It is the province of invention, the supreme faculty of poetic genius, to discover and to collect", but "it is the province of imagination, the very soul of poetry, to bring near distant objects, to unite them into one form, and to give them a glow, as from a painter's hand" (I, 355). He concludes with the Hartleyan idea that "All knowledge is derived from the association of ideas; and man's knowledge is in proportion to his number of ideas" (I, 360).

Dyer asserts that there are "few excellent poets" (II, 249-274) because the motives which make people write often destroy excellence, for "from muddy springs flow muddy waters"—a phrase which, curiously enough, is found in Shelley's poem, "England in 1819", as "mud from a muddy spring". "The principal reason, why . . . there have existed so few excellent poets, is, that the spring and source do not arise in majesty and true greatness" (II, 273). "Genius", he says, "is the towering eagle that soars high, sails on the whirlwind, and sees and feels vast things." (II, 270). Some poets lack the vast capability of associating ideas and the flow of imagination; poetic genius, to Dyer, is not only the vivid perception and sensibility and the ability to associate ideas in the imagination, but also the flash or illumination that comes from nowhere and ignites poetic genius, a combination of the explainable and the unexplainable, of the received impressions plus divine inspiration.

Considered in relation to other periodical essayists of his day, Dyer is "milk and water" when compared to the acidity and acrimony of a Jeffrey or even a Gilchrist; he is not interested in an argument and he avoids the rough and tumble arena of the controversial essay. His articles lack the derogation of others and the exaltation of self so typical of the critical writers of his day, and at the same time have little of the strength which could be there, even without vituperation. In the *Reflector* period Dyer was already middle-aged, his habits were established, and he was not likely to succumb to the Romantic tendency for the subjective or the self-revelatory, the confessional habit that was to become a watermark of the personal essays of Lamb, Hazlitt, DeQuincey, and Hunt. Those days were dawning, and Dyer was not only of a different temperament, but of a different age.

Note

1. P. F. Morgan, "A Note on George Dyer", *CLS Bulletin*, #136 (May 1957), p. 159.

P. M. Zall (essay date January 1974)

SOURCE: Zall, P. M. "Epitaph for George Dyer." *Charles Lamb Bulletin* 5 (January 1974): 104-09.

[*In the following essay, Zall explains how Dyer learned benevolence firsthand, overcoming his own working-class heritage through charitable aid, and by watching his mentor, Robert Robinson, preach to the rural poor.*]

If the essence of an immortal comic hero is a compound of humor, irony, and pathos, George Dyer should live forever. From his shrine in Elia's pantheon he still sheds his grace across the years—reaching for his hat but picking up the coal scuttle, sparkling in conversation with the bust of Diana in mistake for Anna Letitia Barbauld, striding directly out the Lambs' door into the New River. Dyerana still unfit for print could add much more—how, confronting a two-hole loo for the first time, he assumes the holes are meant to accommodate one's legs and sits accordingly. What true Elian cannot but laugh in memory of George Dyer?

To know George Dyer, the man, is to feel the pathos in those tales. His picking up the coal scuttle, his converse with Diana, his walk into the river were all owing to near-blindness from a lifetime's poring over dim print and faded manuscripts in dark archives where he pursued survival through hack-scholarship. Impoverished in pocket—"He would give away his last guinea" (HCR), driven to compulsive benevolence, lashed by self-doubt, he was more to be pitied than laughed at. Until 1801, when Lamb's plastic imagination began to shape the comical legend, the real George Dyer was seldom smiled upon, least of all by Fortune.

This is all the more ironic because from boyhood he was eminently blessed with benevolent friends. Son of a humble but worthy watchman of Wapping, he had been sent to Christ's Hospital at seven by a pair of benevolent Baptist neighbor ladies. At fourteen, he stood a grecian, befriended by Anthony Askew, the school's physician, whose hobby of collecting Greek manuscripts made his library a bank "on which (said Dyer) the most eminent critics, in Greek literature, at home and abroad, were very proud to draw." Given the run of that library, Dyer mixed freely with the literati there, among them another benefactor, the great Shakespearean scholar Richard Farmer, who lived with Askew while preaching at Whitehall.

Like his host, Farmer conscientiously practiced benevolence. He is on record that he would rather do without an epitaph, "He was a great preacher," if he could have one saying, "He was a kind man." When Dyer entered Emmanuel College in 1774, his fees were covered only partly by Christ Hospital funds. The balance came from some "nameless benefactor," most likely Farmer, who followed him to Emmanuel next year as Master of the College.

In his student years, Dyer knit friendships with two outspoken leaders of Dissent, his classmate Gilbert Wakefield and a fellow of Jesus College, William Frend. Because of his own dissenting mind, he would not go on for his MA which would have led to the clergy, but instead—after taking the BA in 1778—taught for a year at Dr Grimwood's academy in Dedham. Encouraged to remain, Dyer declined. He had taught for that year only to provide an annuity for his worthy father of Wapping, and now returned to Cambridge to further his education.

There he served as tutor to the twelve children of the Baptist minister Robert Robinson, "not simply as tutor to his family (he said) but with the view of profiting by his doctrine and learned conversation." Robinson was pre-eminent for his doctrine of benevolence and practising what he preached:

> I feel three pounds gained honestly by the sale of a fat bullock produce more fire in my spirit than all the pretty but poor tassels and spangles can give me. With three pounds I can set fire to ten cold hearts, frozen with infirmity, widowhood, poverty, and fear.

His preaching at the Stoneyard Baptist Chapel would draw 200 from the University alone, and his fame was international. But Robinson's large family kept him close to home, farming 200 acres at Chesterton, dealing in corn and coals, and operating the local ferry.

Still, domestic distractions did not deter Robinson from preaching twice, sometimes thrice, every Sunday, lecturing Sunday evenings and some weekdays, "not only in the evening but at six in the morning," adjusting his schedule to the occupational needs of his congregation. Religiously he would visit the cottagers, smoking his pipe in the chimney corner, discoursing with equal authority on faith, crops, or politics. At least once a month he would travel to outlying villages for public discourses in homes, barns, orchards, paddocks, wherever the faithful could flock.

In 1786 he dictated sixteen of these discourses for publication, "a sort of poor man's broom to sweep his almshouse." As *Village Discourses,* delivered in barnyard-rough rhetoric, they were perfectly suited to the understandings of "the lowest ranks of society." Reprinted at least four times before his death in 1790, they represented for Dyer the essence of Robinson's Christianity. Concluding his biography, he summed up the pattern of this contemporary Christian hero by way of epitaph:

> An amiable, a benevolent, a generous, a learned man, a true philanthropist . . . an invariable friend to liberty.

After Robinson's death, Dyer remained in Cambridge for two years, teaching in the village school at Swavesy while preparing his mentor's works for posthumous publication—the *History of Baptism* (1790) and *Ecclesiastical Researches* (1792). Study under Robinson led also to a book of his own, *An Inquiry into the Nature of Subscription to the Thirty-nine Articles* published by Joseph Johnson in 1792, a discursive work of 439 pages showing that religious and political restrictions were inconsistent with natural rights, free inquiry, the Constitution, and Christian doctrine. The topic was particularly timely in 1792 when Cambridge authorities—including Dr Farmer—were persecuting William Frend as a symbol of campus Dissent. As a Dissenter himself, the pupil and friend of leading Dissenters, Dyer's residence in Cambridge grew precarious.

The French Revolution had excited him—"I experienced energies and exertions by no means congenial to my settled habits of retirement." Now the persecution of Frend mobilized his energies as if in answer to the call of the American Jacobin Joel Barlow: "It is the duty of humanity, to save our fellow-creatures from falling into snares, even those that are spread for them by government." Forsaking his rural retreat, he entrenched at Clifford's Inn, where he would remain for the duration of his life, subsisting on proceeds from reviewing or writing on demand, but also publishing books of his own designed to keep his fellow-creatures from falling into snares, especially those set by government.

Heralding his arrival, he published a thin volume of *Poems* dedicated to Frend and containing an **"Ode on Peace"** celebrating the other Cambridge reformers past and present, along with a complementary **"Ode on Liberty"** celebrating the radical reformers of London, like Richard Price and Tom Paine, whose ranks he had now joined. Then the next year, 1793, he published *Complaints of the Poor,* exposing political snares that the state set for the poor. Taking his lead from Robinson's *Discourses,* he wrote in plain style suited to the poorer classes ("as they will be the principal persons in my eye"), and massed statistics and interviews as well as his beloved books to show how "the *common* people" were kept enthralled because the government kept them in ignorance and thus in apathetic submission. He proposed one solution in free, universal education that would bring rich and poor into the same classroom together and, by means of this integration harmonize their hearts—"The principle which equalizes man dignifies and exalts him."

In 1795 he advanced additional solution in a sequel, *Dissertation on the Theory and Practice of Benevolence,* now writing in a style more suited to middle and upper classes. He urged them to try various vents for benevolent feelings—establishing workhouses, charity schools, Sunday schools, and relief societies. In one chapter, he called for subscribing money to help leaders of reform societies—Thomas Hardy, Horne Tooke, John Thelwall—then on trial for treason. With due circumspection, considering the trials were still in progress, he based his appeal not on politics but on the inconvenience and loss suffered by the defendants as private persons.

In 1796, after those defendants had been gloriously acquitted by a popular jury, Dyer put circumspection behind him and expounded his own political views in his *Memoirs of Robinson.* Returning to the plain style as a badge of democracy, he explained that he was imitating Robinson's *Village Discourses* where the "language of equality" was most appropriate to a "testimony to liberty." In the biography itself he showed that Robinson's views and thus his own were like those of Tom Paine's in seeing government as "an evil that the wickedness of mankind renders necessary," but differed from Paine's in believing that benevolence could correct the inequalities and imperfections inherent in the social state.

In 1797, Dyer carried on in the pattern of his master with another volume of verse, *The Poet's Fate,* a dialogue about how difficult it was to write poetry in an age of party faction. Patent propaganda, the poem celebrated once again the leaders in radical politics and religion, but this time included allusions to young writers rising in their ranks. When he could not squeeze their names into a line of verse, he would generously mention them in explanatory footnotes—succumbing to what Coleridge called DYERHOEA EXPLANATORIA—"a disease not quite so bad to the Patient as Water on the Brain, but more troublesome to his Friends."

An especially unfortunate instance of this disease erupts in a footnote to these lines, as the "Poet" asks his friend "X" how one can survive in such trying times and "X" advises learning to starve:

> When hungry, smoke your pipe, or say your prayers:
> Or plough, in learned pride, the Atlantic main,
> Join PANTISOCRACY'S* harmonious train . . .

The footnote to the last line bears repeating at full length:

> A few years ago some young men of Oxford and Cambridge formed the design of going to America, in order to realise a *pantisocracy*; they intended to devote themselves to literature and agriculture; to accumulate no property, but to have a common stock. Of this number were two very ingenious modern poets, ROBERT SOUTHEY, the author of an epic poem, entitled Joan of Arc, and other poems; and S T COLERIDGE, author of a volume of poems. These two young poets are equally distinguished for their ardent love of liberty; the former more remarkable for his powers of description, and for exciting the softer feelings; the latter for a rich and powerful imagination. In connection with these names, I cannot forbear mentioning those of three young men, who have given early proofs, that they can strike the true chords of poesy; W WORDSWORTH, author of Descriptive Sketches in Verse, taken during a Pedestrian Tour in the Italian, Grison, Swiss and Savoyard Alps; a poem that proves the writer to possess uncommon skill in descriptive poetry; C LLOYD, author of a volume of very elegant sonnets; and CHARLES LAMB, author of some tender sonnets in COLERIDGE'S Poems, of a fine poem in CHARLES LLOYD'S Poems, and of sonnets in an excellent publication, entitled the Monthly Magazine.
>
> (pp. 26-28)

Apologising to Southey, Dyer explained, "I could not bring in Wordsworth, and Lloyd, and Lamb but I put them in a note." "That man," said Southey, "is all benevolence."

But this benevolence, calculated to do good, did immeasurable harm. In concluding its final issue (9 July 1798), the *Anti-Jacobin's* "New Morality" seized upon Dyer's note for one of its most devastating quatrains—

> And ye five other wandering Bards, that move
> In sweet accord of harmony and love,
> Colerdige and Southey, Lloyd and Lambe and Co.
> Tune all your mystic harps to praise Lepaux!—

unjustly endowing Lamb and Lloyd with political notoriety that dogged their days.

In 1799 Dyer, though impoverished, issued *An Address . . . on Libels* at his own expense, "Printed for the Author." (The Huntington Library copy includes a handwritten interpolation, "and sold by him," as though Dyer was trying to shield anyone else from prosecution for selling a libellous book.) The preface claims that though the book had been written over two years, its "suspicions" had been proven by the trials for seditious libel recently decided against his old friend Gilbert Wakefield and his old publisher Joseph Johnson. Wakefield, found guilty of libelling the Bishop of Llandaff, and Johnson, found guilty of selling that libel, both now languished in prison. "The business is over," said Dyer, "and the circumstances I pass in silence, lest I be thought to arraign a court of justice, while I am to interest the friend to humanity" (p. v).

In describing the circumstances of the case that he uses to illustrate his general principles, Dyer acknowledges its similarity to Wakefield's case, but insists, "The principles, on which I shall proceed, will be of a general character, and look beyond the present moment." In passing, he confesses that "retired students" like Wakefield (and himself) "are apt to form opinions that the world reckons extravagant; and an extravagant opinion *sometimes* (I am no advocate for all extravagancies) only means an opinion not fully comprehended" (p. 20). After expressing the hope that some day men will recognize tyrants as tyrannical, unjust judges as unjust, and perfidious priests as perfidious, he concludes with another disclaimer: "I am not here speaking concerning any character in England—my allusions are not directed to any particular quarter:—they are general observations and to be illustrated by the varieties of human character" (p. 119).

In 1800 midst an obituary of the poet William Mason, he erupted, "The cause of reform is the cause of human improvement and will work its own way, whatever becomes of timid poets and short-sighted politicians," yet when he issued his collected *Poems,* it became quite clear that his own fight for freedom was now tempered with timidity. The lines on Pantisocracy that had appeared in *The Poet's Fate* two years earlier were revised to read:

Or plough, in conscious pride, the Atlantic main,
And hail adventurous, Columbia's* plain . . .

The original footnote was replaced by a historical note:

*The first persons that went to England to settle in America, were the Puritans, who afterwards split into different sects, all disaffected to the established religion of their own country, or persecuted for their opposition to it.

(p. 213)

The whole of *The Poet's Fate* was now cleansed of allusions to contemporary politics. Allusions to younger friends of freedom were now mere references to their poetry. A note to the line "Paint the domestic grief, or social bliss" says, "Characteristic of a volume of poems, the joint production of Coleridge, Lloyd and Lamb" (p. 294). A note to the line "Wake, to simpler theme, the lyric lay" simply names *Lyrical Ballads*. Dyer's revisions thus covered his friends as well as himself.

Explaining some of his revisions, the preface said that "the principles of freedom are too sacred, to be surrendered for trifles; too noble, to be exchanged for song"; they required "nobler strains" (p.xxxviii). But Dyer also revised his early political odes, deleting contemporary references while retaining allusions to historical heroes, Milton, Locke, James Harrington, Algernon Sidney. This was more than merely keeping allusions up to date. It was sounding retreat. Dyer made no secret of his timidity, blaming it on an old cast of mind rather than fear of reprisals: "Of early habits of indolence, the effects of which I still feel powerfully, my pursuits and manners are such, as rather belong to a solitary bookworm" (p. xxxii).

With the *Poems* still at the printer's, Dyer suddenly realized the preface contained a statement that might have been misleading—"The public must not be misled!" At an expense he could not afford, he stopped the presses. When the volume eventually appeared in 1802, the revised preface omitted only one statement that could have misled anyone:

A sufficient degree of generosity is found in the world to encourage a useful pursuit . . . the violence of party cannot controul it.

The fate of Frend, Wakefield, Johnson and others had shown otherwise. Henceforth Dyer would follow his own pursuits wrapped in the harmless minutiae of hack scholarship for the rest of his life.

"If I had to write his epitaph," mused "Barry Cornwall" in 1864, "I should say that he was neither much respected nor at all hated; too good to dislike, too inactive to excite great affection; and that he was as simple as the daisy, which we think we admire, and daily tread under foot" (*Memoir of Lamb,* p. 71). Yet his legendary benevolence remained boundless, even to generously submitting to the jokes of Lamb and his friends.

That he was conscious of being a butt is abundantly clear, even before the oblique complaint about his sharp portrait in "Oxford in Vacation"—"You possess so *much wit,* and *that person* so many infirmities, it seemed to be calculated to do what you never intended to do." Thus Dyer at 75. But even thirty years earlier, he had written a stanza accepting his role as Falstaff to Lamb's Hal:

As the Lambs doctored him for malnutrition, Charles played amanuensis, copying out verses for Dyer's *Poems,* including this stanza from **"Democritus Junior; or, the Laughing Philosopher"**—

Thus, Falstaff-like, I'll live and die,
  Laugh long as I can see;
And when Death's busy hand shall close my eye,
  This bag of jokes I leave the doctor's fee:
Then, Doctor, when I'm dead, laugh thou, and think
  of me.

Overstepping his bounds as amanuensis, Lamb crossed it out as (he told Rickman), "An abortive Stanza; very precious—& very false."[1] But when the poem appeared in print, Dyer had restored those lines—a very epitaph of his own.

Note

1. Reproduced from Huntington Library manuscript RS 1250 by gracious permission of the Librarian.

Donald Reiman (essay date 1979)

SOURCE: Reiman, Donald H. Introduction to *The Poet's Fate,* by George Dyer. In *Odes and The Poet's Fate,* pp. v-xii. New York: Garland, 1979.

[*In the following introduction, Reiman summarizes Dyer's life and discusses his poetry, concluding that the poet was one of the bright lights of the era, if not its best poet.*]

George Dyer (1755-1841), friend of Southey, Coleridge, and Wordsworth and beloved by Charles Lamb and William Hazlitt, was one of the great "originals" of his age—a man who, had Thomas Love Peacock known him, would certainly have graced one of his novels of talk as a lovable eccentric. Anecdotes about Dyer fill the letters and essays of Lamb, the writings of Hazlitt, the letters of Southey, and the journals of Henry Crabb Robinson. Dyer wrote a memoir of his friend the Reverend Robert Robinson (1796) that Wordsworth regarded as one of the finest biographies in the language. He was a meticulous scholar, who contributed "whatever was original" to a large series of classical texts published by Valpy, and an assiduous antiquarian, who wrote a *History of the University and Colleges of Cambridge, including Notices Relating to the Founders and Eminent Men* (2 vols., 1814).

Dyer was born in London's Wapping district, the East End shipping slum, where his father was a watchman (the *DNB* [*Dictionary of National Biography*] account, mainly taken from Crabb Robinson, can be expanded greatly by consulting the letters, journals, and publications of Dyer's friends). Sent first to school by charitable women in a dissenting congregation, Dyer was nominated at the age of seven to Christ's Hospital (the endowed charity school that was later the alma mater of Coleridge, Lamb, and Hunt, among others of note). There he was befriended by Anthony Askew (*DNB*) and rose to the head of his class.

As a "Grecian" at Christ's Hospital, he was aided to enter Emmanuel College, Cambridge, in 1774. There Dyer won the favor of Richard Farmer, Master of Emmanuel and Vice-Chancellor of the University. Taking his B.A. in 1778, Dyer first served in 1779 as "usher" (assistant teacher) in a grammar school at Dedham, Essex. He then returned to Cambridge to tutor the children of the Rev. Robert Robinson (1735-1790), a leading Baptist and Unitarian clergyman and political liberal who had a profound influence on scores of Cambridge students. Dyer also won the respect of others in liberal Dissenting circles, including William Frend, Joseph Priestley, Gilbert Wakefield, and Anna Laetitia Aikin Barbauld (the latter two of whom assisted him financially from time to time).

E. V. Lucas' interesting chapter on Dyer in his *Life of Charles Lamb* ([1905], I, 144-167) quotes a full account by Dyer (from the *Mirror of Literature,* XXXVIII) of his service as usher in two schools during his early days. In 1791, after Robert Robinson's death (1790), Dyer was employed as an usher at Dr. Ryland's school at Northampton, where he edited unfinished works by Robinson and where he and John Clarke (later Keats's schoolmaster and father of Charles Cowden Clarke) were friends and rivals for the hand of Ryland's stepdaughter, who married Clarke. Charles Cowden Clarke tells how, after his father's death, Dyer

> asked for a private conference with me, told me of his youthful attachment for my mother, and inquired whether her circumstances were comfortable, because in case, as a widow, she had not been left well off he meant to offer her his hand. Hearing that in point of money she had no cause for concern, he begged me to keep secret what he had confided to me, and he himself never made farther allusion to the subject.
>
> (Lucas, *Life of Charles Lamb,* I, 149)

Dyer's chance for a career in the church having been closed by his unorthodox beliefs, he addressed the philosophical basis of the problem in a pamphlet, *Inquiry into the Nature of Subscription to the Thirty-Nine Articles* (1789; enlarged ed., 1792). With the rising concern for social issues stimulated by the French Revolution, Dyer issued prose works entitled *The Complaints of the Poor People of England* (1793), *Account of New South Wales and the State of the Convicts* (1794), and *A Dissertation on the Theory and Practice of Benevolence* (1795; reprinted 1813), and in 1796 his masterpiece, *Memoirs of the Life and Writings of Robert Robinson.* In 1797 he published *The Poet's Fate,* which proved to be his most interesting poetic work.

Dyer, as *The Poet's Fate* illustrates, was far more a scholar and antiquarian than a poet. He took more interest in gathering the information about poets that fills his notes than in composing his original poem. To Dyer (Lamb once told Coleridge) "All Poems are *good* Poems. . . . *All* men are *fine Geniuses*" (Lamb, *Letters,* ed. Edwin W. Marrs, Jr., I [1975], 240). Such an attitude had definite limitations, as Lamb wrote to Wordsworth on April 26, 1819, while thanking him for *Peter Bell* and saying that he had delivered the gift copy Wordsworth intended for Dyer:

> To G. D. a poem is a poem . . . for I do not think he has the most distant guess of the possibility of one poem being better than another. The Gods by denying him the very faculty itself of discrimination have effectually cut off every seed of envy in his bosom. But with envy, they excided Curiosity also, and if you wish the copy again . . . I think I shall be able to find it again for you—on his third shelf, where he stuffs his presentation copies, uncut [i.e., unopened], in shape and manner resembling a lump of dry dust. . . . I confess I never had any scruple in taking *my own* again wherever I found it, . . . and by this means one Copy of "my Works" served for G. D. and with a little dusting was made over to my good friend Dr. Stoddart.
>
> (Lamb, *Letters,* ed. E. V. Lucas, [1935], II, 242)

In one of his notes to *The Poet's Fate,* Dyer not only praised the aborted experiment in Pantisocracy, but also praised Southey, Coleridge, Wordsworth, Lamb, and Lloyd as up-and-coming writers, thus providing the first united notice of five writers who would eventually be grouped by a variety of commentators, from the satirists of *The Anti-Jacobin* (1797-1798) to modern literary historians.

Dyer lived in cheap lodgings at Clifford's Inn, Fleet Street, from 1792 until his death. He supported himself chiefly by writing for liberal periodicals, including Joseph Johnson's *Analytical Review,* the *Critical Review,* Leigh Hunt's *Reflector,* Southey's and Joseph Cottle's *Annual Anthology,* and Richard Phillips' *Monthly Magazine.* He also contributed biographical sketches of contemporaries to the volumes that Phillips published annually under the title *Public Characters.*

Dyer was so deeply involved in biographical, as well as bibliographical, research in preparing his *History of the University and Colleges of Cambridge* . . . (2 vols., 1814) that I suspect he also contributed to the excellent, anonymous volume entitled *A Biographical Dictionary of the Living Authors of Great Britain and Ireland* (London: Henry Colburn, 1816), the best authors' "who's who" of the period. Though it was dedicated to the Prince Regent, not only was the volume printed by A. J. Valpy, for whom Dyer edited 141 volumes of classical texts between 1809 and 1831, but the biographical sketch of Dyer himself shows no sign of having been written by an objective or unfriendly hand, and it contains detailed information not available in any other biographical sketch:

> Dyer, George, A.B. of Clifford's Inn. This gentleman, a popular writer of considerable genius, and a pleasing poet, was educated at Christ's Hospital, and at Emanuel College, Cambridge. Mr. D. was intended for the church, but having for conscientious motives relinquished all hopes of ecclesiastical preferment, he connected himself with the Baptists and for some years appeared as a preacher in the meeting-houses of various classes of dissenters. He then repaired to the metropolis, where he was at first, for a short time, engaged as a reporter of the Debates of the H. of Commons, and has since employed himself in the business of private instruction, and in writing for Reviews and other periodical works.
>
> (p. 104)

In listing Dyer's publications, the account also adds one not recorded by *DNB, NCBEL* [*New Cambridge Bibliography of English Literature*], or any other bibliography of his works: **"An English Prologue and Epilogue to the Latin comedy of Ignoramus, written by Geo. F. Ruggle, Fellow of Clare Hall, Cambridge, during the reign of K. James I. with notes relating to modern times, 8vo. 1797."** . . .

As a man of letters, Dyer's desire for perfection would not allow him to publish anything that he had second thoughts about. This penchant caused him, sometime ca. 1799-1800, to cancel and have entirely reset (at his expense) an eighty-to-ninety-page preface to his *Poems* that had already been printed. This folly of a poor man led Southey, who dearly loved Dyer ("George the First," as he was called to distinguish him from George Burnett, another character in their circle), to dub him "Cancellarius Magnus" or Lord Chancellor (Southey, *New Letters,* ed. Kenneth Curry [1965], I, 242). In October 1799 Southey wrote to Coleridge that Gilbert Wakefield had devised

> a plan for making George Dyer comfortable—that is his friends were to hold themselves ready to supply him to the amount of a hundred a year, but George was not to know it, for if he did he would always anticipate his resources—and where he publishes one book pub-

lish three, for it seems it is his everlasting corrections of the press that perpetually keep him in debt.

(Southey, *New Letters,* I, 202)

As Lamb found late in 1801, however, Dyer required more than an ample annuity to keep him comfortable, for—absentminded intellectual and antiquarian that he was—the "poor heathen" became sick and nearly died because, as Lamb was informed by Dyer's "little dirty Neice," unless Dyer "dines out he subsists on teas & gruels." Lamb thereupon forced Dyer back from malnutrition to health by persuading Dyer to dine with him each day and, because Lamb was also poor, to pay him a shilling per meal (Lamb, *Letters,* ed. Marrs, II [1976], 28-38).

Besides being feckless about his sustenance, Dyer was also oblivious of the niceties of personal and domestic cleanliness. Writing to Rickman in November 1801, Lamb tells that "G. Dyer . . . has emigrated to Enfield, where some rich man, that has got two country Houses, allows him the use of a very large one, with a Library . . . by *use,* in a sentence back, I mean dirting & littering" (*Letters,* ed. Marrs, II, 33). Lamb, thinking that Dyer needed a wife to take care of him, tried to stir up a romance between Dyer and Elizabeth Ogilvy Benger (1778-1827; her poem against the slave trade is included in this series in a volume of James Montgomery's works). He apparently succeeded in stimulating Dyer's imagination ("He talks of marrying . . ." Lamb, *Letters,* ed. Marrs, II, 38) but not in arousing the lady's interest ("G. Dyer is in love with an Ideot, who loves a Doctor, who is incapable of loving any thing but himself" [*ibid.,* II, 61]). That Lamb's instincts were right was demonstrated in 1825 when Dyer attracted the notice of a Mrs. Mather, widow of a solicitor who lived in Clifford's Inn, who married him and greatly improved his health, happiness, and cleanliness. Crabb Robinson says that Dyer's wife had earlier been his laundress and that she was illiterate; Thomas Sadler, the nineteenth-century editor of *Diary, Reminiscences, and Correspondence of Henry Crabb Robinson,* doubts Robinson's account because Mrs. Dyer (who died in May 1861 in her hundredth year) had married three times before, including the solicitor Mather. But inasmuch as she chose to marry Dyer in order to take care of him, there is no reason to doubt Robinson's firsthand testimony; illiterate or not, she may have earlier married the solicitor to take care of *him,* and while an indigent widow she could have served as Dyer's laundress before deciding that he was a man she wished to live with. In his last few years Dyer went blind, and—writes Crabb Robinson—"I used occasionally to go on a Sunday morning to read to him. A poor man used to render him that service for sixpence an hour" (Robinson, *Diary, Reminiscences,* ed. Sadler, 3rd. ed. [1872], I, 35; Robinson, *On Books and Their Writers,* ed. Edith J. Morley [1938], I, 5). And Matilda Betham (q.v.) was reading to Dyer at the time of his death, March 2, 1841 (E. V. Lucas, *The Life of Charles Lamb,* I, 167). These friends might have performed this loving service, but Dyer would hardly have had to hire someone to read to him had Mrs. Dyer been literate.

In any case, the marriage was a happy one; Lamb wrote to Southey on August 9, 1825: "G. Dyer is in the height of an uxorious paradise. His honeymoon will not wane till he wax cold. Never was a more happy pair, since Acme and Septimus, and longer" (Lamb, *Letters,* ed. Lucas, III, 23). Crabb Robinson also attests to Dyer's happiness, reporting that Dyer told him, "Mrs. Dyer is a woman of excellent natural sense, but she is not literate."

Lamb's Elia essays contain two detailed portraits of Dyer—one at the end of "Oxford in the Vacation," which depicts him as an antiquarian researcher ("With long poring, he is grown almost into a book.") and the other in "Amicus Redivivus," which tells the tragicomical story of how Dyer, nearsighted and (though Lamb could not know it) on his way to becoming blind, left Lamb's cottage on the New River at Islington, walked into the river, and almost drowned. Lamb—though he also quoted approvingly lines from one of Dyer's poems at the end of his "Recollections of Christ's Hospital" (1813) and gloried in his friendship with "the gallless and single-minded Dyer" in his "Letter of Elia to Robert Southey" (1823)—apparently hurt Dyer's feelings, for on February 22, 1831, he had to write to Dyer to explain that "I never writ of you but *con amore.* That if any allusion was made to your near-sightedness, it was not for the purpose of mocking an infirmity, but of connecting it with scholar-like habits . . . (Lamb, *Letters,* ed. Lucas, III, 303-304). Hazlitt, with less humor and awareness of the ridiculous than Lamb possessed, always took Dyer seriously and honored him without condescension. Perhaps William Hazlitt, then, should be given the last word in a portrait of Dyer, whose kindness of heart, dedication to truth, and uncompromised integrity he so honored:

> A man may have the manners of a gentleman without having the look, and he may have the character of a gentleman, in a more abstracted point of view, without the manners. The feelings of a gentleman, in this higher sense, only denote a more refined humanity—a spirit delicate in itself, and unwilling to offend, either in the greatest or the smallest things. This may be coupled with absence of mind, ignorance of forms, and frequent blunders. But the will is good. The spring of gentle offices and true regards is untainted. A person of this stamp blushes at an impropriety he was guilty of twenty years before, though he is, perhaps, liable to repeat it tomorrow. He never forgives himself for even a slip of the tongue, that implies an assumption of superiority over any one. In proportion to the concessions made to him, he lowers his demands. He gives the wall to the beggar: but does not always bow to great men. This class of character has been called "God Almighty's gentlemen."

> ("On the Look of a Gentleman," *The Plain Speaker,* in Hazlitt, *Works,* ed. P. P. Howe, XII [1931], 219)

Dyer as a man, if not as a poet, remains one of the bright lights in the Romantic Context.

Harriet Jump (essay date April 1987)

SOURCE: Jump, Harriet. "'Snatch'd Out of the Fire': Lamb, Coleridge, and George Dyer's Cancelled Preface." *Charles Lamb Bulletin* 58 (April 1987): 54-66.

[*In the following excerpt, originally presented as a lecture on March 1, 1986, Jump speaks in detail about the fate and revisions of Dyer's cancelled preface, using the perspective of Lamb's and Coleridge's amused and critical comments.*]

Born in Wapping, the son of a watchman, in 1755, Dyer was twenty years older than Lamb, seventeen years older than Coleridge. In other words, he belonged to an earlier generation—a fact which becomes obvious when one starts to examine the style of his poetry and the tenor of his literary criticism, both of which are firmly rooted in the eighteenth century. He was educated at Christ's Hospital and Emmanuel College Cambridge. After his graduation in 1778, he worked as an usher at Dedham and later Northampton Grammar Schools, and also for a period as tutor to the family of the reforming baptist minister Robert Robinson. He settled in London in 1792, and remained there for a number of years, actively involved in the early-mid 1790s with political societies and writing a number of political pamphlets, while supporting himself mainly by tutoring and hack-journalism. His chief obsession, however, was the pursuit of knowledge; an obsession which was to be a doubtful blessing when it came to pursuing his literary and critical activities, as we shall see. He met Coleridge in 1794, and, probably through Coleridge, Lamb and Southey sometime during the next year or two.

As far as Lamb's surviving correspondence is concerned, the episode which forms the subject of this paper makes its first appearance in a letter which Lamb wrote to Thomas Manning on August 9 1800.[1] The letter, which is rather jocularly risqué, is dominated by the themes of pregnancy and birth. Lamb starts with a paragraph of semi-serious benediction on the newly-born infant of Charles and Sophia Lloyd, and moves on to the news that 'Coleridge is settled with his Wife (with a child in her Guts) . . . at Keswick' (Marrs I, 221). Literal births now suggest the idea of metaphorical ones: Wordsworth and Coleridge are said to have 'contriv'd to spawn a new volume of Lyrical Balads [sic] which is to see the Light in about a month . . .'; and finally, Lamb goes on,

> George Dyer too—that good natur'd Heathen—is more than 9 months gone with his Twin volumes of Ode, pastoral, sonnet, Elegy, Spenserian, Horatian, akensidish, and Masonic verse—Clio prosper the birth—it will be twelve shillings out of somebody's pocket . . .
>
> (Marrs I, 222).

Dyer was indeed a good deal 'more than 9 months gone' with his poetical project. As early as October 1796—almost four years before Lamb's letter—he had announced in the *Monthly Magazine* that he was 'preparing a course of publications—satire, odes and elegies' to display his 'poetical talents'. The first two of these, he confidently asserted, 'will shortly make their appearance under the title of *Poet's Fate* and "Poetic Sympathies"'.[2] Although the *Poet's Fate* did in fact appear alone in 1797, there was no further sign of the rest of this ambitious project until, slightly more than two years later, the *Monthly* carried an apology:

> Mr. Dyer, in consequence of unforeseen engagements, and the advice of his friends, has been obliged to alter the plan of his Poetical Publications . . . the first volume will appear next month
>
> (*MM* (Nov. 1798) 373).

This announcement appeared in November 1798; and later in the same month Lamb wrote to Southey that he was being 'lectured' by Dyer on 'the distinguishing qualities of the Ode, the Epigram, and the Epic' and that Dyer was correcting the proof sheets of his lyrics (Marrs I, 151). However, another seven months went by before another long apology was printed in the *Monthly* stating that the publication was now to be 'delayed to the winter season' (*MM* (June 1799) 349). Even if Lamb was calculating the length of Dyer's gestation period from the appearance of this announcement, made in June 1799, his 'more than 9 months' was something of an understatement, since fourteen months had elapsed by the time of his August letter to Manning.

In August 1800, however, it really did seem possible that Dyer's works were about to see the light of day. On the 14th, Lamb wrote to Coleridge in Keswick:

> I must announce to you, who doubtless in your remote part of the Island have not heard Tidings of so great a Blessing, that George Dyer hath prepared two ponderous volumes, full of Poetry & Criticism—they impend over the town, and are threaten'd to fall in the Winter . . .
>
> (Marrs I, 226)

Lamb was obviously pleased with the way in which he had described the derivative nature of the poems to Manning ('Spenserian, Horatian, akensidish and Ma-

sonic'), since he repeated the same phrases almost verbatim to Coleridge. He also added a description of the contents of the second volume, which is, he says,

> all Criticism, wherein Dyer demonstrates to the entire satisfaction of the literary world, in a way which must silence all reply for ever, that the Pastoral was introduced by Theocritus & polished by Virgil & Pope—that Gray & Mason (who always hunt in couples in George's brain) have a good deal of poetical fire and true lyric genius; that Cowley was ruined by excess of wit . . . that Charles Lloyd, Charles Lamb and Wm Wordsworth in later days have struck the true chords of Poesy . . .
>
> (Marrs I, 226).

Again, Lamb seems to have been pleased with this periphrastically ironic way of saying that Dyer's volume of criticism contains nothing new or interesting whatsoever, since he echoed it virtually word for word in a letter to Manning on the 21st. To this letter, however, he added further details, evidently gleaned from a visit of Dyer's the night before. Dyer has, it seems,

> touch'd most *deeply* upon the Drama—comparing the English with the modern German stage, their merits and defects . . .
>
> (Marrs I, 229).

Feeling certain that Dyer was somewhat unqualified to discuss these matters, Lamb goes on,

> I modestly enquir'd what plays he had read. I found by George's reply that he *had* read Shakespeare, but that was a great while since . . . (Beaumont & Fletcher, Massinger, Ben Jonson, Shirley, Marlowe, Ford, & the worthies of Dodsley's Collection he confess'd he had read none of them, but profest an *intention* of looking thro' them all, so as to be able to *touch* upon them in his book . . .
>
> (Marrs I, 229).

This rather worrying insight into Dyer's research and composition habits makes it clear that, despite the fast-approaching publication date, his volume of criticism was still far from complete[3]; and Dyer was evidently only too prone to distractions from the serious business of writing it. Indeed, the purpose of this letter from Lamb to Manning is to request for Dyer a copy of Manning's *Introduction to Arithmetic and Algebra* (2 vols.; 1796-1798), since, says Lamb, Dyer is 'just now diverted from the pursuit of the Bell letters by a mathematical paradox which has 'seized violently on [his] Pericranic . . . it is necessary for his health that he should speedily come to a resolution of his doubts'. (Marrs i, 228).

More problems were to follow. On August 26th, Dyer's mathematical ponderings were temporarily displaced by a sudden pressing need to obtain a copy of an obscure

1400 line epic, 'the Epigoniad, by one Wilkie'[4] (Marrs I, 231); while the September issue of the *Monthly,* in addition to a by now predictable announcement that

> The poems of Mr. Dyer are printed, but . . . they will not be published, for obvious reasons, until the winter
>
> *(MM* (Sept. 1800) 157),

contains evidence of further distractions in the form of a letter from Dyer to the Magazine describing in some detail 'a singular kind of verse in the Greek Anthology' (*MM* (Sept. 1800) 134); and another letter on the same subject appears in the October issue (*MM* (Oct. 1800) 212).

On September 22nd, Lamb described a dinner which he and Dyer had been given by an eccentric Dr. Anderson. During the course of the evening the doctor had managed to let fall another 'spark' into the 'inflammable matter' of Dyer's brain, this time in the form of a chance remark about mediaeval Scottish writers, which immediately became

> the dominant sounds in George's pia mater, and their buzzings exclude Politics, Criticism, and Algebra, the Late Lords of that Illustrious Lumber room—
>
> (Marrs I, 238).

Despite all these forays into the more abstruse fields of human knowledge, however, Dyer finally succeeded in getting his volume of criticism (by now referred to as a Preface) actually printed, probably by early December. All, however, was not yet well, as Lamb's letter to Manning of December 27 makes clear:

> At length George Dyer's Phrenesis has come to a crisis, he is raging and furious mad.—I waited upon the Heathen Thursday was a sevn'ight . . . the first symptom which struck my eye, and gave me incontrovertible proof of the fatal truth was a pair of Nankeen Pantaloons, four times too big for him, which the said Heathen did pertinaciously affirm to be *new.*—They were absolutely ingrained with the accumulated dirt of ages. But he affirmed them to be clean. He was going to visit a Lady that was nice about those things, and that's the reason he wore nankeen that day—. And then he danced and capered, and fidgeted, and pulled up his pantaloons, and hugged his intolerable flannel vestment closer about his poetic Loins . . . then he caught at a proof sheet, and catched up a Laundresse's bill instead, made a dart at Bloomfield 's poems, and threw them in agony aside—. I could not bring him to one direct reply, he could not maintain his jumping mind in a right line for the tithe of a moment by Clifford's Inn Clock—he must go to the Printer's immediately—the most unlucky accident—he had struck off five hundred impressions of his Poems, which were ready for delivery to subscribers—and the Preface must all be expunged—there were 80 Pages of Preface, and not till that morning he had discovered that in the very first page of said preface he had set out with a principle of criticism fundamentally wrong, which vitiated all his

following reasoning—the preface must be expunged, altho' it cost him £30——the lowest calculation taking in paper and printing—. In vain have his real friends remonstrated against this. Midsummer madness—. George is as obstinate as a primitive Xtian—and wards and parrys off all our thrusts with one unanswerable fence—"Sir, its of great consequence that the *world* is not *mislead*"—.

> —(Marrs I, 262-3).

When the long-expected happy event finally took place, then, in February 1801, only one of the projected twin volumes was actually published, and its opening page carried a typically rambling, apologetic 'Advertisement', explaining at great length that the Preface 'for many reasons, has been cancelled'.[5] Eight apparently peaceful months now went by until the next episode in this continuing saga. Then, in late October or early November, Lamb wrote to Rickman:

> A letter from G. Dyer will probably accompany this. I wish I could convey to you any notion of the whimsical scenes I have been witness to in this past fortnight. Twas on Tuesday week the poor heathen scrambled up to my door about breakfast time. He came thro' a violent rain with no neckcloth on & a *beard* that made him a spectacle to men and angels and tap'd at the door. Mary open'd it & he stood stark still and held a paper in his hand importing that he had been ill with a fever. He either wouldn't or couldn't speak except by signs. When you went to comfort him he put his hand upon his heart & told us his complaint lay where no medicines could reach it. I was dispatch'd for Dr. Dale, Mr. Phillips of St. Paul's Church yard & Mr. Frend who is to be his executor. George solemnly delivered into Mr. Frend's hands & mine an old burnt preface that had been in the fire with injunctions which we solemnly vow'd to obey that it should be printed after his death with his last corrections & that some account should be given to the world why he had not fulfill'd his engagement with subscribers. Having done this & borrow'd two guineas of his bookseller . . . he laid himself down on my bed in a mood of complacent resignation.
>
> (Marrs II, 29).

Dyer was evidently not so near to death as he had feared, however; indeed, he appeared to be suffering more than anything else from a lack of food and drink. Lamb reported that he complained of 'sensations of gnawing which he felt about his *heart* which he mistook his stomach to be, & sure enough these gnawings were dissipated after a meal or two', and undertook to avoid a recurrence of this state of affairs in future, by proposing that Dyer should 'dine with me . . . whenever he does not go out & pay me. I will take his money beforehand' (Marrs II, 30). These life-saving dinners did take place, as repeated references in Lamb's letters during the rest of this winter make clear.[6] It seems possible, as I hope to show below, that during the course of them, Lamb—who had already 'assisted Dyer in arranging the remainder of what he calls ***Poems***' (Marrs II, 30) for his projected new edition—may also have helped with the considerable revisions which Dyer now made to the 'old burnt preface'. Certainly these revisions appear to have reached their final form during the course of the next four to six weeks, since on November 24th Lamb wrote to Rickman that 'one volume of Dyer's new edition is printing' (Marrs II, 38), and, two weeks or so later, that 'his 1st vol. is nearly printed' (Marrs II, 39). Predictably, however, the second volume, which contained some new critical remarks, seems to have caused problems, since the final revised two volumes did not appear until May or June of the following year (see *MM* (July 1802) 598).

So much, then, for Lamb's contemporary reporting of the events. We are fortunate, however, in having further materials to examine, which add a fascinating and somewhat puzzling dimension to the whole affair. On August 4th 1882 the British Library purchased from a bookseller in Charing Cross—for the sum of £2.10d.—Lamb's copy of Dyer's ***Poems*** of 1801, to which is attached a copy of the cancelled Preface; presumably, indeed, that very same copy which Dyer had consigned to Lamb's care with what he thought to be his dying breath in October 1801. As we saw above, the apologetic 'Advertisment' in Volume II explains that the Preface 'for many reasons, has been cancelled'. In the British Library copy, the last word of this sentence has been underlined in ink; and in the margin, in Lamb's hand, is written

> one copy of this cancelled Preface, snatch'd out of the fire, is prefixed to this volume.

Elsewhere in this copy are several other relatively minor marginalia by Lamb, mostly correcting printing or proofreading errors. It also contains marginalia which are much longer (and much ruder); these are the work of that inveterate scribbler on other people's books, Samuel Taylor Coleridge.[7]

The study of Coleridge's annotations has become a not inconsiderable part of the Coleridge industry. The first two volumes of his *Marginalia* which have been published in the Bollingen *Collected Coleridge* series[8] are together over two thousand pages long and cover less than a third of the alphabet. Their editor, George Whalley, suggests that Coleridge wrote very little marginalia before he settled at Greta Hall in 1800, and goes on to argue that the notes on Dyer's poems are possibly the first example of the 'rather more sustained' note writing which characterised his later habits. Their importance in this respect leads Whalley to go on to speculate as to the probable date of their writing; and he concludes that this was either 'in November 1801-February 1802, when [Coleridge] saw much of Lamb in London, or in March 1803, when he stayed with Lamb to console him on the

recurrence of Mary's insanity' (Whalley I, lxxx). Taking into account the complicated history of events which we have just been examining, I think that one can fix with a fair degree of certainty on the earlier of these two periods, the winter of 1801-2. As we saw earlier, Lamb had been presented with the 'old burnt preface' in October 1801, and was still full of the news a month or so later when Coleridge arrived in London from Keswick, after which he undoubtedly spent a good deal of time with Lamb; visits are definitely recorded on November 19th and February 21st, but there were almost certainly other unrecorded ones before Coleridge returned to the north in late February. The later date—the beginning of 1803—seems much less likely, since the original version of the preface was by then very old news, having been revised and published in its altered version more than six months before.

Whalley also suggests that 'a variety of discernable purposes' lay behind Coleridge's note-writing, among them that of providing 'critical advice for an author . . .' (Whalley I lxii). It would be convenient if one could argue that the notes on Dyers ***Poems*** had been written in order to assist Dyer in the course of his revisions. Unfortunately, however, this does not seem to have been the case, as we shall see.

As far as the volume of poetry is concerned, Coleridge's marginal notes are restricted to the longer poems (described by Dyer as 'satires') which end the volume. Dyer's habit of footnoting his own work becomes particularly marked in the case of these long poems; and it is to these footnotes that Coleridge takes exception. The first of his marginalia is a relatively minor one, correcting a wrong attribution by Dyer of a translation into Greek verse.[9] Next on page 299, Dyer footnotes a rather obscure line in ***Poetic Sympathies*** which refers to the classical Greek poet Sappho as follows:

> Sappho, loved by Anacreon. Her celebrated ode, beginning Φαινεται μοι κηνος ισος θεοισιν, is produced by Longinus as one of the noblest and completest examples of the sublime.

Coleridge disagrees profoundly with this statement. In the text the word 'sublime' is heavily underlined, and down the side and along the bottom of the page, he has written

> No such thing. Longinus was no very profound critic; but he was no Blunderer. Of the energetic, of the language of high excitement, elevated from passion, in short υψοτητος παθητικης, of this indeed it was, & probably ever will be, the most perfect specimen. But as to Sublime you might as well call it Blue, or Snubnosed.

Longinus certainly does cite the poem of Sappho's which Dyer quotes as an example of a quality which in Greek is called το υψος. Coleridge's objection rests on the interpretation of this Greek phrase. Dyer has followed many eighteenth-century translators in taking it to mean 'the sublime', a practice which is still followed in some twentieth century editions of Longinus. Coleridge, however, is suggesting that a more accurate translation of the phrase would be 'the elevated style of writing'; an interpretation which is followed by the editor of the *Loeb Classical Texts* edition of Longinus.[10] In other words, Coleridge sees Dyer as perpetrating a typically eighteenth-century anachronistic interpretation of Longinus (see Whalley II, 355).

The other note which Coleridge made on this volume is a comment on one of Dyer's footnotes to the final poem, **"The Redress: To a Young Poet."** Here, Dyer asserts

> That the principle and immediate aim of poetry is, to please, has been opposed by Julius Scaliger, and some other critics . . . Yet will I still abide by Aristotle's and Plutarch's opinion, that the immediate object of poetry is, to please, and that even in solemn subjects poetry is used to render them more engaging and agreeable.
>
> (*1801* 325-6).

This statement attracts an irritable response from Coleridge:

> Damned nonsense! But *why* does it please? Because it pleases! O mystery!—If not, some cause out of itself must be found. Mere utility it certainly is not—not mere goodness—therefore there must be some third power—& that is Beauty, i.e. that which *ought* to please. My benevolent friend seems not to have made an obvious distinction, between end and means—The Poet *must* always aim at Pleasure as *his* specific *means*; but surely Milton did & all ought to aim at something nobler as their end—viz—to cultivate and predispose the heart of the Reader &c.—

Coleridge's objection here is illuminated by reference to another, rather more significant, piece of contemporary critical prose, Wordsworth's Preface to the *Lyrical Ballads,* which had first appeared in October 1800. In it Wordsworth emphatically states that poetry has a definite purpose, towards which the giving of pleasure is the means rather than the end. He asserts that truly valuable poems—that is, those which are written by 'a man who being possessed of more than organic sensibility, has also thought long and deeply' will naturally elevate and culture the mind and feelings of the reader; in Wordsworth's words,

> the understanding of the being to whom we address ourselves . . . must necessarily be in some degree enlightened, his taste exalted, and his affections ameliorated.[11]

Indeed, the discussion of the higher forms of pleasure which poetry is able to give, their ultimate purpose, and their connection with beauty, is much enlarged on in the revised and extended version of Wordsworth's Preface which was published in April 1802. Since it is probable that the revisions were planned during the previous winter, the subject may well have been under discussion by Wordsworth and Coleridge just before Coleridge's visit to London in November. In this case, Coleridge would have been particularly alert to the lack of clear reasoning on the same subject which was demonstrated by Dyer's footnote.

Even if one puts the earliest possible date on these marginalia—that is, about the middle of November 1801, just after Coleridge's arrival in London—it is hard to see that they could have been influential as far as the selection of poems for Dyer's 1802 edition was concerned. Certainly the poems on which the comments appear were left out of the 1802 edition; but so were a great many others. Indeed, while the 1801 edition contained 53 poems, the 1802 version only contained 23, of which 13 were not in the earlier edition. In other words, only ten poems from *1801* found their way into *1802*; and it seems far more likely that these were selected under the guidance of Lamb, who in any case was writing 'I have assisted him in arranging the remainder of what he calls Poems' approximately two weeks before Coleridge's arrival in London.

One more of Coleridge's notes remains to be considered. This is the one which he wrote at the point in the cancelled Preface where Dyer is extrapolating on the subject of panegyric:

> Panegyric, in the hands of a mere rhymster, is almost sure to sink into insipidity; in the hands of a poet, it may swell into flattery. Here, probably, Pindar and Horace grew extravagant.
>
> (*1800* xxvi-xxvii).

In the margin beside this statement, Coleridge has written:

> PINDAR—and—who?—*Horace*!!! and pray, good George Dyer! in what ode or fragment of the Theban Republican do you find Flattery? I can remember no one word, that justifies the charge. As to Horace, praise be to him as an amiable gentleman, & man of fine courtly sense—thanks & thanks for his Satires & Epistles, and whatever is "sermoni proprius"—& his little translations or originals of light & social growth, thanks for them too!—But as a Poet, a Lyric Poet, a companion of *Pindar,* or the Author of the Atys—(be he Catullus or some unknown Greek—)—it won't do! No!—

The source of Coleridge's indignation here is that Dyer's note seems to him to diminish Pindar in two ways: first by linking him so casually with Horace, and second by accusing him of extravagant flattery. Horace himself would appear to have agreed with this judgment, since he not only described Pindar's poetry as being 'like a torrent rushing down rain swollen from the mountains, boiling and roaring', but also said that he felt it was too dangerous to try and rival Pindar.[12]

If Coleridge's comments had been written with the intention of providing critical advice to Dyer on how to revise his Preface, one would expect to find that this paragraph had been considerably altered in the later version, if not removed entirely. However, this proves not to have been the case. The paragraph remains substantially the same in *1802,* and one source of Coleridge's irritation—the linking of Pindar and Horace—still remains. As for the other source, the accusation of panegyric in their hands 'swelling into flattery', this has been slightly modified; Dyer has replaced 'here, probably, Pindar and Horace grew extravagant' with the more modestly phrased 'as, probably, it did in the hands of Pindar and Horace' (*1802* xxxvi-xxxvii). This kind of modification of statements which in the early version tend to be clumsily phrased and verging on the extreme in their judgments is characteristic of the revisions which Dyer made throughout the Preface, however, so that it would be difficult to prove that Coleridge's comments had any influence in this particular instance. In any case, his notes sound much more like explosions of personal outrage (possibly somewhat exaggerated for the amusement of Lamb) than reasoned critical advice, and his 'addresses' to Dyer almost certainly rhetorical rather than literal.

Nevertheless, that Dyer did have some quite substantial and valuable help with his revisions of the Preface seems a strong probability. Indeed, he says as much in one of the introductory paragraphs which he prefixed to the 1802 Preface. Apologising for the difference 'both in form and contents, from what were originally intended', Dyer explains that 'the present plan has been adopted' following

> the counsel of persons . . . very competent to give advice, because not likely to be mistaken in their judgment; persons, who had not interest of their own to serve, but were well acquainted with the taste of the public . . .
>
> (*1802* ii)

Who, one must ask, were these 'very competent' and disinterested 'persons'? If, as I have suggested, Coleridge must be discounted, then Lamb seems to be the most likely candidate for the main protagonist. He undoubtedly had the opportunity; during the crucial period between late October and the last week of November 1801 when the revisions were probably made, Dyer was dining with him almost daily. Certainly a survey of the revisions themselves suggests that they were carried out under the supervision of someone with a clearer sense of structural logic and a better ear for prose style than Dyer appears to have possessed, at least when it came to writing literary criticism.

A comparison between the two versions of the Preface is interesting. Very little has been removed in the later version; indeed, further examples are frequently added in order to clarify some of its main points. Dyer's overall purpose in writing the Preface seems to be an attempt to justify his decision to present the public with a collection of his lyric poems, since, as his opening paragraph puts it,

> An author never, perhaps, more naturally falls into anxiety, than on presenting the public with poetic compositions.
>
> (*1800* iii)

Characteristically, he hastens to assure his readers that he is well aware of the 'peculiar delicacy and appropriate difficulties' of lyric poetry (*1800* iv); and he goes on to demonstrate this by means of an historical survey of all the poets—both classical and British or European—who have attempted this form in the past. Interspersed throughout this survey are a number of disclaimers to the effect that 'the reader must not conclude from this that I think highly of the following performances: far very far, am I from great pretensions . . .' (*1800* xxvii), and also a number of attempts to anticipate any possible objections which might be made to the poetry. One such attempt produces one of the most appealing passages in the Preface in which Dyer answers the putative objection that 'some of the poems are rural and descriptive but the author lives in the Great City' with several paragraphs of explanatory autobiography:

> But, will it necessarily follow, that the person, who lives in London at a particular time, must have resided there always? Suffice it to say, that of the years of my life since I left college, the greater part have been spent entirely in the country; and, that since I have lived in town, I have usually past some part of the year in a course of constant rambling, or at the rural seat of some friend. The environs of London, too, will bear witness, how regular have been my solitary devotions in her modest retreats; so that, I hope, the critics will not treat my Muse too ungallantly, at least, on this account, as if she were a mere London trollop, always sauntering, or gadding about the streets of London, sallow with city smoke, and listening to the sound of Bow-bells . . .
>
> (*1800* xxxi).

This passage, which was left almost unchanged in the later version, makes one wish that the autobiography which Dyer apparently wrote had not been lost after his death[13], as does the passage towards the end of the Preface in which Dyer confronts another possible objection:

> With regard to the ladies, whose names are mentioned . . . let it be publicly understood, as it has always been privately, that my language has been the expression of a simple, though sincere, respect . . . when the heart is most subdued, it sometimes loves to worship in silence. These feelings may, perhaps, since have broken out into verse . . .
>
> (*1800* lxiii-lxiv).

This passage also remains, though with some alterations in language and structure, in *1802,* and indeed is even expanded upon in the later version, so that it concludes rather touchingly

> But if nothing short of declaring, that I have been in love with every woman who has set my muse to work, will do, I will submit; and here declare, that, though I may not have paid court to any of them, that I have, however, been in love with them all: a confession, it is to be feared, which will not be reckoned prudent.
>
> (*1802* lxxxiv).

Elsewhere, in the more objective critical passages of the Preface, more noticeable changes have been made. For one thing, there have been a number of major structural alterations; whole paragraphs have been uprooted from their original positions and replaced in order to make for greater logical sense in the flow of the argument. An attempt has also been made to flesh out Dyer's frequently rather sketchy generalisations about a particular period of poetry or group of poets by adding further examples. Also, as in the case of the passage which was annotated by Coleridge, extreme statements have been modified; and a general stylistic smoothness and polish has been given to Dyer's often harsh and syntactically irrational prose style. Finally, one very interesting three page addition has been made:

> There is a species of lyric poetry that may be thought somewhat different from those already mentioned, and to have obtained but little sanction from such as we consider the models of this sort of composition, the Greek and Roman poets: I mean that which studiously searches for subjects in what are deemed the most ordinary concerns of life, and where language is characterised by the greatest simplicity . . . to do justice to a subject in this way requires something of the Shakespearean genius, to hold the mirror up to life, and to make nature speak to the heart. In such hands the loftiness of an idea gives dignity to the language; and, in the simplicity of style, we contemplate the true sublime.
>
> (*1802* xxxix, xli).

Clearly it had been pointed out to Dyer that his original Preface had one important omission: he had failed to take account of the recently published *Lyrical Ballads.* The terms in which the deficiency is made up sound to me stylistically quite uncharacteristic of Dyer. One cannot help suspecting that someone—and, again, the strongest candidate would seem to be Lamb—stood over him and told him exactly what to say.

Before we leave the subject of Dyer's revisions, it remains to be said that there is one rather mysterious problem in their complicated history. As we have seen, Lamb's account of Dyer's 'phrenesis', in December 1800, gave as Dyer's reason for his declaration that 'the Preface must all be expunged' the fact that

that very morning he had discovered that in the very first page of said preface he had set out with a principle of criticism fundamentally wrong, which vitiated all his following reasoning . . .

(Marrs I, 263).

The problem here is that although a number of minor stylistic alterations have been made to the 'very first page' of the Preface in the 1802 version, nothing has been substantially changed or removed which fits Dyer's description. Both versions do, in fact, 'set out with a principle of criticism'; this is how the 1800 version begins:

> That poetry will allow no mediocrity, is a formidable principle of criticism; a principle, however, which, as laid down by an accurate critic and elegant poet, may be plausibly quoted and even malignantly applied . . .
>
> (*1800* ii).

The 'accurate critic and elegant poet' referred to here is Horace, and Dyer's reference is to his *Ars Poetica* I. 372-3. In Latin, the lines read:

> Medeocribus esse poetis Non homines, non Di, non concessare columnae.

The *Loeb Classical Edition*'s editor translates this as 'But that poets should be of middling rank, neither men, nor gods, nor booksellers ever brooked'.[14] While it is true that Horace's dictum against mediocrity appears to refer to poets rather than to poetry, it is difficult to see why Dyer should have felt his version of it to be so fundamentally wrong as to warrant the destruction of his entire Preface. Furthermore, if one turns to *1802,* one finds that the passage remains substantially the same, although a 'therefore' has replaced a 'however' in the second phrase.

E. V. Lucas, whose chapter on Dyer in his *Life* of Lamb includes a discussion of some of the events which have been discussed in this paper, notes the curious fact that the first page of the Preface remains more or less the same in *1802,* and points out that the first *omitted* passage, which occurs on the second page of *1800,* is one which reads:

> A sufficient degree of generosity is found in the world to encourage a useful pursuit, and even an attempt to please: the violence of party cannot controul it; nor will it be overrated by the manoeuverings of pride, or the feebleness of ignorance.
>
> (*1800* iv)

'Can this be the benevolent opinion', asks Lucas, 'which poor George Dyer found to be a fatal error?'[15]

To me, this seems rather unlikely. It is, after all, as Lucas says, an opinion rather than a 'principle of criticism' which Dyer is offering here. However, as we saw above,

Dyer's revisions consist almost entirely of additions rather than excisions; and even after a painstaking search I am forced to agree with Lucas that there does not appear to be anywhere in the Preface 'any discrepancy amounting to a false principle' (*Life* 187). One could, of course, simply conclude that Lamb had invented this part of the story; but the fact that the Preface does indeed 'set out with a principle of criticism' does much to support his account. Given Dyer's highly unstable state of mind during the months preceding his decision to destroy the Preface, almost anything seems possible, including, perhaps, his simply misjudging the magnitude of his misquotation from Horace.

When one realises how much time Lamb spent with Dyer throughout this period, and what a prolonged exposure to his habits of composition and their fruits he endured as a result, it seems hardly surprising that his affection for Dyer became considerably tempered with a certain amount of gentle mockery. As for Coleridge and Southey, who had been so much influenced by 'radical George' in the early 1790s, it is clear that for them, too, the episode of the Preface marked the start of a very noticeable change of attitude.

In Coleridge's case, this manifested itself not only in the tone of his marginalia, but also in the fact that Dyer became a standing joke in the Grasmere and Keswick circle at this time: as Coleridge wrote to Southey (who was staying in Bristol) on August 1 1801, the chance remark of a 'little quaker Girl' to the effect that '"Yan belks when yan's fu', & when yan's empty"—that is "One belches when one's full & when one's empty"' had become 'a favourite piece of slang at Grasmere & Greta Hall—whenever we talk of . . . George Dyer, & other Perseverents in the noble Trade of Scriblerism'.[16] Earlier in the same year, too, we find Southey—who as little as nine months before had been writing to Dyer in terms of the greatest admiration and respect—describing him in a letter to Danvers as 'Cancellarius Magnus', the great canceller.[17]

All this being said, however, it is clear that Dyer was still regarded with genuine affection. As a poet and a literary critic, he had proved himself to be something of a failure; but it says much for his qualities of warmth and gentleness that even in the midst of his frenzied last throes of composition in August 1800 Lamb could write of him:

> The oftener I see him, the more deeply I admire him. He is goodness itself.
>
> (Marrs I, 235)

Notes

1. *The Letters of Charles and Mary Anne Lamb,* ed. E.J. Marrs (Ithaca, N.Y., 1975—) i 221-2. Hereafter cited as Marrs.

2. *Monthly Magazine* (October 1796) 735. Hereafter cited as *MM*.

3. The disquisitions on the drama which Lamb describes were not, in fact, included in either the first or second versions of Dyer's Preface.

4. William Wilkie (1721-72), known as 'the Scottish Homer', had published this nine book epic in 1757 (2nd. edn. 1759).

5. George Dyer: *Poems* (1801) lxiii. Hereafter cited as *1801*. The 'cancelled' Preface will be cited as *1800*; and the first volume of the second edition (which contains the revised Preface) as *1802*.

6. See for example Marrs ii 37-8, 39, 51, 53.

7. For Lamb's comments on Coleridge as an annotator, see 'The Two Races of Men', *Works* ii, 31.

8. *Collected Coleridge* Bollingen Series lxxv (Princeton, N.J.), xii. *Marginalia* i and ii, ed. George Whalley (1980, 1985). Hereafter cited as Whalley.

9. Dyer assigns the translation to Josiah Barnes (1654-1712), which Coleridge points out is incorrect. He does not, however, say who did translate the verse in question (see Whalley ii 354).

10. The passage is from Longinus: περι υψους 10. 1-3. The *Loeb Classical Library* translation is by W. Hamilton Fyfe (1927). For a twentieth century translation which follows Dyer's practice, see for example Longinus: *On Sublimity,* trans. D. A. Russell (Oxford, 1965) 14-15.

11. *The Prose Works of William Wordsworth,* ed. W. J. B. Owen and Jane Worthington Smyser (3 vols., Oxford, 1974) i 126.

12. Horace: *Carminedes* 4. 2. For a discussion of the relation of Pindar and Horace, and of the influence of both poets on eighteenth century poetry, see Gilbert Highet: *The Classical Tradition: Greek and Roman Influences on Western Literature* (Oxford, 1949) 224-5.

13. This autobiography is referred to in Dyer's Obituary, which appeared in *The Gentleman's Magazine* N.S. 15 (May 1841) 545.

14. Horace: *Ars Poetica,* 372-3; trans. H. Rushton Fairclough (*Leob Classical Library,* 1970) 480-1.

15. E. V. Lucas: *The Life of Charles Lamb* (2 vols., London, 1907) 187. Hereafter referred to as *Life*.

16. E. L. Griggs (ed): *Collected Letters of Samuel Taylor Coleridge* (6 vols., Oxford, 1956-71) ii 407.

17. Southey to C. Danvers, Jan. 20 1801. K. Curry (ed): *New Letters of Robert Southey* (2 vols., New

York and London, 1965) i 237. The earlier letter from Southey to Dyer is dated Mar. 27 1800, and can be found in *Notes & Queries* N.S. VIII (Jan. 1961) 14-15.

Nicholas Roe (essay date 1992)

SOURCE: Roe, Nicholas. "'Unremembered Kindness': George Dyer and English Romanticism." In *The Politics of Nature: Wordsworth and Some Contemporaries*, pp. 17-35. London: Macmillan, 1992.

[*In the following essay, Roe suggests how the doctrine of benevolence in Dyer's writings foreshadows Wordsworth's morality of benevolence in "Tintern Abbey."*]

> *His kind heart most warmly sympathised at all times with the cause of civil and religious liberty, which he uniformly espoused by his writings . . .*
>
> The Gentleman's Magazine, NS 15 (1841), 545

> *—feelings too*
> *Of unremembered pleasure; such, perhaps,*
> *As may have had no trivial influence*
> *On that best portion of a good man's life;*
> *His little, nameless, unremembered acts*
> *Of kindness and of love.*
>
> "Tintern Abbey," 31-6

'The oftener I see him, the more deeply I admire him. He is goodness itself.' So Charles Lamb described his esteem for George Dyer in a letter to Coleridge, 26 August 1800 (Marrs, i. 235). Elsewhere, however, Dyer frequently turns up in a joke at his own expense. His short sight and chronic absent-mindedness contributed to a number of humorous stories, such as Leigh Hunt's recollection that Dyer had once left a dinner wearing only one shoe, and had not discovered his loss until half way home. Best known of these tales about Dyer are Elia's two essays 'Oxford in the Vacation' and 'Amicus Redivivus'. The former essay indulges Dyer's pedantic scholarship,

> busy as a moth over some rotten archive, rummaged out of some seldom-explored press, in a nook at Oriel. With long poring, he is grown almost into a book. He stood as passive as one by the side of the old shelves. I longed to new-coat him in Russia, and assign him his place.

In 'Amicus Redivivus' Elia gives an affectionate account of his 'strange sensation'

> on seeing my old friend G. D., who had been paying me a morning visit a few Sundays back, at my cottage at Islington, upon taking leave, instead of turning down the right hand path by which he had entered—with staff in hand, and at noon day, deliberately march right forwards into the midst of the stream that runs by us, and totally disappear.[1]

Elia's 'G. D.' is a slapstick hero, a holy fool. Yet when Dyer is mentioned elsewhere, in more sober contexts, the same characteristics often emerge. E. V. Lucas's chapter on Dyer in his *Life of Charles Lamb,* for example, is essentially a list of whimsical anecdotes and his footnotes to 'Amicus Redivivus' offer a map of Dyer's trajectory from Lamb's front door to the point where he had fallen into the New River. All of these stories reflect Dyer's eccentricity as an old man, but they underestimate him by concentrating exclusively on his later years. In Romantic studies, too, his reputation as a minor poet and man of letters has obscured other important aspects of his early career as a writer.[2]

As a unitarian and reformist in the early 1790s, Dyer was active in metropolitan radical circles where he was acquainted with Wordsworth, Coleridge, Southey and Lamb: young jacobins whose literary lives then lay some years in the future. Their creativity coincided with the failure of the French Revolution, and with the decline of Dyer's reputation. As reformist activities gave place to poetry, Dyer—who had been a formative presence in the political and imaginative lives of these writers—was gradually marginalised to become the eccentric personality celebrated by Elia. Dyer remains important, then, as a figure whose medial presence yields an awareness of how revolution and Romantic poetry were related. He focuses a historical perspective, and enables one to see ideological continuities between the political milieux of the 1790s and the ideal universe of the poet's imagination.

Between 1792 and 1795 Dyer published three substantial political pamphlets: the second edition of his ***Inquiry into the Nature of Subscription*** (1792), ***The Complaints of the Poor People of England*** (1793) and ***A Dissertation on the Theory and Practice of Benevolence*** (1795)[3]. Dyer's pamphlets show him to have been as militant as Tom Paine in his criticism of the British government, and practical in his arguments for social change along lines advocated by Paine in his chapter on 'Ways and Means' in *The Rights of Man Part II.* Dyer's political and social idealism was matched by his concern for the realities of opposition and reform in contemporary London. When members of the reformist Constitution and Corresponding Societies were arrested and charged with treason in 1794 Dyer responded, in his ***Dissertation,*** with a plan to coordinate relief for the defendants and their families: 'their real object was the publick good: and they were evidently placed at the post of danger' (***Dissertation,*** p. 77). Elsewhere in his ***Dissertation,*** he remarked that he was acquainted with 'most' of the persons 'lately indicted for treason and sedition' (***Dissertation,*** p. 100), including John Bonney whose 'Prison Diary' is reproduced in Chapter Four of this study.

These publications and activities meant that Dyer was one of the most prominent reformists in London at a time when Wordsworth, Coleridge and Southey were frequently living in, or passing through, the city. For them, he would have been a familiar presence from an early date in London reform societies and among Godwin's intellectual circle. Coleridge, Lamb and Dyer attended Christ's Hospital, and Coleridge and Dyer had both gone on to Cambridge University. All three subsequently became unitarians and reformists. So it was not a coincidence that Dyer was one of Coleridge's first contacts in London in 1794, and that Dyer's thinking about society should have been strikingly similar to Coleridge's, Wordsworth's and indeed Lamb's over the next years.[4]

In his relation to Coleridge and in his response to contemporary political issues Dyer was certainly not a passive or marginal figure in the 1790s. My first chapter explores this period of his life, to show how Dyer's kindly politics were shared and interpreted by other young jacobins and poets, and ultimately came to inform Wordsworth's poetry of compassionate sublimity in 'Tintern Abbey'. In so doing, this recovery of Dyer's presence in the 1790s serves to question recent interpretations of Romantic poetry as a pure 'displacement', or 'erasure' of historical processes.

'War with the Establishment'

Dyer was born in 1755 in East London, where his father worked as a shipwright. He attended Christ's Hospital from 1762, went up to Emmanuel College, Cambridge in 1774, and graduated four years later. He then worked for a short time as usher (assistant teacher) at Dedham Grammar School and Northampton Grammar School before returning to Cambridge as tutor to the family of Robert Robinson, the baptist minister, 'with the view of profiting by [Robinson's] doctrine and learned conversation'. Robinson supported John Jebb's petitions for university reform and, in 1780, he founded the Cambridge Constitutional Society in order to further the aims of its parent society in London.[5] Robinson's society acted as a focus for liberal opinion in Cambridge and its neighbourhood in the 1780s, so that Dyer's presence in Robinson's house placed him at the centre of dissenting and reformist activity in town and university. And given his esteem for Robinson, this obviously had a bearing on the way in which his political and religious opinions took shape during the decade.[6]

Robinson's *A Political Catechism,* published in 1784, suggests how he acted as Dyer's spiritual and political mentor. The *Catechism* uses a simple dialogue to present Robinson's ideal government as a combination of monarchy, a 'select council' of aristocracy, and democratic representatives of the people who would exert their rightful influence after a reform of parliament. A father explains British politics to his son 'George': 'When we speak of administration George, we speak of what is;

but when we speak of representation, we speak of what *ought to be*'.[7] George gained from Robinson's 'doctrine and conversation' as he had hoped. He emerged from this period of his life as a reformist and religious dissenter, and he moved—like Robinson—from the baptist church to become a unitarian by the time he left Cambridge for London in 1792. During the years immediately following, Dyer acknowledged Robinson's influence by quoting from, and recommending his writings in his own pamphlets. And in 1796 he published his *Memoirs of the Life and Writings of Robert Robinson,* as a substantial tribute to his old friend who had died in 1790 while on a visit to Joseph Priestley at Birmingham.

The dissenters' participation in political controversy, and their welcome for the French Revolution in 1789, were misrepresented by Edmund Burke as a revolutionary conspiracy in his *Reflections on the Revolution in France,* and in debates at the House of Commons. In his speech in the debate on Fox's motion for the repeal of the Test Acts, 11 May 1792, Burke claimed that the petitioners urging repeal were 'not confined to a theological sect, but [were] also a political faction'. He cautioned the House against being 'dictated to . . . by the Constitutional, the Revolution, and the Unitarian Societies':

> the dissent on their part is fundamental, goes to the very root: and it is at issue not upon this rite or that ceremony, on this or that school opinion, but upon this one question of an establishment, as unchristian, unlawful, contrary to the Gospel, and to natural right, popish and idolatrous. These are the principles violently and fanatically held and pursued—taught to their children, who are sworn at the altar like Hannibal. The war is with the establishment itself, no quarter, no compromise. As a party, they are infinitely mischievous: see the declarations of Priestley and Price—declarations, you will say, of hot men: likely enough, but who are the cool men, who have disclaimed them?[8]

One man cool enough to answer Burke was George Dyer. In the second edition of his *Inquiry into the Nature of Subscription,* Dyer announced that his immediate reason for republishing his pamphlet was to make 'copious remarks' on Burke's 'extremely ill-informed . . . misrepresentation' of France in his *Reflections.* But finding that Paine, Mackintosh, and Priestley had already done so, he 'dropped [his] original design' (*Inquiry,* p. vii-viii). Nevertheless, Dyer's wish to answer Burke had encouraged his first public declaration of opposition in the 1790s. When Fox's motion to repeal the Test Acts was defeated, there appeared to be no further reason to expect that the government might be influenced to reform by petition. This explains why Dyer (like Frend, Coleridge, and others) was subsequently attracted by the London Corresponding Society's popular campaign for reform, and by the ideas in Paine's *Rights of Man* and Godwin's *Political Justice.*

And in this London milieu, Dyer in particular stands out as an individual who mediates between radical politics and the Romantic imaginations of Wordsworth, Coleridge and Southey.

From 1792, Dyer's political development moved along a middle way between the radical careers of Wordsworth and Coleridge. Like Wordsworth in 1792, Dyer was a republican who anticipated that 'the present convulsions' in France 'will terminate in a complete republic'—a prophecy that was fulfilled in September of that year (*Inquiry,* p. 285). Furthermore, Dyer recommended the French Revolution as an appropriate model for change in Britain, and claimed that nothing 'short of a national convention can remedy the evil' of unequal representation in parliament (*Inquiry,* p. 276). His *Inquiry* is keenly republican, sympathetic to France, and it reveals how much Dyer had been impressed by Paine's *Rights of Man.* As such, the pamphlet is very close indeed to Wordsworth's position in his *Letter to the Bishop of Llandaff,* written early in 1793. The similarities between Dyer and Wordsworth continued over the next three years when both responded favourably to *Political Justice,* and on 27 February 1795 Dyer was present in the company that witnessed Wordsworth's first meeting with Godwin at William Frend's house. By this time Coleridge was already familiar with Godwin and with Dyer, and he had been aware of Wordsworth's poetry since his Cambridge days. So Dyer was well-known to both Wordsworth and Coleridge before the poets' first meeting in August or September 1795, and his friendship with Coleridge helps to clarify some aspects of Coleridge and Wordsworth's creative relationship thereafter.[9]

Coleridge was briefly attracted by the necessarian optimism of *Political Justice,* and his sonnet to William Godwin—

> Nor will I not thy holy guidance bless
> And hymn thee, GODWIN! with an ardent lay
>
> (*CL,* i. 141)

—is a memorial to this brief phase of his intellectual career. By early 1795, though, Coleridge had recognised Godwin's philosophy—and particularly his atheism—as a threat to the emotional and spiritual fabric of human society. Dyer would have differed with Coleridge's estimate of Godwin, whom he regarded as a 'sensible writer' in some respects, but—like Coleridge—his political and social thinking was determined by his unitarianism and his belief in the equality of all humanity in God. 'By considering the relation, which all men bear to the common Parent', Dyer wrote, 'I immediately see the relation, which subsists among all mankind, as a family' (*Inquiry,* p. 13).

The sanctity of this 'relation' was irrelevant to the rationalist theory of *Political Justice* and Godwin's abstract

concept of human benevolence. For Dyer, however, the christian idea of 'mankind, as a family' was essential to a renovated society in which

> there would be no opposition of interests; no exclusive privileges would be enjoyed; no invidious distinctions kept up. In proportion to the smalness of these societies, and the narrowness of their territories, the fraternal spirit would exert itself in all its simplicity and glory.
>
> (*Inquiry,* p. 13).

Dyer's argument for the kinship of humanity under God was similar in many ways to Coleridge's thinking about society from 1794. But Coleridge was especially concerned to identify a dynamic *process* in which 'private Attachments' become a 'necessary *habit* of the Soul', and form the principle of '*Concretion*' that would assimilate mankind into a unified society (*CL,* i. 86). On these grounds Coleridge believed that he could offer a prospect of social renovation which was genuinely in touch with human nature unlike the philosophy of *Political Justice.*

Two years after the publication of Dyer's *Inquiry,* in 1792, his ideal 'fraternal' society was projected in Southey and Coleridge's scheme of Pantisocracy, a small community to be established in America 'on the principles of an abolition of individual property' (*CL,* i. 96). Southey's plan of emigration late in 1793 was an immediate source for the Pantisocracy project, as will be seen in Chapter Two. But the similarities between Dyer's 'fraternal society' and the philosophical bases of Pantisocracy also explain why Dyer was 'enraptured' with the scheme when Coleridge explained it to him at their first meeting in August 1794 (*CL,* i. 98). The emigration scheme all came to nothing, of course, but Pantisocracy formed the basis of Coleridge and Dyer's friendship, and this was to have important consequences for both of them during the next year or so.

INTERLUDE: THE WAKEFIELD CONNECTION

Dyer recalled in 1836 that 'when Mr C. and Dr. Southey were young men & first came to London they were in the habit of calling upon me & I remember introducing the former to Mr Gilbert Wakefield'.[10] Wakefield was a graduate of Jesus College, Cambridge: a brilliant classicist, unitarian dissenter and a reformist of singular extremity. 'He was not one of those Socinians who brought to Coleridge's mind the image of cold moonlight', E. P. Thompson has said, 'for some strange stove raged inside him'. In January 1798, three years after he first met Coleridge, Wakefield wrote and published a *Reply* to Richard Watson's defence of the Pitt government in his *Address to the People of Great Britain.* On a previous occasion, early in 1793, the same Richard Watson had provoked Wordsworth to write his *Letter to the Bishop of Llandaff.* At the other end of the decade, Wakefield 'was almost the last public voice out of Jacobin England' as Thompson has put it. He was charged with seditious libel in his *Reply,* along with three booksellers who had sold his pamphlet: John Cuthell, J. S. Jordan and Joseph Johnson. Jordan and Johnson—both well-known radical publishers—were sentenced on 11 February 1799 and jailed for one year and for six months respectively. Cuthell was fined £20 and discharged. And on 30 May 1799 Wakefield was sentenced to imprisonment in Dorchester Gaol for two years. He was released in May 1801, and died only four months afterwards.[11]

The imprisonment of Wakefield and Johnson, who had both figured in the radical careers of Wordsworth and Coleridge earlier in the 1790s, provides evidence enough of the 'times of fear' that encouraged the poets' move from Nether Stowey to Germany in September 1798. Johnson had of course published Wordsworth's *An Evening Walk* and *Descriptive Sketches* in 1793. And Coleridge, passing through London on his way to Germany, had introduced himself to Johnson and arranged for him to publish *Fears in Solitude* (*CL,* i. 417-8). At the close of the revolutionary decade persecution and imprisonment, or the imaginative introspection of 'Frost at Midnight', 'Tintern Abbey' and the early *Prelude,* appear as alternative consequences of political repression—a relationship to which I shall return later in this book. Indeed Wordsworth's 'Glad Preamble', which dates from 1800, defines his creative 'enfranchisement' as liberation from

> a house
> Of bondage, from yon city's walls set free,
> A prison where he hath been long immured.
>
> (i. 6-8).

In one respect the association of the city with imprisonment was familiar to Wordsworth from the Old Testament, from Milton, Thomson, Cowper, and from Coleridge's poems.[12] But this full literary background to Wordsworth's metaphor is further enriched by the recognition that, as Wordsworth began his 'poem to Coleridge' in the winter of 1798-9, the poets' mutual acquaintances Wakefield and Johnson were tried and imprisoned. In the 'Glad Preamble', literary allusion places Wordsworth's imaginative election within a context of political meaning: Wakefield was 'the last public voice out of Jacobin England', but repression had also contributed to Wordsworth's discovery of his calling as poet of *The Prelude* and *The Recluse.*

Dyer's 1836 recollection that he had introduced Coleridge to Wakefield also offers a glimpse into Coleridge's involvement with metropolitan radicalism in the mid-1790s—a participation that Coleridge was later at pains to deny. Above all, Dyer's anecdote emphasises his important role in enabling Coleridge and Southey to make contact with London reformists from 1794 on-

wards. Indeed, the closer one looks into Coleridge and Southey's involvements with the reform movement at this time, the more significant Dyer appears to have been in their developing political and literary lives.

PROTEST, HISTORY, AND 'THE RUINED COTTAGE'

In 1793 Dyer published his **Complaints of the Poor People of England,** which followed *The Rights of Man Part II* in demanding a wide-ranging reform of government and society. Dyer's earlier **Inquiry,** had been limited to problems of representation and freedom of conscience (the two most obvious issues for religious dissenters in Britain), but his **Complaints** treated these fundamental problems as part of a much broader restructuring of society:

> in a country where one man possesses three or four magnificent houses, and 60 or 80,000 l. a year, or perhaps more, while many of the industrious poor can scarcely get the necessaries of life; in such a country, I say, the government is defective in wisdom, in justice, in mercy.
>
> (*Complaints,* p. 44)

A reform of the government, Dyer argues here, is a necessary precedent for more widespread changes in taxation, the legal system, in prisons, poor-rates, workhouses, schools, the army and navy. He introduces his pamphlet as a work of 'compassion' and 'friendship' for the poor, and is concerned throughout to demonstrate that their contribution to the nation's economy is an argument for political rights:

> The prosperity of nations depends on the poor. They dig the ore out of the mine, and the stone out of the quarry. They build our houses, work our vessels, and fight our battles: yet, while the rich enjoy almost all the benefits, the poor undergo all the labour.
>
> (*Complaints,* p. 4)

This is Dyer at his strongest, drawing encouragement from Paine's example in *The Rights of Man,* and lending Paine's democratic theories his own sympathetic involvement: 'It is not always owing to idleness or to profligacy, that we see many a poor sailor, at the close of a long war, begging his bread in the streets' (*Complaints,* p. 131). In Wordsworth's poems, the emotional force of protest enabled his imaginative mediation with poor soldiers and sailors, in successive versions of *Salisbury Plain,*

> he with the Soldier's life had striven
> And Soldier's wrongs . . .

—and, later, in 'The Discharged Soldier':

> I could mark
> That he was clad in military garb,
> Though faded yet entire. His face was turn'd

Towards the road, yet not as if he sought
For any living thing. He appeared
Forlorn and desolate, a man cut off
From all his kind, and more than half detached
For his own nature.[13]

For Dyer—as for many other pamphleteers in the 1790s—poverty was evidence of injustice and an appropriate cause of protest. But for Wordsworth the soldier's extremity told of spiritual isolation, a ghastly reflex of the poet's comfortable 'self-possession' in the opening lines of 'The Discharged Soldier'. As protest gave place to imaginative poetry in Wordsworth's career up to 1798, political reform was succeeded by a drama of psychic reproach and insight. But this process of turning inward, involving jacobinism with the poet's imaginative growth, did not constitute a full eclipse of history. It was Wordsworth's creative use of some aspects of protest literature that set him apart from Dyer, Frend, Thelwall and other jacobins. All of them were capable of a compassionate identification with social victims, as their pamphlets and lectures show, but it was Wordsworth who moved beyond the idiom of protest to think more deeply 'into the human heart'.

So, Margaret's story in *The Ruined Cottage* was a tragic intensification of earlier protest literature. Wordsworth's poem does not in this case displace the world of political complaint, 'the historical origins and circumstantial causes of Margaret's tragedy' as Jerome McGann has expressed it.[14] Rather, the poem arises from an imagination that comprehends the circumstances of historical change and, simultaneously, a vision of ideal nature: the poem embraces 'a time of trouble', Margaret's 'sore heart-wasting', and nature's 'plants . . . weeds, and flowers' as a unity of life in which the 'spirit of humanity . . . still survived'. This is literally a democratic vision, a radical imagining of human life that reveals the transcendent dwelling within the mundane. In Wordsworth's *Ruined Cottage* the 'passing shews' of history and the 'silent overgrowings' of nature are revealed as a profound continuity.

DYER AND COLERIDGE: ACTS OF KINDNESS

In 1793, Dyer's *Complaints* was particularly timely in that it addressed the fears of ordinary people in Britain following the outbreak of war with France. Dyer vindicated the reform movement in a long **"Address to the Friends of Liberty"**, and described the troubled mood of French sympathisers at this time with extraordinary power:

> The friends of liberty approved and disapproved; they rejoiced, and they wept. In the midst of an event new in the history of the world . . . they were divided, perplexed, confounded: always disposed to rejoice at the conquests of liberty, yet frequently mistaking, amidst the number, the suddenness, and the embarrassment of events, the tendency both of defeats and conquests.
>
> (*Complaints* p. 207)

These extremities of hope and bafflement contribute to an understanding of the 'conflict of sensations' that assailed Wordsworth after his return from France (x. 265). Wordsworth's personal uneasiness reflected widespread unrest, and his perplexity 'amidst the embarrassment of events' offers a further explanation for his decision not to publish his republican pamphlet.

Wordsworth kept quiet, then, but late in 1793 Dyer made an outspoken statement of support for France and the revolution. At the end of his **"Address"**, Dyer reaffirmed his own position:

> Yes! . . . I approved, and still approve, the doctrine of the Rights of Man; and the french revolution I contemplated, and still contemplate, as the most important aera in the history of NATIONS.—But because men rejoiced to see so many millions of people enslaved struggling for liberty, does it follow, that they are enemies to their country?[15]

Dyer's effort to reconcile revolutionary sympathies with his identity as a British citizen indicates tensions working on other friends of liberty during 1793, Wordsworth included. Dyer sought to maintain self-coherence at a period when, as a republican in London, he was increasingly isolated by reactionary policies and opinion. Looking back to this period in *The Prelude,* Wordsworth recalled a dreadful fracturing of his inner self; broken between love of his native country and his emotional and intellectual commitments to France he experienced acute self-alienation, 'cut off' from his kind (x. 257). This psychic trauma can be traced, perhaps, in the strange and overwrought poetry of *Salisbury Plain,* which dates from summer 1793. It also explains Wordsworth's wandering through England and Wales, discussed later in Chapter Six, and his failure—so far as one can tell—to make a 'common cause' with the reformists in London.

Unlike Wordsworth, Dyer consolidated his involvement with the reform movement. He was an active member of the Constitutional Society in London and 'almost constantly attended one of their committees' (*Complaints,* p. 203). He met prominent members of the society such as John Horne Tooke and John Augustus Bonney, both of whom were imprisoned in May 1794, and these acquaintances explain why Dyer organised subscriptions to defray the costs of the defendants when the treason trials came on at the Old Bailey later that year. In addition to his activities in the Constitutional Society, Dyer was much in company with Godwin, Holcroft, Thelwall, Frend and other radicals and dissenters in London. So the man that Coleridge and Southey 'were in the habit of calling upon' at this time was very well placed to introduce both of them to the political and intellectual circles of London, and to act as a London agent for their writings.

At his first meeting with Coleridge in August 1794, Dyer offered to find a publisher for *The Fall of Robe-*

spierre, which he 'liked hugely' (*CL,* i. 98). He called on three London publishers—Robinson, Johnson, and Kearsley—but evidently without success since the play was later published at Cambridge by Benjamin Flower. Nevertheless Dyer also encouraged Coleridge by offering to 'dispose of' fifty copies of the play, although he later found this 'inconvenient'—as Coleridge told Southey—and took only twenty-five (*CL,* i. 101, 117). His enthusiasm for Coleridge's work evidently lost touch with the practicalities of publication and bookselling, so that his initial generosity had to be trimmed. But the interest and support of a published poet, pamphleteer and reviewer must have been vital esteem for Coleridge as a young writer who had yet to make his own contacts in the publishing world.

Coleridge and Dyer's publishing alliance continued during the following year, when Coleridge started his political lectures at Bristol. In February 1795, he wrote to Dyer claiming that 'the opposition of the Aristocrats is . . . furious and determined', adding that he had been '*obliged* to publish' his *Moral and Political Lecture,* 'it having been confidently asserted that there was Treason in it' (*CL,* i. 152). Perhaps Coleridge exaggerated the aristocratic 'fury' to impress his reformist friend. But in the same letter Coleridge begged Dyer's 'acceptance of as many Copies [of the lecture] as [he] may choose to give away', and mentioned that he had seen Dyer's **Dissertation on the Theory and Practice of Benevolence** advertised, and had ordered ten copies from the Bristol bookseller Joseph Cottle. One month later, in March 1795, Coleridge wrote again to Dyer enquiring about the possibility of work on a new London political journal, *The Citizen.* In this letter he also thanked Dyer for his comments on *A Moral and Political Lecture,* sent his 'respects' to Gilbert Wakefield, and concluded by asking: 'Is Mr Frend in Town?' (*CL,* i. 155-6).[16]

Following these letters the correspondence seems to have lapsed for a year, and was only resumed after the failure of Coleridge's *Watchman.* On 10 May 1796, John Thelwall wrote encouraging Coleridge that London booksellers 'would engage with [him] gladly', and suggested that Coleridge's 'old, & very very worthy friend Dyer and friends will give [him] something like similar advice'.[17] Later in the same month Coleridge wrote to Dyer thanking him for a gift of money: 'You have already sent a sum amply sufficient to extricate me from my difficulties, & to provide for my expences till such time as my literary Industry will, I trust, find employment' (*CL,* i. 218). The letter is, understandably, slightly awkward and stilted. But Coleridge was evidently rescued by Dyer's tactful recommendation of his case to the Committee of the Literary Fund. One of Dyer's correspondents, a Mr Scott, wrote to him on 16 May in response to his application to the fund on Coleridge's behalf: 'I will stretch a point to advance what may be expected from the Literary Fund', Scott writes,

'at the same time, trying what I can do further for S: Taylor'. He was successful in those further efforts, for in June 1796 Coleridge wrote thanking the Literary Fund 'for this relief so liberally and delicately afforded me' (*CL,* i. 220).[18]

THE POLITICS OF KINDNESS IN 'TINTERN ABBEY'

that best portion of a good man's life . . .

Coleridge's friendship with Dyer was rooted in their early lives at Christ's Hospital and Cambridge and their mutual political and literary interests. It was also encouraged by Dyer's willingness to find a market for Coleridge's writings in London. Their thinking about society coincided at their first meeting in 1794, when both were eagerly projecting Pantisocracy. Mutual influence explains the continued similarities in their political and social ideas over the following year. During 1795 Dyer and Coleridge were both moving towards a belief in the 'one life' of the universe, the beneficent power of which was mediated through nature to the human mind as a cause of moral good. 'The pleasures, which we receive from rural beauties', Coleridge wrote to Dyer on 10 March,

> are of little Consequence compared with the Moral Effect of these pleasures—beholding constantly the Best possible we at last become ourselves the best possible. In the country, all around us smile Good and Beauty . . .
>
> (*CL,* i. 154)

For Coleridge human behaviour was necessarily 'shaped & coloured' by the surrounding environment: a 'demonstrative proof', he told Dyer, 'that Man was not made to live in Great Cities!' (*CL,* i. 154). But whereas Coleridge's letter reflected the mechanical processes of Hartley's (and, incidentally, Godwin's) necessarianism, Dyer identified the 'Moral Effect' of nature as the 'universal voice' of benevolence. His *Dissertation on Benevolence* was published in February or March 1795, and it contained passages that strikingly resembled Coleridge's thinking at this time. 'In whatever point of the universe we take our stand', Dyer wrote in his pamphlet,

> and to whatever spot we turn our eyes, how fertile and glowing the landscape! In a system so contrived, that one part sheds its influence on, and promotes the harmony of, the other, this cannot be otherwise: There is a kind of voice that speaks through the universe.
>
> (*Dissertation,* p. 15)

Dyer argues, in terms close to Coleridge's letter of 10 March 1795, that this mysterious unity of creation has a moral effect upon individuals:

> The GOOD MAN from the appearances of nature derives tender affections, generous principles, and humane conduct. From the glowing and variegated scenes

around him he derives something which warms his heart, and throws a smile over his countenance. . . . The good man thus acquires universal tenderness.

*(**Dissertation**, p. 19)*

For Dyer as for Coleridge, receptivity to 'the appearance of nature' leads to moral goodness: 'beholding . . . the Best possible we . . . become ourselves the best possible'. One is not far, here, from the '"wise passiveness"' of Wordsworth's 'Expostulation and Reply', or the 'universal tenderness' of 'Lines Written at a Small Distance from my House':

And from the blessed power that rolls
About, below, above;
We'll frame the measure of our souls,
They shall be tuned to love.

(11. 37-40)

Here, Wordsworth's joy in companionship resembled Dyer's belief that natural benevolence was a social virtue, realised through acts of practical compassion. 'True benevolence', he wrote in his *Dissertation,*

is desirous of advancing human beings to all the innocent comforts of which their nature is capable, and of mitigating those distresses, to which by their own frailties, or the injustice of others, they are exposed—Ignorance, slavery, imprisonment, sickness, disappointment, and old age, have their distinct claims, and form a separate interest in a good man's heart.

*(**Dissertation**, p. 21)*

Dyer's radical career and his friendship with Coleridge show that he lived up to these humane ideals. And given Wordsworth's acquaintance with Dyer in London during spring 1795, and Coleridge's intimacy with Wordsworth after 1797, it is not surprising that Dyer's pamphlet should in some ways foreshadow Wordsworth's poetry of 1798. The resemblance appears in the lyrics he wrote in the spring of that year, but also in a central passage of 'Tintern Abbey':

Though absent long,
These forms of beauty have not been to me,
As is a landscape to a blind man's eye:
But oft, in lonely rooms, and mid the din
Of towns and cities, I have owed to them,
In hours of weariness, sensations sweet,
Felt in the blood, and felt along the heart,
And passing even into my purer mind
With tranquil restoration:—feelings too
Of unremembered pleasure; such, perhaps,
As may have had no trivial influence
On that best portion of a good man's life;
His little, nameless, unremembered acts
Of kindness and of love.

(11. 23-36)

For Dyer, the 'appearances of nature' had encouraged 'tender affections, generous principles, and humane conduct'. Three years later, in July 1798, Wordsworth's poem offered a similarly benign morality, mediated through the workings of memory and the inscrutable process of 'unremembered pleasure' to 'unremembered acts / Of kindness and of love': *kindness,* that is, with the sense of human relationship or kinship—what Coleridge would have termed the 'fabric' of society. In 'Tintern Abbey', however, the 'universal tenderness' that Wordsworth shared with Dyer merges with 'another gift, / Of aspect more sublime': the 'serene and blessed mood' in which the feeling soul is led to 'see into the life of things'. In that moment of Romantic exaltation, the kindly aspect of George Dyer's dissent is fulfilled in a vision of transcendent harmony.

DYER'S TRUE GENIUS

The ***Dissertation on Benevolence*** marks the period, in 1795, when Dyer turned away from immediate political action to explore an alternative possibility of human amelioration. The first section of his pamphlet offered a theory of universal benevolence which 'directs its energies to alleviate the distresses incident to humanity, and to remedy the evils forced on the world by a vicious state of society' (*Dissertation,* p. 23). Three years previously, he had anticipated an identical prospect from a national convention and a republican government in London. The second part of the pamphlet examined the consequences of repression in 'the cases of those, lately put on their Trials for Treason or Sedition; which, though the last in the order of this Dissertation, were the first in [the author's] mind' (*Dissertation,* p. 76). So the *Dissertation* looked in two directions. In reviewing the plight of the reform movement, Dyer surveyed the crisis of his own cause as reformist and dissenter. But his recognition of a benevolent tendency in the nature of things opened a fresh prospect, and asserted a fundamental continuity in his political and intellectual life.

Others were moving in this direction during 1795 too. Coleridge's *Lecture on the Slave Trade,* delivered in June that year, began with a vision which showed how the imagination 'stimulates' human progress (*Lects 1795,* 235). The stages of Wordsworth's intellectual development at this time are less readily documented. His settlement in the Dorset countryside effectively severed his immediate links with Godwin and London, although this did not mean that Wordsworth lost touch with contemporary politics altogether. For Wordsworth and Coleridge these personal and intellectual changes eventually led to the mutual achievements of 1797-8, an imaginative triumph Dyer did not share. He did not fulfil the promise of his *Dissertation* by writing a poem, like 'Tintern Abbey', that resolved political failure in the transcendent democracy to which his pamphlet had looked.

In subsequent years, Dyer's prolific output of undistinguished poetry and criticism was a subject of amusement (and sometimes irritation) to Coleridge, Lamb and other friends. Their attitude is an indication of how, in changed times and circumstances, he no longer appeared intellectually or creatively significant. In his lifetime he produced five substantial collections of verse: *Poems* (1792), *The Poet's Fate* (1797) and *Poems* (1801) were followed by two collections of verse with supporting essays, *Poems and Critical Essays* (1802) and *Poetics* (1812). The poetry is most kindly described as 'occasional' verse and Charles Lamb listed its motley, derivative qualities in a letter to Thomas Manning: 'Ode, pastoral, sonnet, Elegy, Spenserian, Horation, akensidish, & Masonic, verse' (Marrs, i. 222). Dyer's early friendship with Coleridge is evidence of his generosity to other writers, but his own ambitions as a literary critic and theorist met with disappointment. Having prepared during 1800 a volume of critical essays to accompany his forthcoming *Poems,* Dyer discovered (as Lamb recalled) 'that in the very first page of [the] preface he had set out with a principle of criticism fundamentally wrong, which vitiated all his following reasoning' (Marrs, i. 262-3). As a result he delayed publication of the volume of essays until 1802, but a single copy of his cancelled preface survives in the British Library bound with Dyer's *Poems* (1801), and containing manuscript notes by Lamb and Coleridge.[19] In this 1800 preface Dyer announced his intention to give 'free rein to [his] imagination . . . to impose no restraint on [his] feelings; to let [his] thoughts run loose to what extent they please; to seize the rudest ideas, while yet lively and warm'. Dyer's indulgence of spontaneity, and his casual attitude to his published poetry, caused Lamb much amusement—especially so in one of the copious footnotes to his 1801 *Poems:* '"Discrimination is not the *aim* of the present volume. It will be more strictly attended to in the next"' (quoted with delight by Lamb in a letter to Manning, 15 February 1801, Marrs, i. 274).

Despite the setback of his cancelled preface Dyer persevered with writing poems, and in 1812 he published *Poetics* in two volumes, as 'a systematic edition of [his] poetical writings' supported by critical 'disquisitions' on 'Arts and Sciences', 'Poetical Genius', 'The Number of Excellent Poets' and 'The Use of Topography in Poetry'. In the same year he also published as a small pamphlet *Four Letters on the English Constitution.* These letters first appeared in Leigh Hunt's *Reflector* and, as this connection suggests, their subject was parliamentary reform. Wordsworth, Coleridge, and Southey had by now moved to the centre of the establishment, but Dyer retained his dissenting opinions to a period when parliamentary reform was once again on the political agenda. At this moment, as Chapter Two will show, Southey and Coleridge were particularly anxious to disown their early reformist opinions, actions and publications. But in his *Letters on the English Constitution,* Dyer looked back in order to gather encouragement for the present:

A second period, when the question concerning the English Constitution became much agitated, commenced with the Revolution of France. That event gave an unusual interest to the question. A new epoch seemed to be forming.[20]

Unlike his former jacobin associates, Dyer wished to affirm the links between the revolutionary decade and the reform movement's revival in the nineteenth century: 'Civil and religious liberty, is the only true cement of the English Constitution: penal laws are wedges driven violently into it . . . Liberty of conscience is every man's inalienable birthright' (pp. 127, 129). His pamphlet is a testament to his consistency through decades when liberal and reformist politics had been energetically suppressed. It was surely Dyer's generous humanity that Lamb had in mind when he told Coleridge that the 'oftener' he saw Dyer 'the more deeply [he] admired him'. His admiration warms Elia's later stories about his 'old friend G. D.'. It transforms those stories into a celebration of Dyer's true genius: an affirmation of the spirit in which Dyer himself—like other, greater Romantic poets—had formerly sought 'to alleviate the distresses incident to humanity'.

Notes

1. Charles Lamb, *Elia and the Last Essays of Elia,* ed. J. Bate (Oxford, 1987) 11, 237-8.

2. See E. V. Lucas, *The Life of Charles Lamb,* (2 vols, London, 1905) i. 144-67, and for Hunt's anecdote, i. 162. For Dyer's trajectory, see *The Works of Charles and Mary Lamb,* ed. E. V. Lucas (7 vols, London, 1903-5) ii. 433, cited in future as Lamb, *Works.* Two studies which take Dyer seriously are Winifred Courtney, *Young Charles Lamb 1775-1802* (London, 1982) hereafter *Young Charles Lamb,* and M. Ray Adams, *Studies in the Literary Backgrounds of English Radicalism* (Lancaster Pa., 1947).

3. Dyer also wrote the 'Preliminary Remarks' to George Thompson, *Slavery and Famine, Punishments for Sedition* (London, 1794).

4. For Dyer and Lamb, see Chapter Three, p. 60 below.

5. See the memoir of Jebb in *The Works of John Jebb,* ed. J. Disney (3 vols, London, 1794) i. 1-227.

6. See Dyer's obituary in *The Gentleman's Magazine* NS 15 (May 1841), 545-7. For Dyer's father, see S. Butterworth, 'Charles Lamb: Some new Biographical and other Details', *The Bookman* 60 (July 1921) 165-70.

7. Robert Robinson, *A Political Catechism* (London, 1784) 57.

8. *The Parliamentary History of England from the Earliest Period to the Year 1803* (36 vols, London, 1806-20) xxix. 1385, 1388, 1392, hereafter *Parliamentary History.*

9. For a more detailed analysis of Wordsworth, Coleridge, Dyer and Godwin see *RY,* 175-98. For a discussion of how Coleridge's response to Godwin affected *The Recluse* scheme, see Nicola Trott, 'The Coleridge Circle and the "Answer to Godwin"', *Review of English Studies* 41 (May 1990) 212-229, hereafter cited as Trott, Godwin.

10. George Dyer to Rev. Mr. Carey, 24 May 1836. Archive of Emmanuel College, Cambridge, Col. 9, 13.

11. For Wakefield see Thompson, 'Disenchantment', 162-7. For Wakefield's and Johnson's trials, see Jane Worthington Smyser, 'The Trial and Imprisonment of Joseph Johnson, Bookseller', *Bulletin of the New York Public Library* 78 (1974), 418-35, hereafter, Smyser, *Johnson*; see also F. K. Prochaska, 'English State Trials in the 1790s: A Case Study', *Journal of British Studies* 13 (November 1973), 63-82. For Henry Crabb Robinson on visiting Johnson—a 'wise man'—in King's Bench Prison, 1799, see *Henry Crabb Robinson's Diary,* ed. T. Sadler (3 vols, London, 1869) i. 57-8.

12. See especially Lucy Newlyn, '"In City Pent": Echo and Allusion in Wordsworth, Coleridge, and Lamb, 1797-1801', *Review of English Studies* 32 (November 1981) 408-428.

13. 'Adventures on Salisbury Plain' in *The Salisbury Plain Poems of William Wordsworth,* ed. Stephen Gill, Cornell Wordsworth Series (Ithaca, New York, and Hassocks, Sussex, 1975). Beth Darlington, 'Two Early Texts', *Bicentenary Wordsworth Studies in Memory of John Alban Finch,* ed. Jonathan Wordsworth (Ithaca and London, 1970) 425-48.

14. See McGann, 83.

15. *The Complaints of the Poor People of England* (2nd edn., London, 1793) 83.

16. *The Citizen* may have been a provisional title for *The Philanthropist,* published in 42 issues by Daniel Isaac Eaton between 16 March 1795 and 18 January 1796. Coleridge's letter is postmarked 10 March 1795, six days before the first issue of *The Philanthropist* appeared in London. For Wordsworth and Eaton's *Philanthropist* see Kenneth R. Johnston, 'Philanthropy or Treason? Wordsworth as "Active Partisan"', *Studies in Romanticism,* 25 (1986) 371-409, hereafter Johnston, 'Philanthropy or Treason?'; *RY,* 276-9; E. P. Thompson, 'Wordsworth's Crisis', *London Review of Books* (8 December 1988) 3-6, hereafter 'Wordsworth's Crisis'.

17. W. E. Gibbs, 'An Unpublished Letter from John Thelwall to S. T. Coleridge', *Modern Language Review* 25 (1930) 85-90.

18. A. Scott to George Dyer, 16 May 1796. Archive of Emmanuel College Cambridge, Col. 9, 13.

19. British Library Catalogue reference C. 45 f. 18. (1). See also Harriet Jump, '"Snatch'd out of the Fire"; Lamb, Coleridge, and George Dyer's Cancelled Preface', *Charles Lamb Bulletin* NS 58 (1987) 54-67.

20. George Dyer, *Four Letters on the English Constitution* (London, 1812) 7. Subsequent page references given in the text.

Abbreviations

BSL: Manuscript letters of Robert Southey in the Bodleian Library, Oxford.

CL: The Collected Letters of Samuel Taylor Coleridge, ed, E. L. Griggs (6 vols, Oxford, 1956-71).

Complaints: George Dyer, *The Complaints of the Poor People of England* (London, 1793).

Curry: *New Letters of Robert Southey,* ed. K. Curry (2 vols, New York and London, 1965).

Dissertation: George Dyer, *A Dissertation on the Theory and Practice of Benevolence* (London, 1795).

EY: The Letters of William and Dorothy Wordsworth, ed. E. de Selincourt, 2nd edn, *The Early Years, 1787-1805,* rev. C. L. Shaver (Oxford, 1967).

Howe: *The Complete Works of William Hazlitt,* ed. P. P. Howe (21 vols, London, 1930-34).

Inquiry: George Dyer, *An Inquiry into the Nature of Subscription* (2nd edn, London, 1792).

Lects 1795: S. T. Coleridge, *Lectures 1795 on Politics and Religion,* ed. L. Patton and P. Mann, Bollingen Collected Coleridge (Princeton, 1971).

Marrs: *The Letters of Charles and Mary Anne Lamb,* ed. E. W. Marrs, Jr. (3 vols, Ithaca, NY, 1975-8).

PJ: William Godwin, *Political Justice* (2 vols, London, 1793).

PrW: The Prose Works of William Wordsworth, ed. W. J. B. Owen and J. W. Smyser (3 vols, Oxford, 1974).

RM, i, ii: Thomas Paine, *The Rights of Man, Part One and Part Two,* ed. H. Collins (Harmondsworth, 1969).

RY: Nicholas Roe, *Wordsworth and Coleridge, The Radical Years* (Oxford, 1988).

A Note on Texts

All references to *The Prelude* will be to William Wordsworth, *The Prelude, 1799, 1805, 1850,* ed. J. Wordsworth, M. H. Abrams, and S. Gill (New York, 1979). Quotations will be from the 1805 text, unless designated 1799 or 1850.

Quotations from Wordsworth's and Coleridge's poems in *Lyrical Ballads,* 1798, will be from *Lyrical Ballads,* ed. R. L. Brett and A. R. Jones (London, 1963). Quotations from Coleridge's 'Monody on the Death of Chatterton' and *Religious Musings* will be from the text in S. T. Coleridge, *Poems on Various Subjects* (London and Bristol, 1796).

Quotations from Blake are from *The Complete Poems* ed. W. H. Stevenson (2nd edn., Harlow, Essex, 1989). Quotations from Milton are from *Paradise Lost,* ed. A. Fowler (London, 1968) and *Complete Shorter Poems,* ed. J. Carey (London, 1968). Quotations from Shakespeare are from *The Complete Works,* ed. S. Wells and G. Taylor (Oxford, 1986).

Square brackets in this book are editorial.

Bibliography

1. Manuscripts Cited

Bodleian Library, Oxford

Manuscript English Letters:

c.22: Letters of Robert Southey.

c.453: Letter from George Burnett to Nicholas Lightfoot, 22 October 1796.

The British Library

Autogr. 46870: Poems by John Augustus Bonney.

Edinburgh University Library

MS Gen 748/4: Prison Diary of John Augustus Bonney.

Emmanuel College, Cambridge

Col. 9.13: Correspondence of George Dyer.

Public Record Office

Treasury Solicitor's Papers:

TS 11 961 3507: Minutes of the SCI, Volume One.

TS 11 961 3508: Minutes of the SCI, Volume Two.

2. Primary Sources

Burke, Edmund, *Reflections on the Revolution in France,* ed. C. C. O'Brien (Harmondsworth, 1968).

Coleridge, Samuel Taylor, *Collected Coleridge* (Bollingen Series 75; Princeton, NJ) i. *Lectures 1795 on Politics and Religion,* ed. L. Patton and P. Mann (1971) ii. *The Watchman,* ed. L. Patton (1970) iii. *Essays on his Times,* ed. D. V. Erdman (3 vols. 1978) vii. *Biographia Literaria,* ed. J. Engell and W. Jackson Bate (2 vols, 1983).

———.*Collected Letters,* ed. E. L. Griggs (6 vols, Oxford, 1956-71).

Dyer, George, *The Complaints of the Poor People of England* (London, 1793; 2nd edn. London, 1793).

———.*A Dissertation on the Theory and Practice of Benevolence* (London, 1795).

———.*Four Letters on the English Constitution* (London, 1812).

———.*An Inquiry into the Nature of Subscription* (2nd edn., London 1792).

Jebb, John, *Works,* ed. John Disney (3 vols, London, 1794).

Lamb, Charles, *Elia and the Last Essays of Elia,* ed. J. Bate (Oxford, 1987).

Paine, Thomas, *The Rights of Man,* ed. H. Collins (Harmondsworth, 1969).

Parliamentary Debates from the Year 1803, to the Present Time (41 vols, London, 1804-20).

Robinson, Henry Crabb, *Diary,* ed. T. Sadler (3 vols, London, 1869).

Robinson, Robert, *A Political Catechism* (London, 1784).

Thompson, George, *Slavery and Famine. Punishments for Sedition* (London, 1794).

Wordsworth, William, *A Letter to the Bishop of Llandaff on the Extraordinary Avowal of his Political Principles Contained in the Appendix to his late Sermon. By a Republican* (London, 1793).

———.*An Evening Walk,* ed. J. Averill, Cornell Wordsworth Series (Ithaca and London, 1984).

———.*The Pedlar, Tintern Abbey, The Two-Part Prelude,* ed. J. Wordsworth (Cambridge, 1985).

———.*The Prelude, 1799, 1805, 1850,* ed. J. Wordsworth, M. H. Abrams, S. Gill (New York and London, 1979).

———.*The Salisbury Plain Poems,* ed. S. Gill, Cornell Wordsworth Series (Ithaca, NY, and Hassocks, Sussex, 1975).

3. Secondary Sources

Adams, M. Ray, *Studies in the Literary Backgrounds of English Radicalism* (Lancaster, Pa., 1947).

Butterworth, S., 'Charles Lamb: Some New Biographical and other Details', *The Bookman* 60 (July 1921).

Courtney, Winifred, *Young Charles Lamb, 1775-1802* (London, 1982).

Darlington, Beth, 'Two Early Texts', *Bicentenary Wordsworth Studies in Memory of John Alban Finch,* ed. J. Wordsworth (Ithaca and London, 1970).

Gibbs, W. E., 'An Unpublished Letter from John Thelwall to S. T. Coleridge', *Modern Language Review* 25 (1930).

Johnston, K. R., 'Philanthropy or Treason? Wordsworth as "Active Partisan"', *Studies in Romanticism* 25 (1986).

Jump, Harriet, '"Snatch'd out of the Fire"; Lamb, Coleridge, and George Dyer's Cancelled Preface', *The Charles Lamb Bulletin* NS 58 (1987).

Lucas, E. V., *The Life of Charles Lamb* (2 vols, London, 1905).

McGann, Jerome J., *The Romantic Ideology. A Critical Investigation* (Chicago and London, 1983).

Newlyn, Lucy, '"In City Pent": Echo and Allusion in Wordsworth, Coleridge, and Lamb, 1797-1801', *Review of English Studies* 32 (1981).

Prochaska, F. K., 'English State Trials in the 1790s: A Case Study', *Journal of British Studies* 13 (1973).

Smyser, J. W., 'The Trial and Imprisonment of Joseph Johnson, Bookseller', *Bulletin of the New York Public Library,* 78 (1974).

Thompson, E. P., 'Disenchantment or Default? A Lay Sermon', *Power and Consciousness,* ed. C. C. O'Brien and W. D. Vanech (London and New York, 1969).

————.'Wordsworth's Crisis', *London Review of Books* (8 December 1988).

Trott, Nicola, 'The Coleridge Circle and the "Answer to Godwin"', *Review of English Studies* 41 (1990).

4. Newspapers and Journals

The Gentleman's Magazine.

The Philanthropist.

Robin Jarvis (essay date summer 1998)

SOURCE: Jarvis, Robin. "Poetry in Motion: George Dyer's Pedestrian Tour." *Wordsworth Circle* 29, no. 3 (summer 1998): 142-51.

[*In the following excerpt, Jarvis discusses one of Dyer's poems about a walking tour with his friend Arthur Aikin, arguing that at least some of his poetry was at the forefront of Romantic and revolutionary sentiment.*]

It is the fate of George Dyer, at least among scholars working outside the eighteenth century and early nineteenth century, permanently to be confused with the author of *The Fleece* and "Grongar Hill." John Dyer (1699-1757), anthologised in popular volumes like *The Norton Anthology of Poetry,* is reputedly—to borrow the imagery once loved by publishers—a "silver poet" of the eighteenth century; by contrast, George Dyer's metallurgical status must be bronze at best. Even among specialists in the Romantic period, his work is little-known and seldom read. He is remembered chiefly as an intimate of Charles Lamb, and Lamb's own amusing caricatures of his friend in the *Elia* essays set the tone for most observations, both contemporary and more recent. "Oxford in the Vacation" portrays Dyer as a deep denizen of the Bodleian Library, the kind of "Herculanean raker" of archives which Lamb himself is not. The image of an absentminded scholar is accentuated by an anecdote of Dyer calling twice the same day at a friend's town house, only realising his error when he saw his own name in the visitor's book. Lamb points out, however, that when "absent from the body" in this way Dyer is habitually meditating some general scheme or individual act of benevolence. The general terms of this humorous raillery reappear in "Amicus Redivivus," which presents the celebrated story of Dyer's leaving Lamb's house in Islington and walking—indeed, completely submerging himself in—the nearby river; Lamb's mock-heroic protest at this near calamity extracts every ounce of satiric potential (*Elia* 11, 13, 237-42). It is tempting to think that Lamb's well-known objection to Coleridge's description of him as "gentle-hearted" in "This Lime-Tree Bower My Prison" stemmed from its resemblance to the image of amiable buffoon he was constructing for Dyer. At any rate, the obituary of the "simple-hearted" Dyer in *The Gentleman's Magazine* in 1841 shows how perfectly this image had crystallised: "The memory of George Dyer will be ever cherished by his friends as of one who passed through the world without having contracted one blemish of wordliness; his guileless simplicity endeared him especially to his friend Charles Lamb, who would often indeed indulge his humorous vein at the expense of one whom he knew to be an invulnerable innocency . . ." (546).

The purpose of the present essay is to examine one particular poem he wrote in 1798, which offers a series of windows onto the literary and political culture of the revolutionary decade. It is also a poem which connects directly to a late eighteenth-century phenomenon—namely, the rise of pedestrian touring and the attendant travel literature—in which I have a special interest. By undertaking a close reading of this poem, I hope to further the efforts made by a small number of critics to restore to Dyer the "worldliness" of which Lamb persuaded posterity to deprive him.

In his *Studies in the Literary Backgrounds of English Radicalism* (1947; 1968), M. Ray Adams vigorously contested Lamb's representation of Dyer as "a queer specimen in the laboratory of human nature" (228), re-establishing his credentials as a key figure in Cambridge dissenting circles in the 1780s and in the metropolitan radical movement of the 1790s. Adams's account, which resonates with good sense and still reads well today, gives generous consideration to Dyer's main political writings, especially his *Inquiry into the Nature of Subscription.* He gives much less attention to Dyer's poetry, although interestingly he does single out, in a footnote, as a rare synthesis of "unaffected simplicity" and "humanitarian fervour" (232), the very blank-verse poem, **"To Mr. Arthur Aikin,"** which I reproduce below. (This is the only reference to the poem I have come across.) Adams's valuable labours towards recovering Dyer's seriousness as a political writer and reformer have sponsored very fresh critical interest. Winifred Courtney, in her biography of Lamb, emphasises Dyer's role in bringing people together (helping introduce Wollstonecraft to Godwin, for example) and acting as "informal coordinator and catalyst for many of his radical generation" (204); and Harriet Jump has cast fresh light on the notorious incident of the cancellation of Dyer's Preface to a volume of essays planned for 1800, which he had thrown into the fire on discovering a "principle of criticism" that was "fundamentally wrong" on the first page (A copy which Dyer rescued is prefixed to the British Library's edition of *Poems,* 1801). Nicholas Roe, however, has done most to resuscitate Dyer's reputation not only as a radical dissenter embroiled in contemporary issues but as a significant player in the literary culture of the day.[1] Roe is particularly enlightening on Dyer's role in introducing Wordsworth, Coleridge and Southey to broader political and intellectual circles in London, and on the continuities between Dyer's moral philosophy and Wordsworth's and Coleridge's developing poetic vision in 1795-98. Roe's chief interest is, in common with Adams, in Dyer's major prose works, and he offers no reason to disturb the general neglect of his subject's "prolific output of undistinguished poetry" (*Politics* 33). While it would be a brave critic who sought to overturn this weight of critical judgment, there is, I believe, a case for giving serious attention to one quite accomplished poem which offers some different connections and contexts for evaluating his achievement.

Dyer was born in 1755, the son of a shipwright in Bridewell, East London, and received charitable support to go to Christ's Hospital, the school later attended by Lamb and Coleridge. Funded by the school, he entered Emmanuel College, Cambridge, in 1774, and graduated four years later, overcoming any scruples he may have had about subscription. A fragment of his lost autobiography preserved in the *Gentleman's Magazine* obituary suggests he was lonely at Cambridge, but it was here that he got acquainted with intellectual dissenters who confirmed his disapproval of the Established Church and politicised his thinking. The Baptist minister, Robert Robinson, who had supported the local campaign for the abolition of subscription and who founded the Cambridge branch of the Society for Constitutional Information in 1780, was one of his close friends. After a

spell of tuition at Dedham Grammar School, Dyer returned to take up lodgings in Robinson's house, both to act as tutor to his children and to be trained for the dissenting ministry himself. In 1781, he preached for a while at Oxford, but soon returned to Cambridge where, in the words of M. Ray Adams, he was "for the next ten years . . . one of that influential group of Cambridge Dissenters which for more than thirty years made a valiant fight for the removal of political and religious disabilities" (234). During this period both Dyer and Robinson were converted to Unitarianism. Dyer's *Inquiry into the Nature of Subscription to the Thirty-nine Articles,* first published in 1789, was the culmination of this phase of his career as a political reformer, a phase which also saw the failure of a scheme to establish a dissenter's college at Cambridge, with Dyer as tutor.

In 1792, Dyer moved permanently to London, a transition made at different times by other prominent Cambridge dissenters, such as John Jebb, Gilbert Wakefield and William Frend. In London, as Nicholas Roe vividly describes, Dyer deepened his involvement in radical politics, associating himself not only with the Society for Constitutional Information but also with the more radical Paineite London Corresponding Society, and publicly maintained liberal, anti-government, pro-republican views through the years which saw the suppression of the revolutionary societies and the growth of a nervous, suspicious conservatism in the culture at large. Dyer supported himself in London by private tuition and writing, and, although his income was modest, he came to the financial help of others, like Coleridge, whose publishing career he materially aided. He seems to have had an irrepressible talent for making introductions, both commercial (as in introducing young writers to booksellers and publishers) and personal: Lamb remarked that "George brings all sorts of people together, setting up a sort of Agrarian Law or common property in matter of society" (*Letters* 1:243).

Dyer's main political writings in the revolutionary decade were the *Inquiry into the Nature of Subscription, Complaints of the Poor People of England* (1793), and *A Dissertation on the Theory and Practice of Benevolence* (1795). The *Complaints* is a comprehensive indictment of "things as they are," taking in the iniquities of parliamentary representation, fiscal policy, crime and punishment, the poor law, the defects of national education, the scandal of public expenditure on the royal household and the civil list, the need to disestablish the Church, and so on. In his penultimate chapter, the "Address to the Friends of Liberty," Dyer contrasts the present British government unfavourably with ancient Athenian democracy, defends the activities of the corresponding societies as consistent with the "genius of english liberty," and, directly attacking the many government-sponsored, counter-propagandist organisations, concludes that 'BRITAIN is ENSLAVED by FRIENDS to LIBERTY and PROPERTY' (198, 211). Dyer carried his principles into practice by raising subscriptions to assist with the legal expenses of the defendants in the treason trials in the final quarter of 1794.

Dyer is still concerned with the situation of these men—acquitted, but materially injured by their treatment by the state—in his *Dissertation on the Theory and Practice of Benevolence,* published in 1795. He puts them forward as worthy objects of the moral disposition of which he speaks, defined as "a gentle and human propensity, that inclines to sympathy, and moves those who possess it to be interested in the happiness of others" (3). Although the *Dissertation* is a less obviously controversial and interventionist work—concentrating more on individual than on collective remedies for social evils—in stressing the independence and objectivity of true benevolence, Dyer maintains his focus on the degenerate state of political morality: "In a system, where besides the regular salaries of office, sinecures and douceurs are held out, corruption is inseparable" (7).

Among Dyer's later prose works, his *Address to the People of Great Britain on the Doctrine of Libels and the Office of Juror,* published in 1799 in the climate of fear, persecution, and war-fever that forced many radicals into silence or reaction, was a defence of fellow-classicist and reformer Gilbert Wakefield, recently prosecuted for publishing a work which suggested that the labouring classes of Britain had nothing to lose from a French invasion (Thompson 192). In 1802, Dyer took part in Sir Francis Burdett's successful election campaign. In 1814, he published *Four Letters on the English Constitution,* which resumed the confrontational political approach of his earlier writings—attacking, for example, the Test and Corporation Acts which still discriminated against dissenters. Nicholas Roe claims this pamphlet as "a testament to [Dyer's] consistency through decades when liberal and reformist politics had been energetically suppressed" (*Politics* 35), underlining the contrast with former jacobins like Wordsworth and Southey. And although M. Ray Adams rightly points to Dyer's guardedness on immediate questions of government policy, and his general disinclination for political activism, he concedes too that fighting the ideological war for reform in counter-revolutionary Britain demanded courage and commitment (263-64, 266)—something more than the watery benevolence with which Dyer, as the kindly, absent-minded clown satirised by Lamb, became too exclusively associated.

Roe, building on the work of Adams and others, has performed valuable service in resurrecting this alternative face of George Dyer. The poetic output, however, which runs to five volumes, several of them substantial, remains completely obscured. The seriousness with which Dyer took his poetry himself, which became

something of a standing joke in the Lamb circle,[2] has not helped him in this regard. Nevertheless, it is worth noting that Dyer himself saw a continuity between democratic politics and poetic excellence: in the cancelled Preface of 1800, for example, he claims that Milton, Marvell, Akenside, Gray and Mason "raised their most rapturous notes" when "under the influence of good political principle," and laments the tendency of illiberal or decadent society to subdue all speech, including poetic utterance, to "the service of the oppressor," so that the poet becomes "a retailer of trifles, if not the propagator of scandal" (*Poems* [1801] xxxviii-xl). His first volume of poems, published in 1792, demonstrates his opposition to such repression: the **"Ode to Liberty,"** for example, surveys the various terrestrial homes of Liberty, including the writings of Mary Wollstonecraft and Helen Maria Williams, declares that he will emigrate to America if need be, and concludes by celebrating the "sacred day" of liberty in France. His **"Monody on the Death of a Friend"** is an elegy for his friends and mentor Robert Robinson, which in its consolatory final movement invokes the "sweet fields of vivid light" where the "sons of freedom" will meet again. Dyer appends an extra stanza to this poem at the end of the volume, which includes a reference to British liberty. In a footnote which displays his characteristic blend of political earnestness, pedantry and strained humour, he adds: "Where I speak on British liberty I speak in a comparative sense, and many grains of allowance must be made. It becomes this nation to give us a reality for a fiction, and not to force bards to use the *licentia poetica.*" This suggests that poetic license is a rhetorical sublimation of freedoms which the British people celebrate, but overestimate, in the constitution of their own country.

The 1792 collection is by no means exclusively political. Other poems variously anticipate strands within the later poem on which the present essay is focused. **"Ode on the Spring"** is conventional praise of the beauties of the season, notably common wild flowers which are the work of "a master's matchless hand," and predictably looks ahead to "a brighter spring above." **"Ode on Pity,"** in a review of situations where "virtue lies distress'd" or "blooming beauty sinks oppress'd," rehearses in stock sentimental language the compassionate feelings to which *Complaints of the Poor People of England* gave concrete, practical application. **"Ode on Pity"** finds its subject nowhere on earth but in the soul of the man "who walks in holy fear / With God, and views him ever near," and invokes fellow Protestant reformers such as Thomas Cranmer, Robert Tyrwhitt and William Frend. Enthusiasm for nature, sentimentalism, and contemplative devotion are common traits in Dyer's poetry, though not usually within a single text.

Dyer's 1800 Preface has other germane things to say about poetry. One such passage appears when he attempts to preempt criticism that his poems, as the product of an ardent scholar, will necessarily be imitative. In the face of the amused consensus among his contemporaries regarding his otherworldly bookishness, he claims that he has been "too wild to be confined to books" and "too confident . . . to be dictated to by pedantic rules"; he has determined, he says, "to impose no restraint on my feelings; to let my thought run loose to what extent they please; to seize the rudest ideas, while yet living and warm; and to invite impressions, in a kind of extemporaneous observation, from real objects, and breathing pictures. . . . Indeed, most of my little pieces are a kind of perambulatory amusements, meditated, when I have been rambling, and, generally, written on the spot" (xxxiv). Improbable as this last claim appears (it is, of course, a rhetorical commonplace), the notion of Dyer's poems possessing a "perambulatory" quality, whether of thought or execution, chimes with my analysis of **"To Mr. Arthur Aikin"** below. Dyer's defensive remarks here suggest that a perambulatory poetics is one which produces effects of spontaneity and practises verisimilitude with respect to external objects and events. There is also a sensuality present in the references to "the rudest ideas . . . yet living and warm" and "breathing pictures" which perhaps offers one gloss on Lamb's characterisation of Dyer as a "goodnatur'd Heathen" (*Letters* 1:222).

The idea of perambulation resurfaces later in the 1800 Preface when Dyer describes himself as a castle-builder who gets absorbed in lateral, digressive aspects of the project in hand: "He resembles a traveller, who is ever striking into byroads; at one time amusing himself in fields and gardens; at others bewildering himself in labyrinths; and then stumbling over rocks, or looking down precipices; when, on striking again into the old track, he finds himself but in the middle of the road, when he ought to have arrived at his journey's end" (lvi-lvii). (Typically, Dyer then apologises for the length of his apology.) This use of pedestrianism as a metaphor for mental wandering gives locomotive particularity to the centuries-old comparison between exterior and interior journeys, and is a familiar trope in late eighteenth-century literature. Dyer would doubtless have been aware, for example, of Rousseau's *Reveries of the Solitary Walker* (1782), which announce his intention to "keep a faithful record of my solitary walks and the reveries that occupy them, when I give free rein to my thoughts and let my ideas follow their natural course, unrestricted and unconfined" (30). Rousseau's association of perambulatory freedom with "unconfined" meditation, which itself alludes to the ancient tradition of the Greek peripatetic philosophers, was congenial to Romantic writers: John Thelwall, in his idiosyncratic but influential work, *The Peripatetic,* sets out with similar intent to "pursue [his] meditations on foot, and can find occasion for philosophic reflection, wherever yon fretted vault . . . extends its glorious covering" (1:9); like Dyer, he represents digression as a departure from the main road into lonely paths and lanes.

In answer to possible objections that his London existence sits oddly against the rural themes of many of his poems, Dyer notes that he spends a good part of each year "rambling, or at the rural seat of some friend." He adds, though, that his perambulations "have been made subservient to some ardent pursuit" (xxxi-xxxii). The same note is struck in the Preface to his last collection of poems, *Poetics* (1812), where he states that, although poetry "easily rivets one to places," he has also been "a great rover through England, Scotland, and Wales"; and though his wanderings were undertaken with a variety of aims and in a variety of moods, they were "generally in sober earnest" (xv). The unnecessary elaboration and scrupulous qualification, the moral earnestness offsetting the quixotic self-display, characterise the man. But it would be interesting to know more about Dyer's annual peregrinations, since contemporary references are mostly from his London acquaintance, and most biographical treatments convey the impression that from 1792, he became a fixture in the capital.

The 1812 Preface announces a forthcoming poem called "The Pedestrian, a descriptive poem in blank verse." This poem was never written, so far as I know. The title, however, might equally well apply to the verse epistle on which this essay is focused. Another earlier poem from the 1801 collection, **"Perambulatory Musings, from Blenheim House, at Woodstock, in Oxfordshire, the Seat of the Duke of Marlborough, to Titley House, in Herefordshire, the Seat of William Greenly,"** gives credence to Dyer's self-representation as a rural rambler. This poem records, in a very idealised manner, the poet's pedestrian progress from Blenheim, where Vanbrugh's masterpiece recalls the splendours of the classical past; to the pastoral simplicity of Shenstone's residence at Leasowes; to Hagley, home of Lord Littleton and famously associated with Pope and Thomson, and which is praised as a setting for poetic composition; and finally to Titley House, where all pleasure in either nature or art is transcended by the joys of female company. (In the 1812 version, Dyer replaced this "melodious maid," somewhat absurdly, with the more abstract virtues of "Fairy-Hall" as the grail of his expedition.) Dyer's pedestrian excursion in this poem is strictly subordinated to a programmatic exploration of the contrary attractions of a various landscape and landscapes improved by art; and the poet performatively mirrors this rapid scene-shifting in his oscillating moods:

> Ever musing, ever ranging,
> Ever pleas'd, yet ever changing,
> Murmuring onward still I go,
> As brooks thro' winding vallies flow. . . .

(lines 55-64)

Both the generalized nature-images and the representation of the loitering poet ("sometimes sad, sometimes as gay") place the poem firmly within the tradition of eighteenth-century landscape verse, and beyond that the seminal instance of a divided nature-sensibility, Milton's companion-poems "L'Allegro" and "Il Penseroso." What is perhaps distinctive is that Dyer's walk takes him from great houses of high social standing and cultural resonance, where he is no more than a disempowered, admiring tourist, to the modest "seat" of a friend where he is a welcome guest on equal terms. The levelling function of walking is thus mirrored in the horizontal progress of the text.

Something more needs to be said about the contemporary (Romantic) meanings of walking before discussing **"To Mr Arthur Aikin,"** a poem more rooted in the material realities of rural pedestrianism than **"Perambulatory Musing."** The full title of Dyer's poem is **"To Mr Arthur Aikin, on Taking Leave of him at Dunkel, in Perthshire, after a Pedestrian Tour."** The pedestrian tour, of which I have given a fuller account in *Romantic Writing and Pedestrian Travel* (1997) was very much in vogue in 1798, the year in which the poem was published in the radical *Monthly Magazine.* The last quarter of the eighteenth century witnessed a rapid rise in recreational walking among the middle classes, the pedestrian tour being the most personally and socially challenging form of such activity. Such tours were taking place on the Continent in the 1780s—William Bowles and William Frend both made notable expeditions—and were not arrested by the upheavals of the revolutionary decade: William Wordsworth's famous walking tour of 1790 was repeated in most particulars by his schoolfriend Joshua Wilkinson in two tours in 1791 and 1793, the latter undertaken after the outbreak of hostilities between England and France.

The Revolutionary wars did, however, accelerate the growth of domestic touring, much of which was pedestrian. The Wye Valley, North Wales, the Lake District and the Highlands of Scotland were the most popular destinations, and a considerable body of travel-writing grew out of it. By 1798, the author of the *Monthly Magazine*'s half-yearly retrospect of British literature takes the opportunity of reviewing Richard Warner's *A Walk Through Wales* to "observe [with pleasure] an increasing frequency of these pedestrian tours"; "it grieves one," he says, "to see a man of taste at the mercy of a postilion." Since walking had historically been identified with poverty, unrespectability and possible criminality, to recommend pedestrian travel to the "man of taste" indicates a decisive reversal of opinion regarding the social acceptability of walking. Ten years later, Robert Southey, in his *Letters from England,* writes to his imaginary Spanish correspondent of the convergence of pedestrianism with the cult of the picturesque, and observes that "Young Englishmen have discovered

that they can walk as well as the well-girt Greeks in the days of old, and they have taught me the use of my legs" (166). By 1810, written tours for all parts of Britain, and specific information for pedestrians in general tourist guidebooks demonstrate that the unconventional or rebellious has become safely institutionalised, and, in 1815, the editor of the *Bristol Journal,* reporting the completion of a walk of 1000 miles in twenty days by a local resident, referred to it smugly as "the climax of what this age of Pedestrianism has afforded" (Gilbert and Howell 10).

The variety of motives that impelled the first generation of pedestrian tourists cannot be reduced to any simple formula. Undoubtedly there was an element of deliberate social nonconformism in the self-levelling expeditions of early pedestrians, many of whom were either undergraduates, as yet unincorporated into professional value systems and economic subservience, or members of the lower clergy, a famously impecunious and disaffected social group. In some cases, as in John Thelwall's tour of the southern counties of England in 1797, or Coleridge's tour of North Wales with Joseph Hucks in 1794, this nonconformism, a democratic urge to see life among the lower orders, amounted to an ideology of radical walking. Other motivations include, first, the Enlightenment model of scientific or philosophical travel, which required walking for the discipline of observation, note-taking and record-keeping; and, secondly, the evolving culture of aesthetic travel, in which walking exposed the spectator to the might of the sublime and to the stationary perspectives of the picturesque.

At the most general level, the origins of voluntary, pleasurable walking are related to changes in cultural semiotics which fashioned individuals as much as they fashioned the changes. The first pedestrians were intent upon challenging social complacencies and clearing an ideological space in which their actions could help redefine their identity. In a cultural landscape where there was strong peer and class pressure to declare one's status in the manner of one's travelling, walking was a performance of dissent: it signified a desired freedom from the context of their upbringing and education, of parental expectations and class etiquette, of a hierarchical and segregated society, and of a culturally defined and circumscribed self. The second generation of Romantic pedestrians inherited this ideology of walking readymade, and could be more relaxed, reflective and ironic about it, as Hazlitt was in his seminal piece of walking literature, "On Going a Journey." But at the time when Dyer and Aikin went on their tour of Scotland it was still being forged and contested in the face of traditional attitudes and a public mood suspicious of anything resembling "French principles"—as the judge says at the end of Mary Wollstonecraft's *Maria.* The *Monthly Magazine* supported pedestrian tours by publishing prose and poetry devoted to pedestrian travel. . . .

Arthur Aikin was probably twenty-four when he and Dyer went on their pedestrian tour in Scotland. Like his father, he had attended the Warrington Academy as a child, later moving to his aunt Mrs. Barbauld's school at Palgrave in Sussex. He showed an early bent towards scientific pursuits, stimulated by acquaintance with Joseph Priestley, whom he helped in setting up a new laboratory. Following his family's religious traditions, he trained as a Unitarian minister, but soon resigned his post on conscientious grounds (I have been unable to establish whether he had this faith in common with Dyer in 1797). In 1796, he made a pedestrian tour of North Wales with his brother Charles and another friend, publishing an account of it the following year. His motives for this tour were partly recreational, and partly to assist the mineralogical studies to which he was now committed. Although he considered going on foot essential to his researches, he recommended it more generally to his readers: "On foot a man feels perfectly at ease and independent; he may deviate from the road to climb any mountain, or descend to any torrent that attracts his notice; whereas on horseback in many cases this is impossible . . ." (x). He is primarily a scientific traveller, and his occasional efforts to aestheticise his account are rather half-hearted: on the top of Snowdon, for instance, lost in cloud, he experiences frustration and inconvenience rather than sublimity. He is interested chiefly in three ring-ouzels discovered in the thickest of the clouds, and hurries on to describe in detail the basaltic columns which he observed on his descent.

Between 1803 and 1808, Aikin edited an *Annual Review and History of Literature,* which aimed to provide early reviews of books across a huge range of subjects straddling the arts and sciences. With the exception of the *Review,* however, his publications were almost exclusively scientific, and the story of his later life is one of growing professional distinction in his chosen field. In 1807 he was one of the co-founders of the Geological Society of London, and contributed to its *Transactions,* on his death in 1855, the Society published a generous obituary which recalled the observation of another early member that Aikin "had a very logical head, and a calm and imperturbable temper" (xlii). He died a bachelor—a prospect Dyer, at age sixty-nine, avoided by marrying his laundress.

On their tour of Scotland in 1797, Aikin and Dyer were compatible. Both came from Dissenting backgrounds, sided politically with the English "Friends of Liberty," had broad, inquiring minds, and shared literary enthusiasms. Indeed, in 1797, Aikin's father, whom Dyer had praised in his **"Ode to Liberty"** in the *Poems* of 1792,

was literary editor of the *Monthly Magazine,* a periodical to which Dyer had already contributed and in which he published the following commemorative poem.

"To Mr. Arthur Aikin, on taking Leave of him at Dunkeld, in Perthshire, after a Pedestrian Tour"

AIKIN, there breathes in friendship what beguiles
The heavy hours, when dark distended clouds
Burst o'er the head in torrents, or high heaven
Rolls muttering deep-mouth'd thunder, and from far
The forked lightning darts athwart the sky,
Quick travelling down to th'eye with dazzling rays:
Then, darkness all around, how sweet the voice
Of friend! In converse kind there dwells a charm,
That wakes a smile, and mocks the sounding storm.
Nor less, when 'mid the barren dreary heath
The traveller strays, where scarce a heath-flower blooms
Yellow, or purple, as where Pentland lifts
His ridge, or spread the poor unthrifty plains
Of Cardigan, (where Pity's eye surveys
Rude heaps of lime and stone, which industry
But mock, and scarce a hedge-rew deigns to smile,
Save the poor furze;—) or toiling when he climbs
Snowdon or hoar Plinlimmon's craggy sides,
Brecnoc, or Grampian summits:—Who surveys
Nature's grand scenery, may not always hope
To view the cultur'd garden, or the lawn
Of verdure softly smooth, or daisied vale:
Nor always may he meet the wilder charms
Of brighter picturesque; nor gaze entranced
The lake, whose fair expanse, like mirror clear,
What smiles upon the bank, of bush, or tree,
And heaven's blue vault, reflects; for nature's tints,
Various as bold, display no common tone.
She, skilful painter, from the wide extremes
Of rough and smooth, of light and shade, effects
The clair obscure, the glory of her work.

Oh! ye who court the silent, calm retreats
Of contemplation, and who most prefer
The solitary walk, as suiting best
Their views, who sigh to pierce the secret haunts
Of nature, marking her vagaries strange,
And bold, and unrestrained as she, to muse
The free, the rapturous lay; still pace along
Your lonely way; and be your musings sweet!
Friendship has too its charms: for kindred minds,
Reflecting thought for thought, like travellers,
Bring each to each some unknown treasures home.

Whether embosom'd deep in ocean's flood,
Or scaling high the cliff, or piercing deep
The secret mine, or silver-winding stream
Skimming in wanton vessel, or with staff,
Like jolly pilgrim, pacing with slow step
The pathless muir, where the short windlestray
Of silvery brown, dispersed with many a knob
And green tall rush, obstruct the doubtful foot;
Converse is doubly sweet—and such, my friend,
We have enjoyed; but now agree to take
A long farewell: and thus through human life;
For what is human life? a day's short journey,
With changes fraught;—now up the wond'rous height
Hope climbs, and wistful views, and views again
The lengthening prospect—calls the prospect fair;—
Now, like the lightsome kid, o'er verdant lawn

She springs; then, 'midst the solitary waste
Sings chearful, though no voice she hears around,
Save the rude north-east, or the querulous brook,
Or screaming eagle: then rude ocean heaves,
Ocean of griefs and cares, the boisterous wave,
Till, prison'd round, she sickens. Oh! my friend,
Sweet then is converse; for to man 'tis given
To chear the soul with converse: nobler man
Nature has diff'renced from the speechless brute
By voice, by reason:—how he rises high,
Proudly prospective! How he looks around,
With nobler front, and soul-inspiring joy!

 But, Aikin, now we part; tho' scene so sweet
Might tempt us still t'extend our social walk.
DUNKELD, oh! lov'd retreat, embosom'd deep
In boldest rocks, and woods, that graceful clothe
The mountain side, beside whose smiling cots
Rolls his pellucid stream the sprightly Tay,
Scotia's divider stream, descending quick,
Meand'ring wide, Braidalbin's silver lake,
Fast hastening to the Frith: Here browner elms,
The greener pine, and larch of paler hue
Spread their most wanton branches: every tree
A language borrows, as proclaiming thee,
DUNKELD, its favourite sweetest residence.

 Enchanting scene! farewell—So blest a spot
Might well allure the priest of ancient time;
(For prudent well he knew to choose the soil
Of fairest, sweetest promise, as most apt
For holy musings) well might it allure,
To rase his temple here: and still appears
The sainted abbey, whose time-moulder'd walls
Bring to the memory the fair Gothic haunts
Of Tintern, Monmouth's fair sequester'd ruin,
Near which Wye pours the wild romantic flood.

 Low sunk in earth the gates! and round the stones
The shining ivy twines its wanton arms
In close embrace; and through the windows howl
Rude winds, and no fair fretted roof is seen,
Heav'ns arch its only roof,—and pavement none
Save the green grass, with here and there between
The moss clad monument, these still announce
Who liv'd, and—sleep, and wake to sleep no more.
The priest no more here chaunts, as measuring out
The hour, his matin and his ev'ning song,
Though still a portion of the stately dome
The Presbyter has claimed, and here he pours
The fervent prayer, thankful in happier hour
That popery sleeps;—and thus turns strangely round
The world, and thus to contemplation's eye
Appears to play the wanton, fickle game.

 But ere were part, my friend, let us ascend
Yon stately mountain, and trace back our course.
Gentle th'ascent, and many a grateful herb
Has nature scatter'd round with skilful hand.
The modest heath-flower here its purple tints
Displays, and broom its yellow splendours; here
The fern spreads broad, and here the juniper
Puts forth its berry, by the prickly green
Guarded, and many a flower of rarer hue
With her own hand she waters:—pleasing heights!

 Now we have gain'd the mountain's sacred brow!
How glows the landskape! for no shadowing cloud
Obstructs the sight: How heav'ns own varying hues
Shine on the face of nature! Mount on mount
Here climbs, and there the lessening hills retire!

The towering wood, where trees innumerous spread,
Shrinks to the slender copse, while stately Tay
Seems a poor streamlet to the astonish'd sight!
How many a day's long journey now appears
To th'eye, quick traveller, a short summers walk!
As fades a series of long wasting cares,
When joy mounts high, and distance veils the scene.
 Now pleas'd each roves a lonely traveller.
For need not seem the solitary path
Or sad, or irksome:—for what voice so sweet
As natures' songsters! And what scene so gay
As the still changing, still delightful change
Of hill and dale, and deep romantic glen,
Quick-gliding stream, and ever babbling brook!
And, oh! what sound so sweet as western gales
Kissing the trembling trees! And fancy can
Wake sounds still sweeter, can create new scenes,
Fresh, gay, ambrosial, such as purer sense
Of museful bard sees, hears, and grows inspir'd.

 There are t'whom humbler walks have charms: their
  feet
Can visit the close cot, where poverty
Sits patient, and where industry retired
From daily toil, drinks-in the poisoned air.
Nor need they scorn to tread the dark retreat
Of prison, and point out to Britain's sons
What may demand redress: subjects like these
Soften the heart: nor shall the humble muse
Blush at these themes, though now perchance
  compell'd
To different musings:—there she learnt to scorn
The low disdains of contumely, there caught
The fire of indignation, there the glow
Of mercy, and the mercy tunes her lyre.

 Ye generous rich, for 'mid the numerous tribe
Of gold-gorg'd wealthy, Britain boasts her few
Of rich, and generous, scorn not to contrive
How best to house the labourer,[3] let him taste
The sweets of cleanliness, and know to breathe
Pure air; nor let him tremble at th'approach
Of every wind that rides the pelting storm.
He, for your luxuries labours, he to you
Like the poor patient ox, and gentle sheep,
Raiment and food supplies: ah! say, shall he
Meet nothing but contempt, and low neglect?
Who deems his fellow mean, for man's his fellow,
Himself is mean—is worthless—a mere nothing,
And though he force the poor man's outward worship
Knee-bent to th'earth, shall have his heart's contempt.

 My friend, be thine to rove no fruitless path
For science guides thee, and thyself hast rais'd
Fair hope,[4] and pointing thee to rural haunts
And pleasing themes, thy parent leads the way.
The months, with all their songs, and fruits and
  flow'rs,
Vapours, and sullen clouds, and frosts, and snows,
In ceaseless change, to Britain's studious youth,
Well he describes; and Britain's studious youth
Shall bless his toils—nor less with EV'NING TALES,[5]
With critic rules, and soft poetic lays,
Moulds tender hearts, than with a modest skill
To art and science lifts the manly breast.
Nature's fair walks invite the various mind
Of man, who all around, beneath, above,
Views what may fire the genius, to pursue
Studies diverse, yet useful, which unite,

Like the rich hues, whose fair varieties
Each into other melting, all conspire
To crown with one grand arch the lofty heav'n;
Or, like the many-darting rays of light,
Which quick converge, and form one lustrous point.
Thy task is toil and patience to survey[6]
The form, position, and proportions due
Of mountains, and their natures thence deduce.
Hence shall determine well the distant eye,
What treasures sleep within, or slates or lime,
Granites, or porph'ries, nor shall vain ascent
Thy feet beguile; to thee research shall bring
Its pleasures due, to others profit bring.
'Twas thus, where circled in immortal snow,
Alps rear their tow'ring summits, Saussure[7] rais'd
His fam'd high monument; nor less shalt thou
On Scotia's barren rocks, though not to thee
Those rocks shall long prove barren, thou shalt gain
From Scotland's sons, the meed of fair renown.

The poem begins with a tribute to the comforts of friendship. The reference to 'heavy hours' in line 2 encourages a metaphorical reading of the ensuing storm images, as though the virtues of friendship will be defined against the background of a conventionally moralised landscape. And indeed, a little further on Dyer openly deploys the life-as-journey allegory, following the progress of Hope from its youthful "prospect fair" to its show of resistance in the "solitary waste" of adult life, and then to its final defeat in the "Ocean of griefs and cares" (57, 59, 63). However, there is a counter-tendency with the introduction of place-names in lines 12-19, and amplified in the second apostrophe to Aikin in lines 71-83, where the picturesque images evoke a local rather than ideal landscape. This tension between rhetorical strategies derived from the topographical poetic tradition, which seeks to extract moral lessons from the "clair obscure" (31) of nature's works, and a representational attachment to the physical realities of place which I would identify as the Romantic, pedestrianising impulse, is one example of the peculiar congeries of voices in this poem.

The overarching theme of the first seventy lines is companionate travel: Dyer does not decry solitary walking, which he associates with the "bold unrestrained" mental excursiveness of the poet, but his overt preference is for the comforts of the "social walk" (72). In later Romantic travel writing, sociability is widely commended: in "On Going a Journey," Hazlitt cannot "see the wit of walking and talking at the same time" (136), but welcomes companions on any form of foreign travel: "In such situations, so opposite to one's ordinary train of ideas, one seems a species by one's-self, a limb torn off from society, unless one can meet with instant fellowship and support" (146). Leigh Hunt writes of "weekly voyages of discovery into green lanes and rustic houses of entertainment" (77) with a friend, and typically addresses his reader as a surrogate of the companion whom he considers indispensable to his excursions.

And the record which Keats has left in his letters of his northern tour in 1818 is coloured importantly by the exuberant, bantering relationship he enjoyed with his companion, Charles Armitage Brown, a relationship in key with the "programme of cheerfulness and sociality" which Jeffrey Cox has aligned with the Cockney School (*Romanticism* 2 [1996]:27-29). In Romantic travel writing of the 1790's, however, the companion is usually a nominal presence, invisible and inarticulate, alongside the central and normative narrating subject. In writing so openly and warmly of the pleasures of companionate travel, Dyer anticipates the socialising literary tendencies of the next generation.

Taking leave of Dunkeld in line 84, Dyer finds that the Abbey and the wooded valley in which it stands call to mind another monastic site, Tintern (89-93). Like Dunkeld, Tintern was by this time on the tourist trail, a station on the picturesque Wye tour, though Wordsworth was yet to make his defining visit. Dyer's description of Dunkeld offers the image of human structures partially reclaimed by nature—"round the stones / The shining ivy twines its wanton arms / In close embrace" (94-96)—central to the picturesque appreciation of ruins. He also incorporates two other forms of conventional response to ruins, as helpfully categorised by Malcolm Andrews (45-46): the moral *memento mori* which the poet reads in the monuments announcing "Who liv'd, and—sleep, and wake to sleep no more" (101), and the political celebration of Britain's emancipation from Catholicism (102-107).

The picturesque calm is disturbed from line 144 onwards, as Dyer engages in a sentimental digression on social deprivation and injustice. He takes a mental walk to "visit the close cot, where poverty / Sits patient, and where industry retired / From daily toil, drinks-in the poisoned air" (145-47). He mentions, and defends as poetic subject-matter, the "dark retreat / Of prison" (148-49), perhaps recalling for readers of the *Monthly Magazine* his humanitarian critique of crime and punishment in *Complaints of the Poor People of England,* where he condemned the imprisonment of teenagers in "seminaries of vice," where they were "instructed in a knowledge which led them to the gallows" (62). Dyer appeals to the better instincts of the "generous rich" (157) to give more attention to housing the poor, underlining the point with a prose note, and shifts the tone from one of social compassion to one of political morality in pleading the labourer's rights (164-69). Again, Dyer echoes sentiments he expressed in *Complaints* five years earlier: "The prosperity of nations depends on the poor. They dig the ore out of the mine, and the stone out of the quarry. They build our houses, work our vessels, and fight our battles: yet, while the rich enjoy almost all the benefit, the poor undergo all the labour. The rich have little to do, but to give orders, or to sign their names, and sometimes not even that" (4-5).

While the introduction of such radical sentiments occlude the topographical functions of the poem, they are consistent with the views Dyer had expressed on the role of nature in promoting "universal tenderness": "The GOOD MAN from the appearances of nature derives tender affections, generous principles, and humane conduct. From the glowing and variegated scenes around him he derives something which warms his heart, and throws a smile over his countenance" (*Dissertation* 19). In the *Dissertation*, the sentimental pietism of these assertions is girded by the writer's detailed knowledge of the way public life is organised in Britain, and by his concern with the material and contemporary distress, such as the plight of the defendants in the Treason Trials of 1794. Similarly, in **"To Mr. Arthur Aikin,"** Dyer translates the "language" (82) of nature, essentially one of delight, into the rhetoric of social protest.

If the progress of Dyer's poem up to this point has been, in pedestrian terms, a meandering one, then his final verse paragraph, which begins with another valedictory apostrophe to Aikin, strikes off in equally unpredictable directions. He notes that Aikin's travels are motivated by science, and that in this, as well as other ways, his father "leads the way" (176-83). As his footnote makes clear, Dyer is alluding to John Aikin's *Calendar of Nature,* an instructional book for ten to fourteen-year-olds which gives, with some poetic embroidery, general views of the "grand system" of nature; his *Essay on the Application of Natural History to Poetry*; and his compilation of children's stories, fables and dialogues, *Evenings at Home.* Dyer's reminder of John Aikin's diverse literary accomplishments points to the combination of poetic sensibility and "manly science" to which he believes his son Arthur should aspire. This exemplarily "various mind" (184) is figured in two strikingly apposite images: nature, he says, inspires different forms of attention, which conspire happily towards mental growth just as the several colours are harmonised in a rainbow, or as scattered light can converge in "one lustrous point" (192). Although either analogy would misrepresent the uneven, progressional structure of Dyer's poem, both demonstrate his belief in the importance of "Studies diverse" in the fashioning of a self. **"To Mr. Arthur Aikin"** shows that an educated person could be simultaneously a man of feeling, a picturesque tourist, a scientist and a political controversialist. Dyer's loose, conversational blank verse displaces these elements into a simple narrative chain, revealing a self driven to perform its differences.

In the concluding lines (193-206), after hoping that Arthur Aikin will be as variously endowed and accomplished as his father, Dyer acknowledges the real interest of the future founder of the Geological Society. In a last eulogistic act, he compares Aikin in anticipation to Horace Benedict de Saussure—a "celebrated Mineralogist," as his note says, and author of the *Voyages dans les Alpes,* a mixture of travel writing, geology and scientific essays published between 1779 and 1796. For both mountaineers and geologists, this innocuous note would do Saussure too little justice. As a mountaineer, he has a distinguished place in the history of Mont Blanc: he promised a big reward to the first man to climb the mountain, and took part in two unsuccessful attempts himself before losing the race to Balmat and Paccard in July, 1786. Saussure became the third man to complete the ascent the following year, and typically regarded the observations he made with his thermometer, hygrometer and electrometer, over a period of four and a half hours on the top, as the main point of his achievement. As a geologist, Saussure asserted the value of fieldwork over speculative theory, advanced the nascent discipline of paleontology, studied the relations of different strata, and approached an understanding of geophysical processes. In the *Voyages,* which Dyer cites, dealing with his conquest of Mont Blanc, he blended aesthetic delight and intellectual excitement which Dyer preferred to a dispassionate 'distant eye' (196): "I could hardly believe my eyes, it seemed a dream, when I saw under my feet these majestic peaks, these formidable Aiguilles du Midi, d'Argentiere, du Géant, of which I had found even the bases so difficult and dangerous of approach. I seized their connections, their relation, their structure, and a single glance cleared away doubts which years of work had not sufficed to remove" (Freshfield 232).

Saussure, great-grandfather of Ferdinand de Saussure, who was to revolutionise the study of language in the twentieth century, came from a prominent Genevan family whose forebears had been religious refugees from France in the mid-sixteenth century. Like Aikin, he showed an early bent towards science, becoming Chair of Philosophy (incorporating natural sciences as well as logic, ethics, and so on) at the age of twenty-two. Although a member of the city's patrician elite, he advocated reform, welcomed the fall of the Bastille, urged the ruling Council to draft a new constitution acceptable to the common people, guided the new-model administration, and withdrew from active politics only after the local Reign of Terror in 1794. In political terms, therefore, there is good reason for Dyer to advert to Saussure with the same respect he shows for the scientific "monument" (203) he left behind.

There is, moreover, a personal link between Dyer and Saussure: they had a common acquaintance in Charles, third Earl of Stanhope (1753-1816), another prominent British reformer and distinguished inventor. Stanhope began his education at Eton, but lived from 1764 to 1774 in Geneva, where he learned both revolutionary sympathies and a love of science, and where his family socialised with the Saussures. His consumptive brother, Philip, was treated by the Saussures' close friend and family doctor, Theodore Tronchin. Later, Stanhope married William Pitt's sister, became an MP, supported the parliamentary reform, and championed religious liberty, chaired the Revolution society meeting in November, 1789, at which Richard Price delivered his famous sermon on the love of country, and, having succeeded to his peerage, brought pro-French motions before the House of Lords as late as 1795, earning his nicknames of "Citizen" Stanhope and "The minority of one." In another life, he was a celebrated inventor, producing innovations in fire-prevention, marine steam-engines, printing presses and calculating machines (see Stanhope and Gooch). At some stage in this colourful life, perhaps as early as the 1780s (Adams 233-4), he became acquainted with Dyer, and employed him for a while as tutor to his sons. When Stanhope made his will in 1805, he appointed Dyer an executor and left him £200—much to the amusement and bafflement of commentators then and since. Crabb Robinson writes: "One day Mrs. Barbauld said to me, 'Have you heard whom Lord Stanhope has made executor?'—'No! Your Brother'—'No, there would have been nothing in that. The very worst imaginable.'—'Oh, then it is Buonaparte.'—'No, guess again.'—'George Dyer?'—'You are right. Lord Stanhope was clearly insane!'" (Robinson 1:62).

However, if Dyer seemed a comical choice for someone charged with executing a will, Stanhope's partiality is more explicable when put in the context of Dyer's public activities in the 1780s and 1790s. Stanhope would have found common political cause with Dyer on a wide range of issues, not least the campaign to remove discrimination against Dissenters, and he would have known that there was a lot more to Dyer than the lovable eccentric caricatured by Lamb. It is tempting, therefore, to see a transnational, cross-class fellowship of minds, and a certain commonality of experience, being invoked between the lines of Dyer's valedictory address. Saussure, Dyer, and their mutual acquaintance, Stanhope, were all industrious, public-spirited men, active in reforming politics, and catalysts for a radical generation, though all were in retreat, at least temporarily, from political life at the time of Dyer's tour in 1797. They all achieved considerable distinction in their particular fields of learning, and offer themselves as perfect exemplars of the "various mind" of which Dyer speaks in **"To Mr. Arthur Aikin."** In addressing the younger Aikin within this context of personal and public allusions, Dyer flatters his companion by incorporating him poetically into the universal brotherhood of the friends of liberty, thereby effecting a continuity of belief and commitment across the generations.

Notes

1. Roe first looked at Dyer in his essay, "Radical George: Dyer in the 1790s," and later in chapter 3 of *Wordsworth and Coleridge: The Radical Years,*

and as "'Unremembered Kindness: George Dyer and English Romanticism',' in *The Politics of Nature* 17-35.

2. Lamb, for instance, writes to Coleridge in August, 1800, "George Dyer hath prepared two ponderous volumes, full of Poetry and Criticism—they impend over the Town, and are threaten'd to fall in the winter" (*Letters* 1:226).

3. [Dyer note] To those who have visited the wretched unhealthy hovels in the Highlands of Scotland, and in Ireland, it cannot be deemed unseasonable to recommend an attention to the more decent accommodation of the cotters, or cottagers. Men of fortune, who in future may build on their estates habitations for their poor tenants, would do well to study a most interesting publication entitled, "*Heights and Elevations for Cottages,*" by Wood.

4. [Dyer note] See a *Journal of a Tour through North Wales and part of Shropshire, with Observations on Mineralogy, and other branches of Natural History,* by Arthur Aikin.

5. [Dyer note] "*Calendar of Nature,*" "*The Use of Natural History in Poetry,*" and "*Evenings at Home,*" etc. by Dr. Aikin.

6. [Dyer note] The leading object of Mr. A.'s Tour into Scotland, was a mineralogy survey of the country.

7. [Dyer note] A celebrated Mineralogist, Author of a work entitled, "*Voyage dans les Alpes.*"

Works Cited

Aikin, Arthur. *Journal of a Tour through North Wales and Part of Shropshire: with Observations on Mineralogy.* 1797; *An Address to the Dissidents of England on their Late Defeat.* 1790; Adams, M. Ray. *Studies in the Literary Backgrounds of English Radicalism.* 1947; Andrews, Malcolm. *The Search for the Picturesque: Landscape Aesthetics and Tourism in Britain, 1760-1800.* 1989; Cox, Jeffrey N. "Keats in the Cockney School," *Romanticism* 2 (1996):27-39; Dyer, George. *Complaints of the Poor People of England.* 1793; *A Dissertation on the Theory and Practice of Benevolence.* 1795; *Poems.* 1792; *Poems.* 1801; *Poetics; or a Series of Poems, and of Disquisitions on Poetry.* 2 vols. 1812; Freshfield, Douglas W. *The Life of Horace Benedict de Saussure.* 1920; Gilbert, Joseph, and Thomas Howell. *A Correct and Minute Journal of the Time Occupied in Every Mile By Mr John Stokes, of Bristol, During his Walk of Fifty Miles per Day for Twenty Successive Days, making One Thousand Miles.* 1815; Hazlitt, William. "On Going a Journey." *Selected Writings.* 1970; Hucks, Joseph. *A Pedestrian Tour through North Wales, in a Series of*

Letters. 1795; Hunt, Leigh "A Walk from Dulwich to Brockham," *Selected Essays.* Ed. J. B. Priestley. 1929; Jarvis, Robin. *Romantic Writing and Pedestrian Travel.* 1997; Jump, Harriet. "'Snatch'd out of the Fire': Lamb, Coleridge, and George Dyer's Cancelled Preface." *Charles Lamb Bulletin* 58 (1987):54-67; Lamb, Charles. *Elia and The Last Essays of Elia.* Ed. Jonathan Bate. 1987; *The Letters of Charles and Mary Anne Lamb.* Ed. Edwin W. Marrs, Jr. 3 vols. 1975-78; Obituary of Arthur Aikin. *The Quarterly Journal of the Geological Society of London* 2 (1855):xli-xlii; Obituary of George Dyer. *The Gentleman's Magazine* ns 15 (1841):546-47; Rousseau, Jean-Jacques. *Reveries of the Solitary Walker.* Trans. Peter France. 1979; Southey, Robert. *Letters from England.* 1807. Ed. Jack Simmons. 1951; Thelwall, John. *The Peripatetic; or, Sketches of the Heart, of Nature and Society.* 1793; Thompson, E. P. *The Making of the English Working Class.* 2nd ed. 1968; Rev. of *A Walk through Wales, in August 1797,* by Richard Warner. *Monthly Magazine* 5 (1798):492; Wilbur, Earl Morse. *A History of Unitarianism: In Transylvania, England, and America.* 1945.

J. R. Watson (essay date October 1999)

SOURCE: Watson, J. R. "'My Benevolent Friend': George Dyer and His 1800 Preface." *Charles Lamb Bulletin* 108 (October 1999): 170-77.

[*In the following essay, Watson examines the dual perception of Dyer as both benevolent and irritating, asserting that the author's poetry and preface are tiresome and old-fashioned compared to his contemporaries.*]

Readers of Charles Lamb will be familiar with the figure of George Dyer, whose eccentric person appears in 'Oxford in the Vacation' and in 'Amicus Redivivus' (after falling into the river outside Lamb's house at Islington). He was an endless source of delight (as well as inconvenience) to Lamb, as he is to the modern reader of Lamb's letters, where he appears in various absurd situations. His absent-mindedness was legendary: perhaps the best story told about it concerns Dyer's time as a Baptist, and William Frend's teasing him in later years about having drowned a woman by dipping her in the water and then forgetting about her. Frend, like Lamb, was a good friend to Dyer at the same time as he had much amusement from him; Lucas, and Winifred Courtney, quote Lamb's charming and tender verses on the subject:

> Friend of the friendless, friend of all mankind,
> To thy wide friendships I have not been blind;
> But looking at them nearly, in the end
> I love thee most that thou art Dyer's Frend.

But Dyer was a learned man as well as an eccentric: he laboured for years over James Valpy's edition of the Classical Authors, published in 141 volumes between 1809 and 1831; and he wrote a fine biography, ***Memoirs of the Life and Writings of Robert Robinson.*** Robinson, who was a Baptist minister and then a Unitarian, is best known today for a hymn which is still sung in some nonconformist churches:

> Come, thou fount of every blessing,
>   Tune my heart to sing thy grace;
> Streams of mercy never ceasing
>   Call for songs of loudest praise.
> Teach me some melodious sonnet,
>   Sung by flaming tongues above;
> Praise the mount; I'm fixed upon it,
>   Mount of God's unchanging love.

The second verse of this hymn begins with a striking image (I sang it with awe and wonder in my youth, but it is now, in the days of ignorance, deemed too obscure):

> Here I'll raise my Ebenezer;
>   Hither by thy help I'm come;
> And I hope, by thy good pleasure,
>   Safely to arrive at home.

The reference to 1 Samuel 7:12, and the general tone of the verses, suggest that Dyer (who was tutor to Robinson's children at one time) moved in circles in which a certain excited enthusiasm was normal, and in which a knowledge of Holy Scripture was taken for granted. And certainly Dyer's nonconformity was part of his independent way of seeing the world—serious, utterly truthful, careless of appearances, unsophisticated and ingenuous, even naive.

The reason for this roundabout opening is that, as an hymnologist, I was drawn back to Lamb's friend George Dyer by discovering that he was the chief source of information about Robinson. The biography, published in 1796, is a good one: Wordsworth admired it. The only element in it that suggests a lack of what the psychologists call 'insight' is the Preface, which states that 'This volume being already swollen to a sufficient bulk, it would be unreasonable to distend it further by a tedious preface': which is what Dyer then proceeds to do, following it with a two-page introductory note, beginning in a rather inflated imitation of Johnsonian grandeur— 'The history of nations, by the extent of its views, and the variety of its objects, may be reckoned the most important subject of human survey'.

Dyer, who moved in the radical circles of the London of the 1790s, had previously written ***The Complaints of the Poor People of England*** (second edition, 1793). Together with the biography of Robinson, it suggests a writer who was more acute and self-aware than might be thought from the portrait of him in Lamb's essays. ***The Complaints,*** for example, describes the sufferings of the poor without condescension: 'But if I love and pity the poor, I also respect them' (p. 2). Again, Johnson comes to mind: whatever Dyer's limitations were, cant was not one of them. He had visited the Marshalsea, the debtors' prison, and seen the disproportion between crimes and their punishments. He describes the corrupt political system, with rotten boroughs such as Old Sarum and Midhurst, and the general inequality of society—'How are the poor oppressed, to enrich our nobles!' (p. 13). The rich held sinecures, and were the beneficiaries of an unequal tax system; in addition, 'a great part of the taxes laid on the people, are not employed merely in great salaries to magistrates and officers in public service, but are wasted on placemen and pensioners' (p. 14). Dyer goes on to write of the Church, the Army, and the education system, with special reference to Christ's Hospital, where he had been a Grecian (before Lamb's time, but it made a bond between them). His common theme is that each has become corrupt. In the Church, for example, the Bishop of Durham had an income of £10,000; a poor curate, in the neighbourhood of Durham, not above £20 a year. 'A sensible man, who had been a justice of the peace, had seen such dreadful instances of oppression in this matter, that he flapped his hat, and became a Quaker' (p. 39). The army ('made up, in great measure, of effeminate coxcombs, or of bold profligates', p. 42) was 'overstocked with officers', whose commissions were bought and sold (pp. 45,43), while the ordinary soldiers survived on very little: 'within a few months past, they have had two-pence farthing a day added, as *bread-money*. What a wretched pittance! Yet for this a poor fellow lets himself to be shot at, and is a slave for life, 'till he is either bought off, or becomes an invalid' (p. 45). As far as education was concerned, Christ's Hospital he thought a good school, but 'not a public school': 'a nobler institution does not exist, in theory, than Christ-Hospital, in London' (p. 18). It had been designed originally for poor orphans, but 'the poor man's bread is frequently put into the rich man's cupboard' (p. 55).

Dyer was a radical in the Godwinian style. He was against the war with France: 'Let those, then, who thrive by the impoverishment of the nation, speak the praises of the present war' (p. 77). He was (naturally, for a nonconformist) against the slave trade: 'the slave-trade teaches us to treat our fellow-creatures like dogs' (p. 63). He was against flogging in the army and navy, and thought the poor houses were 'worse than prisons' (p. 61).

Dyer's radicalism would have endeared him to Lamb; so would his attachment to his old University of Cambridge, which Lamb visited in 1819 to 'play the gentleman, enact the student'. And we have Lamb's own affectionate letter of 1831, which praises Dyer's gentle and unmalicious disposition: 'You mistake your heart if you think you *can* write a lampoon. Your whips are rods of roses. Your spleen has ever had for its objects vices, not the vicious—abstract offences, not the concrete sinner.'[1] This was the Dyer whom Lamb found in 'Oxford in the Vacation', 'busy as a moth over some rotten archive'. The poetic accuracy of that image is so astonishingly evocative of a certain kind of scholarly attention, that it is no surprise when Lamb's fancy goes on to play with the idea that Dyer is no longer quite human: 'With long poring, he is grown almost into a book. He stood as passive as one by the side of the old shelves. I longed to new-coat him in Russia, and assign him his place.'[2]

Dyer 'started like an unbroken heifer' on being interrupted by Lamb in the old library. It is another of those brilliant images, which depends for its humour upon its ability to make Dyer resemble something non-human: first a moth, then an unbroken heifer. But the essay ends with a lovely tribute to Dyer's affection for Cambridge:

> D. is delightful any where, but he is much the best in such places as these. He cares not much for Bath. He is out of his element at Buxton, at Scarborough, or Harrowgate. The Cam and the Isis are to him 'better than all the waters of Damascus'. On the Muses' hill he is happy and good, as one of the Shepherds on the Delectable Mountains; and when he goes about with you to show you the halls and colleges, you think you have with you the Interpreter at the House Beautiful.'[3]

This recognition of a kindred spirit (for Lamb too would surely have been out of his element in a fashionable watering-place) is part of the respect which Lamb felt for Dyer. Lamb's sense of the ridiculous was tempered by something more than affection, and he viewed Dyer's ingenuous personality not only as a rich source of comedy but also as something genuinely good in this world of sharp and self-aware and fashionable people. The portrait of Dyer which I am trying to present, therefore, is more complex than that of the amiable buffoon who walked into the river by mistake, and who left his shoe under Leigh Hunt's table. As an example, I turn to the Preface which Dyer wrote for his *Poems* of 1800. It reveals Dyer as a learned and well-intentioned man, but also a clumsy one, an unbroken heifer clumping about in the yard of literary criticism.

According to Lucas, Dyer's *Poems* were first advertised in the *Monthly Magazine* for October 1796. They were to include satires, odes, and elegies, 'two of which will shortly make their appearance'. A further advertisement appeared in November 1798, promising 'instead of three volumes at a guinea, two only, consisting of poems and poetical essays, will be published at twelve shillings.' The first volume was promised 'next month', but it did not appear. Instead, in June 1799, Dyer produced an apology (printed by Lucas), informing the subscribers 'with great concern', that the publication would be delayed until the following winter. He now promised two volumes, one of prose and one of poetry:

After mature deliberation, therefore, he [the author] thinks it most advisable to print his two volumes at the same time; and his criticisms, extended as they are to an unexpected length, will form a distinct volume, comprehending free remarks on every species of poetry, and illustrations from the mythology of different nations.[4]

The criticisms did not appear in the volume which finally made its way into the world, dated 1801. It dealt with none of the promised subjects, but concerned itself with lyric poetry. It contained an 'Advertisement' (unpaginated, so it had been stuck in):

> In page 321 an allusion is made to a preface. It may be proper, therefore, to inform the reader, that an Essay on the Nature of Lyric Poetry, and on the Characters of Ancient and Modern Lyric Poets, was not only written, but actually printed off; and, from the pages of the introductory poems it will appear, that it run out to a considerable length. This, however, for many reasons, has been cancelled.

In the British Library copy Charles Lamb has written 'one copy of this cancelled preface, snatch'd out of the fire, is prefixed to this volume'. It follows a title page dated 1800.

As Lucas points out, it is hard to know what caused Dyer to withdraw the preface: as it is, the whole episode is part of a sorry narrative of promises, apologies and cancellations. It seems that Dyer, so confident in biography and social commentary, had unusual anxieties about his poetry. That is the theme of his opening remarks:

> That poetry will allow no mediocrity, is a formidable principle of criticism; a principle, however, which, as laid down by an accurate critic and elegant poet, may be plausibly quoted, and even malignantly applied.
>
> I grant, that I experience some portion of this anxiety at present: though I am by no means—however moderately soever I think of my talents—overawed by the strictness of this rule, and still less by the terror of malicious criticism.

(p. iii)

His anxiety, Dyer thinks, 'may proceed from a conviction, that a particular species of poetry hath its particular delicacy, and appropriate difficulties'. This is 'lyrical poetry'. Some people think that it is easy, but it is actually very hard:

> Such sort of compositions may be reckoned of slender contrivance, and easy of execution. And—it is true— any gentleman or lady may cap rhymes at their ease: as any child can blow bladders, or catch a ball in a cup, so may almost any trifler make mere verses. . . . But will they satisfy a correct or refined taste? Or, will what proceeds not from the heart, be likely to reach it?

(pp. iv-v)

Anyone who really knows about the subject, says Dyer, will admit that the writing of good lyric poetry is very difficult:

> Yet who are they, that speak of the easy composition of lyric poetry? Assuredly not such, as have made any successful attempts that way themselves, or are properly acquainted with the opinions of others. Had they made more experiments, let me say, had they been more successful, they would have been better acquainted with their own imbecility.

(pp. v-vi)

The word 'experiments' recalls the 'Advertisement' to *Lyrical Ballads,* which Dyer would almost certainly have known, although there is no sign of it in his preface. His remarks on English poetry are conventional and neo-classical. He quotes Horace on Pindar and on the difficulties of lyric poetry (Ode 2 of Book IV, 'Pindarum quisquis studet aemulari'), and uses Gray and Collins as his modern examples:

> And how slow our two best English lyrists, Gray and Collins, were in their poetical movements, before they could seize on an idea, which they thought sufficiently brilliant, or adapt to it language sufficiently impressive, is well known to all their readers.

(p. vii)

The Greek lyrists were 'the most excellent', followed by Horace; and Dyer notes that Scaliger awarded 'the nobleness of lyric poetry the next place to the majesty of the heroic' (p. ix). This penumbra of classical knowledge which surrounds Dyer's criticism makes him follow Johnson in condemning the 'unnaturalness' of Metaphysical Poetry, especially of Cowley, who was 'a wonderful genius, unquestionably; but a writer always catching at brilliancy, and toiling, as it were, after wit' (p. xvii). 'His metaphysical poetry, unworthy the perspicuity and charm of this kind of poetry, I leave to the tomahawk of Johnson, that has deservedly cleft it asunder' (p. xviii).

The image of Dr Johnson with a tomahawk is one of those ill-judged metaphors that invites what Johnson himself called 'risibility', and Dyer's preface is full of moments that might encourage a certain levity in the reader. He swings into an amiable discussion of eighteenth-century poets, with Shenstone as 'the lady's poet', Akenside as 'a great poet', and Gray's 'On the Progress of Poesy' described as 'exquisite' (pp. xix, xxiii). Then, oddly, he develops an argument that associates lyric poetry with panegyric:

> Panegyric, in the hands of a mere rhymster, is almost sure to sink into insipidity; in the hands of a poet, it may swell into flattery. Here, probably, Pindar and Horace grew extravagant.

(p. xxvi)

This provoked an outburst from Coleridge in the margin, protesting against the bracketing of Pindar with lesser poets:

> *Pindar*—and—who?———*Horace*!!!
>
> and pray, good George Dyer! in what ode or fragment of the Theban Republican do you find Flattery? I can remember no one word, that justifies the charge. As to Horace, praise be to him as an amiable gentleman, & man of fine courtly sense—thanks & thanks for his Satires & Epistles, & whatever is 'sermone proprius'—& his little translations or originals of light & social growth, thanks for them too!—But as a Poet, a Lyric Poet, a Companion of *Pindar,* or the Author of the Atys—(be he Catullus, or some unknown Greek—)—it won't do!—No![5]

Coleridge, like Lamb, shared interests with Dyer—Christ's Hospital, Unitarianism—and one wonders when he made the marginal note. Perhaps Lamb showed him the preface, 'snatch'd from the fire', in 1801, when Coleridge was back in London.

Dyer's critical survey takes him to the end of page 27 of his preface. He then turns to his own work:

> As to the following volume, its very professions are moderate: it is, indeed, but an effort at the lighter excesses of lyric poetry; and how far even any of these pieces are successful attempts, the learned will judge.
>
> But having gone thus far, I am now compelled to go further; and to meet such objections, as the mere reading of the preceding pages may, perhaps, prepare some readers to advance, had they not even occurred to them before.
>
> (pp. xxvii-xxviii)

This modest beginning leads Dyer into a verbose and ramshackle account of his own verse that goes on for another 40 pages. It begins grandly with reflections on lyric poetry in relation to tragedy and comedy, and in connection with musical expression; then suddenly it descends into the bathetic:

> As to particular objections that may be made to the *following* work; I know it may be urged, that some of the poems are rural and descriptive; whereas the author resides in the Great City.
>
> But, will it necessarily follow, that the person, who lives in London at a particular period, must have resided there always? suffice it to say, that of the years of my life, passed since I left college, the greater part have been spent entirely in the country; and, that since I have lived in town, I have usually spent some part of the year in a course of constant rambling, or at the rural seat of some friend. The environs of London, too, will bear witness, how regular have been my solitary devotions in her modest retreats; so that, I hope, the critics will not treat my muse too ungallantly, at least, on this account, as though she were a mere London

> trollop, always sauntering, or gadding, about the streets of London, sallow with city smoke, and listening to the sound of Bow-bells.
>
> (pp. xxx-xxxi)

With this kind of discourse, Dyer's preface descends from the heights of a neo-classical survey of lyric poetry to a sad triviality. If one of his defects as a writer is that he does not know when to stop, another is a failure of decorum. The personal continues to intrude:

> But, though I have been an occasional wanderer, my habits and pursuits are those of a retired, abstracted, though, I will add, of a some what trifling, desultory, and unprofitable student: and, that even my perambulations have been made subservient to some ardent pursuit. Independently, then, of early habits of indolence, the effects of which I still feel powerfully, my pursuits and manners are such, as rather belong to a solitary bookworm, than to one, agreeably relaxing in society. Those hours, which others have spent in the ordinary amusements of life, have been devoted by me to literary visions and speculations, as often, indeed, trifling, and unimportant, as dignified or serious.
>
> This character discovers itself in all my publications; and may lead to an improper conclusion, on the style of my writings.
>
> (pp. xxi-xxii)

It is not easy to see what the 'improper conclusion' might be: but there is an element of self-congratulation here which is tiresome. It suggests that Dyer, ingenuous though he was, took a certain pleasure in his scholarly impracticableness (as academics do, when they say that they cannot boil an egg). He anticipates Lamb's description of him as one who would be out of place in Bath or Harrogate, by claiming that he has been a bookworm rather than one 'agreeably relaxing in society'.

But, of course, his poetry is not always so personally expressive as these revelations suggest. 'I mean not, however, to assert that all my poems either in this volume, or in that which will follow, describe my genuine, at least my present feelings. Some are merely poetical or dramatic' (p. xxxv). One that does represent a mingling of the personal and the classical is **"Gaia, or Willy Rhymer's Address to his London Landladies"**, in which Gaia is 'A landlady honest and true'. At other times there are conventional subjects of eighteenth-century verse, treated in traditional ways: landscape, childhood, friendship. Some of them are clearly influenced by Gray and Collins: the Ode **"Written in the Cloisters of Christ's Hospital"** is Dyer's version of the 'Ode on a Distant Prospect of Eton College', and the poem **"On the Evening, Meditated on the Welsh Coast."** Addressed to Theophilus Lindsay [The respected friend of Dr Priestley]' contains an obvious echo of Gray's 'Elegy':

> Or if, perchance, you church-yard drear
>   Where slowly tolls the passing bell . . .

Others celebrate personified qualities, such as friendship or genius (**"On Genius. On taking leave of Dr Priestley, when preparing to go to America"**), or the seasons (**"Approaching Spring"**, **"Autumn"**), or places such as the River Cam, or traditional poetic emblems such as the nightingale. There is a **"Monody on the Death of Robert Robinson [A celebrated Dissenting Preacher, formerly of Cambridge]"**.

These poems suggest that Dyer was firmly in the tradition of his time, and the contrast with that other 1800 volume of lyric poetry, *Lyrical Ballads,* with its own radical agenda and its manifesto of a preface, could hardly be greater. But Dyer lived in a perpetual state of sanguine expectation. This volume will be the beginning: 'In the second volume I shall attempt, at least, a brighter strain' (p. xxxvii). He proposed to concentrate on liberty. Polonius-like, he promises that these poems 'will be enhanced and coloured, as it were, with various topics, historical, oeconomical, philological, critical, topographical, and commercial. There will also be an attempt, in that volume, at some pictures of poetry and painting' (p. xlii).

But if Dyer's promises are tiresome, his apologies are worse. He spends a good deal of time in the latter half of the preface weaving patterns of self-accusation and breast-beating:

> One word relative to the delay of this publication: and an apology, is, certainly, due, if not to the world at large, who would probably endure the loss of these poems without murmuring, at least to my friends and subscribers. For I have certainly trifled with my engagements, if not with their patience; and so truly blameworthy has been my dilatoriness, that in the very act of apologizing, I must be my own accuser. Apologizing is at all times an irksome and unpleasant business; but it is generally more painful to him who is constrained to make it, than even to him who has patience to hear it.

> (pp. lv-lvi)

This leads into a lengthy discussion of 'castle-building', by which Dyer means building castles in the air. And when this is finished he irritates the reader still further by announcing 'And now while at confessions, I will confess more' (p. lvii). This turns out to be an admission that he has been busy writing other books, and thus distracted from the main task in hand.

After a promising beginning, therefore, Dyer's preface becomes a tedious exercise in self-justification. Nor do his poems provide more than traditional exercises in an eighteenth-century mode. The problem is that Dyer (perhaps because of his amiable character) was trying too hard to please conventional taste. He lacks Wordsworth's awareness, expressed in the 1800 preface to *Lyrical Ballads* (written, one supposes, contemporaneously with Dyer's preface) that his and Coleridge's poems in the 1798 volume could, and should, stir up strong feeling:

I flattered myself that they who should be pleased with them would read them with more than common pleasure: and on the other hand I was well aware that by those who should dislike them they would be read with more than common dislike.[6]

This concept of 'pleasure' is referred to by Dyer in a footnote to one of his poems, **"The Redress"**, which contains the line 'But genuine wit is sure to find a sale'. Typically, Dyer, who could never resist a footnote, adds a comment:

> That the principal and immediate aim of poetry is, to please, has been opposed by Julius Scaliger, and some other critics. But though I must admit that,

> *Omne* tulit punctum, qui miscuit utile dulci,

> yet will I still abide by Aristotle's and Plutarch's opinion, that the immediate object of poetry is, to please, and that even in solemn subjects poetry is used to render them more engaging and agreeable.

Coleridge was aggravated by this into another annotation:

> Damned Nonsense! But *why* does it please? Because it pleases! O mystery!—If not, some cause out of itself must be found. Mere utility it certainly is not—& that is beauty, i.e. that which *ought* to please.

> My benevolent Friend seems not to have made an obvious distinction, between end and means—The Poet *must* always aim at Pleasure as his specific *means,* but surely—Milton did & all ought to aim at something nobler as their end—viz—to cultivate and predispose the heart of the Reader &c.[7]

Coleridge's response is symptomatic. He represents all those readers who find Dyer irritating; yet within a sentence or two he is recalling Dyer as 'My benevolent Friend'. This mixture of exasperation and admiration is something which might be found in all dealings with Dyer, whether those of his friends and contemporaries or those of his readers, then and now. Dyer's learning, sincerity, and genuinely good intentions are never in doubt; what is often missing is tact, literary decorum, and sheer practical sense. It suggests that we should admire William Frend even more than we do for being Dyer's friend; and Charles Lamb also.

Notes

1. Quoted in E. V. Lucas, *The Life of Charles Lamb* (4th ed., London, 1907), p. 147.

2. *The Works of Charles Lamb* ed. Thomas Hutchinson (London, 1924), p. 483. 'Russia' was Russian leather, used for bookbinding. I am not sure what the following sentence, 'He might have mustered for a tall Scapula' means (a scapula is a shoulder blade, or a garment worn by monks).

3. Ibid., p. 485. The essay is dated 'Aug. 5th, 1820. From my rooms facing the Bodleian.'

4. Lucas, *Life,* p. 154.

5. *The Collected Works of Samuel Taylor Coleridge: Marginalia II* ed. George Whalley (Princeton, NJ, 1984), pp. 353-4.

6. *Lyrical Ballads, and Other Poems, 1797-1800* ed. James Butler and Karen Green (Ithaca, NY, 1992), p. 741.

7. *Coleridge: Marginalia II,* pp. 355-6.

FURTHER READING

Biography

Wright, Dudley. "Charles Lamb and George Dyer." *English Review* 39 (September 1924): 390-97.

Relates familiar anecdotes about Dyer's absent-mindedness, using quotes and reminiscences from contemporaries of Dyer, such as Talfourd, Cottle, Barry Cornwall, Leigh Hunt, Benjamin Ellis Martin, and Lamb.

Criticism

Ades, John I., and Winifred Courtney. "'Gentle Charles' and Rick Burners." *Charles Lamb Bulletin* 76 (October 1991): 132-37.

Examines different interpretations of a letter by Charles Lamb to Dyer in which the former complains to Dyer about the increasingly discontented poor.

Roe, Nicholas. "Radical George: Dyer in the 1790s." *Charles Lamb Bulletin* 49 (January 1985): 17-26.

Discusses Dyer's political development in the 1790s in relation to Wordsworth, Coleridge, and other London radicals.

Wellens, Oscar. "George Dyer in Support of Coleridge in the *Critical Review.*" *Wordsworth Circle* 10 (autumn 1979): 376-78.

Treats Dyer's support for Coleridge's play, "The Fall of Robespierre," and the possibility of his having authored some of the anonymous reviews in the *Critical Review.*

Additional coverage of Dyer's life and career is contained in the following sources published by the Gale Group: *Dictionary of Literary Biography,* Vol. 93; *Literature Resource Center.*

Aleksandr Sergeevich Griboedov
c. 1795-1829

Russian playwright, poet, and essayist.

INTRODUCTION

One of Russia's most intelligent and highly educated aristocrats in the early nineteenth century, Griboedov was an accomplished playwright best known for *Gore ot uma* (1831; *Woe from Wit*), which many critics consider the greatest comedy in Russian literary history. The play quickly transcended critical favor and became part of the cultural fabric of the country. Fellow Russian writer Ivan Goncharov described the phenomenon: "Immediately grasping its beauty, and not finding any faults in it, the literate masses wore the manuscript down to tatters, to verses, to hemistiches; they distributed all its pith and wisdom into colloquial speech; they turned a million into kopecks."

BIOGRAPHICAL INFORMATION

Although there is a great deal of contradictory information regarding the date of Griboedov's birth, many sources maintain that he was born on January 4, 1795—others place his birth as early as 1790. His father, Sergei Ivanovich Griboedov, lived apart from his family and had little contact with his son. Griboedov was raised by his mother, Nastas'ia Fedorovna Griboedova, who saw to it that her son received a first-rate education. Griboedov entered the Moscow University Preparatory School for Nobles in 1803, receiving a literature degree in 1808 and a law degree in 1810. He began writing poetry while still a student, and one of his poems was published in the Moscow journal *Vestnik Evropy* in 1809.

Griboedov enlisted in the Russian army in 1812 and served as a general's aide for the next four years. During this time he published pieces of war correspondence in *Vestnik Evropy*. After leaving the army Griboedov entered the diplomatic service in St. Petersburg. He began writing plays at this time, some in collaboration with other playwrights. As part of his work in the Office of Foreign Affairs, Griboedov was assigned to the Russian diplomatic mission in Persia in 1818. He studied the Persian language while living there and was decorated by the shah for his service. In November of 1821 he was sent to Tiflis to serve under General Aleksei Petrovich Ermolov, the minister of foreign affairs.

Griboedov apparently formulated the idea for his masterpiece *Woe from Wit* as early as 1816, but the play was not actually completed until 1823 at the earliest, and it was not performed in its entirety until 1831. The play's many references to contemporary Russian politics attracted the attention of the censors, who thwarted attempts to publish or stage the work for several years. Those who read the play, including Aleksandr Pushkin, widely praised the work and the increasing critical and popular success eventually forced the Russian government to remove the ban. Although the full extent of his involvement is unknown, Griboedov was associated with the leaders of the Decembrists' revolt of 1825, and some critics have linked the republican ideals of the revolutionaries with the social criticism in *Woe from Wit*. He was imprisoned for four months, but was eventually pardoned and released, receiving an annual salary and a promotion to court councillor in compensation for his internment. He returned to service in the Caucasus, his experience proving invaluable in negotiating a peaceful settlement of Russia's war with Persia. The treaty, written by Griboedov, was signed in April of 1828. Shortly thereafter he was assigned to lead the Russian mission to Persia as the new ambassador. Before assuming his post, he visited Tiflis and renewed his acquaintance with Nina Chavchavadze, the daughter of a poet; they were married in August of 1828, and he continued on to Teheran. In January of 1829, all the members of the Russian mission, including Griboedov, were killed by a Persian mob. He is buried on a mountaintop in Tiflis.

MAJOR WORKS

Griboedov's only famous work is *Woe from Wit,* which has often been compared to Molière's *Le Misanthrope.* The play's double plot involves, on one level, a classic love triangle between Chatsky, Sofia, and Molchalin, and on another level, a serious critique of Moscow society. The social criticism and the allusions to political figures and events resulted in heavy censorship and only portions of the play were published during Griboedov's lifetime; handwritten copies of the expurgated version, though, were widely circulated throughout Russia's literary community.

Although Griboedov wrote several plays, some in collaboration with other playwrights, as well as a number of poems and essays, the remainder of his work is virtually unknown today. Some of his manuscripts perished with him in the Persian massacre, others remain untranslated. Only *Woe from Wit* continues to attract critical and popular attention.

CRITICAL RECEPTION

Griboedov's comedy *Woe from Wit* was a tremendous success during the playwright's lifetime, although it was more often read than viewed. Pushkin, who called Griboedov "one of the smartest people in Russia," reportedly considered the play a great accomplishment. Much of the critical attention on the work has centered on the influence of Molière's highly intelligent protagonist in *Le Misanthrope,* Alceste, and the character's disgust with the hypocrisy of contemporary society. Yvette Louria suggests that Griboedov's debt to Molière is considerable and it is a debt often unacknowledged by Russian scholars. She concedes, however, that both Soviet critics and Russian critics of an earlier era may have been concentrating more intensely on the work's political message, which is specific to Moscow's social and political scene and which in no way resembles Molière's play.

William Edward Brown praises *Woe from Wit* for its innovative portrayal of characters who are complex and "psychologically alive." According to Brown: "Griboedov's people are all of a piece; they are intuited as complete psychological entities, and their language, their gestures, their modes of thinking, are all inseparable parts of their personalities." Alexander Gershkovich also discusses Griboedov's characterization, specifically of Chatsky, maintaining that he is not only the first, but the only "effective and consistent portrait of individualism in Russian literature on a European scale." For Gershkovich, the fact that Chatsky is completely alone and "at war with everyone," makes him more like a Western hero or anti-hero than a Russian one.

PRINCIPAL WORKS

*Molodye suprugi: Komediia v odnom deistvii, v stikhakh [Young Wives] (play) 1815
†Svoia sem'ia, ili Zamuzhniaia nevesta [All in the Family, or the Married Fiancée] [with Aleksandr Aleksandrovich Shakhovskoi and Nikolai Ivanovich Khmel'nitsky] (play) 1818
Gore ot uma [Woe from Wit] (play) 1831
Polnoe sobranie sochinenii [Collected Works]. 3 vols. (plays, essays, poems, and letters) 1911-17

*The Russian title is sometimes translated as *The Young Married Couple.*

†The Russian title is sometimes translated as *Pretended Infidelity.*

CRITICISM

Yvette Louria (essay date 1975)

SOURCE: Louria, Yvette. "Molière and Griboiedov." In *Molière and the Commonwealth of Letters: Patrimony and Posterity,* edited by Roger Johnson, Jr., Editha S. Neumann, and Guy T. Trail, pp. 379-82. Jackson: University Press of Mississippi, 1975.

[*In the following essay, Louria discusses the influence of Molière's* The Misanthrope *on Griboedov's* Woe from Wit *and the failure of many critics to acknowledge that influence.*]

The year 1672 is generally considered the official beginning of the Russian theater. The first play to be performed was *The Comedy of Artaxerxes* by Johann Gottfried Gregorii, an Esther play written at the behest of Tsar Alexei, who had a theater built in Moscow especially for this performance. Subsequently, in addition to the original Russian plays, both German and Italian comedies and tragedies found their way to the Moscow stage. After a while its repertory included also several of Molière's plays: *Amphitryon, Le Médecin malgré lui,* and *Les Précieuses ridicules.* Somewhat later, in 1782, Fonvizin's famous comedy, *The Minor* (*Nedorosl',* 1781), in which Molière's influence is discernible, was presented.

It was at the beginning of the nineteenth century that Alexandr Sergeevich Griboiedov wrote what has been since considered the greatest Russian comedy of all times: *Gore ot Uma* (1823), translated into English as *Woe from Wit, Wit Works Woe, The Mischief of Being Clever,* and *'Tis Folly to be Wise.* The title *Woe from Wit* seems to be the nearest to its Russian original both in its brevity and its meaning.

A. S. Griboiedov's family belonged to ancient Russian aristocracy. He received an excellent education and knew several foreign languages, among them French. Born in 1795, Griboiedov was so gifted that he entered the university in 1808 at the age of thirteen. By that time he was not only thoroughly familiar with the greatest works of European literature but also accomplished in music. He received his law degree at sixteen, but remained at the university to study natural sciences. Later, he owed his reputation as one of the best educated men of his time in Russia to his knowledge of the most important European languages, as well as Latin, Persian, and Sanskrit. His great love of literature did not prevent him from joining the Foreign Office and following a brilliant diplomatic career, during which he was made Russian Minister to Persia. Before going to Teheran in 1828, Griboiedov married the lovely sixteen-year-old

Georgian Princess Nina Chavchavadze. She stayed in Tabriz while he went to negotiate directly with the Persian Shah. The members of the Russian legation in Teheran—Grioiedov among them—were savagely killed by an irate crowd which misunderstood certain of their proposals, and his widow is said to have remained faithful to Griboiedov's memory until her death thirty years later.

Although critics justly consider Griboiedov a *homo unius libri,* he also wrote poetry, essays, and a dozen or so other plays. All these are but inferior literary endeavours compared to *Woe from Wit.* Upon reading his *magnum opus* without any preconceived notions, one is immediately struck with the similarity that exists between Griboiedov's comedy and Molière's *Le Misanthrope.* Chatsky, the hero of *Woe from Wit,* is a Russian Alceste, deploring the hypocrisy that surrounds him, antagonizing everybody, and adoring a woman who does not reciprocate his love. This second *atrabiliaire amoureux* is accused by the woman he loves of being always "ready to pour his bile on anyone" whom he encounters.[1] One could, of course, space permitting, introduce innumerable examples of the affinity between the major characters and the plots of Griboiedov's and Molière's plays, for it has already been proven conclusively that Chatsky was patterned upon Alceste and that Griboiedov's debt to Molière is evident. What is surprising, therefore, is the paucity of references to Molière in the critical essays dealing with *Woe from Wit,* both by Griboiedov's contemporaries and the Soviet critics. As a matter of fact, one gains the impression of a conspiracy of silence, so much the more so astonishing since *Woe from Wit* is likened to *Don Quixote* (V. Belinsky, 1840), to *Faust* and *Hamlet* (S. M. Petrov, 1950), and referred to as being similar in its impact on the public to Beaumarchais' *The Marriage of Figaro* (O. I. Senkovsky, 1834).

While the correspondences between Chatsky and Alceste are mostly ignored, a momentous controversy has raged since the play's appearance in manuscript form and continues until today. Scholars debate whether Chatsky is a "positive hero" or a so-called "superfluous man," whether he can be considered a predecessor of the "Decembrists" or simply an unhappy lover, whether he is a clever man himself or only a puppet in the hands of a clever writer. In his famous essay "A Thousand Tortures" ("Milion Terzany," 1871) I. A. Goncharov, the author of *Oblomov,* suggests that Chatsky is not a "positive hero," but an extremely intelligent man whose *bon sens* (*zdravy um*) has deserted him; yet even Goncharov does not refer to Molière.

Veselovsky, on the other hand, is one of the rare critics who suggests that those journalists and writers whose reaction to *Woe from Wit* was favorable were afraid that Griboiedov's originality would be doubted were *Le Misanthrope* to be mentioned. Be that as it may, in his *Etiudy i Kharakteristiki* (1903), Veselovsky asserts that a simple derogatory sketch of the Moscow society which Griboiedov had contemplated writing underwent a thorough change due, not only to the writer's maturing, but also to his discovery of a prototype in Molière's hero, with whom he could completely sympathize.[2]

One would have hoped that contemporary scholarship in Soviet Russia, in view of the unchallenged position that *Woe from Wit* has held and still is holding in Russian literature and theater, would not hesitate to acknowledge Griboiedov's debt to Molière. This, however, is not the case: in one of the latest scholarly editions of the comedy (1969), N. K. Piksanov, in a lengthy essay, vaguely states that "*Woe from Wit* represents a dialectic unity of several elements and energies. One can feel in it the beginning of classicism, Molièrism [*sic*], which can be seen in a multitude of monologues, in the traditional character traits of Lisa [the *soubrette*], in the dynamic development of action . . ." (p. 260). And then he hastens to add that Griboiedov had written "the first Russian comedy which was in no way imitative" (277).[3] It is mostly twentieth-century non-Soviet scholars, among them the Russian émigrés Mirsky and Slonim, the American Harkins, and the Dane Stender-Petersen, who firmly acknowledge Molière's *Le Misanthrope* as the source of Griboiedov's *Woe from Wit.*

Two curious facts surrounding Molière and Griboiedov might be briefly mentioned: first, that just as there seems to be a strong affinity between Molière's work and that of the French fable writer La Fontaine, it is generally considered that Griboiedov's work has a strong affinity with that of Krylov (the Russian fable writer whose emulation of La Fontaine is generally recognized); and second, that just as the part of Alceste is one of the greatest opportunities for a French actor, so is that of Chatsky sought after by the Russian actor. Thus one of the great triumphs of the Moscow Art Theater was the 1906 staging of *Woe from Wit* by Nemirovich-Danchenko, in which the famous actor Kachalov played Chatsky.

Nemirovich-Danchenko (the originator, with Stanislavsky, of the Moscow Art Theater) suggests in an article on *Woe from Wit* in 1910 that it was a tremendous mistake in former productions of the comedy to transfer "the center of the play" from the intimate relationship between Sofya, Chatsky, Famusov (Sofya's father) and Molchalin (the man Sofya loves) to a gallery of types which have only a social significance and to commentaries which may carry political implications. In this way, Nemirovich-Danchenko indicates that the literary critics in their conception of *Woe from Wit* as a socially-conscious and quasi-revolutionary work, had influenced the directors producing it: even before the Soviets, the Russian "intellectual élite" had always sought to discover the political message in great works of art. It is this particular attitude which could have induced the critics not to acknowledge Molière's influence upon Griboiedov. The Misanthrope, in his forthrightness, may deplore the ways of the world but he is by no means a revolutionary. If Alceste were accepted as the *Vorbild,* the prototype, of Chatsky, then the opposition of Alceste as a "negative" hero to Philinte the "positive" character would become cumbersome to critics desirous of discerning a revolutionary note in *Woe from Wit.* It is this political concern which may well be the reason for the paucity of acknowledgement by Russian scholars of Griboiedov's debt to Molière.

Notes

1. Act III, scene 1. The translation is mine.

2. For an excellent translation of Alexei Veselovsky's essay comparing in detail both plays, see Andrew Field, *The Complection of Russian Literature* (New York, 1971).

3. A. S. Griboiedov, *Gore ot Uma,* ed. N. K. Piksanov (Moscow, 1969). The translation is mine.

Gerald Janecek (essay date fall 1977)

SOURCE: Janecek, Gerald. "A Defense of Sof'ja in *Woe from Wit." Slavic and East European Journal* 21, no. 3 (fall 1977): 318-31.

[*In the following essay, Janecek asserts that many critics neither appreciate the complexity of Sofia's character nor how the ambiguity associated with her enhances* Woe from Wit.]

"Sof'ja is unclearly drawn. . . ."

A. S. Puškin

Critiques of *Woe from Wit* (*Gore ot uma*) usually center on Čackij. Mirsky's attitude is, in this respect, typical: "Chatsky is the principal thing in the play. He is its imaginative and emotional focus, its yeast and its zest." But Mirsky precedes this with a remark on Sof'ja which is not typical and which highlights a feature of the play that is peculiar, if not paradoxical:

> Sophia is not a type, but she is a person. She is a rare phenomenon in classical comedy: a heroine that is neither idealized not caricatured. There is a strange, drily romantic flavor in her, with her fixity of purpose, her ready wit, and her deep, but reticent, passionateness. She is the principal *active* force in the play, and the plot is advanced mainly by her actions.[1]

With this brief but pointed statement, Mirsky is more generous to her than most other critics. Many critics, Soviet critics in particular, give Sof'ja much less note—

some even omitting mention of her in fairly extensive articles.[2] Yet Mirsky sees her, not the purported hero, Čackij, as "the principal *active* force in the play." Certainly, then, Sof'ja's position in *Woe from Wit* deserves reexamination.

In spite of its early status as a classic, Griboedov's play continued to be controversial until Soviet times when a narrow view, based on the usual political considerations, became canonized. Early critics representing the conservative, Neoclassical tradition found that the play was not a typical comedy of manners with love intrigue, but a mixed form involving elements not only of serious social criticism, but also of tragedy.[3] From a different perspective, Belinskij considered the play a failure as a work of art because of internal disorganization and inconsistency, but ultimately gave the play high marks since the author's "external goal" was admirable. Commenting on Čackij as one of the author's mouthpieces, Belinskij concluded: "He has many ridiculous and false ideas, but they all issue from a noble source, from the hot spring of pulsing life."[4] Belinskij's provocative critique contains a number of points in regard to Sof'ja and Čackij that bear repeating.

It is striking that Belinskij characterizes Čackij as "half-witted" (*poloumnyi,* 472), whereupon follows a description of Čackij's *faux pas* and ill-considered actions, all of which are justly so described.[5] Čackij, in a word, makes a fool of himself. Belinskij sees the problem in that Čackij is expected to be both "high-society" (*svetskij*) and "profound" (*glubokij*), and neither the character nor the author can manage the combination successfully in a situation where high society is shallow. In this view, Čackij comes off poorly as a character, although the implied criticism of society is nonetheless effective. With such a weakening of the moral position of the hero, his relationship to Sof'ja is cast in a different light. If he is not as obviously admirable as he (and perhaps the author) thinks, then it is understandable that Sof'ja does not dismiss Molčalin at the first sight of Čackij, and does not fall into Čackij's arms even at the end.

The question of who loves whom is always seen as a problem for Čackij, namely: "Does she or does she not love me?" Most critics assume that Sof'ja does not and would never come to love Čackij;[6] and the denouement merely involves his final establishment of that fact. However, if one were to change the traditional focus so as to read the play from Sof'ja's viewpoint, then a more interesting question arises for her: "Should I, or should I not love him?" It is then Čackij, and not just Sof'ja, who is on the scales. Puškin's remark, quoted as an epigraph to this article, is remarkably perspicacious, considering his admission of having heard the play only once and without full attention.[7] Sof'ja is indeed ambiguously drawn in that her attitude to Čackij and her moral essence are unclear. However, this is not necessarily a weakness—it is just what makes her fascinating and worthy of closer attention.

Piksanov's excellent study compares the several extant drafts of the play in an attempt to understand some of the anomalies in the figure of Sof'ja. He uncovers a number of inconsistencies, and concludes that the image of Sof'ja is not fully worked out even in the "final" draft:

> The image of Sof'ja was conceived with unusual originality and complexity. As is now clear from the collation of variants from different times, the poet wanted to accomplish a two-fold task: to depict a nature deep and complex, but combined with traces of sentimentality. This conception was in the poet's consciousness from the very beginning, from the earliest drafts of the comedy. However, it is not worked out, not achieved in the final text. On the contrary, certain characteristic traits sketched in the early versions subsequently disappeared as a result of which the image lost clarity. This smoothing out, this dimming of sharp traits is an interesting peculiarity of the play's creative genesis.
>
> (65.)

Granted this alternative view is of some merit, nevertheless an attempt will be made here to examine only the final draft and to see it in its best light. So positive an approach is well supported by Nemirovič-Dančenko, who comments:

> Is it perhaps that Griboedov failed with Sof'ja, as many critics have suggested? Not in the least, Griboedov has drawn Sof'ja with extreme subtlety and finish, with great care for artistic proportion. But the whole sketch is so subtle, delicate and careful that it easily pales in the crude art known as theatre.
>
> (51.)

Čackij's entrance in Act I is prepared with considerable subtlety in the scenes preceding it. Sof'ja is the central figure in these scenes, and the characterizations of Čackij's two rivals are given from her point of view and mainly in her words. She dismisses Skalozub with irony and a tone of finality in response to Liza's remark on his desirability as a wealthy man with a promising military career ahead of him (."A bag of gold and he's aiming to be a general"):

> Куда как мил! и весело мне страх
> Выслушивать о фрунте и рядах;
> Он слова умного не выговорил сроду,—
>
> Мне все равно, что за него, что в воду.
>
> (I.5.)[8]

How nice he is! and I dearly enjoy / listening about the front and the ranks; / He hasn't uttered a witty word from birth,— / I'd just as soon jump in the lake as marry him.

The main ground for rejection relates to the lack of *um* which characterizes not only Čackij, but also Molčalin. Considering Sof'ja's own wit, just demonstrated in her handling of her indulgent but not unintelligent father in Scene 4, it is hard to feel that she would be happily matched with anyone lacking comparable wit. Thus, from the start Skalozub is not a serious alternative, although Sof'ja might later settle for him if necessary.

Sof'ja's attitude to Molčalin is more complex. One version of the *dramatis personae* (Nemirovič-Dančenko, 28) includes the comment "in love with Molčalin" after her name. Is this accurate? To a degree. Sof'ja's remarks on parting from Molčalin (I. 3.) have the ring of sentimental clichés taken from continental Sentimental novels: "Ah, it has indeed dawned! Both light and sadness. How quick the nights!" ("Ax, v samom dele rassvelo! I svet i grust'. Kak bystry noči!") "The happy don't count the hours." ("Ščastlivye časov ne nabljudajut.") "Go; we will the whole day yet bear our boredom." ("Idite; celyj den' ešče poterpim skuku.") She appears to be living a self-made romance modelled on the books she reads. One wonders whether it is merely a sentimental game to pass the time, or whether she is serious. The issue is not completely resolved even at the end of the play.

The dream invented as a ruse to distract Famusov contains Sof'ja's characterization of Molčalin: ". . . a dear person . . . both ingratiating and intelligent, But shy. . . . You know, one born in poverty. . . ." (". . . milij čelovek . . . i vkradčiv, i umen, No robok. . . . Znaete, kto v bednosti rožden. . . .") (I. 4.) The poverty fits well the part of the dream where "Some creatures, neither people nor beasts, Separated us—and tormented the one sitting with me." (IV. 1.). (The lovers are social outcasts because of their rejection of social norms.) The lover is, of course, *umen*. However, the other two traits are hardly flattering for a man, although they are part only of Molčalin's *public* character, for which Sof'ja is the main audience. Evidently Sof'ja values precisely the security and simplicity of the relationship: "It's as if fate protected us; No troubles, no doubts. . . . While woe waits around the corner." (I. 5.) Sof'ja is as clearly in control of the affair as she is of the household.

Liza eventually turns the conversation to Čackij as a third possibility who has the liveliness and wit that Sof'ja misses in Skalozub. Sof'ja agrees that Čackij is amusing, but ends with a caustic comment, "Laughter one can share with anyone" ("Delit' so vsjakim možno smex"), which smacks of the wounded pride that emerges more clearly in the ensuing prehistory of Čackij. Liza's implication that Sof'ja has "betrayed" Čackij's love elicits from Sof'ja a defense of her actions in which one can read a sense of hurt at having been abandoned without good reason:

Он сьехал, уж у нас ему казалось скучно, . . .
Вот об себе задумал он высоко— — — — — —
Охота странствовать напала на него,
     Ах, если любит кто кого,
Зачем ума искать, и ездить так далеко?

(I.5.)

He left, by now he found us boring, . . . / He held a
high opinion of himself— — — — — — / A yen to travel
fell upon him, / Ah, if one person loves another, / Why
look for wit and go so far away?

Sof'ja feels she has been rejected by Čackij because his
pride and intellectual aspirations could not be satisfied
by her—in other words, because she is not good enough
for him. His departure is a wound that still festers. In
the intervening three years she has matured remarkably
and is certainly his equal, but she has also come to enjoy her position of power and superiority in the house,
and so is more comfortable with the bland, subordinate
Molčalin than she might be with the passionate, unpredictable, and willful Čackij.[9]

Sof'ja may be conscious that her relationship with Molčalin is unworthy of her, and this is hinted at in the in-
terchange at the end of Scene 5 when Liza is caught
smiling at Sof'ja's description of her nights spent with
Molčalin. There is indeed something for a sophisticated
maid to smile at in the evidently chaste handholding
and flute-playing that seem to be the substance of the
night-long rendezvous in Sof'ja's room. But it is precisely in the innocence of these sessions of chaste ado-
ration that their charm lies for Sof'ja. There is, however, a fault in the script in regard to the nocturnal
flute-playing which, in even a large house, could not
but be overheard by other inhabitants (Piksanov, 49).

Liza produces (invents?) an explanation for the merri-
ment in a recollection of a love affair between Sof'ja's
aunt and a young Frenchman who eventually abandoned
her. Sof'ja's annoyance at this ("This is how they'll talk
about me later, too") indicates an appreciation of the
potential parallel between her present situation and that
of her aunt.

At the point of Čackij's arrival, then, the following disposition of thoughts and feelings can be perceived in
Sof'ja: she has reviewed and rejected the most socially
satisfactory suitor, Skalozub; she has been reminded of
Čackij's departure and the hurt it caused her, which revives her anger and sense of wounded pride; she has reviewed her relationship with Molčalin and found it comforting but not overly flattering to her self-esteem and
also possibly not as secure as she had assumed—she
may have sensed that it cannot be permanent. At the
same time the audience can perceive that Čackij is the
only one of the three choices that could be a good
match, provided Sof'ja is willing to enter into a relationship between equals in which she would have a

great deal to contribute but in which she would have to
surrender some of her exclusive control. Her position is
so perfectly balanced between youth (she is only seventeen years old) and maturity (she has evidently ruled
the house for some time) that the choice is a difficult
one.

Čackij enters unexpectedly, and launches on a chatty
speech about the hardships of the journey. Evidently
without giving Sof'ja a chance to get a word in, he begins to reproach her for her cold reception. Her first
words to him are not cold, but only reserved and dignified: "Ah! Čackij, I'm very glad to see you" ("Ax!
Čackij, ja vam očen' rada"). Čackij is unreasonable to
expect her to throw herself on his neck at this first surprise meeting, considering the past history of their relationship. Čackij's reproaches continue. Liza objects and
then even Sof'ja defends herself:

Не можете мне сделать вы упрека.
    Кто промелькнет, отворит дверьь,
Проездом, случаем, из чужа, из далека—
    С вопросом я, хоть будь моряк:
Не повстречал ли где в почтовой вас карете?

(I.7.)

You cannot reproach me. / Whomever flitted by, opened
the door, / passing through, by chance, from distant
lands— / I would ask, though he might only be a sailor:
/ Did he not perhaps meet you somewhere in a post
carriage?

This could be said with irony or obvious insincerity, but
there is no reason why it could not be said in seriousness. In any case, Čackij dismisses her defense with a
skeptical remark: "Let us assume it's so. Blessed is he
who believes, the world is a warm place for him!—"
("Položimte, čto tak. Blažen, kto veruet, teplo emu na
svete!—"). He begins to reminisce about the good old
days, which Sof'ja in her turn dismisses as "Childish-
ness!" (*Rebjačestvo*) so as to serve notice that things
are different now (she is a mature woman and not to be
treated as before).[10] However, Čackij does not take the
hint and crudely asks: "Are you not in love? I ask you
to give me an answer, Without reflection, there's been
enough confusion" ("Ne vljubleny li vy? prošu mne
dat' otvet, Bez dumy, polnote smuščat'sja"). To this she
is justifiably evasive. He interrupts with a few jabs at
Moscow but she counters with, "What's the point of
seeing the world! Where is it better?" ("Čto značit vi-
det' svet! Gde ž lučše?"). This is perhaps not so much a
defense of Moscow as a reference to the conventional
wisdom about finding happiness in one's own backyard.
But Čackij continues with a series of rhetorical questions (which drip with contempt) about her family, relatives, and friends. This speech ends with an insulting
epigram directed at Molčalin—"No doubt he'll reach illustrious ranks, For nowadays they love the *meek*"—
which provokes Sof'ja into a wholly justified counterat-
tack:

Софья

(в сторону)
Не человек, змея!
(Громко и принужденно)
Хочу у вас спросить
Случилось ли, чтоб вы, смеясь? или в печали?
Ошибкою? Добро о ком-нибудь сказали?
Хоть не теперь, а в детстве может быть.

Sof'ja

(aside): / Not a man, a viper! / (Loudly and forcedly): / I want to ask you / whether it ever happened that you, in laughter?, or in sadness? / By mistake? Said something good about anyone? / Perhaps not now, but maybe in childhood.

After all, who is Čackij to be making endless nasty cracks about everyone in sight? He is being plainly rude!

This reaction has an effect on Čackij: he retreats to the theme of hardships of the journey and the cold reception, and indicates that his love is so strong that he is willing to be patient:

И как вас нахожу? в каком-то строгом чине!
Вот полчаса [!] холодности терплю!
Лицо святейшей богомолки! . . .—
И все-таки я вас без памяти люблю.—

And how do I find you? in some sort of stern demeanor! / Alright, I bear a half-hour of coldness! / The face of the holiest pilgrim! . . .— / And all the same I love you madly.—

In fact, after a moment of further reflection, he seems to realize that he has perhaps gone too far with the speech and tries to rationalize it away:

Послушайте, ужли тлова мои все колки?
И клонытсю к чьему-нибудь вреду?
Но если так: ум с сердцем не в ладу.
Я в чудаках иному чуду
Раз посмеюсь, потом забуду:
Велите ж мне в огонь: попду как на обед.

Say, are all my words sharp, really? / And tending to anyone's harm? / If so: my mind is not in harmony with my heart. / Among oddballs at another oddity / I'll laugh once and then forget it: / Order me into the fire; I'll go as if to dinner.

Famusov interrupts and Sof'ja escapes with a puzzling remark, "Oh, Daddy, the dream's come true" ("Ax, batjuška, son v ruku").[11] These words are intended to refer to the dream in Scene 4. How so? Possibly Sof'ja is beginning to perceive the disruptive effect of Čackij and number him among the "neither people nor beasts" of the dream.[12] (Remember that she has already called him "a viper.") On the other hand, Famusov, in the final scene of the act wonders why she said this to him *aloud,* evidently perceiving that the remark might have been intentionally directed to Čackij. In that case, since Čackij was not present for the narration of the invented dream, he could not have been expected to understand the reference, but only to understand her in the more general meaning of "a nightmare (or dream) come true," which could be negative or positive.[13] Thus the remark is piquantly ambiguous and quite coy.[14] However, Čackij refuses to rise to the challenge of this sort of game ("I'm not an interpreter of dreams") and goes off to brood—but not before indicating the wonderful impression she has made on him, "How lovely!"

On the other hand, Čackij has clearly made a poor first impression on Sof'ja. He has shown himself to be insulting, abrupt, aggressive, sardonic, inconsiderate, demanding, and egotistical. This behavior is perhaps to be attributed to the impetuosity of youthful ardor,[15] but it does nothing to draw Sof'ja away from remembering her wounded pride and Čackij's upsetting, impetuous departure. In short, he has *deserved* the cold reception.

In Act II, after Čackij has refused Famusov's request to keep his tongue in rein while Famusov plays host to Skalozub, Sof'ja bursts in, runs to the window, and faints at the sight of Molčalin falling from a horse. The scenes that follow (8-11) seem almost unequivocal proof that Sof'ja not only does not love Čackij, but has nearly come to despise him. Yet a close reading yields uncertainties. Čackij skillfully revives Sof'ja, and for this receives a rebuff—perhaps deserved again, since his reply to her immediate inquiries about Molčalin upon regaining consciousness is: "So what if he might have broken his neck, he was almost the death of you" ("Puskaj sebe slomil by šeju, Vas čut' bylo ne umoril," II. 8). The comment rightly angers her again. He is remarkably insensitive and unsolicitous. She says to everyone present that misfortunes to others, even those not close to her, upset her greatly. Yet who would believe this? Least of all, Čackij. This "scene" is perhaps contrived by Sof'ja to dramatize her relationship to Molčalin in front of Čackij. One might also wonder whether it is part of the Sentimental secret romance in which "depth" of emotion is shown by accidental revelation of the secret in a moment of danger for the beloved. Is it part of the game, or a sincere unguarded moment? The lines to Molčalin could be either, depending on whether they were read with slight exaggeration or pure sincerity:

Откуда скрытость почерпнуть!
Готова я была в окошко, к вам прыгнуть.
Да что мне до кого? до них? до всей вселенны?
Смешно?—пусть шутят их; досадно?—пусть бранят.

(II.11.)

Why this secretiveness! / I was ready to jump out the window to you. / About whom should I worry? them? the whole universe? / Is it ridiculous?—Let it amuse them; a nuisance?—let them scold.

Sof'ja wants to be open about their affair, but Molčalin is a coward, perhaps realizing better than she the consequences that such an admission might have for *him* (dismissal from the house). Sof'ja is, of course, willing to "suffer the consequences" as part of the game, since they would be not so material for *her*. On the other hand, Čackij has complicated her life by his presence: "You want to? . . . I'll go and be gracious through my tears; I'm afraid I can't maintain the pretense. Why did God bring Čackij here!" ("Xotite vy? . . . Pojdu ljubezničat' skvoz' slez; Bojus', čto vyderžat' pritvorstva ne sumeju. Začem sjuda bog Čackogo prines!"). (II. 11.)

In the very next scene (12) it becomes obvious that one other pretense in the situation involves the genuineness of Molčalin's love for Sof'ja. Molčalin makes a pass at Liza. This lays the foundation for a dramatic irony in the next act when Čackij forces Sof'ja into a defense of Molčalin's character. Act III, Scene 1 is the key scene in the love intrigue of the play. Čackij confronts Sof'ja with the blunt question: "Whom do you love?" The interrogation has already gotten off to a bad start with Čackij's haughty-sounding opening words to Sof'ja: "You're here? I'm very glad, this is what I desired" ("Vy zdes'? ja očen' rad, Ja ètogo želal"). Sof'ja reacts with proper hostility: in answer to Čackij's emotion-laden (but rude) question, she is again suitably evasive and, as before, she counterattacks her aggressive interlocutor:

Софья

> Хотите ли знать истины два слова?
> Малейшая в ком странность чуть видна,
> Веселость ваша не скромна,
> У вас тотчас уж острота готова,
> А сами вы . . .

Чацкий

> Я сам? не правда ли, смешон?

Софья

> Да! грозный взгляд, и резкий тон,
> И этих в вас особенностей бездна;
> А над собой гроза куда не безполезна.

Чацкий

> Я странен, а не странен кто ж?
> Тот, кто на всех глупцов похож;
> Молчалин например . . .

Софья

> Примеры мне не новы;
> Заметно, что вы желчь на всех излить готовы;
> А я, чтоб не мешать, отсюда уклонюсь.

Sof'ja:

> You want to hear a few words of truth? / If the faintest strangeness is just visible in someone, / Your merriness

is not modest, / You've right away a witticism ready, / Yet you yourself . . .

Čackij:

> I, myself? you don't say, am ridiculous?

Sof'ja:

> Yes! the stormy gaze, and caustic tone, / you've no end of these things; / But a storm against a storm is of little value.

Čackij:

> I'm strange, but who isn't? / One who is just like all the other idiots; / Molčalin, for example . . .

Sof'ja:

> The examples are not new to me; / I notice you are ready to pour your spleen on everyone; / But I, so as not to interfere, will bow out.

Seeing the tables turned Čackij pretends "for once in a lifetime" to a certain mental distraction caused by an excess of love and passion. Here again he makes the tactical error of drawing an invidious comparison between himself and Molčalin:

> Нускай в Молчалине ум бойкий, гений смелый,
> Но есть ли в нем та страсть? то чувство? пылкость га?
> Чтоб кроме вас ему мир целый
> Казался прах и суета?

> Let's grant Molčalin a nimble mind, a brave spirit, / But is there in him the passion? the feeling? the ardor? / That except for you the whole world / Seems to him but vanity and dust?

He ends by wondering aloud if Molčalin is worthy of her, while demonstrating (even if in pretense) an unstable personality of questionable sanity and maturity. In fact this whole speech is a grave error on Čackij's part because he lowers himself to Molčalin's level instead of showing the nobility and reserve that might have won her over. By trying to prove Molčalin's unworthiness, he has only proved his own.

Sof'ja reacts with significant directness, revealing to him his failures. He objected to her being upset over Molčalin's fall, that is, objected to the idea that "one can be kind to all without exception." He has shown he can not keep control of his nasty tongue, and never stops joking at the expense of others. He showers contempt even on the meek. Hidden in this is an indication that her main objection might be that he does not take her relationship with Molčalin seriously—which is a profound insult to her womanhood and sense of dignity. He does not treat her as an equal worthy of respect. This is partly because he has not had time to adjust psychologically to the maturity she has acquired in three years. No doubt, however, he *does* love her.

Sof'ja's defense of Molčalin involves presenting him as a model of how Čackij ought to act if he is to gain her sympathy. Molčalin is solicitous, mild-mannered and taciturn, polite even to boring elders. She concludes that these features are better qualifications for family life than the traits Čackij has displayed.

Very interesting are Čackij's three asides during this defense: "She doesn't respect him. . . . She doesn't think him worth a penny. . . . She jests, she doesn't love him." ("*Ona ego ne uvažaet. . . . Ona ne stavit v groš ego. . . . Šalit, ona ego ne ljubit.*") They might be an accurate assessment of Sof'ja's true feelings and show that Čackij perceives a subtext to her argument. But this is a perception of the mind, not the heart. His mind's accurate perception produces a continuation of the same behavior as before, which results in further alienating Sof'ja. There are more sarcasms, witticisms, and attacks on Molčalin and other members of Sof'ja's circle. Instead of learning the lesson Sof'ja hoped he would, Čackij, in his investigation of Molčalin's personality in Scene 3, reaches the conclusion: "With these feelings, this soul, Loved . . . ! Deceiver, she is mocking me!" ("*S takimi čuvstvami, s takoj dušoju Ljubim . . . ! Obmanščica smejalas' nado mnoju!*") The dramatic irony is further intensified here. Čackij's assessment of Molčalin is more penetrating than Sof'ja's own. Yet this knowledge leads to the wrong conclusion and to further misbehavior, thus justifying Sof'ja's rejection of Čackij as a potential mate.

Two episodes germane to this investigation remain to be examined. The first occurs in Scenes 13 and 14 of Act III. Čackij and Sof'ja meet at the ball, and the stupidities surrounding Čackij have irritated him into another sarcastic comment on Molčalin in Sof'ja's presence. She reacts as usual: "Ah! This man is always the cause of terrible upset in me! He loves to humiliate, to jab; he's envious, proud and nasty!" One might ask, if Sof'ja's love of Molčalin is secure and divinely ordained ("God brought us together" she says about him in Act III Scene 1 to Čackij), and her contempt for Čackij so clear-cut, why are Čackij's witticisms the cause of "terrible upset"? One would expect her to ignore or dismiss them with less emotion. That she cannot do so is another indication that she harbors real doubts about Molčalin and feels that Čackij's criticisms are perhaps justified. In her pique, she takes advantage of a slight misunderstanding by Mr. N. of her statement that "he is not in his right mind" ("*on ne v svoem ume*") to have her revenge on Čackij by subtly and deliberately initiating the rumor of his insanity. Here she shows herself to be a brilliant society lady in complete command of her milieu.

The second episode is, of course, the denouement. Within earshot of the hidden Čackij, Sof'ja discovers Molčalin's deception and confesses her error: "It's as if

I hadn't known you until now." However, instead of playing the gentleman and stealing away unnoticed, perhaps to use this knowledge to press his suit on a more graceful occasion, and instead of feeling sympathy for her painful plight, Čackij attacks her without justification.[16] He accuses her of deception merely because she has told Molčalin she was glad Čackij was not present to see her shame. And he attacks her merely because she had preferred Molčalin to him: "So it's for him I've been sacrificed! I don't know how I controlled my rage!" ("*Vot ja požertvovan komu! Ne znaju, kak v sebe ja bešenstvo umeril!*"). (IV. 13.) In tears at this unfairness, Sof'ja again confesses her mistake: "Don't continue, I blame myself completely. But who could have thought that he was so perfidious!" ("*Ne prodolžajte, ja vinju sebja krugom. No kto by dumat' mog, čtob byl on tak kovaren!*"). At this point they are interrupted and Čackij concludes with a tirade in which he accuses her of having betrayed the relationship he assumed still to exist between them. Interestingly, Griboedov does not allow Sof'ja to reply to Čackij's indictment. Or perhaps it is Čackij who, in his passionate indignation, does not allow it, because he immediately (and thus prematurely) storms out. Had she replied, the final ambiguity of her view of Čackij might have been resolved in the mind of the audience. Essentially, however, her negative view of Čackij is amply justified by his final, ungallant actions. In any case, she has lost both Molčalin and Čackij, her only fault being a lack of perfect simplicity in her behavior, a fault common to Molčalin and Čackij as well. And so she is an object of pity, perhaps even a tragic figure.

It is possible that Sof'ja sincerely loved Čackij or Molčalin, or both, or neither. It is also possible that she did not clearly understand what her true feelings were in regard to either man. It should be obvious that critics who unequivocally assume one position or another for Sof'ja do not adequately account for the complexity and ambiguity of her character, and thus underestimate the play's dramatic interest. It is further arguable that this ambiguity is a great asset to the play and one of the factors contributing to its longevity. The role of Sof'ja, if subtly played by a gifted actress, can be one of great richness and grace.[17] Sof'ja might be made a commanding presence and the focal point of the dramatic action.

Finally, another aspect of this situation is noteworthy. In a previous study of character, the "undetermined" character of Ol'ga Il'inskaja in *Oblomov* was seen as the most artistically advanced in that novel.[18] Perhaps the same can be said about the female lead in this play of forty years earlier. (There are also certain obvious parallels between Sof'ja and the married Tat'jana when she is confronted by Onegin, also newly returned from abroad.) Piksanov aptly points out in this regard the limitation imposed on Griboedov by the genre in which he was working (65-66). The psychological depth toward which the author seems to have been striving in the figure of Sof'ja might have found a better medium of expression in the novel. In any case, perhaps it is time to shift our attention from Čackij who stands at an opposite pole from Moscow society because of his radical rejection of that society, and turn to Sof'ja who holds the moderate and wise central position that is expressed in her very name.[19]

Notes

1. D. S. Mirsky, *A History of Russian Literature from its Beginnings to 1900* (New York: Vintage, 1958), 116.

2. See for instance the articles by Lunačarskij and Leonov in A. L. Gordin, ed., *A. S. Griboedov v russkoj kritike. Sbornik statej* (M.: GIXL, 1958), 324-42 and 343-56. Lunačarskij discusses all the other major characters, including Liza, without mentioning Sof'ja. In the entry on Griboedov by O. I. Popova for the *Kratkaja literaturnaja ènciklopedija* (M.: Sov. ènciklopedija, 1964), II, 366-72, even the existence of the love intrigue itself is not mentioned. The major exceptions to this neglect of Sof'ja in the history of Griboedov criticism are the book by V. I. Nemirovič-Dančenko, *Gore ot uma v postanovke Moskovskogo xudožestvennogo teatra* (M.-SPb.: Gos. Izd., 1923), and a little known study by N. Piksanov, "Sof'ja Pavlovna Famusova," *Atenej,* I-II (1924), 37-71, which will be discussed below. In recent criticism, a balanced view is presented by Jean Bonamour, *A. S. Griboedov et la vie littéraire de son temps* (Paris: Presses Universitaires de France, 1965) 264-69. I. Medvedeva, "'Gore ot uma' A. C. Griboedova" [published together with G. Makogonenko, "'Evgenij Onegin' A. S. Puškina"] (M.: GIXL, 1971), 8-19, reviews the relationship of Sof'ja to Čackij with considerable subtlety, but does not fundamentally depart from a negative view of her.

3. For a discussion of early major critics (Puškin, Belinskij, Gogol', Gončarov) on the question of genre see the article by V. Asmus, "'Gore ot uma' kak èstetičeskaja problema," *Literaturnoe nasledstvo,* 47-48 (1946), 189-212.

4. V. G. Belinskij, *Polnoe sobranie sočinenij* (13 vols.; M.: AN SSSR, 1953), III, 484.

5. The places that Belinskij singles out as instances that do not do credit to Čackij's intelligence are several. He arrives at Famusov's at 6:00 A.M. and begins to reproach Sof'ja for receiving him coldly. He thereafter launches into an attack on the "good old times" in the presence of Famusov, who does not understand him and refuses to listen. He undertakes the meaningless task of discovering

whom Sof'ja loves, Molčalin or Skalozub. After confessing his love for her in trite clichés, he bluntly asks Sof'ja if she loves him. He delivers his most acid liberal attacks to a Moscow society gathering of people not smart or deep enough to follow his meaning. He fails to take Sof'ja's actions in Act IV as the "bitter truth," and does not steal away unnoticed, but insists on confronting her with an unjust accusation of duplicity—thus making himself appear to be a sneaky, eavesdropping fool. (475-80.)

6. This judgment depends on whether one assumes that Sof'ja is a part of the Moscow circle (even though its highest manifestation) or somehow an exception—an outsider like Čackij. If the former position is taken, then one concludes with most critics that there can be no permanent grounds for a relationship between her and the bitter enemy of that circle, Čackij. In its simplest terms, the argument runs: "Sof'ja belongs completely to Famusov's world. She cannot love Čackij, who is in opposition to this world with the whole make-up of his mind and soul." See V. Orlov, "Xudožestvennaja problematika Griboedova," *Literaturnoe nasledstvo,* 47-48 (1946), 50. The opposing position is held by the actress V. A. Mičurina-Samojlova, *Šest'desjat let v iskusstve,* (M.-L.: Iskusstvo, 1946), 104. "[Sof'ja] continues to love Čackij. Sof'ja's feminine self-love is wounded by his leaving her. In order to forget Čackij, she tries to love Molčalin, but she does not succeed in this." It is interesting that to step into the role conceived in this way the actress resorts to a fantasy: "So, to find and define the place of my Sof'ja among the other characters of *Gore ot uma* it helped me to think that she was not Famusov's daughter, but that her mother conceived her by someone else." In any case, it is necessary to posit in Sof'ja a certain degree of independence from her environment. This is not unreasonable when we think of the fact that there must be *some* reason why Čackij loves her. She must once have had, and probably still has some qualities in common with him.

7. A. S. Puškin, *Polnoe sobranie sočinenij* (16 vols. and suppl. vol.; M.-L.: AN SSSR, 1937-55), XIII, 138. Letter to A. A. Bestužev (Jan. 1825): "Sof'ja načertana ne jasno. . . ." In fact, Puškin's remarks are very close to Belinskij's views. On Čackij Puškin says: "Everything he says is very witty. But to whom is he saying all this? To Famusov? To Skalozub? To the Moscow grannies at the ball? To Molčalin? This is unforgivable. The first sign of an intelligent person is to know at first glance with whom he is dealing and not to cast pearls before Repetilovs and the like." Interestingly, he also notes: "Čackij's lack of confi-

dence in Sof'ja's love of Molčalin is charming!—and how natural! That's what the whole comedy should have centered on, but Griboedov evidently didn't want to—that's his decision."

8. The text used here is A. S. Griboedov, *Sočinenija* (M.: GIXL, 1956). References are to act and scene.

9. A similar view of Sof'ja's reasons for preferring Molčalin is presented by Vasil'ev, in *Aleksandr Sergeevič Griboedov: ego žizn' i sočinenija,* ed. V. Pokrovskij, 2nd ed. (M., 1908), 94-98.

10. A point made also by V. A. Ušakov, "Moskovskij bal, tret'e dejstvie iz komedii 'Gore ot uma,'" *A. S. Griboedov v russkoj kritike,* 51.

11. Although the expression *son v ruku* is ambiguous—*son* can be either pleasant or unpleasant in content—it often has the meaning "the nightmare has come true."

12. This view is advanced by S. Vasil'ev (Flerov), as quoted in Piksanov, 60.

13. The view that the phrase is intended to confuse Čackij rather than just Famusov is advanced by P. P. Gnedič, as cited in Piksanov, 60.

14. Piksanov, 58-61, devotes much attention to this line. On the basis of earlier drafts, he considers the line to be a reflex of the dream which was intended, it seems, originally to be a test on Sof'ja's part to see if Famusov would react favorably to a match with Molčalin, in which case she would confess her love for Molčalin openly to her father. Of course, Famusov reacts negatively. In any event, this motivation for the invention of the dream has been so obliterated in the final draft as to be negligible. The subtle complexities of the phrase are also noted by Nemirovič-Dančenko, 73.

15. Nemirovič-Dančenko, 136, emphasizes that Čackij is indeed a young man and not suitably played by the senior actors who often claimed the role.

16. I. A. Gončarov also makes this point: "He eavesdropped on the rendezvous of Sof'ja and Molčalin and played the role of Othello, having no right to do so." See "'Mil'on terzanij'," *Sobranie sočinenij* (8 vols.; M.: GIXL, 1955), VIII, 24.

17. I direct the reader to Nemirovič-Dančenko's book for a full description of a conception and theatrical realization of the play that appears to be wholly in consonance with the interpretation presented here. This production received a fairly positive review by Sergej Jablonovskij, *O teatre* (M., 1909), 139-64. MXAT's version stimulated that critic to reread the role of Sof'ja with much greater

sympathy. On the other hand, Mejerxol'd's famous revivals of the play (1928 and 1935) emphasized social criticism and the heroic qualities of Čackij, and are less consonant with this view. See Marjorie L. Hoover, *Meyerhold: The Art of Conscious Theater* (Amherst: Univ. of Massachusetts Press, 1974), 171-79, for a description of these productions.

18. Gerald Janecek, "Some Comments on Character in Oblomov," *Scando-Slavica,* 21 (1975), 41-50.

19. For this last insight I am indebted to Jesse Zeldin, who acted as discussant when I read this paper at the Southern Conference on Slavic Studies, Charlottesville, Virginia, 22 October 1976.

Mieczyslaw Giergielewicz (essay date 1979)

SOURCE: Giergielewicz, Mieczyslaw. "Structural Footnotes to Griboedov's *Woe from Wit.*" *The Polish Review* 24, no. 1 (1979): 3-21.

[*In the following essay, Giergielewicz discusses the structure of Griboedov's play, maintaining that the playwright skillfully manipulated theatrical conventions to convey a double plot: one involving a personal domestic dispute and the other involving a larger conflict the hero faces with Moscow society collectively.*]

Aleksandr S. Griboedov's masterpiece, the comedy **Gore ot uma** (**Woe from Wit**) has been translated into many languages, including English, French, German and Italian. It roused warm acclaim among the Poles. Fragments of the play in Polish rendition were printed in the Polish periodical *Bałamut* (*The Philanderer*), published in Petersburg (1831, Nos. 24-26). In 1857 two complete Polish translations of **Gore ot uma** were made available. In 1858 its first Polish theatrical performance took place in Lwów. Eight years later, in 1866, still another translation of the comedy appeared. In modern times the prominent poet Julian Tuwim, fascinated with Griboedov's play, did a Polish rendition in verse which was published and performed in 1951 in Warsaw.

I

Impressive literary criticism dedicated to Griboedov's dramatic masterpiece **Woe from Wit** pointed to certain unusual features of its structural framework. The famous Russian novelist, Ivan A. Goncharov, intimated that this comedy gives the impression that two different comedies have been blended together in this work: one is a domestic skit involving Sofia, Chatski, Molchalin, and Lisa, in which petty incidents are focused around a love intrigue;[1] the other is a more formidable plot, which embraces many people of Muscovite high society and introduces a more general conflict. Goncharov's observation is basically correct and deserves closer attention.

The initial scenes of the comedy establish a traditional farcical scheme. Lisa, a pretty and clever servant girl, keeps vigilance at the door of the bedroom where her mistress Sofia and the house clerk, Molchalin, have spent a sleepless night together. Lisa's concern is to protect the lovers from any sudden incursion of Sofia's father, Famusov. Indeed, the old man appears in person, but instead of dealing with his daughter, he cajoles the servant girl who defends herself against these unwanted advances by warning Famusov that his wheedling might be overheard by his daughter. He vanishes for a while, but soon returns and sees Sofia in the company of Molchalin, his own clerk. Sofia disarms her father's anger by telling him the content of her alleged nightdream, in which his voice was distinctly heard.

Such is the starting episode of *Woe from Wit.* Under the very nose of the watchful father, his daughter manages to arrange a nightly rendez-vous and succeeds in mitigating his suspicions. The respectable parent, who is so anxious about his daughter's potential misdemeanor, solicits Lisa's favors at the very threshold of Sofia's room. And the alert soubrette not only escapes the lust of her employer but helps the couple in avoiding unpleasant discredit. This course of events distinctly resembles the typical French farcical repertory of the period concerned.

Of the four actors involved, Lisa initially plays the most active part. She enjoys the confidence of her mistress, and deserves this trust. She dominates the risky situation and behaves with sober composure even in the presence of her master. She dares to give Sofia some sensible advice, and it is not her fault that it is disregarded. She is the only person in the whole cast of the play speaking with respect of Chatski, of whom she reminds her mistress just before his unexpected arrival. Her natural grace impresses not only the oldish Famusov but also Molchalin, who ultimately prefers her to Sofia. She acts like a *spiritus movens* of the domestic comedy which would become more sluggish without her animating presence. Moreover, this clever soubrette realizes well her social standing, and she chooses the barman Petrushka as her true favorite.

There is much reason for the assumption that the character of Lisa owed her theatrical existence to French playwriting.[2] She certainly looks, speaks, and behaves like a typical soubrette from the French theatrical repertory, which abounded in similar characters (though they were often more frivolous). She might look out of place in Russian surroundings during the reign of Alexander I, where peasant serfdom remained unshakable and would last for half a century more. But it is doubtful whether the author would have approved of such an objection. He might have underscored the brave public spirit of Muscovite servants during the occupation of the capital by the French aggressors. While the landlords hastened to flee, their serfs took care of the abandoned estates, displaying gallantry and dedication. Occasional hints about the plight of the peasants in Russia scattered in the text of the comedy never cast discredit on their morale.

The playwright's treatment of Lisa's mistress is more puzzling. Sofia's childhood was handicapped by the lack of maternal care, but her French governess earned her father's recognition. Chatski admired Sofia's beauty and charm. Her choice of beau proved to be an error, but psychologically it was not unjustified: active, dynamic persons, like Famusov's daughter, are often fond of passive and submissive companions. Sofia's youth and lack of experience also deserve some indulgence. Nevertheless, Griboedov exposed her to severe castigation. She had chances of becoming a success, and her guilt was not quite manifest; yet, in the comedy she is submitted to painful humiliation.

The inadequacies of Russian womanhood seemed to intrigue Griboedov when he compiled his minor plays. In the earlier one-act comedy *Molodye Suprugi* (*The Young Married Couple*), a free paraphrase of a French play,[3] he introduced Ariste and Elmira, soon after their wedding. Both love each other, nevertheless the husband soon finds his charming wife boring, and their verbal clashes reveal that apparently they have little to say to each other. The author intimates that their emotional coolness is Elmira's fault. She takes her husband's reciprocal love for granted; she adopts a passive attitude, neglects her clothes, and shuns the company of other men. Fortunately a friend of the couple opens Elmira's eyes to her situation and teaches her proper behavior. She begins to wear exciting dresses and pretends to receive mysterious letters, making her husband jealous. Casual quarrels add spice to their relationship, and the former emotional crisis is quickly forgotten. In *Woe from Wit* Sofia's blunders are of course different; she alienates not only Chatski but also Molchalin.

A surprising aspect of misogyny was also demonstrated in the vaudeville written jointly by Griboedov and his friend Pyotr Andreevich Vyazemsky and performed on September 1, 1824, in Petersburg.[4] Its protagonist, the Russian officer Roslavlev, disappointed by some girl, begins to dislike women so violently that he disapproves of any marriage. When he learns that his younger brother intends to marry a Polish girl, he becomes furious and decides to intervene. Unaware that the wedding had already taken place, he leaves for Poland. Both brothers stop in the same locality. The attractive daughters of the local postmaster do not dispel Roslavlev's ire; but Julia, his sister-in-law, disguised as a boy, captivates his sentiments and arouses his admiration; even when she divulges her true identity, she still enchants him to such a degree that he discards his anti-feminist grudge, and a happy reunion of the brothers is the inescapable result. Roslavlev senior not only reconciles himself to his brother's marriage, but renounces his former prejudice against women.

A peculiar national undertone sounds in this carefree vaudeville. Roslavlev junior pays a compliment to Polish girls by marrying one of them. His senior brother is less complacent, but he also indulges in their ambiguous praise. He voices his opinion to Julia before finding out her real identity:

JULIA (DISGUISED AS A BOY)

Just imagine—to get married at his age!

ROSLAVLEV SR.

And to a Polish girl! This is most dangerous.

JULIA.

Why? I am Polish myself.

ROSLAVLEV SR.

Let us be just, taking patriotism aside. Our coquettes are mere school-girls if compared with the Polish women.[5]

Julia still expresses the fear that Polish women may meet with hostility in Russia, but her brother-in-law assures her that all men in Russia adore girls arriving from Poland.[6] This emphatic homage sounds like a discreet sally against the alleged drabness of the native fair sex in Russia.

Griboedov's jest may reflect the popular fad as well as some real episodes. The story of Mme. Walewska, who became Napoleon's mistress, was widely known. Russian people were not unaware that the temporary heir to the Russian throne, Grand Duke Konstantin, married the Polish beauty Joanna Grudzińska. Marriages of other prominent Russians with Polish women were not infrequent.[7] And only a few years after the performance of Griboedov's vaudeville, Russian readers would be amused by a humorous ballad of Mickiewicz, "The Three Budrys Brothers." It was the story of an old Lithuanian warrior who advised his three sons departing on military expeditions to bring back silver rubles from Novgorod, amber from the Teutonic Knights at the Baltic seashore, and a bride from Poland. Naturally all three lads returned home with Polish brides. The translation by Aleksandr Sergeevich Pushkin popularized this ballad among the Russians.

Notwithstanding the Russian eulogies, some Polish playwrights subjected their native girls to a censure reminiscent of Griboedov's attitude towards Russian

women. In 1822 the first performance of the comedy *Mąż i żona* (*Husband and Wife*) by Aleksander Fredro was staged.[8] It is a sprightly and entertaining play in three acts with only four actors. The major role is entrusted to the servant girl Justysia (Justine) who in many respects resembles Griboedov's Lisa, lacking, however, her honesty and integrity. Justine acts as a confidante of her mistress, Elwira, who has established a liaison with her husband's cordial friend, Alfred. On her part Justine has an affair both with the lady's husband, Wacław, and with her lover, Alfred. Thus every imaginable heterosexual triangle links the members of the cast. Justine's treachery is ultimately discovered; Wacław decides to get rid of her, severs his friendship with Alfred and seeks reconciliation with his wife.

What were the reasons of Elwira's neglect—not only by her husband but also by her lover? She commits almost the same mistakes which Griboedov attributes to the forsaken wife in *The Young Married Couple*. She does little to please her husband, and her maudlin, monotonous sentimentality dampens the passion of her lover. Justine has no difficulty in making romantic conquests, because her vivacious, carefree, infectious gaiety is a delightful contrast with the moody behavior of her mistress. Besides, Fredro makes her victories more carefully motivated than those of her Russian counterpart, as Justysia had received some education and was well acquainted with the French language.

Fredro's apparent structural goal was to reduce the well-known farcical plot to the most economical drawing-room scale. Griboedov completed the cast of four basic actors with two additional characters. Apart from the main competitors—Sofia and Lisa, Chatski and Molchalin—he introduced Sofia's father, Famusov, and another potential suitor, Colonel Skalozub. However, the essential partners in the initial, farcical episode of *Woe from Wit* and Fredro's *Husband and Wife* are of patent similarity.

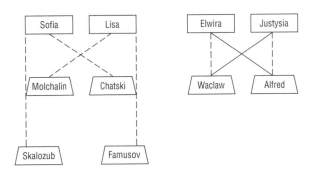

The interplay among Sofia and Lisa—Chatski and Molchalin, with Skalozub and Famusov as stage partners, was theatrically self-sufficient and contained enough potential for a small, three-act comedy comparable to

Fredro's *Husband and Wife.* Various ramifications of the intrigue were conceivable within the framework of such traditional farcical plots. Fortunately Griboedov leaned towards vigorous expansion of the conflict. He made the protagonist of the comedy rather an exponent of the growing protest against social evils than a mere clumsy partner in the entertaining game of love.

Even though the early episodes of **Woe from Wit** were overshadowed by further developments, the initial farcical nucleus was not completely discarded. Lisa continued to act as a faithful confidante of her mistress, and in the second act of the play extricated her once more from an embarrassing situation. Molchalin alluded casually to his fancy for Lisa, and his amorous intentions would be revealed in the final act of the play, precipitating the dénouement. Famusov still displayed the amusing shortsightedness of a comical figure: in spite of his cleverness, he completely misunderstood the conduct of his daughter and even accused Chatski of misdemeanor which had never occurred, while ignoring the involvement of Molchalin. Thanks to these ties the structural continuity of the comedy was maintained.

II

Curiously enough, in his own resumé of the play (written to Pavel Aleksandrovich Katenin in response to his critical remarks) Griboedov did not mention Lisa, as if he disregarded her structural role. When he looked at her from the perspective of his work as a whole, her presence lost some of its initial prominence. He simply recorded that Sofia, though not stupid, preferred a fool to the man who voiced his antagonism towards the social milieu:

> Nobody understands him, nobody wishes to condone his superiority over other people. At first he is just hilarious, and this is also a vice. "To joke all the time, how can you afford this!" He mildly castigates the oddities of his former acquaintances; but how could he behave otherwise, if they lack any sizable noble features? His mockery is not vicious until he gets infuriated; nonetheless he evokes a negative judgment: "He is not a man but a snake!" And later, when personal interests are menaced—our own people are being attacked—he is subjected to an anathema: "He enjoys humiliating people; he is jealous, conceited and wicked! . . ." Somebody remarked from spite that he was a lunatic; nobody believes it, but all repeat the rumor. The sound of general disapproval reaches his ears, and he also realizes the complete indifference of the girl who was the only reason for his arrival in Moscow; he spits in her and everybody's eyes and departs. The chess queen is also disappointed with her honey sugar.[9]

In this manner the playwright interprets the mechanism of further incidents in the comedy and the behavior of its protagonist. If one, however, knew only the four initial scenes of the play (preceding the appearance of Chatski), one would hardly anticipate such a continuation. The arrival of Chatski results in concentrating all floodlights on the newcomer. Structurally this was the favorite pattern of comedy writing by many seventeenth- and eighteenth-century playwrights, above all Molière.

As far as Molière is concerned, Chatski's stubborn belligerence shows some apparent kinship with Alceste from *Le Misanthrope,* and certain analogies between both characters could be easily traced. However, the background of Chatski's anger was basically different. His attitude is to be associated with Russian underground brooding, which found such an impressive outlet in the Decembrist rebellion and its tragic finale. Moreover, Chatski's dignified isolation, his emotional élan and passionate outbursts link him with the incipient Romantic rebellion which swept the European communities in the first half of the nineteenth century. He behaves as if he were a spiritual relative of the Byronic heroes. Like most of them, he seeks refuge in love, and as soon as his hopes are disillusioned, he disappears from the stage. The period of the playwright's work on **Woe from Wit** coincides with the rapid ascent of the Byronic star which fascinated so many European poets. Griboedov's knowledge of English enabled him to become one of the early harbingers of Byronism in Russian literature.

Various devices were exploited by the author in order to underscore the prominence of the protagonist in the comedy. Chatski is the first person from the outside world visiting the Famusovs in their home. His surprising entrance has been distinctly signaled. The exchange of opinions between Sofia and Lisa before his visit stirs the attention of the audience. Then the butler announces his entrée. Griboedov does not submit the audience to such protracted suspense as Nikolai Vasilievich Gogol did in *Revizor* (*The Inspector-General*) where Khlestakov appears only in the second act; however, both playwrights manipulated a similar structural stratagem. And as soon as Chatski enters the stage, his prominence becomes incontestable. His vigorous effusions are contrasted against the farcical atmosphere of the initial scenes. Presently he will become involved in acrimonious verbal skirmishes, revealing his firm, resolute convictions and an explosive fighting spirit. Gradually petty squabbles are replaced by more significant confrontations.

Chatski is received by both Famusov and his daughter with ostentatious coolness, but he cannot be easily discouraged. Although hardly conceited, he is well aware of his advantages and believes in his cause. He does not fear social isolation, and seems to be a good fighter. However, the course of events turns disastrous for him. He does not make converts and provokes general disapproval. He fails as a lover and must savor the bitterness of the defeat, although his competitor is a nonentity whom he heartily despises. He learns that people have proclaimed him a lunatic. His last gesture of defiance is the decision to abandon the capital.

In spite of these humiliating mishaps it may be acknowledged that the protagonist gains a moral victory. Chatski might draw some consolation from casual clashes with the opponents whom he makes victims of his acidulous wit. Until the very end of the play he remains the focus of general attention. Even if he stays behind the scenes, his influence is felt. In his defeat he looks more impressive than his triumphant tormentors. He is allowed by the author to indulge in a few long, violent soliloquies which enhance his stature. In the last scene of the third act he recites a monologue among a crowd of the guests, none of whom pays any attention to him; this wasted effort makes his diatribe even more conspicuous to the public. The role of a prophet crying in the wilderness does not make him ridiculous. Confronted with a mute, impersonal society, the protagonist looks like the only human being distinguishable in the mob of nondescript creatures.

Some of Chatski's passionate invectives refer to his amorous misadventure, but most of them have no personal motivation. Chatski's judgments sound like an objective assessment of the shortcomings and vices of Muscovite community. The playwright's biography indicates his connection with the clandestine political brooding; yet in **Woe from Wit** Chatski ridicules the silly conspirators whose reckless clamoring becomes a public secret, and speaks with scorn of the meetings at the English Club where Famusov is one of the members.

Chatski's aggressive fierceness soon creates the impression that the Famusov drawing room is too narrow a milieu for his militant sallies. Griboedov finds a bold solution to the resulting artistic dilemma. He discards the Classicist's habit of manipulating a strictly limited number of actors. In order to provide a more convincing psychological justification for his hero's belligerence, he arranges a reception to which many guests are invited. The initial cast of five actors (plus Skalozub who is added in the second act) will grow to twenty-four participants; moreover, a number of anonymous people will appear on the stage, including casual, unnamed visitors, servants, butlers, footmen, et al.

Owing to this growth of the cast, Chatski's behavior acquires a more adequate perspective. The reasons for his animosity become more convincing as soon as he is confronted with a more representative body of Muscovite high society. The mechanism of meaningless chattering and slanderous gossiping which animates the crowd contrasts effectively with Chatski's bold straightforwardness and intellectual honesty. Especially instructive in this respect is the late introduction of Repetilov, the indefatigable windbag eagerly avoided by his acquaintances.

III

Even the greatly increased cast did not represent adequately the social target subjected to the playwright's satirical castigation. The message of the comedy was not limited to a superficial layer of the Muscovite community, but attacked the system with manifold social implications. Griboedov displayed much creative courage by straining the technical limits of traditional stagecraft. But the resources available were not unlimited. Further increase of the cast might create confusion and could be embarrassing for the producers.

The writer resorted to an expedient for conveying the images of individual persons and collective groups without overcrowding the stage. He boldly exploited the device moderately tested by Classicist playwrights. He let the actors evoke images of people and incidents attributed to the real life beyond the stage. In this respect Molière was one of his worthy predecessors. In *Le Misanthrope* Acaste and Celimène indulge in free gossiping, drawing sketchy caricatures of their common acquaintances. Acaste points to the talkative Damon who abuses the patience of his friends even under the hottest sun, and Celimène adds her malicious comment:

> C'est un parleur étrange, et qui trouve toujours
> L'art de ne vous rien dire avec de grands discours;
> Dans le propos qu'il tient on ne voit jamais une goutte
> Et ce n'est que du bruit que tout ce qu'on écoute.[10]

This quotation was selected among a dozen of others, as it introduces a man who resembles to some extent Repetilov, equally loquacious and repugnant to his listeners. Appropriate use of the same technique was made by some English playwrights, e.g., by Sheridan in his *School for Scandal*. A. Fredro exploited the same method in *Husband and Wife* to extend his own satirical portrayal of high society. Both Wacław and his friend, Alfred, excel in witty backbiting. They ridicule the Pantler's wife who concocted clumsy anecdotes, generously spread them around—and was the only person laughing at them. They speak of Angela, so enamoured of her husband that whenever he left for his country estate, she would dress herself in mourning garb; of the Baron who dearly loved his wife—and considered her lover his closest friend. These caustic remarks refer to the habitués of the local drawing rooms, and Wacław's wife, Elwira, justly brands their wickedness.[11]

Griboedov visualized the almost unlimited potential of such apparently casual cues pointing to the outer world. He found in them the vehicle for communicating to the public the meaningful information which could not be conveyed visually on the stage. Even though such hints may appear less expressive, they leave some definite imprint in the memory and imagination of the spectators and enrich the texture of the play. In some respects such inserted data may be even more versatile and instructive, as they are independent of the limitations of time and space to which the theatrical stage is submitted. The actors acquire an opportunity for conveying distant incidents which happened in the past or are expected in the more or less distant future.

Certain cues of this category may refer to the characters of the play. Some earlier playwrights indulged in describing the leading personages before their appearance on the stage. In the comedies this rather conventional, introductory function was sometimes performed by conventional servants, anticipating the entrée of their masters. In **Woe from Wit** Sofia and Lisa provide some information about Famusov, as well as of Chatski and Skalozub, who will appear only in subsequent scenes.[12] The informative significance of such utterances may be modest, but is not superfluous. Sofia's criticism of her father reveals some disrespect reflecting the habitual generation gap; her remarks about Molchalin indicate the degree of her infatuation. In the third act of the comedy ironic hints by several persons concerning Zagoretski reveal the general scorn for this unsavory gentleman.

Owing to abundant information conveyed inconspicuously by the cast the cumulative portrayal of Muscovite high society was enriched by many significant traits. On the other hand a number of inserted messages refer to various painful grievances involving the lower classes. Many individuals and groups mentioned in carefree chats among the actors take on definite literary existence, even though they do not appear on the stage. They may be considered as a supplementary phantom cast, firmly anchored in the text.

To weigh properly the significance of the technical device concerned, a complete register of them should be helpful, priority being accorded to the individuals.

1. Madame Rosier, Sofia's governess and "second mother," overpaid by another employer. (I, 4, p. 10).

2. Sofia's aunt, abandoned by her French lover; she forgot to dye her hair, and in three days grew grayhaired. (I, 5, p. 17).

3. The mysterious Turk or Greek, anonymous. (I, 7, p. 19).

4. Another aunt of Sofia, lady-in-waiting of Catherine I, whose home was full of her wards and of little dogs. (I, 7, p. 20).

5. Sofia's tubercular uncle, enemy of books who joined the learned Committee for Liquidating Schools. (I, 8, p. 20).

6. A peasant hidden behind the screen, imitating a nightingale during the winter reception. (I, 8, pp. 19-20).

7. The German mentor of Sofia and Chatski. (I, 7, p. 20).

8. Princess Pulkheria Andreevna, Guillomé's eventual bride-to-be. (*Ibid.*).

9. Guillomé, dancing master, a potential husband for some Russian princess. (*Ibid.*).

10. Praskovia Fedorovna, inviting Famusov to a trout dinner. (II, 1, p. 25).

11. The late chamberlain Kuzma Petrovich, wealthy and respected in Moscow. (II, 1, p. 25).

12. Famusov's uncle Maxim Petrovich, who speeded up his career by stumbling at the court. (II, 5, p. 27).

13. Skalozub's brother, who received a military distinction, but retired from the Army, and turned to books. (II, 5, pp. 33-34).

14. An anonymous magnate, the Nestor of glorious scoundrels, whom Chatski had to visit as a boy. (II, 5, p. 38).

15. A ballet fan, bringing the dancing peasants from his country estate to Moscow. (II, 5, p. 38).

16. Princess Lasova, a widow who fell from a horse and broke a rib, seeking another husband for support. (II, 9, p. 43).

17. Tatiana Yurievna, an influential lady glorified by Molchalin. (II, 5, p. 36 and III, 3, pp. 55-56). The names of three other ladies are mentioned.

18. Foma Fomich, chief of departments in three ministries, an alleged writer, praised by Molchalin and scorned by Chatski. (III, 8, pp. 56-57).

19. Khlestova's Negro girl. (III, 10, p. 67).

20. Another Negro girl of Khlestova's sister, bought at the fair by Zagoretski. (III, 10, p. 68).

21. Monsieur Kok, partner at the card game with Molchalin and Khlestova. (III, 12, p. 70).

22. Prince Fedor, who studied at the Institute in Petersburg, expert in botany, shunning women. (III, 21, p. 79).

23. The anonymous little Frenchman from Bordeaux. (III, 22, p. 79).

24. Prince Grigori, enthusiast of English ways of life. (IV, 4, pp. 89-91).

25. Evdokim Vorkulov, allegedly a fine singer. (IV, 4, p. 89).

26. Ippolit Markelych Udushiev, gambler and alleged writer. (IV, 4, pp. 89-90).

27. Baron von Klotz, Repetilov's father-in-law, a high-ranking civil servant. (IV, 5, p. 92).

28. Lokhmot'jev, an alleged radical politician. (IV, 5, p. 153).

29. The husband—a mere boy acting as his wife's page (with reference to Molchalin. (IV, 14, p. 104).

As can be seen, the register of persons introduced indirectly in the comedy (to which a few less significant, anonymous figures might be added) exceeds numerically the cast of the play. Even more abundant are references to collective groups and to various incidents involving such groups:

1. Advice to the servant girls to avoid both ire and love of their squires. (I, 2, p. 7, Lisa).

2. French tramps and vagrants employed by the Russian squires to teach their daughters dancing, singing, and making love, as if they were expected to marry comedians. (I, 3, p. 9).

3. Method of getting rid of burdensome official business by bureaucrats: once the letter is signed, the matter is over. (I, 4, p. 13).

4. Evening-dress balls, idle gossiping, and writing verse in the albums as usual pastimes for girls. (I, 7, p. 19).

5. The stout landlord fond of theatrical performances and his lean serf actors. (I, 7, p. 19).

6. The three senile boulevard heroes, rejuvenating themselves for half a century, and a million of their relatives dispersed all over Europe. (*Ibid.*).

7. The wards kept in the manor of an old lady-in-waiting of the Imperial Court. (*Ibid.,* p. 20).

8. Large provincial gatherings of the Russian gentry where a mixture of French and the Russian provincial dialects can be heard. (*Ibid.,* p. 21).

9. Regiments of bad, but inexpensive teachers. (*Ibid.,* p. 20).

10. Statement that in Russia everyone is an alleged scholar, an historian or a geographer. (*Ibid.*).

11. Children taught by their German teachers that no salvation is possible without the Germans. (*Ibid.*).

12. A gourmet trout dinner. (II, 1, p. 25).

13. The solemn funeral of a prominent dignitary. (*Ibid.*).

14. An invitation to the baptism of a baby by a doctor's widow, included in Famusov's timetable. (*Ibid.*).

15. A glimpse of life at the Imperial Court in the epoch of Catherine I. (II, 2, p. 27).

16. Crowds of sycophants, eager to please, in the past and the present. (II, 2, p. 27).

17. Buffoons eager to please their patrons. (*Ibid.,* p. 29).

18. Nepotism: employment of nephews and cousins of dignitaries, outsiders being a rare exception. (II, 5, p. 33).

19. The propitious disappearance of Skalozub's competitors in his military career: some were killed, some retired. (II, 5, p. 34).

20. The abundance of brides-to-be in Moscow. (II, 5, p. 35).

21. Worthless suitors, yet acceptable if they possessed two thousand peasant serfs. (II, 5, p. 35).

22. Uninvited guests, taking advantage of the foolish hospitality of the hosts. (*Ibid.*).

23. Young lads, so clever that they are capable of teaching their own teachers. (II, 5, p. 36).

24. Sterile discussions of elderly statesmen. (II, 5, p. 36).

25. Ladies as supreme judges of the community, deserving to sit in the Senate, educated in the French fashion, but still very patriotic and therefore fond of the military. (*Ibid.*).

26. The onesided revival of Moscow after the disaster of 1812: the houses are new, but the prejudices are old. (II, 5, pp. 36-37).

27. Magnates hating freedom, drawing information from obsolete gazettes, relying on the help of influential relatives, enriched by robbery, indulging in waste and sumptuous banquets. (II, 5, p. 37).

28. Foreign sycophants, cultivating the basest traditions of the past. (II, 5, p. 38).

29. Devoted servants of the Nestor of the noble scoundrels, bartered by him for three greyhounds. (*Ibid.,* p. 38).

30. Peasant boys and girls, brought to Moscow as performers in the ballet, and subsequently sold to cover their owner's debts. (*Ibid.*).

31. Universal persecution of gifted young men whose talents aroused apprehension. (*Ibid.*).

32. The uniform as a guise concealing shortcomings of character and mind. (*Ibid.*).

33. Enthusiastic ladies who welcomed uniformed officers by throwing their bonnets in the air. (II, 5, p. 39).

34. Officers of the First Army, competing successfully with the Guards: elegant, with narrow waists, some even speaking French. (II, 1, p. 45).

35. People in Moscow fond of joking, with evil tongues more menacing than pistols. (II, 11, p. 45).

36. Abundance of influential fools, some serving in the Armed Forces, some bad poets, some civil servants. (III, 1, p. 50).

37. People capable of mixing work with amusements, praised by Molchalin and despised by Chatski.

38. Nostalgic memories of the abandoned military camp comrades after the officer's retirement and marriage. (III, 6, p. 62).

39. Girls and their parents depressed at the balls in view of the scarcity of dancers. (III, 6, p. 62).

40. Men abroad marrying salesgirls in fashionable stores, justified by Chatski for preferring the originals to their clumsy Russian copies. (III, 8, p. 65).

41. Excitable ladies, deftly pacified by Molchalin. (III, 13, p. 71).

42. Learning as social calamity, responsible for the fact that more insane people and foolish affairs are to be found than ever before. (III, 21, p. 78).

43. Stultifying boarding schools and lyceums. (III, 21, p. 79, Skalozub).

44. Rebellious schools, especially the Pedagogical Institute, where the professors allegedly teach their students conspiracy and atheism. (III, 21, pp. 78-79).

45. Skalozub's project to make all schools military-like, practising drill and turning to books only on special occasions. (III, 21, p. 79).

46. Famusov's suggestion to burn all books as the source of all social evil. (III, 21, p. 79).

47. Assertion that lunacy may result from book reading as well as from drunkenness. (*Ibid.*).

48. A man (Chatski) lost in the indifferent crowd and subjected to a million tortures: pseudo-friendly embraces, meaningless shouting and sterile ideas. (III, 22, p. 81).

49. A crowd of Russian people approving of the insolent Frenchman from Bordeaux and listening to his conceited chant that there is no better country than France. (*Ibid.*).

50. Venerable customs, language, tradition, clothing, grooming foolishly changed by the Russians. (III, 22, p. 82).

51. General condemnation of everyone who dares to proclaim new ideas. (III, 22, pp. 82-83).

52. Secret gatherings in the English Club; clandestine meetings at which the participants shout so loudly that nobody understands the speakers. (IV, 4, p. 88).

53. The English acquaintances surrounding Prince Grigori. (IV, 4, p. 89).

54. Collective cooperation on a vaudeville making it impossible to compile a valuable work. (IV, 4, p. 90).

55. A gathering at Prince Grigori's: twenty people attend, but they shout for a hundred. (IV, 5, p. 91).

56. Skalozub's suggestion to submit the discussants to the command of a corporal as their intellectual Voltaire. (*Ibid.*).

57. The prosperous clerks of Baron Klotz, vulgar and venal. (IV, 5, pp. 91-92, Repetilov).

58. The prescription of Molchalin's father to please everybody: the landowner, the chief of the Office, the butler brushing the clothes, the janitor, and the dog, in order to acquire general benevolence. (IV, 12, p. 99).

59. Throngs of Molchalin, thriving in the world. (IV, 13, p. 102).

60. Glimpses of life in an obscure village where Sofia would be eventually exiled by her father with Lisa, and where the only pastimes available are knitting and weaving. (IV, 14, p. 10).

IV

The examination of the comedy's structural texture leaves the impression not only of surprising abundance but also of ingenious planning. Its content may be arranged in a concentric way. The central position of Chatski remains uncontestable. The second circle embraces the persons directly participating in the farcical plot. In the third circle the guests attending the reception in the Famusov house can be placed. The fourth circle will enclose all other persons mentioned individually in the text. And the fifth circle will include the groups of different social standing.

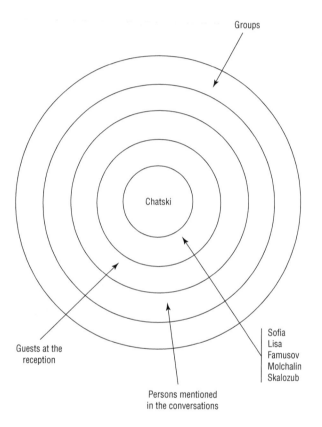

In the first act of **Woe from Wit** farcical entertainment seems to prevail. The arrival of Chatski changes its mood. Gradually, owing to the wealth of information provided by the cast of the comedy, a vision of grim, complicated, turbulent existence emerges from the text. The work sounds like an urgent, alarming social message. This effect has been achieved without didactic pomp. The ironic twist of the final *coda* signals the apparent suppression of the temporary excitement and the eventual return to the atmosphere of the initial scenes.

The playwright's unorthodox technique viewed from the psychological standpoint may be subjected to some doubt. It was certainly difficult to reconcile two different artistic goals: to write a lively, spirited dialogue meeting the standards of theatrical diction and to provide a miniature social encyclopedia of the calamities worrying the Russian progressives of the period concerned.

In order to pay due tribute to Griboedov's mastery, the specific quality of Russian high society should be assessed. The actors of the comedy belong—with only minimal exceptions—to the privileged class whose patchy and rather superficial education was not impressive, but which was well adapted to the exigencies of the drawing room. Conversational skill, mastery of *bons mots,* and witty riposte were almost necessary for societal survival. This ability was expected from both men and women, from civil servants and army officers, from courtiers, intellectuals, and artists. Chatski and Famusov belonged to different generations and political creeds, but both displayed a good command of *bons mots.* Even Skalozub, an obvious sot, uttered a few sayings which revealed his hopeless backwardness, but which sounded like apt epigrams. Lisa, who was a clever girl and learned much from her masters, said of Skalozub, "He is also capable of joking; who is not today?" Pushkin concurred with this opinion by acknowledging the existence of brilliant fools (*"blistatel'nykh gluptsov"*).[13]

Griboedov was well aware of this curious phenomenon and made excellent use of it in his comedy. A similar artistic endeavor would be disastrous if the social milieu consisted mainly of taciturn, uncommunicative growlers. Conversational fencing in **Woe from Wit,** in which practically the whole cast is allowed to participate, makes the cumulative exchange of information and opinions natural and unobtrusive. The actors are sufficiently well equipped for carrying out their respective communicative assignments without any ostentatious prompting by the playwright.

Within the cast, of which every member is capable of conversing in an articulate, entertaining manner, Chatski's prominence is not overemphatic. His dialectical sallies do not crush the opposition and occasionally meet with witty response. Even if some of his adversaries express the opinion of which the playwright definitely disapproves and which the audience may find wrong, they perform a constructive function by conjuring up an atmosphere of authentic verbal strifes.

Naturally enough, Chatski's spirited, ebullient eloquence prevails in the text, and he is involved in drawing ten individual portrayals and twenty-seven group sketches, mainly of satirical content. But he does not silence the opposition; on the contrary, he arouses the objections of other actors and animates their repartées. In several scenes he recedes into the background, while other speakers come to the fore. It was a hazardous task to maintain the proper balance; but Griboedov solved his dilemma with admirable skill, distributing the communicative duties among nine actors. Their register in-

cludes not only the leading performers, but also a few casual guests at the Famusov reception, who did not participate in the plot of the comedy, but still were given a chance to voice certain individual contributions.

	Individual portraits	Collective portraits		
Chatski	10	27	=	37
Famusov	5	16	=	21
Repetilov	5	5	=	10
Skalozub	2	4	=	6
Molchalin	3	1	=	4
Khlestova	2	2	=	4
Princess	1	2	=	3
Lisa	1	2	=	3
Granddaughter of Princess (with Chatski)		1	=	1
Total:	**29**	**60**	**=**	**89**

It would be erroneous to assume that in order to make his own points the playwright felt compelled to rely on Chatski as the exponent of his own opinion. In most cases the writer seemed to identify himself with his main protagonist (but he was also in basic agreement with Lisa). Moreover, if some actor expresses an idea incompatible with the views of the playwright, the audience obtains enough indication to make the proper judgment. Occasionally an ironic accent adds poignancy to the dialogues, making Griboedov's stand even more emphatic. This applies to such characters as Famusov, Skalozub, and Repetilov.

Indirect sketches and episodes conveyed by the cast of the play resulted not only in the bold expansion of the social panorama, but also in some precious qualitative contribution. It was justly remarked that the pageant of the individuals included in the dialogues and monologues of **Woe from Wit** surpasses the prestige of the actors appearing on the stage.[14] Griboedov's ability to maintain the lively tempo of the play in spite of its communicative message is certainly an outstanding achievement.

The comedy was written for alert and imaginative audiences, capable of transferring conversational hints into adequate images during the course of the performance. Recently some modern techniques were experimentally tested in similar instances. The producers of the Romantic drama, *Cyrano de Bergerac,* by Edmond Rostand in Paris exploited film pictures. While all roles of this drama were performed on the normal stage, the atmosphere of the chivalrous period was conveyed by the addition of filmed scenes showing the fantastic exploits of fearless knights. These supplements were added mainly during the intervals.

Griboedov's close acquaintance with European playwriting helped him to start the comedy rolling. He adopted the individualistic method of the Romantic era by concentrating the spotlights on the lonely fighter and by emphasizing his ferocious conflict with Muscovite society. On the other hand he conceived a design to reflect this society in a comprehensive and explicit way, thus dramatizing the isolation of his hero. In order to reach this goal he did not shun the traditional devices of the classic repertory, but manipulated them in an ingenious way, creative and refreshing. He found a masterful application for the Classicist habit of conversational portrayal, rejuvenating its expressiveness and expanding its use.

Notes

1. I. A. Goncharov, "Million terzanii. Kritichesskii etiud" (A Million Torments, a Critical Study), in *A. S. Griboedov v russkoi kritike (Griboedov in Russian Criticism)*, Moscow, 1958, pp. 271-72.

2. About twenty private theaters were active in Moscow at the beginning of the nineteenth century; some of them survived the French occupation in 1812. Cf. Jean Bonamour, *A. S. Griboedov et la vie liiéraire de son temps,* Paris, 1965, pp. 38-41 and 60-69. A member of the Green Lamp Circle (considered the literary branch of the Decembrist movement), probably A. D. Ulybashev, the noted historian of music, published anonymously an essay criticizing the supremacy of French influence in Russian drama. (Cf. B. V. Orlov, "Khudozhestvennaya problematika Griboedova," in *Literaturnoe Nasledstvo (Literary Heritage)*, 1947-48, pp. 18-19). As to the comedy *Gore ot uma,* Ju. N. Tynianov pointed to the ties between this play and Beaumarchais ("Sjuzhet *Goria ot uma,*" in *Literaturnoe Nasledstvo, op. cit.,* pp. 149-150). The critic referred to the eulogy of slander by Don Bazile in *Le barbier de Seville ou La précaution inutile.*

3. *Le secret du ménage,* by Augustin-François Creuse de Lesser, published in 1809 and performed in the same year in Paris. According to F. V. Bulharin and S. N. Bagichev, Griboedov's paraphrase of this three-act play was written in 1814. Cf. A. S. Griboedov, *Sochineniia (Works)*, Moscow, 1959, comments by Vl. Orlov, p. 670. All subsequent quotations from Griboedov's writings were taken from this edition.

4. *Kto brat, kto sestra, ili obman za obmanom (Who Is Brother and Who Is Sister, or One Hoax after Another).* According to the co-author P. A. Vyazemskii, the prose text was provided by Griboedov. See *Sochinenia, op. cit.,* p. 675.

5. *Ibid.,* scene 10, p. 286.

6. *Ibid.,* scene 17, p. 297.

7. One member of the influential Nesselrode family (Frederic, subsequent chief of military police in the Warsaw district), married Tekla Nałęcz Górska. A. S. Shishkov, minister of education, married the widow, Julia Lobarzewska (née Narbutt); during his stay in Russia Mickiewicz attended her receptions. The book by Maria Czapska, *Europa w rodzinie (Europe in the Family)*, Paris, 1970, contains much information on the international ties among prominent European clans, including Russians and Poles.

8. Aleksander Fredro, *Pisma wszystkie (Complete Works)*, vol. I, Warsaw, 1955. The text of the Polish comedy is available in the prose translation into English by Harold Segel. (*The Major Comedies of Alexander Fredro,* Princeton, 1969, pp. 63-115).

9. Letter to P. A. Katenin, in *Sochineniya, op. cit.,* p. 557.

10. Molière, *Le Misanthrope,* act II, scene 5.

11. A. Fredro, *op. cit.,* act I, scene 8.

12. A. S. Griboedov, *op. cit.,* act I, scene 5, pp. 14-15.

13. A. S. Pushkin, *Evgenii Onegin,* canto XLVI, line 14.

14. A. S. Griboedov, *Gore ot uma,* ed. N. K. Piksanov and A. L. Grishin, Moscow, 1969, p. 263.

William Edward Brown (essay date 1986)

SOURCE: Brown, William Edward. "Alexander Griboedov and *Woe from Wit.*" In *A History of Russian Literature of the Romantic Period,* Vol. 1, pp. 105-15. Ann Arbor: Ardis Publishers, 1986.

[*In the following excerpt, Brown claims that* Woe from Wit *marked a turning point in Russian drama in which many of the conventions of classical comedy were modified or overturned.*]

As has been remarked several times in the course of our survey of the Russian comedy of the early nineteenth century, a decisive landmark, dividing the old from the new, is Griboedov's famous piece **Gore ot uma.** The translation of this title has been a stumbling-block from the beginning. Literally rendered, it would be "sorrow (or misfortune) out of intelligence." Sir Bernard Pares in his verse translation dubbed it epigrammatically **Woe from Wit;** this has become the common translation and we shall use it here, although it is too stilted and literary to serve as a modern title for a really very modern piece. F. D. Reeve in his prose translation entitles it *The Trouble with Reason.* I would offer *Grief from Brains* as a tentative rendering. I realize that "brains" as a synonym of "intelligence" is colloquial and perhaps an Americanism; but "intelligence" is too long and too bookish, and "wit" in the meaning of "intelligence" is an archaism which would inevitably give a modern reader the false impression that Chatsky's "grief" was a result of his verbal quips rather than of a superior mind. Griboedov, I take comfort in remembering, was by no means averse, at least in his masterpiece, to employing colloquialisms. In any case, *Grief from Brains* has the merit of conveying succinctly the play's theme: the bitter truth that in a society of fools, intelligence brings its possessor to grief.

The composition of **Woe from Wit**[1] occupied many years of Griboedov's life. Indirect evidence indicates that the comedy was begun as early as 1816; and there are scholars who are convinced that the germs of it go back even to 1812. The earliest manuscript version dates to 1823, the latest to 1828. Only a heavily censored version of Act I, scenes 7-10, and of Act III was ever published in the author's lifetime (1825). The whole comedy, however, circulated freely in handwritten copies and was perfectly familiar to the Russian literate public long before the first complete publication in 1862.

Externally, **Woe from Wit** is a classical comedy with few and unimportant irregularities. It conforms meticulously to the three unities: the action all takes place in several rooms of Famusov's Moscow home; it begins about seven o'clock in the morning, and ends about midnight of the same day. The action centers on the familiar classical love-triangle: Chatsky loves Sofia, who loves Molchalin. Although besides the principal characters Chatsky, Sofia, her father, Molchalin and the maid Liza, there are over twenty minor figures, these are all parts of the single plot-line, whose presence is required to make concrete the "woe" of the title—society's verdict that Chatsky, its caustic critic, is out of his mind. There is one slight irrelevance, not sufficient to breach the unity of action—Chatsky's encounter with Repetilov in the last act. This is extraneous to the plot, but serves to add the pseudo-liberal to the other types of stupidity and hypocrisy which evoke Chatsky's contempt and hatred for all Moscow society. Two minor irregularities concern the form of the comedy: it is in four instead of the customary five acts; and although in verse, employs the free iambic, rather than the classical Alexandrine. It may be recalled that Shakhovskoi's *If You Don't Like It, Don't Listen* (1818) was the first Russian comedy to use the free iambic verse, otherwise the medium for the fable and the verse tale, e.g., *Dushenka*. Griboedov's earlier verse comedies (*The Young Married Couple, Pretended Infidelity,* and his parts of Shakhovskoi's *Her Own Family*) had all made use of the conventional Alexandrine. In this connection it must be remarked that the free iambic verse, with its lines of unpredictable length and its unpredictable rhyme scheme, has a far greater flexibility than even the most skillful Alexandrines. The best comic Alexandrines in Russian are

those of Kapnist's *Chicane* [*Iabeda*], but even they cannot be compared, for smoothness, grace, natural ease and frequently epigrammatic point, with Griboedov's verse. It is puzzling that this superlative medium should have had few sequels; most later Russian comedies, e.g., Gogol's *The Inspector General,* are written in prose, and when verse does recur, it is usually the unrhymed iambic pentameter.

Russian classical comedy, beginning with Sumarokov, had frequently embodied elements of satire—most notable in this regard are of course Fonvizin's *The Minor* and Kapnist's *Chicane*—but with the exception of Shakhovskoi's anti-Karamzinist plays (e.g., *A New Sterne, A Lesson for Coquettes, The Mismanagers,* etc.) early nineteenth-century comedy was for the most part comedy of intrigue or of character, with little or no sting. The drawing-room comedies of Shakhovskoi and Griboedov himself, before **Woe from Wit,** are bland and innocuous.

In his essay on **Woe from Wit** ("A Million Lacerations," 1870)[2] the novelist Goncharov claims that the comedy has two plots—the conventional love-triangle plot, and a socio-political one, in which Chatsky and his "radical" ideas are pitted against the reactionary and philistine world of Famusov, Skalozub, Molchalin, Khlestova and the rest. The denouement of this second plot would be the acceptance by all Moscow society of the calumny that "Chatsky is mad," just as the denouement of the first comes with Sofia's realization that Molchalin is a worthless philanderer and Chatsky's realization that his beloved Sofia is not for him. It is of course not to be questioned that the theme of the play is the conflict between "one intelligent man and twenty-five fools," as Griboedov himself put it, and as the title succinctly expresses it. It is better, however, to confine the concept of plot to an actual succession of incidents with concrete results. Chatsky's several outbursts, to Famusov, to Skalozub, to Sofia, etc., serve to illuminate the complete irreconcilability of their two worlds of thought, but result in no concrete change of situation. Even the gossip about Chatsky's madness is begun by Sofia, in a pique over his contempt for her beloved Molchalin, and thus belongs to the first plot line. The satirical element thus belongs to the comedy as a whole, and is the carrier of the new element of realism, as we shall see, essential to the new concept of character which is the play's most salient feature. The satirical element thus serves two purposes: it provides the concrete exemplification of the woe or grief which intelligence brings— the grief of not only social estrangement and isolation, but of the keenest kind of personal affliction, the recognition of the unworthiness of the object of one's deepest love; and it stands as the background which alone can explain the characters which people the comedy.

Viewed from the standpoint of external structure, **Woe from Wit** is a classical comedy; but at once internal features belie the appearance. One of the most solidly established of all classical canons of comedy is the convention of *bonnes moeurs*—the comedy must end with the triumph of the good and the discomfiture of evil, and this, in a comedy with the requisite love intrigue as its structural core, must mean that hero and heroine must be happily united in the last act. To be sure, Molière's *Le Misanthrope* is a classical example of exception to this rule, but it would be hard to find any other important breach of the canon. *Woe from Wit* is constructed upon precisely the opposite outcome: the good, i.e., intelligent, hero is ridiculed, discomfited and loses his sweetheart, while the evil, that is, the stupid, servile, mean and venomous Muscovite society is apparently triumphant. If only in this reversal of the conventions one might recognize the comedy as a pioneering monument of realism. To be sure, the hero's discomfiture does not go so far as to include the triumph of his contemptible rival—Molchalin at the end loses both his position and the sentimental affections of Sofia, but the damage has already been done in the mere possibility of Sofia's having found such a creature to be of interest.

The impression of realism is greatly strengthened by a consideration of the language. The language of classical comedy in Russian has never been fixed with the rigidity of French convention. From the delightful colloquialism of Sumarokov's old couple in *The Imaginary Cuckold* to the natural small talk of Shakhovskoi's *Her Own Family,* comic language has always embodied a good deal of the vernacular. Nevertheless, one has only to look at Griboedov's own earlier comedies, *The Young Married Couple* and *Pretended Infidelity,* to see the French convention in Russian guise—a completely colorless medium based upon upper-class usage, but divested of everything local and individual. There can be no greater contrast than between the Russian of *Pretended Infidelity* (1818) and of *Woe from Wit* (1823-24). Famusov and his guests, especially Khlestova, express themselves in the most vivid, idiomatic, and specifically Muscovite dialect. Even Chatsky and Sofia, who as members of the younger generation employ a less colorfully local idiom, speak naturally, unconstrainedly, and with innumerable locutions which classical comedy scrupulously avoided as vulgar, even though they were in common vernacular use among the upper classes. Moreover, each person in the comedy speaks a brand of Russian colored by his or her own position in society. Famusov speaks bureaucratese, Skalozub an abrupt, explosive military language (he also speaks in an affectedly thick and rumbling bass, as the stage directions specify, so that he is once contemptuously referred to as a "bassoon"); Molchalin, the cringing lower-grade official whom his father has taught to be obliging to everyone, even his superior's dog, uses a genteel, bookish style, liberally laced with that peculiarly Russian mark of subservience, the "s" sound appended to a word: Molchalin's first utterance on the stage, when Famusov discovers him in his drawing-room with Sofia at a suspiciously early hour of the morning, and accosts him abruptly with: "You here, Molchalin, brother?" is the fawning: "Ia-s" ["I, Sir"].

But to pick out the individualization of language as an external feature of Griboedov's style in *Woe from Wit* conveys a false impression. The colloquial language which Shakhovskoi gives to his four old women in *Her Own Family,* vivid and lifelike though it may be, seems to be the result of an intellectual calculation, as though the playwright said to himself: "See what, for instance, Fyokla, a hard-bitten and stingy old thing, would say under such and such conditions?" and then contrived her speeches to fit his conception. Griboedov's people are all of a piece; they are intuited as complete psychological entities, and their language, their gestures, their modes of thinking, are all inseparable parts of their personalities: it is unthinkable that Famusov, for example, could express himself other than as he does. It is the difference which we see between Ben Jonson's foxy miser Volpone and Shakespeare's Shylock—the one coldly and rationally contrived, the other instantly apprehended in his totality, complex, contradictory, and warmly alive.

Classical literary theory presupposes the universality of human character. Certain types exist, such as Theophrastus and La Bruyère have described, and such as comic writers from Menander on have utilized for the construction of comedies of character. Conformably with Peripatetic philosophy, these types are envisaged as analogous to the species of the natural world—immutable and independent of environment. A lion is a lion because such is the principle of form which nature has imposed on him; he has never been and never will be anything else. Similarly, a miser is a miser because such is his specifying difference, not because of a faulty education, the influence of a money-loving society, or any other influence operating from without. To this conception of the nature of character Griboedov's classical comedies, *The Young Married Couple* and *Pretended Infidelity* conform entirely. The boredom, for example, of the young husband in *The Young Married Couple* is seen not as the result of an idle and parasitic existence imposed by a particular kind of social structure, but as an immutable part of a human character type which cannot indeed be eradicated but palliated by the intervention of another immutable characteristic—jealousy.

But the characters who people *Woe from Wit* are not such universal types: they are, and are presented as, precisely the products of a perfectly specific and sharply defined social structure, to wit, the aristocratic and bureaucratic society of early-nineteenth-century Russian autocracy. Sofia's conduct, for example, is not that of "any woman, any time," but results specifically from the kind of up-bringing which her father's position in society imposes: a frivolous existence centered on clothes, fancy balls, and flirtations, devoid of intellectual interests beyond the reading of trashy French sentimental novels. And so with Molchalin: he is what he is not because nature has imprinted him with an indelible stamp of servility, but because, as he tells Liza, his father has imbued him from childhood with the principle of always ingratiating himself with everyone in order to get ahead in the world. But this radically innovative concept of character is what criticism defines as "realism," that is, character is determined not by an abstract principle of form, but by real, that is, external, circumstances of society, themselves differing from one age to another and from one place to another. And the realist writer will be chiefly concerned to depict such a social background in order to explain the qualities of the characters he chooses to portray.

What is least classical about **Woe from Wit** is precisely the psychological verisimilitude of the characterization. Again, reference to Griboedov's own early comedies is instructive. Roslavlev, for example (**Pretended Infidelity**) is the jealous lover; he is unrestrainedly passionate and irrationally suspicious and afraid of deception. Does he have any other characteristics whatever? If so, the playwright keeps them concealed. Liza is timid, submissive and genuinely in love with Roslavlev, but aroused to the point of angry protest by his groundless jealousy. This sums up all of her character, as far as Griboedov (or Barthe) lets us know. The classical comedy is founded upon such simplification of character: only the traits that are immediately to be utilized in the elaboration of the plot are ever displayed. Classicism regards complex or contradictory character, such as every living human being inevitably is, as useless and confusing. It would be quite reasonable to add to the canonical three unities a fourth: unity of character. Just as the classical legislators insist on unity of place on the grounds that the spectator will be confused and thrown off if the scene shifts "from Paris to Peking," so although unformulated as a law, classical character must show only one side, lest the spectator be baffled and unable to form a firm appraisal of it. Harpagon, for example, is "the miser" par excellence, just as Roslavlev is "the jealous lover." But Chatsky—what is he? The intelligent man in a society of fools—but far, far more. He is an ardent lover, who idealizes his sweetheart; he is an ardent patriot, who despises the Russian adulation of all things foreign; he is a warm friend (note his affection for the henpecked Platon Mikhailovich); he has romantic, almost sentimental recollections of his childhood; he values his independence and hates servility: "To serve I would be glad, but to be subservient is nauseating." He is conceited enough to believe it impossible that Sofia should prefer the cringing toady Molchalin to him, and he is naive enough to imagine, apparently, that his outbursts to Famusov, Skalozub, et

al. may carry conviction. It is on this score that Pushkin takes him to task, in a letter early in 1825 to A. A. Bestuzhev:[3] "Everything he says is very clever. But to whom does he say all this? To Famusov? Skalozub? To the old ladies of Moscow at the ball? To Molchalin? This is inexcusable." Chatsky, moreover, has another very human trait that adds to his complexity and furthers the plot: clever as he is, he cannot resist the temptation to let fly some of his barbed quips, even when he must know that they will further arm his beloved Sofia against him, to say nothing of her father. It is after one such gratuitous witticism at the expense of her Molchalin that Sofia loses patience and asks Chatsky the ironical question (Act I, scene 7): "Has it ever happened that you, in jest or in sorrow, quite by mistake, have ever said something good about someone? Even if not now, perhaps in childhood?" Chatsky's reply to this reveals his complete incomprehension of the degree to which his smart banter can be irritating. It is the piling up of this irritation that leads Sofia in the third act to retaliate by spreading the rumor that Chatsky is mad.

Sofia is just as complex a character. Her father, in the final scene of the play, reproaches her with repeating her mother's scandalous conduct: "it used to be, I would no sooner be parted from my dearest better half than she would be off somewhere with a man!" Griboedov's friend Begichev testifies that early variations of the play included Mme Famusova as a character: "a sentimental lady of fashion, and Moscow aristocrat." Sofia certainly inherits some of her deceased mother's sentimentality. She and Molchalin spend the night together before the play opens, she playing the piano and he the flute; according to her recital to her confidante Liza, Molchalin gazes into her eyes, sighs, and holds her hand—but nothing more! She idealizes his character, and spiritedly defends him to the mocking Chatsky: earnestly and naively she describes his meekness:

> I made no effort: God brought us together. Just see, he has won the friendship of everyone in the house. He has been serving with father for three years; father is often angry without reason, but Molchalin disarms him with his wordlessness. Out of the goodness of his soul he forgives. Besides, he might look for entertainment: but not at all. He doesn't stir away from old people's thresholds. We joke and laugh, but he will sit with them all day long, whether he enjoys it or not, and plays . . . Of course, he hasn't that intellect that is genius for some people, but a plague for others—a wit that is quick, brilliant, ready to oppose, that abuses the world roundly so that the world may at least have something to say about it . . . finally, his is the most marvelous of qualities—he is compliant, modest, quiet; his face has no trace of restlessness, nor his soul any wrong. He doesn't abuse others up and down—that's what I love about him.[4]

It is typical of Chatsky's character that this most self-revealing of Sofia's speeches elicits only the aside: "She's joking, she doesn't love him." The very picture which she draws of Molchalin's admirable meekness and complaisance portrays to Chatsky a mean, servile nature which he finds it wholly unbelievable that she could love.

But there are other sides to Sofia's character than this sentimental, almost motherly one. Several times she remarks to her confidante almost defiantly that she would like to avow her love for Molchalin to all and sundry. When, after her tell-tale faint at seeing Molchalin thrown by his horse, Liza advises her to go to her father and Skalozub as if nothing had happened, in order to dispel suspicion, Sofia says (Act II, scene 10): "But what do I care for any of them? I'll love if I want to and tell if I want to. Molchalin! Didn't I restrain myself? You came in, I didn't say a word. With them around, I didn't dare so much as sigh, or ask you a question, or look at you!" It is evident from Molchalin's words to Liza in the last act that all the advances in this strange love affair were made by Sofia—he submitted passively without "daring to lift his eyes to her."

And finally, Sofia's spirit and self-possession are revealed in the painful last scene of the play; as she finds herself unsuspectingly the witness of her lover's advances to her own maid, she suddenly intervenes:

SOFIA

(almost in a whisper; the whole scene is in a low voice): Go no further, I've heard a great deal. Dreadful man! I'm ashamed of myself, ashamed of the very walls.

MOCHALIN:

What! Sofia Pavlovna—

SOFIA:

Not a word, for God's sake. Be silent: I'm capable of anything!

MOLCHALIN

(throws himself on his knees. Sofia repulses him): Oh! remember! Don't be angry. Look at me . . .

SOFIA:

I remember nothing, don't importune me. Remembrances: They're like a sharp knife.

MOLCHALIN

(crawls to her feet): Have mercy . . .

SOFIA:

Don't be base; stand up. I want no answer. I know your answer,—you'll lie . . .

MOLCHALIN:

Do me the kindness . . .

SOFIA:

No! No! No!

MOLCHALIN:

I was joking! I didn't say anything, except . . .

SOFIA:

Stop it, I say, or I'll shout and rouse everyone in the house, and ruin myself and you. *(Molchalin stands up).* From this time forth it is as if I had never known you. Do not dare to expect reproaches, complaints, or tears from me: you aren't worth them. But see to it that the dawn does not find you in this house: see to it that I never hear of you again.

MOLCHALIN:

As you command.[5]

The angry woman of this scene is far from the scatter-brained girl of the play's opening, surprised by the dawn with her lover, and quick with a cock-and-bull story to her father of a frightening dream—but she is the same person, and the truth of her characterization is perfectly manifest. Goncharov can rightly compare her to Pushkin's Tatyana—but between her and such earlier comedy heroines as Griboedov's own Elmira, Yeledina or Liza there is no comparison: they are mechanical dolls, Sofia is a woman of flesh and blood.

Chatsky and Sofia are complex characters with facets that mark them psychologically alive, but which have no immediate relevance to the plot of the comedy. But where, one may ask, did Griboedov learn this entirely new technique of character portrayal? Pushkin at just about the same time was using it in the novel: the "first chapter" of *Eugene Onegin* was published in 1826, but begun in 1823. In western literature Balzac's first novel of the *Comédie humaine* cycle was published in 1829, Stendhal's *Le Rouge et le noir* in 1831. The real pioneer was probably Sir Walter Scott, whose *Waverley,* opening his series of historical novels, was issued in 1814. Historicism (the doctrine that historical differences of time and place do determine character, despite classical denial) and realism were in the air, and it would be time wasted to attempt to specify any single source from which Griboedov might have derived them. He was an extremely well read and intelligent person, and the discovery may not have involved anything but his own observation and intuition. In this connection, his work offers an interesting parallel with that of another great pioneer of an earlier date—Cervantes. In the Spanish master's early novel *Galatea,* in his tragedy *Numancia,* in his *Novelas ejemplares,* and in his last novel *Persiles y Sigismundo,* there is hardly a suggestion of the startling psychological profundity of *Don Quixote*; the "ingenious hidalgo" and Sancho Panza are made of absolutely different stuff from the conventional people of the other works. To be sure, the rascals Rinconete and Cortadillo, in the *novela* of that name, are strikingly naturalistic portraits, as is "El Licenciado Vidriera" in his *novela*—but they are isolated and seen from outside, while the Don and his squire are, as it were, intuited. They come from within the man, and critics almost universally regard the famous pair as a kind of dual projection of different sides of Cervantes's own personality. Much the same seems to be the case with Griboedov. Chatsky is the poet himself, not of course an autobiographical portrait in detail, but endowed with Griboedov's own intelligence, passionate feelings, sensibility, and all the other conflicting and contradictory characteristics that mark him. But I think it is equally true that the despised and hated Muscovite officialdom that Famusov represents is also a part of Griboedov himself—a part which he passionately rejects and exorcises by objectifying it as Chatsky's antagonist, just as Cervantes objectifies the prosaic world of common sense in Sancho Panza. There is an "anti-Chatsky" as well as a Chatsky in Griboedov. But such characters as Ariste and Safir, Lensky and Roslavlev, Benevolsky and Zvezdov are intellectual constructs, seen from outside, without background, moved by a puppeteer's strings, with no life of their own.

The theme of *Woe from Wit* is, as Goncharov rightly observed, two-fold: Chatsky against society, and Chatsky's "woe" (the annihilation of his love affair with Sofia) resulting from his intellectual superiority to Sofia's entire milieu. A large part of the comedy, and indeed the most memorable part, is devoted to a merciless exposure of this reactionary bureaucratic and aristocratic milieu in a life-and-death struggle with Chatsky and his modern ideas of personal freedom and intellectual and moral honesty. In presenting this milieu on the stage, Griboedov boldly transgresses the classical principle that a cast of characters should be small, and lists, exclusive of servants, twenty-three persons. Of these, seventeen belong exclusively to Acts III and IV, and their function is precisely that of representing in miniature the high society of Moscow: they are the "grande dame" of Catherine's day, Khlestova—imperious, rude, intelligent but uncultured, her latter-day interests confined to a pet dog and a tigerish little negro slave-girl: Platon Mikhailovich, a once sturdy and dashing hussar, now the docile husband of his sweetly tyrannical wife, the one-time coquette Natalya Dmitrievna; the ancient relic Prince Tugoukhovsky (his name comes from the phrase *tugoi na ukho,* "hard of hearing"), who shuffles about with an ear-trumpet and throughout the play mutters nothing more intelligible than "oh-hm" and "ah-hm"; his wife, whose sole preoccupation is finding husbands for her six undifferentiated daughters, whose sole preoccupations in turn, as revealed in their remarks, are fine clothes and gossip; the Countesses Khryumina, grandmother and granddaughter, who share a surly and cattish disposition, with minor variations—the old lady is deaf and impatient, her granddaughter is peevish and

spouts French; and Anton Antonovich Zagoretsky, a complicated and particularly unpleasant character. He is recognized by everyone as a dangerous swindler and cardsharper, a contemptible repeater and inventor of gossip—and yet he is accepted by everyone because of his indefatigable services, by which he ingratiates himself with all and sundry. At his first appearance he rushes to Sofia with an unsolicited present—a ticket to "tomorrow's spectacle," practically wrested by force, as he admits, from a decrepit old friend of his, "who doesn't go out much anyway." Zagoretsky's pride in knowing all the scandal is touched to the quick when one of the guests, specified only as "G. D.," queries about the rumor of Chatsky's madness, and Zagoretsky, to whom the rumor is completely new, at once claims previous knowledge and adds a number of embellishments of his own. Finally, and somewhat apart from the rest, is Repetilov, who stumbles into the Famusov vestibule just as the guests are leaving, and corners Chatsky with some of the most remarkable drivel in the whole comedy. He is a drunk, a notorious spendthrift, despised and avoided by everyone, who at last has found himself a place in society of which he is inordinately and naively proud—he is a member of an unofficial "secret society" connected with Moscow's conservative English Club, whose members drink hard, converse furiously and quarrel noisily, display their wits and dazzle poor Repetilov, who hardly dares raise his voice in such a brilliant environment. They discuss chambers (legislative) and jurors and other arcane political subjects, too deep for their admiring hanger-on. It is, of course, a cruel and unflattering caricature of such a discussion group as the Arzamas to which Pushkin and most of the young literary set of innovators—Zhukovsky, Batyushkov, Vyazemsky, Daskov, et. al.—belonged and which Griboedov disliked and distrusted.

Together with Famusov and Molchalin, to represent two aspects, two ends, as it were, of the bureaucratic ladder, and Skalozub to represent the unpleasant Arakcheev type of behind-the-lines militarism (Skalozub's service, pointedly, has been in reserve regiments, his decorations honor not campaigns but ceremonial state occasions, and his conversation revolves around epaulets and "pipings on full-dress tunics"), the guests at the ball offer a microcosm of the society of lies, hypocrisy, servility and tyranny that Chatsky despises and that his creator is concerned with exposing as responsible for the misfortune of his hero. But it must be emphasized that in drawing his vivid picture of upper-class Russian society, Griboedov is in no way whatever being a revolutionary. Most Marxist discussions of *Woe from Wit* begin with a lengthy and tiresome exposition of Griboedov's relations with the abortive revolutionary movement which the government crushed on December 14, 1825. Most of the leading intellectuals and literary figures of the age, including Griboedov and Pushkin, were in fact in some fashion connected with the Decembrists, as the participants in this movement are familiarly known. Griboedov had belonged to an earlier society—the Union of Salvation—which was disbanded before the disastrous coup of December 14, but there is no evidence that he at any time meditated an overthrow of the autocracy and the institution of a republican constitution, such as the active conspirators envisaged—and least of all can **Woe from Wit** be considered in any sense a revolutionary document, even if the "Decembrists" did revere it and regard it as an inspiration. The "Woe" of the title is a private and personal one; Chatsky's impassioned monologues are exposes of hypocrisy, tyranny and stupidity, but wholly devoid of political overtones; and when at the play's end its defeated hero makes his last speech, he ends it, not with any noble vow to devote the rest of his life to combatting the manifest evil, but with the resolve to seek purely personal repose far from the hated Russian reality:

> Where has destiny thrown me! They all pursue, they all curse me! A gang of tormentors, of traitors in love, tireless in hatred, inexorable tale-bearers, impotent brains, cunning simpletons, evil-tongued old women, old men grown decrepit over their inventions and their twaddle. You all, in chorus, hailed me as witless. You're right: that man will come unscathed out of the fire, who manages to spend a day with you, breathes the same atmosphere, and in it keeps his wits intact. Away from Moscow! To this place I shall never journey again. I shall flee without a backward look, go seek the world over for a nook for outraged feelings! My carriage! My carriage![6]

If evil triumphs and good is discomfited, as it is in **Woe from Wit,** even more emphatically than in Molière's *Le Misanthrope,* is Griboedov justified in calling his play a comedy? Merzlyakov, as was noted above, denied that Kapnist's *Chicane* was a proper comedy, because of its predominantly satirical content,—and yet formally, at least, Kapnist shows his positive hero and heroine triumphant over the swindlers and pettifoggers. No doubt Griboedov's positive hero loses the girl he loves and has to retreat to some nook in the world (where will he find it?) where he can nurse his wounded heart. But as Goncharov, in 1870, astutely observed, "Chatsky is crushed by the quantity of the old power, while in his turn dealing it a mortal blow by the quality of the new power." Elsewhere he refers to Chatsky as "victor," but remarks that "the warrior in the front ranks, the sharpshooter," is always a victim. Chatsky *is* the victor in the duel with Moscow society, even if also its victim; Famusov and his crowd can brand him as a madman, but their society is doomed, and they know it. The usual comedy happy ending is postponed to an indefinite future, but it is sure, none the less; the feeling that the play leaves, in spite of Chatsky's "million lacerations," is after all optimistic, The piece *is* a comedy.

Notes

1. A. S. Griboedov, *Sochineniia v dvukh tomakh* (M. Pravda, Biblioteka "Ogonek," 1971), I, 57-163; A. S. Griboedov, *Sochineniia v stikhakh* (L. Sovetskii pisatel', Biblioteka poeta, bol'shaia seriia, 1967), pp. 63-172. V. P. Meshcheriakov, *A. S. Griboedov. Literaturnoe okruzhenie i vospriiatie* (L. Nauka, 1983), has a good deal to say about *Gore ot uma* throughout the volume; but see particularly chapters 6 (V. F. Odoevsky), 7 (A. I. Odoevsky), 8 (A. A. Bestuzhev), 9 (F. V. Bulgarin) and 11 (Komediia "Gore ot uma" i ee avtor v literaturnom soznanii XIX-nachala XX veka). See also L. A. Stepanov, "Dramaturgiia A. S. Griboedova" in *Istoriia russkoi dramaturgii XVII-pervaia polivina XIX veka* (L. Nauka, 1982), pp. 296-326. Vladimir Nabokov (*Alexander Pushkin: Eugene Onegin, A Novel in Verse,* translated from the Russian with a Commentary by Vladimir Nabokov, 4 volumes [New York: Bollingen Series LXXII, Pantheon Books, 1964], III, 17-18) notes that Pushkin quotes a line from Griboedov's play (*Eugene Onegin,* VI, stanza 11, 1. 12), and proceeds to a brief discussion and circumstances of its partial publication. "The fate of Russian letters seems to have timed things in such a way," Nabokov remarks, "as to have the two greatest verse masterpieces in Russian appear in print simultaneously." (The first complete publication of *Eugene Onegin* was issued in March 1833.)

2. I. A. Goncharov, *Sobranie sochinenii v shesti tomakh* (M. Gosudarstvennoe izdatel'stvo khudozhestvennoi literatury, 1960), VI, 355-382.

3. A. S. Pushkin, *Sobranie sochinenii v desiati tomakh* (M.-L. Gosudarstvennoe izdatel'stvo khudozhestvennoi literatury, 1962), IX, 134.

4. A. S. Griboedov, *Sochineniia v dvukh tomakh,* I, 108-109.

5. A. S. Griboedov, *Sochineniia v dvukh tomakh,* I, 158-159.

6. A. S. Griboedov, *Sochineniia v dvukh tomakh,* I, 163.

Alexander Gershkovich (essay date 1994)

SOURCE: Gershkovich, Alexander. "Russian Romantic Drama: The Case of Griboedov."[1] In *Romantic Drama,* edited by Gerald Gillespie, pp. 273-85. Amsterdam: John Benjamins, 1994.

[*In the following essay, Gershkovich discusses Griboedov's position within the Russian Romantic tradition and claims that in the character of Chatsky, Griboedov created the first true individual in Russian literature.*]

I

The fate of Romantic drama in Russia took shape in an unusual manner. Its highest achievements, **Gore ot Uma** (**Woe from Wit**) and *Boris Godunov,* inspired by the new Romantic poetics, were not classified as Romantic plays in Russian criticism even though Griboedov spoke of his comedy as a "stage poem," and Pushkin of his *Boris* as a "true Romantic tragedy."[2] On the other hand, standard literary history, without any particular regret, assigned artistically weaker plays such as the pathetic tragedies of Ryleyev and Küchelbecker and the pseudo-patriotic melodramas of N. Kukolnik and N. Polevoy, to the Romantic School. Such a view has suited the purpose of "official" twentieth-century criticism to prove the immutable realistic nature of Russian art, its originality and separateness from the Western literary process.[3] The impression was created that the ideas of Romanticism, having come from the West, were pathogenic for Russia, did not deeply affect Russian drama, and did not strike root in Russian soil in a pure form. As anomalies of "secondary" poets, these ideas supposedly did not apply to the "shaft-horses" of Russian literature, from Griboedov to Gogol, pulling the main cart of national drama.

But the development of Russian drama from Griboedov to Chekhov, and even further to M. Bulgakov, cannot be adequately understood without taking account of the beneficial influence of Romanticism. First, it is important to establish what the Russians understood about Romanticism. The closest understanding was formulated by the leader of Russian critical thought, V. Belinsky (1811-48), who from a philosophical viewpoint looked at Romanticism as one natural characteristic not only of art but of the human spirit, as "the concealed life of the heart,"—"where the human being is, there also is Romanticism."[4] From a historical/literary vantage, he found Romanticism among ancient Greeks (Euripides), in the East, and the Middle Ages. In the nineteenth century, however, it had been born completely transformed as "an organic unity of all the moments of the Romanticism which had been developed in the history of humanity."[5] On this basis, Belinsky considered that "Romanticism is not the property or belonging of any one country or epoch: it is an eternal side of nature and of the human spirit—it didn't die after the Middle Ages, but rather only underwent a transformation."[6]

Analyzing the newest Romanticism from an aesthetic point of view, Belinsky calls it, "a war with a deathly imitation of the assertive form" of Classicism and "a striving for freedom and originality of form."[7] In another place (in an article about Griboedov) he sums up his idea even more succinctly: "*Classical* art has a complete and harmonious *balance between idea and form,* and Romantic (art) placed idea over form."[8] Finally, Belinsky adheres to the opinion that Russian experience, in contrast to that of the West which vainly tried to revive the Romanticism of the Middle Ages artificially, represents an organic process of development. Russia "did not have her own Middle Ages," and therefore, her literature could not possess an original Romanticism. However, since "without Romanticism poetry is the same as a body without a soul," when Russia joined the life of Europe, and felt the influence of the intellectual movements which were arising, Russian literature was not able *not* to give birth to Romanticism. This occurred, however, without those complexes of anachronisms which the West had experienced. Of all the Western Romanticists, Belinsky especially singled out Byron, who, like Prometheus, inflicted the mortal blow on this useless attempt to revive the old and became the herald of the new Romanticism, Romanticism which was also close to Russian aspirations.[9]

Belinsky was essentially correct in seeing that Russian Romanticism, especially in the area of drama, although born out of the battle with Classicism, did inherit much from the preceding literary schools, selecting building-materials from them. In this sense it is possible to understand Belinsky's ironic observation about "the Romantic classics" of Russian literature (he referred here to second-rate artists such as N. Kukolnik and N. Polevoy) which, in essence, are representative of the "eclectic reconciliation of Classicism with Romanticism, in which a little something is held over from Classicism and something is taken from Romanticism."[10] This is an old song with new words, that is, Classical absurdities in new Romantic clothing take place when the poet, calling himself a Romantic and an opponent of Classicism, as if it were a criminal offense, is actually continuing to look on the subject from without and not from within. Therefore, says Belinsky, it only seems to the poet that he is nimbly running forward, while he is actually turning in the same place, going around himself in circles. In contrast, because Belinsky considered Griboedov and Pushkin authentic representatives of the new Romantic direction in Russian drama and poetry, he explored the nature of Romanticism in large theoretical essays devoted to their work.

In the 1820s Russian drama took a striking leap. At the beginning of the century it was still in imitative apprenticeship to Western classicist modes, with rudiments of the Enlightenment and Sentimentalism. In the genre of tragedy, the pompous V. A. Ozerov (1769-1816) was still in complete favor, with subjects taken from Greek, Roman, medieval Western, and Russian history (*Oedipus in Athens,* 1804, *Fingal,* 1805, and *Dimitry Donskoy,* 1807). In enlightened comedy, the mocking fabulist I. Krylov (1768-1844) wrote the edifying *Fashionable Store* (1806) and *Lessons for the Daughters* (1807). In vaudeville, the light-minded M. N. Zagoskin (1789-1852) enjoyed success by showing *The Provincial in the Capital* (1817) and in reverse, the metropolitan resident in a village in *Bagatonov, or the Surprise to Himself* (1821). Comedies of manners, usually remakes of French plays, were written by the "anti-sentimentalists," N. A. Zhander, N. I. Khmelnitsky, and A. A. Shakhovskoy. These were all close friends of Griboedov who, at the beginning, was often a co-author of these playwrights.

Russian drama was just barely unfurling its sticky light-green leaves. Suddenly, in the atmosphere of the Pre-Decembrist storm it was as if an electric spark discharged: *Gore ot Uma* (1823-24) and *Boris Godunov* (1825)—unsurpassed examples of Russian comedy and tragedy up until that time—appeared on the scene one right after the other. Unexpected and innovative in design, deeply national in their character, humanist in content, they immediately raised Russian drama to an unprecedented artistic and public level, placing it in European ranks alongside the best of world Romantic drama. Attentive Western observers immediately took note, and thus the first complete edition of *Gore ot Uma* appeared not in Russian but in a German translation by Karl von Knorring in Revel in 1831, while the first deeply objective, scholarly analysis of *Boris Godunov* was done by the German scholar Varnhagen von Ense. "We will be still more surprised at the dramatic strength of the genius Pushkin, if we take into consideration the slender means by which the poet reached his goals," he wrote in 1843 from Leipzig.[11] He valued *Gore ot Uma* highly as did the first English translator and populizer, Nicholas Benardaky who in 1857 wrote that Griboedov's talent was "more closely akin to Juvenal than to Molière," and that the character Chatsky, with his biting irony, is a result of heart and sensitivity and not cold calculation.[12] More recently, although still stipulating some measure of Classicism, I. Sőtér has re-affirmed the connection of *Gore ot Uma,* along with early Pushkin, to the flowering of Romanticism in Russia; and the same view has been put forth by J. Bonamour in his fundamental work on Griboedov.[13]

It was more difficult for Russian Romantic drama to gain recognition in its homeland. It was forbidden and distorted by the censors. None of the authors of the above-mentioned plays ever did see their works on stage, and Griboedov and Lermontov did not even live to see their work published. The critics brought humiliating fire down upon them, having become acquainted with them through notes passing from hand to hand. Nevertheless, they became known to the public and exerted a deep and growing influence on all of Russian culture, still important in our time. In the Soviet era, the officially sanctioned approach to art narrowed the understanding of Romanticism to such an extent that not only the early Pushkin, all of Griboedov, and the early Gogol did not fit in, but even Lermontov's *Masquerade*—a work Romantic to the core. In the two-volume

History of Romanticism in Russian Literature (1979), *Gore ot Uma* is not even referred to, as if Griboedov never existed.[14] On the other hand, it examines in detail young Belinsky's scholarly composition *Dmitry Kalinin* which is of marginal significance.

The swift development of Russian drama at the beginning of the nineteenth century began in an atmosphere of spiritual ascent in Russian culture after the victory over Napoleon in 1812. It was accompanied by the crossing and interlacings of the most heterogenous artistic currents. Russian drama, thanks to its backwardness in relation to the West's development, in a short ten years transversed a path on which Western European theater spent a century. Thus the accelerated development of a national culture let to the birth of works of mixed stylistic form. "Classicist by form, drama inscribes a sentimental spirit; sentimental poetry assimilates Romantic motifs; the Enlightenment grows into revolutionary Romanticism; sentimentalism yields realistic fruit. It is not difficult for a historian of literature and drama to become entangled in this mixture of artistic ideas and tendencies. It [the mixture] came into existence because [. . .] the Russian artistic idea, trying on the one hand to remain in national traditions, at the same time hurried to master all the newness which had arisen in the West [. . .],"[15] the Soviet theoretician, Anikst, has justifiably written.

This process was also rather typical for other Eastern European countries which were experiencing their own national renaissance. The interdependency of various artistic styles was inherent in Polish, Hungarian, and Czech drama of the age of Romanticism.[16] Far from being eclectic, this mixture of styles in all its specificity contained an inner logic; it paralleled the search for a national drama, answering to the spirit and needs of its people.

II

Gore ot Uma clearly reflected this search. Its author, Alexander Sergeevich Griboedov (1795-1829), was one of the mysterious figures of Russian and world literature. He stepped into history as a literary man focused single-mindedly on one idea, a creator of one masterpiece. Griboedov's life and work exhibit the fate of a fiery dreamer in "a country of eternal snows," who having established his remarkable abilities by serving falsely chosen goals, recognizes this too late.[17] An individualist by nature, Griboedov's lofty poetic spirit was interwoven with contradictions. Hating slavery more than anything, especially slavery of the spirit ("According to my times and taste / I hate the word slave"), Griboedov, perhaps more than other poets of his time, was a slave of the society in which he lived. He "made a career," despite his inner convictions and dream to "be independent of people," and despised himself for this, having a foreboding that it would end badly. Thus into Russian literature was born the type of the implacable Chatsky—the first Romantic hero of Russian drama—no doubt based on the author himself.

Griboedov was a descendant of an old, noble family, rich, and one of the most educated people in Russia and Europe at the beginning of the new age, having studied with Göttingen Professors I. T. Booulet, B. Ion, and Schletzer Junior. He spoke many European languages fluently, reading and translating Shakespeare, Goethe, and Schiller. He knew Latin and Greek, Persian, Arabic, and Turkish. Graduating with ease simultaneously in philology, law, physics and mathematics from Moscow University, he was awarded the title of Doctor of Law. He was an excellent pianist and a composer of sentimental romances. He participated in the War of 1812 against Napoleon. He was a member of the Freemason Lodges in Moscow and Saint Petersburg; mixed in higher circles, had friendships with Decembrists; was involved in the uprising of 1825, but was pardoned by the Tsar; was acquainted with the disgraced Pushkin and close to the gendarme informer Fadey Bulgarin, to whom fell the trouble of publishing *Gore ot Uma.* And finally, Griboedov became an official of "the diplomatic unit" of the Russian colonial army in Transcaucasia and progressed as a specialist in the assimilation of subjected territories of the Eastern peoples. He became a bearer of the Order of Lev and of the Sun, second degree, and of Saint Ann with diamonds. Subsequently, by royal decree, he was named state advisor and Ambassador Plenipotentiary of the Russian Empire in Persia, where he was killed by Shi'ite fanatics in Teheran during the destruction of the Russian embassy on January 30, 1829, at thirty-four years of age.

The discord between dream and reality, subjective desires and objective circumstances, in the final analysis, between word and deed, became the main theme of Griboedov's creative work. His lyrical "I" continually strives to overcome this contradiction in the only sphere where it is still possible to be relatively independent of outer circumstances—in the sphere of art. His work wonderfully illustrates the idea of Madame de Staël, whose works were well known in Russian: "In our days, a poet must forfeit both his hopes and faith to intelligence; only then can his philosophical mind make a large impression [. . .] In the age in which we live, melancholia represents the authentic source of talent."[18] Griboedov's poetic credo was expressed in the free translation of the "Prologue in the Theater" from the first part of Goethe's *Faust.* He took up this translation immediately upon the completion of *Gore ot Uma* in 1824, or even possibly while still working on the play. In any case, Griboedov's exposition of Goethe appeared as an aesthetic prologue in the almanac *Arctic Star* in 1825, long before the publication of his comedy.

The relationship of Griboedov to Goethe is known to us through his conversation with the Decembrist A. Bestuzhev.[19] Goethe's dramatic poem drew Griboedov's attention to the idea of the inevitability of compromise, not only in life but in art as well, and to the age-old conflict between high poetic intention and the earthbound needs of "the masses," in the form of didactic discussion between the sober-minded Theater Director and the immeasurably ardent Poet. Griboedov, however, changes the outcome completely in Chatsky's accusatory speeches:

> No, no, his Poet rejects the Director's reason,
> Go away, go look for others to serve you.

Characteristically, Griboedov also enriches Goethe's theatrical crowd with new personages, with an openly Russian character:

> Here villains gaze around in the darkness
> To lie in wait for a word and ruin with a denunciation.
>
> **(G.** 356-60)

Pushkin was more honest and consistent on this score. Literally during the same days that Griboedov was working on the "Prologue," Pushkin turned to the same Goethean theme of the "poet" and "the multitudes"—evidence of how acute this problem was in Russian literature—and wrote his famous "Conversation between the Bookseller and the Poet" along with the first chapter of *Eugene Onegin,* in which the distinctive preface not unlike Goethe's appeared (1825). He solves the worrisome problem of the relationship of art and life through open compromise between the Bookseller and the Poet, in the words of the Bookseller:

> Позвольте просто вам сказать:
> Не продается вдохновенье,
> Но можно рукопись продать.[20]
>
> (Let me simply say to you:
> Inspiration is not sold
> But to sell a manuscript
> possible.)

In response to this mercenary declaration, Pushkin's Poet, in contrast to Griboedov's Poet, does not explode with righteous indignation, but rather answers completely reasonably and accommodatingly, in low prose—as if emphasizing the reality of what is going on: "Вы совершенно правы. Вот вам моя рукопись. Условимся." (You are absolutely correct. Here you are—my manuscript. Let's settle it.) This dual relationship of creative work is the key theme of Russian Romantic drama. The difference in the positions of Griboedov and Pushkin, on the surface, nonetheless turns out to be purely outward, declarative. Actually through all of his writing, Griboedov confirmed Pushkin's concept of Russian art—the inevitability of compromise between the high calling of the artist, as the Romantics understood him, and lowly Russian everyday reality.

III

The project *Gore ot Uma* was conceived by Griboedov at the turning point of his life, after the scandalous duel of 1818 when he abandoned Moscow with a train of high-society aspersions behind him. His hasty exit from Moscow with the Russian diplomatic mission to Persia was more like an escape from a society which he thoroughly knew, loved, and hated. He left for the East against his will, with an evil foreboding. Henceforth, his life would be made up of continual "leavings," and "crossings."[21] Yet the reason for his break from Moscow society was rooted more deeply. The results of the Patriotic War of 1812, in which Griboedov took part firsthand, were disappointing in the end. The unusual rise of patriotism, especially among the noble army officers, who had become accustomed to Western freedom, changed to general apathy. "The expectations, that the fall of slavery follows in answer to the exploits of the people, were not realized."[22] In 1812, heroes were replaced by people indifferent to everything, except their own careers. A "female regime" was established; "wives" acquired power, and this reverberated throughout the whole societal organism. Former gallant commanders became ladies' pages at balls. In this deathly pause during the last years of the "liberal" Alexander I's reign, the sole rational word heard in the worldly drawing room was: "Ах! боже мой! что станет говорить / Княгиня Марья Алексевна!" (Oh my God! What is the Princess going to say!)[23] This ironic remark by Famusov concluded Griboedov's comedy. Not only did it contain the comedy's main idea, the mainspring of the plot; it is reasonable to suggest that *Gore ot Uma* as the author first conceived it, grew out of this kernel. Two incomplete drafts of letters by Griboedov to unknown people have survived written in November 1820 from Tavriz. In one of them, marked 1:00 a.m., Griboedov writes about a dream he had which resembles, just like two peas in a pod, the atmosphere of Famusov's Moscow in Acts III and IV of *Gore ot Uma.* The hero of this dream was Griboedov himself, who finds himself at a ball and is made to vow that he will write "something or other." Even the remark with which Griboedov's acquaintances meet him is given in detailed description. Unmistakably the actors of his future comedy, meeting Chatsky upon entering the hall, repeat this remark nearly word for word.[24]

We can understand Griboedov's method as a dramatist modifying his Romanticism to accord with the Realism of the day if we distinguish the original version of *Gore ot Uma,* which apparently pleased the Romantic Küchelbecker so much, from the final edition. The author himself unequivocally pointed out this difference in his notes as he was preparing it for publication in 1824-25:

> The first inscription of this *stage poem,* as it was born inside of me, was much greater and of *higher* meaning than now, in the vain apparel in which *I was compelled*

to clothe it. The childish pleasure of listening to my poems in the theater [. . .] forced me to *spoil* my creation, as much as possible [. . .]. And besides, there are so many customs and conditions, not in the least connected with the aesthetic side of creation, with which *it is necessary to conform* [. . .]. There is a genre of theory (on which many pride themselves) that art is to please her [the public], that is, to create stupidity.

> (*G.* 400)

From this acknowledgement it obviously follows that in its original conception, the comedy was a "purely" Romantic drama. The compromise with ruling tastes or deliberate "ruining" of the play lasted a few years, right up to the summer of 1824 when Griboedov wrote to his closest friend, S. I. Begichev:

> I am cutting it down, changing the whole business to rubbish, so that in many places my dramatic pictures' bright colors have completely faded. I get angry and put back that which I have just crossed out so that it seems, that for my work there is no end [. . .].

> (*G.* 498)

Begichev was asked not to share the first version with anyone but to burn it if he thought it was necessary; for "it is as imperfect as it is impure," wrote Griboedov. The author aimed at achieving a plot of maximum transparency and simplicity (at the last minute he put in the domestic scene, "Sofia with a Candle") and unifying the poem. In June 1824 he already was writing to Begichev, "I have changed more than 80 lines; now it is as smooth as glass."

But Griboedov had little success in "ruining" his comedy, no matter how hard he tried. His aspiration "to conform" to the customs and conventions of the public of those times, "not connected with the aesthetic side of creation," even became strangely useful to the play. Having been freed from the grip of Classicist rules, Griboedov was inspired as he worked, and the further he got the more he was satisfied with what he was doing: "an alive, quick thing, recalling the final version of the comedy, the verses poured out in sparks." In the same letter to Begichev, he reports on the success of the readings of the comedy in Petersburg ("Eight readings, no I miscounted—twelve [. . .] I pound, make noise, there is no end to delight, curiosity") and admits that "in many places he improvises and experiences passion for a new invention, a new theory, a change of place and occupation, people and unusual pursuits." (*G.* 498-99)

The main reproach against Griboedov which was presented by his friend Katenin, was precisely his abandonment of rules, in favor of the game of imagination: "Talent rather than art." Griboedov answered his friend's criticism, completely in the spirit of Romanticism, "The most complimentary praise [is that] Art exists only *to be subordinate to talent* [. . .]." Griboedov clearly rejected the Classicist era:

> The one [. . .] who had more ability to please with schoolish requirements, conditions, habits, grandmotherly traditions, than with one's own creative strength—is not an artist—let him throw away his palette and brush, his knife or pen—out the window.
>
> (*G.* 511)

Nevertheless, he opted for the path of compromise: "I know that any craft has its ruses." As an experienced diplomat, he attached great meaning to these ruses, calling them in Latin, *nudae difficiles* (difficult trifles). Now his task was a combination of Romantic design and Realistic analysis unusual for Russian literature. "There is no action in it!" an exasperated critic raged indignantly. "The scenes are strung together arbitrarily," said even well-wishing friends—professionals. Griboedov did not dispute all this; he did not strive for obvious scene connections according to the rules of French drama, but to excite curiosity.[25]

The reproach that *Gore ot Uma* lacked action was answered by the like-minded Küchelbecker:

> I will not begin to insist that this is unjust, although it would not be difficult to prove that there is more action or movement in this comedy [i.e., inner action, movement of the soul in the hero's development], than in the majority of those comedies in which all the entertainment is built into the plot. In *Gore ot Uma,* precisely the whole plot is made up of the opposition of Chatsky to the other characters [. . .].[26]

Later, Küchelbecker gives a shining formula of the inner, heartfelt conflict of Romantic drama:

> Take Chatsky, the given characteristics; they are considered together and show what kind of meeting there will be, without fail, of these antipodes—and only. This is very simple, but in all this simplicity is newness, bravery, greater than that poetic consideration which they didn't understand.[27]

Griboedov actually preserved two of the Classical unities: time and place. The evolution of his hero, from the moment when he arrives at his beloved's after a three-year separation, and up until the final break from her and the escape from Moscow, fits strictly into twenty-four hours, from morning to midnight. The place of action is as strictly bounded in the drawing room of the rich Moscovite, Famusov. But the absence of unity of action, the creation of an exceptionally Romantic hero and the new kind of dramatic conflict veer from Classicism. The play's action, beginning with a trivial lover's intrigue, shifts grounds in the third act, when his beloved's fiasco becomes evident to Chatsky. The main action commences, for which the play really was written—the single-handed combat of Chatsky against society, hateful to him with its stagnation and hypocrisy.

This seeming inner contraction in the play evoked surprise and censure in many contemporaries.[28] What especially annoyed Belinsky was Chatsky's reasonableness and coldness in expressing living sentiments: when the hero finds out the bitter truth, that he is not loved, instead of leaving quietly, he begins "to rage against all of society" and uses the time "to read a few homilies." About what happens later in the play Belinsky did not even care to write, for him the play was already exhausted with the love intrigue, "And so, the comedy has no wholeness, since it has no idea." Nonetheless, Belinsky grasped at the significant negative definition: "The opposition of an intelligent and deep person against the society in which he lives" cannot form the positive idea of Russian drama. If the Famusovs were hated by Chatsky, why should they meet together? Let them look for their own circle, reasons the great critic and comes to an odd conclusion: "Society is *always righter and higher* than the private person, and the private individual is real and not a phantom only to the degree that he is expressed by society."[29] On this basis Belinsky announces further that because Chatsky as a personality expresses no one besides himself, he is foolish, like "an image without a face," like a "'phantom,' like something imaginary and unreal."[30] Here we have arrived at the core of the play itself—at the problem of the Romantic hero in Russian drama, and the theme of the Russian treatment of individualism. Chatsky is antithetical not only according to the utilitarian view of Belinsky, but even to the ideas of Decembrist aesthetics, to which Griboedov was close at one time.

IV

The idea of the free individual was common to Russian and Western European literature of the 1820s. The vogue for Byron in Russia was as great as in the West. However, the Russian ideal of the person under an authoritarian regime did not really accord with the understanding of the personality's value which had been developed in the generally more liberal West. It has been noted long ago, that the process of the individual's development in Russia took place under conditions completely different from those in the West.[31] In Russia, from the time of Peter, and with a few interruptions during the intervals of liberalism under Alexander I and Alexander II, social development was accompanied by far-reaching enslavement of personality, by an attack on its sovereignty, by the subordination of the private person to public or state interests. The famous Russian historian S. M. Solov'ev said that Nicholas I wanted to behead all those who rose above the average—to make them all equal.

It is significant that the Decembrists, though having supported personal freedom, also demonstrated the destructiveness of the philosophy of individualism. Their ideal was "a saintly offering of oneself for the common good of the people," and the higher manifestation of personal freedom was in service to the commonweal.[32] During the same years and months that Griboedov was creating his character Chatsky in Tiflis, completely different requirements for the ideal Russian hero were heard in bitter arguments about the meaning of art in Saint Petersburg. On June 13, 1821, in the main headquarters of literary free thought, in the unrestricted society of amateurs of Russian literature, the Romantic poet N. Gnedich delivered a famous speech in which he rejected the ideal person as put forward in German and English Romanticism.[33] Having Byron in mind, Gnedich condemned the individualistic character of his poetry and philosophy:

> Shunning, like a cold wall, the society of those who are like-minded, a person sees himself—a cheerless spectacle!—alone in the world and the world for him alone.[34]

He argued further that individualism destroys the person, implants disdain towards society, leads to egotism and spiritual emptiness of the soul. This was said at the time when Byron, having been torn from English society and having given free rein to his individualism, joined the Italian Carbonari movement and participated in the liberation battle of the Greek peoples.

In contrast, Griboedov was basing on Byron not only the features of his hero Chatsky's world outlook, but also the main conflict in the plot, Sofia's invention of Chatsky's craziness.[35]

The Decembrist theory, finding expression in the dramas of Ryleev, Küchelbecker, and others, in essence, controverted European Romanticism with its cult of inner, individual, "egotistic" life. Taken to the extreme, this theory, as the American historian of Russian culture, Richard Pipes, justly observed, began to work against itself:

> The quarrel [. . .] was not over aesthetics but over the freedom of the creative artist—and, ultimately, that of every human being—to be himself. The radical intelligentsia [. . .] began to develop a service mentality of its own. The belief that literature and art [. . .] had a primary responsibility to society became axiomatic in Russian left-wing circles.[36]

One long-range result was the lifelessness of literature, its subordination to openly propagandistic goals.

Griboedov's different road for Russian literature turned out to be impracticable under Russian conditions. The image of Chatsky is the first and—alas!—right up to the present the only effective and consistent portrait of individualism in Russian literature on a European scale. It is an image not so much of a hero as of a Romantic anti-hero in Russian life, *not the rule,* but an *exception.* Proud, smart, caustic, open, unprotected, detesting lies and hypocrisy, Chatsky finds himself in a state of war with everyone. He has no allies; he is "a lone soldier in the field," and hence much closer to the Romantic hero of Western literature than even to the Russian Onegin and Pechorin. Goncharov has written about Chatsky that he was a full head higher than those who also had once shone as a fashionable idea, though like a stylish suit. But "Onegin and Pechorin turned out to be unfit for the matter, for the active role, although both vaguely understood that all around them had been reduced to ashes."[37] Despising the emptiness of life, the festive lordliness, these "progressive personalities," as Goncharov judges, yielded to it. Their general dissatisfaction did not keep them from playing the dandy, "to shine," to flirt, and Pechorin, in addition, to be wretched in his laziness and melancholy. Despising both society and themselves in society, they adapted to life in it. In this resided both their Russianness and their typicalness.

Chatsky, in contrast, does not wish to be reconciled with anything, does not wish to pretend, does not wish to look "like everyone else." The only time that he does pretend in the play—in the scene of the resolute explanation with Sofia (III.i), he considers it his duty to play a part—"Just for this once I am going to pretend." Chatsky appears happy, energetic, witty, self-confident, deeply sensitive, open to the whole world, similar to Hamlet before the meeting with the ghost of his father. He craves activity; he is full of optimistic hopes. He jokes, entertains. His enthusiasm, lifting the soul a little, his rare gift of eloquence a result of constant work on his ideas and spiritual development. And if such "related souls" in society are, in fact, non-existent? If each of your jokes is met as a flaw? If your mockery of peoples obvious defects, of stupidity, self-conceit, emptiness, and laziness is assessed as "a snake's bite?" If your indignation at human baseness, cajolery, hypocrisy meets society's response, "Oh my God, is he a Carbonaro?" If you are deceived by a loved woman and want to have it out with her and she lets a rumor out that "you are not in your right senses" which is snatched up by everyone? And then they are already shunning you like they would a madman? Then how should you act?

Having drunk the cup of agony to the bottom, not finding in a single soul, the "sympathy of the living," at first, Chatsky more and more loses self-control. Disappointingly, it turns out that there are too many antagonists—the whole Moscow world. He feels that the battle in isolation has exhausted him. But, he doesn't give up. Experiencing "a million agonies," squeezing his chest, he becomes jaundiced, nagging, immeasurably irritable and, boiling with rage, continues to expose the lie, flinging himself on everyone and everything indiscriminately, passing a merciless sentence on Moscow before abandoning her forever:

I've no more dreams, the scales have fallen from my
   eyes.
Now it would do no harm to take them all in turn—
Daughter and father,
And the brainless lover,
And the whole world, and pour upon them
All of my bitterness, all my frustration.
Who was I with? Where did Fate cast me up?
Tormentors, all of them; Cursing and persecuting,
[. . .]
You all with one accord declared that I was mad—
And you were right! A man could go through fire un-
   harmed,
If he could spend a single day with you,
Breathe the same air as you.
And keep his reason.
Out, out from Moscow! Now, no more I'll ride this
   way;
I am off, I'm running, I'm not looking back,
I've gone to search the world,
To find some niche where outraged sense can shel-
   ter!—
My carriage! Get my carriage![38]

In Chatsky's last monologue we find, in essence, a model for the whole play. The monologue actually brings to mind a gryphon—that fantastic winged being with a lion's body and eagle's head—with which Griboedov compared his comedy, emphasizing two beginnings in it, the real and ideal, from which latter alone appears a "wonderful, ideal nature, higher than is visible to us."[39] From another perspective, in the monologue is reflected a completely realistic, even emphatically common everyday background, upon recognition of which occurs "the sobering" of the hero—he finds a concrete world of sinister old women and men, grown decrepit over made-up things, nonsense, in the poisoned air of the Moscow *beau monde*.

Griboedov's picture of Moscow is dominated by the Romantic image of Chatsky's coach, the real emblem of the daily life of the city's nobility, and simultaneously, the symbol of the wandering, searching, eternal dissatisfaction of the suffering and staggering hero. Chatsky's coach, as theatrical metaphor, suggests rushing off somewhere, not finding one's destiny in Russia. Not in vain was this image of Griboedov's snatched up afterwards with such lyrical strength by N. V. Gogol. In the final part of the first volume of *Dead Souls,* he transforms the *kibitka* (a hooded cart) of his arch-Realistic hero Chichikov into an unexpected Romantic symbol of all of Russian life:

Eh, thou troika, thou that art a bird! Who conceived thee? Methinks it is only among a spirited fold that thou couldst have come into being [. . .] Whither art thou soaring away to, then, Russia? Give me thy answer! But Russia gives none [. . .] all things on earth fly past and, eyeing it askance, all the other peoples and nations stand aside and give it the right of way.[40]

Notes

1. This essay was begun in Moscow and completed in Boston. The author is grateful to Tracy Rich for translating the original Russian draft into English. The first English version has been revised by Gerald Gillespie. Unless otherwise noted, emphasis in quotations have been added.

2. A. S. Pushkin, *Polnoe Sobranie Sochinenie v Desvati Tomakh* (*Complete Collection of Compositions in 10 volumes*) (Leningrad: Nauka, 1978), VII, 52. Pushkin also called *Boris Godunov* a Romantic tragedy in a letter to P. A. Vyazensky (X, 146) and in other places in his correspondence.

3. This point of view finds even more complete expression in the works of the official commentator of Russian classics in the Soviet period, Academician D. D. Blagoy. During more than half a century, from the 1920s to the 1980s he tried to "round off" and at the same time to distort the authentic picture of Russian literature's contradictory development which characterizes his two-volume composite work, *Ot Kantemira do Nashikh Dney* (*From Kantemir to Our Days*) (Moscow: Hudozhestvennaya Literatura, 1979).

4. V. G. Belinsky, *Sobranie Sochinenie v Trekh Tomakh* (*Collection of Compositions in Three Volumes*) (Moscow: OGIZ, 1948), III, 217. The Soviet editor considers it necessary to add the following commentary here: "However, the social essence of Romanticism slips away from Belinsky; therefore, the design of Romanticism's development carries a still too formal-logical character. However, with all the inadequacies thrown at us, Belinsky's concept [. . .] was the first attempt to examine Romanticism in a historical context as a whole complex of problems interconnected by a deep inner unity" (III, 872). See also the valuable research of Donald Fanger in *Dostoevsky and Romantic Realism* (Cambridge, Mass.: Harvard Univ. Press, 1967).

5. Belinsky, II, 232.

6. Belinsky, II, 245.

7. Belinsky, II, 176.

8. Belinsky, I, 461 and 466.

9. Belinsky, III, 255-236

10. Belinsky, I, 463.

11. K. A. Varnhagen von Ense, *Denkwürdigkeiten und vermischte Schriften,* (Leipzig: Brockhaus, 1843), V, 592-635.

12. A. S. Griboedov, *Gore ot Ouma,* trans. by Nicholas Benardaky (London: Simpkin, Marshall & Co.,

1857), pp. i-iv. Further references to this edition are enclosed in the text in parentheses after the symbol *G*.

13. István Sőtér, "A romantika Elötörténete és Korszákolása," in *Az Europa Romantika* (Moscow: Nauka, 1973), pp. 79-80. Jean Bonamour, *A. S. Griboedov et la vie littéraire de son temps* (Paris: Presses Universitaires de France, 1965).

14. A. S. Kurilov, ed. in chief, *Istoria Romantizam v Russkoi Literature* (*History of Romanticism in Russian Literature*) (Moscow: Nauka, 1979). Prepared by the Gorky Institute of World Literature of the USSR Academy of Sciences.

15. A. Anikst, *Istoria Uchenii o Drame. Teoria Drami v Rossii ot Pushkina do Chekhova* (*History of Studies on Drama. Theory of Drama in Russia from Pushkin to Chekhov*) (Moscow: Nauka, 1972), p. 10. See also the brilliant essay of Roman Jakobson, "Pushkin in a Realistic Light," in *Pushkin and His Sculptural Myth* (The Hague and Paris: Mouton, 1975), p. 63.

16. A. A. Gershkovich, "Teatr i natsional'naya Kul'tura (k postanovke problemi)" (Theater and National Culture [Relating to the Statement of the Problem]), in *Teatr v National'noy Kul'ture Stan Tsentral'noy i Ugovostochnoy Evropi XVIII-XIX vv* (*Theater in the National Culture of Central and South-Eastern European Countries of the XVIII-XIX centuries*) (Moscow: Nauka, 1976), pp. 7-25. Also in French: "Le Théâtre Est-Européen à la charnière des Lumières et du Romantisme," *Neohelicon*, 3, Nos. 3-4 (1975), 51-67.

17. Near the end of his life he confessed to his closest friend, Begichev (in a letter dated December 9, 1826, from Tiflis), "Will I ever not be dependent on people? Dependency on family, secondly on service, thirdly on life's goals which I created for myself, and perhaps I will defy fate. Poetry! I love her without memory, passionately, but is love alone enough to bring fame to oneself? [. . .] Who of us respects singers sincerely inspired, in that land where dignity is valued in direct relationships to the number of medals and enslaved serfs. *It's torture to be a fiery dreamer* in a land of eternal snows." V. Orlov, ed., *Griboedov: Sochinenia* (*Griboedov: Compositions*) (Leningrad: Hudozhestvennaya Literatura, 1940), p. 534.

18. *Literaturnie Manifesti Zapadnoevropeyskikh Romantikov* (*Literary Manifestos of Western European Romantics*) (Moscow: Nauka, 1980), p. 382. From the original French of de Staël, *De la littérature considérée dans ses rapports avec les institutions sociales* (1800). Concerning sources of de Staël's literary theory, see R. Wellek, *A History of Modern Criticism: The Romantic Age* (New Haven and London: Yale Univ. Press, 1955), p. 220.

19. A. Bestuzhev (Marlinsky), *Znakomstvo moë s Grivoedovim* (*My Acquaintance with Griboedov*) (Otechestvennie Zapiski, 1860), CXXXII, 635. "You called them both (Goethe and Byron) great, and in relation just to them this is fair, but between the two of them all superiority in greatness must be assigned to Goethe—who with his own idea explains all of humanity; Byron, with all sorts of diverse thoughts, a single person."

20. Pushkin, II, 179.

21. In 1820, describing his life in the East, he noted that "and here my wits are in shock." Speaking ironically of Moscow life, he grieved over it with all the passion of a Romantic nature ("Gone is happiness, I am not writing poetry [. . .],") and he called his departure "political banishment." Griboedov, p. 481.

22. U. Tinyanov, *Pushkin i ego Sovremenniki* (*Pushkin and His Contemporaries*) (Moscow: Nauka, 1969), p. 359.

23. Orlov, ed., p. 133. Of several English translations, we prefer that by Joshua Cooper in his book, *Four Russian Plays* (New York: Penguin Books, 1982), p. 210.

24. In the dream: "Is that really you, Alexander Sergeevich? How you've changed! It's impossible to recognize you." Griboedov, pp. 487-88. In the play (III.v): "Ah, Alexander Andreich, is it you?—Is it possible three years have changed me as much?" Griboedov, p. 86.

Three years is exactly the time period which separates Griboedov's departure/escape from Moscow and the beginning of work on the play. His friend, a witness to the creation of *Gore ot Uma* and its first audience, the Romantic poet Küchelbecker, came to Tiflis from Western Europe. He left evidence that Griboedov read him "each separate scene immediately after it had been written." V. K. Küchelbecker, "Dnevnik, 1833" (Diary, 1833), in *Puteshestive, Dnevnik, Stat'i* (*Travels, Diary, Articles*) (Leningrad: Nauka, 1979), p. 227. He certifies, in addition, that the poet did not intend to write simple portraits, as the contemporary critics thought: "His wonderful soul," writes Küchelbecker, "was higher than such trifles." However, he takes note of the critics, "qui se sent galeux qu'il se gratte." Küchelbecker, 227-28. The French saying which Küchelbecker uses means "The cat knows whose meat he ate." Küchelbecker here defends Griboedov from the unjust attacks of the critics on *Gore ot Uma* in conjunction with the publication of a short excerpt in the almanac *Russkaya Taliya* in 1825. He suggested that M. Dmitriev, the writer of the criticisms, be tried in a court of honor for "the perfidious praises to the lucky portrait" in Griboedov's comedy, which Küchelbecker considered a conscious distortion of the author's intention.

25. The more "outside" of the West that the events are, as he explained his principles, the more they entice curiosity: "I write for those like myself—when by the first scene I am already guessing the tenth, I am filled with yawns and then I run from the theater." (*G.* 498)

26. Küchelbecker, p. 228.

27. Küchelbecker, p. 228.

28. Even Pushkin, the admired master of convoluted love intrigues, was sorry that "the whole comedy did not revolve around it; it seems Griboedov didn't want it—his will." (Pushkin, X, 97.) Belinsky expressed it still more categorically. Chatsky for him was, in general, "a silly character" as a 'lover.' All the words expressing his feelings for Sofia are so ordinary, in order not to utter banalities!" (Belinsky, I, 508.) It is necessary to admit Belinsky had a point.

29. Belinsky, I, 508.

30. Belinsky, I, 515.

31. Recently the Hungarian scholar Erzsebet Köves offered an interesting comparison between the Western and Russian paths of development in the first half of the nineteenth century in his book *Kelet és Nyugat* (Budapest: Magvető, 1983).

32. Cf. passim Richard Pipes, *Russia under the Old Regime* (London: Weidenfeld & Nicolson, 1977); ch. 1, pp. 20-30 in Adam B. Ulam, *In the Name of the People* (New York: Viking Press, 1977); James H. Billington, *The Ikon and the Axe: An Interpretive History of Russian Culture* (New York: Vintage Books, 1970).

33. Russian Romantics of the Decembrist doctrine placed the problem of the Romantic hero in antiquity and far from the contemporary Slavic/historical material on the abstract/heroic plane, rejecting "the useless" Byronesque individualism. "It is more necessary to overmeasure, that is, to exaggerate the greatness of a person than to belittle him," demanded the same N. Gnedich, inviting Russian literature to exhibit "a saintly offering of the self for the good of the people." *Dekabristi i Ikh Vremya* (*Decembrists and Their Time*) (Moscow and Leningrad: Nauka, 1951), p. 134. Serious Soviet scholars, e.g., G. P. Makogonenko and E. N. Kupreyanova, with their valuable book

National'noe Soveobrazie Russkoy Literaturi (*National Distinctiveness of Russian Literature*) (Leningrad: Nauka, 1976), expound on Gnedich's view but without giving it its full value.

34. Gnedich, pp. 133-34.

35. Based on the story of Lord Byron, which was making itself heard in the West and in Russia. Byron was blamed for his wife's mental illness, which served as a reason for his break from society and his running away from England. "As he himself says, he had to fight alone against all," wrote the Russian press in the 1820s. *Sin Otechestva* (*Son of the Fatherland*), 1822, no. 21, p. 24. For more details on Byron and Griboedov, see U. Tinyanov's article "Suzhet *Gore ot Uma*" (The Plot of *Gore ot Uma*) in *Pushkin i ego Sovremenniki*, pp. 347-379.

36. Pipes, pp. 279-80. In Russian translation: *Rossia pri Starom Rezhime* (Cambridge, Mass.: Harvard Univ. Press, 1980), pp. 374-75.

37. I. A. Goncharov, *Million Terzanii (Kriticheskii Etud)* (*A Million Agonies—A Critical Study*), cited from *Gore ot Uma* (Moscow: Pravda, 1980), p. 110.

38. Griboedov, p. 147. In the first edition of *Gore ot Uma,* this second to last line was different: "Where there is a cosy corner both for reason and sense." In our view it expresses the main idea of the comedy more exactly (which in its original version was titled "Gore Umu" (Tragedy to the Reason). The accepted, smoothed over version, "Where for the insulted one there is a corner for sense," puts the accent on the lover's intrigue and relates, in our opinion, to the corrections in the text which in Griboedov's own words, "spoiled" the comedy and made it poorer. Here the remarks of the American translator J. Cooper are appropriate. In the latest edition of his translation (*Four Russian Plays [. . .], p. 213), he suggests to compare this line with the words of Alceste in Molière's *Le Misanthrope* (V.iv): "Et chercher sur la terre un endroit écarté Où d'estre homme d'honneur on ait la liberté." Although Cooper (who titled his translation of "Gore ot Uma," *Chatsky*) follows the Russian text exactly, his remark that Chatsky, like Alceste, promotes consideration of "reason" strengthens our supposition.

39. I am citing from the innovative work of I. Medvedev, *A. S. Griboedov: Gore ot Uma,* (Moscow: Hudozhestvennaya Literatura, 1971), p. 71, which presents a rare analysis of the elements of Romanticism in Griboedov's work. The author comes to the conclusion, in this work, that in *Gore ot Uma,* developing a new poetics, "Griboedov

masterfully carried out [. . .] the inner fused unification of two styles: Romantic and Classical" (p. 68).

40. Nikolai Gogol, *Dead Souls,* trans. B. Guerney, introd. by René Wellek (New York: Rinehart, 1948), pp. 303-4.

George Kalbouss (essay date spring 1995)

SOURCE: Kalbouss, George. "Rhyming Patterns in Griboedov's *Gore ot uma." Slavic and East European Journal* 39, no. 1 (spring 1995): 1-13.

[*In the following essay, Kalbouss analyzes the rhyming patterns of* Woe from Wit, *claiming that Griboedov skillfully demonstrated the importance of rhyming as a form of entertainment in early nineteenth-century Moscow.*]

1994 marked 200 years since the birth of Aleksandr Sergeevič Griboedov, the author known primarily for one significant work, ***Gore ot uma*** (***Woe From Wit***). The fame of this play has generated scores of studies, ranging from biographies of Griboedov's life to more formal analyses of the play's poetics. This study focuses on one formal aspect of this play—its rhyming patterns. In Griboedov's day, rhyming was a form of social entertainment. A person was considered only as clever as his rhymes. Since historians agree that in ***Woe From Wit*** Griboedov captures much of the essence of Muscovite culture of the 1820's, this study intends to show that Griboedov likewise captures the various practices of rhyming of that time in his play. Hopefully, the paper will show that the play's principle characters may be evaluated by the "quality" of their rhyme, especially Čatskij and Sofija. With regard to these two, can one determine who is the better rhymer? This study relies on the work done by Professor J. Thomas Shaw in his studies of rhyming patterns in the works of Puškin, Batjuškov and Baratynskij.[1]

The rhyming schemes of this work may be compared to a symphonic composition. The work is dominated by "solo" rhyming, in which various characters deliver monologues while others listen. A second kind of rhyming could best be called "fugue" rhyming, in which three characters or more—both principle and secondary—engage in rhyming together, each interrupting the other, and each rhyming lines begun by another. The best example of this is the rumor scene (III:14-22) where various characters at the ball conclude erroneously that Čatskij has gone mad. The third kind of rhyming is a combination of the two, in which the characters' dialogues with each other could also be regarded as a rhyming *repartee,* where one character rhymes lines started by another, engage each other not only by

discussing and arguing, but also in trying to best each other through rhyming. Such *repartees* occur between Čatskij and Sofija at various moments in the play.

The play's verse structure enables these different kinds of rhyming. Written in variable length, rhyming iambic verse, the lines are reminiscent of Krylov's *basennij stix.* Alternating between masculine and feminine, the rhymes signal both the end of a line and, for the most part, the end of a phrase. Since the lines vary in length, the rhymes occur at irregular frequencies, giving the impression of conversation rather than spoken poetry. Also, rhymes do not necessarily immediately follow line-after-line. Characters frequently "share" lines between each other, so that one character begins a line, a second adds several more words, and a third completes the line. This typical device for eighteenth and nineteenth century verse drama is also found in the operas of this time, and has been termed, "подхватывание стиха" by Tomaševskij.[2] All of these conventions imbue the dialogue with a conversational tone. Three possible rhyming patterns are found in the play: AA (adjacent/смежные), AB AB (alternate/перекрестные), and AB BA (enclosing/охватные). The rhymes do not repeat predictably—there is no equivalent in this play to an *Onegin* stanza—yet the longer monologues at least shift rhyming patterns. There are seven instances of triple rhyme (i.e. ABBACAC). For the purposes of this study, the rhyming is identified as A, B, or occasionally C (in capital letters); masculine and feminine rhymes are not addressed.

The rhymes may be also classified according to their "quality" against standards established in the 1820's. These may be summarized as follows:

1. "Canonical" rhymes. These are the permissible rhymes for the time as delineated in various works on how to rhyme (see ftn. 1 above). In general, Shaw observes that permissable rhyming prefers the declinables to the verbals, and discourages mixing parts of speech.

2. "Non-canonical" rhymes. These rhymes do not adhere to the canons of the rhyming books. Shaw observes that Puškin and his contemporaries already showed derision in their works by not adhering to the canons, especially by mixing parts of speech.

3. "Clever" rhymes. These are rhymes which rely on words which one would not expect could provide a rhyme, i.e., names of persons, towns, foreign words, mispronunciations and regionalisms. Griboedov is particularly fond of rhyming with particles, adverbs, and other parts of speech.[3]

When Griboedov's rhymes are compared to those of Puškin, Batjuškov and Baratynskij (again using Shaw's statistics), Griboedov tends to be slightly more conservative in mixing parts of speech, that is, rhyming nouns with verbs, etc. Shaw reports that 33% of Puškin's rhymes are "mixed" (Dictionary, xxxix). With Griboedov, only 25% are mixed, but the "mixed rhymes" are not evenly divided among the various characters.

For the record, here is how Griboedov's rhyming compares to the statistics from Shaw's figures published in "Parts of Speech . . ." on the rhyming of Puškin, Batjuškov and Baratynskij by parts of speech:

	Batjuškov	Puškin 1813-17	Puškin-later
	(in percents)		
Nouns	51.48	52.38	50.42
Pronouns	6.16	6.51	8.21
Adjectives	12.44	13.91	12.65
Participles	1.55	2.42	1.66
Verbs	25.38	20.94	20.13
Adverbs	1.98	1.93	3.82

	Baratynskij	*Gore ot uma*
Nouns	46.17	42.62
Pronouns	13.49	6.89
Adjectives	13.57	11.11
Participles	2.34	1.20
Verbs	17.61	26.04
Adverbs	3.49	8.93 (5)

Summaring noun-forms (declinables) and verb-forms (verbals) we have:

	Batjuškov	Puškin-1813-17	*Puškin-later*
	(in percents)		
Declinables	71.65	75.21	72.94
Verbals	25.38	20.94	20.13
Others	2.99	3.84	6.91

	Baratynskij	*Gore ot uma*
Declinables	75.58	61.78
Verbals	17.61	26.04
Others	6.81	12.18[4]

The statistics provide some interesting revelations. Griboedov tends to be "more canonical" by not mixing parts of speech, yet is significantly less canonical in terms of using verbal forms. Verbs are the "dynamic" parts of speech and Griboedov puts verbs at the ends of phrases and thus in rhyming positions, to endow the dialogue with a dynamism which declinables might not bring about as theatrically. The "others" category for his work is much higher than those of the other poets. Griboedov's rhymes many more adverbs as well as words which do not easily submit themselves to classification as "parts of speech" (например, недосуг любо). This "other" category is the source of much clever rhyming.

Rhyming in drama can also provide some theatrical effects. It has been observed that the most theatrical rhyme is AA. This rhyme enables effective, immediate contrasts, comic effects, and what would be called "punch lines" (here, more accurately, punch "words").

The more complex ABAB rhyme is used more for orchestration and flow of thought. The ABBA rhyme is a mixture of the two above. The BB part enables making the strong contrast, the A . . . A, separated by the BB, "sandwiches" the contrast into a context and a flow of thought.[5]

It is possible to make some assumptions about rhyming and individual characters. A character is a better rhymer if he varies his rhymes. For example, if a character only uses ABABAB rhymes, he would tend to be more tedious, less original than one who varied his lines, i.e. AABB/ABBA/ABBA/ABAB, etc. On the other hand, a character is the least interesting if he only uses AA rhymes.

In *repartees,* the above patterns enable various verbal-interplays between the characters. The simplest is when one character "feeds" another a line, and the other rhymes it with an AA rhyme, but more complicated patterns exist. An AB line is "fed" and is responded to by an "AB" rhyme. Other variations are possible: a character may begin a line, and a second character will provide the rhyme. Also, a character may "feed himself" a line, i.e., he will provide the A line, a second character will give a "B" line, the first will rhyme with the "A" line he gave himself and then will rhyme the second character's "B" line as well.

There may also be semantic differences in the rhyming. In many cases, the semantic "load" is neutral, that is, each word in the rhyming pair is equal in its significance; however, in many rhymed pairs the semantic "load" is not neutral. Some rhymewords carry additional semantic loads, forcing a comparison by the very fact of the rhyme. In this case, the second rhyming word is usually stronger than the first. This device is particularly effective in comedy where the first line serves as a "straight" line and the second as a "punch" line, i.e. дурацкий/Чацкий (I:5-6).

Using the above assumptions, a character's rhyming may be evaluated in the following two ways: 1. by the rhyming patterns they choose and how they vary them, and 2. by the types of words they rhyme according to the above-mentioned parameters (are they canonical? do they mix parts of speech?). The monologues of the principle characters provide the best opportunities for such evaluations. One of Famusov's early monologues (I:3) is typical of his rhyming patterns:

FAMUSOV'S RHYMING PATTERNS (I:3)

AA: adv-verb (проворно[Sofija's line]—покорно [F. rhymes line from Sofija])

AA: verb-verb (вбежал-испужал)

AA: adj-adj (целый-угорелый)

AA: noun-pronoun (хлопотня-до меня)

AA: verb-verb (обманут-станут [Sofija starts line, Famusov completes it])

AA: verb-verb (журю-говорю)

AA: verb-noun (радели-колыбели)

AA: verb-noun (принанять-мать)

AA: pronoun-noun (приставил-правил)

AA: noun-noun (допустила-сила)

AA: noun-noun (образца-отца)

AB: noun-noun (сложеньем-седни)

BA: noun-noun (господни-поведеньем)

AA: verb-verb (Молчать![Famusov completes line started by Liza]-начать)

AB: noun-noun (летам-добряки)

BA: noun-noun (языки-билетам)

AB: pronoun-noun (всему-вздохам)

BA: noun-pronoun (скоморохам-к чему?)

AB: noun-noun (семейство-секретари)

AB: noun-noun (содейство-В Твери)

Famusov's rhymes are not that remarkable. He prefers the AA rhymes, which he repeats throughout most of the monologue. Only in the end does he vary his rhymes with ABBA, ABBA. ABAB. Out of the 42 rhymewords, 14 are verbals (33%), and of the 21 pairs of rhymes, 4 mix parts of speech (19%), but this percentage is much higher in later speeches. There is one rhyme which could qualify as interesting or even outrageous: секретари/в Твери. Compare this rhyming pattern to a typical one of Čatskij's from II:5:

CATSKIJ'S RHYMING PATTERNS (II:5)

AB: noun-adj (лет-непримирима)

AB: noun-noun (газет-Крыма)

AB: noun-particle (журьбе-и ту же)

AB: pronoun-adj (об себе- хуже)

AA: noun-noun (отчы-образчы)

AB: adj-noun (богаты- родстве)

AB: noun-noun (палаты-мотовстве)

AB: noun-noun (клиенты-иностранцы-черты)

BA: noun-noun (рты-танцы)

AB: noun-adj (пелен-непонятных)

BA: noun-adj (поклон-знатных)

AB: noun-noun (слуг-драки)

AB: adv-noun (вдруг-собаки)

AB: noun-noun (затей-фурах)

AB: noun-noun (детей-Амурах)

AB: noun-noun (красе-отсрочке)

AB: pronoun-noun (все-в одиночке)

AB: noun-noun (седин-безлюьи)

BA: noun-adj (суди-один)

CA: noun-noun (исканий-чин)

C: noun (познаний)

AB: noun-adj (жар-прекрасным)

AB: noun-noun (пожар-опасным)

AB: noun-adj (быту-красивый)

AB: noun-adj (нищету-счастливый)

AB: noun-verb (страсть-отрекся)

AB: verb-verb (впасть-повлекся)

AB: noun-verb (двора-приезжали)

AB: interj-verb (ура!-бросали)

In comparing these two monologues, we see right away that Čatskij is the more versatile rhymer. Famusov's rhymes tend to repeat rhyming patterns almost monotonously, with AA being the most frequent type of rhyme. When one looks at all of his longer monologues, his rhyming appears to "atrophy" from a variety of ABAB or ABBA rhymes to the simpler AA patterns. Čatskij varies his rhymes more frequently, demonstrating his creativity and versatility. Čatskij uses declinables almost exclusively (82% in the above monologue) and rarely mixes part of speech. He does venture a few clever rhymes, i.e. и ту же/хуже, двора/ура! Both Famusov and Čatskij use triple rhymes, but Čatskij's, in the above monologue, is the most complex in the entire play: ABBACAC. Indeed, Čatskij's meticulous rhyming adds further proof to his image as a truly cultured man of the 1820's.

Repetilov's rhymes are more versatile as witnessed in his one long monologue in IV:4. Repetilov's rhyming patterns have a greater symmetry to them than that of the other characters, yet, towards the end, also suffer from an atrophy into AA rhyme, similar to Famusov's.

REPETILOV'S RHYMING PATTERNS (IV:4)

AB: "other"-noun (недосуг-дело)

BA: verb-adv (созрело-вдруг)

AA: noun-noun (историй-Григорий)

AB: verb-noun (морит-складка)

AB: verb-noun (говорит-порядка)

AA: pronoun-noun (с ним-Евдоким)

AA: noun-noun (диво-особливо)

AA: adj-particle, foreign wd. (одно- но, но, но)

AA: noun-noun (брата-ребята)

AA: verb-verb (сказать-назвать)

AB: noun-pronoun (Маркелыч-его)

AB: noun-noun (мелочь-ничего)

AB: pronoun, particle-verb (сечь-то—писать)

BA: verb-pronoun (отыскать-нечто)

AA: pronoun-verb (обо всем-пасем)

AA: particle-noun (нету-портрету)

AB: noun-noun (дуэлист-алеутом)

AB: noun-noun (нечист-плутом)

AB: verb-verb (говорит-внушаем)

AB: verb-verb (лорит-рыдаем)

AA: noun-adv (Навряд . . . -зауряд)

AA: noun-verb (ужас-понатужась)

AA: verb-verb (сижу-рожу)

AA: verb-verb (лодчеплят-слепят)

AA: verb-verb (кладут-дают)

AB: "other"-verb (любо-нарядил)

BA: verb-noun (мил-Скалозуба[rhyme made by servant])

Like Čatskij, Repetilov tends to not mix parts of speech. Yet, he uses more verbal forms than Čatskij. True to his character as liberal and party-goer, Repetilov produces more of the clever rhymes than the other characters, including rhyming names and foreign words: историй/ Григорий; с ним/ Евдоким; одно/"А! нон лашьяр ми, но, но, но"; Маркелыч/ мелочь; дуэлст/нечист; алеутом/плутом.

The rhyming of the two main female characters, Liza and Sofija is not as "proper" as is Čatskij's, and many of their longer discourses use a high percentage of verbal forms for rhymes. It is difficult to make a rule for Sofija's rhyming pattern, as some speeches do use declinables. However, others are almost exclusively verbal, for example, in I:5.

Возмет он руку, к сердцу жмет,	verb
Из глубины души вздохнет	verb
Ни слова вольного, и так вся ночь проходит,	verb
Рука с рукой, и глаз с меня не сводит.—	verb
Смеешся! Можно ли! чем повод подала	verb
Тебе я к хохоту такому!	adj. (16).

Of the other characters, Skalozub's rhyming is usually simple, of the AA variety. In contrast, Molčalin's two faces are exposed by his rhyming, e.g. when he is pretending to be humble before his superiors, he avoids participating in the rhyming. For example, in I:9, where there are 36 lines shared by Skalozub, Sofija, Čatskij and Molčalin, he only completes one line, which he rhymes with Skalozub's previous line. His rhyming becomes much more lively when he attempts to seduce Liza in I:12 [pp. 46-47] as well as in IV:11-12 [pp. 97-99]. In these scenes, Molčalin commands the situation. In contrast, when Sofija discovers his hypocrisy in IV:12, Molčalin reverts to his "humble self" by only starting the lines which Sofija completes:

София:

> Не помню ничего, не докучайте мне.
> Воспоминания! как острый нож оне.

Молчалин

> (ползает у ног ее): Помилуйте . . .

София:

>   Не
> подличайте, встаньте.
> Ответа не хочу, я знаю ваш ответ,
> Солжете . . .

Молчалин:

> Сделайте мне милость . . .

София:

>   Нет. Нет.
> Нет

(100)

As stated above, individual or "solo" rhyming is only one of three types in this play. The shorter speeches are frequently integrated into ensemble or "fugue" rhyming, where various characters interact with each other. This kind of rhyming is best seen in *Act III* in the ball scene, where various secondary characters decide that Čatskij is going mad. In a classical musical fugue, all instruments appear to be playing their own melodies, and the combinations produce interesting harmonies and combinations. Yet, one instrument, usually the first violin, still has the dominant role in the fugue. The same thing is true in these rhyming scenes. While numerous characters appear on the stage and all are interacting with each other, close observation shows that only several perform the rhyming as in III:7:

1-я княжня:

> Какой фасон прекрасный!

2-я кнкжня:

> Какие складочки!

1-я княжня:

> Обшито бахрамой.

Наталья Дмитриевна:

> Нет, если б виделн мой тюрлюрлю атласный!

3-я княжня:

> Какой эшарп cousin мой подарил!

4-я княжня:

> Ах! Да, барежевый!

5-я княжня:

> Ах! прелесть!

6-я княжня:

> Ах! как мил!

(62-63)

Note that only three rhymers are used in this fugue while there are seven voices.

It is rhyming which causes Čatskij's downfall in this episode, notably in the scene where Grafinja Babuška, who is both deaf and has an accent, misunderstands other's lines and arrives at the fatal conclusions (III:19):

Графиня Бабушка:

> Что? Что? уж нет ли здесь пои ара?

Загореукий:

> Нет, Чакий произвел всю эту кутерьму.

Графиня Бабушка:

> Как, Чацкого? Кто свел в тюрьму?

Загореукий:

> В горах изранен в лоб, сошел с ума от раны.

Графиня Бабушка:

> Что? К фармазонам в клоб? Пошел он в ηусурманы?

(75)[7]

Griboedov intensifies the effect of the traditional comic device of "dialogue of the deaf" to both create comic lines as well as a fatal misunderstanding.

The most interesting comparisons in rhyming are the rhyming *repartees* between Čatskij and Sofija, where one of them begins a rhyme, and the other completes or "caps" it, the "подхватывание стиха." Griboedov creates a *repartee* immediately in I:7, when Čatskij first arrives, but the *repartees* intensify throughout the scene. For example, at Catskij's first entrance, we have a fairly civil exchange which Sofija rhymes:

Ч:

> И вот подвиги награда!

С:

> Ах, Чаукий, я вам рада

(17-18).

A few lines later, Čatskij rhymes with a little more versatility in performing an AB rhyme to Sofija's AB:

С:

> С вопросом я, хоть будь моряк
> Не повстречал ли где в почтовой вас карете?

Ч:

> Положите, что так
> Блажен, кто верует, тепло ему на свете

(18).

A few lines later, Čatskij interrupts an utterance of Sofija's and "steals" her rhyme:

С:

> Гоненье на Москву. Что значит видеть свет!
> Где ж лучше?

Ч:

> Где нас нет

(19).

Sofija then shows Čatskij that she can interrupt his lines just as well:

Ч:

> А Гильоме, фраиууз, подбитый ветерком
> Он не женат еше?

С:

> На ком?

(20).

Sofija counters with two rhyming exchanges. The first is a creative, clever rhyme:

Ч:

> Да двух, без этого нельзя ж

С:

> Но мудрено из них скроить, как ваш

(21).

In the next exchange, Sofija continues being the rhymer, using rhyme words to insult Čatskij, revealing her low view of him and her suspicions of his high-flown sentiments. With Sofija's rhyming, the semantic load of the phrase is definitely on the rhyming word:

Ч:

> Велите мне в огонь, пойду как на обед

С:

> Да хорошо—сгорите если ж нет?

(22).

In II:8, she further reveals her versatility as an accomplished rhymer:

Ч:

> Пускай себе сломил бы шею
> Вас чуть было не уморил

С:

> Убийствен холодностью своею!
> Смотреть на вас, вас слушать нету сил.

Ч:

> Прикажете, мне за него терзаться?

С:

> Туда бежать, там быт, помочь ему стараться

[p. 41]

In II:9 Sofija demonstrates her versatility and inventiveness she knowingly injects a line continuing the meter and rhyming exchange after Čatsky mutters something she is not intended to hear:

С:

> Ах! очень вижу, из пустого,
> А вся еше теперь дрожу

Ч

> (про себя): С Молчалиным ни слова!

С:

> Однако о себе скажу.

[p. 43]

Čatskij's muttering quietly signals his withdrawal from the repartee. Afterwards, Sofija continues to rhyme at Čatskij's expense, including stealing two lines from him in III:1:

Ч:

> Вы здесь, я очень рад
> А этого желал.

С:

> (про себя):   И очень невпопад

[p. 48]

And (also in III:1)

Ч:

> Хоть некстати, нужды нет
> Кого бы любите?

С:

> Ах, Боже мой, весь свет.

[p. 48]

In III:2, Sofija steals a "B" rhyme away from Čatskij:

Ч:

> И прими знаю стана
> Лицом и голосом герой

С:

> Не моего романа

(52).

And, in her last rhyming exchange in III:13, again completes a line begun by Čatskij:

Ч:

> За то, что он смягчил разгневанную гостью
> Хотел япохвалить

С:

> А кончим бы злостью

(70-71).

In evaluating Čatskij and Sofija's rhyming, we find that Čatskij is most clever when rhyming with himself; he does not possess the quickness of wit to provide colorful rhymes for Sofija's lines. On the contrary, Sofija's rhymewords carry significant semantic loads: they are barbed, angry and in sharp contrast to the lines supplied by others; for example, to her "нельзя ж / как ваш; во огонь пойду как на обед / сгорите, если ж нет?; сломил бы шею / холодностью твоею; не уморил / вас слушать нету сил; терзаться / стараться; нужды нет / весь свет; знаю стана / не моего романа; гостью / злостью."

In addition, the rhyming exchanges point out a significant set of images which are used to define Čatskij, first by himself, and then by Sofija. Repeatedly, Čatskij describes himself with images of warmth: hot, ardent, on fire, etc.; to the contrary, Sofija observes his coldness and detachment.

In summary, it has been shown that Griboedov's rhyming adds significantly to the definition of the characters in this play. The rhymes certainly provide a final artistic touch to the principle characters. Molčalin, who is reticent to talk to people in his own social level, is reluctant to rhyme, yet when he encounters a possible victim from a lower station, he rhymes eloquently. Skalozub, whose world view is limited by his atrophying military mind, performs mostly AA rhymes. Famusov who is pompous and pretentious, varies some rhyme patterns but invariably uses mostly AA rhymes. He also mixes various parts of speech in his rhyming. Repetilov's lines are more "eclectic" revealing his dilettantish personality. Čatskij speaks well and is clever, but is predictable in his rhyming. His best rhymes are in his monologues, when he is making speeches and not engaged with other characters.

It is Sofija, then, whose rhymes are the most interesting. Sofija's rhyming is the most flexible and adaptable to the situation about her. Her rhyming reflects her feelings, particularly her great anger at Čatskij. Moreover, Sofija is a survivor, and the flexibility in her rhyme reflects the flexibility she needs to survive in Famusov's Moscow. Her rhyming takes advantage of the weaknesses of others as do the decisions in her life. While she tends to rhyme with verbs, she does not mix her rhymes, and, there is promise, in her last speech, that she will now be rhyming in declinables, more like a man. Indeed, for Sofija to be independent, she needs to marry a Molcalin whom she can blackmail and control at any moment.

In his book, *Griboedov i Mol'er,* N. K. Piksanov compares this play to Molière's *Le Misanthrope.* While the comparisons between characters and situations are certainly convincing, the rhyming patterns do not seem to correspond. N. D. Howarth, a scholar of Molière's poetics comments that while Moliere did tend to use local language, fractured lines were rare, as were examples of comic neologisms. Indeed, Molière appeared to prefer ordinary expected rhymes (when he did rhyme—he often did not) (236-241). We may surmise that the rhyming poetics of *Gore ot uma* are even more so a testimony to Griboedov's originality and creativity.

Certainly, the terms "orchestration" and "instrumentation" fit this work perhaps better than any other in Russian dramaturgy. Each character speaks with his own voice, not only in terms of content, but also with a distinctive rhyming pattern. At the same time all the voices intertwine into a polyphonic work; the individual voices create a harmonic whole which is greater than the sum of the individual voices. Conversely, the harmonic whole could not be created without each individual voice's contribution.

Yet, there is perhaps a more interesting and significant conclusion that may be drawn from these observations. It has often been commented that the characters in this work curiously do not seem to "connect" with each other; each speaks his or her lines as if into the void, while the others are present. Surely this is true if one

only pays attention to the *content* of their speeches. On this level, characters are intensely reacting to each other, especially when one character feeds a potential end-rhyme to another. On this level, the characters are commenting on each other, reacting, and revealing their true natures. Hopefully this study has shown that Griboedov's "code" for the plot, is not constructed on the lines of simply exchanging words in the dialogue, rather it is constructed on the level of poetics, and specifically on rhyme.

Notes

1. "Rhyming" was a significant cultural and social pastime in early 19th century Russian society. Shaw cites one rhyming "guide" from that time that established norms for various parts of speech as rhymewords, Ivan Levitskij, *Kurs rossijskoj literatury dlja devic,* SPB, 1819, in J. Thomas Shaw, "Parts of Speech in Puškin's Rhymewords and Nonrhymed Endwords," *SEEJ* [*Slavic and East European Journal*] 37:1 (1993). Rhyming took the form of *repartees* at various social events, with persons trying to best each other by the more clever rhymes. William Mills Todd III, *Fiction and Society in the Age of Pushkin.* Cambridge: Harvard, 1986, 56. "Kuplety" were frequently performed at various parties and balls. Geršenzon cites one such in his *Griboedovskaja Moskva.* Moskva-Berlin: 1922. 99-100. Trike reads such to Tatjana in *Onegin.* (5:XXXIII) and Čajkovskij gives him "kuplety" to read in his opera. I am indebted to Ms. Constance Cherok for helping gather the statistics on rhyming and parts of speech. I am likewise grateful to Dr. Anelya Rugaleva for her philological expertise in helping identify those more slippery parts of speech.

2. Tomaševskij, "Stixotvornaja sistema 'Gore ot uma'," in I. Klabunovskij and A. Slonimskij, eds. *A. S. Griboedov. Sbornik statej.* Moskva: Gosudarstvennyj literaturnyj muzej, 1946. 97. These kinds of rhymes may be found in most Russian 18th century plays, including Sumarokov's *Xorev, Semira,* and *Dmitrij Samozvanec,* and Kapnist's *Jabeda.* A. P. Sumarokov, *Izbrannye proizvedenija.* Leningrad: Sovetskij pisatel', 1957; V. V. Kapnist, *Izbrannye proizvedenija.* Leningrad: Sovetskij pisatel', 1973. 33-462.

3. Tomaševskij calls these "sostavnye rifmy." Tomaševskij, *Ibid.*

4. Shaw classifies adverbs in the "others" category. This study does the same.

5. Tomaševskij's terms these rhymes as: AA = aphoristic, ABAB = for more developed conversation. Tomaševskij, 100.

6. All quotes from *Gore ot uma* are taken from A. S. Griboedov, *Sočinenija,* Moskva-Leningrad, 1959.

7. The italics are Griboedov's to cast attention to the mispronunciation.

Works Cited

Bonamour, Jean. *A. S. Griboedov et la Vie Littéraire de Son Temps.* Paris: Presses Universitaires de France, 1965.

Fomičev, S. A. *Komedija A. S. Griboedova,* Gore ot uma. Moskva: Prosveščenie, 1983.

Geršenzon, Mixail. *Griboedovskaja Moskva.* Moskva-Berlin: Gelikon, 1922.

Gordina, A. M., ed. *A. S. Griboedov v russkoj kritike. Sbornik statej.* Moscow: Goslitizdat, 1958.

Griboedov, A. S. *Sočininenija.* Moskva-Leningrad, 1959.

Harden, Evelyn Jasiulko. "Griboedov and the Willock Affair." *Slavic Review* March (1971): 74-92.

Howarth, N. D. *Molière. A Playwright and His Audience.* Cambridge: Cambridge University Press, 1982.

Klabunovskij, I. and A. Slonimskij, eds. *A. S. Griboedov. Sbornik Statej.* Moskva: Gosudarstvennyj literaturnyj muzej, 1946.

Janecek, G. "A Defense of Sof'ja." *SEEJ* 20 (1977): 318-331.

Piksanov, N. K. *Griboedov i Mol'er.* Moskva: Gosudarstvennoe izdatel'stvo, 1922. Reprinted, Letchworth: Prideau Press, 1979.

Shaw, J. Thomas. "Rhymes in a 'Prose' Context: Varlaam's Rhyming in Puškin's *Boris Godunov.*" *SEEJ* 32.4 (1988): 542-561.

———. "Parts of Speech in Puškin's Rhymewords and Nonrhymed Endwords." *SEEJ* 37:1 (1993): 1-22.

———. *Pushkin's Rhymes, A Dictionary.* Madison: University of Wisconsin Press, 1974.

Tomaševskij, B. "Stixotvornaja sistema 'Gore ot uma'" *A. S. Griboedov, Jbornik Statej.* Eds. I. Klabunovskij and A. Slonimskij. Moskva: Gosudarstvennyj literaturnyj muzej, 1946.

Stephen Baehr (essay date 1998)

SOURCE: Baehr, Stephen. "Is Moscow Burning? Fire in Griboedov's *Woe from Wit.*" In *Russian Subjects: Empire, Nation, and the Culture of the Golden Age,* edited by Monika Greenleaf and Stephen Moeller-Sally, pp. 229-42. Evanston, Ill. : Northwestern University Press, 1998.

[*In the following essay, Baehr explores the importance of fire imagery in the events and themes of* Woe from Wit.]

And Moscow is burning up.
The black smoke spreads and curls.
And, behold, the brilliant head of Moscow
Stops gleaming.
Poor Moscow is ablaze,
Moscow has been burning for 12 days . . .

—N. M. Shatrov, "The Fire of Moscow: To the Year 1812"

In A. S. Griboedov's comedy **Woe from Wit** (**Gore ot uma,** completed 1824),[1] fire imagery plays a central structural role. Fire is polysemous in the play, summarizing many essential themes and conflicts, connecting and capsuling major events and themes, and serving as a "master image" for the play as a whole. Through frequent references to fire, flame, fumes, and smoke, the idea is implicit that both Moscow and its inhabitants are "burning" with several very different fires. In this essay I shall attempt to uncover the meanings of this essential (but largely unnoticed) fire imagery in Griboedov's play, which provides a fitting frame for the period portrayed, beginning with the 1812 burning of Moscow that saved the city from Napoleon and ending just before the revolutionary "fire" of the 1825 Decembrist uprising.[2] As I shall argue, Griboedov in this play parodically reverses the apocalyptic fire imagery of post-1812 Russian chauvinistic literature (which was often based on the oxymoron of a destructive conflagration that *saved* the nation), replacing it with a satiric vision of a hellish Moscow, burning with the prejudices of its post-Petrine past and scorching anyone trying to "rebuild" the city with new ideas.[3]

Much of Griboedov's comedy is structured on the punning interplay between words formed from two similar-sounding (and etymologically linked) roots: *goret'* (to burn) and *gore* (woe—one of the two key words of the title).[4] Even several character names reflect this interplay. In the original draft of the play, for example, the main character (called Chatsky in later drafts) was named Chadsky, reflecting immediately a connection with *chad* (fumes, smoke), and thus with fire, that became somewhat more oblique in the published version of the play.[5] His "woe" is caused in part by the gossip, liar, and cardsharp Zagoretsky, whose name derives from *zagoret'sia* (to catch fire)—a name justified when he fans the flames of rumor that Chatsky "has gone out of his mind" (a rumor begun at the ball by Sophia as vengeance against Chatsky's caustic tongue, 3.438-44).[6] The only other character besides Chatsky who feels "woe" in and is "burned" by fiery Moscow is Chatsky's old friend Platon Mikhailovich *Gorich,* whose name comes from *gorech'* (bitterness), which derives from *gore* (woe).[7]

As in much world literature, fire is connected with change on one level of Griboedov's play. Indeed, the play can be read as being about the impossibility of change in Moscow, a city that even "fire" (both the historical fire of 1812 and the symbolic fire of "intelligent" ["umnye"] critics like Chatsky) cannot change.[8] In this article, I shall explore three distinct layers of fire imagery in **Woe from Wit** and their interaction: the fire of passion associated with Chatsky; the portrayal of Moscow as a hellish "burning city"; and the attempt of the Moscow upper classes to extinguish the "fire" of revolution and, with it, any form of "enlightenment."

THE FIRE OF PASSION: CHATSKY

Throughout Griboedov's play, Chatsky is associated with passion, heat, and fire. He is described by himself and others through nouns like *zhar* (heat), *pylkost'* (ardor [etymologically: "burning"]), *dym* (smoke), and *chad* (fumes). This "fire" with which Chatsky is linked has at least three distinct meanings: love, choler, and enlightenment. In the first part of the play, much of the fire imagery is commonplace, reflecting the "sacred fire of love" felt by Chatsky for Sophia.[9] At Chatsky's first entrance, the stage directions indicate that he immediately kisses Sophia's hand "with passion" (*s zharom*; literally, "with heat"). When Chatsky realizes that a similar "fire" is no longer burning in Sophia, he says to her that he would not even wish on an enemy what is now "*boiling*, agitating, raging (*kipit, volnuet, besit*)" in him (3.52).[10] Indeed, he criticizes his rival Molchalin for *lacking* this fiery passion.[11] He explicitly uses imagery of fire in stressing his love for her: "Order me to walk through *fire*, and I'll go as if to dinner (*Velite zh mne v ogon': poidu, kak na obed*) (1.445). Sophia's caustic retort—"*All well and good if you burn up*, but what will happen if you don't?" (*Da, khorosho sgorite, esli zh net?* 1.446)—unwittingly portends a later truth: that Chatsky will be "burned" by the "fire" raging in Moscow society. Sophia's father, Famusov, also identifies Chatsky with fire when he says (after realizing that not simply one but two "undesirable" suitors—his clerk Molchalin and now Chatsky—are in love with his daughter): "Now, *out of the fire and into the flame*" (*v polmia iz ognia*, 1.482 [the equivalent of "out of the frying-pan and into the fire"]).

On a second level, Chatsky's connection with fire may also be explained through the famous theory of "humors" that saw the healthy body—paralleling the universe—as containing a balance between four fluids or "humors," each of which corresponded to one of the elements: black bile (earth), blood (air), phlegm (water), and yellow bile/choler (fire).[12] According to this theory, a person's character could be explained by the prominence of one humor. In Chatsky's case, the dominant humor is clearly yellow bile (*zhelch'*), giving him his "fiery" character.[13] Chatsky's link with yellow bile is made explicit several times during the play. As Sophia says to him, "It is obvious that you are ready to pour your bile (*zhelch' . . . izlit'*) on everyone" (3.30-31). And in his last speech in act 4, Chatsky states:

Теперь не худо б было сряду
На дочь и на отца
И на любовника глупца,
И на весь нир *чзлчмь бсю жслчь* и всю досаду.

(4.503-6)

(Now it's not a bad idea
To vent all my bile and fury
On the daughter, on the father,
On the stupid lover, and on all the world.)

Chatsky's "yellow bile"/fire is implicitly opposed to the "phlegm"/water of his foil and rival, the "stupid lover" Molchalin, whose name derives from the root for "silence" (*molch—*), recalling the widespread Russian idea that a life without trouble is possible only by being "*quieter* than *water*, lower than *grass*" (*tishe vody, nizhe travy*).[14]

Chatsky's fiery choler is directed largely against the servile spirit of self-advancement among Moscow's bureaucrats and the virulent hatred of change among its decrepit doyens. Already in his first appearance on stage, he sarcastically expresses his certainty that no change has occurred there during the three years he has been absent:

Что нового покажет мне Москва?
Вчера был бал, а завтра будет два.
Тот сватался—успел, а тот дал промах
Всё тот же толк, и те ж стихи в альбомах.

(1.353-56)

(What new things can Moscow show me?
There was a ball yesterday and there will be two tomorrow.
One man has managed to get engaged, and one man has failed.
The conversations are the same, as are the verses in the albums.)

Throughout the play, this unchanging Moscow is associated with "the old," metonymically represented by its "gerontocracy" (the malicious old aristocracy who dominate the city); for the young Chatsky "what is older is worse" (*Chto staree, to khuzhe*, 2.345-46). This Moscow gerontocracy is so hateful to Griboedov and his fiery hero that Simon Karlinsky has fairly stated that one of the main themes of the play is "gerontophobia."[15] The attempts of this gerontocracy, and of the bureaucracy with which it is linked, to thwart change and to retain the standards of the past (specifically those of the epoch of Catherine II) are symbolically prefigured in the first scene of the play when the servant Liza sets a clock forward at daybreak so that it will chime the hour and signal Molchalin to leave Sophia's room. But Liza is caught by Famusov, who stops the clock—an emblem for his actions in the rest of the play.

In Griboedov's play, the Moscow gerontocracy fights the fire of change, challenge, and nonconformity in Chatsky and tries to "extinguish" it, declaring Chatsky

194

mad and thus trying to eliminate the harm that his fire can bring;[16] in Moscow, only those who *lack* fire (like Molchalin) can be successful. As Chatsky states:

> Теперь пускай из нас один,
> Из молодых людей, найдется—враи исканйб,
> Не треяуя ни мест, ни повышенья в чин,
> В науки он вперит ум, алчущий познаний.
> Или в душе его сам боя возбудит *жар*
> К искусствам творческим, высоким и прекрасным,—
> Они тотчас: разбой! *уожар!*
> И прослывет у них мечтателем! опасным!!

> (2.376-83)

(Now, let's suppose that one of us,
One of the younger people, could be found who was an enemy of
    self-advancement,
Who did not demand a position or promotion to a higher rank,
Who would focus his mind on scholarship, in quest of knowledge.
If God himself should awaken a *passion* in his soul
For the creative arts, sublime and lofty,
These people would immediately yell: "Robbery!" "*Fire!*"
And among them he would gain the reputation as a dreamer and a danger.)

As this speech reflects, the fire burning in Chatsky is, on another level, the fire of "enlightenment" and learning—a "passion" (*zhar*) that challenges the obscurantist upper classes, who cry "fire" at any sign of deviation from their unchanging bureaucratic norm. In an earlier draft of this speech, the clash between Chatsky and these groups is even stronger, with Chatsky emphasizing their intolerance of anyone "who *burns with a different fire*" (*inym ognem goriashchii*: Griboedov, *Gore ot uma*, 1969, 164). As is clear from this version, even at an early stage of writing, Griboedov was opposing two very different fires: one raging in Chatsky and one burning in Moscow.

THE BURNING CITY

From Chatsky's first scene in the play (act 1, scene 7) through his last (act 4, scene 14), he describes Moscow society through imagery of fire and smoke. When he returns to the city after his three-year absence, he is even prepared to forget its foibles, although he well remembers the repulsive and ridiculous characters who have peopled it. His desire to see Sophia has even created a degree of homesickness in him, expressed through a Latin proverb about smoke:

> Опять увидеть их мне суждено судьбой!
> Жить ними надоест, и в ком не сыщем пятен?
> Когда ж постранствуем, воротимся домой,
> *И уым омечесмва нам сдауок ч урчя мен!*

> (1.383-86; emphasis in original)

(I am again fated to see them all again!
I'll be bored by living among them, but in whom can one not find fault?
When you have been traveling, and you finally return home
Even the smoke of one's Fatherland is sweet and pleasant.)

The expression used by Chatsky about the "smoke of one's Fatherland" being "sweet and pleasant" comes from a Latin proverb (Et fumus patriae est dulcis), taken from Ovid, which had its ultimate origin in Homer's *Odyssey*.[17] As Griboedov's play develops, this expression acquires clear irony: the play becomes a kind of "anti-*Odyssey*," where the hero, who (like Odysseus) had pined for the "smoke of his fatherland," cannot tolerate the place for even a single day.

Within Griboedov's play, the "*smoke of the fatherland*" is linked, on one level, with the Moscow *fire* of 1812—that "pyric victory" that saved the city from Napoleon, destroying more than 6,000 of its 9,000 buildings. In Russian literature and culture in the years after 1812, this "great fire" was a symbol of hope and salvation. As Tsar Alexander I proclaimed after the burning of Moscow: "God has chosen the venerable capital of Russia to save not just Russia but all of Europe through her sufferings. Her fire was the *conflagration of freedom* for all the kingdoms of the earth."[18] In literature like N. M. Shatrov's panegyric "The Fire of Moscow: To the Year 1812" ("Pozhar Moskvy: 1812 godu," 1813 or 1814), this fire had been similarly praised as a savior of Europe from Napoleon. As Shatrov describes the fire:

> И *зауораемя* Москва.
> *Дым* черный стелется, клубится,
> И се перестает светиться
> Москвы блестящая глава.

> Москва несчастная *уылаем*
> Москва *уорчм* двенадцать дней.

> (Lotman and Al'tshuller, *Poety,* 589)

(And Moscow is *burning up.*
The black *smoke* spreads and curls
And, behold, the brilliant head of Moscow
Stops gleaming.

Poor Moscow is *ablaze,*
Moscow has been *burning* for 12 days.)

I would argue that Griboedov takes fire imagery like that in much chauvinistic literature and rhetoric appearing after the "Great Patriotic War" of 1812—imagery of an apocalyptic, purgative fire creating the "new earth" foreseen in Revelation—and uses it ironically to challenge, rather than to praise, contemporary Russia.

The fire of 1812 is discussed explicitly in act 2 in a conversation among Famusov, Skalozub, and Chatsky. Skalozub describes the massive rebuilding project that has taken place in Moscow: "In my judgment, / The *fire* greatly helped improve its looks" (*Po moemu suzhdeniiu / Pozhar sposobstvoval ei mnogo k ukrasheniiu*, 2.319-20).[19] To this, Famusov responds in agreement: "Since then the roads, the sidewalks, / The houses, and everything has been built anew" (*na novyi lad*; 2.322-23). But Chatsky immediately rejoins:

> Дома новы, но предрассудки стары.
> Порадуйтесь, не истребят
> Ни годы их, ни моды, ни *уожары.*
>
> (2.324-26)

(The houses are new, but the prejudices old.
Rejoice, that neither years
Nor modes, nor *fires* will wipe them out.")

Thus, while Skalozub sees the fire as purgative—the current commonplace—Chatsky argues that even "fire" cannot change Moscow, a city that has, paradoxically, been "captured" by the customs and language of the defeated French.

Chatsky prays for a "spark" that will start a different fire—one that would consume Russia's habit of blindly imitating foreign customs and ignoring its own native traditions:

> Я одаль воссылал желанья
> Смиренные, однако вслух,
> Чтоб истребил господь нечистый этот дух
> Пустого, рабского, слепого подражанья;
> Чтоб искру заронил он в ком-нибудь с душой,
> Кто мог бы словом и примером
> Нас удержать, как крепкою вожжой,
> От жалкой тошноты по стороне чужой.
>
> (3.592-99)

(I, at a distance, sent up my wishes,
Which were humble but said aloud,
That God should destroy that unclean spirit
Of empty, slavish, blind imitation;
That He should place a *spark* in someone with a soul
Who could by his example and his word
Restrain us, as with strong reins,
From pitiful yearning for some foreign land.)

Chatsky's words (in a speech that at points prefigures views of the later Slavophiles) describe a prayer to God ("desires sent upward") to "destroy the unclean spirit / . . . / of empty, slavish, blind imitation" in Moscow.[20] The use of the phrase "the *unclean* spirit" ("*nechistyi dukh*") links Moscow's "spirit of imitation" with the devil, who was often called "the *unclean* force" ("*nechistaia sila*") in Russian culture; it thus creates an implicit comparison of Moscow to hell.

I would argue that this implicit image of Moscow as hell assumes three different but related forms in Griboedov's play: a generic "burning city"; Babylon; and Sodom. This Muscovite "inferno" is described by Chatsky (in almost Dantean terms) as populated by:

> . . . Мучителей толпа,
> В любви предателей, в вражде неутомимых,
> Рассказчиков неукротимых,
> Нескладных умников, лукавых простяков,
> Старух зловещих, стариков,
> Дряхлеющих над выдумками, вздором.
>
> (4.508-13)

(. . . A crowd of torturers,
Of betrayers of love who are indefatigable in hatred,
Of indomitable tellers of false tales,
Unsuccessful wits, cunning simpletons,
Malicious old ladies and old men,
Who are growing senile over their made-up tales and nonsense.)[21]

Immediately following this description of upper-class Muscovites, Chatsky describes their Moscow through the implicit metaphor of a burning city in his last speech in the play:

> Безумным вы меня прославили всем хором.
> Вы правы: из *оуня* тот выйдет невредим,
> Кто с вами день пробыть успеет,
> Подышит воздухом одним
> И в нем рассукок уцелеет.
>
> (4.514-18)[22]

(You have pronounced me mad in a single chorus.
Correct you are. Any person will escape from *fire* unscathed
Who succeeds in spending a day with you,
Who breathes the same air that you do,
And whose reason remains intact.)

Here Chatsky compares Moscow society to a fire that chars any reasonable person who comes into contact with it; he leaves Moscow, having been "burned" by its senseless fire of malice, rumor, lies, and servile self-advancement.

On a second level, Moscow is implicitly compared to the burning city of Babylon—a symbol of a "fallen and corrupt existence, the *opposite* of the Heavenly Jerusalem and of Paradise."[23] Indeed, this comparison may help explain the important interplay between grief and burning (between *gore* and *goret*') that runs throughout the play. In Revelation 18, the burning of Babylon by God in retribution for the sins of the city is described in the Russian Bible through several famous verses intertwining imagery of grief and fire:

> . . . *горе, горе* тебе, великий город Вавилон, город крепкий! Ибо в один час пришел суд твой. . . .
> И видя *дым* от ηожара ее, возопили, говоря: какой город подобен городу великому!
>
> (Откровение 18:10 and 18)

Since the King James version of the English Bible does not correspond exactly to the Russian Bible here, I shall translate into literal English:

> *Woe, woe* unto you, o great city of Babylon, o mighty city. For in one hour your judgment has come. . . . And when [the merchants and ship captains] saw the *smoke* from its *fire,* they cried out, What city is like this great city?
>
> (Revelation, 18:10 and 18)[24]

In originally naming his play **Gore umu** (**Woe to wit**)—a phrase that creates a direct parallel to the first phrase of this biblical quotation with its use of the word *Gore* plus the dative case—and in strongly emphasizing fire imagery throughout his drafts, Griboedov was, I argue, making an implicit comparison between the "great city" of Moscow and the burning city of Babylon.

Within the play there is also an implicit comparison of Moscow to Sodom, where God "*rain[ed] brimstone and fire*" (*dozhdem seru i ogon'*) and "the *smoke* [*dym*] was rising from the earth like smoke from a furnace" (Gen. 19:24, 28). The word *sodom* (with a small "s," meaning "disorder," "chaos," or "noise" in early nineteenth-century Russia) is used explicitly in act 2 of the play. After Chatsky criticizes fawning courtiers like Famusov's late uncle Maksim Petrovich (who was promoted for the fact that after once accidentally falling while bowing to Empress Catherine the Great, he purposefully fell a second and a third time upon seeing her amusement; 2.78ff.), Famusov chastises Chatsky and his "radical" ideas: "Well, I expect disorder from this" ("Nu, tak i zhdu *sodoma*," 2.155-56). To an audience that is watching (as opposed to reading) the play, the word *sodom* is clearly ambiguous ("disorder" or "Sodom" itself).[25] Given this hint, it may not be coincidental that Chatsky says in his last speech, "Von iz Moskvy! Siuda ia bol'she ne ezdok / Begu, *ne oglianus*'" (I'm leaving Moscow! I won't come here again. / I rush and *won't look back,*" 4.519-20). The overtones of the words *ne oglianus'* recall the warning of one of the angels to Lot as they were leading them out of Sodom: "Save your soul; don't look back" (*ne ogliadyvaisia nazad*) (Gen. 19:17). Like Lot, Chatsky dares not look back on the "burning city" of Moscow.

Griboedov's play in effect reverses a cultural tradition that had been frequent in Russia from the mid-fifteenth through the late eighteenth century and had arisen, once again, after the Russian victory over Napoleon in 1812: that of depicting Moscow, or Russia as a whole, as the Third Rome, paradise, heaven-on-earth, or New Jerusalem. This tradition was graphically represented in a famous mid-sixteenth-century icon called "The Church Militant" (*Tserkov' voinstvuiushchaia*), which celebrated

Ivan IV's victory over the Tartar horde and his capture of the city of Kazan by depicting the Archangel Michael leading troops from the burning city of Sodom (Kazan), to a paradise or holy city, a "city on a hill" (Moscow), where the Mother of God sits enthroned.[26] In depicting *Moscow* as the burning city, Griboedov joined a number of other important writers of Russia's Golden Age (including, at times, Pushkin and Lermontov) who were *reversing* such traditions, portraying Moscow and/or Russia not as paradise but as hell.[27]

THE FIRE OF REVOLUTION

A third layer of pyric imagery in Griboedov's play centers around the symbolic "fire" of revolution. As the French Revolutionary writer Sylvain Maréchal wrote in his 1799 *Voyages of Pythagoras* (the six volumes of which were translated into Russian from 1804 to 1809 and achieved great popularity): "with the smallest *spark* a *great fire* can be ignited."[28] This image of the fire of revolution spread throughout nineteenth- and twentieth-century Russian literature and culture, used by writers as diverse as Petr Viazemsky, Aleksandr Odoevsky, Dostoevsky, and Blok, among others, and provided the title for several journals advocating revolution (including Lenin's *Iskra* [*The Spark*]).

The connection of fire with revolution in original Russian literature and culture goes back at least to Count Rostopchin's anti-Napoleonic placards and brochures. In one 1807 brochure, for example, he stated about the French Revolution: "*The Revolution is a fire (pozhar), the French are pieces of smoldering wood (goloveshki), and Napoleon is the stoker (kochegar).*"[29] This link of fire with revolution is also implied in Petr Viazemsky's fable "The Conflagration" ("Pozhar," 1820), which was not printed at the time because of its Aesopian fire imagery. The poem tells of a conversation between the owner of a house that is burning and a "councillor" (*sovetnik*). The councillor tells the owner that he himself avoids such risks by not using fire to light his house at night or to heat it in winter. The owner, however, retorts that "man was not born to go numb in the dark" (*kostenet' vpot'makh*): "*Fire can be a danger but more often brings use to us. And your tomblike house is suitable only to make wolves freeze to death (chtob v nem morit' volkov)* and for owls to weave their nests" (*gnezda vit' sycham*).[30] As V. S. Nechaeva notes in her commentary to this poem: "Conflagration (*pozhar*) is often a symbol of revolt, of revolution, the reason for which is fire (*ogon'*)—a symbol of knowledge and enlightenment, both of which are opposed to the 'tomblike house' of Russia, in which reactionaries suppressed knowledge out of fear of revolutionary activity"[31] Imagery of revolutionary fire was also used by Aleksandr Odoevsky in his response to some verses sent by Pushkin in 1827 to the Decembrists imprisoned in Siberia:

Наш скорбный труд не пропадет:
Из ыскры возгорчмся ᵤлам̈я,
И ᴛлам̈я вновь зажжем *свободы.*[32]

. . . . .

(Our mournful labors won't be in vain,
From a spark there will flash a flame

. . . .

And once again we will light the *fire of freedom.*)

In short, it was not without precedent when Dostoevsky in his famous antirevolutionary novel *The Possessed (Besy,* 1872) had his provincial governor, Lembke, say about the fires being set by revolutionaries: "The *conflagration* is in people's minds, and not on the roofs of houses" ("*Pozhar* v umakh, a ne na kryshakh domov"); or when Aleksandr Blok wrote in his notebooks about the "terrible tongues of the revolutionary flame" ("strashnykh iazykov *revoliutsionogo plameni*").[33]

In Griboedov's play, "fire" is often a symbol of enlightenment, education, or new ideas, which obscurantist, upper-class Muscovites frequently mistook for revolution. Thus, **Woe from Wit** attacks the crusade against enlightenment that often accompanied the chauvinism arising after the war of 1812. As Anatole Mazour has written:

> The war of 1812-14 . . . and especially the burning of Moscow, greatly stimulated the chauvinistic sentiment. It was a call to die-hard conservatives to raise their banner . . . and declare open warfare against the . . . "Jacobin spirit." . . . Fighting political windmills everywhere, the authorities saw revolution in the most timorous opposition. . . . The government . . . considered all societies potential *Carbonari* and forbade them entirely, except those sponsored by itself. Hence the crusade against revolution in Russia turned into a petty persecution of various developments of national life, destroying thus the finest elements within the state.[34]

Griboedov's play depicts just such "petty persecution," portraying Famusov, his friends and colleagues as what contemporaries like the future Decembrist N. I. Turgenev dubbed "gasil'niki" (Extinguishers)—people who, in the conservative reaction occurring after the fire of 1812, tried to "extinguish" the fires of change and enlightenment within Russian society by opposing any new ideas.[35] Famusov embodies typical views of these *gasil'niki* when he states:

> Ученье—вот чума, ученость—вот причина,
> Что нынче, пуще, чем когда,
> Безумных развелось людей, и дел, и мнений.
>
> (3.522-24)

(Learning—that's the plague; erudition—that's the
    reason
That now, more than ever,
There are more mad people, mad deeds, and mad
    opinions.)[36]

Others at the ball support this attack on learning, justifying their "noms parlants" as they blame education for all contemporary evils: Khlestova (Famusov's sister-in-law, whose name comes from the word "to whip") blames schooling of all kinds, especially the Lancaster System "of mutual education" (a system associated with liberal ideas and freethinking at the time, which, in the manner of Mrs. Malaprop in Sheridan's *The Rivals,* she mistakenly calls the "Landcart [= map] system"); Princess Tugoukhovskaya ("Princess Hard-of-Hearing") blames the Pedagogical Institute (where "they give exercises in schism and atheism"—reflecting the fact that four professors had recently been fired for godlessness and other subversive activities); and Colonel Skalozub (whose name comes from the phrase *skalit' zuby* ["to bare one's teeth," "to laugh in a threatening way"]) advocates an Arakcheev-type project for education:

> Я вас обрадую: всеобщая молва,
> Что есть проект насчет лицеев, школ, гимназий;
> Там будут лишь учить по-нашему: раз, два;
> А книги сохранят так, для больших оказий.
>
> (3.535-39)

(I've got good news: there's a rumor circulating
That there is a plan for lycées, schools, gymnasia,
Where they will only teach in our own Russian way—
    left, right, left—
And books will be reserved for special occasions.)

This interpretation of the society surrounding Famusov as a group of "Extinguishers" is further justified when Famusov urges an obscurantist "auto-da-fé": "[I]f you want to stop all evil / Gather all the books, and *burn them all at once*" (Uzh koli zlo presech'; / Zabrat' vse knigi by, da *szhech',* 3.540-41).

Griboedov establishes a context of absurd suspicions by upper-class Muscovites of any intelligent nonconformist or critic, who is immediately taken for a revolutionary. Thus, Famusov declares Chatsky a "Carbonarist" (2.121)—a member of the revolutionary group striving for a constitutional system of government in countries throughout Europe[37]—after he hears Chatsky decry Famusov's beloved ideal, the age of Catherine, as "a regiment of jesters" (*polk shutov,* 2.124) and listens to him disparage Famusov's favorite role model, his uncle Maksim Petrovich:

> Хоть есть охотники поподлгчать веьде,
> Да ныоче смех страшит и держит стыд в узде;
> Недаром жалуют их скупо государи.
>
> (2.118-20)

(Although there still are people who would grovel everywhere,
Now laughter frightens them, and shame holds them in check.
It is not in vain that rulers now reward them poorly.)

Famusov concludes that with statements like this Chatsky will "inevitably be dragged into court" (*upekut pod sud*) and calls him "a dangerous man" (2.152-53, 123). Indeed, Famusov is so convinced of Chatsky's revolutionary intentions that when a servant comes in announcing the arrival of Skalozub, Famusov—in one of the classic Freudian slips in Russian literature—is too upset to understand, taking Chatsky's words "Vas zovut" (You are being called) for the words "A? bunt?" (What? A rebellion?) and declaiming (as was discussed above): "Indeed, I expect disorder" (*sodom*) (2.155-56).

The supposed connection of Chatsky with the "fire" of subversive groups—specifically the Masons and the Carbonarists—is humorously asserted again at the ball, when Zagoretsky (who "burns" with the fire of rumor) spreads the word that Chatsky is mad, even though he at first cannot remember who Chatsky is. In trying to tell this rumor to the old Countess Khriumina (a hard-of-hearing dotard, whose name combines the well-known noble name Riumina with the sound made by a grunting pig [*khriuk*]), Zagoretsky is asked by her: "What's going on? What's going on? Is there a *fire* here ("uzh net li zdes' *poshara* [*sic*])?" (3.478) After being told by Zagoretsky that Chatsky "was wounded in the forehead while in the mountains (*v gorakh izranen v lob*) and went crazy from his wound," the countess says, "What? He's joined the club of Freemasons (*k farmazonam v klob*)? He's become a heathen!" (3.482).[38] This same Khriumina later spreads a rumor to Prince Tugoukhovsky (Prince "Hard-of-Hearing," who can understand even less than she) that the chief of police has come to jail Chatsky and will conscript him into the army as a private because he broke the law and is, to boot, a heathen and "a damned freethinker" (*okaiannyi vol'ter'ianets*); later the Prince's wife says of Chatsky: "[I]t's even dangerous to speak with him / He should have been locked up long ago / . . . / I think that he's simply a Jacobin" (4.252-56, with omissions). In short, Griboedov is satirizing the tendency of upper-class Russian society after the burning of Moscow to confuse the frequently distinct "fires" of enlightenment and revolution.[39]

Those actually trying to light the "fire" of revolution are portrayed as absurd or comical in Griboedov's play (which was completed in May 1824, about nineteen months before the Decembrist revolt). Although Griboedov was friendly with such future Decembrists as Kiukhel'beker, Ryleev, and Bestuzhev, their influence (despite some pre- and post-revolutionary Russian interpretations) seems minimal here.[40] Indeed, the only "revolutionary" in the play is the ludicrous Repetilov, who describes his "most secret union" (*sekretneishii soiuz*) in act 4 using several images of fire. In Repetilov's words his unit consists of "a dozen *hot-heads*" (*Goriachikh* diuzhina golov") (4.96, 116), whose leader, "when he speaks about high honor" has "eyes [that] turn bloodshot" and a face that "is on *fire*" (*gorit*), "as though he was possessed by a demon" (4.156-58). Given the inanity of this "most secret union," it is most unlikely that Griboedov intended this group as a portrait of the future Decembrists (as some commentators have proposed); conversely, it is unlikely that Griboedov is portraying Chatsky as a future Decembrist (as others have argued, beginning with Herzen and continuing with Dostoevsky, Goncharov, and Grigor'ev, among others). It is more likely, I would argue, that the imagery of revolutionary "fire" in Griboedov's play is used more as a portrait of the Moscow "Extinguishers" and their intolerance of any new ideas than as a serious portrait of the revolutionary movement itself.[41]

In sum, I have argued that through the imagery of fire Griboedov is describing the obscurantist Moscow of the upper classes (including both bureaucrats like Famusov and army officers like Skalozub), who opposed any change in Russia after the war of 1812 yet continued to borrow their language, conduct, and clothing from the French whom they had defeated. Griboedov depicts a stagnant Moscow that is burning with servility and malice, a city that has become a modern Babylon or Sodom and that, in turn, "burns" any idealist who hopes for change. The imagery of fire connects and capsulizes several of the main events and themes of the play: the return to Moscow of Chatsky, burning with love for Sophia; the lack of change in Moscow after its rebuilding (indicating that the fire of 1812 was not the fire of purification that many had hoped for); and the absurdity of the *gasil'niki* of Moscow high society, who saw the fire of revolution in every act of nonconformity and individuality.

Chatsky's hopes at his return to Moscow are charred by a single day there. As he states in a speech at the beginning of act 4, which makes his original name (Chadskii) into another of the many *noms parlants* in the play:

Ну вот и день прошел, и с ним
Все призраки, весь *чад ч дым*
Надежд, которые мне душу наполняли.
· · · · ·

В повозке так-то на пути
Необозримою равниной, сидя праздно,
Всё что-то видно впереди
Светло, синё, разнообразно.
И едешь час, и два, день целый, вот резво,
Домчались к отдыху, ночлег: куда ни взглянешь,
Всё та же гласы и степь, и пусто и мертво! . . .
Досадно, мочи нет, чем больше думать станешь.

(4.24-37, with omissions)

(Well, the day has passed, and with it
All the ghosts, all the *fume and smoke*
Of hope which filled my soul.

. . . . .

In just this way, you drive in your carriage along the
   road,
Sitting idly across the boundless plain.
All the time something is visible ahead,
Bright, blue, and varied.
You drive an hour, two, and then a day,
And finally you've reached your rest, your lodging
   place, but wherever you
      look
There's the same old plain and steppe, and it's empty
   and dead.
The more you begin to think, the more maddening it
   becomes.)

Chatsky's emphasis on the "extinguishing" of the "smoke of hope" in him by Moscow society uses the image of *chad* (the hazardous smoke of a coal that has almost—but not fully—burned out) to imply that the "fire" that had burned in him in the morning has been virtually extinguished by the end of the night and that Moscow has "burned him out."[42] His bitter comparison of Moscow (the "lodging place," to which he has been looking forward and "rushing" on his long trip) to a mirage—a place that from a distance looks "bright, blue, and varied" but in reality is as dull, "dead," and "empty" as the Russian steppe—represents the essence of the city as depicted in the play.[43] By act 4, Chatsky says about his native land, which he had praised earlier by stating that even its smoke is "sweet and pleasant": "And this is my native land. . . . No, for this trip, / I see that I will soon have taken all that I can" (*Net, v nyneshnii priezd, / Ia vizhu, chto ona mne skoro nadoest*) (4.287-88). It is fitting that the stage directions for this scene state that the speech takes place when "the last light is extinguished" (*posledniaia lampa gasnet*) (act 4, scene 10). For the *gasil'niki* of Moscow society have fully "extinguished" the fire of hope that had fueled Chatsky's return to this "burning city"—a hellish place that is "empty" and "dead," a place that even fire cannot change.

Notes

1. The play was first published posthumously, with cuts, in 1833 but not published in full until 1861. Unless indicated otherwise, all emphases in quotations from the play are my addition.

2. The importance of the events of 1812 to Griboedov during the mid-1820s is reflected not only by the overt references to the fire of 1812 in the play but also by the fact that in 1824 (the year that he completed *Gore ot uma*) he even began a tragedy about 1812 (which he never completed). In the surviving sections of this latter play, fire imagery also plays an important role. In the sec-

ond part, Griboedov planned to show the destruction wrought by the 1812 fire and to depict the burning houses of Moscow; in his sketches, he notes that the events of 1812 will arouse in later generations "an *inextinguishable flame* (*ogn' neugasimyi*), a zeal for the glory and freedom of their fatherland" (A. S. Griboedov, *Sochineniia v stikhakh,* ed. I. N. Medvedeva [Leningrad: Sovetskii pisatel', 1967], 328).

3. My argument about Griboedov's parody of the apocalyptic fire imagery in contemporary chauvinistic literature is not intended to challenge the well-known fact that Griboedov was himself a nationalist. Indeed, much of his criticism of upper-class Moscow society reflects his feeling that Russia was ignoring its own native traditions and favoring those of the France it had defeated; he implicitly blames the reforms of Peter the Great for this blind imitation of the West. Indeed, as will be noted below, some of Chatsky's speeches prefigure ideas of the Slavophiles and other nationalists.

Models for this apocalyptic fire imagery had already appeared in Russian literature before the conflagration of 1812. For example, M. A. Dmitriev-Mamonov's 1811 ode to fire called "Ogon'" (Fire) uses the biblical image of creation of "a new heaven and a new earth" out of the apocalyptic destruction of the old as "an allegory for the moral and political rebirth of Russia" (Iu. M. Lotman and M. G. Al'tshuller, eds., *Poety 1790-1810-x godov* [Leningrad: Sovetskii pisatel', 1971], 872). As Dmitriev-Mamonov wrote: "Fire, you devour the impure, / And can beautify the pure / And embrace everything in yourself" (Lotman and Al'tshuller, *Poety,* 721). As David Bethea has observed, this work uses the image of an apocalyptic "great fire" (*ekpyrosis*) resulting in the creation of a new world (*The Shape of Apocalypse in Modern Russian Fiction* [Princeton: Princeton University Press, 1989], 29 n). Works like Dmitriev-Mamonov's to some extent justify Frank Kermode's overbroad generalization that "the mythology of Empire and of Apocalypse are very closely related" (*The Sense of an Ending* [Oxford: Oxford University Press, 1967], 10).

4. Words formed from *gore* and *goret'* in turn interact with the other major word in the title, *um* ("mind," "wit"), to punningly show how the "intelligent" (*um-nyi*) Chatsky is "burned" and receives "woe" (*gore*) when he comes into contact with Moscow's idle, rumormongering high society. As I shall show later in discussing the problems of Moscow, Griboedov's witty punning throughout the play reflects the truth of A. W.

Schlegel's observation in his *Lectures on Dramatic Art and Literature* that "indignation makes a man witty."

Several critics have observed that during Griboedov's time, the word *um* often connoted freethinkers, members of secret societies, and other independent citizens. See Vladimir Orlov, *Griboedov: Ocherk zhizni i tvorchestva* (Moscow: Gosudarstvennoe izdanie khudozhestvennoi literatury, 1954), 127; and Wladimir Troubetzkoy, "Tchatski, ou la Répétition," in *Le Misanthrope au Théâtre: Ménandre, Molière, Griboiedov,* ed. Daniel-Henri Pageaux (Mugron, France: Editions José Feijóo 1990), 281-83. On the role of *umniki* in Russian comedies of Griboedov's time, see Jean Bonamour, *A. S. Griboedov et la vie littéraire de son temps* (Paris: Presses universitaires de France, 1965), 278. On Griboedov's text as a "long conceit or pun on the meaning of the word *um*," see J. Douglas Clayton, "'Tis folly to be wise: The Semantics of *um-* in Griboedov's *Gore ot uma,*" in *Text and Context: Essays to Honor Nils Åke Nilsson,* ed. Peter Alberg Jensen et al. (Stockholm: Almqvist and Wiksell International, 1987), 8ff.

Clayton argues quite convincingly that the title summarizes the main problems of the play, which he sees as a clash between two opposing types of *um*: the "common wisdom" of Moscow society that demands conformity with its values of "nepotism, corruption, [and] foreign fashions" and declares anyone mad who does not share these values; and the *um* of Chatsky, which "criticizes the hypocrisy of Famusov's [i.e. Moscow high society's] *um*" and is often associated with education and enlightenment. As Clayton has suggested, Griboedov's switch from his original title *Gore umu* ("Woe to Wit") to *Gore ot uma* allowed purposeful ambiguity (7 and 9).

5. There has been major controversy surrounding Griboedov's naming of his "Chadsky"/Chatsky. Although Piksanov sees the name as "purely invented" and views the derivation of Chatsky from *chad* as "artificial," Medvedeva argues that this derivation is likely (reflecting Chatsky's tendency to live in "the fumes—*chad*—of ideas and enthusiasm"). Karlinsky sees the name "Chadsky" as suggesting "both that the young man fumes a lot and that his head is in a daze," but El'zon proposes that "Chatsky" is linked with *chaiushchii* (thinking, hoping), recalling the proverb "Zhdut Fomu, chaiut, byt' umu" (which means, very roughly, "They are waiting for Foma, hoping for brains"). Tynianov even suggests that the name reflects a link with that of the philosopher Chaadaev (which was occasionally written as "Chadaev"). As I shall argue below, I believe that the text explains Chatsky's name in act 4, associating it with the "burning" of the hopes with which Chatsky had returned to Moscow in act 1. On this controversy, see V. I. Korovin, commentary to Griboedov, *Gore ot uma* (Moscow: Russkii iazyk, 1984), 132-33; Simon Karlinsky, *Russian Drama from Its Beginnings to the Age of Pushkin* (Berkeley and Los Angeles: University of California Press, 1985), 288; M. D. El'zon, "'Chad'" ili 'chaiat'? O smysle familii 'Chatskii,'" *Russkaia literatura* 24, no. 2 (1981): 182-83; Iu. N. Tynianov, "Siuzhet 'Goria ot uma',"" in *Pushkin i ego sovremenniki,* ed. V. A. Kaverin and Z. A. Nikitina (Moscow: Nauka, 1968), 360-68.

6. All quotes throughout this article are from A. S. Griboedov, *Gore ot uma,* ed. N. K. Piksanov and A. L. Grishulin (Moscow: Nauka, 1969). References will be given to act and line number. Thus, "3.52" is act 3, line 52.

7. Gorich is tied to Moscow because of his wife, Natal'ia Dmitrievna, who, unlike him, loves Moscow's balls, social life, and style. Her constant henpecking reflects the broader theme of misogyny in the play, which Simon Karlinsky has identified as one of its two main themes (the other, "gerontophobia," will be discussed below). As Karlinsky argues: "What is really wrong with Moscow is that it is run by corrupt old men ('the older the worse') and by domineering women of all ages" (292).

It is significant that Gorich longs to leave Moscow and return to the country. Thus, a second theme raised by Gorich and Chatsky (the only two male characters who can be seen as positive) is the opposition between the negative Moscow and the positive rural areas (the home of what Chatsky calls "our bold, intelligent folk" [*umnyi, bodryi nash narod,* 3.615]). Griboedov, therefore, is probably being ironic when he has Famusov threaten to punish Sophia by sending her "to the country (*v derevniu*), to your aunt's, to the backwoods (*glush'*)," where (in her father's words) she will "grieve *woe*" ("*Tam budesh' gore gorevat'*")."

8. On fire and change, see Gaston Bachelard, *The Psychoanalysis of Fire,* trans. Alan C. M. Ross (Boston: Beacon, 1964), 7, 16.

One early indication that change/lack of change will be central to Griboedov's play is the repeated emphasis in the early scenes on clocks and time. The words *chasy* (clock) and *chas* (hour) are repeated four times in the first scene (21 lines) and six times in the first 75 lines. Indeed, the first prop mentioned in the stage directions to act 1, scene 1 is the "large clock."

9. The commonplace image of love as a "sacred fire" was rather frequently used in Russia during the

Golden Age—especially by Romantic writers. For example Lermontov in the "Princess Mary" section of *Hero of our Time* (*Geroi nashego vremeni*, 1840) has Pechorin write in his diary for 3 June: "[A]n electric *spark* ran from my hand to hers; almost all passions begin this way, and we often deceive ourselves greatly in thinking that a woman loves us for our physical or moral qualities. Of course, these qualities prepare and incline their hearts for the reception of the *sacred fire,* but nevertheless it is the first contact that decides the matter" (M. Iu. Lermontov, *Sobranie sochinenii v chetyrekh tomakh* [Moscow: Izdatel'stvo Akademii nauk, 1958-59], 4:406-7).

10. Chatsky's search for a passion that will match his own is reflected in the use of fire imagery for women whom he finds attractive. For example, in an early manuscript for the play, Griboedov had Sophia respond to Chatsky's accusations of Molchalin by "hotly" (*goriacho*) defending the latter, presenting a clear parallelism between her and Chatsky (Griboedov, *Gore ot uma,* 1969, 182). After his rejection by Sophia, Chatsky is attracted to Natal'ia Dmitrievna at the ball: "[Y]ou're such a lot prettier / You've become younger, fresher; / There's *fire,* color, laughter, play in all your features" ("[P]okhorosheli strakh; / Molozhe vy, svezhee stali; / *Ogon',* rumianets, smekh, igra vo vsekh chertakh," 3.233-35).

11. In this speech about his "boiling" love, Chatsky pretends to admire Molchalin, saying to Sophia: "Let's grant him a lively wit, a bold genius. / But is there that passion in him? That feeling? That *ardor* (*pylkost'*) / That would make all the world except for you / Seem just vanity and dust?" (3.43-46). In an earlier draft, Griboedov had emphasized the phlegmatic Molchalin's *lack* of fire even more explicitly, continuing after the penultimate line just quoted: "Seem just laughter and dust? Just *smoke* and trivia and vanity?" (*dym,* meloch' i tscheta) (Griboedov, *Gore ot uma,* 1969, 181).

12. On the theory of humors, which predominated in medicine from Galen through the medieval period and was a frequent source of metaphors in literature from the Renaissance through the early nineteenth century, see E. M. W. Tillyard, *The Elizabethan World Picture* (New York: Vintage Books, n.d), 69-79.

13. The term "fiery" (*ognennyi*) was used for Chatsky by critics from the first appearance of the play. For example, Pushkin in 1825 called Chatsky "fervent" (*pylkii,* etymologically "flaming"), and one 1833 commentary said he was "animated by fiery passions" and "fervid." On such criticism, see A. M. Gordin, ed., *A. S. Griboedov v russkoi kritike* (Moscow: Gosudarstvennoe izdatel'stvo khu-

dozhestvennoi literatury, 1958), 40. According to Orlov, passion and "zeal" (*goriachnost'*, etymologically "hotness") were frequent characteristics of the liberal youth of the 1810s-1820s (*Griboedov,* 121).

14. In the theory of humors, the "cold and moist" phlegmatic type opposes the "warm and dry" choleric type (Tillyard, *Elizabethan World Picture,* 69). Molchalin has some of the typical characteristics of the "phlegmatic" individual: unemotional, even-tempered, calm. His name may also reflect the saying that "silence is a mark of assent" (*molchanie—znak soglasiia*), which originated with Pope Boniface VIII but was popular in Russia (N. S. Ashukin and M. G. Ashukina. *Krylatye slova: Literaturnye tsitaty, obraznye vyrazheniia,* 2d ed. [Moscow: Gosudarstvennoe izdatel'stvo khudozhestvennoi literatury, 1960], 370-71). I am grateful to Monika Greenleaf and Stephen Moeller-Sally for suggesting Molchalin's possible connection with the phlegmatic personality.

15. Karlinsky argues that "all of Chatsky's speeches that identify old age with corruption—beginning with his famous Act II monologue 'And who are the judges'—are quite specifically aimed at the situation in Moscow." He goes on to say that "the trouble with the aged" in this play is that "they shut out the modern world and still see things in eighteenth-century terms" (*Russian Drama,* 292).

16. In a famous January 1825 letter to Katenin, Griboedov himself stressed the opposition between the "intelligent" Chatsky and Moscow society as a whole. As he wrote: "[I]n my comedy there are 25 fools (*gluptsov*) for one intelligent (*zdravomysliashchego*) person. And this person, of course, contradicts the society which surrounds him" (quoted in Tynianov, "Siuzhet 'Goria ot uma'," 348). Pushkin, in a letter to Bestuzhev of the same month, disagreed with Griboedov, stating that the only "intelligent" (*umnoe*) character in the comedy is Griboedov himself; he criticized Chatsky by noting that "the first sign of an intelligent man is to know from the first glance with whom he is dealing and not to cast pearls before Repetilovs"—perhaps an unwitting draft of his own future lines to his muse in "Exegi monumentum" (1836); "And do not contradict the fool" (*I ne osparivai gluptsa*) (letter excerpted in Gordin, *A. S. Griboedov v russkoi kritike,* 40).

17. The image of the "smoke of the fatherland" probably first occurs in Homer's *Odyssey* (book 1, lines 57-59), in a prayer by Athena to Cronus asking him to release Odysseus from the spell of Calypso, who "charms him to forget Ithaca." As Athena states: "Odysseus, however, wanting to catch sight even of *smoke* leaping up from his father-

land, is longing to die" (*The Odyssey,* trans. and ed. Albert Cook [New York: Norton, 1974], 5). The phrase was later used by Ovid (*Epistulae ex Ponto,* 1.3.33), from whom the Latin proverb came (Ashukin and Ashukina, *Krylatye slova,* 243).

In Russia, this phrase had been used as an epigraph for the journal *Rossiiskii muzeum* (*The Russian museum,* 1792-94) and was quoted in a number of poems at the turn of the century, including Derzhavin's poem "The Harp" ("Arfa," 1798)—the probable immediate source of Chatsky's quote. Griboedov has Chatsky quote the last line of Derzhavin's poem in the version that appeared in the journal *Aonidy* (1798-99, book 3, p. 14) (V. I. Korovin, commentary to Griboedov, *Gore ot uma,* 1984, 135). For an interesting short history of this phrase in Russian literature from Derzhavin through Mayakovsky, see Ashukin and Ashukina, *Krylatye slova,* 242-43.

18. Quoted in Ernst Benz, *The Eastern Orthodox Church: Its Thought and Life,* trans. Richard and Clara Winston (New York: Anchor Books, 1963), 188.

19. In an early manuscript of the play, Skalozub made even stronger comments about the effects of the Moscow fire: "In my judgment, the fire flamed as if someone ordered it (*Pozhar kak na zakaz pylal*). It helped to beautify the city. And the style of life has improved." But Chatsky responds, "It was a gloomy year (*chernyi god*) for us and served no purpose" (Griboedov, *Gore ot uma,* 1969, 161).

20. Given the association of Chatsky with fire (as discussed earlier), it would at first appear that Griboedov has Chatsky in mind as the person "with a soul" in whom a "spark" would be placed to destroy the "spirit of . . . blind imitation" in Russia. But as the speech progresses, Griboedov uses imagery implying that such changes could be made in Russia only by a powerful monarch. Indeed, the image of restraint "with strong reins" recalls the iconographic tradition—used in the West since Roman times and in Russia since the eighteenth century—of the emperor as horseman, controlling the "horse" of his empire with strong "reins." This tradition was used, for example, by the sculptor Falconet some fifty years before *Woe from Wit* when he depicted Peter the Great as "the Bronze Horseman." On the symbolism of horsemanship in Russian literature and culture of the eighteenth century, see Stephen Baehr, *The Paradise Myth in Eighteenth-Century Russia: Utopian Patterns in Early Secular Russian Literature and Culture* (Stanford: Stanford University Press, 1991), 50, 58, 213.

The need for a monarch who could eliminate the "harm" caused by Peter's westernizing reforms is implied several lines after this speech when Chatsky says that "for me our North [Russia] has become a hundred times worse" since Peter's reforms, requiring Russians to change their ways and imitate the West: "he gave everything away for a new style— / Our morals and our language and our holy past— / And changed our majestic clothing for another, / Which was like that of a jester (*po shutovskomu obraztsu*)" (3.602-5). Chatsky makes a clear opposition in his speeches between "copies" (*spiski*) or "imitations" (*podrazhan'ia*) and "originals" (*originaly*) (for example, 3.323-24; 3.595), and stresses that Russia should be returned to its own original path and should stop copying the foreign.

21. Since completing this section, I have seen Apollon Grigor'ev's 1862 comment that "Griboedov's comedy is a true *divina commedia*" (Gordin, *A. S. Griboedov* 225).

22. It is probably not coincidental that this last speech (act 4, scene 14) is pronounced on a stage lit with a large number of lanterns and candles—the "fire" illuminating the truth. Famusov at the beginning of the scene explicitly calls for "more candles, more lanterns" (4.420). Indeed, Griboedov seems to have designed the play to move from darkness (the play begins at the first sign of dawn) to light (the "exposure scene" that we are discussing, where Famusov discovers the rendezvous between Sophia and her lover, Sophia realizes the truth about Molchalin, and Chatsky, finally, realizes that Sophia loves Molchalin). The candles and lanterns reveal Moscow's old aristocrats as liars, cheaters, double-dealers, and so forth. On one level, Chatsky is like the raisonneur of eighteenth-century Russian drama, "illuminating" society for what it is.

23. J. E. Cirlot, *A Dictionary of Symbols,* trans. Jack Sage (New York: Philosophical Library, 1962), 21.

24. These verses were (and still are) extremely well known in Russia. Ivan Bunin even used Revelation 18:10 as an epigraph to one edition of his 1915 "The Gentleman from San Francisco."

Chapter 18 of Revelation may provide a clue to the overall meaning of Griboedov's play, uniting the major themes of "fire" and "woe" with the theme of judgment, which is also central to the play (as reflected in important speeches like "A sud'i kto? [Who are the Judges], 2.340ff.). Indeed, like the *gor-* roots (fire, woe) and the *um-* roots (intelligence, mind, wit), the *sud-* root (judgment) is extremely important in the play, reflecting, once again, Griboedov's tendency to stress central themes through a repetition of roots.

25. According to Dal', the phrase "u nikh Sodom i Gomorra" meant "the epitome of disorder." Compare also the proverb "Takoi sodom, chto dym koromyslom" (There is such disorder that all hell is breaking loose; literally, There is such a Sodom that smoke is like a yoke). See Vladimir Dal', *Tolkovyi slovar' zhivogo velikorusskogo iazyka,* 4 vols. (Moscow: Gosudarstvennoe izdatel'stvo inostrannykh i natsional'nikh slovarei, 1956), 4.260; 1.506.

26. In this icon, the victory of Ivan IV at Kazan is allegorically depicted as the victory of Christianity over Islam. As Olga Dacenko has observed, "Christ's armed horsemen advancing in triple rank toward the Heavenly City symbolize the Russian people, God's chosen ones, the 'new Israel.'" See M. W. Alpatov and Olga Dacenko, *Art Treasures of Russia,* trans. Norbert Guterman (New York: Abrams, 1967), 142. I am grateful to Michael Flier of Harvard University for pointing out the possible relevance of this icon in a March 1995 discussion.

27. For a discussion of this tradition of Russia as paradise, third Rome, or a place enjoying the Golden Age, see Baehr, *The Paradise Myth.* On the reversal of this tradition in the early nineteenth century, see ibid., 162-67.

28. James H. Billington, *Fire in the Minds of Men: Origins of the Revolutionary Faith* (New York: Basic Books, 1980), 104.

29. F. V. Rostopchin, *Okh, Frantsuzy!* ed. G. D. Ovchinnikov (Moscow: Russkaia kniga, 1992), 151; Irina Mess-Baehr, "'Soldattskaia' satira i allegoriia v neizdannykh antinapoleonovskikh stikhakh Derzhavina," *Study Group on Eighteenth-Century Russia Newsletter* 8 (1980): 82 n.

30. P. A. Viazemskii, *Stikhotvoreniia,* ed. L. Ia. Ginzburg and K. A. Kumpan (Leningrad: Sovetskii pisatel', 1986), 142.

31. P. A. Viazemskii, *Izbrannye stikhotvoreniia,* ed. V. S. Nechaeva (Moscow: Academia, 1935), 540. Viazemskii, in a letter of 22 March 1820 to A. I. Turgenev that included this poem, encouraged such political readings of the poem, stating that he wondered if this fable would pass the censors because of its allusions (Viazemskii, *Stikhotvoreniia,* 472). His fears proved justified when the censors rejected its publication.

32. Aleksandr Odoevskii, "Strun veshchikh plamennye zvuki," cited in A. S. Pushkin, *Stikhotvoreniia,* ed. B. V. Tomashevskii (Leningrad: Sovetskii pisatel', 1955), 3:819. Odoevskii's acknowledgment of receipt of the "*flaming* sounds of prophetic strings" of Pushkin's poetic lyre (that is, the 1827 poem Pushkin sent to the Decembrists, entitled "Vo glubine sibirskikh rud") in its very first line already signals the relevance of revolutionary fire symbolism. The last four lines of the poem affirm this, stating that the Decembrists (and, implicitly, other freedom fighters) will "forge swords from chains / And once again light the *fire* of freedom / And with this freedom we will pounce upon rulers (*grianem na tsarei*), / And nations (*narody*) will sigh with joy." For Pushkin's text and additional commentary, see 392 and 819.

33. F. M. Dostoevskii, *Polnoe sobranie sochinenii,* 30 vols., ed. B. G. Bazanov et al. (Leningrad: Nauka, 1972-90), 10:395; Aleksandr Blok, *Sobranie sochinenii,* 8 vols. (Moscow: Gosudarstvennoe izdatel'stvo khudozhestvennoi literatury, 1960-63), 7:279. The theme of revolutionary fire in Dostoevsky already begins in *Crime and Punishment,* when Raskol'nikov goes to a tavern to read newspaper accounts about the murder that he has committed and can find only material on (revolutionary) fires being set throughout Petersburg (and, as Luzhin notes, throughout the country); see Dostoevsky, 6:117, 124-25.

34. Anatole Mazour, *The First Russian Revolution, 1825: The Decembrist Movement* (Stanford: Stanford University Press, 1961), 29.

35. See N. I. Turgenev, *Dekabrist N. I. Turgenev,* ed. N. G. Svirin (Moscow: Izdatel'stvo Akademii nauk SSSR, 1936), 396 n. The term "Extinguisher" came from a liberal French newspaper, *Nain Jaune,* which satirized the Old Regime (Turgenev, *Dekabrist,* 387 n). In the 5 January 1815 issue there appeared "The Organic Statutes of the Order of Extinguisher," providing the bylaws of this "group," supposedly created on the order of Mizofan the 2367th: "Wishing to restrain 'the oppressive progress of enlightenment,' Mizofan announces the founding of this order, [which] consists of a grand master, judges or grand extinguisher, commanders, and knights of the double extinguisher." According to these bylaws, "every person entering this order must take a vow of hatred for philosophy, for liberal ideas, and for any constitutional charter" (quoted in Turgenev, *Dekabrist,* 396 n). In his letters, Turgenev sometimes used two cone-shaped candlesnuffers instead of the word "extinguisher" to signify this group (e.g. Turgenev, *Dekabrist,* 193, letter 76); at least once he called the movement by the French equivalent name, describing contemporary Russia as being dominated by "egoism, laziness, and in addition a lack of trust of anything good, a coarse mysticism, and *éteignorisme* (*eten'uarizm*)" (288). I am grateful to Savely Senderovich for giving me the reference to this volume.

36. I. Medvedeva notes that the "learned committee" (*uchenyi komitet*) satirized by Chatsky in his first diatribe against Moscow—a committee on which Sophia's "tubercular relative, an enemy of books" served, and which "demanded with a shout that no one should be literate or should learn" (1.379-82)—was effectively under the control of the "extinguisher of enlightenment M. L. Magnitskii" (*Gore ot uma A. S. Griboedova,* 2d ed. [Moscow: Khudozhestvennaia literatura, 1974], 32).

37. The Carbonarists, faithful to their name (which meant "charcoal-burners"), used imagery of fire throughout their ritual: new members were referred to as sticks or pieces of wood who were to be transformed into "the purer, more useful form of charcoal." Meetings were depicted as "a ritual purification by fire in the furnaces of a secret grotto." Guards standing at the door where the Grand Master entered were called "flames," and two sabers "like flames of fire," were placed on either side of the door (Billington, *Fire in the Minds of Men,* 133).

38. As a Mason (an active member of the lodge *Soedinennye druz'ia* / "Des Amis Réunis" from 1816), Griboedov would have known from Masonic songs that Freemasonry was often called a "sacred fire" by its members. So the old countess's error had an element of truth. This association of Freemasonry with a "sacred fire" appears in Russian Masonic songs as early as the reign of Empress Elizabeth. One song, for example, says that James Keith (the founder of Freemasonry in Russia) "*lit the sacred fire*" of Freemasonry in Russia (*Pesni,* n.p., n.d., 66). Within the Masonic lodge fire imagery (especially images of "sparks" and of burning) was frequent.

It may (or may not) be coincidental that the first question asked by Sophia to Liza in act 1 and repeated by Repetilov in act 4—"What time is it? (*Kotoryi chas?,* 1.15, 17; 4.69)—was also a question asked at the opening of the initiation ceremony into Freemasonry (asked by the grand master to the officers of the lodge). (In the opening of the lodge, the answer is "five minutes to seven"; in the play Liza answers "seven, eight, nine.") Both in the play and in the lodge, the question reflects the important theme of time and of change. See, for example, Harry B. Weber, "*Pikovaia dama*: A Case for Freemasonry in Russian Literature," *Slavic and East European Journal* 12 (1968): 438.

39. It is likely that in this play the Mason Griboedov is reacting against the popular contamination of the Masonic quest for enlightenment and moral change with the revolutionary quest for violent political change.

40. On Griboedov's friendship with future Decembrists, see Karlinsky, *Russian Drama,* 284; Harold B. Segel, "Griboedov, Aleksandr Sergeevich," in *Handbook of Russian Literature,* ed. Victor Terras (New Haven: Yale University Press, 1985), 184-85; and M. Nechkina, *Griboedov i dekabristy,* 3d ed. (Moscow: Khudozhestvennaia literatura, 1977).

41. For a summary of the views of Dostoevsky, Goncharov, and Grigor'ev on this "most secret union," see: A. V. Arkhipova, "Dvorianskaia revoliutsionnost' v vospriiatii F. M. Dostoevskogo," in *Literaturnoe nasledie dekabristov,* ed. V. G. Bazanov and V. E. Vatsuro (Leningrad: Nauka, 1975), 221-24; Bonamour, *A. S. Griboedov,* 318; Medvedeva introduction to Griboedov, *Sochineniia v stikhakh,* 45.

D. P. Costello has suggested that this "most secret union" is a parody of Arzamas (the "mock-secret" society to which Pushkin, Zhukovsky, Batiushkov, and other important literary figures belonged), a group that Griboedov had previously parodied in his 1817 comedy *The Student* and that, like Repetilov's, also met "on Thursdays" (4.96), discussed Byron, and at points created impromptu vaudevilles (4.167); see his argument in his edition of *Gore ot uma* (Oxford: Clarendon Press, 1951), 192.

Simon Karlinsky, on the other hand, sees the "most secret union" as a parody of the secret societies that prepared for the Decembrist rebellion; he argues on the basis of the satire in act 4—including the discussion of themes like legislative chambers (implying constitutional government) and juries (4.101-2)—that Griboedov "must have been aware of the . . . societies that fomented the [Decembrist] rebellion," even though he did not know of their specific plans for rebellion, as an investigation disclosed after Griboedov was arrested (284-85). Following V. Filippov, Karlinsky argues that "Griboedov's familiarity with the inner workings of the Decembrist societies extends even to having Repetilov cite a phrase from Baldassare Galuppi's opera *Didone abbandonata* 'A! non lasciar mi, no, no, no,' which was used by the Decembrists as a password" (295).

For additional material on the supposed Decembrist references in act 4 to Byron and his revolutionary activities, as well as to chambers of deputies (parliamentary systems) and the jury system, see V. I. Korovin's notes to his edition of *Gore ot uma,* 153. For an exhaustive analysis of possible Decembrist connections, see Nechkina, *Griboedov i dekabristy.*

42. The harmfulness of *chad* is expressed in Russian through such proverbs as "S khudoi golovoi, ne

suisia v chad" (If you have a headache, stay away from the fumes), and "Zharko topit', ne boiat'sia chadu" (Those who heat a place warmly are not afraid of the fumes) (Dal', *Tolkovyi slovar'*, 4.580).

43. Another emblem for the unchanging city is the ball, where (as the stage directions state at the end of act 3), "everyone goes round and round" (*vse kruzhatsia*). As I have mentioned, several stage props in the play are also implicit metaphors. See the discussions of the clock (above and note 8) and of the candles and lanterns in the "discovery" scene (note 22).

Adrian Wanner (essay date June 1999)

SOURCE: Wanner, Adrian. "The Misanthrope as Revolutionary Hero: Revisiting Griboedov's Chatskii and Molière's Alceste." *Canadian Slavonic Papers* 41, no. 2 (June 1999): 177-88.

[*In the following essay, Wanner discusses the frequent comparisons between the main characters in Molière's* The Misanthrope *and Griboedov's* Woe from Wit.]

It has been the fate of Chatskii, the hero of Griboedov's comedy *Gore ot uma* (*Woe from Wit*, 1825), to be eternally compared to Alceste, the hero of Molière's *Le misanthrope* (*The Misanthrope*, 1667). At least at first sight, Chatskii and Alceste indeed seem to have much in common. Both of them could be described as aggressively frank personalities who make no secret of the fact that they find their respective aristocratic milieu distasteful. Both have unrequited feelings of love for a woman from that society, and both, with deeply wounded self-esteem, escape to pursue a solitary existence far from the company which they despise. Perhaps not surprisingly in light of these parallels, the juxtaposition of the two characters has become a shopworn cliché in the critical literature devoted to *Woe from Wit*. The French comparatist Maurice Colin went so far as to claim that "one cannot talk about Griboedov without going back to Molière."[1]

The goal of this article is not to review once again all the arguments that could be adduced for or against such a contention.[2] In an age where the author has been declared dead and the locus of meaning has shifted from the text producer to the text recipient, studies of "sources" and "influence" have become a somewhat problematic endeavor. To quote Linda Hutcheon's formulation, "on the one hand, we are dealing with *authorial* intent and with the historical issue of sources and influences; on the other, it is a question of *reader* interpretation whereby visible sources become signs of plagiarism, and influences yield to 'intertextual' echoes."[3]

In accordance with the shift of critical attention from the author to the reader, the discussion that follows will approach the tortuous interrelationship between Alceste and Chatskii as a phenomenon of reader response.[4] A comparison of the reception history of *The Misanthrope* and *Woe from Wit* will demonstrate that the strongest link between Chatskii and Alceste exists less on the textual level, which has been the focus of previous criticism, than in the parallel pattern of (mis)readings generated by the two plays.

To be sure, there can be no "innocent" reading. Every act of assigning meaning to a literary text is conditioned by a variety of external factors, including a host of unspoken ideological presuppositions. It is important to note that this observation applies not only to the naive amateur reader, but also, and perhaps even more so, to the seemingly disinterested literary scholar. The relationship between Chatskii and Alceste presents a case in point: far from being an "objective" fact of comparative literature, the similarity between the two characters is in fact eternally constructed and disconstructed in the discourse of literary criticism. Beyond asserting a parallel or difference between two literary figures, this discourse frequently pursues an unstated political or nationalist agenda. At its core, the comparison involves questions of national prestige, since it positions one's own cultural heritage against that of the other. In this process, the Russian position evolves over time from a feeling of inferiority vis-à-vis the French toward the proclamation of Russian superiority.

It is noteworthy that the connection between Chatskii and Alceste was drawn already by the earliest readers of *Woe from Wit*. Alceste's name emerged in the critical response following the first, fragmentary publication of the play in the almanac *Russkaia Talia* (1825). This first rapprochement between the two characters was dominated by a sense of Russian cultural backwardness. A comparison between Molière and Griboedov could only highlight the latter's inferior status. The journalist M. A. Dmitriev, who had a negative opinion of Griboedov's comedy, went so far as to accuse the author of plagiarism. He claimed in *Vestnik Evropy* that Chatskii was nothing but a "caricature" of Molière's Alceste. The vaudeville writer A. I. Pisarev expressed a similar opinion. According to him Griboedov tried in vain to copy Molière's immortal hero: whereas Alceste is a noble character, chastising the "real, eternal reasons" of human misery, Chatskii is nothing but a paltry malcontent upset over futile trifles.[5] This judgement was somewhat mitigated by V. A. Ushakov, who also stressed the secondary character of *Woe from Wit*, but this time showed Chatskii in a positive light. He claimed that, far from being misanthropes, the two characters are in fact secret lovers of humanity. As he states: "Neither Alceste nor Chatskii can be accused of hating people. On the contrary: the wish to better the lot of humanity was the only reason for their rude behavior."[6]

The idea of Chatskii as a copy of Alceste assumed canonical status with A. N. Veselovskii's article "Al'tsest i Chatskii," which was later reprinted several times and became a widely read and quoted "classic" in its field.[7] Whereas none of the earlier critics had deemed it necessary to validate their claims with a concrete comparison of Griboedov's and Molière's texts, Veselovskii based his interpretation on a close reading of the two plays. He saw not only similarities between the heroes and the plots of *Woe from Wit* and *The Misanthrope,* but detected a whole row of verse quotations which Griboedov allegedly borrowed from *The Misanthrope* and other comedies of Molière. Veselovskii's findings did not go uncontested, however. His article provoked several polemic retaliations, the most authoritative of which is N. K. Piksanov's monograph on Griboedov and Molière.[8] Piksanov strives to demonstrate the arbitrariness of most of Veselovskii's parallels. After discussing the body of critical literature devoted to foreign influences on Griboedov, Piksanov himself undertakes a detailed comparison of *Woe from Wit* and *The Misanthrope.* At the end, only a very few uncontested points remain concerning the character of the central hero and certain elements of the plot. Even here, Piksanov maintains that it is difficult to assert whether these parallels are the result of a conscious borrowing or of pure coincidence.

Piksanov ends his book with a resounding statement of Griboedov's independence and originality. *Woe from Wit,* in his opinion, is a highly original Russian creation which by far transcends its possible French source of inspiration. This patriotic approach was later to prevail in Soviet criticism, especially after the recognition of Western influence on Russian classics became anathema under Stalin. In a curious reversal of A. I. Pisarev's position quoted above, the Soviet critic A. L. Shtein, in a 1962 study on critical realism in Russian drama, declared Alceste to be a negative and Chatskii a positive hero. Although Alceste criticizes certain aspects of French society, he is himself a ridiculous figure, whereas Chatskii, in Shtein's opinion, incorporates the best "progressive" and "revolutionary" tendencies of the Russian people. In Shtein's treatment Griboedov becomes something like an honorary Socialist Realist *avant la lettre.* As he states: "The image of Chatskii with his forceful striving away from routine to a free life prophetically pointed to the direction in which our history would develop, prophetically pointed to the great revolutionary potential of the people *(narod)*."[9]

The pursuit of a nationalist agenda is by no means the monopoly of Soviet scholarship. Whereas the Soviets tended to belittle or to dismiss the French influence on Russian literature for reasons of national prestige, the French regard the impact of their literature in Russia and other countries as a matter of pride. This becomes evident in the work of the French scholar Jean Bonamour, who studied the problem of Molière's influence on *Woe from Wit* in his 1965 monograph on Griboedov. Since the textual parallels between *The Misanthrope* and *Woe from Wit* had been convincingly dismissed by Piksanov, it was necessary to look for correspondences on another level. Bonamour finds them in what he calls the "primary intuition" of both plays—a conception which is sufficiently vague that it can be proved neither right nor wrong. As Bonamour puts it: "It is not impossible that in his concept of *Woe from Wit* Griboedov wanted to be the Molière of his age, not by imitating him, but by going back to the primary and profound intuition of the author of *The Misanthrope*."[10]

We simply do not know whether Molière was for Griboedov a "frère intérieur," as Bonamour believes. If we understand the relationship between Alceste and Chatskii as a problem of "influence," we are left with unprovable speculations. A close comparison of the texts produces, as Piksanov has demonstrated, only dim insights. Having no clear evidence for a connection between Alceste and Chatskii *a priori,* the only fact that we can assert with certainty are the strong links created *a posteriori* by the reading public. Curiously enough, certain textual parallels serving as evidence for a connection between the two plays were in fact, as Piksanov has shown, *created* by people who believed in this connection in the first place.

The history of translations offers a case in point. *Woe from Wit* had a clear impact on the form and spirit of the Russian translations of Molière. The French alexandrines were rendered, using Griboedov's meter as a model, into iambic lines of varying length.[11] Of special interest are Alceste's last words, uttered when he is about to leave Parisian society to set out for the "desert:"

> . . . chercher sur la terre un endroit écarté
> où d'être homme d'honneur on ait la liberté.
>
> (To look for a remote place on earth
> Where one has the liberty to be a man of honor)

I. P. Elagin, the first Russian translator of *The Misanthrope,* rendered this passage as follows: ". . . stanu iskat' na zemle takogo dikogo mesta, gde ne vospreshchaetsia byt' chestnym chelovekom."[12] After the appearance of *Woe from Wit,* Alceste's words were translated by T. Shchepkina-Kupernik as:

> I budu ugolka iskat' vdali ot vsekh,
> Gde mog by chelovek byt' chestnym bez pomekh.

and by N. Kholodkovskii as:

> I budu ia iskat',—naidetsia l' ugolok
> Gde chestnyi chelovek svobodno zhit' by mog.[13]

The translation of "endroit" with "ugolok" is clearly modeled after Chatskii's final exclamation:

> poidu iskat' po svetu,
> Gde oskorblennomu est' chuvstvu ugolok.

The similarity between Alceste's and Chatskii's last words, a cornerstone of Veselovskii's textual rapprochement between *The Misanthrope* and *Woe from Wit,* was thus artificially reinforced by the translators. Exactly the same phenomenon, but the other way around, can be observed in the French translation of Chatskii's last statement, included in a critical article by Mikhail Achkinazi:

> Je vais chercher sur la terre un endroit écarté
> où puisse s'abriter le sentiment outragé.[14]

A French reader with no knowledge of Russian must have been struck by the similarity of these lines with Molière's and would probably have concluded that this is clear evidence of a literary borrowing.

This example shows that the relationship between *The Misanthrope* and *Woe from Wit* has less to do with influence and authorial intention than with literary reception. If we compare the reader response to Alceste and Chatskii, we discover some rather striking parallels. Both heroes were canonized as fighters for "truth" and "progress" for reasons which depended more on social and political history than on their intrinsic literary qualities. If there are indeed considerable differences between the two plays, the reception of Alceste and Chatskii, or rather their *myth,* developed very much along the same lines. While both characters were originally understood by their contemporary public in a multidimensional way, leaving room for considerably divergent interpretations and polemics between clashing viewpoints, they were later streamlined in a unidimensional sense to fit into preconceived ideological patterns.

Both *The Misanthrope* and *Woe from Wit* are characterised by a certain semantic indeterminacy. While Chatskii and Alceste criticize the shortcomings of their society and therefore could be seen as the mouthpiece of the author, they are at the same time discredited by their excessive behavior, their "blind spots," and by the development of the plot. Both plays end with the defeat of the protagonist, who leaves in disgrace, unable to realize any of his ideals. The society which ostracizes him and was the target of his critical attack remains unimpressed by his harangues and unaltered by his moral

preaching. For a traditional "raisonneur," this is certainly an unusual fate, and his criticism seems, at least dramaturgically speaking, considerably weakened. This is a rather bewildering outcome for a reader who wants to identify Alceste or Chatskii as the positive character embodying the play's "message."

As a result, both *The Misanthrope* and *Woe from Wit* initially provoked a certain confusion and consternation. None of Molière's other characters incited a greater spate of contradictory interpretations than Alceste. Is he a comic or a tragic figure, a negative or a positive hero? There can be little doubt, especially if we look at the original subtitle of Molière's play, "L'atrabilaire amoureux" (The Grumbles in Love), that Alceste was conceived as the comic incarnation of a specific vice (or mental illness): misanthropy—in the same way as "L'avare" (The Miser) represents covetousness or "Le malade imaginaire" (The Imaginary Invalid) hypochondria. In a society as strictly ruled by conventions and "bienséance" as France under Louis XIV, misanthropy was indeed perceived as a reprehensible aberration, defined by the *Dictionnaire de l'Académie* (1694) as follows: "This word, coming from the Greek, signifies 'hatred of people.' It is used for a sullen, irritable person, who seems to be the enemy of society."[15] Rather than Alceste with his exaggerated moral ideals, the positive hero of Molière's play seems to be Philinte, a perfect "honnête homme" who incorporates common sense and advocates the necessity of compromise with society.

Interestingly enough, however, even Molière's contemporaries did not see Alceste as an entirely negative figure. They recognized that he was justified to some extent in exposing the hypocrisy of high society. Loret wrote in 1666, the year the play was staged for the first time:

> Et ce misanthrope est si sage
> En frondant les moeurs de notre âge
> Que l'on dirait, benoît lecteur,
> Qu'on entend un prédicateur[16]
>
> (And this misanthrope is so wise
> In criticizing the customs of our age
> That one could think, dear reader,
> Of hearing a preacher)

The view of Alceste as a moralist was later to prevail, especially after J. J. Rousseau came to his defense in his famous "Lettre à d'Alembert sur les spectacles" (Letter to d'Alembert on Spectacles, 1758), in which he accused Molière of willfully ridiculing a virtuous man in order to please a depraved audience. Alceste became a forebearer of "progressive" ideas, and after the outbreak of the French Revolution, he was even made a Jacobin in Fabre d'Eglantine's play "Philinte de Molière ou la suite du Misanthrope" (Molière's Philinte, or the Confirmation of the Misanthrope, 1790). Philinte, faithful to Rousseau's view, was shown here as an execrable egoist and a royalist in the bargain. The same opinion was shared by the revolutionary Camille Desmoulins, who declared that "Molière, in *Le misanthrope,* has painted in sublime colors the character of the republican and the royalist. Alceste is a Jacobin, Philinte, a complete *feuillant* [member of a royalist faction]."[17]

The romantic interpretation of *The Misanthrope* basically maintained the view of Alceste as a virtuous moralist, but rehabilitated Molière who was now seen as a victim of seventeenth-century Classicism, the strict rules of which forbade him to develop his genius as he would have liked and forced him to use a comic mask to critically expose of the vices of society. The "real" Alceste was a serious person devoid of all comic elements. In fact he was seen as a self-portrait of Molière struggling with a hypocritical world, as he was immortalized by Alfred de Musset in his poem "Une Soirée perdue" (A Lost Evening):

> J'admirais quel amour pour l'âpre vérité
> Eut cet homme si fier en sa naïveté,
> Quel grand et vrai savoir des choses de ce monde,
> Quelle mâle gaieté, si triste et si profonde
> Que, lorsque' on vient d'en rire, on devrait en pleurer![18]

> (I admired what love for the bitter truth
> Had this man, so proud in his naiveté,
> What great and true knowledge of the things of this world,
> What masculine gaiety, so sad and so profound,
> That, when one laughs about it, one should cry instead!)

Echoes of this romantic Alceste can be found also in Russia, as we have seen in the earlier quotations from A. I. Pisarev and V. A. Ushakov, who presented Alceste as a noble lover of humanity. *The Misanthrope* was staged for the first time in Russia on December 22, 1757, in I. P. Elagin's translation,[19] which was published in 1788. In 1789, a flamboyant defense of Alceste appeared in Ivan Krylov's journal *Pochta dukhov,* where Molière hero was presented in the best Rousseauian fashion as an inspired fighter for honesty and justice: "May they condemn as much as they want the coarseness and strange behavior of those misanthropes—I will always maintain that it is almost impossible to be a totally honest man without resembling them a bit."[20] In his foreword to the comedy "Polubarskie zatei" (Semi-Lordly Fancies, 1808), A. A. Shakhovskoi defined *The Misanthrope* as a comedy of manners comparable to Fonvizin's "Nedoros!'" (The Minor). Not the virtuous Alceste is a ridiculous figure, but the society which laughs at him.[21]

Turning now to the Russian response to *Woe from Wit,* we can observe a similar pattern. The reception of Griboedov's comedy by its contemporary audience has been analyzed in great detail by the German scholar Witold Kosny in his 1985 *Habilitationsschrift.* According to Kosny's findings, the originally predominant "aesthetic reception-style" favored by Griboedov himself, i.e., the appreciation of *Woe from Wit* as a work of verbal art, was quickly overshadowed by other readings which were potentially inherent in the text, but ancillary to its aesthetic function: an "instrumental reception-style" (seeing the text as a medium to promote a certain ideology), a "mimetic reception-style" (the text as a representation of a certain societal reality) and an "expressive reception-style" (the text as an expression of the author's personality).[22]

Certain external circumstances contributed to the growing impact of non-aesthetic readings. The fact that Griboedov's comedy was censored induced the public to emphasize its political meaning and therefore to either celebrate or reject it as a political pamphlet. Moreover, Griboedov's adventurous life and his violent death in Teheran in 1829 made him somewhat of a legendary figure and encouraged the interpretation of Chatskii as self-expression of the author. The immense popularity of the play also reinforced its non-aesthetic reception. As Kosny points out, it was not the professional literati, but mostly the less competent "mass readers" who favored a non-aesthetic interpretation of *Woe from Wit.* This was not, however, the public for which the play was originally written.[23]

A specific case of "mimetic" reading, namely the identification of the protagonist with a model from real life, occurred in the reception of both Griboedov's and Molière's plays. For both Alceste and Chatskii, the public immediately started searching for prototypes in their contemporary society. Alceste was seen as a representation of the preceptor of the Dauphin, the somewhat eccentric M. de Montausier.[24] Griboedov's contemporaries understood Chatskii as a portrait of Petr Chaadaev.[25] For later generations of readers who were more removed from the original historical and sociological context of *The Misanthrope* and *Woe from Wit,* the search for models was supplanted by an "expressive" reception-style. Alceste and Chatskii were increasingly seen as self-portraits of Molière and Griboedov. At the same time, the "instrumental" reception-style, i.e., the political reading of the plays, acquired a predominant role. It has been shown earlier how Alceste became a Jacobin in the French Revolution. A very similar fate befell Chatskii after the Decembrist uprising. Whereas early readers like Pushkin, Viazemskii or Gogol' still expressed considerable reservations about him,[26] he later became a sacrosanct positive hero through his association with the Decembrist movement and thus with the "progressive forces" in Russian history. The explicit identification of Chatskii as a Decembrist, propagated by Apollon Grigor'ev and Alexander Herzen, later became a locus communis of Russian and Soviet criticism.[27]

In the same way as Rousseau was instrumental in promoting Alceste as a positive hero, Chatskii received his "lettre de noblesse" from another famous writer: Ivan Goncharov. In his article "Mil'on terzanii" (A million tortures), first published in *Vestnik Evropy* in 1872, Goncharov tried to dispel the impression that Chatskii, a fighter for the common good, might be a "superfluous man." Goncharov assures us that he is "incomparably higher and more intelligent than Onegin and Lermontov's Pechorin. He is a sincere and ardent activist, while they are parasites, amazingly drawn by great talents as the sickly creatures of an obsolete age."[28] Goncharov's essay, which, in D. S. Mirsky's words, "has had the good, or ill, fortune of being singled out by schoolmasters and professors of literature for special admiration,"[29] exerted a considerable influence on the teaching and reading of Griboedov's comedy in Russia.

For the reception of both Alceste and Chatskii, political events played a crucial role. In Alceste's case, it was J. J. Rousseau's philosophy of social protest and the abolition of the ancient régime in the French Revolution; in Chatskii's, the Decembrist uprising, the political radicalization of Russian thought and criticism in the eighteen-fifties and sixties and, last but not least, the advent of Soviet totalitarianism. The earlier quote from A. L. Shtein, who celebrated Griboedov as a "critical realist," is typical for the post-revolutionary approach. Even a serious Griboedov scholar like N. K. Piksanov deemed it necessary to promote *Woe from Wit* by engaging in the political rhetoric of Soviet criticism. As Piksanov put it:

> The Great October Revolution deepened our understanding of art and all the historical forces of its creation. The organic link between *Woe from Wit* and its protagonist Chatskii and the Decembrist period became much more deeply felt. Chatskii's patriotic emotionalism became more understandable. The high ideological and moral significance of *Woe from Wit,* its typicality, the universality of its images were duly appreciated by V. I. Lenin. In Lenin's works we find dozens of quotes and references to *Woe from Wit*."[30]

It is interesting to compare this and similar Soviet commentaries on *Woe from Wit* with French statements about *The Misanthrope* made under the dictatorship of Napoleon III in the 1860s. Like the later Soviet State, Louis Napoleon's Second Empire was an autocratic regime which justified its existence by claiming the glorious mantle of a progressive, revolutionary tradition. The Napoleonic Alceste looks strikingly similar to the Soviet Chatskii. The French critic F. Sarcey, for ex-

ample, wrote in 1868: "Alceste is the first and most radical of republicans. I tell you that Alceste, at the court of Louis XIV, typifies the revolutionary and republican."[31] The "Jacobin" Alceste and the "Decembrist" Chatskii thus both became supporting pillars of authoritarian regimes with a revolutionary pedigree.[32]

How can we account for this overlap in the reception of the two plays? As has been mentioned earlier, both *The Misanthrope* and *Woe from Wit* make it impossible for the reader to simply rely on a reassuring moral perspective offered by the author as a guarantee of an unequivocal meaning. Such ambivalence was, of course, not to everybody's liking. Especially dictatorial regimes asserting progressive agendas tend to be bothered by manifestations of semantic indeterminacy, ambiguity or irony. The distortions which the plays suffered in their reception could be explained as a desperate attempt to invest the text with a reassuring, clearcut, unmistakable "message." Ironically enough, it was precisely the negative features of Alceste and Chatskii—their intolerance, stubbornness, self-righteousness, inflexibility and general "misanthropy"—which were valorized positively as steadfastness and ideological firmness in the presumably philanthropic revolutionary enterprise. Paradoxically, the greatest similarity between Alceste and Chatskii was thus created in their ultimate distortion by the propaganda organs of repressive states, when they became the interchangeable figures of the revolutionary "positive hero."

Notes

An earlier version of this paper was presented at the 1997 Conference on "Russia's Golden Age" at Ohio State University. I am indebted to an anonymous reviewer of *Canadian Slavonic Papers* for constructive criticism.

1. Maurice Colin, "Tchatski un Alceste russe?" *Revue de littérature comparée* 46.4 (1972): 481.

2. For a useful summary of the debate, see Wladimir Troubetzkoy, "Griboedov et Molière," *Littératures* 21 (Fall 1989): 83-93.

3. Linda Hutcheon, "Literary Borrowing . . . and Stealing: Plagiarism, Sources, Influences, and Intertexts," *English Studies in Canada* 12.2 (1986): 230.

4. The stage history of *The Misanthrope* and *Woe from Wit* will largely remain beyond the scope of this study. Such an approach seems legitimate inasmuch as the two plays have become canonical works of French and Russian literature which enjoy a privileged status as literary texts beyond and independently from any theatrical production.

5. On Dmitriev's and Pisarev's articles, see N. K. Piksanov, "'Gore ot uma' v kritike i v nauchnoi

literature," in A. S. Griboedov, *Gore ot uma* (Moscow: Nauka, 1969) 168-69.

6. *Moskovskii telegraf,* 1830. Quoted in A. M. Gordin, ed., *A. S. Griboedov v russkoi kritike: Sbornik statei* (Moscow: Gos. izd-vo khudozhestvennoi literatury, 1958) 53. All translation are my own.

7. See A. N. Veselovskii, "Al'tsest i Chatskii," in *Etiudy i kharakteristiki* (Moscow, 1894) 144-69 (first published in *Vestnik Evropy* 3 [1881]: 91-112).

8. N. K. Piksanov, *Griboedov i Mol'er: Pereotsenka traditsii* (Moscow: Gosizdat, 1922). Repr. ed. Letchworth: Prideaux Press, 1979.

9. A. L. Shtein, *Kriticheskii realizm i russkaia drama XIX veka* (Moscow: Khudozhestvennaia literatura, 1962) 142.

10. Jean Bonamour, *A. S. Griboedov et la vie littéraire de son temps* (Paris: Presses Universitaires de France, 1965) 297. Bonamour's assumption is shared by his fellow French scholars Maurice Colin and Wladimir Troubetzkoy, although both of them also point to differences between the two plays. The concrete evidence about Griboedov's attitude toward Molière is in fact rather scant. There can be no doubt, of course, that Griboedov, like any educated Russian of his time, was familiar with Molière's plays. If we are to believe P. P. Gnedich, he even had a special predilection for Alceste and played this role in amateur productions of *The Misanthrope* (see "O Griboedovskom 'Gore ot uma'," *Russkii vestnik* 1890, quoted in Piksanov, *Griboedov i Mol'er,* 16). We have, however, no written testimony by Griboedov about Molière's influence on *Woe from Wit.* The only time he mentions Molière in his letters, it is to commend him for his art of creating "portraits" and to express a preference for "Le bourgeois gentilhomme" and "Le malade imaginaire" over "L'avare" (see the letter to P. A. Katenin, January 1825, in A. S. Griboedov, *Polnoe sobranie sochinenii,* 3 vols. Ed. N. K. Piksanov [Petrograd: Akademiia nauk, 1917] 3: 168.

11. See E. A. Maimin, "Russkii vol'nyi iamb i stikh 'Goria ot uma'," in *A. S. Griboedov. Tvorchestvo, biografiia, traditsii* (Leningrad: Nauka, 1977) 85.

12. Zh.-B. Mol'er, *Mizantrop ili Neliudim. Komediia v 5 deistviiakh.* Per. I. Elagina (Moscow, 1788) 121-22.

13. Quoted in Piksanov, *Griboedov i Mol'er* 47.

14. Ibid., 48. Originally published in Mikhaïl Achkinazi, "Les influences françaises en Russie: Molière, *"Le Livre,"* Revue du monde littéraire 11 (59) (November 1884): 360-62.

15. Quoted in René Jasinski, *Molière et Le Misanthrope* (Paris: Armand Colin, 1951) 125.

16. Quoted in Molière, *Le misanthrope* (Paris: Classiques Larousse, n.d.) 96.

17. Quoted in Peter Schunk, "Zur Wirkungsgeschichte des Misanthrope". *Germanisch-Romanische Monatsschrift,* Neue Folge, 21 (1971) 7. It is interesting to note that Chatskii, too, is declared a Jacobin by the Princess Tugoukhovskaia:

    Ia dumaiu, on prosto iakobinets,
    Vash Chatskii!!!

    (Act IV, scene 7)

18. Alfred de Musset, *Poésies complètes* (Paris: Gallimard, 1957) 389.

19. See Veselovskii, "Al'tsest i Chatskii" 145. Bonamour (*A. S. Griboedov,* 293) erroneously dates Elagin's translation with 1807.

20. "Pis'mo chetvertoe, ot Sil'fa Dal'novida k vol'shebniku Malikul'mul'ku," quoted in Veselovskii, "Al'tsest i Chatskii" 149.

21. See Bonamour, *A. S. Griboedov* 295-296. Bonamour claims, without supplying any material evidence, that Shakhovskoi's article is a faithful expression of Griboedov's opinion about *The Misanthrope,* that it was perhaps even written under his influence (295).

22. See Witold Kosny, *A. S. Griboedov—Poet und Minister: Die zeitgenössische Rezeption seiner Komödie "Gore ot uma" (1824-1832)* (Berlin-Wiesbaden: Otto Harassowitz, 1985) 17-18.

23. Ibid. 259.

24. According to legend, Montausier, alerted by his friends that Molière lampooned him in his play, arrived fuming with rage at the theatre to thrash the author. But after he saw the performance, he felt so flattered by his alleged portrait that he hurried backstage to embrace the startled Molière. For a Russian account of this episode, see Mikhail Bulgakov, *Zhizn' gospodina de Mol'era,* repr. ed. (Letchworth: Prideaux Press, 1978) 121.

25. See Pushkin's letter to Viazemskii in December 1823: "What is Griboedov doing? I have been told that he wrote a comedy on Chaadaev: under the current circumstances that is very noble of him" (A. S. Pushkin, *Polnoe sobranie sochinenii,* 17 vols. [Leningrad: Akademiia nauk, 1937-58] 13: 81). As Iu. N. Tynianov has shown, Chaadaev, indeed, has certain features in common with Chatskii: besides the similar name (Chatskii was originally spelled "Chadskii"), he shares with him certain political ideas and is also a victim of mali-

cious rumours (see Iurii Tynianov, "Siuzhet 'Goria ot uma'," in *Pushkin i ego sovremenniki* [Moscow: Nauka, 1969] 360-67).

26. "Chatskii is not an intelligent man at all—but Griboedov is very intelligent" (Pushkin, Letter to Viazemskii, January 1825, *Polnoe sobranie sochinenii* 13:137). "In this lies the main flaw of the author, that among idiots of various characteristics he depicted only one intelligent man, and even this one is mad and annoying. In comparison with Chatskii, Molière's Alceste is a veritable Philinte, a model of patience." (Viazemskii, "Fon-Vizin," quoted in Gordin, *A. S. Griboedov v russkoi kritike* 96). "In his anger and justified indignation against everybody Chatskii goes to excess, not noticing, that through this and through his unrestrained tongue he makes himself unbearable and even ridiculous" (N. V. Gogol', "V chem zhe, nakonets, sushchestvo russkoi poezii i v chem ee osobennost'," *Sobranie sochinenii*. 7 vols. [Moscow: Khudozhestvennaia literatura, 1978] 6: 362).

27. There exists a considerable body of literature on Griboedov's alleged connection with the Decembrists. M. V. Nechkina, in her book *Griboedov i dekabristy* (Moscow: Khudozhestvennaia literatura, 1947, reprinted in 1951 and 1977), tried to prove both Chatskii's and Griboedov's "Decembrism" with arguments mostly relying on the text of *Woe from Wit*. Her findings were later criticized by Piksanov (see A. S. Griboedov, *Gore ot uma* 291-298) and more recently by A. A. Lebedev, *Griboedov. Fakty i gipotezy* (Moscow: Iskusstvo, 1980).

As Kosny points out, the only solid observations that we can make about *Gore ot uma* and the Decembrists are to be found not in Griboedov's alleged intentions (on which we can only speculate), but in the reception of the play. Independently of Griboedov's intentions, *Woe from Wit* found in the Decembrists an audience that tended to identify itself with the protagonist (see Kosny, *A. S. Griboedov* 125).

28. I. A. Goncharov, *Sobranie sochinenii*. 8 vols. (Moscow: Khudozhestvennaia literatura, 1955) 8:13-14.

29. D. S. Mirsky, *A History of Russian Literature: From its Beginnings to 1900* (New York: Vintage Books, 1958) 190.

30. A. S. Griboedov, *Gore ot uma* 289. Piksanov forgets to mention that many quotes from *Woe from Wit* have become common Russian proverbs, which means that such "references" are not necessarily proof of a particular appreciation or predilection for the play.

31. Quoted in René Doumic, *Le Misanthrope de Molière: Etude et analyse* (Paris: Edition de la Pensée Moderne, 1966) 227.

32. The German scholar Erich Köhler has noted that there is perhaps indeed an at least potentially totalitarian element in Alceste's character, a "pathological obstinacy" which he shares with later revolutionary activists: "The hybris of the idea that one is an exceptional human being, the only righteous one in a world of crooks, hypocrites, cowards and opportunists, transforms the solemnity of moral protest into the pathological case of the dogmatist, who acknowledges no truth except his own absolute truth, and whom only society prevents from tyrannically subjugating this society under his will" (Erich Koehler, *Vorlesungen zur Geschichte der französischen Literatur: Klassik II* [Stuttgart: Kohlhammer Verlag, 1983] 77). The same could probably be said about Chatskii. In *this* sense, he is perhaps indeed a forerunner of the Soviet ideology. The Soviet canonization of Chatskii provoked R. Pletnev to launch a polemical attack against the character which reads like an inverted mirror image of the Soviet glorification (see "A. A. Chatskii v 'Gore ot uma' Griboedova: Popytka razvenchaniia geroia," *Novyi Zhurnal* 139 [1980]: 92-102).

FURTHER READING

Biography

Harden, Evelyn Jasiulko. "Griboedov and the Willock Affair." *Slavic Review* 30, no. 1 (March 1971): 74-92.

Discusses an unpublished Griboedov letter believed to be his final correspondence prior to the Persian massacre of the Russian mission in Tehran in February, 1829.

Criticism

Clayton, J. Douglas. "'Tis Folly To Be Wise: The Semantics of *um-* in Griboedov's *Gore ot uma*." In *Text and Context: Essays to Honor Nils Åke Nilsson,* edited by Peter Alberg Jensen, Barbara Lönnqvist, Fiona Björling, Lars Kleberg, and Anders Sjöberg, pp. 7-15. Stockholm: Almqvist & Wiksell International, 1987.

Analyzes the semantics of *um* and the frequency of its use in Griboedov's play, suggesting that such an analysis provides insight into the hero's primary dilemma.

Hammerbeck, David. "Opposition and Transformation: Dialogism in Russian and Soviet Satire." *European Studies Journal* 17-18, nos. 2-1 (fall-spring 2000-2001): 163-82.

Examines three Russian satirical plays—Griboedov's *Woe from Wit,* Sukhovo-Kobylin's *The Death of Tarelkin,* and Erdman's *The Suicide*—and the oppositional strategies employed in each as they attempted to reform the inequalities of Russian society.

Mirsky, Prince D. S. Introduction to *The Mischief of Being Clever (Gore ot Uma),* by Aleksandr Sergeevich-Griboedov, translated by Sir Bernard Pares, pp. iii-xv. London: School of Slavonic Studies in the University of London, King's College, 1925.

Provides a brief overview of Griboedov's life and praises the realism of various facets of his work.

Additional coverage of Griboedov's life and career is contained in the following sources published by the Gale Group: *Dictionary of Literary Biography,* **Vol. 205;** *Literature Resource Center;* *Reference Guide to World Literature,* **Eds. 2, 3.**

Giacomo Leopardi
1798-1837

(Full name Conte Giacomo Talegardo Francesco di Sales Saverio Pietro Leopardi) Italian poet, prose writer, translator, and editor.

The following entry presents criticism on Leopardi from 1963 through 2000. For additional information on Leopardi's life and career, see *NCLC*, Volume 22.

INTRODUCTION

An important figure of Italian Romanticism, Leopardi is best remembered for his profoundly pessimistic outlook on the human condition and his exquisite lyricism. Not widely known in his own time, Leopardi has since been acclaimed as the greatest Italian poet of the nineteenth century.

BIOGRAPHICAL INFORMATION

Leopardi was born June 29, 1798, in Recanati, an isolated rural village in Italy. He was the eldest of five surviving children of Count Monaldo Leopardi and the Marquess Adelaide Antici Leopardi. His father was interested in literature, philosophy, and politics, and he established an impressive personal library that covered a wide variety of subjects. Anxious for his talented son to succeed as a classical scholar, Leopardi's father provided the best possible private tutors for the boy, and by the age of sixteen, Leopardi had mastered Latin, Greek, and Hebrew, as well as English, French, and Spanish. Leopardi's mother, who controlled the family's finances due to her husband's inability to manage money, encouraged her children to lead the same austere, religious life she led. The boy spent hours reading, writing, and translating, which contributed to his poor health and exacerbated his numerous physical ailments, including poor vision and a deformity of the spine. The atmosphere created by his domineering mother and overprotective father was stifling and constricted, and Leopardi spent an isolated and boring childhood. Although he professed great love for the rest of Italy, he grew to despise Recanati, referring to it as a "horrible, detestable, execrated sepulcher, where the dead are happier than the living."

In 1817 Leopardi began recording his thoughts in a notebook that would become one of his most celebrated works, and also began corresponding with several im-

portant European writers. After an unsuccessful attempt to leave the family home in 1819, Leopardi continued his studies but increasingly devoted time to his own writing. In 1822 he was finally able to leave Recanati and visit Rome, which proved a bitter disappointment to him. He was unable to find suitable employment in the clerical or academic fields, in part due to his physical limitations, but also because of his agnosticism and avowed patriotism, both unpopular positions at the time. After returning for a time to his family, he began traveling throughout Italy, settling first in Florence, where an unhappy love affair inspired some of his most mournful verse, and then in Naples, where he took up residence with his friend and companion Antonio Ranieri. Supporting himself through his writing was a constant struggle and at times he was forced to depend on the generosity of friends. In his last years he became increasingly despondent over his failed romance, deteriorating health, and the Italian government's suppression of his writings. He died in 1837 of pulmonary failure.

MAJOR WORKS

Leopardi's early works consist of translations of the texts of Horace and Moschus, and sections of the *Aeneid* and the *Odyssey.* His first original works were *Storia della astronomia* (1813; *History of Astronomy*), which he wrote at the age of fifteen, and *Saggio sopra gli errori popolari degli antichi* (1815; *Essay on the Popular Errors of the Ancients*).

In 1816, according to some scholars, Leopardi experienced what he called his "literary conversion," after which he concentrated on the production of creative pieces rather than critical writings. The poems "All'Italia" ("To Italy") and "Sopra il monumento di Dante" ("On Dante's Monument") were inspired by a visit from his friend and first literary mentor Pietro Giordani in 1818. Some time after 1819 he composed some of his most admired poetry, including "L'Infinito ("The Infinite"), "Alla luna" ("To the Moon"), and "Alla Primavera" (To the Spring"). His first collection of poetry, *Canzoni,* was published in 1824, and in 1831 a second collection, *Canti,* appeared.

One of Leopardi's most important works was his seven-volume notebook, *Pensieri di varia filosofia e di bella letteratura,* better known as *Zibaldone,* published in 1898-1900, but written between 1817 and sometime in the 1830s. Influenced by classical poetry as well as by Enlightenment rationalism and skepticism, the work represents Leopardi's philosophical speculations and reflects his profoundly pessimistic belief in the meaninglessness of life. In his later poems and in the *Operette morali* (1827), a series of dialogues outlining his philosophy, Leopardi tempered some of the nihilism expressed earlier in the *Zibaldone.* Leopardi's final poem, "La ginestra" ("The Broom"), dealt with the hostile relationship between nature and mankind, but offered a slight glimmer of hope—unlike most of his earlier pieces.

CRITICAL RECEPTION

Leopardi's oeuvre has received considerable scholarly attention in Italy while garnering steady and diverse criticism from other Western critics as well. Many scholars have commented on the despair inherent in Leopardi's work. Sergio Pacifici compares Leopardi to Alessandro Manzoni, but where the latter's work is infused with Christian optimism, the former's verse is characterized by a "bleak pessimism." Yet due to this, Pacifici believes that Leopardi's work is more likely to appeal to modern readers because he explores the fundamental questions of life with an unblinking eye. Kenelm Foster also compares Manzoni and Leopardi, but finds that despite their differences, both poets were concerned with the essential nature of truth. Alfredo Bonadeo has examined Leopardi's treatment of death in his prose works and contends that "contrary to what one may surmise from his somber vision of life, neither the fact nor the idea of death bears negatively upon his evaluation of human existence nor do they constitute a desirable escape from life."

Numerous critics have noted the importance of illusion in Leopardi's thought and in his writing. Erasmo G. Gerato maintains that it is a crucial concept in understanding the poet because for Leopardi illusion was the one thing that could make life bearable, not just for him but for all of humanity. But as the poet was increasingly making use of illusion, he was at the same time, according to Gerato, viewing reason more and more negatively. G. Singh believes that illusions were an important part of Leopardi's early life, as they are with most people. However, Singh reports that "the crucial difference between him and any other person . . . was the extraordinarily swift and unimpeded transition from illusions, however agreeable and even necessary, to truth, however bitter. His journey from the one to the other could not have been briefer or more decisive." Alan S. Rosenthal asserts that Leopardi's concept of nature also became increasingly negative over time: "In Leopardi's poetry, Nature is at first indifferent to mankind, then cruel, increasingly hostile, and finally viciously destructive." Bonadeo traces a similar evolution in Leopardi's concept of nature, although he finds that the poet first held a positive conception of the link between man and nature.

In recent years the *Zibaldone* has received increasing attention from literary critics, including Martha King and Daniela Bini. "Leopardi's meditations on the creative process and his statements on style and the psychological effect of certain words are a rare testimony of a great poet," according to King and Bini. Despite this renewed interest, however, Leopardi's poetry remains relatively unknown outside Italy; in the English-speaking world, the study of his work is largely restricted to academic circles where he is considered by many the greatest Italian poet of the nineteenth century. In his own country, according to Nicolas J. Perella "the critical literature on Leopardi has, in the last forty years, been massive, perhaps exceeding even what has been written on Dante." Perella believes that Leopardi has been a significant influence on Western literature since his death but the acknowledgement of that impact has not been sufficient to secure his reputation, outside scholarly circles, as one of Italy's greatest poets and thinkers.

PRINCIPAL WORKS

Storia della astronomia (essay) 1813

Saggio sopra gli errori popolari degli antichi (essay) 1815

Canzoni del conte Giacomo Leopardi (poetry) 1824; revised and enlarged as *Versi del Conte Giacomo Leopardi* 1826

Operette morali [*Essays and Dialogues of Giacomo Leopardi*; also published as *Essays, Dialogues and Thoughts of Giacomo Leopardi*] (essays, fictional dialogues, and prose poetry) 1827; enlarged edition, 1836

Canti (poetry) 1831; enlarged edition, 1835

Opere di Giacomo Leopardi. 6 vols. (poetry, essays, fictional dialogues, aphorisms, and letters) 1845-49

Pensieri di varia filosofia e di bella letteratura [*Zibaldone*]. 7 vols. (prose) 1898-1900

The poems of Leopardi (poetry) 1923

Epistolario di Giacomo Leopardi. 7 vols. (letters) 1934-41

Tutte le opere di Giacomo Leopardi. 5 vols. (poetry, prose, fictional dialogues, essays, aphorisms, prose poetry, and letters) 1937-49

Poems from Giacomo Leopardi (poetry) 1946

Giacomo Leopardi: Selected Prose and Poetry (poetry, prose, and fictional dialogues) 1966

A Leopardi Reader (poetry, prose, aphorisms, and letters) 1981

CRITICISM

Beatrice Corrigan (essay date 1963)

SOURCE: Corrigan, Beatrice. "The Poetry of Leopardi in Victorian England 1837-1878." *English Miscellany* 14 (1963): 171-84.

[*In the following essay, Corrigan discusses Leopardi's reputation in England in the mid-nineteenth century.*]

«The first time an Englishman ever mentioned the name of Leopardi in print was, we believe, in a recent novel», wrote George Henry Lewes in an anonymous contribution to *Fraser's Magazine* in 1848[1]. «Yet Germany has long known and cherished Leopardi. Even France, generally so backward in acknowledging a foreigner, has, on several occasions, paid tribute to his genius».

Some of Leopardi's poems had indeed been translated into German as early as 1823[2], and he had been the subject of an article in France in 1833[3]. But during his lifetime an unfortunate barrier had already risen between English and Italian men of letters. No longer did English poets seek out, as Byron had done in Milan in 1816, their Italian confreres, and the English periodicals were interested in Italian politics rather than in Italian literature.

Leopardi was himself conscious of this lack of intellectual intercourse. Of the two Leopardi brothers, it was Carlo who had devoted himself to English literature, and who was urged by his uncle to win fame as a translator[4]; yet it was Giacomo who in 1826 wrote to the publisher Stella telling him about a newly founded English journal, the *Panoramic Miscellany,* and offering to translate some of its articles for the *Ricoglitore.* The *Miscellany,* he explains, «promette di accordare una particolare attenzione alla nostra letteratura trascurata generalmente dagli altri giornali inglesi, e si annunzia che i redattori sono, per opportune corrispondenze, in grado di ricevere sopra le nostre produzioni letterarie maggiori e più numerose informazioni che non si sogliono avere in Inghilterra»[5]. If the *Ricoglitore* published a selection of these articles, translated and annotated, «acquisterebbe un grado d'interesse dei maggiori possibili, ed anche una grande utilità, pei dibattimenti urbani a cui darebbe luogo tra una nazione e l'altra; pel confronto delle opinioni letterarie delle due nazioni, ec.».

However the *Panoramic Miscellany* survived only one year, and in any case Stella discouraged the project, which he considered too precarious because it was difficult to import foreign periodicals into the Austrian and Papal territories with any regularity[6].

Leopardi seems to have made the acquaintance of only two English men of letters. In 1831 he sent a copy of his edition of Petrarch's *Canzoniere* to the distinguished Anglo-Italian scholar George Frederick Nott, whom he had probably met that year in Rome[7]. Nott praised the edition as «semplice e dotta», and added: «A mio avviso essa è la più utile, e perciò la migliore edizione, che forse finora sia mai comparsa di quell'illustre Poeta»[8]. He also suggested an interpretation of a passage that had puzzled Leopardi, who included Nott's explanation, with a grateful acknowledgement, in the 1839 reprint of his *interpretazione.*

The second surviving letter from Nott to Leopardi shows that they were on cordial terms, and that they met again in Florence in 1832 before the English scholar's departure from Italy[9].

The only contemporary description of Leopardi in English occurs in the diary of Henry Crabb Robinson, distinguished like John Cam Hobhouse for his literary friendships rather than for his own achievements. He met Leopardi in Florence in 1831, and wrote under the date of June 13:

«I occasionally saw Leopardi the poet, a man of acknowledged genius and of irreproachable character. He was a man of family, and a scholar, but he had a feeble frame, was sickly, and deformed. He was also poor, so that his excellent qualities and superior talents were, to a great degree, lost to the world. He wanted a field for display—an organ to exercise»[10].

More than twenty years later Robinson was reminded of his Florentine acquaintance, and was more frank about his own estimate of the poet. «Finished the last Prospective Review», he wrote on June 2, 1854, «by reading on Leopardi—a sickly poet of great reputation whose *Odes* I found unreadable—that is, obscure. He, Leopardi, was the friend of Poerio the Neapolitan victim. And Ranieri his friend is a name I recall and find in my journal. The praise is extravagant but more of the philosopher than poet. His person not unlike De Quincey in the impression left of it, like mother of pearl»[11].

However Robinson's diary was not published until 1869, and the novel to which George Henry Lewes referred in the passage which I have quoted at the beginning of this article, his own *Ranthorpe,* appeared in 1847. One of the themes of *Ranthorpe* is, appropriately enough, the formative influence of suffering on a poet, and though Leopardi is not mentioned in the text quotations from his poems and prose are used as epigraphs for four chapters[12]. Yet Lewes' cautiously worded statement was misleading, for Leopardi's name had been mentioned in print in England, though not by an Englishman, as early as 1837. An article by Giuseppe Mazzini, entitled «Italian Literature since 1830», which appeared in the *Westminster Review*[13] divides contemporary Italian men of letters into two camps, the followers of Manzoni and the followers of Guerrazzi. Then it continues: «Between these two opposite tendencies in the literary world, answering to two which exist in great activity in the social world, but with which we have no concern here, is placed making advances sometimes to one, sometimes to the other, a sect without a name—a certain number of individuals professing a literary eclecticism, who hesitate between imitation and innovation, between the ancient and the modern. Some, as Nicolini . . . clothe a classic outline with drapery of Romanticism. Others, as Leopardi of Recanati (who died at Naples on the 14th of June) endeavour to express the feelings and the thoughts of the present day in a form and style savouring of the classics. Neither the dramas of the first nor the Petrarchan songs of the second at all deserve, in our opinion, the high reputation they have acquired from the sentiments of patriotism with which they abound. The former contain pieces of exquisite poetry, and the latter breathe a spirit of profound melancholy, a characteristic of the age, but they are nevertheless the efforts of a transitory period, which the future is destined to efface».

This ungenerous consignment to oblivion of the greatest Italian poet of his age may perhaps be explained by Mazzini's own bias to political optimism, probably in particular need of encouragement during the first bitter moments of exile when the article was written. But it was one of the ironies of Leopardi's fate that the only record in England of his death should be set down in this casual tone by his own compatriot, unwilling or unable to appreciate his genius.

In any case, Mazzini's article preceded *Ranthorpe* by ten years, and Lewes' own article in *Fraser's* was inspired, as he himself says, by an article by Sainte-Beuve which had appeared in the *Revue des Deux Mondes* in 1844, and by the publication in 1845 and 1846 of Leopardi's prose works in four volumes.

Lewes begins his article with a biographical sketch, touching lightly on the fact that Leopardi had passed, «by what steps is now unknown, from the submission of a fervent piety to the freedom of unlimited scepticism». He classes him with the Romantic school, though he points out that there is no German influence on Leopardi's work. «The distinctive characteristic of Leopardi's poetry», he says, «is despair over the present accompanied with a mournful regret for the past».

«As the 'poet of despair' we know of no equal to Leopardi», he continues. «But he is too limited ever to become popular. His own experience of life had been restrained within a small sphere by his misfortunes: it was intense but not extensive; consequently his lyre had but few strings. He had thought and suffered, but he had not lived; and his poems utter his thoughts and sufferings, but give no image of the universal life. Yet he is never tiresome, though always the same. His grief is so real and so profound, that it is inexhaustible in expression; to say nothing of the beauty in which he embalms it. Something of the magic of his verse he doubtless owes to that language which ennobles the most trivial thoughts, and throws its musical spell over the merest nothings; but more to the exquisite choice of diction, which his poet's instinct and his classic tastes alike taught him».

It is evident however that Lewes was not always capable of judging either Leopardi's mastery of his art or the profundity of his thought, and this is evident in his comments on one of the most perfect of Italian lyrics. «When not roused to indignation his Muse has but one low plaint—a yearning for release from life. In one of his smaller pieces this is delicately touched: every reader who has known the luxury of reverie when contemplating a setting sun will recognize the yearning for the Infinite Silence in his lines *L'Infinito*».

But though his discussion of the poems is slight, and he is, characteristically, much more interested in the philosophical prose works, Lewes did earn the distinction of being the first to translate into English one of Leopardi's poems. He chose *Amore e morte* (translated by

Sainte-Beuve into French at the close of his own article) which was to prove a favourite with English translators. He made no attempt to follow the metric form of the original; his aim was rather a line by line translation which should be as faithful as possible, and at the same time rhythmic and poetical.

Lewes concluded his article by saying: «Our task is done. We have introduced the name of a great writer and most unhappy man, and, in a general way, indicated the nature of his genius and the cast of his thoughts. It remains for those who can enjoy the one, without being ungenerous towards the other,—who can admire the writer while condemning his opinions, and who, in the calm serenity of their own minds can still recognize a corner of doubt, and believe thas so long as doubt and sorrow shall be the lot of mankind, the poet whose lyre vibrates powerfully with their accents will deserve a place amongst the musical teachers,—it remains for them to seek in Leopardi's works a clearer, fuller knowledge of the man».

In 1849 Leopardi's *Poesie* and Viani's edition of his letters appeared, and the six volumes of his published works were the subject of a long review article by William Ewart Gladstone in the *Quarterly Review* for 1850[14]. Unlike Lewes, Gladstone indicates no covert sympathy with Leopardi's bleak philosophical speculations, but he admires him as a «powerful and lofty poet», unequalled by any Italian in his generation with the exception of Manzoni. Yet he found the abundant beauties of his poems often «scarred and blighted by emanations from the pit of his shoreless and bottomless despair», and he illustrated his essay with translations from the prose works alone.

A second account of «Giacomo Leopardi: His Life and Writings» appeared anonymously in *The Prospective Review* in 1854, and was the article to which Crabb Robinson referred. It was based on the *Epistolario* alone, which accounts for the greater emphasis laid on Leopardi's philosophy, but it contained translations of twenty lines of *All'Italia* and of the major part of *Il risorgimento*[15]. Like Lewes' article in 1848, it opened with a claim to discovery. «Few of our countrymen we imagine», says the author, «have read the writings, not many even heard the name, of one of the most remarkable men of modern Italy, who passed away to his rest some fifteen years ago, after a life into whose short space was crowded an almost superhuman amount of labour, of wrecked ambition, and of physical suffering».

It is perhaps not without significance that Lewes' article appeared in the same number of *Fraser's* as one on «The Austrian-Italian Question». It was undoubtedly the political events of 1848 that kindled English interest in Italian poetry, and an Italian political exile was the next to play a part in introducing Leopardi to an En-

glish audience. Count Carlo Arrivabene, who had fought in Venice in 1848, came to London and in 1854 became deputy professor of Italian at University College, London, during the absence of Antonio Gallenga, who had returned to Italy as a member of the Subalpine Parliament. In 1855 Arrivabene published an anthology of Italian verse, with brief biographies of the poets included, for the benefit of students of the Italian language in England[16]. In it he printed the whole of *All'Italia,* and stanzas 2 and 3 of *La ginestra*—a characteristic and appropriate choice for a hero of the Risorgimento.

In 1859 an anonymous writer in the *Westminster Review*[17] set down with unsparing candour the reason for the low esteem in which Italian letters had been held for some years. «The contempt which, rightly or wrongly, has fallen on the Italians as a people has extended itself to their literature. In England especially it is little valued; our poetic affinities incline us towards the north, towards Goethe, Schiller, and the poets of the 'Fatherland'. Another reason for the neglect into which Italian poetry has fallen among us, is the difficulty attending its study. The Italian minstrels have adopted a language peculiar to themselves, abounding in the most daring inversions, which demand a long and careful study, and for this few of us have either time or patience. So we turn coldly away, and take for granted what detractors both abroad and at home are continually repeating, or at least have been repeating till the present moment, that Italian modern poetry is weak, affected, and inflated; even as we have been in the habit of repeating that modern Italians, the countrymen of Balbo, Gioberti, Manin, Cavour, are all either triflers or conspirators, opera-singers or revolutionists».

He calls Leopardi «the poet and the philosopher of grief», but makes no mention of his nihilism; and he describes his poetry as «marked by the rare purity, the nervous eloquence, the energetic conciseness which characterizes his style, and which renders all translations incapable of conveying a just idea of its beauty». He ventures however to translate the first three stanzas of *All'Italia,* and concludes his article by saying that «no work of imagination, however admirable in itself, which does not touch the chord of patriotism and national independence, can expect popular sympathy. This is a hopeful symptom; it proves that Italy has awoke from its slumbers—awoke to a new and healthy existence».

This view was shared by Louisa Anne Merivale, daughter of the distinguished Italian scholar, John Hermann Merivale. In 1863 she published in *Fraser's Magazine* a two-part article entitled «Italian Poetry and Patriotism»[18]. She is the first writer to recognize Leopardi's stature as a poet; she calls him superior to both Giusti and Manzoni, and says that he has had no equal for three hundred years. She points out his debt to Petrarch, and compares him to Foscolo in the Greek quality of his genius. She mentions, without deploring, that he was «deeply penetrated with the querulous, ironical, melancholy views of life, characteristic of modern scepticism», and explains this by the unhappy circumstances of his own life and the country into which he was born. She illustrates her comments by quoting in Italian fragments from the *Monumento di Dante* and from *Ad Angelo Mai.*

In 1865 Miss Merivale published an anthology, *I poeti moderni italiani*[19], modelled to some extent on Arrivabene's, and using for the biographical notes, as she herself acknowledged, much of the material which she had already published in *Fraser's.* Like the writer in the *Westminster,* she feels that the modern poetical idiom is difficult for the English reader, and her anthology, containing thirty-two poets of the past hundred years, is meant for «a class of readers, common I believe in this country, who, knowing Italian in a general way, and sufficiently able to construe it in prose or in a classical poet of the olden time, are not at home in the involutions of the modern style, and are wont to be repelled from the study of more recent authors by the labour it often requires to master their precise meaning».

She includes nine poems by Leopardi in her anthology, and in a prefatory note attempts to justify his philosophical attitude. «As Dante is the Poet of Scorn, Petrarch of Love, Ariosto of Adventure, so Leopardi is preeminently the Poet of Ennui: not of the mere self-indulgent listlessness to which the name is commonly applied but of that deep dissatisfaction with human life and its paltry results, which is in fact the noblest argument for man's immortal nature—for while the gloom of this dissatisfaction has often thrown its shadow over other aspiring and speculative minds besides his, the better balanced and the happier have been cheered by the consolation that lies beyond it. It was Leopardi's portion to feel the gloom but not the consolation. Yet his was far from the calculating misbelief of the Atheist. His heart clung to love and truth and virtue; and even the scepticism which his writings profess was, as has been said of it, a scepticism which led men to happiness».

An anonymous reviewer of Miss Merivale's anthology in the *Athenaeum*[20] praised Leopardi even more highly. «He is to be classed among the most complete and elect poets of our time; he is one of the typical writers of the nineteenth century, and, among Italians, closer than any contemporary to the compactness, eloquence grace and dignity of the great mediaevalists who remain to this day, and will to all ages remain, the constellations of the poetic horizon of Italy. As finished as Tennyson, as sensitive as Victor Hugo, as sombre as Byron, Leopardi would alone avail to render the poetry of the present

age of permanent value and weight among the rich, but for a long while past decreasingly rich, literature of his noble country».

This reviewer commented on the monotony of the patriotic theme in Italian poetry, but it was true that, as it had been through the centuries, Italy's literary reputation was still closely linked to her political fortunes. Mazzini in 1837 had first introduced Leopardi to the English public, Arrivabene had first included him in an anthology published in England, and one of Mazzini's fellow-exiles, Giovanni Ruffini, was to be responsible for the first extensive translations of his poems into English.

After a few hungry years in England, and a quarrel with Mazzini, from whom he differed violently on more than literary matters, Ruffini had taken up residence in Paris in 1842. There in the winter of 1864 he met the Scottish novelist, Mrs. Margaret Oliphant, and became a regular weekly visitor to her salon. When she left Paris for Avranches in May 1865 he gave her as a parting present a copy of Leopardi's poems. In June of the same year Mrs. Oliphant wrote to Mr. Blackwood the publisher: «I send you with this a paper upon the Italian Leopardi, which I hope very much you may like. I am so destitute of anybody to speak to here, on literary subjects, that I cannot feel sure whether my author will impress you as he does me, or whether I have done him anything like justice. The paper is very long, I am afraid»[21]. Her article appeared anonymously in *Blackwood's Magazine* in October[22]. It began with a semi-apology for the obscurity of its subject, who, Mrs. Oliphant says, «has neither the breadth nor the depth of the great masters of Italian song». He may however, she suggests, provide for the English reader a stepping stone to Dante after he leaves «the little well-known round furnished by Manzoni and Silvio Pellico». The modern mind after all needs help to pass from «Manzoni's limpid narrative to the great depths of the majestic Florentine». The works of Leopardi, she continues, «are so little known in England that it is scarcely presumption to fancy that it is a new poet whom we are about to introduce to a large number of our readers; and though it would be vain to pretend that they are of an order which can be called popular, they express at least the emotions of a mind of our own century, whose thoughts run in a more modern channel than those of the greater poets of Italy, and by means of whom the reader may perhaps ascend more easily to those great and solemn heights».

But she compensates for her patronizing tone by translating the whole of *A se stesso, A Silvia, Le ricordanze,* and *Il sabato del villaggio*; almost the whole of *Amore e Morte*; and fragments from *All'Italia, Nelle nozze della sorella Paolina,* and *La quiete dopo la tempesta.*

During the next ten years, though James Thompson's translation of the prose works was printed in *The National Reformer* between 1867 and 1868[23], only one translation of a poem appeared in England[24]. This was John Addington Symonds' version of *A se stesso,* published in the semi-obscurity of a school magazine, *The Cliftonian,* in 1870[25]. In 1878, as I have described elsewhere[26], Giovanni Ruffini was responsible for the translation by Eugene Lee-Hamilton of a second group of poems, six in number. These appeared in Lee-Hamilton's *Poems and Transcripts,* published by Blackwood.

In the same year, 1878, another member of the Merivale family, Herman C. Merivale, the prolific Victorian dramatist, grandson of John and nephew of Louisa Merivale, translated for *Blackwood's Magazine* the **Canto notturno** under the title of **Song of the Night**[27]. Like Mrs. Oliphant, he half apologized for the obscurity of his subject, quoting, without acknowledgement, his aunt's remark that Leopardi «as a constant victim to disease and suffering, was incapacitated from sustained composition on a large scale, so that his principal poems were *canti* and *canzoni*» Merivale further forestalled criticism with the following footnote: «The translator, while anxious to introduce to the English-reading public a version of so fine a poem as the **'Canto Notturno'**, desires at the same time, happy as he is in a simpler faith, to disclaim on his own account all sympathy with the gloomy 'nihilism' which pervades it».

Thus during the first phase of Leopardi's fortunes in England, the thirty years from 1848 to 1878, only thirteen of his poems had been translated in full or in part: *A se stesso, Amore e morte,* and *All'Italia* three times each, the others once. *Il passero solitario* had never found a translator, though it was one of Ruffini's favourites and should have had a special appeal for the bird-loving English. The two great final poems, *Il tramonto della luna* and *La ginestra,* still remained unknown except in Italian to a generation of readers unprepared to accept Leopardi's resolute denial that future happiness for man might lie beyond the black abyss of death.

A philosopher, a statesman, two descendants of an Anglo-Italian scholar, three Italian patriotic exiles, a popular novelist and two poets had shared in the attempt to make Leopardi known to an English public. None of them apparently had any great success: most seem to have been unaware of their predecessors' efforts, though Herman C. Merivale does refer to Mrs. Oliphant's article, as well as quoting from his aunt's; many reiterate apologies for the poet's obscurity and pessimism, and seem doubtful of his merit. At least two regard him as a student's training ground for poetry more elevated or more elaborate.

Indeed it was not until 1887 that the first complete English translation of the poems, by Frederick Townsend,

was published[28] though according to Ruffini Mrs. Oliphant had hoped to produce such a work in 1865. This marked the beginning of a second period for Leopardi. In 1888 Matthew Arnold accorded him the serious attention due to a major poet, comparing him with Wordsworth and Byron. From then on, he was to belie the predictions of Mazzini, Lewes and Mrs. Oliphant by proving the most popular and the most frequently translated Italian poet of the nineteenth century.

Notes

1. «Life and Works of Leopardi», *Fraser's Magazine,* XXXVII, ccxxvii (Dec. 1848), 659-669. I am indebted to Professor Walter Houghton of Wellesley College for this identification, which is based on *The George Eliot Letters,* ed. G. S. Haight, New Haven and London, 1955, p. 369.

2. Franz Spunda, *G. Leopardi, Gedichte,* Leipzig.

3. G. Charlier, «Le premier article français sur Leopardi», *Revue des Études Italiennes,* Jan-Mar. 1938, 13-20.

4. *Epistolario di Giacomo Leopardi,* ed. Francesco Moroncini, Firenze, Le Monnier, 1934-41, I, 200, 204.

5. *Ibid.,* IV, 177-178.

6. *Ibid.,* IV, 179-180.

7. In 1808 Nott had published in London *Petrarch Translated: in a Selection of his Sonnets and Odes Accompanied with Notes and the Original Italian.*

8. *Epistolario,* VI, 129.

9. *Ibid.,* VI, 191.

10. *Diary, Reminiscences and Correspondence of Henry Crabb Robinson,* ed. Thomas Sadler, Boston, 1871, II, 154.

11. Published by permission of the Trustees of the Dr. Williams's Library from the Henry Crabb Robinson Collection. A portion of this entry in the Journal had been previously published in *Henry Crabb Robinson on Books and their Writers,* ed. Edith Morley, London, Dent, 1938, II, 740.

12. Book III, chap. xi («Despair»), lines 27-36 of the *Ultimo canto di Saffo. Book IV,* ch. viii («The Miseries of Genius»), quotation from the *Operette morali.* Book IV, ch. vii («The Dream»), lines 4-8 of *Il sogno,* and 25-31 of *Il primo amore.* Book IV, ch. viii («Waking Dreams and Waking Sadness»), lines 19-23 of the *Ultimo canto.*

13. *Westminster Review,* XXVIII (1837-38), 132-168. The article is signed A. U., probably as a compliment to Mazzini's companion in exile, Angelo Usiglio. It was the first article published by

Mazzini in English. He was paid £ 36 for it, but had to give half this sum to the translator.

14. LXXXVI, clxxii (March, 1850), 295-336. Cf D. E. RHODES, «Mr Gladstone's Essay on Leopardi», *Italian Studies,* VIII (1953), 59-70. Also Professor J. H. Whitfield's introduction to his translation of *I Canti,* Naples, Scalabrini, 1962.

15. X, xxxviii (1854), 157-194.

16. *I Poeti Italiani. Selections from the Italian Poets,* London, 1855.

17. «Modern Poets and Poetry of Italy», *Westminster Review,* LXXII, cxlii (Oct. 1859, American ed.), 237-253. This is a review of three works: Fosco-lo's *Opere* (Florence, 1857); *Rime scelte di vari poeti moderni* (Paris, 1857); *Poeti italiani* (Lugano, 1859).

18. LX (Jan.-June, 1863), 383-395; LXVIII (July-Dec., 1863), 603-618. Leopardi is discussed in the second part, which covers the period from Alfieri to Guerrazzi.

19. London, Williams and Norgate. The poems included are: *All'Italia, Ad Angelo Mai, Canto notturno, La sera del dì di festa, Frammento* («Spento il diurno raggio»), *Consalvo, Le ricordanze, Alla luna, A Silvia, Il sogno.*

20. May 20, 1865, pp. 681-2.

21. *The Autobiography and Letters of Mrs M. O. W. Oliphant.* 3rd ed., Edinburgh, Blackwood, 1899, p. 71.

22. XCVIII, 459-480.

23. Though he translated none of Leopardi's poems, his own poetry shows the influence of the Italian poet. For Thompson's interest in Leopardi, see IMOGENE B. WALLER's *James Thompson (B. V.),* Cornell University Press, 1950, pp. 86-88.

24. I am dealing here only with translations published in England. But mention should be made of William Dean Howell's article, «Modern Italian Poets», *North American Review,* CIII, 213 (Oct. 1868), 313-345. In a perceptive discussion of Leopardi, he translates *A se stesso, A Silvia, Imitazione, Sopra un bassorilievo antico sepolcrale,* and lines 96-107 of *Amore e morte.*

25. II, I (July 1870), 11.

26. *English Miscellany,* 13 (1962).

27. CXXIV, dcclv (Sept. 1878), 336-339.

28. *The Poems of Giacomo Leopardi,* translated by Frederick Townsend: New York and London, G. P. Putnam's Sons, The Knickerbocker Press, 1887.

Townsend, an American born in New York, spent the last ten years of his life in Italy. His translation was published posthumously with an introduction by Octavius Brook Frothingham. It begins, inevitably: «Giacomo Leopardi is a great name in Italy among philosophers' and poets, but is quite unknown in this country». The translation is complete except for the *Coro dei morti, I nuovi credenti,* and three *Frammenti.*

Kenelm Foster (essay date 1967)

SOURCE: Foster, Kenelm. "The Idea of Truth in Manzoni and Leopardi." *Proceedings of the British Academy* 53 (1967): 243-57.

[*In the following essay, Foster compares the philosophies of Manzoni and Leopardi, who, despite their extreme differences, were both concerned with the nature of truth.*]

There is a danger in being honoured beyond one's expectations; one may try a little too hard to rise to the occasion, and I fear I have run the risk of doing that in choosing to address so distinguished an audience on so difficult, though fascinating, a topic. Two men of genius and their idea of truth would always be a large subject for one lecture, and the matter is certainly made no easier in the present case by the fact that the two minds and mentalities I have chosen as my theme are not only complex but also exceedingly different. As thinkers—which is how I have to consider them—Alessandro Manzoni and Giacomo Leopardi differ all along the line—in temperament, outlook, method, and conclusions, in their entire view of things; to which it seems almost trivial to add that intellectually each was wholly independent of, indeed almost unaffected by the other, though they were contemporaries and slightly acquainted. As thinkers they had almost nothing in common except the concern to think truthfully. That certainly they shared in some sense. But what does a common truth-concern imply? Manzoni, writing to Victor Cousin, insisted that every history of philosophy presupposes a philosophy 'exposée ou simplement indiquée'.[1] And this I am sure is true; but even were it not, the historian of philosophy is of course obliged to philosophize just because and to the extent that he is giving an account of philosophies. And this in a modest way is what I am attempting now: a small essay in—or on the frontiers of—the history of ideas; and so touching, inevitably, on matters in which my technical competence is, I fear, extremely limited.

It is then in a way heartening to recall that neither Manzoni nor Leopardi ever took a university course in philosophy or has the general name and fame of a philosopher. Both are remembered as creative writers, the one as author of a great novel, the other as a lyric poet. And it is true that both philosophized as it were on the side—though with passion and persistence, for both were intellectually very serious men and serious about the ultimate questions. Indeed it is likely that both set more store by their relatively little-known philosophical speculations than by their triumphant achievements in imaginative literature. Leopardi's lyric poems were but a tiny part of his writings (counting the unpublished with the published) and he never spoke of them anything like so tenderly as he spoke of the ***Operette morali,*** the dialogues by which he hoped for a time to recommend his bitter philosophy—'my system' as he liked to call it—to the world.[2] His strongest ambition may well have been to win glory precisely as a philosopher. As for Manzoni, we all know how he liked to mock at himself as poet and novelist ('i miei venticinque lettori'!)[3] but it is an error, I think, to ascribe this only to modesty and a humorous gentlemanly detachment; it sprang as much from that speculative bent in him which, after the glorious but short-lived spell of creative writing (say, 1818-27), increasingly predominated and found its apt expression in dry prose of reflection and analysis; in those letters, essays, and dialogues of his later years, which can all be described as directly or indirectly philosophical. Italian critics used to speak of Don Alessandro's gradual lapse into silence and sterility, a judgement which has little to recommend it except that Manzoni always found composition difficult, was intellectually very scrupulous, and that much of this later writing was left unfinished or unpublished. But today—with the excellent editions we now have of the 'Lettre à Victor Cousin', of the draft of Part II of the *Morale cattolica,* of the Appendix to Part I (the refutation of Utilitarianism), of the *Discorso* on the historical novel and other scattered reflections on art and truth, of the *Dell'Invenzione,* Manzoni's clearest statement on the relation between the individual mind and universal ideas—today there is no excuse for ignoring his philosophy, unless perhaps it is not worth studying; which obviously is not my own view and which I am encouraged to discount by signs in recent Italian criticism of a growing interest in this aspect of Manzoni.[4] This 'élève de rhétorique', as he once described himself, 'qui *a* écouté, quelquefois et en passant, à la porte de la salle de philosophie'[5] is himself now being listened to and is found to have pertinent things to say about those *sousentendus,* as he called them, those ideas underlying all language and discourse, which he thought it the proper business of philosophers to examine.[6] I observe too that the thought of Leopardi also has attracted a growing attention since the war.[7] These renewals of interest tend to represent, understandably, rather different backgrounds: Catholic in Manzoni's case and humanist or Marxist in Leopardi's; but not without some overlapping.

Since comparison presupposes definition, let me now try briefly to define or describe, in their salient characteristics as I see them, these two poetico-philosophical mentalities, beginning with the older man Manzoni. This done, I shall attempt to draw the threads together and compare and contrast the two in terms of what seems to me most characteristic and essential in the way each used and applied the concept of truth.

Everyone knows that Manzoni was a Christian, and discerning readers will know that in him an ardent faith went hand in hand with a very rational cast of mind and a conviction of the rightness, indeed the duty of using reason freely and vigorously on all serious matters, not excluding the issue of religious belief. This rational temper, reflected in the persistent logical finesse of his prose, is a constant in Manzoni's work, in his approach to every topic without exception. His return to the Church in youth was the decisive event of his long life and an absolutely religious event; yet he remained, and consciously so, a child of the Enlightenment, even in a sense, of the Revolution: the *Promessi Sposi* from one point of view is all a searching critique of the *ancien régime.* Indeed in a sense he always remained a rationalist, if this term can be used without its negative connotation of disbelief in revelation.[8] He rejected with horror the idea that Christian faith involves any sort of loss or reduction of rationality; and—given the powers he possessed and the interests he came to pursue—this meant that Christianity, as he conceived it, was not only capable of, but demanded, the utmost extension of those powers and interests; which again meant, in particular, an exploration, both rational and poetic, of what I would call the special manzonian problem, the relation between history and morality, man as he has been and man as he should be.

In a way this is only a variant on the age-old issue of the real and the ideal; but the form it took in Manzoni was determined, I think, by the interaction of three personal factors: by his deep interest in history; by an extreme moral sensibility;[9] and by what I would call his intellectualism. His interest in history and his profound and exact knowledge of certain historical periods are generally admitted. It is more relevant to note that this historical bent implied a certain concentration on human nature as social, such as one does not, I think, find in Leopardi, for all the many and acute reflections in the ***Zibaldone*** on social life and customs, and not forgetting the famous call for human brotherhood in the ***Ginestra.*** The difference is not a matter of themes or topics but of fundamental outlook. Nor do I wish, in affirming that in one sense Manzoni's thought was socially orientated and Leopardi's was not, to dispute the general rightness of the post-war reaction in Italy, chiefly in Marxist circles, against the old, rather facile stress on Leopardi's solitude and misanthropy; nor even at present to dispute Salvatorelli's and Luporini's judgement that the thought of Manzoni is politically sterile whereas Leopardi's has an enduring vitality.[10] I am concerned, now, not to evaluate attitudes but to define them; and by attitudes here I mean characteristic and basic ways of taking stock of the human situation. Both our subjects were poets but for Leopardi poetry meant chiefly lyrical utterance, for Manzoni poetic drama which was to Leopardi the least poetic form of poetry. Again, for Manzoni incomparably the richest material for poetry was historical fact—what existing men have actually thought and done; and his best lyrics—the first chorus of *Adelchi, Cinque maggio, Marzo 1821, La Pentecoste*—are themselves brief distilled histories; whereas whatever Leopardi said about poetry even allowing, I think, for the final realistic phase, presupposed the position he had adopted in adolescence, that poetry is born of illusion—'l'illusione senza cui non ci sarà poesia in sempiterno'.[11] I say 'said *about* poetry', for of course the leopardian lyric itself represents, both in theme and in tone, a persistent *rejection* of illusion; so that paradoxically it is in fact dominated by an ideal of truth, by a continual taking the measure, so to say, of a human and cosmic reality which simply *is what it is*. But the 'realities' envisaged by the two men differ *toto coelo*; and a very important factor in the difference, and one that is not reducible to the opposition between Christianity and atheism, is Manzoni's special concern with morality. His historical curiosity was entirely governed by an interest in the relations between men as involving justice and injustice; so that through the study of laws, institutions, etc., it always came round in the end to ethical matter, to a preoccupation with right and wrong, to a contemplation of actions as at once interpersonal and morally responsible; whereas in general the relationship Leopardi was most deeply concerned with was only unilaterally personal and not, I would say, properly ethical at all. I will return to this last point, only asking you for the moment to try to imagine Manzoni even conceiving the basic situation expressed in the *Canto notturno d'un pastore errante,* where all mankind speaks through one solitary shepherd alone with the moon and stars and his indifferent sheep. All mankind—yes, for half the theme of that great poem is the common human lot ('la vita mortale, lo stato mortale'), the other half being, to adopt Pascal's phrase, 'ces espaces infinis (la stanza / smisurata e superba)' and their 'silence éternel (silenziosa luna)'; but it is a humanity facing outwards, away from itself; facing a world not merely unknown but *unconscious*. And that is never Manzoni's attitude: the universe outside man did not greatly interest him; when he faces outwards, away from humanity, it is towards God alone, whose traces he thought he discerned *within* humanity.

But such a 'facing outwards' is Manzoni's attitude as believer and thinker, not—or not immediately—as an artist; witness the *Promessi Sposi* in which Manzoni the artist found his *complete* expression. And what in the

novel Manzoni aimed at achieving was precisely that which he had already defined as the proper and only adequate aim of the historian: to represent as far as possible the *whole* condition of a given society in a given period.[12] The aims of historian and novelist (or poet) are so far identical: to represent man in his whole social reality. Yet obviously poetry is not history, as art is not science. And yet again, if there is one thing which characterizes Manzoni's intellectual procedures from first to last it is a tendency to relate every aspect of the human spirit as closely as possible to *knowing*; to see every human activity as an expression of some aspect of truth. It is this that I call his intellectualism, and from it sprang his special problem about poetry and his two chief attempts at a solution: the *Lettre à M. Chauvet* of 1820 and the *Del romanzo storico* a dozen years later.

Manzoni's instinctive starting-point, what he felt in his bones from the first, was that poetry simply could not be an interesting, an 'adult' matter at all—it was a refined and disguised frivolity—if and in the degree that it could be separated from reason, the faculty of truth, and regarded as a product of mere sensibility and imagination. Now just this separation was vehemently affirmed by the young Leopardi, and affirmed in the name of 'holy Nature', the source of all poetry as of all that was great and good in man; but also, alas, and by the same token the source of illusions, for reason, and knowledge its bitter fruit ('l'acerba verità'), was Nature's enemy; and though in his later years (notably in his great poetic testament *La ginestra*) Leopardi came round implicitly to a certain reconciliation between reason and poetry, it was on grounds that are anything but manzonian, as we shall see. His usual explicit view is recorded, for example, in the *Zibaldone,* in June 1821: poetry has nothing to do with philosophy or science, since 'its proper object is the beautiful, which is to say the false, for the truth (such is our sad human lot) has never been beautiful'.[13] Or again in the following March, speaking of a philosopher he admired, 'his aim was not beauty but the thing most contrary to it, truth'.[14] For Manzoni, however, 'only the true is beautiful'.[15] It is truth that is holy—'il santo vero'[16]—and while poetry and science represent different approaches to truth and illustrate different aspects of it, nevertheless the poet, so far as he is genuinely one, is guided in his own way by reason and arrives in the end at reason's proper objective, true knowledge. Hence the essential element of reflection in great poetry: 'To those who say poetry is based on imagination and feeling and reflection only chills and numbs it, I answer that the more deeply one explores the human heart for truth, the more true poetry one will find.'[17] Or again, with characteristic pugnacity: 'Literature (les belles-lettres) will be accurately considered only when it comes to be regarded as a branch of the moral sciences';[18] which, along with the previous allusion to the 'human heart', points us towards the kind of truth Manzoni expects poetry to reveal: it is truth about man, both man as a moral agent, balanced between right and wrong, and man as a feeling, desiring subject. This human complexity is the matter of poetry. But first of all it has been history itself, it has happened or is happening: let the poet only look and see; what could he imagine, make up, invent more interesting than that which exists?[19] More *interesting*—that is the right manzonian word here, with its connotations of attending, considering, thinking; Manzoni's theory of art, though in one sense 'romantic', is thoroughly intellectualist. Poetry depicts passion because it depicts man, and the poet cannot depict what he does not feel; but that is only his starting-point. The purpose of his art is not to feel or make others feel but to induce a state wherein feeling is contemplated;[20] to bring about certain states of contemplation of which the poet alone has the secret; and he has this secret, he is truly a poet, in the degree that, besides a special capacity for feeling, he has also the capacity to achieve an *idea* of his emotion, and so discern the 'truth' of it: 'la verità insomma di quell'affetto'.

But what, more precisely, is this poet's truth? How does it differ from the historian's or the scientist's? This question gave Manzoni a deal of trouble. His first answer came with the defence, in the *Lettre,* of romantic drama. Poetry is essentially an insight into history and the poet *par excellence* is Shakespeare. Now history is apprehended under two aspects: as a connected series of objective events and as subjective experience: the first is the province of ordinary historiography, the second the special field of poetry. The poet's task then is to complete man's possession of his past by bringing out its inward subjective side, the part the historian cannot reach to, 'la partie perdue', the felt experience of countless human individuals.[21] But this was only an *ad hoc* answer, it could not satisfy Manzoni for long. For, first, it defined poetry in terms of a special subject-matter, not as a special way of treating *any* subjective matter; and secondly, by so stressing the historical aspect it seemed to leave poetry still confused with positive factual knowledge (albeit 'spiritual' facts), thus discounting the element of imagination and invention. Hence in the *Del romanzo storico* the idea of 'inwardness' is tacitly dropped, and with it the stress on the common subject-matter of poetry and history. The specific imaginative factor of invention in poetry is frankly accepted: and the proper *res* of poetry, the object the poet *qua* poet produces for contemplation, is specified as 'il verosimile', a verisimilitude, something quite distinct from the historian's factual truth, 'il vero positivo', and claiming a quite distinct kind of assent from the mind.[22] In fact, this brief dense essay all turns on a distinction between historical assent, given to truth of fact, and poetic assent, given to verisimilitude;[23] and the ground is cleared for an unconfused consideration of the latter. But here, just when we expect at last a positive definition of poetry and the poetic, Manzoni

breaks off, leaving us only tantalizing hints and suggestions—brilliant, seminal, no more. Two points, however, have emerged clearly. First, the 'verosimile', the proper matter of art, may be an illusion in respect precisely of its mere *likeness* to factual truth (as Don Abbondio is only 'like' a country priest in seventeenth-century Lombardy), but considered in a wider perspective it is unquestionably *true*; a genuine object in its own right offered, for contemplation, to the truth-seeing faculty of intellect. And secondly, we can say what truth this is, what area of reality it shows: for on this point the teaching of the *Lettre* is maintained, that poetry's function is to give knowledge of man; but it does so by the creation of truth-likenesses, where the truth presupposed and implicit is an idea of man as a being open to all the possibilities inherent in a nature that requires to be defined in terms of *indeterminacy*—driven by an indeterminate desire for happiness and able at any moment freely—that is, out of a previous indeterminacy—to determine itself by an act of will. Now every act of the will for Manzoni is governed by truth or falsehood, as is every act of the mind; and as thinking is either true or false, so in its own order, the practical order, is voluntary action. It is either a conforming or a not conforming to the full reality of a given situation; it is either, that is, just (practical truthfulness) or unjust (practical mendacity). If then every act of will is either just or unjust, the truth about man, which is poetry's truth, 'il vero poetico', will be a showing of justice and injustice, good and evil, a 'vero morale'.

Thus implicitly poetry is a lesson, it suggests an ideal. But looking out on history, on reality, Manzoni, like Newman, was appalled by that same 'heart-piercing, reason-bewildering fact' of human misery which Newman summarized in an inspired page of the *Apologia*. Only, perhaps Manzoni's reason was less bewildered than that of his great contemporary. He did not pretend to discern God's ways in history; nor even think it was his business to try. But he did think he discerned in man himself the fundamental cause of human distress—namely, that, within the limits of this life, man's natural desire for happiness is basically irreconcilable with his equally natural (if often less obvious) sense of moral obligation. The 'drive' for happiness and the claims of justice—reducible to the claims of truth as governing not intellect alone but also will—these two things can perfectly unite only in another life, an immortal life, where justice is transformed into and rewarded by the vision of its divine source, truth itself.[24]

Human history then is borne onward by an inward conflict which cannot be resolved within history itself; the forces involved—the subject's urge to happiness, the objective demands of justice—these are reconciled only outside history. Ultimately they will, they must unite, but this is a truth taught not by history but by religion.

To this view of things the only serious alternative, for Manzoni, was Utilitarianism, the reduction of the two conflicting forces to one by simply absorbing morality into the desire for happiness, making it a mere calculation of utilities to that end. But this, he said, was to solve the problem by denying its existence; and its existence was as undeniable intellectually as the difference between the concept of the useful and the concept of the just; a difference he thought self-evident.[25]

In a sense Leopardi's ideas lend themselves more easily than Manzoni's to a treatment in line with my general aim, which is not so much to analyse two philosophical systems as to describe and contrast two different mentalities or outlooks; an undertaking that perhaps suits Leopardi's case better than Manzoni's just because on particular topics his thought is usually less rigorous and precise—its characteristic procedure being a kind of extension into the poet's growing experience of the world of certain primary intuitions, strongly emotive in character, which themselves are never closely or dispassionately analysed.[26] This is not to say that Leopardi is not self-critical; it is only to say that dialectically he is less so than Manzoni. He is content with vaguer concepts and looser reasoning. His intellect is less detached (on the conscious level at any rate) from subjective emotional factors; one sign, I suggest, of this being that Leopardi is hardly ever, as Manzoni constantly is, ironical at his own expense. His mind developed and changed; indeed it remained to the end open to change, to a degree impossible for Manzoni, so that even Leopardi's apparently final conclusions and most cherished positions have always something provisional about them, but it is a feature of his mind that it never kept pace logically with its own development. His ideas are 'tried out'—reasoned about up to a point and then left for another occasion: which of course suits the diary form he gave them—or rather, no doubt, it was the diary form which profoundly agreed with his original cast of mind. Leopardi is a blend of visionary and philosophical essayist; and perhaps his best essays, and certainly the greater number, were written for himself alone, in a private journal of unique range and richness and candour. But the philosophy in it is always somehow 'essays'.

I said that his mind remained open to the end, contrasting him in this with Manzoni. It is broadly the difference between an empiricist and a philosophical realist. For Manzoni to possess an intellect was to be always *able* to possess some absolutely irrefragable certainties. Intellect is the faculty that records logical necessities, and whatever is logically necessary is an eternal and universal truth—irrevocable: 'to know some things for certain', he said, 'there's no need to be omniscient; enough to be intelligent'.[27] Now at first sight Leopardi too seems full of certainties—even dogmatic (and far more so than Manzoni); but the deeper one gets into the

Zibaldone the more the profoundly *provisional* nature of this thought comes home to one. Deep down Leopardi—the essayist Leopardi—is a relativist; and this because from first to last it was at least his intention, *when philosophizing,* simply to stick to facts as he saw them, to be thoroughly empirical, to eschew metaphysics. Anything might ultimately be true, but ultimate truth is beyond our range. The universe may even, ultimately, be more good than evil (or the reverse); but relative to us evil predominates; that is the *fact*.[28] As I have said, this tentative empirical 'intention' is not evident prima facie in the *Zibaldone*; especially in the earlier sections it is offset and obscured by the great dramatizing stresses on the visionary starting-points (life and the threat to life, nature and rationality): it is none the less, I think, the very soul of the work considered as philosophy. In what follows I shall be concerned to state certain main positions taken up successively by Leopardi. But I would wish it to be understood that in my view he attached, implicitly, a proviso to every such position (even to the final vision of *La ginestra*), the proviso, 'this is truth *as I see it*'.

His development presents three constant features: sensism and pessimism and a habit of representing reality in oppositions or contradictions. Leopardi's sensist theory of knowledge derived from Locke through the French 'philosophes'.[29] It took root in him before he was out of his teens and I do not think he ever clearly thought it out. To say that all thinking derives from sensation seemed to him virtually the same as to say that all thought *is* sensation of some kind; for the only alternative he seems ever to have envisaged—only to reject it as early as 1821—was the theory of innate ideas, which he thought Locke had finally refuted.[30] And if innatism was false, belief in God lost its rational basis: 'Certainly, now that the Platonic pre-existing forms are destroyed, God is destroyed.'[31] Sensism opened the way to materialism, and—after some early hesitations—to the lucid atheism of *La ginestra.*

'Lucid', but only in a sense: what is lucid in the *Ginestra,* Leopardi's final—in the sense indicated—vision of man and Nature, are the contours of the picture, not the ideas they presuppose and give shape to: on the one side the vast mindless universe, utterly indifferent to man; on the other side mankind united in a common scorn and defiance of this dreadful and yet contemptible environment, and called to fight, literally to the death, against it—mankind doomed yet indomitable. The picture is indeed tremendously clear; but the ideas involved—matter, existence, man, reason, truth, happiness—each of these notions has become in the poet's mind a focus of thought and feeling expressing attitudes of attraction or revulsion; each lives in him by the emotional charge it carries; and what it expresses in the last resort is Leopardi's personal misery and his struggle to come to terms intellectually with it. He was not a metaphysical materialist for he was not a metaphysician. On the other hand—and here Timpanaro is surely right against the Marxists—you cannot explain Leopardi's pessimism as an extrapolation of politico-social discontent.[32] The declared basis of his final cosmic pessimism is a radical opposition between life and existence: 'life', represented chiefly by man, necessarily desires happiness; 'existence', i.e. the mindless material cosmos, takes no account of this desire and continually frustrates it and from time to time simply stamps it out. Man's fight against existence (called 'Natura' in the ***Ginestra***) is decided in advance, and against man. Defeat is inevitable (as in Marxism it presumably is not): meanwhile humanity's only nobility consists in fighting. But what is humanity?

To this question Leopardi gives always, implicitly, one answer: man is the being who *stands in opposition.* In his earlier meditations it is a human self-opposition that he stresses; later, and with increasing intensity, man's opposition to the universe. Each stage expresses a reaction to evil and suffering; and the change from the first stage to the second consisted essentially in a shifting the blame for this from human nature to Nature generally, to the whole cosmic order. In Leopardi's early, 'rousseauistic' phase the agent of evil is located in reason itself. Reason arising—inexplicably—within man has withered his natural life at the root, destroying the natural illusions which are the precondition of all that is noble in him—moral vigour, generosity, enthusiasm, poetry: 'reason is the enemy of all greatness'.[33] But gradually a different attitude prevails, affecting first the concept of Nature and eventually that of reason also. Bit by bit Leopardi separates Nature from man; until, with the ***Operette morali,*** composed for the most part in 1824, 'she' is virtually identified with the non-human, with the indifferent cosmos 'outside'. The 'Mother Nature' illusion is destroyed. But this separation is not yet a fully declared opposition: mankind, in the poet's vision, is still more a victim than a rebel; more to be scorned or pitied than admired. By 1829, however, Leopardi had taken sides unconditionally with man against Nature, in terms which anticipate his call to mankind, in *La ginestra,* to declare itself innocent of all evil and lay the blame squarely on 'a higher principle' (. . . 'ma dà la colpa a quella / che veramente è rea' . . .).[34] His revolt had found its moral principle. All that was needed now to complete the poet's self-identification with the human against the non-human was that he fully accept reason and reason's abhorrence of illusion, and so become, in Luporini's phrase, 'a hero of the truth'.[35] And this acceptance of truth, the leopardian truthfulness, is complete in *La ginestra.*

How shall we characterize it, finally? Its dominant ethical note is a proud sincerity: its contrary, the theistic and Christian 'illusion' ('le superbe fole'), is rejected with contempt. But precisely as cognitive, as a declaration of or aspiration to knowledge, this final Leopardian 'truth' is essentially, it seems to me, an acceptance of *fact,* a statement that man's solitude within an utterly alien reality is *simply the case.* For here the term 'truth' does not imply, in the poet's intention, anything other than sheer fact—not any demand that the universe should make sense, for that has been ruled out from the start; not any aspiration towards some light on the total darkness; not even any protest against the absence of light; only a recognition that things are as they are, followed by a call to mankind to shoulder the consequences and join in a common war against 'pitiless Nature'. Thus the object implied by Leopardi's 'vero' is primarily extramental material fact, and then the irreconcilable opposition between this and human nature. But observe—not in the ***Ginestra*** but in the background ***Zibaldone***—one further essential point. As he considered and reconsidered the opposition between the universe and man a new horror took shape in Leopardi's mind: did not that opposition perhaps not only doom man to death and extinction but make nonsense of logic itself? The discrepancy between the mind's pretensions and material fact, already in a way implicit in Leopardi's sensism, now turns into a deeper, a more radical opposition between rationality and existence. Nature or existence goes its own way, indifferent to the *natural* desire for happiness inborn in living things; and this is a contradiction written into existence itself, 'terrifying but none the less true; a great mystery, an inexplicable mystery unless one denies that anything is absolutely either true or false (and my system involves this denial) and unless one in a sense even gives up the principle of contradiction, *non potest simul esse et non esse'.*[36] His philosophy of opposition could hardly go further than that.

And now perhaps the broad contrast between his outlook and Manzoni's is clear enough for our purpose. In Leopardi's thought a double tendency has been noted: to the affirmation of empirical fact and to the affirmation of opposition or contradiction; leading in the end to the self-questioning materialism of the last poems—the positive note sounding in *La ginestra,* while the nuance of doubt is heard in the closing lines of *Sopra il ritratto d'una bella donna.* His 'truth' opposes man to the universe as it is in fact, and existence to reason. But for Manzoni fact, empirical fact, is only a medium through which the mind passes so as to return to itself and to the discovery within itself, underlying all its activities, of certain inchoate 'showings' of absolutely necessary and universal truth. These showings are not 'innate ideas'; that view of their origin in us Manzoni expressly rejects, though he offers no thoroughly formulated view of his own. But two points were for him certain: first, that the truth we apprehend in these ideas is absolutely objective—we do not cause it, we simply receive it;[37] and secondly (but this point is left more obscure), that these ideas represent a sort of contact between our finite minds and the infinite Mind; a contact which for Manzoni (as for Dante) adumbrates the possibility, even for us, of sharing eternally in the vision of infinite truth.[38] Both he and Leopardi were children of the Enlightenment and of rationalism, and both loved reason (though Leopardi in youth thought he did not) and they followed reason wherever it seemed to lead; and it led them in opposite directions. And perhaps these are the only possible directions open, in the end, to human thought. It is not for me to say, here and now, which I think the right one.

Notes

1. *Tutte le opere di A. M.,* ed. A. Chiari and F. Ghisalberti, Milan, 1963, iii, p. 596. For works by M other than the 'Lettre à Cousin' references will be to *Opere di A. M.,* ed. M. Barbi and F. Ghisalberti, 3 vols., Milan, 1942-50; and in the case of the *Osservazioni sulla morale cattolica* also to the critical edition, with commentary, of R. Armerio, 3 vols., Milan-Naples, 1966.

2. See L's letters to his publisher Stella in 1826, *Epistolario di G. L.,* ed. F. Moroncini, iv, pp. 63, 78, 85, 101, 119; cf. M. Porena, *Scritti leopardiani,* Bologna, 1959, pp. 393-5.

3. *Promessi Sposi,* c. I; and cf. his description of *Adelchi*: 'mon petit monstre romantique' (letter to Fauriel, 6 Mar. 1826, *Carteggio,* ed. Sforza and Callavresi, p. 10).

4. e.g. the new edition of *Osservazioni sulla morale cattolica* by R. Armerio, mentioned in n. 1, p. 243, the third volume of which, *Studio delle Dottrine,* is the most careful analysis yet made of M's thought in general. Other noteworthy recent studies: B. Boldrini, *La formazione del pensiero etico-storico del M,* Florence, 1954; R. Montano, *M o del lieto fine,* Naples, 1950; N. Sapegno, *Ritratto di M,* Bari, 1961; L. Derla, *Il realismo storico di A. M.,* Milan-Varese, 1965.

5. 'Lettre à V. Cousin', ed. cit., p. 583.

6. Ibid., p. 597.

7. Some noteworthy studies within this period: C. Luporini, 'L progressivo', in *Filosofi vecchi e nuovi,* Florence, 1947; W. Binni, *La nuova poetica leopardiana,* Florence, 1947; L. Salvatorelli, *Il pensiero politico italiano dal 1700 al 1870,* Turin, 1949 (5th ed.); G. A. Levi, *Fra Arimane e Cristo,* Naples, 1953; B. Biral, *La 'posizione storica' di G. L.,* Venice, 1962; G. Berardi, 'Ragione e stile in L', *Belfagor,* xviii, 1963, nos. 4-6; *L e il Settecento. Atti del I Convegno internazionale di studi leopardiani,* Recanati, 1964; S. Timpanaro, 'Alcune osservazioni sul pensiero di L' and 'Il L e i filosofi antichi', in *Classicismo e illuminismo nell'Ottocento italiano,* Pisa, 1965.

8. See R. Armerio, op. cit. iii, espec. pp. 51-7, 66-90; R. Montano, op. cit., pp. 139-46.

9. 'E in verità è la visione morale, l'attenzione volta non ai dati fisici o sentimentali o d'altro genere ma all'essenza peccaminosa o virtuosa degli atti che costituisce la natura vera della visione manzoniana. Dove altri sentono il distacco dei colori, i rilievi fisici, il Manzoni vede qualità morali.' R. Montano, op. cit., pp. 88-9.

10. Cf. L. Salvatorelli, op. cit., p. 189 (in 2nd ed.); C. Luporini, op. cit., p. 273.

11. *Zibaldone* 17 (ed. Flora, i, p. 23). For the pre-eminence given by L to lyric poetry, see *Zibaldone* 4234-6, 4367, 4475-7 (ed. Flora, ii, pp. 1063-5, 1191, 1283-4).

12. Cf. *Del romanzo storico,* p. 626 of vol. ii of *Opere,* ed. Barbi and Ghisalberti; *Osservazioni sulla morale cattolica,* ibid., pp. 34-5 (in R. Armerio, op. cit. ii, p. 10). It is, of course, relevant to note that in the *Lettre à M. Chauvet,* defending romantic drama against neo-classicist objections, M calls the general method of such drama 'le système historique', *Opere,* ii, p. 322. Cf. also *Carteggio,* ed. cit. i, p. 541.

13. *Zibaldone* 1228-31 (ed. Flora, i, pp. 828-30); cf. ibid. 168 (ed. cit. i, p. 184): 'La cognizione del vero cioè dei limiti e definizioni delle cose, circoscrive l'immaginazione.' It is the theme of the canzone *Ad Angelo Mai.*

14. *Comparazione delle sentenze di Bruto minore e di Teofrasto,* in *G. L., Opere,* ed. S. Solmi, 'La Letteratura Italiana: Storie e Testi', Milan-Naples, 1966, ii, t. 1, pp. 682-3.

15. *Del romanzo storico,* in *Opere,* ed. cit. ii, p. 631.

16. *In morte di Carlo Imbonati,* in *Opere,* ed. cit. iii, p. 213.

17. *Opere,* ed. cit. iii, p. 618; cf. p. 488.

18. *Opere,* ed. cit. iii, p. 617.

19. *Lettre à M. Chauvet,* in *Opere,* ed. cit. ii, pp. 344-6, 351.

20. *Lettre à M. Chauvet,* in *Opere,* ed. cit. ii, pp. 368-9; cf. R. Armerio, op. cit. iii, pp. 225-31, 237-40.

21. *Lettre à M. Chauvet,* in *Opere,* ed. cit., p. 347.

22. *Del romanzo storico,* in *Opere,* ed. cit. ii, pp. 627, 630.

23. This is R. Armerio's view and I accept it; see ed. cit. iii, p. 248; and cf. R. Montano, op. cit., pp. 34-7.

24. See the very important ch. 3 of *Osservazioni sulla morale cattolica,* in *Opere,* ed. cit. ii, pp. 48 ff. (in R. Armerio's critical ed. cit., ii, pp. 45 ff.); and the Appendix to this chapter, the critique of Utilitarianism—which in fact is a short treatise on the subject—in *Opere,* ed. cit. ii, espec. pp. 185-92 (R. Armerio, ed. cit. ii, pp. 349-67).

25. See the Appendix on Utilitarianism referred to in n. 1, above: *Opere,* ed. cit. ii, pp. 175-213; R. Armerio, ed. cit. ii, pp. 323-410.

26. See the acute observations of S. Solmi (beginning 'Leopardi è, e non è, un filosofo') on pp. xiv-xvii of the Introduction to vol. ii of his edition referred to in n. 2, p. 249 above.

27. Appendix on Utilitarianism, *Opere,* ed. cit. ii, p. 177; R. Armerio, ed. cit., p. 331.

28. *Zibaldone* 4258, cf. 1340-1, 4134 (ed. Flora, ii, pp. 1090-1; i, p. 902; ii, p. 960).

29. See in *Leopardi e il Settecento: Atti,* etc. (cf. n. 4, p. 245 above), the contributions of M. Sansone, pp. 133-72, of A. Frattini, pp. 253-82, and of A. L. de Castris, pp. 399-413. Cf. also M. Losacco, *Indagini leopardiane,* Carabba, 1937, pp. 165 ff., S. Timpanaro, op. cit., pp. 145-6.

30. *Zibaldone* 1339 (ed. Flora, i, p. 902).

31. Ibid. 1342 (ed. Flora, i, p. 903).

32. S. Timpanaro, op. cit., pp. 174-82.

33. *Zibaldone* 14-15; cf. 37, 44-5 (ed. Flora, i, pp. 19-68).

34. *La ginestra,* 123-4; *Zibaldone* 4428 (ed. Flora, ii, p. 1239)

35. C. Luporini, op. cit., p. 252.

36. *Zibaldone* 4128-9 (ed. Flora, ii, pp. 955-6). This is L's clearest assertion of the contradiction *in nature and existence* between man and the universe: cf. the powerful summary by Luporini, op. cit., pp. 246-51.

37. This is the argument of *Dell'Invenzione, Opere,* ed. cit. ii, pp. 675 ff.

38. *Dell'Invenzione,* ed. cit., pp. 690-701; cf. R. Armerio, op. cit. iii, pp. 88-90, 120-3. Dante, *Paradiso,* iv, 124 ff., v, 7-9.

Nicolas James Perella (essay date 1970)

SOURCE: Perella, Nicolas James. "The Sun and Midday in Leopardi." In *Night and the Sublime in Giacomo Leopardi,* pp. 139-51. Berkeley: University of California Press, 1970.

[*In the following excerpt, Perella examines Leopardi's many references in his lyric poetry to light, which he equated with happiness.*]

1

Taking both day and night settings, the number of references to light in Leopardi's not very large output of lyric poetry is strikingly high. We have seen that brightness and clarity have for him a significant affective value of a positive kind (chapter I). In this connection, an entry made in the *Zibaldone* on August 19, 1823, explicitly equates light with happiness, and darkness with melancholy. The affirmation is made by way of illustrating the idea that the "spirit" of man is affected by external physical causes independently of habit:

> Così, per esempio, la luce è *naturalmente* cagione di allegria, siccome le tenebre di malinconia; quella eccita sovente l'immaginazione, ed ispira; queste la deprimono. Un luogo, un appartamento, un clima chiaro e sereno, o torbido e fosco, influiscono sulla immaginativa, sull'ingegno, sull'indole degli abitanti, sieno individui o popoli, indipendentemente dall'assuefazione. Così una stagione, una giornata, un'ora nuvolosa o serena; il trovarsi per più o men tempo in un luogo qualunque oscuro o luminoso, senza però abitarvi, tutte queste   circostanze   fisiche,   indipendenti dall'assuefazione e dalle circostanze morali, affettano, quali momentaneamente quali durevolmente, lo spirito dell'uomo, e variamente lo dispongono.[1]

We would also recall here Leopardi's observation that the sight of sunlight or moonlight in a vast open landscape with a deep clear sky causes in us a pleasurable idea-sensation.[2] Though it seems to shine on his world less frequently than does the moon, the sun is by no means absent from Leopardi's poetry. In his most famous poem—*L'infinito*—there is no specific reference to the sun, but it is certainly on a bright, *serene* day that there takes place the psychologico-sublime experience recorded by that poem. It will be remembered that the poet tells us that he can see a part of the far-off landscape. The hedge that keeps him from seeing the rest of it leaves him gazing into an immense and serene expanse of sky.

So too the bliss recalled in the beautiful canzone *A Silvia* is associated with that time when the boy Leopardi, moved by the singing of the girl, would look out from his window, upon a cloudless sky, the sun-gilded streets and orchards of the village, and, in the brightness of a vast expanse, see as far as the distant sea on the one side and as far as the distant mountains on the other:

> Mirava il ciel sereno,
> Le vie dorate e gli orti,
> E quinci il mar da lungi, e quindi il monte.
> Lingua mortal non dice
> Quel ch'io sentiva in seno.

> (23-27)

This same image and its accompanying emotion are evoked in *Le ricordanze* in a way that involves a curious feature in the poem's first stanza (lines 1-27). At the outset, the poet addresses the night sky with its lovely stars of the Bear. Hence the time is night (or evening) and the poet recollects specifically an earlier time of his life when he would pass the evenings (or early part of the night) seated (the typical attitude suggesting meditation) on the grass, looking up at a stellated sky that brought him enchanting fantasies.

> Vaghe stelle dell'Orsa, io non credea
> Tornare ancor per uso a contemplarvi
> Sul paterno giardino scintillanti,
> E ragionar con voi dalle finestre
> Di questo albergo ove abitai fanciullo,
> E delle gioie mie vidi la fine.
> Quante immagini un tempo, e quante fole
> Creommi nel pensier l'aspetto vostro
> E delle luci a voi compagne! allora
> Che, tacito, seduto in verde zolla,
> Delle sere io solea passar gran parte
> Mirando il cielo, ed ascoltando il canto
> Della rana rimota alla campagna!
>
> (1-13)

There follows a reference to the presence of fireflies in those earlier evenings, and the voices of members of the household heard from a distance:

> E la lucciola errava appo le siepi
> E in su l'aiuole, susurrando al vento
> I viali odorati, ed i cipressi
> Là nella selva; e sotto al patrio tetto
> Sonavan voci alterne, e le tranquille
> Opre de' servi.
>
> (14-19)

But just here the poet introduces a reference to the vast (immense) thoughts and sweet dreams and hopes that once were inspired in him by the sight of the far-off sea and the mountains that appear *azure* in the distance, which sight the poet says he makes out from the very spot in which he now again finds himself.

> E che pensieri immensi,
> Che dolci sogni mi spirò la vista
> Di quel lontano mar, quei monti azzurri,
> Che di qua scopro, e che varcare un giorno
> Io mi pensava, arcani mondi, arcana
> Felicità fingendo al viver mio!
>
> (19-24)

This can only be a vast panorama seen in the clarity of a bright yet serene sunlit day, the same as that in lines 23-27 of *A Silvia*. The phrase "Che di qua scopro" ("which I discern from here") cannot mean that the poet sees that view in the present tense time of the poem, during his evening meditation. Rather, into his "night thoughts" has come, quite naturally as it were, the memory of an affecting view which *on a clear day* can be seen from the spot he now occupies. The connection between this remembered view and the nocturnal images that are actually present is an affective one.[3]

In *La quiete dopo la tempesta* a bright sun breaks through patches of blue sky at the end of a rainstorm; its light "smiles" on hills, fields, and houses, and causes the river to appear clearly in the distant (once again) valley:

> Ecco il sereno
> Rompe là da ponente, alla montagna;
> Sgombrasi la campagna,
> E chiaro nella valle il fiume appare.
> . . . . .
>
> Ecco il Sol che ritorna, ecco *sorride*
> Per li poggi e le ville.
>
> (4-7; 19-20)

In *Il passero solitario,* the sun is radiant in the springtime that the poet says "sparkles" in the air and "exults" in the fields so that in beholding it his heart melts:

> Primavera d'intorno
> Brilla nell'aria, e per li campi esulta,
> Sì ch'a mirarla intenerisce il core.
>
> (5-7)

And later in the same poem the poet stands gazing into the bright air (*l'aria aprica*) at the sun setting behind the distant (yet again) mountains at the end of a clear sunny day (*giorno sereno*), a sun that because it sets symbolizes the waning of the happy time of childhood or early youth:

> e intanto il guardo
> Steso nell'aria aprica
> Mi fere il Sol che tra lontani monti,
> Dopo il giorno sereno,
> Cadendo si dilegua, e par che dica
> Che la beata gioventù vien meno.
>
> (40-44)

That clear sunny day—"il giorno sereno"—appears also at the end of *Il sabato del villaggio* as a metaphor for the happy time of childhood that will pass all too soon:

> Garzoncello scherzoso,
> Cotesta età fiorita
> è come un *giorno d'allegrezza pieno,*
> *Giorno chiaro, sereno.*
>
> (43-46)

In *La vita solitaria* much the same components of the moonlit scene of *La sera del dì di festa* (but they are components common to most of Leopardi's landscapes) are seen to "sparkle" (again) in the light of the sun; and such a moment, especially if the poet then chances to espy a pretty maiden, has the beneficial if temporary effect of stirring the poet's listless heart. In typical Leopardian fashion, this momentary benignancy is also experienced in the silence of a clear serene summer night:

Pur se talvolta per le piagge apriche,
Su la tacita aurora o quando al sole
Brillano i tetti e i poggi e le campagne,
Scontro di vaga donzelletta il viso;
O qualor nella placida quiete
D'estiva notte, il vagabondo passo
Di rincontro alle ville soffermando,
L'erma terra contemplo, e di fanciulla
Che all'opre di sua man la notte aggiunge
Odo sonar nelle romite stanze
L'arguto canto; a palpitar si move
Questo mio cor di sasso.

(56-67)

2

But it is the second stanza of *La vita solitaria* that presents us with the sun in the context of what is surely as remarkable a passage as one will find in Leopardi's poetry. The experience described therein takes place at midday under a sun that does not vivify but silently reflects itself in a motionless lake on the banks of which the poet sits. All around is absolute stillness; there is no sound and no motion in the grass and trees. The lake itself is without a ripple; no bird flutters, no butterfly sports, and not even the cicada is heard. Attuning himself to the setting, the poet feels himself absorbed into the surroundings until all trace of consciousness and sensation is drained from him, whereupon he becomes one with the uncanny stillness:

Talor m'assido in solitaria parte,
Sovra un rialto, al margine d'un lago
Di taciturne piante incoronato.
Ivi, quando il meriggio in ciel si volve,
La sua tranquilla imago il Sol dipinge,
Ed erba o foglia non si crolla al vento,
E non onda incresparsi, e non cicala
Strider nè batter penna augello in ramo,
Nè farfalla ronzar, ne voce o moto
Da presso nè da lunge odi nè vedi.
Tien quelle rive altissima quiete;
Ond'io quasi me stesso e il mondo obblio
Sedendo immoto; e già mi par che sciolte
Giaccian le membra mie, nè spirto o senso
Più le commova, e lor quiete antica
Co' silenzi del loco si confonde.

(23-38)

How different then is this sun and this landscape from what we have met with in the previous quotations. Here it will be instructive to compare the midday hour of the poem with that described by Leopardi in chapter VII of his adolescent compilation *Saggio sopra gli errori popolari degli antichi* (1815):

Tutto brilla nella natura all'istante del meriggio. L'agricoltore, che prende cibo e riposo; i buoi sdraiati e coperti d'insetti volanti, che, flagellandosi colle code per cacciarli, chinano di tratto in tratto il muso, sopra cui risplendono interrottamente spesse stille di sudore, e abboccano negligentemente e con pausa il cibo sparso

innanzi ad essi; il gregge assetato, che col capo basso si affolla, e si rannicchia sotto l'ombra; la lucerta, che corre timida a rimbucarsi, strisciando rapidamente e per intervalli lungo una siepe; la cicala, che riempie l'aria di uno stridore continuo e monotono; la zanzara, che passa ronzando vicino all'orecchio; l'ape, che vola incerta, e si ferma su di un fiore, e parte, e torna al luogo donde è partita; tutto è bello, tutto è delicato e toccante.[4]

The most striking thing about the two descriptions lies in their contrasting moods and the different affective value they attribute to the midday hour. In the prose passage there is nothing of the dead stillness evoked in the verses. At the very outset is that significant Leopardian verb *brillare* suggesting a confident and even joyful value in nature; and, indeed, the paragraph closes with a reference to the "sentimental" (in a positive sense, of course) quality of the scene which is said, in those equally significant and "eighteenth-century" words, to be "tender and touching"—*delicato e toccante.*[5] Rather than the absolute immobility of the midday of *La vita solitaria,* we find what might be referred to as a luxurious torpor or languor, the sense of which is conveyed by way of the signs of life that do exist at that hour.

The poem, on the other hand, develops its description of the midday hour by way of a series of negatives referring to the absence of life, even of those same reduced signs of life that might be expected to prevail at midday. The prose description, in short, is what the verses are not, an *idyll,* and as such is much more in keeping with the idyllic treatment of midday in the poetic tradition from classical antiquity. It is with cause that Leopardi follows his paragraph with a quotation from Virgil.

One of the first bibliographical references made by Leopardi in his *Zibaldone* is to a review of Ignazio Martignoni's study on the beautiful and the sublime. Among the sources of the sublime listed by the reviewer is light such as occurs at midday when the sun is felt as immense and oppressive.[6] But this theme of the oppressiveness of the scorching heat of the sun, which is found so frequently in references to midday, has no place in the experience recounted in *La vita solitaria.* Its presence, in fact, would be at odds with and most likely make that experience impossible. And what Leopardi describes is perhaps not even the uncanny in the usual sense, but rather the sense of a vast deadness that pervades all things. It is as though the whole were bathed in the light of a sun that was without warmth.[7] Symptomatically, the same vision of a lifeless world lying beneath an apparently cold sun is evoked in the *Cantico del gallo silvestre*:

Se sotto l'astro diurno [i.e., the sun], languendo per la terra in profondissima quiete tutti i viventi, non apparisse opera alcuna; non muggito di buoi per li prati, nè strepito di fiere per le foreste, nè canto di uccelli per l'aria, nè sussuro d'api o di farfalle scorresse per la campagna; non voce, non moto alcuno, se non delle acque, del vento e delle tempeste, sorgesse in alcuna banda; certo l'universo sarebbe inutile; ma forse che vi si troverebbe o copia minore di felicità, o più di miseria, che oggi non vi si trova?[8]

Thus Leopardi's midday sun is quite unlike the noon-day sun that Shelley saw descend around him amidst the Euganean Hills. In Shelley's midday, although the plains below lie silent and the air is windless, the Alps around him, all *living* things, and with them his own *spirit* (cf. Leopardi's *spirto*)

> Interpenetrated lie
> By the *glory* of the sky.

And for Wordsworth, as we learn from his poem on Peter Bell, noon should be the hour when one feels "The witchery of the soft blue sky." Least of all is there in Leopardi's midday sun the Panic invitation to immersion in a rich life, even a "divine" life of sensations such as that sung by D'Annunzio who could feel the heat of the sun course through his veins, and the sun itself lodged in his heart. In *La vita solitaria,* midday, the hour of Pan, is entirely without the hushed sense of that august god's presence.

The following stanza from D'Annunzio's poem *L'Annunzio*—and the announcement is that Pan is not dead—is remarkable for its quality of antithesis to Leopardi's stanza in the matter of the effect derived from the same spot of time. While in Leopardi the light and silence of the midday hour are associated with immobility and death, they cause D'Annunzio to throb with the expectancy of a superhuman, cosmic energy:

> Tutto era silenzio, luce, forza, desio.
> L'attesa del prodigio gonfiava questo mio
> Cuore come il cuor del mondo.
> Era questa carne mortale impaziente
> Di risplendere, come se d'un sangue fulgente
> L'astro ne rigasse il pondo.
> La sostanza del Sole era la mia sostanza.
> Erano in me i cieli infiniti, l'abondanza
> Dei piani, il Mar profondo.

(44-52)

Given these verses—and many more like them—it will not surprise us to learn that in an interview granted to Filippo Surico in June 1921, D'Annunzio parried the question whether he liked Leopardi by saying: "È molto lontano dal mio temperamento: la mia arte è solare."[9] And in this respect, even more like and unlike Leopardi's midday experience is what we find in D'Annunzio's poem entitled precisely *Meriggio*. At the noon hour when all seems stagnant and stifling, the poet feels himself dissolving into the objects of nature that surround him until he is lost unto himself and without his former

name (i.e., no longer a mortal human); but now his name is Midday itself, and he *lives* in all things, as silently as death, a life that is divine.[10]

In Leopardi's verses we have anything but panpsychism; as we have seen, there we are far removed from the thrilling sense of a union with a pulsating universe. We are witness to a release of the self from sentiency and a passing into the utter immobility of death.[11] There is no trace of the rhapsodic feeling associated with the sense of a "deeper meaning," that nature mystics claim to experience "while gazing at the sky in the azure noon, and in the starlit evening."[12] And yet Leopardi so often gazed at the sky and at vast expanses of landscapes, both in the azure noon and in the starlit and moonlit evening, that it is perhaps this picture of him that most readily comes to mind at the mention of his poetry. The quality of the emotion associated with that gesture is one of the things we are here concerned with. For this reason we may further ponder the verses from *La vita solitaria.*

Although it is not a Wordsworthian intimation of "a sense sublime / Of something far more deeply interfused" [*Tintern Abbey*] that Leopardi recounts, yet there is something about Leopardi's description that is not without a suggestion of the sublime, precisely in the characterization of the "deep" and "ancient" silence that pervades the whole scene. It is in this feature, if in anything, that Leopardi creates (but unwittingly, if at all) the sense of something like the uncanny. As the *Saggio sopra gli errori popolari degli antichi* shows us, Leopardi knew full well that midday could be experienced as a sacred, awesome hour.

It is this concept, in fact, that his chapter on midday in the *Saggio* is meant to illustrate. The first paragraph with its "idyllic" midday scene is given as an anticipatory contrast to the rest of the discourse, which is introduced with the comment: "Chi crederebbe che quello del mezzogiorno fosse stato per gli antichi un tempo di terrore, se essi stessi non avessero avuto cura d'informarcene con precisione?"[13] There follow several pages of references (from classical, biblical, and early Christian sources) to midday as the hour of Pan and of Panic terror, the midday demon, the apparition of gods and goddesses at noon, etc., in support of the thesis that "È dunque evidente che gli antichi aveano del tempo del meriggio una grande idea, e lo riguardavano come sacro e terribile."[14]

But all this is discounted by the young Leopardi—still firm at that time in his faith in reason and in Christian revealed truths—as superstition which modern enlightened man can happily claim to have eradicated. Though the "later" Leopardi was to lament the passing of such "popular errors" and "superstitions," the rationalist in him always remained too vigilant to allow him to write a poetry that might reactivate them in some mythical way. It is in perfect coherence with this rationalism that in his verse the only evocation of midday as a time when sylvan deities and the goddess Diana appear occurs in the poem *Alla primavera* which, as its subtitle (*o delle favole antiche*) suggests, is a nostalgic farewell to the happy age of fable:

> Già di candide ninfe i rivi albergo,
> Placido albergo e specchio
> Furo i liquidi fonti. Arcane danze
> D'immortal piede i ruinosi gioghi
> Scossero e l'ardue selve (oggi romito
> Nido de' venti): e il pastorel ch' all'ombre
> Meridiane incerte ed al fiorito
> Margo adducea de' fiumi
> Le sitibonde agnelle, arguto carme
> Sonar d'agresti Pani
> Udì lungo le ripe; e tremar l'onda
> Vide, e stupì che non palese al guardo
> La faretrata Diva
> Scendea ne' caldi flutti, e dall'immonda
> Polve tergea della sanguigna caccia
> Il niveo lato e le verginee braccia.
>
> (23-38)

Characteristically, Leopardi himself annotated these verses with the observation that "anticamente correvano parecchie false immaginazioni appartenenti all'ora del mezzogiorno, e fra l'altre, che gli Dei, le ninfe, i silvani, i fauni e simili, aggiunto le anime de' morti, si lasciassero vedere o sentire particolarmente su quell'ora." It is this inerasable rationalism and skepticism that make it impossible to talk of the weird or the eerie in connection with the midday experience of *La vita solitaria.* For the same reason, it is difficult to consider that experience as being characterized by the feeling of the numinous save in a primitive sense.[15]

3

By the same token, we have suggested that Leopardi's midday sun is not the occasion for an ecstasy. The profound quiet is even unlike that which we find at the end of *La sera del dì di festa* where it has the nature of an ominous dread (see above pp. 52-53). For there is no doubt that the experience spoken of in *La vita solitaria* (and the title fits the poem's second stanza to perfection) was one that the solitary poet sought out and welcomed.

This, of course, is also true of the experience described in *L'infinito,* and it is in this connection that both poems reveal a characteristic that distinguishes their respective experiences from that of the mystics. I refer to the conscious subjectivity of the experiences in Leopardi. His words allow us no possibility of assuming that he merged into or was united with a personal God or with a transcendental Reality of any sort. Even if we admit that mystical experiences need not be intrinsically or necessarily connected with these specifically

religious concepts, and that a mystic experience is possible for atheists (e.g., the case of the Buddhistic Nirvana), we are obliged to exclude Leopardi from the category of the mystical. At least we must do so if we assume—and there is good reason for this assumption—that a significant feature of the mystic's belief or his psychology is that "it nearly always includes an unshakable conviction that his experience is not merely a subjective mental state, but that it is objective in the sense that it constitutes a revelation of some transcendental reality. He may call this reality God or Nirvana or the Absolute, but the point is that no mystic will ever admit that his experience is merely a subjective state of his own consciousness, and no more."[16]

The experiences described by Leopardi, on the other hand, are knowingly self-induced and even explicitly declared to be a subjective state. The vast silent spaces beyond the horizon, and the immense sky-sea in which he sweetly drowns have nothing to do with the Christian unified sea of Being or any other notion of a transcendental reality; they are the creation of the poet's own imagination, building, to be sure, on certain natural phenomena: "Io nel pensier mi fingo." The phrase, coming almost at the halfway mark of *L'infinito,* does not belittle Leopardi's experience; rather it signals the triumph of the poetic imagination over a limited reality.

"Un silence absolu porte à la tristesse. Il offre une image de la mort." So wrote Rousseau in the famous fifth promenade of *Les Rêveries du promeneur solitaire.*[17] For Leopardi, however, there were moments when this image of death was terrifying (e.g., *La sera del dì di festa*), and other times when it was friendly and cultivated by him (e.g., *La vita solitaria, L'infinito*). All in all the second stanza of *La vita solitaria* bespeaks an experience that resembles not so much that of *L'infinito* as it does the condition said to be theirs by the chorus of the dead in the stupendous verses sung at the opening of Leopardi's prose composition *Dialogo di Federico Ruysch e delle sue mummie.* Bliss as a state of active and perfect happiness is denied to man in life and in death alike. Yet these dead who are not "returned" to life as sentiency but to consciousness of a sort for a brief quarter hour, make it known that they are safe from that former pain that was life. They have, in death, attained to that condition in which all hope and all desire are stilled, as are all anxiety and fear. Here then is that hymn to death:

> Sola nel mondo eterna, a cui si volve
> Ogni creata cosa,
> In te, morte, si posa
> Nostra ignuda natura;
> Lieta no, ma sicura
> Dall'antico dolor. Profonda notte
> Nella confusa mente
> Il pensier grave oscura;
> Alla speme, al desio, l'arido spirto

Lena mancar si sente:
Così d'affanno e di temenza è sciolto,
E l'età vote e lente
Senza tedio consuma.
Vivemmo: e qual di paurosa larva,
E di sudato sogno,
A lattante fanciullo erra nell'alma
Confusa ricordanza;
Tal memoria n'avanza
Del viver nostro; ma da tema è lunge
Il rimembrar. Che fummo?
Che fu quel punto acerbo
Che di vita ebbe nome?
Cosa arcana e stupenda
Oggi è la vita al pensier nostro, e tale
Qual de' vivi al pensiero
L'ignota morte appar. Come da morte
Vivendo rifuggia, così rifugge
Dalla fiamma vitale
Nostra ignuda natura;
Lieta no ma sicura,
Però ch'esser beato
Nega ai mortali e nega a' morti il fato.

These verses bring to mind a lesser poem that has in common with them the voice of one who has died expressing relief that "the fever called 'Living' / Is conquered at last." But there is nothing in Leopardi's verses of the lilting yet morbid sentimentality that characterizes Poe's *For Annie*. And since Poe has once again found his way into these pages, I should like to suggest a comparison between the "Midday" stanza of **La vita solitaria** and the American poet's early poem *The Lake*:

In spring of youth it was my lot
To haunt of the wide world a spot
The which I could not love the less—
So lovely was the loneliness
Of a wild lake, with black rock bound,
And the tall pines that towered around.

But when the Night had thrown her pall
Upon that spot, as upon all,
And the mystic wind went by
Murmuring in melody—
Then—ah then I would awake
To the terror of the lone lake.

Yet the terror was not fright,
But a tremulous delight—
A feeling not the jewelled mine
Could teach or bribe me to define—
Nor Love—although the Love were thine.

Death was in that poisonous wave,
And in its gulf a fitting grave
For him who thence could solace bring
To his lone imagining—
Whose solitary soul could make
An Eden of that dim lake.

Poe's attempt to create a sense of the eerie is a puerile one here; he was wont to abuse the word "mystic" which, in this case, applied to wind, is ineffectual if not gratuitous. But it is not my intention to comment on the poetic value of the poem which is certainly not one of Poe's best.

Let us simply note that both poems are possessed of a "solitary soul" and that in the two poets we find the same searching out of a lonely spot in which a lake is a fundamental element and where nature reflects an image of and inspires a desire for death. The particular moment in Poe's poem is night; in Leopardi's verses it is midday, that is, the moment when daylight is most intense. It is not the least remarkable thing about the Leopardi example that no less than the blackness of night, the brightness of day could be made to assume the face of death.

Notes

1. *Zibaldone di Pensieri,* 3206; ed. F. Flora (Milan, 1945), II, 321. Compare the following entry made in August 1822: "Le stelle, i pianeti ec. si chiamano più o meno belle secondo che sono più o meno lucide. Così il sole e la luna secondo che son chiari e nitidi. Questa così detta bellezza non appartiene alla speculazione del bello, e vuol dir solamente che il lucido, per natura, è dilettevole all'occhio nostro, e rallegra l'animo ec. ec. *Zibaldone,* 2592; ed. Flora, I, 1540.

2. *Zibaldone,* 1745; ed. Flora, I, 1123-1124.

3. That the poem continues as an evening meditation is made clear by lines 50-55 where the poet hears the village bell-tower sound the hour, whereupon he recalls that the sound used to comfort him as a child during his night fears.

4. Giacomo Leopardi. *Le poesie e le prose,* ed. Francesco Flora (Milan, Mondadori, 1953), II, 280-281.

5. See above, p. 86.

6. *Annali di scienze e lettere* (Milan, 1811), III, 359. See above, p, 85, n. 41.

7. Emilio Peruzzi acutely observed that the blinding glare and heavy sultriness of the midday sun are not present in Leopardi: "In Leopardi non si trova mai l'acceccante fulgore del sole meridiano, l'aria che fiammeggia senza respiro. . . . Leopardi non riesce a sentire l'immobile calura meridiana ed anche quando si prova ad esprimerla finisce per descrivere proprio l'opposto come nella *Vita solitaria* 28-32 (nè gli vale servirsi della negazione perchè questa, come tutti i morfemi, non ha valore poetico)." "Saggio di lettura leopardiana," *Vox Romanica,* 15 (July-Dec. 1956), 148-149. I do not agree, however, with Peruzzi's judgment that Leopardi's utilization of negatives is ipso facto without poetic value.

8. The passage is immediately followed by questions of deep but calm despair, put not to the moon, as is the usual case in Leopardi (in the poetry), but to the sun.

9. F. Surico, *Ora luminosa: Conversazioni letterari con Gabriele D'Annunzio* (Rome, 1939), p. 50.

10. At the beginning of an essay on Giorgione, D'Annunzio makes reference to the idea that the immobility of the midday hour derives from a concentrated passion and a repressed violence: "Soprastava a Venezia una di quelle ore che si potrebbero chiamar paniche, in cui la vita sembra sospesa ma non è, chè anzi la sua immobilità risulta da passione concentrata e da violenza repressa." *Prose scelte* (Milan, 1920), p. 17.

A different and, I believe, consciously anti-D'Annunzian midday experience has been prominent in twentieth-century Italian poetry. The most famous and most significant poem of this later development in Eugenio Montale's *Meriggiare pallido e assorto* where the scorching and blinding noonday sun beats relentlessly on a world of drought.

11. We may compare the verses with the following words, dated Oct. 21, 1820. "Io bene spesso trovandomi in gravi travagli o corporali o morali, ho desiderato non solamente il riposo, ma la mia anima senza sforzo, e senza eroismo, si compiaceva naturalmente nell'idea di un'insensibilità illimitata e perpetua, di un riposo, di una continua inazione dell'anima e del corpo, la qual cosa desiderata in quei momenti dalla mia natura, mi era nominata dalla ragione col nome espresso di morte, nè mi spaventava punto." *Zibaldone,* 291-292; ed. Flora I 272.

12. The words are those of Richard Jeffries, from *The Story of my Heart* (London, 1968), p. 140.

13. *Poesie e prose,* II, 281.

14. *Poesie e prose,* II, 290.

15. Adriano Tilgher first spoke of the feeling of the numinous in connection with Leopardi's *Infinito*. On the *Vita solitaria* he has the following remarks: "Nell'immobilità e nel silenzio profondi del poeta e del mondo si produce la preparata—dunque attesa e desiderata—esperienza spirituale. Il poeta oblia sè stesso e il mondo: cioè con maggior precisione, la barriera tra l'Io e il Non-Io cade, ed egli vive un'esperienza di unità, di naufragio mistico dell'io nel tutto (la stessa con cui si chiude *l'Infinito*). Ma in lui quest'esperienza ha un carattere speciale: egli sente le membra sue come sciolte e senza più spirto nè senso, cioè senza più vita *individuale* e senso dell'*individualità*, e con-

fuse da tempo infinito (lor *quiete* antica) ai silenzi del loco, cioè della Natura. Egli si sente natura e sente la natura come immobilità assoluta. è l'esperienza della Morte." *La filosofia di Leopardi* (Rome, 1940), pp. 156-157. My own view of the question of "mysticism" in Leopardi's experience follows in the text. See also my second essay above.

16. W. T. Stace, *Man against Darkness* (University of Pittsburgh, 1967), p. 33.

17. Ed. J. S. Spink (Paris, 1948), p. 102.

Alfredo Bonadeo (essay date 1974)

SOURCE: Bonadeo, Alfredo. "Death in Leopardi's Prose." *Italian Quarterly* 70 (1974): 3-19.

[*In the following essay, Bonadeo discusses Leopardi's concept of death in the* Zibaldone, *maintaining that the poet was more concerned with life and its purpose than with death.*]

"What meaning and significance can be attached to the fact that man must die?"[1] What meaning and significance, consequently, can be attached to life in view of its extinction? These are the questions that may help to understand Leopardi's concept of death embodied in the prose of the *Zibaldone*. If one bears in mind the pessimism and the unhappiness that pervaded the life and work of the poet from Recanati, one would be inclined to think that he held life into little account, and viewed death as a welcome and liberating event. The glorification of death is indeed said to be part and parcel of romantic thought and sensibility;[2] death was Ugo Foscolo's answer to the narrowness and emptiness of life as conceived in *Le ultime lettere di Jacopo Ortis*. For Leopardi, however, contrary to what one may surmise from his somber vision of life, neither the fact nor the idea of death bears negatively upon his evaluation of human existence nor do they constitute a desirable escape from life. The idea of death brings Leopardi's mind back constantly to the idea of life and to a search for its meaning and purpose; in the end only after the poet has succeeded in imparting positive values to human existence, will mortality become acceptable as a natural occurrence, inspiring neither fear nor attraction.[3]

According to contemporary views there are different ways "in which human beings have sought to reconcile themselves to the fact of death." Three of these ways are: the endeavor on the part of man to make himself "the master of death" by committing suicide; to deny "the reality of death through the belief in . . . immortality"; to conquer "the reality of death through the immortality of the world" man leaves behind.[4] To understand the meaning of life in relation to mortality, and the meaning of death itself, and certainly to reconcile himself to it, Leopardi explored the three approaches to the problem: suicide, immortality of the soul, and immortality of man's work and achievements.

In 1823 Leopardi noted that man, due to "un sentimento naturale della sua propria eternità e indestruttibilità," always "mira alla posterità." This goal, however, Leopardi dismisses as a manifestation of an egotistic and escapist tendency, namely the "desiderio dell'infinito." This desire derives "dal continuo ricorrer che l'uomo fa colla speranza al futuro, non potendo esser mai soddisfatto del presente, né trovandovi piacere alcuno." There is also a practical reason for man's wish to survive death: it lies in the "esperienza già fatta, che la memoria degli uomini insigni si conserva, dal veder noi medesimi conservata presentemente e celebrata la memoria di tal uomini." As a result of this human experience, the concept of, and yearning for, the "fama superstite alla morte" has been introduced among men, and they have avidly sought lasting fame. But this aspiration and search Leopardi finds unnatural to man for the precise reason that nature had not created in man that desire. In fact, in the early times of society, when nature still prevailed among men, "non v'era esempio di rammemorazioni e di lodi tributate ai morti." In those times men were less egotistical, and "neppur gli uomini coraggiosi e magnanimi, quando anche desiderassero la stima dé loro compagni e contemporanei, pensarono mai a travagliare per la posterità, nè molto meno, a trascurare il giudizio de' presenti per proccurarsi quello de' futuri, o rimettersi alla stima de' futuri."[5] Thus, these thoughts do not seem to reveal on the part of Leopardi any particularly keen interest or concern about man's survival through achievements and fame; furthermore, human aspiration to immortality carries in this context the stigma of egotism and unnaturalness.

But if one turns from this detached, cold assessment to the meditations on immortality of four years later, one finds that the problem of death and survival through man's achievements on earth has become a matter of personal concern to the poet from Recanati. The problem is approached by considering the present and the future value of books and writers in Leopardi's times. The considerations evoke a note of pessimism, but they also embody a firm denial of the belief and hope for man's survival through work and fame. The starting point of the ***Zibaldone***'s entry dated 1827 is a reflection on the relationship between the intrinsic and the extrinsic value of books, ancient and modern. "Quanto lo stile peggiora, e divien più vile, più incolto, . . . di meno spesa; tanto cresce l'eleganza, la nitidezza, lo splendore, la magnificenza, il costo e vero pregio e valore delle edizioni." Many works of his time, Leopardi recognized, seemed to be perfect, as far as external workmanship such as printing, is concerned. The em-

phasis on the external value of modern printed works was intended to compensate for the scarcity of internal worth. In fact, "l'arte e lo studio son cose oramai ignote e sbandite dalla professione di scriver libri," and "gli stili moderni" answer only the passing needs of the moment. But there is a more cogent and deep seated reason for modern neglect in writing: modern books are destined to have a very short life because "troppa è la copia dei libri o buoni o cattivi o mediocri che escono ogni giorno, e che per necessita fanno dimenticare quelli del giorno innanzi, sian pure eccellenti." No doubt, the works of the classics will retain the fame, hence the immortality that they have deservedly acquired, but it is utterly impossible for contemporary writers to gain immortal fame, exclaimed dishearteningly Leopardi. Thus, "se mai fu chimerica la speranza dell'immortalità, essa lo è oggi per gli scrittori. . . . Tutti i posti dell'immortalità . . . sono gia occupati." As for modern books in particular, their fate is "come quella degl'insetti chiamati effimeri . . . : alcune specie vivono poche ore, alcune una notte, altre tre o quattro giorni; ma sempre si tratta di giorni." Man's fate is the same as that of the books he writes, and this fate precludes immortality: "Noi siamo veramente oggidi passeggeri e pellegrini sulla terra: veramente caduchi: esseri di un giorno: la mattina in fiore, la sera appassiti o secchi: soggetti anche a sopravvivere alla propria fama, e più longevi che la memoria di noi." There is a final reason that to Leopardi's mind renders the achievement of immortality and hopeless endeavor and goal: the conviction that, no matter how important the single event and individual might have been, they will, in the course of time, be drowned by the complexity and vastness of the perennially unfolding history of human civilization: "Non ai soli letterati ma ormai a tutte le professioni è fatta impossibile l'immortalità, in tanta infinita moltitudine di fatti e di vicende umane, dapoi che la civiltà, la vita dell'uomo civile, e la ricordanza della storia ha abbracciato tutta la terra." Leopardi had in fact no doubt that within "dugent'anni non sia per essere più noto il nome di Achille . . . [e] quello di Napoleone, vincitore e signore del mondo civile" (**Z**, II, 1102-1104).[6] Thus, even though these reflections were certainly erroneous, at least as far as the place in posterity that the name and work of Leopardi himself were to occupy, they nonetheless reveal an extremely skeptical attitude toward man's survival through his achievements after physical annihilation. But, as it will be seen, this negative and hopeless attitude was perhaps due to a solution on much different terms that Leopardi had given to the problem four years earlier.

The idea and belief in the immortality of the soul as an explanation and reconciliation to the impermanence of human existence held some interest and positive value in Leopardi's early life, but they were in the end rejected. In 1820 the poet compared man's immortality and unhappiness with that of the beasts. Whereas the latter are able to achieve a degree of happiness in the course of their lives, man, the most perfect animal, the master of his own world and of all the animals, cannot. Yet, the fulfillment of human existence lies precisely in man's happiness. Then, the fact that man "racchiuda in sè una sostanziale infelicità, è una specie di contraddizione colla sua esistenza al compimento della quale non è dubbio che si richieda la felicità proporzionata all'essere di quella tale sostanza." To Leopardi the way out of this tragic contradiction must be that "la nostra esistenza non è finita dentro questo spazio temporale come quella dei bruti, perche ripugna alle leggi seguite constantemente in tutte le opere della natura." Thus Leopardi grants the human soul immortality as a compensating factor for man's earthly unhappiness: "Una delle grandi prove dell'immortalità dell'anima è la infelicità dell'uomo paragonato alle bestie che sono felici o quasi felici." The happiness that was denied man on earth would be achieved by that part of his being that was to survive him after the destruction of the body. To Leopardi the thought that man would not be able to enjoy at least the same degree of happiness that beasts did enjoy must have been wholly incomprehensible and terrifying; man had to be able to be happy in some way, sometimes. Thus, he reiterated that same year: "L'infelicità nostra è una prova della nostra immortalità, considerandola per questo verso, che i bruti e in certo modo tutti gli esseri della natura possono essere felici e sono, noi soli non siamo né possiamo" (**Z,** I, 61-62, 68).

But such rationalizations were not deeply and lastingly convincing to Leopardi's sensibility and intellect. Why would man have to wait for the otherworldly life to achieve happiness? If this were true, then it was necessary to explain what was man doing in this life, what was the meaning of earthly life, if there was one. The rejection of immortality on the part of Leopardi is partly due to his interpretation of the development of Christian ideas on the subject. The belief in the life of the spirit appeared to him rather shaky, for it was the product of reason, hence artificial. That belief was thoroughly unacceptable to a thinker who deeply believed that man's excellence was based on nature and that reason was its enemy number one. After the original sin, which according to Leopardi consisted precisely in the acquisition and use of an exorbitant amount of reasoning power on the part of Adam (**Z,** I, 338-339), man found himself in a condition where "la ragione aveva preso il disopra sulla natura: e quindi l'uomo era divenuto . . . infelice." Man had become unhappy because the supremacy of reason had made his "natura primitiva . . . alterata e guasta, ed egli era decaduto dalla sua perfezione primigenia" (**Z,** I, 342). Most ironically, however, to show mercy for man's fall and unhappiness God perfected his reason, which then became the tool that substituted nature in the government of man's existence. There followed two consequences. First, since the perfection of reason is not "la perfezione dell'uomo assolutamente, ma bensì dell'uomo tal qual è dopo la corruzione," and since the original essence of man "supponeva e conteneva l'ubbidienza della ragione, in somma tutto l'opposto della perfezione della ragione," man was hopelessly de-naturalized. Secondly, and most important, "la perfezione della ragione consiste in conoscere la sua propria insufficienza a felicitarci, anzi l'opposizione intrinseca ch'ella ha colla nostra felicità." Therefore, the perfection of reason could not but lead man to the conviction that "non poteva essere la sua felicità in questa vita," that "la sua felicità" was "in un'altra vita." It is thus understandable why unhappiness became, and still is, the ideal and a style of life among Christians, why "il Cristianesimo chiama beato chi piange, predica i patimenti, li rende utili e necessari; in una parola suppone essenzialmente l'infelicità di questa vita." God's revelation, finally, disclosed to man his divine nature and predestination. But man's destiny, Leopardi objected, was to achieve happiness on earth by following nature's dictates (**Z,** I, 342-344). Thus, according to Leopardi, Christianity has in a sense taken advantage of man's fall from the state of nature in that it has not endeavored to lead man back to nature where he could recapture his primitive essence and happiness; Christianity seized instead upon man's weakness and unhappiness to persuade him through reason that the fulfillment of his destiny and his happiness lay in a world outside his earthly existence.

Without the expectation of a future, happy life, approaching death cannot be conceived of as the imminent beginning of eternal bliss; hence Leopardi regards it as an agonizing and terrifying event. Let us consider, Leopardi suggested, the situation of an eighty-year-old man; he positively knows that "dentro dieci anni al più egli sarà sicuramente estinto, cosa che ravvicina la sua condizione a quella di un condannato." But even from the point of view of a younger man, the knowledge that some day he will find himself in that situation "basterebbe per istupidire di spavento, e scoraggiare tutta la nostra vita" (**Z,** I, 128). The poet, however, pulls his thoughts out of that bleak picture by envisioning life after death among the ancients. These supposed that the dead "non avessero altri pensieri che de' negozi di questa vita, e la rimembranza de' loro fatti gli occupasse continuamente, e s'attristassero o rallegrassero secondo che aveano goduto o patito quassù, in maniera che, secondo essi, questo mondo era la patria degli uomini, e l'altra vita un esilio, al contrario de' cristiani" (**Z,** I, 147).[7] Thus, the ancients placed "la consolazione, anche della morte, non in altro che nella vita," and judged death "una sventura appunto in quanto privazione della vita, e che il morto fosse avido della vita e dell'azione, e prendesse assai più parte, almeno col desiderio e coll'interesse, alle cose di questo mondo" (**Z,** II, 183).[8] These reflections seemed to provide some comfort to Leopardi's mind and sensibility by conjuring

up an immortality of sort, so much more believable because it was entertained by the deeply admired ancients,
and because it was wholly independent from the "reasoned" tenets of the Christian religion.

But Leopardi was unable to escape the thought of death
and immortality as shaped by Christian thought; in fact
he was haunted by it, and to it he reacted in painful disbelief. In 1827 he approached the problem again from a
practical and emotional standpoint. A person, he pondered, feels tenderness and sorrow for his fellow men
who pass away, in a natural and impulsive manner: "Gli
stimiamo infelici, gli abbiamo per compassionevoli,
tenghiamo per misero il loro caso, e la morte per una
sciagura." But, Leopardi argued, "se l'uomo è immortale, perchè i morti si piangono? . . .

Perchè aver compassione ai morti, perchè stimarli infelici, se gli animi sono immortali?" In truth, man's sorrow and compassion for the dead rest on the instinctual
assumption that they have truly lost "la vita e
l'essere; . . . le quali cose, pur senza ragionare, e in
dispetto della ragione, da noi si tengono naturalmente
per un bene." Those who outlive the deceased believe
that "i morti sieno morti veramente e non vivi; e che
colui ch'è morto, non sia più"; they grieve him because
"ha cessato di vivere, perchè ora non vive e non è. Ci
duole . . . che egli abbia sofferta quest'ultima e irrepa-
rabile disgrazia . . . di essere privato della vita e
dell'essere. Questa disgrazia accadutagli è la causa e il
soggetto della nostra compassione e del nostro pianto."

What bearing do the grief and compassion of the living
for the dead have on the idea of immortality? If immortality implies the survival of the individual soul in the
other world, this means that the souls of the living and
those of the dead will eventually be reunited in that
world. Death would, then, be a temporary separation of
the souls, and as such only a slightly painful event, in
view especially of the eternity that men's souls will live
together. But has any man ever been consoled by the
thought of an eternal life in the company of the soul
who had been taken away from him in this world, asks
Leopardi. On the occurrence of death, he replies, "le
nostre opinioni, la natura e il sentimento in simili occa-
sioni ci portano senza nostro consenso o sconsenso a
giudicare e tenere per dato, che il morto sia spento e
passato del tutto e per sempre." In conclusion, when
men are bereft of those who are close to them, "nel
fondo del loro cuore, piuttosto consentono in credere la
estinzione totale dell'uomo, che la immortalità
dell'animo" (**Z,** II, 1111-1113).[9] Death means man's total extinction.

The idea and act of suicide drew considerable attention
from Leopardi. The vanity and unhappiness of human
life are the causes of modern man's desperation and
yearning to end his own life. The ancients "si uccidevano e disperavano . . . per l'opinione e la persuasione
di non potere, a causa di sventure individuali, conseguire e godere quei beni ch'essi stimavano
ch'esistessero." Modern man, on the other hand, has acquired the notion that nothing good and valuable can be
achieved in life; the idea that "la vita nostra per sè
stessa non sia un bene, ma un peso e un male" prevails
in him (**Z,** I, 389); hence, modern man tends to disparage, and even to hate, his own life. "Che cosa dimos-
trano tante morti volontarie," Leopardi asked himself in
1820 (or 1823), "se non che gli uomini sono stanchi e
disperati di questa esistenza?"[10] In adversity the ancients
conceived "odio e furore contro il fato, e bestemmia-
vano gli Dei, dichiarandosi . . . nemici del cielo, impo-
tenti bensì, e incapaci di vittoria o di vendetta," but did
not turn against themselves. Modern man, on the other
hand, rages against, and hates, himself; we conceive,
wrote Leopardi of contemporary fellow men, "contro la
nostra persona un odio veramente micidiale, come del
più feroce e capitale nemico, e ci compiaciamo nell'idea
della morte volontaria" (**Z,** I, 399).[11] Of his personal
sense of emptiness and desperation he said: "Concepiva
un desiderio ardente di vendicarmi sopra me stesso e
colla mia vita della mia necessaria infelicità insepara-
bile dall'esistenza mia, e provava una gioia feroce ma
somma nell'idea del suicidio" (**Z,** I, 400).

It would seem, then, that the misery of this life, as
Leopardi saw it and experienced himself, wholly explained and justified a clear cut and final solution to human existence, suicide. Yet, the number of suicides,
Leopardi must have realized, was not such as to support
this extremely pessimistic conclusion. To explain this
contradiction he argued that reason, that is religion and
related ideas and feelings about the "incertezza della
nostra origine, destino, ultimo fine, e di quello che ci
possa attendere dopo la morte," were restraints to the
suicidal impulses of modern man. It was distressing
that man could not achieve what under the circumstances was the best solution to his life, Leopardi added;
indeed, what "maggior miseria che il trovarsi impediti
di morire e di conseguire quel bene che è sommo," that
is, self-destruction. It is true that "la natura ripugna con
tutte le sue forze al suicidio"; however, since "la natura
è del tutto alterata, da che la nostra vita ha cessato di
esser naturale, da che la felicità che la natura ci aveva
destinata è fuggita per sempre," and since "quel desiderio della morte, che non dovevamo mai, secondo
natura, neppur concepire, . . . e per forza di ragione,
s'è anzi impossessato di noi," man ought to be able to
choose death freely. Thus religion with the moral inhi-
bitions it imposed upon man's determination appeared
to Leopardi as "un'idea concepita dalla nostra misera
ragione, . . . la più barbara cosa che possa esser nata
nella mente dell'uomo: è il parto mostruoso della ragione il più spietato; . . . il più gran male dell'uomo"
(**Z,** I, 555-557).

To the conflict between what Leopardi regards as modern man's plausible and logical inclination, self-destruction, and self-preservation owing to reason's restraint, the poet returns time and again in the course of his meditations without, however, reaching a solution. "Il suicidio," he wrote in 1821, "è contro natura. Ma . . . non l'abbiamo del tutto abbandonata per seguir la ragione? Perche dunque dovendo vivere contro natura, non possiamo morire contro natura? . . . La presente condizione dell'uomo obligandolo a vivere e pensare ed operare secondo ragione, e vietandogli di uccidersi, è contraddittoria" (**Z**, I, 1240). He acknowledged a year later with more logical and positive certainty that the only possible denouement to life is indeed suicide. Nature forbids it, but human nature is altered; this second nature that governs modern man's life "invece d'opporsi al suicidio, non può far che non lo consigli, e non lo brami intensamente; perchè anch'ella odia sopratutto l'infelicità, e sente che non la può fuggire se non con la morte . . . Dunque la vera natura nostra, . . . permette, anzi richiede il suicidio" (**Z**, I, 1446-1447). Leopardi's firm conviction does not, however, succeed in explaining why most men, after all, prefer to live an unhappy life rather than eliminate their sufferings by an act of the will. "Intorno al suicidio. È cosa assurda che . . . si possa e si debba viver contro natura . . . e non si possa morir contro natura. E che sia lecito d'essere infelice contro natura (che non aveva fatto l'uomo infelice), e non sia lecito di liberarsi della infelicità in un modo contro natura" (**Z**, I, 1494). Elsewhere, meditations on human suffering seem to carry a decisive weight in favor of suicide: "La questione se il suicidio giovi o non giovi all'uomo . . . si restringe in questi puri termini. Qual delle due cose è la migliore, il patire o il non patire? . . . E si conchiude ch'essendo all'uomo più giovevole il non patire che il patire, è matematicamente vero e certo che l'assoluto non essere giova e conviene all'uomo più dell'essere" (**Z**, I, 1521-1523).[12] Not suffering would be better than suffering, and suicide would, therefore, be the best alternative to life. But this choice could not provide a meaning to life, nor support an attitude toward death.

Thus, Leopardi could not reach a definite conclusion, neither practical nor ideological, about the problem of death even though his meditations stood on some well defined assumptions and beliefs. Death for him, on the one hand, was truly the end of physical and spiritual man, for the immortality of man's work and soul had no place in his intellectual and sentimental world. Death through suicide clearly held interest for Leopardi, but not as a final solution; rather, it raised uncertainties and doubts about the human condition. This kind of death was a most suitable way to get rid of the unhappiness and suffering that he saw inexorably associated with modern man's condition. It did not, however, in any way insure the survival, intellectual or spiritual, of the human being; it ultimately meant the total rejection of man's life and value. The authentic reason Leopardi could not accept suicide was not reason's restraints, moral or religious tenets, but a deep-seated, albeit tenuous, faith in the inherent value of human life.

In 1820 he stated that old men love life and fear death much more than young men do. With old age the former experience a decrease in the intensity and vitality of existence; hence, "si estingue o scema il coraggio, e quindi a proporzione che l'esistenza è meno gagliarda, l'uomo è meno forte per poterla disprezzare" (**Z**, I, 274). However, two years later, when he returned to that theme, Leopardi added that craving for life among old men increases "quasi come l'amor del denaio, e, . . . cresce in proporzione che dovrebbe scemare." Thus, they dread death "sommamente e sono gelosissimi della propria vita, ch'è miserabilissima, e che ad ogni modo poco hanno a poter conservare," and they accumulate and preserve as many goods as possible, as if they had to provide for a lengthy existence (**Z**, II, 19-20). Old men's excessive love for life has a more universal reason: "Il timor dei pericoli è tanto maggiore quanto maggiore è l'infelicità e il fastidio di cui la morte ci libererebbe, . . . quanto è più nullo quello che morendo abbiamo a perdere." Paradoxically enough, yearning for life and fear of death have increased everywhere proportionately as the significance of life has decreased. This strange relationship between life and death was borne out, according to Leopardi, by those countries and classes which were under political oppression. These were the least brave, the most fearful of death, and clung desperately to life. The explanation of the phenomenon on the part of Leopardi was that modern man's life, devoid of worthwhile endeavors and purpose, is unhappy; such life is very much like living death, it bears a close resemblance to real death, and it gives man a sharp presentiment of death itself. Thus, "quanto più la vita dell'uomo è simile alla morte, tanto più la morte [è] temuta e fuggita, quasi ce ne spaventasse quella continua immagine che nella vita medesima ne abbiamo e contempliamo" (**Z**, II, 229).

Young men, on the other hand, are perhaps no less unhappy than the old, but they hold the potential for a much more meaningful and purposeful existence; hence, they have no fear of death. For one thing, young people are "più facili a disprezzar la vita, coraggiosissimi nelle battaglie e in ogni rischio." Since the goods of this life "si disprezzano quando si possiedono sicuramente, e si apprezzano quando sono perduti," the young are in this sense the true "possessor della vita", and are more willing to sacrifice it (**Z**, I, 274-275).[13] In fact, they "disprezzano e prodigano la vita loro, ch'è pur dolce, e di cui molto avanza loro, e non temono la morte"; they are willing to sacrifice everything they hold almost as if they were going to die shortly (**Z**, II, 19-20). More importantly, young people possess "più vita o più vitalità" than old ones; they are irresistibly led to use their "forza vitale, di darle sfogo e uscita, . . . di versarla fuori." Unfortunately, the "presente stato degli uomini" and "questa presente mortificazione della vita umana, che contrastano colla vitalità ed energia della giovinezza," cause a stagnation of young men's sentimental and intellectual life, and prevent the potential energy and vitality of the young from being transformed into actual accomplishments (**Z**, II, 68-69).[14] The significance of these reflections lies in this implication: if the conditions of life during Leopardi's time had been favorable, the young people could have lived a purposeful, meaningful existence, the expression of an exuberant and generous vitality. Were the manifestation of such a favorable condition present, the meaning of death for man would, according to Leopardi, be completely altered in such a way that the intense existence allowing for self-expression and purposefulness would nullify to a large extent that fear of death entertained by old men and oppressed people that lead a precarious, worthless existence. It is in the name of an existence that man loves that he is willing to sacrifice his life; a meaningful existence is not only worth living for but also worth dying for. "La vita non fu mai più felice che quando fu stimato poter esser bella e dolce anche la morte"; for instance, "mai gli uomini vissero più volentieri che quando furono apparecchiati e desiderosi di morire per la patria e per la gloria." Thus, "quando gli uomini avevano pur qualche mezzo di felicità o di minore infelicità ch'al presente, quando perdendo la vita, perdevano pur qualche cosa, essi l'avventuravano spesso e facilmente e di buona voglia, non temevano, anzi cercavano i pericoli, non si spaventavano della morte, anzi l'affrontavano tutto dì o coi nemici o tra loro, e godevano sopra ogni cosa e stimavano il sommo bene, di morire gloriosamente" (**Z**, II, 229).[15]

With these considerations Leopardi has, at least partially, solved the problem of human death in terms of the value of existence. Death becomes a less fearful and agonizing eventuality in proportion as life acquires intensity, meaning and purpose, and as death serves to preserve and better that style of life. On these terms death becomes acceptable because it is viewed as an integral part of the living process and it no longer constitutes one final irreversible step into infinite nothingness, it does not evoke a sense of uselessness about life and despair of the mind. If it is a worthwhile existence that makes death acceptable, then it is easy to understand why Leopardi was unable to embrace suicide: the act was to his mind and sensibility simply the expression of a sterile and useless existence. In the poet's conception, then, the attitude and ideas about death depend largely upon the value man places upon existence. The statement of a critic cited at the beginning to the effect that even though Leopardi was convinced that "pain and suffering predominate in life," he was unable to overcome his fear of death[16] should be, first, reversed in this sense: it was Leopardi's fear of living a worthless

existence that led him to foreknow the excruciating pain of dying. Then, it should be rejected, because Leopardi, by holding out the ideal of an intense, meaningful life, successfully aimed to suppress fear in man and thus to help him to master death.

Notes

1. J. G. Gray, "The Problem of Death in Modern Philosophy," in N. A. Scott, ed., *The Modern Vision of Death* (Richmond, 1967), p. 47.

2. Jacques Choron, *Death and Western Thought* (New York, 1963), p. 156. This author states that Leopardi, like Byron, was convinced that "pain and suffering predominate in life," but he was unable "to overcome . . . fear of death." *Ibid.,* p. 298.

3. Except for the inconsequential work of Antonio Borriello, *La visione della morte in Giacomo Leopardi* (Napoli, 1937), no systematic treatment of Leopardi's concept of death is available. But useful observations are scattered throughout critical works on Leopardi. See, for instance, Francesco De Sanctis's remark, based however on works other than the *Zibaldone,* to the effect that Leopardi's intellect longed for death, but sentiment rejected it: *Leopardi,* ed. C. Muscetta, A. Perna (Torino, 1960), pp. 271-272; Eugenio Donadoni, *Scritti e discorsi letterari* (Firenze, 1921), p. 32, stated that "da tutta l'opera del Leopardi non emerge l'apoteosi della morte; si la brama dolorosa della vita." Contrarywise, Sergio Solmi, *Scritti leopardiani* (Milano, 1969), pp. 88-89, sees the idea of death in Leopardi as "l'ultimo rifugio, la suprema valvola di sicurezza, . . . aspirazione al riposo." According to G. A. Levi, "Il suicidio nelle meditazioni del Rousseau e del Leopardi," *Humanitas,* II (1947), 1122-1127, the poet from Recanati rejected the idea of suicide. Raffaele Giolli, "L'occhio di Leopardi," in *La disfatta dell'Ottocento* (Torino, 1961), p. 117, has this interesting observation: "Della morte, Leopardi ebbe solo il ribrezzo, sentendola così vivergli attorno, minaccia del mondo ostile." On Leopardi's deeply disturbing feeling about the ephemeral nature of human things and life see Bruno Biral, "Il sentimento del tempo: Leopardi, Baudelaire, Montale," *Il Ponte,* XXI (1965), 1156-1160. On death as a loss of the "amante compagnia" for the individual, see Umberto Bosco, *Titanismo e pietà in Giacomo Leopardi* (Roma, 1965), p. 84, and Sebastiano Timpanaro, *Classicismo e Illuminismo nell'Ottocento italiano* (Pisa, 1965), p. 162. Finally, on the Christian character of Leopardi's concept of death see Bruno Biral, *La posizione storica di Giacomo Leopardi* (Venezia, 1962), p.38.

4. Arnold Toynbee, "Traditional Attitudes Towards Death," in A. Toynbee et al., *Man's Concern with Death* (New York, 1969), pp. 69, 72, 75-77, 84; Hans Morgenthau, "Death in the Nuclear Age," *The Modern Vision of Death,* pp. 69-70.

5. *Zibaldone di pensieri,* in *Tutte le opere di Giacomo Leopardi,* ed. F. Flora (Milano, 1937), II, 227-228. All quotations from the *Zibaldone* are from this edition and are referred to in the text by Z, followed by the number of the volume, and page.

6. Cf. further the reciprocal relationship between neglect in writing and want of immortality: "Come la impossibilità di divenire immortali giustifica la odierna negligenza dello stile nei libri, così questa negligenza dal canto suo, inabilita, e fa impossibile ai libri, il conseguimento della immortalità." Z, II, 1104.

7. Cf. Z, II, 265-266: ". . . non supponendo gli antichi maggiori beni che quelli di questa vita, fino a credere che i morti, anche posti nell'Elisio, s'interessassero più della terra che dell'Averno, e che gli Dei fossero più solleciti delle cose terrene che delle celesti."

8. Leopardi supports this view by referring to the meaning of funereal games among the ancients. The games were "le opere più vivaci, più forti, più energiche, più solenni, più giovanili, più vigorose, più vitali che si potessero fare." It seems as if the ancients wanted "intrattenere il morto collo spettacolo più energico della più energica e florida vivida vita, e credessero che poich'egli non poteva più prender parte attiva in essa vita, si dilettasse e disannoiasse a contemplarne gli effetti e l'esercizio in altrui" (Z, II, 183). Cf. Z, II, 1224: in death "le consolazioni degli antichi non erano che nella vita; i loro morti non avevano altro conforto che d'imitar la vita perduta."

9. Leopardi had indirectly attacked the idea of immortality by representing the aberrant attitude of a mother "saldissima ed esattissima nella credenza cristiana, e negli esercizi della religione." She felt no compassion for those parents who lost their children; on the contrary, "gl'invidiava intimamente e sinceramente, perchè questi erano volati al paradiso senza pericoli." Diseases and deaths among the young did not affect her in the least "perchè diceva che non importa l'età della morte, ma il modo: e perciò soleva sempre informarsi curiosamente se erano morti bene secondo la religione" (Z, I, 309-311).

10. *Frammento sul suicidio,* in *Tutte le opere di Giacomo Leopardi, Le poesie e le prose,* ed. F. Flora (Milano, 1940), I, 1082. In 1821 Leopardi wrote:

"Noi desideriamo bene spesso la morte, e ardentemente, e come unico evidente e calcolato rimedio delle nostre infelicità, in maniera che noi la desideriamo spesso, e con piena ragione, e siamo costretti a desiderarla e considerarla come il sommo nostro bene" (Z, I, 555).

11. In the *Frammento sul suicidio* Leopardi differentiated suicide among the ancients and modern men thus: "Anticamente gli uomini si uccidevano per eroismo per illusioni per passioni violente . . . e le morti loro erano illustri. Ma ora che l'eroismo e le illusioni sono sparite, e le passioni così indebolite, che vuole dire che il numero dei suicidi è tanto maggiore?" It means that wherever people use reason a great deal "senza immaginazione ed entusiasmo, si detesta la vita; vuol dire che la cognizione delle cose conduce il desiderio della morte." In conclusion, in antiquity "si viveva anche morendo, e ora si muore vivendo." *Le poesie e le prose,* I, 1082, 1084.

12. On the contrast between nature and suicide see further Z, I, 1360: "Se la natura è oggi fatta impotente a felicitarci, . . . perchè dev'ella essere ancora potente ad interdirci l'uscita da quella infelicità che non viene da lei, non dipende da lei, non ubbidisce a lei, non può rimediarsi se non con la morte? S'ella non è più l'arbitrio né la regola della nostra vita, perchè dev'esserlo della nostra morte?" Cf. substantially identical reflections in the "Dialogo di Plotino e di Porfirio" (1827), *Operette morali,* in *Le poesie e le prose,* I, 1008-1010. On Leopardi's apparent yearning for death and powerlessness to embrace it see his *Lettere,* ed. F. Flora (Milano, 1949), pp. 301, 310.

13. The young, however, are likely to experience the same fear of death as old men do, if their life is weakened by diseases; this disability causes a "minor forza del corpo, e quindi dell'animo" (Z, I, 274).

14. Contrarywise, cf. Leopardi on the ancients, their vitality and death: "La vitalità negli stati antichi era tanto maggiore che nei presenti, non solo da compensare abbondantemente ogni cagione o principio di mortalità, ma da preponderare, e far pendere la bilancia dalla parte della vita . . . Così che non è vero che le cagioni di morte . . . fossero maggiori anticamente, anzi all'opposto sono maggiori oggidì" (Z, I, 463).

15. On self love leading to a selfish death, see Z, I, 101: "Effetto dell'amor proprio che preferisce la morte alla cognizione del proprio niente, . . . onde quanto più uno sarà egoista tanto più fortemente e costantemente sarà spinto in questo caso ad uccidersi."

16. Choron, *Death and Western Thought,* p. 298.

Erasmo G. Gerato (essay date May 1976)

SOURCE: Gerato, Erasmo G. "Reality of Illusion and Illusion of Reality in Leopardi's *Zibaldone*." *South Atlantic Bulletin* 41, no. 2 (May 1976): 117-25.

[*In the following essay, Gerato traces Leopardi's increasingly negative assessment of reason, which the poet came to identify as the source of humanity's unhappiness.*]

Illusion is perhaps the most essential element in the *pensiero* of Leopardi, becoming in the end the sole concept capable of rendering life bearable not only for the poet himself but for all of humanity as well.

This study aims at tracing the theme of illusion in the development of Leopardi's thought, especially in relation to one of the poet's least-known works, the ***Zibaldone***. We shall further attempt to show how momentous the presence of illusion was for the poet and how with the passing of time its importance increased.[1]

Reflecting on reason as it contrasts with nature, Leopardi mentions, for the first time the word *illusione* in the ***Zibaldone***, which bears the date 1818. From this point on, it is evident that in the opinion of the poet, illusion is not only desirable and gratifying to man, but absolutely necessary if he is to achieve any greatness in life: "Voglio dire che uno uomo tanto meno o tanto più difficilmente sarà grande, quanto più sarà dominato dalla ragione: chè pochi possono essere grandi (e nelle arti e nella poesia forse nessuno) se non dominati dalle illusioni."[2] Thus, not only must there be illusion, "e senza le illusioni qual grandezza ci può essere o sperarsi?" (***Zib.*** I, p. 20), but nature itself, which in his later writings Leopardi will transform into a malevolent and deceiving element,[3] at this point is still friendly towards man and is "big" in contrast to the "smallness" of reason: "La ragione è nemica d' ogni grandezza: la ragione è nemica della natura: la natura è grande, la ragione è piccola" (***Zib.*** I, p. 19). For Leopardi not only will reason always remain "small" but with the passing of time and with the progression of his thought, reason will acquire an ever more negative aspect and will be identified by the poet as the true source of all man's miseries. In order to illustrate further the contrast between nature and reason, the poet gives the example of a sickly boy who is "assolutamente sfidato e morrà di certo fra pochi giorni" (***Zib.*** I, p. 20). According to reason, the family of the dying boy should stop feeding him, for not only will the nourishment be useless to the boy, but it will also be detrimental to his family which is utterly destitute. Yet according to nature, on whose side firmly also stands religion, to let this young man starve to death would be a most cruel and barbarous act. The result is, therefore, that man places himself on the side of religion and of nature inasmuch as "essa è grande."

Although at this point Leopardi extols nature and still considers her benevolent toward man, we begin to discern a new concept of nature; that is, of nature which, as a malevolent force, is constantly oppressing mankind. Thus, the young man is kept alive and consequently in a state of constant suffering on account of this malevolent nature.

The theme of illusion was first treated in a poem entitled, ***l'Appressamento della morte***. He wrote it, so he says: "in undici giorni tutta senza interruzioni . . . nel Novembre e Dicembre del 1816" (***Op.*** I, p. 281). Feeling death close to him, Leopardi is suddenly, and for the first time in his life, faced with the emptiness of his existence and with the total shattering of his childhood illusions of love and glory. In order to leave a testimonial of his erudition, the poet earnestly sets out to write the *cantica*.

The poem, written in the Dantean *terza rima,* is divided in five cantos and is allegorical in content. Finding himself in a delightful field too beautiful even to describe (***Op.*** I, p. 256), the young poet is caught by a sudden and terrifying storm. An angel appears to him announcing his imminent death and beckoning him to contemplate a vision whereby the poet sees those who are damned because of love, avarice, errors, war, and tyranny. In the fourth canto the poet watches a procession during which oblivion mounts an obscure cart pulled by turtles, followed by those who in life strove for fame and glory. Before the final admonishment of the angel, the poet sees the blessed souls among whom are: Dante, Petrarch, Tasso, and finally Christ Himself. The last canto, which contains the inspirational motive of the poem, presents Leopardi in a state of continuous despair. Even though he has been shown by the symbolic vision how vain the acquisition of earthly ideals or substances really is, the poet cannot help but despair: his life has passed so swiftly and he will soon die without having created any literary masterpiece.

The poem has little poetic value, and perhaps this is the reason why Pietro Giordani, to whom Leopardi had sent a copy, after praising the poetic composition, discouraged his young friend from publishing it. Commenting on the same poem, inasmuch as it is the first original poetic composition of Leopardi, Piero Bigongiari states that it is on account of the very presence of illusion that poetry is born in Leopardi, "col sentimento dell'illusione nasce proprio quella presentita illusione che è la poesia."[4]

As for the many places in the poem where Leopardi imitates directly Dante, Petrarch, or Tasso,[5] we wish to relate at least one example. From the Dantesque episode of Paolo and Francesca, Leopardi draws the episode of Ugo d'Este, in which Ugo's father Niccolò kills his wife and Ugo, who had fallen into incestuous love:

> Ma un dì fui sol con quella in muto loco
> e bramava in lontano e non volea,
> e palpitava, e 'l volto era di foco,
> e al fine un punto fu che 'l cor non resse,
> tanto ch'i' dissi: T'amo, e 'l dir fu roco.
>
> (*Op.* I, p. 263, ll. 116-120)

Yet, unlike the Dantean episode where it is a woman who speaks, namely Francesca, here it is a man who narrates his tragic adventure. In addition, the double murder committed by the husband is a much more cruel and deplorable action since the real act of love had never taken place,

> Poi nulla i' fei, ma tanto più che pria
> divampò 'l foco al soffio di speranza,
> ch'arder le vene e i polsi i' mi sentia.
>
> (*Op.* I, p. 263, ll. 124-126)

Clearly, one cannot speak of a sin that has been committed as in the episode of Paolo and Francesca; if anything, if we wish to consider one, it would be the sin of hope or of illusion; whereby the lover deludes himself in believing that perhaps soon he will have the love of his lady, "divampò 'l foco al soffio di speranza."

Returning to the theme of illusion, we may conclude by stating that the poem marks the first momentous step in Leopardi's development of the "illusion" motif. The poet, who at this time still retains much of his childhood Christian beliefs, is suddenly faced with the picture of his true existence; that is, the shattering of all his juvenile illusions, his desire for glory, love, happiness, and calls out to them:

> Addio speranze, addio vago conforto
> del poco viver mio già trapassa: . . .
> E tu pur Gloria, addio, che già s'abbassa
> mio tenebroso giorno e cade omai,
> e mia vita sul mondo ombra non lassa.
>
> (*Op.* I, p. 280, ll. 79-80; 82-84)

An attentive reading reveals that the above is not to be considered a desperate call; on the contrary, the above verses show the sincerity of the poet, as do the following ones with which he calls on his Creator and his Virgin Mother for help and comfort:

> A te mi volgo, O Padre, o Re supremo
> o Creatore o Servatore o Santo.
> Tutto son tuo . . .
> O Vergin Diva . . .
> deh tu soccorri lo spirito lasso.
>
> (*Op.* I, p. 281, ll. 95-97; 106; 109)

Thus, Leopardi accepts death but only because man is powerless against it; for in the end, as Chiarini also noted, he still prefers the miseries of this world to the beatitudes of the next, "Si sente che il poeta anche dopo la visione, preferisce le miserie di questo mondo alla beatitudine celeste. Verrà tempo, e non lontano, ch'egli invocherà la morte sinceramente ma allora ahimè non crederà più nella vita futura."[6]

With the partial return of his health, Leopardi realizes that his life is not over, as he had feared, and that once again he must find the strength to face the bitter reality of existence. Just as he had been in his childhood, Leopardi is aware of the fact that the only possible way out is the return to illusions for, "l'avvenire è come le cose lontane, bello nell' incertezza, misero nella realtà."[7]

Having come face to face with the bitter reality, which he calls "l'arido vero," from this moment on Leopardi finds that his existence, and the strength and will to continue this wretched and miserable life of his, rest purely on a paradoxical concept which will govern the remainder of his days, namely, the vanity of illusion as contrasted with the harshness of reality.

> Il più solido piacere di questa vita è il piacere vano delle illusioni. Io considero, le illusioni come cosa in certo modo reale stante ch'elle sono ingredienti essenziali del sistema della natura umana, e date dalla natura a tutti quanti gli uomini, in maniera che non è lecito spregiarlo come sogni di un solo, ma propri veramente dell'uomo e voluti dalla natura, e senza cui la vita nostra sarebbe la più misera e barbara cosa ec. . . ."
>
> (*Zib.* I, p. 78)

This, I feel, is the most exalted and refined statement that the poet leaves us in all of his works with regard to the importance of illusion in man's life. If we analyze more closely the above citation, we find that his thought rests basically on the paradox "solido piacere—piacere vano." It is precisely in that word *vano* where lies all the misery and unhappiness of the poet. Up to this moment, Leopardi had found in illusion a true escape and has believed in its existence and importance in life. At the present, however, although he still considers illusion necessary to his survival and does still believe in it, how different is this belief! Contrary to the past, the poet is fully conscious of himself. In short, we might say that Leopardi has reached a point when his *ragione* is certainly overshadowing his *sentimento*. The poet knows that the only possible pleasure left to mankind is the illusion of that pleasure; however, and this is the dreadful paradox, he is also conscious of the fact that this illusion is vain because in itself it is nothing but illusion within an illusion.

Here lies the tragedy of Leopardi's life: All of his pleasures stem from a knowledge of the nonexistence of these pleasures; all of his optimism stems from an utter acceptance of a pessimistic reality of things. It would be true to say that from this time on, ironically enough, the more the poet comes to realize the vanity of a certain illusion, the greater pleasure this illusion will bring him.

Using the above statement as a basic premise, we can almost[8] arrive at the formulation of a logical system in Leopardi's thought: Illusions become indispensable for man if he is to achieve any great deeds, for as we saw already, without illusions there will never be greatness of thought nor great deeds—"senza le quali non cisarà quasi mai grandezza di pensieri, nè forza e impeto e ardore d'animo, nè grandi azioni che per lo più son pazzie" (*Zib.* I, p. 31). Indeed the absence of illusions coupled with the progress of reason generates barbarism in man: "E però non c'è dubbio che i progressi della ragione e lo spegnimento delle illusioni producono le barbarie" (*Zib.* I, p. 32). Not only are illusions necessary to keep mankind from becoming barbarous, but they are inherent to the natural system of the world: "Le illusioni sono in natura, inerenti al sistema del mondo, tolte via affatto o quasi affatto, l'uomo è snaturato" (*Zib.* I, p. 32). As a part of the system of the world, illusions are necessary for the happiness and perfection of mankind: "Vengo a dimostrare ch'elle appartengono sostanzialmente al sistema naturale, e all'ordine delle cose, e sono essenziali e necessarie alla felicità e perfezione dell'uomo" (*Zib.* I, p. 728). Thus Leopardi concludes by saying that, since pleasure cannot be found in reality, one turns to imagination, which is the source of both hope and illusion: "Il piacere infinito che non si può trovare nella realtà si trova così nella immaginazione, della quale derivano la speranza, le illusioni" (*Zib.* I, p. 183). Man lives only because of religion and illusion, for if we were to take these elements away from him, the human race would willingly destroy itself, a concept which Leopardi will once again take up when he writes his first *Operetta Morale,* **"Storia del Genere Umano."** "L'uomo non vive che di religione o d'illusioni . . . tolta la religione e le illusioni radicalmente, ogni uomo, anzi ogni fanciullo alla prima facoltà di ragionare . . . si ucciderebbe infallibilmente di propria mano, e la razza nostra sarebbe spenta nel suo nascere per necessità ingenita, e sostanziale" (*Zib.* I, p. 223).

Leopardi sees himself as an integral part of mankind and his suffering as part of the universal suffering of man. In fact, like the shepherd of one of his later poems, Leopardi goes as far as to say that life is full of sorrow and anguish:

> Questo io conosco e sento,
> che degli eterni giri,
> che dell'esser mio frale,
> qualche bene o contento
> avrà fors'altri; a me la vita è male.

> (*Op.* I, p. 106, ll. 100-104)

As the above quoted poem ends, the poet becomes ever more aware that his suffering is not at all different from that of any other man and that perhaps even the *gregge* towards which the poet had felt envy before, "quanta invidia ti porto!" is not really free of pain and toil. Realizing all this, the poet not only joins his suffering to that of every other human being but also to that of every living creature to be found in nature. Thus he concludes pessimistically, but still preserving a ray of hope masterfully expressed by the word *forse*:

> Forse in qual forma, in quale
> stato che sia, dentro covile o cuna,
> è funesto a chi nasce il dì natale.

> (*Op.* I, p. 108, ll. 141-143)

It is on account of the poet's constant and complete awareness that "è funesto a chi nasce il dì natale" that illusions acquire an even more extraordinary value and importance for man, and even though they may be only vanity, the poet will incessantly strive to defend them and to keep them alive.

Thus in speaking to the *garzoncello scherzoso* of **"Il Sabato del Villaggio"** and realizing that life will certainly not be as beautiful nor as free from toil and pain as it is at this moment, the poet wishes to hide the bitter truth of reality from the boy and therefore tells him to enjoy himself: "Godi, fanciullo mio; stato soave, / stagion lieta è cotesta" (*Op.* I, p. 113, ll. 48-49). The poet urges the child to enjoy his world, thus keeping illusions alive in his mind: "Altro dirti non vo'; ma la tua festa / ch'anco tardi a venir non ti sia grave" (*Op.* I, p. 113, ll. 50-51).

Perhaps the example which best shows us Leopardi's concern for humanity and his heartfelt desire to keep illusions alive in man, since they are his only salvation, can be found in one of his *Operette Morali* entitled **"Dialogo di un venditore d'almanacchi e di un passaggero,"** which he wrote in 1832, five years before his death. Leopardi draws the material for his *operetta* from his own reflections on a passage of the *Zibaldone.*[9] When the dialogue begins, we find a vendor of almanacs who is in a happy frame of mind mainly because he remains in his natural and primitive state of a "non-thinker." This relates to a passage in the *Zibaldone* where the author, speaking on the nature of man, says that, "ci sono tre maniere di veder le cose" (*Zib.* I, p. 128). In other words, there are in this world three different kinds of men: the genius, the vulgar man and the philosopher, or man of sentiments (*Zib.* I, p. 129).

It is to the second group, or to the vulgar men, that the vendor of almanacs belongs. This group, according to the poet, is the most natural of all and the most happy, although doomed to accomplish no great deeds (*Zib.* I, p. 129).

The dialogue may be divided into three distinct parts. The first, shows us the vendor in his "natural state of contentedness"; the second part may be called the "shattering of the illusions," brought about by the questions of the passerby; and the third, "the return of the illusions" and of happiness itself.

As long as the vendor does not reason or think about his existence, he is relatively happy, and optimism reigns in all of his answers: "Più, più assai," he answers, for instance, to the passerby's questions on whether the coming year is going to be happier than the one just ended.

The second stage of the dialogue occurs when the vendor is forced to use his *ragione* in answering the question: "Non vi piacerebb'egli che l'anno nuovo fosse come qualcuno di questi anni ultimi?" In fact, through the use of reason, activated by the questions of the passerby, the vendor of almanacs is forced to see more and more clearly how unhappy the past has been, not only for himself, but probably for all of mankind as well. It is at this point that we reach the nadir of the once optimistic outlook of the vendor.

The passerby, who undoubtedly represents Leopardi himself, begins to feel pity and compassion for this man once he has succeeded in casting him into such a wretched state of mind. At this point he advises him to do what he will counsel other men to do in his **Ginestra,** that is, to join in sorrow with his fellow man and do his utmost to comfort and to aid him against the adverse blows of nature. Thus the passerby renders to the vendor his previously lost illusion:

> Quella vita ch'è una cosa bella, non è la vita che si conosce, ma quella che non si conosce; non la vita passata, ma la futura. Coll'anno nuovo, il caso incomincerà a trattar bene voi e me e tutti gli altri, e si principierà la vita felice. Non è vero?
>
> (***Op.*** I, p. 662)

It is not necessary to ask ourselves if the passerby truly believed in the above statement for, if forced to answer, he would probably answer negatively. What matters at this point is that he does succeed in his intentions. The vendor in fact does answer with the word *speriamo,* which is all we desire to hear.

For a moment we seem to be present at the opening of Pandora's box—all evils have been cast loose all over the world—but at the sight of hope, which lingers helplessly behind, we too utter that one word: *speriamo.*

In Leopardi we see therefore the clear distinction between two realities: the *true* reality, or the world in which we live (nature), and the *false* reality, which is the world of illusion. The first is characterized by the life of man, who is doomed to suffering and pain; the second is characterized by our aspirations and ideals which, even though they will never be fulfilled, at least bring to man temporary joy and relief from the never ending *noia.*

In the end, even though "religione, natura o l'esistenza medesima" might be considered evil forces by Leopardi, he remains an apostle of optimism precisely because of his strong faith in illusions.

In fact, illusions, especially *le grandi illusioni* of love and glory, remain in the end the element which not only will give the poet the strength to go on living, but will also endear him to us. Through them he leaves us a ray of hope, even though the darkness of *l'arido vero,* the true barrenness, is all around us.

Notes

1. As Chiarini states in his book, *Vita di Giacomo Leopardi* (Firenze, 1921), p. 131; "Leggendo lo *Zibaldone,* noi assistiamo giorno per giorno agli studi dell'autore, all'erudirsi della sua mente, allo svolgersi del suo pensiero, e per affetto di esso, alla trasformazione della sua coscienza."

2. Giacomo Leopardi, *Zibaldone di Pensieri* (Verona, 1945), I, p. 19. Hereafter cited in the text as *Zib.*

3. "O natura, natura, / perchè non rendi poi / quel che prometti allor? Perchè di tanto / inganni i figli tuoi?" Giacomo Leopardi, *Opere* (Milano—Napoli, 1956), I, p. 94. Hereafter cited in the text as *Op.*

4. Piero Bigongiari, *Leopardi* (Firenze, 1962), p. 37.

5. This may recall to our mind what Galimberti once wrote: "Il Leopardi raccolse assai presto l'eredità dei poeti che lo precedettero, prima ancora di formulare una sua teoria dello stile." Cesare Galimberti, *Linguaggio del vero in Leopardi* (Firenze, 1959), p. 156.

6. Chiarini, *Vita,* p. 31.

7. Lino Lazzarini, *Storia della crisi di Giacomo Leopardi* (Padova, 1941), p. 113.

8. I have said "almost" because Leopardi never did arrive at a formulation of this system or any other logical deductive or inductive correlated system. For this reason Leopardi cannot be considered a philosopher. The thoughts that I have here tried to collect do not logically follow each other in the *Zibaldone* but were expressed at random by the poet without any intentional connection with each other.

9. "Io ho dimandato a parecchi se sarebbero stati contenti di tornare a rifare la vita passata, con patto di rifarla né più né meno quale la prima volta. L'ho dimandato anche sovente a me stesso. Quanto al tornare indietro a vivere, ed io e tutti gli altri sarebbero stati contentissimi; ma con questo patto, nessuno . . . Vuol dire che nella vita che abbiamo sperimentata e che conosciamo con

certezza, tutti abbiamo provato più male che bene; e che se non ci contentiamo ed anche desideriamo di vivere ancora, ciò non è per l'ignoranza del futuro, *è per una illusione della speranza,* senza la quale illusione e ignoranza non vorremmo più vivere, come mai non vorremmo rivivere nel mondo che siamo vissuti." (*Zibaldone,* II, p. 1118). Underlining in text is mine.

Alan S. Rosenthal (essay date fall 1976)

SOURCE: Rosenthal, Alan S. "Baudelaire and Leopardi: An Affinity in Anguish." *Essays in Literature* 3, no. 2 (fall 1976): 251-67.

[*In the following essay, Rosenthal discusses similarities in themes, imagery, and even phrasing in the work of Leopardi and Baudelaire.*]

Considering the differences in their respective backgrounds, the likelihood of parallels between Charles Baudelaire (1821-1867) and Giacomo Leopardi (1798-1837) would, at first glance, appear remote. Yet, in spite of the obvious contrasts, there does indeed exist between the two poets a remarkable and largely unheralded literary affinity.[1] Surprisingly, these seemingly dissimilar individuals treated many of the same themes and ideas, employed analogous imagery, and at times used almost identical phraseology. There has been, up to now, little tangible evidence to support the possibility of direct influence. Nevertheless, the parallels are undeniable; and their very nature and number suggest that they are not the product of mere coincidence. They seem, instead, to represent significant points of congruence in two otherwise contrasting personalities.

Baudelaire was undoubtedly familiar with Leopardi to a certain extent, as he ranked him among the finest modern poets.[2] One can not be absolutely sure where Baudelaire read him, but there was an abundance of material available. In 1841, for example, an edition of Leopardi's poems in the original Italian was published in Paris by Baudry and soon became well-known. Opinions vary, but I believe that Baudelaire had some ability to read Italian, sufficient at least (with the possible aid of a dictionary) to avail himself of the Baudry edition.[3] Even if—for the sake of argument—the original text were beyond his comprehension, French translations of Leopardi appeared in increasing number during Baudelaire's lifetime. By 1867 most of the thirty-four *Canti* poems had been translated. Quite notably, translations from twelve important poems were presented by Sainte-Beuve in his sensitive and penetrating study of Leopardi, which appeared in 1844 in the *Revue des Deux Mondes.* It is a well-known fact that Baudelaire idolized Sainte-Beuve, especially during that period, and

was also an avid reader of, and future contributor to, the *Revue des Deux Mondes.* If he read nothing else, Baudelaire unquestionably saw Sainte-Beuve's translations and analyses.

Further evidence concerning Baudelaire's knowledge of Leopardi is furnished by Henri Hignard, his most intimate friend at the *lycée* in Lyon (where Baudelaire studied from 1832 to 1836) and an acquaintance until 1846, when he saw the poet for the last time. The two shared a profound love for literature and spent endless hours discussing modern writers. In a biographical article Hignard recounts their experiences at school and goes on to describe his subsequent meetings with him in Paris. Discussing Baudelaire's poetic tastes, he reproaches him for his deliberate cultivation of the bizarre and for his "blasphèmes à froid imitées de Leopardi"[4] [cold blasphemies imitated from Leopardi]. Because Hignard wrote his study long after his last personal contacts with Baudelaire, and because a few of his judgments are questionable, this statement—in the absence of further supportive evidence—can not be considered in itself totally conclusive. Nevertheless, we must approach Hignard's testimony seriously; for it is indisputable that he was Baudelaire's closest friend at Lyon, that he was the only one of Baudelaire's acquaintances from this period who remained on close terms with him for any length of time thereafter, and that his recollection of several small details has been corroborated by the accounts of others. The similarities in the works of Baudelaire and Leopardi render Hignard's observation all the more provocative.

The affinity I propose to show is above all a spiritual kinship between two tortured souls. The poets found themselves in much the same predicament—that of the high-minded individual who strives to find beauty and meaning in a life marked by pain and emptiness, and who attempts to resist the oppression caused by the mysterious forces which control man's destiny. Their personal dramas took them through shattered illusions, unfulfilled dreams, pain, despair, and numbness; but they each sought some kind of affirmation with which to close their respective volumes of poetry. This spiritual kinship is especially observable in their attitudes toward Nature, death, evil and suffering, and rebellion, and in their use of metaphor and choice of symbols to express these themes in their works.

Baudelaire and Leopardi were both born with a keen sensitivity to Nature's beauty and, initially, found themselves in relative harmony with their surroundings. Traces of this receptivity appear in their works. They suggest in several places that Nature is, or was, alive and communicative; and both point to the poet's function as decipherer of Nature's secrets. Baudelaire's idea of *correspondances* is widely-known, but Leopardi also felt that hidden relationships exist between Nature's diverse parts; and, significantly enough, he used the Italian counterpart (*corrispondenza*) to expound his particular conception of the analogies in Nature.[5] Interestingly, similar images are presented in two poems of essentially different character. Baudelaire notes in "Correspondances" (1857) that the woods are alive—the *vivants piliers* [living pillars] emit words as Man passes through. Leopardi tells us much the same thing in **"Alla primavera"** (1824). Although this poem expresses nostalgic regret for the innocent illusions of classical antiquity and is thus far-removed from the allusions to synesthesia and corruption in "Correspondances," the portrait of a Nature that once was (and could possibly again be) alive and aware of mankind lies quite close to the Baudelairean concept:

> Vissero i fiori e l'erbe,
> vissero i boschi un dì. Conscie le molli
> aure, le nubi e la titania lampa
> fur dell'umana gente.[6]

> [The flowers and grass were alive,
> the woods were alive once. Conscious were the soft
>   breezes,
> the clouds and the titanic lamp
> of mankind.]

The aura of classical antiquity in **"Alla primavera"** can also be found to an extent in "Correspondances," where Nature is likened to a temple with pillars, and where the quite classical concept of Man in the universal sense (*L'homme*) is introduced:

> La Nature est un temple où de vivants piliers
> Laissent parfois sortir de confuses paroles;
> L'homme y passe à travers des forêts de symboles
> Qui l'observent avec des regards familiers.
>
> (*Oeuvres*, p. 11)

> [Nature is a temple in which living pillars
> Sometimes emit indistinct words;
> Man walks there through forests of symbols
> That watch him with familiar looks.]

Perhaps no aspect of Nature struck so responsive a chord in the poets as the sea, images of which abound in their verse. Both write of their desire to commune with the ocean, which conjures up visions of the infinite and the boundless. Striking parallels can be found, for example, between Leopardi's **"Sopra il ritratto di una bella donna"** (1835) or **"L'Infinito"** (1826) and Baudelaire's "Elévation" (1857). Though, again, the settings of the poems differ, the sea—in all three—is an abstract one suggesting rapt meditation and a feeling of immensity. Baudelaire writes:

> Mon esprit, tu te meus avec agilité,
> Et, comme un bon nageur qui se pâme dans l'onde,
> Tu sillonnes gaiement l'immensité profonde
> Avec une indicible et mâle volupté.
>
> (*Oeuvres*, p. 10)

> [My spirit, you move with agility,
> And, like a skillful swimmer who swoons within the
>   wave
> You gaily furrow the profound immensity
> With an indescribably, male voluptuous delight.]

Leopardi writes in **"Sopra il ritratto"**:

> Onde per mar delizioso, arcano
> erra lo spirto umano,
> quasi come a diporto
> ardito notator per l'Oceano.
>
> (*Opere*, I, 137)

> [Whereby on a delicious, mysterious sea
> the human spirit wanders,
> almost as if in sport
> like a bold swimmer on the Ocean.]

And in **"L'Infinito"**:

> Così tra questa
> immensità s'annega il pensier mio:
> e il naufragar m'e'dolce in questo mare.
>
> (*Opere* I. 58)

> [Thus in this
> immensity my thought drowns:
> and shipwreck within this sea is sweet to me.]

We note that the imagery and use of metaphor are similar, though marked by each writer's individual personality. Baudelaire presents a more personal point of view as he addresses his own spirit ("mon esprit"), which he likens to a swimmer ("nageur"). Leopardi depicts a more universal human spirit ("spirto umano"), which he also styles a swimmer ("notator"). The choice of verbs and adverbs relating to Baudelaire's swimmer contain distinct sexual overtones—he swoons ("se pâme"), and furrows ("sillonnes"), moves with agility, gaily, with a "mâle volupté." Leopardi's swimmer in **"Sopra il ritratto"** is not so aggressive, nor does he convey sensuality, as he wanders about almost as if in sport ("quasi come a diporto"). And while Leopardi points affectively to a delightful, mysterious sea ("mar delizioso, arcano"), he paints his swimmer in classical abstraction, with the single adjective—bold ("ardito"). In **"L'infinito,"** Leopardi does express the personal point of view, stating that his mind, or thought, is drowned, ecstatically shipwrecked as it were, in a sea of immensity ("immensità"). One may compare this with "Elévation," where Baudelaire conveys the sensation of rapture by writing that his mind, floating through "l'immensité profonde," is like a swimmer who swoons within the wave. However, Leopardi's verbal metaphors of drowning and shipwreck again reveal a more passive and resigned nature, in contrast to Baudelaire's verbs and adverbs which suggest a dynamic, aggressive spirit.

Thus there are times—especially in the poets' early years—when Nature appears to be an endless source of pleasure; but they eventually experience a profound aversion, which turns to fear and hatred. While Baudelaire more and more stresses the ugliness he finds in Nature, Leopardi continues for some time to find a mysterious, cold beauty in her, as he considers her exterior appearance separately from her innate malevolent force. Indeed, it is because of this beauty that she seems to promise so much to mankind; but she deceives her children, man's hopes remain unfulfilled, and she is resented as a vicious stepmother.[7] In Leopardi's poetry, Nature is at first indifferent to mankind, then cruel, increasingly hostile, and finally viciously destructive. She builds up humanity and then, as if following a whim, tears it down again like a spiteful child. A basic difference here is that Leopardi's hatred encompasses the entire scheme of things in the universe, and it reacts primarily to forces exterior to man himself. Baudelaire's hatred does not entirely result from the hostility of Nature to man. It springs in large part from the poet's own interior being, as he projects his own despair on the world around him and sees it reflected in Nature. Ultimately, however, both Leopardi and Baudelaire arrive at the same antipathy to Nature; and the bond between poet and Nature is dissolved.

The destruction of the myth of a benevolent Nature lays bare man's condition on earth. Surrounded by a hostile environment, bewildered by the mysteries of the universe, he recognizes that his own existence is but an infinitesimal part of things. Thus Leopardi's shepherd in **"Canto notturno"** (1831) ponders the purpose of life, a harrowing, miserable journey to death, which is man's only hope:

> Vecchierel bianco, infermo,
> mezzo vestito e scalzo,
> con gravissimo fascio in su le spalle,
> per montagna e per valle,
> per sassi acuti, ed alta rena, e fratte,
> al vento, alla tempesta, e quando avvampa
> l'ora, e quando poi gela
> corre via, corre, anela,
> varca torrenti e stagni,
> cade, risorge, e più e più s'affretta,
> senza posa o ristoro,
> lacero, sanguinoso; infin ch'arriva
> colà dove la via
> e dove il tanto affaticar fu vòlto:
> abisso orrido, immenso,
> ov'ei precipitando, il tutto obblia.

> (*Opere,* I, 103-104)

> [A whitehaired old man, ill,
> half-clothed and barefoot,
> with a heavy load on his shoulders,
> over mountains and valleys,
> over sharp stones, deep sand, through bushes
> through wind, through storm, when the hour blazes

> and when it freezes,
> runs, runs, pants,
> crosses streams and ponds,
> falls, rises again, and hurries more and more,
> without rest or refreshment,
> torn, bloody, until he arrives
> there where his path
> and where so much wearying toil were aimed:
> a dreadful, immense abyss,
> where he, falling in, forgets all.]

Some of the concepts found in **"Canto notturno"** are almost identical to those in Baudelaire's "La Mort des pauvres" (1857), which, despite its title, deals with death in general. It is true that this piece presents a contrast to **"Canto notturno,"** one that foreshadows the conclusions of their respective collections: for Leopardi, death is essentially oblivion; for Baudelaire, it is also the gateway to the Unknown. Yet, as in the Leopardi poem, death is portrayed as the goal of life. It is man's only hope for rest, just as the shepherd hopes only to rest at evening. Similarly, to reach this ultimate end one must travel life's unhappy road, through wind and snow, through obstacles and untold misery, until death permits one to forget what life was like, as Baudelaire writes:

> C'est la Mort qui console, hélas! et qui fait vivre;
> C'est le but de la vie, et c'est le seul espoir
> Qui, comme un élixir, nous monte et nous enivre,
> Et nous donne le coeur de marcher jusqu'au soir;
> A travers la tempête, et la neige, et le givre,
> C'est la clarté vibrante à notre horizon noir.

> (*Oeuvres,* pp. 119-20)

> [It is Death who consoles us, alas! and makes us go
>   on living;
> It is the goal of life, and the only hope
> Which, like an elixir, excites and intoxicates us,
> And gives us heart to go on until evening;
> Through tempest, and snow, and frost,
> It is the glittering light on our black horizon.]

The next-to-last verse cited above furnishes, in particular, a significant parallel to lines in the Leopardi poem ("al vento, alla tempesta, e quando avvampa / l'ora, e quando poi gela").

Because death appears to be the only aim of man's existence, life itself seems devoid of meaning. Baudelaire and Leopardi, seeking a metaphysical reason for all this useless misery, formulated quite similar theories. As Leopardi explained in the **"Dialogo della Natura e di un Islandese"** (1827), life is a constant cycle of production and destruction. For the universe to continue, destruction and consequently man's suffering are necessary: "La vita di quest'universo è un perpetuo circuito di produzione e distruzione, collegate ambedue tra sé di maniera, che ciascheduna serve continuamente all'altra, ed alla conservazione del mondo" (*Opere,* I, 534) [Life in this universe is a perpetual circuit of production and destruction, both interconnected in such a way that each one continuously serves the other, for the preservation of the world]. In August of 1860, in a letter to Poulet-Malassis, Baudelaire expressed essentially the same idea in referring to the continuous cycle of creation and destruction in the universe: "Enfin, s'il est vrai que beaucoup de races (d'animaux) ont disparu, il est vrai aussi que d'autres sont nées, destinées à manager leurs voisines ou à être mangées par elles . . . suivant une loi éternelle de nombres et de forces proportionnels."[8] [In conclusion, if it is true that many races (of animals) have disappeared, it is true also that others have been born, destined to eat their neighbors or to be eaten by them . . . following an eternal law of proportional numbers and strength.]

We are now at the heart of the matter: man's suffering in a mysterious, hostile universe is ordained by an eternal law; an all-embracing force has decreed that all men shall be by necessity unhappy. Convinced of the inevitability of suffering, both poets conclude that everything in the universe is governed by evil. When used by Baudelaire and Leopardi, this term (*le mal, il male*) ordinarily refers to that force which works to the detriment of all living things, a malevolent influence which pervades every part of creation and is a source of the anguish so keenly felt by the poets. Both men were vitally concerned with the problem of evil. Baudelaire once described his great work as "un livre destiné à représenter l'agitation de l'esprit dans le mal" (*Oeuvres,* p. 181) [a book designed to depict the spirit's agitation in evil]. Moreover, a basic aspect of Baudelairean esthetics is the poet's desire to extract beauty from evil and suffering. Marcel Ruff has noted that this *esthétique* "est toute entière fondée sur la résonance poétique du mal, inséparable de la condition humaine"[9] [is based entirely on the poetic resonance of *le mal,* which is inseparable from the human condition]. It is significant that evil is also an essential part of Leopardi's esthetic plan and that here, too, it is intimately linked with the human condition.[10] One need look no further that the following passage from the *Zibaldone* (1898, posth.) to ascertain the place of *il male* in Leopardi's view of the universe. Noting the unrelenting pain found in all aspects of existence, he makes a sweeping, bitter assertion: "Tutto è male. Cioè tutto quello che è, è male; ciascuna cosa esiste per fin di male; l'esistenza è un male e ordinata al male; il fine dell'universo è il male; l'ordine e lo stato, le leggi, l'andamento naturale dell'universo non sono altro che male nè diretti ad altro che al male" (*Zib,* II, 1004). [Everything is *male.* That is to say, everything that is, is *male*; each thing exists for the purpose of *male*; existence is a *male* and is arranged according to *male*; order, the state, laws, the natural course of the universe are none other than *male* nor aimed at other than *male*.] This passage could just as easily have been written by Baudelaire himself.

Another entry in the *Zibaldone* graphically demonstrates the extent of suffering in the universe. Leopardi describes a garden during the springtime; but instead of concentrating on the beauty of the flowers and plants he uncovers the misery beneath the surface. In a scene that calls to mind the image of the ravaged, eroded garden in Baudelaire's "L'Ennemi" Leopardi depicts the sickly flowers (one is in fact, reminded that Baudelaire referred to his verses as "ces fleurs maladives") and thus demonstrates how evil attacks every living thing.[11] He begins by inviting the reader to enter the garden and behold the spectacle: a rose is burned by the sun and withers, a lily is cruelly sucked dry by a bee, everything is in torment. After portraying the inconceivable misery experienced by each species of plant life in the garden, Leopardi expands his view to encompass human life. Like a beautiful garden it may appear to be a realm of joy, he relates, "ma in verità questa vita è trista e infelice, ogni giardino è quasi un vasto ospitale (luogo ben più deplorabile che un cemeterio), e se questi esseri sentono o, vogliamo dire, sentissero, certo è che il non essere sarebbe per loro assai meglio che l'essere" (*Zib,* II, 1006) [but actually this life is gloomy and miserable, every garden is almost like a vast hospital (a much more deplorable place than a cemetery), and if these beings feel or, rather, if they could feel, then certainly non-being would be for them much better than being].

Leopardi's conclusion coincides with Baudelaire's conception of existence. Though he has experienced moments of happiness Baudelaire sees life essentially as continuing torment, as he states in a letter to Nadar: "La vie doit être une perpétuelle douleur" (*CG,* II, 320-21). [Life must be perpetual pain.] Like Leopardi he uses the hospital as a metaphor to indicate that life is a place of suffering, in the prose poem "Anywhere out of this world": "Cette vie est un hôpital où chaque malade est possédé du désir de changer de lit" (*Oeuvres,* p. 303). [This life is a hospital where each patient is obsessed with the desire to change beds.] Like the Italian he attempts to suggest the universality of evil and proclaims in the poem "L'Irrémédiable" that his dilemma is indeed without remedy (*Oeuvres,* p. 76), just as Leopardi had called the human condition irremediable ("insanabile") in his poem **"Palinodia,"** (*Opere,* I, 146). Thus, for both of them, life is evil; and man's means of resistance seem virtually non-existent.[12]

In a world where everyone suffers without exception, both Leopardi and Baudelaire hold to the Romantic notion that the superior man—especially the artist—suffers more intensely than ordinary men. Fame, glory, and excellence go hand-in-hand with unhappiness. The poet, whose soul is endowed with divine powers, is a superior being; but his very greatness brings with it a legacy of suffering.[13]

It is noteworthy that both Leopardi and Baudelaire found in Tasso a symbol of the poet's tragic situation in life. Leopardi considered him to be the most unhappy of poets. In his poem to Angelo Mai (1820), he pictures Tasso's wretchedness, the malevolence which was directed against him, and the gradual disintegration of his mind and spirit:

> Oh misero Torquato! il dolce canto
> non valse a consolarti o a sciôrre il gelo
> onde l'alma t'avvean, ch'era sì calda,
> cinta l'odio e l'immondo
> livor privato e de' tiranni. Amore,
> amor, di nostra vita ultimo inganno,
> t'abbandonava. Ombra reale e salda
> ti parve il nulla, e il mondo
> inabitata piaggia.
>
> (*Opere,* I, 21)

> [Oh miserable Torquato! your sweet song
> could not console you or melt the frost
> with which the hatred and filthy spite
> of common citizens and tyrants
> covered your soul, which was so warm. Love,
> love, the last illusion of our life,
> abandoned you. Nothingness appeared a real,
> tangible shade to you, and the world
> an uninhabited domain.]

The poignancy of this passage is matched by the sentiment which inspired "sur le Tasse en prison" (1864). Baudelaire portrays Tasso in the same misery; and furthermore, he suggests that the great poet's mind has wandered into a realm of fantasy, as a result of the incessant abuse he is forced to bear:

> Le poète au cachot, débraillé, maladif,
> Roulant un manuscrit sous son pied convulsif,
> Mesure d'un regard que la terreur enflamme
> L'escalier de vertige où s'abime son âme.
>
> Les rires enivrants dont s'emplit la prison
> Vers l'étrange et l'absurde invitent sa raison;
> Le Doute l'environne, et la Peur ridicule,
> Hideuse et multiforme, autour de lui circule.
>
> (*Oeuvres,* p. 152)

> [The poet in his cell, unkempt, sickly,
> Rolling a manuscript under his convulsive foot,
> Measures with a gaze that terror inflames
> The dizzying stairway where his soul is swallowed up.
>
> The intoxicating laughs which fill the prison
> Entice his reason toward the strange and the absurd;
> Doubt surrounds him and ridiculous Fear,
> Hideous and multiform, moves in circles round him.]

There can be no doubt that Baudelaire and Leopardi found Tasso's plight analogous to their own. Just as he had been doomed to misery, they both felt that their own lives were cursed from the very start. Most probably, very real anguish—beginning with the tribulations of their youth—led to this conviction. Leopardi, for instance, wrote to Pietro Brighenti that he was conscious of the fact that he had been born with "la sacra indelebile maledizione del destino"[14] [the awesome, everlasting curse of Fate]. Baudelaire, also convinced that he was doomed to suffer, wrote to his mother: "En somme, je crois que ma vie a été damnée dès le commencement, et qu'elle l'est pour toujours" (*CG,* I, 317). [In short, I believe that my life has been damned from the beginning, and that it will be so forever.] They believed that, as poets, their exceptional powers (and their singular misfortune) set them apart from the rest of society. Baudelaire often expressed the feeling of solitude he had always experienced, especially when contact with others accentuated the singularity of his condition.[15] Leopardi recognized his own solitary destiny in much the same way. He had only to observe the townspeople who surrounded him to see the disparity of their respective conditions. This led him to observe in **"Il passero solitario"** (1835):

> Quasi romito, e strano
> al mio loco natio,
> passo del viver mio la primavera.
>
> (*Opere,* I, 56)

> [Virtually secluded, and foreign
> to my native place,
> I pass the springtime of my life.]

It is of interest that in their poetry Leopardi and Baudelaire both employ the image of a bird to evoke the solitude of the poet and his isolation from society. Like his *passero solitario,* Leopardi is alone in life. The sparrow has no companions; he stays off by himself on a tower and sings as he observes the other birds. This is essentially the poet's condition: he is a solitary figure who observes life from a superior vantage point and sings in his poetry of what he sees. Such is the situation Baudelaire describes in "L'Albatros" (1859). As Leopardi's sparrow remained at the top of the tower, aloof from society, the albatross prefers to dwell in his own domain—the sky. He spends his time following ships on ocean voyages. Just as the huge sea bird pursues the vessels from above, the poet follows the ship of society as it glides across the sea of life, but he is forever alienated from the life he observes. And when, like the majestic albatross, he is brought down to earth, he finds himself out of his element, tormented by a contemptuous and ignorant society, as Baudelaire depicts through the symbolic imagery of the poem:

> Ce voyageur ailé, comme il est gauche et veule!
> Lui, naguère si beau, qu'il est comique et laid!

L'un agace son bec avec un brûle-gueule,
L'autre mime, en boitant, l'infirme qui volait!

(*Oeuvres*, p. 10)

[This winged voyager, how awkward and feeble he is!
A short while ago so beautiful, now how ludicrous
   and ugly!
One (sailor) teases his beak with a short pipe,
Another, limping, mimics the cripple who once flew.]

Similarly, Leopardi relates how envy, scorn, and derision pursue the superior man. In **"Le ricordanze"** (1831), he laments his own situation as an outcast who leads a bitter existence amid a vicious multitude:

Qui passo gli anni, abbandonato, occulto,
senz'amor, senza vita; ed aspro a forze
tra lo stuol de' malevoli divengo.

(*Opere*, I, 97)

[Here I pass the years, abandoned and hidden away,
deprived of love, deprived of life; and I perforce
grow bitter amid a multitude of malicious people.]

Thus, in a world filled with suffering, it is the man of genius whose life is marked by the most tragic destiny. Blessed with the power to perceive and to feel more intensely than others, he is consequently more profoundly aware of man's dreadful condition, in general, and of his own lot, in particular. However, deep within his anguished soul rises the desire to rebel against the cruel fate which oppresses mankind and which regulates heaven and earth. If *le mal* is universal, he can at least resist its force within himself.

There are several figures representing or suggesting revolt in the poetry of Leopardi and Baudelaire. Although the methods of revolt sometimes vary, the objective is always to cast off the shackles of man's oppressive condition and to give meaning to one's own existence. Leopardi conceives of the superior soul in revolt as the *magnanimo*—a noble, unselfish, courageous being who recognizes man's unhappiness but who stands firm against this tragic destiny. He continues to defy fate and in a certain manner revolts against his condition.[16] Two significant figures of magnanimous revolt in Leopardi's poetry are borrowed from classical antiquity: Brutus and Sappho. *Bruto minore* represents the strong and brave who wage constant war against their destiny, although they know they are alone in their struggle. Brutus chooses death, or more specifically suicide, as his means of revolt, because it deprives fate of the final blow (*Opere*, I, 33). Sappho, cursed with an ugly body which evokes repulsion, also chooses death in defiance of the harsh fate that has been accorded to her. Rather than continuing in misery with the *velo indegno* which shrouds the beauty of her soul, she will cast it to the ground and thus overcome her unjust lot in death. She greets the final act as a definitive remedy:

Morremo. Il velo indegno a gerra sparto,
rifuggirà l'ignudo animo a Dite,
e il crudo fallo emenderà del cieco
dispensator de' casi.

(*Opere*, I, 50)

[We shall die. Its unworthy veil shed upon the ground,
the naked soul will flee to Dis,
and amend the cruel fault of the blind
dispenser of events.]

The *ginestra*, or broom-plant, is another symbol of the *magnanimo* who resists his fate; and it represents another manner of revolt. The frail plant, clinging to the edges of Vesuvius, knows its condition but does not submit to fate. It will soon be engulfed by flaming lava, but it will have acquired dignity by not bending in supplication to the destructive river of fire. In this instance, the *magnanimo* does not actively seek death but stands firm, true to himself, to the very end; and in so doing, he gives meaning to his existence. The ultimate result of this philosophy is the humanistic conviction that perhaps the best way to combat the evil condition allotted to mankind is to encourage others and help them face their own destinies. Suicide is not the answer, after all; men should live in order to unite against the common enemy—Nature, as Leopardi proclaims in the **"Dialogo di Plotino e di Porfirio"** and then again in **"La ginestra"**:

Costei chiama inimica; e incontro a questa
congiunta esser pensando,
siccome è il vero, ed ordinata in pria
l'umana compagnia,
tutti fra sé confederati estima
gli uomini, e tutti abbraccia
con vero amor, porgendo
valida e pronta ed aspettando aita
negli alterni perigli e nelle angosce
della guerra comune.

(*Opere*, I, 157-58)

[Her he calls enemy;
and thinking the company of humans joined,
as is the truth, and drawn up against her,
he considers all men confederates among themselves,
and embraces all with true love, offering
and expecting valid and ready help
in the alternating perils and distresses
of the common war.]

The Baudelairean figures of revolt are more solitary individuals; and although some are based on classical models, as were Brutus and Sappho, their manner of revolt is quite different and evinces the ideas of sin and punishment, so characteristic of Baudelaire. Rather than contemplating suicide or joining with others to face a common foe, they rebel by trying to rise above their condition, by attempting to lift themselves to a higher plane of existence. Such a person is seen in "Don Juan aux enfers." He is a hero of superhuman proportions who is above all pity and remorse. In the boat which carries him to Hell, Don Juan does not even lift his eyes to defy the heavens; he ignores them with contempt: "Mais le calme héros, courbé sur sa rapière, / Regardait le sillage et ne daignait rien voir" (*Oeuvres*, p. 19). [But the calm hero, bent over his rapier, / Gazed at the wake and deigned to look at nothing else.]

A time-honored symbol of man's aspiration to exceed his condition is Icarus. Like Icarus, the poet rebels against his condition by attempting to go beyond the limits prescribed for man. His presumption is punished, as Baudelaire describes in "Les Plaintes d'un Icare":

> En vain j'ai voulu de L'espace
> Trouver la fin et le milieu;
> Sous je ne sais quel oeil de feu
> Je sens mon aile qui se casse.
>
> (*Oeuvres*, p. 173)

> [In vain have I attempted
> To find the end and the center of space;
> Under I know not what eye of fire
> I feel my wing break apart.]

Then, there are the *femmes damnées*, the Baudelairean counterpart of Leopardi's Sappho. Baudelaire, with a distinct feeling of empathy, looks upon these tormented creatures as superiour women. They despise the human condition and, in seeking what Baudelaire considered to be a higher existence (as lesbianism was beyond the constraining social norm), have in a sense revolted. He cries out to them in a burst of admiration and affection:

> O vierges, ô démons, ô monstres, ô martyres,
> De la réalité grands esprits contempteurs,
> Chercheuses d'infini, dévotes et satyres,
> Tantôt pleines de cris, tantôt pleines de pleurs.
>
> (*Oeuvres*, p. 108)

> [Oh virgins, oh demons, oh monsters, oh martyrs,
> Great spirits contemptuous of reality,
> Seekers of the infinite, devout and satyric,
> Sometimes full of screams, sometimes filled with wailing.]

And, of course, the poem "Lesbos" contains a passage which specifically concerns Sappho, herself:

> De la mâle Sapho, l'amante et le poète,
> Plus belle que Vénus par ses mornes pâleurs!
> —L'oeil d'azur est vaincu par l'oeil noir que tachète
> Le cercle ténébreux tracé par les douleurs
> De la mâle Sapho, l'amante et le poète!
>
> (*Oeuvres*, p. 136)

> [Of the virile Sappho, lover and poet,
> More beautiful than Venus in her dreary paleness!

> The eye of azure is vanquished by the dark eye which is ringed
> By the shadowy circle traced by the sorrows
> Of the virile Sappho, lover and poet!]

Finally, there is the supreme symbol of revolt in the poetry of Baudelaire—Satan. The prince of darkness, who was punished for having risen up to challenge the authority of God, typifies man's desperate struggle to overcome his condition. Baudelaire's Satanism is well-known and is intimately linked with his Catholic concept of the duality of man; it is surprising, however, to discover that Leopardi, despite his innate atheism, also felt the impulse to flirt with this cult. The analogies in their respective attitudes are striking; and we are reminded of the "blasphèmes à froid imitès de Leopardi" mentioned by Hignard, above.

Baudelaire rejects the notion of a just God. In "Le Reniement de saint Pierre," he pictures God as a cruel tyrant who delights in the suffering of humanity while men curse him (*Oeuvres*, p. 114). The heavens actually seem empty and oblivious of man, an observation that Baudelaire also emphasizes in "Les Aveugles," where the blind men stare at the sky with vacuous eyes while he compares this to the void he discovers in the heavens: "Vois! je me traine aussi! mais, plus qu'eux hébété, / Je dis: Que cherchent-ils au Ciel, tous ces aveugles?" (*Oeuvres*, p. 88). [See! I also drag myself along! but, even more stupefied than they, / I say: What are they looking for in the heavens, all those blind men?] And in "L'Amour du mensonge" (1860), he speaks of eyes that are "more empty than the heavens" (*Oeuvres*, p. 95). Leopardi portrays in **"Alla primavera"** (1824) the same emptiness of the heavens, albeit couched in classical terms, and also rejects the idea of a just and consoling Deity:

> Ahi ahi, poscia che vòte
> son le stanze d'Olimpo, e cieco il tuono
> per l'atre nubi e le montagne errando,
> gl'iniqui petti e gl'innocenti a paro
> in freddo orror dissolve.
>
> (*Opere*, I, 40)

> [Alas, alas, then empty
> are the rooms of Olympus, and blind thunder,
> wandering through the black clouds and the mountains,
> dissolves wicked and innocent breasts alike
> in cold horror.]

His bitterness grows until it spills over in the verses of **"A se stesso"** (1835).[17] In a benumbed state he expresses his disgust at the vanity of a meaningless existence and scorns life on earth, where genius is not rewarded. He tells his heart that life is not worth grieving about:

> Non val cosa nessuna
> i moti tuoi, né di sospiri è degna

la terra, Amaro e noia
la vita, altro mai nulla; e fango è il mondo.

(*Opere,* I, 125)

[Nothing is worth
your stirrings, nor is the earth
deserving of your sighs. Bitter and tedious
is life, and nothing else; and the world is mud.]

Baudelaire, who also feels that his qualities have not been rewarded, writes of his disgust with life on this earth in "Abel et Caïn" (1857). He commiserates with the unfortunate race of Cain, those condemned to a miserable existence. As Leopardi wrote that the world was "mud" (*fango*), so Baudelaire in his poem sees the progress of the pariah as a wretched trek through mire: "Race de Caïn, dans la fange / Rampe et meurs misérablement" (*Oeuvres,* p. 115). [Race of Cain, in the mire / Crawl and die miserably.] He exhorts the outcasts of life to revolt and throw God off his lofty perch: "Race de Caïn, au ciel monte / Et sur la terre jette Dieu!" (*Oeuvres,* p. 116). [Race of Cain, to the sky ascend / And upon the ground cast God!]

In his movement of rebellion, Baudelaire replaces God with the myth of the Devil.[18] Similarly, in a moment of extreme bitterness, Leopardi drew up the plan for a proposed hymn to the power of evil, to whom he gave the name "Arimane." The plan was written in 1833, but was never developed into a poem. Arimanes was actually the ancient Persian god of evil, but Riccardo Bacchelli confirms that to Leopardi he represented Satan.[19] There are distinct parallels between Leopardi's proposed prayer to Arimanes and several Baudelairean works, notably "Les Litanies de Satan," which is itself an appeal to the Devil. In form and purpose both are hymns of supplication to the prince of darkness by outcasts who are burdened with an accursed destiny.

In the opening lines of **"Ad Arimane"** (1845, posth.), Leopardi addresses the god of evil as the king of all earthly things. He is the prime mover, the supreme intelligence, the ultimate power:

Re delle cose, autor del mondo, arcana
malvagità, sommo potere e somma
intelligenza, eterno
dator de' mali e reggitor del moto.

(*Opere,* I, 326)

[King of things, author of the world, mysterious
wickedness, supreme power and highest
intelligence, eternal
giver of evil and governor of all movement.]

We are reminded of "Au Lecteur" (1855) where Baudelaire paints an analogous image when he pictures Satan as the Being which manipulates all men: "C'est le Di-

able qui tient les fils qui nous remuent!" (*Oeuvres,* p. 5). [It is the Devil who holds the strings that move us!] In "Les Litanies de Satan" (1857), the parallel becomes even more evident, with three passages suggesting the supreme intelligence of Satan. Baudelaire invokes him in the opening verse: "O toi, le plus savant et le plus beau des Anges" (*Oeuvres,* p. 116) [You, the wisest and most beautiful of Angels]. Like Leopardi, he considers him an all-knowing, all-powerful king: "Toi qui sais tout, grand roi des choses souterraines" (*Oeuvres,* p. 117) [You who know everything, great king of subterranean things]. (We note a near-parallel in the choice of words: "Re delle cose" and "Roi des choses souterraines.") Finally, he prays to Satan, the guardian of knowledge:

Fais que mon âme un jour, sous l'Arbre de Science,
Près de toi se repose, à l'heure où sur ton front
Comme un Temple nouveau ses rameaux s'épandront!

(*Oeuvres,* p. 118)

[Cause my soul one day under the Tree of Knowledge,
To rest near you, at the hour when on your brow,
Like a new Temple, its branches will spread forth!]

Leopardi hails Arimanes, who lives and triumphs: "Vivi, Arimane e trionfi, e sempre trionferai" (*Opere,* I, 326). [You live, Arimanes, and triumph, and will always triumph.] Baudelaire also salutes the Devil and proclaims his glory in "Les Litanies de Satan." In this poem, though Satan is defeated, he is more worthy of admiration than his oppressor, as Baudelaire exclaims: "O Prince de l'exil, à qui l'on a fait tort, / Et qui, vaincu, toujours te redresses plus fort" (*Oeuvres,* p. 116) [Oh Prince of exile, to whom wrong was done, / And who, though defeated, bridles ever more proudly]; and then again:

Gloire et louange à toi, Satan, dans les hauteurs
Du Ciel, où tu regnas, et dans les profondeurs
De l'Enfer, où, vaincu, tu rêves en silence!

(*Oeuvres,* p. 118)

[Glory and praise to you, Satan, in the heights
Of Heaven, where you reigned, and in the depths
Of Hell, where, vanquished, you dream in silence!]

Finally, Leopardi claims that he has been Arimanes' apostle and preacher. He asks a reward for his faithfulness—death; for he can no longer bear this life: "Io sono stato, vivendo, il tuo maggior predicatore . . . l'apostolo della tua religione. Ricompensami. Non ti chiedo nessuno di quelli che il mondo chiama beni: ti chiedo quello che è creduto il massimo de' mali, la morte. . . . Non posso, non posso più della vita" (*Opere,* I. 327). [I have been, during my life, your greatest preacher . . . the apostle of your religion. Reward me. I ask for none of what the world calls blessings: I ask for what is thought to be the greatest of evils, death. . . . I can not, I can not stand life any longer.] In "Les Litanies de Satan," Baudelaire also states that he has suffered unbearably, and he hopes only for death:

> O toi qui de la Mort, ta vieille et forte amante,
> Engendras l'Espérance,—une folle charmante!
> O Satan, prends pitié de ma longue misère!
>
> (*Oeuvres*, p. 117)

> [You who through Death, your old and strong lover,
> Begot Hope—a charming madwoman!
> Oh Satan, take pity on my long misery!]

The revolt thus reaches a frenetic peak with the celebration of Satan. To be sure, Satanism is a transitory attitude and represents an extreme measure of rebellion. Yet, what Satan has in common with all the other figures of revolt in the works of Leopardi and Baudelaire—Brutus, Sappho, the broom-plant, Don Juan, Icarus, the *femmes damnées*—is a consciousness of his own condition and a desire to stand nobly in face of the lot accorded him. Ultimately, both poets find in this consciousness a manner of redemption for mankind. They state in remarkably similar terms that this awareness of one's situation in life, however unhappy it may be, constitutes man's grandeur.[20] *Le mal* is inexorable and pervasive; but, as Leopardi proposes in **"La ginestra"** (1845, posth.), there is glory in recognizing our condition:

> Nobil natura è quella
> che a sollevar s'ardisce
> gli occhi mortali incontra
> al comun fato, e con franca lingua,
> nulla al ver detraendo,
> confessa il mal che ci fu dato in sorte,
> e il basso stato e frale.
>
> (***Opere***, I, 157)

> [A noble nature is that
> which dares to lift up
> mortal eyes to
> our common fate, and with a frank tongue,
> detracting in no way from the truth,
> admits the evil that was given to us as our destiny,
> and our low and fragile state.]

Baudelaire advances the same idea in "L'Irrémédiable" (1857). He claims that in this horrible existence, man's consciousness of his condition tortures him; but it is the source of his glory because he is fully aware of humanity's evil lot, and he acknowledges it openly:

> Un phare ironique, infernal,
> Flambeau des grâces sataniques,
> Soulagement et gloire uniques,
> —La conscience dans le Mal!
>
> (*Oeuvres*, p. 76)

> [An ironic, infernal beacon,
> Torch of satanic graces,
> Sole comfort and glory,
> —Consciousness in Evil!]

At the end of their respective collections of poetry, we find Baudelaire and Leopardi awaiting death, the great liberator, but with somewhat different outlooks. In "Le Voyage," which indeed represents Baudelaire's final attitude, he calls on death to take him, hoping for a new and possibly better existence beyond the grave. Above all, he is attracted to the unknown element in death, which holds much promise for a more interesting world than the endless spectacle of sin, corruption, and suffering which he knew in this one. Leopardi, on the other hand, does not concern himself so much with the possibilities of life after death. As we read in **"La ginestra,"** written at the very end of his life, he stands firm, resisting Fate, while waiting for the final liberation from this sorry condition. As with Baudelaire, death will certainly be a form of escape; but Leopardi does not hope for any better existence after he dies. While Baudelaire, at the conclusion of his work, detaches himself from reality in the contemplation of an unknown future world, Leopardi remains attached to this life, even though he suffers from it. For the former, death is the anticipated beginning; for the latter, it is the awaited end. Yet in both cases, death justifies their hopes and struggles. It is the fitting climax for two lives spent in combat with the overwhelming forces which oppress humanity and strip life of vitality and meaning.

Notes

1. There have been very few studies devoted exclusively to the affinities between Baudelaire and Leopardi. Most have been quite superficial; and this article is, to the best of my knowledge, the first substantive treatment of parallels between the two writers. See, for example: Vittorio Arullani, "Leggendo il Leopardi e il Baudelaire," *Fanfulla della domenica*. 11 Aug. 1901, p. 13; Valentino Piccoli, "Leopardi e Baudelaire," in *Anime e ombre* (Milan: Treves, 1927), pp. 200-215; Lionello Fiumi, "Leopardi et Baudelaire," *Nouvelles littéraires* 21 Aug. 1937, p. 6; and Bruno Biral, "Il sentimento del tempo: Leopardi, Baudelaire, Montale," *Il Ponte* 21 (1965), 1156-76.

2. In his writings, Baudelaire mentioned Leopardi only once, but in quite a laudatory context. As part of his planned rebuttal to an article (Feb. 13, 1865) by Jules Janin, who had attacked modern foreign poets in general, Baudelaire himself proposed a list of the greatest foreign poets, among whom he included Leopardi. He wrote first: "Byron, Tennyson, Poe et Cie. Ciel mélancolique de la poésie moderne. Etoiles de première grandeur." [Byron, Tennyson, Poe and Co. Melancholy sky

of modern poetry. Stars of the first magnitude.] Then, he completed the list: "Byron. Tennyson. E. Poe. Lermontoff. Leopardi. Esproncéda . . . Eh! quoi! je n'ai pas cité un Français La France est pauvre." [Byron. Tennyson. E. Poe. Lermontoff. Leopardi. Espronceda . . . What's that! I haven't mentioned a Frenchman. France is impoverished.] The above quotes appear in *Oeuvres complètes* (Paris: Pléiade, 1961), pp. 805-06—hereafter cited as *Oeuvres*. Except for his correspondence, all citations from Baudelaire's works are to this edition.

3. See my article, "Baudelaire's Knowledge of Italian," *Romance Notes* 14 (Autumn 1972), 71-74. For other views see J. S. Patty, "Baudelaire's Knowledge and Use of Dante," *Studies in Philology,* 53 (1956), 604, and W. T. Bandy, "Baudelaire, Masini et le Tasse," *Bulletin Baudelairien,* 10 (Eté 1974), 6-15.

4. Henri Hignard would eventually become Dean of the Faculty of Letters at Lyon. His article "Charles Baudelaire, sa vie, ses oeuvres, souvenirs personnels" appeared in the *Revue du Lyonnais,* 5th Ser., 13 (June 1892), 418-34. The passage cited in my text appears on p. 432.

5. In *Zibaldone di pensieri* (Milan: Mondadori, 1937), I, 1179-80—hereafter cited as *Zib*—Leopardi speaks of flashes of insight which reveal to the poet "i misteri più nascosti, gli abissi più cupi della natura, i rapporti più lontani o segreti, le cagioni più inaspettate e remote" [the most hidden mysteries, the deepest abysses of nature, the most distant and secret relationships, the most unexpected and remote causes]. On p. 732 of the same volume, he suggests the idea of *correspondances* by stating: "Certo è che l'idea del sistema, cioè di armonia, di convenienza, di corrispondenza, di relazioni, di rapporti, è idea reale." [It is certain that the idea of a system, that is, of harmony, of suitability, of correspondence, of relations, of connections, is a real idea.]

6. Giacomo Leopardi, *Opere* (Milan: Ricciardi, 1956), I, 38.

7. Maurice Mignon, in "Giacomo Leopardi et la France," *Revue des Deux Mondes,* 1 Nov. 1959, p. 125, notes that Leopardi reaches this conclusion and mentions a parallel with Baudelaire: "Ainsi devance-t-il, par son affirmation de la nature marâtre, le Vigny de la *Maison du Berger,* et Baudelaire, qui n'est pas sans affinités avec lui." [Thus he anticipates, by his affirmation of a Nature that is like a harsh stepmother, the Vigny of *La Maison du Berger,* and Baudelaire, who is not without affinities to him.]

8. Charles Baudelaire, *Correspondance générale,* 3 (Paris; Conard, 1948), 179—hereafter cited as *CG.*

9. Marcel Ruff, *L'Esprit du mal et l'esthétique baudelairienne* (Paris: Colin, 1955), p. 350.

10. Francesco Flora, "Poetica del Leopardi," in *Saggi di poetica moderna* (Messina: D'Anno, 1949), p. 11, makes a comment about Leopardi's poetry which is quite similar to Ruff's statement concerning Baudelaire's esthetic plan: "Poiché una poetica è necessariamente un rapporto con la concezione totale della vita, la poetica leopardiana si leva sul concetto primordiale del male cosmico e della vanità d'ogni cosa." [As a poetic plan necessarily is related to the total conception of life, Leopardian poetics is erected on the primeval concept of cosmic evil and the vanity of everything.]

11. Gustavo Rodolfo Ceriello pointed to the significance of this "giardino malato" in *Saggi di varia letteratura* (Milan: Ceschina, 1943), p. 176, and found in this description the ultimate encroachment of *le mal* upon all forms of life.

12. It should be added that, of all the various travails of life depicted in common by Baudelaire and Leopardi, the one most often cited by scholars is ennui. Each knew well this debilitating moral ailment which attacks the will and robs the soul of vitality and hope. Afflicted by the monotonous emptiness of existence and the seeming vanity of all activity, they expressed on numerous occasions their despair as ennui gained an ever-greater foothold in their spirit; and they contemplated in horror the apparently immortal proportions of the monster. Leopardi wrote, for instance: "Come colonna adamantina, siede / noia immortale" (*Opere,* I, 81) [Like an adamantine column, sits / immortal ennui]; and Baudelaire: "L'ennui, fruit de la morne incuriosité, / Prend les proportions de l'immortalité" (*Oeuvres,* p. 69) [Ennui, fruit of dismal incuriosity, / Assumes the proportions of immortality.]

13. One should note, however, Baudelaire's conception of the ennobling element in suffering. The poet's torment guarantees his greatness. He considers suffering "un divin remède à nos impuretés" and also "la noblesse unique," as he states in "Bénédiction" (*Oeuvres,* p. 9).

14. Giacomo Leopardi, *Epistolario* (Florence: Le Monnier, 1892), I, 265.

15. In *Mon Coeur mis à nu* (1886, posth.), for instance, Baudelaire notes: "Sentiment de solitude, dès mon enfance. Malgré la famille,—et au milieu des camarades surtout,—sentiment de destinée

éternellement solitaire" (*Oeuvres,* p. 1275). [Sentiment of isolation, since my childhood. In spite of my family—and in the midst of companions, especially—a sentiment of an eternally solitary destiny.] The idea is set forth once more in the prose poem "Les Vocations" (*Oeuvres,* pp. 281-84).

16. Leopardi described the nature of the *Magnanimo* in the preamble to the *Manuale di Epitteto* (1845, posth.): "E proprio degli spiriti grandi e forti . . . il contrastare, almeno dentro se medesimi, alla necessità, e far guerra feroce e mortale al destino, come i sette a Tebe di Eschilo, e come gli algri magnanimi degli antichi tempi" (*Opere,* I, 1066). [Characteristic of great and strong spirits is the resistance, at least within one's self, to necessity, and fierce and mortal war against fate, like the Seven against Thebes of Aeschylus, and like the other magnanimous individuals of ancient times.]

17. Giovanni Gentile calls this poem a "satanic moment." It represents an attitude of rebellion and tends to recur, as Gentile notes in *Poesia e filosofia di Giacomo Leopardi* (Florence: Sansoni, 1939), pp. 13-14: "Il momento satanico ricorre spesso nel Leopardi. Ma esso è la prima e fondamentale ribellione di questa forza incoercibile che egli sente insorgere di dentro a se medesimo, di fronte e a dispetto della natura, ossia di questo universal meccanismo che regge il mondo concepito." [The satanic moment recurs often in Leopardi. But it is the first and fundamental rebellion of that incoercible force that he feels rising within himself, in face of and in defiance of Nature, that is, of that universal mechanism which governs the known world.]

18. P. Mansell Jones feels that Baudelaire actually believed in the presence of Satan on earth. In *Baudelaire* (Cambridge, England: Bowes and Bowes, 1952), p. 19, Jones points to the poet's Catholic background and states that he believed in the Devil "with a conviction compared to which Gide's was that of a recent convert."

19. Riccardo Bachelli, *Leopardi* (Milan: Mondadori, 1960), p. 73. Mr. Bacchelli also points out, correctly, the forces at work in European literature during the lifetime of Leopardi and Baudelaire which made the cult of Satan a highlight of the romantic era.

20. The notion that man's consciousness of his condition is an indication of his grandeur comes directly from Pascal. It is highly probable that both Baudelaire and Leopardi found this idea at its source.

Alfredo Bonadeo (essay date 1977)

SOURCE: Bonadeo, Alfredo. "Leopardi's Concept of Nature." In *The Two Hesperias: Literary Studies in Honor of Joseph G. Fucilla,* edited by Americo Bugliani, pp. 69-87. Madrid: José Porrúa Turanzas, 1977.

[*In the following essay, Bonadeo explores the two phases of Leopardi's views on nature; the poet originally considered nature a benign force, but later began to see nature as hostile toward humanity.*]

The concept of nature in Leopardi's work has been, and still is controversial. Nature, and fate in Leopardi's poetical works were interpreted by De Sanctis as «due persone poetiche sotto le quali si nasconde una concezione del mondo essenzialmente materialista»[1]. This materialistic view of nature as an impersonal force governing blindly man's life met with great favor among future critics, and was also applied to Leopardi's prose, specifically to that part that is said to represent the last phase of his thought. Recent and current criticism does in fact refer to two phases in the development of Leopardi's concept of nature: an earlier one representing nature as beneficial to man, and a later one representing it as hostile to mankind[2]. This second phase has considerably exercised the imagination of the critics. According to Blasucci, for instance, in the ***Dialogo della natura e di un Islandese*** (1824) «natura rivela finalmente il suo volto malefico, assumendo definitivamente su di sé . . . attributi di crudeltà o indifferenza»[3]. The type of nature represented by Leopardi's meditations between 1825 and 1829 has been defined as «un meccanismo incosciente e non-provvidenziale,» responsible for the «inevitabile vicenda biologica che condanna gli esseri viventi o alla morte immatura . . . o ad una sopravvivenza non più allietata dalla speranza»[4]. Nature's antagonism toward man has been characterized not only as a physical entity, but also as a negative social force[5]. Very recently a critic, Sergio Solmi, has sought to break down the prevailing stark chronological dichotomy between the concept of a benevolent nature shaped by Leopardi during the years preceding the composition of the ***Operette morali*** and a malevolent one emerging first from the ***Operette*** and again in the later entries of the ***Zibaldone.*** This critic suggested that two dissimilar notions of nature are indeed detectable, but that they do not belong to separate chronological phases because they are traceable throughout the whole development of Leopardi's thought. One notion, defined by Solmi as «principio informatore» of life, represents «lo sviluppo vitale nella sua spontaneità»; the other is the «inesplicabile potenza creatrice e distruggitrice.» Solmi's hypothesis seems to be the most valid and fruitful among those advanced so far by the interpreters of Leopardi's thought. One reason, the critic explains, for the relevance of the thesis is the following: if two opposite concepts of nature, one belonging to an early phase and the other to a later one, are postulated, then the tacit assumption that Leopardi in his later years had repudiated the idea of a «natura provvidenziale, fondamentalmente benigna» has to be made. To make this assumption it would in turn mean to conclude that the whole Leopardian system had broken down: that Leopardi eventually repudiated the superiority of the primitive condition of man, that he rejected the importance of the «illusioni» nurtured by nature, that he had given up his fundamental idea of man's decadence due to the relinquishment of his natural condition[6]. Thus, an interpretation postulating a negative concept of nature following chronologically a positive one entails an unjustifiable mutilation of Leopardi's thought.

The two meanings of «natura» that can be traced in Leopardi's prose are the following: nature as the ideal complex of man's moral and sentimental energies that, when operative, allow him to lead a relatively happy life; implicit in this meaning is the idea that since modern man has abandoned his original nature to adopt a spurious one, he has relinquished the essential means to happiness. The second meaning of nature consists in the actual negative impact of those physical forces that act upon man in an impersonal and random manner, such as diseases and the environment. The two concepts cannot be separated by a chronological criterion; even less, the second meaning cannot be regarded as a modified extension of the first. The two concepts originate and develop wholly independently throughout Leopardi's work.

The first connotation of nature is already present in the *Discorso di un italiano intorno alla poesia romantica* (1818). Nature was here identified as the indispensable source of poetical inspiration and power, and defined as «invariata e primitiva, . . . schietta e inviolata,» the kind that appears in children and among primitive men. However, the forces of this nature, Leopardi proceeded, no longer operate among modern men, because they have been overcome by reason and civilization. Therefore, he added, in a world where everything that once existed according to nature has been altered by men, that inner primitive and genuine nature appears only «a somiglianza di lampo rarissimo, dovunque coperta e inviluppata come nel più grosso e fitto panno che si possa pensare»[7]. That original nature with which man was endowed, so vitally important to his feeling and imagination, has become corrupt and useless to him. The distinction between a nature originally benign and a corrupt one reappeared in a note of the *Zibaldone* of 1820 devoted to the subject of human happiness and to man's responsibility in nature's corruption. It should not be assumed, the poet cautioned, that unhappiness is a condition congenital to man, determined «dalla natura asso-

luta dell' uomo»; on the contrary, unhappiness is the product of our own present nature, «rispettiva e corrotta.» Many circumstances supporting this secondary, corrupt nature were not willed by original nature, but by man himself[8]. The corruption of nature is partly a reflection of the degeneration of reason. That year Leopardi declared that nature and reason had become enemies since the latter had lost its natural primitive character. Man in his natural and pristine condition availed himself of a reason given to him by «la stessa natura, e nella natura non si trovano contraddizioni. Nemico della natura è quell'uso della ragione che non è naturale, quell'uso eccessivo ch'è proprio solamente dell'uomo, e dell'uomo corrotto: nemico della natura, perciò appunto che non è naturale, nè proprio dell'uomo primitivo» (**Z**, I, 324). The passage from a primitive, wholesome inner human nature to a corrupt one is thus underscored by the transformation in the character of human reason. «In proporzione che l'uomo si allontana dalla natura,» the poet again observed, the power of reason increases as the force of natural instinct, the essential means to happiness, decreases. But why does man tend to abandon that condition in which nature had originally placed him? Because he erroneously believes that he is destined to reach a condition incomparably more perfect than that in which he finds himself in his primitive state. To this Leopardi retorted that human beings need not seek perfection simply because nature had made them perfect already; «l'uomo aveva naturalmente tutto il necessario.» It is precisely the belief in, and vain search for, a phantomatic perfection that caused man to experience a sense of inadequacy of his condition; hence a constant, unappeased yearning for a goal that will forever elude him. Thus, man «ha perduto la perfezione, volendosi perfezionare»; «si allontana dalla natura,» and in the process he his «alterato, cioè divenuto imperfetto relativamente alla sua natura» (**Z**, I, 363-364, 366-367)[9].

Some considerations on the problem of suicide bring out again the significance of the distinction between a benign, primitive nature and a spurious one acquired by man in the course of civilization. It is said, Leopardi noted, that nature forbids suicide; but, he asked, which nature is one referring to? It must be «questa nostra presente» nature, for «noi siamo di tutt'altra natura da quella ch'ervamo.» Men are now subject to the dictates of a «natura che . . . non è nostra.» This corrupt nature Leopardi defines as a «seconda natura, ch'è veramente nostra e presente,» thus distinguishing it once more from the primitive, congenital one. Nature in the latter sense truly forbade suicide, but because the fictitious «seconda natura» is the source of the corrupt, unhappy condition of modern man, he is led to attempt escaping that undesirable condition through self-destruction (**Z**, I, 1446-1447). Even the problem of «noia» finds, according to Leopardi, its origin in man's surrender to the dictates of a fictitious, inferior nature. Why do animals, who toil much less than man, and who would seem therefore exposed to the curse of «noia» to a larger extent than man, not experience ennui, he asked somewhat paradoxically. The answer was that «l'uomo si annoia e sente il suo nulla ogni momento» because «fa e pensa cose non volute dalla natura» (**Z**, I, 1351). The impact of the change for the worse in man's inner nature is reflected in his outward features. In discussing the changing physical characteristics of mankind through time Leopardi cited the «gran differenza fisica che s'incontra fra gli uomini da individuo a individuo,» especially among those individuals living in a same country and climate. No other animal species, he observed, exhibits the staggering variety in physical traits as the human species does. Since nature, Leopardi argued, had originally assigned to each and every species certain uniform physical traits, the extreme physical irregularities discernible nowadays among individuals belonging to the same species points to a decline in humanity's physical quality; it reveals «quanto gli uomini sieno allontanati dalla loro vera natura» (**Z**, I, 1525-1526).

The relinquishment of man's original nature was not due to some obscure force beyond his control; the responsibility rests with man himself. Nature has shown a studied generosity toward man in placing many carefully designed obstacles to his decadence; so much so that the fall of mankind to the present calamitous condition has taken place only through the exercise of extreme violence upon nature itself and the primitive order of things. Thus, no matter how serious and universal the fallen condition of mankind, corruption and unhappiness cannot be considered evils inherent in what Leopardi calls «il sistema della natura» (**Z**, I, 726). Progress and civilization have created new needs in man and society which the natural environment is unable to satisfy. Those «stesse cose che la natura aveva destinate al suo [man's] uso» are no longer of any use to man in the civilized state. Therefore, in order to fulfill the wide range of modern needs, man sought to modify those «cose» to render them serviceable again; but in doing so, he has only succeeded in reducing them «a una condizione diversissima e anche opposta alla naturale.» The fact that man has experienced needs that the available means in his environment were unable to satisfy, and therefore had to resort to the manipulation of the available resources in order to meet the increased requirements, was, according to Leopardi, an unmistakable symptom of his incipient decadence. It did not mean, as it might seem to imply, that man's natural environment was imperfect; rather, it signifies that «l'uomo non è qual doveva,» for man, having himself changed, was compelled to seek to modify external nature; hence «è ridotto a tale stato che non gli basta più la natura di gran lunga; e ciò prova che questo stato non gli conviene.» This condition does not fit him because his natural environment no longer suits his needs;

man «trova la natura renitente, ripugnante, mal disposta a' suoi vantaggi, a' suoi piacere, a' suoi desiderii, a' suoi fini, e gli conviene rifabbricarla,» but with little success and much grief (**Z**, I, 1022-1023). Because man's life style has changed in an unnatural manner, he has elicited nature's hostility. The responsibility for humanity's sunken state belongs to man: nature has not endowed man with any quality that would render him corrupt and unhappy, and that hindered his welfare; on the contrary, he was given the ability to preserve himself in the «stato suo primitivo puro» (**Z**, II, 159)[10]. It is true, Leopardi conceded in the course of some meditations on society, that nature placed in men the tendency to hate one another; nature, however, also willed that men should live in «società larga,» that is, in a loosely organized society allowing for considerable individual autonomy and little reciprocal interference. Therefore, the poet concluded, perhaps stretching somewhat the argument, the tendency to hatred that exists among men is to be considered only as unrealized potential, not as an actual evil; hence, «come tanti altri mali, che essendo sempre, o secondo natura, solamente in potenza, la natura non ne ha colpa alcuna» (**Z**, II, 768).

The distinction between an artificial nature that man has allowed to develop within himself and the primitive one he has relinquished became sharper as time went by. In the **Operette morali** (1824), for instance, the poet from Recanati attributed the inability on the part of mankind to find a modicum of peace and happiness to an «inquieta, insaziabile, immoderata natura umana.» Men, Leopardi further asserted, have gone «in perdizione» on account of wars, idleness, and knowledge because they did not follow the path set by nature: they studiously tried «tutte le vie di far contro la propria natura e di capitar male»[11]. A counterpart to this reflection can be found sometime later in a meditation concerned with emotional life. Modern men, Leopardi argued, have lost the ability to rid themselves swiftly of sorrow. The ancients well knew how to do it: when oppressed by pain they cried aloud, rolled on the ground, banged their heads on the walls. Through these impulsive, uninhibited physical reactions they let pain and sorrow out, relieving themselves, because such acts, taught man by «natura medesima, . . . sono a chi li pratica naturalmente un conforto grandissimo.» Such primitive animal-like reactions are repressed in modern man who, unable to find an outlet for his grief and suffering, is oppressed by these painful feelings within his being. Whereas nothing else could have helped him endure human suffering better than that nature man once possessed (**Z**, II, 1074-1075), now his nature has changed to such an extent that he can no longer alleviate his suffering. «Tanto è mutata, vinta cancellata in noi la natura dall'assuefazione.» Modern man no longer retains his primitive nature, but is governed by a corrupt one. The differentiation between these two types of human nature finds perhaps its thorough expression in the **Dialogo di**

Plotino e di Porfirio (1827). Here Leopardi aptly distinguished a «natura primitiva degli uomini antichi, e delle genti selvagge e incolte,» which, however, «non è più la natura nostra,» from a «nostra natura nuova.» The poet used the distinction, as he had done a few years earlier, to discuss anew the problem of suicide. Whereas among the primitive and ancient peoples both the desire for, and the act of, suicide was uncommon because it was not natural, among modern peoples it is common and natural. The difference in outlook depends on the different character of human nature: ancients' nature was supported by «illusioni,» but moderns' nature is sustained by reason. When brought to bear on the condition of modern life the ruthless power of reason inexorably leads to the conclusion that the only efficacious remedy to the unhappy life of civilized man is death. Modern man's nature, Leopardi gloomily acknowledged, «noi abbiamo, ed avremo sempre, in luogo di quella prima»[12].

The idea that in the course of progress mankind has sunk to a state in which those qualities and energies, with which it had naturally been endowed, were muted owing to man's deviation from the life style set by nature, finds a counterpart and substantiation in the conviction that man's life, in the progress of time and civilization, will again be lived according to the tenets of primigenial nature. Leopardi had already defined man's return to nature in the first pages of the *Zibaldone* as «ultrafilosofia»[13]. Since the shrinkage of natural life is a condition of barbarity, the mankind's regeneration, the poet admonished as early as 1820, «dipende da una . . . ultrafilosofia, che . . . ci ravvicini alla natura» (*Z,* I, 140). The «ultrafilosofia» would aim at overcoming the harmful consequences of the «filosofia,» by bringing man to the realization that he was indeed wise and learned when he was living according to his original condition, and that he should never have relinquished it. The «ultrafilosofia,» then, will help «a rimetter l'uomo in quella condizione in cui sarebbe sempre stato» before philosophy sidetracked him (*Z,* I, 280). Reason itself will unwittingly assist mankind in its journey back to nature, for reason will eventually reach the stage where it will have to acknowledge «che quanto ella ci ha insegnato al di là della natura, tutto è inutile e dannoso, e quanto ci ha insegnato di buono, tutto già lo sapevamo dalla natura» (*Z,* I, 924)[14]. In this context knowledge and civilization shaped up in Leopardi's mind as a force capable of amending the errors committed by humanity, and of bridging the extant breach between man and nature. Learning's most useful function, he asserted with unusual force, consists «nel ricondurre l'intelletto umano . . . appresso a poco a quello stato in cui era prima del di lei [knowledge] nascimento,» that is, back to the stage of natural life (*Z,* I, 56). An entry of 1823 confronts the reader with this stupefying statement: «Non è dubbio che l'uomo civile è più vicino alla natura che l'uomo selvaggio e sociale.» The asser-

tion is unsettling because Leopardi's prevalent claim is that civilized man is farther from the natural condition than the savage. But this thought becomes clear when one considers the rationalization on the cycle of humanity's corruption and healing that the poet derived from it: «Che vuol dire questo? La società è corruzione. In processo di tempo e di lumi l'uomo cerca di ravvicinaris a quella natura onde s'è allontanato. . . . Quindi la civiltà è un ravvicinamento alla natura» (*Z,* II, 665). Finally, a letter of 1829 predicted a hard and long way yet ahead before humanity could reacquire the condition of the ancients; but there was an unmistakable glimmer of optimism in the presage. If the poet could write to Pietro Colletta that «resta ancora molto a ricuperare della civiltà degli antichi,» this meant that some of the ancients' condition had already been regained, and that the return of man to nature had begun and was in the process of unfolding[15].

Leopardi's other concept of nature as an external material force hostile to mankind is traceable throughout the development of the poet's thought, not merely in a later stage. In an early, famous page of the *Zibaldone* the author analyzed the change that in 1819 had occurred in his physical condition; to this corresponded a modification in his moral and poetical outlook. «La mutazione totale in me, e il passaggio dallo stato antico al moderno, seguí si può dire dentro un anno, cioè nel 1819 dove privato dell'uso della vista, . . . cominciai a sentire la mia infelicità in un modo assai più tenebroso, cominciai . . . a riflettere profondamente sopra le cose (in questi ho scritto . . . sopra materie appartenenti sopra tutto alla nostra natura, a differenza dei pensieri passati, quasi tutti di letteratura), a divenir filosofo di professione (di poeta ch'io era), a sentire l'infelicità certa del mondo, in luogo di conoscerla, e questo anche per uno stato di languore corporale, che tanto più mi allontanava dagli antichi e mi avvicinava ai moderni» (*Z,* I, 162). The impact of physical deterioration led Leopardi to meditate assiduously on nature, a nature manifestly no longer benign, as it was toward the ancients, but hostile; he came then to recognize that unhappiness was no longer a strictly personal experience, but universal. The poet admitted in that same page that he had «stato sempre sventurato,» but, whereas before the impairment of the vision, he believed that unhappiness was a condition peculiar to this being[16] while everybody else enjoyed happiness, after the onset of the disease he became convinced that unhappiness was the common lot of men[17].

The working of a malefic nature as an external force affecting the physical condition of both man and his world reappears throughout the meditations of the *Zibaldone* and other works time and again. It will be sufficient to indicate here a few significant occurrences. As early as March 1821 he observed that a great many individuals were exposed to considerable health hazards due to the nature of their work; this, he added, was ordinary work, performed to produce ordinary things indispensable to modern life. In this respect, then, production and consumption amounted to the subsistence of certain individuals, the consumers, at the expense of others, the producers. Leopardi was dismayed at the price exacted by the exigencies of modern life. What do you think about this, he sardonically asked the reader. It is understandable that it is nature's plan to have one species survive at the expense, and even destruction, of another, he conceded. But that nature «abbia disposta ed ordinata precisamente la distruzione di una parte della stessa specie, al comodo, anzi alla perfezione essenziale dell'altra parte . . . , questo chi si potrà indurre a crederlo?» (**Z**, I, 582-583). In the progress of time the poet's awareness of nature's hostility became more intense. The peculiar condition of man, to exist unhappily, Leopardi wrote in 1824, is mind-boggling. No more anguishing a contradiction is conceivable than that of existence and unhappiness. «L'essere, unito all'infelicità . . . , è cosa contraria direttamente a se stessa . . . Dunque l'essere dei viventi è una contraddizione . . . con se medesimo.» The poet regarded this cruel antithesis as one of the «contraddizioni che sono in natura,» and as part of the «orribile mistero delle cose e della esistenza universale.» To explain unhappiness in this context Leopardi referred the reader to the *Dialogo della natura e di un islandese* (1824) (**Z**, II, 924). In order to escape the evils of civilization a man withdrew from society to Iceland. He lived isolated, in a condition very close to nature. Leopardi's concern, however, is not with any romantic notion of man's return to his natural state and to a wholesome mode of inner existence. On the contrary, he dwells on the unenduring physical pain the man from Iceland underwent owing to his exposure to the elements. His body was afflicted in various ways, by «la lunghezza del verno, l'intensità del freddo, e l'ardore estremo della state . . . e il fuoco» near which he was forced to spend a great deal of his time. Diseases oppressed his «corpo e l'animo con mille stenti e mille dolori.» Exasperated and extenuated by the excruciating experience, the man from Iceland turned to nature, accusing it of deliberately denying humankind even short periods of physical wellbeing. You, the poet addressed nature, «ora c'insidii, ora ci minacci ora ci assalti ora ci pungi ora ci percuoti ora ci laceri, e sempre o ci offendi o ci perseguiti.» Nature replied to confirm the accusation and to claim responsibility for the character of existence: «La vita di quest'universo è un perpetuo circuito di produzione e distruzione»[18].

The year following the *Operette morali* Leopardi wrote again about the cycle of creation and destruction of animals and things as the «fine della natura universale.» He concluded then that «la natura tutta, e l'ordine eterno delle cose non è in alcun modo diretto alla felicità degli esseri sensibili o degli animali. Esso vi è anzi con-

trario» (**Z**, II, 956, 959). In a page which exceeded all others in somberness and despair one year later Leopardi brooded: «Il fine dell'universo è il male . . . ; le leggi, l'andamento naturale dell'universo non sono altro che male. . . . L'esistenza, per sua natura ed essenza propria e generale, è un'imperfezione, un'irregolarità, una mostruosità.» He sought to minimize the annihilating force of these meditations by surmising that man's world was only one of the many worlds of which the universe is composed, but his thought had apparently lost the ability to lift a profoundly demoralized being out of the depression created by his own rationalizations. He continued in the same page: «Non gli uomini solamente, ma il genere umano fu e sarà sempre infelice di necessità. Non il genere umano solamente ma tutti gli animali. Non gli animali soltanto ma tutti gli altri esseri al loro modo. Non gl'individui ma le specie, i generi, i regni, i globi, i sistemi, i mondi.» Evidently inspired by the previous idea of the process of creation and destruction inexorably ordained by nature, Leopardi concluded by explaining the nature of unhappiness with the memorable passage on the garden in a perennial state of *souffrance*. The prosperous aspect of plants and flowers, he meditated, is only apparent. They are certainly living, may be growing, but to do so they fiercely compete among themselves for air, sun, and space; they are also exposed to damage wrought by winds, insects, birds, and to the wounds of the gardener that prune them; «ogni giardino è quasi un vasto ospitale (luogo ben più deplorabile che un cemeterio)» (**Z**, II, 1004-1006). The quality of life given living organisms by a remote, impersonal nature could not be considered as a gift, but a curse. The same type of transformation, Leopardi observed, prevails among animals; some of them are endowed with great aggressive drive and power to offend, others only with the art of defense. Because «la natura ha dato agli uni la tendenza a distruggere, agli altri la tendenza a conservarsi,» a ceaseless struggle accompanied by an unending production and destruction process occurs among them. At this point Leopardi asked with a note of anguish: «Qual'è il fine, qual'è il voler sincero e l'intenzione vera della natura?» Nature is responsible for the cruelty inherent in the ruthless contests for life and death, he replied. Was it not in nature's power «il non crear queste tali offese?» Yet nature chose to make these offenses a part of life; it is «l'autrice unica delle difese e delle offese, del male e del rimedio» (**Z**, II, 1032-1033). The working of nature with regard to the physical existence of its creatures seemed to have become incomprehensible to the author of the *Zibaldone*.

Six months later Leopardi turned his attention again to the fate of all living creatures, and in particular to the process of destruction which they are ineluctably subjected to: «Tutte si distruggono scambievolmente, tutte periscono, e, quel ch'è peggio, tutte deperiscono, tutte patiscono a lor modo.» Is, then, «il gran magisterio della natura, l'ordine incomparabile dell'universo» to be praised? Let us admire nature's order, he urged with bitter irony: «io l'ammiro più degli altri: lo ammiro per la sua pravità e deformità, che a me paiono estreme» (**Z,** II, 1090-1091)[19]. Nature's way in the process of production and destruction struck Leopardi as being particularly profligate: «La natura è come un fanciullo: con grandissima cura ella si affatica a produrre e a condurre il prodotto alla sua perfezione; ma non appena ve l'ha condotto, ch'ella pensa e comincia a distruggerlo, a travagliare alla sua dissoluzione. Così nell'uomo, così negli altri animali, ne' vegetabili, in ogni genere di cose» (**Z,** II, 1.233)[20]. The last pages of the ***Zibaldone*** on the relationship between nature and the physical condition of man follow the pattern outlined above, but also reveal some reluctance to holding nature completely responsible for mankind's suffering. The process of material creation and destruction among men and animals attracted Leopardi's attention again in 1829. He recognized it as a horrible disorder, «che fa fremere, [e] tende dirittamente e più efficacemente d'ogni altro alla distruzione della specie.» It is impossible, he concluded, to ascribe such frightening operation to nature's intention, for, he argued, if nature proceeded this way mankind would have ceased to exist long ago (**Z,** II, 1269). But only two months later the poet seemed to have already changed his mind; he wrote then: «La natura, per necessità della legge di distruzione e riproduzione, . . . è essenzialmente regolarmente e perpetuamente persecutrice e nemica mortale di tutti gl'individui d'ogni genere e specie, ch'ella dà in luce; e comincia a perseguitarli dal punto medesimo in cui li ha prodotti» (**Z,** II, 1293)[21].

Leopardi's meditations upon the ceaseless cycle of physical creation and destruction willed and carried out by nature do not reveal anything new and different from what he had written many years before. Nature, he noted in 1820, has denied men the possibility to coexist peacefully, has placed no restraint upon their inclination to harm one another. Nature «non ha dettato nessuna regola di onestà e di rettitudine, perchè l'uomo non prova nessuna ripugnanza nel far male agli altri animali. . . . Ma eziandio nella propria specie l'uomo . . . non sente ingenitamente nessuna colpa a far male a' suoi per suo vantaggio, come non la sentono gli altri animali, che maltrattano, combattono» (**Z,** I, 246). The closeness of this early view to the later ones just examined is such as to show again that Leopardi's thought on that particular aspect of nature flowed with remarkable consistency throughout time.

The importance of Leopardi's concept of nature as a complex of laws and forces hostile to the material and moral happiness of mankind is revealed by the vigorous and emotional response it inspired in his writing, and especially in his most celebrated poem ***La ginestra.*** In 1823 he noted that in the beginning man's mortal enemies were the wild animals and the elements; these made the primitives' life extremely precarious. Instead of spawning pessimism and despair, the primitive, but extremely vulnerable condition acted as an incentive for men to form a brotherhood in a common defensive cause. Leopardi saw the emergence of this fellowship as coinciding with the golden age. Then man «amò e ricercò lo scontro, la compagnia, l'aiuto del suo simile, senz'odio alcuno, senza invidia, senza sospetto. . . . Quella fu veramente l'età dell'oro, e l'uomo era sicuro tra gli uomini: non per altro se non perch'esso e gli altri uomini odiavano e temevano de' viventi e degli oggetti stranieri al genere umano; e queste passioni non lasciavano luogo all'odio o invidia o timore verso i loro simili» (**Z,** II, 40). But, even though the golden age and primitive life are things of the past, the defensive struggle against a malevolent nature goes on. Who will carry on the fight? Men, of course, men united by the common bond of an ever expanding civilization. This «tende naturalmente a propagarsi, e a far sempre nuove conquiste, e non può star ferma, nè contenersi dentro alcun termine, . . . finchè vi sieno creature civilizzabili, e associabili al gran corpo della civilizzazione, alla grande alleanza degli esseri intelligenti contro alla natura, e contro alle cose non intelligenti» (**Z,** II, 1114). In this sense civilization with its ability to bring humanity together in a common endeavor became in Leopardi's eyes the substitute for the mythical and unreachable state of nature. In ***La ginestra*** (1836), finally, nature reappeared in its function of wicked generator. It was, the poet sarcastically meditated, our «amante natura» that has placed the frail ginestra, symbol of the precariousness of the human condition, defenseless on the barren slope of the «formidabil monte / Sterminator Vesevo.» There the lonely reed exists in wait of certain death, and as such, it indeed reflects the «aspra sorte e . . . depresso loco / Che natura ci diè.» The nature that has presided over the birth and existence of the ginestra is the same entity that through volcanic eruptions has brought about destruction of lives and things, a devastation extensive both in time and space. It was the most diabolic and vicious nature represented by Leopardi so far. Yet, to the work of this fiendish generator the poet reacted at the same time with uncommon vigor and optimism. With the last cited passage of the ***Zibaldone*** evidently in mind, Leopardi again represented the fellowship of primitive man for defense against a hostile nature as an example to be imitated by the moderns. This solidarity no longer would take shape under the terror of the unleashed forces of nature, but through a conscious and concerted effort springing from a civil and social organization, to bring about and maintain the material and moral welfare of its members:

> E quell'orror che primo
> Contro l'empia natura
> Strinse i mortali in social catena,
> Fia ricondotto in parte

Da verace saper, l'onesto e il retto
Conversar cittadino,
E giustizia e pietade, altra radice
Avranno allor che non superbe fole.

The conclusions drawn from two different concepts of nature justify the legitimacy and usefulness of the distinction made on the basis of an ideological, rather than a chronological criterion. Man must return to nature to recapture the tone and rhythm of life the primitives and ancients enjoyed. Man must protect himself against a perfidious nature that gave him life, but denied him happiness by endowing him with an insidiously vulnerable and insecure physical existence. To accept the prevalent, undifferentiated interpretation of Leopardi's idea of nature, an entity inimical to man over which he has no control, means to deny man's responsibility in the shaping of his own moral and physical existence[22]. That interpretation does Leopardi and his work a grave injustice because it attributes to them a pessimism and fatalism that make the poet's outlook deathlike[23]. Beyond any doubt the issue in Leopardi's concept of nature is whether man does, or does not, have power over his own existence. By appealing to a beneficial nature to whom man must return to improve the quality of his life, and to a common human cause against a malefic nature, Leopardi resolved the issue by squarely placing the responsibility for mankind's destiny upon man, and rejecting, conversely, resignation to fatalism.

It should be noted, finally, that the reason for conjuring up the notion of a cruel, hostile nature with whom man must contend, precisely as Leopardi himself had to contend for most of his life, was perhaps not due solely to his intent of asserting the ideal of a humanity united in a common cause. It was possibly due in part to the poet's disguised ambition to enhance his own fame. Leopardi achieved the stature of a genius in the course of only a brief life and in the face of overwhelming odds. What was to appear more heroic and worthy of admiration to posterity than the success and fame that that physical ruin of a man was able to reach by defying and overcoming the staggering pain and suffering that nature had placed in his way? What greater victory than defeating that very nature that the poet had once designated as an invincible enemy?

Notes

1. Francesco De Sanctis, *Leopardi,* ed. C. Muscetta, A. Perna (Turin, 1960), p. 263.

2. See Michele Losacco, *Indagini leopardiane* (Lanciano, 1937), p. 311; G. A. Levi, *Storia del pensiero di Giacomo Leopardi* (Turin, 1911), p. 123; Lorenzo Giusso, *Leopardi e le sue ideologie* (Florence, 1935), pp. 57, 207, 208; Giulio Reichenbach, *Studi sulle Operette morali di Giacomo Leopardi* (Florence, 1934), p. 81; Manfredi

Porena, *Scritti leopardiani* (Bologna, 1959), pp. 157-158; Antonello Gerbi, *La disputa del nuovo mondo* (Milan-Naples, 1955), p. 429; Bruno Biral, «Il significato di 'natura' nel pensiero di Leopardi,» *Il ponte,* XV, (1959), 1271, states that nature according to Leopardi completely ignores the destiny and happiness of mankind. Ferdinando Neri, «Il pensiero del Rousseau nelle prime chiose dello *Zibaldone,»* in *Letteratura e leggende* (Turin, 1951), p. 270, refused to acknowledge a positive concept of nature whatsoever in Leopardi's work: «La natura non è mai stata considerata davvero dal Leopardi come buona in sé: . . . la natura è malvagia.» See, finally, Piero Bigongiari, «Leopardi e il senso dell'animo,» in *Leopardi e l'Ottocento. Atti del II convegno internazionale di studi leopardiani* (Florence, 1970), p. 39.

3. Luigi Blasucci, «La posizione ideologica delle *Operette morali,»* in *Critica e storia letteraria* (Padua, 1970), I, 663.

4. Sebastiano Timpanaro, *Classicismo e Illuminismo nell'Ottocento italiano* (Pisa, 1969), pp. 401, 403.

5. Michele Kerbaker, *Scritti inediti* (Rome, 1932), I, 146-148; Cesare Luporini, «Leopardi progressivo,» in *Filosofi vecchi e nuovi* (Florence, 1947), p. 222. Conversely, that nature that Leopardi saw as beneficial to mankind embodies values opposite to those of the society in which the poet lived: Biral, «Il significato di 'natura' nel pensiero di Leopardi,» p. 1226.

6. Sergio Solmi, *Scritti leopardiani* (Milan, 1969), pp. 109, 116-121. But see Timpanaro's objections to Solmi's hypothesis in *Classicismo e Illuminismo,* pp. 387, 401-403.

7. Leopardi, *Discorso di un italiano intorno alla poesia romantica,* in *Tutte le opere di Giacomo Leopardi: Le poesie e le prose,* ed. F. Flora (Milan, 1940), II, 481-482. On nature as a source of poetical imagination see Leopardi's very significant letter of March 1820 in *Lettere,* ed. F. Flora (Milan, 1963), p. 246.

8. Leopardi, *Zibaldone di pensieri,* in *Tutte le opere di Giacomo Leopardi,* ed. F. Flora (Milan, 1937), I, 193. All quotations from the *Zibaldone* will be from this edition and referred to in the text by *Z,* followed by the volume's number and page.

9. Cf. *Z,* I, 393: «La natura era quella che noi sentivamo senza studiarla, trovavamo senza cercarla, seguivamo senza osservarla, ci parlava senza interrogarla.» Humanity, however, has painstakingly sought «quella condizione conveniente a noi . . . : e non s'è trovata»; it could only realize that the superior condition believed to befit man was precisely «quella che avevamo prima di pensare a cercarla,» that is, the primitive one.

10. In this entry Leopardi mitigated the responsibility of man by pointing out that nature made him «il più mutabile e quindi il più corruttibile di tutti gli esseri terrestri,» hence the most prone to relinquish his natural state. Since man is like a perfect machine with a very complex and delicate mechanism, he, like the machine, tends to break down easily, that is, he possesses «una disposizione maggiore . . . a perdere il suo stato primitivo e la sua perfezione naturale» (Z, II, 159-160).

11. *Storia del genere umano. Dialogo di un folletto e di un gnomo,* in *Le poesie e le prose,* I, 820, 840.

12. *Operette morali,* in *Le poesie e le prose,* I, 1010-1011. Five years later Leopardi returned to the problem of suicide in the *Frammento sul suicidio,* and noting that suicides have multiplied with the development of civilization and the corresponding decline of happiness, he concluded that «la felicità che la natura ci ha destinata, e le vie d'otternerla . . . immutabili e sole» have been abandoned. The poet underscored the responsibility of man by adding that nature's ways had not changed: *Le poesie e le prose,* I, 1082-1084.

13. A negative, but biased interpretation of the term «ultrafilosofia» was offered by Romano Amerio. According to him the term means «riduzione della ragione alla natura»; but since to Amerio «natura» means a primeval state without morals and religion, the return to nature advocated by Leopardi is seen as an «inversione del Cristianesimo,» for man «adeguandosi alla pura esistenzialità . . . rifa la natura, cioè il nulla»; «L'ultrafilosofia di Giacomo Leopardi,» *Filosofia,* IV (1953), 455, 482.

14. Even earlier Leopardi assigned to reason, corrupt however it may be, the task of leading man back to nature. He was not, however, very sanguine about the outcome. Such a return, he admitted, «essendo fatto mediante quella ragione stessa che ha corrotto l'uomo, ed avendo il suo fondamento in questa medesima corruttrice, non può più equivalere allo stato naturale, nè per conseguenza alla nostra perfezion primitiva, nè quindi procurarci quella felicità che si era destinata» (Z, I, 344).

15. *Lettere,* p. 906.

16. On nature affecting Leopardi's life in particular rather than humanity as a whole, see *Lettere,* p. 290. In retrospect he will represent himself being old and decrepit even before being young; this, he will argue, was the sure indication that nature had destined him to be a nonentity: *Lettere,* p. 449.

17. Timpanaro, *Classicismo e Illuminismo,* p. 389, stated that in the period between 1819 and 1820

Leopardi was still far away from the «concezione della natura nemica dell'intero genere umano.» The evidence in the passage just cited of the *Zibaldone* suggests, however, that the hostility of nature toward the physical well-being of mankind as a whole is to be dated from 1819. The early, cosmic character of nature's negative impact is also detectable in the poetry. In *La sera del dì di festa,* for instance, the poet recognized the working of «l'antica natura onnipossente, / Che mi fece all'affanno.» This nature has denied the poet even hope in a better future, and condemned him to tears. The representation of this personal condition of sorrow, however, merges, and finds an explanation, in a much more universal predicament, the natural cycle of life and death:

> E fieramente mi si stringe il core,
> A pensar come tutto al mondo passa,
> E quasi orma non lascia . . .

18. *Operette morali,* in *Le poesie e le prose,* I, 883, 885, 886, 888. Cf. *Z,* I, 1351 (1821), where the poet is already aware, but still indifferent, to nature's process of production and destruction.

19. This decisive turn in Leopardi's attitude toward nature as the entity responsible for mankind's physical existence is doubtlessly tied to the rapid decline in the poet's personal condition, a further deterioration of the eyesight: *Lettere,* pp. 763, 764, 778. He defined the illness as «la più grave ed ostinata che . . . abbia sofferto da otto anni in qua»: *Ibid.,* p. 783. For the progress and effects of the disease in the following years, see *Ibid.,* pp. 897, 904, 927, 933. On the impact of Leopardi's infirmity upon his «morale», see generally Bonaventura Zumbini, *Studi sul Leopardi* (Florence, 1902), p. 111, and Timpanaro, *Classicismo e Illuminismo,* p. 156.

20. Cf. the *Palinodia al marchese Gino Capponi* (1835):

> La natura crudel, fanciullo invitto,
> Il suo pariccio adempie, e senza posa
> Distruggendo e formando si trastulla.

21. Cf. *Ad Arimane* (1833): «Produzione e distruzione ec. per uccider partorisce ec. sistema del mondo, tutto patimen. Natura è come un bambino che disfa subito il fatto.» *Le poesie e le prose,* I, 434.

22. This is what Eugène Anagnine implies in «Giacomo Leopardi et Jean-Jacques Rousseau,» *Annales de la Société Jean-Jacques Rousseau,* XXVIII (1939-1940), 68, 72.

23. Francesco De Sanctis already warned against an interpretation of this sort: *Leopardi,* p. 466.

Margaret Brose (essay date 1983)

SOURCE: Brose, Margaret. "Leopardi's 'L'Infinito' and the Language of the Romantic Sublime." *Poetics Today* 4, no. 1 (1983): 47-71.

[*In the following essay, Brose examines the relationship of Leopardi's lyrics to the aesthetics of European romanticism in general and of the romantic sublime in particular.*]

"L'Infinito"

Sempre caro mi fu quest'ermo colle,
E questa siepe, che da tanta parte
Dell'ultimo orizzonte il guardo esclude.
Ma sedendo e mirando, interminati
Spazi di là da quella, e sovrumani
Silenzi, e profondissima quiete
Io nel pensier mi fingo; ove per poco
Il cor non si spaura. E come il vento
Odo stormir tra queste piante, io quello
Infinito silenzio a questa voce
Vo comparando: e mi sovvien l'eterno,
E le morte stagioni, e la presente
E viva, e il suon di lei. Così tra questa
Immensità s'annega il pensier mio:
E il naufragar m'è dolce in questo mare.

(Giacomo Leopardi, 1819)

[(1) Always dear to me was this solitary hill, (2) And this hedge, which from so great a part (3) Of the farthest horizon excludes the gaze. (4) But sitting and gazing, boundless (5) Spaces beyond that, and superhuman (6) Silences, and profoundest quiet (7) I in my mind imagine (create); wherefore (8) The heart is almost filled with fear. And as (9) I hear the wind rustle through these plants, that (10) Infinite silence to this voice (11) I go on comparing: and I recall to mind the eternal, (12) And the dead seasons, and the present (13) And living one, and the sound of it. So in this (14) Immensity my thought is drowned: (15) And the shipwreck is sweet to me in this sea.]

This appears to be a propitious moment to reconsider the lyrics of Giacomo Leopardi (1798-1837). Or rather, more to the point, it is time to consider the lyric structure of Leopardi's idylls in the light of current discussions of Romanticism. For these discussions, to which Bloom, de Man, Abrams, Hartman, and the late Thomas Weiskel have made important contributions, have all been marked by an inexplicable inattention to the one Italian poet who reflected most systematically on the aesthetic of the sublime. To be sure, a number of Italian critics have given us studies which greatly elucidate our understanding of Leopardi's work, but the relationship of that work to the poetics of the Romantic Sublime, and thus to European Romanticism in general, remains undetermined.[1] Since Leopardi was not only a great poet but also a philologist, rhetorician, and critic—one who, moreover, reflected on the nature of language in terms consonant with the spirit of modern linguistically oriented stylistics—his theory and poetic practice of the sublime are of especial interest to studies of Romantic literature. What follows are the prolegomena to a re-reading of the Leopardian *idillio* with a close look at **"L'Infinito"** (1819) as a self-conscious demonstration of lyric transcendence.

I

A discussion of the Leopardian sublime permits us to circumvent a typical critical impasse: the *cul-de-sac* of dichotomous terminological pairs. Romantic poets lend themselves easily to classificatory dyads such as subject-object, mind-nature, poet-landscape. And this because not only do Romantic poets tend to characterize their own poetic theory in these terms, but because the reader is ineluctably drawn to a description of the moment of Romantic transcendence as a passage from one state or pole to another. The danger lies, of course, in our tendency to hypostatize these poles as mutually exclusive places: to de-linguistify, in other words, or to transfer from the domain of language to that of spatial-temporal *loci*. By so doing, we necessarily create binary oppositions. Rather than seek to isolate an extra-textual *locus*, we need to explicate the rhetorical moves involved in this intra-textual transference: the tropological shifts by which one mode of discourse is substituted for another.

In his discussion of the Romantic subject-object dyad, Paul de Man comments that whichever term is given priority by the critics, we come to a persistent contradiction. Critics are obliged, on the one hand, "to assert the priority of object over subject that is implicit in an organic conception of language." And yet, continues de Man, if we examine theoretical passages from Wordsworth or Coleridge, we find that these poets "confer an equally absolute priority to the self over nature." What are we to believe? de Man disingenuously queries. Is Romanticism "a subjective idealism" or "a return to a certain form of naturalism?" (de Man, 1969:182). To such a query, posed as it is in terms which are mutually exclusive, we would have to answer that Romanticism is neither. Or that it is both. Binary pairs may be useful, however, if we examine the linguistic protocols characterizing each pole. In fact, it would be possible to borrow any number of binary pairs to describe the specific nature of the rhetorical transference of the Romantic Sublime. I am thinking here of de Man's own insightful distinction between the temporality of allegory and that of irony; or the metaphoric-metonymic axes of language as formulated by Roman Jakobson; or the Saussurian algorithm of *signifié* and *signifiant*. In terms of the Leopardian lyric, we could formulate a dialectic of presence and absence—a poetics of *rimembranza*.

De Man's query about the nature of Romanticism quoted above concerns contradictions which surface when we consider Romantic theory and praxis as a static entity. Consider, for example, the apparently contradictory nature of these two axiomatic phrases of Wordsworth: "I have at all times endeavored to look steadily at my subject"; and "The mind is lord and master—outward sense / the obedient servant of her will" (*The Prelude* [1850], XII, 222-223). It is not the priority of object or of subject that concerns us, but rather the dynamic relationship between the two, which occurs only within language itself. It is, therefore, a *rhetorical* relationship.

Let us look for a moment at the structure of the Romantic lyric—the "greater Romantic lyric" as it is labeled by M. Abrams as the form which replaced what neoclassical critics had called "the greater ode" (the elevated Pindaric). Abrams sees the many instances of this form yielding a discernible paradigm: a "determinate speaker in a particularized . . . outdoor setting," who carries on a colloquy with himself, or the outer scene, or an absent or silent human auditor. "The speaker begins with a description of the landscape; . . . an aspect in the landscape evokes a varied but integral process of memory, thought, anticipation, and feeling. . . . In the course of this meditation the lyric speaker achieves an insight, faces up to a tragic loss, comes to a moral decision, or resolves an emotional problem. Often the poem rounds upon itself to end where it began, at the outer scene, but with an altered mood. . . ." This structure, "the repeated out-in-out process, in which mind confronts nature and their interplay constitutes the poem," is, according to Abrams, a remarkable phenomenon in literary history (Abrams, 1970:201-202). The poetic structure is actually a *transcodage* of this thematic interplay: in other words, the Romantic lyric resolves itself in the *exchange* of linguistic attitudes. Perhaps the uniqueness of the greater Romantic lyric lies in its exposure of the rhetorical transference that constitutes transcendence, for this exposure suggests that transcendence belongs to language alone and thus puts into question the ontology of *both* subject *and* object.

It is this desire to disrobe rhetorically that renders useless to our present discussion the notions of both mimetic and expressive theories of poetry. The sublime moment is located in the interstices between expression and mimesis. Or, to recall Thomas Weiskel's formulation, it is located in the breakdown of discourse itself, in the incommensurability between signifier and signified, which gives rise to a radical shift in language which transcends a merely mimetic or expressive mode of poetry (Weiskel, 1976). This breakdown is not a problem, but, rather, the solution to a problem. The Romantic lyric requires this indeterminacy of language and meaning to make possible a new meaning: the transcendental significance of the sublime.

Leopardi's **"L'Infinito"** adheres to the tripartite paradigm described by Abrams. What is more, Leopardi

himself conceived of this *idillio* as a concise demonstration of the poetic sublime. **"L'Infinito"** actually exemplifies most aspects of Leopardi's theories of the sublime set forth in various forms throughout the numerous pages of his notebooks, the *Zibaldone*. In **"L'Infinito"** the sense of the sublime (Leopardi's *indefinito* or *infinito*) is created by a metaleptic substitution in which all spatial and temporal deictics are shifted from one mode of figuration to another. (We could also speak of this as a breakdown or transference of the referent; or as a shift from a metonymic to a metaphorical axis; or as a metaleptic reversal of absence and presence.) But let us turn now to Leopardi's own statements about the nature of the sublime.

Leopardi seems to have had a rather consistent notion of the poetic process for creating a sense of the sublime, although his several descriptions of the process appear on the surface to indicate a reversal of thought. His first theoretical statements appear in 1818, in his anti-Romanticist essay *Il discorso di un italiano intorno alla poesia romantica,* written before the composition of his great lyrics.[2] Here Leopardi defends Classicism (the ancients) against Romanticism (the moderns) on the grounds that the ancients wrote superior "affective" verse. The ancients (the true poets) achieved poetic sublimity by means of an imitation of nature in which nature becomes transumed by its linguistic encoding into a more forceful representation than it possesses in naked perception. "The ancient poets," argues Leopardi, "imitated Nature, and they imitated it in such a way that it appeared to be transposed (*trasportata*) in their verses, not merely imitated." Leopardi then claims that such imitated objects of Nature are actually more affective than real ones. "In fact, it is manifest that the most ordinary things, and especially when they are common, affect our minds and imaginations with much more force when they are imitated than when they are real" (*Discorso*:67).

Although Leopardi appears to be speaking from within a mimetic theory of poetry, his theory, developed and made explicit in later comments, emphasizes poetic trans-figuration. And indeed, ten years later, in the *Zibaldone* entries of 1828, Leopardi rejects the notion that poetry is an imitative act.

> It is completely erroneous to judge and to define poetry as an imitative art, to place it along side of painting, etc. The poet imagines [*imagina*]: the Imagination sees the world as it is not, fashions for itself [*si fabbrica*] a world which does not exist, creates [*finge*], invents [*inventa*], but does not imitate . . . a creator, an inventor, but not an imitator; this is the essential character of the poet
>
> (*Zib.*, II:1182-83; August 1828).[3]

In the Leopardian lexicon, verbs such as *fingere, immaginare, fabbricare, inventare* all describe the rhetorical act of substituting the infinite for the finite, memory for the present, the sublime for the ordinary. Neither mimetic nor expressive theory locates the origin of this process in language's illusion-making power. But Leopardi understood this well. In fact, Leopardi triumphs over a paradoxical adherence to both a mimetic and an expressive theory of poetry in his **Discorso** by adopting a Vichian resolution: Leopardi posits a "poetic imagination" of primitive man in which mimesis is primarily a rhetoricization or *transpositio* of nature into language.

Like Vico's first men, Leopardi's ancients were inherently poetic because they were ignorant. They had free reign of the fantasy because they lacked reason, which, like the super-ego, could censor and subordinate their imaginative capacities. The ancients were blessed with *illusion*. For Leopardi, the powers of reason and the imagination are antithetical and inversely correlative: the more extensively reason sees, the less precisely it can see ("ella tanto meno vede quanto più vede," **Zib.,** II:183; July 1823); the more powerful reason, the more impotent the reasoner ("ma ella [Ragione] è dannosa, ella rende impotente colui che l'usa, è tanto più quanto maggiore uso ei ne fa," **Zib.,** II:182; July 1823). So too, reason and nature are opposed ("la ragione . . . è nemica formale della natura . . . dove la natura è grande, la ragione è piccola," **Discorso**:26).

The ancients, blissfully ignorant, thought themselves intended for happiness by nature and ascribed to nature a teleology. Their fall from this edenic state was due to man's desire to know the truth. Reason, according to Leopardi, reveals the meaninglessness of life and its merely random patterns, and the illusion of illusion. Not only does Leopardi recount this drama of Genesis in his **"Storia del genere umano,"** the first of the ironic prose pieces of the **Operette morali,**[4] but he also posits it as the representative anecdote of his own poetic *iter* ("In my poetic career, my soul has followed the same path as that of Mankind in general," **Zib.,** II:161; June 1820). It is a passage from the domain of the imagination to that of reason, from poet to philosopher. Or, we might add, it is a passage from a metaphoric to a metonymic linguistic axis. Leopardi's poetic career does evince, in fact, the Vichian anamorphosis of the tropes. The task of the poetic, for Leopardi, is to reverse by metalepsis that inevitable passage. The structure of metalepsis as a poetic strategy also provides the model for the relationship between Leopardi's early *piccoli idilli* and his later *grandi idilli* in that the latter idylls attempt to re-figure the more metaphoric experience of the first period.[5]

In his **Discorso** of 1818 Leopardi likens the ancient poets to childhood: "that which the ancient poets were, we have all been, and that which the world was for several centuries we have all been for several years—that is to say, children." As children, Leopardi continues, we, like the ancient poets, "were active participants in a world

of ignorance—of fears and pleasures and hopes"—and above all "in the infinite workings of the Imagination [*fantasia*]" (**Discorso**:20). The reappropriation of that earlier mode of *fantasia* (later designated by Leopardi as illusion) becomes the source of the sublime in poetry: a return to the state of consciousness in which the first men had to invent or figure [*fingere*] the meaning of the world, because everything was mysterious and sublime (**Discorso**:21). By this same rhetorical process [*fingere*] Leopardi invents the "infinito" in his famous eponymous lyric. This reappropriation is only possible by means of the memory [*rimembranza*] of a childhood illusion which, despatialized and detemporalized, metaleptically returns inviolate. The return is also an illusion—("the poet is the artificer of illusions," **Discorso**:57)—a rhetorical sleight-of-hand, but one which provides in the textual actuality of the poem the presence and plenitude that life denies.

II

Central to the Leopardian conception of the sublime is the notion of the indefinite (*l'indefinito,* **Zib.,** I:1202; October 1821)—the conviction that true poetry evokes the indefinite, and is syntactically and semantically grounded in the vague (*il vago,* with the Italian connotation of the beautiful). The content of indefinite apprehensions of reality derives from childhood illusion, brought back to consciousness through memory. Poetic language seeks to emulate primitive language: dereifying, we might say, it seeks to dispel a purely fictitious clarity which modern language imposes on our experience of the world in order to put us in touch not with "reality," but with a childlike apprehension of it.

Now, this notion of poetry as dealing in the indefinite is certainly consonant with most theories of the sublime, from Longinus through Joseph Addison, Edmund Burke, Hugh Blair, and so on, the writers who had preceded Leopardi in the discussion of the sublime. The **Zibaldone** attests to Leopardi's careful reading of Longinus, and in terms consonant with περί ὕψους Leopardi perceived that orators and poets seek different means to achieve their different ends. Poetic power is identified with the domain of the affective (*il patetico*), while that of the orator is the plausible. It is for this reason that the poet's image must be obscure or indefinite while that of the orator must be clear and precise. Leopardi, assimilating the sensation of indeterminacy to that of the sublime, postulates a condition of blockage or obstruction as prerequisite to the creation of the sense of the infinite. Like Burke, Leopardi recognized that when the eye is blocked, the imagination is liberated to envision that which Nature denies—the vast, the vague, the infinite.[6] This is so, Leopardi states, because "man's desire for the infinite" is innate and irrepressible, and when the imagination has free rein it will inevitably figure forth infinity (**Zib.,** I:187; July 1820). The sense of the infinite can only be attained, however, as a projection against the finite, in opposition/apposition to the *hic et nunc.* Such is the Leopardian valorization, albeit ironic, of the utility of the present. This dialectic of the bound and the unbound posits a moment *in limine,* a threshold state when perception, limited, becomes disfunctional and before imagination assumes control. Here the Leopardian metaleptic substitution occurs. This return to a past mode of figuration is one of several alternatives open at the liminal moment: Eugenio Montale's early lyrics, for example, exploit the epiphanic potentiality of the concrete objects of liminality. However, Leopardi's infinity is material in nature, without a trace of the Montalian noumenality, and objects of the *hic et nunc* can never be epiphanic.

From this nexus of the indefinite, the infinite, and the sublime, Leopardi elaborates a theory of the poeticity of language itself. He classifies the lexicon into two basic categories, *termini* (terms) and *parole* (words) (**Zib.,** I:135-137; April 1820). Scientific and philosophical languages deal in terms which present a univocal idea of a given object or concept: these *termini* fix meaning and delimit semantic flexibility. *Parole,* conversely, do not present a precise idea of an object, but are polysemic and call up clusters of images that, by virtue of their indefiniteness, suggest the infinite and the sublime.[7] When a given language has a preponderance of *termini* it becomes incapable of poetic expression. Such was the condition, Leopardi thought, of the French language of his time. It was, in his view, a language which *desublimated* experience.

Parole, poetical words as Leopardi describes them, are, I would suggest, semantically metaleptic. Such words not only refer literally to indeterminacy in a spatial or temporal sense; they necessarily depend upon a leap backward (and forward) for any poetic signification whatsoever. To adopt contemporary semiotic terminology, we might say that Leopardi perceived not only the distinction between the signifier and the signified as prime elements of the sign in which they are united, but that he saw *parole* as signifiers possessing an overabundance of signifieds. *Parole* are the mark of true poetry; semantically metaleptic, their indeterminacy makes them susceptible even to future semantic permutations, and thus they possess that "eternal" quality which is to be found in the language of all great poetry.

Leopardi believed that in ancient languages words were charged with endless signification; the ancient poets signified many things with one word, rather than using many words for the same thing. All ancient lexemes were therefore semantically infinite and indefinite. The proliferation of synonyms in modern languages suggested to Leopardi a decline in meaning. The lexicon passes, we might say, from an original condition of pure "metaphoricity" to one of "metonymicity": an endless accretion of terms linked, finally, by contiguity alone. What many of his contemporaries viewed, then, as the progress of civilization, Leopardi envisioned as merely the progressive restriction of consciousness, specifically the desiccation of the imagination. The growing precision of our language for describing the world is attended by the growing apprehension of the world's essential nullity. Synonymy is the death of difference. The expansion of reason (and thus *termini*) effects a semantic reduction, in the same way that the filling out of the map of the world resulting from the age of exploration necessarily destroyed the field where imagination at an earlier time could write: "Here be monsters." In a *canzone* written in 1820, **"Ad Angelo Mai,"** Leopardi reflects on this cartographic analogy in a verse on the expedition of Columbus:

> Ecco svaniro a un punto,
> E figurato è il mondo in breve carta;
> Ecco tutto è simile, e discoprendo,
> Solo il nulla s'accresce. A noi ti vieta
> Il vero appena è giunto,
> O caro immaginar; de te s'apparta
> Nostra mente in eterno; allo stupendo
> Poter tuo primo ne sottraggon gli anni;
> E il conforto perì de' nostri affanni.

(vv. 97-105)

[Now they (our dreams) have vanished in an instant, and the world can be outlined on a small sheet of paper; Now everything is the same, and by these discoveries only Nothingness has increased. O dear Imagination, at the advent of Truth you are lost to us; Truth separates forever our spirit from yours; the passage of time removes us from your once stupendous power; and thus has perished the only consolation for our woes.]

Leopardi's own brand of Romantic Irony takes the form of asking the reader to help him perform a rhetorical sleight-of-hand by which the *apprehension* of metaphysical absence would be turned into the *illusion* of presence.

Leopardi's theory of the sublime and poetic of the indefinite are grounded in his view of man's insatiable desire for pleasure. Man's desire for pleasure is limitless (and Leopardi equates pleasure with happiness and happiness with illusion—there is no credence in a morally informed condition of happiness). Frustration is thus inevitable, for there is no infinite object with which this desire could be united and endless pleasure thereby attained. Yet man's imagination permits him to conceive of things which do not exist in reality, and to imagine that infinity which an insatiable desire for pleasure presupposes. The imagination can do this by "figuring" a pleasure which is limitless in one of three ways: in number, in duration, in extension.

> Let us turn now to man's desire for the infinite. Independently from the desire for pleasure, there exists in man an imaginative faculty, which can conceive of

things that do not exist, and can imagine them in ways that do not obtain for real things. Considering man's innate drive towards pleasure, it is natural that one of the principal occupations of the Imagination should be the imagining of pleasure . . . and the Imagination can represent [*figurarsi*] pleasures which do not exist at all, and it can represent them as infinite: 1) in number, 2) in duration, 3) in extension

(***Zib.,*** I:183; July 1820).

Although this, too, is in perfect accord with numerous earlier treatises on the sublime, Leopardi is echoing here a sensationist psychology, and more specifically, that of Locke. For Locke, the idea of infinity is actually derived from sensation: the mind extrapolates from empirical experience the sensations of space, duration, and number, and then reconceptualizes these in terms of an *endless* repetition (Locke, 1975:II, 17). When combined with the notion of the human being as a creature of insatiable desire, this idea of the sensationist origin of the infinite results in an elevation of imagination over reason as the faculty which saves us from despair by the production of illusions. The object of desire and thereby the occasion of the feeling of pleasure is always spatially and temporally elsewhere than the ostensible *locus* of the poetic discourse; but the object of desire can be magically transposed, i.e., rhetorically transumed into the poetic text by means of the poet's manipulation of the human capacity to hope and to remember.

Pleasure is never in the present. Only the hope for future happiness or the remembrance of past happiness can approximate that condition of the infinite which is correlative to happiness. In fact, Leopardi ironically concludes, happiness itself is the most unhappy moment of life.

> The remembrance of pleasure can be compared to hope, and produces almost the same effects. Like hope, remembrance is more pleasing than pleasure itself . . . and one can conclude that the most miserable moment of life is that of pleasure or of enjoyment
>
> (***Zib.,*** I:702; May 1821).

The dynamics of this transference of desire is explicated in one of the *Operette morali,* the **"Dialogo di Torquato Tasso e del suo genio familiare."** Here Tasso's genius explains that pleasure is constituted by *desire* alone, and that during any one ostensible moment of pleasure, there exists a truer, latent pleasure: the expectation of a future greater pleasure. Pleasure derives from a continuous transference to the future moments of the same delight.

> Pleasure is a speculative subject, and not something real; a desire and not a fact; a sentiment of which man conceives with his thought, but does not experience; or, rather, a concept and not a sentiment. Do you not realize that during the very moment of your delight, even if it is infinitely desired, and obtained by indescribable

labor . . . you are expecting a greater and truer enjoyment, in which that pleasure really consists; and you are always continuously transferring yourself to future moments of the same delight? . . . For pleasure is always past or future, but never present

(***O. M.***:90).

Pleasure is always either past or future, but never present. Such is this Derridian *différence* of desire, forever displaced or deferred, accessible only by the re-evocation of another (putative) moment of pleasure which also eludes our grasp. We should remember that there is absolutely no hint of the transcendental in any of this; there is no teleology in nature, no ontological reality to infinity. Our desire for the infinite is not implanted by God to bring man's thought from nature to nature's Creator; the sublime is not proof of man's immortality. According to Leopardi, our desire for the infinite is actually a desire for "an infinity of material *pleasures*" (*una infinità materiale,* ***Zib.,*** I:194; July 1820). Man is condemned to live, think and desire only within the limits of a purely physical universe. This universe, according to Leopardi, is mere matter forever decomposing and recomposing. And in a Pascalian vein, albeit without the consolation of religion, Leopardi conceived of man's grandeur as precisely his ability to recognize his insignificance in the face of an immense and ateleological universe. Within this Leopardian *antitopia,* the apotheosis of *rimembranza* is the only viable alternative to despair.

By 1829, Leopardi explicitly equates the poetic and the sublime throughout the ***Zibaldone*** (***Zib.,*** II:1300; April 1829). Leopardi then posits remembrance as the axial concept for his poetics of the sublime. Images of the vast and the beautiful elicit the sensation of *sublimity* because they evoke our most remote memories, those of childhood, when the indefinite was ubiquitous and when we believed in the advent of happiness (***Zib.,*** II:1321; May 1829). The poetic consists only in memory.

> Remembrance is the essential and principal element in poetic sentiment if for no other reason than because the present, no matter what it may be, can never be poetic
>
> (***Zib.,*** II:1237; December 1828).

Our adult experiences of the infinite and of the sublime are inextricably tied to childhood memory. Our adult image-making, then, is a sort of *déjà-vu,* or better still, a metaleptic return of these earliest illusions. The image is re-presented.[8] Memory, mimesis, and poetic invention are thus bound together in a complex symbiotic relationship. Memory is an imitation (a transfiguration) of a past sensation, and subsequent remembrances are imitations of prior remembrances. Thus Leopardi tells us, "memory imitates itself" (***Zib.,*** I:1098; September 1821). Man necessarily imitates while he is inventing—

or, continues Leopardi, he imitates his *invenzioni* with other *invenzioni*. Man's imaginative capacity is limited in the sense that it can only *transfer* (in the etymological sense of μετάφορα) remembered images into a present. It re-tropes, by metalepsis, a prior figuration (the *rimembranza,* itself invention or illusion) into a present figuration. But according to Leopardi's mythology, the *figurative* (linguistic) potentiality of that Edenic anteriority is limitless in nature.

Leopardi's conception of memory is thus more complex than Wordsworth's "emotion recollected in tranquility." For, like Petrarch, Leopardi's true precursor, Leopardi understood that memory and desire are the source of all poetic figuration. However, Leopardi recognized in a way that Petrarch could not, that behind any memory was another figuration; and that *that* other figuration was itself a repetition or doubling; and thus, that the poetic image was the very spirit of the letter that Petrarch had sought.

III

Infinity, wrote Leopardi, "is an optical illusion" (**Zib.,** II:1126; September 1827). What *is* infinite, he continues, however, is thought; and thus, we might add, it is the linguistic protocols which encode thought that provide us with the sensation of the infinite. This Leopardi intuited: two years after writing **"L'Infinito"** he described it as a poem which demonstrates the *production* of the experience of the sublime by means of contrasts between the *finito* and the *indefinito* (**Zib.,** I:953; August 1821). The contrastive structure of the lyric, recognized and variously described by most critics of Leopardi,[9] involves not only an alternation between two fields, one visual and one imaginative, but more importantly, a substitution of one for the other. This is a metaleptic substitution, made possible within the perimeters of the 15-line lyric by means of a reversal of deictics.

Metalepsis may be defined heuristically here as a trope or figure of thought—a strategy—as distinguished from figure of speech. Metalepsis is the trope which takes *substitution* (the literal meaning of μετάληψις) of one word for another, one meaning for another, one mode of figuration for another, etc., as an end in itself. It does not presuppose any specific structure of relationships or hierarchy between words, or between sign and referent (metaphor, for example, presupposes the notion of similarity as a valid mode of relation; metonymy, that of contiguity). Metalepsis presupposes an *other* of some sort, thus engendering a dialectic of presence and absence.

Quintilian (1976:VIII, vi) describes metalepsis (Latin *transumptio*) as the trope which provides a transition from one trope to another. He writes:

> It is the nature of metalepsis to form a kind of intermediate step between the term transferred and the thing to

which it is transferred, having no meaning in itself, but merely providing the transition.

Metalepsis has no *semantic* meaning in the way metaphor, for example, does; metalepsis is a strategy of transition in discourse and effects its own operations, a self-consuming trope. Metalepsis means, therefore, that some mode of figuration, of perceiving or knowing the world, is insufficient and that another mode is needed for resolution (psychological, epistemological, or rhetorical). It signals a problematic relation to the present and to presence, a need for avoidance, evasion, deferral, *coupure*. It signals rupture and recovery of discourse by means of displacement of word, thought, or affect. Metalepsis, the logician Chaim Perelman (1969:181) tells us, is a trope by which we can substitute one mode of argumentation for another, especially in those discourses whose aim it is to facilitate "the transposition of values into facts" or the attribution of "a certain behavior to some remembered phenomenon."

Above all, however, metalepsis permits us to wrestle with the past, to form a bridge or continuity with it, to transform priority into acceptable presentness, absence into figurative presence. If we wish to suggest a rhetoric of the psyche, as Freud often did, we would call metaleptic the way in which the Unconscious slips into Consciousness: the way in which some childhood memory, repressed and returned, is transformed into the experience of the uncanny. It is because metalepsis is the bridge between one mode of figuration and another that Harold Bloom (1975:74) fondly calls it "the trope of a trope"; it is an allusive scheme "that refers the reader back to any previous figurative scheme."

Bloom's "map of misreading" presents a paradigm of the Romantic lyric which is at once rhetorical, psychological, and cognitive, with a six-phase process, each phase of which features a different trope of figuration. The paradigmatic Romantic lyric, he argues, begins in irony (the trope of the interplay of absence and presence in consciousness) and ends in metalepsis (the trope of substitution of the early for the late and the late for the early) (Bloom, 1975:84; 1976:ch. 14). Since all great Romantic lyrics deal with time and death, metalepsis is necessary for that bridging of the gap between origin and end, the poet and his predecessors. Only by metalepsis can we reverse temporality and make the present vanish. For, Bloom (1975:103) concludes,

> metalepsis leaps over the heads of other tropes and becomes a representation set against time, sacrificing the present for an *idealized past* or a *hoped for future.*

Rimembranza and *speranza* are the cathodic poles of the Leopardian poetic also, to which the present must succumb if the sublime is to exist at all.

Of course, metalepsis understood *strictu sensu* is also a specific figure, localizable on the surface structure of the text. And in Bloom's system it is primarily that: one trope only of a six-phase progression. But in terms of the Leopardian corpus, metalepsis would describe the underlying poetic strategy by means of which the affective (always *other*) can be activated within the presence of the text; the substitution of an absent plenitude for a present void.

The present, according to Leopardi, can never be imbued with sublimity. Yet the Leopardian *idillio* typically opens with the denomination of specific natural objects pertaining to the *hic et nunc*—the idyllic landscape—thus suggesting a fullness and a plenitude. However, we immediately recognize that these objects are valued not in and for themselves, but only inasmuch as they function as signs pointing beyond themselves. They refer to a priority—the hypostatized original moment of plenitude in the past. Signs in Leopardi (objects, words, sensations, memory) all refer to something absent; the present reveals only ubiquitous transience. As in Leopardi's dual personal and social mythology, these traces indicate a loss of Edenic presence. But there is never an *unmediated* experience of that presence; there are only desires for and memories of such a condition.[10]

The very first line of **"L'Infinito"** signals the impossibility of an unmediated present. The allusion to the topographical identity of the solitary hill (Mt. Tabor) thrusts the speaker back into childhood reveries. The poem unfolds with a metaleptic gesture back to an anteriority and an origin: a prior mode of figuration and affect. The opening line immediately initiates this complex interplay of temporalities: the first word (*sempre*) conveys an indeterminate continuity and atemporality which is juxtaposed to the central word in the line, the aorist *fu* indicating a completed, time-bound distant action. These two modes of temporality are conjoined in the present by means of the pronomial indicator *mi* and the demonstrative adjective *questo*. The indefinite (*sempre*) and the past (*fu*), both axial to the Leopardian sublime, are transfigured in a spatial and temporal presence (*questo*) which otherwise would have been an affective absence. This metaleptic leap depends upon Leopardi's careful control of deixis.

Deixis, the linguistic category of spatial-temporal indicators (Jakobson's "shifters"), is described by Emile Benveniste (1971:218-19) as forming a specific linguistic class, because these markers do not refer to reality or to objective positions in space or time. They refer "to the utterance, unique each time, that contains them." Benveniste illustrates this with a discussion of the pronomial pair *I-you,* which also lacks objective referents; this pair refers only to a reality of discourse. The pronoun *I* can only mean, therefore, "the individual who utters the present instance of discourse containing the linguistic instance *I*." This is true, Benveniste continues, for deixis in general: deictics "delimit only the spatial and temporal instance coextensive and contemporary with the present instance of discourse containing *I*." Thus, according to Benveniste, deixis constitutes

> an ensemble of *empty* signs that are non-referential with respect to reality. These signs are always available and become *full* as soon as a speaker introduces them into each instance of discourse. Since they lack material reference they cannot be misused. . . . Their role is to provide the instrument of a *conversion* of language into discourse.

Leopardi intuitively grasped this conversional power of deixis. This is all the more remarkable given his theory of the sublime as residing in the indefinite. We *ought* to expect his poetry to be devoid of deictics, and yet the *idilli* contain an overabundance of these spatial-temporal markers. Their quantitative weight signals their qualitative importance as a major stylistic device. Leopardi uses a deictic reversal to convert the affectively empty present into the fullness of the remembered (i.e., refigured) past. Not only are deictics empty signs, but so are all the putatively real objects described in a Leopardian idyll, as I have already suggested—they all function as signifiers without signifieds. The Leopardian natural object has no intrinsic meaning: the hill (*colle*) is significant only insofar as it is reappropriated by memory; the hedge (*siepe*), only insofar as it is a boundary to be transcended by the imagination. But all these signs become full when the speaker's animus participates in the localizing and temporalizing act of converting language into discourse. The poem itself, then, is the *locus* of the conversion of the finite into the infinite. Rather than a dichotomy between subject and object, what we see is a text which serves as the arena for the speaking subject to activate the latent potentialities in a series of empty signs.

Even on its most basic semantic level, **"L'Infinito"** is a calmly delineated prescription for the experience of the sublime. It is a precisely articulated progression of contrasts and juxtapositions, from the visible and bound to the limitless and infinite. The speaker's eye moves from hill to hedge to an inward imagining of infinity beyond, the poetic faculty liberated at last by the blockage (how importantly does the verb *esclude* figure here). The speaker conceives of an infinite space in plural terms, "as an endless succession of spaces beyond spaces," to quote Renato Poggioli (1962:277). Then, the speaker shifts from the intuition of limitless space to that of limitless time, and this eternity is also envisioned in plural terms as the superhuman silences of the universe. This epiphanic vision almost fills the speaker with terror. He compares the infinite silence with the ephemeral rustling of the wind. From this comparison he shifts by metalepsis to a *remembrance* of eternity—a shift to a prior mode of figuration—and from eternity back to the present season. This is the reverse of that progression we noted earlier, from the sound of the wind (1. 9) to the infinite silence (1. 10): finite → infinite. Now we move from the eternal (1. 10) to the present season (1. 13): infinite → finite. The progression reverses itself around the remembrance (1. 11, "*mi sovvien*"), which is a metaleptic reappropriation of an affective presence. The actual present is experienced as mere trace (the voice of the wind, the sound of the present season). This vertiginous alternation of presence and absence permits a conflation of time and space into the image of a sublime sea of immensity in which the poet sweetly drowns. And yet, there is no mystical delirium, no rape of the senses here. All the affective, visual, auditory, and imaginative operations within **"L'Infinito"** are fully consonant with Leopardi's theories cited above. The poem illustrates with great precision how the infinite can be derived from physical sensation (figuring it "limitless in number, duration, and extension"). The poem progresses through a geometrical pattern of concentric circles which, by successively larger alternations of memory and imagination, exponentially leaps beyond the very confines of time and space. The progression is programmatic, and the lyric has often been called an *itinerarium mentis in infinitum.*

The structure of the poem progresses by a metaleptic reversal of the spatial deictics and by a reversal of time-frames. The first three lines of the lyric form one unit containing two deictics (1. 1, "*quest*'ermo colle"; 1. 1, "*questa* siepe"). They are markers of a temporal, spatial present, but one which is affectively empty, as if in suspension. So too, the suspension of the proposition until the verb *esclude* at the end of 1. 3 corroborates the spatial attenuation semantically indicated as "da tanta parte / Dell'ultimo orizzonte" (11. 2-3). The second section of the poem, lines 4-13, is introduced by the adversative conjunction *Ma.* This marks more than a grammatical break (although it is noteworthy that 1. 3 is the only end-stopped line in the poem). The conjunction *Ma* is, on the syntactical level, a sign of opposition and blockage, just as the "hedge" is on the imaginative level. It is a rhetorical and affective swerve into an interiority. The intransitive gerunds "sedendo e mirando" (1. 4) signal this suspended temporality; a processual state of liminality, a *durée* beyond chronological markers.

The syntax and cadence of the second section are markedly lengthened, replicating the durational quality of the gerunds. The three adjective-substantive pairs ("interminati/Spazi," 11. 4-5; "sovrumani/Silenzi," 11. 5-6; "profondissima quiete," 1. 6) precede their verbal phrase ("Io nel pensier mi fingo," 1. 7), thus suspending the closure of the line. The polysyllabism of the three adjectives contributes to this lengthening. In each of the three cases, the adjective precedes its substantive so that affect rather than essence is stressed. The enjambements of the first two of these pairs transcend the metric boundaries of these semantically indefinite and pho-

netically protracted words. This sense of suspension and cosmic awe is fostered by dieresis ("qui-e-te," 1. 6; "spa-u-ra," 1. 8).

The radical break at the conjunction *Ma* is strengthened by a deictic. In line 6 the demonstrative *quella* is syntactically and semantically ambiguous, able to refer to either "da tanta parte" (1. 2) or "questa siepe" (1. 2). But the overall linguistic structure of the poem indicates that *quella* refers to the hedge, which was earlier marked by *questa*. This is a metaleptic substitution, in which a once present object is spatially and temporally distanced. The abstract interior figuration—the poet's *fingere* (1. 7)—has supplanted the specific natural scene first described: the infinite obliterates the finite.

There is another inversion, between lines 9 and 11, one which at first seems like a return to the spatial-temporal *loci* of the opening description. The wind rustling through *these* plants ("*queste* piante," 1. 9) is compared to *that* infinite silence ("*quello* / Infinito silenzio," 11. 9-10). Again, apparently, the infinite is abstract and distant, the landscape concrete and near. But in fact, as the powerful lexeme "voce" (1. 10) suggests, the present is affectively absent: as we have seen, the elements of the landscape are reduced to signs such as memory (the hill), boundary (the hedge), or trace (the voice of the wind). Leopardi masterfully manipulates an auditory sensation to indicate the ephemerality of the present.[11] The present can only be appropriated as the experience of passage and dissolution. This inversion recurs—inversely—in the appellation of the present season as sound ("il suon di lei," 1. 13). The long enjambement of "quello / Infinito silenzio" (11. 9-10) gives phonetic weight to the infinite, while "questa voce" (1. 10) is syntactically and rhythmically neutral. The syntax of this entire section is attenuated by means of polysyndeton. There are no subordinate clauses and the lyric floats in an oneiric continuum.

The aulic gerund of line 11, "vo comparando," describes the contrastive structure of the poem, itself a series of similes. The juxtaposition of infinite and finite, of silence and sound, *recalls* to Leopardi ("mi sovvien," 1. 11) the eternal, the dead seasons, the present season and its sound. The movement seems to progress from abstract to concrete, but the concrete is revealed to be an illusion, graspable only through memory, and the present has form only as *vestigium*.

The third and last section of the poem, lines 13-15, signals the definitive triumph of the imagined over the real, the final displacement of the present. In this section, the two deictics signifying "this"—"*questa* / Immensità" (11. 13-14) "*questo* mare" (1. 15)—indicate an immediate present, but their referents have undergone a metaleptic substitution: these deictics now designate the imagined infinite realm. The "incommensurable, inaudible, and invisible," to borrow again from Renato Poggioli's discussion of **"L'Infinito"** (1960:277), now becomes the only presence in the poem. The symmetrical alignment of "tra queste piante" (1. 9) and "tra questa / Immensità" (11. 13-14) reinforces the efficacy of this final deictic reversal. These parallelisms suggest that the poem moves upon a chiastic pattern and that all the inversions we have noted converge upon a central axis.

The axis is centrally located with regard to the form of the lyric (lines 7 and 8 of the 15-line poem), as well as to the content, that is, it corroborates that the metaleptic substitution which engenders the sublime is the product of the linguistic capacities of the speaker ("il nel pensier mi fingo," 1. 7). The power of this imaging of the sublime instills a rupture, an almost-loss of self, the linguistic breakdown. It is the affective center of *L'Infinito,* "over per poco / Il cor non si spaura" (11. 7-8). The powerful lexeme "spaura" is followed by the poem's first true caesura. At the outermost perimeters of the lyric we find the only two other affective syntagmas, which undergo a metaleptic exchange at this center, radiating out in a chiastic pattern. In the first line: "caro-mi-fu-questo-colle"; in the last line: "mi-è-dolce-questo-mare." Not only does the temporality radically alter (aorist to present of *essere: fu → è*), but the two adjectives, *caro* and *dolce* (so typical of the intimate lexicon of the Leopardian *idillio*) are almost identical semantically and syntactically, but joined to two diametrically opposed realms: the specific hill and the abstract sea of sublimity. Presence and absence are now suddenly metaleptically reversed.

There is a masterful phonetic paranomastic play in this pattern. Or perhaps we should employ Kenneth Burke's terminology for this type of formal recurrence. Burke (1957:298) speaks of an "acrostic" structure of alliteration, where a sequence of consonants or vowels reappears in a scrambled order. What we actually find in **"L'Infinito"** is a phonetic chiasmus between the first and last lines:

This phonetic chiasmus is intensified by the euphonic recurrence of *ar* in the last line: "naufrag*ar* [. . .] m*ar*e"; as well as its inversion in the virtual center of the poem's central line: "spau*ra*." It recurs again (in an extended form conflating *ar + ra*) in the key verb denoting the poem's structure: "comp*ara*ndo" (1. 11). This complex euphonic exchange permits, simultaneously, two other patterns to emerge. We have on the one hand, a structural homology:

caro: colle:: dolce: mare

and, on the other hand, a virtual affective identification of hill and sea, of finite and infinite:

colle=mare.

In the poem's central section another phonetic chiasmus instantiates the Leopardian sublime: the process of sensation becoming memory while metaleptically reversing itself. Between the acrostic alliteration of "*v*ento" (1. 8) and "*e*terno" (1. 11)—both substantives symmetrically placed at the end of their respective lines—we follow the progression of "*vo*ce" to "*vo* comparando" to "mi s*ov*vien": a chiastic reversal of *vo ↔ ov,* in which sensation through memory is refigured as infinite. These phonetic recurrences not only emphasize a relationship obtaining between the words which contain them but also, and more importantly, confirm a sense of closure made possible by the reader's compliance in the linguistic exchange.[12]

This same process is revealed when we trace the progression of the four first-person pronominal indicators (*mi*) in the poem:

Again, by means of a chiastic movement, the past is refigured through memory and returns to inhabit the presence of the poem. This trajectory has also been noted by the poet Giuseppe Ungaretti. Ungaretti comments that in the first section of **"L'Infinito,"** a remembrance returns to make a visual sensation alive (to make the hill "dear"), whereas in the second section, by means of a "process which reverses that of the first part," a live auditory sensation, the sound of the wind, leads back to memory.[13] This ebb-like motion from memory to sensation and back again is fully consonant with Leopardi's empiricist notion that our concept of infinity is derived from the duration of material phenomena.

This substitutionary pattern of memory and sensation is reflected in the meter of **"L'Infinito,"** which is *endecasillabo sciolto*—a metric system of lines of eleven syllables without a fixed rhyme scheme, but usually with a regular stress pattern. But Leopardi has so manipulated the actual rhythm of his poem that it approximates free verse. The polysyndeton, enjambements, dieresis, synaloepha (the elision of adjacent vowels), and assonance work together to create a continuous melic flow. So too, the absence of hypotactical constructions and the long series of coordinated copulas (as for example, 11. 1 and 2, "quest'ermo colle / E questa siepe"; 1. 4, "sedendo e mirando") open up the poem's metric form. Thus the *actual* stress-patterns of the poem reinforce the parallelisms and reversals of the *questo/quello* deictics. In fact, in a detailed analysis of the rhythmic structure of **"L'Infinito,"** Giuseppe Sansone (1970:337) has revealed a highly balanced pattern of accentuation—a "symmetrical bilaterality"—which actually constitutes a chiastic accentual exchange.

The chiastic affective transformation which occurs in the poem's center is intensified by the repetition and reversal of the substantive "pensiero" in two key phrases. In line 7 we have "Io nel pensier mi fingo"; and in line 14, "s'annega il pensier mio." In the first instance the poet carefully controls the figurative capacity of his thought, whereas in the second, the poetic figuration controls the poet. This, of course, is Leopardi's intention. The structural recurrence is now a chiastic reversal:

> thought: poet:: poet: thought.

"L'Infinito" closes, then, with the apotheosis of the poetic figuration.

The tripartite structure of **"L'Infinito"** has been noted by many of Leopardi's best critics.[14] What is more, several contemporary critics of Romanticism discern a tripartite structure as the paradigm for lyrics of Romantic transcendence. In his study of the poetry of Wallace Stevens, Harold Bloom (1976:404) designates these three moments as poetic "crossings," and describes the three stages as follows: 1) "a dialectical movement of the senses, usually between sight and hearing"; 2) "a movement of oscillation between mimetic and expressive theories of poetic representation"; 3) "a movement toward an even greater degree of internalization of the self, no matter how inward the starting point was." These crossings are, for Bloom, the transition from trope to trope; they are achieved by what I would call metaleptic leaps.

These three phases are also delineated in Thomas Weiskel's *The Romantic Sublime.* Weiskel calls the first phase the mind "in a determinate relation to the object and this relation is habitual, more or less unconscious." In the second phase, "the habitual relation of mind and object suddenly breaks down." This second phase is characterized, according to Weiskel, by a sense of astonishment, and by a disproportion between inner and outer. "Either mind or object is suddenly in excess." And, Weiskel concludes, in the third phase of the sublime, "the mind recovers the balance of outer and inner by constituting a fresh relation between itself and the object such that the very indeterminacy which erupted in phase two is taken as symbolizing the mind's relation to a transcendent order."[15] So too, Marjorie Hope Nicolson (1959:321) in her study on the aesthetics of

the infinite discerns "a threefold process" in the experience of the sublime. And since **"L'Infinito"** has been referred to as an *itinerarium mentis in infinitum,* we should recall that St. Bonaventura's *itinerarium mentis in Deum* is also a conversional progression in a tripartite structure.

We could easily explain the affect of **"L'Infinito"** by adopting Leopardi's own terminology. The poem is brief—what he called a *canto* or short lyrical flow. The infinite is called forth from a visually blocked landscape, almost, we might say, as a counter-image produced by the retina (the "optical illusion" referred to by Leopardi himself). The lexicon consists primarily of *parole*—words which are themselves antique, indeterminate, poetically suggestive (*sempre, ermo, ultimo, interminati, sovrumani, profondissima,* etc.). Leopardi also favored as inherently poetic the juxtaposition of these *parole* to more common and concrete substantives (*colle, siepe*). Leopardi noted that the sky's horizon and the sea are the two most important archetypal *topoi* for the evocation of the sublime (**Zib.,** I:1165; October 1821). We witness the process by which *rimembranza* reappropriates the past (childhood illusion) and refigures it as the sublime. **"L'Infinito,"** in short, fully exemplifies Leopardi's theories of the indefinite, childhood, remembrance, and the sublime.

What is remarkable in all this, however, is that Leopardi's perceptions are so consonant with contemporary stylistics, as well as with traditional treatises on the sublime. In terms of lexis, for example, we should note the preponderance of hyperbolic terms in **"L'Infinito"**: terms of excess and extreme, superlatives. Hyperbole, according to Longinus (1935:139, 101-103), is, along with anaphora and hyperbaton, one of the crucial figures for the sublime. And according to Harold Bloom (1975:73), it is the most important trope for the Romantic Sublime. It is the trope of excess and finds its imagery in height and depth (Leopardi's sky and sea). In Bloom's view, hyperbole is aligned with the psychic defense of repression, and, he notes, "the glory of repression, poetically speaking, is that *memory* and *desire* have no place to go in language except up onto the heights of sublimity" (1975:100; my italics). Leopardi's great insight was that this sublimity was the gift of language itself.

* * *

Whereas the specific temporal indices of **"L'Infinito"** undergo a metaleptic substitution, we could speak of the overall temporality of the Leopardian *idillio* as a form of diachrony. This mode is best described by Paul de Man as the temporality of allegory. The temporal structure of allegory, according to de Man (1969:203, 206-207), involves successive stages of consciousness, "one belonging to the past and mystified, the other to the *now* of the poem, the stage that has recovered from the mystification of a past now presented as being in error." The poem presents this demystification as a temporal sequence: the difference does not occur within the subject (which is a unified self in the poem) but is instead "spread out over a temporality." Irony, according to de Man, has an opposite structure to that of allegory. In irony, the difference "resides in the subject, whereas time is reduced to one single moment." Irony is the mode of the present: "It knows neither memory nor prefigurative duration, whereas allegory exists entirely within an ideal time that is never here and now but always a *past* or an *endless future*. Irony is a synchronic structure, while allegory appears as a successive mode capable of engendering duration as the illusion of a continuity that it knows to be illusionary." Allegory, comments de Man, always implies "an unreachable anteriority." That anteriority is, for Leopardi, a mystified conception of childhood and its mode of prelapsarian consciousness.

We could describe the early Leopardian *idillio* as resulting from compensating and attempting to compensate for this allegorical mode of temporality. It seeks, in other words, to reverse by metalepsis this successive demystification and to return to a previous unified moment of non-error, of presence. The early *idilli* attempt to negate their inherent diachrony by reappropriating the poetic images of purely fictive prior time-frame. But the anteriority is unreachable. There are only displacements through memory to images of that image.

The later Leopardian *idillio* (the *grandi idilli*) suggests that the moment of the first *idilli* might be poetically constituted as that hypostatized anteriority. For, if all we have is an infinite series of displacements, one of those displaced images might serve as the illusion of anteriority. Here the speaking subject does not try to replace the present with the notion of a prelapsarian plenitude, but rather fills the poem with his allegorizing of the simultaneous insight into the disparity between life's emptiness and his own earlier mystified vision of fullness. Here memory serves not to re-figure the past, but to allegorize it as error or illusion (*inganni, errori, illusioni*).

The last Leopardian poems, the great *odi* and *canzoni* of the 1830's (from the *ciclo di Aspasia* to **"La Ginestra"** in 1836) exhibit a structure of temporality more akin to that of irony. Irony, according to de Man (1969:203), "divides the flow of temporal experience into a past that is pure mystification and a future that remains harassed forever by a relapse within the inauthentic." Here the difference between error and truth is not allegorized as successive, but is coextensive with the present of the speaking subject. The speaker understands the illusionary nature of all origin and closure. What is first conceived of as merely *deferred* is now

recognized as forever *other*. Life's truth, this condition of boredom, pain, and, finally, death (*noia, dolore, morte*), is unmitigated by hope or remembrance, or even by the bittersweet pleasure of allegorizing. Leopardi's last lyrics signal the ironic acceptance of presence as image or trace and the contingent nature of all life. The last poems function, then, as the de-mystification of the *idilli*. The synchrony of the ironic temporality abrogates any possibility of illusion, including the rhetorical illusion on which the experience of the Romantic Sublime is based.

Notes

1. See, among others, such classic early studies as Croce's essay on Leopardi (1946) and De Sanctis (1925). An analysis of the *idillio* alone is presented by Figurelli (1941). Among critics who discuss the "binary" nature of the Leopardian corpus (aside from the Crocean "poesia e non-poesia" distinction), see Binni (1971) and Bosco (1965). On Leopardi's philology and his cultural milieu, see Timpanaro (1955; 1969). I found the most provocative study of Leopardi's *Canti* to be that of Bigongiari (1976).

2. Leopardi (1970). All subsequent quotations are from this 1970 Capelli edition, referred to hereafter as *Discorso*.

3. Leopardi (1967). All subsequent quotations are from this 1967 Mondadori edition, referred to hereafter as *Zib*.

4. Leopardi (1951:7-22). All subsequent quotations are from this 1951 Rizzoli edition, referred to hereafter as *O. M.*

5. It is interesting that Leopardi ascribes this passage in his own life to a neurological crisis, when in 1819 his sight failed him (*Zib.*, I:162; July 1820). Deprived of sight, he was forced to abandon all hope. This transition from hope to memory, then, so axial to Leopardi's poetics, is connected to the operation of the *visual* faculty. Thus, Bigongiari's apt denomination of the *ottica leopardiana* to describe the permutations of the *idillio* (1976:267-377).

6. Burke (1909, II, iv). For a discussion of the Leopardian sublime in relationship to other theories of the sublime, see Perella (1970). Blockage in terms of the sublime should be understood, of course, as visual, psychological, and rhetorical at the same time.

7. This adherence to the concept of the *indefinito* recalls the theories of Edgar Allan Poe, although in practice Poe and Leopardi are strikingly dissimilar. It also seems to anticipate Mallarmé's famous dictum: "Nommer un objet, c'est supprimer le trois-

quarts de la jouissance du poème qui est faite de deviner peu à peu: le suggérer voilà la rêve." Leopardi also prescribes that images and relationships be merely "suggested" (*Zib.*, I:1275; November 1821). But if we may speak of both poets employing a dialectic of presence and absence, it should be stressed that Leopardi never aspired to a Mallarmean linguistic transparency but, rather, to the opacity of language as a surrogate for the density of presence which life denies. See, for example, Leopardi's notion of the multiplicatory power of metaphor (*Zib.*, I:1482-83; June 1822).

8. It is only in this sense of doubling that Leopardi speaks about seeing "correspondences," or a second order of things. In a famous passage in the *Zibaldone* Leopardi speaks of seeing the world and objects first with the eyes and then seeing reduplicated by the imagination the same phenomena ("il mondo e gli oggetti sono in certo modo doppi," *Zib.*, II:1200-31; November 1828). This notion does seem to anticipate certain tenets of Symbolist theories of poetry. But Leopardi does not suggest—as do Baudelaire, Poe, Rimbaud, etc.—that these are correspondences between a physical and a spiritual order. Rather, for Leopardi, things exist poetically only insofar as they can be *re-figured*. Leopardi's notion is more austere and cynical than Wordsworth's concept of the "two consciousnesses" (a landscape is seen, then its remembered image is superimposed upon the landscape re-visited). This double awareness of things as they are and as they were carries, in the later Leopardi, the bitter apprehension that things "as they were" can only have been an illusion.

9. Among other critics who discuss "L'Infinito" as contrastive, see especially Bigongiari (1976:253-265); Dolfi (1973); Herczeg (1962:321-365); Sansone (1970); Ungaretti (1943).

10. At first glance, the speaker in a Leopardian *idillio* appears to exhibit what de Man has called "the nostalgia for the object" (1970:69-70): the desire, in Romantic poetry, for language to possess the ontological status of the natural object. Language, continues de Man, is capable of endless origination, but can never have an ontological foundation. And yet, it is "the absolute identity with itself that exists in the natural object" which for Leopardi constitutes the object's *delimiting nature*. Ironically, the speaker in the Leopardian *idillio* exhibits instead a nostalgia for language, in that he would wish upon the present object the infinite open-endedness of consciousness. Leopardi's last poems, however, are marked by the absence of all nostalgia for ontological priority of either object or word.

11. See also the contrapuntal (metaleptic) use of the song of the artisan and the clamor of the Roman Empire in "La Sera del di dì festa."

12. Bigongiari (1976:87) describes another pattern of phonetic chiasmus in "L'Infinito": the repetition and reversal of the *io* sound; the hammering insistence on the first-person singular speaking subject which underlines the purely mental or, if you will, linguistic foundation of the sublime. This neatly fits Bigongiari's major contention (1976:28) that the entire *Canti* form a chiasmus around the variations of the "desiderio dell'io": *canzoni-odi: primi idilli = grandi idilli: odi-canzoni.*

13. Ungaretti (1950:19-22). Ungaretti goes on to note that eternity is only "a memory, and thus the past", and that the present, accessible only through memory, "is already dead." Thus, the sweet sea of sublimity is the most grotesque of ironies—it is actually "the sea of the finite, of nothingness." "L'Infinito" is, according to Ungaretti, "an ironic idyll"—it is actually a representation of the finite. Ungaretti, a poet committed to a Christian notion of the resacralizing power of language, viewed the Leopardian solution of the rhetorical illusion of infinity as an anathema, and yet, it was the spectre which haunted Ungaretti's own poetry.

14. Among the critics who delineate a tripartite structure in "L'Infinito" see especially De Sanctis (1925:126); Ungaretti (1943:227); Bigongiari (1976:87-88); Dolfi (1973:75). Both Bigongiari and Dolfi see this typical Leopardian tripartite movement as involving a chiastic reversal in the center phase (the chiasmus may be conceptual, rhetorical, psychological, or phonetic).

15. Weiskel (1976:23-24). Weiskel's study posits a distinction between a "metaphorical" or negative sublime, and a "metonymical" or positive sublime. The "metonymical" sublime—that of Wordsworth, and of Leopardi too I suggest—results from an excess of signifieds within the mind of the poet. This causes a breakdown of discourse. The recovery of discourse is effected by a displacement of this excess of signifieds onto a dimension of contiguity (spatial or temporal). This version of the sublime exhibits, according to Weiskel, Jakobson's famous "contiguity disorder." We should remember at this point that Leopardi's notion of *parole* might also be characterized in terms of an excess of signifieds.

References

Abrams, M. H., 1970. "Structure and Style in the Greater Romantic Lyric," in: Harold Bloom, ed. *Romanticism and Consciousness* (New York: Norton).

Benveniste, Émile, 1971. *Problems in General Linguistics,* trans. Mary Elizabeth Meek (Coral Gables: Univ. Miami Press).

Bigongiari, Piero, 1976. *Leopardi* (Firenze: La Nuova Italia).

Binni, Walter, 1971. *La nuova poetica leopardiana* (Firenze: Sansoni).

Bloom, Harold, 1975. *A Map of Misreading* (New York: Oxford UP).

———, 1976. *Wallace Stevens, The Poems of our Climate* (Ithaca: Cornell UP).

Bosco, Umberto, 1965. *Titanismo e pietà in Giacomo Leopardi* (Roma: E. De Sanctis).

Burke, Edmund, 1909. *On the Sublime and the Beautiful,* ed. Charles W. Eliot (New York: Collier).

Burke, Kenneth, 1957. *The Philosophy of Literary Form* (New York: Random House).

Croce, Benedetto, 1946. *Poesia e non-poesia* (Bari: Laterza).

de Man, Paul, 1969. "The Rhetoric of Temporality," in: Charles S. Singleton, ed., *Interpretation: Theory and Practice* (Baltimore: Johns Hopkins UP).

———, 1970. "Intentional Structure of the Romantic Image," in: Harold Bloom, ed. *Romanticism and Consciousness* (New York: Norton).

De Sanctis, Francesco, 1925. *Studio su Giacomo Leopardi,* ed. Raeffaele Bonari (Napoli: Alberto Morano).

Dolfi, Anna, 1973. *Leopardi tra negazione e utopia* (Padova: Liviana).

Figurelli, Francesco, 1941. *Giacomo Leopardi, poeta dell'idillio* (Bari: Laterza).

Herczeg, Giulio, 1962. "Premesse teoriche per un'interpretazione stilistica della frase leopardiana," in: *Leopardi e il Settecento,* Atti del I convegno internazionale di studi leopardiani (Firenze: Olschki).

Leopardi, Giacomo, 1951. *Le Operette morali,* ed. Mario Oliveri (Milano: Rizzoli).

———, 1967. *Zibaldone di pensieri,* V. I and II, ed. Francesco Flora, 2nd ed. (Milano: Mondadori).

———, 1970. *Discorso di un italiano intorno alla poesia romantica,* ed. Ettore Mazzali (Bologna: Capelli).

Locke, John, 1975. *An Essay Concerning Human Understanding,* ed. Peter H. Nidditch Oxford: Oxford UP).

Longinus, 1935. *On the Sublime,* ed. and trans. W. Rhys Roberts (London: Cambridge UP).

Nicolson, Marjorie Hope, 1959. *Mountain Gloom and Mountain Glory: The Development of the Aesthetics of the Infinite* (Ithaca: Cornell UP).

Perella, Nicolas James, 1970. *Night and the Sublime in Giacomo Leopardi* (Berkeley: California UP).

Perelman, Chaim and Obrechts-Tyteca, L., 1969. *The New Rhetoric* (Notre Dame UP).

Poggioli, Renato, 1962. On "L'Infinito" in: Stanley Burnshaw, ed. *The Poem Itself* (Cleveland/New York: Merridon/World Publishing).

Quintillian, 1976. *The Institutio Oratoria,* trans. H.E. Butler (Cambridge: Harvard UP).

Sansone, Giuseppe, 1970. "La struttura ritmica dell' *Infinito,*" *Forum Italicum* 4, 331-337.

Timpanaro, Sebastiano, 1955. *La filologia di Giacomo Leopardi* (Firenze: Le Monnier).

———, 1969. *Classicismo e Illuminismo nell'Ottocento italiano* (Pisa: Nistri-Lischi).

Ungaretti, Giuseppe, 1943. "Immagini del Leopardi e nostre," *Nuova Antologia* 78 (16 febbraio), 221-232.

———, 1950. "Secondo discorso su Leopardi," *Paragone* 10, letteratura, 3-35.

Weiskel, Thomas, 1976. *The Romantic Sublime: Studies in the Structure and Psychology of Transcendence* (Baltimore: Johns Hopkins UP).

Daniela Bini (essay date 1983)

SOURCE: Bini, Daniela. "Introduction: A Synthesis for Leopardi." In *A Fragrance from the Desert: Poetry and Philosophy in Giacomo Leopardi,* pp. 1-21. Saratoga, Calif.: ANMA Libri, 1983.

[*In the following excerpt, Bini discusses Leopardi's writings as a synthesis between poetry and philosophy, maintaining that earlier critics have mistakenly considered the two aspects of his work incompatible.*]

> The imagination takes its flight only after the void, the inauthenticity of the existential project has been revealed; literature begins where the existential demystification ends.
>
> (Paul de Man, *Blindness & Insight*)[1]

> Life itself . . . has no meaning. But so what? "What are the meanings in our lives?" is the only question.
>
> (Robert Solomon, *The Passions*)[2]

> Tout ce qui est beau et tout ce qui est grand, ne soit qu'une illusion. Mais si cette illusion était commune . . . n'en serait-on pas plus heureux? . . . En effet il n'appartient qu'à l'imagination de procurer à l'homme la seule espèce de bonheur positif dont il soit capable. C'est la véritable sagesse que de chercher ce bonheur dans l'idéal.
>
> (Giacomo Leopardi, *Lettere*)[3]

The 1959 Taylorian lecture "Schiller: Poet or Philosopher?" by Elizabeth Wilkinson began with the recollection of a previous paper which Paul Valéry had given in the same series twenty years before. The revolutionary aspect of Valéry's lecture consisted in showing the public "that the stock opposition of Poetry and Abstract Thought is one of those seductively simple schematizations so beloved of the human mind and so conveniently crystallized by language."[4] To accomplish his purpose Valéry had revealed the complexity of his own inner life, showing how "an idea which starts off with all the appearance of developing into philosophical discourse may well become entirely metamorphosed *en route* and emerge as that species of linguistic specialization we call a poem."[5]

Wilkinson used Valéry's lecture as a starting point for her discussion of the twofold personality of Schiller, poet and philosopher. Schiller himself, as will be seen in the third chapter, was well aware of it, and this awareness was the cause of a psychological trauma which lasted many years and made him reflect over and over on the subject. Wilkinson, however, noted, "what to Schiller seems a hybrid is for Valéry the norm: a man becomes now poet, now philosopher, by one of those successive specializations which are characteristic of human behaviour."[6] Valéry wanted to put an end to the "romantic heresy," that is to "the notion that the poet and the thinker are two utterly opposed types of mind."[7] Since Leopardi, like Schiller, made of the relationship between philosophy and poetry the central issue of his life, they should, in this respect, be considered in advance of the Romantics.

The concern met in Wilkinson's essay on Schiller motivates Naddei's book *L'eterno e il tempo in Giacomo Leopardi poeta e filosofo.* The aim of the book is, in fact, to study Leopardi's personality and work as a whole. The author rejects the "Romantic heresy" attacked by Valéry, which had become much more deeply entrenched in Italy through the influence of Benedetto Croce. Croce, in fact, not only stated the incompatibility of poetry and philosophy, but went so far as to consider philosophical thought harmful to poetry, and thus to be dismissed altogether from the artistic activity. Croce's established antithesis between the artistic and the philosophical faculties made their collaboration in the human spirit impossible. "The poet and the thinker are," for him undoubtedly, "two utterly opposed types of mind." In his criticism of Leopardi he remained consistent with his principles and approved only that part of his poetical production which he called purely idyllic, that is, detached, in his view, from speculative thought.[8] By so doing Croce not only reduced Leopardi's poetry to a minimum, but he also made it impossible to understand the poetry he wanted to save. None of Leopardi's poetry, in fact, is totally devoid of philosophical thought. Even the so-called idyllic phase is a

moment which is posited only to be negated by rational thought. In the dialectical process of Leopardi's poetical creation the idyll represents the negative moment, and thus its value consists in its negation.

The merit of Naddei's book is, principally, to have recognized the legitimate role of Leopardi's philosophy in all his production and to have seen its value together with the unquestioned value of his poetry. In pursuing this task Naddei applied the aesthetic theory of Carmelo Ottaviano which requires that a concept be present in poetry. As she herself admitted, the theory was not new. Gentile had already stated that art should have a philosophical content, when he argued, against Croce, that art and philosophy are not things in themselves but "prospettive mentali che nascono con l'atto stesso del pensiero giudicante e si configurano con quella struttura che accompagna il giudizio concreto."[9] Following Gentile's example, Naddei writes that "lo stesso contenuto della mente . . . può rappresentarsi al poeta come al critico suo interprete, una volta come immagine, un'altra come discorso . . . come poesia . . . come filosofia."[10] In support of her thesis Naddei could have found in the ***Zibaldone,*** in the ***Pensieri*** and in the ***Operette morali*** the philosophical correlatives for all Leopardi's poems.

Naddei's book also offers an almost complete annotated bibliography of the critical works related to Leopardi's philosophy, which began at the end of the last century, immediately after the publication of the ***Zibaldone,*** with the massive work of Zumbini.[11] The philosophical line in Leopardian scholarship stopped with the Crocian reaction, which was continued by the literary movement "La Ronda." Only since the late forties, thanks to the pioneer works of Sapegno, Binni, Luporini, and Timpanaro has the interest in Leopardi's philosophical thought been revived and pursued in a more critical fashion.

Naddei, finally, rejected the superficial argument which denied the presence of a philosophy in Leopardi on the basis that Leopardi lacked a system; as if philosophy could only exist in an orderly and systematized form. "L'asistematicità" of Leopardi, she writes, "è liberamente voluta e non rappresenta perciò un limite criticamente riscontrabile."[12] To support her claim she quotes several passages from the ***Zibaldone*** and paraphrases a statement made by Luporini in his study on Leopardi. A philosopher is, in Luporini's view, he who has a critical consciousness; "chi vede la vita sotto un particolare punto di vista e ne ha coscienza ed è capace di condurre un ragionamento dimostrativo che conferisca validità al suo assunto."[13]

Naddei, however, did not develop her intuition. She did not explain why "l'asistematicità [sia] liberamente voluta e non rappresent[i] perciò un limite." Yet the reason is of great importance. Leopardi, in fact, freely chose to "lack a system," since the use of a system would have implied a belief in the possibility of finding a logical order in reality. But reality is illogical and absurd, and escapes any attempt at systematization. Thus a philosophy of life must represent it as it is. Leopardi sees a world in which chaos reigns. He laughs at the human weakness which still attempts to see the purpose and order where there are none. This is his philosophical message and he uses, in order to convey it, a procedure which is determined by that very message. The content and the structure of his message are the same. The discovery of the paradoxical essence of life is conveyed to the reader through a style which is built on syntactical as well as logical opposition and paradox. They fill the *Zibaldone* and find their apodictic form in his *Pensieri*.[14]

In Naddei's analysis of Leopardi's philosophy the Crocian heritage paradoxically still survives. She diagnoses, in fact, a "psychological fracture" whereby Leopardi "crede nella verità e presta fede alla menzogna"[15] and she sees Leopardi's way out of this impasse in his conscious separation "dell'immaginazione e del sentimento dall'intelletto."[16] In her view, when Leopardi succeeds in silencing his speculative mind he is a poet, but a philosopher when his intellect takes over and stifles poetical inspiration. If this were true, his late poetry would be incomprehensible. Leopardi never abandoned reason, not even in the idyllic phase. Through its dialectical force the poetical process takes place. Rationalism, about which more will be said shortly, is the key concept in understanding Leopardi. It constantly performs a mediating role.

The "psychological fracture" that Naddei finds in Leopardi is the same device which Italian scholars after Croce and "La Ronda" needed in order to justify the presence in Leopardi of both philosophical and poetical thought. The psychological fracture is the precondition to Flora's statement that "al di là del riscatto supremo dell'arte . . . la sua [Leopardi's] filosofia, astrattamente considerata è sensistica, roussoviana, settecentesca."[17] But Leopardi's philosophy cannot be considered in the abstract, beyond his art (in fact beyond the "riscatto supremo" of art), for it is the very structure of his art. Even Sansone, who wrote many brilliant pages on Leopardi's philosophy, cannot escape from this psychological fracture. "Il nucleo della spiritualità leopardiana è un sentimento del mondo e non una comprensione teorica di esso."[18] The first half of Sansone's statement is correct, but its truth is contradicted by the second half. The core of Leopardi's spirituality is truly a sentiment of the world, but the word "sentiment" has in Leopardi a profound theoretical implication. It is a sentiment which, far from being opposed to "the theoretical comprehension of the world," derives precisely from it.[19]

1. Purpose and Methodology

Il mezzo filosofo combatte le illusioni perchè . . . è illuso, il vero filosofo le ama e predica, perchè non è illuso: e il combattere le illusioni in genere è il più certo segno d'imperfettissimo e insufficientissimo sapere, e di notabile illusione.

(**Z** I, 1107-08)

The purpose of the present work is to show the presence in Leopardi of a dialectical inner relationship between philosophy and poetry, seen not as separate moments which exclude each other, but as mutually necessary. The analysis of Leopardi's philosophy will follow the traditional distinctions of ethics, metaphysics, and aesthetics; they will be treated in this order in the three following chapters. Furthermore a philosophical justification will be given to the commonly recognized priority of poetry in Leopardi's life. Aesthetics will appear as the supreme category in Leopardi's phenomenology, dialectically resolving, and thus assuming by transformation, the preceding ethical and theoretical moments.

The methodology used will also be dialectical, for it is the most appropriate in a study which aims at the disclosure of a dialectical thought. The division of the work into three chapters corresponds also to the triadic pattern of dialectics.

The first chapter will deal with the subjective moment of the dialectical process. The emphasis will, therefore, be placed on the experiencing subject and on its modifications by means of external reality. The starting point of Leopardi's self-analysis is sensation which presents itself as the first and unquestionable element of experience. Sensation is also the parameter by which Leopardi analyzes the formation and functions of the human faculties and by which he arrives at the establishment of a hedonistic ethic. Leopardi's sensationalism is, therefore, here considered first for it is the methodology Leopardi himself used in his philosophical inquiry and for it represents, chronologically, the first moment of his philosophical experience.

Leopardi's interest in philosophical speculation was raised by the puzzling nature of sensation. He was a sensationalist by a sentimental adhesion even before becoming a sensationalist through a rational choice. His main concern was with the various and complex ways in which external reality affects the senses. Nature had given him an overly acute sensibility which made him extremely receptive to any contact with the external world and which was the cause of a life of intense suffering. His letters to friends and family are filled with remarks and complaints about the disadvantages which his sensibility had caused him. The short letter he wrote to Antonietta Tommasini on June 19, 1830, is emblematic of his physical and psychological state. "Tutti i miei organi, dicono i medici, sono sani; ma nessuno può essere adoperato senza gran pena, a causa di una estrema, inaudita sensibilità, che . . . ostinatissimamente cresce ogni giorno: quasi ogni azione, e quasi ogni sensazione mi dà dolore" (*Lettere,* p. 941).

Remarks of this sort were the basis for the opinion, widely diffused among scholars, that Leopardi's pessimistic philosophy was nothing but the consequence of his personal unhappiness.[20] Croce added his weight to the belief, using the letters as evidence. When they were first published, he remarked, they proved that "codeste dottrine alle quali avevamo attribuito valore speculativo, non erano altro che il riflesso e delle sofferenze e delle miserie dell'individuo . . . delle infermità che lo travagliarono, delle compressioni familiari ed angustie economiche, del vano desiderio di un amore di donna non mai ottenuto."[21] Nobody could deny that at the beginning "la cosiddetta filosofia di Leopardi è un movimento piuttosto affettivo che razionale"[22] as Sapegno put it. It is impossible not to see "la nettissima dipendenza della metafisica materialistica dallo sviluppo dell'etica pessimistica [of Leopardi]" as Sansone remarked.[23] De Sanctis, in fact, had already noticed this when he wrote that "l'infelicità sua propria [Leopardi's] . . . lo condusse di buon'ora alla meditazione sul male e sul dolore."[24] The personal condition, however, was only the starting point of Leopardi's philosophical speculation, and exemplifies a natural intellectual procedure. Any speculative inquiry starts from a personal need.[25] Croce made an arbitrary inference when he accused Leopardi of having universalized that personal need which was, instead, only the efficient cause of a logical series of empirical observations.[26] Nobody ever defended Leopardi from this accusation better than he did himself, and even now his argument certainly deserves more credit than the hypothetical guesses made by scholars through the years. His words are not only for De Sinner, to whom he directly addressed them, but for his contemporaries and for posterity as well. "Quels que soient mes malheurs . . . j'ai eu assez de courage pour ne pas chercher à en diminuer le poids ni par de frivoles espérances d'une prétendue félicité future et inconnue, ni par une lâche résignation . . . Ç'a été par suite de ce même courage, qu'étant amené par mes recherches à une philosophie désespérante, je n'ai pas hésité à l'embrasser toute entière; tandis que de l'autre côté ce n'a été que par effet de la lâcheté des hommes, qui ont besoin d'être persuadés du mérite de l'existence, que l'on a voulu considérer mes opinions philosophiques comme le résultat de mes souffrances particulières, et que l'on s'obstine à attribuer à mes circonstances matérielles ce qu'on ne doit qu'à mon entendement. Avant de mourir, je vais protester contre cette invention de la faiblesse et de la vulgarité, et prier mes lecteurs de s'attacher à détruire mes observations et mes raisonnements plutôt que d'accuser mes maladies" (*Lettere,* p. 1033). His "protest," however, remained unheard for a long time.

The second chapter of this work will deal with the second and complementary moment of the dialectical process. It will, thus, place the emphasis on the object experienced in an attempt to arrive at the formulation of a theoretical system. The sensationalistic methodology which Leopardi followed strictly led him to a materialistic view of the world. If all knowledge is reducible to physical sensation, it is a logical consequence to consider all its objects as matter. Materialism, thus, appears as the complementary aspect of sensationalism. Many orthodox sensationalists of the eighteenth century would have protested—and some actually did—against the reduction of sensationalism to materialism. Nevertheless this reduction was made by Leopardi and was implicit in a coherent development of the sensationalistic doctrine. La Mettrie, Diderot, Cabanis were, in fact, both sensationalists and materialists. They also had arrived at materialism through a serious sensationalistic study of reality. The suspicion of materialism which many sensationalists shared was based, as Diderot well understood, on the simple-minded concept that traditional philosophical thought had of matter and handed down to his own times. "Le vice de tous ces raisonnements est toujours de confondre une matière activement sensible avec une matière brute, inerte, inorganisée, inanimalisée, le bois avec la chair."[27] Such an argument, however, was to encounter many obstacles since it was opposed to the well-established classical tradition of the Manichean dualism of body and soul, matter and spirit. To give to matter the attributes once considered as belonging exclusively to the spirit meant to do without the spirit altogether. And with spirit the soul would also disappear. The analysis of sensation had brought the rigorous mind of Diderot to the conclusion that "il n'y a qu'une seule opération dans l'homme: c'est sentir. Cette opération, qui n'est jamais libre, se résout en pensée, raisonnement, délibération, désir ou aversion."[28] "Vivre c'est sentir," Cabanis was to write in his famous book *Rapports du physique et du moral de l'homme,* published in 1802.[29] This major work to which Cabanis contributed the basis of his scientific training, brought together all the speculative efforts of the *idéologues.* In his brilliant book *Il pensiero degli idéologues* Sergio Moravia explains the reason for the confusion and polemic surrounding the newly established materialistic thought. Most of the *Idéologues* who contributed to it lacked scientific training and were, therefore, easy prey for their opponents. Diderot was an exception. "La lettura di tante opere," writes Moravia, "la discussione coi *confrères* dell'ambiente filosofico lo [Diderot] ha[nno] reso persuaso che il tipo di discorso . . . condotto fin allora sopra certi temi è ormai superato"[30]—Diderot, in fact, understood that "da un discorso ancora generale bisogna passare a un discorso particolare e scientifico . . . La 'filosofia' della vita e della materia deve lasciare il campo alla 'scienza' dell'*organisation* dell'uomo."[31] Leopardi, like most of the *Idéologues,* remained in the realm of the "philosophy of life and matter" since he lacked the necessary technical training and probably also the desire to enter the field of science. His logical speculations, however, took him very close to those which Diderot, Cabanis, and their followers elaborated with the help of scientific knowledge.

Leopardi knew that sensationalism and materialism owed much to John Locke. The problem of the origin of knowledge and of the formation of ideas had not yet been resolved when Locke decided that a solution could be found only through a detailed analysis of the human intellect and its operations. His *Essay Concerning Human Understanding* which began as an examination of the ways in which the intellect operates, arrived at the rejection of innatism, thus at the reduction of all ideas to sensation. From it every intellectual operation begins. Even the most abstract ideas, which may seem at first to lack any correlative object in reality, are nothing but the highest levels of abstraction of a series of other ideas, whose first source must be sought in sensation. Hence Locke was considered the founder of empiricism.

From Locke, Leopardi took his criticism of any form of innatism and his reduction of all ideas to sensation. Empiricism was also a part of Leopardi's methodology since experience is at the origin and at the end of every knowing process. It is in fact experience, on the one hand, which supplies the material to the intellect which, without it, is simply a *tabula rasa.* Intellect, thus, organizes and catalogues the material presented to it by experience. On the other hand, experience is also at the conclusion of any knowing process, for it is the only parameter which we possess for measuring and verifying the obtained results. This discovery led the *Idéologues* to proclaim the death of metaphysics.[32] If human knowledge must limit itself to physical experience, it is vain and pointless to search for the origin of mankind or of the world. It is absurd to try to answer the metaphysical questions with which the human mind has been preoccupied for centuries. Leopardi accepted the criticism of innatism. He branded the monades, the innate ideas and the optimism of Leibnitz, "fables" and praised instead Descartes, Galileo, and Newton as the philosophers who "hanno veramente mutato faccia alla filosofia" (*Z* I, 1180). Agreeing with Locke and the *Idéologues,* he wrote: "È già stabilito dagli ideologi che il progresso delle cognizioni umane consiste nel conoscere che un'idea ne contiene un'altra (così Locke, Tracy ec.) e questa un'altra ec" (*Z* I, 832). And he concludes: "In-

somma dal detto qui sopra e da mille altre cose che si potrebbero dire, si deduce quanto giustamente i moderni ideologisti abbiano abolite le idee innate" (*Z* I, 217-18).

Having rejected innatism and abolished metaphysics the *Idéologues* turned their philosophical inquiry into an operative tool and began to deal with the social aspect of man. For Leopardi, however, the abolition of metaphysics did not imply an involvement with social problems. What interested him was the individual and the type of philosophical inquiry he pursued was psychological. Like Schiller he believed that "any individual soul, unfolding its inner strength is better than the greatest human society."[33]

The interest in psychology was widespread among materialists. Leopardi shared their conviction that society and education can do little to erase the differences among men created by nature. His personal experience was the best possible proof in support of this belief. Physical makeup cannot be changed either by laws or by education. Society cannot make equal those whom nature created different. This strong belief in natural determinism is what differentiates Leopardi from many of the French writers who influenced him and primarily from Helvétius, despite the frequency with which his name appears in the *Zibaldone*. Diderot's "Réfutation suivie de l'ouvrage intitulé *L'Homme*" would have found a great supporter in Leopardi. The focus of Leopardi's philosophical inquiry remained constantly circumscribed to the understanding of the individual man, and if he "conclude con una negazione sempre più decisa dell'anima come essenza immateriale, questo gli consente una più spregiudicata analisi della vita interiore dell'uomo e del suo comportamento."[34]

The presence of sensationalistic and materialistic ideas in Leopardi has been long recognized by most of the scholars who have been involved in the analysis of his thought. What they have not yet attempted, however, is the study of these two philosophical elements in the light of a dialectical development leading to a third stage of Leopardi's phenomenology, namely, that of an idealistic aesthetics. This will be the central and final aim of the present work. Only in the light of the third chapter, in fact, will the first two find their real place and acquire their true significance. The three moments of sensationalism, materialism, and idealism are dialectically intertwined and only the necessity of writing about them can justify their division into separate chapters. Writing, as a process of reflecting and analyzing is, as Schiller said, the separating of things from one another. It cannot be avoided; even if it might seem ironical in a work whose aim is to show the impossibility of this very separation.

The idealistic moment in Leopardi's philosophy concerns only his poetry; yet it will be shown that art becomes the highest stage of his philosophic development, the final synthesis, dialectically embodying and resolving the preceding ethical and theoretical moments. For some modern scholars, still reacting against Croce's aesthetic tradition, and concerned with the reactionary implications of idealism in politics, this conclusion may be hard to accept. Yet it will appear as a natural consequence of the development of those materialistic ideas which most critics in Italy today agree are present in Leopardi.

The necessary link between sensationalism, materialism, and idealism was Leopardi's loyalty to rationalism.[35] Despite his innumerable attacks on reason and his insistence on the opposition between reason and nature, to the apparent benefit of the latter, Leopardi never abandoned or betrayed reason; even at the cost of his own happiness. He owed much to Descartes and was fascinated by his discovery of the methodological 'doubt,' which he transformed into an existential doubt, reversing the Cartesian meaning. "Il mio sistema," he wrote in the *Zibaldone,* "introduce non solo uno Scetticismo ragionato e dimostrato, ma tale che . . . la ragione umana per qualsivoglia progresso possibile, non potrà mai spogliarsi di questo scetticismo . . . e che non solo il dubbio giova a scoprire il vero . . . ma il vero consiste essenzialmente nel dubbio" (**Z** I, 1075-76). It was this loyalty to reason at any cost which made reason perish in his hands.

The reason which perished was the goddess the seventeenth century worshiped, who knew all the answers and found all the solutions. Yet, through his devout worship of this goddess, Leopardi found himself both more enlightened and more *souffrant.* Reason had appeared as a destructive tool which, having removed past errors, as Bayle said, left man before a bare and cold truth. It had destroyed the pseudo-answers invented by superstition, religion, and fantasy, but had offered no substitute which could replace them. The reality that appeared at the end of this process was meaningless and absurd. Yet, even at this point Leopardi could not abandon reason. What Robert Solomon said for Camus can here be applied to Leopardi. "The Absurd, for him, is a strictly rational conclusion, and it is in the name of reason that he will not attempt to deny or transcend this Absurd."[36] Taken to its extreme consequences, rationalism had destroyed itself for it had discovered the irrationality of existence. Yet this self-defeat was necessary if man was to be freed from the myth of reason. Nietzsche and the existentialists meant precisely this when they spoke of the destruction of reason by means of reason. And this is also what Leopardi meant in the various passages of his *Zibaldone* where he made the paradoxical statement that "il miglior uso ed effetto della ragione e della riflessione, è distruggere o mi-

norare nell'uomo la ragione e la riflessione" (**Z** I, 784).[37] Only through the use of reason can man discover its deficiencies.

This pessimistic conclusion, however, did not force Leopardi to take the opposite position, namely, to a praise of irrationalism, as it was to do with many romantics. As Solmi rightly pointed out, Leopardi's pessimism was not the romantic outpouring of a Byron or of a Musset. On the contrary, "egli ci offre ferme, esatte, glaciali ricognizioni della realtà."[38] Man is bound to his rational condition and, thus, to suffering. Sentiment is the new force which springs forth from this state. It is a feeling which results from the act of reason and is thus a rational feeling. It represents man's recognition of the inadequacy of reality and his legitimate quest for meanings.[39] Sentiment is, therefore, the synthesis of reason and feeling. It brings forth a lament which finds its expression in poetry. In poetry man has created a new reality or better a "surreality," as Solomon would call it; and like Solomon he can now say "Life itself has no meaning. But so what? 'What are the meanings in our lives?' is the only question."[40] The world thus created will be a man-made product and will last forever untouchable by nature's destructive forces. "What my world includes that the world does not is value"[41] and this value is "my" own creation. The insufficiency of reality, its lack of purpose allows man to create his own meaningful world, and in so doing he manifests his superiority over nature. The negative moment of Leopardi's dialectics, that of senseless matter, can be overcome only through the exploitation of that very recognition.

Leopardi had always said, in order to exemplify the paradoxical mechanism of existence, that life perpetuates itself through death. The garden which, to those who enter it, evokes images of beauty and harmony, hides in itself suffering and death.[42] Leopardi, however, does not stop at the recognition of this paradoxical principle. He overcomes it by subsuming it into a higher paradox: that of a beautiful poetry which is born out of an ugly truth. The correlation of philosophy and poetry could not have been more absolute.[43]

2. CONDILLAC, LA METTRIE, AND SCHILLER

The works of Condillac have been chosen as the parameter for the analysis of Leopardi's sensationalism in the first chapter. The choice was determined by two reasons. In the first place Leopardi's acquaintance with Condillac is easy to prove. The influence of the French philosopher in Italy was deeply felt, especially in Parma where he lived and where Pietro Giordani was educated. The Italian sensationalists with whom Leopardi was acquainted took Condillac as their spiritual father. Furthermore, some of his works were present in the Leopardi family library. To compare him with the founder of the sensationalist movement in France is perhaps the best way to judge Leopardi's own sensationalism. Restricting the comparative analysis to Condillac does not, of course, imply that he was the only sensationalistic influence on Leopardi.

The methodology used in this comparative analysis is strictly positivistic. Condillac's texts are placed side by side with those of Leopardi in order to emphasize their similarity. Some differences are also shown with the purpose of pointing out Leopardi's own individual position and to make the peculiar turn he gave to sensationalism more understandable. This peculiar turn was in the direction of materialism which Condillac would never have accepted.

The comparanda for the analysis of Leopardi's materialism are the works of La Mettrie; yet something will also be said about d'Holbach, Frederick the Great, Diderot, and Sade. The founder of French materialism was chosen to demonstrate clearly the materialistic aspect of Leopardi's philosophy.[44] A peculiarity of La Mettrie's nature further justifies this choice. His, like Leopardi's, was alien to any type of systematic and rigid theorization and was very receptive to the infinite suggestions of intuition and imagination.

Much has been written on the influence on Leopardi of Rousseau, Voltaire, d'Alembert, Helvétius, d'Holbach, Maupertuis, Montesquieu, and Mme de Staël, from Serban's book *Leopardi et la France,* published in 1913, up to the recent essays by Frattini.[45] No extensive comparative analysis, however, has yet been done on Leopardi and Condillac or on Leopardi and La Mettrie. The present study was inspired by a remark by Frattini. After giving an extensive list of the French thinkers quoted by Leopardi in his *Zibaldone* he writes: "Altri ideologi, come il Condillac e il La Mettrie—nelle cui dottrine morali eudemonistiche, edonistiche e relativistiche si potrebbe ricercare un preludio o preannuncio di certe posizioni del L.—non risultano mai citati nello *Zibaldone.*"[46] Since a comparative analysis is not, or at least not exclusively, a search for sources, this work will try to prove that in Condillac and La Mettrie there was much more than "un preludio . . . di certe posizioni del L."

In the third chapter, which is the core of the whole work, the acknowledged founder of idealism has been passed over in favor of Schiller for the comparative analysis. Kant (who in any case will not be ignored here) made his major contribution to philosophy in metaphysics and ethics, namely in his *Critique of Pure Reason* and in his *Critique of Practical Reason.* Although the importance of his third critique, which deals with aesthetics, should not be minimized, nevertheless it was Schiller, the poet and philosopher, who developed Kantian aesthetics in the direction which is rel-

evant to Leopardi. Furthermore, Schiller's personality is much closer to Leopardi's than Kant's. Both men had to struggle with what they called the two conflicting impulses of human nature: reason and feeling, in order to find a balance between their philosophical minds and their poetical needs.

The comparative analysis of the third chapter does not aim at establishing any direct influence of Schiller on Leopardi. This would be hard to prove, just as it would be hard to prove any direct idealistic influence on Leopardi. If he knew German he knew it very poorly and he was therefore not directly acquainted with Schiller's philosophical writings, which are the basis of the present comparative analysis.[47]

It is legitimate to suppose that what he knew of Schiller and Kant came from his reading of *De l'Allemagne.* His study of most of Mme de Staël's works is well documented by the many explicit references Leopardi made in the *Zibaldone* and also by the lists of the readings he himself drew up.[48] The third section of *De l'Allemagne* dealt with philosophy in general and German philosophy in particular. Mme de Staël dedicated a whole chapter in that section to Kant. It is interesting, however, to note that of the forty pages devoted to Kant (not too many to begin with) only a few paragraphs were on his *Critique of Pure Reason.* The rest dealt with his aesthetics and in particular with his ethics, whose rigorism must have made a profound impression on the French writer. Leopardi could not have learned much about Kant's metaphysics from Mme de Staël's pages. His superficial judgment is probably derived from the equally superficial treatment given to it in *De l'Allemagne.*[49] The only part of Kant's philosophy which was sufficiently explained, the *Critique of Practical Reason,* could not have impressed Leopardi since little space was given to man's individual and material happiness.

Leopardi probably read about Schiller in that section of *De l'Allemagne* called "La littérature et les arts" where a chapter was dedicated to every major German author.[50] Even in the chapter on Schiller, however, Mme de Staël was much more interested in his moral merit than in his poetical value. Schiller was probably right when, after meeting her, he wrote to Goethe: "Elle est parfaitement insensible à ce que nous appelons la poésie."[51] Schiller's remark about her 'philosophical' mind is also worthy of noting: "Sa nature et son coeur valent mieux que sa métaphysique."[52] Yet the chapter which probably influenced Leopardi the most was another. He learned more about Schiller from "Poésie classique et poésie romantique" than from the section devoted exclusively to him. The title of this chapter is already evocative enough. Without knowing it Leopardi was reading in those pages a superficial summary of the first section of Schiller's "Naive and Sentimental Poetry."[53]

Leopardi read profusely and without system. The criteria he followed were subjective and selective. He took from what he read only that part which would support his ideas, which were well established early in his life. In his cultural formation one can, therefore, hear the echo of many ideas of the time, as well as of many from the Greek and Roman classics.[54] There was no contemporary thinker from whom he did not take something. Della Giovanna is right when he says: "[Leopardi] trasse il concetto della natura, della società e della civiltà dal Rousseau, derivò il principio universale dell'egoismo da Helvétius, apprese a dubitar di tutto da Cartesio, e a deridere l'ottimismo leibniziano dal Voltaire . . . dedusse la teoria dell'assuefazione dal sensismo del Locke." The list could go on and on.[55] Yet such syncretism was possible only insofar as he already had those ideas at least in an embryonic form. If many parallels can be drawn between Leopardi and French thought of the eighteenth century, none, however, could be exceptionally relevant. All that has been written on this topic is valid and helpful in the understanding of Leopardi only if it is considered as a whole, without isolating one particular source. De Sanctis long ago had already noticed this when, commenting on the various aspects of Leopardi's philosophy, he wrote: "Trovi nelle sue diverse parti reminiscenze stoiche, platoniche, sensiste, una erudizione varia . . . Ma il tutto è pensiero originale, e per la inesorabilità delle conclusioni e per la sua compenetrazione in tutte le forze della vita."[56] Today, this interpretation is still valid and it has been taken up again by Frattini: "Le sterminate letture [Leopardi's] . . . avevano principalmente la funzione di offrire come un ricchissimo ideario su cui alimentare alcuni approssimativi nuclei dottrinari che si venivano nel suo pensiero gradualmente formando."[57] Finally, Leopardi himself had something to say on this topic: "La lettura dei libri non ha veramente prodotto in me nè affetti o sentimenti che non avessi, né anche verun effetto di questi, che senza esse letture non avesse dovuto nascere da sé" (**Z** I, 94). For this reason also the present study is not a search for sources. The intention, instead, is to try to reconstruct a spiritual tie among various trends of thought, to see them as the necessary steps of a logical development which points to the continuity between Enlightenment and Romanticism and to the unity between philosophy and art.

Notes

1. Paul De Man, *Blindness & Insight. Essays in the Rhetoric of Contemporary Criticism* (New York: Oxford University Press, 1971), pp. 34-35.

2. Robert C. Solomon, *The Passions* (New York: Anchor Books, 1977), p. 44.

3. Giacomo Leopardi, *Tutte le opere di Giacomo Leopardi,* ed. Francesco Flora, 5 vols. (Verona: Mondadori, 1968-1973), *Lettere,* pp. 439-40. The

five volumes are so divided: *Lettere* (1 vol.), *Zibaldone di pensieri* (2 vols.), *Le poesie e le prose* (2 vols.). They will be referred to, respectively, as *Lettere, Z* I, *Z* II, and *PP* I, *PP* II.

4. Elizabeth M. Wilkinson, *Schiller, Poet or Philosopher?* Special Taylorian Lecture (Oxford: Clarendon Press, 1961), p. 3.

5. *Ibid.*

6. *Ibid.,* p. 4.

7. *Ibid.,* p. 5.

8. "È stato considerato talvolta il Leopardi come un poeta filosofo, cosa che . . . si dimostra non esatta per lui come è sempre inesatta per ogni poeta. La sua fondamentale condizione di spirito non solo era sentimentale e non già filosofica, ma si potrebbe addirittura definirla un ingorgo sentimentale" (Benedetto Croce, *La letteratura italiana,* III, ed. Mario Sansone, *L'Ottocento* [Bari: Laterza, 1957], 74). As a reply to Croce here is a quote from Frattini's book on Leopardi: l'idillio leopardiano nasce come "il compenetrarsi della facoltà poetica avente per oggetto il bello (cioè . . . il falso, la finzione) e il diletto con la facoltà filosofica che mira alla conquista del vero" (Alberto Frattini, *Giacomo Leopardi* [Bologna: Cappelli, 1969], p. 66).

9. Quoted by Mirella Carbonara Naddei, *L'eterno e il tempo in Giacomo Leopardi poeta filosofo* (Naples: Libreria Scientifica, 1973), p. 51. Her references are mainly to Giovanni Gentile, *Poesia e filosofia di Giacomo Leopardi* (Florence: Sansoni, 1939).

10. *Ibid.,* p. 133.

11. Bonaventura Zumbini, *Studi sul Leopardi,* 2 vols. (Florence: Barbera, 1902, 1904). However, in her bibliographical list Naddei forgets to mention the name of Cantella who had also stated the presence in Leopardi of the philosopher as well as of the poet (Francesco Cantella, *Giacomo Leopardi filosofo* [Palermo: Alberto Reber, 1907], pp. 89-90, 92). Cantella, however, saw in Leopardi's philosophy a prelude of pragmatism.

12. Naddei, p. 162.

13. *Ibid.,* p. 22. She summarizes the first page of the essay by Cesare Luporini, "Leopardi progressivo" in his book *Filosofi vecchi e nuovi* (Florence: Sansoni, 1947), pp. 185-274; p. 185. Hans Zint also remarks that "una qualità di Leopardi pensatore . . . lo attesta anche metodologicamente come vero spirito filosofico: la sua prontezza, cioè, e la sua attitudine a circuire gli oggetti presi in esame, osservarli sotto vari angoli visuali" (Hans Zint,

"Giacomo Leopardi filosofo," *Rivista di psicologia normale, patologica e applicata,* 23, no. 1-2 [Jan.-June 1942], p. 97).

14. A few examples will suffice. "Nessun segno d'essere poco filosofo e poco savio, che volere savia e filosofica tutta la vita" ("Pensiero" 27). "Gli uomini sono miseri per necessità, e risoluti di credersi miseri per accidente" ("Pensiero" 31). "Nessuna qualità umana è più intollerabile nella vita ordinaria, né in fatti tollerata meno, che l'intolleranza" ("Pensiero" 37). "L'uomo è condannato o a consumare la gioventù senza proposito, la quale è il solo tempo di far frutto per l'età che viene, e di provvedere al proprio stato; o a spenderla in procacciare godimenti a quella parte della sua vita, nella quale egli non sarà più atto a godere" ("Pensiero" 47). "La natura, benignamente come suole, ha ordinato che l'uomo non impari a vivere se non a proporzione che le cause di vivere gli s'involano" ("Pensiero" 79) (*PP* II, 21, 23, 25, 33, 49).

In the most recent years the value of Leopardi's philosophical thought has been restored, and Antonio Prete's last book *Il pensiero poetante* (Milano: Feltrinelli, 1980), although limited to the analysis of the *Zibaldone,* is an effort to show the reciprocal influence and close relationship between philosophy and poetry, with the emphasis placed precisely on Leopardi's conscious refusal at systematization. This line of thought is continued by Burchi in her analysis of *I pensieri,* where the very literary form chosen by Leopardi—that of thoughts, reflections, "pensées"—reflects, in her view, "la crisi di una vision sistematica della realtà" (Elisabetta Burchi, *Il progetto leopardiano: I pensieri* [Roma: Bulzoni, 1981], p. 105).

15. Naddei, p. 153.

16. *Ibid.*

17. Francesco Flora, *Leopardi e la letteratura francese* (Milan: Rodolfo Malfasi, 1947), pp. 20-21.

18. Mario Sansone, "Il carattere delle *Operette morali* e il 'Dialogo della Natura e di un islandese,'" *Nuova antologia,* 466, no. 91 (Jan. 1956):30.

19. In his review of Battaglia's book *L'ideologia letteraria di Giacomo Leopardi,* Ernesto Caserta also aims at the dismissal of the old Crocian fallacy. He rejects, in fact, in Battaglia's book "il riconoscimento di una duplice direzione della poesia leopardiana . . . uno dell'anima . . . e uno intellettuale . . . Questa distinzione di due livelli di coscienza," he continues, "estetica e concettuale, di evidente derivazione crociana, non è convincente . . . A causa della stessa unità dello spirito . . . lo svolgimento non può avvenire che in en-

trambe le coscienze; quindi a misura che il pensiero del Leopardi matura, anche la sua arte matura e si sviluppa: si tratta di un processo dialettico in cui il pensiero non è assente nella poesia ma piuttosto domato, superato, guardato *sub specie intuitionis*" (Ernesto G. Caserta, "Pensiero, estetica e poesia del Leopardi: una soluzione critica," *Italica,* no. 1 [1972], pp. 71-72).

20. This thesis was brought up by the neopositivistic school at the end of the last century. A list of the best known studies of the school can be found in Naddei's book.

21. Croce, p. 70.

22. Natalino Sapegno, "Leopardi," in *Disegno storico della letteratura italiana,* ch. 26 (Florence: La Nuova Italia, 1948), p. 643.

23. Mario Sansone, "Leopardi e la filosofia del Settecento," in *Leopardi e il Settecento. Atti del I Convegno internazionale di studi leopardiani* (Florence: Olschki, 1964), p. 148.

24. Francesco De Sanctis, *Opere complete,* IV, *La letteratura italiana nel secolo decimonono* (Naples: Alberto Morano, 1933), 240.

25. "Non per questo tuttavia la filosofia che nasca dalla situazione personale sarà espressione della situazione personale: lo sarà, se ne nasca e vi rimanga." "Noi crediamo . . . che la situazione personale del Leopardi non pregiudichi alla teoricità dei suoi pensamenti, poichè la consideriamo come la base . . . e non la risultanza del filosofare" (Romano Amerio, "L' 'ultrafilosofia' di Giacomo Leopardi," *Filosofia* [July 1953], pp. 452, 453).

26. The following passage from the *Zibaldone* is one of the many in which Leopardi exemplified his philosophical procedure. "Il sentimento della nullità di tutte le cose, la insufficienza di tutti i piaceri . . . la tendenza verso un infinito che non comprendiamo, forse proviene da una cagione semplicissima e più materiale che spirituale. L'anima umana desidera sempre essenzialmente e mira unicamente . . . al piacere, ossia alla felicità, che considerandola bene, è tutt'uno col piacere . . . Questo desiderio e questa tendenza non ha limiti, perch'è ingenita o congenita coll'esistenza" (*Z* I, 181-82).

27. Quoted in Sergio Moravia, *Il pensiero degli idéologues: Scienza e filosofia in Francia (1780-1815)* (Florence: La Nuova Italia, 1974), p. 161.

28. *Ibid.*

29. P. G. Cabanis, *Oeuvres philosophiques,* 2 vols. (Paris: Lehec-Cazeneuve, 1956), I, 168. "La sensi-

bilité physique est le dernier terme auquel on arrive dans l'étude des phénomènes de la vie, et dans la recherche méthodique de leur véritable enchaînement: c'est aussi le dernier résultat, ou . . . le plus général que fournit l'analyse des facultés intellectuelles et des affections de l'âme" (p. 142; also quoted by Moravia, p. 187). Cabanis' name is mentioned twice in the *Zibaldone* together with the names of Newton, Leibnitz, Locke, Rousseau, Tracy, Vico, Descartes, Malebranche, and Kant (*Z* I, 633; *Z* II, 7).

30. Moravia, p. 162.

31. *Ibid.*

32. The word "metaphysics" is here used with the modern meaning of the study of things transcending nature, which was given to the word in medieval times.

33. Quoted in F. W. Kaufman, *Schiller, Poet of Philosophical Idealism* (Oberlin, Ohio: The Academy Press, 1942), p. 36. In his drama *Fiesko,* Schiller wrote: "The state is a creature of chance, but man is a necessary being, and what else makes a state great and venerable but the moral energies of its individuals" (p. 40).

34. Sansone, "Leopardi e la filosofia del Settecento," p. 141.

35. Amelotti explains the relationship between sensationalism and rationalism in the eighteenth century. "All'epoca del Leopardi sarebbe improprio parlare di razionalismo e sensismo contrapposti . . . Razionalismo e sensismo non sono che due modi dell'unico indirizzo scientifico, poiché ormai si è del tutto affermata una scienza, dotata di una propria logica e fondata sull'esperienza sensibile, che ha unito in sé le due correnti." He also sees the strict connection between sensationalism and materialism (Giovanni Amelotti, *Filosofia del Leopardi* [Genoa: Dante Alighieri, 1939], p. 17). According to Savarese, "l'argomentare rigorosamente deduttivo" is a characteristic of eighteenth-century materialism (Gennaro Savarese, *Saggio sui "Paralipomeni" di Giacomo Leopardi* [Florence: La Nuova Italia, 1967], pp. 142-43).

36. Solomon, p. 40.

37. The same concept is expressed in *Z* I, 140, 280, 924; *Z* II, 56. Amerio understood this important dialectical turn in Leopardi when he wrote that "la filosofia può restituire l'uomo alla sua naturalità soltanto annullando se stessa . . . cioè concludendo la propria necessaria distruzione" (p. 455). This is the conclusion at which Eleandro arrives. "L'ultima conclusione che si ricava dalla filosofia vera e perfetta si è che non bisogna filosofare"

(*PP* I, 986). If philosophy, Amerio said, "è il sistema della natura appreso dalla ragione, affinché l'uomo che è ragione, torni alla natura," "l'ultrafilosofia è il ritorno dello spirito alla natura, la ridiscesa dal reale all'illusione" (pp. 455, 461). Gentile was the first scholar who spoke of this dialectical turn, and who saw the point of arrival of Leopardi's dialectics "in questa filosofia superiore che è negazione della negazione, e che afferma perciò come abbiamo udito da Eleandro, ultima conclusione della filosofia vera e perfetta esser quella, che non bisogna filosofare" (*Poesia e filosofia,* pp. 36-37).

38. Sergio Solmi, *Scritti leopardiani* (Milan: All'insegna del pesce d'oro, 1969), p. 56.

39. Commenting on the "Dialogo della Natura e di un islandese" Garin writes: "Il dolore umano nasce da questa sproporzione, dal saperci natura e dal sentirci oltre la natura" (Eugenio Garin, *La filosofia,* II [Milan: Vallardi, 1947], 415).

40. Solomon, p. 44.

41. *Ibid.,* p. 67.

42. "Entrate in un giardino di piante, d'erbe, di fiori. Sia pur quanto volete ridente. Sia nella più mite stagione dell'anno. Voi non potete volger lo sguardo in nessuna parte che voi non vi troviate del patimento. Tutta quella famiglia di vegetali è in istato di *souffrance* . . . Là quella rosa è *offesa* dal sole, che gli ha *dato la vita*; si corruga, langue, appassisce. Là quel giglio è succhiato crudelmente da un'ape, nelle sue parti più sensibili, più vitali. Il *dolce mele* non si fabbrica dalle industriose . . . *virtuose api* senza *indicibili tormenti* di quelle fibre delicatissime, senza *strage* spietata di teneri fiorellini . . . Quella *donzelletta sensibile e gentile,* va *dolcemente sterpando* e *infrangendo* steli. Il giardiniere va *saggiamente troncando,* tagliando membra sensibili, colle unghie, col ferro . . . Lo spettacolo di tanta copia di vita all'entrare in questo giardino ci rallegra l'anima e di qui è che questo ci pare essere un soggiorno di gioia" (*Z* II, 1005-06; italics mine). The paradoxical principle of existence applies to nature and to man. However "kind" and "wise" an action might be in its intention, its effect will necessarily be suffering and destruction. Every element of existence needs its opposite and it is forever tied to it. At the end of his philosophical speculation in the *Zibaldone,* Leopardi is still faithful to its beginning. "La ragione ha bisogno delle immaginazioni e delle illusioni ch'ella distrugge; il vero del falso; il sostanziale dell'apparente . . . il ghiaccio del fuoco . . . l'impotenza della somma potenza; il piccolissimo del grandissimo" (*Z* I, 1171).

43. If the content of Leopardi's early poetry was the ideal seen, and thus celebrated, as inexistent in re-

ality, the content of his late poetry is the real seen in its bareness and devoid of the ideal. It was Binni who first pointed out the poetical value of Leopardi's late poetry, whose inspiration springs from the analytical mind of the poet-philosopher. "Il presente è affrontato e risolto in fantasma poetico, non allontanato, aggirato come momento deteriore ed impoetico. Sì che il pensiero . . . è sempre al centro dell'ispirazione" (Walter Binni, *La nuova poetica leopardiana* [Florence: Sansoni, 1971], p. 38). The first edition was in 1947. This important trend in Leopardi's poetry is what Binni called "la tendenza antidillica" which was to find its apotheosis in the lines of "La ginestra" (p. 163). In "La ginestra," Amelotti wrote, "il Leopardi sente finalmente la bellezza della stessa ragione, della conoscenza chiara e disillusa" (p. 23). The only objection which can be raised to this statement is against the restrictive implication of the adverb "finally." The discovery of the "beauty" of reason was an early one in Leopardi's life. If it had not been, he would never have arrived at the creation of "La ginestra."

44. Even though the present work does not concern itself with the influence on Leopardi of classical thought, his profound knowledge of classical philosophy cannot be ignored. A serious study of the topic is the essay "Il Leopardi e i filosofi antichi" by Timpanaro. Here he points out the same characteristic as did Sansone and De Sanctis before him, namely Leopardi's sympathy for all those thinkers in whom he could find the confirmation of his own ideas. Timpanaro, however, wonders about the fact that in a materialist and a hedonist like Leopardi so few references are made to Democritus, Epicurus, and Lucretius. There is no doubt, he says, about the spiritual affinity between Leopardi and Lucretius. "Non possiamo leggere la Ginestra senza pensare al *De Rerum Natura*," yet, he concludes, "altro è l'affinità spirituale, altro la lettura e la derivazione diretta." The *manifesto* of Leopardi's materialism is the "Frammento apocrifo di Stratone di Lampsaco." Timpanaro writes that Strato was "il filosofo peripatetico che aveva accentuato, ancor più di Teofrasto, la componente scientifica dell'aristotelismo, fino a ritornare, in sostanza, all'atomismo democriteo." The choice of Strato, therefore, was "una professione di materialismo e di ateismo." However, after having examined the influence of Greek philosophy on Leopardi, Timpanaro concludes: "I maestri prediletti di filosofia furono sempre per il Leopardi i materialisti e i sensisti del secolo XVIII" (Sebastiano Timpanaro, "Il Leopardi e i filosofi antichi," in *Classicismo e illuminismo nell'Ottocento italiano* [Pisa: Nistri-Lischi, 1969], pp. 222-24, 228).

45. A list of the major works on this topic may be found in ch. 1, n. 9.

46. Alberto Frattini, "Leopardi e gli ideologi del Settecento," in *Leopardi e il Settecento* (*op. cit.,* n. 23), p. 266.

47. Twice in his letters Leopardi speaks of his ignorance of German. Answering to Carlo Antici on March 5, 1825, he comments with good humor on the trick played on him by Antici in sending him a passage "in una lingua per me inintelligibile." "Il buono è, ch'io non ho alcuno a cui ricorrere per intenderlo, ed ora appunto muore in questo spedale un tedesco senza potersi confessare, perchè in tutta la nostra colta provincia non si trova un prete che sappia quella lingua." Between 1825 and 1829 Leopardi perhaps tried to learn German, but he must not have made much progress if he answered De Sinner, who had apologized to the poet for his limited knowledge of Italian, "Piacesse al cielo ch'io sapessi o avessi mai saputo altrettanto di lingua tedesca" (*Lettere*, pp. 518, 965).

48. For information on the publication of those lists, see ch. 2, n. 8.

49. Leopardi mentions Kant's name in his *Zibaldone* for the first time together with the names of other distinguished philosophers (see n. 29) in order to show the necessity for philosophers to have a system (Z I, 633). He mentions him again, and this time as an example of obscurity—in his view peculiar to German thought (Z I, 1180). A third time in the *Zibaldone* he mentions Kant as an example of a metaphysician (Z II, 1138). In the same way he speaks about him in a footnote of his "Discorso sopra lo stato presente dei costumi degl'Italiani" where he refers to the "setta e scuola . . . metafisica, di Kant, suddivisa ancora in diverse sette" (*PP* II, 587). I do not agree with Sansone's remark that Leopardi did not even try to learn Kantian criticism because "quella filosofia non poteva offrirgli nulla." Not knowing German he could not even have made this guess. The judgment that it was "la filosofia di attardati metafisici" is superficial and gratuitous. It would have taken Leopardi a lot of hard work just to become able to decide that Kant's philosophy "non poteva offrirgli nulla" ("Leopardi e la filosofia del Settecento," p. 163).

50. The only two works by Schiller which were present in the Leopardi library during the poet's lifetime were acquired after 1830. Leopardi could not have seen them since he spent the last seven years of his life in Rome, Florence, and Naples and never went back to Recanati. In the catalog of the library they appear in the following form: Schiller, Federico: *Storia della guerra dei*

Trent'anni, tradotta dal tedesco da Antonio Benci, Capolago 1831; *I Masnadieri,* dramma, Capolago 1832. Schiller's name appears only once in the *Zibaldone* and it is brought in merely as an example in support of Leopardi's disbelief in friendship: "Anche la possibile amicizia è difficilissima . . . Schiller uomo di gran sentimento era nemico di Goethe (giacchè non solo fra tali [with the same profession] non v'è amicizia . . . ma v'è più odio che fra le persone poste in altre circostanze)" (*Z* I, 1112).

51. Quoted in French by the curator of the 1958 edition of *De l'Allemagne,* Contesse de Pange. Anne Louise Staël-Holstein, *De l'Allemagne,* II, *La Litterature et les arts* (Paris: Librairie Hachette, 1958), 92.

52. *Ibid.*

53. Speaking about Greek art, she writes: "L'homme personnifioit la nature; des nymphes habitoient les eaux, des hamadryades les forêts: mais la nature à son tour s'emparoit de l'homme, et l'on eût dit qu'il ressembloit au torrent, à la foudre, au volcan, tant il agissoit par une impulsion involontaire, et sans que la réflexion pût en rien altérer les motifs ni les suites de ses actions" (*ibid.,* p. 132). In the third chapter similar passages written by Leopardi and Schiller will be analyzed.

54. It is important to point out what Timpanaro wrote about Leopardi's interest in Epictetus and in the philosophy of the Hellenistic period. "L'interesse per Epitteto, e per la filosofia ellenistica . . . si accord[a] realmente con una fase di disempegno politico e di tentativo di adattamento alla realtà della vita, che il Leopardi attraversò all'incirca dal '24 al '27" (p. 219). This topic will be treated in the second chapter.

55. Quoted by Frattini in "Leopardi e gli Ideologi," pp. 256-57.

56. De Sanctis, p. 240.

57. Frattini, "Leopardi e gli Ideologi," p. 259.

Michael Caesar (essay date winter 1991)

SOURCE: Caesar, Michael. "Leopardi and the Knowledge of the Body." *Romance Studies* 19 (winter 1991): 21-36.

[*In the following essay, Caesar rejects earlier critical views that equated Leopardi's own physical limitations with his pessimism and agnosticism, focusing instead on the body as "disputed territory in Leopardi's work."*]

Natura umana, or come,
Se frale in tutto e vile,

Se polve ed ombra sei, tant'alto senti?
Se in parte anco gentile,
Come i più degni tuoi moti e pensieri
Son così di leggeri
Da sì basse cagioni e desti e spenti?

Englished by Ezra Pound with due pathos—O mortal nature, / If thou art / Frail and so vile in all, / How canst thou reach so high with thy poor sense; / Yet if thou art / Noble in any part / How is the noblest of thy speech and thought / So lightly wrought / Or to such base occasion lit and quenched?'—these lines complete one of the last of the canti composed by Leopardi,[2] and take on the redundancy of a great and final question. I do not think that I will be giving anything away if I say that the answer to such a question posed by a poet whose atheism and whose pessimism fascinated and horrified his contemporaries and successors, in Victorian England as in Risorgimento Italy, in about equal measure,[3] is not that despite the baseness of the body we are yet capable of exquisite feeling and right thought because we have an immortal soul, or because there is some other thing in us, which exalts us, some other, transcendental principle. That is not the answer to which Leopardi is tending with his last question. But I am not going to try and produce the answer which Leopardi does not give in the poem; rather, taking those lines as a destination towards which to argue, I shall try to explore and illustrate the gap which he speaks there; and shall attempt to show how large that gap is and how it is constituted in his writing.

There is one area of discussion concerning the body in Leopardi, regarding in particular that knowledge of the body—in the double sense of what the body knows and what we know of the body—one chapter in this story which I intend to open and then close again very quickly. It has to do with Leopardi's reputation precisely as a pessimist, as the author of a pessimism which historically always has been linked in one form or another to illness, to his deformity, to the weakness of his eyes, to his endless gastric difficulties and complaints, not to mention the particular illnesses which occur in his bodily career from time to time.[4] An early Catholic enemy of Leopardi, Niccolò Tommaseo, is remembered for his cruel summary of the poet's creed along the lines, 'There is no God because I am a hunchback, I am a hunchback because there is no God'.[5] Tommaseo's jibe mattered, because he was instrumental in blocking for many years an edition of Leopardi's complete works in Paris which might have had considerable impact on his European reputation. He was a real enemy. And this idea of the body, the sick body, as having some fundamental responsibility in the formation of Leopardi's thought recurs in different guises through the decades following Leopardi's death in 1837. At the end of the last century, there were positivist readings of Leopardi which did not hesitate to make the crude equation between illness and deformity on the one hand and a dis-torted view of reality on the other. He had a twisted body and therefore he had a twisted sense of the world; if he had been straightened out, then perhaps a clearer and more acceptable view would have resulted.[6]

More recently—and I mention this because it has had a limited but perhaps significant impact among at least some English-speaking readers—there has been the po-sition of a Marxist materialist, Sebastiano Timpanaro. Timpanaro published two books with New Left Books in the Seventies, *The Freudian Slip* and *On Material-ism,* after which he also published—it seems rather ex-traordinary at first sight—an essay on Leopardi's pessi-mistic materialism in *New Left Review,* not the place you would have expected at the time to find an essay on Leopardi.[7] But this was really part of Timpanaro's general strategy and part also of his relation with the editorial board of New Left Books, which was to re-inject a form of modern materialism into Marxism. To this end he drew strongly on Leopardi, whom he saw as a complement to Marx, in this way: that the illness here, far from being an impediment to an understanding of the world, enables Leopardi to see the world, to see the reality of life as it is. It contributes to the forma-tion—I quote from the *New Left Review* article—of 'Leopardi's sense of the heavy weight of determination exercised by nature over man, of the unhappiness of man as a physical being' (p. 36). And again (p. 38), the "human unhappiness of which Leopardi speaks is not a romantic *mal du siècle,* nor a vague existentialist *angst*: it is [. . .] above all a physical unhappiness, based on highly concrete givens: illness, old age, the ephemeral-ity of pleasure" (part of Leopardi's sense that we are both predisposed naturally to seek pleasure, to seek sat-isfaction, and always denied the full achievement of it). For Timpanaro, Leopardi was a model for a sort of ma-terialism which he was eager to present as an antidote to a Marxism which in his view was fixated on the su-perstructure. 'We cannot,' he argued in *On Materialism,* 'deny or evade the element of passivity in experience [. . .] The results of scientific research teach us that man occupies a marginal position in the universe [this is a very Leopardian lesson]; that for a very long time life did not exist on earth, and that its origin depended on very special conditions; that human thought is con-ditioned by determinate anatomical and physiological structures, and is clouded or impeded by determinate pathological alterations of these; and so on'.[8] Now this presents an alternative view of the way in which the pa-thology, the illness, the dis-ability of the body in the particular case of Leopardi can open the way to truth. The heightened awareness of the body afforded by sick-ness allows privileged insight into the material nature of the world. This view certainly comes closer than that of the positivists to how Leopardi himself probably un-derstood the relationship between his own body and his knowledge, except that Leopardi, especially the younger Leopardi, makes it clear that the sick, deformed or ugly body is a *ruined* body, something broken, which cries out for compensating ideals of wholeness and nobility, clarity and self-control.[9]

Now I am not going to follow this line any further; as I say, I want to close this particular chapter. Timpanaro's position is a Leopardian one, not because of its deter-minism which is I think a method which Leopardi would not endorse, but because of its recognition of an extreme possibility, that is to say that at the edges and at the very base of human experience is a physical limi-tation, which may or may not take pathological forms, but in any case a physical limitation which we cannot talk away. Neither Leopardi nor Timpanaro attempts to talk it away; as they would see it, it is left to others to do that.

Going beyond that, and I suppose in going beyond it trying also to reject a certain biographism in accounting for Leopardi's views of the body and uses of the body, and allowing that there is this fundamental conscious-ness of the body, I would like to argue that the body as-sumes different meanings in Leopardi's writing: it is both present and absent; and it is this presence and ab-sence which I would like to explore, in both his thought and his poetry. The body is in some sense disputed ter-ritory in Leopardi's work, in part because the cultural heritage to which Leopardi has recourse is itself a com-plex and sometimes contradictory one, in part because much depends on the angle from which one approaches his writing, whether it be as an empiricist, as a materi-alist, as an anthropologist, or as an aesthetician. In or-der to guide our discussion, I would like to keep in mind not only the question with which we started, but four broad areas which are opened up by the different points of view just mentioned: sensation, matter, ab-sence and appearance.

Let us start then from *sensation.* Leopardi comes from and draws on the heritage of eighteenth-century empiri-cism. He takes Locke for granted; he argues, and re-argues, Locke's and Hume's and then the *philosophes'* position against received ideas or innate ideas. Nothing, in Leopardian psychology, is given in the form of in-nate ideas. There are natural dispositions, but these may or may not be realized in the course of an individual life. Everything in this empiricist psychology is learned through experience. The human being becomes what he or she is through the lessons of experience. Experience is garnered first and foremost through the senses and then, following Locke and other empiricists, through the practice of internal reflections and memory. We learn to be who we are, and what we are, according to our different dispositions, according to different circum-stances. We learn to learn. Everything about the human being, everything, thoughts, feelings, is acquired and is therefore losable. On a variation of Locke's *tabula rasa,* man is described by Leopardi as a soft paste, a 'pasta molle' which is available, susceptible, to every possible shape, figure and impression and which then hardens with time. In this empiricist psychology, habituation—what Leopardi calls *assuefazione*—is all-important: we learn through practice, through repetition, through exercise, modification and adaptation of what we have already learnt to the circumstances. All differences between human beings are to be understood not in terms of what is pre-given, but in terms of the outcome of habituation, the development of this or that faculty as opposed to another, to this or that degree as opposed to another.[10]

We are told that everything about us is subsequent to existence, that is, to our own existence as species and as individuals:

> [. . .] veduto che le nostre idee non dipendono da altro che dal modo in cui le cose realmente sono, che non hanno alcuna ragione indipendente nè fuori di esso, e quindi potevano esser tutt'altre, e contrarie; ch'elle derivano in tutto e per tutto dalle nostre sensazioni, dalle assuefazioni ec.; che i nostri giudizi non hanno quindi verun fondamento universale ed eterno e immutabile ec. p. essenza; è forza che, riconoscendo tutto per relativo, e relativamente vero, rinunziamo a quell'immenso numero di opinioni che si fondano sulla falsa, benchè naturale, idea dell'assoluto, la quale, come ho detto, non ha più ragione alcuna possibile, da che non è innata, nè *indipendente dalle cose quali elle sono,* e dall'esistenza.

> ([. . .]) given that our ideas depend on nothing other than the way in which things actually are, that they have no independent or extrinsic cause, and therefore they could be entirely different, or opposite; given that they derive wholly and entirely from our sensations, from habituation, etc.; given that our judgements therefore have no essentially universal or eternal or immutable foundation; it follows of necessity that, in recognizing that all is relative, and true relatively, we should surrender that huge number of opinions which are based on the false, though natural idea of the absolute, which idea, as I have said, has no possible reason for being, seeing that it is not innate, nor *independent from things as they are,* or from existence.)[11]

Everything that we know, everything that we are, is formed within what Leopardi appears to think of as an envelope, an envelope which is human existence, which is human experience, within which not only everything that we know, but everything that we can possibly imagine is formed. There is nothing outside the envelope which influences, which penetrates it, or which gives us an answer or gives us an indication of how things are. Everything is formed from within the envelope of our experience, and whatever there might be outside that envelope—and of course there may be a multiplicity of alternative models—whatever there might be outside is precisely that which we are not and which we cannot be. That envelope, through which everything that we

know, that we can be, that we can possibly imagine, is mediated, is first and foremost constituted by sensation, the registering and communication of sensations by the senses. In this kind of empiricism, not only is all knowledge acquired originally, both for the species and for the individual, through the senses—that is not to say that it remains at the level of the senses, but the senses are as it were the limit and the first port of call of experience—but, furthermore, knowledge is perceived as coextensive with experience and habituation which in turn are perceived to be coextensive with the individual's sense of his or her own physical body. There is no human knowledge, no human experience outside the body, which for each one of us means our own body.

The body is pervasive in eighteenth-century empiricism. In the absence of a pre-given self, it is frequently the vocabulary of the body which seems best suited to describe the mysteries of interiority. The reach of the physical is extended to account for sensations, feelings, emotions ('movements of the heart' in Leopardi's words) which are clearly not occasioned directly by the five senses, but which are part and parcel of our intimate sense of ourselves. Together they form that 'other sense' for which the *philosophes* had difficulty in finding a name ('tact intérieur', 'sentiment intime', sixième sens'), but whose recognition is fundamentally constitutive of an 'age of sensibility': '[. . .] les douleurs qu'on ressent quelquefois dans l'intérieur des chairs, dans la capacité des intestins, & dans les os mêmes; les nausées, le mal-aise qui précède l'évanouïssement, la faim, la soif, l'émotion qui accompagne toutes les passions; les frissonemens, soit de douleur, soit de volupté; enfin cette multitude de sensations confuses qui ne nous abandonnent jamais, qui nous circonscrivent en quelque sorte notre corps, qui nous le rendent toûjours présent, & que par cette raison quelques metaphysiciens ont appellées *sens de la coexistence de notre corps*'.[12] For Leopardi, this radical sense of our being 'with' the body, of its ever-presence and its ubiquity, is a significant accomplishment of eighteenth-century empiricist thought, and one that he repeatedly underlines in his own reflections on self and selfhood. The body, especially when conceived of in terms of sensation, both 'external' and 'internal', is us, we are body.

Now *materialism* is not a necessary concomitant of empiricism, but in Leopardi the two do come together, and they come together in fairly radical ways. Our mind, says Leopardi, cannot either know or conceive of anything beyond the limits of matter. Even the purest and most spiritual, the most imaginary and indeterminate happiness that we can experience or desire can never be anything but material, for our every faculty is confined within the terms of matter. We cannot conceive of any emotion unless it be expressed in material form or material likeness. Arguing against the followers of Leibniz, he affirms that once you go beyond matter, once matter has been broken down into its smallest components, you find not spirit but nothing; you cannot argue the existence of spirit from that of matter. And on another occasion, in a lapidary sentence, 'I limiti della materia sono i limiti delle umane idee', the limits of matter are the limits of human ideas.[13]

Some years on, Leopardi adopts an even more radical formulation for the relationship between matter and thought:

> Parrebbe che secondo ogni ragione, secondo l'andamento naturale dell'intelletto e del discorso, noi avessimo dovuto dire e tenere p. indubitato, *la materia può pensare, la materia pensa e sente*. Se io non conoscessi alcun corpo elastico, forse io direi: la materia non può, in dispetto della sua gravità, muoversi in tale o tal direzione ec. Così se io non conoscessi la elettricità, la proprietà dell'aria di essere instrumento del suono; io direi la materia non è capace di tali e tali azioni e fenomeni, l'aria non può fare i tali effetti. Ma perchè io conosco dei corpi elastici, elettrici ec. io dico, e nessuno me lo contrasta: la materia può far questo e questo, è capace di tali e tali fenomeni. Io veggo dei corpi che pensano e che sentono. Dico dei corpi; cioè uomini ed animali; che io non veggo, non sento, non so nè posso sapere che sieno altro che corpi. Dunque dirò: la materia può pensare e sentire; pensa e sente.

> (It would seem that by all reason and following the natural line of thought and speech we should say, and hold to it unwaveringly, that matter can think, that *matter thinks and feels*. If I did not know of any body possessing elasticity, perhaps I would say: matter cannot act against its own gravity and move in such or such direction etc. Similarly, if I did not know about electricity, or the property of air as an instrument of sound; I would say that matter is not capable of such and such actions or phenomena, air cannot produce these effects. But because I am acquainted with elastic or electric bodies, I say, and no-one contradicts me: Matter can do this or that, it is capable of such and such phenomena. I see bodies which think and feel. I say bodies, that is to say human beings and animals, for I do not see, I do not hear, I do not know nor can I know that they are anything other than bodies. So I say: matter can think and feel; it does think and feel.)[14]

Not only then do we have a psychology which is body-bound, in the sense that whatever is the extent of our senses of ourselves is the extent of human presence in the world, but this body is material, this presence is an entirely material one, it is something that is confined within, or coextensive with, matter. People think that 'thinking matter' is a paradox. But the fact that matter thinks is indisputable, declares Leopardi; given that we, when we think, cannot know or conceive anything but matter, we feel thought physically ('noi sentiamo corporalmente il pensiero'), and we can see that the modifications of thought depend wholly on sensations and on the state of our physical being.[15]

So to conclude this first half of the paper, on the presence of the body, I would argue that for Leopardi our whole sense of ourselves and our whole sense of the world is coextensive with our bodies, our bodies are matter, which in turn is the limit of everything that we know, think and feel—not a limit to be overcome, in a Platonist or a Christian sense, as a prison or a barrier, but that which sets the limit, beyond which we cannot conceivably cross. The ultimate destiny of matter is another question to which Leopardi turns on various occasions—perhaps matter will disappear in some way, leaving space for what we can only conceive of as emptiness, a desert, or perhaps matter is eternal, perhaps it always reconstitutes and renews itself.[16] But leaving that aside, as a question beyond the scope of this paper, we are left with the sense of the absolute indispensability for Leopardi's thought, and for Leopardi's conception of ourselves and the world, of a material, physical, corporeal universe.

Now it is one thing to consider the role of the body in the formation of consciousness, to consider it psychologically, which is what we have been doing so far. It is another thing to look at it historically and socially, and this is where we come to that sense of the gap which I illustrated with the lines from *Sopra il ritratto* at the beginning. In the first case, psychologically, the body, as I have tried to argue, is ubiquitous, pervasive; it is our only way of knowing, it is knowledge. In the second, looked at historically and socially, the body is more often a barrier to knowing and is itself frequently unknown. This is not only a matter of the same topic being examined from different perspectives, with a different 'disciplinary' emphasis. The shift of attention away from the presence of the body to its absence is also a measure of Leopardi's complex relation to the tradition of Enlightenment thought to which he was in many respects an heir; for while Leopardi willingly accepted, as we have seen, the most radical consequences of a rationally inferred psychology, he did not share any of the optimism or confidence of those who imagined that ever greater understanding must lead to ever greater happiness. Thus for Leopardi, the Fall, in a re-reading of *Genesis,* is not, as Christian apologists would have it, the triumph of the senses over some other state, which he polemically calls reason, but exactly the opposite: the story of the Fall is the story of the triumph of reason over the senses, so that what is lost in that historical, mythological, account is some special sense of the body.[17] Psychologically we work within a bodily universe, but historically there is in Leopardi a sense of a loss of the special status of the body. There was a time, in that Genesis story, a pre-lapsarian time, an elsewhere, a time that is described as ancient *(antico),* in Leopardi's very elastic term (it means pre-civilized, it may mean primitive, it may mean antique, it may mean something as close to us as the Augustan age, a classical time), an ancient time in which the body was far more important than the spirit. Or, to put it conversely, the characteristic of modernity is that spirit, spiritualization has occurred and that spirit has taken over, or is taking over, from the body as a means of social intercourse, as a means of social communication. Moderns are far less physically vigorous and active than the ancients, the body is weaker in modern society than it is in primitive societies or than it was in ancient society, modern society takes no care for the physical education of the body, and so on.[18] There is a sense then in which attention to the body has become less in modern times, and this is a loss; and at the same time the communicative power of the body, historically, has weakened. Leopardi talks about imaginative poetry as though it were a physical thing, that is to say, what is characteristic about imaginative poetry, the poetry of the ancients, is that it communicates directly through the senses, images being seen precisely as sensistic creations, as opposed to modern poetry which reflects, and which explores feelings and which ruminates on feeling.[19] So that the body in this version of things has, or had, a function of direct communication between human beings. It was the way in which people—Leopardi now drawing on a Rousseauesque distinction mediated through Mme de Staël—acted more naturally; nature required, as it were, a more direct use and a more direct presence of the body, and that is disappearing. The body, therefore, becomes, in this account, that which modernity has lost; in other words, it becomes the name for something which is invisible or at least which is very difficult to find.

Of the two poems to which I now wish to draw attention, the first one, *Alla sua donna,* 'To his lady',[20] seems to revel in the *absence* of a body, a desired body, a loved body. When Leopardi published it, he announced it as a love poem, but as a love poem that was unusual in that it would not arouse jealousy, he thought, because it was addressed to a woman 'che non si trova', who doesn't exist.[21] Now this poem has been read as almost a Platonizing poem, so something quite unexpected in the Leopardi who was a materialist and an empiricist and who does not believe in innate ideas. But if we read through even just the first two stanzas, we can perhaps qualify that judgement.

> Cara beltà che amore
> Lunge m'inspiri o nascondendo il viso,
> Fuor se nel sonno il core
> Ombra diva mi scuoti,
> O ne' campi ove splenda
> Più vago il giorno e di natura il riso;
> Forse tu l'innocente
> Secol beasti che dall'oro ha nome,
> Or leve intra la gente
> Anima voli? o te la sorte avara
> Ch'a noi t'asconde, agli avvenir prepara?
>
> Viva mirarti omai
> Nulla spene m'avanza;
> S'allor non fosse, allor che ignudo e solo
> Per novo calle a peregrina stanza

> Verrà lo spirto mio. Già sul novello
> Aprir di mia giornata incerta e bruna,
> Te viatrice in questo arido suolo
> Io mi pensai. Ma non è cosa in terra
> Che ti somigli; e s'anco pari alcuna
> Ti fosse al volto, agli atti, alla favella,
> Saria, così conforme, assai men bella.

> Gentle beauty, who with love
> inspires me from afar, though near your face is hid,
> save when, image divine,
> you thrill my heart in sleep,
> or in the fields
> where nature's smile beams most and day is handsomer;
> once perhaps you blessed
> the so-called golden age of innocence,
> and now, ethereal soul,
> you flit among mankind? or does begrudging fate,
> hiding you from us, reserve you for a future date?
>
> By now I have no hope
> to see your living form;
> unless perhaps one of these years my soul,
> when stripped and lone, over an untrod path
> shall reach an unfamiliar distant land.
> Once at the dawn of my uncertain, gloomy days,
> I fancied you a fellow-traveler
> on this sterile soil. But nothing on this earth
> resembles you; and even if one were your like
> in countenance, in gesture, and in voice,
> though she be so similar, she would be much less fair.[22]

Now this is a woman who can not be found, who does not exist, who is conceived of precisely as not having body, or if there is a body, it is a body that we are never going to see in this mortal life. If it were possible, the poem says, for this mortal vision to take form, then of course I would be enraptured; but it is not possible. 'If' ('se') is the key word in this poem; it is repeated in all five stanzas (above, in lines 3, 14, 20) and it quickly becomes clear that in this love-poem addressed to a vision, it is the vision itself, the image, which is the object of desire, as well as the object of address.

It may be useful now to consider this attitude of the poet alongside reflections in the *Zibaldone* which he penned just a few days before writing the poem in August-September 1823. These are pages in which Leopardi continues his thought about the way in which all of our knowledge is based on experience and in which the physical is taken as the bedrock of everything that we know; but also, in these same pages, he is linking that argument with the point about how, historically and anthropologically, we have lost a sense of the body. He talks about the transition from direct knowledge of the bodies of others, in primitive society, ancient society, when nakedness was the rule, to what happens when human beings begin to clothe themselves—so this again, I suppose, is a further comment on the Genesis story.

Ma introdotto l'uso de' vestimenti [. . .] la donna all'uomo (massime al giovane inesperto) e l'uomo alla donna sono divenuti esseri quasi misteriosi. Le loro forme nascoste hanno lasciato luogo all'immaginazione di chi le mira così vestite. Per l'altra parte l'inclinazion e il desiderio naturale dell'un sesso verso l'altro non ha, per questo cangiamento di circostanze esteriori, potuto nè cessare nè scemare nel genere umano, niente più che negli altri animali. L'uomo dunque (e così la donna verso l'uomo) si è veduto sommamente e sopra tutte le cose trasportato [. . .] verso un essere quasi tutto a lui nascosto, un essere che sin dalla sua nascita non se gli è rappresentato nè agli occhi nè al pensiero, o non suole rappresentarsegli, che velato tutto e quasi arcano.

(But with the introduction of clothing [. . .] women have become as it were a mystery in the eyes of men (especially the young and inexperienced) and likewise men in the eyes of women. Their hidden forms have given way to the imagination of the one who regards them thus clothed. On the other hand, the natural inclination and desire that one sex has for the other has not been diminished or annulled by this change in exterior circumstances in human beings any more than in any other animal. So men (and women likewise) have found themselves drawn above all things [. . .] towards a being which is almost wholly hidden to them, a being which since their birth they have as a rule never seen or thought of other than entirely veiled and almost arcane.)[23]

So we see—and this is an argument about how physical causes give rise to vast spiritual effects—how a purely extrinsic circumstance, something that is a matter of choice or decision (Leopardi's word is 'removibile'), something as 'accidental' as the adoption of clothing can lead to fundamental changes in the relations between the sexes; the concealment of the body has rendered each sex mysterious to the other, with perhaps predictable but no less far-reaching consequences:

> [. . .] il pensiero dico e la vista e il consorzio di questo essere l'immerge in una quantità di concezioni, d'immaginazioni, d'illusioni, di sentimenti, vivissimi e profondissimi perchè quell'essere gli è per natura dolcissimo e carissimo, ma nel tempo stesso confusissimi, incertissimi, per lo più falsissimi, sublimi, vasti, perchè quel medesimo essere trovandosi essergli quasi tutto misterioso e quasi cosa segreta ed occulta, i pensieri e i sentimenti ch'esso gli desta, sono tutti capitalmente e quasi esclusivamente governati e modificati e figurati, e in gran parte prodotti e creati, dalla fantasia.

> ([. . .] so seeing, thinking of, being with this creature immerses them in a great quantity of profound and vital thoughts and images and illusions and feelings, for that being is eminently sweet and dear to them, but at the same time those thoughts and images and illusions and feelings are confused, uncertain, for the most part completely false, vast and sublime, because, since that same being is almost wholly mysterious to them, as it were a secret and hidden thing, all the thoughts and feelings which he or she inspires in them are almost exclusively governed and modified and shaped, and to a large extent produced and created, by the imagination.)[24]

'The thoughts and the feelings which arise from this mixture of extreme desire and natural tendency on the one hand and the obscure idea of the object of such desire and tendency on the other are almost mystical,' he goes on to argue (*Zib* 3308), adding in a footnote that 'it is for this reason that a man thinks of women in general, and especially the woman he loves, as something divine, as a being of a different race from his own, etc.'

I quote these pages partly in order to provide a linkage, a possible support to this poem which allows the hypothesis, as he says in the final stanza, of an eternal idea, of a Platonic idea: 'Se dell'eterne idee / L'una sei tu [. . .]', If you are one of the eternal ideas [. . .], ll. 45 ff. The combination of the passage from the *Zibaldone* and the poem would allow a 'naturalistic' interpretation of the poem, as the actual writing-out of a fantasy, the origins of which are explained in the *Zibaldone*, origins deriving from the condition of clothedness. In fact, in the poem we have a situation where an idea is imagined as looking for a body, which it is unable to reach, or to find ('if I could imagine you as a body, then that would be a rapturous event'). In the *Zibaldone* we have the description of bodies which are unable to be bodies because the modern sensibility requires, or has taken the form of, an extreme spiritualization. But this refusal of the body, or this absence of the body, may be expressed still in sensistic and empiricist terms, for one can read the poem in this way: if you exist, as indeed you do exist in my imagination, my attention focusses not on the spirit, not on the Platonic alternative to the body, but on the image. What emerges in the absence of the body, both in modern society, and in the poem *Alla sua donna,* is not a religious or spiritual alternative to bodiliness, but something which is like a shadow of the body, which is the *appearance* of body. What in fact we deal with in reality, in relations with others, is something which takes the place of that original substantial sense of the body which belonged to antiquity, or which belonged to the pre-lapsarian age, to the Garden of Eden, and we deal instead with a veil, or with a shadow, or with something that is more apparent than real, and yet which is, still, all that we can know.

So we come finally to the poem from which I took my original point of departure, *Sopra il ritratto di una bella donna scolpito nel monumento sepolcrale della medesima,* faced with which we might ask: Where is the body in this text?

> Tal fosti: or qui sotterra
> Polve e scheletro sei. Su l'ossa e il fango
> Immobilmente collocato invano,
> Muto, mirando dell'etadi il volo,
> 05 Sta, di memoria solo
> E di dolor custode, il simulacro
> Della scorsa beltà. Quel dolcé sguardo,
> Che tremar fe', se, come or sembra, immoto

In altrui s'affisò; quel labbro, ond'alto
10 Par, come d'urna piena,
    Traboccare il piacer; quel collo, cinto
    Già di desio; quell'amorosa mano,
    Che spesso, ove fu porta,
    Sentì gelida far la man che strinse;
15 E il seno, onde la gente
    Visibilmente di pallor si tinse,
    Furo alcun tempo: or fango
    Ed ossa sei: la vista
    Vituperosa e trista un sasso asconde.

20 Così riduce il fato
    Qual sembianza fra noi parve più viva
    Immagine del ciel. Misterio eterno
    Dell'esser nostro. Oggi d'eccelsi, immensi
    Pensieri e sensi inenarrabil fonte,
25 Beltà grandeggia, e pare,
    Quale splendor vibrato
    Da natura immortal su queste arene,
    Di sovrumani fati,
    Di fortunati regni e d'aurei mondi
30 Segno e sicura spene
    Dare al mortale stato:
    Diman, per lieve forza,
    Sozzo a vedere, abominoso, abbietto
    Divien quel che fu dianzi
35 Quasi angelico aspetto,
    E dalle menti insieme
    Quel che da lui moveva
    Ammirabil concetto, si dilegua.

    Desiderii infiniti
40 E visioni altere
    Crea nel vago pensiere,
    Per natural virtù, dotto concento;
    Onde per mar delizioso, arcano
    Erra lo spirto umano,
45 Quasi come a diporto
    Ardito notator per l'Oceano:
    Ma se un discorde accento
    Fere l'orecchio, in nulla
    Torna quel paradiso in un momento.

50 Natura umana, or come,
    Se frale in tutto e vile,
    Se polve ed ombra sei, tant'alto senti?

    Se in parte anco gentile,
    Come i più degni tuoi moti e pensieri
55 Son così di leggeri
    Da sì basse cagioni e desti e spenti?

Such you were: who now underground
Are skeleton and dust. Above the bones and dirt,
Immobile and useless, a silent
Witness to the flight of years,

05 Sole guardian of memory and grief,
    Stands this image of past beauty.
    That gentle gaze, if bent fixedly on others,
    (As it seems now) made them tremble;
    That lip, whence deep pleasure seems to over-
10 Flow, as from a brimming urn; that neck,
    Once girt with desire; that loving hand,
    That often, where it touched,
    Felt the hand it grasped grow chill;

And the breast, whose pallor
15 Visibly tinged the beholder—
    All these once were: and now are only
    Dirt and bones; the sad
    And infamous sight a tomb conceals.

    Thus does Fate bring low
20 That form that among us seemed Heaven's
    Liveliest image. Eternal mystery
    Of our being: today the ineffable source
    Of vast, lofty thoughts and feelings,
    Beauty grows big, and appears
25 Like the tremulous glory
    Of immortal nature above these shores,
    Giving to man's estate
    The sign and certain hope
    Of superhuman destiny,
30 Of blessed realms and worlds of gold.
    Tomorrow, at a light blow,
    It becomes abominable, abject,
    Dreadful to behold, that before
    Had almost an angel's face;
35 And that which joined the mind
    To inspire it with
    Marvelous conceits, has vanished.

    Infinite desires
    And lofty visions
40 Are bred in eager thought
    By learned harmony's inherent power;
    Whence, mysterious, through a delightful sea,
    The human spirit wanders,
    As a bold swimmer wanders
45 Through the ocean for his sport;
    But if a note of discord
    Strike the ear, instantly
    That paradise is turned to naught.

    Ah, human nature, how
50 If utterly base and frail,
    If dust and shadow, can you feel deep sentiment?

    If you are yet partly noble
    How can your finest impulses and thoughts
    Thus so easily,
55 By such causes, be aroused and spent?[25]

We do not have the space here for the detailed reading which this poem requires. It is perfectly clear that the open questions of the last stanza with which I began depend in part for their context, if not for their explanation, on the lines which immediately precede them, on the joy of music, and on the potential for 'that paradise' to be instantaneously annulled. To focus on the body in the poem is to set on its way a reading that is certainly partial but no less indispensable to the poem's outcome. The body is there as a corpse and a rotting corpse, one, however, that is hidden; the 'sasso', the tombstone, has the function of concealing the body in that aspect. The body is also, at a 'higher' level, perceived in the form of a monument, or there is a monument which has the function of reevoking the body of the dead woman. All the details about the effect of the woman's beauty in the world in which she lived are inferred from the monument, from the carving. All that remains of that effect is the sepulchral monument itself. The rest can only be inferred. What is inferred is a presence which is noticeable above all, indeed uniquely, for its effect upon others, and its effect, as in **Alla sua donna,** upon the imagination. This ghostly body, evoked through the stone, contained within the stone, is an 'image' (l. 22), a 'source' (l. 24), a 'sign' (l. 30).

Thus we return to the paradoxical interplay between presence and absence already described; the body here portrayed is that which absolutely we cannot see and which is taboo in a sense, that which is put away and hidden, just as the body of the ancients is something that in modernity we cover; and it is at the same time an image, an appearance, a source of effects.

And that is as far as I can go at the moment in thinking about, and trying to comment on, that last question: if you are nothing, in the Horatian words, but dust and shadow (*pulvis et umbra*), how can you think or feel so high, or so deep? The question does not lend itself to paraphrase, precisely because it is the outcome of a way of thinking about the self which tends towards disintegration. All that I can do, as I hope that I have done, is to illustrate the space, the gap—to which that question it seems to me addresses itself—between a body on the one hand conceived of as ubiquity, as everything that we are, and at the same time a body conceived of as nothing, as an absence, or as something that we cannot any longer feel ourselves at ease in, and as something that is replaced, by a shadow, by a presence, by what is actually distinctly not body.

Notes

1. Ezra Pound, 'Her Monument, the Image Cut thereon. From the Italian of Leopardi', in his *Canzoni* (London, 1911), pp. 28-29.

2. 'Sopra il ritratto di una bella donna scolpito nel monumento sepolcrale della medesima', written some time between 1831 and 1835, first published in Giacomo Leopardi, *Canti,* Napoli, Starita, 1835; no. XXXI in modern editions of the *Canti.* The edition referred to here is Giacomo Leopardi, *Poesie e prose* vol. I, *Poesie,* a cura di M. A. Rigoni (Milano, 1987). The lines quoted are ll. 50-56.

3. For Leopardi's fortunes in Victorian England, see B. Corrigan, 'The poetry of Leopardi in Victorian England, 1837-1878', in *English Miscellany* XIV, 1963, pp. 171-84.

4. See V. Gazzola Stacchini, *Alle origini del 'sentimento' leopardiano* (Napoli 1974); R. Di Fernando, *L'amarezza del lauro. Storia clinica di Giacomo Leopardi* (Bologna, 1987).

5. 'On vit sortir du sein des flots [. . .] un petit comte, qui chantait comme une grenouille de Ce-phisse, et disait en chantant: "Il n'y a pas de Dieu, parce que je suis bossu, je suis bossu parce qu'il n'y a pas de Dieu." Quoted in Iris Origo, *Leopardi. A study in solitude* (London, 1953), p. 171. Origo's biography, which remains the most authoritative in English, also lays great stress on the contribution of Leopardi's 'physical sufferings' to his thought and poetry.

6. For the full story of the clinical appropriation of Leopardi's symptoms after his death and the medicalization of his writing in the nineteenth century and beyond, see Mario Picchi, *Storie di casa Leopardi,* (Milano, 1986), especially pp. 291-326.

7. Sebastiano Timpanaro, *On materialism* (London, 1975 [tr. of *Sul materialismo,* Pisa 1970]); *The Freudian slip; psychoanalysis and textual criticism,* (London, 1976 [tr. of *Il lapsus freudiano: psicanalisi e critica testuale,* Firenze, 1975]); 'The pessimistic materialism of Giacomo Leopardi', in *New Left Review* 116, July-Aug. 1979, pp. 29-50. See also, more recently, *Antileopardiani e neo-moderati nella sinistra italiana* (Pisa, 1985), especially pp. 188-97.

8. S. Timpanaro, *On materialism,* pp. 35-36.

9. On the ruined body see the famous declaration in a letter to Pietro Giordani of 2 March 1818: 'io mi sono rovinato con sette anni di studio matto e disperatissimo in quel tempo che mi s'andava formando e mi si doveva assodare la complessione', 'I ruined myself with seven years of mad and desperate study just at the time that my constitution was forming and should have been strengthened' (*Epistolario di Giacomo Leopardi,* nuova ed. a cura di F. Moroncini, vol. I (Firenze, 1934), p. 162; and especially the poem *Ultimo canto di Saffo,* 'Sappho's last song', written in May 1822, *Canti* IX.

10. Most of the observations in this and the following paragraphs are derived from Leopardi's notebooks, known as the *Zibaldone,* some four-and-a-half thousand pages of reading notes, diary entries, aphorisms, reflections, essays, recollections, dialogues with himself, which Leopardi began when he had just turned nineteen in the summer of 1817 and went on adding to up until December 1832, but with the great bulk of the writing done between 1820 and 1823—the *Zibaldone,* as Neuro Bonifazi has observed, is 'an early work'. In accordance with normal practice, the page-references are to the numeration of Leopardi's autograph. The edition referred to is Giacomo Leopardi, *Zibaldone di pensieri,* Edizione critica e annotata a cura di Giuseppe Pacella, 3 vols. (Milano, 1991).

For the critique of innate ideas, see *Zib* 443-445 (n.d.); on the sensations as "sole nostre maestre", our only teachers, see *Zib* 1339-1341 (17 July

1821); on *assuefazione,* including the habit of habituation, see *Zib* 1370-71 (22 July 1821), 1628-29 (4 Sept. 1821), 2162-65 (24 Nov. 1821), and *passim*; on the 'conformability' of human beings, cf. *Zib* 2599 (6 August 1822 and addendum of 1827), 3807-08 (Oct. 1823), 3892-93 (18 Nov. 1823). The 'soft paste' is referred to in *Zib* 1452 (4 August 1821); 'Ciascun uomo è come una pasta molle, suscettiva d'ogni possibile figura, impronta ec. S'indurisce col tempo [. . .].'

11. *Zib* 1617-18 (3 Sept. 1821); emphases are Leopardi's.

12. [A.-R.-J. Turgot], article on 'Existence', in the *Encyclopédie, ou dictionnaire raisonné des sciences, des arts et des métiers . . .* , vol. VI (Paris, 1756), p. 261; emphases are Turgot's.

13. 'La mente nostra non può non solamente conoscere, ma neppur concepire alcuna cosa oltre i limiti della materia' (*Zib* 601, 4 Feb. 1821); '[. . .] ogni qualunque facoltà dell'animo nostro finisce assolutamente sull'ultimo confine della materia, ed è confinata intieramente dentro i termini della materia' (*Zib* 1025-26, 9 May 1821); 'noi non possiamo concepire verun affetto dell'animo nostro se non sotto forme o simiglianze materiali' (*Zib* 1262, 2 July 1821); 'Arrivate anche se potete, agli atomi o particelle indivisibili e senza parti. Saranno sempre materia. Al di là non troverete mica lo spirito ma il nulla' (*Zib* 1635-36, 5 Sept. 1821). The thought on the limits of human ideas is dated 3 Sept. 1823 (*Zib* 3341).

14. *Zib* 4251-52 (9 March 1827); emphases are Leopardi's.

15. 'Che la materia pensi, è un fatto. Un fatto, perchè noi pensiamo; e noi non sappiamo, non conosciamo di essere, non possiamo conoscere, concepire, altro che materia. Un fatto, perchè noi veggiamo che le modificazioni del pensiero dipendono totalm. dalle sensazioni, dallo stato del nostro fisico; che l'animo nostro corrisponde in tutto alle varietà ed alle variazoni del nostro corpo. Un fatto, perchè noi sentiamo corporalm. il pensiero [. . .]' (*Zib* 4288-89, 18 Sept. 1827).

16. The alternatives are explored in two of Leopardi's *Operette morali,* respectively 'Cantico del gallo silvestre' (Nov. 1824) and 'Frammento apocrifo di Stratone da Lampsaco' (autumn 1825). In a note at the end of the earlier piece, Leopardi writes: 'This is a poetic, not a philosophical conclusion. Philosophically speaking existence, which never began, will never end.' Cf. Giacomo Leopardi, *Moral Tales,* tr. Patrick Creagh (Manchester, 1983), p. 258, n. 12.

17. See *Zib* 433-435 (n.d.) and 2939-41 (11 July 1823); and, more extensively, the 'founding' fable

of the *Operette morali,* 'Storia del genere umano', Story of the human race (Jan.-Feb. 1824).

18. There are frequent references to these phenomena *passim* in the *Zibaldone*; they are summarized in A. Bonadeo, 'Il corpo e il vigore nello *Zibaldone* di Leopardi', in *Italianistica* V, 1976, pp. 55-65.

19. The failure of the Italian Romantic theorists to acknowledge the 'commercio co' sensi' ('commerce with the senses') which characterized all true poetry, and ancient poetry in particular, was one of the reasons which provoked Leopardi to compose his youthful, unpublished, critique of the pro-Romantic arguments advanced by the critic Ludovico Di Breme. See Leopardi's 'Discorso di un italiano intorno alla poesia romantica' (1818) in *Poesie e prose,* ed. cit., vol. II (Milano, 1988), p. 350.

20. Written in September 1823, no. XVIII in modern editions of the *Canti*.

21. See *Poesie e prose,* ed. cit., vol. I, pp. 163-65.

22. Translated by Jean-Pierre Barricelli, in *Leopardi. Poems and Prose,* ed. A. Flores (Bloomington and London, 1966), pp. 72-74.

23. *Zib* 3305-06 (29-30 August 1823).

24. *Zib* 3307.

25. Translated by Muriel Kittel, in *Leopardi. Poems and Prose* cit., pp. 142-47.

Massimo Mandolini Pesaresi (essay date 1992)

SOURCE: Pesaresi, Massimo Mandolini. "Leopardi's Platonic Temper." In *Giacomo Leopardi: Estetica e Poesia,* edited by Emilio Speciale, pp. 57-75. Ravenna, Italy: Longo Editore, 1992.

[*In the following essay, Pesaresi discusses the critical debate on whether or not Leopardi was a Platonic thinker, noting that the relationship between ethics and aesthetics in the poet's work was complicated and ambiguous.*]

The dispute on Leopardi's Platonism, being partly a terminological one, risks to be marred with nominalistic elusiveness. Before deciding to which extent Leopardi was a "Platonic" thinker, one should have a fairly precise and consistent definition of Platonism: which, of course, is not always the case, and, in a sense, cannot be the case, because such an apodeictic clarity is rarely the lot of historical discussions.

Out of the extreme complexity and ambiguity of the notion of Platonism, therefore, I will simply point to a few aspects that have been notably relevant to Leopardi's own reflection.

In his youth, when barely sixteen, Leopardi had translated Porphyry's *Vita Plotini:*[1] a monument of classical scholarship which earned him the praises of the German philologist Friedrich Creuzer. A few years later, in 1823, he accepted a proposal from the printer De Romanis to translate Plato's entire work[2].

In spite of this deep familiarity with the Platonic and Neo-Platonic traditions, however, Leopardi's observations on the subject are very rare, and mostly devoted to philological and linguistic matters. Among them, however, is a dense and illuminating page of the *Zibaldone,* written in September 1821, two years before the composition of the Platonic canzone *Alla sua donna*:

> Il sistema di Platone delle idee preesistenti alle cose, esistenti per se, eterne, necessarie, indipendenti e dalle cose e da Dio: non solo non è chimerico, bizzarro capriccioso, arbitrario, fantastico, ma tale che fa meraviglia come un antico sia potuto giungere all'ultimo fondo dell'astrazione, e vedere sin dove necessariamente conduceva la nostra opinione intorno all'essenza delle cose e nostra, alla natura astratta del bello e brutto, buono e cattivo, vero e falso. Platone scoprì quello ch'è infatti, che la nostra opinione intorno alle cose, che le tiene indubitabilmente per assolute, che riguarda come assolute le affermazioni, e negazioni, non poteva né potrà mai salvarsi se non supponendo delle immagini e delle ragioni di tutto ciò ch'esiste, eterne necessarie ec. e indipendenti dallo stesso Dio, perché altrimenti:
> 1. si dovrà cercare la ragione di Dio, il quale se il bello il buono il vero ec. non è assoluto né necessario, non avrà nessuna ragione di essere, né di essere tale o tale;
> 2. posto pur che l'avesse, tutto ciò che noi crediamo assoluto e necessario non avrebbe altra ragione che il voler di Dio; e quindi il bello il buono il vero, a cui l'uomo suppone un'astratta essenza, assoluta, indipendente non sarebbe tale, se non perché Dio volesse, potendo volere altrimenti, e al contrario. Ora, trovate false e insussistenti le idee di Platone, è certissimo che qualunque negazione e affermazione assoluta, rovina interamente da se, ed è maraviglioso come abbiamo distrutte quelle, senza punto dubitar di queste.

> (16 Settembre 1821)[3].

Leopardi's poignant remark gets to the core of a fundamental *vexata quaestio* in Western philosophy. As it appears from a previous note in the *Zibaldone,* written on that same day[4], Leopardi is concerned with the notion of a God, which be the origin of moral law: the creative act can be conceived either as the result of volition (in a personal God) or as the necessary unfolding of a perfect essence. The former hypothesis, which accounts for different moral laws, given to mankind in the course of time, implies a contradiction (the idea of a God which may not choose perfection) usually overlooked (or dismissed) by theologians.

Within this frame of reference, Plato's philosophy of Ideas appeared to Leopardi as the most abstract (and most genuinely philosophical) theory about the neces-

sary progression from essence to existence. The very fact that the Ideas are independent of God delivers them from the condition of possibility, inherent to the act of volition itself. Envisaging the Platonic doctrine within the scope of the metaphysical issue of the relation between essence and existence, Leopardi emphasizes the rational legacy of a philosopher who has often been all too easily confused with the mystical thinking of some epigons of his. The world of Ideas is not to be viewed, therefore, as the imaginary counterpart of the real world, but rather as a powerful abstraction, aimed at preserving the essences of truth, goodness, and beauty by—figuratively—separating them from their actual occurrences (their absoluteness, in fact, would be endangered even by the arbitrariness of God's will).

There is also another aspect of Plato's philosophy which sets him aside from his followers: his capacity of conceiving abstractions with all the color and warmth of living persons. In the *Phaedrus,* for instance, Plato celebrates the absolute Beauty with such an enthusiasm that may sound inappropriate for an Idea. Indeed, a certain philosophical tradition has accustomed us to see abstraction as something colorless, cold, and motionless: an entity bereft, by way of negation, of all the qualities that belong to the warm turbulence of life. Plato, instead, although inheriting from Parmenides the notion of absolute eternal essence (the world of Ideas may be conceived as a plural reflection of the Eleatic One) makes it vivid with all the characters—I would say the charms—of phenomena. Outstripped of the colorful garment of Pythagorean metempsychosis, Plato's doctrine can be construed as a theory of knowledge in which memory makes the One vibrate with all the richness of the Many, reflected and almost contained in it. Precisely to this quality of remembering was referring Leopardi in his scattered and extraordinarily insightful remarks on the poetic nature of reminiscence. In a note of the *Zibaldone,* dated September 11, 1821, Leopardi writes:

> *Scire nostrum est reminisci* dicono i platonici. Male nel loro intendimento, cioè che l'anima non faccia che ricordarsi di ciò che seppe innanzi di unirsi al corpo. Benissimo però può applicarsi al nostro sistema e di Locke. Perché infatti l'uomo, (e l'animale) niente sapendo per natura ec. tanto sa, quanto si ricorda, cioè quanto ha imparato mediante le esperienze de' sensi. Si può dire che la memoria sia l'unica fonte del sapere, ch'ella sia legata, e quasi costituisca tutte le nostre cognizioni ed abilità materiali e mentali, e che senza memoria l'uomo non saprebbe nulla, e non saprebbe far nulla. E siccome ho detto che la memoria non è altro che assuefazione, nasce (benché prestissimo) da lei, ed è contenuta in lei, così vicendevolmente può dirsi ch'ella contiene tutte le assuefazioni, ed è il fondamento di tutte, vale a dire d'ogni nostra scienza e attitudine. Anche le materiali sono legate in gran parte colla memoria. Insomma, siccome la memoria è essenzialmente assuefazione dell'intelletto, così può dirsi

che tutte le assuefazioni dell'animale sieno quasi memorie proprie de' respettivi organi che si assuefanno[5].

Leopardi uses the technical language of the empiricists and the notion of "assuefazione" is as crucial to him as, perhaps, it is uninteresting to us. Besides that parlance, however, there is a remarkable insistence, in his notes, on the intellectual nature[6] of memory and, more specifically, on the creative character[7] of it (for which he uses the word "imitativo," in which the sensism of the Enlightenment seems to meet with the old Platonic prejudice). This concept of remembrance as faculty of the intellect may seem to be inconsistent with its fundamentally poetic nature, which is supposed to rest on the very vagueness and indistinctness produced by the act of remembering:

> Un oggetto qualunque, per esempio un luogo, un sito, una campagna, per bella che sia, se non desta alcuna rimembranza, non è poetica punto a vederla. La medesima, ed anche un sito, un oggetto qualunque, affatto poetico in sé, sarà poetichissimo a rimembrarlo. La rimembranza è essenziale e principale nel sentimento poetico, non per altro, se non perché il presente, qual ch'egli sia, non può essere poetico; e il poetico, in uno o in altro modo, si trova sempre consistere nel lontano, nell'indefinito, nel vago.

> (Recanati, 14 Dicembre, Domenica, 1828)[8].

The particular quality of this vagueness, however, is more clearly expressed in another entry of the *Zibaldone,* about three months later:

> Notano quelli che hanno molto viaggiato (Viesseux parlando meco), che per loro una causa di piacere viaggiando è questa: che, avendo veduto molti luoghi, facilmente quelli per cui si abbattono a passare di mano in mano, ne richiamano loro alla mente degli altri già veduti innanzi, e questa reminiscenza per se e semplicemente li diletta (e così li diletta poi, per la stessa causa, l'osservare i luoghi, passeggiando ec., dove fissano il loro soggiorno. Così accade: un luogo ci riesce romantico e sentimentale, se non per sé, che non ha nulla di ciò, ma perché ci desta la memoria di un altro luogo da noi conosciuto, nel quale poi se noi ci troveremo attualmente, non ci riescirà (né mai ci riuscì) punto romantico né sentimentale.

> (10 Marzo 1829)[9]

In this passage, remembrance appears, besides the sentimental overtones, as a complex cognitive act, which is capable of giving a multifarious resonance to an otherwise simple (or even insignificant) sensation.

The Platonic unity of the One and the Many, achieved by way of reminiscence, is restored by Leopardi at a more explicitly (though not more intrinsically) aesthetic level.

This capacity of giving warmth and quickness to an idea (and conversely of freezing a sensation in the crystal sphere of immutable essences) can be contrastively observed in a poem, which, in its very title, expresses an almost religious devotion for an abstract entity: Shelley's *Hymn to the Intellectual Beauty* (1816).

Although the phrase "intellectual beauty" is not found in Plato's dialogues, the notion is unmistakably Platonic[10]. In the *Symposium,* the Mantinean stranger describes the stages of an aesthetic education, which leads the soul from the love of beautiful bodies up to the contemplation of Beauty itself[11]. This ascension, although announced with the colors of a mysteric revelation (*epoptie*), is rather a dialectic progression from the particular to the general[12]. The process of abstraction does not imply a subtraction of the sensuous elements: they are preserved at a higher level of generality, delivered from the intermingling with imperfections (as it is the case in reality) and, most important, freed from the constraints of particularity[13]. It is, therefore, an ideal concept of form devoid of content, and its best figuration is perhaps music, in which the aesthetic emotion issues from a most rigorous and abstract order expressed in a sensuous medium.

In Plotinus, this abstractive process is tinged with a new sensitivity to the inner self. Rather than in the generality of the Idea, Beauty is to be sought in the aesthetic experience of the subject. In the eighth treatise of the *Ennead* V, entitled *Peri tou noetou kallous,* Plotinus remarks that "as long as it [beauty] remains outside, we do not perceive it, but only when comes inside it moves us."[14] In the same chapter, the author goes as far as viewing an inner mirroring, or reverberation on the subject, of the contemplated beauty[15].

Far from acquiring intimistic connotations, however, this attention to interiority is always marked by the clarity of philosophical reasoning. In a later chapter of the same treatise, is discussed the possibility of an inner vision of the world (the only veritable knowledge) that be not disjoined from self-awareness. A paradoxical balance of internalization and distancing is proposed in order to depict, in quasi-mysteric terms, the consciousness of being absorbed by the whole. In the last paragraph, however, the fundamental skepticism of the external perception (*aisthesis*) is contrasted with the inner vision, about which, on the contrary, no doubt can subsist because that is the only mode of self-awareness—given the impossibility for the subject to perceive itself with the eyes of the body[16]. The distinctly Cartesian character of this argument has been emphasized by Bréhier in his introduction to the treatise[17].

This love for abstraction, one of the purest scents of the Hellenic mind, could lead to the conceits of the late Neo-Platonist known to the Middle Ages under the name of the first Athenian convert of St. Paul, Dionysius the Areopagite[18]. His apophatic doctrine, when wedded to the asceticism of renunciation in the Christian religion, engendered a concept of abstraction as blood-less and grim as the purgatorial mortifications that went with it. A whole panoply of paradoxes was mobilized to conjure up ghastly visions of emptiness.

The admonition that "poesy alone can tell her dreams" had been clearly, though indirectly, intimated by Plato himself, when he tells, with flaring eloquence, the en-counter of man with the earthly vestiges of Beauty.

Through reminiscence, Beauty itself (*auto to kallos*) is capable of stirring a frenzy in the heart of man[19].

The contemplation of the Ideal Beauty is a mental act not devoid of sensuous fervor and thrill. And to this particular sense of "mental" refers the phrase "intellec-tual beauty," which Shelley derived from a well estab-lished Platonic and Neo-Platonic tradition. As it was shown, in fact, "intellectual" renders the Greek "*no-etos*," which properly means "pertaining to the mind (*nous*)."[20] It is not incongruent with the title, therefore, the tone of rapture and enthusiasm that pervades Shel-ley's hymn from its very beginning[21].

A disquietude runs through the poem, and is often fig-ured with images of inconstant and restless swiftness. It is the anxiety for the evanescent visitations of thought and feeling ("elevating and delightful beyond all expression"), evoked as the intermittent glowing of a fading coal in *A Defense of Poetry*. The almost obses-sive presence of the shadow, however, may not simply be a reminiscence of the Platonic (and Neo-Platonic) dialectics of light (as truth of the Ideas) and shadow (as falsehood of the earth). The word is so deeply—and ambiguously—charged with a sense of thrilling (almost dreadful) joy, that it seems to mirror the cryptic am-bivalence of another equally obsessive adjective: "aw-ful." The notion of numinous experience that "awful" intimates in the poem can be glossed with the deep—sacral—ambiguity of the Greek *deinos*[22], which from the original semantic duplicity of "terrible" and "power-ful" (already in Homer) passed to denote the forceful-ness and vehemence of a rhetorical style, (thus becom-ing almost synonymous to *hypselos* "sublime").

And it is still a shadow ("ombra diva") that haunts the opening lines of *Alla sua donna,* as well as Leopardi's dreams. In the closing stanza, moreover, the canzone is referred to as "inno," not unlike Shelley's own poem. Besides such verbal similarities, the analogy might be extended a little further: at least to the sense of loss af-ter the sudden, unpredictable epiphany, and to the inti-mation of the almost supernatural bliss that would grace the human condition, if such supernal power had a steady abode among us. Shelley, however, unlike Leop-ardi, is rather saddened by the inconsistency of such visitations than by their elusive, "unreal" nature; and the final augur of calm for his onward life alludes to a

hopeful possibility which is totally alien to Leopardi's disenchanted landscape. Moreover, Shelley's diction is still inflamed with visionary enthusiasm, while the often discursive speech of *Alla sua donna* seems to prelude to the long season of prose that was about to follow.

Leopardi's reference to imagination as the only giver of some positive joy, in the famous letter (June 23, 1823) to Jacopssen[23], and such a telling phrase as "che dell'imago, / poi che del ver m'è tolto assai m'appago" (which according to a convincing hypothesis proposed by Moroncini and accepted by many critics, concluded the poem in an earlier draft)[24] may overemphasize the idea of contentment with the delusional world of shad-ows, and even insinuate the doubt of some compla-cency in it. Such a supine resignation was alien to Leop-ardi's titanic spirit (the commonplace of Leopardi's frailty is a fiction of his adversaries and does not even deserve a confutation). The very sense of dejection verging on despair, only vaguely intimated by the poem—but supported by contemporary evidence and confirmed by the ensuing poetic silence—should make us suspicious of any hasty conclusion about Leopardi's "idealism." His materialism, the legacy of the Enlight-enment, could not let him be appeased with an escape from reality. Leopardi's defence of the illusions (aesthetic and poetic illusions) is rather a polemical move against the vulgar (and often fanatical) myths of religion and politics, than an advocation of solipsistic contentment. He did not defend the notion of illusion per se, as with a sort of nihilistic self-indulgence: he ac-cepted it as a temporary repose amidst the often unbear-able toil of his existence. In the *Storia del genere umano,* composed in January and February of 1824[25], the Italian poet does not deny that Love—the real god and not its specious phantom—occasionally visits the abodes of the mortals[26]. From this perspective one can say that there is irony in *Alla sua donna*; but that is not to be understood as superficial irrision, rather as inner duplicity: while depicting his loving reverie, Leopardi is at the same time drawing a horizon in which that rev-erie appears less as a triumph of the imagination than an existential *échec*.

Like Dante, Leopardi does not yield to the temptation of a subjectivistic reduction of love (neither Guinizelli's idealization of "cor gentile," nor Cavalcanti's psycho-physiological mechanism of the spirits). For them both—saved the macroscopic, but not essential, differ-ences—love is still an objective cosmic power: the roar-ing god of the Greek mythology. And for this unremit-ting realism, Dante and Leopardi can be called—*absit ironia verbo*—Platonic[27].

We have examined so far Leopardi's dealing with a few different aspects of that constellation of topics, referred to as Platonism: the relevance of abstraction in the theory of knowledge, the overwhelming power of

Beauty in human affairs, and the sentimental idealization of the woman. Leopardi's sense of the infinite (often mystically interpreted) and, moreover, his own individual sensitiveness (his *schöne Seele,* one might say) have been purported to be distinctly Platonic (and Neo-Platonic) traits. I will not discuss the plausibility of such an appreciation, and will rather point to an element which, in my opinion, is more intrinsically constitutive of Leopardi's Platonic temper (if such a phrase is tenable at all).

In the closing chapter of *Plato and Platonism,* Pater dwells on the place attributed to aesthetics in the perfect education of man, in the Ideal City[28]. The prodigious eloquence of Pater's prose would almost dispense us from retrieving the passages in the *Republic*[29]: paraphrasing his own words, one might say that the main interest of those pages lies in the fact that in them we read what Pater actually said on a subject concerning which readers have been so ready to put themselves under his authority.

An important element in Pater's argument is the Platonic self-restraint towards beauty and the key concept is *askesis*[30]. Unforgettable, in particular, is the uncanny image of dry beauty, at the very end of the chapter, probably inspired by the following passage, in book X of the *Republic*: "*Socrates*: [. . .] When you take the greatest pleasure in things so low that you would be full of shame about them if they were yours, you are doing just what you do at the tragedy. [. . .] The effect of such poetry is the same. It waters and cares for these feelings when what we have to do is dry them up. It makes into our rulers the very things which have to be ruled, if we are to become happier and better men."[31]

The word *askesis,* however, before acquiring its common connotation of self-curtailing and stillness, referred to the idea of energetic exercising of the athletes[32]: one of the several aspects of that preeminent pagan virtue, which was *andreia,* or manliness. This *askesis,* of which *sophrosyne* (temperance) was an integral component, can, therefore, aptly refer to Plato's (and Leopardi's) grave reverence for Beauty: the heedful calmness of the true artist, who (as the true lover, Pater would add) has learned patience by waiting for the rare epiphanies in which joy must enhance—not hinder—control (as the perfect musician, who is able to transmute, with divine easiness, the inner fervor into forms of pure terseness). We are reminded of the almost colorless and tasteless sense of beauty conveyed by classical art to Winckelmann, who could not find any more appropriate image for it than a gush of spring water, pure and fresh.

So far as the *lexis* is concerned, Leopardi can be unquestionably considered a "Platonic" poet. The sublime simplicity of his style is so antonomastically Leopardian that the critics often deem devoting much attention

to it an unnecessary concern. We may just draw attention to a few observations in the ***Zibaldone*** on what Leopardi called "semplicità," or, with a Rousseauian echo, "naturalezza."

In the notes of the year 1821 (in which more than one third of the entire ***Zibaldone*** was drafted) is outlined a fairly consistent aesthetic theory, based on the concepts of "semplicità" and "natura." Although skeptical of any absolute principle or idea, Leopardi retains the notion of a stable, universal criterion for aesthetic judgment, founded on a concept of nature which was obtained, in a subtractive way (*à la Rousseau*), by stripping humanity bare of all artifices (or believed such) produced by societal corruption[33].

Leopardi's "semplicità" appears to be the necessary garb of a poetry which is aware of its own impotence to heal the tragedy of human existence. The poverty of poetry, therefore, regards the very essence of poetry as a human activity (not simply its modes of expression).

In this a whole philosophy of man is adumbrated. Limited, constrained, ineffectual activity seems to be the fate of man. This condition, often deeply (and obliquely) exploited by religion, is at times serenely (and stoically) accepted by a humanistic philosophy, which views limits rather as harmonious finitude than as diminution. Likewise, in the arts a luxuriant expressive abundance is the frequent sign of a protervous refusal of man's fated frailty: quite rarer, on the contrary, is the conscious acceptance of it under the guises of an austere discipline of self-curtailment. Such an *askesis* may be recognized in the voluntary imposition of rigid and difficult formal patterns (such as complex rhyme schemes, or, in music, the labyrinthine plaits of counterpoint) or in a dramatic reduction of the expressive means in order to distill the tenuous essence of it. This latter form of *askesis* was Leopardi's own discipline: a native sensitivity and piety for all frail beauty (be it Silvia or the broom flower) was the secret undercurrent of his expressive choices.

Within such an intrinsic—and almost organic—unity it seems artificious and inappropriate to separate the domains of ethics and aesthetics, even for the purpose of reconciling them.

Pater incidentally remarked the ethical bearing of Plato's aesthetic discipline[34]. Another passionate reader of Plato's dialogues rather obscurely admonishes that ethics and aesthetics are one and their unity is "mystic," that is to say "ineffable," because it lies outside the domain of representational discourse[35]: in other words, it is something philosophy is almost embarrassed to talk about, since it can do that only with an indirect allusion (the paradoxical unity preceding and transcending the inevitable distinctions). At a less general and abstract level we may assume that such an elusive unity be found in the aesthetic experience itself, or, more precisely, in a lifelong education to the appreciation of beauty. Evidently, the argument is circular: one can find only what one has been taught to look for. But perhaps we should accept the paradox, with all its theoretical power, as such, without attempting any simplification: let it be another (and not the least) unresolved element in our adventure of existing.

Notes

1. The *Porphyrii de vita Plotini* is listed in the "Indici delle opere composte da Giacomo Leopardi compilati da lui stesso", under the heading "Da bruciare senz'altro". (Cf. Giacomo Leopardi, *Poesie e Prose,* ed. Francesco Flora; 2 vol., Milano: Mondadori, 1957, p. 1112).

2. In a letter to his father (January 13, 1823), Leopardi writes: "[. . .] ho presso di me un Platone di Lipsia 1819-22 in 8, volumi, finora, 3, datomi da De Romanis gratis" (Giacomo Leopardi, *Lettere,* ed. Francesco Flora, Milano: Mondadori, 1957, p. 377).

3. Giacomo Leopardi, *Zibaldone,* ed. Francesco Flora, 2 vols. (Milano: Mondadori, 1957, 1712-1714).

4. "[. . .] Or domando io; se quella morale che Dio ci ha dato mediante il suo verbo era, come noi diciamo, la vera, e se Dio non solo n'è il tipo, e la ragione, ma ragione necessaria; dunque quando egli stesso dava una morale diversissima, e quasi contraria a questa, in punti essenzialissimi, egli operava contro la sua essenza. Non v'è taglio. [. . .] Checché dicano i teologi per ispiegare, per concordare, tutto insomma si riduce a questi termini: ed è forza convenire che Dio non solo è il tipo e la ragione, ma l'autore, la fonte, il padrone, l'arbitro della morale, e che questa, e tutti i suoi principii più astratti, nascono assolutamente, non dall'essenza, ma dalla volontà di Dio, che determina le convenienze, e secondo quelle che ha determinate, e create, secondo che le mantiene o le cangia o le modifica, detta, mantiene, cangia o altera le sue leggi. Egli è il creatore della morale, del buono e del cattivo, e della loro astratta idea, come di tutto il resto. (16 Settembre 1821)" (*Zibaldone*: 1711-1712)

5. *Zibaldone*: 1675-1676

6. "Malamente si distingue la memoria dell'intelletto, quasi avesse una ragione a parte nel nostro cervello. La memoria non è altro che una facoltà che l'intelletto ha di assuefarsi alle concezioni, diversa dalla facoltà di concepire o d'intendere. Ed. Ec. è tanto necessaria all'intelletto, ch'egli, senza di essa, non è capace di verun'azione, (l'azione dell'intelletto è diversa dalla semplice concezione ec.) perché ogni azione dell'intelletto è composta (cioè di premesse e conseguenza) né può tirarsi la conseguenza senza la memoria delle premesse. [. . .] (4 Agosto 1821)" (*Zibaldone*: 1453-1454).

7. "La memoria non è quasi altro che virtù imitativa, giacché ciascuna reminiscenza è quasi un'imitazione che la memoria, cioè gli organi suoi propri fanno delle sensazioni passate, (ripetendole, rifacendole, e quasi contraffacendole); e acquistano l'abilità di farla, mediante un'apposita e particolare assuefazione diversa dalla generale, o esercizio della memoria [. . .] Dal sopraddetto si vede che la proprietà della memoria non è propriamente di richiamare, il che è impossibile, trattandosi di cose poste fuori di lei e della sua forza, ma di contrattare, rappresentare, imitare, il che non dipende dalle cose, ma dall'assuefazioni alle cose e impressioni loro, cioè alle sensazioni, ed è proprio anche degli altri organi nel loro genere. E le ricordanze non sono richiami, ma imitazioni, o ripetizioni delle sensazioni, mediante l'assuefazione. Similmente (e notate) si può discorrere della natura delle idee. Questa osservazione rischiara assai la natura della memoria, che molti impossibilmente hanno fatto consistere in una forza di dipingere, o ricevere le impressioni stabili di ciascuna sensazione o immagine ec. laddove l'impressione non è stabile né può. [. . .] (24 Luglio 1821)" (*Zibaldone*: 1383-1384).

8. *Zibaldone*: 4426.

9. *Zibaldone*: 4471.

10. The title of Shelley's poem may have been suggested by a reading of Spenser's "An Hymne of Heavenly Beautie". For a detailed discussion of the possible sources of the Shelleyan phrase, see James A. Notopoulos, *The Platonism of Shelley. A Study of Platonism and the Poetic Mind.* (Durham: Duke UP, 1949, pp. 196-197).

11. First of all, it is everexistent and neither comes to be nor perishes, neither waxes nor wanes; next, it is not beautiful and in part ugly, nor is it such a time and other at another, nor in one respect beautiful and in another ugly, nor so affected by position as to seem beautiful to some and ugly to others. Nor again will our initiate find the beautiful presented to him in the guise of a face or of hands or any other portion of the body, nor as a particular description or piece of knowledge, nor as existing somewhere in another substance, such as an animal or the earth or sky or any other thing; but existing ever in singularity of form independent by itself, while all the multitude of beautiful things partake of it in such wise that, though all of them are coming to be and perishing, it grows neither

greater nor less, and is affected by nothing". (Plato, *Plato* III: *Lysis, Symposium, Gorgias,* trans. W. R. M. Lamb, Cambridge: Harvard U P; London: William Heinemann, 1983. *Symposium*: 211a-b, p. 205). The attribute monoeides refers to the formal unicity which characterizes the Idea, as opposed to the multiplicity of the body.

12. "Bien que cette élévation de l'âme jusqu'au Beau intelligible revête l'aspect d'un mystère, elle n'est pas à proprement parler un élan mystique; c'est une sorte de dialectique ascendante, car elle consiste, on l'a vu, à gravir une série d'échelons, sur chacun desquels s'opère une unification de la multiplicité determinée qui caractérise cet échelon (cf. 210e-211c), une sorte de rassemblement synoptique (synagoge). Il y a donc une remarquable analogie entre la méthode de l'*Erotique* et cette méthode dialectique qui est décrite brièvement dans le *Phédon* (101d), plus longuement dans la *République* à la fin du livre VI, puis au début ou vers la fin du livre VII". (Plato, *Oeuvres complètes,* Tome IV, 2ᵉ Partie: *Le Banquet,* ed. with an introduction by Léon Robin, Paris: Les Belles Lettres, 1951, p. xciv).

13. *Symposium*: 211a.

14. "oti exo men eos estin, oupo eidonem, otan de eiso genetai, dietheken". (Plotinus, *Ennéades,* ed. with translation and an introduction by Emile Bréhier, Paris: Les Belles Lettres, 1956, V 8, 2: 24-26).

15. "Da quel dì innanzi a me medesimo piacqui", as Petrarch said in his canzone *Gentil mia donna, i' veggio.*

16. "The doubting element, therefore, is perception, and the other one is the beholder; but, if that one too doubted, he could not believe his own existence. In fact, he cannot look from outside at himself, as a perceptible entity, with the eyes of the body". (*Ennéades,* V, 8, 11: 35-39).

17. "Mais, pour saisir dans son ampleur la pensée de Plotin, il ne faut pas oublier les dernières lignes du chapitre, qui, abandonnant le ton dévot du début, énonce avec fermetè une pensée qui sera celle de Descartes: on fait de la vision des choses sensibles, nous dit Plotin, le type même de la connaissance; il n'est pas étonnant que l'on ne puisse croire à une vision intérieure: mais douter de cette vision, ce serait douter de soi-même; car on ne se connaît pas comme un être sensible, mais par l'intérieur (xi, 33-39). N'est-ce pas ainsi que, chez Descartes, le Cogito, expurgé grâce au doute méthodique de toute trace de connaissance sensible, a servi de modèle à la connaissance intellectuelle?" (*Ennéades,* V: 133).

18. The corpus of Neo-Platonic writings that came to us under his name dates from the end of the V and the early VI century. Among them are *De divinis nominibus, De theologia mystica, De coelesti hierarchia,* and *De ecclesiastica hierarchia.* Dionysius' fundamental doctrine of negative theology stresses the absolute difformity between a transcendent entity and its possible representations. Any attempt at approaching such a reality should involve a progressive detachment from material representations (anagogy) in order to reach the intellectual void of mystic experience, the illuminating darkness of the final contemplation ("in obscurissimo, quod est supermanifestissimum", as it sounds in Scotus Eriugena's translation).

19. "But he who is newly initiated, who beheld many of those realities, when he sees a godlike face or form wich is a good image of beauty, shudders at first, and something of the old awe comes over him, then, as he gazes, he reveres the beautiful one as a god, and if he did not fear to be thought stark mad, he would offer sacrifice to his beloved as to an idol or a god". (Plato, *Plato* I: *Euthyphro, Apology, Crito, Phaedo, Phaedrus,* trans. Harold North Fowler and with an introduction by W. R. M. Lamb, Cambridge: Harvard U P; London: William Heinemann, 1982. *Phaedrus*: 251a, p. 487).

20. For the opposition of *noetos* to *haptos* (tangibile) and *horatos* (visible), see the following passage: "Hos de geometrai paisin oupo dunaimenois eph' heauton ta noeta myethenay tes asomatou kai apathous ousias eide, plattontes hapta kai horata mimemata sphairon kai kubon kai dodekaedron proteinousin". (Plato, *Republic,* trans. I. A. Richards, New York: Norton, 1942, VI: 509d).

21. See, on the other hand, Notopoulos' remark: "Though it is titled *Intellectual Beauty,* Shelley's poem is emotional and mystic rather than intellectual and objective, as in Plato's conception." (*The Platonism of Shelley*: 202).

22. For the etymology of the word see P. Chantraine's *Dictionnaire étymologique de la langue grecque* (s.v. deido): "Il est probable enfin que *dwei "craindre" est issu en définitive du thème *dwei "deux", exprimant l'idée de division, de doute cf. *Il.,* 9, 229-230 "deidimen en doie de saosemen e apolesthai": cf. en français "doute" et "redouter". (*Dictionnaire*: 257).

23. "En effet il n'appartient qu'à l'imagination de procurer à l'homme la seule espèce de bonheur positif dont il soit capable. C'est la véritable sagesse que de chercher ce bonheur dans l'idéal, comme vous faites. Pour moi, je regrette le temps où il m'était permis de l'y chercher, et je vois avec une

sort d'effroi que mon imagination devient stérile, et me refuse tous les secours qu'elle me prêtait autrefois." (*Lettere*: 440).

24. Francesco Moroncini, *Canti di Giacomo Leopardi*, Critical edition, 2 vols. (Bologna: Cappelli, 1927, II: pp. 455-477).

25. "Cominciata ai 19 di gennaio del 1824, finita ai 7 di Febbraio" (*Poesie e Prose*, I: pp. 1146).

26. *Poesie e Prose*, I: pp. 824-825.

27. By "realism" we mean the imputation of objective reality to the abstraction, independently of its particular instances and of the mind which entertains it: a philosophical stance that appears over and over again, often without an explicit genealogical link to the Platonic doctrine.

28. "Before him [Plato], you know, there had been no theorising about the beautiful, its place in life, and the like; and as a matter of fact he is the earliest critic of the fine arts. He anticipates the modern notion that art as such has no end but its own perfection,—'art for art's sake.' [. . .] The loveliness of virtue as a harmony, the winning aspect of those 'images' of the absolute and unseen Temperance, Bravery, Justice, shed around us in the visible world for eyes that can see, the claim of the virtues as a visible representation by human persons and their acts of the eternal qualities of 'the eternal,' after all far out-weigh, as he thinks, the claim of their mere utility. And accordingly, in education, all will begin and end in 'music,' in the promotion of qualities to which no truer name can be given than symmetry, aesthetic fitness, tone. Philosophy itself indeed, as he conceives it, is but the sympathetic appreciation of a kind of music in the very nature of things." (Walter Pater, *Plato and Platonism*, London: MacMillan, 1901, pp. 267-268).

29. A verification, however, will but confirm his words. See, for instance, the following passage, from book III of the *Republic*: "Socrates:" [. . .] Wouldn't it be better to get workers of another stamp, with the natural power to see very clearly what is good and beautiful so that our young men and women, living, as it were, in a healthy country, would all the time be drinking in good from every side; so may it come upon their eye or ear like a sweet wind from a cleaner land and from their earliest days secretly make like to and friends with and in harmony with the beautiful measure of reason? *Glaucon*: Such an education would be by far the best. *Socrates*: That, Glaucon, is why music is so all-important in education. Because rhythm and harmony go down most deeply into the hollows of the soul, and take the strongest grip upon it, and are able to give a man order, if he is rightly trained in them; but if not he will be without it." (*Republic*: 64 [401]).

30. "Imitation then, imitation through the eye and ear, is irresistible in its influence over human nature. And secondly, we, the founders, the people, of the Republic, of the city that shall be perfect, have for our peculiar purpose the simplification of human nature: a purpose somewhat costly, for it follows, thirdly, that the only kind of music, of art and poetry, we shall permit ourselves, our citizens, will be of a very austere character, under a sort of 'self-denying ordinance'. We shall be a fervently aesthetic community, if you will; but therewith also very fervent 'renunciants,' or 'ascetics'." (*Plato and Platonism*: pp. 270-271).

31. *Republic*: 196 [606].

32. From the original meaning, in classical Attic, of "exercise, practice, training" (with a shift from the Homeric semantic value of the related verb *askeo* "to work"), it came to signify "mode of life" (he kynike askesis, in Lucian's *Toxaris,* 27), and more specifically "mode of life of a religious sect" (in Philo Judaeus, I: 643). See *Thesaurus Linguae Latinae*, Lipsiae: in aedibus B. G. Teubneri, 1900-1906, II: 2183-2184.

33. See for instance the long entry of July 30, 1821 (*Zibaldone*: 1412-1415), and also the following passage, in a note of July 21: "Un falso pregio, cioè non naturale, in fatto di bellezza, non può dunque né lungamente né comunemente essere stimato, e la mia teoria che distrugge il bello assoluto, lascia salda questa massima, e quella che il giudizio conforme delle nazioni e de' secoli circa il bello d'ogni genere, non erra mai; e lascia interi e inviolati i diritti che i grandi scrittori, poeti, artisti, hanno alla immortalità, ed alla universalità della fama." (*Zibaldone*: 1425).

34. "[. . .] we have here, in outline and tendency at least, the mind of Plato in regard to the ethical influence of aesthetic qualities [. . .]" (*Plato and Platonism*: p. 270).

35. "6.421 Es ist klar, dass sich die Ethik nicht aussprechen lässt. Die Ethik ist traszendental." (Ethik und Ästhetik sind Eins). [It is clear that ethics cannot be put into words. Ethics is transcendental. (Ethics and aesthetics are one and the same.)"] (Ludwig Wittgenstein, *Tractatus Logico-philosophicus*. The German text of Ludwig Wittgenstein's *Logisch-philosophische Abhandlung,* with a new edition of the translation by D. F. Pears & B. F. McGuinness and with the introduction by Bertrand Russell." London: Routledge & Kegan Paul; New York: The Humanities Press, 1972, pp. 146-147).

Martha King and Daniela Bini (essay date 1992)

SOURCE: King, Martha, and Daniela Bini. Introduction to *Zibaldone: A Selection,* translated by Martha King and Daniela Bini, pp. xiii-xxii. New York: Peter Lang, 1992.

[*In the following essay, King and Bini provide an overview of the composition of Leopardi's multivolume record of his thoughts on poetry and philosophy.*]

Giacomo Leopardi, the author of this collection of thoughts, this hodge-podge or medley, as the Italian word **Zibaldone** signifies, was beginning to win renown as a precocious young philologist when the three poets whose names are identical with English romantic poetry took up residence in Italy. In fact, Byron, Shelley, and Keats came to Italy between 1816 and 1820, during the crucial years of Leopardi's intellectual development, the years of his "conversion" [143-144] (Numbers correspond to Leopardi's pagination in the **Zibaldone.**) to poetry which would eventually make him not only Italy's greatest poet of the Romantic period, but one of the greatest poets of Italian literary history.

Of the three English expatriots, Leopardi had heard only of Byron, whose fame preceded his arrival, and which became even more widespread as word of his physical, amorous, revolutionary, and literary activities got around. It was Byron's poetry, particularly *The Giaour,* that one Italian romantic, Ludovico di Breme, touted as the great exemplar of modern poetry—modern in its invention of new myths, its freedom from traditional forms, and its predilection for the melancholy tone. The praise lavished upon Byron's poetry moved the young Leopardi, a devotee of Greek and Latin poetry, to defend the classical equilibrium, craftsmanship, and rules, and to regard modern poetry over emotional and affected. [**Zibaldone** 15-21]

After years of study in the isolation of his father's extensive library, the young Count Leopardi revised his estimation of the illustrious English lord's poetry, and deemed *The Giaour* symbolic of a new force roaming the European literary landscape which was the antithesis of Greek restraint and suggestiveness. This revision coincided with Leopardi's developing sense of poetic vocation, *The Giaour* providing an exemplary model of a new poetics.

In 1823, Leopardi wrote in his **Zibaldone**: "The only poetry suitable for our time is the melancholy, and it is the only poetic tone possible for every subject."[3976] Such modifications of his thought are what give interest and value to these notebooks, and in this case indicate his reluctant acceptance of the unavoidable shift in nineteenth century poetic sensibility.

Leopardi was nineteen when he began making notes in his **Zibaldone** (July or August of 1817) to record images, words, and ideas for his poetry and prose, to jot down his etymological explorations, to develop his philosophical speculations, to clarify his thoughts. He continued writing in it over the next fifteen years, as he resided in Rome, Bologna, Pisa, Florence, after finally escaping from his restrictive family life in Recanati. The last entry is dated December 4, 1832, seven years before his death in Naples, though most of the **Zibaldone** was written between 1819 and 1823, the years of self-examination and philosophical speculation.

In 1819, after a period of poetic inspiration and production, in which the thriving force was his fantasy, Leopardi became in his own words "filosofo di professione" (philosopher by profession) [**Zibaldone** 144]. A temporary illness kept him away from books and he began to reflect on human suffering and on his own. It was during this period that he realized the impossibility for modern man to recreate the naive poetry of the ancients, after reason had produced a fracture between man and nature. Just as Schiller had done in 1789, Leopardi came to the conclusion that only sentimental, that is, *philosophical* poetry was now possible; this poetry was nurtured by the discovery of the opposition between the poetical I and nature, the other. "Sentimental poetry belongs exclusively to this century, just as the true and simple imaginative . . . poetry belonged exclusively to the Homeric age . . . the sentimental is based upon and rises out of philosophy, experience, knowledge . . . in other words, out of the truth, whereas the primitive essence of poetry was to be inspired by falsehoods." [**Zibaldone** 734-5]

Though poetry and poetics were his main concern, Leopardi's speculations did not slight any field of human enquiry. The crisis of poetry coincided with the development of man and society, and therefore with human progress. In criticizing the naive trust in scientific and social progress of his day, Leopardi was in line with much contemporary thinking. If the **Operette morali** are the accomplished realization of such criticism and the **Pensieri** the apodictic statement of it, the **Zibaldone** was the place of its birth, growth, and full development

Rapidly, in the attempt to keep up with the complexity of his thoughts (hence a reliance on etceteras to indicate their unfinished state), or without always bothering to form complete sentences, in an informal style often laced with colloquialisms, he recorded the journey of his mind. At times, however, this journey was arduous, and the issues at stake obscure, as his thoughts unfolded in long and complex sentences. Leopardi recorded his ideas in the process of their being born; thus the complexity of his style mirrored the movements of his mind.

From an unusually early age he explored and defined a variety of subjects, including astronomy, superstition, history, philosophy, in carefully written, scholarly essays. But he needed a vehicle for expressing his own ideas, a place to record poetic images as they spontaneously came to him, a repository for the thoughts he wanted to mull over as they occurred during his wide and constant reading in Greek, Latin, Hebrew, and modern European languages.

Few poets have left such a complete record of the matter which sparked their creativity. Leopardi's meditations on the creative process and his statements on style and the psychological effect of certain words are a rare testimony of a great poet. The letters of Keats, the criticism of Eliot, Wordsworth's Preface to *Lyrical Ballads* are equally illuminating, but nowhere else is the dramatic development of a creative artist so well documented as on these 4526 pages. Aesthetics and poetry are Leopardi's life-long concern, since art—and poetry in particular—are for him the only solace for life's suffering.

From the first publication of the *Zibaldone* in 1897 these notes have been read as a key to his poetry: critics have combed these pages for clues to explicate his poetic themes. For a long time, however, they also dismissed his most complex reflections on ethical and social issues as pedantic and disorderly, in the attempt to arrive exclusively to the heart of his poetics. Only in the last few decades have scholars begun to value the philosophical weight of Leopardi's thought and to see it not as a hindrance to his poetry, as the leading voice of Italian aesthetics Benedetto Croce had affirmed, but as its *conditio sine qua non*. In fact, with his philosophy of "distinti," (strict separation of mental faculties), Croce was the cause of the long-lasting misinterpretation of Leopardi. Philosophy and poetry, as products of different mental faculties, could not coexist, but were mutually exclusive to Croce. Therefore a philosophical poet was a contradiction in terms. Of Leopardi's extensive works, Croce sanctioned only his lyric poetry, the "Idylls" and rejected everything else, especially the *Zibaldone.*

The resistance to recognizing the presence of a real philosophy in Leopardi's work also had another cause: the longtime tradition in Western thought, from Aristotle to Hegel, that had established the identity or coincidence of philosophy with systematic thought. At its basis there was, of course, a faith in the readability of the world, in the existence of stable and immutable principles by which every human and natural phenomenon could be explained. Only recently scholars who nurtured their thoughts on Nietzsche, Heidegger, and Freud, were able to re-read Leopardi and discover in the asystematic quality of his thoughts not the lack of a philosophical mind, but the trait of a modern philosophical mind akin to those of the philosophers just mentioned.

After spending a lifetime on the study of Greek philosophy, Emanuele Severino, one of Italy's leading contemporary philosophers, turned to Leopardi and wrote the first of a two volume study on his thought, which he defines as the core of Western philosophy that opened the path to modern man (*Il nulla e la poesia. Alla fine dell'età della tecnica: Leopardi.*)

The fragmentary quality of the *Zibaldone* must therefore be seen as Antonio Prete remarked, as a statement about the impossibility of the Opus, of the final, definitive work, given the absence of final answers and absolute truths (*Il pensiero poetante*). The only possible philosophical work is always recreating itself, questioning everything that has previously been done. The *Zibaldone* becomes the anti-philosophical opus, where the traditional division of philosophy into ethics, metaphysics and aesthetics has been destroyed. Metaphysics is defeated by a materialistic view of the world where everything is reduced to matter and from which the spirit has been banned forever. Ethics and aesthetics are now intertwined since the source of pleasure can be found only in illusions, thus in man's own creations.

The foundation of Leopardi's world view, upon which all his suppositions are based, is his theory of pleasure derived from the French sensationalists and materialists of the eighteenth century (Condillac and La Mettrie above all). Pleasure is what everyone seeks but never finds, because we do not want a particular, short-lived pleasure; we want pleasure that lasts forever. The responsibility for this unhappy necessity lies with Nature that has given her creatures the everlasting need for pleasure and happiness without the means of achieving it (because nothing in the world is infinite or limitless). She has, however, granted him illusions—of love, glory, virtue—that can only give him a temporary, precarious happiness, for reason's task is to destroy these illusions. Leopardi, in fact, soon becomes aware of the contradictory character of illusions whose power lies precisely in their nonbeing. Were they to be realized, they would necessarily cease to be ideals, illusions, and thus lose their essence. The ideal exists only insofar as it is not realized.

The final logical and bitter conclusion of these thoughts is that life is composed of nothing but suffering, which makes death the preferable and only reasonable alternative.

Leopardi dramatized his interrogations of reality by dividing every issue into antitheses: Nature and Reason, Pleasure and Pain, Happiness and Unhappiness, Existence and Nothingness, Life and Death. These dichotomous entities comprising his "philosophy" or "system" (as he called these theoretical passages) are "the incompatible and irreconcilable elements of the human system"[1982]. No synthesis is possible.

In his scheme Nature plays a large part and has more than one role. On the one hand she is responsible for all suffering, illness, misfortune; but "nature" also refers to the enthusiasm, intuition, poetic spontaneity belonging to the ancients, children, and the naive. Reason, nature's opposite, represents intellectual coldness and analysis. Reason is the progenitor of progress that causes undue suffering, but that must nevertheless be pursued as the moral duty of modern man.

These same antitheses are at work in his poems; in fact, the very opposition between the real and the ideal is their inspiring and propelling force. In his poetry the painful philosophical truths he had discovered in the *Zibaldone* are metaphorically rendered through images that temper the polemic tone present in his prose: the moon over a desert, the morning rain on the roof, a quiet evening after the festivities of the day have ended, muffled sounds at night of a lovely young woman working at her loom. The stony harshness of his philosophical conclusions is often softened by a bitter-sweet nostalgia. A nostalgia for times past—for the simpler, naive (that wisdom lies in ignorance is one of his paradoxes) life of those who were innocent of civilization spawned by reason, and for youth and beauty which, in the sorrowful nature of things, is always momentary. His great "Idylls" (as he called them), and numerous poems making up the *Canti* share the image of youthful beauty (Silvia, the woman in the *Dream, Aspasia, Nerina*) that soon fades and dies, symbol of the precariousness and brevity of the ideal. Behind the illusory world is the irrefutable bedrock of nothingness and indifference to individual existence.

In one of his final poems, *La ginestra,* Leopardi suggests the possibility of hope in this absurd existence, perhaps the only reasonable one to expect—hope in feelings of confraternity. The image of a broom plant—a rugged yellow blossom on a long broom-like stem that grows wild in the Italian countryside—represents stubbornly resistant life at the edge of a volcano that will certainly destroy it. The appearance of Mount Vesuvius, reminiscent of Sade's description of erupting Etna in *La Nouvelle Justine,* represents nature's irrational destruction that leaves man facing a vast desert. The broom symbolizes the individual who "takes all men as his allies, and men / Embraces in deep love" (trans. Ottavio M. Casale) and no longer blames them for his suffering for which Nature alone is responsible.

The germ of this poem is in a passage of the *Zibaldone* written years earlier and serves as an example of how Leopardi's desperate philosophy is sublimated, and thus rescued by its poetical transformation. In this passage he defends himself against the accusation of misanthropy when he writes that his philosophy does not foster hatred for mankind, but it "makes nature guilty of everything, and excusing men completely, directs the hate, or at least the lament, to the highest principle, to the true origin of the evils of existence . . ."[4428].

The *Zibaldone.*gives the readers of Leopardi's poetry and prose a rare look into the mind of a great poet: a great poet and a moralist, an advocate of illusions and an advocate of nothingness, a man of sensibility and a man of reason. This work is untidy with inconsistencies, complexities, and repetitions, but fearless in following a thought to its logical conclusion. As the poet created himself, in the Keatsian sense, he went from a kind of residual faith in Christianity, to an anguished declaration of the nothingness of everything, a philosophical nihilism that refuses all solace and accepts only desperation. Hence the truly heroic position that comes to terms with the inevitable loneliness and emptiness of this life and finds in man's creative power the only means to cope with life's evils. Leopardi was able to look squarely at human life—short, difficult, often painful, often boring—as few have done. He understood both the harshness of reality and the human need to mask that harshness with illusions. But above all he discovered man's superiority in his capability to create Beauty, Happiness, and Immortality in his world of fiction.

It is ironic that one so opposed to the desperate heroism of *The Giaour* and other Promethean protagonists of the romantics would so resemble them in his psychological make-up. A certain heroism is achieved by refusing the illusory comforts that most men seek. "Man would be omnipotent if he could be desperate all his life, or at least for a long time: that is, if his desperation were a condition that could endure"[4090]. It was the relatively inexperienced, relatively untraveled Leopardi, with few friendships and loves to claim, physically weakened and misshapen by years of persistent study, who took a solitary, heroic position against the refuge of hope and illusion, and the expectation of pleasure and happiness—in effect much like a brooding Giaour or Manfred.

Yet Leopardi was not a poet only for his time. It is no coincidence that philosophers like Schopenhauer and Nietzsche praised him above other poets of the romantic age. His insights about the risk of dehumanization that modern civilization and technology provoke (*Operette morali*), his reflections of the dialectical principles of life—thought and action—bring him into the twentieth century and set him side by side with Pirandello, Musil, Svevo, and Montale.

Furthermore, Leopardi contributed to contemporary thought the discovery of the cognitive power of the imagination. Tearing down the barrier between poetry and philosophy, he saw them working together toward the discovery of new truths as well as toward the creation of art. At the center of the *Operette morali* stands

"Il Parini," a didactic composition whose importance lies in the character of Parini, the eighteenth-century Italian poet and philosopher. Parini "was . . . one of the very few Italians who, in addition to literary excellence, possessed depth of thinking and great familiarity with contemporary philosophy." (Trans. by G. Cecchetti) The ideal modern poet is he who is endowed with a philosophical mind, that is, he who seeks out truth. In a parallel way the true philosopher is he who is endowed with "eccellente ingegno" (greatest intelligence), but also with "ardentissimo cuore" (warmest heart). The latter truth is delivered by the authority of Filippo Ottonieri the philosopher who taught "that the most real pleasures in life are those produced by false imagining." (Cecchetti). In these two compositions Leopardi had two illustrious speakers repeating and summarizing what he had been reflecting on in so many pages of the *Zibaldone,* and it was not by chance that the praise of philosophy was undertaken by a poet and that of poetry by a philosopher. Philosophy and poetry must proceed together because they depend upon each other. "You can be certain," Parini says, "that subtlety of intellect and great power of reasoning are not enough to make substantial progress in philosophy; great power of imagination is also necessary." And he concludes that "both poet and philosopher penetrate the depths of human nature and bring to light its innermost qualities and moods, its hidden emotions and impulses, and its causes and effects." (Cecchetti) Only a year earlier Leopardi had written in his notebooks: "It is as astonishing as true that poetry which by its very nature seeks out the beautiful, and philosophy which by its very essence seeks out the true, that is the very opposite of the beautiful, are the closest faculties . . . poetry and philosophy are equally at the summit of the human spirit." [3382]

In making our selections we have tried to choose passages that reflect the variety of thought sketched above, while keeping in mind the important fact that the *Zibaldone* should facilitate the understanding of his literary works. And with the conviction that biography is useful when it can illuminate the reader's imagination, we have included passages that reveal the poet's personality, such as the well-known description of his strict, narrowly religious mother, Countess Adelaide Antici [353-356]. It increases our overall understanding to know that he liked solitude [670], that he was a faithful friend [4274], that study and creativity were the single absorbing joys of his life [4417], and yet that he felt regret for the other pleasures of life that he missed because of these pursuits [4421].

We have made a large selection of his observations of his own method of creating a poem, and his opinions about the psychological effects of certain words and images. Not only did he have an abiding interest in the origins and meaning of words, but he was highly sensitive to their emotional effect, just as he was to suggestive sights and sounds [1744], and he analyzed these effects carefully. Leopardi states repeatedly that words selected for their many associative meanings set up reverberations of memories that go back to childhood, as do sights when they recall other scenes, and sounds when muffled or diffused. His important division of words into *termini* and *parole* is a prelude to modern linguistic theory.

Using examples from other poets' work (Petrarch in particular) and his own, he writes that the words a poet chooses should be vague as well as suggestive, to allow the reader to expand the poem's meaning within his own range of experience [1701-1706, 2054]. In addition, particular images may arouse the pleasurable sense of infinity that extends one's mental vision and can produce a transcendental experience [185, 1430]. His poem *L'infinito* exemplifies this supposition.

Well over a third of the notebook entries deal with his constant preoccupation with the tools of his craft, words. However, we have included none of the etymological or philological passages, as we felt that, although brilliant, they would not be of general interest.

In Leopardi's comments on the creative act of writing poetry, students of English literature will recognize similarities to another English poet. In his Preface to *Lyrical Ballads,* Wordsworth wrote that "poetry is the spontaneous overflow of powerful feelings: it takes its origin from emotion recollected in tranquility . . ." Quite unaware of this famous statement of nineteenth century poetics, Leopardi writes of the enthusiasm that is necessary for the conception of a poem, but which can be "actually harmful" for its execution. "Often we can best create at that moment following an enthusiasm of a powerful emotion when the soul, though quiet, sways like an undulating sea after a storm and recalls the experience with pleasure."[257-259].

It is Leopardi the poet-philosopher who speaks in the *Zibaldone,* no matter what the subject, couching his thoughts in metaphor and simile, ever conscious of the imaginative language forming those thoughts. The paths of reasoning recorded in this book give form to his poetry and prose, and recognition of this creative reciprocity gives an undeniable value and importance to the study of this work.

G. Singh (essay date 1994)

SOURCE: Singh, G. "Giacomo Leopardi: Journey from Illusions to Truth." In *The Motif of the Journey in Nineteenth-Century Italian Literature,* edited by Bruno Magliocchetti and Anthony Verna, pp. 53-69. Gainesville: University Press of Florida, 1994.

[In the following essay, Singh traces Leopardi's brief journey from a period of youthful and comforting illu-

sions to maturity and the necessity of abandoning those illusions in favor of a pursuit of truth.]

Illusions—or what he considered to be such—were to play as important a part in Giacomo Leopardi's childhood and early life as in that of any other person. The crucial difference between him and any other person, however, was the extraordinarily swift and unimpeded transition from illusions, however agreeable and even necessary, to truth, however bitter. His journey from the one to the other could not have been briefer or more decisive. "I fanciulli trovano il tutto nel nulla, gli uomini il nulla nel tutto" [children find everything in nothing, men nothing in everything], he was to say in *Zibaldone*.[1] But his own journey from a child's position—seeing "il tutto nel nulla"—to an adult's, seeing "il nulla nel tutto," cannot be measured in terms of time; only in terms of a tacit change within himself that amounted to a sort of moral, psychological, and emotional revolution. From 1809 (when he took his first communion and when, according to his father, he was "sommamente inclinato alla divozione" [greatly inclined to devotion] and "voleva sempre ascoltare molte messe, e chiamava felice quel giorno in cui aveva potuto udirne di piú [always wanted to hear many masses, and called a happy day the day he was able to hear the most])[2] until 1821 (when he composed **"Bruto minore,"** which if not the first is certainly the most explicit and unequivocal statement of his moral and philosophical position), the distance may only have been twelve years; but how many invisible milestones Leopardi had passed in his inner journey and how many unrecorded incidents in the development of his soul there had been.

Again, while outlining his poetic development in a note he wrote down in *Zibaldone* in 1820, Leopardi was in a way indicating the various stages of his psychological, philosophical, and emotional journey. "Nella carriera poetica," he tells us, echoing both Vico's thought and terminology, "il mio spirito ha percorso lo stesso stadio che lo spirito umano in generale" [in my poetic career, my spirit has gone through the same stage as the human spirit in general]; that is, from imagination to philosophy when, in 1819,

> cominciai a sentire la mia infelicità in un modo assai piú tenebroso . . . a riflettere profondamente sopra le cose . . . a divenir filosofo di professione (di poeta ch'io era), a sentire l'infelicità certa del mondo, in luogo di conoscerla.

> [I started to feel my unhappiness in a much more somber manner . . . to reflect profoundly on things . . . to become a philosopher by profession (from the poet that I was), to feel the certain unhappiness of the world, instead of knowing it.][3]

This change brought him face-to-face with the goal his mind had been slowly but irresistibly moving toward—the conviction about the "infinita vanità del vero" [the

infinite vanity of truth].[4] Yet the vanity of truth did not contradict what was tragically certain about it. Thus, he describes the truth about human destiny, as he saw it, in inflexibly tragic accents in **"Bruto minore"**:

> A voi, marmorei numi
>
> . . . . .
>
> . . . a voi ludibrio e schermo
> È la prole infelice . . .
>
> . . . . .
>
> Guerra mortale, eterna, o fato indegno,
> Teco il prode guerreggia,
> Di cedere inesperto . . .
>   In peggio
> Precipitano i tempi . . .
>
> [To you, oh marble gods
>
> . . . . .
>
> . . . mere sport and mockery
> Is that unhappy progeny . . .
>
> . . . . .
>
> Mortal war, eternal, oh vile fate
> With you the brave wages,
> Untutored in surrender . . .
>   To the worse
> Our times precipitate . . .]

These accents characterize the desperation of one who has come to his journey's end, having traveled a long way during the span of a mere dozen years.

From now on, Leopardi's journey toward truth would continue to be uninterrupted; his thirst for it insatiable, for all its "infinita vanità"; and his passion for it unmatched except by his passion for love. But once he had discovered "l'infinita vanità del tutto" [the infinite vanity of everything] he was left with nothing else to discover. His only task was to come to grips with his experiences, his hopes, disappointments, and disillusions, using truth as the sole criterion, the only point of reference. In other words, if the discovery of truth became the goal of his disillusioned life, the journey toward that goal could never come to an end, because truth or the application of truth could never be exhausted. And even though his mortal journey was coming to an end and he considered himself to be "un sepolcro ambulante, che porta dentro di me un uomo morto" [a walking sepulcher, carrying a corpse within me][5] his consuming passion for truth knew no abating. For having reached his destination once—the discovery of truth—Leopardi resumed his journey again and again to reach the same goal, to discover the same truth.

In fact, if one were to single out one characteristic that, more than any other, distinguishes Leopardi from any other Italian poet (Dante included) and links him with an altogether different cultural and poetic tradition (namely, the English) it would unquestionably be his passion for truth and the untrammeled freedom of thought and independence of mind with which he pursued it. Leopardi's fortune in Victorian as well as in twentieth-century England—and in terms of the weight and variety of critical thought devoted to him, as well as of the competence and distinction of the numerous translations undertaken of his work, it is unparalleled—owed not a little to the recognition and appreciation of this aspect of his poetry, with which readers of Chaucer, Shakespeare, Donne, and Milton, Wordsworth, and T. S. Eliot were so familiar. Bertrand Russell, the most eminent English philosopher and thinker of this century, enjoyed Leopardi's poetry and had this to say in 1967 in a letter to me: "I consider the poetry and pessimism of Leopardi to be the most beautiful expression of what ought to be the creed of a scientist"; and as to **"La ginestra,"** Russell observed that it expresses "more effectively than any other poem known to me my views about the universe and human passions."

It is not that Leopardi followed or cultivated truth, or a particular kind of truth, as one cultivates a particular creed, doctrine, or ideology. Nor did he father or enunciate any particular philosophy. Pessimism is as old as the hills, and its treatment in poetry is found in all ages and climes. Leopardi was not, nor did he profess to be, a philosopher. But what he offers in his poetry and, in a different form in *Operette morali,* is something more than philosophy: it is a fusion, not a dichotomy as Milton saw it, between calm of mind and passion at its most burning. So that what he desires on a sentimental plane—"lingua mortal non dice / quel ch'io sentiva in seno" [Mortal tongue cannot utter / what I felt in my bosom][6]—does not make him less eager on the rational and intellectual plane about the other and equally dominant passion—the passion for truth that is so vital an ingredient of his thought and poetry.

However, Leopardi for all his power of analytical thought—and it was as considerable as that of Coleridge—did not bring any abstract or metaphysical concepts or criteria to bear upon his attitude to or notion of truth. He identified truth, generally speaking, with nature and the reality of things as they are—or as they are seen to be by a mature, disinterested, and disillusioned mind—and with the feelings and sentiments as well as with the thoughts such a view entails. In this respect his attitude to truth is poles apart from that of Keats or Wordsworth. "What the imagination seizes as beauty," says Keats, "must be the truth—whether it existed before or not."[7] And for Wordsworth, the child is the "best philosopher"—"Mighty prophet! Seer blest!? / On whom those truths do rest, / Which we are toiling all our lives to find."[8] But neither what the imagination seizes as beauty nor what the child, "haunted for ever by the eternal mind,"[9] sees was enough for Leopardi's profoundly cultured and skeptical mind. And he could

have said to both the Wordsworthian child and to Keats, what he says in a vein of poetic irony to the moon in **"Canto notturno"**:

> Ma tu per certo,
> Giovinetta immortal, conosci il tutto,
> Questo io conosco e sento,
> Che degli eterni giri,
> Che dell'esser mio frale,
> Qualche bene o contento
> Avrà fors'altri; a me la vita è male.

> [But you, for certain,
> Immortal maiden, know all,
> This I know and feel,
> That in eternal cycles,
> That in my frail being,
> Some good, some happiness,
> Others perhaps can find; life to me is evil.]

It is, therefore, not what his imagination seizes, but what he knows and what he perceives to be the real truth—the processes of "knowing" and "feeling" being inseparable in Leopardi's perception of truth—that ultimately counts, for one who was free from illusions and who at the same time celebrated eloquently their value and efficacy in human life. But however strongly he might have felt the spell of illusions or envied those who find "qualche bene o contento" in the "eterni giri," it never distracted him from his unswerving quest for truth, his moral integrity, and his belief that "a me la vita è male." The silence of the stars frightened Pascal; the "interminati spazi" [interminable spaces] "sovrumani silenzi" [superhuman silences] and "profondissima quiete" [deepest silence] almost frightened Leopardi and dramatically heightened his sense of the contrast between the finiteness of his "esser mio frale" and the infinity of the universe, which made him cling all the more passionately and determinedly to his own convictions. Leopardi's passion for truth, as he saw it (even though it was inimical to happiness), became for him a matter of personal honor, pride, and integrity; it was not merely a philosophical pursuit but also a moral concern. In all of Leopardi's poetry we find accents of personal moral pride as a result of his total commitment to truth—accents that add a peculiar potency to his lyricism, for which one looks in vain in the works of his contemporaries. In the poetry of Wordsworth, another votary of truth, what we have is something quite different. In Wordsworth's best poetry, as in Leopardi's, moral fervor and poetic fervor almost always go together. But unlike Leopardi, whose gaze remained fixed uncompromisingly on the truths of life really lived, Wordsworth habitually shifted his gaze from the outer to the inner, from the visible to the visionary, from earth to heaven. Not only that, but he sees truth as being in the nature of (to quote his own words) something half-perceived and half-created. It was, in the last analysis, a product of his own mind or, as Leopardi says of love, "la figlia / Della sua mente" [the daughter of his mind].[10] Hence, with regard to the kind of truths that nourished Wordsworth's poetic life, one might say (as Coleridge did) about the various aspects of nature: "O Lady! we receive but what we give, / And in our life alone does Nature live."[11]

But the kind of truth that interested Leopardi, which he celebrated in his poetry and which constitutes its moral and philosophical backbone, is a truth that originates from firsthand experience or from an unbiased and disinterested observation of nature and society. It is not something half-perceived and half-created. The poet has no choice but to present what he sees around him, what he feels within himself, and what his insatiably exploratory and analytical mind presents him with or forces upon him. If Wordsworth was a seer in the idealistic sense and Blake in the visionary sense, Leopardi was a seer in the most rational and realistic sense of the term.

In fact, Wordsworth thought he derived his light from heaven and that he shone to the measure of that heaven-born light, rather than to the measure of the light born out of his everyday experiences and observations. That is why his truths no less than his sense of reality have an essentially idealistic rather than empirical basis, even though he chose to deal with "incidents and situations from common life" and to write about them in "a selection of language really used by men."[12] For Leopardi, on the contrary, the source of inspiration was nothing more than his own thoughts, experiences, and observations concerning life; and there was no consolation for him except in truth, however bitter and unconsolatory it might have been. Leopardi considered truth to be neither beautiful nor conducive to happiness. The knowledge of truth, he tells us, "non sarà mai sorgente di felicità, né oggi; né era allora quando uomo primitivo se la passava nella solitudine, ben lontano certamente dalle meditazioni filosofiche" [will never spring from happiness, neither today, nor did it before when primitive man spent his time in solitude, clearly a long way from philosophical meditations].[13] Nevertheless, so far as he was concerned, however unpalatable or unflattering the truth he pursued it unflinchingly and made it known in his writings, even at the risk of incurring oblivion in his own age or in posterity ("obblio / Preme chi troppo all'età propria increbbe" [oblivion / weighs heavy on he who displeases his own times][14] by telling people what they do not want to know but what a man like him, once he has seen it or known it himself, cannot forbear from telling; any more than he can unsee it or unknow it. Leopardi's English counterpart, Thomas Hardy, after decades of writing and unbaring what people did not want to know promised himself, toward the end of his life that he would not anymore reveal what he saw. In his poem "He Resolves to Say No More," published

posthumously and presumably written in the last year of his life, he tells himself (more or less in the same philosophically disillusioned vein as Leopardi in **"A se stesso"**):

O my soul keep the rest unknown!
It is too like a sound of moan . . .
Why load men's minds with more to bear
That bear already ails to spare?
    From now alway
    Till my last day
What I discern I will not say.[15]

But, for one thing, Leopardi was too young and too passionately interested in the discovery, analysis, and exposition of what he considered to be real to want to or to be able to afford to make such a resolution; for another, his need to attest to the truth and reality of what most people ignore (or prefer to ignore because it is not conducive to their happiness) was too great a necessity of his own soul and being to be set aside. It was something he could live by, and he assumed that spirits congenial to his own could also live by it. I am thinking of the Scottish poet Edwin Muir, who called Leopardi and Baudelaire Romantic, in the bad sense, because for him they merely portrayed the sufferings of existence and merely questioned fate. They expressed an attitude to life, he tells us, "a perfectly genuine one too—but not a principle of life, not something by which one can live."[16] Leopardi would have retorted that for most people the principle they live by is to avoid, as far as possible, facing the unpleasant truths forced upon them in the course of living.

He compared humankind's attitude in general to unpalatable truths, to husbands' attitudes to wives: "I mariti, se vogliono viver tranquilli, è necessario che credano le moglie fedeli, ciascuno la sua; e così fanno; anche quando la metà del mondo sa che il vero è tutt'altro" [Married men, if they want to live in peace, must believe their wives to be faithful, each man his own; and that's what they do; even when half the world knows the truth is totally different]. And this because "il genere umano crede sempre, non il vero, ma quello che è, o pare che sia, piú a proposito suo" [human beings believe, not the truth, but what is, or seems to be, more convenient to them].[17] For Leopardi such pragmatism was utterly out of place and inconceivable, and he could well have said, with Dante, that what he has seen and known, "mentr'io vivo / Convien che nella mia lingua si scerna" [while I live / it is possible to see this in my life and in my art][18]—which is precisely what he did and continued doing until the very end of his life. To camouflage or suppress the bitter truths of life was too ignominious and cowardly for him: "Non io / Con tal vergogna scenderò sotterra" [not I, not with that shame shall I die], he tells us in **"La ginestra."** It was not so much pride in a personal sense as pride on account of his espousing truth at the expense of personal comfort and happiness that mattered to him both as a poet and as a man. Such pride contributed to the tone and timber of his verse as much as did his supreme mastery over style and diction. It also enabled him to accept the common lot of a man, "nato a perir, nutrito in pene" [born to perish, reared in pain], as the subject matter of his poetry rather than the glorification of "eccelsi fati e nove / Felicità, quali il ciel tutto ignora. / Non pur quest'orbe" [sublime destinies and new / Happiness, of a kind that Heaven ignores / not the least of which those of this world].[19]

In this respect, therefore, Leopardi could have turned to Wordsworth, or rather to his spokesman and admirer Matthew Arnold, and said that the joy offered to us in nature that, according to Arnold, constitutes Wordsworth's supremacy over Leopardi, may be "accessible universally," but it needs a particularly gifted nature like Wordsworth's to be able to profit from it. Thus, it can hardly be said to form a part of the "comun fato" [common destiny] that was the "haunt, and the main region" of Leopardi's song.[20] In depicting the lot of common mortals, Leopardi chose the image of the "vecchierel bianco, infermo. / Mezzo vestito e scalzo, / Con gravissimo fascio sulle spalle" [white-haired wise old man, infirm / Barely clad and bare footed / A heavy burden on his shoulders], and not that of one belonging to "a privileged world / Within a world," such as Shakespeare or Milton whom Wordsworth calls "labourers divine!"[21] It is true that the leech-gatherer, protagonist of Wordsworth's great poem "Resolution and Independence," may be regarded as being in some ways a Wordsworthian counterpart, if not equivalent, of Leopardi's "vecchierel bianco, infermo." But although the Leopardian model symbolizes a condition of existence that is all too common, almost universal, the Wordsworthian model embodies qualities one aspires to, or ought to aspire to, but seldom attains. Thus the leech-gatherer is more of an ideal than a symbol of, to quote Wordsworth's own words, "what is to be borne"—and borne by all and sundry without exception.

Hence the ethos as well as the essence of Leopardi's thought and sentiment—and in Leopardi the two are seldom apart—derive from his concern with what is true of human nature and human destiny in general rather than from his interest in what befalls the lot of only some exceptionally gifted and privileged individuals and their not less privileged experience. Take, for instance, such lines as

> Io sono distrutto
> Né schermo alcun ho dal dolore,
> Amore,
> Amor, di nostra vita ultimo inganno

[I am destroyed
No shield whatever have I from pain,
Love,
Love, of our life the ultimate deception][22]

> . . . non le tinte glebe,
> Non gli ululati spechi
> Turbò nostra sciagura,
> Né scolorò le stelle umana cura

[. . . neither the bloodstained lands,
Nor the echoing caves
have been troubled by our misfortune,
Nor have human cares dimmed the stars][23]

> Oh come grato occorre
> Nel tempo giovanil, quando ancor lungo
> La speme e breve ha la memoria il corso,
> Il rimembrar delle passate cose,
> Ancor che triste, e che l'affanno duri!

[Oh how pleasant it is
In time of youth, when hope is still
Long and the span of memory short,
To remember things past,
Though be they sad, and though the anguish endures!][24]

> . . . perché giacendo
> A bell'agio, ozioso,
> S'appaga ogni animale;
> Me, s'io giaccio in riposo, il tedio assale?

[. . . why is
Every animal content
Lying idle at perfect ease;
Why, if I lie down to rest, does boredom seize me?][25]

> Uscir di pena
> È diletto fra noi,

[To overcome hardship
Is for us delight][26]

> Misterio eterno
> Dell'esser nostro

[Eternal mystery
Of our being][27]

> Ma la vita mortal, poi che la bella
> Giovinezza sparí, non si colora
> D'altra luce giammai, né d'altra aurora.

[But mortal life, once fair
Youth has vanished, never takes on the colors
Of another light, nor of another dawn.][28]

> Magnanimo animale
> Non credo io già, ma stolto,
> Quel che nato a perir, nutrito in pene,
> Dice, a goder son fatto.

[I do not, at all believe him
A noble-minded creature who,
Born to perish, reared in pain,
Claims, I was made to find enjoyment.][29]

In such lines, Leopardi's thought and sentiment have all the marks of an intensely personal participation in what he is talking about. But what he is talking about concerns not his own self or situation, but that of mankind in general. And if he generalizes on the basis of his own experience, as one often does, his generalizations are not the less valid for that. The language of these generalizations bears the mark of Leopardi's genius; but the moral as well as the logical cogency behind them confers upon them a universal character, not because he transforms something that has merely a personal validity or relevance into something universally valid, but because—such is his burning passion for truth—he cannot contemplate what has a universal application without identifying himself with it at a personal level. As the "sounding cataract" haunted the young Wordsworth, reflections about human destiny—the nature of what is real and what is to be borne as distinguished from what is illusory and fragile in human life, hopes, and aspirations—haunted Leopardi "like a passion";[30] that is why his thoughts are expressed not so much in philosophical terms, as in poetically charged ones. No philosopher, said Leopardi, can do without a system, but he himself had none. What he did have were those qualities he considered indispensable to a philosopher:

Chi non ha o non ha mai avuto . . . immaginazione, sentimento, capacità di entusiasmo, di eroismo, d'illusioni vive e grandi, di forti e varie passioni, chi non conosce l'immenso sistema del bello, chi non legge o non sente, o non ha mai letto o sentito i poeti, non può assolutamente essere un grande, vero e perfetto filosofo, anzi non sarà mai se non un filosofo dimezzato, di corta vista, di colpo d'occhio assai debole, di penetrazione scarsa, per diligente, paziente, e sottile, e dialettico e matematico ch'ei possa essere; non conoscerà mai il vero, si persuaderà e proverà colla possibile evidenza cose falsissime.

[He who does not have or has never had . . . imagination, feeling, capacity for enthusiasm, for heroism, for grand and ardent illusions, for strong and varied passions, who does not know the vast system of beauty, who does not read or does not feel, or who has never read the poets or listened to them, can certainly never be a great true, or perfect philosopher. In fact, he will never be anything but a cloven philosopher, short-sighted, with dull glance, and feeble insight, however diligent, patient, subtle, dialectical, and mathematical he may be; he will never know the truth, and he will come to believe and prove, as true things that are utterly false.][31]

Leopardi's passion for truth was, therefore, the passion of a philosopher as well as that of a poet. But it was above all the passion of one who found the ultimate confirmation of what he thought in his own experience, observation, and thought, rather than in any theory, dogma, or philosophy.

And although the more he pursued truth the more he found it inimical to happiness, this did not prevent him from carrying on the pursuit intrepidly; nor did it prevent him from celebrating the beauty, sweetness, and soothing power of illusions, because he realized the essential emptiness of life without them (and, in the case of one like himself with his unstinting acceptance of "l'acerbo vero" [the bitter truth] even with them).[32] The contrast between what is true and what is illusory, between what people choose to believe because it is comfortable and conducive to their happiness—as summed up by Browning in "God's in His Heaven, / All's right with the world!"[33]—and what the facts of life in reality are or what they appear to be to an insatiably searching and relentlessly honest mind is the predominant theme in Leopardi's writings, the focal point to which all his moral as well as philosophical reflections and excogitations converge. That is why Leopardi's convictions have the air of incontrovertible certitude about them, which goes a long way toward explaining the masterly simplicity, poise, and perfection of his style. Truth creates its own style, said Ezra Pound, whose translation of Leopardi's **"Sopra il ritratto di una bella donna"** stands out among all the English and American translations of Leopardi's *Canti*. Hence truth and Leopardi's attitude to it determine his style as much as his extraordinary powers of expression and technique.

One of the most conspicuous features of his style and mode of expression is the exceptional degree of calm and even detachment behind them, even when he is dealing with the strongest passions and emotions. It is for this reason that some English critics of Leopardi in the nineteenth century—Charles Edwardes and H. F. Brown, for instance—compared him with Sakyamuni (the Buddha). Seekers of truth, Buddha thought, cannot attain enlightenment unless their passions are calmed. There is, one might say, a dispassionateness in Leopardi's poetry, which is a reflection or consequence of his implicit acceptance of truth, however detrimental that might be to his own peace or happiness. Even in his protestations against nature—

O natura, natura
Perché non rendi poi
Quel che prometti allor?

[Oh nature, nature
Why do you not yield afterward
What you promised then?][34]

—there is an element of stoic calm and dispassionateness that Leopardi associated with the "nobil natura," which, like Leopardi himself,

. . . a sollevar s'ardisce
Gli occhi mortali incontra
Al comun fato, e che con franca lingua,
Nulla al ver detraendo,
Confessa il mal che ci fu dato in sorte.

[. . . that ventures to look up
Through mortal eyes to meet
Our common fate, and with truthful tongue,
Nothing subtracting from the truth,
Admits the evil lot assigned to us as destiny][35]

How many resources of strength this sickly and un-happy poet had at his command can be gauged from his unswerving devotion to and single-minded passion for truth, and from the calm grandeur and crystalline clarity of his style. Each of Leopardi's **Canti** manifests these qualities, but none so superbly as **"Canto notturno di un pastore errante dell'Asia,"** where the silence of the moon may be compared with Buddha's in the face of the unanswerable questions the shepherd—and Leopardi's mouthpiece—confronts it with:

. . . a che vale
Al pastor la sua vita,
La vostra vita a voi? . . . ove tende
Questo vagar mio breve,
Il tuo corso immortale?
Se la vita è sventura,
Perché da noi si dura?
Che fa l'aria infinita, e quel profondo
Infinito seren?

[. . . what is his life worth
To the shepherd,
Or your life to you? . . . where does it lead
This brief wandering of mine,
And your immortal course,
If life is misfortune,
Why do we endure?
What makes the skies infinite, and that infinite
Space serene?][36]

It is of the very essence of Leopardi's integrity as a seeker after truth that he not only asks these questions but also refrains from giving implausible, still less insincere answers to them. Hence the ironical drift of his supposition that what he does not know and therefore cannot answer, the moon, being immortal, might know. But in directing the irony against the moon Leopardi is in fact directing it against himself—insofar as he knows full well that the questions he is asking the moon are by their very nature unanswerable. The silence of the moon cannot be interpreted, as Buddha's silence has sometimes been, as an expression of suspended judgment; for Leopardi it is, as it were, the dumb answering the dumb, and if no answer is given, it is because there is none to give.

Leopardi's passion for truth brought him face-to-face with the unfathomable mystery of life, with the unanswerable questions concerning the universe and human destiny, and he realized, quite early on in life, that the universe is indifferent to man's ethical striving—

Non ha natura al seme
Dell'uom piú stima o cura
Che alla formica.

[Nature has no more regard or care
For the seed of man
Than she does for an ant.][37]

But his view of life "in questo oscuro / Granel di sabbia" [in this obscure grain of sand][38] remained full of its moral content, that is, the values and criteria governing human conduct. Leopardi may not have said with Matthew Arnold that three-fourths of life is conduct, but he would have agreed with him that poetry, and indeed all literature, is at bottom a criticism of life, as his own writings so convincingly demonstrate. Considering man to be "in tutto il nostro globo la cosa piú nobile" [in our entire world the most noble thing],[39] "la principale opera della natura terrestre, o sia del nostro pianeta" [the most important work of earthly nature, that is, of our planet], Leopardi could not but interpret his position both vis-à-vis other men and the "brutto poter . . . ascoso" [brutal power . . . secret] of the universe in broadly moral terms.[40] The very connection between life with illusions and life without them, between illusion and reality, between "uom di povero stato e membra inferme" [man in poor and sickly condition] and "nobil natura" [noble nature], is by its very nature of a profoundly moral order.[41] And "l'acerbo, indegno mistero delle cose" [the bitter, unkind mystery of things],[42] with which Leopardi's passion for truth had to reckon, served only to strengthen his sense of the categorical imperatives of a moral and social life and make his need to embody them in his own daily life all the greater, even though (to quote Omar Khayyám) "tomorrow I may be / Myself with yesterday's Sev'n Thousand Years."[43]

Notes

1. Giacomo Leopardi, *Zibaldone,* 1, 411, ed. Francesco Flora (Milan: Mondadori, 1957).

2. Monaldo Leopardi, in a letter to Antonio Ranieri. Printed by Francesco Flora in his edition of Giacomo Leopardi, *Canti, con una scelta di prosa* (Milan: Mondadori, 1959).

3. Leopardi, *Zibaldone,* 1:161-62.

4. Ibid., 100.

5. Leopardi, *Zibaldone,* 2:976.

6. Leopardi, "A Silvia," in Leopardi, *Canti.* All poems cited are from this work.

7. In a letter to Benjamin Bailey, 22 November 1817. See John Keats, *Complete Poems and Selected Letters,* ed. Clarence DeWitt Thorpe (New York: Doubleday, Doran, 1935), 523-26.

8. William Wordsworth, "Ode on the Intimations of Immortality," in Wordsworth, *Complete Poetical Works* (New York: Crowell, 1962), 403-6.

9. Ibid.

10. Leopardi, "Aspasia."

11. Samuel Taylor Coleridge, "Dejection: An Ode," in *The Poetical Works of Samuel Taylor Coleridge,* ed. James Dykes Campbell (London: Macmillan, 1893), 159-62.

12. Wordsworth, preface to *Lyrical Ballads,* in *Selected Prose,* ed. with intro. and notes by John O. Hayden (Harmondsworth: Penguin, 1988), 278-307.

13. Leopardi, *Zibaldone,* 1:488.

14. Leopardi, "La ginestra."

15. Hardy, "He Resolves to Say No More." See Thomas Hardy, *Winter Words in Various Moods and Metres* (London: Macmillan, 1928), 202.

16. Edwin Muir, *Essays on Literature and Society* (Cambridge, Mass.: Harvard University Press, 1967).

17. Leopardi, "Dialogo di Tristano e di un amico," in Leopardi, *Operette Morali. Essays and Dialogues,* ed. Giovanni Cecchetti (Berkeley and Los Angeles: University of California Press, 1982), 484-507.

18. Dante, *Inferno,* 15.87.

19. Leopardi, "La ginestra."

20. Wordsworth, preface to *The Excursion,* 457-64.

21. Leopardi, "Canto notturno"; Wordsworth, *The Prelude,* 3.291, 5.301.

22. Leopardi, "Ad Angelo Mai."

23. Leopardi, "Bruto minore."

24. Leopardi, "Alla luna."

25. Leopardi, "Canto notturno."

26. Leopardi, "La quiete dopo la tempesta."

27. Leopardi, "Sopra il ritratto di una bella donna."

28. Leopardi, "Il tramonto della luna."

29. Leopardi, "La ginestra."

30. Wordsworth, "Lines Composed a Few Miles above Tintern Abbey," in Wordsworth, 115-18.

31. Leopardi, *Zibaldone,* 1:1169.

32. Leopardi, "Al conte Carlo Pepoli."

33. Robert Browning, *Pippa Passes,* part 1 (London: Duckworth, 1898).

34. Leopardi, "A Silvia."

35. Leopardi, "La ginestra."

36. Leopardi, "Canto notturno."

37. Leopardi, "La ginestra."

38. Ibid.

39. Leopardi, *Zibaldone,* 1:68.

40. Leopardi, "A se stesso."

41. Leopardi, "La ginestra."

42. Leopardi, "Le ricordanze."

43. Edward Fitzgerald, *Rubáiyát of Omar Khayyám and Six Plays of Calderon* (London: J. M. Dent, 1948).

John Alcorn and Dario Del Puppo (essay date spring 1995)

SOURCE: Alcorn, John, and Dario Del Puppo. "Leopardi's Historical Poetics in the *Canzone* 'Ad Angelo Mai.'" *Italica* 72, no. 1 (spring 1995): 21-39.

[*In the following essay, Alcorn and Del Puppo discuss Leopardi's use of figures from Italian history in his poetry.*]

The *canzone,* **"Ad Angelo Mai quand'ebbe trovato i libri di Cicerone della Repubblica"** (1820),[1] raises interesting questions about poetry as a medium for representing history. Though likened to a philosophy of history by Francesco De Sanctis,[2] it is perhaps best analyzed as an expression of what we shall call Leopardi's *historical poetics,* a central element of which is the representation of an idiosyncratic canon of glorious figures in Italian history. In this paper we wish to elucidate Leopardi's historical poetics and make sense of his choice of canon by exploring his philological sensibility and his affinities with the figures whom he evokes. In Section One we consider his philological sensibility through the prism of Friedrich Nietzsche's typology of history, as set out in the essay, "On the Uses and Disadvantages of History for Life." In this light we discuss Leopardi's notions of *truth, reason, beauty,* and *imagination,* and their place in the *canzone.* In Section Two we analyze the poem's framework and its canon of great-hearted spirits. We argue that the poem expresses two, conflicting conceptions of history. In Section Three we return to Leopardi's philological sensibility and discuss his representation of Columbus.

I. LEOPARDI'S PHILOLOGY AND NIETZSCHE'S
TYPOLOGY OF HISTORY

Philology and archaeology contribute to a representation of the past, which in turn can help to create a national identity, or what Benedict Anderson terms "imagined community." An imagined community with the past is a resource in creating a new imagined community in the present. This is apparent in the development of the Risorgimento, and the *canzone* to Mai is an attempt to grapple with these interdependent dimensions of imagined community at the nadir of the Restoration. Nietzsche's discussion of the value of history is a useful, general framework for making sense of Leopardi's vision of history in the *canzone*.

NIETZSCHE'S TYPOLOGY OF HISTORY

It is not by chance that an admirer of Leopardi, Friedrich Nietzsche, himself a philologist, addressed issues which are relevant to Leopardi's poem. Nietzsche writes:

> We need history, certainly, but we need it for reasons different from those for which the idler in the garden of knowledge needs it, even though he may look nobly down on our rough and charmless needs and requirements. We need it, that is to say, for the sake of life and action, not so as to turn comfortably away from life and action, let alone for the purpose of extenuating the self-seeking life and the base and cowardly action. We want to serve history only to the extent that history serves life. . . .
>
> (59)

The German philosopher also provides a useful typology:

> History pertains to the living man in three respects. . . . This threefold relationship corresponds to three species of history—insofar as it is permissible to distinguish between a *monumental*, an *antiquarian* and a *critical* species of history.
>
> (67; textual emphasis)

Let us briefly rehearse Nietzsche's types. Monumental history teaches us that the "greatness that once existed was in any event once *possible* and may thus be possible again" (69; textual emphasis). In this mode, the historian deliberately ignores many deeds which are not considered exemplary. Monumental history has little use for "absolute veracity" and underscores the practical effects of inquiry rather than erudition or explanation. In short, it is less interested in establishing the truth about events, than in creating a meaningful analogy or model for contemporaries.

Antiquarian history, instead, is characterized by the historian's pious reverence for past deeds and by a desire to conserve every artifact which has come down to us through the ages. Nietzsche explains:

> By tending with care that which has existed from of old, he wants to preserve for those who shall come into existence after him the conditions under which he himself came into existence—and thus he serves life.
>
> (72-73)

At first glance, this seems a noble objective, for the antiquarian deems all evidence pertinent and can therefore both satisfy a passion for scholarly pursuits and contribute to our knowledge of the past. Yet Nietzsche's antiquarian closely resembles Leopardi's caricature of pedants:

> Non ho ancora potuto conoscere un letterato Romano che intenda sotto il nome di letteratura altro che l'Archeologia. Filosofia, mor,ale, politica, scienza del cuore umano, eloquenza, poesia, filologia, tutto ciò è straniero in Roma, e pare un giuoco da fanciulli, a paragone del trovare se quel pezzo di rame o di sasso appartenne a Marcantonio o a Marcagrippa.
>
> (Letter to Monaldo Leopardi from Rome, 9 December 1822; *Tutte le opere* 1: 1133-34)

For Nietzsche, the antiquarian's "blind rage for collecting" leaves mankind "encased in the stench of must and mould" (75).

Although Nietzsche overstates his point, he underscores a premise about historical inquiry which is basically true: evidence of past events and actions cannot by itself provide the fullness of meaning. Historical knowledge requires interpretation and judgment. The monumental historian is selective, whereas the antiquarian is incapable of exercising good judgment about what should be preserved and studied. The real problem, continues Nietzsche, is that antiquarianism "knows only how to *preserve* life, not how to engender it; it always undervalues that which is becoming because it has no instinct for divining it—as monumental history, for example" (75; textual emphasis).

Lastly, Nietzsche describes the *critical* mode of historical inquiry as follows:

> If he is to live, man must possess and from time to time employ the strength to break up and dissolve a part of the past: he does this by bringing it before the tribunal, scrupulously examining it and finally condemning it. . . .
>
> (75-76)

Nietzsche's *critical* history is not based on a transcendent sense of justice but on life alone, "that dark driving power that insatiably thirsts for itself" (76). There is of course much overlap among Nietzsche's categories. For example, the *monumental* mode can be as destructive as *critical* history in its selection of phenomena worth perpetuating. The *antiquarian* is also subject to the necessity which compels the *critical* historian to make hard choices. A difference is that the antiquarian does not choose "to break up or dissolve a part of the past." Selection occurs nonetheless because the quantity of artifacts and information taxes a society's capacity for conservation. By placing enormous strain on society's resources, antiquarian overload might lead paradoxically to degeneration of historical memory. In sum, Nietzsche's historical types underscore the subjective uses of information and artifacts from the past, and provide concepts which are manageable and useful for examining Leopardi's philological sensibility.

LEOPARDI'S PHILOLOGICAL SENSIBILITY

In light of Nietzsche's categories, how might one characterize Leopardi's approach to history in the period when he composed **"Ad Angelo Mai"**?[3] We have seen that Leopardi rejects the antiquarian mode. His approach is largely monumental, though with an element of critical history. The monumental approach is manifest in the poem's pageant of great-hearted Italians. The poem's vatic tone corresponds to the "divining" feature of monumental history: "When the past speaks it always speaks as an oracle: only if you are an architect of the future and know the present will you understand it" (Nietzsche 94). In an image which fascinated De Sanctis,[4] monumental history shades over into a twist on critical history, as Leopardi accuses his contemporaries of precluding a future by squandering the past: "ozio circonda / I monumenti vostri" (**"Ad Angelo Mai"** 43-44). The twist is that, whereas Nietzsche defines the critical mode as an effort to "break up and dissolve a part of the past . . . by bringing it before the tribunal" (75-76), Leopardi writes in order to break up and condemn *the present* by recovering a monumental past.

In his modernist critique of Enlightenment and Romantic historiography, Nietzsche dethrones Reason; and in his typology of history, rational belief takes a back seat to desire and will, where it appears to be merely instrumental. Leopardi, too, is a harsh critic of rationalism, witness his argument in the **"Discorso intorno alla poesia Romantica"** (1818), that "La ragione è nemica nelle cose umane di quasi ogni grandezza" (**Tutte le opere** 1: 921). Reason is, however, crucial to understanding the ancient poets' close relationship to nature, the key to artistic creativity:

> Ora da tutto questo e dalle altre cose che si son dette, agevolmente si comprende che la poesia dovette essere agli antichi oltremisura più facile e spontanea che non può essere presentemente a nessuno, e che a' tempi nostri per imitare poetando la natura vergine e primitiva, e parlar il linguaggio della natura (lo dirò con dolore della condizione nostra, con disprezzo delle risa dei romantici) è pressoché necessario lo studio lungo e profondo de' poeti antichi.
>
> (**Tutte le opere** 1: 930-31)

The object of Reason, *il vero,* is thus at once a necessary condition for and a solvent of the object of imagination, *il bello.* In a notebook entry dated 12-23 July 1820, Leopardi states: "La cognizione del vero cioè dei limiti e definizioni delle cose, circoscrive l'immaginaz." (**Zibaldone di pensieri** 1: 167). Correlatively, monu-

mental history can no longer be innocent of an element of critical history. We shall explore the tension within this hybrid in Section Three.

To clarify Leopardi's approach to history, consider how the basic ways of framing historical inquiry differ in their respective objects of scrutiny. When speaking of *history,* for example, we typically mean a process or set of processes of change occurring in a particular time and place, the existence of which we can conjecture from presently available evidence together with our knowledge of how different kinds of processes of change typically occur. *History* is the object of inquiry for the critical historian. The *past,* on the other hand, can be likened to an ocean of actions and events whose murky water we observe from a distance and cannot fathom. This is the realm of the antiquarian, for whom history is a collection of facts. Finally, when we speak of having a *sense of the past,* we attempt to give meaning to events and actions from the perspective of *utility.* We assume that there is a relation between the present and the past and that a sense of the past shapes an individual's or community's identity and informs behavior in the present. For Leopardi, a sense of the past is a poetic understanding of the relation among historical facts. A difference between *history, past,* and *a sense of the past* is that the lattermost concept has room for the objects of the former, whereas the converse is not so readily the case.

NECESSARY ILLUSIONS

Parallel to the tension of *il bello* and *il vero* is the conflict between Leopardi's belief that *illusioni* are necessary and his awareness of their irrationality. This conflict has implications for his understanding of action. In a notebook entry dated 26 March 1820 Leopardi writes:

> Per le grandi azioni che la maggior parte non possono provenire se non da illusione, non basta ordinariamente l'inganno della fantasia come sarebbe quello di un filosofo, e come sono le illusioni de' nostri giorni tanto scarsi di grandi fatti, ma si richiede l'inganno della ragione, come presso gli antichi.
>
> (**Zibaldone di pensieri** 1: 119)

Heroic actions require more than flights of imagination, they demand self-deception. It might be argued that in espousing self-deception Leopardi resolves the conflict between *illusioni* and *ragione* in favor of the former, but the matter is more complicated. In the same notebook entry Leopardi refers to a news report from Germany describing the assassination of the conservative playwright, August-Friedrich Kotzebue, by a young liberal. Leopardi judges that the assassin was motivated by "fanfaluche mistiche," a mindset "che ingombra la ragione," rather than "per effetto della semplice antica illusione di libertà" (1: 119). Leopardi dissociates *illusioni* from delirium and madness, arguing that great deeds spring from stances that leave room for reason. We have come full circle. *Illusioni* are necessary and require *l'inganno della ragione,* yet cannot produce *grandi azioni* if they crowd out reason. Reason appears to be a necessary *negative* component of *grandi azioni*. To complicate matters further, there is a second-order effect: the implications for action of *awareness* of the structure of *grandi azioni*. Does reflexivity undermine the possibility of great actions? Leopardi gives poetic expression to the ideal of 'rational *illusioni*' and the implications of reflexivity in the *canzone* to Mai.

II. THE CANZONE TO MAI

COMPOSITION AND THEMES

"Ad Angelo Mai" is in the tradition of Italian classicist poetry which champions a patriotic cause. One thinks in particular of Ugo Foscolo's *poemetto,* "Dei Sepolcri" (1804),[5] in which tombs and associated rituals prolong the memory of historical events and figures. By contrast, **"Ad Angelo Mai"** expresses Leopardi's plaint at the ineluctable demise of historical imagination.[6]

In the dedication to the first edition of **"Ad Angelo Mai,"** Leopardi writes: "la facoltà dell'immaginare e del ritrovare è spenta in Italia, ancorché gli stranieri ce l'attribuiscano tuttavia come nostra speciale e primaria qualità, ed è secca ogni vena di affetto e di vera eloquenza" (**Tutte le opere** 1: 55-56). He quotes Petrarch, for whom weeping is a natural disposition ("ed io son un di quei che 'l pianger giova," *Canzoniere* 37.69), and states that his own tears are instead caused by historical circumstances and the will of fortune. Like Leopardi's other *canzoni* of this period, the poem to Mai is based on the Petrarchan model. Dante (229-30) explains in the *De vulgari eloquentia* (2.3) that the *canzone* is characterized by a high style and a serious subject matter (229-30). Indeed, in *canzoni* such as "All'Italia" Petrarch combines lyrical expression with political purpose. The *canzone* form enables Leopardi to establish a link to Dante and Petrarch, who open the canon of great-hearted spirits in the poem. Like Petrarch before him, Leopardi describes the abysmal state of contemporary Italy and shames his interlocutors into action.

The poem consists of twelve stanzas of fifteen verses.[7] The first four stanzas (1-60) and the concluding verses of the last stanza (175-80) comprise the poem's conceptual framework. The intermediate stanzas (61-175) represent the pageant of great-hearted spirits and the thoughts they evoke in the poet. In the fifth stanza there are the portraits of Dante (61-66) and Petrarch (66-75). The sixth and seventh stanzas (vv. 76-105) represent Columbus and the consequences of his voyage for humankind. The eighth stanza (106-20) evokes Ariosto. The ninth and tenth stanzas (121-50) summon Tasso from his "sconsolato avello." The eleventh stanza and

introduction to the twelfth portray Alfieri. Leopardi concludes the pageant of great-hearted spirits with an invocation to Angelo Mai, "scopritor famoso," to resurrect the dead since the living are fast asleep.

THE CANZONE'S CONCEPTUAL FRAMEWORK

The poem's exordium conjures the historical context. In an age when Italy is but an imagined polity, Mai is a real-life, modern-day Clio who symbolizes philological inquiry. Leopardi praises Mai's discovery while lambasting the "secol morto" (4) enveloped in a "nebbia di tedio" (5). *Tedio* is the phenomenological equivalent of *il nulla,* which appears in the fifth stanza. Leopardi notes that historical knowledge is subject to the will of the gods:

> Certo senza de' numi alto consiglio
> Non è ch'ove più lento
> E grave è il disperato obblio.
>
> (16-18)

Archaeology and philology are of ambiguous utility if they require the unpredictable cooperation of the gods. In this vein Leopardi suggests that *disperato obblio* (18) can eventually dissolve historical memory.

Rather than view these verses as a nihilistic reflection on historical knowledge and as a critique of free will, we should recognize that Leopardi identifies a constraint which all historians face: the destructive effects of time, nature, and history itself on the artifacts which are the raw material of historical memory. Historical memory thus requires an immense effort to preserve and recover meaningful artifacts. Though this effort is made systematic in the disciplines of archaelogy and philology, the results must be fragmentary, and the fragments unrepresentative. The accidents of time, nature, and history lend a random element to the pattern of historical artifacts, an element which Leopardi represents as the will of the gods. Following a conventional view, Leopardi portrays the gods as fickle, underscoring humankind's frailty and vulnerability; yet he interprets Mai's unexpected discovery as a sign of the gods' good will:

> Ancora è pio
> Dunque all'Italia il cielo; anco si cura
> Di noi qualche immortale.
>
> (20-22)

The young Leopardi clings to a 'centering' view of the universe, in which the gods care (in unpredictable and not necessarily providential ways) for human history.

These verses (16-22) fuel Leopardi's indictment of his contemporaries, whom not even the favor of the gods shakes from cowardly torpor. "Codarda" modifies "patria," Leopardi's imagined community (30), deepening the criticism of national character in verses 24-25: "virtude / rugginosa dell'itala natura." Luigi Blasucci (86) describes concrete poetic images such as *virtude/ rugginosa* and *tedio che n'affoga* as Leopardi's materialization of the abstract.[8] Further excellent examples are *disperato obblio* (18) and *dira / obblivione* (50-51). Here the adjectives (*disperato, dira*) express his subjective, existential condition whereas the nouns (*obblio, obblivione*) reveal Nature's devastating effects on historical memory.

The rhetorical questions in the first three stanzas are a characteristic feature of Leopardi's poetics in this period. The poet also employs this device in **"All'Italia"** and **"Sopra il monumento a Dante."** Luigi Russo (640) and De Sanctis (115) note that the rhetorical questions prepare the poetic impetus of the central stanzas, yet proceed to argue that this part of the *canzone* is less effective than the representation of illustrious cultural figures which follows.

Leopardi dramatically introduces the third stanza with the following questions:

> Di noi serbate, o gloriosi, ancor
> Qualche speranza? in tutto
> Noi siam periti?
>
> (31-33)

The discovery of artifacts provides the material evidence for a comparison between the poet's contemporaries and previous civilizations. The study of past actions and events helps build a sense of imagined community or historical identity. The pressing question for Leopardi is whether his age meets the expectations of previous civilizations. There is a subtle shift in poetic voice from "patria" to "Di noi." The former is objective and ostensive, whereas the latter is subjective and collective.

To understand the deeds and works of a previous civilization requires imagination. Leopardi explains this in the case of old texts in a notebook entry dated 22 November 1820:

> Del resto per intendere i filosofi, e quasi ogni scrittore, è necessario, come per intendere i poeti, aver tanta forza d'immaginazione, e di sentimento, e tanta capacità di riflettere, da potersi porre nei panni dello scrittore, e in quel punto preciso di vista e di situazione, in cui egli si trovava nel considerare le cose di cui scrive; altrimenti non troverete mai che'egli sia chiaro abbastanza, per quanto lo sia in effetto.
>
> (*Zibaldone di pensieri* 1: 227)

The faculty of imagination thus requires the capacity for empathy.

Historical imagination is a kind of vicarious memory. It can therefore be tinged with temporal emotions (the complex emotions associated with memory and anticipation). How one imagines, and forms, a sense of the past is often complicated by the way one's emotions are associated with memory and anticipation. This is evident in verses 33-36:

> A voi forse il futuro
> Conoscer non si toglie. Io son distrutto
> Né schermo alcuno ho dal dolor, che scuro
> M'è l'avvenire, e tutto quanto io scerno.

The image of a dark future is closely related to Leopardi's sense of the past. Awareness of the fragility of historical memory quickens his desire for historical knowledge, for to forget the past is to compromise the future.[9] Leopardi draws attention to a sign of moral decay and atrophied memory, the "ozio" (43) that surrounds the monuments to the past. A sense of historical closure finds formal expression in the rhymes *futuro-scuro* (33; 35) and *viltade-etade* (44-45).

At the beginning of the fourth stanza Leopardi again invokes Mai, "Bennato ingegno," suggesting that the Vatican scholar was destined to great deeds. In his letter to Mai of January 1820, Leopardi writes:

> Ella è proprio un miracolo di mille cose, d'ingegno di gusto di dottrina di diligenza di studio infatigabile, di fortuna tutta nuova ed unica. Insomma, V. S. ci fa tornare ai tempi dei Petrarca e dei Poggi, quando ogni giorno era illustrato da una nuova scoperta classica, e la maraviglia e la gioia de' letterati non trovava riposo.
>
> (*Tutte le opere* 1: 1091)

Leopardi's conception of Mai's contribution and his use of Mai's discovery as an occasion to conjure Dante, Petrarch, Columbus, Ariosto, Tasso, and Alfieri invites a comparison with Dante's use of Virgil in the *Divina Commedia*. In these works Mai and Virgil are more than dramatic characters or interlocutors: Virgil is a symbol of human reason and Mai is a symbol of philology. Dante and Leopardi sit in judgment on their times and aspire to change the behavior of their contemporaries through art. The contrasts are, of course, substantial. In the mimetic scene narrated in *Inferno* IV, Virgil is a direct link between Dante and antiquity. This episode well illustrates Dante's optimism regarding historical recovery and the continuation of a literary tradition. By contrast, Mai is not a guide but a catalyst for historical memory. Moreover, Dante feigns an encounter between modernity and antiquity, whereas Leopardi evokes the great-hearted spirits in a doleful *ubi sunt* which underscores his longing for the values personified in them.

IDENTIFYING WITH THE GREAT-HEARTED SPIRITS

Despite the complexity of Leopardi's affinities with Dante and Petrarch he devotes merely ten verses to them (61-70). By omitting to mention them by name he underscores their prominence in the Italian cultural imagination. Their contemporary interest is spelled out in the remark, "Ahi dal dolor comincia e nasce / L'italo canto" (69-70). Dante is a symbol of the poetry which can spring from political oppression, and Petrarch is a symbol of the song of unrequited love. Leopardi contrasts the life-affirming pain which Dante and Petrarch experienced and the unbearable, destructive pain of "noia" (70-72):[10]

> Oh te beato,
> A cui fu vita il pianto! A noi cinse le fasce
> Cinse il fastidio; a noi presso la culla
> Immoto siede, e su la tomba, il nulla.
>
> (72-75)

Leopardi thus enlarges his lament beyond the Italian question, expressing a sense of a general oppression of humankind by *il nulla*. Leopardi moves from blaming the current state of Italy on the *ozio* of his contemporaries and the unfathomable actions of the gods to argue that political redemption is further undermined by a demoralizing awareness of the human condition. Perhaps Leopardi is saying that the obstacles confronting him are much greater than the ones faced by Dante and Petrarch. To create an imagined community now requires not only a shared historical identity, but a common understanding of the negative effects of *noia*.

Leopardi's representation of Columbus in the sixth and seventh stanzas is more elaborate than his representations of Dante and Petrarch because it is the locus of reflections on myth and imagination, two requirements of great deeds. His representation of the "ligure ardito" can also be seen as a comment on the distinction between two conceptions of the universe: one anthropocentric, the other *decentered*. Columbus represents the destruction of myth. He is the only non-poet in Leopardi's canon. Columbus's voyage is of special interest as a metaphor for Leopardi's predicament and as a clue to Leopardi's use of Mai as a symbol. Hence we shall defer further discussion of Columbus to Section Three and pass directly to Leopardi's representation of Ariosto.

Ariosto is depicted as the "cantor vago dell'arme e degli amori" (108) who fills our lives with "felici errori," a Leopardian synonym for useful *illusioni*. Leopardi's nostalgia for *illusioni* has an element in common with his praise of pain, for both are life-affirming. Leopardi's affinity with Ariosto, the least philosophical among the great-hearted spirits, rests on a distinction between two types of imagination. In a notebook entry dated 5 July 1820 Leopardi explains that Dante and Homer manifest the strength of imagination, Ariosto and Ovid its fecundity:

> Quella facilmente rende l'uomo infelice per la profondità delle sensazioni, questa al contrario lo rallegra colla varietà e colla facilità di fermarsi sopra tutti gli

oggetti e di abbandonarli, e conseguentemente colla copia delle distrazioni.

*(**Zibaldone di pensieri** 1: 154)*

Ariosto's imagination does not produce lasting passions of the kind that sustain great action, but consoles humankind in times of misfortune (1: 154). In the Ariosto stanza the vatic and tormented tone of the previous strophes gives way to a lyrical voice:

> Nascevi ai dolci sogni intanto, e il primo
> Sole splendeati in vista,
> Cantor vago. . . .
>
> (106-08);

> a voi pensando,
> In mille vane amenità si perde
> La mente mia. Di vanità, di belle
> Fole e strani pensieri
> Si componea l'umana vita.
>
> (113-17)

The lyricism is a stylistic complement to the tragic tone of the representations of the other figures, while it reinforces the complex emotions triggered by nostalgia. The evocation dissolves in the stanza's conclusion where Leopardi blames humankind for banishing sweet illusions, the only solace in the face of bitter truths. Though less central than works that encourage one to imagine (historically) possible worlds, Ariosto's fantastic literature also has a place in creating a sense of imagined community.

A sense that everything is vain, except for pain and suffering, is attributed to Tasso, the only figure who is named and the one with whom Leopardi identifies most closely. The altercasting of Tasso in the ninth and tenth stanzas comprises a complex of social and personal themes, namely, a profound sense of social and political alienation (127-28); lack of love (128-30); constant meditation on "il nulla" (130-32); and the knowledge that glory comes late or posthumously ("tardo onore," 132-34); all of which contribute to psychological alienation and madness (141-43). Tasso is a symbol of the Romantic notion of the artist as a misunderstood and tormented visionary (145-46). In evoking Tasso's vicissitudes, Leopardi predicts a similar fate for himself, the consequence of a shared illness ("nostro mal," 135).

The identification with Tasso has implications for Leopardi's views on political action and historical knowledge. In his belief that art has the power to cement an imagined community, Leopardi is a man of his times. He attributes this power not to politicians or to theorists but to artists; in particular, to poets. Perhaps it is for this reason that Machiavelli is not represented in the canon. Indeed, the author of *The Prince* theorized the possibility that base motives can contribute to glorious actions. Leopardi loathes opportunism, a political necessity. Like Machiavelli, he recognizes the importance of *exempla* in political education, but his choice of canonical figures is guided by wholly different principles.

In Leopardi's view, Italian cultural history would have ended with Tasso were it not for the "Allobrogo feroce," Vittorio Alfieri. Leopardi's neglect of other figures conflicts with the traditional literary-historical view of the eighteenth century as a period of political and cultural innovation. He overlooks civic-minded and patriotic figures such as Ludovico Antonio Muratori in historical studies and Cesare Beccaria in political and legal theory. He ignores Carlo Goldoni whose theatrical reform was widely acknowledged and debated. The most surprising lacuna is the omission of Giuseppe Parini, whose conception of glory is the subject of a moral essay written by Leopardi in 1824. Leopardi selects Alfieri as a kindred spirit for his opposition to tyranny and for his tragic temperament. Timpanaro (*Classicismo e illuminismo* 149) explains that Leopardi was also moved by the antitheistic strand in Alfieri's tragedies. By altercasting Alfieri, Leopardi affirms his desire to combat the will of the gods, who in the second stanza act as inscrutable catalysts or obstacles to historical knowledge and who, thereby, either promote or inhibit the development of a collective identity. There, humankind has not been abandoned by the gods. In the poem's conclusion, however, Leopardi's representation of Alfieri suggests that the transcendent is the enemy.[11] In this light Leopardi's criticism of his contemporaries makes sense. If psychological alienation is a given of human existence, then one may either surrender to the inevitable, or combat it by promoting human dignity. With the help of Alfieri, Leopardi finds that the struggle for glory and dignity lends meaning to human existence. Leopardi's imagined community is a community of kindred and noble spirits and not merely a political entity.

In the poem's conclusion Leopardi again invokes Mai, the "scopritor famoso" (175), exhorting him to wake the dead since the living are fast asleep. May this century of mud (179), augurs the poet, thirst for life and rise to do illustrious deeds, or may it wallow in shame. The concluding rhyme "agogni-vergogni" recapitulates the poem's tenor. Leopardi's exhortation turns on a distinction between the ethos of his contemporaries and that of the great-hearted spirits, between a *guilt culture* and a *shame culture*. Bernard Williams ably explains this distinction:

> What arouses guilt in an agent is an act or omission of a sort that typically elicits from other people anger, resentment, or indignation. What the agent may offer in order to turn this away is reparation; he may also fear punishment or may inflict it on himself. What arouses shame, on the other hand, is something that typically elicits from others contempt or derision or avoid-

ance. . . . It will lower the agent's self-respect and diminish him in his own eyes. . . . More positively, shame may be expressed in attempts to reconstruct or improve oneself.

(89-90)

In a notebook entry dated 22 August 1822, Leopardi states that there is nothing more shameful for the spirited individual than shame itself: "Nessuna cosa è vergognosa per l'uomo di spirito nè capace di farlo vergognare, e provare il dispiacevole sentimento di questa passione, se non solamente il vergognarsi e l'arrossire" (*Zibaldone di pensieri* 2: 1397). The structure and conclusion of the *canzone* to Mai indicate that Leopardi predicates the regeneration of Italian history and culture upon the mechanisms of a shame culture. The effective scope of his imagined community can thus be no greater than the grip of such an ethos on his interlocutors. Nevertheless, by expressing his conception in verse, Leopardi reclaims a social purpose for letters. Perhaps this explains Leopardi's exclusion of the Arcadian and Neo-Classical poets who came between Tasso and Alfieri. For Leopardi, poetry stirs the soul and promotes action, much as Alfieri attempts to do with theater. Even in Foscolo's inspiring poem about the civic value of tombs poetry is seen as one among many human activities which contribute to social identity. Leopardi appears to privilege poetry as the most inspirational art form because he believes that poetry speaks the language of the emotions and character, and that it is thus most suited to inspire a sense of imagined community.

III. LEOPARDI'S HISTORICAL POETICS

BETWEEN CLASSICISM AND ROMANTICISM

The passage from *pessimismo storico* to *pessimismo cosmico* occurs when Leopardi appreciates the degree to which nature rather than historical circumstances is responsible for unhappiness. The study of history contributes to this passage insofar as history manifests human frailty before nature. In the *canzone* to Mai Leopardi expresses an intermediate position comprising conflicting strands. One strand is normative: historical knowledge should have the hortatory function of inspiring actions aimed at alleviating *la noia,* and, more ambitiously, at recasting one's imagined community. The other strand is a second-order effect in which recognition of the vulnerability of historical identity, a vulnerability which historical inquiry itself discloses, induces skepticism about the possibility of a new imagined community. The second-order effect undermines the normative function.

Leopardi's treatment of Italian cultural history is different from politically conservative classicism (Mai's current) and progressive Romanticism.[12] Mai takes philology and historical disciplines to lend legitimacy to Catholic doctrine and prestige to the *Ancien regime,* whereas progressive Romantics promote Italian nationalism. Though Leopardi shares the classicists' belief that classical antiquity and mythology are sources of aesthetic inspiration, he rejects their political aims. And, conversely, though he shares the Romantics' aim of national unification, he rejects their repudiation of myths and their optimism.[13]

LEOPARDI'S THREE WAYS OF SEEING

In a notebook entry dated 20 January 1820, written immediately after the completion of the *canzone* to Mai, Leopardi explores a threefold typology of 'ways of seeing': heroic, natural and philosophical (***Zibaldone di pensieri*** 1: 116-18). His typology invites comparison with Nietzsche's threefold typology of history and the everyday ways of framing historical inquiry mentioned above (Section One). The heroic way of seeing closely resembles monumental history and captures a sense of the past because it appeals to the imagination:

> L'una e la più beata, di quelli per li quali esse hanno anche più spirito che corpo, e voglio dire degli uomini di genio e sensibili, ai quali non c'è cosa che non parli all'immaginazione o al cuore, e che trovano da per tutto materia di sublimarsi e di sentire e di vivere, e un rapporto continuo delle cose coll'infinito e coll'uomo, e una vita indefinibile e vaga, in somma di quelli che considerano il tutto sotto un aspetto infinito e in relazione cogli slanci dell'animo loro.
>
> (***Zibaldone*** 1: 116)

The poet ascribes three attributes to the natural way of seeing: it is the most common way of seeing; it is superficial; and it provides the most durable happiness to individuals. Unlike the heroic way of seeing, it does not produce great actions but a sense of complacency:

> e senza dar gran risalto al sentimento dell'esistenza, riempie però la vita di una pienezza non sentita, ma sempre uguale e uniforme, e conduce per una strada piana e in relazione colle circostanze dalla nascita al sepolcro.
>
> (***Zibaldone di pensieri*** 1: 117)

Like Nietzsche's antiquarian mode, the natural way of seeing is nonjudgmental. It thus expresses a static *mediocritas* or complacency which the poet rejects, echoing his criticism of Roman antiquarians.

Leopardi characterizes the philosophical way of seeing as follows:

> La terza e la sola funesta e miserabile, e tuttavia la sola vera, di quelli per cui le cose non hanno nè spirito nè corpo, ma son tutte vane e senza sostanza, e voglio dire dei filosofi e degli uomini per lo più di sentimento che dopo l'esperienza e la lugubre cognizione delle cose, dalla prima maniera passano di salto a quest'ultima senza toccare la seconda, e trovano e sentono da per

> tutto il nulla e il vuoto, e la vanità delle cure umane e dei desideri e delle speranze e di tutte le illusioni inerenti alla vita per modo che senza esse non è vita.
>
> (1: 117)

He argues further that reason, though generally extolled as humankind's distinctive faculty, cannot relieve misery, let alone provide happiness. He admires the heroic way of seeing, but recognizes that post-Enlightenment intellectuals, and he among them, are prone to the philosophical way of seeing. Reason has irreversibly disclosed *il nulla*. The development of civilization issues in the tyranny of rational thinking which in turn diminishes the motivation for *grandezza*. The poet draws the paradoxical conclusion that to dwell on *il nulla* is "una verissima pazzia," but the most reasonable madness known to humankind and therefore the only true wisdom. The philosophical way of seeing resembles Nietzsche's conception of critical history and is close to current notions of history.

The *canzone* to Mai gives poetic representation to a particular conflict between belief and desire: between his belief that monumental history can no longer inspire great action and political change in the age of the philosophical way of seeing, and his desire for such action and change. Leopardi introduces a quandary which goes beyond a subjective, youthful expression of the conflicting emotions of desire for hope and glory, on the one hand, and frustration, anger, bitterness, and despair, on the other. Leopardi's poem illustrates two conflicting views of history: the philosophical perspective (or critical history) and the heroic view (or monumental history). The poet prefers the latter given his desire for action, but recognizes that as a thinker influenced by the Enlightenment he cannot escape the former. It is noteworthy that he reaffirms monumental history precisely in an age when historians are shifting decisively to critical history, witness Leopold von Ranke's (57) celebrated project in 1824 of representing history "wie es eigentlich gewesen." To believe that great actions are still possible, Leopardi must renounce a part of his intellectual formation. Reason has relegated human beings to the role of passive spectators of life; historical inquiry thus serves little purpose. In the *canzone* he expresses this belief but does not fully accept it.

There is another important feature of Leopardi's treatment of past actions and events: the impossibility of detaching the emotional from the rational self. In Leopardi's language, *illusioni* are not only useful, they are necessary. Contemplation of *il nulla* does not enable humankind to dispense with the emotional self: the epicurean ideal of ataraxy eludes us. As moral agents, humans cannot remove the emotional, psychological self from the world. Leopardi cannot reconcile critical and monumental history in the *canzone,* just as he cannot square the philosophical with the heroic way of seeing.

One of the poem's most interesting portraits expresses Leopardi's complex historical sensibility and illumines the poet's intentions. Columbus, the "ligure ardita prole," is a symbol of daring. A modern Ulysses, he personifies the risk-taker who undertakes great actions; he is a figure worthy of both the Romantic notion of hero and the Enlightenment ideal of intellectual progress. Yet in a set of brilliant verses Leopardi tempers his portrait of Columbus by expressing a sense of loss in the great discovery, a perverse effect of Columbus's epistemic journey: "Ecco svaniro a un punto, / E figurato è il mondo in breve carta; / Ecco tutto è simile, e discoprendo, / Solo il nulla s'accresce" (97-100). Leopardi revisits and enlarges this kind of perverse effect in the moral essay, **"Il Copernico,"** in which he underscores the demystifying consequences of knowledge. Columbus unsettles the European view of the world; Copernicus debunks the anthropocentric conception of the Universe. Columbus's journey represents the eradication of myth and the impossibility of creating new myths. In this sense Leopardi is unlike Nietzsche, whose discussion of the advantages and disadvantages of history for life is a brief for will and desire. Instead Leopardi's representation of Columbus affirms the irreversibility of the critical mode guided by reason.[14] There is thus a parallel between Mai's discovery of the ciceronian manuscript and Columbus's discovery of the New World. A sense of a genuinely tragic element in knowledge colors Leopardi's representations of the two discoveries.

Let us gather the threads of our discussion. The *canzone* to Mai and contemporary writings reveal Leopardi's concern with the phenomenology of historical imagination. He historicizes this subject and provides a simple typology for making sense of it. He argues that awareness of the phenomenology of historical imagination is in tension with the psychology of action required for *grandi azioni*. As a moralist, Leopardi wishes his philosophical meditations to issue in art that might influence the attitudes and actions of his readers. The tension between insight and aspiration is represented in the *canzone* in the form of a canon of great actors interwoven with reflections upon the perverse effects of knowledge, itself the product of great actions. Monumental history is interwoven with critical history. The poet's peculiar representation of history at once affirms reason and reveals reason's limits. Poetry, the language of the emotions and the imagination, is life-affirming (like Nietzsche's monumental history), yet also speaks bitter truths.

Notes

1. In Leopardi (1981: 67-106). It was composed in January 1820, published in July of the same year in Bologna, and then revised and published anew during Leopardi's lifetime, in 1824 (Bologna), 1831 (Florence) and 1835 (Naples). In a letter to Pietro Brighenti of 28 April 1820, Leopardi writes that the deliberately innocent title enabled the *canzone* to escape his father's censorship: "Il titolo della seconda inedita si è trovato fortunatamente innocentissimo. Si tratta di un Monsignore. Ma mio padre non s'immagina che vi sia qualcuno che da tutti i soggetti sa trarre occasione di parlar di quello che più gl'importa, e non sospetta punto che sotto quel titolo si nasconda una Canzone piena di orribile fanatismo" (*Tutte le opere* 1: 1100).

2. De Sanctis hailed the poem: "Canzone straordinaria, se mai ce ne fu. . . . Prima c'era l'artista, già maestro di stile; ora c'è anche il poeta, c'è lui" (115) and "La canzone è un primo poema del mondo, cosí com'è visto dal giovine. E' come una filosofia della storia, dove tutto è coordinato, come in uno schema" (119).

3. Roger Baillet states that 'history' is the "materia sofferta del Canto, asservita dalla poesia che se ne giova, trasformata dal filtro della memoria, come di un'esperienza viva della gioventù e mai come meditazione matura, da storico, sui fatti del passato" (95).

4. According to De Sanctis, "Quest'ultima frase è gigantesca: è la piramide nel deserto" (115).

5. Cesare Federico Goffis explains that unlike Leopardi, Foscolo wishes to construct myths. He suggests that Leopardi engages in a veiled polemic with Foscolo and that "Ad Angelo Mai" is an emendation of "Dei Sepolcri" (687-88).

6. Dante Della Terza notes that the poem to Mai is unique among the patriotic poetry of the time "proprio per l'audace simbiosi tra storia letteraria e visione del mondo che essa propone . . ." (10).

7. Unlike Leopardi's previous *canzoni*, "Ad Angelo Mai" has a uniform rhyme scheme. Like the earlier *canzone*, "Sopra il monumento a Dante," "Ad Angelo Mai" exhibits a contrast between regularity of prosody and irregularity of syntax (Fubini 50-51). This contrast is compounded by Leopardi's use of rhymed couplets at the end of each strophe. The stanzas' axiomatic and epigraphic conclusions express his bitterness.

8. Blasucci and Galimberti provide close analyses of linguistic and stylistic features.

9. The negative effects of historical amnesia described by Leopardi recall the *contrapasso* suffered by heretics in Dante's *Inferno*. There is a difference however. In Dante's text the impaired vision which afflicts the souls of heretics is a manifestation of divine justice, whereas in Leopardi the historical blindness which afflicts the liv-

ing is caused by a prosaic *ethos* and is a manifestation of the fragility of historical memory. Galimberti (54-56) suggests that Leopardi was inspired by Dante's representation of Statius's encounter with Virgil in *Purgatorio* XXI.

10. "Anche il dolore che nasce dalla noia e dal sentimento della vanità delle cose è più tollerabile assai che la stessa noia" (*Zibaldone di pensieri* 1: 93).

11. See in particular Alfieri's *Saul*. Vitilio Masiello explains that in the tragedies before *Saul* Alfieri represents political conflict, usually altercasting a dominant and powerful antagonist to a vanquished protagonist. In *Saul,* however, Alfieri represents the protagonist's existential struggle against the backdrop of "un più ampio, cosmico rapporto di forze" (161-62).

12. See Springer (Introduction and chapter three). Springer distinguishes two types of archaeological representation: the encomiastic mode of the Church and the hortatory mode of the democratic opposition (2). Springer describes them in terms that may also readily apply to philology and historiography: "To the nostalgic evocation of an irretrievable past they substitute, respectively, the pious idealization of the present and the apocalyptic projection of a democratic future" (3).

13. Leopardi is not the only "progressive" classicist of the early nineteenth century. Timpanaro (*Classicismo e illuminismo* 40-117) discusses at length the political and cultural views of the poet's friend and mentor, Pietro Giordani, who was certainly the most prominent of the "progressive" classicists.

14. Leopardi underestimates the role of imagination in modern science. For an illuminating comparison of artistic and scientific imagination, and their respective strengths and limits, see O'Hear.

Bibliography

Alcorn, John and Dario Del Puppo. "Memory and Anticipation: The Temporal Structure of the Emotions in the Poetry of Giacomo Leopardi." Unpublished conference paper delivered at the NEMLA Convention. March 27 1993.

Alighieri, Dante. *Tutte le opere.* Ed. Luigi Blasucci. Firenze: Sansoni, 1981.

Anderson, Benedict. *Imagined Communities: Reflections on the Origin and Spread of Nationalism.* London: Verso, 1983.

Baillet, Roger. "La storia, più che coesione, materia sofferta del canto." *Il pensiero storico e politico di Giacomo Leopardi. Atti del VI Convegno internazionale di studi leopardiani.* Firenze: Olschki, 1989. 91-96.

Binni, Walter. *La protesta di Leopardi.* Firenze: Sansoni, 1977.

Blasucci, Luigi. "Livelli e correzioni dell''Angelo Mai'." *Leopardi e i segnali dell'infinito.* Bologna: Il Mulino, 1985. 81-95.

Cohen, L. Jonathan. *An Essay on Belief and Acceptance.* Oxford: Clarendon, 1992.

Della Terza, Dante. "La canzone ad Angelo Mai." *Gradiva* 4.4 (1990-1991): 1-10.

De Sanctis, Francesco. *Giacomo Leopardi.* Ed. E. Ghidetti. Roma: Riuniti, 1983.

Galimberti, Cesare. "Stile 'vago' e linguaggio del vero nella canzone 'Ad Angelo Mai'." *Linguaggio del vero in Leopardi.* Firenze: Olschki, 1959. 11-67.

Giordano, Emilio. "L'età delle macchine: appunti sul concetto leopardiano di 'Storia'." *Il pensiero storico e politico di Giacomo Leopardi.* Firenze: Olschki, 1989. 285-306.

Goffis, Cesare Federico. "La canzone ad Angelo Mai e i 'Sepolcri'." *Miscellanea di studi in onore di Vittore Branca* IV. Firenze: Olschki, 1983. 2: 677-702.

Leopardi, Giacomo. *Tutte le opere.* Ed. W. Binni and E. Ghidetti. 2 vols. Firenze: Sansoni, 1976.

———. *Canti.* Ed. E. Peruzzi. Milano: Rizzoli, 1981.

———. *Canti.* Ed. M. Fubini. Torino: Loescher, 1978.

———. *Zibaldone di pensieri.* Ed. G. Pacella. 3 vols. Milano: Garzanti, 1991.

Luporini, Cesare. *Leopardi progressivo.* Roma: Riuniti, 1980.

Masiello, Vitilio. "Il *Saul* e la crisi interna dell'umanesimo alfieriano." *L'ideologia tragica di Vittorio Alfieri.* Roma: Edizioni dell'Ateneo, 1964. 157-86.

Nietzsche, Friedrich. "On the Uses and Disadvantages of History for Life." *Untimely Meditations.* Trans. R. J. Hollingdale. Cambridge: Cambridge UP, 1983. 57-123.

O'Hear, Anthony. *The Element of Fire: Science, Art and the Human World.* London: Routledge, 1988.

Russo, Luigi, and Riccardo Rugani, eds. *I classici italiani. L'Ottocento.* Vol 3, Part 1. Firenze: Sansoni, 1959.

Springer, Carolyn. *The Marble Wilderness: Ruins and Representation in Italian Romanticism, 1775-1850.* Cambridge: Cambridge UP, 1987.

Talamo, Giuseppe. "Leopardi e la storia d'Italia a lui contemporanea." *Il pensiero storico e politico di Giacomo Leopardi.* Firenze: Olschki, 1989. 69-90.

Timpanaro, Sebastiano. *Classicismo e illuminismo nell'Ottocento italiano*. Pisa: Nistri-Lischi, 1969.

———. *La filologia di Giacomo Leopardi*. Bari: Laterza, 1977.

Treves, Pietro. *Lo studio dell'antichità classica nell'Ottocento*. Milano e Napoli: Ricciardi, 1962. 471-89.

von Ranke, Leopold. Preface. *Histories of Romance and Germanic Peoples. The Varieties of History: From Voltaire to the Present*. Ed. Fritz Stern. New York: Vintage, 1973. 54-62.

Williams, Bernard. *Shame and Necessity*. Berkeley: U of California P, 1993.

Claudia Stancati (essay date 1995)

SOURCE: Stancati, Claudia. "The French Sources of Leopardi's Linguistics." In *Historical Roots of Linguistic Theories*, edited by Lia Formigari and Daniele Gambarara, pp. 129-39. Amsterdam: John Benjamins, 1995.

[*In the following essay, Stancati examines the relationship of Leopardi's linguistic theory to his study of various thinkers of the French Enlightenment.*]

Giacomo Leopardi's "rationally founded and demonstrated scepticism" (**ZIB** [*Zibaldone*]: 1653) draws its nourishment from still-vital elements of Enlightenment thought. This can be seen, for example, if we explore Leopardi's connection with Holbach (cf. Stancati 1979). But it is true in a more general way of his relationship with other French Enlightenment thinkers, also with regard to the question of a national language, the "questione della lingua", which is an important aspect of Leopardi's political and cultural project. As Lo Piparo (1982) and Gensini (1984) have shown, Leopardi's materialist anthropology, based on the discovery of the "adaptive" nature of man, is tightly linked to his linguistic theory, which posits close, reciprocal relations between society, language and culture.

1. LEOPARDI'S USE OF HIS SOURCES

It is very hard to identify the sources of Leopardi's linguistics owing to his extraordinary ability to make highly significant contributions of his own to cultural issues, even when he took his cue from second-hand quotations encountered, perhaps, in minor authors (Gensini 1984:26). To be able to say anything definitive about the sources of Leopardi's linguistics, in fact, we would need to "make a thoroughgoing investigation of the materials stowed away in Leopardi's library" (Ibid.:29): for example, in order to trace the origins of Leopardi's remarks on Sanskrit or Chinese (cf. **ZIB**:929, 942, 950, 978, 982).

As regards his intuitive grasp of the cultural issues of his day and his ability to make his own syntheses of these, Leopardi himself writes:

> Never having read metaphysical writers and being engaged in studies of quite a different nature, having learnt nothing of these matters in the schools (which I have never attended), I had already awoken to the falsity of innate ideas, guessed at the optimism of Leibniz, and discovered the principle that the progress of knowledge consists entirely in conceiving that one idea contains another, which is the summa of the whole of the new ideological science.

(*ZIB*:1347)

His claim never to have read metaphysical writers should of course be taken with a pinch of salt, since we know that Leopardi was a voracious reader—one engaged, moreover, in developing what he himself explicitly referred to as "his philosophical system" (**ZIB**:946-950, 1089-1090).

Although the only available catalogue of Leopardi's library is an old and incomplete one (CAT. 1899), we know that he had at his disposal texts of all kinds, including many of the most challenging works of Enlightenment culture, such as the *Lettre de Trasybule à Leucippe* or the *Examen critique des apologistes de la religion chrétienne* attributed to Fréret, or Holbach's *Bon sens*. There also exists a record of the poet's reading from 1823 to 1830 (cf. Binni, in Leopardi 1969:I. 373 ff.) in which the names of some of the authors I shall later be mentioning appear, as well as numerous Italian works specifically concerning the "questione della lingua" (Lollio, Salvini, Buonmattei).

Since the connection between Leopardi and the *Idéologues* has been fully explored by Gensini and since the poet's references to Constant, Chateaubriand and Madame de Staël are explicit and direct, I will dwell here only on the relationship between Leopardi and a number of exponents of the Enlightenment (Montesquieu, Voltaire, Rousseau, Diderot and D'Alembert) with a view to adding a little to the observations already made by Lo Piparo and Gensini.

2. DIDEROT AND D'ALEMBERT

Diderot is mentioned directly in the *Zibaldone* only as co-author of the *Encyclopédie* (*ZIB*:4299). We can perhaps detect an echo of Diderot in Leopardi's comparison between a baby and a dumb person (*ZIB*:1924, 2960): like a dumb person, a baby has the disposition for but not the faculty of speech. What Leopardi certainly did not share with Diderot was his view of the superiority of the French language: the poet's rejection of this view is one of the central issues in his linguistic enquiries.

Leopardi's links with D'Alembert are much easier to demonstrate since, in the above-mentioned list of works read, we find not only the latter's *Discours prélimi-*

naire, but also his *Observations sur l'art di traduire* and *Sur l'harmonie des langues.* These are listed between 1827 and 1829 and cited in notes dated May 1829. However, the list of readings and the citations in the *Zibaldone* do not always coincide chronologically (for example, in the case of the *Essai sur les éloges de Thomas* which is listed as having been read in 1824 but is mentioned as early as August 1820).

D'Alembert's observations on the difficulty of translating are picked up more than once in the *Zibaldone,* as is his opinion that Italian is more suitable for translation thanks to its flexibility and that French is less easily translated because of the severity of its rules and the uniformity of its construction. Each language, in any case, D'Alembert concludes, has its particular "genius", a view which Leopardi certainly shares.

It is impossible here to cite all the passages in which Leopardi discusses the harmony of languages and the connection between modern European languages and Latin and Greek. But there is no doubt that he agrees with some of D'Alembert's remarks on the impossibility of reconstructing the sounds of dead languages, whose true pronunciation is lost to us. In fact, Leopardi stresses that, as far as Latin is concerned, the most authentic pronunciation is more likely to be found in popular writings and verses than in learned works (***ZIB***:3344).

3. OTHER AUTHORS OF THE *ENCYCLOPÉDIE*

It is certainly possible to find connections between Leopardi the linguist and the *Encyclopédie* if we bear in mind that the work of linguistics most often cited in the ***Zibaldone*** (no fewer than 17 times) is the *Encyclopédie méthodique* of Nicolas Beauzée who succeeded Dumarsais as author of the grammatical articles of the *Encyclopédie* and wrote, among other things, the article on *Langue* itself.

Leopardi did not of course share the linguistic rationalism of Beauzée and the other contributors to the *Encyclopédie.* But when he writes that "usage is acknowledged as the sovereign lord of speech (***ZIB***:1263), he is virtually translating the passage in *Langue* where Beauzée writes: "Tout est usage dans les langues [. . .] l'usage n'est donc pas le tyran des langues, il en est le législateur naturel", since "l'idée de tyrannie emporte chez nous celle d'une usurpation injuste".

In the same article we find another observation which was to be picked up by Leopardi, namely that the old vernaculars are closer to Latin and Greek, and derive from these. Beauzée also incidentally criticises Rousseau for getting entangled in insoluble contradictions with regard to the connection between sociality, needs, and the origin of language. The circularity of Rousseau's approach is pointed out by Leopardi too:

We can thus apply to the alphabet what Rousseau said when he confessed that, in examining language and endeavouring to explain its invention, he was greatly embarrassed, since it did not seem possible for a language to be formed before a society had come to perfection, or for an almost perfect society to exist before it possessed a ready-formed and mature language.

(***ZIB***:2957)

We might add here that another thread links Leopardi with Beauzée and the encyclopedists, namely Girard's work on synonyms frequently cited in the *Encyclopédie* and explicitly mentioned by Leopardi (***ZIB***:367, 978, 994).

There is more than one resemblance between some of Leopardi's jottings and Turgot's article *Etymologie.* Leopardi, in fact, used etymological analyses as a kind of proving-ground for his ideas on language and proclaimed himself "a philologist enlightened by philosophy" (***ZIB***:1205), for whom etymology was one of the main tools of the archaeology of language. Leopardi thus might be seen as agreeing with the article *Dictionnaire* of the *Encyclopédie* where he would be able to read that the earliest words are the "philosophical roots" of a language.

4. VOLTAIRE

In the ***Zibaldone*** there are three direct mentions of Voltaire on language, together with an indirect one via a passage from Vincenzo Monti's *Proposta di correzioni e aggiunte al vocabolario della crusca.* The earliest is dated 17 June 1821 when Leopardi, discussing Chinese language and culture, cites Voltaire in order to stress the difference between words that "fall within the language of conversation", and "technical words" which he calls terms, whose meaning is much more precise and definite (***ZIB***:1180). In another note Leopardi mentions a letter from Voltaire to Frederick II in order to turn upside down Voltaire's view that Latin is a much apter language than French for details and precision. For Leopardi French is a supremely "unnatural" language and hence extremely rich in minute terminology (***ZIB***:3633). There is also a brief note dated March 1824 in which Leopardi makes a reference to Voltaire on the universality of the French language (***ZIB***:4050).

5. MONTESQUIEU

Montesquieu is an important presence in the jottings that form the ***Zibaldone***: he is cited with great frequency and on a variety of topics. It is worth recalling that the idea of investigating human phenomena as products of a web of relationships first appears in Enlightenment culture in the *Esprit des lois* and in the early writings of Montesquieu, with which Leopardi was certainly familiar. In one respect, Leopardi's linguistics may thus be seen as an enquiry into the relationship between languages and "the constitution, customs, climate, religion, commerce etc." as the frontispiece of the *Esprit des lois* has it; an account of the connections between Leopardi and Montesquieu would also be useful for reconstructing Leopardi's political ideas.

In the **Zibaldone** Leopardi talks about the relations of necessity that govern the human world: "man will never be happy till he knows himself and the necessary relations that bind him to other beings" (**ZIB**:379). He had already noted earlier, citing Montesquieu's work on the Romans, that "the human world has become like the natural world; we need to study events as we study phenomena" (**ZIB**:119). It is hardly surprising, then, that when he mentions Madame de Staël (no doubt still with Montesquieu in mind), he sets up a new relationship between languages and climates (**ZIB**:200, 3247), a subject here turns to when he mentions "the infinite number of causes" which give rise to the diversity of languages.

Re-reading the *Pensées* of Montesquieu devoted to language, we come across a number of topics that will later turn up in Leopardi. For example, the antiquity of Hebrew, the prosodic differences between the various languages, the difficulty of accepting a foreigner's pronunciation of our own language; or again, a parallel drawn between Latin and French, a remark on the difficulty of translation, an attack on the academies for attempting to impose norms on languages (cf. Montesquieu, *Pensées*, in *OC* [*Oeuvres complètes*] II:1213 ff.). Moreover, the systematic parallel drawn by Montesquieu between five modern languages (French, English, Italian, German and Spanish), with the inclusion of Greek and Latin, seems to foreshadow Leopardi's project for a "parallelo delle 5 lingue". Similarly, Montesquieu's brief notes on the origin of writing foreshadow Leopardi's observations on this topic and mention among other things the legend of the Phoenician origin of the alphabet.

6. ROUSSEAU

The relationship between Leopardi and Rousseau is a vast, controversial and complex matter. Leopardi seems to echo Rousseau continually when he deals with subjects like the relationship between nature and reason, barbarity and civilisation, individual and community, and their contradictions (see for instance **ZIB**:873-877).

I have already remarked that Leopardi was aware of the circularity of Rousseau's approach to the problem of the origin of language in the *Discours sur l'origine de l'inégalité,* but we do not know whether he also knew the *Essai sur l'origine des langues* directly. This work of Rousseau's is mentioned only once in the **Zibaldone** (**ZIB**:2086) and then only at second-hand, via Madame de Staël's *De l'Allemagne,* where the work from which

the idea is derived is not mentioned explicitly. The passage in question draws a distinction between the "langues du Nord" and the "langues du Midi": the former are seen as the daughters of necessity and the latter the daughters of joy. This contrast between North and South corresponds to that between the ancients and the moderns in Leopardi's notes on language (as a comparison with, for example, **ZIB**:932 and 1026 shows).

For Leopardi as for Rousseau, language "is the most essential feature of man, who is distinguished from animals by the organs of speech" (**ZIB**:1021); "la parole distingue l'homme entre les animaux: le langage distingue les nations entre elles" (Rousseau [1781] 1990:59). "La langue de convention n'appartient qu'à l'homme", writes Rousseau. Leopardi maintains that "the faculty of speech comes from nature but the difference of sounds comes from the force of habit", and that "speech is an art learned by men. The variety of languages is proof of this. Gesture is a natural thing taught by nature" (**ZIB**:65, 51, 141).

As regards the relationship between human and animal language Leopardi may owe something to Lamettrie's *L'Homme machine,* where he would read that the capacities of man and animals are the same but that man possesses many more signs and, above all, arbitrary signs. (We might recall here that Leopardi in his youth wrote a **Dissertazione sopra l'anima delle bestie**).

Another subject which Leopardi and Rousseau have in common is music; it is discussed in the second part of the *Essai sur l'origine des langues* and Leopardi touches on it on various occasions in the **Zibaldone** (**ZIB**:154, 178). It is worth noting in this context that Maupertuis, for example, considered music a kind of universal language like arithmetic. There are no traces of direct or indirect citations of Maupertuis by Leopardi, but a reading of *La dissertation sur les différens moyens dont les hommes se sont servis pour exprimer leurs idées* shows that they have a number of points in common, especially as regards the origin of the alphabet.

To return to Leopardi and Rousseau: each of them holds that languages lose their naturalness as they acquire greater clarity and precision, and that the earliest names are those designating objects (Rousseau [1781] 1990:73; **ZIB**:1356, 1202, 1448, 1388, 1205, 2383).

One difference needs to be recorded here, namely their concepts of synonyms. According to Leopardi primitive languages do not possess synonyms, whereas according to Rousseau they are rich in these. Both however believe that in ancient languages vowels predominated over consonants.

It could of course be argued that these topics are not peculiar to Rousseau, since they appear in most of the literature of the 18th century on the problem of the origin of languages. Yet, like both Rousseau and Vico, Leopardi highlights the imaginative function of language (see for example his rejection of languages that are too geometrical), even though he by no means underestimates language's logical, rational aspects.

7. LEOPARDI AND THE ORIGIN OF THE ALPHABET

Leopardi is less attracted by such typical 18th-century issues as the invention of language, the original tongue, and the quest for a new universal language (*ZIB*:3254, 4374). What seems to interest him more, on the other hand, is the origin of the alphabet. The transition from a spoken to a written language seems extremely important to him, since it is through the alphabet—and the invention of numbers—that we move from the phonetic to the semantic plane, in other words from the oral expression of primordial feelings and needs to the representation and communication of abstract, complex ideas. The more the alphabet is restricted and "stylised", the further it moves from hieroglyphic and ideographic scripts, which are related to objects and not ideas, the more the powers of a language are enhanced and multiplied.

If conventionality is what characterises human language, the main medium of this convention is writing. It is at the point of transition from spoken language to written language that an authentic semantic revolution takes place: the transition from sound to writing. "Sound and structure are independent, so that it is possible to imagine two languages whose words have a common etymology but which are nonetheless very different tongues", Leopardi writes (*ZIB*:965). "An infinity of results and combinations derives from the use of elements in writing and arithmetic" (*ZIB*:808). It is a sort of chemical combination: just as nature, drawing on a large though limited number of elements, mixes an infinite series of compounds, so language is able, through the graphic representation made possible by the alphabet, to make infinite use of finite means. What fascinates Leopardi is the transition to this second phase of language, and his wonder at the invention of the alphabet is expressed on various occasions, with possible echoes of Polybius: "a most abstruse and admirable invention if we reflect a moment on it, one which men have had to do without, not out of chance but out of necessity, for centuries upon centuries" (*ZIB*:940). This "miracle of the human spirit" was born of chance and, according to Leopardi, was the product of the genius of a single person, subsequently spreading throughout the world. In fact, peoples that "have had no commerce with any other literate nation have not had or do not have an alphabet" (*ZIB*:2620).

In a long passage dated 4 June 1823 Leopardi (*ZIB*:2948, 2960) returns to the idea that all alphabets derive from a single, Phoenician original ("I say that all

or nearly all derive from a single one"), illustrating how some letters may have been introduced into our alphabet even if they were absent from Phoenician, Hebrew, other ancient oriental, and Latin alphabets. The "admirable thought" that gave rise to the alphabet consisted in

> applying the signs of writing to the sounds of words, instead of applying them to things or ideas as was done in primitive writing and hieroglyphics and by the Mexicans in their picture-writing, and as is done by savages and the Chinese.

In ascribing the invention of the alphabet to the Phoenicians Leopardi is repeating an ancient legend which he may of course have come across in Lucan's *Pharsalia* or in Hobbes, but which is also mentioned in the articles "Ecriture" and "Encyclopédie" of the *Encyclopédie,* and by Warburton and Condillac, as well as by Rousseau in his *Essai sur l'origine des langues.* Leopardi may also have found in these texts the idea of an evolution from a pictorial to an ideographic to a linear alphabet. In another passage Leopardi writes

> Since man can only think by speaking, it is through the medium of language that ideas are attached to words [. . .] the alphabet is the language with which we conceive sounds and break down language into its simple elements until we are able to reassemble ideas by means of the elements of sound.
>
> (*ZIB*:2949ff.)

Those who do not know the alphabet—children or the illiterate—cannot master those procedures of thought consisting in the analysis of elements into simpler ones and the synthesis of elements into more complex ones. The alphabet gives words wings and enables language to achieve that lightness which makes the understanding of the world accessible to man.

Leopardi returns to the invention of the alphabet—so essential for the "denaturalising" of man—in a comment dated 8 December 1823 referring to Algarotti's *Saggio sugli Incas,* which he had read that year (*ZIB*:3958). To Leopardi, the refined civilisations of the Incas and of China represent a typical example of how the lack of a linear alphabet can cripple a civilisation and culture, giving rise to a rift between the cultivated classes and the people (*ZIB*:942). A very similar thesis is expounded in Condorcet's *Esquisse.* These observations also appear in a long note dated October 1823, which begins with the story of the invention of fire, continues with the invention of navigation and language, and ends with the invention of writing. In the same passage Leopardi refers to the idea that there was a single, original human language, citing as evidence the biblical story of the Tower of Babel, as does Beauzée in his article "Langue" (*ZIB*:3669).

Leopardi also remarks on the lack of graphic representation of vowels in ancient oriental alphabets, in spite of the fact that vowels are widely used in the spoken languages. He notes that "the subtlety and spirituality" of these sounds defy the still rather limited and crude analytical capacities of these alphabets (**ZIB**:2402).

In discussing the origins of the great enterprise of language, Leopardi claims that we can uncover the ancient roots of languages by employing "the discernment and subtlety of the philosopher, and the vast erudition and skill of the philologist, archaeologist and polyglot" (**ZIB**:1263).

Leopardi frequently dwells on the "prodigious and most difficult [art] of writing" and on the changes that the use of a single alphabet brought about in the infinite variety of languages which had already developed, in however rough and ready a form. For writing, after a long process of refinement, succeeds in exalting the creative capacities of a language, encoding its sound, making conventions possible—conventions that can be shared by an ever-growing number of men.

In a passage dated 22 June 1821 Leopardi writes:

> Words in themselves are mere sounds, yet, like languages as a whole, they are signs of ideas; they are able to signify these because men by mutual consent apply them to particular ideas, and recognise them as signs of these. In a fairly developed society the principal medium of this human convention is writing. Languages that entirely lack or are deficient in this medium [. . .] remain either completely impotent, or extremely impoverished and weak [. . .]. All these things are impossible without writing because there is no medium for a universal convention, and without this a language is not a language but mere sound. The living voice of each person does not carry far and carries to few others.
>
> (**ZIB**:1202 ff.)

We may say, then, that convention rather than analyticalness is the key concept of the philosophy of language for Leopardi.

8. CONCLUSIONS

The dream of a general grammar that constitutes a universal logic, the idea of a new single, universal and natural language, the quest for the origin of language or the zero degree of the word—all these are alien to Leopardi in spite of the fact that his culture is deeply rooted in Enlightenment thought. Radically materialist and sensationalist, Leopardi shares above all with Enlightenment thought a descriptive, non-evaluative stance and a comparative approach to languages and cultures, while implicitly acknowledging the superiority of the ancients. Echoes of all the most important 18th-century investigations of language can be found in his works. What Leopardi lacks is the Enlightenment's idea of nature as the source of intelligibility, order, goodness, and universal, absolute values. Rather, he perceives nature as a

tangle of insoluble contradictions which reason struggles to reduce to uniformity, but which cannot be resolved by new, consolatory mythologies. Such mythologies seem to him to be an attempt to reintroduce innate ideas, which have been overthrown "by Locke and by modern ideology" (**ZIB**:1616). This attitude of Leopardi's is confirmed in the opinions he frequently expresses about the idea of natural law as universal law, or about the French Revolution (**ZIB**:312, 160, 358, 725, 1180).

References

Alembert, Jean le Rond (dit d'). [1753] 1967. *Observations sur l'art de traduire*. In *Oeuvres*. IV. 31-42.

———. [1753]1967a. *Sur l'harmonie des langues*. In *Oeuvres* IV. 11 - 27.

———. 1967b. *Oeuvres*. 5 vols. Genève: Slatkine.

CAT. 1899 = *Catalogo della Biblioteca Leopardi in Recanati*, ed. by E. De Paoli. In *Memorie della Deputazione di Storia Patria per la provincia delle Marche*. Roma.

De Stael, Germaine. [1813].1968. *De l'Allemagne*. Paris: Garnier.

Diderot, Denis. 1751-1780. *Encyclopédie*. 35 vols. Paris: Briasson.

Gensini, Stefano. 1984. *Linguistica leopardiana*, Bologna: Il Mulino.

La Mettrie, Julian Offray de. [1747].1960. In *La Mettrie's L'Homme machine. A Study in the origins of an idea*, ed. by A. Vartanian, Princeton: Princeton University Press.

Leopardi, Giacomo. [1817-1832]. *Zibaldone*. In *Opere* III-IV.

———. [1823-1830]. *Memorie e disegni letterari. Elenco di letture*. In *Tutte le opere* I. 367-377.

———. 1937. *Opere*, ed. by F. Flora. 5 vols. Milano: Mondadori.

———. 1969. *Tutte le opere*, 2 vols., ed. by W. Binni e F. Ghidetti, Firenze: Sansoni.

Lo Piparo, Franco. 1982. "Materialisme et linguistique chez Leopardi". *Historiographia Linguistica* IX. 3. 361-387.

Maupertuis, Pierre Moreau de. 1768. *Dissertation sur les differens moyens dont le hommes se sont servis pour exprimer leurs idees*. In *Oeuvres* III. 437-478.

———. *Oeuvres*. Lyon: Bruyset.

Montesquieu, Charles Louis Secondat baron de la Brède de. [1796] 1949. *Les pensées*. In *Oeuvres complètes* I. 973-1574.

———. *Oeuvres complètes,* ed. by R. Callois. 2 vols. Paris: Gallimard.

Monti, Vincenzo. 1817-26. *Proposta di alcune aggiunte e correzioni al Vocabolario della Crusca.* 4 vols. Milano: Imperiale Stamperia Regia.

Rousseau, Jean Jacques. [1781].1990. *Essai sur l'origine des langues,* ed. by J. Starobinski. Paris: Garnier.

Stancati, Claudia. 1979. "Lettura di d'Holbach in Italia nel XIX secolo". *Giornale critico della filosofia italiana* LVIII. 279-285.

Voltaire, F.-M. Arouet de. 1877-1883. *Oeuvres complètes.* 52 vols. Paris: Garnier.

David Castronuovo (essay date December 1998)

SOURCE: Castronuovo, David. "Metamorphosis of the Occasion in 'Nelle Nozze Della Sorella Paolina.'" *Rivista di Studi Italiani* 16, no. 1 (December 1998): 160-84.

[In the following essay, Castronuovo explains Leopardi's poem "Nelle Nozze Della Sorella Paolina," which purports to be a brother's remarks on his sister's marriage, but which is actually a pessimistic assessment of his sister's transition from childhood to adulthood.]

> All literary works are occasioned in some sense; occasional verse differs in having not a private but a public or social occasion.
>
> (Miner *et al.,* 851)

> What *is* poetry's relationship to its occasion? Does poetry imitate it? Merely complement or report it? Recreate it? Create a parallel occasion? Supplant it? Does poetry compensate for it, create the occasion where history neglected or failed to? Or is poetry rather constitutive of the occasion it appears to describe?
>
> (Sugano, 13)

Premise

Among the titles of the *Canti,* surely none suggests the idea of occasional verse more clearly than **"Nelle nozze della sorella Paolina"** (Oct.-Nov. 1821), which proposes the theme of a brother's remarks on the "occasion" of his sister's marriage (in point of fact, never celebrated).[1] As is well-known, however, we cannot discern the poem's true matter from its title. In his **"Preambolo alla ristampa delle 'Annotazioni' nel 'Nuovo Ricoglitore' di Milano"** of 1825, Leopardi himself explains that "[N]essun potrebbe indovinare i soggetti delle Canzoni[2] dai titoli; anzi per lo piú il poeta fino al primo verso entra in materie differentissime da quello che il lettore si sarebbe aspettato. Per esempio, una

Canzone per nozze, non parla né di *talamo* né di *zona* né di *Venere* né di *Imene*" (Damiani and Rigoni, 1. 163, emphasis added).

Thus the poet insists that the title of his **"Canzone per nozze"** prepares us misleadingly for an encounter with social phenomena such as conjugal myths ("Venere," "Imene") and rituals ("talamo," "zona") that are not present in the text. We may therefore expect to take the author at his word, and find in the entire *canzone* that which Luigi Blasucci describes as a "divaricazione" between title and text (159). Indeed, Leopardi does leave behind—"al primo verso"—the theme of Paolina's marriage rites, moving quickly instead to present the moral and historical precepts that constitute his actual discourse: "la decadenza e la barbarie del presente, in cui la fortuna e il valore si sono ormai dissociati per sempre e non si dà altra scelta che quella fra l'infelicità e la viltà. Da qui, per antitesi [. . .] l'evocazione di gloriosi emblemi del mondo antico [. . .]" (Damiani and Rigoni, 1. 295).

Nevertheless, I wish to premise my remarks by observing that although Leopardi abandons the *subject matter* of the titular occasion, the *concept* of occasionality does not simply vanish as the reader moves from title to text. Rather, the titular occasion is transformed in the opening strophe, and is (to borrow Sugano's term) effectively "supplanted" by an occasion of a substantially different nature. This new occasion is Paolina's forced coming-of-age ("Te nella polve della vita e il suono / Tragge il destin," 5-6)—her fatal passage, at destiny's hand, from the imaginative paradise of childhood into the reality of adulthood in the modern era. Stylistic recollections of this "transformed" or "true" occasion serve generally to infuse the remaining text with a tone of increased pessimism, and tend to undermine the sense of hope (for the future of the *patria*) that the *canzone* at times appears to inspire. More importantly, Leopardi presents the poem's true occasion in such a way as to prepare, perhaps even justify, the *canzone*'s eventual rejection of the present age, and its consequent movement backward through time—away from the exhortative passages on civil virtue that address Paolina ("Che di fortuna amici / non crescano i tuoi figli, e non di vile / Timor gioco o di speme," 24-26) and all modern "Italian" mothers ("Madri d'imbelle prole / V'incresca esser nomate," 61-62); toward the description of the anonymous bride of ancient Sparta, an exemplary figure who, in grief, receives with decorum the corpse of her warrior-husband ("Spandea le negre chiome / Sul corpo esangue e nudo," 73-74); and finally, to the apostrophe directed at Virginia, the Roman political martyr and model of patriotic devotion, who willingly sacrificed her own life in the fifth century B. C. ("E all'Erebo scendesti / Volonterosa," 84-85) rather than yield to the carnal desires of a political tyrant. My comments will be centered primarily on the ramifications of Paolina's "occasional" passage into maturity, rather than on the episodes of the Spartan bride and Virginia, which have already received considerable critical attention.

INTENSIFICATION OF THE TITLE'S OCCASIONAL NATURE

Blasucci has clarified a number of points regarding the *canzone*'s occasional title, particularly in so far as it relates to the proximate literary past:[3]

> [Il titolo] **"Nelle nozze della sorella Paolina"** ricorda i vari *Per le nozze di* seguiti dai nomi degli sposi (per es. Parini: "Per le nozze di Rosa Gigliani e Gaetano Fiori"), salvo che in Leopardi, ed è uno scarto significativo, compare solo il nome della sposa (e *pour cause,* dato che la canzone è dedicata alla missione della donna nella società contemporanea [. . .])
>
> (159).

He also notes that on the manuscript, Leopardi crossed out the words originally selected to begin the title—"Negli sponsali"—and replaced them with **"Nelle nozze"** (Peruzzi, 110); always attentive to the conventions of the Italian tradition, Blasucci interprets this *pentimento* as the poet's "ricerca del termine piú topico" (159n).[4] In addition, Leopardi's remarks in the **"Preambolo"**—on the thematic disparity between title and text—cause one to suspect that the lexical change holds importance for the poet as an intensifier of the title's sense of occasion, i.e., its proclamation of Paolina's marriage as an imminent occurrence. The original "sponsali" (from the Latin *spondēre,* "to promise solemnly") had suggested only betrothal—merely the *anticipation* of the marriage rather than the event itself. The substituted term "nozze" is connected more precisely to the ceremonial occasion, for (like the Italian *nubile*) "nozze" is derived from *nūbere* (originally, "to cover"), which came in Latin to mean *sposarsi* "perché la sposa veniva velata" (Zingarelli). Hence the use of "nozze" in the title's final version conjures a more distinct image of the ritualized ceremony that is ostensibly at hand, but which the poet will, to the reader's surprise, abandon as thematic material.[5]

As to the complete *Canti,* Blasucci has noted therein the striking predominance of titles indicative of allocution (**"All'Italia," "Alla Primavera," "A Silvia"** and so forth), as well as the relatively low frequency of occasional titles—of the kind often used by Parini and Monti, and not unknown in Foscolo and Manzoni (163-64): indeed, if we disregard those poems excluded from the *Canti,* we find that Leopardi uses occasional titles in the four successive pieces **"Sopra il monumento di Dante," "Ad Angelo Mai quando ebbe trovato i libri di Cicerone della Repubblica," "Nelle nozze della sorella Paolina"** and **"A un vincitore nel pallone"** (164-65). In addition, Blasucci notes that all of these "circumstantial" titles stand in contrast to the "conte-

nuto effettivo, tutt'altro che celebrativo e occasionale, dei rispettivi testi" (165). Thus he reaffirms our awareness of Leopardi's untiring preference for the use of allocution throughout the *Canti*:

> e non solo nelle liriche con titolo allocutorio; in realtà tanti altri canti leopardiani dovrebbero intitolarsi con una figura allocutiva; **"Sopra il monumento di Dante"** potrebbe almeno in parte intitolarsi "A Dante," **"Nelle nozze della sorella Paolina"** intitolarsi *"Alla sorella Paolina"* [. . .]
>
> (164, emphasis added).

Precisely because it is accurate, however, this observation serves in turn to confirm the significance of Leopardi's decision to include among the canon of his *Canti,* in the singular case of **"Nelle nozze,"** a patently occasional title that begins with the preposition *in* (used in its temporal aspect) rather than the preposition *a* (which could have been used in its terminal or apostrophic aspect). As in the choice of "nozze" over "sponsali," the preference for *in* over *a* appears to stem from the poet's desire to intensify (in the title) the expectation that the *canzone* will treat the ceremonial aspects of an imminent event—rather than present the succession of apostrophic discourses that actually comprise the *canzone* and lead it purposefully into the past, away from any overt discussion of the titular occasion.

CONVENTIONAL INTERPRETATION OF THE OCCASION

Having established a sense of the unique emphasis placed on occasionality in the title of **"Nelle nozze,"** let us turn briefly to comments by Sugano that summarize the various ways in which literary criticism has conventionally interpreted a poem's occasion in relation to the text that the occasion purports to inspire:[6]

> In its simplest form occasional literature presupposes two elements: an occasion and its textual inscription. Traditionally, the occasion is conceived of according to a philosophical hierarchy that places it, as an extratextual origin, *temporally prior to and logically causal* of the poetry it inspires. The occasional poem is then viewed as an *after effect,* an imitation or representation of the original occasion. In its most typical gesture, occasional literature seeks to *recapture the world within its textual confines*
>
> (20, emphasis added).

Along these lines, we might say that in the case of **"Nelle nozze,"** it is customary to interpret the *canzone*'s "divaricazione" between title and text in the following way. Within the context of a strictly "philosophical hierarchy," we have come to read the poem's historical pessimism as the "aftereffect" of its titular occasion (Paolina's decision to marry), i.e., as the *consigli* of a loving brother, whose text "recaptures" the essence of the morally bleak, modern world, in which his married sister will be forced to live, and presumably to bear children.

This is by no means a misguided interpretation of the *canzone*'s relationship to its occasional title, especially in so far as it resolves logically the most salient problem presented by that which we know of the poem's compositional history—namely, that Leopardi's invention of the titular occasion followed (rather than preceded) his composition of the material that forms the germ of the *canzone*'s content. As Carlo Muscetta explains, Leopardi sketched out what was, philosophically, a more positive version of the *canzone*'s subject matter many months (at the least) before he ever thought of connecting it to the "occasion" of Paolina's marriage:

> L'occasione dell'imminente [. . .] matrimonio di Paolina, fece riprendere al poeta precedenti disegni di canzoni abbozzate in altro stato d'animo e in un momento diverso della sua "carriera." "Dell'educare la gioventú italiana" si intitola il primo di questi abbozzi, che al Flora "par da riportare al 1818" contro il parere dello Scarpa, che lo vorrebbe datato "in prossimità" della canzone **"Ad Angelo Mai"** (gennaio 1820) [. . .]. L'argomento dell'abbozzo si risolve tutto positivamente nell'urgenza di una educazione moderna e virile [. . .] "[Q]uando trionferà la verità il diritto la ragione la virtú se non adesso? [. . .] O in questa generazione che nasce, o mai" [. . .] E accennava alla opportunità di rafforzare questa esortazione, richiamandosi agli antichi padri e alle antiche madri, proponendosi di "terminare con l'esempio di Pantea e di Virginia." Accanto a questo primo abbozzo, e forse successivamente, il Leopardi disegnava una canzone **"A Virgina Romana,"** dove "si finga di vedere in sogno l'ombra di Lei, e di parlargli teneramente tanto sul suo fatto quanto sui mali presenti d'Italia"

> (215-16).

In the fall of 1821, Paolina's impending marriage provided the "occasion" that would allow Leopardi—having now entered more deeply into the "approfondimento di quel pessimismo storico ed esistenziale, che aveva avuto la prima enunciazione nella canzone al Mai" (Blasucci, 59-60)—to rework the earlier, sketched material and address it to his sister:

> La canzone era indirizzata a colei che aveva condiviso tanta parte delle sue illusioni e delle sue ribellioni: ora la Paolina andava sposa ed era giusto che il fratello le augurasse, anzi le chiedesse, un'educazione nuova per i suoi figli, diversa da quella che i genitori avevano preteso di imporre a loro

> (Muscetta, 216).

In this way, Leopardi could combine the "public" considerations of the earlier *abbozzi* with the "private" considerations of his sister's (and his own) responsibilities as adults; as Blasucci recounts, this approach created the need for synthesis, for a "grafting" of the occasional theme onto the ideas originally laid out in the *abbozzo* that is the *canzone*'s principle source:

> [I]l passaggio dal soggetto occasionale al soggetto effettivo non fu un'operazione programmata in partenza. L'argomento di fondo della canzone [. . .] era stato infatti concepito [nell'abbozzo **"Dell'educare la gioventú italiana"**] parecchio tempo prima dell'evento (o meglio, del prospettarsi dell'evento, che poi non ebbe luogo) da cui la canzone prende il titolo [. . .]. L'operazione leopardiana nella canzone consisté dunque nell'*innestare* il motivo nuziale e familiare nella trama morale e parenetica offerta da quell'abbozzo

> (54-56, emphasis added).

Clearly, then, the relationship between the titular occasion and the text of **"Nelle nozze"**—even in the simple terms of the "story" of how Leopardi came to create it—is a complicated one. The occasional title of **"Nelle nozze"** is (literally) the *canzone*'s *pre*-text—one that is, according to its compositional history, logical rather than *chrono*-logical. But it is also a "pretext" in the sense that it "cloaks" the poem's "real intention and condition" (Merriam). Thus the *canzone*'s negation of normal chronology is evident both in its compositional history, and in its intention to deposit the reader, ultimately, in an historical past that precedes by more than twenty centuries the poem's ostensible "occasion." The nominal occasion is a misleading starting point, onto which the poet "grafts," as Blasucci says, the exposition, development, and conclusion of that which the critic has described—it bears repeating—as a "contenuto effettivo [. . .] tutt'altro che celebrativo e occasionale" (164-5).

METAMORPHOSIS OF THE OCCASION

As Sugano suggests with respect to the general topic of occasionality, "the relationship between the event and the poem in occasional poetry" is not a simple one; "the phrase 'occasioned by' is perhaps more complex and more interesting than occasional verse has been credited for" (13). What meaning do these comments have in the context of **"Nelle nozze"**?

Like its counterpart in the science of botany, the "operation" that Blasucci describes (above) as the "grafting" ("innestare" / "innesto") of Paolina's marriage proclamation onto the pre-existing textual themes sketched in **"Dell'educare la gioventú italiana"** is a delicate one—especially so, since the two elements that Leopardi joins by graft (the occasional title and the moral-historical content of the *canzone*) are, by his own admission in the **"Preambolo,"** thematically unrelated. If such a graft is to "take" successfully—i.e., if the fusion of title and text is to create a poem that is viable—it would seem that some sense of the title's occasionality must "survive," must continue to live, in the *canzone* proper.

And indeed, it would be incorrect to say that the text of **"Nelle nozze"** repudiates or renounces completely the intentional and intensified sense of occasionality that we have already discovered in the title. From the outset, the poet *does* confront the reader with an occasion—

one that is arguably the central event in the life of Paolina. True, this event (as the **"Preambolo"** warned us) is not the marriage ceremony referred to in the title. It is, rather, the "occasion" of a younger sister's forced entrance into the "dust and noise," into the degraded confusion of adulthood.

> Poi che del patrio nido
> I silenzi lasciando, e le beate
> Larve e l'antico error, celeste dono,
> Ch'abbella agli occhi tuoi quest'ermo lido,
> *Te nella polve della vita e il suono*
> *Tragge il destin;* [. . .]
>
> (1-6, emphasis added).

These lines describe no ceremonial coming-of-age undertaken through an act of will (in other words, they speak not of a sister's decision to marry); instead, as the present indicative "Tragge" indicates with great physicality, they announce the fatal and inexorable pull into maturity that is being imposed by the grammatical subject ("destin") upon a helpless, restive, human object ("Te," i.e., Paolina). And this event is, according to the definition provided by Miner *et al.* (851), truly the stuff of "occasional poetry," for the moment of the unavoidable loss of childhood, of the forced passage "nella polve della vita e il suono," is not "private," but is both "public" and "social":

> [. . .] l'obbrobriosa etate
> Che il duro cielo a noi prescrisse impara,
> Sorella mia, che in gravi
> E luttuosi tempi
> L'infelice famiglia all'infelice
> Italia accrescerai [. . .]
>
> (6-11).

According to Leopardi's pessimistic world-view, Paolina is entering adulthood in the worst of times, and her fate—"Che il duro cielo *a noi prescrisse*"—is common to us all.

For clarity's sake, let us restate the words of lines 5 and 6 to read: "Il destino tragge te [Paolina] nella polve e il suono della vita." Let us also give a name to this, the poem's "true occasion," and call it the "forced coming-of-age" that destiny imposes upon all except those who have the fortune to die young.[7] What we find (again, I borrow Sugano's terms) is that Leopardi has responded to the nominal occasion by "creating" in the *canzone*'s opening lines "a parallel occasion." This "new" occasion is vastly more important than the one announced by the title: it reflects and transforms the essence of the "occasional" sense of the words **"Nelle nozze della sorella Paolina"** in the darkest possible way.

Trarre—the verb that describes what we may now refer to as the *canzone*'s true occasion—is a favorite of the poet's, probably because it is one of those terms ex-

pressive of "un maggior numero d'idee" (*Zibaldone,* p. 1226); in the opening clause of **"Nelle nozze,"** he uses it to intend movement not only *through space* ("del patrio nido / I silenzi lasciando," 1-2), but, in addition, movement *through time* and into a common destiny ("nella polve della vita e il suono," 5; "in grave / E luttuosi tempi," 8-9). As to the use of *trarre* elsewhere in the *Canti,* it should be noted that Leopardi also links the verb with destiny in Simonide's speech from **"All'Italia,"**

> Nell'armi e ne' perigli
> Qual tanto amor le giovanette menti,
> Qual nell'*acerbo fato* amor vi *trasse?*
>
> (88-90, emphasis added)

and again links *trarre* with both destiny and time in **"Il risorgimento,"**

> Cosí quegl'ineffabili
> *Giorni, o mio cor, traevi,*
> Che sí fugaci e brevi
> *Il cielo a noi sortí*
>
> (77-80, emphasis added)

where the discourse on lost youth is addressed to the poet's own heart.

With these examples in mind, we may speculate reasonably that Leopardi's use of *trarre* in both a spatial and a temporal sense reflects a fondness for the second quatrain of Petrarch's *Rime sparse* 16 ("Movesi il vecchierel canuto et biancho"), which describes the Roman pilgrimage of an old man:[8]

> indi *traendo* poi l'antico fianco
> *per l'estreme giornate di sua vita,*
> quanto piú po col buon voler s'aita,
> rotto dagli anni, et dal camino stanco;
>
> (5-8, emphasis added)

Here Petrarch suggests that in order to fulfill a personal destiny, the "vecchierel" is pulling himself through time ("traendo poi l'antico fianco / per l'estreme giornate di sua vita") even as he is journeying through space to Rome—"thence dragging his ancient flanks," as Robert Durling interprets it, "through the last days of his life" (50).[9] Hence *trarre* conveys the same double meaning that it will hold (in the *Canti* cited above) for Leopardi.

Moreover, Leopardi's use in **"Nelle Nozze"** of the gerund "lasciando" (l. 2)—to portray a young woman who is leaving childhood behind—may deliberately recall Petrarch's use of the gerund "traendo" to portray an old man seen leaving his family.[10]

Indeed, the recollection in **"Nelle nozze"** of the quatrain from *Rime sparse* 16 is further strengthened by Leopardi's use of "Tragge," which may represent an intentional transformation of Petrarch's "traendo"—a transformation that renders the verb finite, and places it significantly in the very line that presents the "finite" and unavoidable coming-of-age which is (I have suggested) the poem's true occasion.[11]

AGE AND AGING

With regard to the occasion of Paolina's "forced coming-of-age," it is worth noting that the universal problem of aging—and humanity's complicated understanding thereof—were very much on Leopardi's mind in the period prior to the composition of **"Nelle nozze."** Consider the poet's "psychological" musings on the advantages of maintaining a certain vagueness when thinking about age (*Zibaldone*, p. 102, January 20, 1820):

> È pure un tristo frutto della società e dell'incivilimento umano anche quell'essere precisamente informato dell'età propria e de' nostri cari, e quel sapere con precisione che di qui a tanti anni finirà necessariamente la mia o la loro giovinezza ecc. ecc. invecchierò necessariam, o invecchieranno, morrò senza fallo o morranno, perché la vita umana non potendosi estendere più di tanto, e sapendo formalmente la loro età o la mia io veggo chiaro che dentro un definito tempo essi o io non potremo più viver goder della giovinezza ecc. ecc. Facciamoci un'idea dell'ignoranza della propria età precisa ch'è naturale, e si trova ancora comunemente nelle genti di campagna, e vedremo quanto ella tolga a tutti i mali ordinari e certi che il tempo reca alla nostra vita, mancando la previdenza sicura che determina il male e lo anticipa smisuratamente, rendendoci avvisati del quando dovranno finire indubitabilmente questi e quei vantaggi della tale e tale età di cui godo ecc. Tolta la quale l'idea confusa del nostro inevitabile decadimento e fine, non ha tanta forza di attristarci, né di dileguare le illusioni che d'età in età ci consolano. Ed osserviamo quanto sia terribile in un vecchio p. e. d'80 anni, quel sapere determinatam. che dento [sic] 10, anni al più sarà sicuram. estinto, cosa che ravvicina la sua condizione a quella di un condannato, e toglie infinitam. a quel gran benefiz. della natura d'averci nascoto l'ora precisa della nostra morte che veduta con precisione basterebbe per istupidire di spavento, e scoraggiare tutta la nostra vita.

The passage bears upon **"Nelle nozze"** in a number of ways. First, the tendency toward precision regarding our exact age (and that of our loved ones) is seen in the *Zibaldone* as a product of civilization's unfortunate progress ("un tristo frutto della società e dell'incivilimento umano"); such progress is a basic theme in the *canzone* ("Ahi troppo tardi / E nella sera dell'umane cose, / Acquista oggi chi nasce il moto e il senso," 19-21). Indeed, the *canzone*'s concluding example of Virginia's decision to sacrifice her life constitutes a rejection of the "gran benefiz. della natura d'averci nascoto l'ora precisa della nostra morte che veduta con precisione basterebbe per istupidire di spavento." Thus, at poem's end, Leopardi can point back with longing to the "Golden Age" of Virginia's

heroic deed ("O generosa, ancora / Che più bello a'tuoi dí splendesse il sole / Ch'oggi non fa," 91-93), an epoch in which the moral suicide's "unnatural" knowledge of the precise moment of her death did not inhibit the commission of a virtuous act.

But of equal importance is the passage's relevance to the *canzone*'s "true occasion": phrases such as "di qui a tanti anni finirà necessariamente la mia o la loro giovinezza" and "sapendo formalmente la loro età o la mia io veggo chiaro che dentro un definito tempo essi o io non potremo più viver goder della giovinezza" anticipate clearly the sententious pronouncement of the end of Paolina's childhood that the first strophe presents. Most importantly, perhaps, the *Zibaldone* passage makes us aware of the emotional and moral courage that lie behind Leopardi's decision, in the opening lines of the *canzone,* to "force" his sister to look at her own progress into adulthood, and therefore, at the inevitability of her own death. The *canzone*'s true occasion—"Te nella polve della vita e il suono / Tragge il destin"—wrests forever from Paolina's mind (as it does from the poet's) the soothing balm of "l'idea confusa del nostro inevitabile decadimento" and the illusory "idea dell'ignoranza della propria età." In their stead, this grim certainty from the *Zibaldone* passage is implicitly placed: "morrò senza fallo [. . .]."

GRAFTING THE "TRUE OCCASION" ONTO THE REMAINDER OF THE TEXT

In the opening six lines of the *canzone*, Leopardi speaks only of Paolina's *personal* passage from childhood into adulthood. Immediately thereafter, he tells her that she must become aware ("impara, / Sorella mia") of the "obbrobriosa etate," the "shameful" age in which celestial law forces all adults to live:[12]

> Te nella polve della vita e il suono
> Tragge il destin; l'obbrobriosa etate
> Che il duro cielo a noi prescrisse *impara*,
> Sorella mia [. . .]
>
> (5-8, emphasis added)

At this early point in the strophe, it is of the utmost importance that the *historical* meaning of "obbrobriosa etate"—soon to be used unequivocally as a reference to the modern era—has not yet been made explicit. At first reading, one may be inclined to interpret "etate" in a *personal* sense, as a reference to some sort of shame associated with Paolina's individual entrance into adulthood. Indeed, Leopardi associates such age-related shame and corruption in the *Zibaldone* not with childhood, but with the rational or "reflective" faculties that are among the distinctive (and destructive) signs of impending adulthood:

> Il fanciullo è sempre franco e disinvolto, e perciò pronto ed attissimo all'azione, quanto portano le forze naturali dell'età. Le quali egli adopera in tutta la loro

estensione. Se però non è alterato dall'educazione, il che può succedere piú presto o piú tardi. E tutti notano che la timidità, la diffidenza di se stesso, *la vergogna,* la difficoltà insomma di operare, è segno di riflessione in un fanciullo.[13]

(p. 1063, May 19, 1821, emphasis added)

In **"Nelle nozze,"** the momentary interpretation of "obbrobriosa etate" as a reference to shame associated with *Paolina*'s coming-of-age would be logical, in so far as it would foreground—by contrast—the imaginative faculties ("le beate / Larve e l'antico error," 2-3) just celebrated in the description of her disappearing childhood. At its initial hearing, then, the words "obbrobriosa etate" keep in the reader's mind—by way of antithesis—the childish paradise that is now being lost. Technically, Leopardi holds on to the "sounds" of that paradise by the rhyming of "etate" (line 6) and "beate" (line 2), and by the reference to the "duro cielo" (line 7), which recalls the "celeste dono" described earlier (line 3). Still mindful, then, of Paolina's beatific past, we recoil as Leopardi tells us that the same heaven that had once bestowed the celestial gift of the "antico error" during Paolina's girlhood has, in an instant, turned cruel, and become the "duro cielo" that now marks her maturity with opprobrium.

Indeed, the suggestion that Leopardi is inclined to be ambiguous with regard to the personal and historical meanings of the word "etate" is not contradicted by revisitation of one of the most oft-cited passages of the ***Zibaldone***—pp. 143-4, July 1-2, 1820—which demonstrates a fondness for comparing the "ages" of his own intellectual life to the "ages" of history ("Nella carriera poetica il mio spirito ha percorso lo stesso stadio che lo spirito umano in generale [. . .]").[14] And with respect to uses of "etate" elsewhere in the **Canti,** we find that although it usually means "epoch," there are three examples where the poet uses "etade" to refer to personal rather than historical age (Bufano, 137-8).[15]

Of course, as the clause in question unfolds, we quickly learn that the "obbrobriosa etate" refers explicitly to the modern epoch, and only implicitly to an individual passage into adulthood. The textual occasion has now become part of a wider, historical situation, and Paolina's future role as mother is one that will add not only to her own, but also to a *common* human misery:

> [. . .] che in gravi
> E luttuosi tempi
> L'*infelice* famiglia all'*infelice*
> Italia accrescerai [. . .]

(6-11, emphasis added).

The repetition of "infelice" literally surrounds the notion of "family" with sadness, and through this designation of both the single and the national family as "infelice," the poet joins that which is personal to that which is historical.

Thus the ambiguity that had momentarily surrounded the meaning of "etate"—which at line 6 could still suggest the notion of personal aging and the "occasional" passage to adulthood—has been emphatically resolved by line 11, where we understand "etate" as an unmistakable reference to historical age. Nevertheless, that ambiguity has served an important purpose; its double meaning connects the poems's true occasion—*Paolina*'s "forced coming-of-age"—to the unhappy story of the *world's* "adulthood," i.e., of the modern civilization in which Paolina's days as child bearer will be lived out. Again taking up Blasucci's botanical image, I believe we can point with confidence to the word "etate" as the exact moment when the source materials of **"Nelle nozze"**—the primarily moral and historical idea of **"Dell'educare la gioventú italiana"** and the design for **"A Virginia Romana"**—are *grafted* onto the poem's true occasion, which centers not on history, as we have seen, but on the "familiar" moment of Paolina's entrance into womanhood.

"RISING" TO THE OCCASION

The transformation of the extratextual occasion (marriage) into the textual occasion (adulthood) occurs within the context of an opening strophe that is hypotactically structured; its first six lines imply that *because* ("Poi che," 1) destiny now pulls "Paolina into maturity, a response is warranted."[16] Attempting to "rise" to this fatal occasion, Leopardi reacts ostensibly by meeting it "head on," with the force of moral truths that will be conveyed to Paolina by three imperative verbs.

As we have already noted, his poetic voice swells at the first imperative ("impara," 7), exhorting Paolina not to hide from but to *learn* the harsh reality of the situation she now faces.[17] True, the next imperative, which will be used to implore Paolina to provide ("provvedi") examples of civic virtue for her children, is apparently heroic—and does suggest an amelioration of the poet's initially pessimistic response:

> [. . .] Di forti esempi
> Al tuo sangue *provvedi* [. . .]

(11-12, emphasis added).

But as Blasucci reminds us, it is pessimism that will dominate in this *canzone,* and the opening lines of strophe II demonstrate that the "tema della patria da soccorrere è pur sempre presente, ma non piú dominante" (59);[18]

> O miseri o codardi
> Figliuoli avrai. Miseri *eleggi* [. . .]

(16-17, emphasis added).

Indeed, this third imperative ("eleggi") tips the balance decidedly back toward a pessimistic response, as the poet insists that his sister choose to raise children who

will be unhappy precisely because they will be virtuous. Thus Leopardi's use of the imperative mode in
strophes I and II suggests stylistically that a morally
valid response (the raising of virtuous children) to the
textual occasion (passage into motherhood) *is* possible—but only at the cost of personal happiness.

In strophe III, Leopardi widens the discourse explo-
sively, addressing all modern Italian women in a
straightforward, highly alliterative and sententious passage:

> Donne, da voi non poco
> La patria aspetta; e non in danno e scorno
> Dell'umana progenie al dolce raggio
> Delle pupille vostre il ferro e il foco
> Domar fu dato [. . .]
>
> (31-5).

Rhetorical phrasing ("al dolce raggio / delle pupille
vostre") here gives momentary emphasis to beauty as a
source of feminine power;[19] nevertheless, it is to feminine *wisdom* that the modern *patria* expects all the
world to bow:

> [. . .] A senno vostro il
> saggio
> E il forte adopra e pensa; e quanto il giorno
> Col divo carro accerchia, a voi s'inchina
>
> (35-7).

The reference to Phoebus's chariot anticipates momentarily both the rejection of the historical present and the
consequent passage to the Classical episodes (the Spartan bride, Virginia) that will come in strophes V-VII.

But for now, Leopardi continues to address the women
of the *patria*:

> Ragion di nostra etate
> Io chieggo a voi [. . .]
>
> (38-9).

These verses, normally glossed as a reference to "il mo-
tivo della decadenza della nostra età" (Damiani and
Rigoni, 1. 926), are followed by an interrogative:

> [. . .] La santa
> Fiamma di gioventú dunque si spegne
> Per vostra mano? [. . .]
>
> (39-41).

Critical tradition interprets the interrogative as follows:
"[S]e tanta è la vostra potenza, voi siete responsabili
del nostro decadimento" (Ottolini, 32). Or as Fubini
puts it, "se tanto è il potere delle donne, ad esse si
deve, se non la presente corruzione, almeno la mancanza di tentativi volti a combatterla" (63). And indeed,
the interrogatives that finish the strophe,

> [. . .] attenuata e franta
> Da voi nostra natura? E le assonnate
> Menti, e le voglie indegne,
> E di nervi e di polpe
> Scemo il valor natio, son vostre colpe?
>
> (41-5)

continue to call contemporary women to task.[20]

Are these accusations truly pessimistic, or do they constitute a positive and optimistic exhortation to change
the present state of affairs? Alas, they seem devoid of
any real hope for the future. For even as he cries, "Ra-
gion di nostra *etate* / Io chieggo a voi" (ll. 38-9), Leopardi makes poignant use of the poem's "graft" word
("etate") to put us in mind of Paolina's fatal passage
into the "obbrobriosa etate" (l. 6) that marked the poem's truly pessimistic occasion. And when he asks, "La
santa / Fiamma di gioventú dunque si spegne / Per vostra mano?" (ll. 39-41), the poet accuses contemporary
mothers of having extinguished the "holy flame of
youth" (a phrase that recalls the "celeste dono" of his
sister's childhood); sadly their "crime" is essentially the
same as that perpetrated by destiny on Paolina.

In strophe IV, Leopardi introduces another Classical image, that of an Olympian storm presented as a power
that can be countered only by love:

> [. . .] D'amor digiuna
> Siede l'alma di quello a cui nel petto
> Non si rallegra il cor quando a tenzone
> Scendono i venti, e quando nembi aduna
> L'olimpo, e fiede le montagne il rombo
> Della procella [. . .]
>
> (48-53).

To bolster the recollections of Paolina's occasional
coming-of-age included in the interrogatives of the preceding strophe, the terms "venti," "nembi," and "rombo
/ Della procella" here introduce the mythological coun-
terparts of the modern "polve della vita e il suono" that
were described in the poem's true occasion. Unfortunately, it is only when presented in this remote Classical context that one can imagine the conquering of such
formidable obstacles.

The first part of strophe V presents a series of optative
subjunctives presented as optimistic exhortations:

> Madri d'imbelle prole
> V'incresca esser nomate. I danni e il pianto
> Della virtude a tollerar s'avezzi
> La stirpe vostra, e quel che pregia e cole
> La *vergognosa età* condanni e sprezzi;
> Cresca alla patria, e gli alti gesti, e quanto
> Agli avi suoi deggia la terra *impari*
>
> (61-7, emphasis added).

But pessimistic remembrances of Paolina's occasional
passage to adulthood persist here as well: the phrase
"vergognosa età" (l. 65), now used unambiguously in

an historical sense, recalls almost exactly the graft phrase—"obbrobriosa etate" (l. 6)—which immediately followed the description of Paolina's fateful coming-of-age. In addition, the subjunctive "impari" (l. 67)—ostensibly presented here as a hopeful reference to that which the contemporary world ("terra," 67) might learn—recalls with equal force the first, hopeless imperative directed by the poet to his younger sister ("L'obbrobriosa etate / Che il duro cielo a noi prescrisse *impara*," 6-7).

REACTING TO THE OCCASION

In the remarks that premise the present essay, I suggested that Leopardi's initial presentation of the poem's true occasion prepares, and in a sense, provokes, the *canzone*'s movement backward through historical time (a movement that begins with the Spartan episode at the end of strophe V, and continues in the concluding strophes devoted to Virginia). How is this accomplished?

In the *canzone*'s opening, we gain the sense that Paolina's course through childhood is being ended by an unstoppable destiny: she must be pulled—dragged away—from the utopia of her early life in Recanati. Leopardi adds poignancy to the situation not only by selecting *trarre* as the main verb of the first clause, but also by delaying its arrival (in conjugated form) until the beginning of line 6—and by postponing even further the arrival of the grammatical subject "destin," which he places at the clause's very end. Before these fatal words are sounded in present tense ("Tragge il destin"), we revisit with Paolina, for the last time, the beauties of infancy from which she is about to be forever removed:

> Poi che del patrio nido
> I *silenzi* lasciando, e le beate
> *Larve* e l'*antico error, celeste dono*,
> Ch'abella agli occhi *tuoi* quest'ermo lido,
> *Te* nella polve della vita e il suono
> Tragge il destin; [. . .]
>
> (1-6, emphasis added).

Once the phrase "Tragge il destin" is read, we can only look backward, in time and verse, to review the litany of pleasures—enjoyed by the ear ("silenzi"), by the eye ("beate / Larve"), and by the celestial gift of the imaginative faculty ("l'antico error, celeste dono")—that had made of Paolina's childhood (even in the "ermo lido" of Recanati) a paradise. Her forced removal from the blessed world of infancy represents no Judeo-Christian *cacciata* from some miniature Eden (by 1821, Leopardi would have been loath to associate sinful shame with childhood pleasure); it represents, rather, the fatal "pulling" or "drawing" of the helpless girl into womanhood.[21]

Thus constructing the description of the poem's true occasion—from the perspective of one who is forced to gaze back wistfully at childhood—Leopardi prepares

thematically the "look backward" to past historical ages that in the end offers his only consolation. "Lasciando Recanati Paolina vedeva con il suo matrimonio la fine di quell'età giovanile in cui secondo il mito poetico leopardiano si riproduce la beatitudine primigenia dell'uomo" (Muscetta, 217). It is to this primordial (moral) beauty that the poem's final strophes return. In a sense, this historical "homecoming" constitutes Leopardi's artistic answer to the poem's true occasion. For if, in real life, heaven and destiny can pull his beloved Paolina mercilessly into a corrupt present and future, Leopardi can respond by choosing—in his poetic imagination—to return not to any personal childhood, but to the virtuous "childhood of the world," as it is described in the Spartan and Roman episodes.

Moreover, Leopardi can respond ultimately by invoking a heroine, Virginia, who chooses to commit an act that is, in effect, the exact opposite of the *maturation* represented by the *canzone*'s true occasion. For Virginia chooses *suicide* at her father's (compassionate) hand:

> [. . .] A me disfiori e scioglia
> Vecchiezza i membri, o padre; a me s'appresti,
> Dicea, la tomba, anzi che l'empio letto
> Del tiranno m'accoglia
>
> (85-8).

Thus she calls "pre-maturely" upon "old age," upon "la vecchiaia precoce" (Ottolini, 33), to destroy her body while she is still young, defying a destiny that would have forced her to grow old, and die, under the bonds of tyranny.

CONCLUDING REMARKS

With reference to the relationship between the figures of Paolina and Virginia, Blasucci notes that

> all'eroina virile [del dramma] di Alfieri l'autore della canzone conferisce connotati di vaghezza che l'assimilano per certi aspetti [. . .] al personaggio di Paolina [. . .]. Virginia si pone cosí come il secondo *tu* della canzone dopo quello di Paolina, esattamente all'altro capo del componimento. E anche questo conferma di riflesso il ruolo non occasionale, ma strutturale e poetico di Paolina nella canzone che s'intitola alle sue nozze
>
> (57-8).

Thus he maintains that in **"Nelle nozze,"** Paolina's role is structural rather than occasional, in so far as the "occasion" of her marriage does not enter effectively into the content of the poem.[22] Indeed, he distinguishes clearly the "scarto tra l'occasione significata dal [. . .] titolo e la sostanza della meditazione poetica a cui essa dà l'avvio" (53).

I have not attempted to gainsay this interpretation of the *canzone*'s relationship to the *titular* occasion. Rather, I have endeavored only to broaden our understanding of the poet's "scarto" of the titular occasion, in the case of **"Nelle nozze,"** and have proposed that the opening of the first strophe accomplishes this "scarto," this exclusion, by substituting a different and fatal occasion for the ceremonial one proclaimed by the title.

Were we to raise the problem of how to apply the term "occasional" to the *Canti* in general, we would arrive quickly at temporal complications that remain present throughout Leopardi's poetic journey—and these would surely confirm Blasucci's observation that "La poesia leopardiana è aliena in linea di principio dal porsi come poesia d'occasione (salvo che nel senso trascendentale e goethiano)" (53).[23] For even from childhood, Giacomo Leopardi's mind seems almost never to have been able to exist in a "single" time, i.e., in the "occasion" offered by present experience:

> La cosa piú notabile e forse unica in lui è che in età quasi fanciullesca avea già certezza e squisitezza di giudizio sopra le grandi verità non insegnate agli altri se non dall'esperienza, cognizione quasi intera del mondo, e di se stesso in guisa che conosceva tutto il suo bene e il suo male, e l'andamento della sua natura, e andava sempre *au devant* de' suoi progressi, e secondo queste cognizioni regolava anche le sue azioni [. . .] cosa stranissima ne' giovani istruiti sopra l'età e vivaci [. . .] e tutta propria degli uomini di molto senno e maturi
>
> (Damiani and Rigoni 2. 1200).

These words—the poet's own, taken from the quasi-autobiographical **"Alla vita abbozzata di Silvio Sarno"**—display the clear recognition of a self caught between present occasions and the intuitive knowledge of other states of being.[24]

Notes

1. Binni reminds us (l. 1425) that Leopardi explained the reasons for the dissolution of the marriage contract in a letter to Giordani (Feb. 1, 1823): "Carlo e Paolina stanno bene di corpo e saranno molto contenti d'aver le tue nuove, chè le avranno da me subito. Paolina non fu piú sposa. Voleva, e ciò (lo confesso) per consiglio mio e di Carlo, fare un matrimonio alla moda, cioè d'interesse, pigliando quel signore [Pietro Peroli di Sant'Angelo in Vado], ch'era bruttissimo e di niuno spirito, ma di natura pieghevolissimo e stimato ricco. S'è poi veduto che quest'ultima qualità gli era male attribuita, e il trattato ch'era già conchiuso è stato rotto" (Flora, 3. 391).

2. Leopardi here refers only to the ten *canzoni* published in Bologna in 1824.

3. All readers of "Nelle Nozze" are greatly indebted to Blasucci for his recent, insightful discussions of the *canzone* (see "Works Cited").

4. Leopardi may also have been dissatisfied with the phonic emphasis that the original title, "Negli sponsali della sorella Paolina," would have placed upon the letters *s* and *p*. Cf. his sarcastic criticism, in the "Discorso di un italiano intorno alla poesia romantica" (1818), of a line from Byron's "Giaurro" as it is translated by Pellegrino Rossi. Of the line, "Oh quanto i suoi sospir spargon fragranza!", Leopardi remarks "Ci vuole un tedesco a pronunziare quest'ultimo verso" (Damiani and Rigoni, 2. 418 and 2. 1408).

5. With regard to the change from "sponsali" to "nozze," the most obvious theory would suggest simply that it came about because Paolina's wedding, during the two months in which Leopardi worked on the poem (Oct.-Nov. 1821), was drawing closer in time. But this is contradicted by passages in two letters written by Leopardi to Giordani. On July 13, 1821, he writes, "La mia Paolina questo Gennaio sarà sposa [. . .]" (Flora 3. 323). Then, on October 26, 1821, Leopardi explains that "Paolina andrà sposa di un Signor Peroli a Sant'Angelo in Vado, ma non prima di Gennaio, come già ti scrissi, e forse a primavera" (Flora, 3. 328). Thus it appears that while Leopardi was composing the *canzone* in the fall of 1821, the marriage—rather than drawing nigh—was already entering a phase of postponement.

6. Sugano centers her study on the occasional poetry of Mallarmé, explaining her choice as follows: "I have selected [. . .] a modern rather than a Renaissance poet in order to confront the problem [of the poetics of occasion] in its most complex form. Mallarmé's notorious dismissals of the real world, combined with his early critics' willingness to ignore the occasional nature of his work, radically problematize the question of the relationship between circumstance and writing in his poetry" (14).

7. Cf., the epigraph of "Amore e Morte," which cites Menander: "Muor giovane colui ch'al cielo è caro."

8. This fondness is made explicit in the second strophe of "Canto Notturno" (1829-30), which begins "Vecchierel bianco, infermo" (21); the similarity to *Rime sparse* 16 is noted by Fubini (182).

9. In the notoriously sparse commentary that Leopardi prepared for the edition of the *Rime sparse* published by Stella in 1826 (Dotti, 12), the poet notes merely that in number 16, the "per" in the phrase "per l'estreme giornate" is to be understood literally as "nelle estreme giornate," i.e., "during (the pilgrim's) last days of life" (Dotti, 63).

10. One notes with interest that Leopardi's "imaginative" use of "lasciando" in line 2 of "Nelle nozze"

was defended extensively by the poet in the "Annotazioni" as reprinted in 1825:

> I.1 Poi che del patrio nido
>   I silenzi lasciando,
>   Te ne la polve della vita e il sono
> Tragge il destin [sic].

> Questa e simili figure grammaticali, appartenenti all'uso de' nostri gerondi, sono cosí famigliari e cosí proprie di tutti gli scrittori italiani de' buoni secoli, che volendole rimuovere, non passerebbe quasi foglio di scrittura antica dove non s'avesse a metter le mani [. . .]. E anche oggidí, non che tollerata, [questa figura grammaticale] va custodita e favorita, considerando ch'ella spetta a quel genere di locuzioni e di modi, quanto piú difformi dalla ragione, tanto meglio conformi e corrispondenti alla natura, de' quali abbonda il piú sincero, gentile e squisito parlare italiano e greco [. . .]

(Damiani and Rigoni, 1. 179-80).

Although the use of "traendo" in *Rime sparse* 16 offers a more straightforward use of the gerund than that of the kind Leopardi discusses above, it nevertheless seems plausible that the poet would have been attentive to all uses of the gerund in the works of "gli scrittori italiani de' buoni secoli"; hence, in composing the *canzone,* he may well have had in mind Petrarch's use of "traendo" to describe the old pilgrim's voyage to Rome and into destiny.

11. Muscetta points out the Petrarchan quality of the epithet "patrio lido" in line 1 of "Nelle nozze" (217).

12. Bickersteth translates "obbrobriosa etate" as "shameful lot" (167).

13. Cf., p. 2390 of the *Zibaldone,* written several months (Feb. 16, 1822) after the *canzone*: "[L]a natura ha provveduto in modo che fin che l'uomo è nello stato naturale, come sono i fanciulli, poco e insufficientemente attende, essendo l'attenzione la nutrice della ragione, e la prima ed ultima causa della *corruz.[ione]* ed infelicità umana" (emphasis added).

14. The passage continues: "La mutazione totale in me, e il passaggio dallo stato antico al moderno, seguí si può dire dentro un anno, cioè nel 1819, dove [. . .] cominciai [. . .] a divenir filosofo di professione (di poeta ch'io era) [. . .]. [S]i può ben dire che in rigor di termini, poeti non erano se non gli antichi, e non sono ora se non i fanciulli, o giovanetti, e i moderni che hanno questo nome, non sono altro che filosofi [. . .]."

15. (a) [. . .] Oh giorni orrendi
    In cosí verde *etate* [. . .]

    ("La sera del dí di festa" 23-4, emphasis added)

    (b) [. . .] Ben mille volte
    Fortunato colui che la caduca
    Virtú del caro immaginar non perde
    Per volger d'anni; a cui serbar eterna
    La gioventú del cor diedero i fati;
    Che nella ferma e nella stanca *etade,*
    Cosí come nell'età *verde,*
    In suo chiuso pensier natura abbella,
    Morte, deserto avviva [. . .]

    ("Al Conte Carlo Pepoli" 110-18, emphasis added).

    (c) [. . .] All'inquieta speme,
    Figlia di giovin core,
    Tutti prestiam ricetto.
    Mentre è vermiglio il fiore
    Di nostra *etade* acerba,
    L'alma vota e superba
    Cento dolci pensieri educa invano,
    Né morte aspetta né vecchiezza; [. . .]

    ("Dello stesso" 7-14, emphasis added).

16. The first lines of "Nelle nozze" anticipate closely the opening of "Bruto minore," "Poi che divelta, nella tracia polve" etc. (Dec. 1821).

17. Leopardi confirms these sentiments (rhetorically) some 14 months later in a letter written to Paolina (Jan. 18, 1823). In fact, he makes the point that his sister can only be "happy" by *avoiding* the truth, i.e., only by remaining far away from harsh realities: "[N]on ti ripeterò che la felicità umana è un sogno, che il mondo non è bello, anzi non è sopportabile, se non veduto come tu lo vedi, cioè da lontano; che il piacere è un nome, non una cosa; che la virtú, la sensibilità, la grandezza d'animo sono, non solamente le uniche consolazioni de'nostri mali, ma anche i soli beni possibili in questa vita; e che questi beni, vivendo nel mondo e nella società, non si godono né si mettono a profitto, come sogliono credere i giovani, ma si perdono interamente, restando l'animo in un vuoto spaventevole" (Flora, 3. 385).

18. Blasucci explains that in *Canti* I through III ("All'Italia," "Sopra il monumento di Dante," "Ad Angelo Mai"), it had seemed that the poet's historical pessimism—presented as a position "in cui la negatività del giudizio sullo stato presente dell'Italia era ancora aperta a qualche concessione sulla disposizione dei tempi per una riscossa"— could be tempered, perhaps even conquered, by Leopardi's own generation (58). In "Nelle nozze,"

however, "Il fatto è che tra l'abbozzo e la stesura di 'Nella nozze' sono trascorsi mesi decisivi e per la storia nazionale e per quella leopardiana. La canzone costituisce infatti la ripresa dell'ispirazione civile dopo la stagione 'idillica' riempita dalla 'Sera del dí di festa,' da 'Sogno' e dalla 'Vita solitaria,' caratterizzata sul piano riflessivo dall'approfondimento di quel pessimismo storico ed esistenziale, che aveva avuto la prima enunciazione nella canzone al Mai. È un processo documentato da circa duemila pagine dello *Zibaldone,* stese tra i primi del 1820 e la fine del 1821. Quanto alla storia nazionale, è da registrare nell'intervallo di quei mesi il fallimento dei moti carbonari [. . .] (59-60).

19. Three critics have identified ancient sources that reinforce the notion of women as possessors of a beauty powerful enough to influence men of arms. Ermanno Carini (quoted in Frattini, 118) observes a clear affinity of content between lines 32-5 of "Nelle nozze" and a section of the invocation of Venus that opens Lucretius's *De rerum natura*:

> nam tu sola potes tranquilla pace iuvare
> mortalis, quoniam belli fera moenera Mavors
> armipotens regit, in gremium qui saepe tuum se
> reicit aeterno devictus vulnere amoris,
> atque ita suspiciens tereti cervice reposta
> pascit amore avidos inhians in te, dea, visus,
> eque tuo pendet resupini spiritus ore
>
> (l. 33-9).

Fubini (63) and Straccali (80) note that lines 33-35 of "Nelle Nozze" also recall the last verses of an ode (no. xxiv) attributed to Anacreon: "vince il ferro e il fuoco chi è bella."

20. Straccali confirms the intent of these lines by noting that Leopardi wrote (albeit years later, on March 19, 1828) to Antonietta Tommasini: "Vi ringrazio della vostra affettuosa lettera, piena di cosí nobili sentimenti di amor patrio. Se tutte le donne italiane pensassero e sentissero come voi, e procedessero conforme al loro pensare e sentire, la sorte d'Italia già fin d'ora sarebbe diversa assai da quella che è" (80).

21. "La storia del genere umano con la sua decadenza, non derivante dal peccato originale, ma dall'allontanamento dalla natura attraverso incivilimento, è implicita in questa lirica" (Muscetta, 217).

22. In the case of "Nelle nozze," Geoffrey Bickersteth remained greatly disappointed by the "contenuto effettivo" that Leopardi's efforts produced: "He loved his sister passionately and, moved by this love, he might have justified to our hearts the theory (which is his theme) that all modern Italians are without exception bound to be either cowardly or unfortunate. He prefers to illustrate his argument by evoking pictures of a Spartan warrior and of Virginia, beautiful pictures certainly, but rhetorical, whereas if the heroine of the tragedy had been Paolina his own affection for her would have made him eloquent" (70). Walter Binni is more enthusiastic about the sentimental and formal achievements of the poem, and finds that the compelling apostrophe to Virginia, in which "la canzone raggiunge dinamicamente la sua zona piú alta," does in fact spring from a development of the "toni alti e i toni affettuosi e colloquiali già presenti nel primo rivolgersi alla sorella" (l. liv).

23. Sugano remarks, "Goethe so enlarged the notion of the occasion as to render it meaningless, and the future usefulness of the term 'occasional literature' as a descriptive category was largely diminished" (9).

24. Ottavio Casale has identified this very characteristic, i.e., the presence of *cognizioni* intuited *in anticipo* to the point that they disturb a sense of linear time, as a constant in the first works of the *Canti*: "Except possibly for 'The Infinite,' the lonely poet or persona of the early poems etches the tragic perceptions of one caught between two dimensions or times: time and self *then* as against time and self *now*; the world as seen through illusion, memory, hope, and the affections compared to the world grasped by the disenchanted reason; the desire for love, life, fame, and virtue as opposed to the reality of our transience, pain, and ignominy. These themes repeat again and again in Leopardi" (20-1).

Works Cited

Bickersteth, Geoffrey L. (ed.). *The Poems of Leopardi.* New York: Russell and Russell, 1973.

Binni, Walter (ed.). *Giacomo Leopardi: Tutte le opere.* 2 vols. Florence: Sansoni, 1989.

Blasucci, Luigi. *I Titoli dei "Canti" e altri studi leopardiani.* Naples: Morano, 1989.

Bufano, Antonietta. *Concordanze dei "Canti" del Leopardi.* Florence: Le Monnier, 1969.

Casale, Ottavio. *A Leopardi Reader.* Urbana: University of Illinois Press, 1981.

Damiani, Rolando and Mario Andrea Rigoni (eds.). *Giacomo Leopardi: Poesie e Prose.* 2 vols. Milan: Mondadori, 1991.

Dotti, Ugo (ed.). *Francesco Petrarca. Canzoniere. Commento di Giacomo Leopardi.* Milan: Feltrinelli, 1979.

Durling, Robert M. (trans. and ed.). *Petrarch's Lyric Poems*. Cambridge, MA: Harvard University Press, 1976.

Flora, Francesco (ed.). *Tutte le opere di Giacomo Leopardi*. 3 vols. Milan: Mondadori, 1959.

Frattini, Alberto. *Giacomo Leopardi: Il problema delle "fonti" alla radice della sua opera*. Rome: Coletti, 1990.

Fubini, Mario (ed.). *Giacomo Leopardi: Canti*. Turin: Loescher, 1964.

Merriam, G. and C. *Webster's New International Dictionary*. Second ed. Springfield: Merriam, 1944.

Miner, Earl, A. J. M. Smith, and T. V. F. Brogan. "Occasional Verse," in *The New Princeton Encyclopedia of Poetry and Poetics,* eds. Alex Preminger and T. V. F. Brogan. Princeton: Princeton University Press, 1993.

Muscetta, Carlo. *Ritratti e letture*. Milan: Marzorati, 1961.

Ottolini, Angelo (ed.). *Giacomo Leopardi: I Canti*. Milan: Signorelli, 1982.

Pacella, Giuseppe (ed.). *Giacomo Leopardi: Zibaldone di pensieri*. Milan: Garzanti, 1991.

Peruzzi, Emilio (ed.). *Giacomo Leopardi. "Canti": Edizione critica con la riproduzione degli autografi*. Milan: Rizzoli, 1981.

Straccali, Afredo (ed.). *I Canti di Giacomo Leopardi*. Florence: Sansoni, 1932.

Sugano, Marian Zwerling. *The Poetics of the Occasion: Mallarmé and the Poetry of Circumstance*. Stanford: Stanford University Press, 1992.

Zingarelli, Nicola. *Vocabolario della lingua italiana*. 11th ed. Bologna: Zanichelli, 1984.

Anne Urbancic (essay date December 1998)

SOURCE: Urbancic, Anne. "Reflecting on a Moment of Calm: Leopardi's 'La Quiete Dopo La Tempesta.'"[1] *Rivista di Studi Italiani* 16, no. 1 (December 1998): 519-36.

[*In the following essay, Urbancic discusses an especially tumultuous time in Leopardi's life that was followed by a period of calm during which he composed the lyric poems of the "grandi idilli."*]

On September 5, 1829, an angry and resentful Leopardi begins to write a letter to Carlo Bunsen in Rome,[2] a task which he surmises will take three or four days because of his debilitated physical state. The main purpose of the letter, to congratulate Bunsen on the incep-

tion of the *Giornale archeologico* and to decline the invitation to participate as contributor, is completely overshadowed by the profound bitterness and hopelessness that envelops him. Leopardi writes:

> Non solo i miei occhi, ma tutto il mio fisico, sono in istato peggiore che fosse mai. Non posso né scrivere, né leggere, né dettare, né pensare. Questa lettera sinché non l'avrò terminata, sarà la mia sola occupazione, e con tutto ciò non potrò finirla se fra tre o quattro giorni. Condannato per mancanza di mezzi a quest'orribile e detestata dimora, e già morto ad ogni godimento e ad ogni speranza, non vivo che per patire, e non invoco che il riposo del sepolcro.[3]

Even further on in the letter, in an indicative parenthesis, he reiterates his state of mind, writing of "le pochissime felicità della mia vita (la quale spero o certamente desidero prossima ad estinguersi)."[4] But it is the opening line of the letter that best reveals the atmosphere of frustration and anger which is the source of Leopardi's antagonism. He warns Carlo Bunsen that there are discrepancies between what the latter may have heard of him, and the true situation of his psychological and physical turmoil: "Mio padre il quale ama immaginarsi che nella sua casa paterna io stia meglio che altrove, le ha dato del mio stato un'idea ben diversa dal vero."[5]

Giacomo clearly wishes to undermine his father's authority and his father's attitudes regarding what is best for the eldest Leopardi son. The criticism of Monaldo Leopardi is unmistakable, and likely much to the father's chagrin, almost a public declaration of the deleterious tension between father and son.

The tension was not new, of course. At the time of this letter, however, it marked a period of acquiescence on the part of the younger Leopardi. It seemed, for the moment, that the war of his personal independence, the war over how and where and by what means Giacomo was to live his life had been won by Monaldo. It was a time of imposed calm after a period of physical and psychological upheaval. And it was in this emotional environment that Giacomo was inspired to compose some of his most memorable lyric poetry, the poems of the "grandi idilli," and among them **"La quiete dopo la tempesta."**

This study will explore how the events of Leopardi's daily life culminated in the ambience that inspired the "grandi idilli," with particular emphasis on **"La Quiete [. . .]."** We shall examine how the psychological and physical exile into his father's house reflected a state of seeming absence (absence of turmoil, absence of independence, absence of activity) that follows a period of personal upheaval. Finally we shall examine the poem to show how each stanza illustrates the essence of the calm as physical respite and as metaphor.

Natalino Sapegno, in his seminal essay on Leopardi that appears in the *Storia della Letteratura Italiana*,[6] provides the richly detailed background that helps us understand the genesis of **"La Quiete [. . .]."** The chronological and diachronically validated events that he recounts are important considerations not so much for their biographical relevance but, rather, for their psychological and literary significance.

In November 1822, Giacomo Leopardi had finally made a much desired escape from the stifling bourgeois environment of his home in Recanati. He was invited to be a guest of his maternal uncle Carlo Antici, at the latter's residence in Rome. He returned to his own home in Recanati a few months later, in May of 1823. In the years that followed, he was intent on working on many of the pages that would become the **Operette morali**,[7] and on expanding and elaborating the pages that would constitute the **Zibaldone di pensieri**.[8] Then in 1825, he was invited by the Milanese publisher Stella to supervise an edition of Cicero.[9] Recanati, and the oppressive authority of his father, were left behind, and except for a brief period in the winter of 1826-27, as Sapegno tells us, Leopardi was able to avoid his paternal home until November 1828.[10] The time spent away from Recanati focused on various literary and editorial pursuits in Milan (1825), in Bologna (1826 and 1827) and then in Tuscany, where he came into contact with some of the most influential men of letters of the Ottocento, including Gino Capponi, Alessandro Poerio, Alessandro Manzoni and also Giampietro Vieusseux,[11] who offered to make him a collaborator of the *Antologia*. In a letter that is most significant for our purposes, Leopardi declined the invitation, pointing out:

> La mia vita, prima per necessità di circostanze e contro mia voglia, poi per inclinazione nata dall'abito convertito in natura e divenuto indelebile, è stata sempre, ed è, e sarà perpetuamente solitaria, anche in mezzo alla conversazione, nella quale, per dirlo all'inglese, io sono più *absent* di quel che sarebbe un cieco e sordo. Questo vizio dell'*absence* è in me incorreggibile e disperato.[12]

The concept of absence of which he writes will recur time and again, and will inform the poem **"La Quiete [. . .]."**

By November of 1828, after time spent in the amenable climate of Pisa[13] and then in Florence, Leopardi felt the necessity of returning to Recanati. Sapegno describes the conditions that led the poet to this conclusion. His health continued to be ever more uncertain; he had no means of support and the promises of his friends to try and place him in some official or professorial capacity had come to naught. His brother Luigi had died recently, on May 4 of that year, and Giacomo felt the need to grieve with his family. Furthermore, his father was unwilling to support him financially if he did not reside at the family home. And thus, after a tumultuous

attempt at freedom, where it appeared that truly everything had conspired to impede him from realizing his personal goals, Giacomo returned home, defeated. His father's complete ignorance of the return as a true psychological defeat for his son, in the way Giacomo described in the letter to Bunsen quoted earlier, must have augmented the negative feelings that Leopardi felt toward Recanati, his home, and his family. He considered himself psychologically and intellectually dead, and sought escape in a physical death, which he hoped would come soon.

On the other hand, despite his avowals otherwise, Leopardi was not *"absent"* as he had indicated in his correspondence. Nor was his "vizio dell'*absence*" as incorrigible as he had claimed in the letter to Vieusseux, for all that he had considered it desperate. The year and a half spent in Recanati, his last stay there before a definitive departure, may indeed have been "sedici mesi di notte orribile,"[14] but simultaneously these were months of intensive and fruitful poetic awareness and activity. If we review the literary chronology proposed by Luigi Russo in his edition of the *Canti*,[15] we read that in about the middle of June 1829, Leopardi composed **"Il passero solitario,"** which the critic Fernando Figurelli calls a "canto [. . .] di esilio dalla vita."[16] At the end of August, Leopardi began to write **"Le Ricordanze,"** a poem completed on the 12th day of September, as Russo notes. A week later, between the 17th and 20th of September, he composed **"La Quiete dopo la tempesta,"** followed immediately by **"Il sabato del villaggio,"** which was written in a single day, on the 29th of September 1829. In October and November he worked on the **"Canto notturno di un pastore errante dell'Asia,"** before initiating, in 1830, the cycle of poems intended for his beloved, and then traitorous, Aspasia. In the deepest darkness of his despair were born the "grandi idilli" that bloom as a miraculous flower, as Sapegno has written.[17]

And after the winter of the "grandi idilli," Leopardi seemed to emerge morally fortified and resolved that he would not be defeated either by his health, his home, or his parents. The despondent passivity of his letter to Carlo Bunsen had been replaced with plans of cautious activity, as is evident in his letter to Vieusseux of March 21, 1830:

> Mio carissimo amico. Son risoluto, con quei pochi danari che mi avanzarono quando io potea lavorare, di pormi in viaggio per cercare salute o morire, e a Recanati non ritornare mai più. Non farò distinzion di mestieri; ogni condizione conciliabile colla mia salute mi converrà: non guarderò ad umiliazioni; perché non si dà umiliazione o avvilimento maggiore di quello ch'io soffro vivendo in questo centro dell'inciviltà e dell'ignoranza europea. Io non ho più da perdere, e ponendo anche a rischio questa mia vita, non rischio che di guadagnare.[18]

So intent was he on his decision to leave Recanati once and for all that he even offered his services as a tutor:

> Ditemi *con tutta sincerità* se credete che costí potrei trovar da campare dando lezioni o trattenimenti letterarii *in casa*; e se troverei presto; perché poco tempo mi basteranno i danari per mantenermi del mio. Dico lezioni letterarie di qualunque genere; anche infimo; di lingua, di grammatica e simili. E vorrei che mi rispondeste subito che potrete, perch'io partirò presto, e secondo la vostra risposta determinerò se debbo voltarmi a Firenze, o cercare altri barlumi di speranza in altri luoghi.[19]

The letter is truly fascinating because his Florentine friends—Pietro Giordani, Pietro Colletta, Giuseppe Montani, and Vieusseux—were clearly able to see what Leopardi could not; namely, that he was not cut out for a teaching and tutoring position.[20] Of his own plans in this area he was openly derisory in this letter to Vieusseux. His friends responded with an offer of a monthly stipend that would allow him to work and live in Florence. Leopardi gratefully accepted, writing to Pietro Colletta shortly before his departure from Recanati:

> Mio caro Generale. Né le condizioni mie sosterrebbero ch'io ricusassi il benefizio, d'onde e come che mi venisse, e voi e gli amici vostri sapete beneficare in tal forma, che ogni piú schivo consentirebbe di ricever benefizio da' vostri pari. Accetto pertanto quello che mi offrite; e l'accetto cosí confidentemente, che non potendo (come sapete) scrivere, e poco potendo dettare, differisco il ringraziarvi a quando lo potrò fare a viva voce, che sarà presto, perch'io partirò fra pochi giorni. Per ora vi dirò solo che la vostra lettera, dopo sedici mesi di notte orribile, dopo un vivere dal quale Iddio scampi i miei maggiori nemici, è stata a me come un raggio di luce, piú benedetto che non è il primo barlume del crepuscolo nelle regioni polari.[21]

The letters sent to Recanati from Florence in the year that followed reveal a slight change in tone. Leopardi speaks of feeling appreciated by his friends and plays down his precarious state of health. The quiet, the silence, the absence of activity that he had perceived in his father's house, after some of the more tumultuous events of his life seem to have passed, and Leopardi seems to be open to new events and new activities.

Let us return now to the "orribile notte" of Recanati to focus more closely on **"La Quiete [. . .]."**

Luigi Russo provides some important details regarding the composition of **"La Quiete [. . .]."** As we have mentioned previously, the poem was composed within a period of three days in late September of 1829. It was published in Florence by Piatti in 1831. Although not mentioned specifically in the prefatory note in which Leopardi dedicated the edition to his Tuscan friends, it is striking to see how both the poem and the dedicatory prose focus on a similar moment, and on a similar attitude. This is precisely that brief period of time that follows some frenetic, critical activity, before the undertaking of a new one; it is a moment of simultaneously reflecting back on the crises that have been overcome and cautiously advancing forward. In the dedication, Leopardi writes:

> Amici miei cari. Sia dedicato a voi questo libro, dove io cercava, come si cerca spesso colla poesia, di consacrare il mio dolore, e col quale al presente (né posso già dirlo senza lacrime) prendo comiato dalle lettere e dagli studi. Sperai che questi cari studi avrebbero sostentata la mia vecchiezza, e credetti colla perdita di tutti gli piaceri, di tutti gli altri beni della fanciullezza e della gioventú, avere acquistato un bene che da nessuna forza, da nessuna sventura mi fosse tolto [. . .]. Ho perduto tutto: sono un tronco che sente e pena. Se non che in questo tempo ho acquistato voi: e la compagnia vostra, che m'è in luogo degli studi, e in luogo d'ogni diletto e di ogni speranza, quasi compenserebbe i miei mali [. . .].[22]

Leopardi reflects on the hardships he has experienced, and looks forward to new activities. In these latter too, he knows, he will be beset by difficulties and crises, but at least he will have felt and cherished the love of his friends. To the fact that new troubles will plague him, and that he will not be able to avoid or control them even unto death, he is utterly resigned.

The same sequence of looking back, reflecting and then hesitantly looking forward is also seen in **"La Quiete [. . .]."** Luigi Russo notes that the poem may have been occasioned by Leopardi's observation of meteorological phenomena and a similar sequence there; the area around Recanati, in September 1829, had been hit by several heavy downpours and violent storms. But Leopardi had been fascinated by storms, and the brief moment of respite immediately following, for many years. Russo points out that the **"Ultimo Canto di Saffo,"** composed in 1822, has lines that are thematically analogous:

> Noi l'insueta allor gaudio ravviva
> quando per l'etra liquido si volve
> e per li campi trepidanti il flutto
> polveroso de' Noti, e quando il carro
> grave carro di Giove e noi sul capo,
> tonando, il tenebroso aere divide.

(l. 8-13)

Russo also describes a draft of a poem prepared in 1819, entitled **"Le fanciulle nella tempesta"** in which Leopardi depicts a similar situation. In their translation of selections of the *Zibaldone,* Martha King and Daniela Bini have observed that a precursor of **"La Quiete [. . .]."** had appeared in verse in one of the earliest annotations. There Leopardi expressed his criticism of Ludovico Di Breme's negative opinions of Horace. Leopardi claimed that it is up to the poet to imitate and depict nature as perfectly as possible.[23]

Luigi Russo reads **"La Quiete [. . .]."** as a tripartite composition. He sets apart the first 24 lines as descriptive or idyllic; Part 2, consisting of the next 17 lines (from "Si rallegra ogni core" to "folgori, nembi e vento") is the moment in which Leopardi, according to Russo, renders mythical the storm followed by calm. And in the closing 13 lines, Russo observes how Leopardi bitterly and bitingly expresses his anger against Nature, a Nature which offers to mortals no delight other than temporary relief from pain. Only the finality of death will heal all difficulties and wounds.[24]

Natalino Sapegno, on the other hand, intuits a bipartite structure, both in **"La Quiete [. . .]."** and in the **"Sabato del villaggio,"** which as we will recall were written almost contemporaneously. According to Sapegno, the two poems manifest "una struttura bipartita quasi di apologo o parabola, in cui la rappresentazione prefigura e alla fine si solve in una morale che ne esplicita il senso [. . .]."[25]

Together with the **"Passero solitario,"** these poems highlight the point of "verismo" in Leopardi, writes Sapegno, where moments of reality are relived as if in a clear dream. Conversely, the second part of **"La Quiete [. . .]."** attests to a new stylistic attitude on the part of the poet: "il momento riflessivo s'intona in modi nuovi e piú distaccati in una scansione piú severa e deserta dello stile."[26]

Sapegno's contention that there is a newness of attitude evident in the poem is a valid one. Russo, too, senses a difference between the attitude of the first idyllic poems and the later "grandi idilli," and he focuses upon the idea of the poet's distancing of himself from the poem as its source. No longer are the anxiety and regret for the unrecoverable past a factor in this later poem as they had been previously. Leopardi does not participate in **"La Quiete [. . .]."** at all; he merely observes from distant point. The poet's observations take place on two different levels. First, he observes the effects of the storm on the countryside. Then his observations become metaphysical, perhaps even philosophical, as he expands his comments beyond the immediate environment, extrapolating the lessons of Nature on a much grander scale. For once, Leopardi, the oppressed poet awaiting death, is totally absent from the poem, with the exception of the verb "odo" in line 2. He does not give advice or dire forewarnings of what is yet to be, as he does in the **"Sabato del villaggio,"**[27] nor does he proclaim his own personal bitterness, depression and hopelessness as he does in the **"Canto notturno [. . .],"**[28] in the **"Ricordanze,"**[29] or especially in the **"Pensiero dominante,"** which is an interior monologue. In fact, all autobiographical details that are often revealed in Leopardi's poetry, and which serve to underscore his torment and utter despair are missing in **"La Quiete [. . .]."** Russo has commented that in this poem

"il fascino della poesia consiste in questo suo essere un idillio filosofato, ma la filosofia, dove c'è, è sempre offerta con levità di termini e musica di brevi parolette arcane."[30] Russo's observation is appreciated, and especially in the first stanza are his comments applicable. The images upon which Leopardi draws are of the simplest, most humble elements of life: the birds, the hen,[31] the singing labourer, the young woman, the farmer, the family, the traveller. It is fascinating to consider that all of these "actors," as they take up again the activities that had been interrupted by the storm, are only heard by the poet, and not seen.[32] There is no seeing, no observing in this poem of highly visual images. The poet remains aloof, apart. He only hears the birds, the hen, the everyday noises of usual work, the singing of the craftsman, the shouting of the "erbaiolo," the jingling of bells as the coach starts up again on its travels. The whole of this first verse revolves only around "odo," despite the visual detail that the reader perceives. Russo glosses the verb "odo" as an autobiographical element; he would have Leopardi in his room, with the shutters closed. While this is indeed possible, and is emphasized by the fact that in his correspondence at the time of writing, as well as in later letters, Leopardi referred often to problems with his eyes, it is far more likely that this auditory detail, as Russo also observes, was carefully and deliberately chosen by Leopardi and preferred over "seeing."[33] This type of envisaging through hearing, as Leopardi is wont to do in **"La Quiete [. . .]."** represents a reflective process that he had outlined in the *Zibaldone* only some ten months before composing this poem. He seemed attracted to the process because it afforded him as a poet, a heightened sensorial experience. He wrote:

> For the sensitive and imaginative man who lives as I have lived for a long time, continually feeling and imagining, the world and objects are in a peculiar way double. He will see a tower, a landscape, with his eyes; he will hear the sound of a bell with his ears; and at the same time in his imagination he will see another tower, another landscape, he will hear another sound. In this second mode of perceiving objects resides all the beauty and pleasure of concrete things. How sad is that life (and yet it is the ordinary life) that sees, hears, feels only the simple objects, only those perceived by the eyes, ears, and the other senses.[34]

One is particularly struck by how closely this passage of the *Zibaldone* (when it is represented in verse, as it is in **"La Quiete [. . .]."**), approaches the enquiries into language, into signifier and signified, of poststructuralist theorists, and especially Jacques Derrida. Let us not forget that, in fact, it is the poets of Romanticism who provide the inspirational force from which the poststructuralist theorists elaborate their own ideas.[35] The entry of the *Zibaldone* cited above anticipates the reflections of Derrida today on signifying chains and on *différance* which refer to the ineluctable polysemy of words and concepts. By signifying chain, Derrida has intended the sequential changes in meaning which the value of a particular word, word group or concept (i.e., Signifier) undergoes across space and time. Derrida's theories are far more elaborate than this brief allusion would show, and incorporate epistemological enquiries that Leopardi does not necessarily pose for himself. But it is nevertheless fascinating to see in passages such as the one quoted above, the beginnings of the study of philosophy and discourse that will eventually prepare the way for poststructuralist theory. Similarly with *différance,* a neologism proposed by Derrida (which subsumes within itself the meaning of "to defer," "to differ" and the Latin "differre" = "to scatter"). Derrida's concept refers to the difficulty of establishing a fixed meaning for a word or concept, since each of the signifiers employed in the exercise of stabilizing meaning can be "opened up" and interpreted differently by different interlocutors. Given Leopardi's passage above, we can see that the poet focused on the simplest elements of contemporary life in order to universalize a scene and an emotional environment that could be, if not fixed semantically, then at least shared and understood by all his readers. This was for him a necessary step that would subsequently allow him to reflect philosophically on the symbolic (or even, as Russo would have it) on the allegorical meaning of the poem, as he does in the later stanzas. This universalization is important to the development of the poem because it allows the poet to establish common bonds with his readers. Previously, and later, Leopardi had depended on memory, on nostalgia and yearning for things past in his poems.[36] He had even written just some months before composing this cycle of poetry that "[r]emembrance is essential in poetic feeling for no other reason than the present, whatever it may be, cannot be poetic; and the poetic, in one way or another, always consists of the distant, the indefinite, the vague."[37]

If we examine the images of the first stanza more closely we can see that the scene that has been prepared for us is heard, rather than seen directly, as we have already discussed, and, as well, Leopardi has carefully added references and allusions to distance and to vagueness such as "rompe *là* da ponente alla montagna" (emphasis mine), "il romorio," "l'umido cielo," "di sentiero in sentiero," "odi lontano tintinnio di sonagli."

The idea of distance also attenuates the temporal concept of the present moment, which Leopardi considers difficult and unpoetic. If one can ascribe to Leopardi, once again, ideas that would be further developed by poststructuralists, we can see that, similarly to the first stanza, which depended on the word "odo," the second stanza revolves around "com'or." The questions when is "now"? or what is "now"? lead us also to considerations made by Jacques Derrida, which he termed as indicative of his concept of *aporia.* This concept, also referred to as "mise-en-abyme" or gap, points to the

semantic disparity between signifier and signified, and to the incoherence and impossibility of a one-to-one correspondence between the two elements. When Leopardi refers to the "quiete," the period of calm immediately following a storm, as "now," we can see how fragile and tenuous its referent is. The phrase "com'or" does not mean the time of the storm because "passata è la tempesta." The storm is over. On the other hand, it is not the period after the storm when activity is fully underway. Instead, Leopardi stops to reflect upon that almost fleeting moment that may be glimpsed between the storm's end and full post-storm activity. He expands, or opens up, that brief moment in order to pause for reflection. That particular moment is neither before nor after, neither activity of the storm, nor activity after the storm, neither here nor there. It is in fact a gap, a pause, a silence. And from that silence, the poet stops to consider the life's lesson that he has intuited as he has listened to the world around him come to life again:

> Si rallegra ogni core.
> Sí dolce, sí gradita,
> quand'è com'or la vita?
> quando con tanto amore
> l'uomo ai suoi studi intende?
> o torna all'opre? o cosa nuova imprende?
> quando de' mali suoi men si ricorda?

(ll. 25-31)

The unexpressed answer to the question "when" is, in fact, "now." But "now" is an ephemeral moment. It is over immediately and is supplanted by the dire warning of the true nature of the moment, of the true characteristics of life before and after, of here and there:

> Piacer figlio d'affanno;
> gioia vana, ch'è frutto
> del passato timore, onde si scosse
> e paventò la morte
> che la vita abborria:
> onde in lungo tormento,
> fredde, tacite, smorte,
> sudâr le genti e palpitar, vedendo
> mossi alle nostre offese
> folgori, nembi e vento.

(ll. 32-46)

The moment of awareness of how horrible life can be is found succinctly and heart-rendingly expressed in the simple phrase of utter pathos, "Piacer figlio d'affanno," in which the dichotomous "piacere" and "affanno" no longer express antinomy but instead become synonymous. Even early literary critics, among them Francesco Flora, had noticed and commented upon the tight syntactic structure of this phrase that is at once exclamation, synthesis, and resignation.[38] Lacking any verb that would render it finite, the phrase becomes horrifyingly past, present, and future.

The equivalence of pleasure and pain had been considered by Leopardi at various times previously. On one occasion, in the *Zibaldone,* he had even used the context of the calm after the storm to study this idea. He wrote:

> Therefore with good reason they [infirmities and a hundred other inevitable evils] are contained in the natural order which aims in every way at the aforesaid happiness. This not only because these evils give prominence to the good, and good health is enjoyed more after sickness, and the calm after the storm, but because without these evils, a good thing would not even be good for very long. It would turn into boredom, and would not be enjoyed or felt to be a good thing or a pleasure, and the sensation of pleasure, as far as it is really pleasurable, would not be able to last for a long time etc.[39]

The last few lines of the second stanza illustrate the effects of the "piacer figlio d'affanno" and of the "vain joy" upon mankind:

> onde in lungo tormento,
> fredde, tacite, smorte,
> sudâr le genti e palpitâr, vedendo
> mossi alle nostre offese
> folgori, nembi e vento.
>
> (ll. 37-41)

The stanza ends with the three nouns that refer back to the storm of the title. But unlike the hopeful opening line, "[p]assata è la tempesta," the last line of the second stanza is structured in such a way as to threateningly presage another storm: "folgore, nembi e vento." Russo has pointed out that with the three nouns there is a natural descending order toward the earth, because there are "in alto i folgori, e poi le nuvole tempestose (nembi) e infine il vento."[40] The effect is one of continuing oppression on the part of Nature.

It is worthwhile to observe at this point that generally, in speaking of that reflective space, that gap in which man reconsiders his tremendous lot in life, Leopardi elaborates his concept of "noia." He had written in his *Zibaldone* that

> Chi dice assenza di piacere e dispiacere, dice noia, non che assolutamente queste due cose siano tutt'una, ma rispetto alla natura del vivente, in cui l'una senza l'altra (mentre ch'ei sente di vivere) non può assolutamente stare. La noia corre sempre e immediatamente a riempire tutti i vuoti che lasciano negli animi de' viventi il piacere e il dispiacere.[41]

But in the verses of this poem, which focus directly on that brief, tenuous moment that separates life before the storm from life after the storm, there is curiously no mention of boredom, or lack of awareness. This may be because there is a certain pleasure for the poet as he listens, alone but intent on hearing life renew itself, not participating himself but able to appreciate the participation of others, as he had written in the *Zibaldone.*[42]

The absence of "noia" may also have as its source the impending and certain new pain or displeasure that Leopardi anticipates in the second stanza.[43]

With the closing of this verse, there is a change of attitude with which the poet initiates the third stanza. In the latter, Nature is invoked and addressed directly. As the lines proceed, Leopardi's tone toward Nature becomes more accusatory and even sarcastic, as Russo has justifiably suggested.[44] The stanza poeticizes many of the concepts that the poet had painfully elaborated throughout the *Operette morali* which had been written in the dolorous period just prior to the composition of the "grandi idilli." Paradoxically in 1828, Leopardi had written to his sister Paolina that he had finally succeeded in writing poetry "ma versi all'antica, e con quel mio cuore di una volta."[45] But in truth, the attitude he has shown toward Nature is reiterated in the poetry written after the letter.

The invocation of Nature begins benignly; he calls her "cortese," and a giver of gifts. When, however, he begins to detail what these are ("uscir di pena," "pene tu spargi," "il duolo spontaneo" "piacer nasce d'affanno"—which echoes the painful observation that pleasure is "figlio d'affanno"), his tone becomes mocking; he emphasizes how humanity is completely at the mercy of the whims of Nature:

> Umana
> prole cara agli eterni! assai felice
> se respirar ti lice
> d'alcun dolor; beata
> se te d'ogni dolor morte risana.
>
> (ll. 50-4)

We can see here how the plaintive addressing of Nature, perhaps in the hope of some response, or some justification for her unwavering cruelty to mankind, is no longer a consideration, even as it had been in **"A Silvia."**[46] Instead there is only the resignation that death alone will heal the sufferings imposed on mankind by Nature. Mankind can never know true happiness; only relative happiness is attainable ("assai felice"), and ironically, this joy is dependent on absence of pain, which will never be truly diminished until the moment of death.

The thought of, and desire for, death were recurring themes in Leopardi's personal life at this period of time. It is likely that he even delighted in such considerations for he wrote in the *Zibaldone* in the late winter of 1829 that "distracting the mind forcibly from a bitter or terrible thought is more painful than concentrating on it."[47] As he searched within himself for a release from his psychological pain, he became aware of his need for compassion and was despondent over the realization that there was none for him:

Now [the] concept of one's nobility seems ridiculous and is sadly rejected like a lost illusion when one is regularly or occasionally scorned by those around him. And so, in these cases, the temptation to feel, etc. is painful because it renews the thought of your degradation.[48]

Consequently, can there be compassion from Nature? The answer is negative, of course. Nature disperses pain with a generous hand, suffering is spontaneous. Nature is not compassionate, and instead, demonstrates unfeeling cruelty, as Leopardi had noted:

> Nature, through the necessity of the law of destruction and reproduction, and in order to preserve the present state of the universe, is essentially, regularly, and perpetually the persecutor and mortal enemy of all individuals of every genus and species to which she has given life; and she begins to persecute them from the moment she has produced them.[49]

In this last stanza of **"La Quiete [. . .]."** Leopardi has been able to capture in a few brief verses all the pain and sorrow inflicted by Nature upon the "Islandese" of the **Operette morali,** and he proposes the same solution, death, that he had outlined in the **Dialogo di Federico Ruysch e le sue mummie.**

It is interesting, however, that in the last line of the poem, Leopardi has succeeded in reproposing the whole thematic of **"La Quiete [. . .]."** on a metaphorical plane. At the start of the poem, the meteorological storm has passed, and there is a brief period of calm. At the end of the poem, the storm that is life, buffeted by the uncaring and uninvolved force that is Nature, is over. It is followed by the healing calm of death.

After the horrible sojourn of his "long night" in his father's house in Recanati, this is the calm to which the poet aspires.

Notes

1. This essay is dedicated to Professor M. W. Ukas, Professor Emeritus at the University of Toronto, whose inspiring lectures on Leopardi have touched countless students, both graduate and undergraduate.

2. Bunsen (1791-1860) was an archeologist, philosopher and Protestant theologian. He was the secretary of the Prussian Embassy to the Holy See, and after 1823, ambassador. In this he was the successor of Georg Niebuhr, author of the *Storia romana fino al 241 a C.* which Leopardi praises further on in this letter. The journal to which Leopardi refers is the *Bollettino di corrispondenza archeologica.*

3. In *Giacomo Leopardi. Lettere,* edited by Giorgio Ficara (Milan: Mondadori, 1993), p. 320.

4. *Ibid.,* p. 321.

5. *Ibid.,* p. 320.

6. N. Sapegno, "Giacomo Leopardi," in *Storia della letteratura italiana,* Voll. VII. *L'Ottocento* (Milan: Garzanti, 1969), pp. 733-865.

7. Published in 1827 by Stella (Milan).

8. His literary and philosophical diary was begun in 1817, with entries until December 4, 1832. These were published posthumously in 1845 by Le Monnier of Florence.

9. It is with this commitment that he incurred the wrath and the subsequent enmity of Niccolò Tommaseo (1802-1874). Leopardi had negatively adjudicated Tommaseo's contributions to the project. Although Leopardi did not know who the commentator was, Tommaseo was deeply offended by Leopardi's comments and the advice that Stella abandon the project. Tommaseo began a series of personal and professional attacks on Leopardi that lasted many years after the latter's death. But as late as 1829, Leopardi included Tommaseo as one of the Florentine friends to whom he sent greetings. (Letter to Vieusseux, 12 April 1829.) However, in later correspondence he referred to Tommaseo as the *factotum* of the *Antologia* (Letter to De Sinner, 18 December 1832), and, in 1835, he responded to the verbal attacks in his poem "Palinodia al Marchese Gino Capponi" (ll. 228-239).

10. Sapegno, *op. cit.,* p. 818.

11. Gino Capponi (1792-1876) was a man of politics, a philologist, an educator, economist, and historian. He was an ardent supporter of cultural and patriotic activities. Together with Giampietro Vieusseux (1779-1863), he began publishing the *Antologia* in 1820. Alessandro Poerio (1802-1848) was a poet and patriot, and presented Leopardi to Fanny Targioni-Tozzetti. Alessandro Manzoni (1785-1873), of course, needs no introduction.

12. Leopardi, *Lettere, op. cit.,* p. 250.

13. In his letter to his sister Paolina of November 12, 1827, he described how Pisa enchanted him for its climate. Leopardi, *Lettere, op. cit.,* p. 284.

14. Leopardi, *Lettere, op. cit.,* p. 323.

15. Leopardi, *I Canti,* edited by Luigi Russo (Florence: Sansoni, 1971).

16. F. Figurelli, *Giacomo Leopardi poeta dell'idillio* (Bari: Laterza, 1941), p. 113.

17. Sapegno, *op. cit.,* p. 835.

18. Leopardi, *Lettere, op. cit.,* p. 321-2.

19. *Ibid.*

20. Colletta (1775-1831) was a general who had fought against the Bourbons under Murat and lived

in exile in Florence. Giordani (1774-1848) was an author and researcher/translator of classical literature. Montani (1789-1833) collaborated on the *Antologia* and on the *Conciliatore*. As far as Leopardi's teaching was concerned, we should note that in the *Zibaldone* he had written on December 1, 1828 that "the necessity of living with people, of being outgoing, reacting, living externally made [him] stupid, inept, inwardly dead" [4420] in G. Leopardi, *Zibaldone. A Selection,* trans. and with an introduction by Martha King and Daniela Bini (New York: Peter Lang, 1992), p. 194.

21. Leopardi, *Lettere, op. cit.,* pp. 322-3.

22. *Ibid.,* p. 36.

23. Leopardi, *Zibaldone, op. cit.,* p. 17. The lines of the poem are: "Sí come dopo la procella oscura / Canticchiando gli augelli escon del loco / Dove cacciogli il vento (nembo) e la paura; / E il villanel che presso al patrio foco / Sta sospirando il sol si riconforta (si rasserena) / sentendo il dolce canto e il dolce gioco."

24. Leopardi, *I Canti, op. cit.,* p. 283.

25. Sapegno, *op. cit.,* p. 842.

26. *Ibid.*

27. "Godi fanciullo mio; stato soave / stagion lieta è cotesta. / Altro dirti non vo'; ma la tua festa / ch'anco tardi a venir non ti sia grave" (ll. 48-51).

28. "a me la vita è male. / O greggia mia che posi, oh te beata, / che la miseria tua, credo, non sai! / quanta invidia ti porto!" (ll. 104-7).

29. "E sebben vòti / son gli anni miei, sebben deserto, oscuro / il mio stato mortal, poco mi toglie / la fortuna, ben veggo" (ll. 84-7).

30. Leopardi, *I Canti, ed. cit.,* p. 284.

31. Russo wishes to interpret this image as symbolic, *ibid.*

32. Cf. Leopardi, *Zibaldone, op. cit.,* [1828]. Entry for October 16, 1821, p. 140: "any sound whatever is pleasurable that is diffused far and wide [. . .] especially if we do not see where it comes from [. . .]."

33. Leopardi, *I Canti, op. cit.,* p. 284.

34. Leopardi, *Zibaldone, op. cit.,* [4418]. Entry for November 30, 1828, p. 193.

35. American poststructuralist Geoffrey Hartman has written much on the English Romantic poet, Wordsworth, in this vein. In nineteenth-century Italy, the correspondence between Leopardi's contemporaries Gino Capponi and Niccolò Tommaseo and the latter with Alessandro Manzoni also reveal similar preoccupations with words and their denotative and connotative meanings (i.e., signifiers and signified). For Jacques Derrida, see his study *Of Grammatology,* trans. by Gayatri Chakravorty Spivak (Baltimore-London: The Johns Hopkins University Press, 1974). For Hartman, see Harold Bloom *et al., Deconstruction and Criticism* (New York: Continuum, 1979), pp. 177-216.

36. Among them "Le Ricordanze," "A Silvia," "Il sabato del villaggio," of the "grandi idilli."

37. Leopardi, *Zibaldone, op. cit.,* [4426]. Entry for December 14, 1828, p. 196.

38. Cited by Russo in Leopardi, *I Canti, op. cit.,* n. 32, p. 287.

39. Leopardi, *Zibaldone, op. cit.,* [2602]. Entry for August 17, 1822, p. 156.

40. Leopardi, *I Canti, op. cit.,* p. 288. Tommaseo also experimented with descending and ascending word/image order for the purpose of ultimately creating images that would lead the reader to God. Cf. Niccolò Tommaseo, *Della bellezza educatrice* (Venice: Gondoliere, 1838).

41. Leopardi, *Zibaldone di pensieri. Scelta a cura di Anna Maria Moroni.* Vol. 2 (Milan: Mondadori, 1972), [3714-3715], p. 977. Entry for October 17, 1823.

42. "In my solitary walks through the city, the interior of the rooms that I glimpse from the street through their open windows usually awakens very pleasant sensations and beautiful images. These same rooms would not awaken any feeling in me if I say them from inside," Leopardi, *Zibaldone. A Selection, op. cit.* [4421]. Entry for December 1, 1828, p. 195. Cf. also entry [4061].

43. Cf. also entries [4074-4075].

44. Leopardi, *I Canti, op. cit.,* p. 288.

45. Leopardi, *La vita e le opere. Scelta, introduzione biografica e note di Nico Naldini* (Milan: Garzanti, 1983), p. 412.

46. "O natura, o natura, / perché non rendi poi / quel che prometti allor? perché di tanto / inganni i figli tuoi?" (ll. 36-9).

47. Leopardi, *Zibaldone, op. cit.,* [4492-4493]. Entry for April 22, 1829, p. 197.

48. *Ibid.,* [4493]. Entry for April 22, 1829, p. 199.

49. *Ibid.,* [4485-4486]. Entry April 11, 1829, p. 197.

References

Binni, Walter. *La nuova poetica leopardiana.* Florence: Sansoni, 1947. 3rd. ed, 1971.

Figurelli, F. *Giacomo Leopardi poeta dell'idillio.* Bari: Laterza, 1941.

Frattini, Alberto. *Leopardi nella critica dell'Otto e del Novecento.* Rome: Edizioni Studium, 1989.

Leopardi, Giacomo. *I Canti,* edited by Luigi Russo. Florence: Sansoni, 1971.

―――. *Zibaldone di pensieri. Scelta a cura di Anna Maria Moroni.* 2 voll. Milan: Mondadori, 1937. Edizione Gli Oscar, 1972.

―――. *La Vita e le lettere. Scelta, introduzione biografica e note di Nico Naldini.* Milan: Garzanti, 1983.

―――. *Zibaldone. A Selection,* translated and with an introduction by Martha King and Daniela Bini. New York: Peter Lang, 1992.

―――. *Lettere. Scelta, a cura di Giorgio Ficara.* Milan: Mondadori, 1993.

Georges Barthouil (essay date March 1999)

SOURCE: Barthouil, Georges. "Asia in the Work of Leopardi." *Journal of European Studies* 29, no. 1 (March 1999): 55-60.

[*In the following essay, Barthouil examines the* Zibaldone's *many references to distant lands, particularly in Asia, despite the fact that Leopardi never traveled outside Italy.*]

Leopardi was not a great traveller. In fact he imagined his foreign travels, and it was only his hatred for Recanati that led him to stay elsewhere in Italy. For him, Recanati was a prison from which he wanted to escape. However, escaping from a prison is not the same as giving in to the temptation of travel. He did not feel particularly drawn to it; neither did he feel any powerful sense of curiosity. In this respect, and indeed in many others, he was very similar to Vigny, his contemporary, who felt that foreign travel was simply useless, since one had to transport oneself along with other hindrances. Leopardi, then, did not really travel. He merely *stayed* sometimes in various Italian cities; Rome, Bologna, Milan, Florence, Pisa, Naples . . . The only time he had the chance to leave Italy was when he was offered a chair at Bonn University, which he refused because he had an upset stomach.

Could he have travelled 'around his room' through his imagination? This seems no more likely. Like everything characteristic of Leopardi, his imagination was sentimental. He dreamed of love . . . or of romantic encounters. He had no curiosity for individuals: he was convinced that people were the same everywhere; that in general they were undesirable.

Moreover, he was afraid of anything new and of all human contact. He had very little interest in places. Leopardi was not highly sensitive to aesthetic quality, except that of literature and language. His feeling for nature is generic, and more symbolic than anything. For example, there is never any description in his work. Spring, for Leopardi, is no particular spring but the season which symbolizes youth, hope and carefree romantic bliss. The sun becomes the symbol of sterile lucidity; winter traditionally represents old age and the antechamber of death.

This great poet was more concerned with the meaning of things than with their beauty. Did he not himself state that he had become a 'philosopher' and even that he had been 'converted'? Philosophers are rarely wanderers. However, Leopardi was very hungry for knowledge. Certainly he believed that exploration of the world deromanticized it, and that it was better to dream of paradise than to actually discover it; for reality could only disappoint:

> . . . Ahi, ahi, ma conosciuto il mondo
> Non cresce, anzi si scema, e assai più vasto
> L'etra sonante e l'alma terra e il mare
> Al fanciullin, che non al saggio, appare.
>
> ("**Ad Angelo Mai**," v.86-90)

Neither an explorer, nor interested in different horizons, monuments, societies and races, Leopardi was convinced that there was 'nothing new under the sun' as stated in a passage of the Bible to which he was very attached.[1] He can only have been merely a 'second-hand' traveller. This is what he remarks in *Zibaldone* on 10 March 1829 (p.4471):

> Notano quelli che hanno molto viaggiato (. . .) che per loro una causa di piacere viaggiando, è questa: che, avendo veduto molti luoghi, facilmente quelli per cui si abbattono a passare di mano in mano, ne richiamano loro alla mente degli altri già veduti innanzi, e questa reminiscenza per sé e semplicemente li diletta (. . .). Così accade: un luogo ci riesce romantico e sentimentale, non per sé (. . .) ma perché ci desta la memoria di un altro luogo da noi conosciuto, nel quale poi se noi ci troveremo attualmente, non ci riescirà (ne mai ci riescì) punto romantico nè sentimentale.

As we can see from this quotation, Leopardi did not make a good tourist. He never dreamed of travelling!

However, in the inexhaustible mine of information that is *Zibaldone* we find very many remarks and pieces of information about faraway places, particularly in Asia. Asia is also mentioned in Leopardi's literary work, but never *per se*; what I mean is that he refers to historical and spatial Asia, but never to its sociological and picturesque (or aesthetic) dimension. As for Geography and as for everything, Leopardi is interested because of his convictions, his belief in what he himself calls his 'system'. For example:

> La vita degli orientali e di coloro che vivono nè paesi assai caldi è più breve di quella dei popoli che abitano nè paesi freddi e temperati (. . .) più breve, la vita degli orientali (. . .) è molto più intensa, tanto che in pari spazio di tempo è maggiore la somma della vita che provano gli orientali che non è quella che provano gli altri populi.
>
> (***Zibaldone***, 4062, 8 April 1824).

A life which is 'short and sweet'. For Leopardi, the Orientals are similar to the Ancients who also, according to him, had an enviable 'esuberanza di vita' (***Zibaldone***, 1841). This view is reinforced by another entry dated 17 April 1824: (Oriental people have) 'maggior disposizione naturale alla felicità'. Indeed, they live in 'climi destinati della natura alla specie umana (. . .) i soli in cui l'uomo possa viver nudo, come la natura lo ha posto'.

Climates are conducive to fornication, might one dare add, like that of the Californians mentioned in ***Inno ai patriarchi***. In this Leopardian interest in Oriental people and the Orient, there lies perhaps something of an anthropologist's or an ethnologist's interest. There is no trace of that of a dreamer, poet or adventurer.

In fact, his initial interest was in biblical Asia. In his 'childish' poems the themes are mostly inspired by the Old Testament.[2] This vein of inspiration is to be found in the ***Canti*** (though completely distorted, according to the author himself), in ***Inno ai patriarchi***, of course, where we find the anachronistic American Indians.

The composition of ***La Virtu indiana*** is rather more absorbing. This is a tragedy in three acts, written in 1811. It was given to Monaldo Leopardi, and in it Leopardi declares the intention to rival his father's own tragedy entitled *Montezuma*. The former therefore has no female protagonists, like Monaldo Leopardi's work. It is an historical work. The setting is not distant, as if situated in Mexico at the time of the Spanish Conquest. According to a psychoanalytical interpretation of the circumstances, Leopardi shows the superiority of a generous young man (which we also find, contrary to all historical accuracy, in the character of Tolomeo in the second tragedy entitled ***Pompeo in Egitto***, written in 1812) in relation to older men who are shown to be fearful and ignorant. (Monaldo is in fact the father in this tragedy). The scene is set in Delhi, the capital of the Mogul empire which yielded 150 years of peace and prosperity for India before being defeated by the Marathes's uprising. This was a particularly interesting theme to Leopardi, who was especially moved by the rise and fall and the demise of civilizations, and who saw in the recent case of India (the high point of the Mogul empire was around 1700 during the reign of Aurang-Zeb) a replica of the fate of the Roman empire. Peace, harmony and prosperity, all ruined in but a few years . . .

In ***Zibaldone***, which was started in 1817, we find evidence of Leopardi's reading concerning Asia. Let us put Antiquity aside and concentrate on the present time. Leopardi makes about ten comments about China. He writes about its caste system, the Chinese custom of binding little girls' feet, music and the different alphabet. However, once more, 'Tutto il mundo è paese.' China does not escape the collective fate of all civilizations; that of corruption: 'Populo umano totalmente naturale e incorrotto non esiste. Tutti i populi, tutti gli individui umani sono corrotti o alterati' (***Zibaldone***, 3665). In China's case this is indeed true, except that 'Questa corruzione dico (. . .) si fermò e divenne stazionaria . . .' (***Zibaldone***, 3660). China fell asleep . . . What would Leopardi have thought of its current 'awakening'—if indeed that is what it is?

All the little peculiarities and particularities, at least, are fairly uninteresting compared to the fact that China, like *all* other 'human' societies, complies with the general rule of necessary corruption. It is not surprising, then, that Leopardi should make a dozen or so comments on the Chinese language. As far as India is concerned, which had been his inspiration at the age of thirteen, there are few comments in ***Zibaldone***. Leopardi does, however, note the '*nonviolence*' of the Indians, who 'were never conquerors' (***Zibaldone***, 917-27) but who 'resigned and submissive, due to the climate, are however capable of great feats', as proved by the Marathes's struggle against the English (***Zibaldone***, 95). Thus, allowing himself to prophesy, Leopardi believes that the Indians will one day defeat the English. As he does for the Chinese language, he reflects on Sanskrit, 'a very poetic language full of boldness' (***Zibaldone***, 2419).

Leopardi does not appear to have written a single line about Japan or the Japanese. Neither does he say much about the Arabs. As for Persia, he only concerns himself with its ancient history, as he does for the Assyrians.

Finally, he makes a few comments about the Turks, their music (***Zibaldone***, 8), their use of opium (***Zibaldone***, 172), their 'wish to conquer Europe' (***Zibaldone***, 3173-7), etc. Yet in Leopardi's time, was the Ottoman empire really considered part of Asia? It was certainly Oriental, but was also referred to as 'the sick man of Europe'.

Overall, the representation of Asia in Leopardi's work is minimal, except that of its ancient history and particularly the constant and considerable reference to the Bible. At least this would be so, were it not for a kind of poetic miracle which is to be found in the ***Canti***. I refer to the ***Canto notturno di un pastore errante dell'Asia***, which is surely one of the greatest masterpieces in Western poetry . . .

This poem is perhaps the most serenely pessimistic and the most solemnly desperate of the *Canti.* The trigger for its inspiration was Leopardi's reading of an article in the *Journal des savants* about Georges de Meyendorff's diary of his travels in central Asia, the full title of which was *Voyage d'Orenbourg* (once renamed Tchkalov but now called Orenbourg once more) *à Boukhara; fait en 1820, à travers les steppes qui s'étendent à l'est de la mer d'Aral et au-delà de l'ancien Jaxartes* (Paris, 1826).

Leopardi's *Canto* was composed from 22 October 1829 to 9 April 1830. In *Zibaldone,* he inserts a quotation from Meyendorff's article in the 'Journal des savants':

> Les Kirkis (nazione nomade, al Nord dell'Asia centrale) ont aussi des chants historiques (non scritti) qui rappellent les hauts faits de leurs héros; mais ceux-là ne sont récités que par des chanteurs de profession, et M. de Meyendorff (barone, viaggatore russo, autore d'un 'Voyage d'Orenbourg à Boukhara, fait en 1820', Paris, 1826; dal quale sono estratte queste notizie) eut le regret de ne pouvoir en entendre un seul. *Ibid.,* septembre, p.515. Plusieurs d'entre eux (d'entre les Kirkis), dice M. de Meyendorff, *ibid.,* passent la nuit assis sur une pierre à regarder la lune et à improviser des paroles assez tristes sur des airs qui ne le sont pas moins
>
> (3 octobre 1828, *Zibaldone,* 4399-4000).

As we can see, Leopardi initially comments on two different things: the 'patriotic' songs (which must have reminded him of his own patriotic *Canzoni*) and the solitary ballads sung to the moon, which were the only ones he chose for the composition of his own *Canto.* However, two more quotations from Meyendorff's article can be linked to the poet's work. The first in this: 'J'ai vu le frère du sultan, très considéré chez les Kirkgiz, faire paître ses moutons, monté sur son cheval, en habit de drap rouge, et voyager ainsi pendant une quinzaine de jours, sans croire déroger à sa dignité.' This, then, could be the origin of his *pastore errante.*

The second passage is the following:

> Je me trouvais à la veille d'entreprendre un voyage pendant les froids, les ouragans, les giboulées des mois d'octobre et de novembre (. . .) le ciel n'était qu'un nuage, et la terre qu'un monceau de neige (. . .). Je plaignais nos pauvres soldats qui, sans pelisses, allaient être exposés à toutes les intempéries (. . .) (en) un si long voyage à travers d'immenses déserts.

I think we can recognize in these lines the inspiration for the second verse of the *Canto notturno:*

> Vecchierel bianco, infermo,
> mezzo vestito e scalzo,
> con gravissimo fascio in su le spalle,
> per montagna e per valle,
> per sassi acuti, ed alta rena, e fratte,
> al vento, alla tempesta, e quando avvampa

> l'ora, e quando poi gela,
> corre via, corre, anela,
> varca torrenti e stagni,
> cade, risorge, e più e più s'affretta,
> senza posa o ristoro,
> lacero, sanguinoso; infin ch'arriva
> colà dove la via
> e dove il tanto affaticar fu volto:
> abisso orrido, immenso,
> ov'ei precipitando, il tutto obblia.
> Vergine luna, tale
> è la vita mortale.

We can see that the first nine lines echo Meyendorff's words, in a more poetic way. Of course, in keeping with his temperament, Leopardi makes an allegory of the cruel, exhausting journey. The final conclusion aptly expresses his pessimism regarding the human condition: *'tale/è la vita mortale'*; the statement is reinforced and definitive. Regarding the main quotation, it is worth pointing out that in Leopardi's poem the *Kirkis* 'spend the night gazing at the moon', whereas Meyendorff writes 'la moitié de la nuit', which seems to be a pessimistic and sentimental generalization . . .

Asia as it is represented in Leopardi's work is in fact a timeless and symbolic land which allows him to express the universality of human life and suffering. Everywhere man is alone, a victim of the cruelty of Nature and of Society. And man, solitary but lucid, like Kirkhis, weeps and sings to the moon, his mirror and confidante . . .

Notes

1. See Georges Barthouil, 'Leopardi et la Bible' in *Revue de littérature comparée,* 2/1996

2. Cf. texts compiled and published by Maria Corti, *Entro dipinta gabbia* (Milan, 1972).

Nicolas J. Perella (essay date autumn 2000)

SOURCE: Perella, Nicolas J. "Translating Leopardi?" *Italica* 77, no. 3 (autumn 2000): 357-85.

[In the following essay, Perella ponders Leopardi's relative obscurity outside his native Italy despite the poet's influence on Anglo-American literary culture.]

> *E chiaro nella valle il fiume appare*
>
> —**"La quiete dopo la tempesta"**

"Giacomo Leopardi is a great name in Italy among philosophers and poets, but is quite unknown in this country." So wrote Octavius Brook Frothingham in 1887 at the outset of his prefatory remarks to the first English translation of a truly representative number of the *Canti,* done by Frederick Townsend.[1] Surely, the statement would have to be qualified today, more than one hundred years later. Or would it? Actually, it continues to be a complaint registered over and over by Leopardi's admirers, Italian and non-Italians alike, frustrated that beyond Italy's confines the name of so great a poet and thinker does not often appear save in the most generic way.

Among the reasons adduced for the absence of a fuller appreciation of Leopardi in the English-speaking world, there is one suggested by Ottavio Di Fidio that strikes me as worth pondering. It is not so much that Leopardi has not found an adequate translator into English as it is a fact that there has not been a great history of modern Italian literature written in English that could arouse a more vital interest in our poet by seeing him in a broad cultural context. Nor has there been a critic of eminence in English who has made the case for his greatness.[2]

But was not Leopardi greatly praised already in the nineteenth century by the likes of Matthew Arnold and the French critic Sainte-Beuve? Keeping to English and our own times, we may note that Leopardi shows up in Harold Bloom's widely disseminated book *The Western Canon*. In giving the reasons for his selection of the authors he deals with in some depth, Bloom writes, in the "Preface and Prelude," that they were chosen "for both their sublimity and their representative nature," and that a book about twenty-six writers is possible, but not a book about four-hundred.[3] Hence, Leopardi figures among the distinguished-enough group of four hundred that includes, among others, Petrarch, Ariosto, Spenser, Rousseau, Balzac, Nietzsche, Baudelaire, Yeats, et al. Thus we need not take Bloom's lists amiss. But though Leopardi has not been slighted, his admirers might well regret what must seem a missed opportunity to broadcast to a wide English-speaking audience the virtues of Italy's greatest modern poet.

Italy's most exemplary writer of the second half of the twentieth century, Italo Calvino, was among the many to lament Leopardi's ill fortune abroad, never so tellingly as at a 1979 convention whose theme was the cultural image of Italy as it is perceived abroad:

> Per noi Leopardi è una presenza che diventa sempre più grande e sempre più vicina; da tempo ogni generazione letteraria italiana si costruisce il suo Leopardi, diverso da quello delle generazioni precedenti, e si definisce attraverso la sua definizione di Leopardi; e Leopardi regge a tutte queste esperienze. Ebbene, fuor dei confini dell'Italia Leopardi semplicemente non esiste. Non c'è modo di far capire chi è; non c'è modo di definirlo in rapporto ad altri personaggi, di far capire perché per noi è così importante ed è importante in tanti modi diversi e tutti veri. . . . La trasmissione del contesto culturale italiano nel suo complesso deve fare i conti con zone d'ombra di cui quella di Leopardi è la più impressionante e macroscopica.[4]

The tone of Calvino's words almost sounds defeatist; and though I rebel at the thought, the words themselves seem to suggest, in a broad sense, that perhaps Leopardi is after all an exclusively Italian national treasure, with minimum resonance elsewhere.

Meanwhile, in Italy, the critical literature on Leopardi has, in the last forty years, been massive, perhaps exceeding even what has been written on Dante. But even in the English-speaking world, particularly in Great Britain and the United States, the amount of critical literature has been nothing short of astonishing; and English translations of one sort or another are churned out at a surprising pace. Yet for all that, the interest has been mostly restricted to scholarly or academic circles. It is as though we need only change Frothingham's "quite unknown" to "relatively unknown" to bring his observation (1887) up to date.

Nonetheless, I shall be referring to a number of translations of recent vintage, each of which contains a selection, from ten to about half of the *Canti* poems generally thought of as the more lyrical of Leopardi's poetic gems.[5]

Is it then a matter of poor translations? Reviewing the translations of two of the editions listed in note 5 (those of Grennan and Lawton), Paolo Possiedi approves of the poems selected by the respective translators as being appropriate for an introduction to "un poeta ancora poco conosciuto," but he is less charitable in his judgement of the effectiveness (or lack thereof) of the translations: "Ma son meglio di niente," he writes, an expression that lies somewhere between resignation and disconsolation.[6] This begrudging approval of the translations is on a par with what G. Singh affirms in an essay on Leopardi and his English translators: "Infatti le migliori traduzioni inglesi di Leopardi sembrano piuttosto delle parafrasi in prosa che aspirano ad essere poesia."[7] We can only wince in recalling that Leopardi spoke harshly of paraphrases.

Definitely not of a paraphrastic character are the translations by the Anglo-Irish poet Patrick Creagh, of the ten *canzoni* Leopardi published first in 1824. Indeed, a curious feature of the recent spate of translations of Leopardi's poems is the lively participation of the Irish. In addition to Creagh and other Irish translators who over the years have done English versions of one or more of the *Canti*'s lyrics, there are the previously mentioned two anthologies of poems done by the Irish poet-translators: Eamon Grennan and Paul Lawton.

Interestingly enough, a third anthology—*A Scottish Quair*—is a tribute to our poet done by several Scot poets and scholars who have fashioned this trilingual version (English, Scots, and Gaelic) of eleven poems from the *Canti* plus the **"Coro dei morti"** that introduces the

"Dialogo di Frederico Ruysch e delle sue mummie" of the *Operette morali.* But it is the Irish who, in terms of poetry and translation, may have outdone all others in paying homage to Italy's sovereign lyric poet. Taking its title from a phrase in one of Leopardi's most intimate poems, **"Alla luna,"** the volume *Or volge l'anno / At the Year's Turning* is a commemorative endeavor spearheaded by a young Italian scholar residing in Ireland, who elicited "responses" to Leopardi's poetry from more than 100 Irish poets. This resulted in a thick-enough volume that offers us, first, ten of Leopardi's poems in a bilingual dress, the translations being those included by Eamon Grennan in his slim volume published by Princeton University Press. There follows an introductory word to the Irish poet-playwright John M. Synge's unfinished translation of *A Silvia* and a printing of the text. The bulk of the volume is given over to the "responses," a hundred or more poems (one poem per respondent) directly (but sometimes quite indirectly) inspired by or otherwise connected with Leopardi's poetry and vision of life. Broadly speaking, many of them can be called "Imitations," some of which are indeed like paraphrases of one or another of Leopardi's poems; some of them, less concerned with a literal rendering of a particular poem, express a sympathetic allegiance to the "spirit" of the great poet, while still other "responses" take a combative stance against it. Finally, a few respondents go so far afield as to make Robert Lowell's well-known and much maligned "Imitations" seem the very model of strict adherence to Leopardi's texts. The poetic responses are made in one of three languages: English, colloquial Hiberno-English, or Gaelic, and it all makes for interesting reading.

In the vein of poetic responses vis-à-vis Leopardi's poetry and his vision of life, I would call attention to three non-Irish instances in which the common denominator is **"Canto notturno d'un pastore errante dell'Asia."**

The great modern Portuguese poet Fernando Pessoa dedicated a poem to his Italian predecessor. Dated July 21, 1934, "Canto a Leopardi" pays homage to Leopardi in its very title (one thinks especially of **"Canto notturno"**) and in its content, which is given in the context of a dialogue with the poet's heart, bringing to mind **"A se stesso."** Presented as an anxious metaphysical questioning, the *Canto* ends on a quasi-nihilistic note: "E não há paz nem conclusão; Tudo é como se fora inexistente."[8]

The second instance is the poetic encounter between Leopardi and the contemporary American poet and translator Charles Wright. Wright has been a successful translator of Italian poetic texts, including Montale's difficult *Mottetti* and *La bufera.* After many years of trying and failing to translate Leopardi's poems to his own satisfaction, he salvaged fragments of his efforts

and worked them into a poem of his own called "Giacomo Leopardi in the Sky." As with the title of Pessoa's "Canto a Leopardi," the title of Wright's poem puts us in the questioning mode of the shepherd of **"Canto notturno di un pastore errante dell'Asia."** The poem itself, however, begins by echoing **"Alla sua donna"**: "If you [Leopardi] are become an eternal idea"; it then goes on as a paean/meditation interspersed with Leopardian echoes bespeaking the almost obsessive and sometimes ambiguous (positive/negative) presence of Leopardi in Wright's own intellectual and poetic life. Half-way into the poem occur these lines in which Leopardi's "face" is metamorphosed into the moon, or vice versa:

> You doom us who see your face.
> You force on us your sorrow:
> So frail and vile throughout,
>   as ours is,
> It assails the ear like paradise.[9]

There is assonance and near-rhyme between *frail* and *assails,* words that undoubtedly echo *frale* and *assale* of **"Canto notturno"**; and there is consonance between those words and *vile.* I shall return later to these features of Leopardi's marvelous song of existential anguish. In the meantime I note that it is this same poem that figures centrally in Donald Davie's poem "Pastor errante," which, even more directly than the poems by Pessoa and Wright, takes its title from Leopardi's questioning nomadic shepherd. Addressing a fellow poet (Robert Pinsky) Davie questions the utterances of Leopardi's shepherd. In so doing, he intersperses in his address large sections of the **"Canto notturno"** in verses (unrhymed) that lie somewhere between a free translation and an "imitation." The seventh and eighth stanzas of the address introduce the first stanza of Leopardi's poem in Davie's version:

> I do not expect an answer. The lord Hermes,
>   Tutelary deity
> Of shepherds, no doubt patronizes also
>   Hermetic poetry, ours:
> Wherein we ask unanswerable questions
>   To what man's profit?
>
> Errant though why not America? although Asia
>   Is what Leopardi
> Too plangently imagined, that much nearer
>   The god's faint trace. And
>
>   'Moon'
> He starts out, bald as that, "what are you doing
> There in the sky? Unspeaking moon,
> What are you about? You come
> Up in the evening, and you go
> Looking at deserts; then you stop, stand still.
> What is this all about? Are you
> Pleased to be pacing these eternal alleys?
> Don't you get bored? Or is it
> Still to your liking, looking down on these
> Glens of ours? Ah well, your life is

> Much like a shepherd's. Up he gets before
> Dawn, and moves out
> His sheep to pasture, sees to
> Folds, to water, fodder; then,
> Tired out, snores through the evening:
> Hopes for no more, ever. Tell
> Me, you moon: what is it worth to
> The shepherd, this life of his,
> And what to you, your life? Tell me
> The ends they move to: his brief, vagrant life
> And yours, unending."[10]

One need only recall the Italian of the **"Canto notturno"**'s first stanza to realize that Davie was almost exclusively interested in Leopardi's "thought" and not in the **Song**. Nonetheless, even without rhyme his jazzed-up version has its own music or rhythm and is rather catching. Much (but by no means all) of the music in Leopardi's text is in its echoing rhymes.

I should not pass up the chance, in this context, to call attention to Thomas Hardy's wonderful poem "To the Moon." Though separated by half a century, Hardy and Leopardi were true soul-brothers. Hardy's poem is a brilliant amalgam of two veins of the Leopardian spirit: the lyrical plangency of the **"Canto notturno"** and the satiric wit of the **Operette morali,** in particular the lighter humor of **"Il Copernico"** in which Copernicus is given orders by the Sun. In Hardy's poem the moon does not remain silent.[11]

Absorbing and richly informative, if idiosyncratic, is the volume *Canti by Giacomo Leopardi,* edited by G. Singh. All native English-speaking admirers of Leopardi are indebted to Professor Singh who for decades has championed the cause of our poet, both in studies of Leopardi's writings and, of more immediate interest to us here, in his inquiries into their impact on Anglo-American culture. He would have every right to be chagrined by the frequently expressed complaint that Leopardi is unjustly neglected or simply unknown outside of Italy, for he has repeatedly, as in the volume just referred to, adduced an impressive amount of evidence to show that Leopardi has in fact been a significant presence in the thought of Anglo-American writers and thinkers of both the nineteenth and twentieth centuries. Some names: William Ewart Gladstone, Matthew Arnold, G. H. Lewes, James Thomson "B. V.," John Addington Symonds, Margaret Oliphant, A. C. Swinburne, Arthur Symons, Michael Rossetti, Christina Rossetti, A. E. Housman, Thomas Hardy, William Dean Howells, Richard Garnett, Herman Melville, Ezra Pound, Sir Maurice Bowra, Bertrand Russell, Cyril Connolly, and others, among whom I would add the name of Samuel Beckett.[12]

Thus Singh could begin his bibliographic essay, "Leopardi in the English-Speaking World," with the pronouncement that: "Few Italian poets—with the exception of Dante—have had such a rich and extensive fortune in the English-speaking world as Leopardi" (39). And yet, there remains a nagging suspicion (and, in my own case, a conviction) that Leopardi's presence in the Anglo-American world is not commensurate with his greatness.

The main part of Singh's volume is given to the *Canti,* both in the original Italian and in English translations done by various hands. It differs from other bilingual anthologies of the *Canti* involving multiple translators by virtue of its near completeness. As he himself says, his choice of translations "is necessarily a personal one." Receptive to translations of all periods, he has selected what he takes to be the most satisfying English version of each poem; and there is no point in quarreling with his choices. He has, however, divided Leopardi's poems into two broad categories; "the more intensely lyrical poems" for which he preferred translators who were themselves primarily poets with "creative" and "inventive" resources; and "the longer and more discursive poems" for which he preferred scholarly-minded translators apt to give "a faithful and lucid rendering of Leopardi's thought and intelligence . . . without being too literal or too prosaic." So be it. Such a dichotomy undoubtedly has its dangers, but I think that most of us, despite misgivings, are apt to have some such division in the back of our mind when reading the *Canti.* What we are likely to wonder about most here is the presence of so many translators, for the most obvious (and most important) thing that is bound to be sacrificed or lost in a translation by committee or team of a unified work of art—and the *Canti* are just that—is the work's homogeneity in the sense of its singular voice, its unique tone, whether the mode be lyrical or discursive. It was Paul Celan, I believe, who said that "poetry is the fatal uniqueness of language," which saying brings to mind Robert Frost's rather more caustic remark that "poetry is what gets lost in the translation." Perhaps both remarks are meant to suggest the futility or betrayal inherent in the act of translating poetry. I need not translate the well-worn Italian adage: *tradurre = tradire* (or) *traduttore = traditore.*[13]

Interestingly enough, the first nearly complete translation of the *Canti* was done by an American, Frederick Townsend. It appeared in 1887, and was soon followed by the nearly complete translations of Francis Henry Cliffe (1893) and J. M. Morrison (1900). But the greatest impact of Leopardi's poems was not to be made in English until the ambitious version of the whole appeared in 1923, in a bilingual edition by Geoffrey L. Bickersteth. In speaking of aiming for accuracy of translation Bickersteth meant "faithfulness not only to the content but also to the form (metre, cadence, rhyme, sound, accent, rhythm, tone, style, etc.) of the original" (vii-viii). There is much to admire in Bickersteth's noble effort, and I do not mean to be facetious in saying that the only way to remain faithful in such absolute terms would be to have Leopardi himself dictate his poems to us. Bickersteth's words are a short way of declaring that translation at its best (as Bickersteth's often is) can never be more than a "corrispondenza imperfetta."[14] For my part, I find Bickersteth's translation—in terza rima—of *The Divine Comedy* more satisfying than his version of the *Canti.* But it will surprise nobody if I say that lyric poetry, especially of an intimate kind, is in general more vulnerable to distortion in translation than are other poetic genres. The evocative power of words/ sounds is then usually, but by no means always, much more critical. Moreover, each generation of readers and critics will have its own translation(s) of great works. The original text alone remains, while translations of it come and go. As splendid as Vincenzo Monti's Italian version of the *Iliad* is, it is read today only by scholars and critics. In part, Bickersteth's translation of the *Canti* suffers today because of a language and style that were once characteristic of an earlier era.

The next complete English translation of the *Canti* was published in 1962. Its author, J. H. Whitfield, like Bickersteth a scholar/critic of the Italian poet, translated the poems in verse, but was not wed to Leopardi's rhyme-schemes and musico-magic rhythms. Whitfield's version is supple enough, but it has little of Leopardi's tone.[15]

Leopardi's translators inevitably speak of the dual and apparently antithetical if not antagonistic co-presence of feeling and thought, of lyricism and rhetorical eloquence as the characteristic that makes translation of his poetry so difficult and problematic. More specifically, I think, the difficulty lies in the alternation between a lyricism that tends toward a simplicity of expression even as it avails itself of a quasi-archaic elitist vocabulary, and a classicizing, at times convoluting syntax; at the best moments, there is a magical blend of these apparently discrete elements. Every would-be translator (but even the common reader) of Leopardi's poetry would do well to read Francesco Flora's characterization of Leopardi's poetic language, of the poet's assimilation of a vocabulary and a syntax that, belonging to a long tradition of Italian poetry, become an integral part of his essential and natural expression found in *all* of his poetry: "La presenza del linguaggio poetico tradizionale si avverte non soltanto nel Leopardi più togato delle *Canzoni,* ma anche in quello più dimesso dei *Canti* più puri. . . ." Even so, Flora himself distinguishes between a more solemn, formally classicizing manner and a simpler, more "accessible" one.[16]

Here I must confess to being puzzled by G. Singh's characterization of Leopardi's poetic language, made in his "Introductory Note" to his anthology of translations of the *Canti* poems: "In spite of the apparent simplicity and lucidity of diction in Leopardi *and the conspicuous*

absence of any verbal complexity or interpretative difficulty, his poetry presents certain pitfalls to an English translator" (71; my emphases). There may well be other pitfalls, but surely the most obvious ones involve precisely verbal complexity and interpretative difficulties, and, I may add, a "deceptive simplicity" (in the more intimate or "purer" lyrics) that Singh himself refers to elsewhere.[17] In a round-table discussion on translating the *Canti,* Patrick Creagh, referred to earlier as the translator of the ten *Canzoni* Leopardi published in 1824, speaks despairingly of the problem of translating Leopardi's archaisms and "contortions":

> If you translate **"L'infinito"** into archaic English, you're certainly rendering a great disservice because it's a poem intensely fresh in the original, whereas in [*Le Canzoni*] he uses archaic language; and his contortions . . . what do you do with his contortions? Well they have to stay contorted, you can't iron it all out or you haven't translated the same point.[18]

The scores of annotated Italian editions of *Canti* are filled with attempts at resolving interpretative difficulties and "ironing out" Leopardi's convoluted (classicizing, if one prefers) syntax, especially, but by no means exclusively, as it is found in the early *Canzoni.* In great part this means resorting to paraphrases, and not just in scholastic editions. It is in connection with one such recent edition of the *Canzoni* that paraphrastic rendition has been raised to the "dignity" of a facing-page, running translation in Italian alongside Leopardi's Italian text, an event that has raised the ire of Italy's scandalized academes.[19] Here, from that edition, is the first stanza of the poem **"Alla primavera,"** followed by Santagata's prose paraphrase:

> Perché i celesti danni
> Ristori il sole, e perché l'aure inferme
> Zefiro avvivi, onde fugata e sparta
> Delle nubi la grave ombra s'avvalla;
> Credano il petto inerme
> Gli augelli al vento, e la diurna luce
> Novo d'amor desio, nova speranza
> Ne' penetrati boschi e fra le sciolte
> Pruine induca alle commosse belve;
> Forse alle stanche e nel dolor sepolte
> Umane menti riede
> La bella età, cui la sciagura e l'atra
> Face del ver consunse
> Innanzi tempo? Ottenebrati e spenti
> Di Febo i raggi al misero non sono
> In sempiterno? ed anco,
> Primavera odorata, inspiri e tenti
> Questo gelido cor, questo ch'amara
> Nel fior degli anni suoi vecchiezza impara?

> Per il fatto che il sole venga a riparare
> i danni provocati dal tempo invernale e Zefiro
> rianimi l'aria malsana, cosicché la coltre
> nebbiosa, scacciata e dispersa dal cielo,
> s'abbassa sul fondo delle valli; o perché gli
> uccelli di nuovo affidino al vento il loro

gracile corpo e la luce del giorno, penetrando
nei boschi e sciogliendo le nevi, infonda negli
animali risvegliati rinnovata fiducia nella vita
e rinnovato desiderio d'amore, forse agli uomini
stanchi e infelici ritorna la bella giovinezza,
che le sventure e la funesta luce della
conoscenza hanno consumato ancor prima che fosse
giunta al termine? Per gli uomini afflitti i
raggi del sole non sono oscurati e spenti per
sempre? E ancora una volta, primavera odorosa,
ecciti e seduci questo cuore ghiacciato, che nel
fiore degli anni sperimenta un'amara vecchiaia?

(1-19)

The paraphrase has the unintended virtue of putting into relief the symphony of Leopardi's stanza that, though limited to four rhymes (or eight rhymed lines) in 19 lines, is cohesively interlaced throughout by assonance, and is rhythmically propelled by its intricate Latinizing syntax, so that a tension is created between a forward motion and a retarding factor: fifteen enjambments and (only three of which are end punctuated), in addition to the nineteen metric end-line pauses, nine punctuated internal pauses. To this add the use of archaic and/or Latinizing words. Indeed, what is a translator to do? In a review of two successful English translations of Leopardi's prose compositions **Operette morali** that appeared in 1986, D. C. Carne-Ross remarked that the lines of the first stanza of **Alla primavera** are "almost as hard to construe as one of the knottier odes of Horace."[20] Nonetheless Joseph Tusiani and Patrick Creagh, whose respective translations of the poem first appeared in 1987 and 1982, offer us English versions worthy of notice:

"To Spring or Concerning the Antique Fables" (1822)

Even if the sun redresses
The ravages of heaven, and freshet airs
Rinse the sick atmosphere, and heavy, hanging
Clouds are harried and scattered down the valleys,
And if small birds confide
Defenseless breasts to the wind, and the light of day
Induces hope and new intent for love
In feeling creatures, in the sun-filtering woodlands
And among the loosened snows,
Do wearied human hearts, interred in grief,
Perhaps regain
The lovely time of life that tragedy
And the murderous glare of truth, all too soon
Consumed away? And are the sun's rays
Not overcast, snuffed out in the suffering spirit
For ever and for ever? Is it possible
Sweet-scenting Spring, that you revive and try
This gelid heart, that in its tenderest years
Already studies the acids of old age?

(Creagh)

"To Spring or of ancient fables"

Although once more the sun
Restores the harms of heaven, and the breeze
Revives the sickly air, so that, outcast

And shattered, the black shadow of the clouds
Heavily downward bends;
Although once more the birds
Entrust their breasts unarmed upon the wind,
And the diurnal ray
Spurs the excited animals within
The deep of forests and the loosened frost
With a new hope and new desire for love;
Does to man's weary, anguish-sunken mind
The lovely season once again return,
Which evil fortune and truth's horrid torch
Has prematurely burned?
Are not Apollo's rays
Darkened forever and forever spent
To miserable man?
Do you still, O fragrant Spring, inspire
And tease this gelid heart,
This heart that in the bloom
Of years already learns old age's doom?

(Tusiani)

Creagh's translation (despite his misgivings on the matter) irons out more of the original's "contortions" than does Tusiani's version, and it reads somewhat like a smoothly turned English version without smacking of paraphrase. Yet Tusiani, it seems to me, is better at keeping enough of the original's tone, verbal texture, and rhythm so as to evoke the impression of a life force—and the poet's heart—struggling to extricate itself from a frozen world, outer and inner.

Resorting to paraphrastic solutions or to starkly literal renderings is no guarantee of accuracy even when wishing only to convey the poet's "thought." The most notoriously misconstrued passage from the **Canti** occurs in Leopardi's best-known and most frequently translated poem, **"L'infinito."** At the midway point of a revery (and of the poem) that has led him into a vastness of preternatural silence, the poet is on the verge of being gripped by a sudden fright—or is he?

Ma sedendo e mirando, interminati
   Spazi di là da quella [the limiting hedge] e sovru-
   mani
Silenzi, e profondissima quiete
Io nel pensier mi fingo; *ove per poco*
Il cor non si spaura.

(4-8; my emphases)

There is today almost universal agreement among Italian critics and professional Italianists of all linguistic stripes on the matter of "ove per poco / Il cor non si spaura." But it was not always so, and even today the phrase remains a pitfall for translators who, if without a keen knowledge of Italian, are likely to miss the pleonastic character of the negative, *non*, in the expression *per poco . . . non*, which "simply" means *almost (all but, nearly*, etc.). It is not surprising, then, that many English translations of the poem fall into a countersense when, instead of a fear that "almost" grips the young poet's heart, they speak of his heart being "calm for a while." This, of course, is to miss the point on which the poem turns and to undercut the element of surprise, the happy irony, as it were, of its ending.

It is a pity that this uncertainty should be so clearly exemplified by the English poet John Heath-Stubbs who, among all translators of Leopardi, can still be accounted one of the most elegant. When first published in 1946, his rendering of the poem's pivotal phrase was good enough: "until almost / My heart becomes afraid." But in reprinting his translation in 1966 he changed the wording into the misguided "then for a while / The heart is not afraid." I suspect that he was led astray by an annotated Italian edition of the **Canti**.[21] Whatever the cause, his translation errs no less seriously in yet another way. Leopardi's careful (and astonishing) use of the demonstrative adjectives (and pronouns) *questo* and *quello* to indicate space and distance and an internalized world and an externalized world (with the ultimate triumph of the poet's inner world over the external world) is jumbled up in the second half of the poem, with the disastrous result that Leopardi's

> . . . Così tra *questa*
> Immensità s'annega il pensier mio:
> E il naufragar m'è dolce in *questo* mare.

> (13-15)

becomes an incomprehensible

> . . . And thus it is
> In *that* immensity my thought is drowned:
> And sweet to me the foundering in *that* sea.

Several other translators show a similar lack of understanding of the importance of the demonstratives in this remarkable poem. Robert Lowell's idiosyncratic "Imitation" of the poem starts recklessly by giving us *that* hill and *the* hedges instead of *this* hill and *this hedge*; it then goes on to its blissful countersense: "Here for a little while my heart is quiet inside me."[22]

Morrison is perhaps the earliest (1900) translator to give us a gratuitous substitution of *that* for *this* in the poem's first two lines. And though he understands the meaning of "ove per poco / Il cor non si spaura" ("whereat the breast / In awe doth well-nigh sink"), his version of the original's fifteen unrhymed hendecasyllables is prettified into four rhyming quatrains! Predating Morrison's translation, Townsend (1887) is the first (among nearly complete translations of the **Canti**) to misconstrue the poem's pivotal phrase so as to give us "and for a moment I am calm."

I find it interesting that most English translations reverse the order of the comparative terms stated in the Italian text. Where Leopardi has

> . . . E come il vento
> Odo stormir tra queste piante, Io quello
> Infinito silenzio a questa voce
> Vo comparando. . . .

> (8-11)

Grennan, for example, has

> . . . And hearing the wind
> Rush rustling through these bushes,
> I pit its speech against infinite silence

Besides the curious idea of "pitting" speech against infinite silence, there are too many things wrong with these few lines. In the ill-fated attempt at onomatopoeia ("Rush rustling through these bushes"), *Rush rustling* is either a contradiction in terms or an annoying redundancy, and the translator's *bushes* have usurped the poet's *trees* (*piante*). The original's three demonstratives are reduced to one. The all-important *quello* of "*quello / Infinito silenzio*" is nonchalantly dropped so that we are faced with an abstract infinite silence in place of the personalized infinite silence "feigned" by the poet's imagination. As to the reversal of the order of the comparison's terms, Grennan is far from alone in not recognizing the teleological nature of Leopardi's comparison. *That* infinite silence is mentioned first because it is the end toward which, and into which, the wind's voice and the passing of the seasons (i.e., ages) proceed. The infinite silence is swallowing or engulfing the wind that, like a river on its way to the sea, is a metaphor for time. The teleological character of the image/comparison becomes clearer in the light of the order of the succeeding components that come to the poet's mind; the end comes first—eternity—followed by past ages and the present.

There has been much uncertainty about just what kind of sound is intended by the verb *stormire* in the context of **"L'infinito"**: ". . . E come il vento / Odo *stormir tra queste piante*." Translators have heard it as a sigh, a whisper, a murmur, a rustle, a bluster, a stirring, etc. More and more, however, English versions have been opting for *rustle*, although, not unlike *stormire*, this leaves the question open. Gradations of volume are implied. But one does well to remember that the sound (i.e., voice) of the wind rustling amid the leaves [of the trees] in **"L'infinito"** is not so boisterous or "stormy" as to disorient the poet or to take him completely out of his revery. Its function is to lead the poet into a meditation on the passing of time measured out in terms of seasons (i.e., ages past and present). Thus *rustle* will do nicely; but so too would whisper, hiss, and a few other such terms.

A word about translations of the marvelous last line of **"L'infinito"**: "E il naufragar m'è dolce in questo mare." As becomes the poem, this much translator-tormented line has, in the Italian, sounds that evoke an oceanic expansiveness. (In this it may be equaled, if not surpassed, by the verse serving as an epigraph to this article.) English is undoubtedly at a disadvantage in trying to render it. In place of the openness of the Italian sounds, an English version is apt to be dominated by *ee* sounds, as in John Heath-Stubbs's version quoted above. At its worst it will give us "And it's *easeful* to be wrecked in *seas* like *these*" (Grennan), a procession of sibilants and ee's that compresses the original's amplitude into a tight squeeze. Alas, such lines as this and "Rush rustling through the bushes" are but extreme examples of what seems to me one of the main defects of most English translations of Leopardi's poetry: the failure, for the most part, to notice, much less convey, the aura of unstrained dignity that the great poet's verses breathe.[23]

Nothing in the **Canti** is so starkly straightforward and desolate as the epitaphic **"A se stesso,"** in which Leopardi, announcing the death of hope and desire, commands his heart to stop beating. Nonetheless, the brief poem's ending has proved a stumbling block to more than one translator:

> . . . Dispera
> l'ultima volta. Al gener nostro il fato
> non donò che il morire. *Omai disprezza*
> *te, la natura, il brutto*
> *poter che, ascoso, a commun danno impera,*
> *e l'infinita vanità del tutto.*
>
> (11-16; my emphasis)

If ever there was a poem that demands of a translator the strictest adherence to its every word and its rhythm, it is this one. Whatever one may think of Arturo Vivante's as-literal-as-possible translations of a number of Leopardi's poems, his rendering of **"A se stesso"** is, to my ears, satisfying. Or so it would be, save for what I take to be a serious flaw:

> . . . Despair
> for the last time. Fate to our kind
> gave only dying as a gift.
> *Now scorn nature, the ugly*
> *power which, hidden, rules for the common evil,*
> *and the infinite vanity of it all.*
>
> (my emphasis)

I leave aside the insertion of a pleonastic *it* in the last line, though I feel that it undercuts the poem's linguistic essentiality (or conciseness) and demeans its noble tone. More to my point is the fact that Vivante's literal version surprisingly omits (or misreads) the *te* placed so conspicuously at the beginning of the third from the last line of the poem. And it makes all the difference! "*Ormai disprezza / te . . .*" It seems that Vivante has taken the *te* (a disjunctive pronoun) as an emphatic form for the nominative *tu*: (*disprezza tu* or *tu disprezza . . .*) whereas Leopardi's text is surely meant to say:

disprezza te stesso, etc., with reference to the addressee of the phrase and of the poem—the poet's heart. First in order of the things commanded to be despised is the poet's heart ("stanco mio cor"), the side of the poet prone to desire and hope, the side that even in the face of grim reality and truth is forever sliding back into a life of feeling and beautiful illusions. The dejected and embittered poet, after having invited his heart to rest forever, to despair no more, must yet (in the summing-up of the last sentence) order it, tragically or sardonically, to self-destruct.

The misconstruction of Leopardi's phrase, though not as widespread as the misinterpretation of **"L'infinito"**'s pivotal phrase, "*ove per poco / il cor non si spaura,*" is not uncommon. And one of the most embarrassing cases is that of a paraphrase/translation in Italian prepared by a cultivated Italian for non-Italian students learning the language in Italy. It occurs in a slim volume containing eleven of Leopardi's presumably more accessible lyrics accompanied by facing-page paraphrases, where the last sentence of **"A se stesso"** is rendered as follows:

> . . . Ormai ti disprezza
> la natura, quel potere brutto e nascosto
> che opera a danno di tutti, [e ti disprezza]
> l'infinita inutilità di tutto.[24]

That is: "*Nature,* that ugly and hidden power that works for the common ill, *despises you,* [and you are despised by] the infinite uselessness of all."

The end result of this unfortunate rendering is that the bitterly vehement yet dignified Brutus-like denouncer of the gods and Fate (and Nature), instead of steadfastly commanding his heart to despise and silence itself, is reduced to a whimpering complainer.

But one of the earliest translators of the **Canti** had subjected Leopardi's verses to perhaps an even greater distortion:

> Still, Nature, art thou doomed to fall
> The victim scorned of that blind, brutal power
> That rules and ruins all.
>
> (Townsend, 1887)

In place of the poet's heart, Nature has become addressee and victim, etc. The original's powerful last line, with its Biblical echo, is wholly abandoned, but the translator has managed to come up with a rhyme (*fall/all*) where Leopardi has *brutto/tutto.*

The following examples are representative of the many attempts at translating the poem's ending:

> . . . Now scorn thyself, scorn Nature,
> Scorn the brute Power whose reign

We know but by our woes, which are its pastime;
Scorn all that is, for all is vain, vain, vain.

(Bickersteth)

. . . henceforth despise
Thyself, Nature, the ugly power
Which, hidden, governs for the hurt of all,
And the infinite vanity of all that is.

(Whitfield)

. . . Cast a cold eye now
On yourself, on nature, on that hideous hidden
Force that drives all things to their
Destruction, and the infinite
All is vanity of it all.

(Grennan)

Scorn yourself, Nature, and the ugliness
Of the mysterious night
That for the common fall,
Concealed, outspreads its reign.
And the unbounded vanity of it all.

(Tusiani)

. . . Henceforward you can scorn
yourself and nature, brutal
and hidden force that rules our common doom
and the vast vanity of everything.

(Lawton)

. . . Now, vanquish in your disdain
Nature and the ugly force
That furtively shapes human ill, and the whole
Infinite futility of the universe.

(Morgan)

. . . Henceforth hold in contempt
Not yourself only, but Nature, the arrogant
Power that consigns us in secret to ruin,
And the everlasting emptiness of All.

(Gascoyne)

Bickersteth's repetition of the word "scorn" serves to indicate that the poet's *heart* ("thyself"), *Nature,* and the *brute Power* are three separate elements. Some readers consider (unwisely I think) *il brutto / poter . . . impera* to be in apposition to *Natura.* Repeated for a fourth time, "scorn" introduces the last of the things to be rejected. The poem's final rhyme in the original—*brutto . . . tutto*—is matched by Bickersteth's use of *reign . . . vain*; but "vain, vain, vain" is overly emphatic, whereas the emphatic repetition of "scorn" dilutes the original's lapidary effect. The phrase "which are its pastime" is an interpolation having no counterpart in the Italian text. Whitfield, like Leopardi and most transla-

tors, makes do with one use of the word "despise" to denounce all four entities. His version has the merit of being relatively spare, although the last four words include a redundancy—"of all *that is*"—that, besides lowering the tone, seems to result from a need to make the rhyme *all/all* less conspicuous.

Grennan's "Cast a cold eye now" is flaccid compared to Leopardi's forceful "disprezza," and in similar fashion the last line ("And the infinite *all is vanity of it all*"), intending perhaps to emphasize the concept of infinite vanity, has the opposite effect, here too with a banalizing redundancy.

Tusiani's replacement of Leopardi's "brutto poter" with the "mysterious night" that "outspreads its reign" brings us again, as in Bickersteth's version, to the question of how free we are willing to allow a translation to be. The image of a "mysterious night" or some similar phrase in connection with an evil force can be found elsewhere in Leopardi's writings, but it is not in **"A se stesso."** (Cf. *"arcana malvagità"* in **"Ad Arimana,"** from the ***Argomenti e abbozzi di poesie***; and in **"Le ricordanze"**: *"l'acerbo, indegno / Mistero delle cose."*)

Lawton's use of the indicative, "you *can* scorn . . . ," detracts from the peremptory force of Leopardi's imperative (*disprezza*), and the absence of the definite article before "brutal . . ." along with the omission of commas in the last two lines leads one to construe everything from "brutal" to the end of the poem as being in apposition to "nature." The "vast vanity" of the last line is equivocal at best; *vast* is a word that belongs to Leopardi's vocabulary of words that are deemed poetical because they evoke an aura of the indefinite and the sublime, but it pales next to the text's *infinita,* the most highly charged word/idea/sentiment in Leopardi's writings.

E. Morgan's version apparently fails to see that the poet's heart is itself among the things (indeed, the first) it is ordered to scorn, or, as he so strangely has it, to "vanquish." The word "whole" before "Infinite" is decidedly *de trop.*

Gascoyne's "hold in contempt" intellectualizes the forthright disdain of *disprezza*; similarly "arrogant" dilutes the intensity of *brutto.* The "everlasting emptiness" may be semantically correct, but it lacks the particular Leopardian and Biblical echoes of "infinite vanity."

The preceding versions of a mere few lines from the ***Canti,*** and the "faults" one may find with them, are not meant to denigrate the efforts of the respective translators, but rather to highlight some of the difficulties inherent in rendering Leopardi into English. There are other difficulties, too.

Besides the "contortions" (particularly of the early *canzoni*) and the unique interweaving of archaic (and quasi-archaic) words into a more common lexicon, there are Leopardi's inimitable music and sound patterns. The *Canti* are notorious for being recalcitrant to translation. But what is it that we expect or hope for from a translator of Leopardi into English? Broaching the subject most recently, Alessandro Carrera, in a vein much like Bickersteth's 1923 "Preface," yearns for a "traduzione ideale" that would capture all Leopardian nuances "sia dal punto di vista semantico che da quello fonetico." This, he adds, "è un compito quasi impossibile," where *quasi* perhaps betrays some wishful thinking. Carrera rightly notes that above all what is lacking in English is

> un lavoro complessivo intrapreso da un grande poeta o da un grande traduttore autoctono, *che sia in grado di dare un tono unitario alla progressione dei Canti.* E finché quell'interlocutore non sarà trovato, Leopardi non avrà il suo posto in nessuna *Norton Anthology.*[25]

> (my emphasis)

As for the kind of English poet/translator Carrera despairingly evokes, the poet Stephen Spender had a wistful and tantalizing suggestion of his own that is at once a shattering judgment on the history of English versions of Leopardi's best known lyric and, implicitly, the *Canti* in general: "The ideal translator of Leopardi would have been, I think, Shelley. . . ." One imagines that a version by Shelley of *L'infinito* would have been in the English an "irreplaceable masterpiece."[26] Indeed, as Carrera's parenthetical remark ("perché a volte proprio non si può") reminds us, some poets are simply not translatable, an opinion expressed also by D. S. Carne-Ross who, while registering the old complaint: "Except at home Leopardi is not fully on the literary map," went on to forewarn would-be translators that "only one English poet could have translated the best of Leopardi's poems: the Milton of our lost paradise, of *Lycidas* and parts of *Samson Agonistes.*"[27]

Milton and Shelley, and one thinks of their supreme elegies, respectively *Lycidas* and *Adonais*: fit company for Italy's supreme elegist, the poet of **"A Silvia"** and **"Le ricordanze,"** of **"Alla primavera"** and **"Alla sua donna,"** of the heroically elegiac close of **"Amore e Morte"** (vv. 96-124). The first 29 lines of **"A Silvia"** merit a closer look:

> Silvia, rimembri ancora
> quel tempo della tua vita mortale,
> quando beltà splendea
> negli occhi tuoi ridenti e fuggitivi;
> e tu, lieta e pensosa, il limitare
> di gioventù salivi?
>
> Sonavan le quiete
> stanze, e le vie dintorno,

> al tuo perpetuo canto,
> allor che all'opre femminili intenta
> sedevi, assai contenta
> di quel vago avvenir che in mente avevi.
> Era il maggio odoroso: e tu solevi
> così menare il giorno
>
> Io gli studi leggiadri
> talor lasciando e le sudate carte,
> ove il tempo mio primo
> e di me si spendea la miglior parte,
> d'in su i veroni del paterno ostello
> porgea gli orecchi al suon della tua voce,
> ed alla man veloce
> che percorrea la faticosa tela.
> Mirava il ciel sereno,
> le vie dorate e gli orti,
> e quinci il mar da lungi, e quindi il monte.
> Lingua mortal non dice
> quel ch'io sentiva in seno.
>
> Che pensieri soavi,
> che speranze, che cori, o Silvia mia!

> (1-29)

Among translators who have used rhyme in seeking to match Leopardi's "free" rhymes in **"A Silvia,"** Bickersteth, Townsend, and Tusiani are among the most effective. Bickersteth, not content merely to retain Leopardi's rhyme schemes, felt the need, "where [his] ear demanded it," to introduce extra rhymes. His incidental remark is revealing: "I do not think my ear would have so demanded if the English tongue were by nature as musical as the Italian." Tusiani, too, makes frequent and usually good use of rhyme, but without always trying to follow Leopardi's placements; and like Bickersteth he sometimes introduces more rhymes than the Italian texts have.

In a poet like Leopardi, and perhaps in most if not all lyrical poets, rhyme is a way of accentuating certain words for their concepts and evocative value. But there is more to be said of the sound patterns in **"A Silvia."** The first stanza begins with the name *Silvia* and ends with the verb *salivi,* nothing less than an anagram that echoes obliquely Silvia's name.[28] The echo is subtly muted in terms of resonance by its distance from the name. (*Silvia salivi* would, of course, be intolerable.) Yet *salivi,* with its phonosymbolic value caps the introductory first stanza in the ascendant. Echoes of Silvia's name continue throughout the poem by way of an extraordinary insistence on the *s* and *v* sounds, and, to a lesser degree, the liquid *l,* in various combinations or singly. In the first 29 lines alone we hear: *Silvia, vita, fuggitivi, gioventù, salivi, sonavan, vie, veloce, sedevi, vago, avvenir, che avevi, solevi, sentivi, ostello, veroni, mirava, splendea,* and again, now capping the wistfully rhapsodic first half of the poem, Silvia's name: "Che pensieri *soavi,* / Che *speranze,* che cori, o *Silvia* mia!" This clustering of the sounds connected with Silvia's name (line 20 includes the phrase "al *s*uon de *l*a tua *v*oce") and the alliterative pattern of echoing them and vowel similarities pervasively but wisely, can hardly be fortuitous. Rather, taken with the poem's rhythmical melody and flow and pauses, they create a subtle allusive echoing of sense and musical magic that we perhaps at first perceive only subliminally.[29]

Aside from the impossibility of carrying over into English such sound patterns, *A Silvia* has other difficulties of a more specifically lexical nature. Lines 4-5 seem simple enough: "Negli occhi tuoi ridenti e fuggitivi / E tu, lieta e pensosa . . ." and for the most part, if we leave aside Morrison's overwrought "When in thy bright eyes shone / Soft beauty's witching, laughing, wayward glance / And thou hadst just begun so coyly gay . . .," translators have respected the wistful sobriety of the two antithetical pairings: In Bickersteth's "eyes with laughter lit and shyly glancing / And thou, *serene* and pensive . . . ," *serene* for *lieta* perhaps takes us just a bit more than is desirable in the direction of sedateness and would have been better used for *assai contenta* in line 11. Kittel seems just right in concision and tone: "your laughing, elusive eyes, / And gaily, thoughtfully." Vivante has a perceptive "fleeting" for *fuggitivi*. John Heath-Stubbs perhaps gives up something in precision for a nicely suggestive "elusive laughter of your eyes," and his choice of "wonder" (for *pensosa*) in the second binomial—"And full of joy and wonder"—is, I think, as insightful as it is lovely, for indeed there can be a touch of something half-tremulous in a young girl's wonder. Grennan's reduction of each of the antithetical couplings to an adjective plus noun misses the spontaneous quality of Leopardi's Silvia, and "pensive joy" seems more suited to a Manzonian context and heroine. Whitfield has hit upon a daring but not ineffectual rendering in the first of the two couplings: "Your laughing, *glancing* eyes."

Concerning the lines I have been discussing, it is the most recent English translation of **"A Silvia"** (done by Tom Parks and Jonathan Galassi) that takes us furthest from Silvia's *occhi fuggitivi*.[30] The term *startled*, said of Silvia's eyes, gives us a sudden but frozen stare rather than the shy and quick averting of the eyes suggested by *fuggitivi*. Rather than sift through various translations for problematical renderings, I will refer to this latest translation for a few more hazardous spots that can cause a translator to stumble. The trickiest of these, a conundrum in fact, is the word *vago* as it appears in line 12, where Silvia is pictured sitting at her woman's work, and thinking of her future as a young woman: "Sedevi, assai contenta / Di quel vago avvenir che in mente avevi." Park and Galassi give us "hazy" for *vago*: "Happy enough with the *hazy / Future* in your head." *Vago* is a key word (and concept) in Leopardi's lexicon and in his theory of poetry where, in the sense of *vague*, or indistinct, indefinite, it is considered an essential

quality of poeticalness. But the word has three possible meanings: beautiful, vague (unclear, whence "hazy"), and avid or desirous [of].[31] Leopardi's poetry makes use of the word in all three senses at one time or another. In the context of the serenely rapturous first half of **"A Silvia,"** where the girl is evoked as joyful and hopeful of a "wonderful" future, *vago* clearly has a positive connotation, however undelineated the hope may be. At the same time, I would not discount the hint of uncertainty or trepidation that hovers over Silvia's *vago avvenir*; its presence however, seems to have at best a secondary role, perhaps as an ironic anticipation of the death, before realization, of the hopes of both Silvia and the poet. How then is one to translate here what is both beautiful and vague? For Leopardi the words form an inseparable binomial. Not so in English. Assuming that translators are aware of the pluralistic meaning of *vago*, those who have opted for the sense of something unknown have used such words as *vague, blurred,* or *hazy*. Those accentuating the positive have used words such as *beautiful, fair, bright, pleasant, future bliss*.

Other terms misconstrued by Park and Galassi (who, however, are not alone) are: *perivi*, which is not, in this case, "you were dying"; Italian (especially literary Italian) sometimes uses the imperfect tense where the past absolute would be expected. What is referred to is a specific event in the past: "You [Silvia] died"; *gli sguardi innamorati*, translated as "your lovestruck, guarded glance," is not correct here, where Leopardi uses *innamorati* in an active sense; it is not Silvia who is lovestruck, but the young men (or late-adolescent boys) who, had Silvia lived, would have been "lovestruck," that is, captivated by her "endearing," "enchanting," or "love-inspiring" glances; *ragionare* (to reason, to use one's reason) is commonly used in Italian in the sense of "to discuss" or simply "to talk." Park and Galassi go astray in using "to brood" ("And on Sundays you and your friends / Didn't brood about love"). Why have Silvia and her girlfriends brood over love when they more likely would have only been chattering, or whispering, or even giggling while talking about love—half-tremulously if one likes, but not broodingly; "*Tu, misera, cadesti*": addressed by the poet to his lost hope (personified here), these words are seriously wrenched from their sense in order to come up with "You fell away in misery." In Leopardi's text *misera* is an adjectival noun and would properly be rendered by something like "You, poor (or piteous) creature, fell" (i.e., "died"). The term bespeaks the poet's compassion for his dead hope, which he considers and caresses as though it were a creature. By this point, Silvia dead and the poet's dead hope have merged.

Except in the atypical lilting and sing-song Metastasian-like meter of **"Il risorgimento,"** Leopardi's rhymes for the most part are syntactically contextualized in a rhythm that renders them *relatively* inconspicuous and unemphasized, balanced between calling attention to a particular thought or sentiment and allowing meaning and feeling to flow across them. But in the case of **"Canto notturno di un pastore errante dell'Asia"** (the very title is an example of euphony), a poem rich in rhyme, Leopardi stresses to great effect one rhyme in particular, making of it a phonosymbolic refrain. Indeed, what *is* a translator to do with the echoing of *-àle*, sounding as an existential *wail* and as a submerged metaphor evoking *wings* as a desire to escape from the human predicament. In the nomadic shepherd's complaint this sound binds the poem's six stanzas together. The end words in which the sound/image recurs are the following: *vale, immortale, tale, mortale, cale, frale, male, animale, assale, ale, quale, natale.*

As though to convey the growing anxiety of the shepherd, the intensity of the refrain is expressed by its repetition in the last two lines (131-32) of the penultimate stanza and in the first line of the last stanza, where the phonosymbolic refrain acquires its explicit semantic denotation, *àle [àli] = wings,* yet still sounding in its dual significance of wail and wings:

> O greggia mia, nè di ciò sol mi lagno.
> Se tu parlar sapessi, io chiederei:
> Dimmi: perchè giacendo
> A bell'agio, ozioso,
> S'appaga ogni *animale*;
> Me, s'io giaccio in riposo, il tedio *assale*?
>
>   Forse s'avess'io *l'ale*
> Da volar su le nubi,
> E noverar le stelle ad una ad una,
> O come il tuono errar di giogo in giogo,
> Più felice sarei, dolce mia greggia,
> Più felice sarei, candida luna.
> O forse erra dal vero,
> Mirando all'altrui sorte, il mio pensiero:
> Forse in *qual* forma, in *quale*
> Stato che sia, dentro covile o cuna,
> E' funesto a chi nasce il dì *natale*.

>   (129-43; my emphases)

It is a rare translator who can find an effective English equivalent for the refrain's sound and keep it throughout the poem wherever it occurs in the original. One who does is Bickersteth with the sound A as in *day,* but the inversion he resorts to in the last line of his translation makes for an awkward close:

> Tell me why animals,
> Lying outstretched at ease,
> Repose without *dismay,*
> While I find nothing please, rest as I *may?*
>
>   Chance had I wings, *away*
> Above the clouds to soar,
> And count how many stars thro' heaven are *strewn,*
> Or like the thunder roam from range to range,
> I should be happier, sweet flock of *mine,*

> I should be happier, white-beaming *Moon.*
> Or errs, perchance, my thought
> From truth to aim thus at another's lot?
> Perchance in any *way,*
> To beast or man, in den or cradle, *soon*
> Deadly to all things born proves their *birthday.*

>   (my emphases)

Tusiani, without trying to keep the refrain wherever it occurs in the original, but realizing its importance, ends each of the poem's six stanzas with the sound *āre: thoroughfare, share, care, despair, care, anywhere.* His translation of the poem's ending follows:

> . . . Tell me: why
> Is every animal
> Happy to lie in easy idleness,
> And why, if I lie down, am I *alone*
> Assailed by still new boredom and new care?
>
>   Maybe if I had wings
> To fly above the clouds,
> And count the stars in heaven *one by one,*
> Or like the thunder roam from hill to hill,
> Happier I would be, O my sweet flock,
> I would be happier, my candid moon.
> Or maybe, watching other creature's *fate,*
> My thoughts now stray from truth:
> Maybe in whatsoever form or *state,*
> In cradle or in den,
> The day of birth is fatal any*where.*

Alone and *one by one,* of course, rhyme for the eye, not for the ear. The refrain/sound of *care/anywhere* is echoed by the assonants of the rhyming pair *fāte/stāte* and a number of supporting assonants: *assāiled, strāy, crādle, dāy, fātal.* Except for the one rhyme, *moon/soon* (and *strewn*) in Bickersteth's version, neither translator seeks to match the original's hauntingly beautiful rhyme of *una da una/luna/cuna.* The plaintive *u* sound occurs also in *nubi, altrui,* and *funesto,* which words chime with one another even as they are in assonance with *una, luna,* and *cuna.* These features, along with the rhyming *-àle* words (*animale, assale, ale, quale, natale*), the pervasive (but not invasive) alliteration, assonance and consonance, and the rhythm (with its flow and pauses) combine to make lines 129-43 of the **"Canto notturno"** one of the great moments of Leopardi's lyricism.

Bickersteth and Tusiani are accomplished poets and craftsmen in their own right, and they are, each in his own manner, among the best translators of pre-twentieth-century Italian poetry. Nonetheless, it is inevitable that even they at times show signs of straining for rhyme and of "wresting words from their true calling," as Ben Jonson centuries ago said in connection with the then relatively new use of rhyme among English poets. And as with rhyme, so too with syntactical inversions, which, like rhyme, come not so readily or "naturally" in

English as in Italian, notwithstanding stylistic conventions permitting their use. Bickersteth's self-consciousness on the matter of rhyme as expressed in the Preface to his translation of the **Canti** is quite understandable.

In many ways Tusiani's translation of the **Canti,** the first truly complete American edition, is admirable, and I wish to conclude my excursus by pointing to two passages that show him at his best.

The canzone **"Amore e Morte"** is among the poems of the **Canti** in which copious rhyme is employed, appearing here in free play in alternating lines of septenaries and hendecasyllables. Lines 45-87 of Leopardi's poem describes the propulsive drive of Eros towards Death. The rhymes are almost all line-ending:

> Then, when its boundless might
> Breaks and enwraps all things,
> And the unvanquished care like lightning strikes
> Deep in their hearts, O Death,
> How many times, with what immense desire,
> Are you implored and called
> By lovers out of breath!
> How many times at night,
> How many times, relinquishing at dawn
> His weary limbs, the one in love has deemed
> Himself a blessèd man
> If he should never rise,
> And if his bitter light
> Should nevermore appear before his eyes!
> And often at the sound of somber bells
> And at the dirge that led
> To their eternal nothingness the dead,
> With far more ardent sighs
> From his profoundest heart he envied him
> Who at that moment went
> To dwell among the spent,
> Even the humble throng,
> Even the peasant wholly unaware
> Of every valor that from knowledge springs;
> Even the modest, timid, tender maiden
> Who at the name of death
> Soon felt her hair on end
> Dares halt her glance, irrevocably bold,
> On her own tomb, her own funereal veil,
> And therefore warmly brood
> On poison and on steel
> Now that her simple mind has understood
> The gentleness of Death.
> So much indeed does love's new discipline
> Bend us toward death! And oftentimes to such
> Despair our horrid inner anguish comes—
> When mortal strength can beat it nevermore—
> That either a weak frame
> Yields to its wrecking might, and in this way,
> By her own brother's wishes, Death prevails;
> Or so does Love still prick the heart profound
> That, by themselves, at once,
> The little peasant wholly unaware,
> And the sweet damsel fair,
> With violent hand can lay upon the ground
> Their youthful limbs. The world

> Laughs at their story, and may heaven grant
> To those who laugh contentment and old age.

Finally, here is Tusiani's rendering of the first stanza (lines 1-27) of **"Le ricordanze, Remembrances"** in Tusiani's Englishing of Leopardi's unrhymed hendecasyllables:

> O Bear's so graceful stars, I did not think
> I would once more return to see you shine
> Above the garden of my father's home,
> And to address you from the window-sills
> Of this my place where as a child I dwelt
> And saw my every pleasure quickly end.
> What dear imaginings and what sweet dreams
> Your sight, and that of your escorting lights,
> Would rouse within my mind! It was the time
> When, sitting silent on a verdant clod,
> I used to spend long hours of each new eve
> Watching the sky and listening to the song
> Of a deep-hidden frog far in the field,
> And near the thickets, over flower-beds,
> A firefly wandered while the fragrant lanes
> And, there, the cypresses within the woods
> Murmured upon the wind; alternate words
> Re-echoed down our palace with the sound
> Of servants' easeful chores. What boundless thoughts,
> What fondling dreams were mine, as I could view,
> So far away, the sea, and those blue hills
> I still can glimpse from here, and which I thought
> I was one day to cross, thus feigning worlds
> Unknown and unknown bliss for my new days!
> Still unaware of fate, how many times
> This life of mine, so sorrowful and stark,
> Would I have willingly exchanged with death.

These lines capture as no other of the many versions I have read, all the pathos and, with different words—English words—the magic of Leopardi's music and mood. Think, for example, of the remarkable weaving of the alliterating *w* and *hw* throughout the stanza: *would, once, window, where, dwelt, saw, quickly, What, what, sweet, Would, within, was, when, new, Watching, wandered, while, within, woods, wind, words, down, with, What, were, view, away, which, was, one, worlds, unknown, new, unaware, how, sorrowful, Would, willingly, with.* And accompanying such sounds are the alliterating fricatives *f* and *v*: *graceful, above, of, father's, from, of, every, of, verdant, eve, of, frog, far, field, over, flower, firefly, fragrant, of, servants, easeful, fondling, view, far, from, feigning, for, fate, life, of, sorrowful, have.* Assonance and consonance also share in creating the "dotto concento" of Tusiani's lines.

It would be asking too much to expect a translator to sustain throughout his translation of the **Canti** such excellence as we are treated to in these last two excerpts. But the excellence is not limited to these. The reader of Tusiani's translation will meet again and again with passages that make reading it a rewarding esthetic experience.

Is it merely better than nothing? Better, but better by far, and we are lucky to have it.

Notes

1. *The Poems of Giacomo Leopardi,* translated by Frederick Townsend (New York: Putnam's Sons, 1887) VII.

2. "La fortuna di Leopardi in area anglosassone," *Testo* 29-30 (1995): 122.

3. Harold Bloom, *The Western Canon* (New York: Harcourt Brace, 1994) 2, 548.

4. "L'immagine culturale dell'Italia all'estero," *Atti della conferenza promossa dal Comitato Italiano dell'UNESCO,* 22 febbraio 1979, a cura di A. Bartoli, *Il Veltro* (1980): 72-73.

5. 1) Giacomo Leopardi, *Ten Odes* (the ten *canzoni* Leopardi published in 1824 and subsequently included in the *Canti*), translated by Patrick Creagh, *PN Review* 9.3 (1982): 11-21 (English version only). 2) Giacomo Leopardi, *Poems,* edited by Angel Flores (Bloomington: Indiana UP, 1966). Reprinted in 1987. Bilingual edition of twenty-four poems from the *Canti,* plus the "Chorus of the Dead" from the *Operette morali.* Several translators, among whom Muriel Kittell and Edwin Morgan stand out. 3) *Leopardi: A Scottish Quair* (Edinburgh: Italian Institute, 1987). Translations of eleven poems from the *Canti,* plus the "Chorus of the Dead," done by several hands into English, Scots, and Gaelic. 4) Giacomo Leopardi, *Poems,* translated by Arturo Vivante (Wellfleet, MA: Delphinium, 1988). Bilingual edition of sixteen poems from the *Canti.* 5) *Canti by Giacomo Leopardi: Bibliographic Essay and Anthology of the Translations in the Anglo-Saxon World,* edited by G. Singh, preface by Mario Luzi, foreword by Franco Foschi (Recanati: Centro Nazionale di Studi Leopardiani, 1990). Bilingual edition of thirty-four poems from the *Canti,* plus the "Chorus of the Dead" with various translators. 6) Giacomo Leopardi, *Canti,* selected and introduced by Franco Fortini and translated by Paul Lawton (Dublin: UCD Foundation for Italian Studies, 1996). Bilingual edition of twenty-four poems from the *Canti.* 7) Giacomo Leopardi, *Selected Poems,* translated by Eamon Grennan (Princeton: Princeton UP, 1997). Bilingual edition of fifteen poems from the *Canti* plus the "Chorus of the Dead." 8) *Leopardi's Canti,* translated into English verse by Joseph Tusiani, introduction and notes by Pietro Magno, preface by Franco Foschi (Fasano: Schena, 1998). English version only of all (41) the poems of the *Canti.* 9) *Or volge l'anno / At the Year's Turning: An Anthology of Irish Poets Responding to Leopardi,* edited, introduced and annotated by Marco Sonzogni (Dublin: Dedalus, 1998). The volume includes ten poems from the *Canti,* translated by Eamon Grennan. 10) *La corrispondenza imperfetta: Leopardi tradotto e traduttore,* a cura di Anna Dolfi e Adriana Mitescu (Rome: Bulzoni, 1990), twenty-three articles by as many contributors. 11) *La traduzione poetica nel segno di Giacomo Leopardi,* a cura di Rosario Portale, Atti del primo Simposio Internazionale, Macerata, 29-30 novembre 1988, Università degli Studi di Macerata (Pisa: Giardini, 1992).

6. Possiedi's review appeared in *Forum Italicum* 32.1 (1988): 279-82.

7. G. Singh, "Leopardi e i suoi traduttori inglesi," *La traduzione poetica nel segno di Giacomo Leopardi,* Atti del primo Simposio Internazionale 58. Singh refers specifically to a "mancanza di buone traduzioni [dei *Canti*] in inglese" (59).

8. See Elisabeth Ravoux-Rallo, "Pessoa chante Leopardi," *La Spleen du poète: autour de Fernando Pessoa* (Paris: 1997) 31-39.

9. Charles Wright, "To Giacomo Leopardi in the Sky," *Giacomo Leopardi, poeta e filosofo.* Atti del Convegno dell'Istituto Italiano di Cultura, New York. 31 marzo-1 aprile 1998, a cura di Alessandro Carrera (Fiesole: Cadmo, 1999) 18.

10. Donald Davie, *Collected Poems 1970-1983* (Manchester: Carcanet, 1983) 154.

11. G. Singh, who has written so well on the Leopardi-Hardy kinship, quotes Hardy's "To the Moon" and makes the following comments: "Let us quote Hardy's poem 'To the Moon' (1917) in which, through a closely woven net of Leopardian echoes, reminiscences and affinities, both verbal and conceptual, he deals with the theme of Leopardi's celebrated poem 'Canto notturno' in his own way and in his own accents" ("I *Canti* di Giacomo Leopardi nelle traduzioni inglesi" 62).

12. For Beckett under the influence of Leopardi (especially of the poem "A se stesso"), see my "Leopardi and the Primacy of Desire," in *Giacomo Leopardi.* Proceedings of the Congress held at UCLA, November 10-11, 1988, edited by Giovanni Cecchetti, *Forum Italicum* 9 (1990): Leopardi Supplement 84-85.

13. As a counter to this skepticism vis-à-vis translation, we may ponder Joseph Brodsky's intriguing remark that "poetry, in essence, is itself a certain other language—or a translation from such" ("Footnote to a Poem," *Less than One: Selected Essays* [London: Viking, 1987] 234).

14. Among the things Bickersteth hoped to accomplish in the "Preface" was to "show conclusive

reasons for treating the *Canti* as one coherent work of art expressive of a mind fundamentally at one with itself, rather than as a series of independent poems full of inconsistencies and contradictions, which has been the usual way of regarding them hitherto" (viii).

15. *Leopardi's Canti,* translated into English verse, with parallel text and an introduction (Naples: G. Scalabrini Editore, 1962).

16. Giacomo Leopardi, *Canti,* a cura di Francesco Flora (Milan: Edizioni Scolastiche Mondadori, 1963) 6-9.

17. "Leopardi e i suoi traduttori inglesi" 47.

18. *La traduzione poetica nel segno di Giacomo Leopardi,* a cura di Rosario Portale. Atti del primo Simposio Internazionale. Macerata, 29-30 novembre 1988 (Pisa: Giardini, 1992) 175.

19. I refer to Giacomo Leopardi, *Canzoni,* versione in prosa, note, e postfazione di Marco Santagata (Milan: Mondadori, 1998).

20. "The Strange Case of Leopardi," *New York Review of Books* 29 Jan. 1987: 42-44.

21. Corrado Zacchetti, in his commentary, writes: "Ove per poco il cor non si spaura": Credo sia da intendersi: io in quegli spazi interminati, in quei sovrumani silenzi, in quella profondissima quiete (tutto ciò è da: *ove*), che mi fingo (mi creo) nel pensiero, *per poco tempo,* ossia nel breve tempo che dura la mia interiore contemplazione, non mi sento impaurito dalla brutta realtà della vita, della dolorosa realtà: il mio cuore dimentica per un momento—per poco—che: 'Amaro e noia la vita, altro mai nulla: e fango è il mondo,'" *Canti di Giacomo Leopardi,* scelti e commentati da Corrado Zacchetti (Bologna: Zanichelli, 1927) 68-69. The same interpretation is given by Renzo Frattarolo who writes of the phrase in question: "intendi nel breve tempo che dura la mia contemplazione non mi sento impaurito dalla dolorosa realtà," Giacomo Leopardi, *Canti,* a cura di R. Frattarolo (Rome: Ausoni, 1957) 114. As can be seen by the last part of Zacchetti's statement and by Frattarolo's reference to a "dolorosa realtà," both critics were interpreting "L'infinito" in the light of the much later (by 16 years) and much different poem, "A se stesso." There is no "dolorosa realtà" in "L'infinito," unless it be in the *ubi sunt* motif that follows; but it is not this that provokes the momentary fear that grips the poet's heart, a sensation sparked by the poet's own making, i.e., the "interminati spazi . . . e sovrumani silenzi, e profondissima quiete" that he "feigns" within his mind. In the construction "per poco . . . non,"

per poco has no temporal significance. Heath-Stubbs's translation with the correct rendering of the *per poco . . . non* passage was printed in *Poems from Giacomo Leopardi,* translated and introduced by John Heath-Stubbs (London: Shenval, 1946) 17. The incorrect version appeared in Giacomo Leopardi, *Selected Prose and Poetry,* edited, translated, and introduced by Iris Origo and John Heath-Stubbs (London: Oxford UP, 1966) 213.

22. But Lowell's "Imitation" is in fact a personal poetic exercise. Thus he even casts it in long and short verses of varying syllabic length; and he uses rhyme! We are well beyond "creative translation" here. On the other hand, it is exasperating to find an Italian paraphraser of "L'infinito" separating the poet from his dear hill by tampering with the poet's demonstrative adjective: "Ho sempre amato *quella* collina solitaria / e *questa* siepe. . . ." For the offender see note 22.

23. J. Whitfield, who generally translates Leopardi with a sobriety that comes close to dignity, is one of the few translators who keep the poet's comparative terms intact: "I then compare / That infinite silence to this voice"; but the poem's last line fares almost as poorly as in Grennan's translation: "And shipwreck *sweet* for *me* within this *sea.*" Here the sounds of English are at a disadvantage if one wishes to translate word for word *dolce*—sweet, *m'è*—me, *mare*—sea.

24. G. Leopardi, *Poesie,* a cura di E. Balboni (Rome: Bonacci, 1994). Eleven poems from the *Canti,* original texts with facing page paraphrases in Italian prose.

25. A. Carrera, "Per Leopardi in America," *Giacomo Leopardi poeta e filosofo* XII-XIII.

26. "Translating Leopardi and Hölderlin," *La traduzione poetica nel segno di Giacomo Leopardi* 129. Continuing with Spender's cogent thought: "Lacking a Shelley, Leopardi remains a poet who, for English poets, represents a kind of perfection—our idea of poetry purely poetic both in language and in mood. Perhaps, though, Leopardi belongs too much to the Nineteenth Century for modern English poets, drawn as they are to him—close, indeed, as they feel to him—to be able to translate." This seems to say, I think, that Leopardi is a poet's poet, and this may be so not only for English poets.

27. "The Strange Case of Leopardi," *The New York Review of Books* 29 Jan. 1987: 44.

28. See Giorgio Orelli's meticulous and absorbing article, "Connessioni leopardiane," *Strumenti critici* NS 2.1 (1987): 73-96.

29. On the matter of the labiodental (fricatives) sounds (*v* and *f*) that were so dear to Leopardi and that figure (along with the liquid *l*) so essentially in "A Silvia," we may note that he favored them more than once in creating passages of a particularly high musical quality. It may be that the letter sound v is bound to have a prominent role in Italian. One thinks of the imperfect tense (the tense of memory and duration in the past) and especially of the verbs *avere* and *vedere*. But whether the concentration of v sounds in Leopardi's verses (especially in "A Silvia" and "Canto notturno d'un pastore errante dell'Asia") be deliberate or not, it appears with high frequency and is a marked component of his musical palette. I have noted elsewhere its striking presence in an erotic vein in Giuseppe Ungaretti's poem "L'isola." See my *Midday in Italian Literature* (Princeton: Princeton UP, 1979) 236.

30. The translation, by Tim Parks and Jonathan Galassi, is appended to Park's "In Love with Leopardi," *New York Review of Books* 23 Mar. 2000: 38-41; it is an insightful and subtle review article inspired by the recent new editions of Iris Origo's *Leopardi: A Study in Solitude* and *Images and Shadows: Part of a Life.* Origo's sensitive and finely written biography of Leopardi includes quotations from the poet's work, given in Italian and in her English versions.

31. "Hazy" for *vago* was first used by the Irish dramatist John Synge in his unfinished translation of "To Sylvia." It is also Eamon Grennan's choice in his translation of Leopardi's poem. In Petrarch's poetry *vago* has mostly the meaning of "wandering." Compare *vagare,* which means to wander, as in Foscolo's sonnet "Forse perché della fatal quiete," often given the title "La sera."

FURTHER READING

Criticism

Barricelli, Jean-Pierre. "*Poésie* and *Suono*: Balzac and Leopardi on Music." In *Romanticism across the Disciplines,* edited by Larry H. Peer, pp. 99-113. Lanham, Md.: University Press of America, 1998.
    Explores the relationship between Romanticism and music through the novels of Balzac and the poetry of Leopardi.

Brose, Margaret. "Remembrance and the Rhetorical Sublime in Leopardi's Lyric." *Stanford Literature Review* 6, no. 1 (spring 1989): 115-33.

Discusses the opposition between the temporal present and the poetic imagination in Leopardi's *Zibaldone.*

Carsaniga, Giovanni. *Giacomo Leopardi: The Unheeded Voice.* Edinburgh: Edinburgh University Press, 1977, 129 p.
    Approaches Leopardi's poetry and prose from a variety of critical perspectives.

Cook, Albert. "Leopardi: The Mastery of Diffusing Sorrow." *Canadian Journal of Italian Studies* 4, nos. 1-2 (1980-81): 68-82.
    Examines Leopardi's deep feelings of sorrow which prompted him to combine the romantic themes of love and nature in his writing.

Dasenbrock, Reed Way. "Petrarch, Leopardi, and Pound's Apprehension of the Italian Past." *ELH* 58, no. 1 (spring 1991): 215-32.
    Discusses Leopardi's debt to previous Italian poets, and the influence of these poets and Leopardi on the later work of Ezra Pound.

Frattini, Alberto. "The Leopardian Continent: A Continuing Exploration." *Italian Books and Periodicals* 34, nos. 1-2 (January-December 1991): 5-10.
    Surveys critical research on Leopardi in the years surrounding the bicentennial of his birth.

Garofalo, Silvano. "The Tragic Sense in the Poetry of Leopardi and Unamuno." *Symposium* 26, no. 3 (fall 1972): 197-211.
    Compares themes of joy and despair in the poetry of Unamuno and Leopardi.

Johnson, Trevor. "Hardy, Leopardi and *Tess of the d'Urbervilles.*" *The Thomas Hardy Journal* 9, no. 2 (May 1993): 51-53.
    Explores Leopardi's work as a possible source of specific passages in Hardy's novel.

La Porta, Christina. "Confronting the Artifact: Interrogative Ekphrasis in Keats and Leopardi." *Rivista di Studi Italiani* 14, no. 1 (June 1996): 36-47.
    Studies similarities and differences in Keats's "Ode on a Grecian Urn" (1820) and Leopardi's "Sopra un bassorilievo antico sepolcrale" (1835).

Marroni, Francesco. "The Poetry of Ornithology in Keats, Leopardi and Hardy: A Dialogic Analysis." *Thomas Hardy Journal* 14, no. 2 (May 1998): 35-44.
    Explores commonalities between Hardy's *The Darkling Thrush* and Leopardi's *Il Passero Solitario.*

Molinaro, Julius A. "A Note on Leopardi's *Il Passero Solitario.*" *Studies in Philology* 64, no. 4 (July 1967): 640-53.

Examines the poetic language of *Il Passero Solitario,* maintaining that Leopardi invoked ancient words and phrases associated with Cicero, Horace, and Petronius.

O'Connor, Desmond. "From Venus to Proserpine: 'Sappho's Last Song.'" *Rivista di Studi Italiani* 16, no. 2 (December 1998): 438-53.

Explores Leopardi's admiration for Sappho's poetry and his affinity for her unhappiness—a melancholy attributed to her unattractive physical condition.

Pacifici, Sergio. "Giacomo Leopardi: An Introduction." In *Leopardi: Poems and Prose,* edited by Angel Flores, pp. 9-19. Bloomington: Indiana University Press, 1966.

Maintains that Leopardi's poetry and prose is as relevant today as it was in his own time.

Pesaresi, Massimo Mandolini. "Musing on the Infinite and the Sublime." *Italian Quarterly* 28, nos. 109-11 (summer-fall 1987): 19-24.

Discusses Leopardi's notions of the sublime, both as it is applied to natural phenomena and to aesthetic judgments.

Williams, Pamela. "Leopardi's Aspasia Poems: 'L'inganno estremo.'" In *The Italian Lyric Tradition: Essays in Honor of F. J. Jones,* edited by Gino Bedani, Remo Catani, and Monica Slowikowska, pp. 55-71. Cardiff: University of Wales Press, 1993.

Contends that Leopardi's four works often referred to as the "Aspasia poems" are part of the well-established Italian tradition of love poetry that includes the works of Dante and Petrarch.

How to Use This Index

CMW = *St. James Guide to Crime & Mystery Writers*
CN = *Contemporary Novelists*
CP = *Contemporary Poets*
CPW = *Contemporary Popular Writers*
CSW = *Contemporary Southern Writers*
CWD = *Contemporary Women Dramatists*
CWP = *Contemporary Women Poets*
CWRI = *St. James Guide to Children's Writers*
CWW = *Contemporary World Writers*
DA = *DISCovering Authors*
DA3 = *DISCovering Authors 3.0*
DAB = *DISCovering Authors: British Edition*
DAC = *DISCovering Authors: Canadian Edition*
DAM = *DISCovering Authors: Modules*
   DRAM: *Dramatists Module;* **MST:** *Most-studied Authors Module;*
   MULT: *Multicultural Authors Module;* **NOV:** *Novelists Module;*
   POET: *Poets Module;* **POP:** *Popular Fiction and Genre Authors Module*
DFS = *Drama for Students*
DLB = *Dictionary of Literary Biography*
DLBD = *Dictionary of Literary Biography Documentary Series*
DLBY = *Dictionary of Literary Biography Yearbook*
DNFS = *Literature of Developing Nations for Students*
EFS = *Epics for Students*
EXPN = *Exploring Novels*
EXPP = *Exploring Poetry*
EXPS = *Exploring Short Stories*
EW = *European Writers*
FANT = *St. James Guide to Fantasy Writers*
FW = *Feminist Writers*
GFL = *Guide to French Literature,* Beginnings to 1789, 1798 to the Present
GLL = *Gay and Lesbian Literature*
HGG = *St. James Guide to Horror, Ghost & Gothic Writers*
HW = *Hispanic Writers*
IDFW = *International Dictionary of Films and Filmmakers: Writers and Production Artists*
IDTP = *International Dictionary of Theatre: Playwrights*
LAIT = *Literature and Its Times*
LAW = *Latin American Writers*
JRDA = *Junior DISCovering Authors*
MAICYA = *Major Authors and Illustrators for Children and Young Adults*
MAICYAS = *Major Authors and Illustrators for Children and Young Adults Supplement*
MAWW = *Modern American Women Writers*
MJW = *Modern Japanese Writers*
MTCW = *Major 20th-Century Writers*
NCFS = *Nonfiction Classics for Students*
NFS = *Novels for Students*
PAB = *Poets: American and British*
PFS = *Poetry for Students*
RGAL = *Reference Guide to American Literature*
RGEL = *Reference Guide to English Literature*
RGSF = *Reference Guide to Short Fiction*
RGWL = *Reference Guide to World Literature*
RHW = *Twentieth-Century Romance and Historical Writers*
SAAS = *Something about the Author Autobiography Series*
SATA = *Something about the Author*
SFW = *St. James Guide to Science Fiction Writers*
SSFS = *Short Stories for Students*
TCWW = *Twentieth-Century Western Writers*
WLIT = *World Literature and Its Times*
WP = *World Poets*
YABC = *Yesterday's Authors of Books for Children*
YAW = *St. James Guide to Young Adult Writers*

Literary Criticism Series
Cumulative Author Index

Allen, Sidney H.
See Hartmann, Sadakichi
Allen, Woody 1935- .... **CLC 16, 52**
See also AAYA 10, 51; CA 33-36R; CANR 27, 38, 63; DAM POP; DLB 44; MTCW 1
Allende, Isabel 1942- ... **CLC 39, 57, 97, 170; HLC 1; WLCS**
See also AAYA 18; CA 125; 130; CANR 51, 74; CDWLB 3; CWW 2; DA3; DAM MULT, NOV; DLB 145; DNFS 1; EWL 3; FW; HW 1, 2; INT CA-130; LAIT 5; LAWS 1; LMFS 2; MTCW 1, 2; NCFS 1; NFS 6; RGSF 2; RGWL 3; SSFS 11, 16; WLIT 1
Alleyn, Ellen
See Rossetti, Christina (Georgina)
Alleyne, Carla D. .... **CLC 65**
Allingham, Margery (Louise)
1904-1966 .... **CLC 19**
See also CA 5-8R; 25-28R; CANR 4, 58; CMW 4; DLB 77; MSW; MTCW 1, 2
Allingham, William 1824-1889 ...... **NCLC 25**
See also DLB 35; RGEL 2
Allison, Dorothy E. 1949- .... **CLC 78, 153**
See also AAYA 53; CA 140; CANR 66, 107; CSW; DA3; FW; MTCW 1; NFS 11; RGAL 4
Alloula, Malek .... **CLC 65**
Allston, Washington 1779-1843 .... **NCLC 2**
See also DLB 1, 235
Almedingen, E. M. .... **CLC 12**
See Almedingen, Martha Edith von
See also SATA 3
Almedingen, Martha Edith von 1898-1971
See Almedingen, E. M.
See also CA 1-4R; CANR 1
Almodovar, Pedro 1949(?)- .... **CLC 114; HLCS 1**
See also CA 133; CANR 72; HW 2
Almqvist, Carl Jonas Love
1793-1866 .... **NCLC 42**
Alonso, Damaso 1898-1990 .... **CLC 14**
See also CA 110; 131; 130; CANR 72; DLB 108; EWL 3; HW 1, 2
Alov
See Gogol, Nikolai (Vasilyevich)
Alta 1942- .... **CLC 19**
See also CA 57-60
Alter, Robert B(ernard) 1935- .... **CLC 34**
See also CA 49-52; CANR 1, 47, 100
Alther, Lisa 1944- .... **CLC 7, 41**
See also BPFB 1; CA 65-68; CAAS 30; CANR 12, 30, 51; CN 7; CSW; GLL 2; MTCW 1
Althusser, L.
See Althusser, Louis
Althusser, Louis 1918-1990 .... **CLC 106**
See also CA 131; 132; CANR 102; DLB 242
Altman, Robert 1925- .... **CLC 16, 116**
See also CA 73-76; CANR 43
Alurista .... **HLCS 1**
See Urista, Alberto H.
See also DLB 82
Alvarez, A(lfred) 1929- .... **CLC 5, 13**
See also CA 1-4R; CANR 3, 33, 63, 101; CN 7; CP 7; DLB 14, 40
Alvarez, Alejandro Rodriguez 1903-1965
See Casona, Alejandro
See also CA 131; 93-96; HW 1
Alvarez, Julia 1950- .... **CLC 93; HLCS 1**
See also AAYA 25; AMWS 7; CA 147; CANR 69, 101; DA3; DLB 282; LATS 1; MTCW 1; NFS 5, 9; SATA 129; WLIT 1
Alvaro, Corrado 1896-1956 .... **TCLC 60**
See also CA 163; DLB 264; EWL 3

Amado, Jorge 1912-2001 ... **CLC 13, 40, 106; HLC 1**
See also CA 77-80; 201; CANR 35, 74; DAM MULT, NOV; DLB 113; EWL 3; HW 2; LAW; LAWS 1; MTCW 1, 2; RGWL 2, 3; TWA; WLIT 1
Ambler, Eric 1909-1998 .... **CLC 4, 6, 9**
See also BRWS 4; CA 9-12R; 171; CANR 7, 38, 74; CMW 4; CN 7; DLB 77; MSW; MTCW 1, 2; TEA
Ambrose, Stephen E(dward)
1936-2002 .... **CLC 145**
See also AAYA 44; CA 1-4R; 209; CANR 3, 43, 57, 83, 105; NCFS 2; SATA 40, 138
Amichai, Yehuda 1924-2000 .. **CLC 9, 22, 57, 116; PC 38**
See also CA 85-88; 189; CANR 46, 60, 99; CWW 2; EWL 3; MTCW 1
Amichai, Yehudah
See Amichai, Yehuda
Amiel, Henri Frederic 1821-1881 .... **NCLC 4**
See also DLB 217
Amis, Kingsley (William)
1922-1995 ...... **CLC 1, 2, 3, 5, 8, 13, 40, 44, 129**
See also AITN 2; BPFB 1; BRWS 2; CA 9-12R; 150; CANR 8, 28, 54; CDBLB 1945-1960; CN 7; CP 7; DA; DA3; DAB; DAC; DAM MST, NOV; DLB 15, 27, 100, 139; DLBY 1996; EWL 3; HGG; INT CANR-8; MTCW 1, 2; RGEL 2; RGSF 2; SFW 4
Amis, Martin (Louis) 1949- .... **CLC 4, 9, 38, 62, 101**
See also BEST 90:3; BRWS 4; CA 65-68; CANR 8, 27, 54, 73, 95; CN 7; DA3; DLB 14, 194; EWL 3; INT CANR-27; MTCW 1
Ammianus Marcellinus c. 330-c.
395 .... **CMLC 60**
See also AW 2; DLB 211
Ammons, A(rchie) R(andolph)
1926-2001 ...... **CLC 2, 3, 5, 8, 9, 25, 57, 108; PC 16**
See also AITN 1; AMWS 7; CA 9-12R; 193; CANR 6, 36, 51, 73, 107; CP 7; CSW; DAM POET; DLB 5, 165; EWL 3; MTCW 1, 2; RGAL 4
Amo, Tauraatua i
See Adams, Henry (Brooks)
Amory, Thomas 1691(?)-1788 .... **LC 48**
See also DLB 39
Anand, Mulk Raj 1905- .... **CLC 23, 93**
See also CA 65-68; CANR 32, 64; CN 7; DAM NOV; EWL 3; MTCW 1, 2; RGSF 2
Anatol
See Schnitzler, Arthur
Anaximander c. 611B.C.-c.
546B.C. .... **CMLC 22**
Anaya, Rudolfo A(lfonso) 1937- ...... **CLC 23, 148; HLC 1**
See also AAYA 20; BYA 13; CA 45-48; CAAS 4; CANR 1, 32, 51; CN 7; DAM MULT, NOV; DLB 82, 206, 278; HW 1; LAIT 4; MTCW 1, 2; NFS 12; RGAL 4; RGSF 2; WLIT 1
Andersen, Hans Christian
1805-1875 .... **NCLC 7, 79; SSC 6, 56; WLC**
See also CLR 6; DA; DA3; DAB; DAC; DAM MST, POP; EW 6; MAICYA 1, 2; RGSF 2; RGWL 2, 3; SATA 100; TWA; WCH; YABC 1
Anderson, C. Farley
See Mencken, H(enry) L(ouis); Nathan, George Jean

Anderson, Jessica (Margaret) Queale
1916- .... **CLC 37**
See also CA 9-12R; CANR 4, 62; CN 7
Anderson, Jon (Victor) 1940- .... **CLC 9**
See also CA 25-28R; CANR 20; DAM POET
Anderson, Lindsay (Gordon)
1923-1994 .... **CLC 20**
See also CA 125; 128; 146; CANR 77
Anderson, Maxwell 1888-1959 ...... **TCLC 2**
See also CA 105; 152; DAM DRAM; DFS 16; DLB 7, 228; MTCW 2; RGAL 4
Anderson, Poul (William)
1926-2001 .... **CLC 15**
See also AAYA 5, 34; BPFB 1; BYA 6, 8, 9; CA 1-4R; 181; 199; CAAE 181; CAAS 2; CANR 2, 15, 34, 64, 110; CLR 58; DLB 8; FANT; INT CANR-15; MTCW 1, 2; SATA 90; SATA-Brief 39; SATA-Essay 106; SCFW 2; SFW 4; SUFW 1, 2
Anderson, Robert (Woodruff)
1917- .... **CLC 23**
See also AITN 1; CA 21-24R; CANR 32; DAM DRAM; DLB 7; LAIT 5
Anderson, Roberta Joan
See Mitchell, Joni
Anderson, Sherwood 1876-1941 .. **SSC 1, 46; TCLC 1, 10, 24, 123; WLC**
See also AAYA 30; AMW; BPFB 1; CA 104; 121; CANR 61; CDALB 1917-1929; DA; DA3; DAB; DAC; DAM MST, NOV; DLB 4, 9, 86; DLBD 1; EWL 3; EXPS; GLL 2; MTCW 1, 2; NFS 4; RGAL 4; RGSF 2; SSFS 4, 10, 11; TUS
Andier, Pierre
See Desnos, Robert
Andouard
See Giraudoux, Jean(-Hippolyte)
Andrade, Carlos Drummond de ..... **CLC 18**
See Drummond de Andrade, Carlos
See also EWL 3; RGWL 2, 3
Andrade, Mario de .... **TCLC 43**
See de Andrade, Mario
See also EWL 3; LAW; RGWL 2, 3; WLIT 1
Andreae, Johann V(alentin)
1586-1654 .... **LC 32**
See also DLB 164
Andreas Capellanus fl. c. 1185- .... **CMLC 45**
See also DLB 208
Andreas-Salome, Lou 1861-1937 ... **TCLC 56**
See also CA 178; DLB 66
Andreev, Leonid
See Andreyev, Leonid (Nikolaevich)
See also EWL 3
Andress, Lesley
See Sanders, Lawrence
Andrewes, Lancelot 1555-1626 .... **LC 5**
See also DLB 151, 172
Andrews, Cicily Fairfield
See West, Rebecca
Andrews, Elton V.
See Pohl, Frederik
Andreyev, Leonid (Nikolaevich)
1871-1919 .... **TCLC 3**
See Andreev, Leonid
See also CA 104; 185
Andric, Ivo 1892-1975 .... **CLC 8; SSC 36; TCLC 135**
See also CA 81-84; 57-60; CANR 43, 60; CDWLB 4; DLB 147; EW 11; EWL 3; MTCW 1; RGSF 2; RGWL 2, 3
Androvar
See Prado (Calvo), Pedro
Angelique, Pierre
See Bataille, Georges
Angell, Roger 1920- .... **CLC 26**
See also CA 57-60; CANR 13, 44, 70; DLB 171, 185

Artaud, Antonin (Marie Joseph)
1896-1948 .... **DC 14; TCLC 3, 36**
See also CA 104; 149; DA3; DAM DRAM;
DLB 258; EW 11; EWL 3; GFL 1789 to
the Present; MTCW 1; RGWL 2, 3

Arthur, Ruth M(abel) 1905-1979 ..... **CLC 12**
See also CA 9-12R; 85-88; CANR 4; CWRI
5; SATA 7, 26

Artsybashev, Mikhail (Petrovich)
1878-1927 .... **TCLC 31**
See also CA 170

Arundel, Honor (Morfydd)
1919-1973 .... **CLC 17**
See also CA 21-22; 41-44R; CAP 2; CLR
35; CWRI 5; SATA 4; SATA-Obit 24

Arzner, Dorothy 1900-1979 .... **CLC 98**

Asch, Sholem 1880-1957 .... **TCLC 3**
See also CA 105; EWL 3; GLL 2

Ash, Shalom
See Asch, Sholem

Ashbery, John (Lawrence) 1927- .. **CLC 2, 3,
4, 6, 9, 13, 15, 25, 41, 77, 125; PC 26**
See Berry, Jonas
See also AMWS 3; CA 5-8R; CANR 9, 37,
66, 102; CP 7; DA3; DAM POET; DLB
5, 165; DLBY 1981; EWL 3; INT
CANR-9; MTCW 1, 2; PAB; PFS 11;
RGAL 4; WP

Ashdown, Clifford
See Freeman, R(ichard) Austin

Ashe, Gordon
See Creasey, John

Ashton-Warner, Sylvia (Constance)
1908-1984 .... **CLC 19**
See also CA 69-72; 112; CANR 29; MTCW
1, 2

Asimov, Isaac 1920-1992 ..... **CLC 1, 3, 9, 19,
26, 76, 92**
See also AAYA 13; BEST 90:2; BPFB 1;
BYA 4, 6, 7, 9; CA 1-4R; 137; CANR 2,
19, 36, 60; CLR 12, 79; CMW 4; CPW;
DA3; DAM POP; DLB 8; DLBY 1992;
INT CANR-19; JRDA; LAIT 5; LMFS 2;
MAICYA 1, 2; MTCW 1, 2; RGAL 4;
SATA 1, 26, 74; SCFW 2; SFW 4; SSFS
17; TUS; YAW

Askew, Anne 1521(?)-1546 .... **LC 81**
See also DLB 136

Assis, Joaquim Maria Machado de
See Machado de Assis, Joaquim Maria

Astell, Mary 1666-1731 .... **LC 68**
See also DLB 252; FW

Astley, Thea (Beatrice May) 1925- .. **CLC 41**
See also CA 65-68; CANR 11, 43, 78; CN
7; EWL 3

Astley, William 1855-1911
See Warung, Price

Aston, James
See White, T(erence) H(anbury)

Asturias, Miguel Angel 1899-1974 .... **CLC 3,
8, 13; HLC 1**
See also CA 25-28; 49-52; CANR 32; CAP
2; CDWLB 3; DA3; DAM MULT, NOV;
DLB 113; EWL 3; HW 1; LAW; LMFS
2; MTCW 1, 2; RGWL 2, 3; WLIT 1

Atares, Carlos Saura
See Saura (Atares), Carlos

Athanasius c. 295-c. 373 .... **CMLC 48**

Atheling, William
See Pound, Ezra (Weston Loomis)

Atheling, William, Jr.
See Blish, James (Benjamin)

Atherton, Gertrude (Franklin Horn)
1857-1948 .... **TCLC 2**
See also CA 104; 155; DLB 9, 78, 186;
HGG; RGAL 4; SUFW 1; TCWW 2

Atherton, Lucius
See Masters, Edgar Lee

Atkins, Jack
See Harris, Mark

Atkinson, Kate 1951- .... **CLC 99**
See also CA 166; CANR 101; DLB 267

Attaway, William (Alexander)
1911-1986 .... **BLC 1; CLC 92**
See also BW 2, 3; CA 143; CANR 82;
DAM MULT; DLB 76

Atticus
See Fleming, Ian (Lancaster); Wilson,
(Thomas) Woodrow

Atwood, Margaret (Eleanor) 1939- ... **CLC 2,
3, 4, 8, 13, 15, 25, 44, 84, 135; PC 8;
SSC 2, 46; WLC**
See also AAYA 12, 47; BEST 89:2; BPFB
1; CA 49-52; CANR 3, 24, 33, 59, 95;
CN 7; CP 7; CPW; CWP; DA; DA3;
DAB; DAC; DAM MST, NOV, POET;
DLB 53, 251; EWL 3; EXPN; FW; INT
CANR-24; LAIT 5; MTCW 1, 2; NFS 4,
12, 13, 14; PFS 7; RGSF 2; SATA 50;
SSFS 3, 13; TWA; YAW

Aubigny, Pierre d'
See Mencken, H(enry) L(ouis)

Aubin, Penelope 1685-1731(?) .... **LC 9**
See also DLB 39

Auchincloss, Louis (Stanton) 1917- .. **CLC 4,
6, 9, 18, 45; SSC 22**
See also AMWS 4; CA 1-4R; CANR 6, 29,
55, 87; CN 7; DAM NOV; DLB 2, 244;
DLBY 1980; EWL 3; INT CANR-29;
MTCW 1; RGAL 4

Auden, W(ystan) H(ugh) 1907-1973 . **CLC 1,
2, 3, 4, 6, 9, 11, 14, 43, 123; PC 1;
WLC**
See also AAYA 18; AMWS 2; BRW 7;
BRWR 1; CA 9-12R; 45-48; CANR 5, 61,
105; CDBLB 1914-1945; DA; DA3;
DAB; DAC; DAM DRAM, MST, POET;
DLB 10, 20; EWL 3; EXPP; MTCW 1, 2;
PAB; PFS 1, 3, 4, 10; TUS; WP

Audiberti, Jacques 1900-1965 .... **CLC 38**
See also CA 25-28R; DAM DRAM; EWL 3

Audubon, John James 1785-1851 . **NCLC 47**
See also ANW; DLB 248

Auel, Jean M(arie) 1936- .... **CLC 31, 107**
See also AAYA 7, 51; BEST 90:4; BPFB 1;
CA 103; CANR 21, 64, 115; CPW; DA3;
DAM POP; INT CANR-21; NFS 11;
RHW; SATA 91

Auerbach, Erich 1892-1957 .... **TCLC 43**
See also CA 118; 155; EWL 3

Augier, Emile 1820-1889 .... **NCLC 31**
See also DLB 192; GFL 1789 to the Present

August, John
See De Voto, Bernard (Augustine)

Augustine, St. 354-430 .... **CMLC 6; WLCS**
See also DA; DA3; DAB; DAC; DAM
MST; DLB 115; EW 1; RGWL 2, 3

Aunt Belinda
See Braddon, Mary Elizabeth

Aunt Weedy
See Alcott, Louisa May

Aurelius
See Bourne, Randolph S(illiman)

Aurelius, Marcus 121-180 .... **CMLC 45**
See Marcus Aurelius
See also RGWL 2, 3

Aurobindo, Sri
See Ghose, Aurabinda

Aurobindo Ghose
See Ghose, Aurabinda

Austen, Jane 1775-1817 ...... **NCLC 1, 13, 19,
33, 51, 81, 95, 119; WLC**
See also AAYA 19; BRW 4; BRWC 1;
BRWR 2; BYA 3; CDBLB 1789-1832;
DA; DA3; DAB; DAC; DAM MST, NOV;
DLB 116; EXPN; LAIT 2; LATS 1; LMFS
1; NFS 1, 14; TEA; WLIT 3; WYAS 1

Auster, Paul 1947- .... **CLC 47, 131**
See also AMWS 12; CA 69-72; CANR 23,
52, 75; CMW 4; CN 7; DA3; DLB 227;
MTCW 1; SUFW 2

Austin, Frank
See Faust, Frederick (Schiller)
See also TCWW 2

Austin, Mary (Hunter) 1868-1934 . **TCLC 25**
See Stairs, Gordon
See also ANW; CA 109; 178; DLB 9, 78,
206, 221, 275; FW; TCWW 2

Averroes 1126-1198 .... **CMLC 7**
See also DLB 115

Avicenna 980-1037 .... **CMLC 16**
See also DLB 115

Avison, Margaret 1918- .... **CLC 2, 4, 97**
See also CA 17-20R; CP 7; DAC; DAM
POET; DLB 53; MTCW 1

Axton, David
See Koontz, Dean R(ay)

Ayckbourn, Alan 1939- ...... **CLC 5, 8, 18, 33,
74; DC 13**
See also BRWS 5; CA 21-24R; CANR 31,
59, 118; CBD; CD 5; DAB; DAM DRAM;
DFS 7; DLB 13, 245; EWL 3; MTCW 1,
2

Aydy, Catherine
See Tennant, Emma (Christina)

Ayme, Marcel (Andre) 1902-1967 ... **CLC 11;
SSC 41**
See also CA 89-92; CANR 67; CLR 25;
DLB 72; EW 12; EWL 3; GFL 1789 to
the Present; RGSF 2; RGWL 2, 3; SATA
91

Ayrton, Michael 1921-1975 .... **CLC 7**
See also CA 5-8R; 61-64; CANR 9, 21

Aytmatov, Chingiz
See Aitmatov, Chingiz (Torekulovich)
See also EWL 3

Azorin .... **CLC 11**
See Martinez Ruiz, Jose
See also EW 9; EWL 3

Azuela, Mariano 1873-1952 .. **HLC 1; TCLC
3**
See also CA 104; 131; CANR 81; DAM
MULT; EWL 3; HW 1, 2; LAW; MTCW
1, 2

Ba, Mariama 1929-1981 .... **BLCS**
See also AFW; BW 2; CA 141; CANR 87;
DNFS 2; WLIT 2

Baastad, Babbis Friis
See Friis-Baastad, Babbis Ellinor

Bab
See Gilbert, W(illiam) S(chwenck)

Babbis, Eleanor
See Friis-Baastad, Babbis Ellinor

Babel, Isaac
See Babel, Isaak (Emmanuilovich)
See also EW 11; SSFS 10

Babel, Isaak (Emmanuilovich)
1894-1941(?) .... **SSC 16; TCLC 2, 13**
See Babel, Isaac
See also CA 104; 155; CANR 113; DLB
272; EWL 3; MTCW 1; RGSF 2; RGWL
2, 3; TWA

Babits, Mihaly 1883-1941 .... **TCLC 14**
See also CA 114; CDWLB 4; DLB 215;
EWL 3

Babur 1483-1530 .... **LC 18**

Babylas 1898-1962
See Ghelderode, Michel de

Baca, Jimmy Santiago 1952- . **HLC 1; PC 41**
See also CA 131; CANR 81, 90; CP 7;
DAM MULT; DLB 122; HW 1, 2

Baca, Jose Santiago
See Baca, Jimmy Santiago

Bacchelli, Riccardo 1891-1985 .... **CLC 19**
See also CA 29-32R; 117; DLB 264; EWL 3

Barnes, Peter 1931- .... **CLC 5, 56**
    See also CA 65-68; CAAS 12; CANR 33,
    34, 64, 113; CBD; CD 5; DFS 6; DLB
    13, 233; MTCW 1
Barnes, William 1801-1886 .... **NCLC 75**
    See also DLB 32
Baroja (y Nessi), Pio 1872-1956 .... **HLC 1;**
    TCLC 8
    See also CA 104; EW 9
Baron, David
    See Pinter, Harold
Baron Corvo
    See Rolfe, Frederick (William Serafino Aus-
    tin Lewis Mary)
Barondess, Sue K(aufman)
    1926-1977 .... **CLC 8**
    See Kaufman, Sue
    See also CA 1-4R; 69-72; CANR 1
Baron de Teive
    See Pessoa, Fernando (Antonio Nogueira)
Baroness Von S.
    See Zangwill, Israel
Barres, (Auguste-)Maurice
    1862-1923 .... **TCLC 47**
    See also CA 164; DLB 123; GFL 1789 to
    the Present
Barreto, Afonso Henrique de Lima
    See Lima Barreto, Afonso Henrique de
Barrett, Andrea 1954- .... **CLC 150**
    See also CA 156; CANR 92
Barrett, Michele .... **CLC 65**
Barrett, (Roger) Syd 1946- .... **CLC 35**
Barrett, William (Christopher)
    1913-1992 .... **CLC 27**
    See also CA 13-16R; 139; CANR 11, 67;
    INT CANR-11
Barrie, J(ames) M(atthew)
    1860-1937 .... **TCLC 2**
    See also BRWS 3; BYA 4, 5; CA 104; 136;
    CANR 77; CDBLB 1890-1914; CLR 16;
    CWRI 5; DA3; DAB; DAM DRAM; DFS
    7; DLB 10, 141, 156; EWL 3; FANT;
    MAICYA 1, 2; MTCW 1; SATA 100;
    SUFW; WCH; WLIT 4; YABC 1
Barrington, Michael
    See Moorcock, Michael (John)
Barrol, Grady
    See Bograd, Larry
Barry, Mike
    See Malzberg, Barry N(athaniel)
Barry, Philip 1896-1949 .... **TCLC 11**
    See also CA 109; 199; DFS 9; DLB 7, 228;
    RGAL 4
Bart, Andre Schwarz
    See Schwarz-Bart, Andre
Barth, John (Simmons) 1930- ... **CLC 1, 2, 3,**
    5, 7, 9, 10, 14, 27, 51, 89; SSC 10
    See also AITN 1, 2; AMW; BPFB 1; CA
    1-4R; CABS 1; CANR 5, 23, 49, 64, 113;
    CN 7; DAM NOV; DLB 2, 227; EWL 3;
    FANT; MTCW 1; RGAL 4; RGSF 2;
    RHW; SSFS 6; TUS
Barthelme, Donald 1931-1989 ... **CLC 1, 2, 3,**
    5, 6, 8, 13, 23, 46, 59, 115; SSC 2, 55
    See also AMWS 4; BPFB 1; CA 21-24R;
    129; CANR 20, 58; DA3; DAM NOV;
    DLB 2, 234; DLBY 1980, 1989; EWL 3;
    FANT; LMFS 2; MTCW 1, 2; RGAL 4;
    RGSF 2; SATA 7; SATA-Obit 62; SSFS
    17
Barthelme, Frederick 1943- ...... **CLC 36, 117**
    See also AMWS 11; CA 114; 122; CANR
    77; CN 7; CSW; DLB 244; DLBY 1985;
    EWL 3; INT CA-122
Barthes, Roland (Gerard)
    1915-1980 .... **CLC 24, 83; TCLC 135**
    See also CA 130; 97-100; CANR 66; EW
    13; EWL 3; GFL 1789 to the Present;
    MTCW 1, 2; TWA

Barzun, Jacques (Martin) 1907- ..... **CLC 51,**
    145
    See also CA 61-64; CANR 22, 95
Bashevis, Isaac
    See Singer, Isaac Bashevis
Bashkirtseff, Marie 1859-1884 .... **NCLC 27**
Basho, Matsuo
    See Matsuo Basho
    See also RGWL 2, 3; WP
Basil of Caesaria c. 330-379 .... **CMLC 35**
Bass, Kingsley B., Jr.
    See Bullins, Ed
Bass, Rick 1958- .... **CLC 79, 143; SSC 60**
    See also ANW; CA 126; CANR 53, 93;
    CSW; DLB 212, 275
Bassani, Giorgio 1916-2000 .... **CLC 9**
    See also CA 65-68; 190; CANR 33; CWW
    2; DLB 128, 177; EWL 3; MTCW 1;
    RGWL 2, 3
Bastian, Ann .... **CLC 70**
Bastos, Augusto (Antonio) Roa
    See Roa Bastos, Augusto (Antonio)
Bataille, Georges 1897-1962 .... **CLC 29**
    See also CA 101; 89-92; EWL 3
Bates, H(erbert) E(rnest)
    1905-1974 .... **CLC 46; SSC 10**
    See also CA 93-96; 45-48; CANR 34; DA3;
    DAB; DAM POP; DLB 162, 191; EWL
    3; EXPS; MTCW 1, 2; RGSF 2; SSFS 7
Bauchart
    See Camus, Albert
Baudelaire, Charles 1821-1867 . **NCLC 6, 29,**
    55; PC 1; SSC 18; WLC
    See also DA; DA3; DAB; DAC; DAM
    MST, POET; DLB 217; EW 7; GFL 1789
    to the Present; LMFS 2; RGWL 2, 3;
    TWA
Baudouin, Marcel
    See Peguy, Charles (Pierre)
Baudouin, Pierre
    See Peguy, Charles (Pierre)
Baudrillard, Jean 1929- .... **CLC 60**
Baum, L(yman) Frank 1856-1919 .. **TCLC 7,**
    132
    See also AAYA 46; CA 108; 133; CLR 15;
    CWRI 5; DLB 22; FANT; JRDA; MAI-
    CYA 1, 2; MTCW 1, 2; NFS 13; RGAL
    4; SATA 18, 100; WCH
Baum, Louis F.
    See Baum, L(yman) Frank
Baumbach, Jonathan 1933- .... **CLC 6, 23**
    See also CA 13-16R; CAAS 5; CANR 12,
    66; CN 7; DLBY 1980; INT CANR-12;
    MTCW 1
Bausch, Richard (Carl) 1945- .... **CLC 51**
    See also AMWS 7; CA 101; CAAS 14;
    CANR 43, 61, 87; CSW; DLB 130
Baxter, Charles (Morley) 1947- . **CLC 45, 78**
    See also CA 57-60; CANR 40, 64, 104;
    CPW; DAM POP; DLB 130; MTCW 2
Baxter, George Owen
    See Faust, Frederick (Schiller)
Baxter, James K(eir) 1926-1972 .... **CLC 14**
    See also CA 77-80; EWL 3
Baxter, John
    See Hunt, E(verette) Howard, (Jr.)
Bayer, Sylvia
    See Glassco, John
Baynton, Barbara 1857-1929 .... **TCLC 57**
    See also DLB 230; RGSF 2
Beagle, Peter S(oyer) 1939- .... **CLC 7, 104**
    See also AAYA 47; BPFB 1; BYA 9, 10;
    CA 9-12R; CANR 4, 51, 73, 110; DA3;
    DLBY 1980; FANT; INT CANR-4;
    MTCW 1; SATA 60, 130; SUFW 1, 2;
    YAW
Bean, Normal
    See Burroughs, Edgar Rice

Beard, Charles A(ustin)
    1874-1948 .... **TCLC 15**
    See also CA 115; 189; DLB 17; SATA 18
Beardsley, Aubrey 1872-1898 .... **NCLC 6**
Beattie, Ann 1947- ..... **CLC 8, 13, 18, 40, 63,**
    146; SSC 11
    See also AMWS 5; BEST 90:2; BPFB 1;
    CA 81-84; CANR 53, 73; CN 7; CPW;
    DA3; DAM NOV, POP; DLB 218, 278;
    DLBY 1982; EWL 3; MTCW 1, 2; RGAL
    4; RGSF 2; SSFS 9; TUS
Beattie, James 1735-1803 .... **NCLC 25**
    See also DLB 109
Beauchamp, Kathleen Mansfield 1888-1923
    See Mansfield, Katherine
    See also CA 104; 134; DA; DA3; DAC;
    DAM MST; MTCW 2; TEA
Beaumarchais, Pierre-Augustin Caron de
    1732-1799 .... **DC 4; LC 61**
    See also DAM DRAM; DFS 14, 16; EW 4;
    GFL Beginnings to 1789; RGWL 2, 3
Beaumont, Francis 1584(?)-1616 .. **DC 6; LC**
    33
    See also BRW 2; CDBLB Before 1660;
    DLB 58; TEA
Beauvoir, Simone (Lucie Ernestine Marie
    Bertrand) de 1908-1986 .... **CLC 1, 2, 4,**
    8, 14, 31, 44, 50, 71, 124; SSC 35;
    WLC
    See also BPFB 1; CA 9-12R; 118; CANR
    28, 61; DA; DA3; DAB; DAC; DAM
    MST, NOV; DLB 72; EW 12; EWL 3; FW; GFL 1789 to the Present;
    LMFS 2; MTCW 1, 2; RGSF 2; RGWL
    2, 3; TWA
Becker, Carl (Lotus) 1873-1945 ..... **TCLC 63**
    See also CA 157; DLB 17
Becker, Jurek 1937-1997 .... **CLC 7, 19**
    See also CA 85-88; 157; CANR 60, 117;
    CWW 2; DLB 75; EWL 3
Becker, Walter 1950- .... **CLC 26**
Beckett, Samuel (Barclay)
    1906-1989 .. **CLC 1, 2, 3, 4, 6, 9, 10, 11,**
    14, 18, 29, 57, 59, 83; SSC 16; WLC
    See also BRWR 1; BRWS 1; CA 5-8R; 130;
    CANR 33, 61; CBD; CDBLB 1945-1960;
    DA; DA3; DAB; DAC; DAM DRAM,
    MST, NOV; DFS 2, 7; DLB 13, 15, 233;
    DLBY 1990; EWL 3; GFL 1789 to the
    Present; LATS 1; LMFS 2; MTCW 1, 2;
    RGSF 2; RGWL 2, 3; SSFS 15; TEA;
    WLIT 4
Beckford, William 1760-1844 .... **NCLC 16**
    See also BRW 3; DLB 39, 213; HGG;
    LMFS 1; SUFW
Beckham, Barry (Earl) 1944- .... **BLC 1**
    See also BW 1; CA 29-32R; CANR 26, 62;
    CN 7; DAM MULT; DLB 33
Beckman, Gunnel 1910- .... **CLC 26**
    See also CA 33-36R; CANR 15, 114; CLR
    25; MAICYA 1, 2; SAAS 9; SATA 6
Becque, Henri 1837-1899 .... **DC 21; NCLC 3**
    See also DLB 192; GFL 1789 to the Present
Becquer, Gustavo Adolfo
    1836-1870 .... **HLCS 1; NCLC 106**
    See also DAM MULT
Beddoes, Thomas Lovell 1803-1849 .. **DC 15;**
    NCLC 3
    See also DLB 96
Bede c. 673-735 .... **CMLC 20**
    See also DLB 146; TEA
Bedford, Denton R. 1907-(?) .... **NNAL**
Bedford, Donald F.
    See Fearing, Kenneth (Flexner)
Beecher, Catharine Esther
    1800-1878 .... **NCLC 30**
    See also DLB 1, 243
Beecher, John 1904-1980 .... **CLC 6**
    See also AITN 1; CA 5-8R; 105; CANR 8

Beresford, J(ohn) D(avys)
1873-1947 .... **TCLC 81**
See also CA 112; 155; DLB 162, 178, 197;
SFW 4; SUFW 1

Bergelson, David 1884-1952 .... **TCLC 81**
See Bergelson, Dovid

Bergelson, Dovid
See Bergelson, David
See also EWL 3

Berger, Colonel
See Malraux, (Georges-)Andre

Berger, John (Peter) 1926- .... **CLC 2, 19**
See also BRWS 4; CA 81-84; CANR 51,
78, 117; CN 7; DLB 14, 207

Berger, Melvin H. 1927- .... **CLC 12**
See also CA 5-8R; CANR 4; CLR 32;
SAAS 2; SATA 5, 88; SATA-Essay 124

Berger, Thomas (Louis) 1924- .. **CLC 3, 5, 8,
11, 18, 38**
See also BPFB 1; CA 1-4R; CANR 5, 28,
51; CN 7; DAM NOV; DLB 2; DLBY
1980; EWL 3; FANT; INT CANR-28;
MTCW 1, 2; RHW; TCWW 2

Bergman, (Ernst) Ingmar 1918- ...... **CLC 16,
72**
See also CA 81-84; CANR 33, 70; DLB
257; MTCW 2

Bergson, Henri(-Louis) 1859-1941 . **TCLC 32**
See also CA 164; EW 8; EWL 3; GFL 1789
to the Present

Bergstein, Eleanor 1938- .... **CLC 4**
See also CA 53-56; CANR 5

Berkeley, George 1685-1753 .... **LC 65**
See also DLB 31, 101, 252

Berkoff, Steven 1937- .... **CLC 56**
See also CA 104; CANR 72; CBD; CD 5

Berlin, Isaiah 1909-1997 .... **TCLC 105**
See also CA 85-88; 162

Bermant, Chaim (Icyk) 1929-1998 ... **CLC 40**
See also CA 57-60; CANR 6, 31, 57, 105;
CN 7

Bern, Victoria
See Fisher, M(ary) F(rances) K(ennedy)

Bernanos, (Paul Louis) Georges
1888-1948 .... **TCLC 3**
See also CA 104; 130; CANR 94; DLB 72;
EWL 3; GFL 1789 to the Present; RGWL
2, 3

Bernard, April 1956- .... **CLC 59**
See also CA 131

Berne, Victoria
See Fisher, M(ary) F(rances) K(ennedy)

Bernhard, Thomas 1931-1989 ..... **CLC 3, 32,
61; DC 14**
See also CA 85-88; 127; CANR 32, 57; CD-
WLB 2; DLB 85, 124; EWL 3; MTCW 1;
RGWL 2, 3

Bernhardt, Sarah (Henriette Rosine)
1844-1923 .... **TCLC 75**
See also CA 157

Bernstein, Charles 1950- .... **CLC 142**
See also CA 129; CAAS 24; CANR 90; CP
7; DLB 169

Berriault, Gina 1926-1999 .... **CLC 54, 109;
SSC 30**
See also CA 116; 129; 185; CANR 66; DLB
130; SSFS 7,11

Berrigan, Daniel 1921- .... **CLC 4**
See also CA 33-36R; CAAE 187; CAAS 1;
CANR 11, 43, 78; CP 7; DLB 5

Berrigan, Edmund Joseph Michael, Jr.
1934-1983
See Berrigan, Ted
See also CA 61-64; 110; CANR 14, 102

Berrigan, Ted .... **CLC 37**
See Berrigan, Edmund Joseph Michael, Jr.
See also DLB 5, 169; WP

Berry, Charles Edward Anderson 1931-
See Berry, Chuck
See also CA 115

Berry, Chuck .... **CLC 17**
See Berry, Charles Edward Anderson

Berry, Jonas
See Ashbery, John (Lawrence)
See also GLL 1

Berry, Wendell (Erdman) 1934- ... **CLC 4, 6,
8, 27, 46; PC 28**
See also AITN 1; AMWS 10; ANW; CA
73-76; CANR 50, 73, 101; CP 7; CSW;
DAM POET; DLB 5, 6, 234, 275; MTCW
1

Berryman, John 1914-1972 ... **CLC 1, 2, 3, 4,
6, 8, 10, 13, 25, 62**
See also AMW; CA 13-16; 33-36R; CABS
2; CANR 35; CAP 1; CDALB 1941-1968;
DAM POET; DLB 48; EWL 3; MTCW 1,
2; PAB; RGAL 4; WP

Bertolucci, Bernardo 1940- ...... **CLC 16, 157**
See also CA 106

Berton, Pierre (Francis Demarigny)
1920- .... **CLC 104**
See also CA 1-4R; CANR 2, 56; CPW;
DLB 68; SATA 99

Bertrand, Aloysius 1807-1841 .... **NCLC 31**
See Bertrand, Louis oAloysiusc

Bertrand, Louis oAloysiusc
See Bertrand, Aloysius
See also DLB 217

Bertran de Born c. 1140-1215 .... **CMLC 5**

Besant, Annie (Wood) 1847-1933 ..... **TCLC 9**
See also CA 105; 185

Bessie, Alvah 1904-1985 .... **CLC 23**
See also CA 5-8R; 116; CANR 2, 80; DLB
26

Bethlen, T. D.
See Silverberg, Robert

Beti, Mongo .... **BLC 1; CLC 27**
See Biyidi, Alexandre
See also AFW; CANR 79; DAM MULT;
EWL 3; WLIT 2

Betjeman, John 1906-1984 ...... **CLC 2, 6, 10,
34, 43**
See also BRW 7; CA 9-12R; 112; CANR
33, 56; CDBLB 1945-1960; DA3; DAB;
DAM MST, POET; DLB 20; DLBY 1984;
EWL 3; MTCW 1, 2

Bettelheim, Bruno 1903-1990 .... **CLC 79**
See also CA 81-84; 131; CANR 23, 61;
DA3; MTCW 1, 2

Betti, Ugo 1892-1953 .... **TCLC 5**
See also CA 104; 155; EWL 3; RGWL 2, 3

Betts, Doris (Waugh) 1932- ..... **CLC 3, 6, 28;
SSC 45**
See also CA 13-16R; CANR 9, 66, 77; CN
7; CSW; DLB 218; DLBY 1982; INT
CANR-9; RGAL 4

Bevan, Alistair
See Roberts, Keith (John Kingston)

Bey, Pilaff
See Douglas, (George) Norman

Bialik, Chaim Nachman
1873-1934 .... **TCLC 25**
See also CA 170; EWL 3

Bickerstaff, Isaac
See Swift, Jonathan

Bidart, Frank 1939- .... **CLC 33**
See also CA 140; CANR 106; CP 7

Bienek, Horst 1930- .... **CLC 7, 11**
See also CA 73-76; DLB 75

Bierce, Ambrose (Gwinett)
1842-1914(?) ..... **SSC 9; TCLC 1, 7, 44;
WLC**
See also AMW; BYA 11; CA 104; 139;
CANR 78; CDALB 1865-1917; DA;
DA3; DAC; DAM MST; DLB 11, 12, 23,
71, 74, 186; EWL 3; EXPS; HGG; LAIT
2; RGAL 4; RGSF 2; SSFS 9; SUFW 1

Biggers, Earl Derr 1884-1933 .... **TCLC 65**
See also CA 108; 153

Billiken, Bud
See Motley, Willard (Francis)

Billings, Josh
See Shaw, Henry Wheeler

Billington, (Lady) Rachel (Mary)
1942- .... **CLC 43**
See also AITN 2; CA 33-36R; CANR 44;
CN 7

Binchy, Maeve 1940- .... **CLC 153**
See also BEST 90:1; BPFB 1; CA 127; 134;
CANR 50, 96; CN 7; CPW; DA3; DAM
POP; INT CA-134; MTCW 1; RHW

Binyon, T(imothy) J(ohn) 1936- .... **CLC 34**
See also CA 111; CANR 28

Bion 335B.C.-245B.C. .... **CMLC 39**

Bioy Casares, Adolfo 1914-1999 ... **CLC 4, 8,
13, 88; HLC 1; SSC 17**
See Casares, Adolfo Bioy; Miranda, Javier;
Sacastru, Martin
See also CA 29-32R; 177; CANR 19, 43,
66; DAM MULT; DLB 113; EWL 3; HW
1, 2; LAW; MTCW 1, 2

Birch, Allison .... **CLC 65**

Bird, Cordwainer
See Ellison, Harlan (Jay)

Bird, Robert Montgomery
1806-1854 .... **NCLC 1**
See also DLB 202; RGAL 4

Birkerts, Sven 1951- .... **CLC 116**
See also CA 128; 133, 176; CAAE 176;
CAAS 29; INT 133

Birney, (Alfred) Earle 1904-1995 .. **CLC 1, 4,
6, 11**
See also CA 1-4R; CANR 5, 20; CP 7;
DAC; DAM MST, POET; DLB 88;
MTCW 1; PFS 8; RGEL 2

Biruni, al 973-1048(?) .... **CMLC 28**

Bishop, Elizabeth 1911-1979 ..... **CLC 1, 4, 9,
13, 15, 32; PC 3, 34; TCLC 121**
See also AMWR 2; AMWS 1; CA 5-8R;
89-92; CABS 2; CANR 26, 61, 108;
CDALB 1968-1988; DA; DA3; DAC;
DAM MST, POET; DLB 5, 169; EWL 3;
GLL 2; MAWW; MTCW 1, 2; PAB; PFS
6, 12; RGAL 4; SATA-Obit 24; TUS; WP

Bishop, John 1935- .... **CLC 10**
See also CA 105

Bishop, John Peale 1892-1944 ..... **TCLC 103**
See also CA 107; 155; DLB 4, 9, 45; RGAL
4

Bissett, Bill 1939- .... **CLC 18; PC 14**
See also CA 69-72; CAAS 19; CANR 15;
CCA 1; CP 7; DLB 53; MTCW 1

Bissoondath, Neil (Devindra)
1955- .... **CLC 120**
See also CA 136; CN 7; DAC

Bitov, Andrei (Georgievich) 1937- ... **CLC 57**
See also CA 142

Biyidi, Alexandre 1932-
See Beti, Mongo
See also BW 1, 3; CA 114; 124; CANR 81;
DA3; MTCW 1, 2

Bjarme, Brynjolf
See Ibsen, Henrik (Johan)

Bjoernson, Bjoernstjerne (Martinius)
1832-1910 .... **TCLC 7, 37**
See also CA 104

Black, Robert
See Holdstock, Robert P.

Blackburn, Paul 1926-1971 .... **CLC 9, 43**
See also BG 2; CA 81-84; 33-36R; CANR
34; DLB 16; DLBY 1981

Black Elk 1863-1950 .... **NNAL; TCLC 33**
See also CA 144; DAM MULT; MTCW 1;
WP

Black Hawk 1767-1838 .... **NNAL**

Bontemps, Arna(ud Wendell)
1902-1973 ..... **BLC 1; CLC 1, 18; HR 2**
See also BW 1; CA 1-4R; 41-44R; CANR
4, 35; CLR 6; CWRI 5; DA3; DAM
MULT, NOV, POET; DLB 48, 51; JRDA;
MAICYA 1, 2; MTCW 1, 2; SATA 2, 44;
SATA-Obit 24; WCH; WP

Booth, Martin 1944- .... **CLC 13**
See also CA 93-96; CAAE 188; CAAS 2;
CANR 92

Booth, Philip 1925- .... **CLC 23**
See also CA 5-8R; CANR 5, 88; CP 7;
DLBY 1982

Booth, Wayne C(layson) 1921- .... **CLC 24**
See also CA 1-4R; CAAS 5; CANR 3, 43,
117; DLB 67

Borchert, Wolfgang 1921-1947 .... **TCLC 5**
See also CA 104; 188; DLB 69, 124; EWL
3

Borel, Petrus 1809-1859 .... **NCLC 41**
See also DLB 119; GFL 1789 to the Present

Borges, Jorge Luis 1899-1986 ... **CLC 1, 2, 3,
4, 6, 8, 9, 10, 13, 19, 44, 48, 83; HLC 1;
PC 22, 32; SSC 4, 41; TCLC 109;
WLC**
See also AAYA 26; BPFB 1; CA 21-24R;
CANR 19, 33, 75, 105; CDWLB 3; DA;
DA3; DAB; DAC; DAM MST, MULT;
DLB 113, 283; DLBY 1986; DNFS 1, 2;
EWL 3; HW 1, 2; LAW; LMFS 2; MSW;
MTCW 1, 2; RGSF 2; RGWL 2, 3; SFW
4; SSFS 17; TWA; WLIT 1

Borowski, Tadeusz 1922-1951 .... **SSC 48;
TCLC 9**
See also CA 106; 154; CDWLB 4; DLB
215; EWL 3; RGSF 2; RGWL 3; SSFS
13

Borrow, George (Henry)
1803-1881 .... **NCLC 9**
See also DLB 21, 55, 166

Bosch (Gavino), Juan 1909-2001 ..... **HLCS 1**
See also CA 151; 204; DAM MST, MULT;
DLB 145; HW 1, 2

Bosman, Herman Charles
1905-1951 .... **TCLC 49**
See Malan, Herman
See also CA 160; DLB 225; RGSF 2

Bosschere, Jean de 1878(?)-1953 ... **TCLC 19**
See also CA 115; 186

Boswell, James 1740-1795 ... **LC 4, 50; WLC**
See also BRW 3; CDBLB 1660-1789; DA;
DAB; DAC; DAM MST; DLB 104, 142;
TEA; WLIT 3

Bottomley, Gordon 1874-1948 ..... **TCLC 107**
See also CA 120; 192; DLB 10

Bottoms, David 1949- .... **CLC 53**
See also CA 105; CANR 22; CSW; DLB
120; DLBY 1983

Boucicault, Dion 1820-1890 .... **NCLC 41**

Boucolon, Maryse
See Conde, Maryse

Bourget, Paul (Charles Joseph)
1852-1935 .... **TCLC 12**
See also CA 107; 196; DLB 123; GFL 1789
to the Present

Bourjaily, Vance (Nye) 1922- .... **CLC 8, 62**
See also CA 1-4R; CAAS 1; CANR 2, 72;
CN 7; DLB 2, 143

Bourne, Randolph S(illiman)
1886-1918 .... **TCLC 16**
See also AMW; CA 117; 155; DLB 63

Bova, Ben(jamin William) 1932- ...... **CLC 45**
See also AAYA 16; CA 5-8R; CAAS 18;
CANR 11, 56, 94, 111; CLR 3; DLBY
1981; INT CANR-11; MAICYA 1, 2;
MTCW 1; SATA 6, 68, 133; SFW 4

Bowen, Elizabeth (Dorothea Cole)
1899-1973 . **CLC 1, 3, 6, 11, 15, 22, 118;
SSC 3, 28**
See also BRWS 2; CA 17-18; 41-44R;
CANR 35, 105; CAP 2; CDBLB 1945-
1960; DA3; DAM NOV; DLB 15, 162;
EWL 3; EXPS; FW; HGG; MTCW 1, 2;
NFS 13; RGSF 2; SSFS 5; SUFW 1;
TEA; WLIT 4

Bowering, George 1935- .... **CLC 15, 47**
See also CA 21-24R; CAAS 16; CANR 10;
CP 7; DLB 53

Bowering, Marilyn R(uthe) 1949- .... **CLC 32**
See also CA 101; CANR 49; CP 7; CWP

Bowers, Edgar 1924-2000 .... **CLC 9**
See also CA 5-8R; 188; CANR 24; CP 7;
CSW; DLB 5

Bowers, Mrs. J. Milton 1842-1914
See Bierce, Ambrose (Gwinett)

Bowie, David .... **CLC 17**
See Jones, David Robert

Bowles, Jane (Sydney) 1917-1973 ..... **CLC 3,
68**
See Bowles, Jane Auer
See also CA 19-20; 41-44R; CAP 2

Bowles, Jane Auer
See Bowles, Jane (Sydney)
See also EWL 3

Bowles, Paul (Frederick) 1910-1999 . **CLC 1,
2, 19, 53; SSC 3**
See also AMWS 4; CA 1-4R; 186; CAAS
1; CANR 1, 19, 50, 75; CN 7; DA3; DLB
5, 6, 218; EWL 3; MTCW 1, 2; RGAL 4;
SSFS 17

Bowles, William Lisle 1762-1850 . **NCLC 103**
See also DLB 93

Box, Edgar
See Vidal, Gore
See also GLL 1

Boyd, James 1888-1944 .... **TCLC 115**
See also CA 186; DLB 9; DLBD 16; RGAL
4; RHW

Boyd, Nancy
See Millay, Edna St. Vincent
See also GLL 1

Boyd, Thomas (Alexander)
1898-1935 .... **TCLC 111**
See also CA 111; 183; DLB 9; DLBD 16

Boyd, William 1952- .... **CLC 28, 53, 70**
See also CA 114; 120; CANR 51, 71; CN
7; DLB 231

Boyle, Kay 1902-1992 .... **CLC 1, 5, 19, 58,
121; SSC 5**
See also CA 13-16R; 140; CAAS 1; CANR
29, 61, 110; DLB 4, 9, 48, 86; DLBY
1993; EWL 3; MTCW 1, 2; RGAL 4;
RGSF 2; SSFS 10, 13, 14

Boyle, Mark
See Kienzle, William X(avier)

Boyle, Patrick 1905-1982 .... **CLC 19**
See also CA 127

Boyle, T. C.
See Boyle, T(homas) Coraghessan
See also AMWS 8

Boyle, T(homas) Coraghessan
1948- .... **CLC 36, 55, 90; SSC 16**
See Boyle, T. C.
See also AAYA 47; BEST 90:4; BPFB 1;
CA 120; CANR 44, 76, 89; CN 7; CPW;
DA3; DAM POP; DLB 218, 278; DLBY
1986; EWL 3; MTCW 2; SSFS 13

Boz
See Dickens, Charles (John Huffam)

Brackenridge, Hugh Henry
1748-1816 .... **NCLC 7**
See also DLB 11, 37; RGAL 4

Bradbury, Edward P.
See Moorcock, Michael (John)
See also MTCW 2

Bradbury, Malcolm (Stanley)
1932-2000 .... **CLC 32, 61**
See also CA 1-4R; CANR 1, 33, 91, 98;
CN 7; DA3; DAM NOV; DLB 14, 207;
EWL 3; MTCW 1, 2

Bradbury, Ray (Douglas) 1920- .... **CLC 1, 3,
10, 15, 42, 98; SSC 29, 53; WLC**
See also AAYA 15; AITN 1, 2; AMWS 4;
BPFB 1; BYA 4, 5, 11; CA 1-4R; CANR
2, 30, 75; CDALB 1968-1988; CN 7;
CPW; DA; DA3; DAB; DAC; DAM MST,
NOV, POP; DLB 2, 8; EXPN; EXPS;
HGG; LAIT 3, 5; LATS 1; LMFS 2;
MTCW 1, 2; NFS 1; RGAL 4; RGSF 2;
SATA 11, 64, 123; SCFW 2; SFW 4;
SSFS 1; SUFW 1, 2; TUS; YAW

Braddon, Mary Elizabeth
1837-1915 .... **TCLC 111**
See also BRWS 8; CA 108; 179; CMW 4;
DLB 18, 70, 156; HGG

Bradford, Gamaliel 1863-1932 .... **TCLC 36**
See also CA 160; DLB 17

Bradford, William 1590-1657 .... **LC 64**
See also DLB 24, 30; RGAL 4

Bradley, David (Henry), Jr. 1950- .... **BLC 1;
CLC 23, 118**
See also BW 1, 3; CA 104; CANR 26, 81;
CN 7; DAM MULT; DLB 33

Bradley, John Ed(mund, Jr.) 1958- . **CLC 55**
See also CA 139; CANR 99; CN 7; CSW

Bradley, Marion Zimmer
1930-1999 .... **CLC 30**
See Chapman, Lee; Dexter, John; Gardner,
Miriam; Ives, Morgan; Rivers, Elfrida
See also AAYA 40; BPFB 1; CA 57-60; 185;
CAAS 10; CANR 7, 31, 51, 75, 107;
CPW; DA3; DAM POP; DLB 8; FANT;
FW; MTCW 1, 2; SATA 90, 139; SATA-
Obit 116; SFW 4; SUFW 2; YAW

Bradshaw, John 1933- .... **CLC 70**
See also CA 138; CANR 61

Bradstreet, Anne 1612(?)-1672 ...... **LC 4, 30;
PC 10**
See also AMWS 1; CDALB 1640-1865;
DA; DA3; DAC; DAM MST, POET; DLB
24; EXPP; FW; PFS 6; RGAL 4; TUS;
WP

Brady, Joan 1939- .... **CLC 86**
See also CA 141

Bragg, Melvyn 1939- .... **CLC 10**
See also BEST 89:3; CA 57-60; CANR 10,
48, 89; CN 7; DLB 14, 271; RHW

Brahe, Tycho 1546-1601 .... **LC 45**

Braine, John (Gerard) 1922-1986 . **CLC 1, 3,
41**
See also CA 1-4R; 120; CANR 1, 33; CD-
BLB 1945-1960; DLB 15; DLBY 1986;
EWL 3; MTCW 1

Braithwaite, William Stanley (Beaumont)
1878-1962 .... **BLC 1; HR 2**
See also BW 1; CA 125; DAM MULT; DLB
50, 54

Bramah, Ernest 1868-1942 .... **TCLC 72**
See also CA 156; CMW 4; DLB 70; FANT

Brammer, William 1930(?)-1978 ...... **CLC 31**
See also CA 77-80

Brancati, Vitaliano 1907-1954 .... **TCLC 12**
See also CA 109; DLB 264; EWL 3

Brancato, Robin F(idler) 1936- .... **CLC 35**
See also AAYA 9; BYA 6; CA 69-72; CANR
11, 45; CLR 32; JRDA; MAICYA 2;
MAICYAS 1; SAAS 9; SATA 97; WYA;
YAW

Brand, Max
See Faust, Frederick (Schiller)
See also BPFB 1; TCWW 2

Brand, Millen 1906-1980 .... **CLC 7**
See also CA 21-24R; 97-100; CANR 72

Caldwell, (Janet Miriam) Taylor (Holland)
1900-1985 .... **CLC 2, 28, 39**
See also BPFB 1; CA 5-8R; 116; CANR 5;
DA3; DAM NOV, POP; DLBD 17; RHW

Calhoun, John Caldwell
1782-1850 .... **NCLC 15**
See also DLB 3, 248

Calisher, Hortense 1911- ..... **CLC 2, 4, 8, 38, 134; SSC 15**
See also CA 1-4R; CANR 1, 22, 117; CN
7; DA3; DAM NOV; DLB 2, 218; INT
CANR-22; MTCW 1, 2; RGAL 4; RGSF
2

Callaghan, Morley Edward
1903-1990 .... **CLC 3, 14, 41, 65**
See also CA 9-12R; 132; CANR 33, 73;
DAC; DAM MST; DLB 68; EWL 3;
MTCW 1, 2; RGEL 2; RGSF 2

Callimachus c. 305B.C.-c.
240B.C. .... **CMLC 18**
See also AW 1; DLB 176; RGWL 2, 3

Calvin, Jean
See Calvin, John
See also GFL Beginnings to 1789

Calvin, John 1509-1564 .... **LC 37**
See Calvin, Jean

Calvino, Italo 1923-1985 .... **CLC 5, 8, 11, 22, 33, 39, 73; SSC 3, 48**
See also CA 85-88; 116; CANR 23, 61;
DAM NOV; DLB 196; EW 13; EWL 3;
MTCW 1, 2; RGSF 2; RGWL 2, 3; SFW
4; SSFS 12

Camara Laye
See Laye, Camara
See also EWL 3

Camden, William 1551-1623 .... **LC 77**
See also DLB 172

Cameron, Carey 1952- .... **CLC 59**
See also CA 135

Cameron, Peter 1959- .... **CLC 44**
See also AMWS 12; CA 125; CANR 50,
117; DLB 234; GLL 2

Camoens, Luis Vaz de 1524(?)-1580
See Camoes, Luis de
See also EW 2

Camoes, Luis de 1524(?)-1580 . **HLCS 1; LC 62; PC 31**
See Camoens, Luis Vaz de
See also RGWL 2, 3

Campana, Dino 1885-1932 .... **TCLC 20**
See also CA 117; DLB 114; EWL 3

Campanella, Tommaso 1568-1639 .... **LC 32**
See also RGWL 2, 3

Campbell, John W(ood, Jr.)
1910-1971 .... **CLC 32**
See also CA 21-22; 29-32R; CANR 34;
CAP 2; DLB 8; MTCW 1; SCFW; SFW 4

Campbell, Joseph 1904-1987 .... **CLC 69**
See also AAYA 3; BEST 89:2; CA 1-4R;
124; CANR 3, 28, 61, 107; DA3; MTCW
1, 2

Campbell, Maria 1940- .... **CLC 85; NNAL**
See also CA 102; CANR 54; CCA 1; DAC

Campbell, Paul N. 1923-
See hooks, bell
See also CA 21-24R

Campbell, (John) Ramsey 1946- ..... **CLC 42; SSC 19**
See also AAYA 51; CA 57-60; CANR 7,
102; DLB 261; HGG; INT CANR-7;
SUFW 1, 2

Campbell, (Ignatius) Roy (Dunnachie)
1901-1957 .... **TCLC 5**
See also AFW; CA 104; 155; DLB 20, 225;
EWL 3; MTCW 2; RGEL 2

Campbell, Thomas 1777-1844 .... **NCLC 19**
See also DLB 93, 144; RGEL 2

Campbell, Wilfred .... **TCLC 9**
See Campbell, William

Campbell, William 1858(?)-1918
See Campbell, Wilfred
See also CA 106; DLB 92

Campion, Jane 1954- .... **CLC 95**
See also AAYA 33; CA 138; CANR 87

Campion, Thomas 1567-1620 .... **LC 78**
See also CDBLB Before 1660; DAM POET;
DLB 58, 172; RGEL 2

Camus, Albert 1913-1960 ...... **CLC 1, 2, 4, 9, 11, 14, 32, 63, 69, 124; DC 2; SSC 9; WLC**
See also AAYA 36; AFW; BPFB 1; CA 89-
92; DA; DA3; DAB; DAC; DAM DRAM,
MST, NOV; DLB 72; EW 13; EWL 3;
EXPN; EXPS; GFL 1789 to the Present;
LATS 1; LMFS 2; MTCW 1, 2; NFS 6,
16; RGSF 2; RGWL 2, 3; SSFS 4; TWA

Canby, Vincent 1924-2000 .... **CLC 13**
See also CA 81-84; 191

Cancale
See Desnos, Robert

Canetti, Elias 1905-1994 .. **CLC 3, 14, 25, 75, 86**
See also CA 21-24R; 146; CANR 23, 61;
79; CDWLB 2; CWW 2; DA3; DLB 85,
124; EW 12; EWL 3; MTCW 1, 2; RGWL
2, 3; TWA

Canfield, Dorothea F.
See Fisher, Dorothy (Frances) Canfield

Canfield, Dorothea Frances
See Fisher, Dorothy (Frances) Canfield

Canfield, Dorothy
See Fisher, Dorothy (Frances) Canfield

Canin, Ethan 1960- .... **CLC 55**
See also CA 131; 135

Cankar, Ivan 1876-1918 .... **TCLC 105**
See also CDWLB 4; DLB 147; EWL 3

Cannon, Curt
See Hunter, Evan

Cao, Lan 1961- .... **CLC 109**
See also CA 165

Cape, Judith
See Page, P(atricia) K(athleen)
See also CCA 1

Capek, Karel 1890-1938 .... **DC 1; SSC 36; TCLC 6, 37; WLC**
See also CA 104; 140; CDWLB 4; DA;
DA3; DAB; DAC; DAM DRAM, MST,
NOV; DFS 7, 11; DLB 215; EW 10; EWL
3; MTCW 1; RGSF 2; RGWL 2, 3; SCFW
2; SFW 4

Capote, Truman 1924-1984 . **CLC 1, 3, 8, 13, 19, 34, 38, 58; SSC 2, 47; WLC**
See also AMWS 3; BPFB 1; CA 5-8R; 113;
CANR 18, 62; CDALB 1941-1968; CPW;
DA; DA3; DAB; DAC; DAM MST, NOV,
POP; DLB 2, 185, 227; DLBY 1980,
1984; EWL 3; EXPS; GLL 1; LAIT 3;
MTCW 1, 2; NCFS 2; RGAL 4; RGSF 2;
SATA 91; SSFS 2; TUS

Capra, Frank 1897-1991 .... **CLC 16**
See also AAYA 52; CA 61-64; 135

Caputo, Philip 1941- .... **CLC 32**
See also CA 73-76; CANR 40; YAW

Caragiale, Ion Luca 1852-1912 ...... **TCLC 76**
See also CA 157

Card, Orson Scott 1951- .... **CLC 44, 47, 50**
See also AAYA 11, 42; BPFB 1; BYA 5, 8;
CA 102; CANR 27, 47, 73, 102, 106;
CPW; DA3; DAM POP; FANT; INT
CANR-27; MTCW 1, 2; NFS 5; SATA
83, 127; SCFW 2; SFW 4; SUFW 2; YAW

Cardenal, Ernesto 1925- .... **CLC 31, 161; HLC 1; PC 22**
See also CA 49-52; CANR 2, 32, 66; CWW
2; DAM MULT, POET; EWL 3; HW 1, 2;
LAWS 1; MTCW 1, 2; RGWL 2, 3

Cardozo, Benjamin N(athan)
1870-1938 .... **TCLC 65**
See also CA 117; 164

Carducci, Giosue (Alessandro Giuseppe)
1835-1907 .... **PC 46; TCLC 32**
See also CA 163; EW 7; RGWL 2, 3

Carew, Thomas 1595(?)-1640 . **LC 13; PC 29**
See also BRW 2; DLB 126; PAB; RGEL 2

Carey, Ernestine Gilbreth 1908- ...... **CLC 17**
See also CA 5-8R; CANR 71; SATA 2

Carey, Peter 1943- .... **CLC 40, 55, 96**
See also CA 123; 127; CANR 53, 76, 117;
CN 7; EWL 3; INT CA-127; MTCW 1, 2;
RGSF 2; SATA 94

Carleton, William 1794-1869 .... **NCLC 3**
See also DLB 159; RGEL 2; RGSF 2

Carlisle, Henry (Coffin) 1926- .... **CLC 33**
See also CA 13-16R; CANR 15, 85

Carlsen, Chris
See Holdstock, Robert P.

Carlson, Ron(ald F.) 1947- .... **CLC 54**
See also CA 105; CAAE 189; CANR 27;
DLB 244

Carlyle, Thomas 1795-1881 ..... **NCLC 22, 70**
See also BRW 4; CDBLB 1789-1832; DA;
DAB; DAC; DAM MST; DLB 55, 144,
254; RGEL 2; TEA

Carman, (William) Bliss 1861-1929 ... **PC 34; TCLC 7**
See also CA 104; 152; DAC; DLB 92;
RGEL 2

Carnegie, Dale 1888-1955 .... **TCLC 53**

Carossa, Hans 1878-1956 .... **TCLC 48**
See also CA 170; DLB 66; EWL 3

Carpenter, Don(ald Richard)
1931-1995 .... **CLC 41**
See also CA 45-48; 149; CANR 1, 71

Carpenter, Edward 1844-1929 .... **TCLC 88**
See also CA 163; GLL 1

Carpenter, John (Howard) 1948- ... **CLC 161**
See also AAYA 2; CA 134; SATA 58

Carpenter, Johnny
See Carpenter, John (Howard)

Carpentier (y Valmont), Alejo
1904-1980 . **CLC 8, 11, 38, 110; HLC 1; SSC 35**
See also CA 65-68; 97-100; CANR 11, 70;
CDWLB 3; DAM MULT; DLB 113; EWL
3; HW 1, 2; LAW; LMFS 2; RGSF 2;
RGWL 2, 3; WLIT 1

Carr, Caleb 1955(?)- .... **CLC 86**
See also CA 147; CANR 73; DA3

Carr, Emily 1871-1945 .... **TCLC 32**
See also CA 159; DLB 68; FW; GLL 2

Carr, John Dickson 1906-1977 .... **CLC 3**
See Fairbairn, Roger
See also CA 49-52; 69-72; CANR 3, 33,
60; CMW 4; MSW; MTCW 1, 2

Carr, Philippa
See Hibbert, Eleanor Alice Burford

Carr, Virginia Spencer 1929- .... **CLC 34**
See also CA 61-64; DLB 111

Carrere, Emmanuel 1957- .... **CLC 89**
See also CA 200

Carrier, Roch 1937- .... **CLC 13, 78**
See also CA 130; CANR 61; CCA 1; DAC;
DAM MST; DLB 53; SATA 105

Carroll, James Dennis
See Carroll, Jim

Carroll, James P. 1943(?)- .... **CLC 38**
See also CA 81-84; CANR 73; MTCW 1

Carroll, Jim 1951- .... **CLC 35, 143**
See Carroll, James Dennis
See also AAYA 17; CA 45-48; CANR 42,
115

Chairil Anwar
See Anwar, Chairil
See also EWL 3

Challans, Mary 1905-1983
See Renault, Mary
See also CA 81-84; 111; CANR 74; DA3;
MTCW 2; SATA 23; SATA-Obit 36; TEA

Challis, George
See Faust, Frederick (Schiller)
See also TCWW 2

Chambers, Aidan 1934- .... **CLC 35**
See also AAYA 27; CA 25-28R; CANR 12,
31, 58, 116; JRDA; MAICYA 1, 2; SAAS
12; SATA 1, 69, 108; WYA; YAW

Chambers, James 1948-
See Cliff, Jimmy
See also CA 124

Chambers, Jessie
See Lawrence, D(avid) H(erbert Richards)
See also GLL 1

Chambers, Robert W(illiam)
1865-1933 .... **TCLC 41**
See also CA 165; DLB 202; HGG; SATA
107; SUFW 1

Chambers, (David) Whittaker
1901-1961 .... **TCLC 129**
See also CA 89-92

Chamisso, Adelbert von
1781-1838 .... **NCLC 82**
See also DLB 90; RGWL 2, 3; SUFW 1

Chance, James T.
See Carpenter, John (Howard)

Chance, John T.
See Carpenter, John (Howard)

Chandler, Raymond (Thornton)
1888-1959 .... **SSC 23; TCLC 1, 7**
See also AAYA 25; AMWS 4; BPFB 1; CA
104; 129; CANR 60, 107; CDALB 1929-
1941; CMW 4; DA3; DLB 226, 253;
DLBD 6; EWL 3; MSW; MTCW 1, 2;
NFS 17; RGAL 4; TUS

Chang, Diana 1934- .... **AAL**
See also CWP; EXPP

Chang, Eileen 1921-1995 .... **AAL; SSC 28**
See Chang Ai-Ling
See also CA 166; CWW 2

Chang, Jung 1952- .... **CLC 71**
See also CA 142

Chang Ai-Ling
See Chang, Eileen
See also EWL 3

Channing, William Ellery
1780-1842 .... **NCLC 17**
See also DLB 1, 59, 235; RGAL 4

Chao, Patricia 1955- .... **CLC 119**
See also CA 163

Chaplin, Charles Spencer
1889-1977 .... **CLC 16**
See Chaplin, Charlie
See also CA 81-84; 73-76

Chaplin, Charlie
See Chaplin, Charles Spencer
See also DLB 44

Chapman, George 1559(?)-1634 . **DC 19; LC 22**
See also BRW 1; DAM DRAM; DLB 62,
121; LMFS 1; RGEL 2

Chapman, Graham 1941-1989 .... **CLC 21**
See Monty Python
See also CA 116; 129; CANR 35, 95

Chapman, John Jay 1862-1933 .... **TCLC 7**
See also CA 104; 191

Chapman, Lee
See Bradley, Marion Zimmer
See also GLL 1

Chapman, Walker
See Silverberg, Robert

Chappell, Fred (Davis) 1936- .... **CLC 40, 78, 162**
See also CA 5-8R; CAAE 198; CAAS 4;
CANR 8, 33, 67, 110; CN 7; CP 7; CSW;
DLB 6, 105; HGG

Char, Rene(-Emile) 1907-1988 .... **CLC 9, 11, 14, 55**
See also CA 13-16R; 124; CANR 32; DAM
POET; DLB 258; EWL 3; GFL 1789 to
the Present; MTCW 1, 2; RGWL 2, 3

Charby, Jay
See Ellison, Harlan (Jay)

Chardin, Pierre Teilhard de
See Teilhard de Chardin, (Marie Joseph)
Pierre

Chariton fl. 1st cent. (?)- .... **CMLC 49**

Charlemagne 742-814 .... **CMLC 37**

Charles I 1600-1649 .... **LC 13**

Charriere, Isabelle de 1740-1805 .. **NCLC 66**

Chartier, Emile-Auguste
See Alain

Charyn, Jerome 1937- .... **CLC 5, 8, 18**
See also CA 5-8R; CAAS 1; CANR 7, 61,
101; CMW 4; CN 7; DLBY 1983; MTCW
1

Chase, Adam
See Marlowe, Stephen

Chase, Mary (Coyle) 1907-1981 .... **DC 1**
See also CA 77-80; 105; CAD; CWD; DFS
11; DLB 228; SATA 17; SATA-Obit 29

Chase, Mary Ellen 1887-1973 .... **CLC 2; TCLC 124**
See also CA 13-16; 41-44R; CAP 1; SATA
10

Chase, Nicholas
See Hyde, Anthony
See also CCA 1

Chateaubriand, Francois Rene de
1768-1848 .... **NCLC 3**
See also DLB 119; EW 5; GFL 1789 to the
Present; RGWL 2, 3; TWA

Chatterje, Sarat Chandra 1876-1936(?)
See Chatterji, Saratchandra
See also CA 109

Chatterji, Bankim Chandra
1838-1894 .... **NCLC 19**

Chatterji, Saratchandra .... **TCLC 13**
See Chatterje, Sarat Chandra
See also CA 186; EWL 3

Chatterton, Thomas 1752-1770 .... **LC 3, 54**
See also DAM POET; DLB 109; RGEL 2

Chatwin, (Charles) Bruce
1940-1989 .... **CLC 28, 57, 59**
See also AAYA 4; BEST 90:1; BRWS 4;
CA 85-88; 127; CPW; DAM POP; DLB
194, 204; EWL 3

Chaucer, Daniel
See Ford, Ford Madox
See also RHW

Chaucer, Geoffrey 1340(?)-1400 .. **LC 17, 56; PC 19; WLCS**
See also BRW 1; BRWC 1; BRWR 2; CD-
BLB Before 1660; DA; DA3; DAB;
DAC; DAM MST, POET; DLB 146;
LAIT 1; PAB; PFS 14; RGEL 2; TEA;
WLIT 3; WP

Chavez, Denise (Elia) 1948- .... **HLC 1**
See also CA 131; CANR 56, 81; DAM
MULT; DLB 122; FW; HW 1, 2; MTCW
2

Chaviaras, Strates 1935-
See Haviaras, Stratis
See also CA 105

Chayefsky, Paddy .... **CLC 23**
See Chayefsky, Sidney
See also CAD; DLB 7, 44; DLBY 1981;
RGAL 4

Chayefsky, Sidney 1923-1981
See Chayefsky, Paddy
See also CA 9-12R; 104; CANR 18; DAM
DRAM

Chedid, Andree 1920- .... **CLC 47**
See also CA 145; CANR 95; EWL 3

Cheever, John 1912-1982 ..... **CLC 3, 7, 8, 11, 15, 25, 64; SSC 1, 38, 57; WLC**
See also AMWS 1; BPFB 1; CA 5-8R; 106;
CABS 1; CANR 5, 27, 76; CDALB 1941-
1968; CPW; DA; DA3; DAB; DAC;
DAM MST, NOV, POP; DLB 2, 102, 227;
DLBY 1980, 1982; EWL 3; EXPS; INT
CANR-5; MTCW 1, 2; RGAL 4; RGSF
2; SSFS 2, 14; TUS

Cheever, Susan 1943- .... **CLC 18, 48**
See also CA 103; CANR 27, 51, 92; DLBY
1982; INT CANR-27

Chekhonte, Antosha
See Chekhov, Anton (Pavlovich)

Chekhov, Anton (Pavlovich)
1860-1904 .... **DC 9; SSC 2, 28, 41, 51; TCLC 3, 10, 31, 55, 96; WLC**
See also BYA 14; CA 104; 124; DA; DA3;
DAB; DAC; DAM DRAM, MST; DFS 1,
5, 10, 12; DLB 277; EW 7; EWL 3;
EXPS; LAIT 3; LATS 1; RGSF 2; RGWL
2, 3; SATA 90; SSFS 5, 13, 14; TWA

Cheney, Lynne V. 1941- .... **CLC 70**
See also CA 89-92; CANR 58, 117

Chernyshevsky, Nikolai Gavrilovich
See Chernyshevsky, Nikolay Gavrilovich
See also DLB 238

Chernyshevsky, Nikolay Gavrilovich
1828-1889 .... **NCLC 1**
See Chernyshevsky, Nikolai Gavrilovich

Cherry, Carolyn Janice 1942-
See Cherryh, C. J.
See also CA 65-68; CANR 10

Cherryh, C. J. .... **CLC 35**
See Cherry, Carolyn Janice
See also AAYA 24; BPFB 1; DLBY 1980;
FANT; SATA 93; SCFW 2; SFW 4; YAW

Chesnutt, Charles W(addell)
1858-1932 .... **BLC 1; SSC 7, 54; TCLC 5, 39**
See also AFAW 1, 2; BW 1, 3; CA 106;
125; CANR 76; DAM MULT; DLB 12,
50, 78; EWL 3; MTCW 1, 2; RGAL 4;
RGSF 2; SSFS 11

Chester, Alfred 1929(?)-1971 .... **CLC 49**
See also CA 196; 33-36R; DLB 130

Chesterton, G(ilbert) K(eith)
1874-1936 . **PC 28; SSC 1, 46; TCLC 1, 6, 64**
See also BRW 6; CA 104; 132; CANR 73;
CDBLB 1914-1945; CMW 4; DAM NOV,
POET; DLB 10, 19, 34, 70, 98, 149, 178;
EWL 3; FANT; MSW; MTCW 1, 2;
RGEL 2; RGSF 2; SATA 27; SUFW 1

Chiang, Pin-chin 1904-1986
See Ding Ling
See also CA 118

Chief Joseph 1840-1904 .... **NNAL**
See also CA 152; DA3; DAM MULT

Chief Seattle 1786(?)-1866 .... **NNAL**
See also DA3; DAM MULT

Ch'ien, Chung-shu 1910-1998 .... **CLC 22**
See also CA 130; CANR 73; MTCW 1, 2

Chikamatsu Monzaemon 1653-1724 ... **LC 66**
See also RGWL 2, 3

Child, L. Maria
See Child, Lydia Maria

Child, Lydia Maria 1802-1880 .. **NCLC 6, 73**
See also DLB 1, 74, 243; RGAL 4; SATA
67

Child, Mrs.
See Child, Lydia Maria

Child, Philip 1898-1978 .... **CLC 19, 68**
See also CA 13-14; CAP 1; DLB 68; RHW; SATA 47

Childers, (Robert) Erskine
1870-1922 .... **TCLC 65**
See also CA 113; 153; DLB 70

Childress, Alice 1920-1994 . **BLC 1; CLC 12, 15, 86, 96; DC 4; TCLC 116**
See also AAYA 8; BW 2, 3; BYA 2; CA 45-48; 146; CAD; CANR 3, 27, 50, 74; CLR 14; CWD; DA3; DAM DRAM, MULT, NOV; DFS 2, 8, 14; DLB 7, 38, 249; JRDA; LAIT 5; MAICYA 1, 2; MAICYAS 1; MTCW 1, 2; RGAL 4; SATA 7, 48, 81; TUS; WYA; YAW

Chin, Frank (Chew, Jr.) 1940- ...... **CLC 135; DC 7**
See also CA 33-36R; CANR 71; CD 5; DAM MULT; DLB 206; LAIT 5; RGAL 4

Chin, Marilyn (Mei Ling) 1955- .... **PC 40**
See also CA 129; CANR 70, 113; CWP

Chislett, (Margaret) Anne 1943- ...... **CLC 34**
See also CA 151

Chitty, Thomas Willes 1926- .... **CLC 11**
See Hinde, Thomas
See also CA 5-8R; CN 7

Chivers, Thomas Holley
1809-1858 .... **NCLC 49**
See also DLB 3, 248; RGAL 4

Choi, Susan .... **CLC 119**

Chomette, Rene Lucien 1898-1981
See Clair, Rene
See also CA 103

Chomsky, (Avram) Noam 1928- ..... **CLC 132**
See also CA 17-20R; CANR 28, 62, 110; DA3; DLB 246; MTCW 1, 2

Chona, Maria 1845(?)-1936 .... **NNAL**
See also CA 144

Chopin, Kate ..... **SSC 8; TCLC 127; WLCS**
See Chopin, Katherine
See also AAYA 33; AMWR 2; AMWS 1; CDALB 1865-1917; DA; DAB; DLB 12, 78; EXPN; EXPS; FW; LAIT 3; MAWW; NFS 3; RGAL 4; RGSF 2; SSFS 17; TUS

Chopin, Katherine 1851-1904
See Chopin, Kate
See also CA 104; 122; DA3; DAC; DAM MST, NOV

Chretien de Troyes c. 12th cent. - . **CMLC 10**
See also DLB 208; EW 1; RGWL 2, 3; TWA

Christie
See Ichikawa, Kon

Christie, Agatha (Mary Clarissa)
1890-1976 .. **CLC 1, 6, 8, 12, 39, 48, 110**
See also AAYA 9; AITN 1, 2; BPFB 1; BRWS 2; CA 17-20R; 61-64; CANR 10, 37, 108; CBD; CDBLB 1914-1945; CMW 4; CPW; CWD; DA3; DAB; DAC; DAM NOV; DFS 2; DLB 13, 77, 245; MSW; MTCW 1, 2; NFS 8; RGEL 2; RHW; SATA 36; TEA; YAW

Christie, Philippa .... **CLC 21**
See Pearce, Philippa
See also BYA 5; CANR 109; CLR 9; DLB 161; MAICYA 1; SATA 1, 67, 129

Christine de Pizan 1365(?)-1431(?) .... **LC 9**
See also DLB 208; RGWL 2, 3

Chuang Tzu c. 369B.C.-c.
286B.C. .... **CMLC 57**

Chubb, Elmer
See Masters, Edgar Lee

Chulkov, Mikhail Dmitrievich
1743-1792 .... **LC 2**
See also DLB 150

Churchill, Caryl 1938- .... **CLC 31, 55, 157; DC 5**
See Churchill, Chick
See also BRWS 4; CA 102; CANR 22, 46, 108; CBD; CWD; DFS 12, 16; DLB 13; EWL 3; FW; MTCW 1; RGEL 2

Churchill, Charles 1731-1764 .... **LC 3**
See also DLB 109; RGEL 2

Churchill, Chick 1938-
See Churchill, Caryl
See also CD 5

Churchill, Sir Winston (Leonard Spencer)
1874-1965 .... **TCLC 113**
See also BRW 6; CA 97-100; CDBLB 1890-1914; DA3; DLB 100; DLBD 16; LAIT 4; MTCW 1, 2

Chute, Carolyn 1947- .... **CLC 39**
See also CA 123

Ciardi, John (Anthony) 1916-1986 . **CLC 10, 40, 44, 129**
See also CA 5-8R; 118; CAAS 2; CANR 5, 33; CLR 19; CWRI 5; DAM POET; DLB 5; DLBY 1986; INT CANR-5; MAICYA 1, 2; MTCW 1, 2; RGAL 4; SAAS 26; SATA 1, 65; SATA-Obit 46

Cibber, Colley 1671-1757 .... **LC 66**
See also DLB 84; RGEL 2

Cicero, Marcus Tullius
106B.C.-43B.C. .... **CMLC 3**
See also AW 1; CDWLB 1; DLB 211; RGWL 2, 3

Cimino, Michael 1943- .... **CLC 16**
See also CA 105

Cioran, E(mil) M. 1911-1995 .... **CLC 64**
See also CA 25-28R; 149; CANR 91; DLB 220; EWL 3

Cisneros, Sandra 1954- .. **CLC 69, 118; HLC 1; SSC 32**
See also AAYA 9, 53; AMWS 7; CA 131; CANR 64, 118; CWP; DA3; DAM MULT; DLB 122, 152; EWL 3; EXPN; FW; HW 1, 2; LAIT 5; LATS 1; MAICYA 2; MTCW 2; NFS 2; RGAL 4; RGSF 2; SSFS 3, 13; WLIT 1; YAW

Cixous, Helene 1937- .... **CLC 92**
See also CA 126; CANR 55; CWW 2; DLB 83, 242; EWL 3; FW; GLL 2; MTCW 1, 2; TWA

Clair, Rene .... **CLC 20**
See Chomette, Rene Lucien

Clampitt, Amy 1920-1994 .... **CLC 32; PC 19**
See also AMWS 9; CA 110; 146; CANR 29, 79; DLB 105

Clancy, Thomas L., Jr. 1947-
See Clancy, Tom
See also CA 125; 131; CANR 62, 105; DA3; INT CA-131; MTCW 1, 2

Clancy, Tom .... **CLC 45, 112**
See Clancy, Thomas L., Jr.
See also AAYA 9, 51; BEST 89:1, 90:1; BPFB 1; BYA 10, 11; CMW 4; CPW; DAM NOV, POP; DLB 227

Clare, John 1793-1864 .. **NCLC 9, 86; PC 23**
See also DAB; DAM POET; DLB 55, 96; RGEL 2

Clarin
See Alas (y Urena), Leopoldo (Enrique Garcia)

Clark, Al C.
See Goines, Donald

Clark, (Robert) Brian 1932- .... **CLC 29**
See also CA 41-44R; CANR 67; CBD; CD 5

Clark, Curt
See Westlake, Donald E(dwin)

Clark, Eleanor 1913-1996 .... **CLC 5, 19**
See also CA 9-12R; 151; CANR 41; CN 7; DLB 6

Clark, J. P.
See Clark Bekederemo, J(ohnson) P(epper)
See also CDWLB 3; DLB 117

Clark, John Pepper
See Clark Bekederemo, J(ohnson) P(epper)
See also AFW; CD 5; CP 7; RGEL 2

Clark, M. R.
See Clark, Mavis Thorpe

Clark, Mavis Thorpe 1909-1999 ...... **CLC 12**
See also CA 57-60; CANR 8, 37, 107; CLR 30; CWRI 5; MAICYA 1, 2; SAAS 5; SATA 8, 74

Clark, Walter Van Tilburg
1909-1971 .... **CLC 28**
See also CA 9-12R; 33-36R; CANR 63, 113; DLB 9, 206; LAIT 2; RGAL 4; SATA 8

Clark Bekederemo, J(ohnson) P(epper)
1935- .... **BLC 1; CLC 38; DC 5**
See Clark, J. P.; Clark, John Pepper
See also BW 1; CA 65-68; CANR 16, 72; DAM DRAM, MULT; DFS 13; EWL 3; MTCW 1

Clarke, Arthur C(harles) 1917- .... **CLC 1, 4, 13, 18, 35, 136; SSC 3**
See also AAYA 4, 33; BPFB 1; BYA 13; CA 1-4R; CANR 2, 28, 55, 74; CN 7; CPW; DA3; DAM POP; DLB 261; JRDA; LAIT 5; MAICYA 1, 2; MTCW 1, 2; SATA 13, 70, 115; SCFW; SFW 4; SSFS 4; YAW

Clarke, Austin 1896-1974 .... **CLC 6, 9**
See also CA 29-32; 49-52; CAP 2; DAM POET; DLB 10, 20; EWL 3; RGEL 2

Clarke, Austin C(hesterfield) 1934- .. **BLC 1; CLC 8, 53; SSC 45**
See also BW 1; CA 25-28R; CAAS 16; CANR 14, 32, 68; CN 7; DAC; DAM MULT; DLB 53, 125; DNFS 2; RGSF 2

Clarke, Gillian 1937- .... **CLC 61**
See also CA 106; CP 7; CWP; DLB 40

Clarke, Marcus (Andrew Hislop)
1846-1881 .... **NCLC 19**
See also DLB 230; RGEL 2; RGSF 2

Clarke, Shirley 1925-1997 .... **CLC 16**
See also CA 189

Clash, The
See Headon, (Nicky) Topper; Jones, Mick; Simonon, Paul; Strummer, Joe

Claudel, Paul (Louis Charles Marie)
1868-1955 .... **TCLC 2, 10**
See also CA 104; 165; DLB 192, 258; EW 8; EWL 3; GFL 1789 to the Present; RGWL 2, 3; TWA

Claudian 370(?)-404(?) .... **CMLC 46**
See also RGWL 2, 3

Claudius, Matthias 1740-1815 .... **NCLC 75**
See also DLB 97

Clavell, James (duMaresq)
1925-1994 .... **CLC 6, 25, 87**
See also BPFB 1; CA 25-28R; 146; CANR 26, 48; CPW; DA3; DAM NOV, POP; MTCW 1, 2; NFS 10; RHW

Clayman, Gregory .... **CLC 65**

Cleaver, (Leroy) Eldridge
1935-1998 .... **BLC 1; CLC 30, 119**
See also BW 1, 3; CA 21-24R; 167; CANR 16, 75; DA3; DAM MULT; MTCW 2; YAW

Cleese, John (Marwood) 1939- .... **CLC 21**
See Monty Python
See also CA 112; 116; CANR 35; MTCW 1

Cleishbotham, Jebediah
See Scott, Sir Walter

Cleland, John 1710-1789 .... **LC 2, 48**
See also DLB 39; RGEL 2

Clemens, Samuel Langhorne 1835-1910
See Twain, Mark
See also CA 104; 135; CDALB 1865-1917;
DA; DA3; DAB; DAC; DAM MST, NOV;
DLB 12, 23, 64, 74, 186, 189; JRDA;
LMFS 1; MAICYA 1, 2; NCFS 4; SATA
100; SSFS 16; YABC 2

Clement of Alexandria
150(?)-215(?) .... **CMLC 41**

Cleophil
See Congreve, William

Clerihew, E.
See Bentley, E(dmund) C(lerihew)

Clerk, N. W.
See Lewis, C(live) S(taples)

Cliff, Jimmy .... **CLC 21**
See Chambers, James
See also CA 193

Cliff, Michelle 1946- .... **BLCS; CLC 120**
See also BW 2; CA 116; CANR 39, 72; CD-
WLB 3; DLB 157; FW; GLL 2

Clifford, Lady Anne 1590-1676 .... **LC 76**
See also DLB 151

Clifton, (Thelma) Lucille 1936- .... **BLC 1;
CLC 19, 66, 162; PC 17**
See also AFAW 2; BW 2, 3; CA 49-52;
CANR 2, 24, 42, 76, 97; CLR 5; CP 7;
CSW; CWP; CWRI 5; DA3; DAM MULT,
POET; DLB 5, 41; EXPP; MAICYA 1, 2;
MTCW 1, 2; PFS 1, 14; SATA 20, 69,
128; WP

Clinton, Dirk
See Silverberg, Robert

Clough, Arthur Hugh 1819-1861 ... **NCLC 27**
See also BRW 5; DLB 32; RGEL 2

Clutha, Janet Paterson Frame 1924-
See Frame, Janet
See also CA 1-4R; CANR 2, 36, 76; MTCW
1, 2; SATA 119

Clyne, Terence
See Blatty, William Peter

Cobalt, Martin
See Mayne, William (James Carter)

Cobb, Irvin S(hrewsbury)
1876-1944 .... **TCLC 77**
See also CA 175; DLB 11, 25, 86

Cobbett, William 1763-1835 .... **NCLC 49**
See also DLB 43, 107, 158; RGEL 2

Coburn, D(onald) L(ee) 1938- .... **CLC 10**
See also CA 89-92

Cocteau, Jean (Maurice Eugene Clement)
1889-1963 ...... **CLC 1, 8, 15, 16, 43; DC
17; TCLC 119; WLC**
See also CA 25-28; CANR 40; CAP 2; DA;
DA3; DAB; DAC; DAM DRAM, MST,
NOV; DLB 65, 258; EW 10; EWL 3; GFL
1789 to the Present; MTCW 1, 2; RGWL
2, 3; TWA

Codrescu, Andrei 1946- .... **CLC 46, 121**
See also CA 33-36R; CAAS 19; CANR 13,
34, 53, 76; DA3; DAM POET; MTCW 2

Coe, Max
See Bourne, Randolph S(illiman)

Coe, Tucker
See Westlake, Donald E(dwin)

Coen, Ethan 1958- .... **CLC 108**
See also CA 126; CANR 85

Coen, Joel 1955- .... **CLC 108**
See also CA 126; CANR 119

The Coen Brothers
See Coen, Ethan; Coen, Joel

Coetzee, J(ohn) M(ichael) 1940- ...... **CLC 23,
33, 66, 117, 161, 162**
See also AAYA 37; AFW; BRWS 6; CA 77-
80; CANR 41, 54, 74, 114; CN 7; DA3;
DAM NOV; DLB 225; EWL 3; LMFS 2;
MTCW 1, 2; WLIT 2

Coffey, Brian
See Koontz, Dean R(ay)

Coffin, Robert P(eter) Tristram
1892-1955 .... **TCLC 95**
See also CA 123; 169; DLB 45

Cohan, George M(ichael)
1878-1942 .... **TCLC 60**
See also CA 157; DLB 249; RGAL 4

Cohen, Arthur A(llen) 1928-1986 ...... **CLC 7,
31**
See also CA 1-4R; 120; CANR 1, 17, 42;
DLB 28

Cohen, Leonard (Norman) 1934- ...... **CLC 3,
38**
See also CA 21-24R; CANR 14, 69; CN 7;
CP 7; DAC; DAM MST; DLB 53; EWL
3; MTCW 1

Cohen, Matt(hew) 1942-1999 .... **CLC 19**
See also CA 61-64; 187; CAAS 18; CANR
40; CN 7; DAC; DLB 53

Cohen-Solal, Annie 19(?)- .... **CLC 50**

Colegate, Isabel 1931- .... **CLC 36**
See also CA 17-20R; CANR 8, 22, 74; CN
7; DLB 14, 231; INT CANR-22; MTCW
1

Coleman, Emmett
See Reed, Ishmael

Coleridge, Hartley 1796-1849 .... **NCLC 90**
See also DLB 96

Coleridge, M. E.
See Coleridge, Mary E(lizabeth)

Coleridge, Mary E(lizabeth)
1861-1907 .... **TCLC 73**
See also CA 116; 166; DLB 19, 98

Coleridge, Samuel Taylor
1772-1834 ...... **NCLC 9, 54, 99, 111; PC
11, 39; WLC**
See also BRW 4; BRWR 2; BYA 4; CD-
BLB 1789-1832; DA; DA3; DAB; DAC;
DAM MST, POET; DLB 93, 107; EXPP;
LATS 1; LMFS 1; PAB; PFS 4, 5; RGEL
2; TEA; WLIT 3; WP

Coleridge, Sara 1802-1852 .... **NCLC 31**
See also DLB 199

Coles, Don 1928- .... **CLC 46**
See also CA 115; CANR 38; CP 7

Coles, Robert (Martin) 1929- .... **CLC 108**
See also CA 45-48; CANR 3, 32, 66, 70;
INT CANR-32; SATA 23

Colette, (Sidonie-Gabrielle)
1873-1954 .... **SSC 10; TCLC 1, 5, 16**
See Willy, Colette
See also CA 104; 131; DA3; DAM NOV;
DLB 65; EW 9; EWL 3; GFL 1789 to the
Present; MTCW 1, 2; RGWL 2, 3; TWA

Collett, (Jacobine) Camilla (Wergeland)
1813-1895 .... **NCLC 22**

Collier, Christopher 1930- .... **CLC 30**
See also AAYA 13; BYA 2; CA 33-36R;
CANR 13, 33, 102; JRDA; MAICYA 1,
2; SATA 16, 70; WYA; YAW 1

Collier, James Lincoln 1928- .... **CLC 30**
See also AAYA 13; BYA 2; CA 9-12R;
CANR 4, 33, 60, 102; CLR 3; DAM POP;
JRDA; MAICYA 1, 2; SAAS 21; SATA 8,
70; WYA; YAW 1

Collier, Jeremy 1650-1726 .... **LC 6**

Collier, John 1901-1980 . **SSC 19; TCLC 127**
See also CA 65-68; 97-100; CANR 10;
DLB 77, 255; FANT; SUFW 1

Collier, Mary 1690-1762 .... **LC 86**
See also DLB 95

Collingwood, R(obin) G(eorge)
1889(?)-1943 .... **TCLC 67**
See also CA 117; 155; DLB 262

Collins, Hunt
See Hunter, Evan

Collins, Linda 1931- .... **CLC 44**
See also CA 125

Collins, Tom
See Furphy, Joseph
See also RGEL 2

Collins, (William) Wilkie
1824-1889 .... **NCLC 1, 18, 93**
See also BRWS 6; CDBLB 1832-1890;
CMW 4; DLB 18, 70, 159; MSW; RGEL
2; RGSF 2; SUFW 1; WLIT 4

Collins, William 1721-1759 .... **LC 4, 40**
See also BRW 3; DAM POET; DLB 109;
RGEL 2

Collodi, Carlo .... **NCLC 54**
See Lorenzini, Carlo
See also CLR 5; WCH

Colman, George
See Glassco, John

Colonna, Vittoria 1492-1547 .... **LC 71**
See also RGWL 2, 3

Colt, Winchester Remington
See Hubbard, L(afayette) Ron(ald)

Colter, Cyrus J. 1910-2002 .... **CLC 58**
See also BW 1; CA 65-68; 205; CANR 10,
66; CN 7; DLB 33

Colton, James
See Hansen, Joseph
See also GLL 1

Colum, Padraic 1881-1972 .... **CLC 28**
See also BYA 4; CA 73-76; 33-36R; CANR
35; CLR 36; CWRI 5; DLB 19; MAICYA
1, 2; MTCW 1; RGEL 2; SATA 15; WCH

Colvin, James
See Moorcock, Michael (John)

Colwin, Laurie (E.) 1944-1992 .... **CLC 5, 13,
23, 84**
See also CA 89-92; 139; CANR 20, 46;
DLB 218; DLBY 1980; MTCW 1

Comfort, Alex(ander) 1920-2000 .... **CLC 7**
See also CA 1-4R; 190; CANR 1, 45; CP 7;
DAM POP; MTCW 1

Comfort, Montgomery
See Campbell, (John) Ramsey

Compton-Burnett, I(vy)
1892(?)-1969 ...... **CLC 1, 3, 10, 15, 34**
See also BRW 7; CA 1-4R; 25-28R; CANR
4; DAM NOV; DLB 36; EWL 3; MTCW
1; RGEL 2

Comstock, Anthony 1844-1915 ...... **TCLC 13**
See also CA 110; 169

Comte, Auguste 1798-1857 .... **NCLC 54**

Conan Doyle, Arthur
See Doyle, Sir Arthur Conan
See also BPFB 1; BYA 4, 5, 11

Conde (Abellan), Carmen
1901-1996 .... **HLCS 1**
See also CA 177; DLB 108; EWL 3; HW 2

Conde, Maryse 1937- ..... **BLCS; CLC 52, 92**
See also BW 2, 3; CA 110; CAAE 190;
CANR 30, 53, 76; CWW 2; DAM MULT;
EWL 3; MTCW 1

Condillac, Etienne Bonnot de
1714-1780 .... **LC 26**

Condon, Richard (Thomas)
1915-1996 .... **CLC 4, 6, 8, 10, 45, 100**
See also BEST 90:3; BPFB 1; CA 1-4R;
151; CAAS 1; CANR 2, 23; CMW 4; CN
7; DAM NOV; INT CANR-23; MTCW 1,
2

Confucius 551B.C.-479B.C. .... **CMLC 19;
WLCS**
See also DA; DA3; DAB; DAC; DAM
MST

Congreve, William 1670-1729 ... **DC 2; LC 5,
21; WLC**
See also BRW 2; CDBLB 1660-1789; DA;
DAB; DAC; DAM DRAM, MST, POET;
DFS 15; DLB 39, 84; RGEL 2; WLIT 3

Conley, Robert J(ackson) 1940- .... **NNAL**
See also CA 41-44R; CANR 15, 34, 45, 96;
DAM MULT

Cozzens, James Gould 1903-1978 . **CLC 1, 4, 11, 92**
  See also AMW; BPFB 1; CA 9-12R; 81-84; CANR 19; CDALB 1941-1968; DLB 9; DLBD 2; DLBY 1984, 1997; EWL 3; MTCW 1, 2; RGAL 4

Crabbe, George 1754-1832 .... **NCLC 26, 121**
  See also BRW 3; DLB 93; RGEL 2

Crace, Jim 1946- .... **CLC 157; SSC 61**
  See also CA 128; 135; CANR 55, 70; CN 7; DLB 231; INT CA-135

Craddock, Charles Egbert
  See Murfree, Mary Noailles

Craig, A. A.
  See Anderson, Poul (William)

Craik, Mrs.
  See Craik, Dinah Maria (Mulock)
  See also RGEL 2

Craik, Dinah Maria (Mulock)
  1826-1887 .... **NCLC 38**
  See Craik, Mrs.; Mulock, Dinah Maria
  See also DLB 35, 163; MAICYA 1, 2; SATA 34

Cram, Ralph Adams 1863-1942 ..... **TCLC 45**
  See also CA 160

Cranch, Christopher Pearse
  1813-1892 .... **NCLC 115**
  See also DLB 1, 42, 243

Crane, (Harold) Hart 1899-1932 .... **PC 3; TCLC 2, 5, 80; WLC**
  See also AMW; AMWR 2; CA 104; 127; CDALB 1917-1929; DA; DA3; DAB; DAC; DAM MST, POET; DLB 4, 48; EWL 3; MTCW 1, 2; RGAL 4; TUS

Crane, R(onald) S(almon)
  1886-1967 .... **CLC 27**
  See also CA 85-88; DLB 63

Crane, Stephen (Townley)
  1871-1900 ...... **SSC 7, 56; TCLC 11, 17, 32; WLC**
  See also AAYA 21; AMW; AMWC 1; BPFB 1; BYA 3; CA 109; 140; CANR 84; CDALB 1865-1917; DA; DA3; DAB; DAC; DAM MST, NOV, POET; DLB 12, 54, 78; EXPN; EXPS; LAIT 2; LMFS 2; NFS 4; PFS 9; RGAL 4; RGSF 2; SSFS 4; TUS; WYA; YABC 2

Cranshaw, Stanley
  See Fisher, Dorothy (Frances) Canfield

Crase, Douglas 1944- .... **CLC 58**
  See also CA 106

Crashaw, Richard 1612(?)-1649 .... **LC 24**
  See also BRW 2; DLB 126; PAB; RGEL 2

Cratinus c. 519B.C.-c. 422B.C. ..... **CMLC 54**
  See also LMFS 1

Craven, Margaret 1901-1980 .... **CLC 17**
  See also BYA 2; CA 103; CCA 1; DAC; LAIT 5

Crawford, F(rancis) Marion
  1854-1909 .... **TCLC 10**
  See also CA 107; 168; DLB 71; HGG; RGAL 4; SUFW 1

Crawford, Isabella Valancy
  1850-1887 .... **NCLC 12, 127**
  See also DLB 92; RGEL 2

Crayon, Geoffrey
  See Irving, Washington

Creasey, John 1908-1973 .... **CLC 11**
  See Marric, J. J.
  See also CA 5-8R; 41-44R; CANR 8, 59; CMW 4; DLB 77; MTCW 1

Crebillon, Claude Prosper Jolyot de (fils)
  1707-1777 .... **LC 1, 28**
  See also GFL Beginnings to 1789

Credo
  See Creasey, John

Credo, Alvaro J. de
  See Prado (Calvo), Pedro

Creeley, Robert (White) 1926- .. **CLC 1, 2, 4, 8, 11, 15, 36, 78**
  See also AMWS 4; CA 1-4R; CAAS 10; CANR 23, 43, 89; CP 7; DA3; DAM POET; DLB 5, 16, 169; DLBD 17; EWL 3; MTCW 1, 2; RGAL 4; WP

Crevecoeur, Hector St. John de
  See Crevecoeur, Michel Guillaume Jean de
  See also ANW

Crevecoeur, Michel Guillaume Jean de
  1735-1813 .... **NCLC 105**
  See Crevecoeur, Hector St. John de
  See also AMWS 1; DLB 37

Crevel, Rene 1900-1935 .... **TCLC 112**
  See also GLL 2

Crews, Harry (Eugene) 1935- ..... **CLC 6, 23, 49**
  See also AITN 1; AMWS 11; BPFB 1; CA 25-28R; CANR 20, 57; CN 7; CSW; DA3; DLB 6, 143, 185; MTCW 1, 2; RGAL 4

Crichton, (John) Michael 1942- .... **CLC 2, 6, 54, 90**
  See also AAYA 10, 49; AITN 2; BPFB 1; CA 25-28R; CANR 13, 40, 54, 76; CMW 4; CN 7; CPW; DA3; DAM NOV, POP; DLBY 1981; INT CANR-13; JRDA; MTCW 1, 2; SATA 9, 88; SFW 4; YAW

Crispin, Edmund .... **CLC 22**
  See Montgomery, (Robert) Bruce
  See also DLB 87; MSW

Cristofer, Michael 1945(?)- .... **CLC 28**
  See also CA 110; 152; CAD; CD 5; DAM DRAM; DFS 15; DLB 7

Criton
  See Alain

Croce, Benedetto 1866-1952 .... **TCLC 37**
  See also CA 120; 155; EW 8; EWL 3

Crockett, David 1786-1836 .... **NCLC 8**
  See also DLB 3, 11, 183, 248

Crockett, Davy
  See Crockett, David

Crofts, Freeman Wills 1879-1957 .. **TCLC 55**
  See also CA 115; 195; CMW 4; DLB 77; MSW

Croker, John Wilson 1780-1857 .... **NCLC 10**
  See also DLB 110

Crommelynck, Fernand 1885-1970 .. **CLC 75**
  See also CA 189; 89-92; EWL 3

Cromwell, Oliver 1599-1658 .... **LC 43**

Cronenberg, David 1943- .... **CLC 143**
  See also CA 138; CCA 1

Cronin, A(rchibald) J(oseph)
  1896-1981 .... **CLC 32**
  See also BPFB 1; CA 1-4R; 102; CANR 5; DLB 191; SATA 47; SATA-Obit 25

Cross, Amanda
  See Heilbrun, Carolyn G(old)
  See also BPFB 1; CMW; CPW; MSW

Crothers, Rachel 1878-1958 .... **TCLC 19**
  See also CA 113; 194; CAD; CWD; DLB 7, 266; RGAL 4

Croves, Hal
  See Traven, B.

Crow Dog, Mary (Ellen) (?)- .... **CLC 93**
  See Brave Bird, Mary
  See also CA 154

Crowfield, Christopher
  See Stowe, Harriet (Elizabeth) Beecher

Crowley, Aleister .... **TCLC 7**
  See Crowley, Edward Alexander
  See also GLL 1

Crowley, Edward Alexander 1875-1947
  See Crowley, Aleister
  See also CA 104; HGG

Crowley, John 1942- .... **CLC 57**
  See also BPFB 1; CA 61-64; CANR 43, 98; DLBY 1982; SATA 65, 140; SFW 4; SUFW 2

Crud
  See Crumb, R(obert)

Crumarums
  See Crumb, R(obert)

Crumb, R(obert) 1943- .... **CLC 17**
  See also CA 106; CANR 107

Crumbum
  See Crumb, R(obert)

Crumski
  See Crumb, R(obert)

Crum the Bum
  See Crumb, R(obert)

Crunk
  See Crumb, R(obert)

Crustt
  See Crumb, R(obert)

Crutchfield, Les
  See Trumbo, Dalton

Cruz, Victor Hernandez 1949- ... **HLC 1; PC 37**
  See also BW 2; CA 65-68; CAAS 17; CANR 14, 32, 74; CP 7; DAM MULT, POET; DLB 41; DNFS 1; EXPP; HW 1, 2; MTCW 1; PFS 16; WP

Cryer, Gretchen (Kiger) 1935- .... **CLC 21**
  See also CA 114; 123

Csath, Geza 1887-1919 .... **TCLC 13**
  See also CA 111

Cudlip, David R(ockwell) 1933- .... **CLC 34**
  See also CA 177

Cullen, Countee 1903-1946 .... **BLC 1; HR 2; PC 20; TCLC 4, 37; WLCS**
  See also AFAW 2; AMWS 4; BW 1; CA 108; 124; CDALB 1917-1929; DA; DA3; DAC; DAM MST, MULT, POET; DLB 4, 48, 51; EWL 3; EXPP; LMFS 2; MTCW 1, 2; PFS 3; RGAL 4; SATA 18; WP

Culleton, Beatrice 1949- .... **NNAL**
  See also CA 120; CANR 83; DAC

Cum, R.
  See Crumb, R(obert)

Cummings, Bruce F(rederick) 1889-1919
  See Barbellion, W. N. P.
  See also CA 123

Cummings, E(dward) E(stlin)
  1894-1962 .. **CLC 1, 3, 8, 12, 15, 68; PC 5; TCLC 137; WLC**
  See also AAYA 41; AMW; CA 73-76; CANR 31; CDALB 1929-1941; DA; DA3; DAB; DAC; DAM MST, POET; DLB 4, 48; EWL 3; EXPP; MTCW 1, 2; PAB; PFS 1, 3, 12, 13; RGAL 4; TUS; WP

Cunha, Euclides (Rodrigues Pimenta) da
  1866-1909 .... **TCLC 24**
  See also CA 123; LAW; WLIT 1

Cunningham, E. V.
  See Fast, Howard (Melvin)

Cunningham, J(ames) V(incent)
  1911-1985 .... **CLC 3, 31**
  See also CA 1-4R; 115; CANR 1, 72; DLB 5

Cunningham, Julia (Woolfolk)
  1916- .... **CLC 12**
  See also CA 9-12R; CANR 4, 19, 36; CWRI 5; JRDA; MAICYA 1, 2; SAAS 2; SATA 1, 26, 132

Cunningham, Michael 1952- .... **CLC 34**
  See also CA 136; CANR 96; GLL 2

Cunninghame Graham, R. B.
  See Cunninghame Graham, Robert (Gallnigad) Bontine

Cunninghame Graham, Robert (Gallnigad) Bontine 1852-1936 .... **TCLC 19**
  See Graham, R(obert) B(ontine) Cunninghame
  See also CA 119; 184

Dyer, George 1755-1841 .... **NCLC 129**
See also DLB 93

Dylan, Bob 1941- .... **CLC 3, 4, 6, 12, 77; PC 37**
See also CA 41-44R; CANR 108; CP 7; DLB 16

Dyson, John 1943- .... **CLC 70**
See also CA 144

Dzyubin, Eduard Georgievich 1895-1934
See Bagritsky, Eduard
See also CA 170

E. V. L.
See Lucas, E(dward) V(errall)

Eagleton, Terence (Francis) 1943- .. **CLC 63, 132**
See also CA 57-60; CANR 7, 23, 68, 115; DLB 242; LMFS 2; MTCW 1, 2

Eagleton, Terry
See Eagleton, Terence (Francis)

Early, Jack
See Scoppettone, Sandra
See also GLL 1

East, Michael
See West, Morris L(anglo)

Eastaway, Edward
See Thomas, (Philip) Edward

Eastlake, William (Derry)
1917-1997 .... **CLC 8**
See also CA 5-8R; 158; CAAS 1; CANR 5, 63; CN 7; DLB 6, 206; INT CANR-5; TCWW 2

Eastman, Charles A(lexander)
1858-1939 .... **NNAL; TCLC 55**
See also CA 179; CANR 91; DAM MULT; DLB 175; YABC 1

Eaton, Edith Maude 1865-1914 .... **AAL**
See Far, Sui Sin
See also CA 154; DLB 221; FW

Eaton, Winnifred 1875-1954 .... **AAL**
See also DLB 221; RGAL 4

Eberhart, Richard (Ghormley)
1904- .... **CLC 3, 11, 19, 56**
See also AMW; CA 1-4R; CANR 2; CDALB 1941-1968; CP 7; DAM POET; DLB 48; MTCW 1; RGAL 4

Eberstadt, Fernanda 1960- .... **CLC 39**
See also CA 136; CANR 69

Echegaray (y Eizaguirre), Jose (Maria Waldo) 1832-1916 .... **HLCS 1; TCLC 4**
See also CA 104; CANR 32; EWL 3; HW 1; MTCW 1

Echeverria, (Jose) Esteban (Antonino)
1805-1851 .... **NCLC 18**
See also LAW

Echo
See Proust, (Valentin-Louis-George-Eugene-)Marcel

Eckert, Allan W. 1931- .... **CLC 17**
See also AAYA 18; BYA 2; CA 13-16R; CANR 14, 45; INT CANR-14; MAICYA 2; MAICYAS 1; SAAS 21; SATA 29, 91; SATA-Brief 27

Eckhart, Meister 1260(?)-1327(?) ... **CMLC 9**
See also DLB 115; LMFS 1

Eckmar, F. R.
See de Hartog, Jan

Eco, Umberto 1932- .... **CLC 28, 60, 142**
See also BEST 90:1; BPFB 1; CA 77-80; CANR 12, 33, 55, 110; CPW; CWW 2; DA3; DAM NOV, POP; DLB 196, 242; EWL 3; MSW; MTCW 1, 2; RGWL 3

Eddison, E(ric) R(ucker)
1882-1945 .... **TCLC 15**
See also CA 109; 156; DLB 255; FANT; SFW 4; SUFW 1

Eddy, Mary (Ann Morse) Baker
1821-1910 .... **TCLC 71**
See also CA 113; 174

Edel, (Joseph) Leon 1907-1997 .. **CLC 29, 34**
See also CA 1-4R; 161; CANR 1, 22, 112; DLB 103; INT CANR-22

Eden, Emily 1797-1869 .... **NCLC 10**

Edgar, David 1948- .... **CLC 42**
See also CA 57-60; CANR 12, 61, 112; CBD; CD 5; DAM DRAM; DFS 15; DLB 13, 233; MTCW 1

Edgerton, Clyde (Carlyle) 1944- ...... **CLC 39**
See also AAYA 17; CA 118; CANR 64; CSW; DLB 278; INT 134; YAW

Edgeworth, Maria 1768-1849 .... **NCLC 1, 51**
See also BRWS 3; DLB 116, 159, 163; FW; RGEL 2; SATA 21; TEA; WLIT 3

Edmonds, Paul
See Kuttner, Henry

Edmonds, Walter D(umaux)
1903-1998 .... **CLC 35**
See also BYA 2; CA 5-8R; CANR 2; CWRI 5; DLB 9; LAIT 1; MAICYA 1, 2; RHW; SAAS 4; SATA 1, 27; SATA-Obit 99

Edmondson, Wallace
See Ellison, Harlan (Jay)

Edson, Russell 1935- .... **CLC 13**
See also CA 33-36R; CANR 115; DLB 244; WP

Edwards, Bronwen Elizabeth
See Rose, Wendy

Edwards, G(erald) B(asil)
1899-1976 .... **CLC 25**
See also CA 201; 110

Edwards, Gus 1939- .... **CLC 43**
See also CA 108; INT 108

Edwards, Jonathan 1703-1758 .... **LC 7, 54**
See also AMW; DA; DAC; DAM MST; DLB 24, 270; RGAL 4; TUS

Edwards, Sarah Pierpont 1710-1758 .. **LC 87**
See also DLB 200

Efron, Marina Ivanovna Tsvetaeva
See Tsvetaeva (Efron), Marina (Ivanovna)

Egoyan, Atom 1960- .... **CLC 151**
See also CA 157

Ehle, John (Marsden, Jr.) 1925- ...... **CLC 27**
See also CA 9-12R; CSW

Ehrenbourg, Ilya (Grigoryevich)
See Ehrenburg, Ilya (Grigoryevich)

Ehrenburg, Ilya (Grigoryevich)
1891-1967 .... **CLC 18, 34, 62**
See Erenburg, Il'ia Grigor'evich
See also CA 102; 25-28R; EWL 3

Ehrenburg, Ilyo (Grigoryevich)
See Ehrenburg, Ilya (Grigoryevich)

Ehrenreich, Barbara 1941- .... **CLC 110**
See also BEST 90:4; CA 73-76; CANR 16, 37, 62, 117; DLB 246; FW; MTCW 1, 2

Eich, Gunter
See Eich, Gunter
See also RGWL 2, 3

Eich, Gunter 1907-1972 .... **CLC 15**
See Eich, Gunter
See also CA 111; 93-96; DLB 69, 124; EWL 3

Eichendorff, Joseph 1788-1857 .... **NCLC 8**
See also DLB 90; RGWL 2, 3

Eigner, Larry .... **CLC 9**
See Eigner, Laurence (Joel)
See also CAAS 23; DLB 5; WP

Eigner, Laurence (Joel) 1927-1996
See Eigner, Larry
See also CA 9-12R; 151; CANR 6, 84; CP 7; DLB 193

Einhard c. 770-840 .... **CMLC 50**
See also DLB 148

Einstein, Albert 1879-1955 .... **TCLC 65**
See also CA 121; 133; MTCW 1, 2

Eiseley, Loren
See Eiseley, Loren Corey
See also DLB 275

Eiseley, Loren Corey 1907-1977 .... **CLC 7**
See Eiseley, Loren
See also AAYA 5; ANW; CA 1-4R; 73-76; CANR 6; DLBD 17

Eisenstadt, Jill 1963- .... **CLC 50**
See also CA 140

Eisenstein, Sergei (Mikhailovich)
1898-1948 .... **TCLC 57**
See also CA 114; 149

Eisner, Simon
See Kornbluth, C(yril) M.

Ekeloef, (Bengt) Gunnar
1907-1968 .... **CLC 27; PC 23**
See Ekelof, (Bengt) Gunnar
See also CA 123; 25-28R; DAM POET

Ekelof, (Bengt) Gunnar 1907-1968
See Ekeloef, (Bengt) Gunnar
See also DLB 259; EW 12; EWL 3

Ekelund, Vilhelm 1880-1949 .... **TCLC 75**
See also CA 189; EWL 3

Ekwensi, C. O. D.
See Ekwensi, Cyprian (Odiatu Duaka)

Ekwensi, Cyprian (Odiatu Duaka)
1921- .... **BLC 1; CLC 4**
See also AFW; BW 2, 3; CA 29-32R; CANR 18, 42, 74; CDWLB 3; CN 7; CWRI 5; DAM MULT; DLB 117; EWL 3; MTCW 1, 2; RGEL 2; SATA 66; WLIT 2

Elaine .... **TCLC 18**
See Leverson, Ada Esther

El Crummo
See Crumb, R(obert)

Elder, Lonne III 1931-1996 ..... **BLC 1; DC 8**
See also BW 1, 3; CA 81-84; 152; CAD; CANR 25; DAM MULT; DLB 7, 38, 44

Eleanor of Aquitaine 1122-1204 ... **CMLC 39**

Elia
See Lamb, Charles

Eliade, Mircea 1907-1986 .... **CLC 19**
See also CA 65-68; 119; CANR 30, 62; CDWLB 4; DLB 220; EWL 3; MTCW 1; RGWL 3; SFW 4

Eliot, A. D.
See Jewett, (Theodora) Sarah Orne

Eliot, Alice
See Jewett, (Theodora) Sarah Orne

Eliot, Dan
See Silverberg, Robert

Eliot, George 1819-1880 ...... **NCLC 4, 13, 23, 41, 49, 89, 118; PC 20; WLC**
See also BRW 5; BRWC 1; BRWR 2; CD-BLB 1832-1890; CN 7; CPW; DA; DA3; DAB; DAC; DAM MST, NOV; DLB 21, 35, 55; LATS 1; LMFS 1; NFS 17; RGEL 2; RGSF 2; SSFS 8; TEA; WLIT 3

Eliot, John 1604-1690 .... **LC 5**
See also DLB 24

Eliot, T(homas) S(tearns)
1888-1965 ...... **CLC 1, 2, 3, 6, 9, 10, 13, 15, 24, 34, 41, 55, 57, 113; PC 5, 31; WLC**
See also AAYA 28; AMW; AMWC 1; AMWR 1; BRW 7; BRWR 2; CA 5-8R; 25-28R; CANR 41; CDALB 1929-1941; DA; DA3; DAB; DAC; DAM DRAM, MST, POET; DFS 4, 13; DLB 7, 10, 45, 63, 245; DLBY 1988; EWL 3; EXPP; LAIT 3; LATS 1; LMFS 2; MTCW 1, 2; PAB; PFS 1, 7; RGAL 4; RGEL 2; TUS; WLIT 4; WP

Elizabeth 1866-1941 .... **TCLC 41**

Elkin, Stanley L(awrence)
1930-1995 .. **CLC 4, 6, 9, 14, 27, 51, 91; SSC 12**
See also AMWS 6; BPFB 1; CA 9-12R; 148; CANR 8, 46; CN 7; CPW; DAM NOV, POP; DLB 2, 28, 218, 278; DLBY 1980; EWL 3; INT CANR-8; MTCW 1, 2; RGAL 4

Evans, Marian
    See Eliot, George
Evans, Mary Ann
    See Eliot, George
Evarts, Esther
    See Benson, Sally
Everett, Percival
    See Everett, Percival L.
    See also CSW
Everett, Percival L. 1956- .... **CLC 57**
    See Everett, Percival
    See also BW 2; CA 129; CANR 94
Everson, R(onald) G(ilmour)
    1903-1992 .... **CLC 27**
    See also CA 17-20R; DLB 88
Everson, William (Oliver)
    1912-1994 .... **CLC 1, 5, 14**
    See also BG 2; CA 9-12R; 145; CANR 20;
    DLB 5, 16, 212; MTCW 1
Evtushenko, Evgenii Aleksandrovich
    See Yevtushenko, Yevgeny (Alexandrovich)
    See also RGWL 2, 3
Ewart, Gavin (Buchanan)
    1916-1995 .... **CLC 13, 46**
    See also BRWS 7; CA 89-92; 150; CANR
    17, 46; CP 7; DLB 40; MTCW 1
Ewers, Hanns Heinz 1871-1943 ..... **TCLC 12**
    See also CA 109; 149
Ewing, Frederick R.
    See Sturgeon, Theodore (Hamilton)
Exley, Frederick (Earl) 1929-1992 .... **CLC 6,
    11**
    See also AITN 2; BPFB 1; CA 81-84; 138;
    CANR 117; DLB 143; DLBY 1981
Eynhardt, Guillermo
    See Quiroga, Horacio (Sylvestre)
Ezekiel, Nissim 1924- .... **CLC 61**
    See also CA 61-64; CP 7; EWL 3
Ezekiel, Tish O'Dowd 1943- .... **CLC 34**
    See also CA 129
Fadeev, Aleksandr Aleksandrovich
    See Bulgya, Alexander Alexandrovich
    See also DLB 272
Fadeev, Alexandr Alexandrovich
    See Bulgya, Alexander Alexandrovich
    See also EWL 3
Fadeyev, A.
    See Bulgya, Alexander Alexandrovich
Fadeyev, Alexander .... **TCLC 53**
    See Bulgya, Alexander Alexandrovich
Fagen, Donald 1948- .... **CLC 26**
Fainzilberg, Ilya Arnoldovich 1897-1937
    See Ilf, Ilya
    See also CA 120; 165
Fair, Ronald L. 1932- .... **CLC 18**
    See also BW 1; CA 69-72; CANR 25; DLB
    33
Fairbairn, Roger
    See Carr, John Dickson
Fairbairns, Zoe (Ann) 1948- .... **CLC 32**
    See also CA 103; CANR 21, 85; CN 7
Fairfield, Flora
    See Alcott, Louisa May
Fairman, Paul W. 1916-1977
    See Queen, Ellery
    See also CA 114; SFW 4
Falco, Gian
    See Papini, Giovanni
Falconer, James
    See Kirkup, James
Falconer, Kenneth
    See Kornbluth, C(yril) M.
Falkland, Samuel
    See Heijermans, Herman
Fallaci, Oriana 1930- .... **CLC 11, 110**
    See also CA 77-80; CANR 15, 58; FW;
    MTCW 1

Faludi, Susan 1959- .... **CLC 140**
    See also CA 138; FW; MTCW 1; NCFS 3
Faludy, George 1913- .... **CLC 42**
    See also CA 21-24R
Faludy, Gyoergy
    See Faludy, George
Fanon, Frantz 1925-1961 .... **BLC 2; CLC 74**
    See also BW 1; CA 116; 89-92; DAM
    MULT; LMFS 2; WLIT 2
Fanshawe, Ann 1625-1680 .... **LC 11**
Fante, John (Thomas) 1911-1983 ..... **CLC 60**
    See also AMWS 11; CA 69-72; 109; CANR
    23, 104; DLB 130; DLBY 1983
Far, Sui Sin .... **SSC 62**
    See Eaton, Edith Maude
    See also SSFS 4
Farah, Nuruddin 1945- ...... **BLC 2; CLC 53,
    137**
    See also AFW; BW 2, 3; CA 106; CANR
    81; CDWLB 3; CN 7; DAM MULT; DLB
    125; EWL 3; WLIT 2
Fargue, Leon-Paul 1876(?)-1947 .... **TCLC 11**
    See also CA 109; CANR 107; DLB 258;
    EWL 3
Farigoule, Louis
    See Romains, Jules
Farina, Richard 1936(?)-1966 .... **CLC 9**
    See also CA 81-84; 25-28R
Farley, Walter (Lorimer)
    1915-1989 .... **CLC 17**
    See also BYA 14; CA 17-20R; CANR 8,
    29, 84; DLB 22; JRDA; MAICYA 1, 2;
    SATA 2, 43, 132; YAW
Farmer, Philip Jose 1918- .... **CLC 1, 19**
    See also AAYA 28; BPFB 1; CA 1-4R;
    CANR 4, 35, 111; DLB 8; MTCW 1;
    SATA 93; SCFW 2; SFW 4
Farquhar, George 1677-1707 .... **LC 21**
    See also BRW 2; DAM DRAM; DLB 84;
    RGEL 2
Farrell, J(ames) G(ordon)
    1935-1979 .... **CLC 6**
    See also CA 73-76; 89-92; CANR 36; DLB
    14, 271; MTCW 1; RGEL 2; RHW; WLIT
    4
Farrell, James T(homas) 1904-1979 . **CLC 1,
    4, 8, 11, 66; SSC 28**
    See also AMW; BPFB 1; CA 5-8R; 89-92;
    CANR 9, 61; DLB 4, 9, 86; DLBD 2;
    EWL 3; MTCW 1, 2; RGAL 4
Farrell, Warren (Thomas) 1943- ...... **CLC 70**
    See also CA 146; CANR 120
Farren, Richard J.
    See Betjeman, John
Farren, Richard M.
    See Betjeman, John
Fassbinder, Rainer Werner
    1946-1982 .... **CLC 20**
    See also CA 93-96; 106; CANR 31
Fast, Howard (Melvin) 1914-2003 .. **CLC 23,
    131**
    See also AAYA 16; BPFB 1; CA 1-4R, 181;
    CAAE 181; CAAS 18; CANR 1, 33, 54,
    75, 98; CMW 4; CN 7; CPW; DAM NOV;
    DLB 9; INT CANR-33; LATS 1; MTCW
    1; RHW; SATA 7; SATA-Essay 107;
    TCWW 2; YAW
Faulcon, Robert
    See Holdstock, Robert P.
Faulkner, William (Cuthbert)
    1897-1962 .... **CLC 1, 3, 6, 8, 9, 11, 14,
    18, 28, 52, 68; SSC 1, 35, 42; WLC**
    See also AAYA 7; AMW; AMWR 1; BPFB
    1; BYA 5; CA 81-84; CANR 33; CDALB
    1929-1941; DA; DA3; DAB; DAC; DAM
    MST, NOV; DLB 9, 11, 44, 102; DLBD
    2; DLBY 1986, 1997; EWL 3; EXPN;

EXPS; LAIT 2; LATS 1; LMFS 2; MTCW
    1, 2; NFS 4, 8, 13; RGAL 4; RGSF 2;
    SSFS 2, 5, 6, 12; TUS
Fauset, Jessie Redmon
    1882(?)-1961 .. **BLC 2; CLC 19, 54; HR
    2**
    See also AFAW 2; BW 1; CA 109; CANR
    83; DAM MULT; DLB 51; FW; LMFS 2;
    MAWW
Faust, Frederick (Schiller)
    1892-1944(?) .... **TCLC 49**
    See Austin, Frank; Brand, Max; Challis,
    George; Dawson, Peter; Dexter, Martin;
    Evans, Evan; Frederick, John; Frost, Fred-
    erick; Manning, David; Silver, Nicholas
    See also CA 108; 152; DAM POP; DLB
    256; TUS
Faust, Irvin 1924- .... **CLC 8**
    See also CA 33-36R; CANR 28, 67; CN 7;
    DLB 2, 28, 218, 278; DLBY 1980
Faustino, Domingo 1811-1888 ...... **NCLC 123**
Fawkes, Guy
    See Benchley, Robert (Charles)
Fearing, Kenneth (Flexner)
    1902-1961 .... **CLC 51**
    See also CA 93-96; CANR 59; CMW 4;
    DLB 9; RGAL 4
Fecamps, Elise
    See Creasey, John
Federman, Raymond 1928- .... **CLC 6, 47**
    See also CA 17-20R; CAAE 208; CAAS 8;
    CANR 10, 43, 83, 108; CN 7; DLBY
    1980
Federspiel, J(uerg) F. 1931- .... **CLC 42**
    See also CA 146
Feiffer, Jules (Ralph) 1929- ...... **CLC 2, 8, 64**
    See also AAYA 3; CA 17-20R; CAD; CANR
    30, 59; CD 5; DAM DRAM; DLB 7, 44;
    INT CANR-30; MTCW 1; SATA 8, 61,
    111
Feige, Hermann Albert Otto Maximilian
    See Traven, B.
Feinberg, David B. 1956-1994 .... **CLC 59**
    See also CA 135; 147
Feinstein, Elaine 1930- .... **CLC 36**
    See also CA 69-72; CAAS 1; CANR 31,
    68; CN 7; CP 7; CWP; DLB 14, 40;
    MTCW 1
Feke, Gilbert David .... **CLC 65**
Feldman, Irving (Mordecai) 1928- ..... **CLC 7**
    See also CA 1-4R; CANR 1; CP 7; DLB
    169
Felix-Tchicaya, Gerald
    See Tchicaya, Gerald Felix
Fellini, Federico 1920-1993 .... **CLC 16, 85**
    See also CA 65-68; 143; CANR 33
Felltham, Owen 1602(?)-1668 .... **LC 92**
    See also DLB 126, 151
Felsen, Henry Gregor 1916-1995 ..... **CLC 17**
    See also CA 1-4R; 180; CANR 1; SAAS 2;
    SATA 1
Felski, Rita .... **CLC 65**
Fenno, Jack
    See Calisher, Hortense
Fenollosa, Ernest (Francisco)
    1853-1908 .... **TCLC 91**
Fenton, James Martin 1949- .... **CLC 32**
    See also CA 102; CANR 108; CP 7; DLB
    40; PFS 11
Ferber, Edna 1887-1968 .... **CLC 18, 93**
    See also AITN 1; CA 5-8R; 25-28R; CANR
    68, 105; DLB 9, 28, 86, 266; MTCW 1,
    2; RGAL 4; RHW; SATA 7; TCWW 2
Ferdowsi, Abu'l Qasem 940-1020 . **CMLC 43**
    See also RGWL 2, 3
Ferguson, Helen
    See Kavan, Anna
Ferguson, Niall 1964- .... **CLC 134**
    See also CA 190

Galt, John 1779-1839 .... **NCLC 1, 110**
　　See also DLB 99, 116, 159; RGEL 2; RGSF
　　2
Galvin, James 1951- .... **CLC 38**
　　See also CA 108; CANR 26
Gamboa, Federico 1864-1939 .... **TCLC 36**
　　See also CA 167; HW 2; LAW
Gandhi, M. K.
　　See Gandhi, Mohandas Karamchand
Gandhi, Mahatma
　　See Gandhi, Mohandas Karamchand
Gandhi, Mohandas Karamchand
　　1869-1948 .... **TCLC 59**
　　See also CA 121; 132; DA3; DAM MULT;
　　MTCW 1, 2
Gann, Ernest Kellogg 1910-1991 ..... **CLC 23**
　　See also AITN 1; BPFB 2; CA 1-4R; 136;
　　CANR 1, 83; RHW
Gao Xingjian 1940- .... **CLC 167**
　　See Xingjian, Gao
Garber, Eric 1943(?)-
　　See Holleran, Andrew
　　See also CANR 89
Garcia, Cristina 1958- .... **CLC 76**
　　See also AMWS 11; CA 141; CANR 73;
　　DNFS 1; EWL 3; HW 2
Garcia Lorca, Federico 1898-1936 ...... **DC 2;**
　　HLC 2; PC 3; TCLC 1, 7, 49; WLC
　　See Lorca, Federico Garcia
　　See also AAYA 46; CA 104; 131; CANR
　　81; DA; DA3; DAB; DAC; DAM DRAM,
　　MST, MULT, POET; DFS 4, 10; DLB
　　108; EWL 3; HW 1, 2; LATS 1; MTCW
　　1, 2; TWA
Garcia Marquez, Gabriel (Jose)
　　1928- .... **CLC 2, 3, 8, 10, 15, 27, 47, 55,**
　　68, 170; HLC 1; SSC 8; WLC
　　See also AAYA 3, 33; BEST 89:1, 90:4;
　　BPFB 2; BYA 12; CA 33-36R; CANR 10,
　　28, 50, 75, 82; CDWLB 3; CPW; DA;
　　DA3; DAB; DAC; DAM MST, MULT,
　　NOV, POP; DLB 113; DNFS 1, 2; EWL
　　3; EXPN; EXPS; HW 1, 2; LAIT 2; LATS
　　1; LAW; LAWS 1; LMFS; MTCW 1, 2;
　　NCFS 3; NFS 1, 5, 10; RGSF 2; RGWL
　　2, 3; SSFS 1, 6, 16; TWA; WLIT 1
Garcilaso de la Vega, El Inca
　　1503-1536 .... **HLCS 1**
　　See also LAW
Gard, Janice
　　See Latham, Jean Lee
Gard, Roger Martin du
　　See Martin du Gard, Roger
Gardam, Jane (Mary) 1928- .... **CLC 43**
　　See also CA 49-52; CANR 2, 18, 33, 54,
　　106; CLR 12; DLB 14, 161, 231; MAI-
　　CYA 1, 2; MTCW 1; SAAS 9; SATA 39,
　　76, 130; SATA-Brief 28; YAW
Gardner, Herb(ert) 1934- .... **CLC 44**
　　See also CA 149; CAD; CANR 119; CD 5
Gardner, John (Champlin), Jr.
　　1933-1982 ...... **CLC 2, 3, 5, 7, 8, 10, 18,**
　　28, 34; SSC 7
　　See also AAYA 45; AITN 1; AMWS 6;
　　BPFB 2; CA 65-68; 107; CANR 33, 73;
　　CDALBS; CPW; DA3; DAM NOV, POP;
　　DLB 2; DLBY 1982; EWL 3; FANT;
　　LATS 1; MTCW 1; NFS 3; RGAL 4;
　　RGSF 2; SATA 40; SATA-Obit 31; SSFS
　　8
Gardner, John (Edmund) 1926- .... **CLC 30**
　　See also CA 103; CANR 15, 69; CMW 4;
　　CPW; DAM POP; MTCW 1
Gardner, Miriam
　　See Bradley, Marion Zimmer
　　See also GLL 1
Gardner, Noel
　　See Kuttner, Henry

Gardons, S. S.
　　See Snodgrass, W(illiam) D(e Witt)
Garfield, Leon 1921-1996 .... **CLC 12**
　　See also AAYA 8; BYA 1, 3; CA 17-20R;
　　152; CANR 38, 41, 78; CLR 21; DLB
　　161; JRDA; MAICYA 1, 2; MAICYAS 1;
　　SATA 1, 32, 76; SATA-Obit 90; TEA;
　　WYA; YAW
Garland, (Hannibal) Hamlin
　　1860-1940 .... **SSC 18; TCLC 3**
　　See also CA 104; DLB 12, 71, 78, 186;
　　RGAL 4; RGSF 2; TCWW 2
Garneau, (Hector de) Saint-Denys
　　1912-1943 .... **TCLC 13**
　　See also CA 111; DLB 88
Garner, Alan 1934- .... **CLC 17**
　　See also AAYA 18; BYA 3, 5; CA 73-76,
　　178; CAAE 178; CANR 15, 64; CLR 20;
　　CPW; DAB; DAM POP; DLB 161, 261;
　　FANT; MAICYA 1, 2; MTCW 1, 2; SATA
　　18, 69; SATA-Essay 108; SUFW 1, 2;
　　YAW
Garner, Hugh 1913-1979 .... **CLC 13**
　　See Warwick, Jarvis
　　See also CA 69-72; CANR 31; CCA 1; DLB
　　68
Garnett, David 1892-1981 .... **CLC 3**
　　See also CA 5-8R; 103; CANR 17, 79; DLB
　　34; FANT; MTCW 2; RGEL 2; SFW 4;
　　SUFW 1
Garos, Stephanie
　　See Katz, Steve
Garrett, George (Palmer) 1929- .. **CLC 3, 11,**
　　51; SSC 30
　　See also AMWS 7; BPFB 2; CA 1-4R;
　　CAAE 202; CAAS 5; CANR 1, 42, 67,
　　109; CN 7; CP 7; CSW; DLB 2, 5, 130,
　　152; DLBY 1983
Garrick, David 1717-1779 .... **LC 15**
　　See also DAM DRAM; DLB 84, 213;
　　RGEL 2
Garrigue, Jean 1914-1972 .... **CLC 2, 8**
　　See also CA 5-8R; 37-40R; CANR 20
Garrison, Frederick
　　See Sinclair, Upton (Beall)
Garro, Elena 1920(?)-1998 .... **HLCS 1**
　　See also CA 131; 169; CWW 2; DLB 145;
　　EWL 3; HW 1; LAWS 1; WLIT 1
Garth, Will
　　See Hamilton, Edmond; Kuttner, Henry
Garvey, Marcus (Moziah, Jr.)
　　1887-1940 .... **BLC 2; HR 2; TCLC 41**
　　See also BW 1; CA 120; 124; CANR 79;
　　DAM MULT
Gary, Romain .... **CLC 25**
　　See Kacew, Romain
　　See also DLB 83
Gascar, Pierre .... **CLC 11**
　　See Fournier, Pierre
　　See also EWL 3
Gascoyne, David (Emery)
　　1916-2001 .... **CLC 45**
　　See also CA 65-68; 200; CANR 10, 28, 54;
　　CP 7; DLB 20; MTCW 1; RGEL 2
Gaskell, Elizabeth Cleghorn
　　1810-1865 .... **NCLC 5, 70, 97; SSC 25**
　　See also BRW 5; CDBLB 1832-1890; DAB;
　　DAM MST; DLB 21, 144, 159; RGEL 2;
　　RGSF 2; TEA
Gass, William H(oward) 1924- . **CLC 1, 2, 8,**
　　11, 15, 39, 132; SSC 12
　　See also AMWS 6; CA 17-20R; CANR 30,
　　71, 100; CN 7; DLB 2, 227; EWL 3;
　　MTCW 1, 2; RGAL 4
Gassendi, Pierre 1592-1655 .... **LC 54**
　　See also GFL Beginnings to 1789
Gasset, Jose Ortega y
　　See Ortega y Gasset, Jose

Gates, Henry Louis, Jr. 1950- ... **BLCS; CLC**
　　65
　　See also BW 2, 3; CA 109; CANR 25, 53,
　　75; CSW; DA3; DAM MULT; DLB 67;
　　EWL 3; MTCW 1; RGAL 4
Gautier, Theophile 1811-1872 .. **NCLC 1, 59;**
　　PC 18; SSC 20
　　See also DAM POET; DLB 119; EW 6;
　　GFL 1789 to the Present; RGWL 2, 3;
　　SUFW; TWA
Gawsworth, John
　　See Bates, H(erbert) E(rnest)
Gay, John 1685-1732 .... **LC 49**
　　See also BRW 3; DAM DRAM; DLB 84,
　　95; RGEL 2; WLIT 3
Gay, Oliver
　　See Gogarty, Oliver St. John
Gay, Peter (Jack) 1923- .... **CLC 158**
　　See also CA 13-16R; CANR 18, 41, 77;
　　INT CANR-18
Gaye, Marvin (Pentz, Jr.)
　　1939-1984 .... **CLC 26**
　　See also CA 195; 112
Gebler, Carlo (Ernest) 1954- .... **CLC 39**
　　See also CA 119; 133; CANR 96; DLB 271
Gee, Maggie (Mary) 1948- .... **CLC 57**
　　See also CA 130; CN 7; DLB 207
Gee, Maurice (Gough) 1931- .... **CLC 29**
　　See also AAYA 42; CA 97-100; CANR 67;
　　CLR 56; CN 7; CWRI 5; EWL 3; MAI-
　　CYA 2; RGSF 2; SATA 46, 101
Geiogamah, Hanay 1945- .... **NNAL**
　　See also CA 153; DAM MULT; DLB 175
Gelbart, Larry (Simon) 1928- .... **CLC 21, 61**
　　See Gelbart, Larry
　　See also CA 73-76; CANR 45, 94
Gelbart, Larry 1928-
　　See Gelbart, Larry (Simon)
　　See also CAD; CD 5
Gelber, Jack 1932- .... **CLC 1, 6, 14, 79**
　　See also CA 1-4R; CAD; CANR 2; DLB 7,
　　228
Gellhorn, Martha (Ellis)
　　1908-1998 .... **CLC 14, 60**
　　See also CA 77-80; 164; CANR 44; CN 7;
　　DLBY 1982, 1998
Genet, Jean 1910-1986 .. **CLC 1, 2, 5, 10, 14,**
　　44, 46; TCLC 128
　　See also CA 13-16R; CANR 18; DA3;
　　DAM DRAM; DFS 10; DLB 72; DLBY
　　1986; EW 13; EWL 3; GFL 1789 to the
　　Present; GLL 1; LMFS 2; MTCW 1, 2;
　　RGWL 2, 3; TWA
Gent, Peter 1942- .... **CLC 29**
　　See also AITN 1; CA 89-92; DLBY 1982
Gentile, Giovanni 1875-1944 .... **TCLC 96**
　　See also CA 119
Gentlewoman in New England, A
　　See Bradstreet, Anne
Gentlewoman in Those Parts, A
　　See Bradstreet, Anne
Geoffrey of Monmouth c.
　　1100-1155 .... **CMLC 44**
　　See also DLB 146; TEA
George, Jean
　　See George, Jean Craighead
George, Jean Craighead 1919- .... **CLC 35**
　　See also AAYA 8; BYA 2, 4; CA 5-8R;
　　CANR 25; CLR 1; 80; DLB 52; JRDA;
　　MAICYA 1, 2; SATA 2, 68, 124; WYA;
　　YAW
George, Stefan (Anton) 1868-1933 . **TCLC 2,**
　　14
　　See also CA 104; 193; EW 8; EWL 3
Georges, Georges Martin
　　See Simenon, Georges (Jacques Christian)
Gerald of Wales c. 1146-c. 1223 ... **CMLC 60**
Gerhardi, William Alexander
　　See Gerhardie, William Alexander

Godden, (Margaret) Rumer
 1907-1998 .... **CLC 53**
  See also AAYA 6; BPFB 2; BYA 2, 5; CA
  5-8R; 172; CANR 4, 27, 36, 55, 80; CLR
  20; CN 7; CWRI 5; DLB 161; MAICYA
  1, 2; RHW; SAAS 12; SATA 3, 36; SATA-
  Obit 109; TEA

Godoy Alcayaga, Lucila 1899-1957 .. **HLC 2;**
 PC 32; TCLC 2
  See Mistral, Gabriela
  See also BW 2; CA 104; 131; CANR 81;
  DAM MULT; DNFS; HW 1, 2; MTCW 1,
  2

Godwin, Gail (Kathleen) 1937- ..... **CLC 5, 8,**
 22, 31, 69, 125
  See also BPFB 2; CA 29-32R; CANR 15,
  43, 69; CN 7; CPW; CSW; DA3; DAM
  POP; DLB 6, 234; INT CANR-15;
  MTCW 1, 2

Godwin, William 1756-1836 .... **NCLC 14**
  See also CDBLB 1789-1832; CMW 4; DLB
  39, 104, 142, 158, 163, 262; HGG; RGEL
  2

Goebbels, Josef
  See Goebbels, (Paul) Joseph

Goebbels, (Paul) Joseph
 1897-1945 .... **TCLC 68**
  See also CA 115; 148

Goebbels, Joseph Paul
  See Goebbels, (Paul) Joseph

Goethe, Johann Wolfgang von
 1749-1832 .... **DC 20; NCLC 4, 22, 34,**
 90; PC 5; SSC 38; WLC
  See also CDWLB 2; DA; DA3; DAB;
  DAC; DAM DRAM, MST, POET; DLB
  94; EW 5; LATS 1; LMFS 1; RGWL 2,
  3; TWA

Gogarty, Oliver St. John
 1878-1957 .... **TCLC 15**
  See also CA 109; 150; DLB 15, 19; RGEL
  2

Gogol, Nikolai (Vasilyevich)
 1809-1852 .... **DC 1; NCLC 5, 15, 31;**
 SSC 4, 29, 52; WLC
  See also DA; DAB; DAC; DAM DRAM,
  MST; DFS 12; DLB 198; EW 6; EXPS;
  RGSF 2; RGWL 2, 3; SSFS 7; TWA

Goines, Donald 1937(?)-1974 ... **BLC 2; CLC**
 80
  See also AITN 1; BW 1, 3; CA 124; 114;
  CANR 82; CMW 4; DA3; DAM MULT;
  POP; DLB 33

Gold, Herbert 1924- ... **CLC 4, 7, 14, 42, 152**
  See also CA 9-12R; CANR 17, 45; CN 7;
  DLB 2; DLBY 1981

Goldbarth, Albert 1948- .... **CLC 5, 38**
  See also AMWS 12; CA 53-56; CANR 6,
  40; CP 7; DLB 120

Goldberg, Anatol 1910-1982 .... **CLC 34**
  See also CA 131; 117

Goldemberg, Isaac 1945- .... **CLC 52**
  See also CA 69-72; CAAS 12; CANR 11,
  32; EWL 3; HW 1; WLIT 1

Golding, William (Gerald)
 1911-1993 ..... **CLC 1, 2, 3, 8, 10, 17, 27,**
 58, 81; WLC
  See also AAYA 5, 44; BPFB 2; BRWR 1;
  BRWS 1; BYA 2; CA 5-8R; 141; CANR
  13, 33, 54; CDBLB 1945-1960; DA;
  DA3; DAB; DAC; DAM MST, NOV;
  DLB 15, 100, 255; EWL 3; EXPN; HGG;
  LAIT 4; MTCW 1, 2; NFS 2; RGEL 2;
  RHW; SFW 4; TEA; WLIT 4; YAW

Goldman, Emma 1869-1940 .... **TCLC 13**
  See also CA 110; 150; DLB 221; FW;
  RGAL 4; TUS

Goldman, Francisco 1954- .... **CLC 76**
  See also CA 162

Goldman, William (W.) 1931- ...... **CLC 1, 48**
  See also BPFB 2; CA 9-12R; CANR 29,
  69, 106; CN 7; DLB 44; FANT; IDFW 3,
  4

Goldmann, Lucien 1913-1970 .... **CLC 24**
  See also CA 25-28; CAP 2

Goldoni, Carlo 1707-1793 .... **LC 4**
  See also DAM DRAM; EW 4; RGWL 2, 3

Goldsberry, Steven 1949- .... **CLC 34**
  See also CA 131

Goldsmith, Oliver 1730-1774 .... **DC 8; LC 2,**
 48; WLC
  See also BRW 3; CDBLB 1660-1789; DA;
  DAB; DAC; DAM DRAM, MST, NOV,
  POET; DFS 1; DLB 39, 89, 104, 109, 142;
  IDTP; RGEL 2; SATA 26; TEA; WLIT 3

Goldsmith, Peter
  See Priestley, J(ohn) B(oynton)

Gombrowicz, Witold 1904-1969 .... **CLC 4, 7,**
 11, 49
  See also CA 19-20; 25-28R; CANR 105;
  CAP 2; CDWLB 4; DAM DRAM; DLB
  215; EW 12; EWL 3; RGWL 2, 3; TWA

Gomez de Avellaneda, Gertrudis
 1814-1873 .... **NCLC 111**
  See also LAW

Gomez de la Serna, Ramon
 1888-1963 .... **CLC 9**
  See also CA 153; 116; CANR 79; EWL 3;
  HW 1, 2

Goncharov, Ivan Alexandrovich
 1812-1891 .... **NCLC 1, 63**
  See also DLB 238; EW 6; RGWL 2, 3

Goncourt, Edmond (Louis Antoine Huot) de
 1822-1896 .... **NCLC 7**
  See also DLB 123; EW 7; GFL 1789 to the
  Present; RGWL 2, 3

Goncourt, Jules (Alfred Huot) de
 1830-1870 .... **NCLC 7**
  See also DLB 123; EW 7; GFL 1789 to the
  Present; RGWL 2, 3

Gongora (y Argote), Luis de
 1561-1627 .... **LC 72**
  See also RGWL 2, 3

Gontier, Fernande 19(?)- .... **CLC 50**

Gonzalez Martinez, Enrique
 1871-1952 .... **TCLC 72**
  See also CA 166; CANR 81; EWL 3; HW
  1, 2

Goodison, Lorna 1947- .... **PC 36**
  See also CA 142; CANR 88; CP 7; CWP;
  DLB 157; EWL 3

Goodman, Paul 1911-1972 ..... **CLC 1, 2, 4, 7**
  See also CA 19-20; 37-40R; CAD; CANR
  34; CAP 2; DLB 130, 246; MTCW 1;
  RGAL 4

Gordimer, Nadine 1923- ...... **CLC 3, 5, 7, 10,**
 18, 33, 51, 70, 123, 160, 161; SSC 17;
 WLCS
  See also AAYA 39; AFW; BRWS 2; CA
  5-8R; CANR 3, 28, 56, 88; CN 7; DA;
  DA3; DAB; DAM MST, NOV;
  DLB 225; EWL 3; EXPS; INT CANR-28;
  LATS 1; MTCW 1, 2; NFS 4; RGEL 2;
  RGSF 2; SSFS 2, 14; TWA; WLIT 2;
  YAW

Gordon, Adam Lindsay
 1833-1870 .... **NCLC 21**
  See also DLB 230

Gordon, Caroline 1895-1981 . **CLC 6, 13, 29,**
 83; SSC 15
  See also AMW; CA 11-12; 103; CANR 36;
  CAP 1; DLB 4, 9, 102; DLBD 17; DLBY
  1981; EWL 3; MTCW 1, 2; RGAL 4;
  RGSF 2

Gordon, Charles William 1860-1937
  See Connor, Ralph
  See also CA 109

Gordon, Mary (Catherine) 1949- .... **CLC 13,**
 22, 128; SSC 59
  See also AMWS 4; BPFB 2; CA 102;
  CANR 44, 92; CN 7; DLB 6; DLBY
  1981; FW; INT CA-102; MTCW 1

Gordon, N. J.
  See Bosman, Herman Charles

Gordon, Sol 1923- .... **CLC 26**
  See also CA 53-56; CANR 4; SATA 11

Gordone, Charles 1925-1995 .. **CLC 1, 4; DC**
 8
  See also BW 1, 3; CA 93-96; 180; 150;
  CAAE 180; CAD; CANR 55; DAM
  DRAM; DLB 7; INT 93-96; MTCW 1

Gore, Catherine 1800-1861 .... **NCLC 65**
  See also DLB 116; RGEL 2

Gorenko, Anna Andreevna
  See Akhmatova, Anna

Gorky, Maxim .... **SSC 28; TCLC 8; WLC**
  See Peshkov, Alexei Maximovich
  See also DAB; DFS 9; EW 8; EWL 3;
  MTCW 2; TWA

Goryan, Sirak
  See Saroyan, William

Gosse, Edmund (William)
 1849-1928 .... **TCLC 28**
  See also CA 117; DLB 57, 144, 184; RGEL
  2

Gotlieb, Phyllis Fay (Bloom) 1926- .. **CLC 18**
  See also CA 13-16R; CANR 7; DLB 88,
  251; SFW 4

Gottesman, S. D.
  See Kornbluth, C(yril) M.; Pohl, Frederik

Gottfried von Strassburg fl. c.
 1170-1215 .... **CMLC 10**
  See also CDWLB 2; DLB 138; EW 1;
  RGWL 2, 3

Gotthelf, Jeremias 1797-1854 .... **NCLC 117**
  See also DLB 133; RGWL 2, 3

Gottschalk, Laura Riding
  See Jackson, Laura (Riding)

Gould, Lois 1932(?)-2002 .... **CLC 4, 10**
  See also CA 77-80; 208; CANR 29; MTCW
  1

Gould, Stephen Jay 1941-2002 .... **CLC 163**
  See also AAYA 26; BEST 90:2; CA 77-80;
  205; CANR 10, 27, 56, 75; CPW; INT
  CANR-27; MTCW 1, 2

Gourmont, Remy(-Marie-Charles) de
 1858-1915 .... **TCLC 17**
  See also CA 109; 150; GFL 1789 to the
  Present; MTCW 2

Govier, Katherine 1948- .... **CLC 51**
  See also CA 101; CANR 18, 40; CCA 1

Gower, John c. 1330-1408 .... **LC 76**
  See also BRW 1; DLB 146; RGEL 2

Goyen, (Charles) William
 1915-1983 .... **CLC 5, 8, 14, 40**
  See also AITN 2; CA 5-8R; 110; CANR 6,
  71; DLB 2, 218; DLBY 1983; EWL 3;
  INT CANR-6

Goytisolo, Juan 1931- .... **CLC 5, 10, 23, 133;**
 HLC 1
  See also CA 85-88; CANR 32, 61; CWW
  2; DAM MULT; EWL 3; GLL 2; HW 1,
  2; MTCW 1, 2

Gozzano, Guido 1883-1916 .... **PC 10**
  See also CA 154; DLB 114; EWL 3

Gozzi, (Conte) Carlo 1720-1806 .... **NCLC 23**

Grabbe, Christian Dietrich
 1801-1836 .... **NCLC 2**
  See also DLB 133; RGWL 2, 3

Grace, Patricia Frances 1937- .... **CLC 56**
  See also CA 176; CANR 118; CN 7; EWL
  3; RGSF 2

Gracian y Morales, Baltasar
 1601-1658 .... **LC 15**

Griffin, John Howard 1920-1980 ..... **CLC 68**
　　See also AITN 1; CA 1-4R; 101; CANR 2
Griffin, Peter 1942- .... **CLC 39**
　　See also CA 136
Griffith, D(avid Lewelyn) W(ark)
　　1875(?)-1948 .... **TCLC 68**
　　See also CA 119; 150; CANR 80
Griffith, Lawrence
　　See Griffith, D(avid Lewelyn) W(ark)
Griffiths, Trevor 1935- .... **CLC 13, 52**
　　See also CA 97-100; CANR 45; CBD; CD
　　5; DLB 13, 245
Griggs, Sutton (Elbert)
　　1872-1930 .... **TCLC 77**
　　See also CA 123; 186; DLB 50
Grigson, Geoffrey (Edward Harvey)
　　1905-1985 .... **CLC 7, 39**
　　See also CA 25-28R; 118; CANR 20, 33;
　　DLB 27; MTCW 1, 2
Grile, Dod
　　See Bierce, Ambrose (Gwinett)
Grillparzer, Franz 1791-1872 .... **DC 14;**
　　NCLC 1, 102; SSC 37
　　See also CDWLB 2; DLB 133; EW 5;
　　RGWL 2, 3; TWA
Grimble, Reverend Charles James
　　See Eliot, T(homas) S(tearns)
Grimke, Angelina (Emily) Weld
　　1880-1958 .... **HR 2**
　　See Weld, Angelina (Emily) Grimke
　　See also BW 1; CA 124; DAM POET; DLB
　　50, 54
Grimke, Charlotte L(ottie) Forten
　　1837(?)-1914
　　See Forten, Charlotte L.
　　See also BW 1; CA 117; 124; DAM MULT,
　　POET
Grimm, Jacob Ludwig Karl
　　1785-1863 .... **NCLC 3, 77; SSC 36**
　　See also DLB 90; MAICYA 1, 2; RGSF 2;
　　RGWL 2, 3; SATA 22; WCH
Grimm, Wilhelm Karl 1786-1859 .. **NCLC 3,**
　　77; SSC 36
　　See also CDWLB 2; DLB 90; MAICYA 1,
　　2; RGSF 2; RGWL 2, 3; SATA 22; WCH
Grimmelshausen, Hans Jakob Christoffel
　　von
　　See Grimmelshausen, Johann Jakob Christ-
　　offel von
　　See also RGWL 2, 3
Grimmelshausen, Johann Jakob Christoffel
　　von 1621-1676 .... **LC 6**
　　See Grimmelshausen, Hans Jakob Christof-
　　fel von
　　See also CDWLB 2; DLB 168
Grindel, Eugene 1895-1952
　　See Eluard, Paul
　　See also CA 104; 193; LMFS 2
Grisham, John 1955- .... **CLC 84**
　　See also AAYA 14, 47; BPFB 2; CA 138;
　　CANR 47, 69, 114; CMW 4; CN 7; CPW;
　　CSW; DA3; DAM POP; MSW; MTCW 2
Grossman, David 1954- .... **CLC 67**
　　See also CA 138; CANR 114; CWW 2;
　　EWL 3
Grossman, Vasilii Semenovich
　　See Grossman, Vasily (Semenovich)
　　See also DLB 272
Grossman, Vasily (Semenovich)
　　1905-1964 .... **CLC 41**
　　See Grossman, Vasilii Semenovich
　　See also CA 124; 130; MTCW 1
Grove, Frederick Philip .... **TCLC 4**
　　See Greve, Felix Paul (Berthold Friedrich)
　　See also DLB 92; RGEL 2
Grubb
　　See Crumb, R(obert)

Grumbach, Doris (Isaac) 1918- . **CLC 13, 22,**
　　64
　　See also CA 5-8R; CAAS 2; CANR 9, 42,
　　70; CN 7; INT CANR-9; MTCW 2
Grundtvig, Nicolai Frederik Severin
　　1783-1872 .... **NCLC 1**
Grunge
　　See Crumb, R(obert)
Grunwald, Lisa 1959- .... **CLC 44**
　　See also CA 120
Gryphius, Andreas 1616-1664 .... **LC 89**
　　See also CDWLB 2; DLB 164; RGWL 2, 3
Guare, John 1938- .... **CLC 8, 14, 29, 67; DC**
　　20
　　See also CA 73-76; CAD; CANR 21, 69,
　　118; CD 5; DAM DRAM; DFS 8, 13;
　　DLB 7, 249; EWL 3; MTCW 1, 2; RGAL
　　4
Gubar, Susan (David) 1944- .... **CLC 145**
　　See also CA 108; CANR 45, 70; FW;
　　MTCW 1; RGAL 4
Gudjonsson, Halldor Kiljan 1902-1998
　　See Laxness, Halldor
　　See also CA 103; 164; CWW 2
Guenter, Erich
　　See Eich, Gunter
Guest, Barbara 1920- .... **CLC 34**
　　See also BG 2; CA 25-28R; CANR 11, 44,
　　84; CP 7; CWP; DLB 5, 193
Guest, Edgar A(lbert) 1881-1959 ... **TCLC 95**
　　See also CA 112; 168
Guest, Judith (Ann) 1936- .... **CLC 8, 30**
　　See also AAYA 7; CA 77-80; CANR 15,
　　75; DA3; DAM NOV, POP; EXPN; INT
　　CANR-15; LAIT 5; MTCW 1, 2; NFS 1
Guevara, Che .... **CLC 87; HLC 1**
　　See Guevara (Serna), Ernesto
Guevara (Serna), Ernesto
　　1928-1967 .... **CLC 87; HLC 1**
　　See Guevara, Che
　　See also CA 127; 111; CANR 56; DAM
　　MULT; HW 1
Guicciardini, Francesco 1483-1540 ..... **LC 49**
Guild, Nicholas M. 1944- .... **CLC 33**
　　See also CA 93-96
Guillemin, Jacques
　　See Sartre, Jean-Paul
Guillen, Jorge 1893-1984 . **CLC 11; HLCS 1;**
　　PC 35
　　See also CA 89-92; 112; DAM MULT,
　　POET; DLB 108; EWL 3; HW 1; RGWL
　　2, 3
Guillen, Nicolas (Cristobal)
　　1902-1989 .... **BLC 2; CLC 48, 79; HLC**
　　1; PC 23
　　See also BW 2; CA 116; 125; 129; CANR
　　84; DAM MST, MULT, POET; DLB 283;
　　EWL 3; HW 1; LAW; RGWL 2, 3; WP
Guillen y Alvarez, Jorge
　　See Guillen, Jorge
Guillevic, (Eugene) 1907-1997 .... **CLC 33**
　　See also CA 93-96; CWW 2
Guillois
　　See Desnos, Robert
Guillois, Valentin
　　See Desnos, Robert
Guimaraes Rosa, Joao 1908-1967 .... **HLCS 2**
　　See also CA 175; LAW; RGSF 2; RGWL 2,
　　3
Guiney, Louise Imogen
　　1861-1920 .... **TCLC 41**
　　See also CA 160; DLB 54; RGAL 4
Guinizelli, Guido c. 1230-1276 ...... **CMLC 49**
Guiraldes, Ricardo (Guillermo)
　　1886-1927 .... **TCLC 39**
　　See also CA 131; EWL 3; HW 1; LAW;
　　MTCW 1

Gumilev, Nikolai (Stepanovich)
　　1886-1921 .... **TCLC 60**
　　See Gumilyov, Nikolay Stepanovich
　　See also CA 165
Gumilyov, Nikolay Stepanovich
　　See Gumilev, Nikolai (Stepanovich)
　　See also EWL 3
Gunesekera, Romesh 1954- .... **CLC 91**
　　See also CA 159; CN 7; DLB 267
Gunn, Bill .... **CLC 5**
　　See Gunn, William Harrison
　　See also DLB 38
Gunn, Thom(son William) 1929- .. **CLC 3, 6,**
　　18, 32, 81; PC 26
　　See also BRWS 4; CA 17-20R; CANR 9,
　　33, 116; CDBLB 1960 to Present; CP 7;
　　DAM POET; DLB 27; INT CANR-33;
　　MTCW 1; PFS 9; RGEL 2
Gunn, William Harrison 1934(?)-1989
　　See Gunn, Bill
　　See also AITN 1; BW 1, 3; CA 13-16R;
　　128; CANR 12, 25, 76
Gunn Allen, Paula
　　See Allen, Paula Gunn
Gunnars, Kristjana 1948- .... **CLC 69**
　　See also CA 113; CCA 1; CP 7; CWP; DLB
　　60
Gunter, Erich
　　See Eich, Gunter
Gurdjieff, G(eorgei) I(vanovich)
　　1877(?)-1949 .... **TCLC 71**
　　See also CA 157
Gurganus, Allan 1947- .... **CLC 70**
　　See also BEST 90:1; CA 135; CANR 114;
　　CN 7; CPW; CSW; DAM POP; GLL 1
Gurney, A. R.
　　See Gurney, A(lbert) R(amsdell), Jr.
　　See also DLB 266
Gurney, A(lbert) R(amsdell), Jr.
　　1930- .... **CLC 32, 50, 54**
　　See Gurney, A. R.
　　See also AMWS 5; CA 77-80; CAD; CANR
　　32, 64; CD 5; DAM DRAM; EWL 3
Gurney, Ivor (Bertie) 1890-1937 ... **TCLC 33**
　　See also BRW 6; CA 167; DLBY 2002;
　　PAB; RGEL 2
Gurney, Peter
　　See Gurney, A(lbert) R(amsdell), Jr.
Guro, Elena 1877-1913 .... **TCLC 56**
Gustafson, James M(oody) 1925- ... **CLC 100**
　　See also CA 25-28R; CANR 37
Gustafson, Ralph (Barker)
　　1909-1995 .... **CLC 36**
　　See also CA 21-24R; CANR 8, 45, 84; CP
　　7; DLB 88; RGEL 2
Gut, Gom
　　See Simenon, Georges (Jacques Christian)
Guterson, David 1956- .... **CLC 91**
　　See also CA 132; CANR 73; MTCW 2;
　　NFS 13
Guthrie, A(lfred) B(ertram), Jr.
　　1901-1991 .... **CLC 23**
　　See also CA 57-60; 134; CANR 24; DLB 6,
　　212; SATA 62; SATA-Obit 67
Guthrie, Isobel
　　See Grieve, C(hristopher) M(urray)
Guthrie, Woodrow Wilson 1912-1967
　　See Guthrie, Woody
　　See also CA 113; 93-96
Guthrie, Woody .... **CLC 35**
　　See Guthrie, Woodrow Wilson
　　See also LAIT 3
Gutierrez Najera, Manuel
　　1859-1895 .... **HLCS 2**
　　See also LAW

Harford, Henry
See Hudson, W(illiam) H(enry)

Hargrave, Leonie
See Disch, Thomas M(ichael)

Harjo, Joy 1951- ..... **CLC 83; NNAL; PC 27**
See also AMWS 12; CA 114; CANR 35,
67, 91; CP 7; CWP; DAM MULT; DLB
120, 175; EWL 3; MTCW 2; PFS 15;
RGAL 4

Harlan, Louis R(udolph) 1922- .... **CLC 34**
See also CA 21-24R; CANR 25, 55, 80

Harling, Robert 1951(?)- .... **CLC 53**
See also CA 147

Harmon, William (Ruth) 1938- .... **CLC 38**
See also CA 33-36R; CANR 14, 32, 35;
SATA 65

Harper, F. E. W.
See Harper, Frances Ellen Watkins

Harper, Frances E. W.
See Harper, Frances Ellen Watkins

Harper, Frances E. Watkins
See Harper, Frances Ellen Watkins

Harper, Frances Ellen
See Harper, Frances Ellen Watkins

Harper, Frances Ellen Watkins
1825-1911 ..... **BLC 2; PC 21; TCLC 14**
See also AFAW 1, 2; BW 1, 3; CA 111; 125;
CANR 79; DAM MULT, POET; DLB 50,
221; MAWW; RGAL 4

Harper, Michael S(teven) 1938- ... **CLC 7, 22**
See also AFAW 2; BW 1; CA 33-36R;
CANR 24, 108; CP 7; DLB 41; RGAL 4

Harper, Mrs. F. E. W.
See Harper, Frances Ellen Watkins

Harpur, Charles 1813-1868 .... **NCLC 114**
See also DLB 230; RGEL 2

Harris, Christie 1907-
See Harris, Christie (Lucy) Irwin

Harris, Christie (Lucy) Irwin
1907-2002 .... **CLC 12**
See also CA 5-8R; CANR 6, 83; CLR 47;
DLB 88; JRDA; MAICYA 1, 2; SAAS 10;
SATA 6, 74; SATA-Essay 116

Harris, Frank 1856-1931 .... **TCLC 24**
See also CA 109; 150; CANR 80; DLB 156,
197; RGEL 2

Harris, George Washington
1814-1869 .... **NCLC 23**
See also DLB 3, 11, 248; RGAL 4

Harris, Joel Chandler 1848-1908 ..... **SSC 19;
TCLC 2**
See also CA 104; 137; CANR 80; CLR 49;
DLB 11, 23, 42, 78, 91; LAIT 2; MAI-
CYA 1, 2; RGSF 2; SATA 100; WCH;
YABC 1

**Harris, John (Wyndham Parkes Lucas)
Beynon** 1903-1969
See Wyndham, John
See also CA 102; 89-92; CANR 84; SATA
118; SFW 4

Harris, MacDonald .... **CLC 9**
See Heiney, Donald (William)

Harris, Mark 1922- .... **CLC 19**
See also CA 5-8R; CAAS 3; CANR 2, 55,
83; CN 7; DLB 2; DLBY 1980

Harris, Norman .... **CLC 65**

Harris, (Theodore) Wilson 1921- .... **CLC 25,
159**
See also BRWS 5; BW 2, 3; CA 65-68;
CAAS 16; CANR 11, 27, 69, 114; CD-
WLB 3; CN 7; CP 7; DLB 117; EWL 3;
MTCW 1; RGEL 2

Harrison, Barbara Grizzuti
1934-2002 .... **CLC 144**
See also CA 77-80; 205; CANR 15, 48; INT
CANR-15

Harrison, Elizabeth (Allen) Cavanna
1909-2001
See Cavanna, Betty
See also CA 9-12R; 200; CANR 6, 27, 85,
104; MAICYA 2; YAW

Harrison, Harry (Max) 1925- .... **CLC 42**
See also CA 1-4R; CANR 5, 21, 84; DLB
8; SATA 4; SCFW 2; SFW 4

Harrison, James (Thomas) 1937- ...... **CLC 6,
14, 33, 66, 143; SSC 19**
See Harrison, Jim
See also CA 13-16R; CANR 8, 51, 79; CN
7; CP 7; DLBY 1982; INT CANR-8

Harrison, Jim
See Harrison, James (Thomas)
See also AMWS 8; RGAL 4; TCWW 2;
TUS

Harrison, Kathryn 1961- .... **CLC 70, 151**
See also CA 144; CANR 68

Harrison, Tony 1937- .... **CLC 43, 129**
See also BRWS 5; CA 65-68; CANR 44,
98; CBD; CD 5; CP 7; DLB 40, 245;
MTCW 1; RGEL 2

Harriss, Will(ard Irvin) 1922- .... **CLC 34**
See also CA 111

Hart, Ellis
See Ellison, Harlan (Jay)

Hart, Josephine 1942(?)- .... **CLC 70**
See also CA 138; CANR 70; CPW; DAM
POP

Hart, Moss 1904-1961 .... **CLC 66**
See also CA 109; 89-92; CANR 84; DAM
DRAM; DFS 1; DLB 7, 266; RGAL 4

Harte, (Francis) Bret(t)
1836(?)-1902 ... **SSC 8, 59; TCLC 1, 25;
WLC**
See also AMWS 2; CA 104; 140; CANR
80; CDALB 1865-1917; DA; DA3; DAC;
DAM MST; DLB 12, 64, 74, 79, 186;
EXPS; LAIT 2; RGAL 4; RGSF 2; SATA
26; SSFS 3; TUS

Hartley, L(eslie) P(oles) 1895-1972 ... **CLC 2,
22**
See also BRWS 7; CA 45-48; 37-40R;
CANR 33; DLB 15, 139; EWL 3; HGG;
MTCW 1, 2; RGEL 2; RGSF 2; SUFW 1

Hartman, Geoffrey H. 1929- .... **CLC 27**
See also CA 117; 125; CANR 79; DLB 67

Hartmann, Sadakichi 1869-1944 ... **TCLC 73**
See also CA 157; DLB 54

Hartmann von Aue c. 1170-c.
1210 .... **CMLC 15**
See also CDWLB 2; DLB 138; RGWL 2, 3

Hartog, Jan de
See de Hartog, Jan

Haruf, Kent 1943- .... **CLC 34**
See also AAYA 44; CA 149; CANR 91

Harvey, Gabriel 1550(?)-1631 .... **LC 88**
See also DLB 167, 213, 281

Harwood, Ronald 1934- .... **CLC 32**
See also CA 1-4R; CANR 4, 55; CBD; CD
5; DAM DRAM, MST; DLB 13

Hasegawa Tatsunosuke
See Futabatei, Shimei

Hasek, Jaroslav (Matej Frantisek)
1883-1923 .... **TCLC 4**
See also CA 104; 129; CDWLB 4; DLB
215; EW 9; EWL 3; MTCW 1, 2; RGSF
2; RGWL 2, 3

Hass, Robert 1941- ... **CLC 18, 39, 99; PC 16**
See also AMWS 6; CA 111; CANR 30, 50,
71; CP 7; DLB 105, 206; EWL 3; RGAL
4; SATA 94

Hastings, Hudson
See Kuttner, Henry

Hastings, Selina .... **CLC 44**

Hathorne, John 1641-1717 .... **LC 38**

Hatteras, Amelia
See Mencken, H(enry) L(ouis)

Hatteras, Owen .... **TCLC 18**
See Mencken, H(enry) L(ouis); Nathan,
George Jean

Hauptmann, Gerhart (Johann Robert)
1862-1946 .... **SSC 37; TCLC 4**
See also CA 104; 153; CDWLB 2; DAM
DRAM; DLB 66, 118; EW 8; EWL 3;
RGSF 2; RGWL 2, 3; TWA

Havel, Vaclav 1936- ..... **CLC 25, 58, 65, 123;
DC 6**
See also CA 104; CANR 36, 63; CDWLB
4; CWW 2; DA3; DAM DRAM; DFS 10;
DLB 232; EWL 3; LMFS 2; MTCW 1, 2;
RGWL 3

Haviaras, Stratis .... **CLC 33**
See Chaviaras, Strates

Hawes, Stephen 1475(?)-1529(?) .... **LC 17**
See also DLB 132; RGEL 2

Hawkes, John (Clendennin Burne, Jr.)
1925-1998 .. **CLC 1, 2, 3, 4, 7, 9, 14, 15,
27, 49**
See also BPFB 2; CA 1-4R; 167; CANR 2,
47, 64; CN 7; DLB 2, 7, 227; DLBY
1980, 1998; EWL 3; MTCW 1, 2; RGAL
4

Hawking, S. W.
See Hawking, Stephen W(illiam)

Hawking, Stephen W(illiam) 1942- . **CLC 63,
105**
See also AAYA 13; BEST 89:1; CA 126;
129; CANR 48, 115; CPW; DA3; MTCW
2

Hawkins, Anthony Hope
See Hope, Anthony

Hawthorne, Julian 1846-1934 .... **TCLC 25**
See also CA 165; HGG

Hawthorne, Nathaniel 1804-1864 ... **NCLC 2,
10, 17, 23, 39, 79, 95; SSC 3, 29, 39;
WLC**
See also AAYA 18; AMW; AMWC 1;
AMWR 1; BPFB 2; BYA 3; CDALB
1640-1865; DA; DA3; DAB; DAC; DAM
MST, NOV; DLB 1, 74, 183, 223, 269;
EXPN; EXPS; HGG; LAIT 1; NFS 1;
RGAL 4; RGSF 2; SSFS 1, 7, 11, 15;
SUFW 1; TUS; WCH; YABC 2

Haxton, Josephine Ayres 1921-
See Douglas, Ellen
See also CA 115; CANR 41, 83

Hayaseca y Eizaguirre, Jorge
See Echegaray (y Eizaguirre), Jose (Maria
Waldo)

Hayashi, Fumiko 1904-1951 .... **TCLC 27**
See Hayashi Fumiko
See also CA 161

Hayashi Fumiko
See Hayashi, Fumiko
See also DLB 180; EWL 3

Haycraft, Anna (Margaret) 1932-
See Ellis, Alice Thomas
See also CA 122; CANR 85, 90; MTCW 2

Hayden, Robert E(arl) 1913-1980 ..... **BLC 2;
CLC 5, 9, 14, 37; PC 6**
See also AFAW 1, 2; AMWS 2; BW 1, 3;
CA 69-72; 97-100; CABS 2; CANR 24,
75, 82; CDALB 1941-1968; DA; DAC;
DAM MST, MULT, POET; DLB 5, 76;
EWL 3; EXP; MTCW 1, 2; PFS 1, 3;
RGAL 4; SATA 19; SATA-Obit 26; WP

Hayek, F(riedrich) A(ugust von)
1899-1992 .... **TCLC 109**
See also CA 93-96; 137; CANR 20; MTCW
1, 2

Hayford, J(oseph) E(phraim) Casely
See Casely-Hayford, J(oseph) E(phraim)

Hayman, Ronald 1932- .... **CLC 44**
See also CA 25-28R; CANR 18, 50, 88; CD
5; DLB 155

Hayne, Paul Hamilton 1830-1886 . **NCLC 94**
See also DLB 3, 64, 79, 248; RGAL 4

Herrick, Robert 1591-1674 .... **LC 13; PC 9**
See also BRW 2; DA; DAB; DAC; DAM
MST, POP; DLB 126; EXPP; PFS 13;
RGAL 4; RGEL 2; TEA; WP

Herring, Guilles
See Somerville, Edith Oenone

Herriot, James 1916-1995 .... **CLC 12**
See Wight, James Alfred
See also AAYA 1; BPFB 2; CA 148; CANR
40; CLR 80; CPW; DAM POP; LAIT 3;
MAICYA 2; MAICYAS 1; MTCW 2;
SATA 86, 135; TEA; YAW

Herris, Violet
See Hunt, Violet

Herrmann, Dorothy 1941- .... **CLC 44**
See also CA 107

Herrmann, Taffy
See Herrmann, Dorothy

Hersey, John (Richard) 1914-1993 .... **CLC 1,
2, 7, 9, 40, 81, 97**
See also AAYA 29; BPFB 2; CA 17-20R;
140; CANR 33; CDALBS; CPW; DAM
POP; DLB 6, 185, 278; MTCW 1, 2;
SATA 25; SATA-Obit 76; TUS

Herzen, Aleksandr Ivanovich
1812-1870 .... **NCLC 10, 61**
See Herzen, Alexander

Herzen, Alexander
See Herzen, Aleksandr Ivanovich
See also DLB 277

Herzl, Theodor 1860-1904 .... **TCLC 36**
See also CA 168

Herzog, Werner 1942- .... **CLC 16**
See also CA 89-92

Hesiod c. 8th cent. B.C.- .... **CMLC 5**
See also AW 1; DLB 176; RGWL 2, 3

Hesse, Hermann 1877-1962 ... **CLC 1, 2, 3, 6,
11, 17, 25, 69; SSC 9, 49; WLC**
See also AAYA 43; BPFB 2; CA 17-18;
CAP 2; CDWLB 2; DA; DA3; DAB;
DAC; DAM MST, NOV; DLB 66; EW 9;
EWL 3; EXPN; LAIT 1; MTCW 1, 2;
NFS 6, 15; RGWL 2, 3; SATA 50; TWA

Hewes, Cady
See De Voto, Bernard (Augustine)

Heyen, William 1940- .... **CLC 13, 18**
See also CA 33-36R; CAAS 9; CANR 98;
CP 7; DLB 5

Heyerdahl, Thor 1914-2002 .... **CLC 26**
See also CA 5-8R; 207; CANR 5, 22, 66,
73; LAIT 4; MTCW 1, 2; SATA 2, 52

Heym, Georg (Theodor Franz Arthur)
1887-1912 .... **TCLC 9**
See also CA 106; 181

Heym, Stefan 1913-2001 .... **CLC 41**
See also CA 9-12R; 203; CANR 4; CWW
2; DLB 69; EWL 3

Heyse, Paul (Johann Ludwig von)
1830-1914 .... **TCLC 8**
See also CA 104; 209; DLB 129

Heyward, (Edwin) DuBose
1885-1940 .... **HR 2; TCLC 59**
See also CA 108; 157; DLB 7, 9, 45, 249;
SATA 21

Heywood, John 1497(?)-1580(?) .... **LC 65**
See also DLB 136; RGEL 2

Hibbert, Eleanor Alice Burford
1906-1993 .... **CLC 7**
See Holt, Victoria
See also BEST 90:4; CA 17-20R; 140;
CANR 9, 28, 59; CMW 4; CPW; DAM
POP; MTCW 2; RHW; SATA 2; SATA-
Obit 74

Hichens, Robert (Smythe)
1864-1950 .... **TCLC 64**
See also CA 162; DLB 153; HGG; RHW;
SUFW

Higgins, George V(incent)
1939-1999 .... **CLC 4, 7, 10, 18**
See also BPFB 2; CA 77-80; 186; CAAS 5;
CANR 17, 51, 89, 96; CMW 4; CN 7;
DLB 2; DLBY 1981, 1998; INT CANR-
17; MSW; MTCW 1

Higginson, Thomas Wentworth
1823-1911 .... **TCLC 36**
See also CA 162; DLB 1, 64, 243

Higgonet, Margaret ed. .... **CLC 65**

Highet, Helen
See MacInnes, Helen (Clark)

Highsmith, (Mary) Patricia
1921-1995 .... **CLC 2, 4, 14, 42, 102**
See Morgan, Claire
See also AAYA 48; BRWS 5; CA 1-4R; 147;
CANR 1, 20, 48, 62, 108; CMW 4; CPW;
DA3; DAM NOV, POP; MSW; MTCW 1,
2

Highwater, Jamake (Mamake)
1942(?)-2001 .... **CLC 12**
See also AAYA 7; BPFB 2; BYA 4; CA 65-
68; 199; CAAS 7; CANR 10, 34, 84; CLR
17; CWRI 5; DLB 52; DLBY 1985;
JRDA; MAICYA 1, 2; SATA 32, 69;
SATA-Brief 30

Highway, Tomson 1951- ...... **CLC 92; NNAL**
See also CA 151; CANR 75; CCA 1; CD 5;
DAC; DAM MULT; DFS 2; MTCW 2

Hijuelos, Oscar 1951- .... **CLC 65; HLC 1**
See also AAYA 25; AMWS 8; BEST 90:1;
CA 123; CANR 50, 75; CPW; DA3; DAM
MULT, POP; DLB 145; HW 1, 2; MTCW
2; NFS 17; RGAL 4; WLIT 1

Hikmet, Nazim 1902(?)-1963 .... **CLC 40**
See also CA 141; 93-96; EWL 3

Hildegard von Bingen 1098-1179 . **CMLC 20**
See also DLB 148

Hildesheimer, Wolfgang 1916-1991 .. **CLC 49**
See also CA 101; 135; DLB 69, 124; EWL
3

Hill, Geoffrey (William) 1932- ...... **CLC 5, 8,
18, 45**
See also BRWS 5; CA 81-84; CANR 21,
89; CDBLB 1960 to Present; CP 7; DAM
POET; DLB 40; EWL 3; MTCW 1; RGEL
2

Hill, George Roy 1921- .... **CLC 26**
See also CA 110; 122

Hill, John
See Koontz, Dean R(ay)

Hill, Susan (Elizabeth) 1942- ...... **CLC 4, 113**
See also CA 33-36R; CANR 29, 69; CN 7;
DAB; DAM MST, NOV; DLB 14, 139;
HGG; MTCW 1; RHW

Hillard, Asa G. III .... **CLC 70**

Hillerman, Tony 1925- .... **CLC 62, 170**
See also AAYA 40; BEST 89:1; BPFB 2;
CA 29-32R; CANR 21, 42, 65, 97; CMW
4; CPW; DA3; DAM POP; DLB 206;
MSW; RGAL 4; SATA 6; TCWW 2; YAW

Hillesum, Etty 1914-1943 .... **TCLC 49**
See also CA 137

Hilliard, Noel (Harvey) 1929-1996 ... **CLC 15**
See also CA 9-12R; CANR 7, 69; CN 7

Hillis, Rick 1956- .... **CLC 66**
See also CA 134

Hilton, James 1900-1954 .... **TCLC 21**
See also CA 108; 169; DLB 34, 77; FANT;
SATA 34

Hilton, Walter (?)-1396 .... **CMLC 58**
See also DLB 146; RGEL 2

Himes, Chester (Bomar) 1909-1984 .. **BLC 2;
CLC 2, 4, 7, 18, 58, 108; TCLC 139**
See also AFAW 2; BPFB 2; BW 2; CA 25-
28R; 114; CANR 22, 89; CMW 4; DAM
MULT; DLB 2, 76, 143, 226; EWL 3;
MSW; MTCW 1, 2; RGAL 4

Hinde, Thomas .... **CLC 6, 11**
See Chitty, Thomas Willes
See also EWL 3

Hine, (William) Daryl 1936- .... **CLC 15**
See also CA 1-4R; CAAS 15; CANR 1, 20;
CP 7; DLB 60

Hinkson, Katharine Tynan
See Tynan, Katharine

Hinojosa(-Smith), Rolando (R.)
1929- .... **HLC 1**
See Hinojosa-Smith, Rolando
See also CA 131; CAAS 16; CANR 62;
DAM MULT; DLB 82; HW 1, 2; MTCW
2; RGAL 4

Hinton, S(usan) E(loise) 1950- .. **CLC 30, 111**
See also AAYA 2, 33; BPFB 2; BYA 2, 3;
CA 81-84; CANR 32, 62, 92; CDALBS;
CLR 3, 23; CPW; DA; DA3; DAB; DAC;
DAM MST, NOV; JRDA; LAIT 5; MAI-
CYA 1, 2; MTCW 1, 2; NFS 5, 9, 15, 16;
SATA 19, 58, 115; WYA; YAW

Hippius, Zinaida .... **TCLC 9**
See Gippius, Zinaida (Nikolaevna)
See also EWL 3

Hiraoka, Kimitake 1925-1970
See Mishima, Yukio
See also CA 97-100; 29-32R; DA3; DAM
DRAM; GLL 1; MTCW 1, 2

Hirsch, E(ric) D(onald), Jr. 1928- .... **CLC 79**
See also CA 25-28R; CANR 27, 51; DLB
67; INT CANR-27; MTCW 1

Hirsch, Edward 1950- .... **CLC 31, 50**
See also CA 104; CANR 20, 42, 102; CP 7;
DLB 120

Hitchcock, Alfred (Joseph)
1899-1980 .... **CLC 16**
See also AAYA 22; CA 159; 97-100; SATA
27; SATA-Obit 24

Hitchens, Christopher (Eric)
1949- .... **CLC 157**
See also CA 152; CANR 89

Hitler, Adolf 1889-1945 .... **TCLC 53**
See also CA 117; 147

Hoagland, Edward 1932- .... **CLC 28**
See also ANW; CA 1-4R; CANR 2, 31, 57,
107; CN 7; DLB 6; SATA 51; TCWW 2

Hoban, Russell (Conwell) 1925- ... **CLC 7, 25**
See also BPFB 2; CA 5-8R; CANR 23, 37,
66, 114; CLR 3, 69; CN 7; CWRI 5; DAM
NOV; DLB 52; FANT; MAICYA 1, 2;
MTCW 1, 2; SATA 1, 40, 78, 136; SFW
4; SUFW 2

Hobbes, Thomas 1588-1679 .... **LC 36**
See also DLB 151, 252, 281; RGEL 2

Hobbs, Perry
See Blackmur, R(ichard) P(almer)

Hobson, Laura Z(ametkin)
1900-1986 .... **CLC 7, 25**
See Field, Peter
See also BPFB 2; CA 17-20R; 118; CANR
55; DLB 28; SATA 52

Hoccleve, Thomas c. 1368-c. 1437 ...... **LC 75**
See also DLB 146; RGEL 2

Hoch, Edward D(entinger) 1930-
See Queen, Ellery
See also CA 29-32R; CANR 11, 27, 51, 97;
CMW 4; SFW 4

Hochhuth, Rolf 1931- .... **CLC 4, 11, 18**
See also CA 5-8R; CANR 33, 75; CWW 2;
DAM DRAM; DLB 124; EWL 3; MTCW
1, 2

Hochman, Sandra 1936- .... **CLC 3, 8**
See also CA 5-8R; DLB 5

Hochwaelder, Fritz 1911-1986 .... **CLC 36**
See Hochwalder, Fritz
See also CA 29-32R; 120; CANR 42; DAM
DRAM; MTCW 1; RGWL 3

Houdini
See Lovecraft, H(oward) P(hillips)

Hougan, Carolyn 1943- ...... **CLC 34**
See also CA 139

Household, Geoffrey (Edward West)
1900-1988 .... **CLC 11**
See also CA 77-80; 126; CANR 58; CMW
4; DLB 87; SATA 14; SATA-Obit 59

Housman, A(lfred) E(dward)
1859-1936 .... **PC 2, 43; TCLC 1, 10;**
WLCS
See also BRW 6; CA 104; 125; DA; DA3;
DAB; DAC; DAM MST, POET; DLB 19,
284; EWL 3; EXPP; MTCW 1, 2; PAB;
PFS 4, 7; RGEL 2; TEA; WP

Housman, Laurence 1865-1959 .... **TCLC 7**
See also CA 106; 155; DLB 10; FANT;
RGEL 2; SATA 25

Houston, Jeanne (Toyo) Wakatsuki
1934- .... **AAL**
See also AAYA 49; CA 103; CAAS 16;
CANR 29; LAIT 4; SATA 78

Howard, Elizabeth Jane 1923- ..... **CLC 7, 29**
See also CA 5-8R; CANR 8, 62; CN 7

Howard, Maureen 1930- .... **CLC 5, 14, 46,**
151
See also CA 53-56; CANR 31, 75; CN 7;
DLBY 1983; INT CANR-31; MTCW 1, 2

Howard, Richard 1929- .... **CLC 7, 10, 47**
See also AITN 1; CA 85-88; CANR 25, 80;
CP 7; DLB 5; INT CANR-25

Howard, Robert E(rvin)
1906-1936 .... **TCLC 8**
See also BPFB 2; BYA 5; CA 105; 157;
FANT; SUFW 1

Howard, Warren F.
See Pohl, Frederik

Howe, Fanny (Quincy) 1940- .... **CLC 47**
See also CA 117; CAAE 187; CAAS 27;
CANR 70, 116; CP 7; CWP; SATA-Brief
52

Howe, Irving 1920-1993 .... **CLC 85**
See also AMWS 6; CA 9-12R; 141; CANR
21, 50; DLB 67; EWL 3; MTCW 1, 2

Howe, Julia Ward 1819-1910 .... **TCLC 21**
See also CA 117; 191; DLB 1, 189, 235;
FW

Howe, Susan 1937- .... **CLC 72, 152**
See also AMWS 4; CA 160; CP 7; CWP;
DLB 120; FW; RGAL 4

Howe, Tina 1937- .... **CLC 48**
See also CA 109; CAD; CD 5; CWD

Howell, James 1594(?)-1666 .... **LC 13**
See also DLB 151

Howells, W. D.
See Howells, William Dean

Howells, William D.
See Howells, William Dean

Howells, William Dean 1837-1920 ... **SSC 36;**
TCLC 7, 17, 41
See also AMW; CA 104; 134; CDALB
1865-1917; DLB 12, 64, 74, 79, 189;
LMFS 1; MTCW 2; RGAL 4; TUS

Howes, Barbara 1914-1996 .... **CLC 15**
See also CA 9-12R; 151; CAAS 3; CANR
53; CP 7; SATA 5

Hrabal, Bohumil 1914-1997 .... **CLC 13, 67**
See also CA 106; 156; CAAS 12; CANR
57; CWW 2; DLB 232; EWL 3; RGSF 2

Hrotsvit of Gandersheim c. 935-c.
1000 .... **CMLC 29**
See also DLB 148

Hsi, Chu 1130-1200 .... **CMLC 42**

Hsun, Lu
See Lu Hsun

Hubbard, L(afayette) Ron(ald)
1911-1986 .... **CLC 43**
See also CA 77-80; 118; CANR 52; CPW;
DA3; DAM POP; FANT; MTCW 2; SFW
4

Huch, Ricarda (Octavia)
1864-1947 .... **TCLC 13**
See also CA 111; 189; DLB 66; EWL 3

Huddle, David 1942- .... **CLC 49**
See also CA 57-60; CAAS 20; CANR 89;
DLB 130

Hudson, Jeffrey
See Crichton, (John) Michael

Hudson, W(illiam) H(enry)
1841-1922 .... **TCLC 29**
See also CA 115; 190; DLB 98, 153, 174;
RGEL 2; SATA 35

Hueffer, Ford Madox
See Ford, Ford Madox

Hughart, Barry 1934- .... **CLC 39**
See also CA 137; FANT; SFW 4; SUFW 2

Hughes, Colin
See Creasey, John

Hughes, David (John) 1930- .... **CLC 48**
See also CA 116; 129; CN 7; DLB 14

Hughes, Edward James
See Hughes, Ted
See also DA3; DAM MST, POET

Hughes, (James Mercer) Langston
1902-1967 ..... **BLC 2; CLC 1, 5, 10, 15,**
35, 44, 108; DC 3; HR 2; PC 1; SSC 6;
WLC
See also AAYA 12; AFAW 1, 2; AMWR 1;
AMWS 1; BW 1, 3; CA 1-4R; 25-28R;
CANR 1, 34, 82; CDALB 1929-1941;
CLR 17; DA; DA3; DAB; DAC; DAM
DRAM, MST, MULT, POET; DFS 6;
DLB 4, 7, 48, 51, 86, 228; EWL 3; EXPP;
EXPS; JRDA; LAIT 3; LMFS 2; MAI-
CYA 1, 2; MTCW 1, 2; PAB; PFS 1, 3, 6,
10, 15; RGAL 4; RGSF 2; SATA 4, 33;
SSFS 4, 7; TUS; WCH; WP; YAW

Hughes, Richard (Arthur Warren)
1900-1976 .... **CLC 1, 11**
See also CA 5-8R; 65-68; CANR 4; DAM
NOV; DLB 15, 161; EWL 3; MTCW 1;
RGEL 2; SATA 8; SATA-Obit 25

Hughes, Ted 1930-1998 . **CLC 2, 4, 9, 14, 37,**
119; PC 7
See Hughes, Edward James
See also BRWR 2; BRWS 1; CA 1-4R; 171;
CANR 1, 33, 66, 108; CLR 3; CP 7;
DAB; DAC; DLB 40, 161; EWL 3; EXPP;
MAICYA 1, 2; MTCW 1, 2; PAB; PFS 4;
RGEL 2; SATA 49; SATA-Brief 27;
SATA-Obit 107; TEA; YAW

Hugo, Richard
See Huch, Ricarda (Octavia)

Hugo, Richard F(ranklin)
1923-1982 .... **CLC 6, 18, 32**
See also AMWS 6; CA 49-52; 108; CANR
3; DAM POET; DLB 5, 206; EWL 3; PFS
17; RGAL 4

Hugo, Victor (Marie) 1802-1885 .... **NCLC 3,**
10, 21; PC 17; WLC
See also AAYA 28; DA; DA3; DAB; DAC;
DAM DRAM, MST, NOV, POET; DLB
119, 192, 217; EFS 2; EW 6; EXPN; GFL
1789 to the Present; LAIT 1, 2; NFS 5;
RGWL 2, 3; SATA 47; TWA

Huidobro, Vicente
See Huidobro Fernandez, Vicente Garcia
See also DLB 283; EWL 3; LAW

Huidobro Fernandez, Vicente Garcia
1893-1948 .... **TCLC 31**
See Huidobro, Vicente
See also CA 131; HW 1

Hulme, Keri 1947- .... **CLC 39, 130**
See also CA 125; CANR 69; CN 7; CP 7;
CWP; EWL 3; FW; INT 125

Hulme, T(homas) E(rnest)
1883-1917 .... **TCLC 21**
See also BRWS 6; CA 117; 203; DLB 19

Hume, David 1711-1776 .... **LC 7, 56**
See also BRWS 3; DLB 104, 252; LMFS 1;
TEA

Humphrey, William 1924-1997 .... **CLC 45**
See also AMWS 9; CA 77-80; 160; CANR
68; CN 7; CSW; DLB 6, 212, 234, 278;
TCWW 2

Humphreys, Emyr Owen 1919- .... **CLC 47**
See also CA 5-8R; CANR 3, 24; CN 7;
DLB 15

Humphreys, Josephine 1945- ..... **CLC 34, 57**
See also CA 121; 127; CANR 97; CSW;
INT 127

Huneker, James Gibbons
1860-1921 .... **TCLC 65**
See also CA 193; DLB 71; RGAL 4

Hungerford, Hesba Fay
See Brinsmead, H(esba) F(ay)

Hungerford, Pixie
See Brinsmead, H(esba) F(ay)

Hunt, E(verette) Howard, (Jr.)
1918- .... **CLC 3**
See also AITN 1; CA 45-48; CANR 2, 47,
103; CMW 4

Hunt, Francesca
See Holland, Isabelle (Christian)

Hunt, Howard
See Hunt, E(verette) Howard, (Jr.)

Hunt, Kyle
See Creasey, John

Hunt, (James Henry) Leigh
1784-1859 .... **NCLC 1, 70**
See also DAM POET; DLB 96, 110, 144;
RGEL 2; TEA

Hunt, Marsha 1946- .... **CLC 70**
See also BW 2, 3; CA 143; CANR 79

Hunt, Violet 1866(?)-1942 .... **TCLC 53**
See also CA 184; DLB 162, 197

Hunter, E. Waldo
See Sturgeon, Theodore (Hamilton)

Hunter, Evan 1926- .... **CLC 11, 31**
See McBain, Ed
See also AAYA 39; BPFB 2; CA 5-8R;
CANR 5, 38, 62, 97; CMW 4; CN 7;
CPW; DAM POP; DLBY 1982; INT
CANR-5; MSW; MTCW 1; SATA 25;
SFW 4

Hunter, Kristin 1931-
See Lattany, Kristin (Elaine Eggleston)
Hunter

Hunter, Mary
See Austin, Mary (Hunter)

Hunter, Mollie 1922- .... **CLC 21**
See McIlwraith, Maureen Mollie Hunter
See also AAYA 13; BYA 6; CANR 37, 78;
CLR 25; DLB 161; JRDA; MAICYA 1,
2; SAAS 7; SATA 54, 106, 139; WYA;
YAW

Hunter, Robert (?)-1734 .... **LC 7**

Hurston, Zora Neale 1891-1960 .... **BLC 2;**
CLC 7, 30, 61; DC 12; HR 2; SSC 4;
TCLC 121, 131; WLCS
See also AAYA 15; AFAW 1, 2; AMWS 6;
BW 1, 3; BYA 12; CA 85-88; CANR 61;
CDALBS; DA; DA3; DAC; DAM MST,
MULT, NOV; DFS 6; DLB 51, 86; EWL
3; EXPN; EXPS; FW; LAIT 3; LATS 1;
LMFS 2; MAWW; MTCW 1, 2; NFS 3;
RGAL 4; RGSF 2; SSFS 1, 6, 11; TUS;
YAW

Husserl, E. G.
See Husserl, Edmund (Gustav Albrecht)

Husserl, Edmund (Gustav Albrecht)
1859-1938 .... **TCLC 100**
See also CA 116; 133

Jacobs, W(illiam) W(ymark)
1863-1943 .... **TCLC 22**
See also CA 121; 167; DLB 135; EXPS;
HGG; RGEL 2; RGSF 2; SSFS 2; SUFW
1

Jacobsen, Jens Peter 1847-1885 .... **NCLC 34**

Jacobsen, Josephine 1908- .... **CLC 48, 102**
See also CA 33-36R; CAAS 18; CANR 23,
48; CCA 1; CP 7; DLB 244

Jacobson, Dan 1929- .... **CLC 4, 14**
See also AFW; CA 1-4R; CANR 2, 25, 66;
CN 7; DLB 14, 207, 225; EWL 3; MTCW
1; RGSF 2

Jacqueline
See Carpentier (y Valmont), Alejo

Jagger, Mick 1944- .... **CLC 17**

Jahiz, al- c. 780-c. 869 .... **CMLC 25**

Jakes, John (William) 1932- .... **CLC 29**
See also AAYA 32; BEST 89:4; BPFB 2;
CA 57-60; CANR 10, 43, 66, 111; CPW;
CSW; DA3; DAM NOV, POP; DLB 278;
DLBY 1983; FANT; INT CANR-10;
MTCW 1, 2; RHW; SATA 62; SFW 4;
TCWW 2

James I 1394-1437 .... **LC 20**
See also RGEL 2

James, Andrew
See Kirkup, James

James, C(yril) L(ionel) R(obert)
1901-1989 .... **BLCS; CLC 33**
See also BW 2; CA 117; 125; 128; CANR
62; DLB 125; MTCW 1

James, Daniel (Lewis) 1911-1988
See Santiago, Danny
See also CA 174; 125

James, Dynely
See Mayne, William (James Carter)

James, Henry Sr. 1811-1882 .... **NCLC 53**

James, Henry 1843-1916 ..... **SSC 8, 32, 47;
TCLC 2, 11, 24, 40, 47, 64; WLC**
See also AMW; AMWC 1; AMWR 1; BPFB
2; BRW 6; CA 104; 132; CDALB 1865-
1917; DA; DA3; DAB; DAC; DAM MST,
NOV; DLB 12, 71, 74, 189; DLBD 13;
EWL 3; EXPS; HGG; LAIT 2; MTCW 1,
2; NFS 12, 16; RGAL 4; RGEL 2; RGSF
2; SSFS 9; SUFW 1; TUS

James, M. R.
See James, Montague (Rhodes)
See also DLB 156, 201

James, Montague (Rhodes)
1862-1936 .... **SSC 16; TCLC 6**
See James, M. R.
See also CA 104; 203; HGG; RGEL 2;
RGSF 2; SUFW 1

James, P. D. .... **CLC 18, 46, 122**
See White, Phyllis Dorothy James
See also BEST 90:2; BPFB 2; BRWS 4;
CDBLB 1960 to Present; DLB 87, 276;
DLBD 17; MSW

James, Philip
See Moorcock, Michael (John)

James, Samuel
See Stephens, James

James, Seumas
See Stephens, James

James, Stephen
See Stephens, James

James, William 1842-1910 .... **TCLC 15, 32**
See also AMW; CA 109; 193; DLB 270,
284; RGAL 4

Jameson, Anna 1794-1860 .... **NCLC 43**
See also DLB 99, 166

Jameson, Fredric (R.) 1934- .... **CLC 142**
See also CA 196; DLB 67; LMFS 2

Jami, Nur al-Din 'Abd al-Rahman
1414-1492 .... **LC 9**

Jammes, Francis 1868-1938 .... **TCLC 75**
See also CA 198; EWL 3; GFL 1789 to the
Present

Jandl, Ernst 1925-2000 .... **CLC 34**
See also CA 200; EWL 3

Janowitz, Tama 1957- .... **CLC 43, 145**
See also CA 106; CANR 52, 89; CN 7;
CPW; DAM POP

Japrisot, Sebastien 1931- .... **CLC 90**
See Rossi, Jean Baptiste
See also CMW 4

Jarrell, Randall 1914-1965 .... **CLC 1, 2, 6, 9,
13, 49; PC 41**
See also AMW; BYA 5; CA 5-8R; 25-28R;
CABS 2; CANR 6, 34; CDALB 1941-
1968; CLR 6; CWRI 5; DAM POET;
DLB 48, 52; EWL 3; EXPP; MAICYA 1,
2; MTCW 1, 2; PAB; PFS 2; RGAL 4;
SATA 7

Jarry, Alfred 1873-1907 .... **SSC 20; TCLC 2,
14**
See also CA 104; 153; DA3; DAM DRAM;
DFS 8; DLB 192, 258; EW 9; EWL 3;
GFL 1789 to the Present; RGWL 2, 3;
TWA

Jarvis, E. K.
See Ellison, Harlan (Jay)

Jawien, Andrzej
See John Paul II, Pope

Jaynes, Roderick
See Coen, Ethan

Jeake, Samuel, Jr.
See Aiken, Conrad (Potter)

Jean Paul 1763-1825 .... **NCLC 7**

Jefferies, (John) Richard
1848-1887 .... **NCLC 47**
See also DLB 98, 141; RGEL 2; SATA 16;
SFW 4

Jeffers, (John) Robinson 1887-1962 .. **CLC 2,
3, 11, 15, 54; PC 17; WLC**
See also AMWS 2; CA 85-88; CANR 35;
CDALB 1917-1929; DA; DAC; DAM
MST, POET; DLB 45, 212; EWL 3;
MTCW 1, 2; PAB; PFS 3, 4; RGAL 4

Jefferson, Janet
See Mencken, H(enry) L(ouis)

Jefferson, Thomas 1743-1826 . **NCLC 11, 103**
See also ANW; CDALB 1640-1865; DA3;
DLB 31, 183; LAIT 1; RGAL 4

Jeffrey, Francis 1773-1850 .... **NCLC 33**
See Francis, Lord Jeffrey

Jelakowitch, Ivan
See Heijermans, Herman

Jelinek, Elfriede 1946- .... **CLC 169**
See also CA 154; DLB 85; FW

Jellicoe, (Patricia) Ann 1927- .... **CLC 27**
See also CA 85-88; CBD; CD 5; CWD;
CWRI 5; DLB 13, 233; FW

Jemyma
See Holley, Marietta

Jen, Gish .... **CLC 70**
See Jen, Lillian

Jen, Lillian 1956(?)-
See Jen, Gish
See also CA 135; CANR 89

Jenkins, (John) Robin 1912- .... **CLC 52**
See also CA 1-4R; CANR 1; CN 7; DLB
14, 271

Jennings, Elizabeth (Joan)
1926-2001 .... **CLC 5, 14, 131**
See also BRWS 5; CA 61-64; 200; CAAS
5; CANR 8, 39, 66; CP 7; CWP; DLB 27;
EWL 3; MTCW 1; SATA 66

Jennings, Waylon 1937- .... **CLC 21**

Jensen, Johannes V(ilhelm)
1873-1950 .... **TCLC 41**
See also CA 170; DLB 214; EWL 3;
RGWL 3

Jensen, Laura (Linnea) 1948- .... **CLC 37**
See also CA 103

Jerome, Saint 345-420 .... **CMLC 30**
See also RGWL 3

Jerome, Jerome K(lapka)
1859-1927 .... **TCLC 23**
See also CA 119; 177; DLB 10, 34, 135;
RGEL 2

Jerrold, Douglas William
1803-1857 .... **NCLC 2**
See also DLB 158, 159; RGEL 2

Jewett, (Theodora) Sarah Orne
1849-1909 .... **SSC 6, 44; TCLC 1, 22**
See also AMW; AMWR 2; CA 108; 127;
CANR 71; DLB 12, 74, 221; EXPS; FW;
MAWW; NFS 15; RGAL 4; RGSF 2;
SATA 15; SSFS 4

Jewsbury, Geraldine (Endsor)
1812-1880 .... **NCLC 22**
See also DLB 21

Jhabvala, Ruth Prawer 1927- . **CLC 4, 8, 29,
94, 138**
See also BRWS 5; CA 1-4R; CANR 2, 29,
51, 74, 91; CN 7; DAB; DAM NOV; DLB
139, 194; EWL 3; IDFW 3, 4; INT CANR-
29; MTCW 1, 2; RGSF 2; RGWL 2;
RHW; TEA

Jibran, Kahlil
See Gibran, Kahlil

Jibran, Khalil
See Gibran, Kahlil

Jiles, Paulette 1943- .... **CLC 13, 58**
See also CA 101; CANR 70; CWP

Jimenez (Mantecon), Juan Ramon
1881-1958 .... **HLC 1; PC 7; TCLC 4**
See also CA 104; 131; CANR 74; DAM
MULT, POET; DLB 134; EW 9; EWL 3;
HW 1; MTCW 1, 2; RGWL 2, 3

Jimenez, Ramon
See Jimenez (Mantecon), Juan Ramon

Jimenez Mantecon, Juan
See Jimenez (Mantecon), Juan Ramon

Jin, Ha .... **CLC 109**
See Jin, Xuefei
See also CA 152; DLB 244; SSFS 17

Jin, Xuefei 1956-
See Jin, Ha
See also CANR 91

Joel, Billy .... **CLC 26**
See Joel, William Martin

Joel, William Martin 1949-
See Joel, Billy
See also CA 108

John, Saint 107th cent. -100 .... **CMLC 27**

John of the Cross, St. 1542-1591 .... **LC 18**
See also RGWL 2, 3

John Paul II, Pope 1920- .... **CLC 128**
See also CA 106; 133

Johnson, B(ryan) S(tanley William)
1933-1973 .... **CLC 6, 9**
See also CA 9-12R; 53-56; CANR 9; DLB
14, 40; EWL 3; RGEL 2

Johnson, Benjamin F., of Boone
See Riley, James Whitcomb

Johnson, Charles (Richard) 1948- .... **BLC 2;
CLC 7, 51, 65, 163**
See also AFAW 2; AMWS 6; BW 2, 3; CA
116; CAAS 18; CANR 42, 66, 82; CN 7;
DAM MULT; DLB 33, 278; MTCW 2;
RGAL 4; SSFS 16

Johnson, Charles S(purgeon)
1893-1956 .... **HR 3**
See also BW 1, 3; CA 125; CANR 82; DLB
51, 91

Johnson, Denis 1949- . **CLC 52, 160; SSC 56**
See also CA 117; 121; CANR 71, 99; CN
7; DLB 120

Justice, Donald (Rodney) 1925- .. **CLC 6, 19, 102**
See also AMWS 7; CA 5-8R; CANR 26, 54, 74; CP 7; CSW; DAM POET; DLBY 1983; EWL 3; INT CANR-26; MTCW 2; PFS 14

Juvenal c. 60-c. 130 .... **CMLC 8**
See also AW 2; CDWLB 1; DLB 211; RGWL 2, 3

Juvenis
See Bourne, Randolph S(illiman)

K., Alice
See Knapp, Caroline

Kabakov, Sasha .... **CLC 59**

Kacew, Romain 1914-1980
See Gary, Romain
See also CA 108; 102

Kadare, Ismail 1936- .... **CLC 52**
See also CA 161; EWL 3; RGWL 3

Kadohata, Cynthia .... **CLC 59, 122**
See also CA 140

Kafka, Franz 1883-1924 ... **SSC 5, 29, 35, 60; TCLC 2, 6, 13, 29, 47, 53, 112; WLC**
See also AAYA 31; BPFB 2; CA 105; 126; CDWLB 2; DA; DA3; DAB; DAC; DAM MST, NOV; DLB 81; EW 9; EWL 3; EXPS; LATS 1; LMFS 2; MTCW 1, 2; NFS 7; RGSF 2; RGWL 2, 3; SFW 4; SSFS 3, 7, 12; TWA

Kahanovitsch, Pinkhes
See Der Nister

Kahn, Roger 1927- .... **CLC 30**
See also CA 25-28R; CANR 44, 69; DLB 171; SATA 37

Kain, Saul
See Sassoon, Siegfried (Lorraine)

Kaiser, Georg 1878-1945 .... **TCLC 9**
See also CA 106; 190; CDWLB 2; DLB 124; EWL 3; LMFS 2; RGWL 2, 3

Kaledin, Sergei .... **CLC 59**

Kaletski, Alexander 1946- .... **CLC 39**
See also CA 118; 143

Kalidasa fl. c. 400-455 .... **CMLC 9; PC 22**
See also RGWL 2, 3

Kallman, Chester (Simon)
1921-1975 .... **CLC 2**
See also CA 45-48; 53-56; CANR 3

Kaminsky, Melvin 1926-
See Brooks, Mel
See also CA 65-68; CANR 16

Kaminsky, Stuart M(elvin) 1934- ..... **CLC 59**
See also CA 73-76; CANR 29, 53, 89; CMW 4

Kandinsky, Wassily 1866-1944 .... **TCLC 92**
See also CA 118; 155

Kane, Francis
See Robbins, Harold

Kane, Henry 1918-
See Queen, Ellery
See also CA 156; CMW 4

Kane, Paul
See Simon, Paul (Frederick)

Kanin, Garson 1912-1999 .... **CLC 22**
See also AITN 1; CA 5-8R; 177; CAD; CANR 7, 78; DLB 7; IDFW 3, 4

Kaniuk, Yoram 1930- .... **CLC 19**
See also CA 134

Kant, Immanuel 1724-1804 ..... **NCLC 27, 67**
See also DLB 94

Kantor, MacKinlay 1904-1977 .... **CLC 7**
See also CA 61-64; 73-76; CANR 60, 63; DLB 9, 102; MTCW 2; RHW; TCWW 2

Kanze Motokiyo
See Zeami

Kaplan, David Michael 1946- .... **CLC 50**
See also CA 187

Kaplan, James 1951- .... **CLC 59**
See also CA 135

Karadzic, Vuk Stefanovic
1787-1864 .... **NCLC 115**
See also CDWLB 4; DLB 147

Karageorge, Michael
See Anderson, Poul (William)

Karamzin, Nikolai Mikhailovich
1766-1826 .... **NCLC 3**
See also DLB 150; RGSF 2

Karapanou, Margarita 1946- .... **CLC 13**
See also CA 101

Karinthy, Frigyes 1887-1938 .... **TCLC 47**
See also CA 170; DLB 215; EWL 3

Karl, Frederick R(obert) 1927- .... **CLC 34**
See also CA 5-8R; CANR 3, 44

Kastel, Warren
See Silverberg, Robert

Kataev, Evgeny Petrovich 1903-1942
See Petrov, Evgeny
See also CA 120

Kataphusin
See Ruskin, John

Katz, Steve 1935- .... **CLC 47**
See also CA 25-28R; CAAS 14, 64; CANR 12; CN 7; DLBY 1983

Kauffman, Janet 1945- .... **CLC 42**
See also CA 117; CANR 43, 84; DLB 218; DLBY 1986

Kaufman, Bob (Garnell) 1925-1986 . **CLC 49**
See also BG 3; BW 1; CA 41-44R; 118; CANR 22; DLB 16, 41

Kaufman, George S. 1889-1961 ...... **CLC 38; DC 17**
See also CA 108; 93-96; DAM DRAM; DFS 1, 10; DLB 7; INT CA-108; MTCW 2; RGAL 4; TUS

Kaufman, Sue .... **CLC 3, 8**
See Barondess, Sue K(aufman)

Kavafis, Konstantinos Petrou 1863-1933
See Cavafy, C(onstantine) P(eter)
See also CA 104

Kavan, Anna 1901-1968 .... **CLC 5, 13, 82**
See also BRWS 7; CA 5-8R; CANR 6, 57; DLB 255; MTCW 1; RGEL 2; SFW 4

Kavanagh, Dan
See Barnes, Julian (Patrick)

Kavanagh, Julie 1952- .... **CLC 119**
See also CA 163

Kavanagh, Patrick (Joseph)
1904-1967 .... **CLC 22; PC 33**
See also BRWS 7; CA 123; 25-28R; DLB 15, 20; EWL 3; MTCW 1; RGEL 2

Kawabata, Yasunari 1899-1972 ..... **CLC 2, 5, 9, 18, 107; SSC 17**
See Kawabata Yasunari
See also CA 93-96; 33-36R; CANR 88; DAM MULT; MJW; MTCW 2; RGSF 2; RGWL 2, 3

Kawabata Yasunari
See Kawabata, Yasunari
See also DLB 180; EWL 3

Kaye, M(ary) M(argaret) 1909- .... **CLC 28**
See also CA 89-92; CANR 24, 60, 102; MTCW 1, 2; RHW; SATA 62

Kaye, Mollie
See Kaye, M(ary) M(argaret)

Kaye-Smith, Sheila 1887-1956 .... **TCLC 20**
See also CA 118; 203; DLB 36

Kaymor, Patrice Maguilene
See Senghor, Leopold Sedar

Kazakov, Yuri Pavlovich 1927-1982 . **SSC 43**
See Kazakov, Yury
See also CA 5-8R; CANR 36; MTCW 1; RGSF 2

Kazakov, Yury
See Kazakov, Yuri Pavlovich
See also EWL 3

Kazan, Elia 1909- .... **CLC 6, 16, 63**
See also CA 21-24R; CANR 32, 78

Kazantzakis, Nikos 1883(?)-1957 .... **TCLC 2, 5, 33**
See also BPFB 2; CA 105; 132; DA3; EW 9; EWL 3; MTCW 1, 2; RGWL 2, 3

Kazin, Alfred 1915-1998 ..... **CLC 34, 38, 119**
See also AMWS 8; CA 1-4R; CAAS 7; CANR 1, 45, 79; DLB 67; EWL 3

Keane, Mary Nesta (Skrine) 1904-1996
See Keane, Molly
See also CA 108; 114; 151; CN 7; RHW

Keane, Molly .... **CLC 31**
See Keane, Mary Nesta (Skrine)
See also INT 114

Keates, Jonathan 1946(?)- .... **CLC 34**
See also CA 163

Keaton, Buster 1895-1966 .... **CLC 20**
See also CA 194

Keats, John 1795-1821 ...... **NCLC 8, 73, 121; PC 1; WLC**
See also BRW 4; BRWR 1; CDBLB 1789-1832; DA; DA3; DAB; DAC; DAM MST, POET; DLB 96, 110; EXPP; LMFS 1; PAB; PFS 1, 2, 3, 9, 16; RGEL 2; TEA; WLIT 3; WP

Keble, John 1792-1866 .... **NCLC 87**
See also DLB 32, 55; RGEL 2

Keene, Donald 1922- .... **CLC 34**
See also CA 1-4R; CANR 5, 119

Keillor, Garrison .... **CLC 40, 115**
See Keillor, Gary (Edward)
See also AAYA 2; BEST 89:3; BPFB 2; DLBY 1987; EWL 3; SATA 58; TUS

Keillor, Gary (Edward) 1942-
See Keillor, Garrison
See also CA 111; 117; CANR 36, 59; CPW; DA3; DAM POP; MTCW 1, 2

Keith, Carlos
See Lewton, Val

Keith, Michael
See Hubbard, L(afayette) Ron(ald)

Keller, Gottfried 1819-1890 .... **NCLC 2; SSC 26**
See also CDWLB 2; DLB 129; EW; RGSF 2; RGWL 2, 3

Keller, Nora Okja 1965- .... **CLC 109**
See also CA 187

Kellerman, Jonathan 1949- .... **CLC 44**
See also AAYA 35; BEST 90:1; CA 106; CANR 29, 51; CMW 4; CPW; DA3; DAM POP; INT CANR-29

Kelley, William Melvin 1937- .... **CLC 22**
See also BW 1; CA 77-80; CANR 27, 83; CN 7; DLB 33; EWL 3

Kellogg, Marjorie 1922- .... **CLC 2**
See also CA 81-84

Kellow, Kathleen
See Hibbert, Eleanor Alice Burford

Kelly, M(ilton) T(errence) 1947- ...... **CLC 55**
See also CA 97-100; CAAS 22; CANR 19, 43, 84; CN 7

Kelly, Robert 1935- .... **SSC 50**
See also CA 17-20R; CAAS 19; CANR 47; CP 7; DLB 5, 130, 165

Kelman, James 1946- .... **CLC 58, 86**
See also BRWS 5; CA 148; CANR 85; CN 7; DLB 194; RGSF 2; WLIT 4

Kemal, Yashar 1923- .... **CLC 14, 29**
See also CA 89-92; CANR 44; CWW 2

Kemble, Fanny 1809-1893 .... **NCLC 18**
See also DLB 32

Kemelman, Harry 1908-1996 .... **CLC 2**
See also AITN 1; BPFB 2; CA 9-12R; 155; CANR 6, 71; CMW 4; DLB 28

Kempe, Margery 1373(?)-1440(?) ... **LC 6, 56**
See also DLB 146; RGEL 2

Kempis, Thomas a 1380-1471 .... **LC 11**

Kendall, Henry 1839-1882 .... **NCLC 12**
See also DLB 230

Mann, Abel
See Creasey, John

Mann, Emily 1952- .... **DC 7**
See also CA 130; CAD; CANR 55; CD 5;
CWD; DLB 266

Mann, (Luiz) Heinrich 1871-1950 ... **TCLC 9**
See also CA 106; 164, 181; DLB 66, 118;
EW 8; EWL 3; RGWL 2, 3

Mann, (Paul) Thomas 1875-1955 .... **SSC 5;**
TCLC 2, 8, 14, 21, 35, 44, 60; WLC
See also BPFB 2; CA 104; 128; CDWLB 2;
DA; DA3; DAB; DAC; DAM MST, NOV;
DLB 66; EW 9; EWL 3; GLL 1; LATS 1;
LMFS 1; MTCW 1, 2; NFS 17; RGSF 2;
RGWL 2, 3; SSFS 4, 9; TWA

Mannheim, Karl 1893-1947 .... **TCLC 65**
See also CA 204

Manning, David
See Faust, Frederick (Schiller)
See also TCWW 2

Manning, Frederic 1887(?)-1935 ... **TCLC 25**
See also CA 124; DLB 260

Manning, Olivia 1915-1980 .... **CLC 5, 19**
See also CA 5-8R; 101; CANR 29; EWL 3;
FW; MTCW 1; RGEL 2

Mano, D. Keith 1942- .... **CLC 2, 10**
See also CA 25-28R; CAAS 6; CANR 26,
57; DLB 6

Mansfield, Katherine . **SSC 9, 23, 38; TCLC**
2, 8, 39; WLC
See Beauchamp, Kathleen Mansfield
See also BPFB 2; BRW 7; DAB; DLB 162;
EWL 3; EXPS; FW; GLL 1; RGEL 2;
RGSF 2; SSFS 2, 8, 10, 11

Manso, Peter 1940- .... **CLC 39**
See also CA 29-32R; CANR 44

Mantecon, Juan Jimenez
See Jimenez (Mantecon), Juan Ramon

Mantel, Hilary (Mary) 1952- .... **CLC 144**
See also CA 125; CANR 54, 101; CN 7;
DLB 271; RHW

Manton, Peter
See Creasey, John

Man Without a Spleen, A
See Chekhov, Anton (Pavlovich)

Manzoni, Alessandro 1785-1873 ... **NCLC 29,**
98
See also EW 5; RGWL 2, 3; TWA

Map, Walter 1140-1209 .... **CMLC 32**

Mapu, Abraham (ben Jekutiel)
1808-1867 .... **NCLC 18**

Mara, Sally
See Queneau, Raymond

Maracle, Lee 1950- .... **NNAL**
See also CA 149

Marat, Jean Paul 1743-1793 .... **LC 10**

Marcel, Gabriel Honore 1889-1973 . **CLC 15**
See also CA 102; 45-48; EWL 3; MTCW 1,
2

March, William 1893-1954 .... **TCLC 96**

Marchbanks, Samuel
See Davies, (William) Robertson
See also CCA 1

Marchi, Giacomo
See Bassani, Giorgio

Marcus Aurelius
See Aurelius, Marcus
See also AW 2

Marguerite
See de Navarre, Marguerite

Marguerite d'Angouleme
See de Navarre, Marguerite
See also GFL Beginnings to 1789

Marguerite de Navarre
See de Navarre, Marguerite
See also RGWL 2, 3

Margulies, Donald 1954- .... **CLC 76**
See also CA 200; DFS 13; DLB 228

Marie de France c. 12th cent. - ..... **CMLC 8;**
PC 22
See also DLB 208; FW; RGWL 2, 3

Marie de l'Incarnation 1599-1672 ...... **LC 10**

Marier, Captain Victor
See Griffith, D(avid Lewelyn) W(ark)

Mariner, Scott
See Pohl, Frederik

Marinetti, Filippo Tommaso
1876-1944 .... **TCLC 10**
See also CA 107; DLB 114, 264; EW 9;
EWL 3

Marivaux, Pierre Carlet de Chamblain de
1688-1763 .... **DC 7; LC 4**
See also GFL Beginnings to 1789; RGWL
2, 3; TWA

Markandaya, Kamala .... **CLC 8, 38**
See Taylor, Kamala (Purnaiya)
See also BYA 13; CN 7; EWL 3

Markfield, Wallace 1926-2002 .... **CLC 8**
See also CA 69-72; 208; CAAS 3; CN 7;
DLB 2, 28; DLBY 2002

Markham, Edwin 1852-1940 .... **TCLC 47**
See also CA 160; DLB 54, 186; RGAL 4

Markham, Robert
See Amis, Kingsley (William)

Markoosie .... **NNAL**
See Markoosie, Patsauq
See also CLR 23; DAM MULT

Marks, J
See Highwater, Jamake (Mamake)

Marks, J.
See Highwater, Jamake (Mamake)

Marks-Highwater, J
See Highwater, Jamake (Mamake)

Marks-Highwater, J.
See Highwater, Jamake (Mamake)

Markson, David M(errill) 1927- .... **CLC 67**
See also CA 49-52; CANR 1, 91; CN 7

Marlatt, Daphne (Buckle) 1942- .... **CLC 168**
See also CA 25-28R; CANR 17, 39; CN 7;
CP 7; CWP; DLB 60; FW

Marley, Bob .... **CLC 17**
See Marley, Robert Nesta

Marley, Robert Nesta 1945-1981
See Marley, Bob
See also CA 107; 103

Marlowe, Christopher 1564-1593 . **DC 1; LC**
22, 47; WLC
See also BRW 1; BRWR 1; CDBLB Before
1660; DA; DA3; DAB; DAC; DAM
DRAM, MST; DFS 1, 5, 13; DLB 62;
EXPP; LMFS 1; RGEL 2; TEA; WLIT 3

Marlowe, Stephen 1928- .... **CLC 70**
See Queen, Ellery
See also CA 13-16R; CANR 6, 55; CMW
4; SFW 4

Marmion, Shakerley 1603-1639 .... **LC 89**
See also DLB 58; RGEL 2

Marmontel, Jean-Francois 1723-1799 .. **LC 2**

Maron, Monika 1941- .... **CLC 165**
See also CA 201

Marquand, John P(hillips)
1893-1960 .... **CLC 2, 10**
See also AMW; BPFB 2; CA 85-88; CANR
73; CMW 4; DLB 9, 102; EWL 3; MTCW
2; RGAL 4

Marques, Rene 1919-1979 .. **CLC 96; HLC 2**
See also CA 97-100; 85-88; CANR 78;
DAM MULT; DLB 113; EWL 3; HW 1,
2; LAW; RGSF 2

Marquez, Gabriel (Jose) Garcia
See Garcia Marquez, Gabriel (Jose)

Marquis, Don(ald Robert Perry)
1878-1937 .... **TCLC 7**
See also CA 104; 166; DLB 11, 25; RGAL
4

Marquis de Sade
See Sade, Donatien Alphonse Francois

Marric, J. J.
See Creasey, John
See also MSW

Marryat, Frederick 1792-1848 .... **NCLC 3**
See also DLB 21, 163; RGEL 2; WCH

Marsden, James
See Creasey, John

Marsh, Edward 1872-1953 .... **TCLC 99**

Marsh, (Edith) Ngaio 1899-1982 .. **CLC 7, 53**
See also CA 9-12R; CANR 6, 58; CMW 4;
CPW; DAM POP; DLB 77; MSW;
MTCW 1, 2; RGEL 2; TEA

Marshall, Garry 1934- .... **CLC 17**
See also AAYA 3; CA 111; SATA 60

Marshall, Paule 1929- .. **BLC 3; CLC 27, 72;**
SSC 3
See also AFAW 1, 2; AMWS 11; BPFB 2;
BW 2, 3; CA 77-80; CANR 25, 73; CN 7;
DA3; DAM MULT; DLB 33, 157, 227;
EWL 3; LATS 1; MTCW 1, 2; RGAL 4;
SSFS 15

Marshallik
See Zangwill, Israel

Marsten, Richard
See Hunter, Evan

Marston, John 1576-1634 .... **LC 33**
See also BRW 2; DAM DRAM; DLB 58,
172; RGEL 2

Martha, Henry
See Harris, Mark

Marti (y Perez), Jose (Julian)
1853-1895 .... **HLC 2; NCLC 63**
See also DAM MULT; HW 2; LAW; RGWL
2, 3; WLIT 1

Martial c. 40-c. 104 .... **CMLC 35; PC 10**
See also AW 2; CDWLB 1; DLB 211;
RGWL 2, 3

Martin, Ken
See Hubbard, L(afayette) Ron(ald)

Martin, Richard
See Creasey, John

Martin, Steve 1945- .... **CLC 30**
See also AAYA 53; CA 97-100; CANR 30,
100; MTCW 1

Martin, Valerie 1948- .... **CLC 89**
See also BEST 90:2; CA 85-88; CANR 49,
89

Martin, Violet Florence 1862-1915 .. **SSC 56;**
TCLC 51

Martin, Webber
See Silverberg, Robert

Martindale, Patrick Victor
See White, Patrick (Victor Martindale)

Martin du Gard, Roger
1881-1958 .... **TCLC 24**
See also CA 118; CANR 94; DLB 65; EWL
3; GFL 1789 to the Present; RGWL 2, 3

Martineau, Harriet 1802-1876 .... **NCLC 26**
See also DLB 21, 55, 159, 163, 166, 190;
FW; RGEL 2; YABC 2

Martines, Julia
See O'Faolain, Julia

Martinez, Enrique Gonzalez
See Gonzalez Martinez, Enrique

Martinez, Jacinto Benavente y
See Benavente (y Martinez), Jacinto

Martinez de la Rosa, Francisco de Paula
1787-1862 .... **NCLC 102**
See also TWA

Martinez Ruiz, Jose 1873-1967
See Azorin; Ruiz, Jose Martinez
See also CA 93-96; HW 1

Martinez Sierra, Gregorio
1881-1947 .... **TCLC 6**
See also CA 115; EWL 3

Martinez Sierra, Maria (de la O'LeJarraga)
1874-1974 .... **TCLC 6**
See also CA 115; EWL 3

Martinsen, Martin
See Follett, Ken(neth Martin)
Martinson, Harry (Edmund)
1904-1978 .... **CLC 14**
See also CA 77-80; CANR 34; DLB 259;
EWL 3
Martyn, Edward 1859-1923 .... **TCLC 131**
See also CA 179; DLB 10; RGEL 2
Marut, Ret
See Traven, B.
Marut, Robert
See Traven, B.
Marvell, Andrew 1621-1678 .... **LC 4, 43; PC
10; WLC**
See also BRW 2; BRWR 2; CDBLB 1660-
1789; DA; DAB; DAC; DAM MST,
POET; DLB 131; EXPP; PFS 5; RGEL 2;
TEA; WP
Marx, Karl (Heinrich)
1818-1883 .... **NCLC 17, 114**
See also DLB 129; LATS 1; TWA
Masaoka, Shiki -1902 .... **TCLC 18**
See Masaoka, Tsunenori
See also RGWL 3
Masaoka, Tsunenori 1867-1902
See Masaoka, Shiki
See also CA 117; 191; TWA
Masefield, John (Edward)
1878-1967 .... **CLC 11, 47**
See also CA 19-20; 25-28R; CANR 33;
CAP 2; CDBLB 1890-1914; DAM POET;
DLB 10, 19, 153, 160; EWL 3; EXPP;
FANT; MTCW 1, 2; PFS 5; RGEL 2;
SATA 19
Maso, Carole 19(?)- .... **CLC 44**
See also CA 170; GLL 2; RGAL 4
Mason, Bobbie Ann 1940- ... **CLC 28, 43, 82,
154; SSC 4**
See also AAYA 5, 42; AMWS 8; BPFB 2;
CA 53-56; CANR 11, 31, 58, 83;
CDALBS; CN 7; CSW; DA3; DLB 173;
DLBY 1987; EWL 3; EXPS; INT CANR-
31; MTCW 1, 2; NFS 4; RGAL 4; RGSF
2; SSFS 3,8; YAW
Mason, Ernst
See Pohl, Frederik
Mason, Hunni B.
See Sternheim, (William Adolf) Carl
Mason, Lee W.
See Malzberg, Barry N(athaniel)
Mason, Nick 1945- .... **CLC 35**
Mason, Tally
See Derleth, August (William)
Mass, Anna .... **CLC 59**
Mass, William
See Gibson, William
Massinger, Philip 1583-1640 .... **LC 70**
See also DLB 58; RGEL 2
Master Lao
See Lao Tzu
Masters, Edgar Lee 1868-1950 ...... **PC 1, 36;
TCLC 2, 25; WLCS**
See also AMWS 1; CA 104; 133; CDALB
1865-1917; DA; DAC; DAM MST,
POET; DLB 54; EWL 3; EXPP; MTCW
1, 2; RGAL 4; TUS; WP
Masters, Hilary 1928- .... **CLC 48**
See also CA 25-28R; CANR 13, 47, 97; CN
7; DLB 244
Mastrosimone, William 19(?)- .... **CLC 36**
See also CA 186; CAD; CD 5
Mathe, Albert
See Camus, Albert
Mather, Cotton 1663-1728 .... **LC 38**
See also AMWS 2; CDALB 1640-1865;
DLB 24, 30, 140; RGAL 4; TUS
Mather, Increase 1639-1723 .... **LC 38**
See also DLB 24

Matheson, Richard (Burton) 1926- .. **CLC 37**
See also AAYA 31; CA 97-100; CANR 88,
99; DLB 8, 44; HGG; INT 97-100; SCFW
2; SFW 4; SUFW 2
Mathews, Harry 1930- .... **CLC 6, 52**
See also CA 21-24R; CAAS 6; CANR 18,
40, 98; CN 7
Mathews, John Joseph 1894-1979 .. **CLC 84;
NNAL**
See also CA 19-20; 142; CANR 45; CAP 2;
DAM MULT; DLB 175
Mathias, Roland (Glyn) 1915- .... **CLC 45**
See also CA 97-100; CANR 19, 41; CP 7;
DLB 27
Matsuo Basho 1644-1694 .... **LC 62; PC 3**
See Basho, Matsuo
See also DAM POET; PFS 2, 7
Mattheson, Rodney
See Creasey, John
Matthews, (James) Brander
1852-1929 .... **TCLC 95**
See also DLB 71, 78; DLBD 13
Matthews, Greg 1949- .... **CLC 45**
See also CA 135
Matthews, William (Procter III)
1942-1997 .... **CLC 40**
See also AMWS 9; CA 29-32R; 162; CAAS
18; CANR 12, 57; CP 7; DLB 5
Matthias, John (Edward) 1941- .... **CLC 9**
See also CA 33-36R; CANR 56; CP 7
Matthiessen, F(rancis) O(tto)
1902-1950 .... **TCLC 100**
See also CA 185; DLB 63
Matthiessen, Peter 1927- ... **CLC 5, 7, 11, 32,
64**
See also AAYA 6, 40; AMWS 5; ANW;
BEST 90:4; BPFB 2; CA 9-12R; CANR
21, 50, 73, 100; CN 7; DA3; DAM NOV;
DLB 6, 173, 275; MTCW 1, 2; SATA 27
Maturin, Charles Robert
1780(?)-1824 .... **NCLC 6**
See also BRWS 8; DLB 178; HGG; LMFS
1; RGEL 2; SUFW
Matute (Ausejo), Ana Maria 1925- .. **CLC 11**
See also CA 89-92; EWL 3; MTCW 1;
RGSF 2
Maugham, W. S.
See Maugham, W(illiam) Somerset
Maugham, W(illiam) Somerset
1874-1965 .. **CLC 1, 11, 15, 67, 93; SSC
8; WLC**
See also BPFB 2; BRW 6; CA 5-8R; 25-
28R; CANR 40; CDBLB 1914-1945;
CMW 4; DA; DA3; DAB; DAC; DAM
DRAM, MST, NOV; DLB 10, 36, 77, 100,
162, 195; EWL 3; LAIT 3; MTCW 1, 2;
RGEL 2; RGSF 2; SATA 54; SSFS 17
Maugham, William Somerset
See Maugham, W(illiam) Somerset
Maupassant, (Henri Rene Albert) Guy de
1850-1893 . **NCLC 1, 42, 83; SSC 1, 64;
WLC**
See also BYA 14; DA; DA3; DAB; DAC;
DAM MST; DLB 123; EW 7; EXPS; GFL
1789 to the Present; LAIT 2; LMFS 1;
RGSF 2; RGWL 2, 3; SSFS 4; SUFW;
TWA
Maupin, Armistead (Jones, Jr.)
1944- .... **CLC 95**
See also CA 125; 130; CANR 58, 101;
CPW; DA3; DAM POP; DLB 278; GLL
1; INT 130; MTCW 2
Maurhut, Richard
See Traven, B.
Mauriac, Claude 1914-1996 .... **CLC 9**
See also CA 89-92; 152; CWW 2; DLB 83;
EWL 3; GFL 1789 to the Present

Mauriac, Francois (Charles)
1885-1970 .... **CLC 4, 9, 56; SSC 24**
See also CA 25-28; CAP 2; DLB 65; EW
10; EWL 3; GFL 1789 to the Present;
MTCW 1, 2; RGWL 2, 3; TWA
Mavor, Osborne Henry 1888-1951
See Bridie, James
See also CA 104
Maxwell, William (Keepers, Jr.)
1908-2000 .... **CLC 19**
See also AMWS 8; CA 93-96; 189; CANR
54, 95; CN 7; DLB 218, 278; DLBY
1980; INT CA-93-96; SATA-Obit 128
May, Elaine 1932- .... **CLC 16**
See also CA 124; 142; CAD; CWD; DLB
44
Mayakovski, Vladimir (Vladimirovich)
1893-1930 .... **TCLC 4, 18**
See Maiakovskii, Vladimir; Mayakovsky,
Vladimir
See also CA 104; 158; EWL 3; MTCW 2;
SFW 4; TWA
Mayakovsky, Vladimir
See Mayakovski, Vladimir (Vladimirovich)
See also EW 11; WP
Mayhew, Henry 1812-1887 .... **NCLC 31**
See also DLB 18, 55, 190
Mayle, Peter 1939(?)- .... **CLC 89**
See also CA 139; CANR 64, 109
Maynard, Joyce 1953- .... **CLC 23**
See also CA 111; 129; CANR 64
Mayne, William (James Carter)
1928- .... **CLC 12**
See also AAYA 20; CA 9-12R; CANR 37,
80, 100; CLR 25; FANT; JRDA; MAI-
CYA 1, 2; MAICYAS 1; SAAS 11; SATA
6, 68, 122; SUFW 2; YAW
Mayo, Jim
See L'Amour, Louis (Dearborn)
See also TCWW 2
Maysles, Albert 1926- .... **CLC 16**
See also CA 29-32R
Maysles, David 1932-1987 .... **CLC 16**
See also CA 191
Mazer, Norma Fox 1931- .... **CLC 26**
See also AAYA 5, 36; BYA 1, 8; CA 69-72;
CANR 12, 32, 66; CLR 23; JRDA; MAI-
CYA 1, 2; SAAS 1; SATA 24, 67, 105;
WYA; YAW
Mazzini, Guiseppe 1805-1872 .... **NCLC 34**
McAlmon, Robert (Menzies)
1895-1956 .... **TCLC 97**
See also CA 107; 168; DLB 4, 45; DLBD
15; GLL 1
McAuley, James Phillip 1917-1976 .. **CLC 45**
See also CA 97-100; DLB 260; RGEL 2
McBain, Ed
See Hunter, Evan
See also MSW
McBrien, William (Augustine)
1930- .... **CLC 44**
See also CA 107; CANR 90
McCabe, Patrick 1955- .... **CLC 133**
See also CA 130; CANR 50, 90; CN 7;
DLB 194
McCaffrey, Anne (Inez) 1926- .... **CLC 17**
See also AAYA 6, 34; AITN 2; BEST 89:2;
BPFB 2; BYA 5; CA 25-28R; CANR 15,
35, 55, 96; CLR 49; CPW; DA3; DAM
NOV, POP; DLB 8; JRDA; MAICYA 1,
2; MTCW 1, 2; SAAS 11; SATA 8, 70,
116; SFW 4; SUFW 2; WYA; YAW
McCall, Nathan 1955(?)- .... **CLC 86**
See also BW 3; CA 146; CANR 88
McCann, Arthur
See Campbell, John W(ood, Jr.)
McCann, Edson
See Pohl, Frederik

Millin, Sarah Gertrude 1889-1968 ... **CLC 49**
See also CA 102; 93-96; DLB 225; EWL 3

Milne, A(lan) A(lexander)
1882-1956 .... **TCLC 6, 88**
See also BRWS 5; CA 104; 133; CLR 1, 26; CMW 4; CWRI 5; DA3; DAB; DAC; DAM MST; DLB 10, 77, 100, 160; FANT; MAICYA 1, 2; MTCW 1, 2; RGEL 2; SATA 100; WCH; YABC 1

Milner, Ron(ald) 1938- .... **BLC 3; CLC 56**
See also AITN 1; BW 1; CA 73-76; CAD; CANR 24, 81; CD 5; DAM MULT; DLB 38; MTCW 1

Milnes, Richard Monckton
1809-1885 .... **NCLC 61**
See also DLB 32, 184

Milosz, Czeslaw 1911- ...... **CLC 5, 11, 22, 31, 56, 82; PC 8; WLCS**
See also CA 81-84; CANR 23, 51, 91; CD-WLB 4; CWW 2; DA3; DAM MST, POET; DLB 215; EW 13; EWL 3; MTCW 1, 2; PFS 16; RGWL 2, 3

Milton, John 1608-1674 ..... **LC 9, 43, 92; PC 19, 29; WLC**
See also BRW 2; BRWR 2; CDBLB 1660-1789; DA; DA3; DAB; DAC; DAM MST, POET; DLB 131, 151, 281; EFS 1; EXPP; LAIT 1; PAB; PFS 3, 17; RGEL 2; TEA; WLIT 3; WP

Min, Anchee 1957- .... **CLC 86**
See also CA 146; CANR 94

Minehaha, Cornelius
See Wedekind, (Benjamin) Frank(lin)

Miner, Valerie 1947- .... **CLC 40**
See also CA 97-100; CANR 59; FW; GLL 2

Minimo, Duca
See D'Annunzio, Gabriele

Minot, Susan 1956- .... **CLC 44, 159**
See also AMWS 6; CA 134; CANR 118; CN 7

Minus, Ed 1938- .... **CLC 39**
See also CA 185

Mirabai 1498(?)-1550(?) .... **PC 48**

Miranda, Javier
See Bioy Casares, Adolfo
See also CWW 2

Mirbeau, Octave 1848-1917 .... **TCLC 55**
See also DLB 123, 192; GFL 1789 to the Present

Mirikitani, Janice 1942- .... **AAL**
See also CA 211; RGAL 4

Miro (Ferrer), Gabriel (Francisco Victor)
1879-1930 .... **TCLC 5**
See also CA 104; 185; EWL 3

Misharin, Alexandr .... **CLC 59**

Mishima, Yukio ... **CLC 2, 4, 6, 9, 27; DC 1; SSC 4**
See Hiraoka, Kimitake
See also AAYA 50; BPFB 2; GLL 1; MJW; MTCW 2; RGSF 2; RGWL 2, 3; SSFS 5, 12

Mistral, Frederic 1830-1914 .... **TCLC 51**
See also CA 122; GFL 1789 to the Present

Mistral, Gabriela
See Godoy Alcayaga, Lucila
See also DLB 283; DNFS 1; EWL 3; LAW; RGWL 2, 3; WP

Mistry, Rohinton 1952- .... **CLC 71**
See also CA 141; CANR 86, 114; CCA 1; CN 7; DAC; SSFS 6

Mitchell, Clyde
See Ellison, Harlan (Jay)

Mitchell, Emerson Blackhorse Barney
1945- .... **NNAL**
See also CA 45-48

Mitchell, James Leslie 1901-1935
See Gibbon, Lewis Grassic
See also CA 104; 188; DLB 15

Mitchell, Joni 1943- .... **CLC 12**
See also CA 112; CCA 1

Mitchell, Joseph (Quincy)
1908-1996 .... **CLC 98**
See also CA 77-80; 152; CANR 69; CN 7; CSW; DLB 185; DLBY 1996

Mitchell, Margaret (Munnerlyn)
1900-1949 .... **TCLC 11**
See also AAYA 23; BPFB 2; BYA 1; CA 109; 125; CANR 55, 94; CDALBS; DA3; DAM NOV, POP; DLB 9; LAIT 2; MTCW 1, 2; NFS 9; RGAL 4; RHW; TUS; WYAS 1; YAW

Mitchell, Peggy
See Mitchell, Margaret (Munnerlyn)

Mitchell, S(ilas) Weir 1829-1914 .... **TCLC 36**
See also CA 165; DLB 202; RGAL 4

Mitchell, W(illiam) O(rmond)
1914-1998 .... **CLC 25**
See also CA 77-80; 165; CANR 15, 43; CN 7; DAC; DAM MST; DLB 88

Mitchell, William 1879-1936 .... **TCLC 81**

Mitford, Mary Russell 1787-1855 ... **NCLC 4**
See also DLB 110, 116; RGEL 2

Mitford, Nancy 1904-1973 .... **CLC 44**
See also CA 9-12R; DLB 191; RGEL 2

Miyamoto, (Chujo) Yuriko
1899-1951 .... **TCLC 37**
See Miyamoto Yuriko
See also CA 170, 174

Miyamoto Yuriko
See Miyamoto, (Chujo) Yuriko
See also DLB 180

Miyazawa, Kenji 1896-1933 .... **TCLC 76**
See Miyazawa Kenji
See also CA 157; RGWL 3

Miyazawa Kenji
See Miyazawa, Kenji
See also EWL 3

Mizoguchi, Kenji 1898-1956 .... **TCLC 72**
See also CA 167

Mo, Timothy (Peter) 1950(?)- ... **CLC 46, 134**
See also CA 117; CN 7; DLB 194; MTCW 1; WLIT 4

Modarressi, Taghi (M.) 1931-1997 ... **CLC 44**
See also CA 121; 134; INT 134

Modiano, Patrick (Jean) 1945- .... **CLC 18**
See also CA 85-88; CANR 17, 40, 115; CWW 2; DLB 83; EWL 3

Mofolo, Thomas (Mokopu)
1875(?)-1948 .... **BLC 3; TCLC 22**
See also AFW; CA 121; 153; CANR 83; DAM MULT; DLB 225; EWL 3; MTCW 2; WLIT 2

Mohr, Nicholasa 1938- .... **CLC 12; HLC 2**
See also AAYA 8, 46; CA 49-52; CANR 1, 32, 64; CLR 22; DAM MULT; DLB 145; HW 1, 2; JRDA; LAIT 5; MAICYA 2; MAICYAS 1; RGAL 4; SAAS 8; SATA 8, 97; SATA-Essay 113; WYA; YAW

Moi, Toril 1953- .... **CLC 172**
See also CA 154; CANR 102; FW

Mojtabai, A(nn) G(race) 1938- ..... **CLC 5, 9, 15, 29**
See also CA 85-88; CANR 88

Moliere 1622-1673 ..... **DC 13; LC 10, 28, 64; WLC**
See also DA; DA3; DAB; DAC; DAM DRAM, MST; DFS 13; DLB 268; EW 3; GFL Beginnings to 1789; LATS 1; RGWL 2, 3; TWA

Molin, Charles
See Mayne, William (James Carter)

Molnar, Ferenc 1878-1952 .... **TCLC 20**
See also CA 109; 153; CANR 83; CDWLB 4; DAM DRAM; DLB 215; EWL 3; RGWL 2, 3

Momaday, N(avarre) Scott 1934- ...... **CLC 2, 19, 85, 95, 160; NNAL; PC 25; WLCS**
See also AAYA 11; AMWS 4; ANW; BPFB 2; CA 25-28R; CANR 14, 34, 68; CDALBS; CN 7; CPW; DA; DA3; DAB; DAC; DAM MST, MULT, NOV, POP; DLB 143, 175, 256; EWL 3; EXPP; INT CANR-14; LAIT 4; LATS 1; MTCW 1, 2; NFS 10; PFS 2, 11; RGAL 4; SATA 48; SATA-Brief 30; WP; YAW

Monette, Paul 1945-1995 .... **CLC 82**
See also AMWS 10; CA 139; 147; CN 7; GLL 1

Monroe, Harriet 1860-1936 .... **TCLC 12**
See also CA 109; 204; DLB 54, 91

Monroe, Lyle
See Heinlein, Robert A(nson)

Montagu, Elizabeth 1720-1800 .... **NCLC 7, 117**
See also FW

Montagu, Mary (Pierrepont) Wortley
1689-1762 .... **LC 9, 57; PC 16**
See also DLB 95, 101; RGEL 2

Montagu, W. H.
See Coleridge, Samuel Taylor

Montague, John (Patrick) 1929- ..... **CLC 13, 46**
See also CA 9-12R; CANR 9, 69; CP 7; DLB 40; EWL 3; MTCW 1; PFS 12; RGEL 2

Montaigne, Michel (Eyquem) de
1533-1592 .... **LC 8; WLC**
See also DA; DAB; DAC; DAM MST; EW 2; GFL Beginnings to 1789; LMFS 1; RGWL 2, 3; TWA

Montale, Eugenio 1896-1981 ... **CLC 7, 9, 18; PC 13**
See also CA 17-20R; 104; CANR 30; DLB 114; EW 11; EWL 3; MTCW 1; RGWL 2, 3; TWA

Montesquieu, Charles-Louis de Secondat
1689-1755 .... **LC 7, 69**
See also EW 3; GFL Beginnings to 1789; TWA

Montessori, Maria 1870-1952 ...... **TCLC 103**
See also CA 115; 147

Montgomery, (Robert) Bruce 1921(?)-1978
See Crispin, Edmund
See also CA 179; 104; CMW 4

Montgomery, L(ucy) M(aud)
1874-1942 .... **TCLC 51**
See also AAYA 12; BYA 1; CA 108; 137; CLR 8, 91; DA3; DAC; DAM MST; DLB 92; DLBD 14; JRDA; MAICYA 1, 2; MTCW 2; RGEL 2; SATA 100; TWA; WCH; WYA; YABC 1

Montgomery, Marion H., Jr. 1925- .... **CLC 7**
See also AITN 1; CA 1-4R; CANR 3, 48; CSW; DLB 6

Montgomery, Max
See Davenport, Guy (Mattison, Jr.)

Montherlant, Henry (Milon) de
1896-1972 .... **CLC 8, 19**
See also CA 85-88; 37-40R; DAM DRAM; DLB 72; EW 11; EWL 3; GFL 1789 to the Present; MTCW 1

Monty Python
See Chapman, Graham; Cleese, John (Marwood); Gilliam, Terry (Vance); Idle, Eric; Jones, Terence Graham Parry; Palin, Michael (Edward)
See also AAYA 7

Moodie, Susanna (Strickland)
1803-1885 .... **NCLC 14, 113**
See also DLB 99

Moody, Hiram (F. III) 1961-
See Moody, Rick
See also CA 138; CANR 64, 112

Moody, Minerva
See Alcott, Louisa May

Moyers, Bill 1934- .... **CLC 74**
See also AITN 2; CA 61-64; CANR 31, 52

Mphahlele, Es'kia
See Mphahlele, Ezekiel
See also AFW; CDWLB 3; DLB 125, 225;
RGSF 2; SSFS 11

Mphahlele, Ezekiel 1919- ... **BLC 3; CLC 25, 133**
See Mphahlele, Es'kia
See also BW 2, 3; CA 81-84; CANR 26, 76; CN 7; DA3; DAM MULT; EWL 3;
MTCW 2; SATA 119

Mqhayi, S(amuel) E(dward) K(rune Loliwe)
1875-1945 .... **BLC 3; TCLC 25**
See also CA 153; CANR 87; DAM MULT

Mrozek, Slawomir 1930- .... **CLC 3, 13**
See also CA 13-16R; CAAS 10; CANR 29;
CDWLB 4; CWW 2; DLB 232; EWL 3;
MTCW 1

Mrs. Belloc-Lowndes
See Lowndes, Marie Adelaide (Belloc)

Mrs. Fairstar
See Horne, Richard Henry Hengist

M'Taggart, John M'Taggart Ellis
See McTaggart, John McTaggart Ellis

Mtwa, Percy (?)- .... **CLC 47**

Mueller, Lisel 1924- .... **CLC 13, 51; PC 33**
See also CA 93-96; CP 7; DLB 105; PFS 9, 13

Muggeridge, Malcolm (Thomas)
1903-1990 .... **TCLC 120**
See also AITN 1; CA 101; CANR 33, 63;
MTCW 1, 2

Muhammad 570-632 .... **WLCS**
See also DA; DAB; DAC; DAM MST

Muir, Edwin 1887-1959 . **PC 49; TCLC 2, 87**
See Moore, Edward
See also BRWS 6; CA 104; 193; DLB 20, 100, 191; EWL 3; RGEL 2

Muir, John 1838-1914 .... **TCLC 28**
See also AMWS 9; ANW; CA 165; DLB 186, 275

Mujica Lainez, Manuel 1910-1984 ... **CLC 31**
See Lainez, Manuel Mujica
See also CA 81-84; 112; CANR 32; EWL 3; HW 1

Mukherjee, Bharati 1940- ..... **AAL; CLC 53, 115; SSC 38**
See also AAYA 46; BEST 89:2; CA 107;
CANR 45, 72; CN 7; DAM NOV; DLB 60, 218; DNFS 1, 2; EWL 3; FW; MTCW 1, 2; RGAL 4; RGSF 2; SSFS 7; TUS

Muldoon, Paul 1951- .... **CLC 32, 72, 166**
See also BRWS 4; CA 113; 129; CANR 52, 91; CP 7; DAM POET; DLB 40; INT 129;
PFS 7

Mulisch, Harry 1927- .... **CLC 42**
See also CA 9-12R; CANR 6, 26, 56, 110;
EWL 3

Mull, Martin 1943- .... **CLC 17**
See also CA 105

Muller, Wilhelm .... **NCLC 73**

Mulock, Dinah Maria
See Craik, Dinah Maria (Mulock)
See also RGEL 2

Munday, Anthony 1560-1633 .... **LC 87**
See also DLB 62, 172; RGEL 2

Munford, Robert 1737(?)-1783 .... **LC 5**
See also DLB 31

Mungo, Raymond 1946- .... **CLC 72**
See also CA 49-52; CANR 2

Munro, Alice 1931- .... **CLC 6, 10, 19, 50, 95; SSC 3; WLCS**
See also AITN 2; BPFB 2; CA 33-36R;
CANR 33, 53, 75, 114; CCA 1; CN 7;
DA3; DAC; DAM MST, NOV; DLB 53;
EWL 3; MTCW 1, 2; RGEL 2; RGSF 2;
SATA 29; SSFS 5, 13

Munro, H(ector) H(ugh) 1870-1916 .... **WLC**
See Saki
See also CA 104; 130; CANR 104; CDBLB 1890-1914; DA; DA3; DAB; DAC; DAM MST, NOV; DLB 34, 162; EXPS; MTCW 1, 2; RGEL 2; SSFS 15

Murakami, Haruki 1949- .... **CLC 150**
See Murakami Haruki
See also CA 165; CANR 102; MJW; RGWL 3; SFW 4

Murakami Haruki
See Murakami, Haruki
See also DLB 182; EWL 3

Murasaki, Lady
See Murasaki Shikibu

Murasaki Shikibu 978(?)-1026(?) ... **CMLC 1**
See also EFS 2; LATS 1; RGWL 2, 3

Murdoch, (Jean) Iris 1919-1999 ... **CLC 1, 2, 3, 4, 6, 8, 11, 15, 22, 31, 51**
See also BRWS 1; CA 13-16R; 179; CANR 8, 43, 68, 103; CDBLB 1960 to Present;
CN 7; CWD; DA3; DAB; DAC; DAM MST, NOV; DLB 14, 194, 233; EWL 3;
INT CANR-8; MTCW 1, 2; RGEL 2;
TEA; WLIT 4

Murfree, Mary Noailles 1850-1922 .. **SSC 22; TCLC 135**
See also CA 122; 176; DLB 12, 74; RGAL 4

Murnau, Friedrich Wilhelm
See Plumpe, Friedrich Wilhelm

Murphy, Richard 1927- .... **CLC 41**
See also BRWS 5; CA 29-32R; CP 7; DLB 40; EWL 3

Murphy, Sylvia 1937- .... **CLC 34**
See also CA 121

Murphy, Thomas (Bernard) 1935- ... **CLC 51**
See also CA 101

Murray, Albert L. 1916- .... **CLC 73**
See also BW 2; CA 49-52; CANR 26, 52, 78; CSW; DLB 38

Murray, James Augustus Henry
1837-1915 .... **TCLC 117**

Murray, Judith Sargent
1751-1820 .... **NCLC 63**
See also DLB 37, 200

Murray, Les(lie Allan) 1938- .... **CLC 40**
See also BRWS 7; CA 21-24R; CANR 11, 27, 56, 103; CP 7; DAM POET; DLBY 2001; EWL 3; RGEL 2

Murry, J. Middleton
See Murry, John Middleton

Murry, John Middleton
1889-1957 .... **TCLC 16**
See also CA 118; DLB 149

Musgrave, Susan 1951- .... **CLC 13, 54**
See also CA 69-72; CANR 45, 84; CCA 1;
CP 7; CWP

Musil, Robert (Edler von)
1880-1942 .... **SSC 18; TCLC 12, 68**
See also CA 109; CANR 55, 84; CDWLB 2; DLB 81, 124; EW 9; EWL 3; MTCW 2; RGSF 2; RGWL 2, 3

Muske, Carol .... **CLC 90**
See Muske-Dukes, Carol (Anne)

Muske-Dukes, Carol (Anne) 1945-
See Muske, Carol
See also CA 65-68; CAAE 203; CANR 32, 70; CWP

Musset, (Louis Charles) Alfred de
1810-1857 .... **NCLC 7**
See also DLB 192, 217; EW 6; GFL 1789 to the Present; RGWL 2, 3; TWA

Mussolini, Benito (Amilcare Andrea)
1883-1945 .... **TCLC 96**
See also CA 116

My Brother's Brother
See Chekhov, Anton (Pavlovich)

Myers, L(eopold) H(amilton)
1881-1944 .... **TCLC 59**
See also CA 157; DLB 15; EWL 3; RGEL 2

Myers, Walter Dean 1937- .. **BLC 3; CLC 35**
See also AAYA 4, 23; BW 2; BYA 6, 8, 11;
CA 33-36R; CANR 20, 42, 67, 108; CLR 4, 16, 35; DAM MULT, NOV; DLB 33;
INT CANR-20; JRDA; LAIT 5; MAICYA 1, 2; MAICYAS 1; MTCW 2; SAAS 2;
SATA 41, 71, 109; SATA-Brief 27; WYA;
YAW

Myers, Walter M.
See Myers, Walter Dean

Myles, Symon
See Follett, Ken(neth Martin)

Nabokov, Vladimir (Vladimirovich)
1899-1977 .... **CLC 1, 2, 3, 6, 8, 11, 15, 23, 44, 46, 64; SSC 11; TCLC 108; WLC**
See also AAYA 45; AMW; AMWC 1;
AMWR 1; BPFB 2; CA 5-8R; 69-72;
CANR 20, 102; CDALB 1941-1968; DA;
DA3; DAB; DAC; DAM MST, NOV;
DLB 2, 244, 278; DLBD 3; DLBY 1980, 1991; EWL 3; EXPS; LATS 1; MTCW 1, 2; NCFS 4; NFS 9; RGAL 4; RGSF 2;
SSFS 6, 15; TUS

Naevius c. 265B.C.-201B.C. .... **CMLC 37**
See also DLB 211

Nagai, Kafu .... **TCLC 51**
See Nagai, Sokichi
See also DLB 180

Nagai, Sokichi 1879-1959
See Nagai, Kafu
See also CA 117

Nagy, Laszlo 1925-1978 .... **CLC 7**
See also CA 129; 112

Naidu, Sarojini 1879-1949 .... **TCLC 80**
See also EWL 3; RGEL 2

Naipaul, Shiva(dhar Srinivasa)
1945-1985 .... **CLC 32, 39**
See also CA 110; 112; 116; CANR 33;
DA3; DAM NOV; DLB 157; DLBY 1985;
EWL 3; MTCW 1, 2

Naipaul, V(idiadhar) S(urajprasad)
1932- .... **CLC 4, 7, 9, 13, 18, 37, 105; SSC 38**
See also BPFB 2; BRWS 1; CA 1-4R;
CANR 1, 33, 51, 91; CDBLB 1960 to Present; CDWLB 3; CN 7; DA3; DAB;
DAC; DAM MST, NOV; DLB 125, 204, 207; DLBY 1985, 2001; EWL 3; LATS 1;
MTCW 1, 2; RGEL 2; RGSF 2; TWA;
WLIT 4

Nakos, Lilika 1899(?)- .... **CLC 29**

Narayan, R(asipuram) K(rishnaswami)
1906-2001 . **CLC 7, 28, 47, 121; SSC 25**
See also BPFB 2; CA 81-84; 196; CANR 33, 61, 112; CN 7; DA3; DAM NOV;
DNFS 1; EWL 3; MTCW 1, 2; RGEL 2;
RGSF 2; SATA 62; SSFS 5

Nash, (Frediric) Ogden 1902-1971 . **CLC 23; PC 21; TCLC 109**
See also CA 13-14; 29-32R; CANR 34, 61;
CAP 1; DAM POET; DLB 11; MAICYA 1, 2; MTCW 1, 2; RGAL 4; SATA 2, 46;
WP

Nashe, Thomas 1567-1601(?) .... **LC 41, 89**
See also DLB 167; RGEL 2

Nathan, Daniel
See Dannay, Frederic

Nathan, George Jean 1882-1958 .... **TCLC 18**
See Hatteras, Owen
See also CA 114; 169; DLB 137

Natsume, Kinnosuke
See Natsume, Soseki

Natsume, Soseki 1867-1916 .... **TCLC 2, 10**
See Natsume Soseki; Soseki
See also CA 104; 195; RGWL 2, 3; TWA

Norris, (Benjamin) Frank(lin, Jr.)
1870-1902 .... **SSC 28; TCLC 24**
See also AMW; BPFB 2; CA 110; 160;
CDALB 1865-1917; DLB 12, 71, 186;
LMFS 2; NFS 12; RGAL 4; TCWW 2;
TUS

Norris, Leslie 1921- .... **CLC 14**
See also CA 11-12; CANR 14, 117; CAP 1;
CP 7; DLB 27, 256

North, Andrew
See Norton, Andre

North, Anthony
See Koontz, Dean R(ay)

North, Captain George
See Stevenson, Robert Louis (Balfour)

North, Captain George
See Stevenson, Robert Louis (Balfour)

North, Milou
See Erdrich, Louise

Northrup, B. A.
See Hubbard, L(afayette) Ron(ald)

North Staffs
See Hulme, T(homas) E(rnest)

Northup, Solomon 1808-1863 ...... **NCLC 105**

Norton, Alice Mary
See Norton, Andre
See also MAICYA 1; SATA 1, 43

Norton, Andre 1912- .... **CLC 12**
See Norton, Alice Mary
See also AAYA 14; BPFB 2; BYA 4, 10,
12; CA 1-4R; CANR 68; CLR 50; DLB
8, 52; JRDA; MAICYA 2; MTCW 1;
SATA 91; SUFW 1, 2; YAW

Norton, Caroline 1808-1877 .... **NCLC 47**
See also DLB 21, 159, 199

Norway, Nevil Shute 1899-1960
See Shute, Nevil
See also CA 102; 93-96; CANR 85; MTCW
2

Norwid, Cyprian Kamil
1821-1883 .... **NCLC 17**
See also RGWL 3

Nosille, Nabrah
See Ellison, Harlan (Jay)

Nossack, Hans Erich 1901-1978 .... **CLC 6**
See also CA 93-96; 85-88; DLB 69; EWL 3

Nostradamus 1503-1566 .... **LC 27**

Nosu, Chuji
See Ozu, Yasujiro

Notenburg, Eleanora (Genrikhovna) von
See Guro, Elena

Nova, Craig 1945- .... **CLC 7, 31**
See also CA 45-48; CANR 2, 53

Novak, Joseph
See Kosinski, Jerzy (Nikodem)

Novalis 1772-1801 .... **NCLC 13**
See also CDWLB 2; DLB 90; EW 5; RGWL
2, 3

Novick, Peter 1934- .... **CLC 164**
See also CA 188

Novis, Emile
See Weil, Simone (Adolphine)

Nowlan, Alden (Albert) 1933-1983 ... **CLC 15**
See also CA 9-12R; CANR 5; DAC; DAM
MST; DLB 53; PFS 12

Noyes, Alfred 1880-1958 ...... **PC 27; TCLC 7**
See also CA 104; 188; DLB 20; EXPP;
FANT; PFS 4; RGEL 2

Nugent, Richard Bruce 1906(?)-1987 ... **HR 3**
See also BW 1; CA 125; DLB 51; GLL 2

Nunn, Kem .... **CLC 34**
See also CA 159

Nwapa, Flora (Nwanzuruaha)
1931-1993 .... **BLCS; CLC 133**
See also BW 2; CA 143; CANR 83; CD-
WLB 3; CWRI 5; DLB 125; EWL 3;
WLIT 2

Nye, Robert 1939- .... **CLC 13, 42**
See also CA 33-36R; CANR 29, 67, 107;
CN 7; CP 7; CWRI 5; DAM NOV; DLB
14, 271; FANT; HGG; MTCW 1; RHW;
SATA 6

Nyro, Laura 1947-1997 .... **CLC 17**
See also CA 194

Oates, Joyce Carol 1938- .. **CLC 1, 2, 3, 6, 9,
11, 15, 19, 33, 52, 108, 134; SSC 6;
WLC**
See also AAYA 15, 52; AITN 1; AMWS 2;
BEST 89:2; BPFB 2; BYA 11; CA 5-8R;
CANR 25, 45, 74, 113, 113; CDALB
1968-1988; CN 7; CP 7; CPW; CWP; DA;
DA3; DAB; DAC; DAM MST, NOV,
POP; DLB 2, 5, 130; DLBY 1981; EWL
3; EXPS; FW; HGG; INT CANR-25;
LAIT 4; MAWW; MTCW 1, 2; NFS 8;
RGAL 4; RGSF 2; SSFS 17; SUFW 2;
TUS

O'Brian, E. G.
See Clarke, Arthur C(harles)

O'Brian, Patrick 1914-2000 .... **CLC 152**
See also CA 144; 187; CANR 74; CPW;
MTCW 2; RHW

O'Brien, Darcy 1939-1998 .... **CLC 11**
See also CA 21-24R; 167; CANR 8, 59

O'Brien, Edna 1936- ..... **CLC 3, 5, 8, 13, 36,
65, 116; SSC 10**
See also BRWS 5; CA 1-4R; CANR 6, 41,
65, 102; CDBLB 1960 to Present; CN 7;
DA3; DAM NOV; DLB 14, 231; EWL 3;
FW; MTCW 1, 2; RGSF 2; WLIT 4

O'Brien, Fitz-James 1828-1862 ..... **NCLC 21**
See also DLB 74; RGAL 4; SUFW

O'Brien, Flann .... **CLC 1, 4, 5, 7, 10, 47**
See O Nuallain, Brian
See also BRWS 2; DLB 231; EWL 3;
RGEL 2

O'Brien, Richard 1942- .... **CLC 17**
See also CA 124

O'Brien, (William) Tim(othy) 1946- . **CLC 7,
19, 40, 103**
See also AAYA 16; AMWS 5; CA 85-88;
CANR 40, 58; CDALBS; CN 7; CPW;
DA3; DAM POP; DLB 152; DLBD 9;
DLBY 1980; MTCW 2; RGAL 4; SSFS
5, 15

Obstfelder, Sigbjoern 1866-1900 .... **TCLC 23**
See also CA 123

O'Casey, Sean 1880-1964 .... **CLC 1, 5, 9, 11,
15, 88; DC 12; WLCS**
See also BRW 7; CA 89-92; CANR 62;
CBD; CDBLB 1914-1945; DA3; DAB;
DAC; DAM DRAM, MST; DLB 10;
EWL 3; MTCW 1, 2; RGEL 2; TEA;
WLIT 4

O'Cathasaigh, Sean
See O'Casey, Sean

Occom, Samson 1723-1792 .... **LC 60; NNAL**
See also DLB 175

Ochs, Phil(ip David) 1940-1976 .... **CLC 17**
See also CA 185; 65-68

O'Connor, Edwin (Greene)
1918-1968 .... **CLC 14**
See also CA 93-96; 25-28R

O'Connor, (Mary) Flannery
1925-1964 .... **CLC 1, 2, 3, 6, 10, 13, 15,
21, 66, 104; SSC 1, 23, 61; TCLC 132;
WLC**
See also AAYA 7; AMW; AMWR 2; BPFB
3; CA 1-4R; CANR 3, 41; CDALB 1941-
1968; DA; DA3; DAB; DAC; DAM MST,
NOV; DLB 2, 152; DLBD 12; DLBY
1980; EWL 3; EXPS; LAIT 5; MAWW;
MTCW 1, 2; NFS 3; RGAL 4; RGSF 2;
SSFS 2, 7, 10; TUS

O'Connor, Frank .... **CLC 23; SSC 5**
See O'Donovan, Michael Francis
See also DLB 162; EWL 3; RGSF 2; SSFS
5

O'Dell, Scott 1898-1989 .... **CLC 30**
See also AAYA 3, 44; BPFB 3; BYA 1, 2,
3, 5; CA 61-64; 129; CANR 12, 30, 112;
CLR 1, 16; DLB 52; JRDA; MAICYA 1,
2; SATA 12, 60, 134; WYA; YAW

Odets, Clifford 1906-1963 ..... **CLC 2, 28, 98;
DC 6**
See also AMWS 2; CA 85-88; CAD; CANR
62; DAM DRAM; DFS 17; DLB 7, 26;
EWL 3; MTCW 1, 2; RGAL 4; TUS

O'Doherty, Brian 1928- .... **CLC 76**
See also CA 105; CANR 108

O'Donnell, K. M.
See Malzberg, Barry N(athaniel)

O'Donnell, Lawrence
See Kuttner, Henry

O'Donovan, Michael Francis
1903-1966 .... **CLC 14**
See O'Connor, Frank
See also CA 93-96; CANR 84

Oe, Kenzaburo 1935- .. **CLC 10, 36, 86; SSC
20**
See Oe Kenzaburo
See also CA 97-100; CANR 36, 50, 74;
CWW 2; DA3; DAM NOV; DLB 182;
DLBY 1994; EWL 3; LATS 1; MJW;
MTCW 1, 2; RGSF 2; RGWL 2, 3

Oe Kenzaburo
See Oe, Kenzaburo
See also EWL 3

O'Faolain, Julia 1932- ... **CLC 6, 19, 47, 108**
See also CA 81-84; CAAS 2; CANR 12,
61; CN 7; DLB 14, 231; FW; MTCW 1;
RHW

O'Faolain, Sean 1900-1991 ...... **CLC 1, 7, 14,
32, 70; SSC 13**
See also CA 61-64; 134; CANR 12, 66;
DLB 15, 162; MTCW 1, 2; RGEL 2;
RGSF 2

O'Flaherty, Liam 1896-1984 .... **CLC 5, 34;
SSC 6**
See also CA 101; 113; CANR 35; DLB 36,
162; DLBY 1984; MTCW 1, 2; RGEL 2;
RGSF 2; SSFS 5

Ogai
See Mori Ogai
See also MJW

Ogilvy, Gavin
See Barrie, J(ames) M(atthew)

O'Grady, Standish (James)
1846-1928 .... **TCLC 5**
See also CA 104; 157

O'Grady, Timothy 1951- .... **CLC 59**
See also CA 138

O'Hara, Frank 1926-1966 .... **CLC 2, 5, 13,
78; PC 45**
See also CA 9-12R; 25-28R; CANR 33;
DA3; DAM POET; DLB 5, 16, 193; EWL
3; MTCW 1, 2; PFS 8; 12; RGAL 4; WP

O'Hara, John (Henry) 1905-1970 . **CLC 1, 2,
3, 6, 11, 42; SSC 15**
See also AMW; BPFB 3; CA 5-8R; 25-28R;
CANR 31, 60; CDALB 1929-1941; DAM
NOV; DLB 9, 86; DLBD 2; EWL 3;
MTCW 1, 2; NFS 11; RGAL 4; RGSF 2

O Hehir, Diana 1922- .... **CLC 41**
See also CA 93-96

Ohiyesa
See Eastman, Charles A(lexander)

Okada, John 1923-1971 .... **AAL**
See also BYA 14; CA 212

Pa Chin .... **CLC 18**
  See Li Fei-kan
  See also EWL 3

Pack, Robert 1929- .... **CLC 13**
  See also CA 1-4R; CANR 3, 44, 82; CP 7;
  DLB 5; SATA 118

Padgett, Lewis
  See Kuttner, Henry

Padilla (Lorenzo), Heberto
  1932-2000 .... **CLC 38**
  See also AITN 1; CA 123; 131; 189; EWL
  3; HW 1

Page, James Patrick 1944-
  See Page, Jimmy
  See also CA 204

Page, Jimmy 1944- .... **CLC 12**
  See Page, James Patrick

Page, Louise 1955- .... **CLC 40**
  See also CA 140; CANR 76; CBD; CD 5;
  CWD; DLB 233

Page, P(atricia) K(athleen) 1916- ...... **CLC 7,
  18; PC 12**
  See Cape, Judith
  See also CA 53-56; CANR 4, 22, 65; CP 7;
  DAC; DAM MST; DLB 68; MTCW 1;
  RGEL 2

Page, Stanton
  See Fuller, Henry Blake

Page, Stanton
  See Fuller, Henry Blake

Page, Thomas Nelson 1853-1922 .... **SSC 23**
  See also CA 118; 177; DLB 12, 78; DLBD
  13; RGAL 4

Pagels, Elaine Hiesey 1943- .... **CLC 104**
  See also CA 45-48; CANR 2, 24, 51; FW;
  NCFS 4

Paget, Violet 1856-1935
  See Lee, Vernon
  See also CA 104; 166; GLL 1; HGG

Paget-Lowe, Henry
  See Lovecraft, H(oward) P(hillips)

Paglia, Camille (Anna) 1947- .... **CLC 68**
  See also CA 140; CANR 72; CPW; FW;
  GLL 2; MTCW 2

Paige, Richard
  See Koontz, Dean R(ay)

Paine, Thomas 1737-1809 .... **NCLC 62**
  See also AMWS 1; CDALB 1640-1865;
  DLB 31, 43, 73, 158; LAIT 1; RGAL 4;
  RGEL 2; TUS

Pakenham, Antonia
  See Fraser, Antonia (Pakenham)

Palamas, Costis
  See Palamas, Kostes

Palamas, Kostes 1859-1943 .... **TCLC 5**
  See Palamas, Kostis
  See also CA 105; 190; RGWL 2, 3

Palamas, Kostis
  See Palamas, Kostes
  See also EWL 3

Palazzeschi, Aldo 1885-1974 .... **CLC 11**
  See also CA 89-92; 53-56; DLB 114, 264;
  EWL 3

Pales Matos, Luis 1898-1959 .... **HLCS 2**
  See Pales Matos, Luis
  See also HW 1; LAW

Paley, Grace 1922- .. **CLC 4, 6, 37, 140; SSC
  8**
  See also AMWS 6; CA 25-28R; CANR 13,
  46, 74, 118; CN 7; CPW; DA3; DAM
  POP; DLB 28, 218; EWL 3; EXPS; FW;
  INT CANR-13; MAWW; MTCW 1, 2;
  RGAL 4; RGSF 2; SSFS 3

Palin, Michael (Edward) 1943- .... **CLC 21**
  See Monty Python
  See also CA 107; CANR 35, 109; SATA 67

Palliser, Charles 1947- .... **CLC 65**
  See also CA 136; CANR 76; CN 7

Palma, Ricardo 1833-1919 .... **TCLC 29**
  See also CA 168; LAW

Pancake, Breece Dexter 1952-1979
  See Pancake, Breece D'J
  See also CA 123; 109

Pancake, Breece D'J .... **CLC 29; SSC 61**
  See Pancake, Breece Dexter
  See also DLB 130

Panchenko, Nikolai .... **CLC 59**

Pankhurst, Emmeline (Goulden)
  1858-1928 .... **TCLC 100**
  See also CA 116; FW

Panko, Rudy
  See Gogol, Nikolai (Vasilyevich)

Papadiamantis, Alexandros
  1851-1911 .... **TCLC 29**
  See also CA 168; EWL 3

Papadiamantopoulos, Johannes 1856-1910
  See Moreas, Jean
  See also CA 117

Papini, Giovanni 1881-1956 .... **TCLC 22**
  See also CA 121; 180; DLB 264

Paracelsus 1493-1541 .... **LC 14**
  See also DLB 179

Parasol, Peter
  See Stevens, Wallace

Pardo Bazan, Emilia 1851-1921 .... **SSC 30**
  See also EWL 3; FW; RGSF 2; RGWL 2, 3

Pareto, Vilfredo 1848-1923 .... **TCLC 69**
  See also CA 175

Paretsky, Sara 1947- .... **CLC 135**
  See also AAYA 30; BEST 90:3; CA 125;
  129; CANR 59, 95; CMW 4; CPW; DA3;
  DAM POP; INT CA-129; MSW; RGAL 4

Parfenie, Maria
  See Codrescu, Andrei

Parini, Jay (Lee) 1948- .... **CLC 54, 133**
  See also CA 97-100; CAAS 16; CANR 32,
  87

Park, Jordan
  See Kornbluth, C(yril) M.; Pohl, Frederik

Park, Robert E(zra) 1864-1944 ..... **TCLC 73**
  See also CA 122; 165

Parker, Bert
  See Ellison, Harlan (Jay)

Parker, Dorothy (Rothschild)
  1893-1967 .. **CLC 15, 68; PC 28; SSC 2**
  See also AMWS 9; CA 19-20; 25-28R; CAP
  2; DA3; DAM POET; DLB 11, 45, 86;
  EXPP; FW; MAWW; MTCW 1, 2; RGAL
  4; RGSF 2; TUS

Parker, Robert B(rown) 1932- .... **CLC 27**
  See also AAYA 28; BEST 89:4; BPFB 3;
  CA 49-52; CANR 1, 26, 52, 89; CMW 4;
  CPW; DAM NOV, POP; INT CANR-26;
  MSW; MTCW 1

Parkin, Frank 1940- .... **CLC 43**
  See also CA 147

Parkman, Francis, Jr. 1823-1893 .. **NCLC 12**
  See also AMWS 2; DLB 1, 30, 183, 186,
  235; RGAL 4

Parks, Gordon (Alexander Buchanan)
  1912- .... **BLC 3; CLC 1, 16**
  See also AAYA 36; AITN 2; BW 2, 3; CA
  41-44R; CANR 26, 66; DA3; DAM
  MULT; DLB 33; MTCW 2; SATA 8, 108

Parks, Tim(othy Harold) 1954- ...... **CLC 147**
  See also CA 126; 131; CANR 77; DLB 231;
  INT CA-131

Parmenides c. 515B.C.-c.
  450B.C. .... **CMLC 22**
  See also DLB 176

Parnell, Thomas 1679-1718 .... **LC 3**
  See also DLB 95; RGEL 2

Parr, Catherine c. 1513(?)-1548 .... **LC 86**
  See also DLB 136

Parra, Nicanor 1914- ... **CLC 2, 102; HLC 2;
  PC 39**
  See also CA 85-88; CANR 32; CWW 2;
  DAM MULT; DLB 283; EWL 3; HW 1;
  LAW; MTCW 1

Parra Sanojo, Ana Teresa de la
  1890-1936 .... **HLCS 2**
  See de la Parra, (Ana) Teresa (Sonojo)
  See also LAW

Parrish, Mary Frances
  See Fisher, M(ary) F(rances) K(ennedy)

Parshchikov, Aleksei 1954- .... **CLC 59**
  See Parshchikov, Aleksei Maksimovich

Parshchikov, Aleksei Maksimovich
  See Parshchikov, Aleksei
  See also DLB 285

Parson, Professor
  See Coleridge, Samuel Taylor

Parson Lot
  See Kingsley, Charles

Parton, Sara Payson Willis
  1811-1872 .... **NCLC 86**
  See also DLB 43, 74, 239

Partridge, Anthony
  See Oppenheim, E(dward) Phillips

Pascal, Blaise 1623-1662 .... **LC 35**
  See also DLB 268; EW 3; GFL Beginnings
  to 1789; RGWL 2, 3; TWA

Pascoli, Giovanni 1855-1912 .... **TCLC 45**
  See also CA 170; EW 7; EWL 3

Pasolini, Pier Paolo 1922-1975 .. **CLC 20, 37,
  106; PC 17**
  See also CA 93-96; 61-64; CANR 63; DLB
  128, 177; EWL 3; MTCW 1; RGWL 2, 3

Pasquini
  See Silone, Ignazio

Pastan, Linda (Olenik) 1932- .... **CLC 27**
  See also CA 61-64; CANR 18, 40, 61, 113;
  CP 7; CSW; CWP; DAM POET; DLB 5;
  PFS 8

Pasternak, Boris (Leonidovich)
  1890-1960 ...... **CLC 7, 10, 18, 63; PC 6;
  SSC 31; WLC**
  See also BPFB 3; CA 127; 116; DA; DA3;
  DAB; DAC; DAM MST, NOV, POET;
  EW 10; MTCW 1, 2; RGSF 2; RGWL 2,
  3; TWA; WP

Patchen, Kenneth 1911-1972 .... **CLC 1, 2, 18**
  See also BG 3; CA 1-4R; 33-36R; CANR
  3, 35; DAM POET; DLB 16, 48; EWL 3;
  MTCW 1; RGAL 4

Pater, Walter (Horatio) 1839-1894 . **NCLC 7,
  90**
  See also BRW 5; CDBLB 1832-1890; DLB
  57, 156; RGEL 2; TEA

Paterson, A(ndrew) B(arton)
  1864-1941 .... **TCLC 32**
  See also CA 155; DLB 230; RGEL 2; SATA
  97

Paterson, Banjo
  See Paterson, A(ndrew) B(arton)

Paterson, Katherine (Womeldorf)
  1932- .... **CLC 12, 30**
  See also AAYA 1, 31; BYA 1, 2, 7; CA 21-
  24R; CANR 28, 59, 111; CLR 7, 50;
  CWRI 5; DLB 52; JRDA; LAIT 4; MAI-
  CYA 1, 2; MAICYAS 1; MTCW 1; SATA
  13, 53, 92, 133; WYA; YAW

Patmore, Coventry Kersey Dighton
  1823-1896 .... **NCLC 9**
  See also DLB 35, 98; RGEL 2; TEA

Paton, Alan (Stewart) 1903-1988 ...... **CLC 4,
  10, 25, 55, 106; WLC**
  See also AAYA 26; AFW; BPFB 3; BRWS
  2; BYA 1; CA 13-16; 125; CANR 22;
  CAP 1; DA; DA3; DAB; DAC; DAM

Petry, Ann (Lane) 1908-1997 .. **CLC 1, 7, 18; TCLC 112**
   See also AFAW 1, 2; BPFB 3; BW 1, 3; BYA 2; CA 5-8R; 157; CAAS 6; CANR 4, 46; CLR 12; CN 7; DLB 76; EWL 3; JRDA; LAIT 1; MAICYA 1, 2; MAICYAS 1; MTCW 1; RGAL 4; SATA 5; SATA-Obit 94; TUS

Petursson, Halligrimur 1614-1674 .... **LC 8**

Peychinovich
   See Vazov, Ivan (Minchov)

Phaedrus c. 15B.C.-c. 50 .... **CMLC 25**
   See also DLB 211

Phelps (Ward), Elizabeth Stuart
   See Phelps, Elizabeth Stuart
   See also FW

Phelps, Elizabeth Stuart
   1844-1911 .... **TCLC 113**
   See Phelps (Ward), Elizabeth Stuart
   See also DLB 74

Philips, Katherine 1632-1664 . **LC 30; PC 40**
   See also DLB 131; RGEL 2

Philipson, Morris H. 1926- .... **CLC 53**
   See also CA 1-4R; CANR 4

Phillips, Caryl 1958- .... **BLCS; CLC 96**
   See also BRWS 5; BW 2; CA 141; CANR 63, 104; CBD; CD 5; CN 7; DA3; DAM MULT; DLB 157; EWL 3; MTCW 2; WLIT 4

Phillips, David Graham
   1867-1911 .... **TCLC 44**
   See also CA 108; 176; DLB 9, 12; RGAL 4

Phillips, Jack
   See Sandburg, Carl (August)

Phillips, Jayne Anne 1952- .... **CLC 15, 33, 139; SSC 16**
   See also BPFB 3; CA 101; CANR 24, 50, 96; CN 7; CSW; DLBY 1980; INT CANR-24; MTCW 1, 2; RGAL 4; RGSF 2; SSFS 4

Phillips, Richard
   See Dick, Philip K(indred)

Phillips, Robert (Schaeffer) 1938- .... **CLC 28**
   See also CA 17-20R; CAAS 13; CANR 8; DLB 105

Phillips, Ward
   See Lovecraft, H(oward) P(hillips)

Piccolo, Lucio 1901-1969 .... **CLC 13**
   See also CA 97-100; DLB 114; EWL 3

Pickthall, Marjorie L(owry) C(hristie)
   1883-1922 .... **TCLC 21**
   See also CA 107; DLB 92

Pico della Mirandola, Giovanni
   1463-1494 .... **LC 15**
   See also LMFS 1

Piercy, Marge 1936- .... **CLC 3, 6, 14, 18, 27, 62, 128; PC 29**
   See also BPFB 3; CA 21-24R; CAAE 187; CAAS 1; CANR 13, 43, 66, 111; CN 7; CP 7; CWP; DLB 120, 227; EXPP; FW; MTCW 1, 2; PFS 9; SFW 4

Piers, Robert
   See Anthony, Piers

Pieyre de Mandiargues, Andre 1909-1991
   See Mandiargues, Andre Pieyre de
   See also CA 103; 136; CANR 22, 82; EWL 3; GFL 1789 to the Present

Pilnyak, Boris 1894-1938 . **SSC 48; TCLC 23**
   See Vogau, Boris Andreyevich
   See also EWL 3

Pinchback, Eugene
   See Toomer, Jean

Pincherle, Alberto 1907-1990 ...... **CLC 11, 18**
   See Moravia, Alberto
   See also CA 25-28R; 132; CANR 33, 63; DAM NOV; MTCW 1

Pinckney, Darryl 1953- .... **CLC 76**
   See also BW 2, 3; CA 143; CANR 79

Pindar 518(?)B.C.-438(?)B.C. .... **CMLC 12; PC 19**
   See also AW 1; CDWLB 1; DLB 176; RGWL 2

Pineda, Cecile 1942- .... **CLC 39**
   See also CA 118; DLB 209

Pinero, Arthur Wing 1855-1934 .... **TCLC 32**
   See also CA 110; 153; DAM DRAM; DLB 10; RGEL 2

Pinero, Miguel (Antonio Gomez)
   1946-1988 .... **CLC 4, 55**
   See also CA 61-64; 125; CAD; CANR 29, 90; DLB 266; HW 1

Pinget, Robert 1919-1997 .... **CLC 7, 13, 37**
   See also CA 85-88; 160; CWW 2; DLB 83; EWL 3; GFL 1789 to the Present

Pink Floyd
   See Barrett, (Roger) Syd; Gilmour, David; Mason, Nick; Waters, Roger; Wright, Rick

Pinkney, Edward 1802-1828 .... **NCLC 31**
   See also DLB 248

Pinkwater, Daniel
   See Pinkwater, Daniel Manus

Pinkwater, Daniel Manus 1941- .... **CLC 35**
   See also AAYA 1, 46; BYA 9; CA 29-32R; CANR 12, 38, 89; CLR 4; CSW; FANT; JRDA; MAICYA 1, 2; SAAS 3; SATA 8, 46, 76, 114; SFW 4; YAW

Pinkwater, Manus
   See Pinkwater, Daniel Manus

Pinsky, Robert 1940- .... **CLC 9, 19, 38, 94, 121; PC 27**
   See also AMWS 6; CA 29-32R; CAAS 4; CANR 58, 97; CP 7; DA3; DAM POET; DLBY 1982, 1998; MTCW 2; RGAL 4

Pinta, Harold
   See Pinter, Harold

Pinter, Harold 1930- .. **CLC 1, 3, 6, 9, 11, 15, 27, 58, 73; DC 15; WLC**
   See also BRWR 1; BRWS 1; CA 5-8R; CANR 33, 65, 112; CBD; CD 5; CDBLB 1960 to Present; DA; DA3; DAB; DAC; DAM DRAM, MST; DFS 3, 5, 7, 14; DLB 13; EWL 3; IDFW 3, 4; LMFS 2; MTCW 1, 2; RGEL 2; TEA

Piozzi, Hester Lynch (Thrale)
   1741-1821 .... **NCLC 57**
   See also DLB 104, 142

Pirandello, Luigi 1867-1936 .. **DC 5; SSC 22; TCLC 4, 29; WLC**
   See also CA 104; 153; CANR 103; DA; DA3; DAB; DAC; DAM DRAM, MST; DFS 4, 9; DLB 264; EW 8; EWL 3; MTCW 2; RGSF 2; RGWL 2, 3

Pirsig, Robert M(aynard) 1928- ... **CLC 4, 6, 73**
   See also CA 53-56; CANR 42, 74; CPW 1; DA3; DAM POP; MTCW 1, 2; SATA 39

Pisarev, Dmitrii Ivanovich
   See Pisarev, Dmitry Ivanovich
   See also DLB 277

Pisarev, Dmitry Ivanovich
   1840-1868 .... **NCLC 25**
   See Pisarev, Dmitrii Ivanovich

Pix, Mary (Griffith) 1666-1709 .... **LC 8**
   See also DLB 80

Pixerecourt, (Rene Charles) Guilbert de
   1773-1844 .... **NCLC 39**
   See also DLB 192; GFL 1789 to the Present

Plaatje, Sol(omon) T(shekisho)
   1878-1932 .... **BLCS; TCLC 73**
   See also BW 2, 3; CA 141; CANR 79; DLB 125, 225

Plaidy, Jean
   See Hibbert, Eleanor Alice Burford

Planche, James Robinson
   1796-1880 .... **NCLC 42**
   See also RGEL 2

Plant, Robert 1948- .... **CLC 12**

Plante, David (Robert) 1940- . **CLC 7, 23, 38**
   See also CA 37-40R; CANR 12, 36, 58, 82; CN 7; DAM NOV; DLBY 1983; INT CANR-12; MTCW 1

Plath, Sylvia 1932-1963 ..... **CLC 1, 2, 3, 5, 9, 11, 14, 17, 50, 51, 62, 111; PC 1, 37; WLC**
   See also AAYA 13; AMWR 2; AMWS 1; BPFB 3; CA 19-20; CANR 34, 101; CAP 2; CDALB 1941-1968; DA; DA3; DAB; DAC; DAM MST, POET; DLB 5, 6, 152; EWL 3; EXPN; EXPP; FW; LAIT 4; MAWW; MTCW 1, 2; NFS 1; PAB; PFS 1, 15; RGAL 4; SATA 96; TUS; WP; YAW

Plato c. 428B.C.-347B.C. ... **CMLC 8; WLCS**
   See also AW 1; CDWLB 1; DA; DA3; DAB; DAC; DAM MST; DLB 176; LAIT 1; LATS 1; RGWL 2, 3

Platonov, Andrei
   See Klimentov, Andrei Platonovich

Platonov, Andrei Platonovich
   See Klimentov, Andrei Platonovich
   See also DLB 272

Platonov, Andrey Platonovich
   See Klimentov, Andrei Platonovich
   See also EWL 3

Platt, Kin 1911- .... **CLC 26**
   See also AAYA 11; CA 17-20R; CANR 11; JRDA; SAAS 17; SATA 21, 86; WYA

Plautus c. 254B.C.-c. 184B.C. ...... **CMLC 24; DC 6**
   See also AW 1; CDWLB 1; DLB 211; RGWL 2, 3

Plick et Plock
   See Simenon, Georges (Jacques Christian)

Plieksans, Janis
   See Rainis, Janis

Plimpton, George (Ames) 1927- .... **CLC 36**
   See also AITN 1; CA 21-24R; CANR 32, 70, 103; DLB 185, 241; MTCW 1, 2; SATA 10

Pliny the Elder c. 23-79 .... **CMLC 23**
   See also DLB 211

Plomer, William Charles Franklin
   1903-1973 .... **CLC 4, 8**
   See also AFW; CA 21-22; CANR 34; CAP 2; DLB 20, 162, 191, 225; EWL 3; MTCW 1; RGEL 2; RGSF 2; SATA 24

Plotinus 204-270 .... **CMLC 46**
   See also CDWLB 1; DLB 176

Plowman, Piers
   See Kavanagh, Patrick (Joseph)

Plum, J.
   See Wodehouse, P(elham) G(renville)

Plumly, Stanley (Ross) 1939- .... **CLC 33**
   See also CA 108; 110; CANR 97; CP 7; DLB 5, 193; INT 110

Plumpe, Friedrich Wilhelm
   1888-1931 .... **TCLC 53**
   See also CA 112

Plutarch c. 46-c. 120 .... **CMLC 60**
   See also AW 2; CDWLB 1; DLB 176; RGWL 2, 3; TWA

Po Chu-i 772-846 .... **CMLC 24**

Poe, Edgar Allan 1809-1849 ..... **NCLC 1, 16, 55, 78, 94, 97, 117; PC 1; SSC 1, 22, 34, 35, 54; WLC**
   See also AAYA 14; AMW; AMWC 1; AMWR 2; BPFB 3; BYA 5, 11; CDALB 1640-1865; CMW 4; DA; DA3; DAB; DAC; DAM MST, POET; DLB 3, 59, 73, 74, 248, 254; EXPP; EXPS; HGG; LAIT 2; LATS 1; LMFS 1; MSW; PAB; PFS 1, 3, 9; RGAL 4; RGSF 2; SATA 23; SCFW 2; SFW 4; SSFS 2, 4, 7, 8, 16; SUFW; TUS; WP; WYA

Poet of Titchfield Street, The
   See Pound, Ezra (Weston Loomis)

Prior, Matthew 1664-1721 .... **LC 4**
　See also DLB 95; RGEL 2

Prishvin, Mikhail 1873-1954 .... **TCLC 75**
　See Prishvin, Mikhail Mikhailovich

Prishvin, Mikhail Mikhailovich
　See Prishvin, Mikhail
　See also DLB 272; EWL 3

Pritchard, William H(arrison)
　1932- .... **CLC 34**
　See also CA 65-68; CANR 23, 95; DLB
　111

Pritchett, V(ictor) S(awdon)
　1900-1997 ... **CLC 5, 13, 15, 41; SSC 14**
　See also BPFB 3; BRWS 3; CA 61-64; 157;
　CANR 31, 63; CN 7; DA3; DAM NOV;
　DLB 15, 139; EWL 3; MTCW 1, 2;
　RGEL 2; RGSF 2; TEA

Private 19022
　See Manning, Frederic

Probst, Mark 1925- .... **CLC 59**
　See also CA 130

Prokosch, Frederic 1908-1989 ...... **CLC 4, 48**
　See also CA 73-76; 128; CANR 82; DLB
　48; MTCW 2

Propertius, Sextus c. 50B.C.-c.
　16B.C. .... **CMLC 32**
　See also AW 2; CDWLB 1; DLB 211;
　RGWL 2, 3

Prophet, The
　See Dreiser, Theodore (Herman Albert)

Prose, Francine 1947- .... **CLC 45**
　See also CA 109; 112; CANR 46, 95; DLB
　234; SATA 101

Proudhon
　See Cunha, Euclides (Rodrigues Pimenta)
　da

Proulx, Annie
　See Proulx, E(dna) Annie

Proulx, E(dna) Annie 1935- ...... **CLC 81, 158**
　See also AMWS 7; BPFB 3; CA 145;
　CANR 65, 110; CN 7; CPW 1; DA3;
　DAM POP; MTCW 2

Proust,
　(Valentin-Louis-George-Eugene-)Marcel
　1871-1922 .... **TCLC 7, 13, 33; WLC**
　See also BPFB 3; CA 104; 120; CANR 110;
　DA; DA3; DAB; DAC; DAM MST, NOV;
　DLB 65; EW 8; EWL 3; GFL 1789 to the
　Present; MTCW 1, 2; RGWL 2, 3; TWA

Prowler, Harley
　See Masters, Edgar Lee

Prus, Boleslaw 1845-1912 .... **TCLC 48**
　See also RGWL 2, 3

Pryor, Richard (Franklin Lenox Thomas)
　1940- .... **CLC 26**
　See also CA 122; 152

Przybyszewski, Stanislaw
　1868-1927 .... **TCLC 36**
　See also CA 160; DLB 66; EWL 3

Pteleon
　See Grieve, C(hristopher) M(urray)
　See also DAM POET

Puckett, Lute
　See Masters, Edgar Lee

Puig, Manuel 1932-1990 .... **CLC 3, 5, 10, 28,
　65, 133; HLC 2**
　See also BPFB 3; CA 45-48; CANR 2, 32,
　63; CDWLB 3; DA3; DAM MULT; DLB
　113; DNFS 1; EWL 3; GLL 1; HW 1, 2;
　LAW; MTCW 1, 2; RGWL 2, 3; TWA;
　WLIT 1

Pulitzer, Joseph 1847-1911 .... **TCLC 76**
　See also CA 114; DLB 23

Purchas, Samuel 1577(?)-1626 .... **LC 70**
　See also DLB 151

Purdy, A(lfred) W(ellington)
　1918-2000 .... **CLC 3, 6, 14, 50**
　See also CA 81-84; 189; CAAS 17; CANR
　42, 66; CP 7; DAC; DAM MST, POET;
　DLB 88; PFS 5; RGEL 2

Purdy, James (Amos) 1923- .... **CLC 2, 4, 10,
　28, 52**
　See also AMWS 7; CA 33-36R; CAAS 1;
　CANR 19, 51; CN 7; DLB 2, 218; EWL
　3; INT CANR-19; MTCW 1; RGAL 4

Pure, Simon
　See Swinnerton, Frank Arthur

Pushkin, Aleksandr Sergeevich
　See Pushkin, Alexander (Sergeyevich)
　See also DLB 205

Pushkin, Alexander (Sergeyevich)
　1799-1837 .... **NCLC 3, 27, 83; PC 10;
　SSC 27, 55; WLC**
　See Pushkin, Aleksandr Sergeevich
　See also DA; DA3; DAB; DAC; DAM
　DRAM, MST, POET; EW 5; EXPS; RGSF
　2; RGWL 2, 3; SATA 61; SSFS 9; TWA

P'u Sung-ling 1640-1715 .... **LC 49; SSC 31**

Putnam, Arthur Lee
　See Alger, Horatio, Jr.

Puzo, Mario 1920-1999 .... **CLC 1, 2, 6, 36,
　107**
　See also BPFB 3; CA 65-68; 185; CANR 4,
　42, 65, 99; CN 7; CPW; DA3; DAM
　NOV, POP; DLB 6; MTCW 1, 2; NFS 16;
　RGAL 4

Pygge, Edward
　See Barnes, Julian (Patrick)

Pyle, Ernest Taylor 1900-1945
　See Pyle, Ernie
　See also CA 115; 160

Pyle, Ernie .... **TCLC 75**
　See Pyle, Ernest Taylor
　See also DLB 29; MTCW 2

Pyle, Howard 1853-1911 .... **TCLC 81**
　See also BYA 2, 4; CA 109; 137; CLR 22;
　DLB 42, 188; DLBD 13; LAIT 1; MAI-
　CYA 1, 2; SATA 16, 100; WCH; YAW

Pym, Barbara (Mary Crampton)
　1913-1980 .... **CLC 13, 19, 37, 111**
　See also BPFB 3; BRWS 2; CA 13-14; 97-
　100; CANR 13, 34; CAP 1; DLB 14, 207;
　DLBY 1987; EWL 3; MTCW 1, 2; RGEL
　2; TEA

Pynchon, Thomas (Ruggles, Jr.)
　1937- ...... **CLC 2, 3, 6, 9, 11, 18, 33, 62,
　72, 123; SSC 14; WLC**
　See also AMWS 2; BEST 90:2; BPFB 3;
　CA 17-20R; CANR 22, 46, 73; CN 7;
　CPW 1; DA; DA3; DAB; DAC; DAM
　MST, NOV, POP; DLB 2, 173; EWL 3;
　MTCW 1, 2; RGAL 4; SFW 4; TUS

Pythagoras c. 582B.C.-c. 507B.C. . **CMLC 22**
　See also DLB 176

Q
　See Quiller-Couch, Sir Arthur (Thomas)

Qian, Chongzhu
　See Ch'ien, Chung-shu

Qian Zhongshu
　See Ch'ien, Chung-shu

Qroll
　See Dagerman, Stig (Halvard)

Quarrington, Paul (Lewis) 1953- ..... **CLC 65**
　See also CA 129; CANR 62, 95

Quasimodo, Salvatore 1901-1968 .... **CLC 10;
　PC 47**
　See also CA 13-16; 25-28R; CAP 1; DLB
　114; EW 12; EWL 3; MTCW 1; RGWL
　2, 3

Quatermass, Martin
　See Carpenter, John (Howard)

Quay, Stephen 1947- .... **CLC 95**
　See also CA 189

Quay, Timothy 1947- .... **CLC 95**
　See also CA 189

Queen, Ellery .... **CLC 3, 11**
　See Dannay, Frederic; Davidson, Avram
　(James); Deming, Richard; Fairman, Paul
　W.; Flora, Fletcher; Hoch, Edward
　D(entinger); Kane, Henry; Lee, Manfred
　B(ennington); Marlowe, Stephen; Powell,
　(Oval) Talmage; Sheldon, Walter J(ames);
　Sturgeon, Theodore (Hamilton); Tracy,
　Don(ald Fiske); Vance, John Holbrook
　See also BPFB 3; CMW 4; MSW; RGAL 4

Queen, Ellery, Jr.
　See Dannay, Frederic; Lee, Manfred
　B(ennington)

Queneau, Raymond 1903-1976 ..... **CLC 2, 5,
　10, 42**
　See also CA 77-80; 69-72; CANR 32; DLB
　72, 258; EW 12; EWL 3; GFL 1789 to
　the Present; MTCW 1, 2; RGWL 2, 3

Quevedo, Francisco de 1580-1645 .... **LC 23**

Quiller-Couch, Sir Arthur (Thomas)
　1863-1944 .... **TCLC 53**
　See also CA 118; 166; DLB 135, 153, 190;
　HGG; RGEL 2; SUFW 1

Quin, Ann (Marie) 1936-1973 .... **CLC 6**
　See also CA 9-12R; 45-48; DLB 14, 231

Quincey, Thomas de
　See De Quincey, Thomas

Quinn, Martin
　See Smith, Martin Cruz

Quinn, Peter 1947- .... **CLC 91**
　See also CA 197

Quinn, Simon
　See Smith, Martin Cruz

Quintana, Leroy V. 1944- ...... **HLC 2; PC 36**
　See also CA 131; CANR 65; DAM MULT;
　DLB 82; HW 1, 2

Quiroga, Horacio (Sylvestre)
　1878-1937 .... **HLC 2; TCLC 20**
　See also CA 117; 131; DAM MULT; EWL
　3; HW 1; LAW; MTCW 1; RGSF 2;
　WLIT 1

Quoirez, Francoise 1935- .... **CLC 9**
　See Sagan, Francoise
　See also CA 49-52; CANR 6, 39, 73; CWW
　2; MTCW 1, 2; TWA

Raabe, Wilhelm (Karl) 1831-1910 . **TCLC 45**
　See also CA 167; DLB 129

Rabe, David (William) 1940- .. **CLC 4, 8, 33;
　DC 16**
　See also CA 85-88; CABS 3; CAD; CANR
　59; CD 5; DAM DRAM; DFS 3, 8, 13;
　DLB 7, 228; EWL 3

Rabelais, Francois 1494-1553 .... **LC 5, 60;
　WLC**
　See also DA; DAB; DAC; DAM MST; EW
　2; GFL Beginnings to 1789; LMFS 1;
　RGWL 2, 3; TWA

Rabinovitch, Sholem 1859-1916
　See Aleichem, Sholom
　See also CA 104

Rabinyan, Dorit 1972- .... **CLC 119**
　See also CA 170

Rachilde
　See Vallette, Marguerite Eymery; Vallette,
　Marguerite Eymery
　See also EWL 3

Racine, Jean 1639-1699 .... **LC 28**
　See also DA3; DAB; DAM MST; DLB 268;
　EW 3; GFL Beginnings to 1789; LMFS
　1; RGWL 2, 3; TWA

Radcliffe, Ann (Ward) 1764-1823 ... **NCLC 6,
　55, 106**
　See also DLB 39, 178; HGG; LMFS 1;
　RGEL 2; SUFW; WLIT 3

Radclyffe-Hall, Marguerite
　See Hall, (Marguerite) Radclyffe

Rendell, Ruth (Barbara) 1930- .. **CLC 28, 48**
See Vine, Barbara
See also BPFB 3; CA 109; CANR 32, 52, 74; CN 7; CPW; DAM POP; DLB 87, 276; INT CANR-32; MSW; MTCW 1, 2

Renoir, Jean 1894-1979 .... **CLC 20**
See also CA 129; 85-88

Resnais, Alain 1922- .... **CLC 16**

Revard, Carter (Curtis) 1931- .... **NNAL**
See also CA 144; CANR 81; PFS 5

Reverdy, Pierre 1889-1960 .... **CLC 53**
See also CA 97-100; 89-92; DLB 258; EWL 3; GFL 1789 to the Present

Rexroth, Kenneth 1905-1982 .... **CLC 1, 2, 6, 11, 22, 49, 112; PC 20**
See also BG 3; CA 5-8R; 107; CANR 14, 34, 63; CDALB 1941-1968; DAM POET; DLB 16, 48, 165, 212; DLBY 1982; EWL 3; INT CANR-14; MTCW 1, 2; RGAL 4

Reyes, Alfonso 1889-1959 .... **HLCS 2; TCLC 33**
See also CA 131; EWL 3; HW 1; LAW

Reyes y Basoalto, Ricardo Eliecer Neftali
See Neruda, Pablo

Reymont, Wladyslaw (Stanislaw)
1868(?)-1925 .... **TCLC 5**
See also CA 104; EWL 3

Reynolds, Jonathan 1942- .... **CLC 6, 38**
See also CA 65-68; CANR 28

Reynolds, Joshua 1723-1792 .... **LC 15**
See also DLB 104

Reynolds, Michael S(hane)
1937-2000 .... **CLC 44**
See also CA 65-68; 189; CANR 9, 89, 97

Reznikoff, Charles 1894-1976 .... **CLC 9**
See also CA 33-36; 61-64; CAP 2; DLB 28, 45; WP

Rezzori (d'Arezzo), Gregor von
1914-1998 .... **CLC 25**
See also CA 122; 136; 167

Rhine, Richard
See Silverstein, Alvin; Silverstein, Virginia B(arbara Opshelor)

Rhodes, Eugene Manlove
1869-1934 .... **TCLC 53**
See also CA 198; DLB 256

R'hoone, Lord
See Balzac, Honore de

Rhys, Jean 1894(?)-1979 ...... **CLC 2, 4, 6, 14, 19, 51, 124; SSC 21**
See also BRWS 2; CA 25-28R; 85-88; CANR 35, 62; CDBLB 1945-1960; CD-WLB 3; DA3; DAM NOV; DLB 36, 117, 162; DNFS 2; EWL 3; LATS 1; MTCW 1, 2; RGEL 2; RGSF 2; RHW; TEA

Ribeiro, Darcy 1922-1997 .... **CLC 34**
See also CA 33-36R; 156; EWL 3

Ribeiro, Joao Ubaldo (Osorio Pimentel)
1941- .... **CLC 10, 67**
See also CA 81-84; EWL 3

Ribman, Ronald (Burt) 1932- .... **CLC 7**
See also CA 21-24R; CAD; CANR 46, 80; CD 5

Ricci, Nino 1959- .... **CLC 70**
See also CA 137; CCA 1

Rice, Anne 1941- .... **CLC 41, 128**
See Rampling, Anne
See also AAYA 9, 53; AMWS 7; BEST 89:2; BPFB 3; CA 65-68; CANR 12, 36, 53, 74, 100; CN 7; CPW; CSW; DA3; DAM POP; GLL 2; HGG; MTCW 2; SUFW 2; YAW

Rice, Elmer (Leopold) 1892-1967 ...... **CLC 7, 49**
See Reizenstein, Elmer Leopold
See also CA 21-22; 25-28R; CAP 2; DAM DRAM; DFS 12; DLB 4, 7; MTCW 1, 2; RGAL 4

Rice, Tim(othy Miles Bindon)
1944- .... **CLC 21**
See also CA 103; CANR 46; DFS 7

Rich, Adrienne (Cecile) 1929- ... **CLC 3, 6, 7, 11, 18, 36, 73, 76, 125; PC 5**
See also AMWR 2; AMWS 1; CA 9-12R; CANR 20, 53, 74; CDALBS; CP 7; CSW; CWP; DA3; DAM POET; DLB 5, 67; EWL 3; EXPP; FW; MAWW; MTCW 1, 2; PAB; PFS 15; RGAL 4; WP

Rich, Barbara
See Graves, Robert (von Ranke)

Rich, Robert
See Trumbo, Dalton

Richard, Keith .... **CLC 17**
See Richards, Keith

Richards, David Adams 1950- .... **CLC 59**
See also CA 93-96; CANR 60, 110; DAC; DLB 53

Richards, I(vor) A(rmstrong)
1893-1979 .... **CLC 14, 24**
See also BRWS 2; CA 41-44R; 89-92; CANR 34, 74; DLB 27; EWL 3; MTCW 2; RGEL 2

Richards, Keith 1943-
See Richard, Keith
See also CA 107; CANR 77

Richardson, Anne
See Roiphe, Anne (Richardson)

Richardson, Dorothy Miller
1873-1957 .... **TCLC 3**
See also CA 104; 192; DLB 36; EWL 3; FW; RGEL 2

Richardson (Robertson), Ethel Florence Lindesay 1870-1946
See Richardson, Henry Handel
See also CA 105; 190; DLB 230; RHW

Richardson, Henry Handel .... **TCLC 4**
See Richardson (Robertson), Ethel Florence Lindesay
See also DLB 197; EWL 3; RGEL 2; RGSF 2

Richardson, John 1796-1852 .... **NCLC 55**
See also CCA 1; DAC; DLB 99

Richardson, Samuel 1689-1761 ...... **LC 1, 44; WLC**
See also BRW 3; CDBLB 1660-1789; DA; DAB; DAC; DAM MST, NOV; DLB 39; RGEL 2; TEA; WLIT 3

Richardson, Willis 1889-1977 .... **HR 3**
See also BW 1; CA 124; DLB 51; SATA 60

Richler, Mordecai 1931-2001 .... **CLC 3, 5, 9, 13, 18, 46, 70**
See also AITN 1; CA 65-68; 201; CANR 31, 62, 111; CCA 1; CLR 17; CWRI 5; DAC; DAM MST, NOV; DLB 53; EWL 3; MAICYA 1, 2; MTCW 1, 2; RGEL 2; SATA 44, 98; SATA-Brief 27; TWA

Richter, Conrad (Michael)
1890-1968 .... **CLC 30**
See also AAYA 21; BYA 2; CA 5-8R; 25-28R; CANR 23; DLB 9, 212; LAIT 1; MTCW 1, 2; RGAL 4; SATA 3; TCWW 2; TUS; YAW

Ricostranza, Tom
See Ellis, Trey

Riddell, Charlotte 1832-1906 .... **TCLC 40**
See Riddell, Mrs. J. H.
See also CA 165; DLB 156

Riddell, Mrs. J. H.
See Riddell, Charlotte
See also HGG; SUFW

Ridge, John Rollin 1827-1867 ...... **NCLC 82; NNAL**
See also CA 144; DAM MULT; DLB 175

Ridgeway, Jason
See Marlowe, Stephen

Ridgway, Keith 1965- .... **CLC 119**
See also CA 172

Riding, Laura .... **CLC 3, 7**
See Jackson, Laura (Riding)
See also RGAL 4

Riefenstahl, Berta Helene Amalia 1902-
See Riefenstahl, Leni
See also CA 108

Riefenstahl, Leni .... **CLC 16**
See Riefenstahl, Berta Helene Amalia

Riffe, Ernest
See Bergman, (Ernst) Ingmar

Riggs, (Rolla) Lynn
1899-1954 .... **NNAL; TCLC 56**
See also CA 144; DAM MULT; DLB 175

Riis, Jacob A(ugust) 1849-1914 ..... **TCLC 80**
See also CA 113; 168; DLB 23

Riley, James Whitcomb 1849-1916 .... **PC 48; TCLC 51**
See also CA 118; 137; DAM POET; MAI-CYA 1, 2; RGAL 4; SATA 17

Riley, Tex
See Creasey, John

Rilke, Rainer Maria 1875-1926 .... **PC 2; TCLC 1, 6, 19**
See also CA 104; 132; CANR 62, 99; CD-WLB 2; DA3; DAM POET; DLB 81; EW 9; EWL 3; MTCW 1, 2; RGWL 2, 3; TWA; WP

Rimbaud, (Jean Nicolas) Arthur
1854-1891 .... **NCLC 4, 35, 82; PC 3; WLC**
See also DA; DA3; DAB; DAC; DAM MST, POET; DLB 217; EW 7; GFL 1789 to the Present; LMFS 2; RGWL 2, 3; TWA; WP

Rinehart, Mary Roberts
1876-1958 .... **TCLC 52**
See also BPFB 3; CA 108; 166; RGAL 4; RHW

Ringmaster, The
See Mencken, H(enry) L(ouis)

Ringwood, Gwen(dolyn Margaret) Pharis
1910-1984 .... **CLC 48**
See also CA 148; 112; DLB 88

Rio, Michel 1945(?)- .... **CLC 43**
See also CA 201

Ritsos, Giannes
See Ritsos, Yannis

Ritsos, Yannis 1909-1990 .... **CLC 6, 13, 31**
See also CA 77-80; 133; CANR 39, 61; EW 12; EWL 3; MTCW 1; RGWL 2, 3

Ritter, Erika 1948(?)- .... **CLC 52**
See also CD 5; CWD

Rivera, Jose Eustasio 1889-1928 ... **TCLC 35**
See also CA 162; EWL 3; HW 1, 2; LAW

Rivera, Tomas 1935-1984 .... **HLCS 2**
See also CA 49-52; CANR 32; DLB 82; HW 1; RGAL 4; SSFS 15; TCWW 2; WLIT 1

Rivers, Conrad Kent 1933-1968 .... **CLC 1**
See also BW 1; CA 85-88; DLB 41

Rivers, Elfrida
See Bradley, Marion Zimmer
See also GLL 1

Riverside, John
See Heinlein, Robert A(nson)

Rizal, Jose 1861-1896 .... **NCLC 27**

Roa Bastos, Augusto (Antonio)
1917- .... **CLC 45; HLC 2**
See also CA 131; DAM MULT; DLB 113; EWL 3; HW 1; LAW; RGSF 2; WLIT 1

Robbe-Grillet, Alain 1922- .... **CLC 1, 2, 4, 6, 8, 10, 14, 43, 128**
See also BPFB 3; CA 9-12R; CANR 33, 65, 115; DLB 83; EW 13; EWL 3; GFL 1789 to the Present; IDFW 3, 4; MTCW 1, 2; RGWL 2, 3; SSFS 15

Ross, (James) Sinclair 1908-1996 ... **CLC 13; SSC 24**
See also CA 73-76; CANR 81; CN 7; DAC; DAM MST; DLB 88; RGEL 2; RGSF 2; TCWW 2

Rossetti, Christina (Georgina) 1830-1894 .... **NCLC 2, 50, 66; PC 7; WLC**
See also AAYA 51; BRW 5; BYA 4; DA; DA3; DAB; DAC; DAM MST, POET; DLB 35, 163, 240; EXPP; LATS 1; MAICYA 1, 2; PFS 10, 14; RGEL 2; SATA 20; TEA; WCH

Rossetti, Dante Gabriel 1828-1882 . **NCLC 4, 77; PC 44; WLC**
See also AAYA 51; BRW 5; CDBLB 1832-1890; DA; DAB; DAC; DAM MST, POET; DLB 35; EXPP; RGEL 2; TEA

Rossi, Cristina Peri
See Peri Rossi, Cristina

Rossi, Jean Baptiste 1931-
See Japrisot, Sebastien
See also CA 201

Rossner, Judith (Perelman) 1935- . **CLC 6, 9, 29**
See also AITN 2; BEST 90:3; BPFB 3; CA 17-20R; CANR 18, 51, 73; CN 7; DLB 6; INT CANR-18; MTCW 1, 2

Rostand, Edmond (Eugene Alexis) 1868-1918 .... **DC 10; TCLC 6, 37**
See also CA 104; 126; DA; DA3; DAB; DAC; DAM DRAM, MST; DFS 1; DLB 192; LAIT 1; MTCW 1; RGWL 2, 3; TWA

Roth, Henry 1906-1995 ..... **CLC 2, 6, 11, 104**
See also AMWS 9; CA 11-12; 149; CANR 38, 63; CAP 1; CN 7; DA3; DLB 28; EWL 3; MTCW 1, 2; RGAL 4

Roth, (Moses) Joseph 1894-1939 ... **TCLC 33**
See also CA 160; DLB 85; EWL 3; RGWL 2, 3

Roth, Philip (Milton) 1933- ... **CLC 1, 2, 3, 4, 6, 9, 15, 22, 31, 47, 66, 86, 119; SSC 26; WLC**
See also AMWR 2; AMWS 3; BEST 90:3; BPFB 3; CA 1-4R; CANR 1, 22, 36, 55, 89; CDALB 1968-1988; CN 7; CPW 1; DA; DA3; DAB; DAC; DAM MST, NOV, POP; DLB 2, 28, 173; DLBY 1982; EWL 3; MTCW 1, 2; RGAL 4; RGSF 2; SSFS 12; TUS

Rothenberg, Jerome 1931- .... **CLC 6, 57**
See also CA 45-48; CANR 1, 106; CP 7; DLB 5, 193

Rotter, Pat ed. .... **CLC 65**

Roumain, Jacques (Jean Baptiste) 1907-1944 .... **BLC 3; TCLC 19**
See also BW 1; CA 117; 125; DAM MULT; EWL 3

Rourke, Constance Mayfield 1885-1941 .... **TCLC 12**
See also CA 107; 200; YABC 1

Rousseau, Jean-Baptiste 1671-1741 ...... **LC 9**

Rousseau, Jean-Jacques 1712-1778 .... **LC 14, 36; WLC**
See also DA; DA3; DAB; DAC; DAM MST; EW 4; GFL Beginnings to 1789; LMFS 1; RGWL 2, 3; TWA

Roussel, Raymond 1877-1933 .... **TCLC 20**
See also CA 117; 201; EWL 3; GFL 1789 to the Present

Rovit, Earl (Herbert) 1927- .... **CLC 7**
See also CA 5-8R; CANR 12

Rowe, Elizabeth Singer 1674-1737 ..... **LC 44**
See also DLB 39, 95

Rowe, Nicholas 1674-1718 .... **LC 8**
See also DLB 84; RGEL 2

Rowlandson, Mary 1637(?)-1678 .... **LC 66**
See also DLB 24, 200; RGAL 4

Rowley, Ames Dorrance
See Lovecraft, H(oward) P(hillips)

Rowling, J(oanne) K(athleen) 1965- .... **CLC 137**
See also AAYA 34; BYA 13, 14; CA 173; CLR 66, 80; MAICYA; SATA 109; SUFW 2

Rowson, Susanna Haswell 1762(?)-1824 .... **NCLC 5, 69**
See also DLB 37, 200; RGAL 4

Roy, Arundhati 1960(?)- .... **CLC 109**
See also CA 163; CANR 90; DLBY 1997; EWL 3; LATS 1

Roy, Gabrielle 1909-1983 .... **CLC 10, 14**
See also CA 53-56; 110; CANR 5, 61; CCA 1; DAB; DAC; DAM MST; DLB 68; EWL 3; MTCW 1; RGWL 2, 3; SATA 104

Royko, Mike 1932-1997 .... **CLC 109**
See also CA 89-92; 157; CANR 26, 111; CPW

Rozanov, Vasily Vasilyevich
See Rozanov, Vassili
See also EWL 3

Rozanov, Vassili 1856-1919 .... **TCLC 104**
See Rozanov, Vasily Vasilyevich

Rozewicz, Tadeusz 1921- ...... **CLC 9, 23, 139**
See also CA 108; CANR 36, 66; CWW 2; DA3; DAM POET; DLB 232; EWL 3; MTCW 1, 2; RGWL 3

Ruark, Gibbons 1941- .... **CLC 3**
See also CA 33-36R; CAAS 23; CANR 14, 31, 57; DLB 120

Rubens, Bernice (Ruth) 1923- ... **CLC 19, 31**
See also CA 25-28R; CANR 33, 65; CN 7; DLB 14, 207; MTCW 1

Rubin, Harold
See Robbins, Harold

Rudkin, (James) David 1936- .... **CLC 14**
See also CA 89-92; CBD; CD 5; DLB 13

Rudnik, Raphael 1933- .... **CLC 7**
See also CA 29-32R

Ruffian, M.
See Hasek, Jaroslav (Matej Frantisek)

Ruiz, Jose Martinez .... **CLC 11**
See Martinez Ruiz, Jose

Rukeyser, Muriel 1913-1980 . **CLC 6, 10, 15, 27; PC 12**
See also AMWS 6; CA 5-8R; 93-96; CANR 26, 60; DA3; DAM POET; DLB 48; EWL 3; FW; GLL 2; MTCW 1, 2; PFS 10; RGAL 4; SATA-Obit 22

Rule, Jane (Vance) 1931- .... **CLC 27**
See also CA 25-28R; CAAS 18; CANR 12, 87; CN 7; DLB 60; FW

Rulfo, Juan 1918-1986 .. **CLC 8, 80; HLC 2; SSC 25**
See also CA 85-88; 118; CANR 26; CD-WLB 3; DAM MULT; DLB 113; EWL 3; HW 1, 2; LAW; MTCW 1, 2; RGSF 2; RGWL 2, 3; WLIT 1

Rumi, Jalal al-Din 1207-1273 ...... **CMLC 20; PC 45**
See also RGWL 2, 3; WP

Runeberg, Johan 1804-1877 .... **NCLC 41**

Runyon, (Alfred) Damon 1884(?)-1946 .... **TCLC 10**
See also CA 107; 165; DLB 11, 86, 171; MTCW 2; RGAL 4

Rush, Norman 1933- .... **CLC 44**
See also CA 121; 126; INT 126

Rushdie, (Ahmed) Salman 1947- .... **CLC 23, 31, 55, 100; WLCS**
See also BEST 89:3; BPFB 3; BRWS 4; CA 108; 111; CANR 33, 56, 108; CN 7; CPW 1; DA3; DAB; DAC; DAM MST, NOV, POP; DLB 194; EWL 3; FANT; INT CA-111; LATS 1; LMFS 2; MTCW 1, 2; RGEL 2; RGSF 2; TEA; WLIT 4

Rushforth, Peter (Scott) 1945- .... **CLC 19**
See also CA 101

Ruskin, John 1819-1900 .... **TCLC 63**
See also BRW 5; BYA 5; CA 114; 129; CD-BLB 1832-1890; DLB 55, 163, 190; RGEL 2; SATA 24; TEA; WCH

Russ, Joanna 1937- .... **CLC 15**
See also BPFB 3; CA 5-28R; CANR 11, 31, 65; CN 7; DLB 8; FW; GLL 1; MTCW 1; SCFW 2; SFW 4

Russ, Richard Patrick
See O'Brian, Patrick

Russell, George William 1867-1935
See A.E.; Baker, Jean H.
See also BRWS 8; CA 104; 153; CDBLB 1890-1914; DAM POET; EWL 3; RGEL 2

Russell, Jeffrey Burton 1934- .... **CLC 70**
See also CA 25-28R; CANR 11, 28, 52

Russell, (Henry) Ken(neth Alfred) 1927- .... **CLC 16**
See also CA 105

Russell, William Martin 1947-
See Russell, Willy
See also CA 164; CANR 107

Russell, Willy .... **CLC 60**
See Russell, William Martin
See also CBD; CD 5; DLB 233

Rutherford, Mark .... **TCLC 25**
See White, William Hale
See also DLB 18; RGEL 2

Ruyslinck, Ward .... **CLC 14**
See Belser, Reimond Karel Maria de

Ryan, Cornelius (John) 1920-1974 ..... **CLC 7**
See also CA 69-72; 53-56; CANR 38

Ryan, Michael 1946- .... **CLC 65**
See also CA 49-52; CANR 109; DLBY 1982

Ryan, Tim
See Dent, Lester

Rybakov, Anatoli (Naumovich) 1911-1998 .... **CLC 23, 53**
See also CA 126; 135; 172; SATA 79; SATA-Obit 108

Ryder, Jonathan
See Ludlum, Robert

Ryga, George 1932-1987 .... **CLC 14**
See also CA 101; 124; CANR 43, 90; CCA 1; DAC; DAM MST; DLB 60

S. H.
See Hartmann, Sadakichi

S. S.
See Sassoon, Siegfried (Lorraine)

Saba, Umberto 1883-1957 .... **TCLC 33**
See also CA 144; CANR 79; DLB 114; EWL 3; RGWL 2, 3

Sabatini, Rafael 1875-1950 .... **TCLC 47**
See also BPFB 3; CA 162; RHW

Sabato, Ernesto (R.) 1911- .... **CLC 10, 23; HLC 2**
See also CA 97-100; CANR 32, 65; CD-WLB 3; DAM MULT; DLB 145; EWL 3; HW 1, 2; LAW; MTCW 1, 2

Sa-Carniero, Mario de 1890-1916 . **TCLC 83**
See also EWL 3

Sacastru, Martin
See Bioy Casares, Adolfo
See also CWW 2

Sacher-Masoch, Leopold von 1836(?)-1895 .... **NCLC 31**

Sachs, Marilyn (Stickle) 1927- .... **CLC 35**
See also AAYA 2; BYA 6; CA 17-20R; CANR 13, 47; CLR 2; JRDA; MAICYA 1, 2; SAAS 2; SATA 3, 68; SATA-Essay 110; WYA; YAW

Sachs, Nelly 1891-1970 .... **CLC 14, 98**
See also CA 17-18; 25-28R; CANR 87; CAP 2; EWL 3; MTCW 2; RGWL 2, 3

Shapcott, Thomas W(illiam) 1935- .. **CLC 38**
See also CA 69-72; CANR 49, 83, 103; CP 7

Shapiro, Jane 1942- .... **CLC 76**
See also CA 196

Shapiro, Karl (Jay) 1913-2000 ...... **CLC 4, 8, 15, 53; PC 25**
See also AMWS 2; CA 1-4R; 188; CAAS 6; CANR 1, 36, 66; CP 7; DLB 48; EWL 3; EXPP; MTCW 1, 2; PFS 3; RGAL 4

Sharp, William 1855-1905 .... **TCLC 39**
See Macleod, Fiona
See also CA 160; DLB 156; RGEL 2

Sharpe, Thomas Ridley 1928-
See Sharpe, Tom
See also CA 114; 122; CANR 85; INT CA-122

Sharpe, Tom .... **CLC 36**
See Sharpe, Thomas Ridley
See also CN 7; DLB 14, 231

Shatrov, Mikhail .... **CLC 59**

Shaw, Bernard
See Shaw, George Bernard
See also DLB 190

Shaw, G. Bernard
See Shaw, George Bernard

Shaw, George Bernard 1856-1950 .. **TCLC 3, 9, 21, 45; WLC**
See Shaw, Bernard
See also BRW 6; BRWC 1; BRWR 2; CA 104; 128; CDBLB 1914-1945; DA; DA3; DAB; DAC; DAM DRAM, MST; DFS 1, 3, 6, 11; DLB 10, 57; EWL 3; LAIT 3; LATS 1; MTCW 1, 2; RGEL 2; TEA; WLIT 4

Shaw, Henry Wheeler 1818-1885 .. **NCLC 15**
See also DLB 11; RGAL 4

Shaw, Irwin 1913-1984 .... **CLC 7, 23, 34**
See also AITN 1; BPFB 3; CA 13-16R; 112; CANR 21; CDALB 1941-1968; CPW; DAM DRAM, POP; DLB 6, 102; DLBY 1984; MTCW 1, 21

Shaw, Robert 1927-1978 .... **CLC 5**
See also AITN 1; CA 1-4R; 81-84; CANR 4; DLB 13, 14

Shaw, T. E.
See Lawrence, T(homas) E(dward)

Shawn, Wallace 1943- .... **CLC 41**
See also CA 112; CAD; CD 5; DLB 266

Shchedrin, N.
See Saltykov, Mikhail Evgrafovich

Shea, Lisa 1953- .... **CLC 86**
See also CA 147

Sheed, Wilfrid (John Joseph) 1930- . **CLC 2, 4, 10, 53**
See also CA 65-68; CANR 30, 66; CN 7; DLB 6; MTCW 1, 2

Sheehy, Gail 1937- .... **CLC 171**
See also CA 49-52; CANR 1, 33, 55, 92; CPW; MTCW 1

Sheldon, Alice Hastings Bradley 1915(?)-1987
See Tiptree, James, Jr.
See also CA 108; 122; CANR 34; INT 108; MTCW 1

Sheldon, John
See Bloch, Robert (Albert)

Sheldon, Walter J(ames) 1917-1996
See Queen, Ellery
See also AITN 1; CA 25-28R; CANR 10

Shelley, Mary Wollstonecraft (Godwin) 1797-1851 ...... **NCLC 14, 59, 103; WLC**
See also AAYA 20; BPFB 3; BRW 3; BRWS 3; BYA 5; CDBLB 1789-1832; DA; DA3; DAB; DAC; DAM MST, NOV; DLB 110, 116, 159, 178; EXPN; HGG; LAIT 1; LMFS 1, 2; NFS 1; RGEL 2; SATA 29; SCFW; SFW 4; TEA; WLIT 3

Shelley, Percy Bysshe 1792-1822 .. **NCLC 18, 93; PC 14; WLC**
See also BRW 4; BRWR 1; CDBLB 1789-1832; DA; DA3; DAB; DAC; DAM MST, POET; DLB 96, 110, 158; EXPP; LMFS 1; PAB; PFS 2; RGEL 2; TEA; WLIT 3; WP

Shepard, Jim 1956- .... **CLC 36**
See also CA 137; CANR 59, 104; SATA 90

Shepard, Lucius 1947- .... **CLC 34**
See also CA 128; 141; CANR 81; HGG; SCFW 2; SFW 4; SUFW 2

Shepard, Sam 1943- .... **CLC 4, 6, 17, 34, 41, 44, 169; DC 5**
See also AAYA 1; AMWS 3; CA 69-72; CABS 3; CAD; CANR 22, 120; CD 5; DA3; DAM DRAM; DFS 3, 6, 7, 14; DLB 7, 212; EWL 3; IDFW 3, 4; MTCW 1, 2; RGAL 4

Shepherd, Michael
See Ludlum, Robert

Sherburne, Zoa (Lillian Morin) 1912-1995 .... **CLC 30**
See also AAYA 13; CA 1-4R; 176; CANR 3, 37; MAICYA 1, 2; SAAS 18; SATA 3; YAW

Sheridan, Frances 1724-1766 .... **LC 7**
See also DLB 39, 84

Sheridan, Richard Brinsley 1751-1816 .... **DC 1; NCLC 5, 91; WLC**
See also BRW 3; CDBLB 1660-1789; DA; DAB; DAC; DAM DRAM, MST; DFS 15; DLB 89; WLIT 3

Sherman, Jonathan Marc .... **CLC 55**
Sherman, Martin 1941(?)- .... **CLC 19**
See also CA 116; 123; CAD; CANR 86; CD 5; DLB 228; GLL 1; IDTP

Sherwin, Judith Johnson
See Johnson, Judith (Emlyn)
See also CANR 85; CP 7; CWP

Sherwood, Frances 1940- .... **CLC 81**
See also CA 146

Sherwood, Robert E(mmet) 1896-1955 .... **TCLC 3**
See also CA 104; 153; CANR 86; DAM DRAM; DFS 11, 15, 17; DLB 7, 26, 249; IDFW 3, 4; RGAL 4

Shestov, Lev 1866-1938 .... **TCLC 56**
Shevchenko, Taras 1814-1861 .... **NCLC 54**
Shiel, M(atthew) P(hipps) 1865-1947 .... **TCLC 8**
See Holmes, Gordon
See also CA 106; 160; DLB 153; HGG; MTCW 2; SFW 4; SUFW

Shields, Carol 1935-2003 .... **CLC 91, 113**
See also AMWS 7; CA 81-84; CANR 51, 74, 98; CCA 1; CN 7; CPW; DA3; DAC; MTCW 2

Shields, David 1956- .... **CLC 97**
See also CA 124; CANR 48, 99, 112

Shiga, Naoya 1883-1971 ..... **CLC 33; SSC 23**
See Shiga Naoya
See also CA 101; 33-36R; MJW; RGWL 3

Shiga Naoya
See Shiga, Naoya
See also DLB 180; EWL 3; RGWL 3

Shilts, Randy 1951-1994 .... **CLC 85**
See also AAYA 19; CA 115; 127; 144; CANR 45; DA3; GLL 1; INT 127; MTCW 2

Shimazaki, Haruki 1872-1943
See Shimazaki Toson
See also CA 105; 134; CANR 84; RGWL 3

Shimazaki Toson .... **TCLC 5**
See Shimazaki, Haruki
See also DLB 180; EWL 3

Sholokhov, Mikhail (Aleksandrovich) 1905-1984 .... **CLC 7, 15**
See also CA 101; 112; DLB 272; EWL 3; MTCW 1, 2; RGWL 2, 3; SATA-Obit 36

Shone, Patric
See Hanley, James

Showalter, Elaine 1941- .... **CLC 169**
See also CA 57-60; CANR 58, 106; DLB 67; FW; GLL 2

Shreve, Susan Richards 1939- .... **CLC 23**
See also CA 49-52; CAAS 5; CANR 5, 38, 69, 100; MAICYA 1, 2; SATA 46, 95; SATA-Brief 41

Shue, Larry 1946-1985 .... **CLC 52**
See also CA 145; 117; DAM DRAM; DFS 7

Shu-Jen, Chou 1881-1936
See Lu Hsun
See also CA 104

Shulman, Alix Kates 1932- .... **CLC 2, 10**
See also CA 29-32R; CANR 43; FW; SATA 7

Shusaku, Endo
See Endo, Shusaku

Shuster, Joe 1914-1992 .... **CLC 21**
See also AAYA 50

Shute, Nevil .... **CLC 30**
See Norway, Nevil Shute
See also BPFB 3; DLB 255; NFS 9; RHW; SFW 4

Shuttle, Penelope (Diane) 1947- .... **CLC 7**
See also CA 93-96; CANR 39, 84, 92, 108; CP 7; CWP; DLB 14, 40

Shvarts, Elena 1948- .... **PC 50**
See also CA 147

Sidhwa, Bapsy (N.) 1938- .... **CLC 168**
See also CA 108; CANR 25, 57; CN 7; FW

Sidney, Mary 1561-1621 .... **LC 19, 39**
See Sidney Herbert, Mary

Sidney, Sir Philip 1554-1586 . **LC 19, 39; PC 32**
See also BRW 1; BRWR 2; CDBLB Before 1660; DA; DA3; DAB; DAC; DAM MST, POET; DLB 167; EXPP; PAB; RGEL 2; TEA; WP

Sidney Herbert, Mary
See Sidney, Mary
See also DLB 167

Siegel, Jerome 1914-1996 .... **CLC 21**
See Siegel, Jerry
See also CA 116; 169; 151

Siegel, Jerry
See Siegel, Jerome
See also AAYA 50

Sienkiewicz, Henryk (Adam Alexander Pius) 1846-1916 .... **TCLC 3**
See also CA 104; 134; CANR 84; EWL 3; RGSF 2; RGWL 2, 3

Sierra, Gregorio Martinez
See Martinez Sierra, Gregorio

Sierra, Maria (de la O'LeJarraga) Martinez
See Martinez Sierra, Maria (de la O'LeJarraga)

Sigal, Clancy 1926- .... **CLC 7**
See also CA 1-4R; CANR 85; CN 7

Sigourney, Lydia H.
See Sigourney, Lydia Howard (Huntley)
See also DLB 73, 183

Sigourney, Lydia Howard (Huntley) 1791-1865 .... **NCLC 21, 87**
See Sigourney, Lydia H.; Sigourney, Lydia Huntley
See also DLB 1

Sigourney, Lydia Huntley
See Sigourney, Lydia Howard (Huntley)
See also DLB 42, 239, 243

Siguenza y Gongora, Carlos de 1645-1700 .... **HLCS 2; LC 8**
See also LAW

Slaughter, Frank G(ill) 1908-2001 ... **CLC 29**
See also AITN 2; CA 5-8R; 197; CANR 5, 85; INT CANR-5; RHW

Slavitt, David R(ytman) 1935- ..... **CLC 5, 14**
See also CA 21-24R; CAAS 3; CANR 41, 83; CP 7; DLB 5, 6

Slesinger, Tess 1905-1945 .... **TCLC 10**
See also CA 107; 199; DLB 102

Slessor, Kenneth 1901-1971 .... **CLC 14**
See also CA 102; 89-92; DLB 260; RGEL 2

Slowacki, Juliusz 1809-1849 .... **NCLC 15**
See also RGWL 3

Smart, Christopher 1722-1771 . **LC 3; PC 13**
See also DAM POET; DLB 109; RGEL 2

Smart, Elizabeth 1913-1986 .... **CLC 54**
See also CA 81-84; 118; DLB 88

Smiley, Jane (Graves) 1949- ..... **CLC 53, 76, 144**
See also AMWS 6; BPFB 3; CA 104; CANR 30, 50, 74, 96; CN 7; CPW 1; DA3; DAM POP; DLB 227, 234; EWL 3; INT CANR-30

Smith, A(rthur) J(ames) M(arshall)
1902-1980 .... **CLC 15**
See also CA 1-4R; 102; CANR 4; DAC; DLB 88; RGEL 2

Smith, Adam 1723(?)-1790 .... **LC 36**
See also DLB 104, 252; RGEL 2

Smith, Alexander 1829-1867 .... **NCLC 59**
See also DLB 32, 55

Smith, Anna Deavere 1950- .... **CLC 86**
See also CA 133; CANR 103; CD 5; DFS 2

Smith, Betty (Wehner) 1904-1972 .... **CLC 19**
See also BPFB 3; BYA 3; CA 5-8R; 33-36R; DLBY 1982; LAIT 3; RGAL 4; SATA 6

Smith, Charlotte (Turner)
1749-1806 .... **NCLC 23, 115**
See also DLB 39, 109; RGEL 2; TEA

Smith, Clark Ashton 1893-1961 .... **CLC 43**
See also CA 143; CANR 81; FANT; HGG; MTCW 2; SCFW 2; SFW 4; SUFW

Smith, Dave .... **CLC 22, 42**
See Smith, David (Jeddie)
See also CAAS 7; DLB 5

Smith, David (Jeddie) 1942-
See Smith, Dave
See also CA 49-52; CANR 1, 59, 120; CP 7; CSW; DAM POET

Smith, Florence Margaret 1902-1971
See Smith, Stevie
See also CA 17-18; 29-32R; CANR 35; CAP 2; DAM POET; MTCW 1, 2; TEA

Smith, Iain Crichton 1928-1998 .... **CLC 64**
See also CA 21-24R; 171; CN 7; CP 7; DLB 40, 139; RGSF 2

Smith, John 1580(?)-1631 .... **LC 9**
See also DLB 24, 30; TUS

Smith, Johnston
See Crane, Stephen (Townley)

Smith, Joseph, Jr. 1805-1844 .... **NCLC 53**

Smith, Lee 1944- .... **CLC 25, 73**
See also CA 114; 119; CANR 46, 118; CSW; DLB 143; DLBY 1983; EWL 3; INT CA-119; RGAL 4

Smith, Martin
See Smith, Martin Cruz

Smith, Martin Cruz 1942- .. **CLC 25; NNAL**
See also BEST 89:4; BPFB 3; CA 85-88; CANR 6, 23, 43, 65, 119; CMW 4; CPW; DAM MULT, POP; HGG; INT CANR-23; MTCW 2; RGAL 4

Smith, Patti 1946- .... **CLC 12**
See also CA 93-96; CANR 63

Smith, Pauline (Urmson)
1882-1959 .... **TCLC 25**
See also DLB 225; EWL 3

Smith, Rosamond
See Oates, Joyce Carol

Smith, Sheila Kaye
See Kaye-Smith, Sheila

Smith, Stevie .... **CLC 3, 8, 25, 44; PC 12**
See Smith, Florence Margaret
See also BRWS 2; DLB 20; EWL 3; MTCW 2; PAB; PFS 3; RGEL 2

Smith, Wilbur (Addison) 1933- .... **CLC 33**
See also CA 13-16R; CANR 7, 46, 66; CPW; MTCW 1, 2

Smith, William Jay 1918- .... **CLC 6**
See also CA 5-8R; CANR 44, 106; CP 7; CSW; CWRI 5; DLB 5; MAICYA 1, 2; SAAS 22; SATA 2, 68

Smith, Woodrow Wilson
See Kuttner, Henry

Smith, Zadie 1976- .... **CLC 158**
See also AAYA 50; CA 193

Smolenskin, Peretz 1842-1885 .... **NCLC 30**

Smollett, Tobias (George) 1721-1771 ... **LC 2, 46**
See also BRW 3; CDBLB 1660-1789; DLB 39, 104; RGEL 2; TEA

Snodgrass, W(illiam) D(e Witt)
1926- .... **CLC 2, 6, 10, 18, 68**
See also AMWS 6; CA 1-4R; CANR 6, 36, 65, 85; CP 7; DAM POET; DLB 5; MTCW 1, 2; RGAL 4

Snorri Sturluson 1179-1241 .... **CMLC 56**
See also RGWL 2, 3

Snow, C(harles) P(ercy) 1905-1980 ... **CLC 1, 4, 6, 9, 13, 19**
See also BRW 7; CA 5-8R; 101; CANR 28; CDBLB 1945-1960; DAM NOV; DLB 15, 77; DLBD 17; EWL 3; MTCW 1, 2; RGEL 2; TEA

Snow, Frances Compton
See Adams, Henry (Brooks)

Snyder, Gary (Sherman) 1930- . **CLC 1, 2, 5, 9, 32, 120; PC 21**
See also AMWS 8; ANW; BG 3; CA 17-20R; CANR 30, 60; CP 7; DA3; DAM POET; DLB 5, 16, 165, 212, 237, 275; EWL 3; MTCW 2; PFS 9; RGAL 4; WP

Snyder, Zilpha Keatley 1927- .... **CLC 17**
See also AAYA 15; BYA 1; CA 9-12R; CANR 38; CLR 31; JRDA; MAICYA 1, 2; SAAS 2; SATA 1, 28, 75, 110; SATA-Essay 112; YAW

Soares, Bernardo
See Pessoa, Fernando (Antonio Nogueira)

Sobh, A.
See Shamlu, Ahmad

Sobol, Joshua 1939- .... **CLC 60**
See Sobol, Yehoshua
See also CA 200; CWW 2

Sobol, Yehoshua 1939-
See Sobol, Joshua
See also CWW 2

Socrates 470B.C.-399B.C. .... **CMLC 27**

Soderberg, Hjalmar 1869-1941 ...... **TCLC 39**
See also DLB 259; EWL 3; RGSF 2

Soderbergh, Steven 1963- .... **CLC 154**
See also AAYA 43

Sodergran, Edith (Irene) 1892-1923
See Soedergran, Edith (Irene)
See also CA 202; DLB 259; EW 11; EWL 3; RGWL 2, 3

Soedergran, Edith (Irene)
1892-1923 .... **TCLC 31**
See Sodergran, Edith (Irene)

Softly, Edgar
See Lovecraft, H(oward) P(hillips)

Softly, Edward
See Lovecraft, H(oward) P(hillips)

Sokolov, Alexander V(sevolodovich) 1943-
See Sokolov, Sasha
See also CA 73-76

Sokolov, Raymond 1941- .... **CLC 7**
See also CA 85-88

Sokolov, Sasha .... **CLC 59**
See Sokolov, Alexander V(sevolodovich)
See also CWW 2; DLB 285; EWL 3; RGWL 2, 3

Sokolov, Sasha .... **CLC 59**

Solo, Jay
See Ellison, Harlan (Jay)

Sologub, Fyodor .... **TCLC 9**
See Teternikov, Fyodor Kuzmich
See also EWL 3

Solomons, Ikey Esquir
See Thackeray, William Makepeace

Solomos, Dionysios 1798-1857 .... **NCLC 15**

Solwoska, Mara
See French, Marilyn

Solzhenitsyn, Aleksandr I(sayevich)
1918- .. **CLC 1, 2, 4, 7, 9, 10, 18, 26, 34, 78, 134; SSC 32; WLC**
See Solzhenitsyn, Aleksandr Isaevich
See also AAYA 49; AITN 1; BPFB 3; CA 69-72; CANR 40, 65, 116; DA; DA3; DAB; DAC; DAM MST, NOV; EW 13; EXPS; LAIT 4; MTCW 1, 2; NFS 6; RGSF 2; RGWL 2, 3; SSFS 9; TWA

Solzhenitsyn, Aleksandr Isaevich
See Solzhenitsyn, Aleksandr I(sayevich)
See also EWL 3

Somers, Jane
See Lessing, Doris (May)

Somerville, Edith Oenone
1858-1949 .... **SSC 56; TCLC 51**
See also CA 196; DLB 135; RGEL 2; RGSF 2

Somerville & Ross
See Martin, Violet Florence; Somerville, Edith Oenone

Sommer, Scott 1951- .... **CLC 25**
See also CA 106

Sondheim, Stephen (Joshua) 1930- . **CLC 30, 39, 147**
See also AAYA 11; CA 103; CANR 47, 67; DAM DRAM; LAIT 4

Sone, Monica 1919- .... **AAL**

Song, Cathy 1955- .... **AAL; PC 21**
See also CA 154; CANR 118; CWP; DLB 169; EXPP; FW; PFS 5

Sontag, Susan 1933- .... **CLC 1, 2, 10, 13, 31, 105**
See also AMWS 3; CA 17-20R; CANR 25, 51, 74, 97; CN 7; CPW; DA3; DAM POP; DLB 2, 67; EWL 3; MAWW; MTCW 1, 2; RGAL 4; RHW; SSFS 10

Sophocles 496(?)B.C.-406(?)B.C. ..... **CMLC 2, 47, 51; DC 1; WLCS**
See also AW 1; CDWLB 1; DA; DA3; DAB; DAC; DAM DRAM, MST; DFS 1, 4, 8; DLB 176; LAIT 1; LATS 1; LMFS 1; RGWL 2, 3; TWA

Sordello 1189-1269 .... **CMLC 15**

Sorel, Georges 1847-1922 .... **TCLC 91**
See also CA 118; 188

Sorel, Julia
See Drexler, Rosalyn

Sorokin, Vladimir .... **CLC 59**
See Sorokin, Vladimir Georgievich

Sorokin, Vladimir Georgievich
See Sorokin, Vladimir
See also DLB 285

Sorrentino, Gilbert 1929- .. **CLC 3, 7, 14, 22, 40**
See also CA 77-80; CANR 14, 33, 115; CN 7; CP 7; DLB 5, 173; DLBY 1980; INT CANR-14

Soseki
See Natsume, Soseki
See also MJW

LAIT 3; MTCW 1, 2; NFS 17; RGAL 4;
RGSF 2; RHW; SATA 9; SSFS 3, 6;
TCWW 2; TUS; WYA; YAW

Steinem, Gloria 1934- .... **CLC 63**
See also CA 53-56; CANR 28, 51; DLB
246; FW; MTCW 1, 2

Steiner, George 1929- .... **CLC 24**
See also CA 73-76; CANR 31, 67, 108;
DAM NOV; DLB 67; EWL 3; MTCW 1,
2; SATA 62

Steiner, K. Leslie
See Delany, Samuel R(ay), Jr.

Steiner, Rudolf 1861-1925 .... **TCLC 13**
See also CA 107

Stendhal 1783-1842 .. **NCLC 23, 46; SSC 27;
WLC**
See also DA; DA3; DAB; DAC; DAM
MST, NOV; DLB 119; EW 5; GFL 1789
to the Present; RGWL 2, 3; TWA

Stephen, Adeline Virginia
See Woolf, (Adeline) Virginia

Stephen, Sir Leslie 1832-1904 .... **TCLC 23**
See also BRW 5; CA 123; DLB 57, 144,
190

Stephen, Sir Leslie
See Stephen, Sir Leslie

Stephen, Virginia
See Woolf, (Adeline) Virginia

Stephens, James 1882(?)-1950 .... **SSC 50;
TCLC 4**
See also CA 104; 192; DLB 19, 153, 162;
EWL 3; FANT; RGEL 2; SUFW

Stephens, Reed
See Donaldson, Stephen R(eeder)

Steptoe, Lydia
See Barnes, Djuna
See also GLL 1

Sterchi, Beat 1949- .... **CLC 65**
See also CA 203

Sterling, Brett
See Bradbury, Ray (Douglas); Hamilton,
Edmond

Sterling, Bruce 1954- .... **CLC 72**
See also CA 119; CANR 44; SCFW 2; SFW
4

Sterling, George 1869-1926 .... **TCLC 20**
See also CA 117; 165; DLB 54

Stern, Gerald 1925- .... **CLC 40, 100**
See also AMWS 9; CA 81-84; CANR 28,
94; CP 7; DLB 105; RGAL 4

Stern, Richard (Gustave) 1928- ... **CLC 4, 39**
See also CA 1-4R; CANR 1, 25, 52, 120;
CN 7; DLB 218; DLBY 1987; INT
CANR-25

Sternberg, Josef von 1894-1969 .... **CLC 20**
See also CA 81-84

Sterne, Laurence 1713-1768 .... **LC 2, 48;
WLC**
See also BRW 3; BRWC 1; CDBLB 1660-
1789; DA; DAB; DAC; DAM MST, NOV;
DLB 39; RGEL 2; TEA

Sternheim, (William Adolf) Carl
1878-1942 .... **TCLC 8**
See also CA 105; 193; DLB 56, 118; EWL
3; RGWL 2, 3

Stevens, Mark 1951- .... **CLC 34**
See also CA 122

Stevens, Wallace 1879-1955 . **PC 6; TCLC 3,
12, 45; WLC**
See also AMW; AMWR 1; CA 104; 124;
CDALB 1929-1941; DA; DA3; DAB;
DAC; DAM MST, POET; DLB 54; EWL
3; EXPP; MTCW 1, 2; PAB; PFS 13, 16;
RGAL 4; TUS; WP

Stevenson, Anne (Katharine) 1933- .. **CLC 7,
33**
See also BRWS 6; CA 17-20R; CAAS 9;
CANR 9, 33; CP 7; CWP; DLB 40;
MTCW 1; RHW

Stevenson, Robert Louis (Balfour)
1850-1894 ...... **NCLC 5, 14, 63; SSC 11,
51; WLC**
See also AAYA 24; BPFB 3; BRW 5;
BRWC 1; BRWR 1; BYA 1, 2, 4, 13; CD-
BLB 1890-1914; CLR 10, 11; DA; DA3;
DAB; DAC; DAM MST, NOV; DLB 18,
57, 141, 156, 174; DLBD 13; HGG;
JRDA; LAIT 1, 3; MAICYA 1, 2; NFS
11; RGEL 2; RGSF 2; SATA 100; SUFW;
TEA; WCH; WLIT 4; WYA; YABC 2;
YAW

Stewart, J(ohn) I(nnes) M(ackintosh)
1906-1994 .... **CLC 7, 14, 32**
See Innes, Michael
See also CA 85-88; 147; CAAS 3; CANR
47; CMW 4; MTCW 1, 2

Stewart, Mary (Florence Elinor)
1916- .... **CLC 7, 35, 117**
See also AAYA 29; BPFB 3; CA 1-4R;
CANR 1, 59; CMW 4; CPW; DAB;
FANT; RHW; SATA 12; YAW

Stewart, Mary Rainbow
See Stewart, Mary (Florence Elinor)

Stifle, June
See Campbell, Maria

Stifter, Adalbert 1805-1868 .. **NCLC 41; SSC
28**
See also CDWLB 2; DLB 133; RGSF 2;
RGWL 2, 3

Still, James 1906-2001 .... **CLC 49**
See also CA 65-68; 195; CAAS 17; CANR
10, 26; CSW; DLB 9; DLBY 01; SATA
29; SATA-Obit 127

Sting 1951-
See Sumner, Gordon Matthew
See also CA 167

Stirling, Arthur
See Sinclair, Upton (Beall)

Stitt, Milan 1941- .... **CLC 29**
See also CA 69-72

Stockton, Francis Richard 1834-1902
See Stockton, Frank R.
See also CA 108; 137; MAICYA 1, 2; SATA
44; SFW 4

Stockton, Frank R. .... **TCLC 47**
See Stockton, Francis Richard
See also BYA 4, 13; DLB 42, 74; DLBD
13; EXPS; SATA-Brief 32; SSFS 3;
SUFW; WCH

Stoddard, Charles
See Kuttner, Henry

Stoker, Abraham 1847-1912
See Stoker, Bram
See also CA 105; 150; DA; DA3; DAC;
DAM MST, NOV; HGG; SATA 29

Stoker, Bram .... **SSC 62; TCLC 8; WLC**
See Stoker, Abraham
See also AAYA 23; BPFB 3; BRWS 3; BYA
5; CDBLB 1890-1914; DAB; DLB 36, 70,
178; LATS 1; RGEL 2; SUFW; TEA;
WLIT 4

Stolz, Mary (Slattery) 1920- .... **CLC 12**
See also AAYA 8; AITN 1; CA 5-8R;
CANR 13, 41, 112; JRDA; MAICYA 1,
2; SAAS 3; SATA 10, 71, 133; YAW

Stone, Irving 1903-1989 .... **CLC 7**
See also AITN 1; BPFB 3; CA 1-4R; 129;
CAAS 3; CANR 1, 23; CPW; DA3; DAM
POP; INT CANR-23; MTCW 1, 2; RHW;
SATA 3; SATA-Obit 64

Stone, Oliver (William) 1946- .... **CLC 73**
See also AAYA 15; CA 110; CANR 55

Stone, Robert (Anthony) 1937- ... **CLC 5, 23,
42, 175**
See also AMWS 5; BPFB 3; CA 85-88;
CANR 23, 66, 95; CN 7; DLB 152; EWL
3; INT CANR-23; MTCW 1

Stone, Zachary
See Follett, Ken(neth Martin)

Stoppard, Tom 1937- ... **CLC 1, 3, 4, 5, 8, 15,
29, 34, 63, 91; DC 6; WLC**
See also BRWC 1; BRWR 2; BRWS 1; CA
81-84; CANR 39, 67; CBD; CD 5; CD-
BLB 1960 to Present; DA; DA3; DAB;
DAC; DAM DRAM, MST; DFS 2, 5, 8,
11, 13, 16; DLB 13, 233; DLBY 1985;
EWL 3; LATS 1; MTCW 1, 2; RGEL 2;
TEA; WLIT 4

Storey, David (Malcolm) 1933- . **CLC 2, 4, 5,
8**
See also BRWS 1; CA 81-84; CANR 36;
CBD; CD 5; CN 7; DAM DRAM; DLB
13, 14, 207, 245; EWL 3; MTCW 1;
RGEL 2

Storm, Hyemeyohsts 1935- ... **CLC 3; NNAL**
See also CA 81-84; CANR 45; DAM MULT

Storm, (Hans) Theodor (Woldsen)
1817-1888 .... **NCLC 1; SSC 27**
See also CDWLB 2; DLB 129; EW; RGSF
2; RGWL 2, 3

Storni, Alfonsina 1892-1938 . **HLC 2; PC 33;
TCLC 5**
See also CA 104; 131; DAM MULT; DLB
283; HW 1; LAW

Stoughton, William 1631-1701 .... **LC 38**
See also DLB 24

Stout, Rex (Todhunter) 1886-1975 ..... **CLC 3**
See also AITN 2; BPFB 3; CA 61-64;
CANR 71; CMW 4; MSW; RGAL 4

Stow, (Julian) Randolph 1935- ... **CLC 23, 48**
See also CA 13-16R; CANR 33; CN 7;
DLB 260; MTCW 1; RGEL 2

Stowe, Harriet (Elizabeth) Beecher
1811-1896 .... **NCLC 3, 50; WLC**
See also AAYA 53; AMWS 1; CDALB
1865-1917; DA; DA3; DAB; DAC; DAM
MST, NOV; DLB 1, 12, 42, 74, 189, 239,
243; EXPN; JRDA; LAIT 2; MAICYA 1,
2; NFS 6; RGAL 4; TUS; YABC 1

Strabo c. 64B.C.-c. 25 .... **CMLC 37**
See also DLB 176

Strachey, (Giles) Lytton
1880-1932 .... **TCLC 12**
See also BRWS 2; CA 110; 178; DLB 149;
DLBD 10; EWL 3; MTCW 2; NCFS 4

Stramm, August 1874-1915 .... **PC 50**
See also CA 195; EWL 3

Strand, Mark 1934- .... **CLC 6, 18, 41, 71**
See also AMWS 4; CA 21-24R; CANR 40,
65, 100; CP 7; DAM POET; DLB 5; EWL
3; PAB; PFS 9; RGAL 4; SATA 41

Stratton-Porter, Gene(va Grace) 1863-1924
See Porter, Gene(va Grace) Stratton
See also ANW; CA 137; CLR 87; DLB 221;
DLBD 14; MAICYA 1, 2; SATA 15

Straub, Peter (Francis) 1943- ... **CLC 28, 107**
See also BEST 89:1; BPFB 3; CA 85-88;
CANR 28, 65, 109; CPW; DAM POP;
DLBY 1984; HGG; MTCW 1, 2; SUFW
2

Strauss, Botho 1944- .... **CLC 22**
See also CA 157; CWW 2; DLB 124

Streatfeild, (Mary) Noel
1897(?)-1986 .... **CLC 21**
See also CA 81-84; 120; CANR 31; CLR
17, 83; CWRI 5; DLB 160; MAICYA 1,
2; SATA 20; SATA-Obit 48

Stribling, T(homas) S(igismund)
1881-1965 .... **CLC 23**
See also CA 189; 107; CMW 4; DLB 9;
RGAL 4

Strindberg, (Johan) August
1849-1912 ... **DC 18; TCLC 1, 8, 21, 47;
WLC**
See also CA 104; 135; DA; DA3; DAB;
DAC; DAM DRAM, MST; DFS 4, 9;
DLB 259; EW 7; EWL 3; IDTP; LMFS
2; MTCW 2; RGWL 2, 3; TWA

Tallmountain, Mary 1918-1997 .... **NNAL**
   See also CA 146; 161; DLB 193

Tally, Ted 1952- .... **CLC 42**
   See also CA 120; 124; CAD; CD 5; INT
   124

Talvik, Heiti 1904-1947 .... **TCLC 87**
   See also EWL 3

Tamayo y Baus, Manuel
   1829-1898 .... **NCLC 1**

Tammsaare, A(nton) H(ansen)
   1878-1940 .... **TCLC 27**
   See also CA 164; CDWLB 4; DLB 220;
   EWL 3

Tam'si, Tchicaya U
   See Tchicaya, Gerald Felix

Tan, Amy (Ruth) 1952- . **AAL; CLC 59, 120,**
   151
   See also AAYA 9, 48; AMWS 10; BEST
   89:3; BPFB 3; CA 136; CANR 54, 105;
   CDALBS; CN 7; CPW 1; DA3; DAM
   MULT, NOV, POP; DLB 173; EXPN;
   FW; LAIT 3, 5; MTCW 2; NFS 1, 13, 16;
   RGAL 4; SATA 75; SSFS 9; YAW

Tandem, Felix
   See Spitteler, Carl (Friedrich Georg)

Tanizaki, Jun'ichiro 1886-1965 ... **CLC 8, 14,**
   28; SSC 21
   See Tanizaki Jun'ichiro
   See also CA 93-96; 25-28R; MJW; MTCW
   2; RGSF 2; RGWL 2

Tanizaki Jun'ichiro
   See Tanizaki, Jun'ichiro
   See also DLB 180; EWL 3

Tanner, William
   See Amis, Kingsley (William)

Tao Lao
   See Storni, Alfonsina

Tapahonso, Luci 1953- .... **NNAL**
   See also CA 145; CANR 72; DLB 175

Tarantino, Quentin (Jerome)
   1963- .... **CLC 125**
   See also CA 171

Tarassoff, Lev
   See Troyat, Henri

Tarbell, Ida M(inerva) 1857-1944 . **TCLC 40**
   See also CA 122; 181; DLB 47

Tarkington, (Newton) Booth
   1869-1946 .... **TCLC 9**
   See also BPFB 3; BYA 3; CA 110; 143;
   CWRI 5; DLB 9, 102; MTCW 2; RGAL
   4; SATA 17

Tarkovskii, Andrei Arsen'evich
   See Tarkovsky, Andrei (Arsenyevich)

Tarkovsky, Andrei (Arsenyevich)
   1932-1986 .... **CLC 75**
   See also CA 127

Tartt, Donna 1964(?)- .... **CLC 76**
   See also CA 142

Tasso, Torquato 1544-1595 .... **LC 5**
   See also EFS 2; EW 2; RGWL 2, 3

Tate, (John Orley) Allen 1899-1979 .. **CLC 2,**
   4, 6, 9, 11, 14, 24; PC 50
   See also AMW; CA 5-8R; 85-88; CANR
   32, 108; DLB 4, 45, 63; DLBD 17; EWL
   3; MTCW 1, 2; RGAL 4; RHW

Tate, Ellalice
   See Hibbert, Eleanor Alice Burford

Tate, James (Vincent) 1943- ..... **CLC 2, 6, 25**
   See also CA 21-24R; CANR 29, 57, 114;
   CP 7; DLB 5, 169; EWL 3; PFS 10, 15;
   RGAL 4; WP

Tauler, Johannes c. 1300-1361 ...... **CMLC 37**
   See also DLB 179; LMFS 1

Tavel, Ronald 1940- .... **CLC 6**
   See also CA 21-24R; CAD; CANR 33; CD
   5

Taviani, Paolo 1931- .... **CLC 70**
   See also CA 153

Taylor, Bayard 1825-1878 .... **NCLC 89**
   See also DLB 3, 189, 250, 254; RGAL 4

Taylor, C(ecil) P(hilip) 1929-1981 .... **CLC 27**
   See also CA 25-28R; 105; CANR 47; CBD

Taylor, Edward 1642(?)-1729 .... **LC 11**
   See also AMW; DA; DAB; DAC; DAM
   MST, POET; DLB 24; EXPP; RGAL 4;
   TUS

Taylor, Eleanor Ross 1920- .... **CLC 5**
   See also CA 81-84; CANR 70

Taylor, Elizabeth 1932-1975 ..... **CLC 2, 4, 29**
   See also CA 13-16R; CANR 9, 70; DLB
   139; MTCW 1; RGEL 2; SATA 13

Taylor, Frederick Winslow
   1856-1915 .... **TCLC 76**
   See also CA 188

Taylor, Henry (Splawn) 1942- .... **CLC 44**
   See also CA 33-36R; CAAS 7; CANR 31;
   CP 7; DLB 5; PFS 10

Taylor, Kamala (Purnaiya) 1924-
   See Markandaya, Kamala
   See also CA 77-80; NFS 13

Taylor, Mildred D(elois) 1943- .... **CLC 21**
   See also AAYA 10, 47; BW 1; BYA 3, 8;
   CA 85-88; CANR 25, 115; CLR 9, 59,
   90; CSW; DLB 52; JRDA; LAIT 3; MAI-
   CYA 1, 2; SAAS 5; SATA 135; WYA;
   YAW

Taylor, Peter (Hillsman) 1917-1994 .. **CLC 1,**
   4, 18, 37, 44, 50, 71; SSC 10
   See also AMWS 5; BPFB 3; CA 13-16R;
   147; CANR 9, 50; CSW; DLB 218, 278;
   DLBY 1981, 1994; EWL 3; EXPS; INT
   CANR-9; MTCW 1, 2; RGSF 2; SSFS 9;
   TUS

Taylor, Robert Lewis 1912-1998 .... **CLC 14**
   See also CA 1-4R; 170; CANR 3, 64; SATA
   10

Tchekhov, Anton
   See Chekhov, Anton (Pavlovich)

Tchicaya, Gerald Felix 1931-1988 .. **CLC 101**
   See Tchicaya U Tam'si
   See also CA 129; 125; CANR 81

Tchicaya U Tam'si
   See Tchicaya, Gerald Felix
   See also EWL 3

Teasdale, Sara 1884-1933 .... **PC 31; TCLC 4**
   See also CA 104; 163; DLB 45; GLL 1;
   PFS 14; RGAL 4; SATA 32; TUS

Tecumseh 1768-1813 .... **NNAL**
   See also DAM MULT

Tegner, Esaias 1782-1846 .... **NCLC 2**

Teilhard de Chardin, (Marie Joseph) Pierre
   1881-1955 .... **TCLC 9**
   See also CA 105; 210; GFL 1789 to the
   Present

Temple, Ann
   See Mortimer, Penelope (Ruth)

Tennant, Emma (Christina) 1937- .. **CLC 13,**
   52
   See also CA 65-68; CAAS 9; CANR 10,
   38, 59, 88; CN 7; DLB 14; EWL 3; SFW
   4

Tenneshaw, S. M.
   See Silverberg, Robert

Tenney, Tabitha Gilman
   1762-1837 .... **NCLC 122**
   See also DLB 37, 200

Tennyson, Alfred 1809-1892 ... **NCLC 30, 65,**
   115; PC 6; WLC
   See also AAYA 50; BRW 4; CDBLB 1832-
   1890; DA; DA3; DAB; DAC; DAM MST,
   POET; DLB 32; EXPP; PAB; PFS 1, 2, 4,
   11, 15; RGEL 2; TEA; WLIT 4; WP

Teran, Lisa St. Aubin de .... **CLC 36**
   See St. Aubin de Teran, Lisa

Terence c. 184B.C.-c. 159B.C. ...... **CMLC 14;**
   DC 7
   See also AW 1; CDWLB 1; DLB 211;
   RGWL 2, 3; TWA

Teresa de Jesus, St. 1515-1582 .... **LC 18**

Terkel, Louis 1912-
   See Terkel, Studs
   See also CA 57-60; CANR 18, 45, 67; DA3;
   MTCW 1, 2

Terkel, Studs .... **CLC 38**
   See Terkel, Louis
   See also AAYA 32; AITN 1; MTCW 2; TUS

Terry, C. V.
   See Slaughter, Frank G(ill)

Terry, Megan 1932- .... **CLC 19; DC 13**
   See also CA 77-80; CABS 3; CAD; CANR
   43; CD 5; CWD; DLB 7, 249; GLL 2

Tertullian c. 155-c. 245 .... **CMLC 29**

Tertz, Abram
   See Sinyavsky, Andrei (Donatevich)
   See also CWW 2; RGSF 2

Tesich, Steve 1943(?)-1996 .... **CLC 40, 69**
   See also CA 105; 152; CAD; DLBY 1983

Tesla, Nikola 1856-1943 .... **TCLC 88**

Teternikov, Fyodor Kuzmich 1863-1927
   See Sologub, Fyodor
   See also CA 104

Tevis, Walter 1928-1984 .... **CLC 42**
   See also CA 113; SFW 4

Tey, Josephine .... **TCLC 14**
   See Mackintosh, Elizabeth
   See also DLB 77; MSW

Thackeray, William Makepeace
   1811-1863 .... **NCLC 5, 14, 22, 43; WLC**
   See also BRW 5; CDBLB 1832-1890; DA;
   DA3; DAB; DAC; DAM MST, NOV;
   DLB 21, 55, 159, 163; NFS 13; RGEL 2;
   SATA 23; TEA; WLIT 3

Thakura, Ravindranatha
   See Tagore, Rabindranath

Thames, C. H.
   See Marlowe, Stephen

Tharoor, Shashi 1956- .... **CLC 70**
   See also CA 141; CANR 91; CN 7

Thelwell, Michael Miles 1939- .... **CLC 22**
   See also BW 2; CA 101

Theobald, Lewis, Jr.
   See Lovecraft, H(oward) P(hillips)

Theocritus c. 310B.C.- .... **CMLC 45**
   See also AW 1; DLB 176; RGWL 2, 3

Theodorescu, Ion N. 1880-1967
   See Arghezi, Tudor
   See also CA 116

Theriault, Yves 1915-1983 .... **CLC 79**
   See also CA 102; CCA 1; DAC; DAM
   MST; DLB 88; EWL 3

Theroux, Alexander (Louis) 1939- .... **CLC 2,**
   25
   See also CA 85-88; CANR 20, 63; CN 7

Theroux, Paul (Edward) 1941- ..... **CLC 5, 8,**
   11, 15, 28, 46
   See also AAYA 28; AMWS 8; BEST 89:4;
   BPFB 3; CA 33-36R; CANR 20, 45, 74;
   CDALBS; CN 7; CPW 1; DA3; DAM
   POP; DLB 2, 218; EWL 3; HGG; MTCW
   1, 2; RGAL 4; SATA 44, 109; TUS

Thesen, Sharon 1946- .... **CLC 56**
   See also CA 163; CP 7; CWP

Thespis fl. 6th cent. B.C.- .... **CMLC 51**
   See also LMFS 1

Thevenin, Denis
   See Duhamel, Georges

Thibault, Jacques Anatole Francois
   1844-1924
   See France, Anatole
   See also CA 106; 127; DA3; DAM NOV;
   MTCW 1, 2; TWA

Toole, John Kennedy 1937-1969 ..... **CLC 19, 64**
   See also BPFB 3; CA 104; DLBY 1981; MTCW 2

Toomer, Eugene
   See Toomer, Jean

Toomer, Eugene Pinchback
   See Toomer, Jean

Toomer, Jean 1894-1967 .. **BLC 3; CLC 1, 4, 13, 22; HR 3; PC 7; SSC 1, 45; WLCS**
   See also AFAW 1, 2; AMWS 3, 9; BW 1; CA 85-88; CDALB 1917-1929; DA3; DAM MULT; DLB 45, 51; EWL 3; EXPP; EXPS; LMFS 2; MTCW 1, 2; NFS 11; RGAL 4; RGSF 2; SSFS 5

Toomer, Nathan Jean
   See Toomer, Jean

Toomer, Nathan Pinchback
   See Toomer, Jean

Torley, Luke
   See Blish, James (Benjamin)

Tornimparte, Alessandra
   See Ginzburg, Natalia

Torre, Raoul della
   See Mencken, H(enry) L(ouis)

Torrence, Ridgely 1874-1950 .... **TCLC 97**
   See also DLB 54, 249

Torrey, E(dwin) Fuller 1937- .... **CLC 34**
   See also CA 119; CANR 71

Torsvan, Ben Traven
   See Traven, B.

Torsvan, Benno Traven
   See Traven, B.

Torsvan, Berick Traven
   See Traven, B.

Torsvan, Berwick Traven
   See Traven, B.

Torsvan, Bruno Traven
   See Traven, B.

Torsvan, Traven
   See Traven, B.

Tourneur, Cyril 1575(?)-1626 .... **LC 66**
   See also BRW 2; DAM DRAM; DLB 58; RGEL 2

Tournier, Michel (Edouard) 1924- .... **CLC 6, 23, 36, 95**
   See also CA 49-52; CANR 3, 36, 74; DLB 83; EWL 3; GFL 1789 to the Present; MTCW 1, 2; SATA 23

Tournimparte, Alessandra
   See Ginzburg, Natalia

Towers, Ivar
   See Kornbluth, C(yril) M.

Towne, Robert (Burton) 1936(?)- ..... **CLC 87**
   See also CA 108; DLB 44; IDFW 3, 4

Townsend, Sue .... **CLC 61**
   See Townsend, Susan Lilian
   See also AAYA 28; CA 119; 127; CANR 65, 107; CBD; CD 5; CPW; CWD; DAB; DAC; DAM MST; DLB 271; INT 127; SATA 55, 93; SATA-Brief 48; YAW

Townsend, Susan Lilian 1946-
   See Townsend, Sue

Townshend, Pete
   See Townshend, Peter (Dennis Blandford)

Townshend, Peter (Dennis Blandford) 1945- .... **CLC 17, 42**
   See also CA 107

Tozzi, Federigo 1883-1920 .... **TCLC 31**
   See also CA 160; CANR 110; DLB 264; EWL 3

Tracy, Don(ald Fiske) 1905-1970(?)
   See Queen, Ellery
   See also CA 1-4R; 176; CANR 2

Trafford, F. G.
   See Riddell, Charlotte

Traill, Catharine Parr 1802-1899 .. **NCLC 31**
   See also DLB 99

Trakl, Georg 1887-1914 .... **PC 20; TCLC 5**
   See also CA 104; 165; EW 10; EWL 3; LMFS 2; MTCW 2; RGWL 2, 3

Tranquilli, Secondino
   See Silone, Ignazio

Transtroemer, Tomas Gosta
   See Transtromer, Tomas (Goesta)

Transtromer, Tomas
   See Transtromer, Tomas (Goesta)

Transtromer, Tomas (Goesta) 1931- .... **CLC 52, 65**
   See also CA 117; 129; CAAS 17; CANR 115; DAM POET; DLB 257; EWL 3

Transtromer, Tomas Gosta
   See Transtromer, Tomas (Goesta)

Traven, B. 1882(?)-1969 .... **CLC 8, 11**
   See also CA 19-20; 25-28R; CAP 2; DLB 9, 56; EWL 3; MTCW 1; RGAL 4

Trediakovsky, Vasilii Kirillovich 1703-1769 .... **LC 68**
   See also DLB 150

Treitel, Jonathan 1959- .... **CLC 70**
   See also CA 210; DLB 267

Trelawny, Edward John 1792-1881 .... **NCLC 85**
   See also DLB 110, 116, 144

Tremain, Rose 1943- .... **CLC 42**
   See also CA 97-100; CANR 44, 95; CN 7; DLB 14, 271; RGSF 2; RHW

Tremblay, Michel 1942- .... **CLC 29, 102**
   See also CA 116; 128; CCA 1; CWW 2; DAC; DAM MST; DLB 60; EWL 3; GLL 1; MTCW 1, 2

Trevanian .... **CLC 29**
   See Whitaker, Rod(ney)

Trevor, Glen
   See Hilton, James

Trevor, William .. **CLC 7, 9, 14, 25, 71, 116; SSC 21, 58**
   See Cox, William Trevor
   See also BRWS 4; CBD; CD 5; CN 7; DLB 14, 139; EWL 3; LATS 1; MTCW 2; RGEL 2; RGSF 2; SSFS 10

Trifonov, Iurii (Valentinovich)
   See Trifonov, Yuri (Valentinovich)
   See also RGWL 2, 3

Trifonov, Yuri (Valentinovich) 1925-1981 .... **CLC 45**
   See Trifonov, Iurii (Valentinovich); Trifonov, Yury Valentinovich
   See also CA 126; 103; MTCW 1

Trifonov, Yury Valentinovich
   See Trifonov, Yuri (Valentinovich)
   See also EWL 3

Trilling, Diana (Rubin) 1905-1996 . **CLC 129**
   See also CA 5-8R; 154; CANR 10, 46; INT CANR-10; MTCW 1, 2

Trilling, Lionel 1905-1975 .... **CLC 9, 11, 24**
   See also AMWS 3; CA 9-12R; 61-64; CANR 10, 105; DLB 28, 63; EWL 3; INT CANR-10; MTCW 1, 2; RGAL 4; TUS

Trimball, W. H.
   See Mencken, H(enry) L(ouis)

Tristan
   See Gomez de la Serna, Ramon

Tristram
   See Housman, A(lfred) E(dward)

Trogdon, William (Lewis) 1939-
   See Heat-Moon, William Least
   See also CA 115; 119; CANR 47, 89; CPW; INT CA-119

Trollope, Anthony 1815-1882 .... **NCLC 6, 33, 101; SSC 28; WLC**
   See also BRW 5; CDBLB 1832-1890; DA; DA3; DAB; DAC; DAM MST, NOV; DLB 21, 57, 159; RGEL 2; RGSF 2; SATA 22

Trollope, Frances 1779-1863 .... **NCLC 30**
   See also DLB 21, 166

Trotsky, Leon 1879-1940 .... **TCLC 22**
   See also CA 118; 167

Trotter (Cockburn), Catharine 1679-1749 .... **LC 8**
   See also DLB 84, 252

Trotter, Wilfred 1872-1939 .... **TCLC 97**

Trout, Kilgore
   See Farmer, Philip Jose

Trow, George W. S. 1943- .... **CLC 52**
   See also CA 126; CANR 91

Troyat, Henri 1911- .... **CLC 23**
   See also CA 45-48; CANR 2, 33, 67, 117; GFL 1789 to the Present; MTCW 1

Trudeau, G(arretson) B(eekman) 1948-
   See Trudeau, Garry B.
   See also CA 81-84; CANR 31; SATA 35

Trudeau, Garry B. .... **CLC 12**
   See Trudeau, G(arretson) B(eekman)
   See also AAYA 10; AITN 2

Truffaut, Francois 1932-1984 ... **CLC 20, 101**
   See also CA 81-84; 113; CANR 34

Trumbo, Dalton 1905-1976 .... **CLC 19**
   See also CA 21-24R; 69-72; CANR 10; DLB 26; IDFW 3, 4; YAW

Trumbull, John 1750-1831 .... **NCLC 30**
   See also DLB 31; RGAL 4

Trundlett, Helen B.
   See Eliot, T(homas) S(tearns)

Truth, Sojourner 1797(?)-1883 ...... **NCLC 94**
   See also DLB 239; FW; LAIT 2

Tryon, Thomas 1926-1991 .... **CLC 3, 11**
   See also AITN 1; BPFB 3; CA 29-32R; 135; CANR 32, 77; CPW; DA3; DAM POP; HGG; MTCW 1

Tryon, Tom
   See Tryon, Thomas

Ts'ao Hsueh-ch'in 1715(?)-1763 .... **LC 1**

Tsushima, Shuji 1909-1948
   See Dazai Osamu
   See also CA 107

Tsvetaeva (Efron), Marina (Ivanovna) 1892-1941 .... **PC 14; TCLC 7, 35**
   See also CA 104; 128; CANR 73; EW 11; MTCW 1, 2; RGWL 2, 3

Tuck, Lily 1938- .... **CLC 70**
   See also CA 139; CANR 90

Tu Fu 712-770 .... **PC 9**
   See Du Fu
   See also DAM MULT; TWA; WP

Tunis, John R(oberts) 1889-1975 ..... **CLC 12**
   See also BYA 1; CA 61-64; CANR 62; DLB 22, 171; JRDA; MAICYA 1, 2; SATA 37; SATA-Brief 30; YAW

Tuohy, Frank .... **CLC 37**
   See Tuohy, John Francis
   See also DLB 14, 139

Tuohy, John Francis 1925-
   See Tuohy, Frank
   See also CA 5-8R; 178; CANR 3, 47; CN 7

Turco, Lewis (Putnam) 1934- ..... **CLC 11, 63**
   See also CA 13-16R; CAAS 22; CANR 24, 51; CP 7; DLBY 1984

Turgenev, Ivan (Sergeevich) 1818-1883 ..... **DC 7; NCLC 21, 37, 122; SSC 7, 57; WLC**
   See also DA; DAB; DAC; DAM MST, NOV; DFS 6; DLB 238, 284; EW 6; LATS 1; NFS 16; RGSF 2; RGWL 2, 3; TWA

Turgot, Anne-Robert-Jacques 1727-1781 .... **LC 26**

Turner, Frederick 1943- .... **CLC 48**
   See also CA 73-76; CAAS 10; CANR 12, 30, 56; DLB 40, 282

Turton, James
   See Crace, Jim

Tutu, Desmond M(pilo) 1931- .. **BLC 3; CLC 80**
See also BW 1, 3; CA 125; CANR 67, 81; DAM MULT

Tutuola, Amos 1920-1997 ..... **BLC 3; CLC 5, 14, 29**
See also AFW; BW 2, 3; CA 9-12R; 159; CANR 27, 66; CDWLB 3; CN 7; DA3; DAM MULT; DLB 125; DNFS 2; EWL 3; MTCW 1, 2; RGEL 2; WLIT 2

Twain, Mark .. **SSC 34; TCLC 6, 12, 19, 36, 48, 59; WLC**
See Clemens, Samuel Langhorne
See also AAYA 20; AMW; AMWC 1; BPFB 3; BYA 2, 3, 11, 14; CLR 58, 60, 66; DLB 11; EXPN; EXPS; FANT; LAIT 2; NFS 1, 6; RGAL 4; RGSF 2; SFW 4; SSFS 1, 7; SUFW; TUS; WCH; WYA; YAW

Tyler, Anne 1941- . **CLC 7, 11, 18, 28, 44, 59, 103**
See also AAYA 18; AMWS 4; BEST 89:1; BPFB 3; BYA 12; CA 9-12R; CANR 11, 33, 53, 109; CDALBS; CN 7; CPW; CSW; DAM NOV, POP; DLB 6, 143; DLBY 1982; EWL 3; EXPN; LATS 1; MAWW; MTCW 1, 2; NFS 2, 7, 10; RGAL 4; SATA 7, 90; SSFS 17; TUS; YAW

Tyler, Royall 1757-1826 .... **NCLC 3**
See also DLB 37; RGAL 4

Tynan, Katharine 1861-1931 .... **TCLC 3**
See also CA 104; 167; DLB 153, 240; FW

Tyutchev, Fyodor 1803-1873 .... **NCLC 34**

Tzara, Tristan 1896-1963 ..... **CLC 47; PC 27**
See also CA 153; 89-92; DAM POET; EWL 3; MTCW 2

Uchida, Yoshiko 1921-1992 .... **AAL**
See also AAYA 16; BYA 2, 3; CA 13-16R; 139; CANR 6, 22, 47, 61; CDALBS; CLR 6, 56; CWRI 5; JRDA; MAICYA 1, 2; MTCW 1, 2; SAAS 1; SATA 1, 53; SATA-Obit 72

Udall, Nicholas 1504-1556 .... **LC 84**
See also DLB 62; RGEL 2

Uhry, Alfred 1936- .... **CLC 55**
See also CA 127; 133; CAD; CANR 112; CD 5; CSW; DA3; DAM DRAM, POP; DFS 11, 15; INT CA-133

Ulf, Haerved
See Strindberg, (Johan) August

Ulf, Harved
See Strindberg, (Johan) August

Ulibarri, Sabine R(eyes) 1919- .... **CLC 83; HLCS 2**
See also CA 131; CANR 81; DAM MULT; DLB 82; HW 1, 2; RGSF 2

Unamuno (y Jugo), Miguel de 1864-1936 . **HLC 2; SSC 11; TCLC 2, 9**
See also CA 104; 131; CANR 81; DAM MULT, NOV; DLB 108; EW 8; EWL 3; HW 1, 2; MTCW 1, 2; RGSF 2; RGWL 2, 3; TWA

Uncle Shelby
See Silverstein, Shel(don Allan)

Undercliffe, Errol
See Campbell, (John) Ramsey

Underwood, Miles
See Glassco, John

Undset, Sigrid 1882-1949 ..... **TCLC 3; WLC**
See also CA 104; 129; DA; DA3; DAB; DAC; DAM MST, NOV; EW 9; EWL 3; FW; MTCW 1, 2; RGWL 2, 3

Ungaretti, Giuseppe 1888-1970 ... **CLC 7, 11, 15**
See also CA 19-20; 25-28R; CAP 2; DLB 114; EW 10; EWL 3; RGWL 2, 3

Unger, Douglas 1952- .... **CLC 34**
See also CA 130; CANR 94

Unsworth, Barry (Forster) 1930- .... **CLC 76, 127**
See also BRWS 7; CA 25-28R; CANR 30, 54; CN 7; DLB 194

Updike, John (Hoyer) 1932- . **CLC 1, 2, 3, 5, 7, 9, 13, 15, 23, 34, 43, 70, 139; SSC 13, 27; WLC**
See also AAYA 36; AMW; AMWC 1; AMWR 1; BPFB 3; BYA 12; CA 1-4R; CABS 1; CANR 4, 33, 51, 94; CDALB 1968-1988; CN 7; CP 7; CPW 1; DA; DA3; DAB; DAC; DAM MST, NOV, POET, POP; DLB 2, 5, 143, 218, 227; DLBD 3; DLBY 1980, 1982, 1997; EWL 3; EXPP; HGG; MTCW 1, 2; NFS 12; RGAL 4; RGSF 2; SSFS 3; TUS

Upshaw, Margaret Mitchell
See Mitchell, Margaret (Munnerlyn)

Upton, Mark
See Sanders, Lawrence

Upward, Allen 1863-1926 .... **TCLC 85**
See also CA 117; 187; DLB 36

Urdang, Constance (Henriette) 1922-1996 .... **CLC 47**
See also CA 21-24R; CANR 9, 24; CP 7; CWP

Uriel, Henry
See Faust, Frederick (Schiller)

Uris, Leon (Marcus) 1924-2003 ... **CLC 7, 32**
See also AITN 1, 2; BEST 89:2; BPFB 3; CA 1-4R; CANR 1, 40, 65; CN 7; CPW 1; DA3; DAM NOV, POP; MTCW 1, 2; SATA 49

Urista, Alberto H. 1947- ...... **HLCS 1; PC 34**
See Alurista
See also CA 45-48, 182; CANR 2, 32; HW 1

Urmuz
See Codrescu, Andrei

Urquhart, Guy
See McAlmon, Robert (Menzies)

Urquhart, Jane 1949- .... **CLC 90**
See also CA 113; CANR 32, 68, 116; CCA 1; DAC

Usigli, Rodolfo 1905-1979 .... **HLCS 1**
See also CA 131; EWL 3; HW 1; LAW

Ustinov, Peter (Alexander) 1921- .... **CLC 1**
See also AITN 1; CA 13-16R; CANR 25, 51; CBD; CD 5; DLB 13; MTCW 2

U Tam'si, Gerald Felix Tchicaya
See Tchicaya, Gerald Felix

U Tam'si, Tchicaya
See Tchicaya, Gerald Felix

Vachss, Andrew (Henry) 1942- .... **CLC 106**
See also CA 118; CANR 44, 95; CMW 4

Vachss, Andrew H.
See Vachss, Andrew (Henry)

Vaculik, Ludvik 1926- .... **CLC 7**
See also CA 53-56; CANR 72; CWW 2; DLB 232; EWL 3

Vaihinger, Hans 1852-1933 .... **TCLC 71**
See also CA 116; 166

Valdez, Luis (Miguel) 1940- ..... **CLC 84; DC 10; HLC 2**
See also CA 101; CAD; CANR 32, 81; CD 5; DAM MULT; DFS 5; DLB 122; EWL 3; HW 1; LAIT 4

Valenzuela, Luisa 1938- .... **CLC 31, 104; HLCS 2; SSC 14**
See also CA 101; CANR 32, 65; CDWLB 3; CWW 2; DAM MULT; DLB 113; EWL 3; FW; HW 1, 2; LAW; RGSF 2; RGWL 3

Valera y Alcala-Galiano, Juan 1824-1905 .... **TCLC 10**
See also CA 106

Valery, (Ambroise) Paul (Toussaint Jules) 1871-1945 .... **PC 9; TCLC 4, 15**
See also CA 104; 122; DA3; DAM POET; DLB 258; EW 8; EWL 3; GFL 1789 to the Present; MTCW 1, 2; RGWL 2, 3; TWA

Valle-Inclan, Ramon (Maria) del 1866-1936 .... **HLC 2; TCLC 5**
See also CA 106; 153; CANR 80; DAM MULT; DLB 134; EW 8; EWL 3; HW 2; RGSF 2; RGWL 2, 3

Vallejo, Antonio Buero
See Buero Vallejo, Antonio

Vallejo, Cesar (Abraham) 1892-1938 .... **HLC 2; TCLC 3, 56**
See also CA 105; 153; DAM MULT; EWL 3; HW 1; LAW; RGWL 2, 3

Valles, Jules 1832-1885 .... **NCLC 71**
See also DLB 123; GFL 1789 to the Present

Vallette, Marguerite Eymery 1860-1953 .... **TCLC 67**
See Rachilde
See also CA 182; DLB 123, 192

Valle Y Pena, Ramon del
See Valle-Inclan, Ramon (Maria) del

Van Ash, Cay 1918- .... **CLC 34**

Vanbrugh, Sir John 1664-1726 .... **LC 21**
See also BRW 2; DAM DRAM; DLB 80; IDTP; RGEL 2

Van Campen, Karl
See Campbell, John W(ood, Jr.)

Vance, Gerald
See Silverberg, Robert

Vance, Jack .... **CLC 35**
See Vance, John Holbrook
See also DLB 8; FANT; SCFW 2; SFW 4; SUFW 1, 2

Vance, John Holbrook 1916-
See Queen, Ellery; Vance, Jack
See also CA 29-32R; CANR 17, 65; CMW 4; MTCW 1

Van Den Bogarde, Derek Jules Gaspard Ulric Niven 1921-1999 .... **CLC 14**
See Bogarde, Dirk
See also CA 77-80; 179

Vandenburgh, Jane .... **CLC 59**
See also CA 168

Vanderhaeghe, Guy 1951- .... **CLC 41**
See also BPFB 3; CA 113; CANR 72

van der Post, Laurens (Jan) 1906-1996 .... **CLC 5**
See also AFW; CA 5-8R; 155; CANR 35; CN 7; DLB 204; RGEL 2

van de Wetering, Janwillem 1931- ... **CLC 47**
See also CA 49-52; CANR 4, 62, 90; CMW 4

Van Dine, S. S. .... **TCLC 23**
See Wright, Willard Huntington
See also MSW

Van Doren, Carl (Clinton) 1885-1950 .... **TCLC 18**
See also CA 111; 168

Van Doren, Mark 1894-1972 .... **CLC 6, 10**
See also CA 1-4R; 37-40R; CANR 3; DLB 45, 284; MTCW 1, 2; RGAL 4

Van Druten, John (William) 1901-1957 .... **TCLC 2**
See also CA 104; 161; DLB 10; RGAL 4

Van Duyn, Mona (Jane) 1921- ...... **CLC 3, 7, 63, 116**
See also CA 9-12R; CANR 7, 38, 60, 116; CP 7; CWP; DAM POET; DLB 5

Van Dyne, Edith
See Baum, L(yman) Frank

van Itallie, Jean-Claude 1936- .... **CLC 3**
See also CA 45-48; CAAS 2; CAD; CANR 1, 48; CD 5; DLB 7

Van Loot, Cornelius Obenchain
See Roberts, Kenneth (Lewis)

van Ostaijen, Paul 1896-1928 .... **TCLC 33**
See also CA 163

Van Peebles, Melvin 1932- .... **CLC 2, 20**
See also BW 2, 3; CA 85-88; CANR 27, 67, 82; DAM MULT

van Schendel, Arthur(-Francois-Emile) 1874-1946 .... **TCLC 56**
See also EWL 3

Vansittart, Peter 1920- .... **CLC 42**
See also CA 1-4R; CANR 3, 49, 90; CN 7; RHW

Van Vechten, Carl 1880-1964 ... **CLC 33; HR 3**
See also AMWS 2; CA 183; 89-92; DLB 4, 9, 51; RGAL 4

van Vogt, A(lfred) E(lton) 1912-2000 . **CLC 1**
See also BPFB 3; BYA 13, 14; CA 21-24R; 190; CANR 28; DLB 8, 251; SATA 14; SATA-Obit 124; SCFW; SFW 4

Vara, Madeleine
See Jackson, Laura (Riding)

Varda, Agnes 1928- .... **CLC 16**
See also CA 116; 122

Vargas Llosa, (Jorge) Mario (Pedro) 1939- .... **CLC 3, 6, 9, 10, 15, 31, 42, 85; HLC 2**
See Llosa, (Jorge) Mario (Pedro) Vargas
See also BPFB 3; CA 73-76; CANR 18, 32, 42, 67, 116; CDWLB 3; DA; DA3; DAB; DAC; DAM MST, MULT, NOV; DLB 145; DNFS 2; EWL 3; HW 1, 2; LAIT 5; LATS 1; LAW; LAWS 1; MTCW 1, 2; RGWL 2; SSFS 14; TWA; WLIT 1

Vasiliu, George
See Bacovia, George

Vasiliu, Gheorghe
See Bacovia, George
See also CA 123; 189

Vassa, Gustavus
See Equiano, Olaudah

Vassilikos, Vassilis 1933- .... **CLC 4, 8**
See also CA 81-84; CANR 75; EWL 3

Vaughan, Henry 1621-1695 .... **LC 27**
See also BRW 2; DLB 131; PAB; RGEL 2

Vaughn, Stephanie .... **CLC 62**

Vazov, Ivan (Minchov) 1850-1921 . **TCLC 25**
See also CA 121; 167; CDWLB 4; DLB 147

Veblen, Thorstein B(unde) 1857-1929 .... **TCLC 31**
See also AMWS 1; CA 115; 165; DLB 246

Vega, Lope de 1562-1635 .... **HLCS 2; LC 23**
See also EW 2; RGWL 2, 3

Vendler, Helen (Hennessy) 1933- ... **CLC 138**
See also CA 41-44R; CANR 25, 72; MTCW 1, 2

Venison, Alfred
See Pound, Ezra (Weston Loomis)

Verdi, Marie de
See Mencken, H(enry) L(ouis)

Verdu, Matilde
See Cela, Camilo Jose

Verga, Giovanni (Carmelo) 1840-1922 .... **SSC 21; TCLC 3**
See also CA 104; 123; CANR 101; EW 7; EWL 3; RGSF 2; RGWL 2, 3

Vergil 70B.C.-19B.C. ... **CMLC 9, 40; PC 12; WLCS**
See Virgil
See also AW 2; DA; DA3; DAB; DAC; DAM MST, POET; EFS 1; LMFS 1

Verhaeren, Emile (Adolphe Gustave) 1855-1916 .... **TCLC 12**
See also CA 109; EWL 3; GFL 1789 to the Present

Verlaine, Paul (Marie) 1844-1896 .. **NCLC 2, 51; PC 2, 32**
See also DAM POET; DLB 217; EW 7; GFL 1789 to the Present; LMFS 2; RGWL 2, 3; TWA

Verne, Jules (Gabriel) 1828-1905 ... **TCLC 6, 52**
See also AAYA 16; BYA 4; CA 110; 131; CLR 88; DA3; DLB 123; GFL 1789 to the Present; JRDA; LAIT 2; LMFS 2; MAICYA 1, 2; RGWL 2, 3; SATA 21; SCFW; SFW 4; TWA; WCH

Verus, Marcus Annius
See Aurelius, Marcus

Very, Jones 1813-1880 .... **NCLC 9**
See also DLB 1, 243; RGAL 4

Vesaas, Tarjei 1897-1970 .... **CLC 48**
See also CA 190; 29-32R; EW 11; EWL 3; RGWL 3

Vialis, Gaston
See Simenon, Georges (Jacques Christian)

Vian, Boris 1920-1959(?) .... **TCLC 9**
See also CA 106; 164; CANR 111; DLB 72; EWL 3; GFL 1789 to the Present; MTCW 2; RGWL 2, 3

Viaud, (Louis Marie) Julien 1850-1923
See Loti, Pierre
See also CA 107

Vicar, Henry
See Felsen, Henry Gregor

Vicker, Angus
See Felsen, Henry Gregor

Vidal, Gore 1925- ...... **CLC 2, 4, 6, 8, 10, 22, 33, 72, 142**
See Box, Edgar
See also AITN 1; AMWS 4; BEST 90:2; BPFB 3; CA 5-8R; CAD; CANR 13, 45, 65, 100; CD 5; CDALBS; CN 7; CPW; DA3; DAM NOV, POP; DFS 2; DLB 6, 152; EWL 3; INT CANR-13; MTCW 1, 2; RGAL 4; RHW; TUS

Viereck, Peter (Robert Edwin) 1916- .... **CLC 4; PC 27**
See also CA 1-4R; CANR 1, 47; CP 7; DLB 5; PFS 9, 14

Vigny, Alfred (Victor) de 1797-1863 .... **NCLC 7, 102; PC 26**
See also DAM POET; DLB 119, 192, 217; EW 5; GFL 1789 to the Present; RGWL 2, 3

Vilakazi, Benedict Wallet 1906-1947 .... **TCLC 37**
See also CA 168

Villa, Jose Garcia 1914-1997 .... **AAL; PC 22**
See also CA 25-28R; CANR 12, 118; EWL 3; EXPP

Villa, Jose Garcia 1914-1997
See Villa, Jose Garcia

Villarreal, Jose Antonio 1924- .... **HLC 2**
See also CA 133; CANR 93; DAM MULT; DLB 82; HW 1; LAIT 4; RGAL 4

Villaurrutia, Xavier 1903-1950 ...... **TCLC 80**
See also CA 192; EWL 3; HW 1; LAW

Villaverde, Cirilo 1812-1894 .... **NCLC 121**
See also LAW

Villehardouin, Geoffroi de 1150(?)-1218(?) .... **CMLC 38**

Villiers de l'Isle Adam, Jean Marie Mathias Philippe Auguste 1838-1889 ... **NCLC 3; SSC 14**
See also DLB 123, 192; GFL 1789 to the Present; RGSF 2

Villon, Francois 1431-1463(?) . **LC 62; PC 13**
See also DLB 208; EW 2; RGWL 2, 3; TWA

Vine, Barbara .... **CLC 50**
See Rendell, Ruth (Barbara)
See also BEST 90:4

Vinge, Joan (Carol) D(ennison) 1948- .... **CLC 30; SSC 24**
See also AAYA 32; BPFB 3; CA 93-96; CANR 72; SATA 36, 113; SFW 4; YAW

Viola, Herman J(oseph) 1938- .... **CLC 70**
See also CA 61-64; CANR 8, 23, 48, 91; SATA 126

Violis, G.
See Simenon, Georges (Jacques Christian)

Viramontes, Helena Maria 1954- .... **HLCS 2**
See also CA 159; DLB 122; HW 2

Virgil
See Vergil
See also CDWLB 1; DLB 211; LAIT 1; RGWL 2, 3; WP

Visconti, Luchino 1906-1976 .... **CLC 16**
See also CA 81-84; 65-68; CANR 39

Vittorini, Elio 1908-1966 .... **CLC 6, 9, 14**
See also CA 133; 25-28R; DLB 264; EW 12; EWL 3; RGWL 2, 3

Vivekananda, Swami 1863-1902 .... **TCLC 88**

Vizenor, Gerald Robert 1934- .... **CLC 103; NNAL**
See also CA 13-16R; CAAE 205; CAAS 22; CANR 5, 21, 44, 67; DAM MULT; DLB 175, 227; MTCW 2; TCWW 2

Vizinczey, Stephen 1933- .... **CLC 40**
See also CA 128; CCA 1; INT 128

Vliet, R(ussell) G(ordon) 1929-1984 .... **CLC 22**
See also CA 37-40R; 112; CANR 18

Vogau, Boris Andreyevich 1894-1937(?)
See Pilnyak, Boris
See also CA 123

Vogel, Paula A(nne) 1951- ... **CLC 76; DC 19**
See also CA 108; CAD; CANR 119; CD 5; CWD; DFS 14; RGAL 4

Voigt, Cynthia 1942- .... **CLC 30**
See also AAYA 3, 30; BYA 1, 3, 6, 7, 8; CA 106; CANR 18, 37, 40, 94; CLR 13, 48; INT CANR-18; JRDA; LAIT 5; MAICYA 1, 2; MAICYAS 1; SATA 48, 79, 116; SATA-Brief 33; WYA; YAW

Voigt, Ellen Bryant 1943- .... **CLC 54**
See also CA 69-72; CANR 11, 29, 55, 115; CP 7; CSW; CWP; DLB 120

Voinovich, Vladimir (Nikolaevich) 1932- .... **CLC 10, 49, 147**
See also CA 81-84; CAAS 12; CANR 33, 67; MTCW 1

Vollmann, William T. 1959- .... **CLC 89**
See also CA 134; CANR 67, 116; CPW; DA3; DAM NOV, POP; MTCW 2

Voloshinov, V. N.
See Bakhtin, Mikhail Mikhailovich

Voltaire 1694-1778 .... **LC 14, 79; SSC 12; WLC**
See also BYA 13; DA; DA3; DAB; DAC; DAM DRAM, MST; EW 4; GFL Beginnings to 1789; LATS 1; LMFS 1; NFS 7; RGWL 2, 3; TWA

von Aschendrof, Baron Ignatz
See Ford, Ford Madox

von Chamisso, Adelbert
See Chamisso, Adelbert von

von Daeniken, Erich 1935- .... **CLC 30**
See also AITN 1; CA 37-40R; CANR 17, 44

von Daniken, Erich
See von Daeniken, Erich

von Hartmann, Eduard 1842-1906 .... **TCLC 96**

von Hayek, Friedrich August
See Hayek, F(riedrich) A(ugust von)

von Heidenstam, (Carl Gustaf) Verner
See Heidenstam, (Carl Gustaf) Verner von

von Heyse, Paul (Johann Ludwig)
See Heyse, Paul (Johann Ludwig von)

Warner, Marina 1946- .... **CLC 59**
See also CA 65-68; CANR 21, 55, 118; CN 7; DLB 194

Warner, Rex (Ernest) 1905-1986 ...... **CLC 45**
See also CA 89-92; 119; DLB 15; RGEL 2; RHW

Warner, Susan (Bogert)
1819-1885 .... **NCLC 31**
See also DLB 3, 42, 239, 250, 254

Warner, Sylvia (Constance) Ashton
See Ashton-Warner, Sylvia (Constance)

Warner, Sylvia Townsend
1893-1978 .. **CLC 7, 19; SSC 23; TCLC 131**
See also BRWS 7; CA 61-64; 77-80; CANR 16, 60, 104; DLB 34, 139; EWL 3; FANT; FW; MTCW 1, 2; RGEL 2; RGSF 2; RHW

Warren, Mercy Otis 1728-1814 ..... **NCLC 13**
See also DLB 31, 200; RGAL 4; TUS

Warren, Robert Penn 1905-1989 .. **CLC 1, 4, 6, 8, 10, 13, 18, 39, 53, 59; PC 37; SSC 4, 58; WLC**
See also AITN 1; AMW; BPFB 3; BYA 1; CA 13-16R; 129; CANR 10, 47; CDALB 1968-1988; DA; DA3; DAB; DAC; DAM MST, NOV, POET; DLB 2, 48, 152; DLBY 1980, 1989; EWL 3; INT CANR-10; MTCW 1, 2; NFS 13; RGAL 4; RGSF 2; RHW; SATA 46; SATA-Obit 63; SSFS 8; TUS

Warrigal, Jack
See Furphy, Joseph

Warshofsky, Isaac
See Singer, Isaac Bashevis

Warton, Joseph 1722-1800 .... **NCLC 118**
See also DLB 104, 109; RGEL 2

Warton, Thomas 1728-1790 .... **LC 15, 82**
See also DAM POET; DLB 104, 109; RGEL 2

Waruk, Kona
See Harris, (Theodore) Wilson

Warung, Price .... **TCLC 45**
See Astley, William
See also DLB 230; RGEL 2

Warwick, Jarvis
See Garner, Hugh
See also CCA 1

Washington, Alex
See Harris, Mark

Washington, Booker T(aliaferro)
1856-1915 .... **BLC 3; TCLC 10**
See also BW 1; CA 114; 125; DA3; DAM MULT; LAIT 2; RGAL 4; SATA 28

Washington, George 1732-1799 .... **LC 25**
See also DLB 31

Wassermann, (Karl) Jakob
1873-1934 .... **TCLC 6**
See also CA 104; 163; DLB 66; EWL 3

Wasserstein, Wendy 1950- .. **CLC 32, 59, 90; DC 4**
See also CA 121; 129; CABS 3; CAD; CANR 53, 75; CD 5; CWD; DA3; DAM DRAM; DFS 17; DLB 228; EWL 3; FW; INT CA-129; MTCW 2; SATA 94

Waterhouse, Keith (Spencer) 1929- . **CLC 47**
See also CA 5-8R; CANR 38, 67, 109; CBD; CN 7; DLB 13, 15; MTCW 1, 2

Waters, Frank (Joseph) 1902-1995 .. **CLC 88**
See also CA 5-8R; 149; CAAS 13; CANR 3, 18, 63; DLB 212; DLBY 1986; RGAL 4; TCWW 2

Waters, Mary C. .... **CLC 70**

Waters, Roger 1944- .... **CLC 35**

Watkins, Frances Ellen
See Harper, Frances Ellen Watkins

Watkins, Gerrold
See Malzberg, Barry N(athaniel)

Watkins, Gloria Jean 1952(?)-
See hooks, bell
See also BW 2; CA 143; CANR 87; MTCW 2; SATA 115

Watkins, Paul 1964- .... **CLC 55**
See also CA 132; CANR 62, 98

Watkins, Vernon Phillips
1906-1967 .... **CLC 43**
See also CA 9-10; 25-28R; CAP 1; DLB 20; EWL 3; RGEL 2

Watson, Irving S.
See Mencken, H(enry) L(ouis)

Watson, John H.
See Farmer, Philip Jose

Watson, Richard F.
See Silverberg, Robert

Watts, Ephraim
See Horne, Richard Henry Hengist

Waugh, Auberon (Alexander)
1939-2001 .... **CLC 7**
See also CA 45-48; 192; CANR 6, 22, 92; DLB 14, 194

Waugh, Evelyn (Arthur St. John)
1903-1966 .. **CLC 1, 3, 8, 13, 19, 27, 44, 107; SSC 41; WLC**
See also BPFB 3; BRW 7; CA 85-88; 25-28R; CANR 22; CDBLB 1914-1945; DA; DA3; DAB; DAC; DAM MST, NOV, POP; DLB 15, 162, 195; EWL 3; MTCW 1, 2; NFS 17; RGEL 2; RGSF 2; TEA; WLIT 4

Waugh, Harriet 1944- .... **CLC 6**
See also CA 85-88; CANR 22

Ways, C. R.
See Blount, Roy (Alton), Jr.

Waystaff, Simon
See Swift, Jonathan

Webb, Beatrice (Martha Potter)
1858-1943 .... **TCLC 22**
See also CA 117; 162; DLB 190; FW

Webb, Charles (Richard) 1939- .... **CLC 7**
See also CA 25-28R; CANR 114

Webb, James H(enry), Jr. 1946- ...... **CLC 22**
See also CA 81-84

Webb, Mary Gladys (Meredith)
1881-1927 .... **TCLC 24**
See also CA 182; 123; DLB 34; FW

Webb, Mrs. Sidney
See Webb, Beatrice (Martha Potter)

Webb, Phyllis 1927- .... **CLC 18**
See also CA 104; CANR 23; CCA 1; CP 7; CWP; DLB 53

Webb, Sidney (James) 1859-1947 .. **TCLC 22**
See also CA 117; 163; DLB 190

Webber, Andrew Lloyd .... **CLC 21**
See Lloyd Webber, Andrew
See also DFS 7

Weber, Lenora Mattingly
1895-1971 .... **CLC 12**
See also CA 19-20; 29-32R; CAP 1; SATA 2; SATA-Obit 26

Weber, Max 1864-1920 .... **TCLC 69**
See also CA 109; 189

Webster, John 1580(?)-1634(?) ...... **DC 2; LC 33, 84; WLC**
See also BRW 2; CDBLB Before 1660; DA; DAB; DAC; DAM DRAM, MST; DFS 17; DLB 58; IDTP; RGEL 2; WLIT 3

Webster, Noah 1758-1843 .... **NCLC 30**
See also DLB 1, 37, 42, 43, 73, 243

Wedekind, (Benjamin) Frank(lin)
1864-1918 .... **TCLC 7**
See also CA 104; 153; CDWLB 2; DAM DRAM; DLB 118; EW 8; EWL 3; LMFS 2; RGWL 2, 3

Wehr, Demaris .... **CLC 65**

Weidman, Jerome 1913-1998 .... **CLC 7**
See also AITN 2; CA 1-4R; 171; CAD; CANR 1; DLB 28

Weil, Simone (Adolphine)
1909-1943 .... **TCLC 23**
See also CA 117; 159; EW 12; EWL 3; FW; GFL 1789 to the Present; MTCW 2

Weininger, Otto 1880-1903 .... **TCLC 84**

Weinstein, Nathan
See West, Nathanael

Weinstein, Nathan von Wallenstein
See West, Nathanael

Weir, Peter (Lindsay) 1944- .... **CLC 20**
See also CA 113; 123

Weiss, Peter (Ulrich) 1916-1982 .. **CLC 3, 15, 51**
See also CA 45-48; 106; CANR 3; DAM DRAM; DFS 3; DLB 69, 124; EWL 3; RGWL 2, 3

Weiss, Theodore (Russell) 1916- ... **CLC 3, 8, 14**
See also CA 9-12R; CAAE 189; CAAS 2; CANR 46, 94; CP 7; DLB 5

Welch, (Maurice) Denton
1915-1948 .... **TCLC 22**
See also BRWS 8; CA 121; 148; RGEL 2

Welch, James 1940- ... **CLC 6, 14, 52; NNAL**
See also CA 85-88; CANR 42, 66, 107; CN 7; CP 7; CPW; DAM MULT, POP; DLB 175, 256; LATS 1; RGAL 4; TCWW 2

Weldon, Fay 1931- . **CLC 6, 9, 11, 19, 36, 59, 122**
See also BRWS 4; CA 21-24R; CANR 16, 46, 63, 97; CDBLB 1960 to Present; CN 7; CPW; DAM POP; DLB 14, 194; EWL 3; FW; HGG; INT CANR-16; MTCW 1, 2; RGEL 2; RGSF 2

Wellek, Rene 1903-1995 .... **CLC 28**
See also CA 5-8R; 150; CAAS 7; CANR 8; DLB 63; EWL 3; INT CANR-8

Weller, Michael 1942- .... **CLC 10, 53**
See also CA 85-88; CAD; CD 5

Weller, Paul 1958- .... **CLC 26**

Wellershoff, Dieter 1925- .... **CLC 46**
See also CA 89-92; CANR 16, 37

Welles, (George) Orson 1915-1985 .. **CLC 20, 80**
See also AAYA 40; CA 93-96; 117

Wellman, John McDowell 1945-
See Wellman, Mac
See also CA 166; CD 5

Wellman, Mac .... **CLC 65**
See Wellman, John McDowell; Wellman, John McDowell
See also CAD; RGAL 4

Wellman, Manly Wade 1903-1986 ... **CLC 49**
See also CA 1-4R; 118; CANR 6, 16, 44; FANT; SATA 6; SATA-Obit 47; SFW 4; SUFW

Wells, Carolyn 1869(?)-1942 .... **TCLC 35**
See also CA 113; 185; CMW 4; DLB 11

Wells, H(erbert) G(eorge)
1866-1946 .... **SSC 6; TCLC 6, 12, 19, 133; WLC**
See also AAYA 18; BPFB 3; BRW 6; CA 110; 121; CDBLB 1914-1945; CLR 64; DA; DA3; DAB; DAC; DAM MST, NOV; DLB 34, 70, 156, 178; EWL 3; EXPS; HGG; LAIT 3; LMFS 2; MTCW 1, 2; NFS 17; RGEL 2; RGSF 2; SATA 20; SCFW; SFW 4; SSFS 3; SUFW; TEA; WCH; WLIT 4; YAW

Wells, Rosemary 1943- .... **CLC 12**
See also AAYA 13; BYA 7, 8; CA 85-88; CANR 48, 120; CLR 16, 69; CWRI 5; MAICYA 1, 2; SAAS 1; SATA 18, 69, 114; YAW

Wells-Barnett, Ida B(ell)
1862-1931 .... **TCLC 125**
See also CA 182; DLB 23, 221

Welsh, Irvine 1958- .... **CLC 144**
See also CA 173; DLB 271

Wright, Richard (Nathaniel) 1908-1960 ... **BLC 3; CLC 1, 3, 4, 9, 14, 21, 48, 74; SSC 2; TCLC 136; WLC**
See also AAYA 5, 42; AFAW 1, 2; AMW; BPFB 3; BW 1; BYA 2; CA 108; CANR 64; CDALB 1929-1941; DA; DA3; DAB; DAC; DAM MST, MULT, NOV; DLB 76, 102; DLBD 2; EWL 3; EXPN; LAIT 3, 4; MTCW 1, 2; NCFS 1; NFS 1, 7; RGAL 4; RGSF 2; SSFS 3, 9, 15; TUS; YAW

Wright, Richard B(ruce) 1937- .... **CLC 6**
See also CA 85-88; CANR 120; DLB 53

Wright, Rick 1945- .... **CLC 35**

Wright, Rowland
See Wells, Carolyn

Wright, Stephen 1946- .... **CLC 33**

Wright, Willard Huntington 1888-1939
See Van Dine, S. S.
See also CA 115; 189; CMW 4; DLBD 16

Wright, William 1930- .... **CLC 44**
See also CA 53-56; CANR 7, 23

Wroth, Lady Mary 1587-1653(?) .... **LC 30; PC 38**
See also DLB 121

Wu Ch'eng-en 1500(?)-1582(?) .... **LC 7**

Wu Ching-tzu 1701-1754 .... **LC 2**

Wulfstan c. 10th cent. -1023 .... **CMLC 59**

Wurlitzer, Rudolph 1938(?)- .... **CLC 2, 4, 15**
See also CA 85-88; CN 7; DLB 173

Wyatt, Sir Thomas c. 1503-1542 . **LC 70; PC 27**
See also BRW 1; DLB 132; EXPP; RGEL 2; TEA

Wycherley, William 1640-1716 .... **LC 8, 21**
See also BRW 2; CDBLB 1660-1789; DAM DRAM; DLB 80; RGEL 2

Wylie, Elinor (Morton Hoyt) 1885-1928 .... **PC 23; TCLC 8**
See also AMWS 1; CA 105; 162; DLB 9, 45; EXPP; RGAL 4

Wylie, Philip (Gordon) 1902-1971 ... **CLC 43**
See also CA 21-22; 33-36R; CAP 2; DLB 9; SFW 4

Wyndham, John .... **CLC 19**
See Harris, John (Wyndham Parkes Lucas) Beynon
See also DLB 255; SCFW 2

Wyss, Johann David Von 1743-1818 .... **NCLC 10**
See also JRDA; MAICYA 1, 2; SATA 29; SATA-Brief 27

Xenophon c. 430B.C.-c. 354B.C. ... **CMLC 17**
See also AW 1; DLB 176; RGWL 2, 3

Xingjian, Gao 1940-
See Gao Xingjian
See also CA 193; RGWL 3

Yakamochi 718-785 .... **CMLC 45; PC 48**

Yakumo Koizumi
See Hearn, (Patricio) Lafcadio (Tessima Carlos)

Yamada, Mitsuye (May) 1923- .... **PC 44**
See also CA 77-80

Yamamoto, Hisaye 1921- .... **AAL; SSC 34**
See also DAM MULT; LAIT 4; SSFS 14

Yamauchi, Wakako 1924- .... **AAL**

Yanez, Jose Donoso
See Donoso (Yanez), Jose

Yanovsky, Basile S.
See Yanovsky, V(assily) S(emenovich)

Yanovsky, V(assily) S(emenovich) 1906-1989 .... **CLC 2, 18**
See also CA 97-100; 129

Yates, Richard 1926-1992 .... **CLC 7, 8, 23**
See also AMWS 11; CA 5-8R; 139; CANR 10, 43; DLB 2, 234; DLBY 1981, 1992; INT CANR-10

Yeats, W. B.
See Yeats, William Butler

Yeats, William Butler 1865-1939 .... **PC 20; TCLC 1, 11, 18, 31, 93, 116; WLC**
See also AAYA 48; BRW 6; BRWR 1; CA 104; 127; CANR 45; CDBLB 1890-1914; DA; DA3; DAB; DAC; DAM DRAM, MST, POET; DLB 10, 19, 98, 156; EWL 3; EXPP; MTCW 1, 2; NCFS 3; PAB; PFS 1, 2, 5, 7, 13, 15; RGEL 2; TEA; WLIT 4; WP

Yehoshua, A(braham) B. 1936- ... **CLC 13, 31**
See also CA 33-36R; CANR 43, 90; EWL 3; RGSF 2; RGWL 3

Yellow Bird
See Ridge, John Rollin

Yep, Laurence Michael 1948- .... **CLC 35**
See also AAYA 5, 31; BYA 7; CA 49-52; CANR 1, 46, 92; CLR 3, 17, 54; DLB 52; FANT; JRDA; MAICYA 1, 2; MAICYAS 1; SATA 7, 69, 123; WYA; YAW

Yerby, Frank G(arvin) 1916-1991 ..... **BLC 3; CLC 1, 7, 22**
See also BPFB 3; BW 1, 3; CA 9-12R; 136; CANR 16, 52; DAM MULT; DLB 76; INT CANR-16; MTCW 1; RGAL 4; RHW

Yesenin, Sergei Alexandrovich
See Esenin, Sergei (Alexandrovich)

Yesenin, Sergey
See Esenin, Sergei (Alexandrovich)
See also EWL 3

Yevtushenko, Yevgeny (Alexandrovich) 1933- ...... **CLC 1, 3, 13, 26, 51, 126; PC 40**
See Evtushenko, Evgenii Aleksandrovich
See also CA 81-84; CANR 33, 54; CWW 2; DAM POET; EWL 3; MTCW 1

Yezierska, Anzia 1885(?)-1970 .... **CLC 46**
See also CA 126; 89-92; DLB 28, 221; FW; MTCW 1; RGAL 4; SSFS 15

Yglesias, Helen 1915- .... **CLC 7, 22**
See also CA 37-40R; CAAS 20; CANR 15, 65, 95; CN 7; INT CANR-15; MTCW 1

Yokomitsu, Riichi 1898-1947 .... **TCLC 47**
See also CA 170; EWL 3

Yonge, Charlotte (Mary) 1823-1901 .... **TCLC 48**
See also CA 109; 163; DLB 18, 163; RGEL 2; SATA 17; WCH

York, Jeremy
See Creasey, John

York, Simon
See Heinlein, Robert A(nson)

Yorke, Henry Vincent 1905-1974 ..... **CLC 13**
See Green, Henry
See also CA 85-88; 49-52

Yosano Akiko 1878-1942 .... **PC 11; TCLC 59**
See also CA 161; EWL 3; RGWL 3

Yoshimoto, Banana .... **CLC 84**
See Yoshimoto, Mahoko
See also AAYA 50; NFS 7

Yoshimoto, Mahoko 1964-
See Yoshimoto, Banana
See also CA 144; CANR 98; SSFS 16

Young, Al(bert James) 1939- ... **BLC 3; CLC 19**
See also BW 2, 3; CA 29-32R; CANR 26, 65, 109; CN 7; CP 7; DAM MULT; DLB 33

Young, Andrew (John) 1885-1971 ...... **CLC 5**
See also CA 5-8R; CANR 7, 29; RGEL 2

Young, Collier
See Bloch, Robert (Albert)

Young, Edward 1683-1765 .... **LC 3, 40**
See also DLB 95; RGEL 2

Young, Marguerite (Vivian) 1909-1995 .... **CLC 82**
See also CA 13-16; 150; CAP 1; CN 7

Young, Neil 1945- .... **CLC 17**
See also CA 110; CCA 1

Young Bear, Ray A. 1950- ... **CLC 94; NNAL**
See also CA 146; DAM MULT; DLB 175

Yourcenar, Marguerite 1903-1987 ... **CLC 19, 38, 50, 87**
See also BPFB 3; CA 69-72; CANR 23, 60, 93; DAM NOV; DLB 72; DLBY 1988; EW 12; EWL 3; GFL 1789 to the Present; GLL 1; MTCW 1, 2; RGWL 2, 3

Yuan, Chu 340(?)B.C.-278(?)B.C. . **CMLC 36**

Yurick, Sol 1925- .... **CLC 6**
See also CA 13-16R; CANR 25; CN 7

Zabolotsky, Nikolai Alekseevich 1903-1958 .... **TCLC 52**
See Zabolotsky, Nikolay Alekseevich
See also CA 116; 164

Zabolotsky, Nikolay Alekseevich
See Zabolotsky, Nikolai Alekseevich
See also EWL 3

Zagajewski, Adam 1945- .... **PC 27**
See also CA 186; DLB 232; EWL 3

Zalygin, Sergei -2000 .... **CLC 59**

Zamiatin, Evgenii
See Zamyatin, Evgeny Ivanovich
See also RGSF 2; RGWL 2, 3

Zamiatin, Evgenii Ivanovich
See Zamyatin, Evgeny Ivanovich
See also DLB 272

Zamiatin, Yevgenii
See Zamyatin, Evgeny Ivanovich

Zamora, Bernice (B. Ortiz) 1938- .. **CLC 89; HLC 2**
See also CA 151; CANR 80; DAM MULT; DLB 82; HW 1, 2

Zamyatin, Evgeny Ivanovich 1884-1937 .... **TCLC 8, 37**
See Zamiatin, Evgenii; Zamiatin, Evgenii Ivanovich; Zamyatin, Yevgeny Ivanovich
See also CA 105; 166; EW 10; SFW 4

Zamyatin, Yevgeny Ivanovich
See Zamyatin, Evgeny Ivanovich
See also EWL 3

Zangwill, Israel 1864-1926 ...ˉ**SSC 44; TCLC 16**
See also CA 109; 167; CMW 4; DLB 10, 135, 197; RGEL 2

Zappa, Francis Vincent, Jr. 1940-1993
See Zappa, Frank
See also CA 108; 143; CANR 57

Zappa, Frank .... **CLC 17**
See Zappa, Francis Vincent, Jr.

Zaturenska, Marya 1902-1982 ..... **CLC 6, 11**
See also CA 13-16R; 105; CANR 22

Zeami 1363-1443 .... **DC 7; LC 86**
See also DLB 203; RGWL 2, 3

Zelazny, Roger (Joseph) 1937-1995 . **CLC 21**
See also AAYA 7; BPFB 3; CA 21-24R; 148; CANR 26, 60; CN 7; DLB 8; FANT; MTCW 1, 2; SATA 57; SATA-Brief 39; SCFW 2; SFW 4; SUFW 1, 2

Zhdanov, Andrei Alexandrovich 1896-1948 .... **TCLC 18**
See also CA 117; 167

Zhukovsky, Vasilii Andreevich
See Zhukovsky, Vasily (Andreevich)
See also DLB 205

Zhukovsky, Vasily (Andreevich) 1783-1852 .... **NCLC 35**
See Zhukovsky, Vasilii Andreevich

Ziegenhagen, Eric .... **CLC 55**

Zimmer, Jill Schary
See Robinson, Jill

Zimmerman, Robert
See Dylan, Bob

Literary Criticism Series
Cumulative Topic Index

This index lists all topic entries in Gale's *Classical and Medieval Literature Criticism* (CMLC), *Contemporary Literary Criticism* (CLC), *Drama Criticism* (DC), *Literature Criticism from 1400 to 1800* (LC), *Nineteenth-Century Literature Criticism* (NCLC), *Short Story Criticism* (SSC), and *Twentieth-Century Literary Criticism* (TCLC). The index also lists topic entries in the Gale Critical Companion Collection, which includes the following publications: *The Beat Generation* (BG), and *Harlem Renaissance* (HR).

NCLC Cumulative Nationality Index

AMERICAN

Adams, John **106**
Alcott, Amos Bronson **1**
Alcott, Louisa May **6, 58, 83**
Alger, Horatio Jr. **8, 83**
Allston, Washington **2**
Apess, William **73**
Arnold, Matthew **126**
Audubon, John James **47**
Barlow, Joel **23**
Beecher, Catharine Esther **30**
Bellamy, Edward **4, 86**
Bird, Robert Montgomery **1**
Boker, George Henry **125**
Brackenridge, Hugh Henry **7**
Brentano, Clemens (Maria) **1**
Brown, Charles Brockden **22, 74, 122**
Brown, William Wells **2, 89**
Brownson, Orestes Augustus **50**
Bryant, William Cullen **6, 46**
Calhoun, John Caldwell **15**
Channing, William Ellery **17**
Child, Lydia Maria **6, 73**
Chivers, Thomas Holley **49**
Cooke, John Esten **5**
Cooke, Rose Terry **110**
Cooper, James Fenimore **1, 27, 54**
Cooper, Susan Fenimore **129**
Cranch, Christopher Pearse **115**
Crèvecoeur, Michel Guillaume Jean de **105**
Crockett, David **8**
Dana, Richard Henry Sr. **53**
Delany, Martin Robinson **93**
Dickinson, Emily (Elizabeth) **21, 77**
Douglass, Frederick **7, 55**
Dunlap, William **2**
Dwight, Timothy **13**
Emerson, Mary Moody **66**
Emerson, Ralph Waldo **1, 38, 98**
Field, Eugene **3**
Foster, Hannah Webster **99**
Foster, Stephen Collins **26**
Frederic, Harold **10**
Freneau, Philip Morin **1, 111**
Hale, Sarah Josepha (Buell) **75**
Halleck, Fitz-Greene **47**
Hamilton, Alexander **49**
Hammon, Jupiter **5**
Harris, George Washington **23**
Hawthorne, Nathaniel **2, 10, 17, 23, 39, 79, 95**
Hayne, Paul Hamilton **94**
Holmes, Oliver Wendell **14, 81**
Horton, George Moses **87**
Irving, Washington **2, 19, 95**
Jackson, Helen Hunt **90**
Jacobs, Harriet A(nn) **67**
James, Henry Sr. **53**
Jefferson, Thomas **11, 103**
Kennedy, John Pendleton **2**
Kirkland, Caroline M. **85**
Lanier, Sidney **6, 118**

Lazarus, Emma **8, 109**
Lincoln, Abraham **18**
Longfellow, Henry Wadsworth **2, 45, 101, 103**
Lowell, James Russell **2, 90**
Madison, James **126**
Melville, Herman **3, 12, 29, 45, 49, 91, 93, 123**
Mowatt, Anna Cora **74**
Murray, Judith Sargent **63**
Parkman, Francis Jr. **12**
Parton, Sara Payson Willis **86**
Paulding, James Kirke **2**
Pinkney, Edward **31**
Poe, Edgar Allan **1, 16, 55, 78, 94, 97, 117**
Rowson, Susanna Haswell **5, 69**
Sedgwick, Catharine Maria **19, 98**
Shaw, Henry Wheeler **15**
Sheridan, Richard Brinsley **5, 91**
Sigourney, Lydia Howard (Huntley) **21, 87**
Simms, William Gilmore **3**
Smith, Joseph Jr. **53**
Solomon, Northup **105**
Southworth, Emma Dorothy Eliza Nevitte **26**
Stowe, Harriet (Elizabeth) Beecher **3, 50**
Taylor, Bayard **89**
Tenney, Tabitha Gilman **122**
Thoreau, Henry David **7, 21, 61**
Timrod, Henry **25**
Trumbull, John **30**
Truth, Sojourner **94**
Tyler, Royall **3**
Very, Jones **9**
Warner, Susan (Bogert) **31**
Warren, Mercy Otis **13**
Webster, Noah **30**
Whitman, Sarah Helen (Power) **19**
Whitman, Walt(er) **4, 31, 81**
Whittier, John Greenleaf **8, 59**
Wilson, Harriet E. Adams **78**
Winnemucca, Sarah **79**

ARGENTINIAN

Echeverria, (Jose) Esteban (Antonino) **18**
Hernández, José **17**
Sarmiento, Domingo Faustino **123**

AUSTRALIAN

Adams, Francis **33**
Clarke, Marcus (Andrew Hislop) **19**
Gordon, Adam Lindsay **21**
Harpur, Charles **114**
Kendall, Henry **12**

AUSTRIAN

Grillparzer, Franz **1, 102**
Lenau, Nikolaus **16**
Nestroy, Johann **42**
Raimund, Ferdinand Jakob **69**
Sacher-Masoch, Leopold von **31**
Stifter, Adalbert **41**

CANADIAN

Crawford, Isabella Valancy **12, 127**
De Mille, James **123**
Haliburton, Thomas Chandler **15**
Lampman, Archibald **25**
Moodie, Susanna (Strickland) **14, 113**
Richardson, John **55**
Traill, Catharine Parr **31**

COLOMBIAN

Isaacs, Jorge Ricardo **70**
Silva, José Asunción **114**

CUBAN

Avellaneda, Gertrudis Gómez de **111**
Martí (y Pérez), José (Julian) **63**
Villaverde, Cirilo **121**

CZECH

Macha, Karel Hynek **46**

DANISH

Andersen, Hans Christian **7, 79**
Grundtvig, Nicolai Frederik Severin **1**
Jacobsen, Jens Peter **34**
Kierkegaard, Søren **34, 78, 125**

ENGLISH

Ainsworth, William Harrison **13**
Arnold, Matthew **6, 29, 89**
Arnold, Thomas **18**
Austen, Jane **1, 13, 19, 33, 51, 81, 95, 119**
Bagehot, Walter **10**
Barbauld, Anna Laetitia **50**
Barham, Richard Harris **77**
Barnes, William **75**
Beardsley, Aubrey **6**
Beckford, William **16**
Beddoes, Thomas Lovell **3**
Bentham, Jeremy **38**
Blake, William **13, 37, 57, 127**
Borrow, George (Henry) **9**
Bowles, William Lisle **103**
Brontë, Anne **4, 71, 102**
Brontë, Charlotte **3, 8, 33, 58, 105**
Brontë, Emily (Jane) **16, 35**
Brontë, (Patrick) Branwell **109**
Browning, Elizabeth Barrett **1, 16, 61, 66**
Browning, Robert **19, 79**
Bulwer-Lytton, Edward (George Earle Lytton) **1, 45**
Burney, Fanny **12, 54, 107**
Burton, Richard F(rancis) **42**
Byron, George Gordon (Noel) **2, 12, 109**
Carlyle, Thomas **22, 70**
Clare, John **9, 86**
Clough, Arthur Hugh **27**
Cobbett, William **49**
Coleridge, Hartley **90**
Coleridge, Samuel Taylor **9, 54, 99, 111**
Coleridge, Sara **31**

NCLC-129 Title Index

ISBN 0-7876-6917-2

90000